TROUBLESHOOTING,
MAINTAINING,
AND
REPAIRING MACs

TROUBLESHOOTING, MAINTAINING, AND REPAIRING MACs

Ryan Faas
with
Stuart Brown and Kim Foglia

McGraw-Hill

New York San Francisco Washington, D.C.
Auckland Bogotá Caracas Lisbon London
Madrid Mexico City Milan Montreal New Delhi
San Juan Singapore Sydney Tokyo Toronto

McGraw-Hill

A Division of The McGraw·Hill Companies

1 2 3 4 5 6 7 8 9 0   DOC/DOC   0 5 4 3 2 1 0

P/N 0-07-212624-8
PART OF
ISBN 0-07-212595-0

*The sponsoring editor for this book was Rebekah Young, the editing supervisor
was Penny Linskey, and the production supervisor was Claire Stanley. It was
set in Century Schoolbook by Victoria Khavkina of McGraw-Hill's Professional
Book Group composition unit, in cooperation with Spring Point Publishing
Services.*

Printed and bound by R. R. Donnelley & Sons Company.

*Throughout this book, trademarked names are used. Rather than put a trade-
mark symbol after every occurrence of a trademarked name, we used the names
in an editorial fashion only, and to the benefit of the trademark owner, with no
intention of infringement of the trademark. Where such designations appear in
this book, they have been printed with initial caps.*

This book is printed on recycled, acid-free paper containing a minimum
of 50% recycled, de-inked fiber.

To everyone who has ever been laughed at for, or discouraged from,

Thinking Differently.

Disclaimer and Cautions

It is important that you read and understand the following information. Please read it carefully!

Personal Risk and Limits of Liability

The repair of personal computers and their peripherals involves some amount of personal risk. Use extreme caution when working with AC and high-voltage power sources. Every reasonable effort has been made to identify and reduce areas of personal risk. You are instructed to read this book carefully *before* attempting the procedures discussed. If you are uncomfortable following any of the procedures that are outlined in this book, do not attempt them. Refer your service to qualified service personnel.

NEITHER THE AUTHORS, THE PUBLISHER, NOR ANYONE DIRECTLY OR INDIRECTLY CONNECTED WITH THE PUBLICATION OF THIS BOOK SHALL MAKE ANY WARRANTY EITHER EXPRESSED OR IMPLIED, WITH REGARD TO THIS MATERIAL, INCLUDING, BUT NOT LIMITED TO, THE IMPLIED WARRANTIES OF QUALITY, MERCHANTABILITY, AND FITNESS FOR ANY PARTICULAR PURPOSE.

Further, neither the author, publisher, nor anyone directly or indirectly connected with the publication of this book shall be liable for errors or omissions contained herein, or for incidental or consequential damages, injuries, or financial or material losses (including the loss of data) resulting from the use, or inability to use, the material contained herein. This material is provided *as is,* and the reader bears all responsibilities and risks connected with its use.

CONTENTS

Contents

INTRODUCTION

The Macintosh is often considered to be one of the most stable, trouble-free, and high-performing computers available. In many ways this is due to the elegance of the Macintosh operating system and to the fact that all Macs are built using well-designed motherboards from Apple and other high-quality components. However, there are times when even the most well-designed high-quality products can experience problems, and the Mac is no exception.

This book is devoted to helping solve problems that can occur in the current and recent Macintosh computers and operating system releases. It also stresses preventative maintenance steps that can be taken to keep most problems from occurring or becoming serious. You'll also find detailed coverage and explanations of every major technology that is a part of or can be used with today's Macs.

There are two ways that this book differs from other Macintosh computer books. First, it is focused on a specific set of Macintosh models, those that were released on or after August 15th, 1998 (All iMacs, the iBook, the blue and white Power Mac G3, the Power Mac G4, the PowerBook G3 models with bronze keyboards, and the Power Mac Cube). This allows coverage of details about these computers and the hardware that is a part of or used with them in far greater detail than any other Mac book to date.

Secondly, this book is written to give you a basic understanding of each component or technology of the Mac in as much depth as possible. This includes explanations of the physical parts and functioning of every major Macintosh component and technology so that you can understand the basics behind these components—even if you will never have a need to actually open them up and work with them.

After reading this book, you will have a firm grasp of all the technologies used by the Mac. You will also have an understanding of how to troubleshoot and solve Macintosh problems. And, you'll have an understanding of how to perform common repairs and upgrades of virtually every type on the Mac models covered in this book.

Who Should Read This Book

Although many Mac users can benefit from this book, the core of it is written for intermediate to advanced Mac users. This is not a beginner's book, and it assumes that you have a solid understanding of the bulk of the Mac OS. If you are reading this book, you should already know how to run applications, install software, be familiar with the common Finder menus and commands, and know how to use such things as Apple's Extensions Manager. While this book will walk you through many processes as needed, knowledge of how to use the Mac is required. If you've had six months of Mac experience and/or you have previously read a Macintosh beginner's guidebook, you should be able to understand the concepts and terms set forth in this book.

How This Book Is Organized

This book is divided into four parts. Part One covers the internal components of the Mac and begins with an overview of the user-accessible components of the models covered in this book. Following this overview is a chapter that covers basic diagnostic processes and how to diagnose problems and decide on a course of action as well as other steps to take before beginning any work on a Mac's physical components. Part One then continues with discussion of the primary internal hardware of today's Macintosh computers.

The second part covers expansion and peripheral technologies. This section addresses a wide array of technologies and devices that can be used to expand the internal and external hardware of the Mac. Each technology is included with a basic foundation or history, practical applications, and information for solving problems relating to it.

Part Three covers networking and Internet issues. This part includes details on how to setup and troubleshoot Mac networks and how to integrate Internet services into a network. It also discusses, in detail, Apple's AirPort wireless networking technology as well as high-speed connectivity solutions such as ISDN, DSL, and cable modem technologies.

Part Four is devoted to Mac OS and software issues. Its chapters cover the Macintosh startup process, dealing with freezes and crashes, and preventing and handling computer virus infection. It also contains chapters on working with other computing platforms and regular maintenance that should be performed on every Mac. This book ends with a chapter on recent and future Macintosh technology including the Power Mac G4 Cube and Mac OS X.

Each chapter in this book is organized in a very simple manner. Chapters begin with a basic discussion of the technologies, components, or issues that they cover. Most also end with a special section on troubleshooting the major problems of the technology or devices covered and a collection of Internet resources where you can find additional information and help with the concepts, hardware, and software covered in the chapter.

Additionally, there is a Symptoms at a Glance section following this introduction that can help you quickly and easily locate solutions and explanations for the problems covered in each chapter.

RYAN FAAS

ACKNOWLEDGMENTS

If I tried to remember every person who has helped me in one way or another while I was writing this book to thank, I'd be sitting here for days doing it and thanking them all here by name would take more pages than most chapters in this book. So, I'll stick to the major people and hope anyone not included will forgive the omission (it certainly isn't intentional).

First and foremost, I have to thank Rebekah Young, Penny Linskey, and everyone at McGraw-Hill for giving me the opportunity to write this book and for being patient when I discovered my own limitations along the way. Thank you for the this privilege and for having the faith that I could do this.

Next, Stuart Brown and Kim Foglia for being such honest and straightforward tech editors. You guys didn't hesitate to let me know when I could've said something better and, as irritating as that may be, it did make this a better book and me a better writer. You may not be the most gentle editors out there, but you do get right to the point when correcting work and that is something I truly do appreciate.

Of course, I have to thank everyone at Apple for designing and building such great products. But beyond Apple's engineering departments, I have to say thanks to their press team and to all the people who design and maintain Apple's website for making it easy to find information when you need to. And a special thanks has to go to everyone who maintains the Tech Info. Library (http:///til.info.apple.com). You guys do a phenomenal job providing the mother of all Mac references.

Next on the list are all the devoted users who maintain Macintosh news and reference sites on the Internet. I certainly can't thank you all by name and I won't begin listing your sites here because I'd be afraid of missing one of you, but you all provide excellent sources of information and great resources for Mac users.

And speaking of websites, I have to give a personal thanks to Scott Kurnit (founder and CEO of About.com) for creating a network of sites where I could start and continue writing about the Mac and interacting with so many wonderful users. I'd also like to thank lots of other people at About.com, but I'll settle for just thanking Editorial Manager Avram Piltch for being the best boss I've ever had and being understanding beyond belief while I was writing this book.

I'd also like to thank Tom Smith, my journalism teacher at Guilderland High School all those years ago. Mr. Smith, you made me want to write for a living and you were also responsible for me using a Mac for the first time. I thank you for both, as both have turned out to be so important for me.

Of course, I have to thank my parents. Without them, I wouldn't be here to write this book (or anything else).

And lastly, I have to thank all the employees of the following Albany, NY coffee shops that provided me with all the caffeine I could want while working on this book: Uncommon Grounds, Borders Espresso Bar, and the Barnes and Noble Café. A special thanks goes out to Mandie (former barista at the Borders Espresso Bar) for providing needed distractions and free therapy (as well as coffee) on all those nights I sat hunched over my PowerBook writing.

Symptoms at a Glance

Inside the iMac and PowerMac

This chapter is an introduction to the internal components of the desktop Macintosh computers that are covered by this book and how to gain access to them. Chapter 2 provides a similar introduction to the portable iBook and PowerBook models. Later chapters include specific information on each of the internal components and external peripherals used in or with these computers.

Just looking at the insides of a computer is intimidating for most people. There are a lot of enigmatic components in various shapes and sizes and a lot of wires and cables snaking all over the place without any obvious plan or design. However, the Macintosh computer is distinguished from all other computers by the comprehensive excellence of its design and engineering. You can be confident that every component inside the case of a Mac has been carefully designed to fit in with the functionality of the entire computer. The case design of all recent Macs provides access to components that are likely to require repair, replacement, or upgrading, while preventing you from damaging delicate components or accidentally injuring yourself.

Since this chapter involves a discussion of opening up computers and poking around inside, we should start with a few general points about safety and good habits when working on electronic equipment. You should also read Chapter 3 before beginning repairs and before you open the case of any Macintosh computer. If you plan to work with a specific component of the Mac, also familiarize yourself with that component using the appropriate chapters later in the book before you begin work.

There are a few important rules of thumb to keep in mind regarding maintaining and repairing computers:

- First, never open the case of a computer (or any electrical device) while it is turned on.

- Second, some computer components may heat up or store significant electric charges when the machine is operating, so allow the machine to cool off before beginning to work inside, and avoid touching anything if you are not sure that it is safe.

- Third, static electricity can damage electronic components. Always ground yourself before touching anything inside a computer. This can be done by touching a metal object, or better, by wearing a grounding or anti-static wrist strap that is attached to a metal part of the computer case or to another ground (a grounding strap can be obtained for just a few dollars from any electronics store).

- Finally, if it ain't broke, don't fix it. Even if it the computer *is* broken, randomly adjusting components that "don't look right" is not likely to lead to successful repairs. A systematic approach to repairs is required: remove and test parts that may be broken, or replace them with parts that are known to be okay.

What Desktop Macintosh Computers Are Covered in This Book?

This book contains information specific to only the Macintosh computers released after August of 1998. This includes all iMac models, the Blue and White Power Macintosh G3 (the earlier beige Power Mac G3 models originally released in 1997 are not covered), the Power Mac G4, and the Power Mac G4 Cube (which is covered separately in Chapter 42 because of its very recent release).

The Original iMac Models

The original iMac computers were released in August of 1998. They are the earliest computers covered by this book and were revolutionary Macs in many ways. They began Apple's shift away from earlier interface technologies like serial and SCSI ports, were the first USB Macs, and were the first Macs to feature the now-popular translucent look of virtually all of Apple's products. The iMac was also the first Mac in a long time aimed specifically at consumers and home users.

There were four revisions or changes in the original iMac's design over its 14-month life span. Revision A and B iMacs were available in only the original Bondi Blue color. They also included an infrared port and a special "mezzanine" expansion slot (which Apple discouraged developers from exploiting), which were removed from later revision iMacs. Revision C iMacs introduced the five fruit-flavored iMac colors and an increase in processor speed. Revision D iMacs only increased the iMac processor speed.

Table 1-1 shows the specifications for the original iMac.

The Slot-Loading iMac/iMac DV Models

The entire iMac line was redesigned in the fall of 1999. (It was also updated in July of 2000 with several new colored iMacs and different pricing and hard drive/RAM configurations, but the actual case design

TABLE 1-1

Original iMac Specs.

Processor type: G3

Processor speed: 233 MHz (rev. A and B), 266 MHz (rev. C), or 333 MHz (rev. D)

Backside cache: 512 KB

Installed RAM: 32 MB

RAM slots: 2 (one used by factory installed RAM)

Maximum possible RAM: 256 MB

Video RAM: 6 MB*

Standard hard drive: 4-GB IDE (rev. A and B) 6-GB IDE (rev. C and D)

CD-ROM: 24X

V.90 56-Kbps internal modem

Expansion slots: Mezzanine slot (rev. A and B only)

Built-in display: 15 inch CRT

Ports: Audio in/out, USB (2 ports), 10/100Base-T Ethernet, internal modem phone jack

*The revision A iMac shipped with only 2 MB of video RAM but included a VRAM slot for accepting up to an additional 4 MB of video RAM.

and hardware layout of the iMac was not changed.) These second-generation iMacs are often referred to as the slot-loading iMacs because they use a slot-loading CD-ROM or DVD-ROM drive instead of the more traditional tray-loading drive used in the earlier iMacs. Some models are also referred to as iMac DV (or iMac DV Plus or iMac DV Special Edition) because of the included abilities to work with digital video and, on some models, use a DVD-ROM drive to play DVD movies.

Table 1-2 shows the specifications for the slot-loading iMac.

The Blue and White Power Mac G3

The Blue and White Power Mac G3 was released in January of 1999. It was the first Mac to ship with FireWire ports, as well as the first Power Mac to ship with USB ports and without a SCSI or serial port, and the first Mac to ship with a VGA video out port instead of the older Mac monitor ports. It also featured a revolutionary new case design that makes upgrade or repair work extremely simple.

Table 1-3 shows the specifications for the Blue and White Power Mac.

TABLE 1-2

Slot-Loading iMac
Specs.

Processor type: G3

Processor speed: 350 MHz, 400 MHz, 450 MHz, or 500 MHz (depending on model)

Backside cache: 512 KB

Installed RAM: 64 or 128 MB

RAM slots: 2 (one used by factory-installed RAM)

Maximum possible RAM: 512 MB or 1 GB (depending on model)

Video RAM: 8 MB

Standard hard drive: From 6 GB through 30 GB, depending on model

24X CD-ROM or 4X DVD-ROM

V.90 56-Kbps internal modem

Expansion slots: Air Port Card Slot

Built-in display: 15-inch CRT

Ports (all models): Audio in/out, USB (2 ports), 10/100Base-T Ethernet, internal modem phone jack

Additional ports on DV models: FireWire (2 ports), VGA video out

TABLE 1-3

Blue Power Mac
G3 Specs.

Processor type: G3

Processor speed: 300 MHz, 350 MHz, 400 MHz, or 450 MHz

Backside cache: 512 KB or 1 MB

Installed RAM: 64 or 128 MB

RAM slots: 4 (one used by factory-installed RAM)

Maximum possible RAM: 1 GB

Video RAM: 16 MB*

Standard hard drive: Varies depending on model

32X CD-ROM or 4X DVD-ROM or DVD-RAM

Optional Zip drive included on some models

Expansion slots: Three 33-MHz PCI slots, one 66-MHz PCI slot, comm slot for internal modem

Ports: Audio in/out, USB (2 ports), 10/100Base-T Ethernet, FireWire (2 ports) ADB, VGA Video out

*On factory-installed video card (which can be replaced or supplemented with a second video card)

TABLE 1-4

Early Power Mac G4 Specs.

Processor type: G4

Processor speed: 350 MHz or 400 MHz

Backside cache: 512 KB or 1 MB

Installed RAM: 64 or 128 MB

RAM slots: 4 (one used by factory-installed RAM)

Maximum possible RAM: 1 GB

Video RAM: 16 MB*

Standard hard drive: Varies depending on model

32X CD-ROM or 4X DVD-ROM or DVD-RAM

Optional Zip drive included on some models

Expansion slots: Three 33-MHz PCI slots, one 66-MHz PCI slot, comm slot for internal modem

Ports: Audio in/out, USB (2 ports), 10/100Base-T Ethernet, FireWire (2 ports) ADB, VGA video out

*On factory-installed video card (which can be replaced or supplemented with a second video card)

The Early Power Mac G4 Models (with a PCI Graphics Card)

Apple released the first Power Mac G4 models in September of 1999. These first models were often known by their Apple code name "Yikes." These models were essentially the same case and motherboard design as the Blue and White Power Mac G3 computers, except with a G4 processor. They were only sold briefly before Apple replaced them with a new motherboard-designed G4 model.

Table 1-4 shows the specifications for the early Power Mac G4.

The Later Power Mac G4 Models (with an AGP Graphics Card)

Introduced in October of 1999, the later Power Mac G4 computers featured a new motherboard design that introduced some new features, such as the ability to accept an AirPort card for wireless networking and the use of an Advanced Graphics Port (or AGP) slot for a video card.

TABLE 1-5

Later Power Mac
G4 Specs.

Processor type: G4

Processor speed: 350 MHz, 400 MHz, 450 MHz, or 500 MHz (dual-processor configura
tions are available for 450-MHz and 500-MHz models)

Backside cache: 512 KB or 1 MB

Installed RAM: 64, 128, or 256 MB

RAM slots: 4 (one used by factory-installed RAM)

Maximum possible RAM: 1.5 GB*

Video RAM: 16 MB**

Standard hard drive: Varies depending on model

32X CD-ROM or 4X DVD-ROM*** or DVD-RAM

Optional Zip drive included on some models

Expansion slots: Three 33-MHz PCI slots, one AGP slot for video card, comm slot for
internal modem, AirPort card slot

v.90 56-Kbps internal modem

Ports: Audio in/out, USB (2 ports), 10/100 or Gigabit Base-T Ethernet, FireWire (2 ports),
internal modem phone jack, VGA video out, DVI video out (replaced by ADC video out in
current models)

*These computers can accept higher RAM amounts (up to 2 GB), but only 1.5 GB can be recognized by
the current Mac OS.

**On factory-installed video card (which can be replaced or supplemented with a second video card)

***Current models may feature a 5X DVD-ROM drive.

These later G4 models were often referred to by the Apple code name
"Sawtooth" to differentiate them from the earlier models. In July of 2000,
Apple adjusted the Power Mac G4 line again to include dual-processor
models and Gigabit Ethernet as standard features—a first for any personal computer.

Table 1-5 shows the specifications for the later Power Mac G4.

The Power Mac G4 Cube

The Power Mac G4 Cube is Apple's most recent computer at this writing.
It was released in July of 2000, just prior to the completion of this book.
It is covered separately in Chapter 42 due to its very recent release.

Inside the Power Macintosh G3 and Early G4 Models

With the Power Mac G3/G4 computers there are a number of components that can be installed or replaced by users or technicians. These include the hard drive(s), CD or DVD-ROM drive, removable-media drives (such as a Zip or SuperDisk drive), PCI expansion cards, memory (RAM), processor modules, and an internal modem card. All of these components can be easily accessed when the computer is opened.

The Power Macintosh G3/G4 computers are designed to allow extremely easy access to all of their internal components. Just lift the side latch and lower the side door (see Figure 1-1).

The inside of the G3/G4 is very logically organized. The motherboard, which contains the most frequently accessed components, is located right on the door of the computer. This allows easy access to the components whenever the computer is opened.

The RAM slots are along the edge farthest from the Power Mac's case. There are four RAM slots, at least one of which will contain a RAM module out of the factory. Figure 1-2 shows these slots.

The PCI expansion slots are along the rear of the computer and near the case itself. The PCI slots are easy to identify because there should already be a graphics card in the first slot. If the computer has a SCSI card, then another slot will be occupied. Each PCI slot is adjacent to a metal panel that covers a small opening in the back of the computer. You must remove the metal cover when installing a card, so that one end pokes out the window, then cables can be plugged into the various ports

Figure 1-1
Opening the Power Mac G3/G4 computers is as simple as releasing this latch.

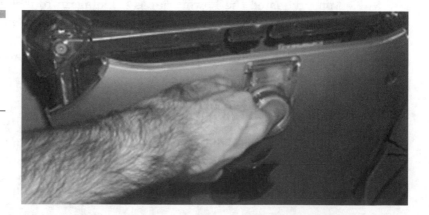

Figure 1-2 The RAM slots in a Power Mac computer.

on the card (this is not required if the card doesn't include any ports) from the rear of the computer.

The internal modem card slot (also called a comm slot) is located along the top edge of the door, near the back of the computer. An internal modem card may or may not be installed in the slot.

The processor is located in the center of the motherboard. It is hidden underneath a heat sink with lots of silver fins poking up. The processor itself is actually plugged into a ZIF (zero insertion force) socket, which is designed to make removal and replacement with processor upgrades very simple. Figure 1-3 shows a diagram of the motherboard of a Blue and White Power Mac G3 or early G4 model.

The hard drives are on the bottom of the main body of the computer's case. There are three standard hard drive bays along the case of the Power Mac G3/G4 models. Unless specially ordered, a standard IDE hard drive is installed in the rearmost bay. On some models, it is possible to mount a second IDE hard drive directly above this hard drive (see Chapters 5 and 13 for details). For IDE hard drives, a cable extends from the hard drive to the connector on the motherboard located right next to the drive. The drives themselves are held in mounting brackets by screws. The brackets can be removed from the computer as discussed in Chapter 5. Each hard drive also must have a power connector attached to it in order to function. Figure 1-4 shows the hard drive bays of a Power Mac G3/G4 computer.

The CD or DVD-ROM drive of the computer is housed in a special carrier that is suspended at the front of the computer's case. This carrier houses both the CD/DVD and the removable-media drive bays. To install

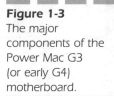

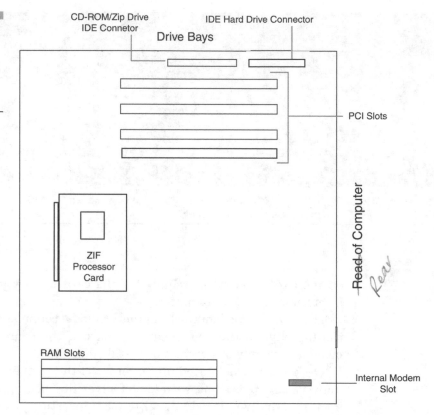

or remove CD/DVD drives or removable-media drives (such as the Zip or SuperDisk), you need to remove the carrier from the computer. This process is described in the chapters relating to CD, DVD, and removable-media drives later in the book.

Directly behind the carrier that holds the CD/DVD and removable-media drives is the Mac's power supply. Extending from it are cables that lead to the motherboard and to each internal drive. There should be extra connectors for installing additional drives. Replacing the power supply, as well as the Mac's motherboard (and ports built into the motherboard), is beyond the scope of this book. This is because doing so is a challenging process that will void the Mac's warranty, and because the required replacement parts can only be ordered from Apple by an Apple Authorized Service Center.

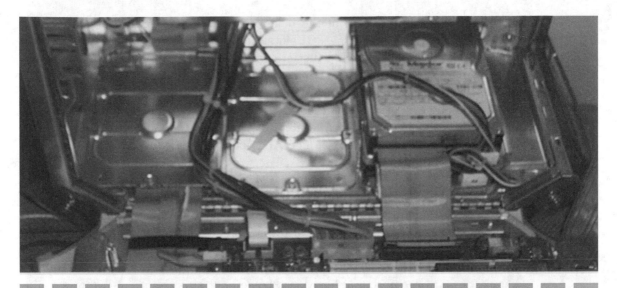

Figure 1-4   The hard drive bays of a Power Mac G3/G4 computer, with two IDE hard drives installed in the rearmost bay.

Inside the Later Power Mac G4 Computers

The second generation of Power Mac G4 computers use the same case design as the Power Mac G3 and early G4 models. However, they have a different-style motherboard. This means that there are differences in the type of video card used, the type of modem card used (and its location on the motherboard), and the type of processor module. These computers also have a special slot for accepting an AirPort wireless networking card. The location of non-motherboard components, such as hard drives and CD/DVD-ROM drives, remains the same as the Power Mac computers discussed earlier.

The later Power Mac G4 computers use an AGP graphics card. This gives them superior graphics capability (as discussed in Chapters 8 and 26). It also means that in place of a fourth PCI slot, these computers have an AGP slot. The location of the remaining PCI slots is the same, however. The location of the RAM slots is also the same.

The modem card of the later Power Mac G4 computers is located directly in front of the PCI slots, along the edge of the computer's case and hard drive bays. This is a major change from the location of the modem slot in the earlier computers. The modem card is also much larger in these computers.

The AirPort card slot is located to the very front of the motherboard, directly behind a large metal guide that holds the inserted card in place, as shown in Figure 1-5. The AirPort antenna cable is secured to this metal guide.

The processor of these later G4 computers is located in roughly the same place on the motherboard as the earlier G3/G4 models. It is not, however, housed on a ZIF module. Rather, it is housed on a special processor daughtercard. Multiprocessor G4 models use the same daughtercard design but have two processors installed on the card instead of one. As with the earlier Power Mac computers, the processor and daughtercard are obscured beneath a large heat sink. Figure 1-6 shows a diagram of the motherboard used in the later G4 computers.

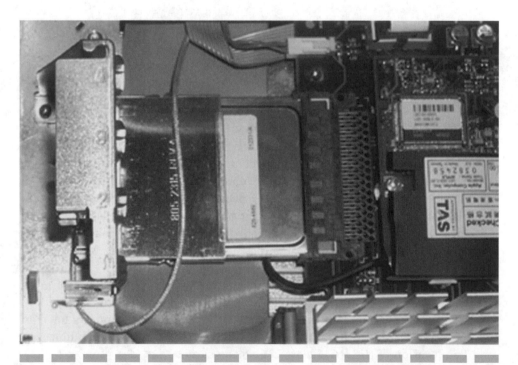

Figure 1-5   An AirPort card inserted in the Power Mac G4's AirPort card guide and slot.

Figure 1-6
The major
components of
the later G4
motherboard.

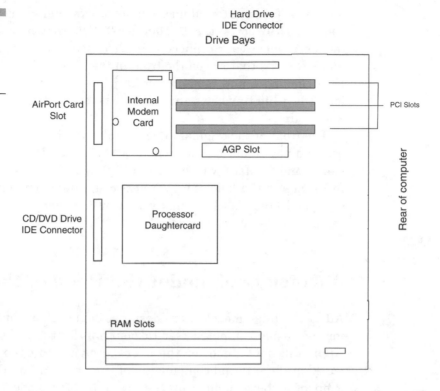

AirPort Card
Slot

CD/DVD Drive
IDE Connector

Internal
Modem
Card

Processor
Daughtercard

Hard Drive
IDE Connector

Drive Bays

AGP Slot

PCI Slots

Rear of computer

RAM Slots

Figure 1-7
The iMac's ports
compartment.

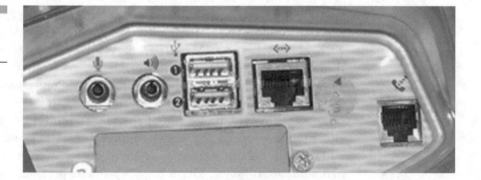

Inside the Original iMac

The original iMac has a special compartment on one side (complete with closable door) where all the external ports are located. These ports, shown in Figure 1-7, include, from left to right, the audio line in and line out ports (for an external microphone or external speakers, respectively), the two USB ports, the 10/100Base-T Ethernet port, and the internal modem's phone jack connector. It also includes the reset and programmer's buttons that are on the front of the Power Mac G3/G4 between the Ethernet port and modem phone jack. However, these buttons are located within tiny holes and can only be pressed with a straightened-out paper clip.

The front of the original iMac includes the built-in display and speakers, the power button, headphone jacks, and CD-ROM drive. The revision A and B iMacs (which are Bondi Blue colored) also include a special infrared port that allows for wireless communication with other infrared-equipped Macs (such as many PowerBook computers). This port was removed in later iMac models.

A Quick Look under the Hood of the iMac

All of the iMac models were designed as consumer machines—that is, for the casual computer user rather than for the professional. As such, Apple did not intend for the average owner to open the case and do work on the internal components of the original iMac. As a result, it is a bit of a chore to open up the original iMac models in order to gain access to any of its internal components. The primary reasons most users will have to open the case of the original iMac are to add RAM, to replace the internal hard drive, or to replace the iMac's processor card with one of the new iMac upgrade cards that have become available this year.

As mentioned, the very first two iMac revisions (A and B), which were Bondi Blue colored, included a special slot called a mezzanine slot that was located on the underside of the iMac's motherboard. Accessing this slot requires you to physically remove the iMac's motherboard, which will void the iMac's warranty. The slot does not exist on any of the later (fruit-flavored) iMacs. There are very few expansion cards that use this slot, and it is unlikely you will need to access it.

All iMac repair work starts the same way: by opening the case and removing the chassis that contains the iMac's motherboard and internal drives. To do this, first unplug the computer, and place it face down (onto the screen). It is a good idea to put a soft cloth down first to protect the screen.

There is a small handle on the underside of the iMac near the back of the computer. Hidden under this handle is a small screw that must be removed before the bottom panel can be removed (see Figure 1-8). Once this screw is out, hold the side of the computer and pull sharply on the handle up and away from the computer until the bottom panel snaps free. This may take more force than you expect.

As you can see in Figure 1-9, once the bottom panel is off, there are three cables (four on revision A and B iMacs). All of these cables must be

Figure 1-8
To remove the bottom panel of the iMac, remove this screw and then pull up on the handle.

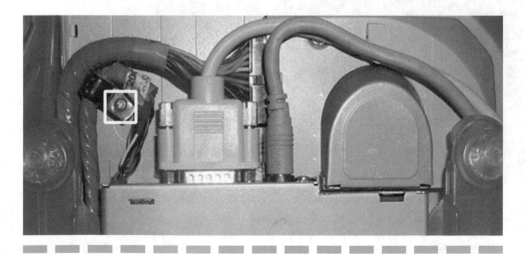

Figure 1-9   The cables (and the screw that secures on cable) that must be removed from the iMac's motherboard/drive chassis.

unplugged. The largest cable is from the internal display. It has small thumbscrews on either side of the plug that must be loosened completely before it can be removed (it also has standard Phillips screw tips, so you loosen the thumbscrews with a screwdriver). The other two cables are power cables that can be removed by pressing on the central portion of the connector and pulling. Revision A and B iMacs have a cable similar to a serial port cable that connects the motherboard to the iMac's IR port. This can just be pulled out. The monitor cable (and IR port cable, if present) are tucked under a clip. You need to move them out from under the clip in order to remove the motherboard/drive chassis. One of the power cables is also secured to the chassis by a screw. This screw also needs to be removed.

All the internal components of the iMac (save the display, power supply, fan, and speakers) are built onto a special chassis that can be removed from the case and display of the iMac. There is a plastic grip near the back of the computer, above the sockets where the cables were attached. There are two screws in this plastic grip, as shown in Figure 1-10, that must be removed (be careful as they are small and can fall into the computer). With the screws removed, grasp the plastic grip and pull straight upward until the entire motherboard/drive chassis slides up and out. Once the motherboard/drive chassis is out, set it down gently on a clean, flat surface. Figure 1-11 shows the chassis once free of the iMac's case.

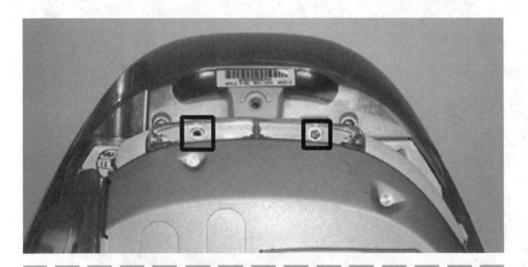

Figure 1-10   These two screws need to be removed before the motherboard/drive chassis can be released from the iMac.

Figure 1-11
The motherboard/
drive chassis once
free of the iMac.

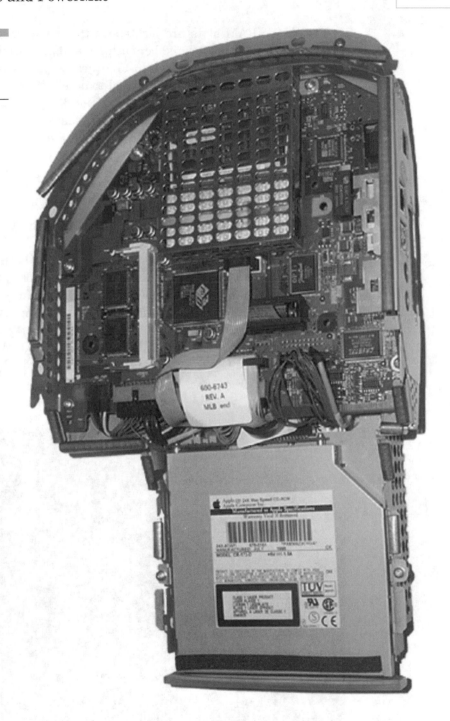

The iMac's RAM slots are located on the same daughtercard as the processor. This card is located beneath a metal grate in the middle of the motherboard. The grate, shown in Figure 1-12, can easily be unsnapped at either side and lifted up if you need to access these components.

There are two RAM slots on the processor daughtercard. One is visible above the processor and is easily accessed once the metal grate is removed. The second, where the factory-installed RAM (usually 32 MB) is located, is on the underside of the processor card. Chapter 6 includes instructions for accessing this lower RAM slot. *Note*: Removing the processor card and accessing the lower RAM slot will void an iMac's warranty.

The CD-ROM drive is at the front of the computer. It must be removed to access the iMac's hard drive, which sits beneath it. To remove the CD-ROM drive, first disconnect the cables leading to both it and the hard drive from the front of the motherboard, shown in Figure 1-13. The CD-ROM drive itself is held in place by a spring and can be removed just by pressing it toward the back of the chassis and lifting it out, as shown in Figure 1-14.

The hard drive is located underneath the CD-ROM drive. It can be accessed after the CD-ROM drive has been removed. Once the CD-ROM

Figure 1-12
The RAM and processor are underneath this metal grate.

Figure 1-13
The CD-ROM and hard drive cable connections on the iMac's motherboard.

Figure 1-14
The CD-ROM drive is easily removed by pushing and lifting.

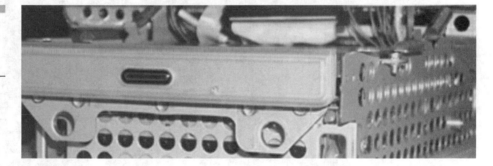

drive is out of the way, you need to remove the screws that secure the hard drive in the mounting bracket below the CD-ROM drive. These are located on either side of the chassis. Once they are removed, you can take out the hard drive.

The motherboard of the iMac can be removed. There are only three reasons to remove it, however. One is to replace it completely (which can only be done by an Apple Authorized Service Center, because individual users or technicians cannot purchase a replacement motherboard from Apple). The second is to replace the modem card (again only Apple Authorized Service Centers can order replacement modem cards). The third reason is to access the mezzanine slot of the revision A and B iMacs (see Chapter 8 for discussion of the mezzanine slot).

To remove the motherboard, first disconnect all cables attached to it. Then remove the five screws that hold it in place, as shown in Figure 1-15. There is a connector on the underside of the motherboard that also holds

Figure 1-15
To remove the iMac's motherboard, you need to remove the five screws indicated and release the connector on the motherboard's underside indicated by the white rectangle.

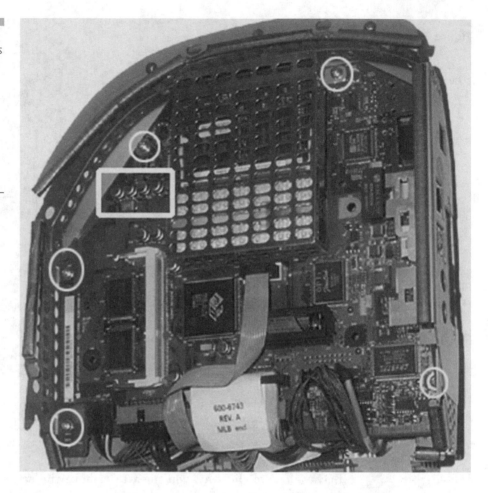

it in place, also shown in Figure 1-15. You need to position your hand so that your fingers can reach beneath the motherboard and release this connector. Once this is done, you can gently lift the motherboard up and set it on a static-free surface.

Note: I strongly caution anyone against removing the iMac's motherboard because it will void the machine's warranty and can easily damage the motherboard or other components of the iMac. This is not a procedure that most users should have a reason to perform, and you should seriously think before doing it.

Replacing or accessing the iMac's built-in display and power supply are considered beyond the scope of this book for two reasons. First, it is impossible to obtain replacement parts unless you are an Apple

Authorized Service Center. Second, the internal monitor of the iMac builds up a lethal electrical charge (as does any monitor), and access to any components of the iMac located in this section of the case can expose you to that charge, meaning that one wrong move could literally kill you. As such, accessing these components should not be attempted by anyone that is not professionally trained.

Putting the motherboard/drive chassis back into the iMac can be tricky. The motherboard assembly slides in on narrow tracks, and it is quite easy to misalign the chassis when inserting it. You'll notice that there are also small plastic tabs that need to fit under the iMac's case when you are inserting the chassis It is also easy for the cables for the power supply and display to get in the way of the chassis. The entire assembly actually has to project right through the case for the CD-ROM drive to seat properly. This process may take some effort to get right, but it can be done. Just take your time.

Once the chassis is inserted and the CD-ROM drive is properly aligned through the front of the iMac's case, you can secure it with the two small screws you removed from the plastic grip at the back of the chassis. After that is completed, insert each of the cables you disconnected (they will reinsert only in the proper places and in the proper direction). Be sure to place the monitor cable (and IR port, if present) under the clip in the bottom of the chassis.

The last step is to reinsert the bottom plastic panel of the iMac. As with reinserting the motherboard/drive chassis, this can be tricky and may take a couple of tries before you get it right. Once it is in place, secure it with the screw.

Inside the Slot-Loading iMac/iMac DV

Like the original iMac models, the slot-loading iMacs have a compartment to one side where any ports are located (although Apple did elect to remove the door from the compartment). These ports include audio line in and out ports, the two USB ports, the 10/100Base-T Ethernet port, the internal modem phone jack, and (on iMac DV models) the two FireWire ports. The ports compartment also includes the reset and programmer's buttons. But unlike the earlier iMacs, these are actual buttons and do not require the use of a paper clip when being pressed. Figure 1-16 shows the ports compartment of an iMac DV computer.

Figure 1-16
The ports in an
iMac DV computer.

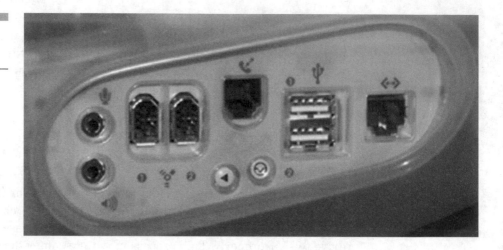

The iMac DV computers also include a VGA monitor port that allows
you to connect an external monitor to the computer. This monitor then
mirrors the built-in display of the iMac. This port is not in the ports compartment. Rather, it is located on the underside of rear of the iMac. It is
covered by a piece of hard plastic with several round holes. This cover can
be removed simply by prying on the indented edge with a flathead screwdriver. Apple also provides a separate plastic piece with a hole for the
monitor port that can be put on if you expect to use an external monitor
with the iMac. The location of the monitor port is shown in Figure 1-17.

A Quick Look under the Hood of the Slot-Loading iMac/iMac DV

As with the earlier iMac models, accessing major components requires
you to tip the iMac forward onto its front (screen) surface. Rather than
removing the entire motherboard assembly, a simple door on the bottom
of the case provides access to the RAM slots and the slot for the AirPort
wireless networking card on the second-generation iMac models. This
door is secured with a large plastic screw the color of the iMac, as shown
in Figure 1-18. You can release this screw by turning it with a coin such
as a quarter. With the door open, you can see the two RAM slots (one of
which contains a RAM module in a factory-standard iMac) and AirPort
card slot above them, as shown in Figure 1-19.

Figure 1-17
The location of the
iMac' video out port,
with the optional
cover that allows
access to the port.

The only components beyond the RAM and AirPort card slots that you are likely to need to access on a slot-loading iMac are the hard drive and CD-ROM or DVD-ROM drive. To access these components, you need to first remove the plastic panel that covers the bottom of the iMac.

To do this, you first need to remove the two screws by the flip-up foot of the iMac, as indicated in Figure 1-20. You then need to remove the plastic

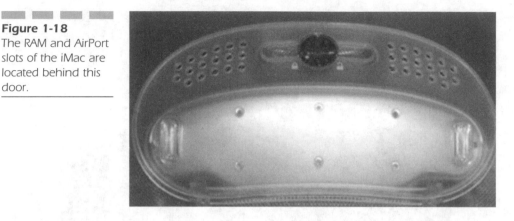

Figure 1-19   The RAM and AirPort card slots of the iMac.

Figure 1-20 These are two of the four screws that secure the bottom panel of the iMac.

panel that covers the video out port. There are two screws beneath this panel that also need to be removed, as shown in Figure 1-21. Once these screws have been removed, you can take off the plastic panel. Begin at the top (or rear) of the iMac near the Apple logo and work downward, as shown in Figure 1-22.

Underneath the bottom cover of the iMac, there is an electromagnetic interference (EMI) shield that must also be removed. The EMI shield is held on by the six screws indicated in Figure 1-23. Be careful when removing or replacing these screws, as they are very small and can easily fall down into the iMac and become difficult, if not impossible, to retrieve. With the screws removed you can then remove the EMI shield, working from the bottom (or front of the iMac) upward. With the EMI shield removed, you need to remove any installed RAM modules and the AirPort card, if one is installed.

Once the RAM modules and AirPort card are removed, you can easily access the carrier unit that contains the hard drive and CD-ROM or

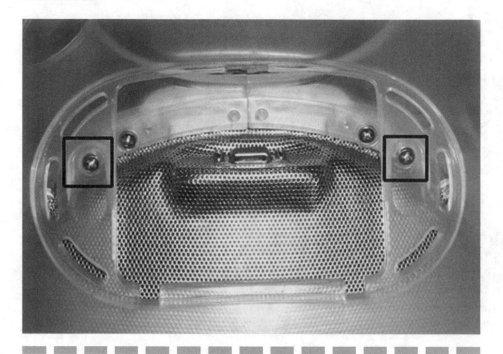

Figure 1-21   These are the other screws that secure the bottom panel of the iMac.

DVD-ROM drive. Before removing the carrier, you need to disconnect the data cables leading to both drives and the power connector attached to the hard drive. The carrier is held in place by four screws, as indicated in Figure 1-24. With the four screws removed and the cables disconnected, you can lift the carrier out of the computer.

The hard drive and the CD/DVD-ROM drive are secured by mounting screws on the bottom and sides of the carrier, respectively.

Access to the motherboard, internal modem card, display, and power supply of the slot-loading iMacs is considered beyond the scope of this book. As with the earlier iMacs, this is because accessing these components can be very challenging and presents a risk to users attempting such work. In addition, only Apple Authorized Service Centers can purchase such replacement components from Apple.

Figure 1-22
Remove the bottom
cover from the iMac.

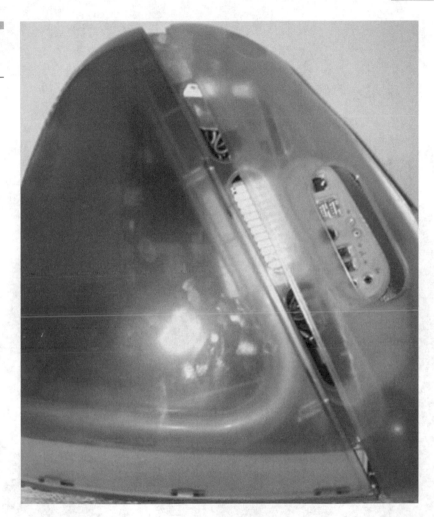

Caution

As you will read in the Chapter 3, there are many areas of the current
Macintosh computers that Apple does not want anyone other than Apple
Authorized Service Centers touching. Performing some of the procedures
described in this chapter may void an Apple warranty. See future chapters for specific procedures and the risk they pose to a Mac's warranty
coverage.

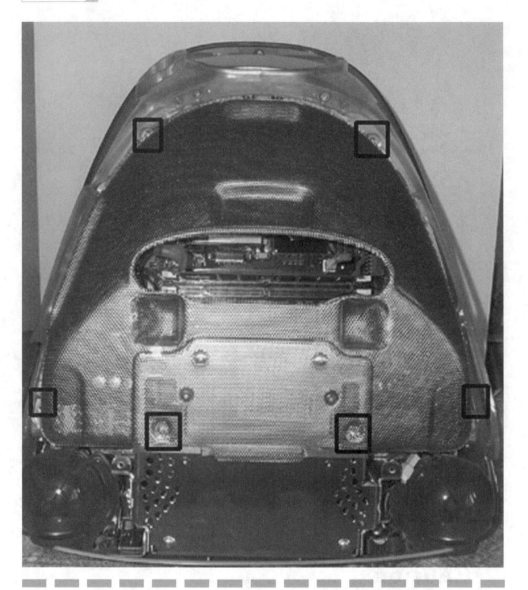

Figure 1-23   The EMI shield is held in place by these six screws.

Figure 1-24 The screws that hold the hard drive and CD/DVD-ROM drive carrier in place are recessed slightly and indicated by the white circles in this figure.

Inside the PowerBooks and the iBook

Chapter 1 introduced you to the desktop Macs covered by this book and showed you how to access their various internal components, which you might have the need or desire to replace. This chapter continues a similar exploration of the portable Macs covered in this book.

Note: It is extremely important that before you access any internal components of a portable Mac, you unplug the Mac from its AC adapter and remove its battery (or batteries). You should also remove any expansion bay modules from PowerBooks before beginning any internal access.

What Portable Macs Are Covered?

This book contains information specific to only the Macintosh computers released after the original iMac in 1998. This means that detailed information on portable Macs is limited to the iBook, the PowerBooks released in February of 2000 with built-in FireWire ports, and the PowerBooks released in May of 1999, which have a built-in SCSI port (although both are technically named the PowerBook G3, along with several earlier PowerBook models). The two PowerBook models covered are often referred to as the PowerBook G3—Bronze keyboard and the PowerBook G3-FireWire.

The PowerBook G3—Bronze Keyboard with a SCSI Port

The PowerBook G3 models from 1999 were designed similarly to the earlier PowerBook G3 computers; however, they were designed to be lighter and more comfortable to carry. They were the first PowerBooks to include built-in USB ports and the first to ship without a serial port. These PowerBooks were available in two basic models, differing only in the speed of the G3 processor they contained and whether or not they shipped with a CD-ROM drive or a DVD-ROM drive. The drive is an expansion bay module that can be used by both models, but only the higher-end version included the ability to view DVD movies. Table 2-1 lists the specifications of these PowerBook computers.

TABLE 2-1

PowerBook G3—
Bronze Keyboard
Specifications

Processor type: G3

Processor speed: 333 or 400 MHz

Backside cache: 512 K (333-MHZ processor models); 1 MB (400-MHZ processor models)

Installed RAM: 64 MB standard (custom configurations could be ordered)

RAM slots: 2 (one used by factory-installed RAM)

Maximum possible RAM: 384 MB

Video RAM: 8 MB

Standard hard drive: 4-GB IDE (custom configurations could be ordered)

24X CD-ROM (333-MHz Models) or 4X DVD-ROM drive (400-MHz models); expansion bay module

v.90 56-Kbps internal modem

Expansion Slots: Type II PC Card slot, expansion bay connector

Battery type: lithium ion (rated for 5 hours of use maximum per battery)

Built-in display: 14.1-inch active-matrix LCD

Dimensions: $1.7 \times 10.4 \times 12.7$

Weight: 5.9 lbs.

Ports: Audio in/out, USB (2 ports), SCSI, 10/100Base-T Ethernet, S-video out, VGA monitor out, internal modem phone jack

Note: Only 400-MHz processor models included DVD video decoding hardware.

The PowerBook G3—Bronze Keyboard with FireWire Ports

The PowerBooks released in 2000 used a case design virtually identical to the PowerBooks released the year before. The major changes were that the new PowerBooks shipped with two FireWire ports built in rather than a SCSI port, the processor speeds were increased (and both models shipped with 1 MB of backside cache), the ability to add an AirPort card was added, and both computers began shipping with DVD-ROM drives and the support for DVD movie viewing. Table 2-2 lists the specifications of these PowerBooks.

TABLE 2-2

PowerBook G3—
FireWire
Specification

Processor type: G3

Processor speed: 400 or 500 MHz

Backside cache: 1 MB

Installed RAM: 64 MB standard (custom configurations can be ordered)

RAM slots: 2 (one used by factory-installed RAM)

Maximum possible RAM: 512 MB

Video RAM: 8 MB

Standard hard drive: 6-GB Ultra-ATA 66 (custom configurations can be ordered)

4X DVD-ROM drive (expansion bay module)

v.90 56-Kbps internal modem

Expansion slots: AirPort card socket, Type II PC Card slot, expansion bay connector

Battery type: Lithium ion (rated for 5 hours of use maximum per battery)

Built-in display: 14.1-inch active-matrix LCD

Dimensions: $1.7 \times 10.4 \times 12.7$

Weight: 5.7 lbs.

Ports: Audio in/out, USB (2 ports), FireWire (2 ports), 10/100Base-T Ethernet, S-video out, VGA monitor out, internal modem phone jack

The iBook

The iBook was released in September of 1999 and is aimed primarily at the consumer market, including students and home users, rather than the professional market. It was also the first Mac to ship with the ability to use Apple's AirPort wireless networking technology. The iBook was initially released in a single model that featured a 3.2-GB hard drive and 32 MB of RAM (and a choice of two colors: Tangerine and Blueberry). In February of 2000, however, Apple made some modifications to the iBook. This included increasing the built-in RAM to 64 MB and the stock hard drive to 6 GB. Apple also added an iBook Special Edition model that featured a graphite color and a faster processor (366 MHz). Table 2-3 lists the specifications of the iBook.

Differences from Desktop Macs

Although portable Macintosh computers use the same operating system and applications and also share much of the same hardware, there are some very important differences between portable and desktop Macs.

TABLE 2-3

iBook Specs

Processor type: G3

Processor speed: 300 MHz (366 MHz—iBook Special Edition)

Backside cache: 512 K

Installed RAM (built into motherboard): 32 MB or 64 MB

RAM slots: 1

Maximum possible RAM: 320 MB (requires 64-MB base RAM and latest firmware update from Apple)

Video RAM: 4 MB

Standard hard drive: 3.2 GB or 6.0 GB IDE

24X CD-ROM drive

v.90 56-Kbps internal modem

Expansion slots: AirPort card socket only

Battery type: Lithium ion (rated for 6 hours of use maximum)

Built-in display: 12.1-inch active-matrix LCD

Dimensions: 1.8 × 13.5 × 11.6

Weight: 6.7 lbs.

Ports: Audio out, USB (1 port), 10/100Base-T Ethernet, internal modem phone jack

These differences include features such as power management and batteries, the LCD displays used in PowerBook and iBook models, and specific types of hardware found only in PowerBook computers.

Power Management and Batteries

Desktop Macs receive a steady stream of electrical power from an electrical outlet. As you will read in Chapter 11, the Mac's power supply continually converts this power from an alternating current into a direct current and then distributes it to the various internal components of the Mac. The power supply is an internal component of a desktop Macintosh.

Portable Macs need to be able to function without being tied to an electrical outlet for power. To do this, they use rechargeable batteries as a power source, a feature not found in desktop computers. They also do not have the internal space for a large power supply to convert alternating current electricity from an outlet into direct current for internal components. On a portable Mac, an external AC adapter performs this function instead. As a result, there is no internal power supply of the type found on a desktop Mac, only a motherboard connection for the AC adapter to provide direct current power. Circuitry built into the motherboard then distributes the power directly to each internal component (such as hard drives, the display, and CD-ROM drives), as well as to the battery bay, which recharges the battery whenever the Mac is plugged in.

Sleep Mode   All Macs today support a low-power sleep mode. Although this mode saves power and monitor life on a desktop Mac, it has a more important function on portable Macs. When a portable Mac enters sleep mode, all the internal components are essentially shut down except for the computer's RAM. A very small trickle of power is used to maintain power to the RAM so that any data currently in use will be available to the computer when it is woken from sleep mode. In this desktop Macs differ because other components of the computer may be powered and active in a desktop Mac while it is in sleep mode.

Reset Buttons and Forced Restarts

Another important difference between desktop Macs and the current PowerBook and iBook computers is the use of the reset button. On a desktop Mac, the reset button is a button built into the front or side of the computer. When pressed, the Mac is forcibly restarted. This is usually done when the Mac has severely crashed or frozen and the traditional restart commands, which should be used under any circumstances other than a crash or freeze, cannot be accessed.

Portable Macs also include a reset button, but the reset button is used primarily to reset the Mac's power management circuitry and/or the Mac's PRAM data (see Chapter 10 for details). Pressing the reset button can be used to shut down a PowerBook or iBook if needed, but this is not the best way to restart the computer. Instead, users of portable Macs should press the Control and Command keys at the same time as the power button above the keyboard, which will cause the Mac to forcibly restart without resetting the power management or PRAM data. Longtime Mac users may remember using this on Macs that predate USB keyboards. Unfortunately, USB does not allow such a reset code to be built into today's external Mac keyboards.

PowerBook-Specific Hardware

There are two pieces of technology that are specific to PowerBook computers and are not included on any other Macintosh model (including the iBook): expansion bays and PC Card slots. Both of these technologies allow the PowerBook to be expanded easily with varying kinds of devices. The following is a brief overview of both expansion bays and PC Card slots. You can find detailed information on these technologies in Chapter 9.

Expansion Bays   The expansion bay is a specially designed connector built into the PowerBook that can be used to easily connect or disconnect a wide range of devices. Since the connector is internal to the PowerBook, any device inserted into it will behave as though it were an internal device. You can easily remove a device from the expansion bay and replace it with another device. Since the devices are internal to the PowerBook and rely on the PowerBook's battery (or AC adapter) for power, this makes expansion bay devices highly portable. The most common expansion bay device is the CD/DVD-ROM drive that is included with a PowerBook. Other common devices include hard drives and Zip and other removable-media drives. The expansion bay can also function as a second battery bay, allowing the PowerBook to use two batteries at once.

PC Card Slots   A PC Card is a device roughly the size of a thick credit card. PC Cards can be inserted into a slot in the side of the PowerBook. Once inserted, the PowerBook can access the device as though it were a built-in, internal feature. This provides PowerBooks with expandability similar to what PCI slots provide for desktop Power Macs. PC Cards can enable a wide range of features and functions. Some common functions can include adding SCSI or FireWire ports, adding a second modem, and adding specialized networking abilities. The PC Card slot itself is an internal component of the PowerBook.

Inside the PowerBook with a SCSI Port

The primary internal components that you'll find yourself wanting or needing access to on these PowerBooks are the processor module where the two RAM slots are located, the hard drive, and possibly the modem card. It's very unlikely that most users or technicians will routinely need to access other parts of the computer. In addition to the internal components, there are some other areas of the PowerBook you may want to familiarize yourself with. These include the external ports along the back

Figure 2-1   The PowerBook's ports. From left to right: Audio in, audio out/headphones, USB (2 ports), 10/100Base-T Ethernet, SCSI, S-video output, VGA monitor output, and modem phone jack.

Figure 2-2
The "battery" side of the PowerBook, including the battery bay and the PC Card slot.

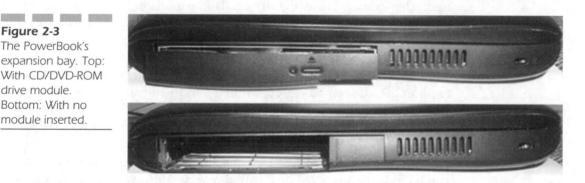

Figure 2-3
The PowerBook's expansion bay. Top: With CD/DVD-ROM drive module. Bottom: With no module inserted.

of the PowerBook (see Figure 2-1), the PC Card slot, and battery bay on one side (Figure 2-2), and the expansion bay on the other side (Figure 2-3).

A Quick Look under the Keyboard

To gain access to virtually all of the PowerBook's internal components, you only need to remove the keyboard. To do so, you release the two tabs (shown in Figure 2-4) that hold the keyboard in place. These are located in the row of half-sized function keys. The first tab is between the Esc and F1 keys, and the second tab is located between the F8 and F9 keys. To release the tabs, simply pull them gently toward the trackpad.

Once the tabs are released, lift the keyboard up slightly and the pull it toward the screen. If you can't lift the keyboard at this point, it is because

Figure 2-4   The tabs that secure the PowerBook's keyboard.

Figure 2-5   The PowerBook's keyboard locking screw.

the locking screw in the ports compartment on the back of the PowerBook is secured, as shown in Figure 2-5. You can release it using a flat-head screwdriver. There are a series of plastic hooks or tabs that hold the keyboard in place along the "bottom" edge where the trackpad is located. Pulling the keyboard toward the screen releases these hooks/tabs. Once it is free of these hooks/tabs, you can flip the keyboard over and rest it on the PowerBook's built-in wrist rests, as shown in Figure 2-6.

You now have access to the internals of the PowerBook. Before going any further, you should ground yourself properly as described in Chapter 3 to avoid damage to the delicate internal components from a static electrical discharge.

As you can see in Figure 2-6, the majority of the PowerBook's components are covered by a metal heat sink. To get at any of the major components, you need to remove this heat sink. It is held in place by the three screws also indicated in Figure 2-6. Once the screws are removed, lift the heat sink straight up and put it aside.

With the heat sink removed, most of the major PowerBook components will be visible. As shown in Figure 2-7, these components are (from left to right) the PC Card slot, the processor module (which has the RAM mounted on it), and the internal hard drive. Located just below the PC

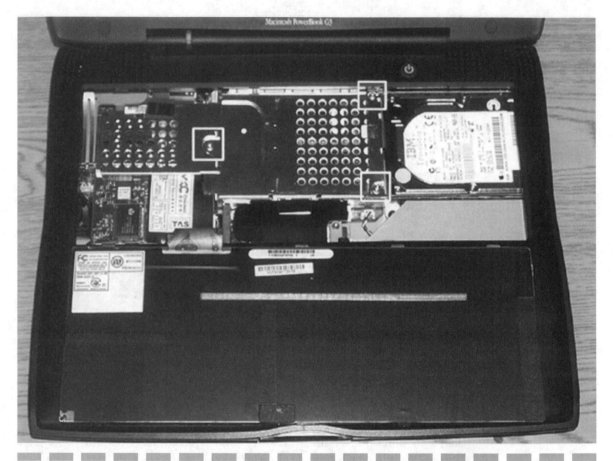

Figure 2-6   The heat sink covers much of the PowerBook's internals and is held in place by the three screws indicated.

Card slot is the internal modem card. Located just below the hard drive is the expansion bay. Located just below the processor module is the keyboard connector. For any work described in this book, you should have no reason to actually disconnect the keyboard cable.

Accessing the Processor Module and RAM Slots

As soon as the heat sink is removed, you have access to the daughtercard module that holds the processor and RAM slots. One RAM slot, shown in Figure 2-8, is located on the upper surface of the daughtercard module

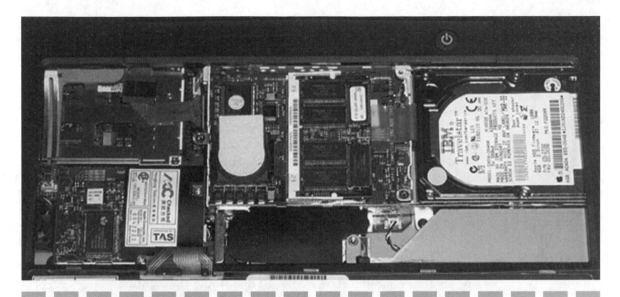

Figure 2-7   The primary internal components of the PowerBook revealed.

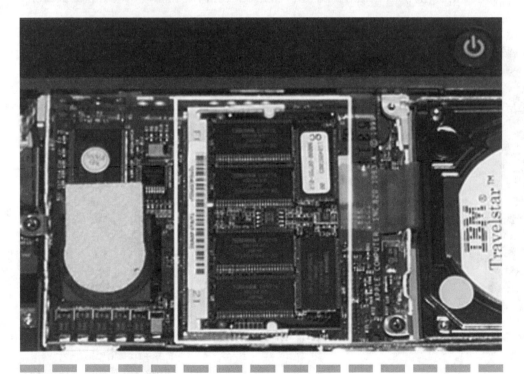

Figure 2-8   The RAM slot on the upper surface of the processor module.

and is easily accessible as soon as the heat sink is removed. Out of the factory, this slot may have a RAM module installed, but most likely it will not. Refer to Chapter 6 for information on the type of RAM used by these PowerBooks and how to install or remove a module into this slot.

The second RAM module is located on the underside of the processor card. To access it, you need to remove the processor module. Before doing this, make certain that you are grounded. The processor module is attached to the motherboard using a connector that is about ¾ inch long and ¼ inch wide. This connector is located in the lower right quadrant of the daughtercard. The daughtercard is also held in place by two tabs that fit into slots in the metal grating that surrounds the module. These tabs are along the leftmost edge.

To remove the daughtercard module, you should lift it gently to release it from the motherboard connector. Do so by carefully lifting on the rightmost edge of the card or by using a smooth and flat tool (preferably plastic or another nonconductive material) under just the rightmost edge and prying the card up very gently, as shown in Figure 2-9. Once the motherboard connector is released, you can lever the card up slightly and pull it out to the right so that the tabs are released from the slots in the metal grate.

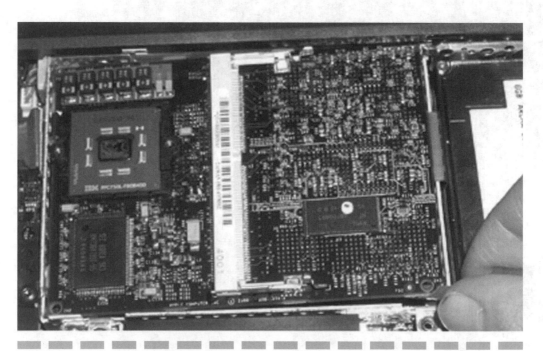

Figure 2-9   Removing the processor card.

Figure 2-10
The underside of the
processor card.

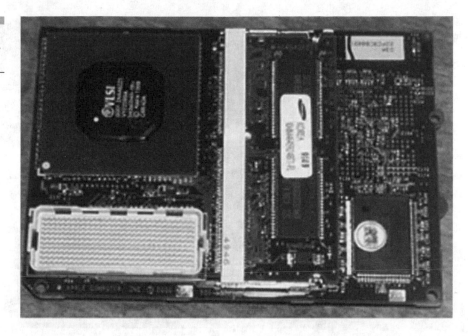

Once the daughtercard is removed, set it on a nonstatic surface. To access the underside RAM slot, simply flip the daughtercard over. *Note:* Removing the daughtercard in this manner can cause you to void a PowerBook's warranty. Figure 2-10 shows the underside of the processor card module.

When you are reinserting the daughtercard, be certain that the tabs fit into the same slots in the metal grate where they were initially inserted. Also, make sure that the processor card's connector is properly aligned and firmly seated into the motherboard connector. This may require it to be pressed down more than you would expect. If the daughtercard module is not fully seated in the motherboard connector, the Mac will not start up. It is also important that the plastic tab attached to the underside of the hard drive is not placed underneath the daughtercard.

Accessing the Hard Drive

Apple designed the hard drives on these PowerBooks to be removed and replaced rather easily. The hard drive is mounted in a metal mounting sled that needs to be removed with the hard drive. With the heat sink removed and with the processor, you can access the hard drive module easily. Pull up on the clear plastic tab, shown in Figure 2-11, that extends

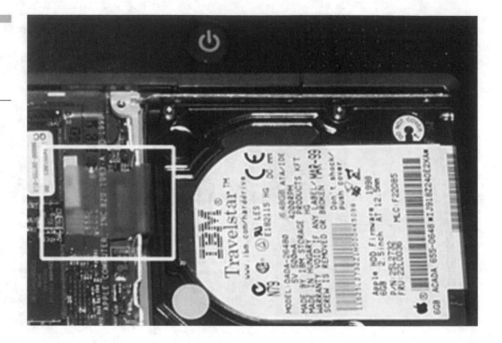

between the hard drive mounting sled and the processor module. This should pull up the left half of the hard drive's mounting sled (and the drive itself) enough for you to easily grasp the sides of the mounting bracket and lift it out.

Before lifting the mounting sled and drive out of the PowerBook, disconnect the cable that runs from the motherboard (under the processor card) to the mounting sled. If the plastic tab comes off when you pull (which happens occasionally), carefully grasp the leftmost section of the mounting sled with a pair of needle-nose pliers and pull it up until you can grasp the sides of the sled to lift it out.

To remove the hard drive from the mounting sled, you need to remove the four torx screws that secure the hard drive in place in the sled. These screws are located in each of the black plastic/rubber circles on the sled, as shown in Figure 2-12. Once the hard drive is removed from the mounting sled, you need to disconnect the hard drive cable from the connector on the mounting sled and pull it out of the slot, shown in Figure 2-13, in the bottom of the sled where it is secured.

When installing a new drive, remember to run the hard drive cable through the slot in the bottom of the mounting sled and connect it to the connector of the sled. When reinserting the mounting sled in the PowerBook, make sure that the alignment tabs on the bottom of the sled

Figure 2-12   The mounting screws of the PowerBook's hard drive.

Figure 2-13
The slot for the hard drive cable in the mounting sled.

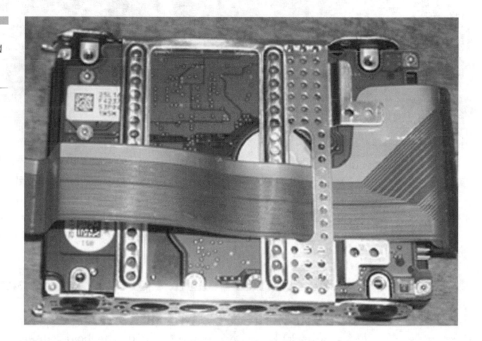

match up with alignment slots in the PowerBook. Also make sure that the clear plastic tab is placed over the heat sink and not under the heat sink or processor module.

Accessing the Modem Card

The internal modem card, shown in Figure 2-14, is plainly visible and easily accessible once the heat sink is removed. To remove the modem, all

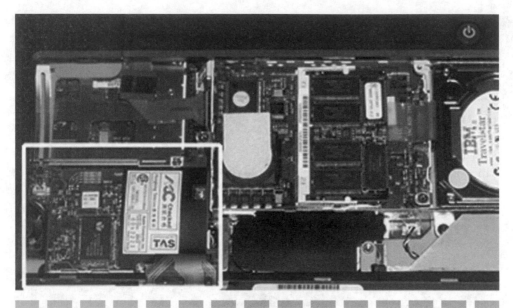

Figure 2-14 The location of the PowerBook's modem card.

you need to do is remove the two screws that hold it in place. Once the screws are removed, the modem card can be lifted directly up to release it from its connector. Once removed, the cable that connects to the phone jack in the back of the PowerBook can be easily disconnected.

The Motherboard, Ports, and Expansion Bay

Accessing the PowerBook's motherboard is considered beyond the scope of this book, because replacing the motherboard itself would require purchasing a replacement motherboard from Apple. This is something that can be done only by Apple Authorized Service Centers and not by individual Mac users, consultants, or technicians who are not employed by an Apple Authorized Service Center. Similarly, the connector for the expansion bay is a proprietary device and cannot be purchased by individuals.

Additionally, replacing the following ports of the PowerBook is beyond the scope of this book simply because these ports are built into the motherboard: the audio in and out, USB, Ethernet, FireWire, S-video out, and VGA monitor out. Also, the AC adapter port is built into the motherboard and considered beyond the scope of this book.

Inside the PowerBook with FireWire Ports

The PowerBooks with FireWire ports are strikingly similar to their earlier cousins. In fact, as you read through this section, you'll find that some areas are virtually identical. The primary internal components that you'll need access to on these PowerBooks are the processor module where the two RAM slots are located, the hard drive, the AirPort card socket, and possibly the modem card. It's very unlikely that you will routinely need to access other parts of the computer. In addition to the internal components, you may want to familiarize yourself with some other areas of the PowerBook, such as the external ports along the back of the PowerBook (see Figure 2-15). You may also want to be familiar with the PC Card slot and battery bay on one side and the expansion bay on the other side. These features are the same as described in the section for the earlier PowerBooks with a SCSI port (refer to Figures 2-2 and 2-3).

A Quick Look under the Keyboard

As with the PowerBook with a SCSI port, you can gain access to virtually all of the PowerBook's internal components by removing the keyboard. Again, this is done by releasing the two tabs that hold it in place. These are located in the row of half-sized function keys. The first tab is between the Esc and F1 keys, and the second tab is located between the F8 and F9 keys. To release the tabs, simply pull them gently toward the trackpad. Refer to Figure 2-4.

Figure 2-15   The PowerBook's ports. From left to right: Audio in, audio out/headphones, USB (2 ports), 10/100Base-T Ethernet, FireWire, S-video output, VGA monitor output, and modem phone jack.

Figure 2-16
The PowerBook's
keyboard locking
screw.

Once the tabs are released, lift the keyboard up slightly and the pull it toward the screen. If you can't lift the keyboard at this point, it is because the locking screw is secured. The locking screw on this PowerBook is located between the F4 and F5 keys, as shown in Figure 2-16. Again, you can release it using a flat-head screwdriver. A series of plastic hooks or tabs hold the keyboard in place along the "bottom" edge where the track-pad is located. Pulling the keyboard toward the screen releases these hooks/tabs. As with the earlier PowerBooks, once the keyboard is free of these hooks/tabs, you can flip it over and rest it on the PowerBook's built-in wrist rests.

You now have access to the internals of the PowerBook. Before going any further, you should ground yourself properly as described in Chapter 3 to avoid damage to the delicate internal components from a static electrical discharge.

There are a pair of heat sinks in these PowerBook models. The first is a metal grate that covers the processor module in the middle of the computer. It is secured with the two screws indicated in Figure 2-17. When this heat sink is removed, you have access to one of the RAM slots on the processor module. However, removing the processor module or accessing the internal modem card requires you to remove the other heat sink.

The second heat sink (see Figure 2-18) extends from the processor module, where it is held by two torx screws directly over the processor itself, in an L-shaped bar to a larger metal heat sink over the modem card, where it is secured with a single screw. Be extremely careful when removing or inserting the screws that are on the processor module itself and when removing the heat sink, as this part of the heat sink rest directly atop the PowerBook's processor. When the second heat sink is removed, you have complete access to the processor module and the internal modem.

With both heat sinks removed, most of the major PowerBook components will be visible. As shown in Figure 2-19, these components are

Figure 2-17   The first heat sink in these PowerBooks is held on by the two screws indicated here.

(clockwise from top left), the PC Card slot and AirPort socket (the AirPort card sits atop the PC Card slot), the processor module (which has the RAM mounted on it), the internal hard drive, the expansion bay, the keyboard connector, and the internal modem card. As with the earlier PowerBook, any work described in this book will not require you to actually disconnect the keyboard cable.

Accessing the Processor Module and RAM Slots

As soon as the first heat sink is removed, you have access to one of the RAM slots. This is the one that is located on the upper surface of the daughtercard module and is easily accessible, as shown in Figure 2-20. Out of the factory, this slot will almost never have a RAM module. Refer to Chapter 6 for information on the type of RAM used by these PowerBooks and how to install or remove a module into this slot.

The second RAM module is located on the underside of the processor

Figure 2-18 The second heat sink of the PowerBook is held in place by the three screws indicated here.

card. To access it, you need to remove the processor module. Before doing this, make certain that you are grounded. To remove the processor module, you need to remove the second heat sink, as described previously. Once both heat sinks are removed, you will have access to the processor module.

The processor module is attached to the motherboard using a connector that is about ¾ inch long and ¼ inch wide. This connector is located in the lower right quadrant of the daughtercard. The daughtercard is also held in place by two tabs that fit into slots in the metal grating that surrounds the module. These tabs are along the leftmost edge.

To remove the daughtercard module, lift it gently to release it from the motherboard connector. Do so by carefully lifting on the rightmost edge of the card or by using a smooth and flat tool (preferably plastic or

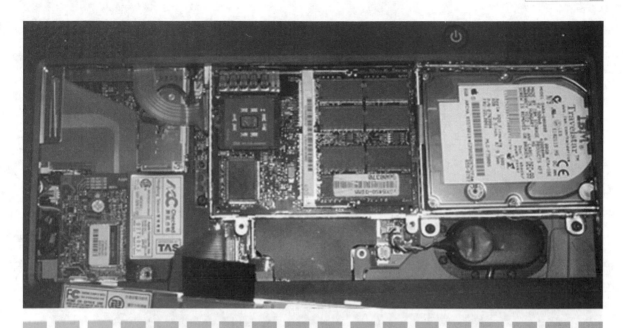

Figure 2-19   The primary internal components of the PowerBook revealed.

Figure 2-20
The RAM slot on the
upper surface of the
processor module.

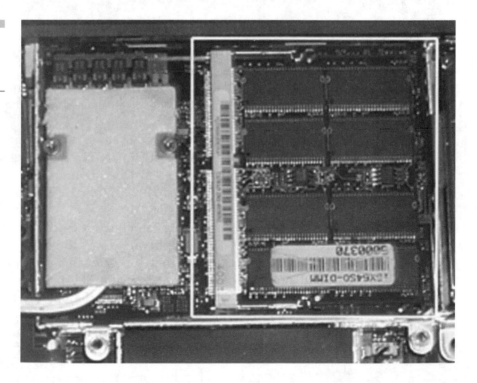

Figure 2-21   Removing the processor card.

another nonconductive material) under just the rightmost edge and prying the card up very gently, as shown in Figure 2-21. Once the motherboard connector is released, you can lever the card up slightly and pull it out to the right so that the tabs are released from the slots in the metal grate.

Once the daughtercard is removed, set it on a nonstatic surface. To access the underside RAM slot, simply flip the daughtercard over. *Note:* Removing the daughtercard in this manner can cause you to void a PowerBook's warranty. Figure 2-22 shows the underside of the daughtercard and the "lower" RAM slot.

When you are reinserting the daughtercard, be certain that the tabs fit into the same slots in the metal grate where they were initially inserted. Also make sure that the processor card's connector is firmly seated into the motherboard connector. This may require it to be pressed down more than you would expect. If the daughtercard module is not fully seated in the motherboard connector, the Mac will not start up. Also be sure not to place the plastic tab attached to the underside of the hard drive underneath the daughtercard or the heat sink.

■■■■ ■■■ ■■■ ■■

Figure 2-22
The underside of the
processor card.

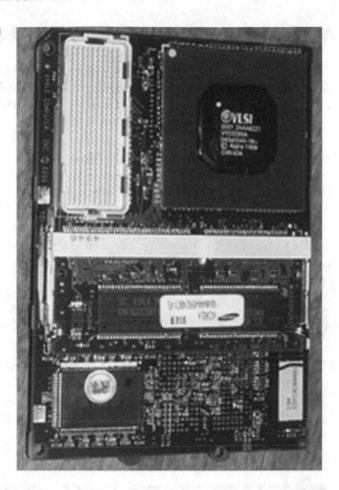

Accessing the Hard Drive

Because both the PowerBooks covered here feature the same case design,
access to the hard drive on both models is identical. To access the hard
drive of the PowerBooks with a FireWire port, follow the instructions in
the earlier section on accessing the hard drive in the PowerBook with a
SCSI port.

Accessing the AirPort Card Socket

The AirPort card socket is located directly atop the PC Card slot module, as indicated in Figure 2-23. The connector for the AirPort card is located under the lip of the PowerBook's case, along the left side of the PowerBook (directly above where the PC Card slot is on the outside of the PowerBook). The cable for attaching the AirPort card to the PowerBook's built-in antenna will be located to the left of the processor module and may be tucked under one of the ribbon cables.

Although you can locate the AirPort socket and cable without removing the first heat sink over the processor module, the space involved is quite tight, and you need to remove the first heat sink (but not the second) in order to install or remove an AirPort card. Chapter 33 includes instructions for installing and setting up an AirPort card in the PowerBook.

Accessing the Modem Card

The modem card of these PowerBooks is located beneath the bulk of the second heat sink. To remove it, you first need to remove the second heat sink as described previously. Once the second heat sink is removed, there will be a black screw that holds a narrow piece of black plastic with a series of holes in place next to the processor module and AirPort card

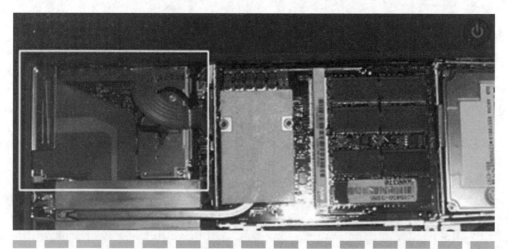

Figure 2-23   The AirPort card socket location. Note the black AirPort antenna cable.

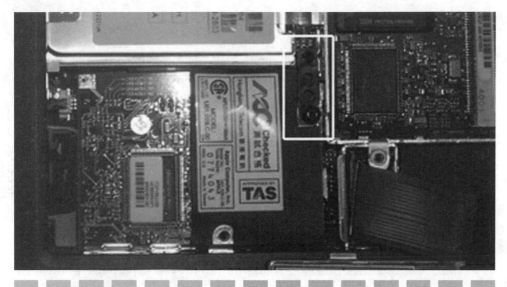

Figure 2-24   The PowerBook's modem card before being removed. Notice the black plastic piece.

socket. Figure 2-24 shows the modem card after the second heat sink has been removed. You need to remove this screw and the black plastic (note how the plastic piece was inserted when removing so you can reinsert it in the same orientation). You can now remove the modem card by lifting it up and disconnecting the cable leading to the phone jack.

The Motherboard, Ports, and Expansion Bay

Accessing the PowerBook's motherboard is considered beyond the scope of this book. As with any Mac, replacing the motherboard itself would require purchasing a replacement motherboard from Apple. This is something that can be done only by Apple Authorized Service Centers and not by individual Mac users, consultants, or technicians who are not employed by an Apple Authorized Service Center. As with the earlier PowerBooks, the connector for the expansion bay is a proprietary device and cannot be purchased by individuals.

Additionally, replacing the following ports of the PowerBook are beyond the scope of this book simply because these ports are built into the motherboard: the audio in and out, USB, Ethernet, FireWire, S-video out, and VGA monitor out.

Inside the iBook

There are only two internal components of the iBook that you should really consider accessing: the RAM slot and AirPort card socket. Apple has designed the iBook so that it is extremely easy to gain access to these. You may also want to familiarize yourself with the ports on one side of the iBook (shown in Figure 2-25).

Accessing any other components of the iBook (including the modem slot, CD-ROM drive, hard drive, motherboard, and internal ports) is considered beyond the scope of this book. Apple discourages even Apple certified technicians from attempting to access any of these components including the hard drive and modem card. This is because accessing any internal components of the iBook besides the RAM and AirPort sockets requires that you literally disassemble the entire iBook. The sheer complexity of this task makes it something that even experienced Mac technicians will find daunting, and damaging the iBook in the process is exceedingly possible. Should you need to replace any of these components, you are advised to return the iBook in question to Apple directly for service. Keep in mind, however, as mentioned, even Apple Authorized Service Centers are discouraged from attempting such work.

Under the iBook's Keyboard

A quick look inside the iBook's means removing the keyboard and accessing the AirPort card socket and RAM slot. To remove the iBook's keyboard, release the three tabs at the edge of the keyboard nearest the screen. The first tab is located between the Esc and F1 keys, the second

Figure 2-25   The iBook's ports. From left to right: Modem phone jack, 10/100 base T Ethernet, USB, audio out/headphones.

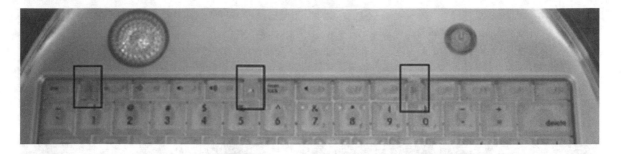

Figure 2-26   The iBook's keyboard release tabs.

between the F4 and F5 keys, and the third between the F8 and F9 keys. These tabs are indicated in Figure 2-26. As with the PowerBook computers, lift the keyboard up slightly and pull it toward the screen to release it from the hooks/tabs that secure it along the opposite edge. Flip the keyboard upside down on the built-in wrist rests.

Located directly in the center of the space beneath the keyboard is the metal bracket on which the AirPort card rests (the socket itself is underneath the lip of the case right behind the trackpad). This bracket is held in place by two screws, indicated in Figure 2-27. To access the RAM expansion slot, you need to remove the bracket. Once the bracket is removed, the RAM slot is perfectly visible and accessible.

Accessing the AirPort Card Socket

When you remove the iBook's keyboard, the space for the AirPort card is immediately visible, as shown in Figure 2-27. The lip of the iBook's case obscures the socket for the AirPort card's connection. It is directly behind the trackpad. The cable from the iBook's built-in antenna should also be visible, though it may be tucked under the wire that is used to hold the AirPort card securely in place. Inserting the AirPort card into the socket can be accomplished without removing any other part of the iBook and is described in Chapter 33.

Accessing the RAM Slot

The iBook has a single slot for adding RAM (unlike the PowerBooks, which have two slots). Out of the factory, there will be no RAM module installed in this slot. To access the RAM slot, you need to remove the

Figure 2-27   The AirPort card bracket, held in place by the screws indicated.

metal bracket on which the AirPort card rests. If an AirPort card is installed, you need to remove it first. Removing the bracket requires that you first remove the two screws indicated in Figure 2-27. Once these screws are removed, simply lift the bracket up and out (along with the wire that secures the AirPort card). As you can see in Figure 2-28, the RAM slot is clearly visible in the opening beneath the bracket. Refer to Chapter 6 for the correct type of RAM to be used in the iBook and how to install it into the slot.

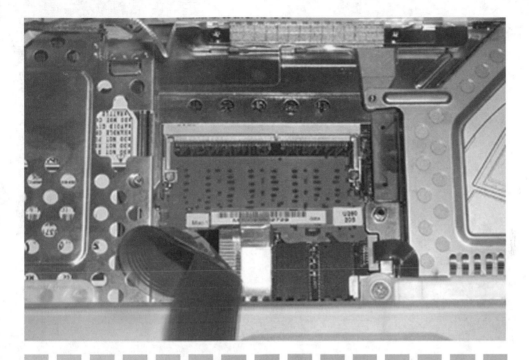

Figure 2-28   The iBook's single RAM slot.

Caution

As you will read in the next chapter, there are many areas of the current Macintosh computers that Apple does not want anyone other than Apple Authorized Service Centers touching. Performing any of the procedures described in this chapter with the exception of installing an AirPort card and RAM into the iBook's single RAM slot or the RAM slot on the upper surface of a PowerBook's processor card module can void a Mac's factory warranty as well as any AppleCare extended service agreement for the Mac.

CHAPTER 3

Before
Beginning
Repairs

Before you can begin solving any problem with a Macintosh, you need to understand what the problem is. You need to observe the problem to determine when it's occurring, what factors are common to each occurrence, and what you are doing when it occurs.

Some people find it helpful to keep a notebook at their desk and write down everything that could be the symptom of a problem. While I think that may be a bit excessive, the principal behind it is a sound one because it involves being aware of just what symptoms are presenting themselves. Before you go rushing off to try any solution, you must know exactly what you're dealing with. Otherwise, you might overlook an obvious and simple solution, or you might even make matters worse by trying to fix things that aren't broken. Figure 3-1 illustrates the basic steps involved in the diagnostic process, from careful observation to solving the problem.

Isolating the Problem

Observing as much as you can about a problem leads right into the first step of solving it: Define as accurately as possible what is happening. In defining the problem, you isolate the various possibilities of the cause. Each of these possibilities can then be tested in a systematic fashion. This allows you to solve the problem more efficiently than if you were to simply make random guesses as to what the problem was to begin with.

Figure 3-1

The main steps in the diagnostic process: observe, isolate, define, verify, and solve.

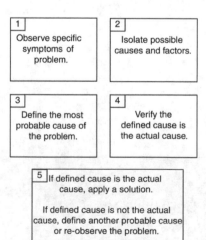

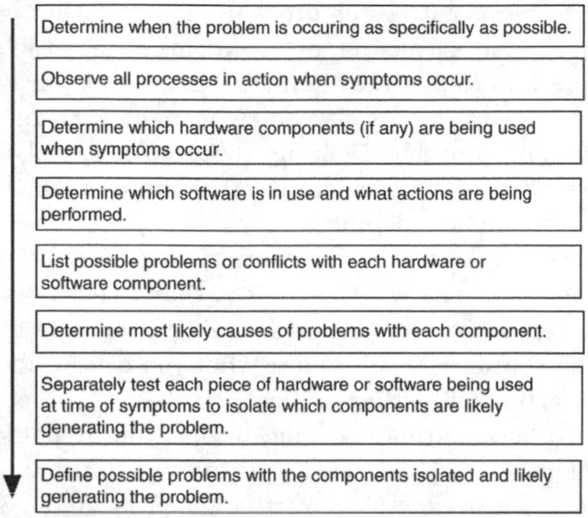

Figure 3-2
The steps in isolating
a problem.

Determine when the problem is occuring as specifically as possible.
Observe all processes in action when symptoms occur.
Determine which hardware components (if any) are being used when symptoms occur.
Determine which software is in use and what actions are being performed.
List possible problems or conflicts with each hardware or software component.
Determine most likely causes of problems with each component.
Separately test each piece of hardware or software being used at time of symptoms to isolate which components are likely generating the problem.
Define possible problems with the components isolated and likely generating the problem.

To isolate the problem and possible causes, observe when the problem is occurring, what error messages (if any) are displayed, what applications are in use when the problem occurs, and so forth. Once you know what individual tasks are occurring or what devices are in use when a problem is presenting itself, you can go about looking at each of them to determine if one of them is the cause of the problem. If so, you can then move on to determining exactly what the problem with the given piece of hardware or software is. Figure 3-2 shows the individual steps involved in isolating a problem.

Defining and Verifying the Problem

Once you've isolated the problem to a given set of causes or to a given selection of software and/or hardware, the next step is to try and define exactly what is happening to cause the problem. This may be something you can figure out from past experience, or you may have to look for additional information on the software or hardware in question. The majority of this book is organized into specific areas of the Mac. Once you know that the problem involves, say, a SCSI chain or hard drive or USB device specifically, you can refer to the chapters specific to those areas for additional information.

Although isolating the problem tells you what isn't functioning properly and what is causing the symptoms of the problem, it doesn't answer the question of why that item (for instance, a hardware component such as a keyboard, or a software component such as an application) isn't functioning properly. Defining the problem involves isolating the item, observing how the problem is manifesting itself, and determining why the problem is happening.

Once you have this hypothetical basis for the problem, you test the hypothesis to see whether or not that hypothesis is correct. This can mean replacing a component, running a software diagnostic, or performing the appropriate solution to what you believe the underlying cause is. These action will either confirm your belief (and possibly solve the problem at the same time) or indicate that your hypothesis was incorrect (at which point you begin looking at the symptoms and observations again).

A very basic example of verifying a problem like this is as follows: Say you notice that one of the applications you recently added to your hard drive shows a generic icon. Your immediate conclusion would be that the desktop file is corrupted. Therefore, your solution is to rebuild the desktop. Here, the conclusion is defining the problem. Actually rebuilding the desktop allows you to verify if this was the problem. If the application has a custom icon after your rebuild the desktop, then you have verified that your definition of the problem was correct, and you've solved the problem at the same time.

A more involved example would be the Finder crashing as soon as startup is completed and freezing the Mac completely. Since you recently installed some new extensions, you decide that must be the problem. You restart with extensions off to verify that this is the case. The Finder still crashes. In this case, your definition of the problem was not verified. This means you need to rethink the situation, but you are a step closer to a solution because you know one issue that you first suspected is not the problem. This further isolates the problem, making it easier to define another cause. Your next thought is that the Finder's preferences file has become corrupt. You start from a Mac OS CD, delete the Finder preferences file on the hard drive in question, and restart. The Finder launches normally without any problems. This time you've verified that your definition of the problem was correct.

In the course of troubleshooting a Mac, you may find yourself going through this process several times: defining what you think is the problem, attempting to solve or verify it, and discovering that what you thought was the problem actually wasn't. Be patient; not all problems are obvious, and some are easily confused. Also, always check the obvious things first. You don't want to spend half a day trying to determine why an external hard drive isn't working only to discover it wasn't plugged in properly. More times than most Mac users or technicians want to admit, the solution was right there in front of them, but it was so obvious that they thought it couldn't possibly be something they missed or forgot.

Types of Problems

The Macintosh consists of both the physical components of the computer, such as the processor, hard drive, and the software that is run on those components. The hardware would be effectively useless without the software to control it and to present the Mac OS. The software would be equally useless without the hardware to run it. This combination is seamless when the computer is running, with both the hardware and software working in concert to deliver the Macintosh user experience. The trick is that this seamlessness quickly disappears when you have to do any amount of troubleshooting.

Hardware problems involve physical components. These components can wear out, break down, be physically damaged, and be connected to each other improperly. When any of this happens, the component in question, and possibly the entire computer, will cease to work as intended.

Software problems, on the other hand, are more subtle. These problems involve lines of code that either don't work as they were designed to, conflict with other lines of code, or become altered and unintelligible. When software problems set in, the computer will usually still function to one degree or another, but specific actions may fail, and behavior may become erratic.

This division of the basic types of Mac problems can be as clear as a summer day with some problems (such as a hard drive not being recognized or an application crashing when you try to enter certain characters from the keyboard). However, it can also be a good deal murkier at times (such as when you are unable to capture video from a source that worked normally the day before). Isolating a problem as either hardware or software lets you know whether to spend your energy disabling extensions and trashing preferences or checking to be sure cables and expansion cards are installed properly. The following two sections discuss what indicates a hardware problem, and what indicates a software problem, as well as the general types of both problems

Hardware Problems

Hardware problems are, as a rule, simpler to recognize than software problems, though the sheer number of hardware problem types dwarfs the few categories of software problems. Hardware problems occur when a piece of hardware doesn't work properly. With the exception of internal components such as the hard drive, RAM, motherboard, and a video circuitry of the Mac, these problems will usually manifest themselves when you try to use a given device. If the device doesn't work, there's a problem with it. The internal components of the Mac are actually tested at startup, so if they are at fault, you will generally know it right away (although it is possible for some problems to escape these self-tests).

Hardware problems can run the gamut from devices being unplugged, to not being configured properly, not having proper cabling, actually being physically damaged and unable to work, being electrically damaged, and not having a properly configured driver. The first two sections of this book are devoted to various hardware components (internal and external) that may be used on a Mac. Each chapter deals with how these components work and what can go wrong with them. If you suspect a device isn't working properly, refer to the appropriate chapter.

Although hardware problems can involve many specific types of issues, the following are common problems that can occur when physical damage of the device itself is not at fault: cabling, power, improper installation, incompatibilities, and driver problems.

Cabling problems can include loose cables, damaged cables, cables that are longer than the maximum allowed for a specific type of device, using the wrong type of cabling, or using low-quality cables. One of the first things to check when a device isn't working is the cabling. It can be the simplest problem to solve and is often one of the most easily overlooked. Always make sure to use good-quality cables and ensure that you are using them appropriately.

Power problems generally mean the device isn't plugged in properly. For external components, plugging in a device can be fairly simple. However, USB (universal serial bus) and FireWire devices that draw power directly from the port on the computer that they are attached to can require more power than is available at that port in order to function. To function properly, internal devices need to be able to get enough power from the computer's power supply. This means that they need to be connected to the power supply properly and that the power supply needs to be capable of providing power to each device inside the computer, both in the actual amount of power required and through the appropriate power connectors and cables.

Improperly installed components may not function at all, or they may not function as intended. It is important to install both internal and external components properly, using the proper cabling, drivers, and connectors and following any rules for that kind of device. Not doing so can lead to damage to your Mac. Often an improperly installed device can be obvious when you look at the device (an expansion card that isn't fully seated or a loose IDE cable), but some things can be far from obvious (an improperly terminated SCSI chain or an IDE [Integrated Device Electronics] device with jumpers/dip switches not set properly). You may need to look at the installation manual to ensure that a device is installed correctly for a given Macintosh.

Sometimes devices, or the drivers needed to use them, simply are incompatible with a computer. Incompatibility can be with either other hardware or with software. If a device is incompatible with your computer or with another device installed on your computer, there usually is little that can be done to force the two to work together. Known incompatibilities should be mentioned in the documentation for a piece of hardware. If you think a device is incompatible with your computer, you may be risking damage by trying to force it to be used with it.

Driver problems deserve special mention here. Drivers are actually software components, usually stored as extensions in the Mac's System Folder, that enable the Mac to be able to recognize, control, and communicate with pieces of hardware. Virtually every piece of hardware outside of the processor and RAM needs a driver for it to function. Because drivers are software, they can suffer from the same types of problems as other pieces of software. However, because drivers deal directly with hardware, they can be thought of as both Mac OS software problems and hardware problems, depending on the situation.

The following sections look at specific pieces of hardware and the symptoms that indicate a problem, as well the common problems that these pieces of hardware are likely to experience. For more-detailed information on each piece of hardware and the problems it is prone to, refer to the appropriate chapter later in this book.

Power Supply Problems   The power supply of a computer converts the power from the wall outlet into something the internal components need in order to function. A problem with the power supply will disrupt the ability of the computer to operate, often preventing the computer from starting up at all.

The most common power supply problem is that the Mac simply will not start up. The fan will not turn on, the hard drive won't begin spinning, and the display will not light up. In less severe cases, the Mac may begin to start up and then mysteriously sit there with the fan going and possibly an internal drive spinning. Less frequently, the Mac will simply shut down or lose all power for no apparent reason. Occasionally, after installing a new internal drive, one or more drives will cease to function because there is not enough power for all the internal devices.

The first step in dealing with a power supply problem is to make sure that the power outlet itself is not the culprit. Make sure there is not a tripped circuit breaker or power outage cutting off power to the outlet the Mac is plugged into. If that doesn't seem to be the problem, try plugging the Mac into another outlet to be certain. If the Mac still refuses to start up or function properly, you can test the power supply with a multimeter (this is described and illustrated in Chapter 11) to determine if it is capable of delivering the power required by the computer. If only specific internal devices are affected, ensure they are plugged in and connected properly. You can test each device's power cable with a multimeter, and you can selectively remove internal devices to determine if you are overtaxing the power supply's capabilities.

Motherboard Problems   The motherboard connects all the internal components of the Mac to each other. If it becomes damaged, the computer will not be able to function properly (if it functions at all). The Mac's startup self-tests should identify motherboard problems at startup and alert you with either a Sad Mac icon, a series of beeps instead of the startup chime, or the sound of a car crash. These can also be symptoms of other problems as well, such as badly installed or damaged RAM, an improperly installed processor, or damaged ROM (read-only memory) chips. If the problem is with either the motherboard or with the ROM chips, there is little solution with the exception of replacing the motherboard. This can only be done by an Apple Authorized Service Center, because Apple does not make these components available to anyone else.

If at startup a Sad Mac icon is displayed instead of a smiling Mac and if any but the following characters appear as the last four digits in the first line of code under the Sad Mac, it is likely a motherboard problem: 0001, 0006, 0007, 0009, 000B (000E can also indicate a motherboard problem or a RAM problem). To be certain, however, attempt to start up the Mac from a separate startup disk, such as a Mac OS CD. If, at startup, you hear a series of either four or five beeps, this also indicates a motherboard or ROM problem (three or fewer beeps indicates a problem with RAM).

It is possible that these self-test failures may indicate problems with expansion or processor upgrade cards. [Before completely assuming the fault is in the motherboard, you should also try removing any PCI or other expansion cards and reinstalling your original processor if you have installed a processor upgrade card.]

Processor Problems   The processor is the heart of the Mac. If it is damaged or installed incorrectly, the Mac will not start up. The Mac will likely either refuse to do anything, leaving the internal hard drives spinning and the fan going but showing no other signs of activity, or it will display a Sad Mac icon or emit a series of beeps similar to what it would do if there was a motherboard problem.

[As with a suspected motherboard problem, you should attempt to start up from an alternate disk to verify the problem is hardware in nature.] If you receive the same results, then it is safe to assume that you have either a processor or motherboard problem. If you have recently installed a processor upgrade, attempt to reinstall your original processor. It is possible that you may have either incorrectly installed the upgrade or that the upgrade is not supported by your Macintosh.

RAM Problems [If there is a problem with the RAM installed in a Mac, the problem will often be caught by the Mac's startup RAM test.] If the Mac begins to start up but then displays an error message indicating that the RAM is either damaged or not installed properly, emits one to three beeps instead of starting up, or displays a Sad Mac icon where the final four characters of the first line of code beneath the Sad Mac are 0002, 0003, 0004, 0005, or 000E (as mentioned, 000E can also indicate a motherboard problem), a RAM problem is indicated. If damaged RAM is not detected by the Mac's self-tests, it may cause apparently random crashes without any noticeable cause. If this is occurring, you can test the RAM with a utility such as Newer Technology's GaugePro or MicroMat's TechTool Pro.

If a RAM problem is indicated, the first thing to do is to ensure that the correct type of RAM was installed in the computer and to ensure that it was installed correctly (see Chapter 6). If all RAM appears to be installed correctly and is the correct type, removing all modules installed and then replacing them until startup is successful will allow you to determine which module is damaged. If the Mac displays an error message regarding the RAM but still starts up, a RAM testing utility can also determine the damaged RAM.

Hard Drive Problems Any number of problems can happen with a hard drive, but the most serious will manifest when you try to start up the Mac. In the most severe cases of hard drive damage or corruption, the drive will not be recognized at all by the Mac and you will see a flashing "?", indicating the Mac cannot start up from the internal hard drive (or the Mac may start up from another hard drive instead). When starting from an alternate disk, you may find that the Mac tells you that it cannot read the hard drive and it asks if you want to initialize (reformat) it. In other cases, the hard drive may not be recognized at all by the Mac (no error, no icon, no sign at all that the drive is even attached to the Mac). Hard drive problems can indicate that the mechanical elements of the drive are not functioning or that the invisible files on the drive that control how and where data is stored on the disk have become corrupted.

If the hard drive does not mount at all and the Mac does not display any error messages regarding it, the drive may not be connected properly or the drive may not be powered properly. First, use a utility such as Adaptec's free SCSIProbe utility or the free Mount Everything utility to attempt to mount the drive manually. It is possible to format a hard drive such that it will not be mounted automatically on startup.

If a mounting utility is unable to detect the drive, it is most likely either not connected properly or physically damaged. Check to be sure it is connected and powered properly. For external drives, make sure they are plugged in, turned on, and attached correctly. For SCSI drives, make sure that all rules regarding SCSI IDs and termination are being followed (see Chapter 12).

For internal drives, ensure that the drive's power cable is securely connected, as well as the ribbon cable connecting the drive to the motherboard or SCSI card. Again, be sure to check that all SCSI rules are followed. If you are using two IDE drives on a single IDE controller/cable, check to be sure one is appropriately set as the slave drive and the other as the master drive. If the drive is not even spinning, chances are that either it is not attached to the power supply correctly, that the power supply isn't capable of powering all the devices attached to it, or that the cable to the power supply may be damaged (all of which can be verified as described in Chapter 11). If the drive is connected and powered properly but is not recognized at all, it is possible that one of the drive's internal components or its control circuitry is damaged and will need to be replaced.

If the Mac displays an error message that the drive is unreadable or is not a Macintosh disk, this indicates damage to the invisible files and directory structures that record what files are stored on a hard drive and where they are stored. This damage is not to the physical parts of the hard drive, but to the important data stored on the drive that controls how information is stored on that drive. Even if the dialog asks if you want to reformat the drive, don't do so. In many cases, a hard drive repair utility can repair such damage to the drive's invisible files and directory structures. Several utilities are on the market, and you should try at least two or three before giving up and reformatting the drive. Chapter 5 includes an overview of many of the utilities on the market, including Apple's free Disk First Aid utility that accompanies every Mac OS CD. If the utility can repair the damage, have it do so. Then run the utility (or utilities if you have more than one on hand) again to be sure that the damage was completely repaired. Continue to run repair utilities until you are able to get a report of no problems with the drive.

If a repair utility is not able to repair the damaged files, it may still be able to mount the drive on the desktop, allowing you to recover files before reformatting. Even if this is not the case, several repair utilities include data recovery software. Once you have recovered files and stored them on an alternate disk, you should reformat the drive and then restore it. This will eliminate directory damage because it will create a new directory and other invisible files for the drive.

Expansion Slot Problems   If an expansion card is damaged or installed incorrectly, the Mac may refuse to start up and may indicate a motherboard problem. More commonly, the Mac will start up, and the card will simply not be recognized or function properly. If the expansion card slot is damaged, the Mac will likely indicate a motherboard problem at startup or it may simply not recognize any cards inserted into the slot.

If the Mac simply does not recognize the card, first check whether the card itself is installed properly (see Chapter 8). If the card appears to be installed correctly, try reinstalling the driver software (as it may have become disabled or corrupted). If this does not seem to help, try moving the card to another expansion slot (if it is a PCI slot). If this solves the problem, the slot itself may be damaged; try installing a different card there to verify if it is a damaged slot. If the card does not work in a different slot or the slot functions with a different card installed, the card in question is likely damaged or defective.

CD-ROM/DVD-ROM Problems   The most common problem you'll find with a CD-ROM or DVD-ROM drive is that a disk will not be recognized. This can happen for a variety of reasons, most resulting from the fact that the drivers or other software are needed for the Mac to recognize and fully use the CD-ROM/DVD-ROM drive.

If the Mac says that an inserted disk is unreadable or is not a Macintosh disk, check to be sure the disk is a Macintosh disk and that there are no signs of scratches, fingerprints, or other debris on the disk that would prevent it from being read properly. If the disk is not a standard Mac-formatted CD-ROM, but rather a PC formatted disk, an audio CD, or a DVD movie, check to make sure the required extensions and control panels necessary for the Mac to read that kind of disk are installed (the File Exchange control panel, Foreign File Access, High Sierra File Access, and ISO 9660 extension for PC disks; the Audio CD Access, Foreign File Access, and High Sierra File Access extensions for audio CDs; the Apple Photo Access for Kodak picture CDs; and the DVD Navigation Manager, DVD Region Manager, and DVDRuntimeLib extensions for DVD movies). If these are installed, they (or their associated preferences files) may have become corrupted and need to be replaced.

If an inserted disk is completely ignored by the Mac and no icon is displayed at all, it may mean that the actual driver for the CD-ROM/DVD-ROM drive is not installed. For Apple-made drives, this will be the Apple CD/DVD Driver extension. For third-party drives, it may be a different extension or control panel that should have come with the drive.

If the driver is installed, the problem may be that the drive is not connected properly. Check to be certain that the drive is powered properly and that any rules for SCSI or IDE devices are being followed correctly as you would with a hard drive. If the drive does not even open properly or show any signs of activity when a disk has been inserted, this indicates that the drive is not getting power.

SCSI Problems   SCSI problems will often result in the Mac beginning to start up but then crashing during the startup process (sometimes with a bomb dialog displaying a bus error). SCSI problems can also occur when one or all of the devices in a SCSI chain is not mounted or recognized, or where the Mac will simply display a blank, gray screen at startup. SCSI problems are generally caused by not following the rules by which SCSI functions. Therefore, the first thing to check is that all these rules are being followed. A less common symptom is that you will see multiple copies of a SCSI drive's icon scattered across the desktop.

First, make sure that every device has a unique SCSI ID number. A SCSI chain can consist of up to seven or fifteen devices, and each device must be set to a separate SCSI ID. Make sure no two devices share the same ID. This can not only cause crashes, it can cause severe loss of data. Also make sure no device uses the same SCSI ID as the SCSI card in the Mac (traditionally set to 7).

In addition, check to be sure that all the devices in the chain are turned on and that the chain is properly terminated. A SCSI chain is a chain of devices, and if one link in the chain is broken (because a device isn't turned on), the chain won't function properly. Each end of the SCSI chain needs to be terminated. Some devices have auto-termination, others have manually set termination, and some have no termination abilities. Make sure that the devices on each end (whether the end is internal or external) are terminated and that no devices in the middle are terminated.

Make sure the SCSI port/card is functioning properly. This can be done with a utilities such as SCSIProbe or TechTool Pro. If it is not, try zapping the PRAM (parameter RAM), as this can often restore correct functioning of a SCSI port. Likewise, as you would with any PCI card, make sure the SCSI card is inserted and recognized properly.

If none of this solves the problem, there may be a problem with a given device on the chain. Turn off and disconnect all the devices in the chain (after shutting down the Macintosh). Then rebuild the chain one device at a time until the problem reoccurs. Sometimes changing the order in which devices are connected to each other can affect SCSI chain performance. Also, be sure that you are using the appropriate type and length of SCSI cable for the SCSI version your SCSI card and devices are using. For additional information and the details of all the SCSI rules, see Chapter 12.

USB and FireWire Problems   The most common symptoms exhibited by USB and FireWire devices are either a device will not be properly recognized or the device will not be able to draw enough power from the port it is attached to in order to function. If the Mac displays an error message saying the drivers needed to use a device were not found, it means that the drivers the Mac needs in order to recognize and communicate with a device are not installed properly. The solution to this is to simply reinstall the drivers. If the Mac displays an error message that there is not enough power for a device, the device either needs to be plugged into a powered hub or directly into the Mac itself. This message can also indicate that too many devices requiring power are attached to the Mac's USB/FireWire ports and that it can't provide enough power for all of them. Externally powered devices or a powered hub will solve this.

If a device is not recognized at all, the problem may be that the cable attaching the device or the hub it is plugged into has become unplugged. Double-check all connections to be certain. If the device has its own power supply, ensure that it is plugged in and powered properly. The problem may be driver-related, and you can try reinstalling the drivers if the device is still not recognized. Lastly, the problem may be that the ports themselves are damaged. Try attaching the device to another port or hub, and try attaching other devices to that port or hub to verify this.

Display Problems   Problems with a Mac's display generally fall into two categories: no or very dim display and low-quality display. If there is no display at all, the first thing to check is that the monitor is powered and connected to the computer properly. If the cabling appears to be connected properly, check to make sure that the Mac itself is turned on and functioning. For Power Macs, check to be sure that the video card is installed properly. For the Power Mac G3 or early G4 models that use PCI video cards, try placing a video card in another slot to rule out damaged slot as the possible problem. This can also be a symptom indicating that the screen resolution chosen in the Monitors or Monitors and Sound control panel is not supported by the display. If this is the case, zapping the PRAM should reset the Mac to the default 640x480 resolution and make the display function again.

If the display is extremely dim, check the contrast and brightness control on the monitor or in the Monitors or Monitors and Sound control panel. For PowerBook and iBook internal displays, check how much battery power is left, as portable Macs will dim the screen to conserve power once a large portion of battery power has been used up.

If the display is bright on startup but then suddenly goes dark, check the cables and the settings in the Energy Saver control panel, which dims or darkens the display as a power-saving feature after a specified amount of time with no user activity.

For display-quality problems, the display will still be visible but will not display at proper quality. If the screen displays blotches, this can be a sign of operating in excessively warm temperatures (the display will be hot to the touch if this is the case) or of electromagnetic interference. If the display contains several thin, vertical lines, this indicates that the video RAM may not be properly installed.

Jittery display, odd color distortions, and scrolling horizontal lines generally indicate electromagnetic interference (from high-power devices, unshielded speakers, other monitors, motors, magnets and magnetic devices, or even fluorescent lights). This is particularly notable in inexpensive monitors that may not have properly electromagnet shielding. Moving the display elsewhere should solve such problems.

For additional display problems and abnormalities, see Chapter 4.

Software Problems

Software problems are more common than hardware problems with the Mac. There are two main categories of software problems: application problems and Mac OS problems, and four main types of software problems: bugs, conflicts, corruption, and viruses. Let's examine these categories separately.

Application Problems   As you might expect, application problems have to do with a given application. These are problems that occur specifically with that application. Most of the time, you'll come across application problems when you begin using an application, and the manufacturer may even include a list of known problems with the documentation of the program.

Application problems are easy to identify because no matter what the problem is it only happens when the application has been launched. The problem may occur when you are actively using the application for a specific task, or it may occur while the application is running in the background. Application problems should be dealt with using any guidelines put forth by the developer, and any serious problems should be reported to the developer.

There is also the case of an application conflicting with an extension or control panel. Technically, this is a Mac OS problem, but it may only be triggered by one application. If this is the case, starting up without extensions or with a limited extension set can determine whether the application itself is at fault or whether it is an extension conflict.

Another common problem with applications is a lack of RAM. As discussed in Chapter 6, applications that are not allocated enough RAM may crash or perform erratically. If an application crashes frequently, check the memory allocated to it using the Finder's Get Info command, and try increasing the memory required by the application (complete instructions for this can be found in Chapter 6).

Mac OS Problems   Mac OS problems are problems that extend beyond the scope of a single application. They occur in any or all applications, system events, and the Finder. Mac OS problems generally point to something in the System Folder being at fault (since this is where the major components of the Mac OS are stored). Although these problems can occur in any aspect of the Mac's operation, they may still be limited to given tasks or events, which can help you diagnose the problem.

Mac OS problems can extend to just about every corner of the Mac's operation, from displaying icons properly to causing programs to crash to erratic error messages. They can be the most difficult problems to figure out because they can be so broad and because they can involve many different components stored in the System Folder—both standard components of the Mac OS and any third-party Mac OS enhancements (such as extensions, fonts, preferences files, and so forth).

Badly Written Software or Bugs   Bugs are lines of code that are part of either the Mac OS (or a subcomponent such as a control panel or extension) or an application that, simply put, don't work the way they should. This is usually because the application wasn't tested in situations where it might later be used or because it simply wasn't developed as completely and properly as possible. Even with the best efforts and testing of developers, bugs can often escape detection before a product ships. Often, developers release updated versions of software that fix bugs.

Because bugs are part of the code that makes up a piece of software, there is very little that can be done if a problem is caused by a bug, short of notifying the developer and waiting for a revision of the software. You can, however, try to find a way to work around a bug, such as not performing a task that will invoke the problem.

Bugs can occur in both applications and Mac OS components (from Apple or third parties). When they occur in an application, they are easy to sort out and locate. When they occur in some Mac OS elements, they can be mistakenly assumed to be the cause of conflicts. If you're not sure if a problem is the result of a bug or a conflict, check with the manufacturer, Macintosh information websites, or mailing lists.

Conflicts   Conflicts occur when various pieces of software don't get along with each other. This can be because both pieces of software are attempting to use the same resources, because their commands contradict each other, or because the Mac simply isn't capable of understanding just how to cope with these two elements asking it to do certain tasks at the same time.

Conflicts often involve extensions—either extensions conflicting with applications or conflicting with other extensions. Because extensions are part of the Mac OS, extension conflicts usually affect the entire Mac OS rather than a single application.

Generally, the only way to deal with extension conflicts is to disable one of the offending extensions. This, of course, means you need to determine which extension is causing the problem. The only way to do that is to disable extension-by-extension until the problem no longer manifests itself. How to handle extension conflicts is discussed in greater detail in Chapter 38.

It is also a good idea to notify the developers of the software components involved in the hopes that they will work out the issue in a future release of their software.

Corruption   Corruption occurs when lines of code become adjusted to the point where they no longer make sense to the Mac. This is most common in preferences files where settings for various items are stored, but it can also happen to Mac OS elements, including the System file, fonts, drivers (particularly for hard drives), the desktop file, and the parameter RAM. The only solution to corruption is to delete the offending code and replace it with the original code that was meant to be there.

In the case of corrupted preferences files, this is simple...locate the file, drag it to the trash, and then relaunch the application and reset any settings that have been lost. With other Mac OS elements, the problem is a little more difficult to solve. With corruption of the System file, you need to reinstall the Mac OS. With the desktop file, you must rebuild the desktop file (fairly simple, actually), and with the PRAM, you need to delete all the information stored in the PRAM chip and reset everything manually. Corrupted fonts must be deleted and replaced with clean originals of the font. For corrupted hard disk drivers, you need to use the formatting utility that was used to format the drive to either update the driver with the correct version or possibly reformat the drive.

More information of corruption is available in later chapters relating to specific components of the Mac OS.

Viruses   Viruses are problem software as much as they are software problems. Viruses are programs, scripts, or other documents that are created to take over and disrupt the functioning of your computer. Viruses are almost always installed without your being aware of it and are usually also self-propagating (meaning that they try to make copies of themselves to cause more problems elsewhere). Although virus scares are a good deal less common for Mac users than they are for users of Windows-based PCs, there are still viruses out there that can inflict severe damage on your Mac. A good antivirus utility should be owned, used, and updated regularly by every Mac owner. Viruses are discussed in detail in Chapter 40.

Replace or Repair

When you do find a hardware problem where a given piece of equipment is at fault, you're often faced with whether or not that device is salvageable. More and more, computer repair is becoming less an issue of repairing problems as it is replacing components that aren't functioning properly. If your Mac's power supply is damaged, chances are it will be easier and cheaper to simply replace it. The same thing applies to many components of the Mac.

Computers today are a collection of easily removed and replaced subassemblies. If the hard drive is damaged, it is generally impossible for most users to repair it. If you wanted to attempt repairs here, you'd need some highly trained specialists and tools. So, keep in mind that many of the repairs you make to the Mac will be done at a component level. Think or repairing a Mac as replacing individual parts of it. In this way, repairing a Mac is similar to repairing a car...if your car's muffler has a hole in it, you replace the muffler rather than trying to weld another piece of metal over the hole. In theory, welding a piece of metal over the hole might work, but it wouldn't work as well as replacing the muffler, and it would take a good deal more effort.

Handling Components

This topic will be discussed again and again throughout this book because proper handling of hardware, particularly internal hardware, is extremely important. It is very easy to damage a large number of hardware components without even realizing it. The only way to avoid doing that is to follow certain precautions.

Static Discharge   Electrostatic discharges are the greatest concern when you are dealing with any electronic component. When working with any internal component of the Mac, be sure you are in an environment that is not conducive to static electricity and that you are properly grounded. Static discharges that are far below the intensity needed for human beings to be aware of them can easily destroy components such as a processor or RAM. Be prepared.

Always use an antistatic wrist strap (see Figure 3-3). I've heard some people claim that touching a metal object before you begin work is enough. That might be true sometimes, but not every time. Don't

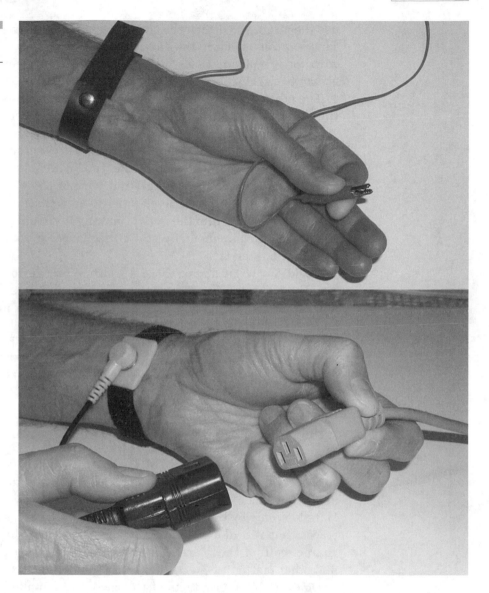

Figure 3-3
Antistatic wrist straps.

take the chance. An antistatic wrist strap is inexpensive, easy to use, and can save you a lot of money by protecting your investment in hardware.

Antistatic wrist straps come in two varieties. Both of these have a thick rubber band that fastens around your wrist. One type, which is less expensive and more common, has wires that lead to an alligator clip. To use the strap, you attach the clip to a metal object (the larger the better). This was convenient in the days when Mac cases were made of metal, but with today's plastic cases, you may have to hunt for a metal object to attach to the clip.

The other, slightly more expensive wrist strap ends in an attachment the same as that of a standard computer power supply. You attach a standard computer power cord to it (such as the one that attaches to a desktop Mac) and plug it into the wall. Don't worry; there's no current coming from the wall to electrocute you. What's actually happening is that you're connected to the ground wire of the electrical outlet. This will ground you from static electricity, as well as grounding anything else that's plugged into the outlet, making it virtually impossible for you to damage a component by static discharge. (Grounding is discussed more in Chapter 11.)

Besides a wrist strap, there are other precautions you can take to avoid static electricity. Never work in a carpeted area. Even static-resistant carpet can build up a mild charge, and even a mild charge can be enough to damage internal components of a computer. Likewise, never work on a surface that has a tablecloth or similar fabric covering.

In addition, never open the computer's case until you are grounded, and never take components out of their antistatic bags until you're grounded. Always use those antistatic bags to store components not in use or that you've removed, and never put packing material in contact with internal components when storing them.

Expansion Cards and RAM Handling   When you're handling any sort of card, be it a PCI card, a ZIF (zero insertion force) processor card, or a RAM module, you need to be careful of how you handle the card. Handle it only by the edges, and don't touch the chips on the card or the traces that run along the card itself. Aside from the risk of static discharge, both of these are sensitive to damage from pressure, skin oils, and other matter.

Don't touch the contacts of the card. This applies to both RAM and expansion cards. The contacts are the area of the card that attaches or contacts with the slot on the motherboard. Anything from skin oil to dust can obstruct the flow of electricity and data across the contacts. And since data is what flows along those contacts as well as electricity, anything on there will impair the card's function.

Don't touch any pins on a ZIF module. The pins are part of the processor itself, which are situated into the ZIF socket and allow the processor to connect with the motherboard. Contact can seriously damage the

Figure 3-4
The correct way to handle expansion cards.

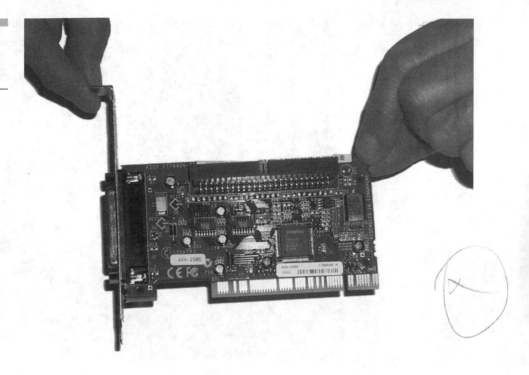

processor. Figure 3-4 shows the correct method of handling expansion cards.

Handling Internal Cables and Internal Drives   Internal ribbon cables, such as those used for internal IDE and SCSI drives, as well as internal power cables, such as those run from the power supply to individual internal components, are not particularly susceptible to accidental damage. When attaching a cable, be gentle but firm if needed, and you should be fine. Make sure that the cable is positioned correctly when you insert it. If a cable seems to resist insertion, check to be sure that you are inserting it correctly, and don't force it, because this can damage the connectors in the cable and device it is being connected to.

When handling internal drives (see Figure 3-5), avoid touching the cable connectors if possible and definitely avoid touching any exposed circuitry. Be sure in advance that a drive will fit in the available space for it, and don't force a drive to fit if the space seems too small for it. Details for working with specific drives are discussed in later chapters.

Figure 3-5
The correct way to
handle an internal
drive.

Figure 3-5
The correct way to handle an internal drive.

Diagnostic and Repair Utilities

Diagnostic and repair utilities are software that can examine components of the Macintosh (both physical hardware and elements of the Mac OS) to locate problems. Most such utilities also include the ability to correct some, though not all, of the problems they are designed to look for. It is important to note that when a utility says "repair," it does not mean that it will repair physical damage to a component (such as a broken read/write head in a hard drive). Rather, these utilities repair damage or corruption to data files essential to the proper functioning of the Mac (such as the invisible files that control and record how data is stored on a hard drive).

In some cases, diagnostic or repair utilities come in packages that include a set of tools for diagnosing and resolving problems with a large number of Mac hardware components or Mac OS elements. An excellent example of this is MicroMat's TechTool Pro, which features diagnostic tools for virtually every Macintosh component. Repair utilities can also come individually, with only a single application that performs a single specific purpose. An example of this is Alsoft's DiskWarrior or Apple's free Disk First Aid, which deal specifically with corruption or damage to a hard drive's invisible files and directory structures.

Diagnostic and repair utilities can also be subdivided into utilities that are launched and run by the user or technician and those that are installed and run regularly by the Mac. Often these self-running tools are installed as extensions or control panels and automatically run once when the Mac shuts down or periodically while the Mac is operating.

The following sections discuss a few of the diagnostic tools available for the Macintosh. This is hardly an exhaustive list and is included simply to give you an idea of the variety of diagnostic tools available and how they function. Diagnostic tools specific to various Macintosh hardware components and Mac OS elements are discussed in the chapters devoted to those components and elements. Additionally, Appendix B includes a large listing of the Macintosh diagnostic and repair tools available and the abilities of each.

Disk First Aid Apple's free disk repair utility, Disk First Aid, is designed to search through hard drives for corruption or damage to the file structure of the disk. This damage and corruption, if undetected, could lead to severe problems with the files stored on the disk and potential loss of data. When you use Disk First Aid to check a drive for problems, it scans the drive, looking for a series of specific criteria. This criteria includes the proper format of the directory structure that the Mac uses to store and retrieve information on the drive. When it finds problems in these areas, it reports them to you or repairs them (depending on the option you chose when you started using the utility). Figure 3-6 shows a report from Disk First Aid.

As an additional precaution, in Mac OS 8.5 and later, Apple made Disk First Aid an automated utility by designing it to run at startup if the Macintosh was not shut down properly the last time it was used (after a forced restart from a crash or starting up following a power outage, for example). This feature is excellent, as such improper shutdowns can cause a severe amount of disk damage. You can, however, turn this feature off in the General Controls control panel.

Disk First Aid is by no means the most powerful hard drive utility on the market, and there are several problems that it can detect but not fix. In many such instances, commercial repair utilities such as Norton Disk Doctor (part of the well-known Norton Utilities for Mac) or Alsoft's DiskWarrior will be able to fix the problem.

Figure 3-6
Disk First Aid
findings.

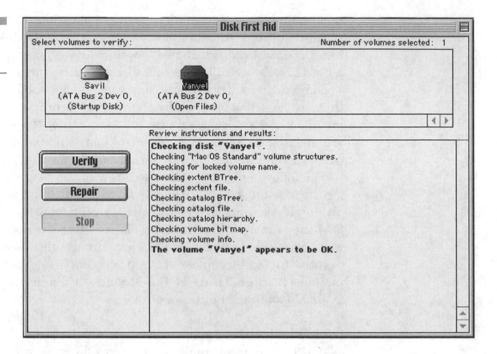

Unique
to
MACs

Font Agent   Font Agent by Insider Software is a utility that allows you to (among a few other features) test fonts for signs of corruption. Font corruption can cause various problems with your Mac, from crashes at startup to intermittent crashes and erratic behavior throughout the Mac OS. Font Agent examines each font file for areas where the file has become nonsensical to the computer, indicating corruption. When corruption in a font is found, it is reported to you along with possible solutions. Other utilities, such as Adobe Type Manager Deluxe, also include this feature. Figure 3-7 shows Font Agent analyzing a main font folder.

TechTool   MicroMat's free utility TechTool (see Figure 3-8) can scan your Mac's System file for signs of corrupted or damaged resources. A damaged System file will inevitably lead to the inability to start up your Mac. Because the System file for any given version of the Mac OS has specific resources and components, TechTool is designed to look for those resources specific to each Mac OS version and ensure that there are no signs of corruption or damage in them.

In addition to its diagnostic abilities, TechTool also provides a simpler and more powerful method for rebuilding the desktop file of a Mac's hard drive and zapping the PRAM. This is discussed more in later chapters.

Figure 3-7
FontAgent at work.

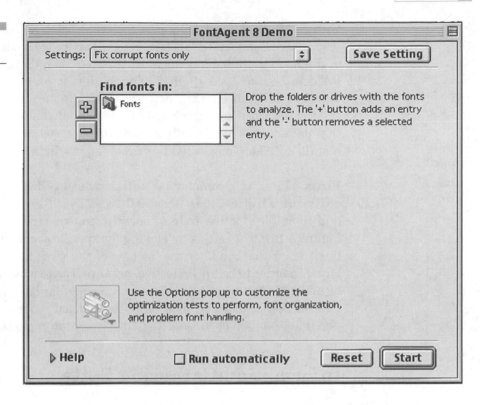

Figure 3-8
Opening screen on
TechTool.

Gauge PRO Gauge PRO is a free tool from Newer Technology that tests your Mac's RAM. This ensures that there is no slight damage to any of the RAM installed in your Mac. It is possible, though not common, for RAM to be damaged slightly enough that it passes the Mac's startup tests but may cause erratic problems while you are using the Mac. Gauge PRO is designed to actively test each part of the Mac's RAM to ensure that data can be successfully stored and accessed in each and every bit of installed RAM. Gauge PRO has provided its finding in Figure 3-9.

Virex Virex is a commercial antivirus utility for the Mac. Like other antivirus utilities, it is designed to search files and folders (visible and invisible) for the code of certain known viruses for the Mac (see Figure 3-10). It does this by looking for specific segments of data in every file it scans that are known to be part of the virus and/or the result of the virus. In order to be fully effective, an antivirus tool such as Virex needs to be updated with new virus definitions on a regular basis (usually companies publish new updates on their websites at least twice a month). For additional information on viruses and antivirus protections, see Chapter 40.

Information-Gathering Software

In addition to diagnostic utilities, there are tools that gather and display information about a Mac. These information-gathering utilities are used

Figure 3-9
Gauge PRO provides system and memory information.

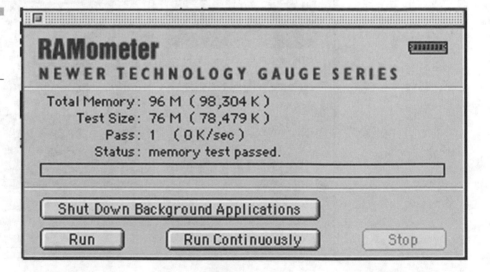

Figure 3-10
Examining all vol-
umes with Virex.

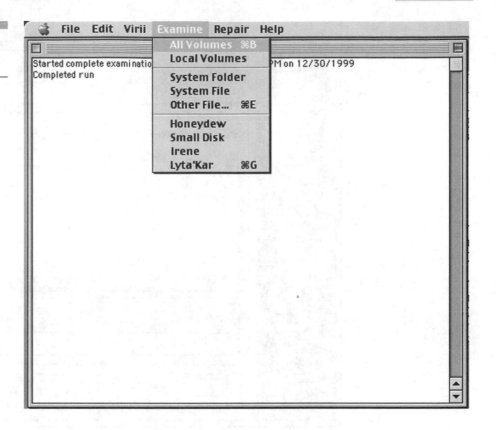

to gain more information about a Mac and can help diagnose a problem that you're experiencing. Information-gathering utilities collect data about a specific area of the Mac and present it to you.

As an example, the SCSIProbe utility from Adaptec simply scans for activity among any SCSI devices attached to your computer and displays what it finds to you (see Figure 3-11). This in itself doesn't tell you whether or not there's a problem with any of the devices, but it does allow you to find out whether one is being recognized. In addition to gathering information, SCSIProbe can also be used to mount SCSI drives in the chain.

Another example of an information-gathering diagnostic utility that ships with every release of the Mac OS is the Apple System Profiler, shown in Figure 3-12. This utility, by default stored in the Apple menu, displays a wealth of information about your Mac and all devices attached to it. The following example illustrates how software that displays information about a Macintosh can sometimes be a useful tool in determining if there is a problem or what components may be involved with that problem.

After purchasing a new Zip drive, one client once complained to me that he could only get the drive to read the Zip disk that was included with the drive and not the other two he had bought to store files on. Since I was talking to him over the phone and couldn't check the drive personally, I had him open the Apple System Profiler. This allowed me to find out if the Mac was recognizing the drive. From that I could isolate the cause as being related to the way the user had attached the drive (perhaps a SCSI termination issue) or if there was a problem with disks he was using (he'd already tried buying two separate packages of disks). The drive was recognized as a physical device, but not specifically as a Zip drive. This tipped me off that the driver software for the Zip drive wasn't installed properly. As it turns out, the user never actually ran the installer from the Zip disk that came with the drive.

As you can see, the Apple System Profiler isn't a complete tool for diagnosing a problem by itself. However, it can be used to confirm a sus-

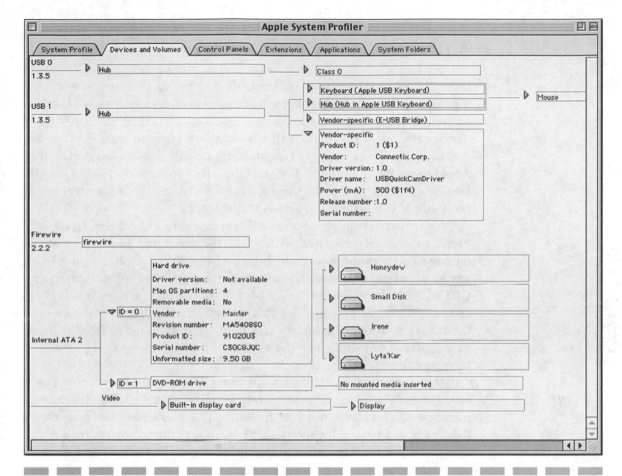

Figure 3-12   The Apple System Profiler utility.

pected cause of a problem or to gather additional information about a problem.

Information-gathering tools can also be helpful in other ways. The Apple System Profiler can tell you exactly which RAM slots are being used by a Mac and what the capacity of each memory module installed is. Since RAM rarely has a capacity listed on the module itself, this may be the only method for determining which of the two installed modules is the 128-MB one and which is the 32-MB one you want to replace. Similarly, SCSIProbe can display the SCSI ID numbers of every device in a SCSI chain. This is a much quicker way of getting the list of SCSI IDs in use than physically looking at the dip switches, dials, or jumpers on each device when you want to add a new device to the chain.

Apple Warranties, Service Agreements, and Authorized Service Providers

Before you open the case of a Mac to do any repair or upgrade work, it's a good idea to be clear that Apple has designated certain areas of the Mac as hands-off to anyone who is not working for an Apple Authorized Service Provider. Throughout this book, when such an area is being discussed, I will make a point of mentioning this. If you are not certified by Apple to repair the Mac and/or working at a repair shop that is not authorized or certified by Apple, you can very well void the warranty on the computer if you attempt to access these areas.

Often, restricting these areas is very practical because those who aren't extensively familiar with what they're doing could very easily damage the computer or even injure themselves. An example of this would be trying to service the internal display of the iMac. Repairing a CRT's internals can be very risky because of the high voltage involved. In fact, some computer shops won't even service displays, opting to send them back to the factory. It is extremely sensible to make this off-limits to discourage any untrained persons from putting themselves, as well as the computer, at risk.

Other times the reason is less technically motivated and more based on business objectives or plans. An example of this would be the mezzanine slot on the revision A and B iMacs. The mezzanine slot was slated to be removed from iMac motherboards. In an effort to discourage development of products for the slot, Apple made installing any device into it a warranty-voiding task.

Whatever the task involves, it is a good idea to be aware in advance of warranty-jeopardizing areas. Be aware that there are quite possibly reasons that Apple feels you should only attempt certain repairs if you are working for an Apple Authorized Service Provider (which are privy to repair information and programs that the general public may not be).

Also keep in mind that Apple Authorized Service Providers are the only entities capable of performing repairs covered by a warranty who can then submit the bill for such repairs to Apple. Independent Mac consultants and computer repair companies that aren't Apple-certified will not be able to repair issues covered under a warranty free of charge.

This is not to say that all repair shops authorized by Apple are reputable. I have seen first-hand some Apple-authorized repair shops where the staff was incompetent and actually created more problems than they fixed. In addition, I do not intend to imply that you need to work for an

Apple Authorized Service Provider in order to open the case of your Mac to perform repairs and upgrades. I do, however, want to make clear that there are times, particularly with machines under warranty, that it may be in your best interest to use such a shop.

There are some cases when you will need to work with an Apple Authorized Service Provider for another reason: parts. Some components to the Mac are of proprietary designs and can only be bought from Apple. The most obvious example of this is a Mac's motherboard. Only Apple manufactures motherboards, and Apple doesn't make them available except to its own factories and to Apple Authorized Service Providers. Therefore, if the problem with a Mac is in the motherboard, there's little option for fixing it yourself. Another example of this includes the LCD screens of the PowerBook and iBook.

Apple Warranties and AppleCare

Apple generally ships Macs with a one-year warranty covering factory defects on the original hardware. Apple also has an extended service program known as AppleCare. AppleCare can be for a variable number of years and varies in price depending on the item being covered. It can be purchased at any time before the expiration of the factory warranty and can be renewed when it expires. If you register a Mac with Apple after purchase, you will receive a notice about a month before the factory warranty expires asking you if you want to purchase AppleCare.

Apple's standard warranty is limited to the hardware that was manufactured by Apple or for Apple that is part of the computer. Any additional hardware, such as additional or replacement hard drives, added RAM, processor upgrade modules, or expansion cards, are not covered under the Apple warranty. If any other hardware is installed and damages the computer during installation or use, that damage will not be covered under warranty. Apple's warranty also does not cover any software-related issues. Damage caused by accidents or deliberate abuse is not covered. In essence, the warranty only applies to Macs that have factory defects and have been modified or upgraded only in the most basic sense.

When you install new components into a Mac, these components will be covered under a warranty from their manufacturer. So don't worry too much that the new hard drive you want to install won't be covered by Apple's warranty, because it will be covered by the warranty from its own manufacturer. Some companies that manufacture devices that can void an Apple warranty when installed have actually gone so far as to provide their own warranty coverage of the entire computer into which these components are installed. Always check out the warranty policies for any piece of hardware you work with. Know exactly what is covered, what isn't covered, and what will void the warranty.

AppleCare generally has the same limitations as the original warranty—both in terms of what is covered and what acts will void the extended coverage AppleCare affords. As with the factory warranty, repairs done under AppleCare must be performed by an Apple Service Provider to be free of charge. AppleCare does, however, seem to be a bit pricier than some store-sold extended service options.

Two of AppleCare's biggest advantages are that you can purchase it at any time during the length of ownership and that repairs can be performed by any repair shop authorized by Apple. Unlike the extended service agreements many stores offer, you aren't limited to dealing with a single company, nor do you have to sign up at the time of purchase.

Another interesting option is computer insurance. A number of companies now make it possible for you to ensure all of your computer hardware as you do a car or house. These coverage policies vary, but they rarely exclude any areas of use and rarely penalize you for performing a task that would void an Apple warranty. With premiums being low and almost anything being covered, these policies are something I encourage anyone to look into (see the following section for resources on locating computer insurance companies). The only downside is that they often require you to provide estimates from two repair shops when filing a claim. This may or may not make things difficult if you wish to perform repairs yourself and still receive money under the policy.

Resources for Further Study

The following URLs provide additional information on some of the concepts, issues, and products discussed in this chapter:

Apple Warranty Information—http://www.info.apple.com/support/supportoptions/warr.html

AppleCare Extended Service—http://support.info.apple.com/support/supportoptions/extservice.html

SafeWare Computer Insurance—http://www.safeware-ins.com

Monitors and Displays

The monitor or display (these terms are used interchangeably, although technically a *monitor* refers to a CRT screen and *display* tends to refer to an LCD screen) is one of the most important parts of a computer. Along with the keyboard and the mouse, it is the component that users will have the most interaction with. The display is literally the way that the Mac communicates with users, and it is, of course, an essential peripheral.

The display is also something that Mac users will spend hours a day looking at. For this reason, choosing a high-quality display is important. Apple produces some truly extraordinary displays that are perfect for many uses, including desktop publishing, graphics design, gaming, and multimedia. Many other companies also produce excellent displays, but not all do.

When choosing a display, try to balance cost and quality. You will be looking at the display much of the time, so you should choose one that is of at least decent quality. Also, the better the display, the less strain it will place on your eyes. Eyestrain can lead to vision problems, so choosing a high-quality display can be an investment in your health. Remember, however, that specifications alone don't define a display. When shopping for a new monitor, go to a store and examine the options. This is the only way you can get a real idea of the quality of a display. If it isn't possible, read as many reviews of the displays you're considering as you can.

This chapter examines how displays function and how to connect and configure a display on the Mac. It also introduces many of the concepts and specifications used in creating and advertising a display. In addition, a section is included on troubleshooting common display problems.

CRT Monitors

Cathode-ray tube or CRT monitors, such as the one in Figure 4-1, are what most people think of when they hear the term *monitor*. A CRT monitor is a large, boxlike unit for displaying images that resembles a television set to some degree. CRT monitors have been used for computer displays for decades now. With the exception of portable Macs and the most recent display offerings from Apple, almost every Mac has used a CRT monitor.

How CRT Monitors Work

The screen of a CRT monitor is coated with special materials called *phosphors*. When phosphors are exposed to the appropriate level of electrical charge, they glow. This is the basic principle on which CRT monitors (and televisions as well) function. An electron gun built into the back of

Figure 4-1
A typical CRT
monitor.

the monitor continually fires off pulses of electrons to the screen of the monitor. When the electrons from each pulse strike a phosphor, it glows.

The electrons fired from the gun are directed by strong magnetic fields inside the monitor. These fields are generated by a series of magnetic coils. As the gun fires each electron pulse, the magnetic fields inside the monitor are adjusted so that the electrons strike a specific point on the surface of the screen. This way, only the phosphors at a specific point on the screen will be illuminated. The components are illustrated in Figure 4-2.

Phosphor Triads and Dot Pitch In color monitors, the surface of the screen is coated with three different-colored phosphors. These colors are red, blue, and green, which are the three primary colors of light. By illuminating these colors to different levels, any individual color of the spectrum can be created (white is created when all three are combined and black when none is illuminated).

The three colored phosphors are arranged in groups called *triads,* such as the one illustrated in Figure 4-3. Each triad is a triangle containing

Figure 4-2
The basic components
and operation of
a CRT monitor.

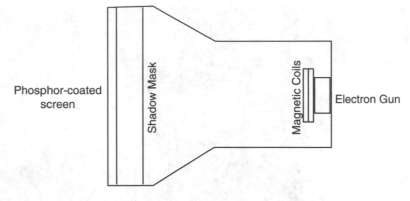

CRT Monitor Components

Figure 4-3
Triads and dot pitch.

One Triad

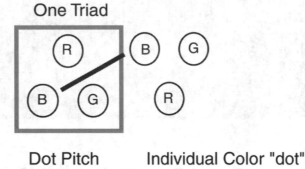

Dot Pitch   Individual Color "dot"

three phosphor dots, one of each color. For practical purposes, each triad represents one dot on the screen surface that can be displayed as any color that the Mac needs to generate. The closer the individual phosphor dots in a triad, the truer the colors will look. If the individual dots in a triad are too far away from one another, the human eye will be able to pick up the distinctions between them, and lines will look curved and colors impure.

The distance from a dot of one color in a triad (say, blue) to the dot of the same color in the triad next to it is referred to as the monitor's *dot pitch*. The smaller the dot pitch, the better the image quality of anything displayed on the monitor. A dot pitch of 0.30 millimeters is considered adequate for many people. Most Apple-made monitors (including those in the iMacs) have a dot pitch of 0.28 mm or lower, giving them superior image quality to other low-cost monitors. Today, it is not uncommon to see high-quality monitors offer a dot pitch of 0.25 mm.

Triads are used to generate pixels. A *pixel* (short for "picture element") is the smallest element that a Mac's video circuitry can generate. Pixels are individual dots of color, created by the blending of the three color phosphors in each triad. The Mac uses hundreds of thousands of individual pixels to generate the images you see on a display. The number of pixels being used to generate the entire display on a Mac's screen is referred to as the Mac's *screen size* or *resolution* (resolution is discussed in more detail later in this chapter).

Burn-in and Brightness Fading   The phosphors used in a CRT monitor have two drawbacks. First, if an unchanging image is displayed on the screen for a length of time, the phosphors can burn that image onto the screen. This effect, called *burn-in,* eventually leaves a shadow of the unchanging image on the screen all the time. Burn-in is not common (if it happens at all) on most recent monitors because of advances in CRT design. One solution to burn-in is to simply keep the display from remaining static for too long. This is why screen saver applications became popular, because they continually change what is being displayed without user input. However, simply dimming the screen so that nothing is displayed or even turning the monitor off functions equally well. Dimming the screen also offers a power conservation function and can be triggered by the Energy Saver control panel on the Mac. However, you may then have to wait a moment for the screen to power back up. Many users find using both a screen saver and monitor dimming to be a good approach.

The second drawback is that over time the phosphors tend to wear out and lose some of their brightness. Even after only a year, a CRT screen's phosphors aren't going to be able to produce the level of brightness they did when the monitor was purchased. This fading takes time before it really becomes noticeable, and adjusting the brightness controls of the monitor can compensate for the effect somewhat. Better-produced monitors, such as Apple's Studio Display line, tend to have longer phosphor life than lower-quality monitors.

Shadow Masks and Convergence   A CRT monitor uses separate electron pulses to trigger each color phosphor in a triad. This means that there are three "guns" firing electrons at the same time, with each pulse being aimed at one of the three phosphors in a triad. To make sure stray electrons don't trigger the wrong phosphors, a piece of perforated metal called the *shadow mask* is placed behind the screen. This way, if there is a stray electron flying around, it will be absorbed by the shadow mask without triggering any other phosphors and distorting the color on the display.

The electrons converge together as they pass through the shadow mask. This convergence means that the electrons accurately strike the correct phosphors in the same triad. If the electrons do not converge properly at the shadow mask, the result will be colored shadows around a line or object. This distortion is known as *misconvergence*. Many monitors can be adjusted for proper convergence. However, adjusting a monitor for convergence can mean opening up the monitor and exposing yourself to components that build and maintain a *lethal* charge of electricity even after the monitor has been unplugged for days. In these cases, you should let trained professionals deal with resetting a monitor's convergence. Also, not all monitors can have their convergence reset, and the process can vary significantly from one monitor to another.

Aperture Grill Displays   Some companies use a technology called *aperture grill displays*. These monitors do not place phosphors in the traditional triangle shape. Rather, these monitors place the individual color dots in rows or lines. Instead of using a shadow mask to ensure that only the appropriate phosphors are triggered, these displays use a series of very thin wires called an *aperture grill*. Aperture grill monitors otherwise function the same as traditional CRT monitors. Proponents of aperture grill displays claim that they provide brighter and clearer images and colors. Some companies also use their own names for aperture grill displays, such as Sony's Trinitron and Mitsubishi's DiamondTron.

Painting the Display in Horizontal and Vertical Scans   A CRT monitor creates an image on-screen by firing an electron pulse that causes each and every phosphor triad to be displayed as a specific color. This process is sometimes called "drawing" or "painting" the screen. A monitor paints the screen one triad at a time in a specific format.

The monitor paints the display one horizontal line at a time, beginning in the upper left corner of the monitor. As each horizontal line is painted, the monitor paints the line below it, beginning with the leftmost triad in that line. This continues until the monitor has painted every part of the screen and reached the bottom right-hand corner. At this point, it begins the process again at the upper left of the screen.

The painting of the entire screen is called a *vertical scan*. The number of vertical scans (or complete screen redraws) the monitor is capable of performing is known as the *vertical scan rate* or *vertical refresh rate*. This is expressed in Hz, indicating the number of scans it performs in a second. The higher the vertical refresh rate, the better the display. The lower the refresh rate, the easier it is for the human eye to perceive the process and notice a flickering in the screen with each scan. A vertical refresh rate of lower than 70 Hz is too poor for comfortable viewing.

Each line is called a *horizontal scan,* and the time it takes the monitor to complete each horizontal scan is referred to as its *horizontal refresh rate* or *horizontal sync rate.* The horizontal refresh rate is expressed in KHz, meaning how many thousandths of a second it takes for each line to be drawn. Most monitor specifications tend to quote the vertical refresh rate as the general refresh rate for the monitor, however.

Interlaced Monitors   Interlaced monitors are an exception to this rule. Rather than painting one line after another, an interlaced monitor only paints every other line on the screen's surface in each pass. On the first pass, it will paint the first line of triads, then the third, then the fifth, and so on. On its second pass, it will paint the second, the fourth, the sixth, and so on. Interlaced monitors are less expensive to produce and therefore cheaper. However, interlacing results in a distinctly lower-quality display, even at higher refresh rates, because you are essentially looking at a display that has half the refresh rate it claims. Apple has never produced an interlaced monitor, and I don't recommend any Mac user (or any PC user, for that matter) to even consider an interlaced monitor because of the lower quality and the increased eyestrain associated with them.

Syncing at Each Scan   As the monitor draws each line on the screen, it needs to sync with the Mac's video circuitry to be certain that it is drawing the proper colors on-screen at the proper times. This is accomplished by means of a sync pulse that is sent between the video circuitry and the monitor. In most monitors, the sync pulse is sent along a separate wire in the video cable from any other data. However, some older monitors are designed to communicate a sync pulse along the same wire that transmits data for a specific color, usually green. This technique is called *sync on color* or *sync on green* (presuming green the color being used).

Today's Macs do not offer support for sync on color monitors. If you need to use such an older monitor, you must purchase an adapter to use it with today's Macs, such as the adapter available from Griffin Technology. Your only other option would be to use a video card that supports syncing on the color of the monitor (an option only available to Power Mac computers).

Because the monitor needs to sync at each scan, it needs to scan at a rate that is supported by the video circuitry in the Mac. Many monitors today are called *multisync monitors,* meaning that they can perform at any one of several scan rates and can function at any one of several screen resolutions. This allows them to support a range of computers. Some older monitors, however, may only support one scan rate or a very limited range of rates. Power Mac and PowerBook computers also support a wide range of range of sync rates, enabling them to be used with a wide range of monitors. The iMac DV computers, however, offer only three scan rates when supporting an external monitor. When buying a monitor, you should check to see what sync rates it supports and note whether your Mac's video circuitry also supports them. It can damage your monitor if you try to use a scan rate that it does not support.

Magnetic Distortions and Degaussing a Monitor   The electron pulses used to trigger the phosphors on a screen are directed by magnetic fields, which are generated by a series of electromagnetic coils. If objects that generate electrical or magnetic fields are placed near the monitor, such as unshielded speakers or even refrigerator magnets, these fields may distort the direction of the electron pulses of the monitor. This can result in wavering images or a distorted picture. Magnetic distortions can even be generated by objects like fluorescent lights.

The obvious solution to this is to position the monitor away from sources of magnetic interference. If this isn't an option (for example, you may not be able to replace your office's fluorescent lights), you can usually degauss a monitor when it experiences distortions. Many monitors include a degauss button that will reset the magnetic coils of the monitor. If your monitor does not have such a button, you can degauss it manually by turning the monitor off, waiting a few seconds, and turning it back on.

Flat-Screen CRT Monitors   The actual glass screen of most CRT monitors is curved slightly. This makes producing the screens simpler and less expensive. However, projecting a flat image onto a curved surface results in an image that has some distortions of actual shape at the edges of the display. Most CRT monitors today include circuitry to compensate for these distortions to a relatively good degree. However, many new CRT monitors are built with flat glass screens rather than curved screens. This results in a less distorted image, particularly on larger monitors.

LCD Displays

Liquid crystal or LCD displays were initially used for portable computers, such as the PowerBook and iBook, because they are flat, lightweight, generate less heat, and require considerably less power to operate than a

CRT monitor. For quite some time, LCD screens were limited to use in portable computers, for two primary reasons. First, LCD screens are much more expensive to produce (and therefore purchase) than CRT monitors. In addition, as LCD screens became larger, they became more expensive to produce per inch of screen space.

Second, LCD screens are more difficult to produce in high quality at large sizes. For several years, the technology to mass-produce large LCD screens (say, over 14 inches) simply wasn't available or wasn't cost-effective enough for manufacturers to consider. Times change, however, and today LCD screens are becoming increasingly popular options for desktop displays, such as the impressive 22-inch Apple Cinema Display shown in Figure 4-4.

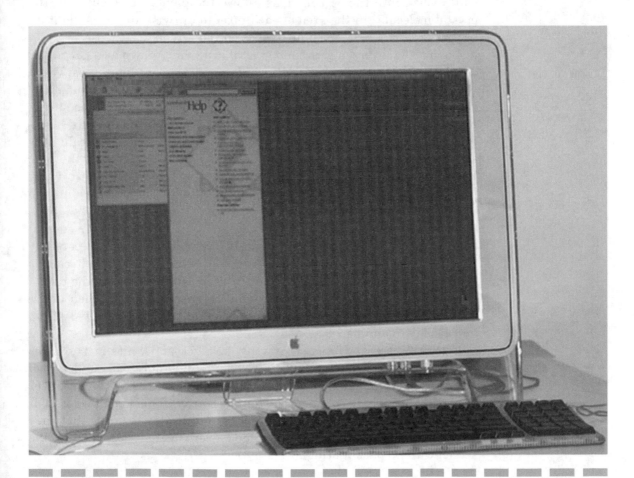

Figure 4-4   The Apple Cinema Display, Apple's extremely impressive 22-inch LCD display.

How LCD Displays Work

The technology for LCD displays differs from CRT in several ways. The basic component of an LCD screen is a liquid crystal compound. Liquid crystal molecules have a spiral structure that allows them to remain permeable to light under most circumstances. However, when an electrical charge is applied to them, the molecules untwist from their usual state. When this happens, they either block light completely or allow very little light to pass through.

A black-and-white LCD screen consists of two very thin sheets of glass with a layer of liquid crystal compound sandwiched between them. A grid allowing the display to pass electrical signals into the compound is also sandwiched into the screen. This allows the display to trigger all the crystal molecules in the area of each pixel to untwist and block light (to appear gray or black), forming images on the screen.

Behind the layers of glass and crystal is a lamp known as a *backlight*. The backlight uses very narrow, low-power fluorescent lightbulbs. When the backlight is illuminated, the light shines through the areas of the screen where the crystal molecules are not blocking light. These areas appear as white, while the areas where the crystal molecules are blocking light appear black. In actuality, a black-and-white or grayscale LCD screen can be used without a backlight (Apple's first laptop, the Mac Portable, didn't come with any backlighting initially). Without a backlight, however, you need to rely on the ambient light in your work area to illuminate parts of the display.

Because the backlight is a fluorescent light, it will last for several years. In most cases, a backlight in an LCD display will remain perfectly functional for at least five years. If the backlight does fail, it can be replaced. This is best done by trained professionals because of the risk of damaging the layers of glass and liquid crystal compound when disassembling the display. The process (and the light needed) also vary from one display to another.

Color LCD screens function exactly like black-and-white LCD screens except that where a black-and-white display has only one sandwich of glass, crystal compound, and electrode grid, a color LCD has four (one for each of the primary colors plus one for black/gray). This makes color LCD screens much more expensive to produce, and it also requires that they have a stronger backlight (and the added layers make it harder to see the screen with no backlighting).

Active Matrix versus Passive Matrix

There are two primary types of LCD displays: active-matrix (also called TFT) and passive-matrix displays. The difference between active- and passive-matrix displays centers on the grid used to send electrical signals to the liquid crystal molecules in the display. Beyond that, the two are functionally the same.

In an active-matrix screen, each pixel on the screen is assigned an individual transistor. This transistor delivers an electrical signal to the liquid crystal molecules making up its pixel whenever the pixel needs to be darkened. Each of these transistors can be activated or deactivated very quickly by the display's control circuitry. This allows the pixels in the display to react to changes so quickly that the action appears instantaneous.

Placing a transistor for each pixel on the screen is a difficult process, however. There are almost 800,000 pixels in a standard PowerBook screen today and 480,000 in an iBook screen (desktop LCD screens may have even more). For each of these, a transistor needs to be bonded or etched into the glass panels in the display. For color LCD screens, this needs to be done for each of the four color liquid crystal layers. The cost of doing this, and the cost incurred by manufacturers for units that fail to be produced properly, makes active-matrix screens much more expensive to produce than passive-matrix screens.

Passive-matrix screens, which predate active-matrix screen technology, use a grid of electrodes to send signals to each pixel. This grid consists of electrodes running horizontally and vertically. An electrical signal of sufficient strength along the horizontal and vertical electrodes associated with a particular pixel will produce a signal strong enough at that pixel to trigger the crystal molecules to become opaque.

Because passive-matrix screens operate with a much easier-to-produce grid of electrodes, they are much less expensive than active-matrix screens. However, there are ways in which a grid of electrodes lowers the quality of passive-matrix screens. First and foremost, passive-matrix screens have a slower reaction time. It takes just a fraction of a second longer for a pixel to be triggered by a grid of electrodes than it does by a single transistor. This means that any fast movement on the screen will appear blurred as the pixels try to keep up with the changing display. Quickly moving the mouse can result in the cursor blurring or even disappearing (an effect referred to as "submarining"). Similarly, it is difficult to read text when scrolling through a document because it blurs as it goes by.

Another common drawback to passive-matrix screens is that they are much more difficult to view at an angle. In fact, if you aren't sitting right in front of a passive-matrix screen, it can be difficult to make out any text. Ironically, some people actually prefer passive-matrix screen laptops because this gives them a measure of privacy when using the computer in public.

Some passive-matrix screens are also less crisp than active-matrix screens, though this is usually limited to only older screens. This happens because the signal being used to trigger a specific pixel may trigger the pixels near it to partially darken. The result is that there aren't clearly defined edges to dark and light areas.

Dual-Scan, Passive-Matrix Displays   Laptop manufacturers, including Apple, have always been faced with the issue of balancing cost with quality when manufacturing laptop screens. One way to improve upon the quality of a passive-matrix screen without reaching the costs involved in creating an active-matrix screen was to split the area of the screen in two. This approach, called a *dual-scan screen,* divides the physical screen into two separate sections. Each section has an independent grid of electrodes to trigger the crystal molecules in specific areas of the screen. Although this is still a passive-matrix screen, it does react much better than a passive-matrix screen of the same size that isn't split into segments. However, a dual-scan screen is still a passive-matrix screen, and it still has many of the inherent weaknesses of a traditional passive-matrix screen. Also, the line dividing the screen in two can be visible in some lighting conditions or screen contrast settings.

Dead Pixels on Active-Matrix Displays   Active-matrix screens suffer from a condition known as "dead" or "voided" pixels. A dead pixel occurs when one of the transistors assigned to a given pixel fails. The failure of at least one transistor is inevitable over time (although most active-matrix screens are likely to function for years or even decades before a transistor fails). It is also possible that a screen will come out of the factory with one or two dead pixels.

When a screen has a dead pixel, that pixel is unable to change color properly and will usually be stuck on one color. This is because it is only one transistor in one of the four color layers of an LCD screen that is stuck. When the area of the display is generating certain colors, the dead pixel may not even be visible. The only way to be certain you have a dead pixel is to turn the entire screen completely one color after another and see if the pixel remains.

There is no way to fix a dead pixel short of replacing the LCD screen. For this reason, many LCD manufacturers will devote two transistors to each pixel rather than one. The second transistor can serve as a backup should one fail, which will keep the screen displaying perfectly.

If you have a PowerBook or iBook with a dead pixel, you may have to fight to even get a replacement screen from Apple. Laptop manufacturers, including Apple, have traditionally required that a screen have five dead pixels before they will sell you a replacement. The exception is if you have two dead pixels within an inch of each other or if one is located in the center of the screen.

Native Resolutions for LCD Displays   While most CRT monitors offer you a wide range of screen resolutions (how many pixels wide by how many pixels high the screen is), LCD screens tend to have a single native resolution. This is because LCD screens are constructed such that each pixel is identified in the screen's hardware (each transistor in an active-matrix screen or each electrode grid intersection in a passive-matrix screen). Changing the size of the pixels (the effect in changing the resolution) means that the screen needs to combine individual pixels in a way that LCD technology wasn't originally designed to do. Today's LCD screens do support multiple resolutions (they didn't do so a few years ago). This is important because some applications and games will only run at certain (usually smaller) resolutions. However, when a LCD screen is run at a lower resolution than its native resolution, text, the edges of images, and other smaller features of the screen often appear blurry or slightly blocky.

Advantages of Both CRT and LCD Displays

Both CRT and LCD screen technologies offer advantages. This section compares the advantages of both types of displays. You'll note that some of these advantages may be more or less important depending on how you intend to use the display.

Advantages of CRT Monitors

Consistent Image Regardless of Viewing Angle   When you look at an LCD screen from an angle instead of head-on, the image on the screen will appear slightly different. Usually this will just be a slight change in the color or the brightness and contrast of the screen. Most desktop LCD screens are of high enough quality that this won't be dramatic, but it will happen. CRT monitors, on the other hand, will look the same regardless of the angle you view them at.

Consistent Color   CRT monitors have consistent coloring. The red in Apple's logo will look the same, regardless of the angle you see it at or the environment around the monitor. This is not true for LCD displays. The nature of LCD displays means that viewing angle can affect the brightness or shade of colors on the display. Also, the temperatures where they are being used can affect LCD screens, resulting in varying levels of contrast at very cold or very warm temperatures. This is one reason LCD screens have not taken an immediate foothold in many graphics or desktop publishing houses.

Lower Cost   CRT monitors simply cost less than LCD displays. This is because the CRT monitor technology is more established and because LCD screens are more labor-intensive to produce. The result is that a CRT monitor with a 17-inch viewable area will cost one-half to one-third what an LCD screen with the same viewable area costs.

Better Support for Multiple Resolutions   As discussed in the previous section, LCD screens tend to have one native resolution at which they display text and other items best. CRT monitors can handle several different resolutions with equal quality. If you expect to need to switch between several resolutions, using a CRT monitor may be your better option.

LCD Advantages on the Desktop

Sharper Displays   LCD screens, when used at their native resolution, offer extremely sharp and crisp display. Lines are perfectly straight without any distortion at all. The distinctions between one object and another are equally clear. This makes looking at images on an LCD display somewhat more pleasing in most cases. There is also no need to worry about screen geometry as there is with most moderate- to large-size CRT monitors.

No Refresh Rates   The image on an LCD screen is completely free of any flicker that can be seen in even the best CRT monitors. This is because the screen is not refreshed many times each second as in a CRT monitor. The image is rock solid and very much like looking at a piece of paper. This is one of the best advantages of LCD screens. Without any refresh flickering, an LCD display is extremely easy on the eyes and comfortable to look at.

Advertised Size and Actual Size When you look at a CRT monitor, you'll see the advertised size of the monitor (17 inches, 19 inches, 21 inches, and so on) and then you'll see the viewable area. The viewable area is the actual size of the screen used for display purposes, and it is always an inch or more less than the size of the monitor (most 15-inch CRT monitors have a viewable area of 13.5 to 14 inches, for example). LCD displays have a viewable area that is equal to their advertised size (i.e., a 15-inch LCD screen has a viewable area of 15 inches). This is something to be aware of when comparing CRT monitors and LCD screens of the same or similar sizes.

No Risk of Burn-in There is no risk of burn-in on an LCD screen. It simply can't happen because, unlike CRT monitors, there are no phosphors to retain an image. This means that the usable life span of an LCD display, particularly when used in public settings, is likely to be longer than a CRT monitor.

No Degradation over Time While CRT monitors tend to lose brightness over time as the phosphors are triggered repeatedly, day after day, LCD displays don't suffer from this. The liquid crystal compound isn't affected by the passage of time. Colors remain as vibrant when a LCD screen is five years old as they were when it was brand-new. Combined with the freedom from burn-in, this gives LCD screens a much longer life span than CRT monitors.

No Effect from Magnetic Fields While a CRT monitor can have its images distorted by nearby magnetic or electrical fields or objects, an LCD screen doesn't rely on magnetic fields to help generate an image. As a result, LCD displays cannot suffer image distortion from magnetic fields. This can be helpful if you plan to use a monitor in an area where there are several electrical or magnetic devices in use.

Smaller Footprint LCD displays are physically smaller than CRT monitors are. Because they are essentially flat, they require a great deal less desk space than a CRT monitor does. This is one of the most immediately attractive features of LCD displays.

Less Power A CRT monitor needs a good amount of power to generate continuous electron pulses strong enough to trigger its phosphor-coated screen. This consumes a lot of electricity and generates a lot of heat (which is why, physical size aside, CRT monitors are unsuitable to use in portable computers). LCD displays require a virtual trickle of electrical power to trigger liquid crystal molecules and not a great deal of power for the fluorescent backlight. They also generate almost no heat. This can have a positive, if not dramatic, effect on your electricity bill.

Resolution

A monitor's resolution is the number of individual pixels used to display images on the Mac's screen. The Mac OS and the Mac's video circuitry interact with the monitor to control the resolution. Most monitors support several resolutions (though LCD screens generally have one native resolution that they work best with). Each of these resolutions that is supported by the video circuitry of a Mac will be available to a Mac user. Different resolutions will also usually use different refresh rates on CRT monitors. This will vary depending on the monitor. However, some higher resolutions may refresh too slowly to be comfortable for viewing.

As the resolution or number of pixels used on-screen is increased, the apparent size of each individual object on-screen (icons, windows, letters of text, and so on) decreases. The items themselves are the same logical size because they continue to be made up of the same number of pixels, but because each pixel is now smaller, they have a smaller apparent size.

Higher resolutions allow you to have more items, windows, and large images on-screen, which can result in a better work environment. However, higher resolutions also require the Mac to work harder because it needs to provide more image data to the display. This requires additional video RAM be used and can cause the Mac's display performance to be reduced at very high resolutions. Some higher resolutions are also not appropriate for smaller monitors simply because icons, text, and other objects become too small to be easily visible. The resolution you choose to use will depend on the size monitor you are using, what you are displaying on the monitor, and your personal preference.

Changing Resolutions

You can change the resolution of the Mac's display via two methods. The first is the Monitors control panel (or the Monitors and Sound control panel on some older Mac OS versions). The second is to use the Monitor Resolution control strip module.

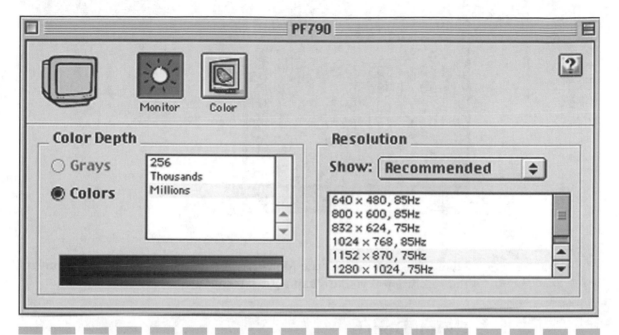

Figure 4-5   The main section of the Monitors control panel.

The Monitors Control Panel   The resolution section of the Monitors control panel, shown in Figure 4-5, displays the resolutions currently available with the attached monitor and the Mac's video circuitry. CRT monitors also display the refresh rate used with each resolution. To change the resolution, simply click on the resolution you wish to use. The Mac changes to the new resolution immediately. For external displays, the Mac also displays a dialog asking you to confirm that you want to use the new resolution. If so, click on OK. If you do not click on OK within 30 seconds, the Mac will revert to the previous resolution. This is a useful safeguard if you change to a resolution that results in a blank or unreadable display. If you are using multiple monitors with a Mac, as described in Chapter 26, each monitor will display the control panel's window so you can adjust resolution and other settings for it separate from the others.

The Monitor Resolution Control Strip Module   The Monitor Resolution control strip module looks like a monitor with a black-and-white checkerboard pattern on it. When clicked, it provides a menu displaying the available resolutions for the chosen display, as shown in Figure 4-6 (if multiple monitors are in use, each monitor is identified for selection by its description in italics within the menu). To choose a new resolution, simply select the new resolution using the menu. As with the

Figure 4-6
The Monitor
Resolution control
strip module.

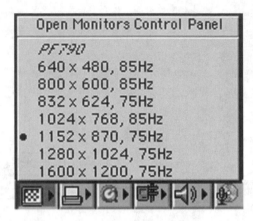

Monitors control panel, the Mac presents a dialog asking you to confirm the resolution if you are using an external display.

Color Depth

Often associated with resolution (though not completely related to it), is color depth (sometimes called bit depth). *Color depth* refers to the level of color accuracy the Mac will produce on a display and is actually a function of the Mac's video circuitry and not the display itself. The higher the color depth, the greater the number of individual colors the Mac is capable of producing. The more individual colors, the more natural looking the gradations from one color to another appear and the more realistic an image can be displayed.

Color depth is given either in terms of the number of individual colors being produced or in terms of the number of bits of memory required to store image data for each pixel of the screen at a color depth. The most common color depths used are 8-bit (256 separate colors), 16-bit (thousands of colors, about 16 thousand), and 24-bit (millions of colors). These three color depths are supported on all recent Mac models. There is also 32-bit (billions of color), which requires an additional, higher-end video card for the Mac to produce.

Although each additional color depth increases the true-life quality of the Mac's display, most people aren't capable of perceiving differences when moving higher than 16-bit color. This is because of the limitations of the human eye when distinguishing individual colors from each other in most still two-dimensional images. Higher color depths may provide better quality in certain situations, however.

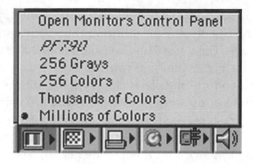

Figure 4-7
The BitDepth control strip module.

Color Depth, Video RAM, and Higher Resolutions   One way in which color depth and screen resolution are related is that they both require video RAM. Video RAM is part of the Mac's video circuitry that holds the data for what is being displayed onscreen. Higher resolutions require more video RAM because there are more pixels to generate data for. Higher color depths require more video RAM because each pixel requires more data. At some higher resolutions, the amount of video RAM installed in a Mac may limit what color depths can be used. A 1600x1200 resolution may limit you to 16-bit color as opposed to 24-bit color on some Macs, for example.

Changing Color Depth   Color depth can be changed in pretty much the same way as resolution, either using the Monitors control panel (see Figure 4-5), where available color depths at a chosen resolution are listed to the left of the resolutions section, or using the BitDepth control strip module. This module, shown in Figure 4-7, looks like a monitor with blue, yellow, red, and green vertical lines. When clicked, it provides a menu with the available color depths. Simply select one from the menu to change the color depth of a display. As with changing the resolution, when using multiple monitors, you need to change the color depth of each monitor separately.

Connecting and Configuring a Monitor

Connecting a monitor or display to the Mac is relatively easy and straightforward. First, unpack and position the display. Plug the display into a power outlet (if needed), and attach it to the appropriate port on the Mac (using an adapter if needed). Follow any special instructions that accompany the display for additional features such as USB ports or built-in speakers. Then start up the Mac and select the appropriate resolution and color depth that you want to use.

Some older monitors (and other display devices, such as LCD projectors) may only function at certain resolutions. If you are using an older monitor as your primary display, you need to be sure it operates at a resolution supported by your Mac. Also, depending on the resolution being used, you may need to start up the Mac with a newer display to select the older monitor's resolution before you are able to connect and use the older monitor.

Following this, however, you may need or want to configure other settings of the display. These can include calibrating the color output of the display and adjusting the brightness, contrast, and other screen geometry settings. This section first examines the types of monitor ports used available for Mac displays and then examines the other monitor configuration issues.

Monitor Ports

There are four primary types of monitor ports that are currently used with the Mac: the standard VGA-style port used on PCs that is now the standard Mac monitor port, the earlier Mac-specific monitor port that is not currently used, and the new digital video interface port and the even newer Apple Display connectors.

VGA-Style All the current Macs that support video-out (the Power Mac, PowerBook, and iMac DV models) use an industry-standard VGA monitor port, shown in Figure 4-8. The big advantage to using this type of port is that it is used in virtually any monitor currently made and allows you to connect an extremely wide variety of monitors to the Mac with no effort at all. This is a change from the proprietary-style monitor port that was standard on earlier Macintosh models.

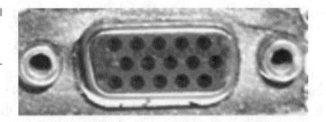

Figure 4-8
A standard VGA monitor port.

Figure 4-9
The older Mac
monitor port.

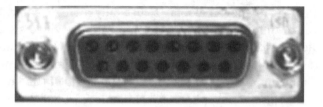

Older Mac-Style Port   For many years, Apple used a proprietary monitor interface. This interface used a 15-pin DB connector, as shown in Figure 4-9. The pins were arranged in two rows, making the connector longer than the one used for VGA and SVGA monitors used with PCs. Although Apple abandoned this connector in favor of the industry-standard VGA connector with the Blue and White Power Mac G3, any older Macs and several Mac video cards still use this interface. Additionally, all Apple monitors before the Studio Displays introduced along with the Blue G3 used the same interface. If you wish to use one of these older monitors with a current Mac, you need to use an adapter. (One is included with the PowerBook computers and one was included with the Power Mac G3; others can be purchased from various companies.) Similarly, if you have an older Mac or are installing a video card with the older connectors and wish to use a VGA or SVGA monitor with it, you need a special adapter (different from the one used with new Macs) to connect it to the older-style video port.

Digital Ports   DVI (Digital Video Interface) ports are a new development in the world of computer displays. LCD displays do not display images by painting the screen in the same manner as a CRT monitor. A CRT monitor requires an analog video signal for each of the three colors it paints on the screen. This means that the Mac's video circuitry needs to convert the digital data for the display into an analog signal. Since LCD displays do not paint a screen in a method that requires an analog signal, it is possible for them to accept digital data directly and display it on-screen. This adds to the sharpness and clarity of the resulting image. DVI ports are ports designed specifically for use with digital LCD displays to send the digital data directly to the display without any analog conversion. It is possible to use an adapter that converts between VGA and DVI ports, and a number of such adapters are on the market.

Apple's ADC Monitor Port   Apple recently unveiled a new proprietary monitor port that combines the standard video output features of earlier ports with a USB channel and a power supply connection. The purpose of this port is to allow a display to use only a single cable. This cable provides power to the display from the computer, the video signal and data, and a connection for USB ports that may be built into a monitor (many monitors, including all of Apple's current displays, include a built-in USB hub).

The new monitor port is included on some of the latest Macintosh models and is used on Apple's newest displays. As of this writing, the technology is extremely new and the port has yet to be adopted by any other monitors or video card manufacturers. The Macs supporting the new port also include a standard VGA port as well. It is likely that an adapter will be produced to convert between the port and a VGA or DVI standard port for using monitors that rely solely on the ADC port with older Macs.

Monitor Settings and Screen Geometry

Once the monitor is plugged and powered (either from the wall outlet, Apple's ADC port, or the second power connector included in the Power Macs for a monitor) and connected to the Mac, it can be used. Unlike other computing platforms, the Mac does not use or require driver software to be installed for individual monitors. Assuming the monitor is a multisync display, it should function with the Mac without any problem.

However, once the display is functioning, there may be several items you need to configure for it to display optimally. You configure these settings either by using controls built into the monitor, which will generate a menu on-screen, or by using the Geometry section of the Monitors control panel, as shown in Figure 4-10 (usually this only applies to built-in displays or some Apple-made monitors).

The following sections cover the major options for configuring a monitor. Not all monitors have all of these features, and you may not need to adjust them on every monitor (in fact, many are only used on CRT monitors and not LCD displays). Also, many of these factors interact with each other. Changing one setting may affect how another setting looks. It is a good idea to write down the original settings before changing them in case the results of your changes don't look as good as you'd expected (some monitors also allow you to save settings in advance). Settings are also resolution-dependent, meaning your settings may be perfect for 800×600 screen display but look positively awful at a higher resolution such as 1600×1200.

Brightness Brightness is something you'll find on almost every monitor. As you might expect, it controls the overall brightness of the entire display. You can adjust the brightness to whatever level you find comfortable, though most people tend to prefer somewhere in the middle of

Figure 4-10
The Geometry section
of the Monitors
control panel.

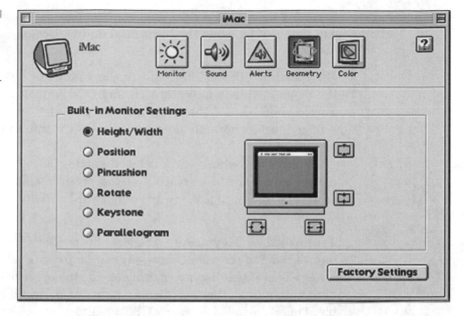

the range for CRT displays and near the high end of the display for LCD displays. If you are using ColorSync or another monitor calibration technology (see later in this chapter for details on monitor calibration), you should stick to the brightness setting implemented when calibrating your display unless it is uncomfortable for you.

Contrast   Contrast is also found on the vast majority of CRT and LCD monitors. It controls the brightness of an image in comparison to the background of the screen. As a general rule, contrast is best left at its highest setting, though you can change it if that seems too dramatic.

Horizontal and Vertical Positioning   Horizontal and vertical positioning are only found on CRT monitors, and they are on almost all CRT monitors. Simply put, *positioning* refers to how and where on the screen's surface images are displayed (or how far left or right or up or down the electrons are being directed to the screen's surface). You can move the image around so that it is as perfectly centered as possible using the positioning controls.

Related to positioning (and sometimes considered to be the same feature) is horizontal and vertical sizing. This controls how much of the available right-to-left and top-to-bottom space on the screen's surface a CRT display is using. Most CRT monitors have some black space surrounding the actual screen image. This space is simply wasted, and you can reduce it by using the horizontal and vertical sizing controls.

Pincushion   Pincushion adjusts the inward or outward curvature of the display. This is important on large CRT monitors where the image may bow outward or bend inward along the left and right edges of the screen. Most moderately large or large CRT monitors include pincushion adjustment.

Pincushion balance is a related setting on several monitors that allows adjusting the curvature of the entire display to one side or the other in addition to just inward or outward curvature.

Trapezoid or Keystone   Trapezoidal or keystone adjustment (both names refer to the same function) can be used to adjust the upper and lower edges of the display, making one or the other wider or narrower as needed to ensure that the display forms as perfect a rectangle as possible. This is included on many CRT monitors.

Rotation   This setting allows you to rotate the entire image clockwise or counterclockwise as needed in order to ensure that the image is as horizontal as possible. It is included on a number of CRT displays.

Corner Correction   Some larger CRT displays include this setting. It allows you to correct the geometry of each corner of the monitor to ensure that the display is as perfect a rectangle as possible. Corner correction can also include the ability to adjust the coloring in a corner of the display on larger monitors if the brightness and shading seems to fade in one or more corners.

Linearity   Linearity is a setting included only on large or high-end displays. It can be used to adjust the entire screen to ensure that lines are displayed completely straight and that circles are displayed with completely even curves.

Moiré   Many displays may produce a waving pattern that seems to overlay a screen image at times. Most of the time, this pattern is not particularly noticeable. However, some displays now include a setting called Moiré that allows you to adjust the display to reduce this effect.

Monitor Calibration

Once the monitor is displaying an image as optimally as possible, you should consider calibrating it to display colors consistently. Color calibration ensures that from one monitor to another, the colors display on-screen with the same shading and tinting and that colors look the same. Calibration can also go a step further because you can calibrate printers and scanners. This ensures that when scanned images are displayed, they retain their actual coloring as accurately as possible. Similarly, printers can be calibrated to ensure that when images are printed, their colors are as close as possible to the colors of the image on-screen.

Several color calibration technologies are available, ranging from Apple's free ColorSync technology, which is included with the Mac OS, to expensive and high-end hardware designed for professional graphic design, publishing, and printing. The following paragraphs overview Apple's ColorSync as well as the Adobe Gamma calibration software. It also includes some general information on higher-end options.

ColorSync Apple's ColorSync is the easiest-to-use monitor calibration technology. It ships with every Mac and includes predefined settings for many Apple monitors, printers, and scanners. If you are in a hurry, you can simply select the appropriate presets in Apple's ColorSync control panel (or choose the Generic settings if you are using a non-Apple product). Many Mac-specific devices, such as scanners and printers include ColorSync calibration profiles along with their driver software. If these are installed by default, they will be displayed in the appropriate menus in the ColorSync control panel. If they are not installed by default, search the installation CDs for the ColorSync Profiles (or contact the manufacturer if you can't locate any) and drag them into the ColorSync Profiles folder inside the System Folder.

For displays that are not made by Apple or intended for Mac use, you need to calibrate the display to create a profile. You can also create customized profiles for an existing Apple display to account for differences between your display and the standard Apple profile.

To create a ColorSync profile, open the Monitors control panel and select the color button at the top of the window. Then click on the Calibrate button. This leads you through a series of questions and options that allow you to calibrate your display. It then allows you to save a custom ColorSync Profile for the display.

Adobe Gamma   Adobe makes several image editing and desktop publishing applications, including the popular programs Photoshop, Illustrator, and PageMaker. It therefore shouldn't come as surprise that Adobe has created their own monitor calibration control panel. The Adobe Gamma control panel is installed as part of multiple Adobe applications and offers many of the same functions as ColorSync. Adobe Gamma also includes additional abilities to auto-detect a monitor and includes additional profile information for monitors that aren't Mac-specific. Although Adobe Gamma is not the most powerful calibration tool available, it does offer some abilities beyond ColorSync and is compatible with ColorSync and some Windows-based color calibration technologies. Adobe Gamma also offers an assistant mode that walks you through the setup process.

Other Calibration Tools   If you are providing graphics or other work for professional publication, you will almost certainly need more precise calibration than is possible with either ColorSync or Adobe Gamma. To achieve these levels of color calibration for your monitor and other hardware, you must invest in a higher-end calibration option. These include higher-end calibration software suites, as well as specialized hardware designed for color calibration. See the "Resources for Further Study" section at the end of this chapter for additional sources of information on color calibration and management.

Troubleshooting Display Problems

Following are common display problems and their solutions.

The Monitor Displays No Image at All

If the monitor is completely blank, first make certain that the monitor is turned on and plugged in properly. Assuming this is the case, check the cable connecting the monitor to the Mac. Also, make sure the Mac is turned on and functioning correctly. In addition, check all cables for any signs of wear, damage, or crimping. If there appear to be no obvious cabling or Mac problems, check to be certain that the Mac's video card (for Power Mac computers only) is inserted properly as discussed in Chapter 8.

It is also possible that the chosen resolution is not supported by the monitor being used. This can often be the case when a new monitor is attached to a Mac for the first time or if a monitor is attached after the startup process begins. Restarting the Mac should resolve this. If not, restarting the Mac and zapping the PRAM will force the Mac to revert to the lowest-possible resolution supported by the monitor (usually 640x480). Another resolution can be chosen once the Mac finishes starting up.

If this doesn't appear to be the problem, the monitor itself is probably damaged. Try using it with another Mac (if it is an external monitor) to be certain, or try using another monitor with that Mac. Using an external monitor can help determine if the built-in display of an iMac DV or PowerBook computer has failed. Assuming the monitor remains non-functional, contact the manufacturer for an appropriate service facility. Repairing CRT monitors yourself can be very dangerous because of lethal electrical charge they can maintain even after weeks of inactivity.

For an LCD screen monitor, you may also want to make sure the screen's backlighting has been turned down completely. For PowerBook/iBook displays, this can be done using the keyboard. For external LCD displays, controls should be on the display itself. If this doesn't help, it is possible that an LCD screen's backlight has failed. Again, you should contact the manufacturer regarding a service facility, as backlights will be device-specific parts and are most likely available only to authorized repair shops.

The Monitor Display Is Jittery or Flickering

This symptom usually only occurs with CRT monitors and can be the result of magnetic interference. Try moving the monitor to another location or seeing if there are any obvious causes of interference (magnets, stereo speakers, motors of any kind, or fluorescent lamps) in the area that could be moved. You can also use the degauss button on a monitor (or turn the monitor off and then on if there is no degauss feature) to alleviate some magnetic effects.

Electrical devices plugged into the same circuit of a building's electrical wiring as a monitor can generate electrical "noise" that can cause screen flicker. You can alleviate this by using an uninterruptible power supply (as discussed in Chapter 11) or by moving the device that is generating the problem to an electrical outlet that is on another circuit of the building's wiring.

If this is not caused by magnetic interference, it can be a sign that the monitor's power supply is beginning to fail. You can determine that this is likely because moving the monitor will not solve the problem. If the power supply is beginning to fail, the monitor must be professionally serviced (again, contact the manufacturer for service providers) or replaced.

The Size of the Display Seems to Shrink during Use or over Time

This problem is also a sign that a CRT monitor's power supply is failing. Contact the manufacturer regarding servicing the monitor or replace it. *Note:* There is also a practical joke extension that will cause a similar effect on the Mac, which can be circumvented simply by starting with extensions off.

The Shape of the Image on the Monitor Seems Distorted

This symptom generally indicates that the monitor's geometry needs to be adjusted. This is particularly true with large monitors or anytime you change screen resolutions. Refer to the section on configuring a monitor earlier in this chapter.

This can also be due to magnetic interference in some cases, though it is less likely than other indications of magnetic interference. Again, moving the monitor or removing the obvious source of magnetic interference can alleviate this condition.

The Monitor Goes Blank after You Select a New Resolution

This problem usually indicates that the monitor doesn't support the resolution you have chosen. Simply wait 30 seconds for the Mac to realize you haven't confirmed the new resolution, and your previous resolution will be reselected.

An Application Says It Cannot Run because of the Current Resolution or Color Depth

A number of programs, mostly games, are designed to run at a specific monitor resolution or color depth. Depending on how the application is designed, it may automatically change your monitor settings when launched or it may simply tell you that it requires different settings and then quit. If it requires different settings, change your screen resolution and/or color depth to accommodate the application or game.

The Monitor Displays One Color Predominantly over the Others

This problem tends to occur with monitors that are designed to sync on a specific color signal (usually green) when used with today's Macs, because today's Mac's don't support sync-on-color. You need to use an appropriate adapter with the monitor to enable it to function properly.

However, this can also occur when using lower-quality monitor cables or cables that are not appropriate for a specific monitor model. If it occurs with a new monitor that does not use sync-on-color, chances are there is a conflict with the monitor cable being used and replacing it should solve the problem.

The Monitor's Picture Seems to Roll or Look Snowy

This problem indicates that the monitor is not syncing properly with the Mac. It tends to occur with monitors that are not multisync (i.e., they support only one resolution and refresh rate), with monitors that use sync-on-color, or with a monitor when a refresh rate that isn't supported by the monitor is chosen in the Monitors control panel (refresh rates are chosen along with screen resolutions). For the first two possibilities, there is little hope other than an appropriate adapter product.

In the case of the third situation, restarting the Mac may solve the problem. If not, restarting the Mac and zapping the PRAM (as the chosen resolution is stored in the PRAM) will force the Mac to use the lowest resolution and refresh rate supported by the monitor, usually 640x480 at 60Hz. Once the Mac starts up, you can choose another resolution and refresh rate as described earlier in this chapter.

All Colors and/or White Appear Blurred or Faded

This symptom can be an effect of magnetic interference (check for usual interference sources as discussed earlier). It can also be due to interference from the Earth's magnetic field. Most monitors are designed to function within a specific hemisphere of the Earth's magnetic field. If the problem is not solved by removing the obvious magnetic interference sources, try turning the monitor at a 45- or 90-degree angle to its current positioning.

Images Appear Blurry or Have a Ghosting or Halo Effect of Other Colors

This symptom usually indicates misconvergence of the electron pulses of the monitor, as discussed earlier in this chapter. Some monitors may have an external control labeled convergence or focus that can be used to adjust for these symptoms. Many, however, place such a control inside the monitor or don't offer it at all. In both of these cases, you should contact the monitor's manufacturer for instructions or locations of service centers (again, CRT monitors build up a lethal electrical charge, and you can injure or kill yourself if you open one up).

There Are Blotches On-Screen

The most common cause of one or a few blotches on a CRT screen is overheating. If you are in a hot climate or building and the monitor has been running steadily for some time, it may begin to overheat and blotches may appear on the screen as a result, growing worse the longer the monitor is running. This can be remedied by turning the monitor off and allowing it to cool down.

Icons and Windows Position Themselves Strangely On-Screen

This problem often occurs if the resolution of the monitor is changed unexpectedly, such as an application automatically switching the resolution before running. The icons and other items may not return to their original places when the monitor is restored to its original resolution. If this happens, you can move the items back to their original positions by hand. Some shareware utilities are available that will reposition icons automatically after changes in screen resolution.

A Blank Screen Appears at Startup when Two Video Cards Are Installed

If you have a Mac with multiple video cards installed but only one monitor connected, you may find that the monitor displays only a blank blue or gray screen when the Mac is started. This happens because the Mac is using the second video card for the startup screen and primary display, even though no monitor is attached to it. This can often occur after zapping the PRAM, because the PRAM data contains the settings for multiple monitors. You can fix this by attaching a monitor to the video card and then changing the primary display and startup screen to the monitor you normally wish to use.

Resources for Further Study

The following URLs provide additional information on some of the concepts, issues, and products discussed in this chapter.

Apple's Studio Displays Home Page—http://www.apple.com/displays

Apple's ColorSync Home Page—http://www.apple.com/colorsync

The Monitor Buyer's Guide—http://www.monitorbuyersguide.com

Griffin Technology—http://www.griffintechnology.com

About.com Mac Hardware Monitor Resources—
   http://machardware.about.com/msubmonitors.htm

About.com Mac Support Monitor Resources—
   http://macsupport.about.com/msub26.htm

About.com Computer Peripherals Monitor Resources—
   http://peripherals.about.com/msub_monitor_top.htm

Hard Drives

A Mac's internal hard drive is its primary place for storing files and applications. It is also the primary startup disk from which the Mac OS will be loaded during startup. Hard drives have the greatest data capacity of any type of disk that can be used to store data, and they also offer greater performance in saving and retrieving files than any other type of disk. Hard drives come in fixed sizes that cannot be expanded without physically removing and replacing the disk (or adding an additional hard drive to a Mac).

All Macs ship with at least one internal hard drive. The Power Mac G3 and G4 models can contain up to three internal hard drives, while all other current Macs can only support a single internal hard drive. In addition to internal hard drives, there are a external hard drives that can be attached to a Macintosh. External hard drives are functionally the same as an internal hard drive, but they are mounted inside an external case that is connected to the Mac, and they often require their own independent power supply.

This chapter examines the physical components of a hard drive: how hard drives organize, store, and retrieve data; how to install an internal hard drive in the Mac models covered in this book; how to format a hard drive for use with the Macintosh (including custom formatting options); and how to use hard drive repair utilities on damaged or corrupted hard drives.

How Hard Drives Work

The name *hard drive* is derived from the use of a platter (usually made of an aluminum alloy) that is coated with a thin magnetic film very similar to the coating on the tape inside an audio cassette. The magnetic film stores information in tiny spots that are alternately turned on or off (magnetized or demagnetized) by an electronic mechanism known as the *drive head* or *read/write head*. The read/write head also reads the magnetic qualities of each spot on a platter without adjusting it, allowing the hard drive to retrieve stored data.

The read/write head is affixed to a mechanical arm called an *actuator arm* that allows the head to be moved across the entire surface of a platter of a hard drive. The read/write head actually floats a few millionths of a centimeter over the platter (a height about equal to the size of an individual smoke particle), never actually touching it. The head is kept floating above the platter by the air current generated whenever the drive is running. When the drive is not running, the head is moved to a safe space in the drive known as the *parking area*. If the head were to come into contact with the platter, it would erase any data stored where the contact occurred, and both the platter and the head could be damaged by the impact. Because of the minute distance between the head and the platter, hard drives are sealed airtight to keep any dust or smoke particle from entering and damaging the drive. Figure 5-1 shows the inside of a typical hard drive.

Most hard drives have multiple platters in them, giving the drive more space on which to store data. Hard drives also almost always use both sides of each platter to store data. Each side of each platter has its own read/write head, but all the read/write heads in a hard drive are affixed to a single actuator arm that scans across the surface of the hard drive as a single unit. The platters of the hard drive all spin together at a constant speed (common speeds include 3600 rpm, 5400 rpm, and 7200 rpm). The faster the platters spin, the faster the actuator arm can position read/write heads at specific points on the platters.

Besides the platters, heads, and the actuator arm that actually store data, hard drives contain a motor that spins the platters and another that moves the actuator arm across their surface. They also contain dedicated circuitry that controls the action of the all the drive components and acts as the interface between the hard drive and the Mac's motherboard and processor.

Figure 5-1

The inside of a hard drive. Notice the round platter and the metal actuator arm that contain the read/write head.

This control circuitry contains all the instructions that the drive needs to locate data on the hard drive and respond to commands issued by the Mac's processor. Most hard drives also contain a special piece of dedicated RAM known as a *cache*. This cache is designed to serve as a buffer to smooth out the flow of data between the drive and the computer. The next chapter contains additional information on caches, such as those used in hard drives.

Internal versus External Hard Drives

Internal hard drives look like small metal cases with one side containing a circuit board and one end containing a connector for the drive's interface cable and a power connector. Figure 5-2 shows a typical internal hard drive. Internal hard drives also often contain jumpers that allow you to configure various settings for the drive. Jumpers, such as those in Figure 5-3, are pairs of narrow metal pins that are set by placing a special plastic or metal sleeve over two specific pins. Which jumpers are used to set which options will vary among drives, and you should check the manual that came with the drive for details. Jumpers are typically used to set a hard drive's SCSI ID number and termination or to set an IDE drive as either the master or slave drive (see Chapters 12 and 13 for additional information on configuring SCSI or IDE drives).

Figure 5-2
An internal hard drive.

Figure 5-3
Jumpers on
an internal drive.

Internal drives need to be connected to the inside of a computer and need to be powered from its internal power supply. Most Macs can support only a single internal hard drive. The exception is the Power Mac G3 and G4 computers, which can accept up to three internal hard drives. Also, every Mac covered in this book requires an IDE internal hard drive. The Power Mac computers are the exception as they can accept internal SCSI hard drives if a SCSI expansion card is installed in them (see Chapter 12).

External hard drives are mounted or built into external cases. These cases often include a separate power supply to power the drive (though some newer drive types, such as USB and FireWire, can draw power directly from the Mac). External hard drives can use a number of interfaces, though FireWire and USB are the most common today.

Hard Drive Interfaces

A hard drive's interface is the means by which a hard drive's control circuitry communicates with the Mac's processor. The interface provides a means by which the processor can send data to the hard drive to be stored, and for the processor to request data. The drive's control circuitry then performs the actual work of storing and retrieving the data.

There have been a number of interface technologies used for hard drives over the years. Each of these interfaces delivers different levels of performance, and each has its own inherent advantages and disadvantages.

SCSI   SCSI (Small Computer System Interface) is the oldest technology used for attaching hard drives to the Mac. It has been, and continues to be, used for many high-performance hard drives. SCSI offers excellent performance for hard drives of any type. It allows the full performance abilities of the drive to be utilized, and it can be used for both external and internal drives, although most internal drives today use the IDE interface instead.

SCSI also has several specific rules in terms of how devices need to be connected to the Mac and configured. Each SCSI device (whether a hard drive or another type of peripheral) needs to be set to a unique SCSI ID number. SCSI also requires the use termination for devices at the end of a chain of SCSI devices (whether internal or external). This makes SCSI more complicated for new users than any other hard drive interface. There are also a variety of SCSI standards and cable types that you need to understand when choosing a SCSI hard drive. These issues, as well as SCSI performance advantages, are discussed in Chapter 12.

NOTE: *Unfortunately, SCSI is not an option for most of the recent Macintosh models. The iMac and iBook models do not have any option for attaching SCSI devices. The Power Mac models can use SCSI, but you need to add a SCSI card to them. The most recent PowerBook models with FireWire ports built in can accept a SCSI PC Card, which allows you to attach SCSI devices to them, but at the added cost of the SCSI card. The older PowerBooks do include a built-in SCSI port, which makes them best candidate for using an external SCSI-based hard drive.*

IDE   The current Macs (and most Macs for the past several years) use the IDE interface for internal hard drives. IDE hard drives offer the advantage of being cheaper than SCSI drives. IDE is also free of many of the rules involved when using SCSI. Although there are some variations in the IDE standard with regard to performance (see Chapter 13 for details on IDE types), most IDE hard drives offer good performance for consumer uses, and the more powerful Ultra ATA/66 IDE hard drives offer better performance than some SCSI variations.

IDE supports the use of up to two hard drives per connector in what is known as a *master/slave* drive configuration. This is only relevant to the Power Mac computers because the iMac, PowerBook, and iBook computers simply do not have room for more than one internal hard drive. All Power Macs covered in this book (except for the Blue Power Mac G3s with a revision 1 motherboard) support the use of master/slave drive configurations.

These early Power Mac G3 models can be identified in two ways. First, the hard drive IDE cable have only a single connector, whereas Macs supporting master/slave configurations have two connectors. Second,

Power Macs supporting master and slave configurations have a hard drive mounting bracket with a rounded or U-shaped upper ridge that allows a second hard drive to be mounted in the bracket above the factory-installed hard drive, as shown in Figure 5-4. The early Power Mac G3s, which did not support the use of master/slave drive configurations, do not ship with this U-shaped bracket.

When you are using two IDE hard drives on a single connector in a master/slave configuration, one of the two drives must be set as the master drive and the other as the slave drive. There is no real difference between which drive is set as master or slave. If there is only a single hard drive attached to the connector, it must be set as the master drive.

Hard drives ship from the factory set to master. To change this setting, you need to adjust the jumpers on the hard drive. The exact jumpers used for setting a hard drive as a slave drive vary depending on the model and manufacturer of the drive. The documentation that accompanies an IDE hard drive should include a diagram indicating the various jumper settings. If not, you can contact the drive's manufacturer or website to obtain information on the jumper settings. See Chapter 13 for more information on master/slave configurations, IDE types, performance, and other considerations.

Figure 5-4
This rounded-edge hard drive bracket identifies Power Macs that support master/slave configurations for IDE hard drives.

USB   USB is one of the primary technologies for attaching external devices of any kind to the current Macs. For some iMac and iBook models, it is the only option for connecting external devices at all. USB hard drives are on the market and they perform well as backup drives. Unfortunately, USB is also very slow. You can use USB drives for backups and for storing files that you don't use regularly, but if you try to run an application or open a large file from a USB drive, you'll find that performance distinctly lacking.

USB offers the ability to connect and disconnect devices at will (known as being hot pluggable). However, you should unmount a USB hard drive by selecting its icon in the Finder and either dragging it to the trash or using the Put Away command in the Special menu before disconnecting it. This ensures that any open files are closed and that the Mac is not accessing the drive when it is disconnected. If the Mac or any application is accessing a hard drive when it is disconnected, open files on the drive can be corrupted, as can the drive's directory structures. Chapter 15 covers USB in greater detail.

FireWire   FireWire is a powerful interface that combines good data transfer performance with an easy-to-use interface. FireWire is hot pluggable, like USB, so you can connect and disconnect FireWire hard drives at will (again, unmount the drive before disconnecting it). FireWire also provides enough power through its cabling to supply the majority of external FireWire hard drives, so there is no need for an external power adapter.

The ease of use, high level of performance, and ability to be powered directly from the Mac all contribute to making FireWire a very attractive interface for hard drives. FireWire also ensures that a specific amount of bandwidth is available to a hard drive when it is being accessed, which makes FireWire hard drives extremely attractive for multimedia work, in which digital audio or video must be recorded at a constant rate to maintain quality. FireWire is covered in detail in Chapter 14.

PowerBook Expansion Bays   As you will read in Chapter 9, PowerBooks include a special bay that normally houses a CD-ROM or DVD-ROM drive module. However, this module is removable and can be replaced with other types of drives, including hard drives. This provides a convenient way to add a second hard drive to a PowerBook that is powered by its power source (battery or AC adapter). PowerBook expansion bay hard drives do not deliver the performance of some of the faster IDE types (such as the PowerBook's internal hard drive) or FireWire, but they do deliver performance that is fine for most uses and perfectly suited to running applications and storing moderately large files.

PC Cards   Also covered in Chapter 9 are PC Card hard drives. These are either very small hard drives that insert into a PowerBook's PC Card slot or hard drives that use a built-in PC Card as an interface. The performance and capacities of these drives vary, but they are generally on par with the PowerBook's expansion bay or better.

Both expansion bay and PC Card hard drives are hot pluggable in the current PowerBooks (though earlier models require the computer to be put into sleep mode while swapping expansion bay drives). However, as mentioned with USB and FireWire hard drives, you should unmount the drive before removing it.

How Hard Drives Organize Data

Before a hard drive can be used to store data, it needs to be formatted. There are two levels of formatting: physical formatting and logical formatting.

Physical Formatting

The platters of a hard drive are organized into circular tracks. Each track is then divided up into individual sections called *sectors*. Each sector is assigned specific addressing information by the hard drive's control circuitry. It is the address of each sector that allows the control circuitry to know which sectors contain data and how to locate that data on the hard drive. On most hard drives, each sector is 512 bytes large, so there are literally billions of sectors on a hard drive. This is known as *physical formatting* (sometimes called low-level formatting), and it allows the drive's control circuitry to be able to identify each sector of the drive so that each sector can be used to store data.

Physical formatting allows the hard drive's control circuitry to store data on the drive and locate stored data when requested by the computer's processor. Physical formatting is performed in the factory when the hard drive is manufactured. It is not something you usually need to worry about, aside from knowing that it has been performed. Even when a hard drive is divided into tracks and sectors for its control circuitry, it needs to be logically formatted or initialized before it can be used by the Mac (or any other computer) to store data.

Logical Formatting

Logical formatting, on the other hand, is something that you do need to be concerned with, and it is what is often meant by "formatting" or initializing a hard drive. Logical formatting is the process of creating index and directory structures on the drive so that the Mac can read data from or write data to the drive. It also creates a driver (instructions that tell the Mac how to access the drive) and places it at the very beginning of the drive. This enables the Mac to recognize and access the hard drive as soon as it sees it at startup. Logical formatting is performed with a hard drive formatting utility such as Apple's Drive Setup (or one of several third-party formatting utilities).

Logical formatting also establishes allocation blocks on the hard drive. *Allocation blocks* are collections of sectors on a hard drive that are used by the Mac's disk format or file system to store files. Each allocation block can contain an entire file or an individual piece of a file.

The directory structures created when formatting a hard drive are the files that allow the Mac to access the hard drive properly. Several different files make up the directory structures, and each performs an important function in allowing the Mac to access the drive. If any of these files are damaged, corrupted, or erased, the Mac may not be able to access the hard drive, or it may not be able to do so reliably. If this happens, a hard drive repair utility (which repairs the directory structures of the drive, rather than the drive's physical components) may be able to restore these important files. Hard drive repair utilities are discussed in detail toward the end of this chapter.

The directory structures for a hard drive include boot blocks, a volume information block, a volume bit map, a catalog tree, and an extents tree. Every disk (hard drive, CD, floppy, and so on) formatted for use with the Macintosh contain these directory structures. Let's take a quick look at the function performed by each of these files, so that you will have an idea of what diagnostic messages relating to them from a hard drive repair utility actually mean.

Boot Blocks The *boot blocks* are the first two allocation blocks of the drive or disk. If no System Folder is installed on the disk, then the boot blocks remain empty of any data. When a System Folder is placed on the disk, however, the boot blocks are changed to include information that the Mac will use when starting up from the disk. The primary information in the boot blocks is the location of the System Folder on the hard drive. This tells the Mac's processor where to find the System Folder at start up so that it can load the Mac OS. If the boot blocks of a drive become corrupted or erased, the Mac will not be able to start up from that drive. Installing a new System Folder on a drive will rewrite the boot blocks, removing any problems.

Volume Information Block   The *volume information block* follows the boot blocks and is a single allocation block that contains data about the drive and its format. This includes the drive's name, the number of files stored on it, the number of folders contained on the drive, the size of the allocation blocks, and other information that is needed for the Mac to interact with the drive. If the volume information block is corrupted or erased, the Mac will not be able to access a hard drive.

Because corruption of the volume information block is a very real possibility, a copy of it, called the alternate volume information block, is created and maintained on a drive as well. The alternate volume information block is located in the second-to-last allocation block of a drive and is used by the Mac if the volume information block is corrupted. If both the volume information block and the alternate block are damaged, the Mac will not be able to access the drive. The Mac will not inform users if the volume information block is damaged and it is using the alternate block, however. Access to the drive will continue without any indication of trouble. This is one reason you should regularly run a hard drive repair utility to check for trouble, as it will detect damage to the volume information block and repair it.

Volume Bit Map   The *volume bit map* is a map of the allocation blocks of a drive. Each allocation block is indicated by one bit of data (a single 1 or 0) that tells the Mac which blocks have files stored in them and which ones are free to use for storing files. If the volume bit map becomes corrupted or damaged, the Mac will be able to access the drive, but it will not know which allocation blocks already have data stored in them. This means that it may replace existing files with new files (deleting the originals). If this happens, there will be no warning until you try to access the original files. This is another reason to run a disk repair utility regularly to compare the actual allocation blocks on a drive with the volume bit map to verify that it is correct (and repair it, if it isn't). It is also a good reason to back up your data regularly (as discussed in Chapter 39).

Catalog Tree   The *catalog tree* (sometimes referred to as the catalog BTree or catalog file) is a database that contains a record for every file (document, application, extension, and so on) and folder on a Mac's hard drive. A catalog tree record for a file includes the name of the file, a special file identification number, the file's type and creator, any Finder flags (such as labels) for the file, and dates relating to that file. A catalog tree record for a folder contains similar information, although not as detailed.

Extents Tree   Files that take up more than one allocation block are split up into pieces known as *extents*. Each extent is stored in a separate allocation block on the hard drive. If a hard drive is nearly full, extents of a file may be stored in allocation blocks across the hard drive rather then in allocation blocks that are next to each other (this is known as fragmentation and is discussed in the next section). The *extents tree* (sometimes referred to as the extents BTree or extents file) is a database that tracks all of the extents stored on a hard drive. An extents tree record contains where an extent begins and ends, as well as what file each extent belongs to and the number of extents in a file.

The extents tree and the catalog tree work together, enabling the Mac to locate each of the pieces of a file on a hard drive. If either one becomes corrupted, the Mac will not be able to locate or access data properly.

Fragmentation

Files that are larger than a hard drive's allocation block size are divided into extents so that they can be stored in multiple allocation blocks on the drive. When a hard drive is first used, each extent of a file is stored in the allocation block right after the extent before it. When the drive needs to retrieve the file, it reads the blocks sequentially, one after the other. If no files were ever deleted from the drive, the drive would quickly become full. But when a file is deleted, there is suddenly a gap of allocation blocks that is usable. The hard drive can use these allocation blocks to store new files. However, a file may require more blocks than are in that particular gap, so the file may need to be broken up, placing extents in different locations on the drive. When this happens a file is said to be fragmented.

Fragmented files take longer for the drive to read and write because the drive heads need to seek across the surface of the drive to locate and read each piece of the file. The more fragmented a file is, the longer it takes to access. Likewise, the more fragmented files there are on a hard drive, the slower the drive (and thus the Mac) will perform.

In addition to individual files being fragmented, a hard drive itself becomes fragmented when there are many series of gaps where old files have been deleted. This leads to strips of used disk space punctuated by areas of available disk space. When a hard drive becomes fragmented, it becomes harder for the drive to find large areas of sequential allocation blocks in which to store files, resulting in more fragmented files.

Defragmenting a Hard Drive It is possible to defragment a drive, placing all the individual extents of files into sequential allocation blocks and/or placing all the files in contiguous blocks so that performance is improved. Figure 5-5 compares the available space on a drive before and after being defragmented.

Defragmentation can be done one of two ways. The first method is to copy all the files to another hard drive (or another storage device), reformat the hard drive, and then copy the files back to it. As the files are resaved on the reformatted hard drive, they will be saved in sequential allocation blocks on the drive.

The second method is to use a hard drive defragmentation utility. These utilities, which are included with most commercial hard drive repair packages like Norton Utilities and TechTool Pro, will defragment files and drive space by copying all the extents of a file into the Mac's RAM, deleting them from the hard drive, and then resaving them elsewhere on the drive, effectively removing any fragmentation from the files. Some utilities automatically resave the files in such a way as to defragment the disk space of a hard drive at the same time, while others do not.

Defragmentation tools offer the ability of not requiring you to back up and then reformat a drive, which can be helpful, but they also pose a risk. If there is a power failure or the Mac crashes for some reason while the utility is working, any files or extents that are being held in the Mac's RAM at that time will be lost. This can cause a loss of data, corrupt individual files, and corrupt the directory structures of the hard drive. For this reason, it is wise to have a current backup of data on the hard drive before defragmenting it.

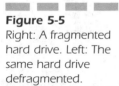

Figure 5-5
Right: A fragmented hard drive. Left: The same hard drive defragmented.

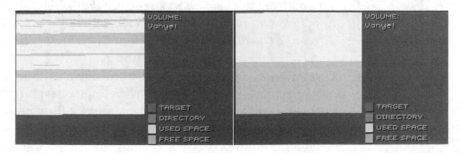

Defragmentation tools also have some limitations. If a drive is too full or individual files are too large, they may not be able to find enough free RAM or disk space to effectively defragment the entire hard drive or its files. Most utilities will alert you to this fact before beginning to defragment a drive.

There is some debate as to how important it is to defragment a hard drive. The hard drive formats used by the Mac are not prone to great degrees of file fragmentation as the formats used by other computing platforms are. The real question, however, is how much of a performance decrease does fragmentation cause. The answer varies, depending on a number of factors, chiefly what tasks are being done on the Mac, and how great the degree of fragmentation.

Severely fragmented drives tend to make the Mac's startup time about 5 percent longer than a defragmented drive. Accessing large (10-MB or larger) files with an application such as Adobe Photoshop can take a performance hit of more than 15 percent when using a severely fragmented drive. Most consumers can probably get away with never defragmenting their hard drive, but most professional users and anyone working with large graphic files or multimedia content should defragment their drives on a regular basis.

An important practice to keep in mind is that you should run a hard drive repair utility before defragmenting a hard drive. Attempting to defragment a hard drive that is suffering even minor corruption can severely damage the drive's directory structures and data. Do not defragment a drive if it is experiencing any other problems. Also, do not try to defragment a hard drive that is more than 85 percent full. This can also lead to problems (and many defragmentation utilities won't even let you attempt it). At this point, you are better off buying a new, larger hard drive and avoiding fragmentation.

NOTE: *When defragmenting a hard drive formatted in the HFS+ disk format (see the next section for information on disk formats), be absolutely sure that you are using a recent utility that supports HFS+. Older utilities (1998 and prior) that do not support HFS+ can severely damage the directory structures on an HFS+ hard drive, often beyond repair.*

Optimization Optimizing a hard drive is a separate process from defragmenting it, although many defragmentation utilities can perform both functions and the two terms are often used interchangeably. Optimizing a hard drive means storing related files in sequential allocation blocks on the drive. For example, placing all the System Folder items at the beginning of the drive (after the directory structures and boot blocks) and placing them in the order they are loaded during the startup process. Optimizing a hard drive can deliver some additional perform-ance, though this is usually limited to the startup process and is typically insignificant. However, even if there isn't a great benefit, there isn't any real reason not to optimize your hard drive while defragmenting it.

Disk Formats

When you use a utility such as Apple's Drive Setup to format a hard drive, you will be asked to choose the format you wish the drive to use. For hard drives (or other disks) intended for use by the Mac, there are two primary formats: the Mac OS Standard Format (also commonly called the hierarchical file system or HFS) and the Mac OS Extended Format (also commonly called HFS+).

Mac OS Standard Format (HFS)   The Mac OS Standard Format was the primary format for all Mac disks from the mid-1980s through the beginning of 1998. It provided a very good file system for the Macintosh to use, but was subject to a major limitation. HFS includes a limit on the number of allocation blocks each drive can have in it (65,536). As multi-gigabyte hard drives became commonplace, this created two problems. With a finite amount of allocation blocks per drive, the size of individual blocks depends on the overall capacity of the hard drive. As individual drives became larger, so did the size of each allocation block. Since each file must take up at least one complete allocation block, small files that fit within each block were taking up extra disk space. For example, on a 4-GB hard drive, each allocation block would be 64 KB. If you have a short word-processing document that is only 20 KB and you save to that hard drive, it needs to take up an entire allocation block, meaning the file is effectively 64 KB in size (more the triple the actual amount of data in the file). On a large HFS hard drive, this wasted space can add up quickly. On even a 1-GB hard drive, this wasted space can add up to 100 MB.

HFS was superseded for use on larger hard drives by an updated for-mat in 1998 called HFS+. However, there are several situations in which HFS is still the preferred format. One of these is on smaller disks. Disks under 100 MB will not see an advantage when using HFS+, and HFS+ does not support disks under 32 MB. This means most removable-media drives and smaller hard drives or hard drive partitions should be for-matted in HFS.

Also HFS1 hard drives can only be accessed by Macs running Mac OS 8.1 or later. If you are using an older Mac, it will not be able to access the hard drive. Also, any Mac based on a processor before the PowerPC processor (circa 1994 or earlier) will not be able to use an HFS1 hard drive as a startup disk, regardless of the Mac OS version it is using.

Mac OS Extended Format (HFS+)   The Mac OS Extended Format was introduced in early 1998 along with Mac OS 8.1. It adjusted the way the Mac creates allocation blocks on a hard drive, meaning that block size is not restricted because of the total capacity of the hard drive (some third-party formatting utilities, such as La Cie's Silverlining, even allow you to choose the size of allocation blocks). This removed the problem of wasted disk space that the HFS file format was prone to. HFS+ can also format larger hard drives than HFS, up to 2 terabytes (2048 GB), although no hard drives of this size are likely to be available for a few years at least. If you are formatting a hard drive (or removable-media disk) of 1 GB or larger, you should use the HFS+ format, unless you are planning to use the drive with an older Macintosh computer or one running Mac OS 8.1 or earlier.

PC Disk Formats   In addition to the disk formats created by Apple for the Mac, there are formats used by other computing platforms. The most common of these include the FAT (file allocation table) and FAT32 formats used for PC disks and hard drives. There is also the NTFS format used by Windows NT/2000 and the formats used by UNIX/Linux computers. The Mac can read the FAT and FAT32 formats used by PCs, provided that the File Exchange control panel is installed on the Mac. Other disk formats generally require the addition of special software utilities for the Mac to access. Chapter 41 covers PC disks and other cross-platform issues in detail.

Hard Drive Partitions

When a hard drive is formatted, it can be divided into volumes known as *partitions*. Each partition behaves as a separate hard drive, with its own name, icon, and directory structures. Each partition can be in either the HFS or HFS+ format (or another format, such as those used by computers running Linux). Because each partition has its own directory structures, corruption of a single partition will not affect other partitions. However, a physical problem with the drive, such as a mechanical failure, loose cable, or loss of power, will affect all of the partitions on the hard drive.

Partitioning hard drives was more common before Apple introduced the HFS+ format. This was because by partitioning a large hard drive to behave as multiple smaller drives, each partition would have a lower capacity and thus smaller allocation blocks, reducing the impact of the wasted space problem inherent in HFS hard drives.

Even though HFS+ removed the primary reason that Mac users tended to partition their drives, there are still some reasons that hard drive partitioning is done today. The most common reasons are to use multiple operating systems on a single Mac and to function as a kind of emergency system backup.

Multiple Operating Systems   A hard drive can only have one version of the Mac OS installed on it. For most users, this isn't a problem, since you only want to run one version (usually, the most recent) of the Mac OS. However, there may be times when you want the ability to easily switch between two Mac OS versions—OS 9 and OS 8, for example. Some discontinued software you regularly use might conflict with Mac OS 9 and not have been updated in a couple of years. By partitioning a hard drive and installing Mac OS 9 on one partition and Mac OS 8 on the other, you can easily switch between the versions as necessary by changing your startup disk or holding down the Option key at startup, as described in Chapter 37.

More likely, you would partition a hard drive if you wanted to install an operating system other than the Mac OS on your computer, such as a version of Linux. Linux cannot be installed on either an HFS or HFS1 hard drive because it is a variation of the UNIX operating system. In this case, you would need to partition your hard drive and create a UNIX-format partition on which to install Linux. You would also need to use another partition for the Mac OS.

Having other operating systems, such as Mac OS X (when it is released) and Mac OS X Server available alongside with the contemporary Mac OS might lead you to partition your hard drive as well. See Chapter 42 for information on both Mac OSX and OSX Server.

Emergency System Backups   Since each partition has its own directory structures, it is possible and likely that if one partition suffers corruption that prevents the Mac from starting up, another partition can serve as a startup disk. This can enable you to keep on working if your typical startup partition no longer functions. This is a limited emergency solution, as it will not help if a hard drive physically fails, but it can be very helpful in some situations, particularly for portable Mac users who are on the road without a Mac OS CD to start up from in the event of trouble. To use a partition like this, you should install a copy of the Mac OS onto it, along with the applications you expect to use regularly. You should also regularly copy important files to that partition so that they will be available should your primary partition fail. Also include your commonly used hard drive repair and antivirus utilities (see Chapter 40 for information on viruses) so that you can diagnose and, hopefully, repair the problems that have occurred on your primary partition.

Formatting/Initializing a Hard Drive

As discussed earlier, you need to initialize or format a hard drive when it is installed on a Mac for the first time. This is done using a formatting utility. Formatting utilities will set up the Mac's disk format (HFS or HFS+), create allocation blocks on and directory structures for a drive, and install the driver that will allow the Mac to recognize the hard drive. You may also need to reformat a hard drive if its directory structures are so badly corrupted that they cannot be repaired. Formatting or reformatting a hard drive will erase any existing data because doing so rewrites the allocation blocks and directory structures of the hard drive. Formatting utilities can also be used to partition a hard drive.

For most user's Apple's free Drive Setup utility is the best formatting utility to use. It will recognize and format most IDE and SCSI hard drives, and it is usually free of any compatibility problems. However, Drive Setup does not recognize all third-party hard drives, and Apple does not guarantee that it will work properly with any non-Apple brand hard drive. Also, Drive Setup does not offer any advanced features such as password protecting hard drives, choosing the allocation block size, data encryption, and other functions.

Using Drive Setup

Drive Setup is a fairly straight-forward application. When launched, it searches for any drives attached the Mac that it is capable of formatting. It displays these drives in a window, as shown in Figure 5-6. If a hard drive is divided into multiple partitions, it lists the name of partitions all as a single hard drive. It also tells you what type each hard drive is and any identification numbers that are associated with the drive.

Figure 5-6
The main Drive Setup
window.

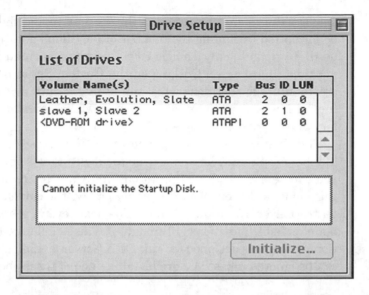

Figure 5-6
The main Drive Setup
window.

Figure 5-7
The Drive Setup
Initialize dialog box.

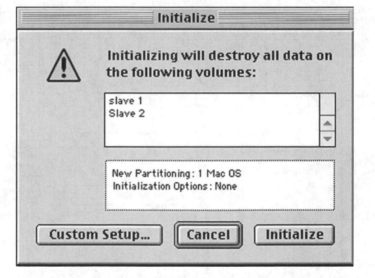

When you select a drive from this list, additional information about the drive is displayed below the list. This information includes the number or partitions the hard drive has been divided into and what formats are used for each. If the hard drive you selected is the current startup disk, you will be told that it cannot be initialized (formatted).

Once you've selected a hard drive from the list, you can format it by clicking on the Initialize button in the window. When you click on the Initialize button, you are presented with the dialog box shown in Figure 5-7, which displays the current partitions of the hard drive and the way the drive will be formatted (including the number of partitions and the file format to be used). By default, only a single HFS+ partition is created when you are formatting a hard drive. Clicking on the Custom Setup button allows you to create multiple partitions when you format a hard drive (if you don't want to partition a hard drive, you can simply click on the Initialize button to format the drive as a single HFS+ partition).

The Custom Setup dialog, shown in Figure 5-8, presents you with a number of options. The first is a menu labeled Partitioning Scheme that lets you choose the number of partitions you want to create. The first item in this menu is Current Volume, and it displays the current partitioning setup for the hard drive (if there is one). The next several items are just the number of possible partitions (1 through 8). This is followed by a series of partitioning schemes designed for Mac OS X Server or Linux installations. These can be ignored unless you are installing one of these operating systems.

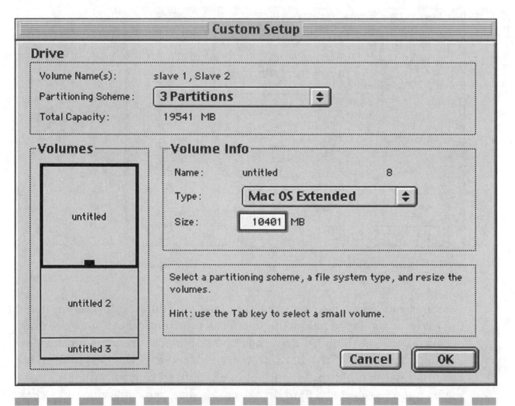

Figure 5-8   The Drive Setup Custom Setup dialog.

The last two items in the Custom Setup menu include ProDOS formats and can be ignored by almost everyone, as ProDOS is the disk format used on the now-antiquated Apple II computers.

Directly below this menu is the total capacity of the hard drive.

Below the Partitioning Scheme menu, the dialog box is divided into two primary sections: Volumes and Volume Info. Volumes simply displays a large rectangle, which is a representation of the hard drive being formatted. Each partition being created is indicated as a smaller box within this rectangle. You can select each partition by clicking on the box representing it. As each partition is selected, you can adjust some of the settings for it in the Volume Info section of the dialog. You can also resize each partition by dragging the black indents that appear on its border when it is selected.

The Volume Info section displays the name of each partition (these will be variations on Untitled, such as Untitled 1, which can be changed after the drive is formatted by clicking on the name beneath each partition's icon and typing the new name) and a number. This number is an identification number for the internal partition map of the hard drive. Unless you are installing the Linux operating system on a Mac, you can ignore this number.

Below the name of each partition is a menu that allows you to select the type of disk format that you want to use for each partition. This menu contains the Mac OS Standard (HFS) and Mac OS Extended (HFS+) formats, the Mac OS UFS (UNIX File System) and Mac OS Server UFS (both of these are only on the recent version of Drive Setup, and both of these should only be used on Macs running Mac OS X or Mac OS X Server), a series of Linux-related formats, ProDOS, and Unallocated. For almost any use, you should select either Mac OS Standard or Mac OS Extended, as discussed earlier. If you are installing Linux, use the Linux options as indicated in the instructions for your Linux version.

Below this menu is a text box displaying the exact size in megabytes of each partition. If you have a specific size you want a partition to be, you can enter it in this box, and the partition rectangle to the right will be adjusted to match this.

The Mac will reserve about 5 MB of hard drive space as a partition named Extra that is designated as Unallocated. This space is used for copying files and performing other disk-related activities. On some smaller hard drives you may notice this partition in the Custom Setup dialog, but on most moderate or large hard drives used today, it is negligible and you won't even see it.

Once you have chosen your partition setup, click on the Okay button to return to the Initialize dialog, and then click on the Initialize button to actually format the hard drive.

In addition to formatting and partitioning hard drives, there are some additional functions that you can perform with Drive Setup. This is done by selecting the various items in the Functions menu. Let's look at each of these menu items separately.

Initialization Options   This is the first item in the Function menu, and it brings up a dialog box, shown in Figure 5-9, that offers two options: Low Level Format and Zero All Data. The first option performs a physical format of the hard drive, creating new sector addressing information for the platters of the hard drive. You shouldn't need to use this option. The only reason a low-level format is done is if there are bad sectors on a hard drive (areas where the drive is physically damaged and can no longer reliably store data). If there are such problems, Drive Setup will detect them and perform a low-level format on its own. They can also be detected by some hard drive repair utilities. Drive Setup may not be able to perform a low-level format on some hard drives.

The second option is Zero All Data. When you format a hard drive without checking any options, the directory structures of the drive are re-created, telling the Mac that the entire hard drive is now available for use, but existing data is not actually erased until new data is written in place of it. This means that some hard drive utilities such as Norton

Figure 5-9
The Initialization
Options dialog.

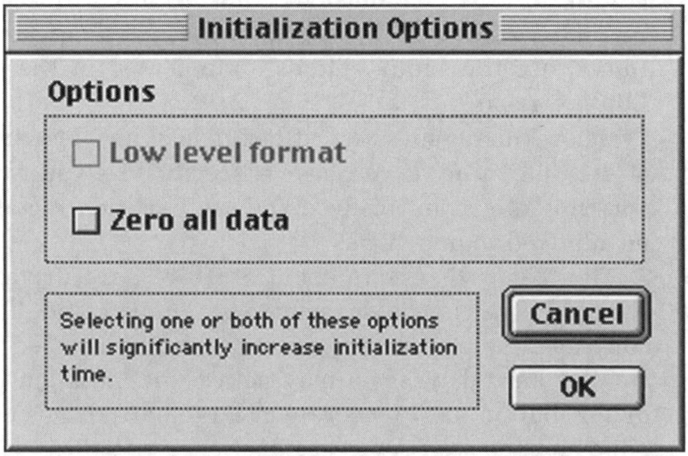

Utilities can recover data even after a hard drive has been formatted. The Zero All Data option actually deletes the existing data, as well as creating new directory structures for the hard drive, which prevents anyone from being able to recover old files. Both Zero All Data and Low Level Format will cause the Mac to take much longer to reformat a hard drive because they need to actually rewrite every part of the hard drive rather than just the directory structures.

Update Driver   The Update Driver option updates the driver of a hard drive without reformatting the drive. This can be useful if Apple releases a new version of the Mac OS or Drive Setup with an improved driver for hard drives. Updated drivers can offer increased performance and compatibility. Actually, the current Mac OS installer programs will automatically update the driver on a hard drive.

Updating the driver can also help solve problems when the original driver has become corrupted. When this happens, the hard drive may become inaccessible to the Mac. Using Drive Setup's Update Driver command will replace the existing driver, which will remove any corruption.

Customize Volumes   The Customize Volumes command displays the dialog box shown in Figure 5-10, and allows you to adjust two settings of a hard drive or the partitions of a hard drive. It is used after selecting one of the hard drives in the Drive Setup window. The two settings you can adjust are Automount on Startup and Write Protected. Automount on Startup is the default state for any hard drive or partition and means that it will automatically be mounted on the Mac's desktop for use when the computer finishes starting up.

Write Protected means that the drive or partition will not be able to be changed. When this is selected, files on the hard drive can still be opened and read by the Mac, but you will not be able to move or delete or change files. Nor will you be able to save changes to files on the drive or create new files on it. Both of these options can be turned on or off for any partition of the selected hard drive (individual partitions are listed in the window). You do not need to reformat or in any way modify the contents of a hard drive to use these options.

Test Disk   Test Disk scans the hard drive selected in the Drive Setup window for any bad blocks or other errors. It does this by copying a piece of existing data to another block on the hard drive and then by copying it across the hard drive in a pattern. Testing a hard drive, can determine if

Figure 5-10
The Customizes
Volumes dialog box.

there are any bad sectors on the hard drive and it can detect some other physical problems with the drive. However, the Test Disk command will not repair any problems, nor will it map out any bad sectors it finds on the drive. Upon completion of testing the drive (which can take quite some time for moderate to large hard drives), Drive Setup displays any problems it found. If bad sectors or blocks are found, you may want to consider backing up your data and performing a low-level format of the hard drive so that these sectors are mapped out by the drive's control circuitry and are not used to store any data in the future.

Rescan Bus   This command causes Drive Setup to look for drives connected to the Mac again. This can be useful if it doesn't display a drive initially and you fix a cabling problem that may be keeping the drive from being recognized.

Mount Volumes   Although hard drives and partitions are usually mounted on the Mac's desktop when the computer starts up or when connected to the Mac, some drives or partitions can be set to not mount automatically. Similarly, a hard drive that is not functioning properly may not mount automatically. Also, as mentioned regarding USB and FireWire hard drives, you can unmount a drive while the computer is running by dragging its icon to the Trash or using the Finder's Put Away command. The Mount Volumes command allows you to select a hard drive listed in the Drive Setup window and mount it on the desktop immediately.

Eject Disk   This is only present if you are using Drive Setup to format or test removable-media disks. Although you can format Zip disks or SuperDisks using Drive Setup, you rarely need to do so. However, larger-capacity removable-media disks, such as the Jaz or Orb disks, are effectively small (2 GB or so) hard drives, and you might want to format or partition them as such. When you use Drive Setup on these disks, the Eject Disk command will eject the disk from the removable-media drive.

Third-Party Formatters

In addition to Drive Setup, there are a number of commercial hard drive formatting utilities on the market for the Mac. The most common of these are listed in Table 5-1. Third-party formatting utilities are needed for hard drives that are not supported by Apple's Drive Setup. Some hard drive manufacturers even include a copy of a third-party formatting utility with their hard drives.

In addition to being able to format a wider variety of hard drives, third-party formatting utilities often enable you great flexibility in formatting a hard drive, including more advanced options for partitioning, as well as for adding password protection and other security options. All current third-party Macintosh formatting utilities use the HFS and HFS+ disk formats. They all create the same types of directory structures as Apple's

TABLE 5-1

Third-Party Hard Drive Formatting Utilities.

Manufacturer	Utility
La Cie	Silverlining
FWB	Hard Disk Toolkit
SoftArch	Formatter Five
CharisMac	Anubis
Intech	Hard Drive Speedtools
APS Technologies	APS Speedtools

Drive Setup. However, they each install their own unique driver, which is the true distinguishing feature among formatting utilities.

Many third-party formatting options claim that their driver provides increased performance over Apple's (and other competitors). There can be some truth to this argument. However, most consumer-level users won't notice much of a performance benefit when using a third-party formatting utility.

There are also some concerns you should be aware of before deciding to use a third-party formatting utility. You will need to update the formatting utility and its driver on your own. Updated versions will not be included with a new Mac OS release, and it will not be updated automatically when you are installing a new Mac OS version. Usually, you can download minor updates free from the manufacturer's website, but some major updates may require you to actually purchase a new version of the utility.

There can also be compatibility issues with drivers installed by third-party formatting utilities. These problems can be with individual extensions or applications, with some pieces of hardware such as some SCSI cards, and even with new versions of the Mac OS. They can also sometimes be very severe, leading to corruption of the hard drive that uses the driver.

Although compatibility issues are usually minor, you should check with the manufacturer before choosing a third-party formatter to be sure it is compatible with your Mac and any expansion cards or software you are using. You should also wait before installing a new Mac OS version to be certain that there is no compatibility concern with the driver and that Mac OS release.

RAID

RAID (redundant array of independent disks) is a technology that allows multiple physical hard drives to be combined so that they appear as a single hard drive to the Mac. This single drive that the Mac sees is called an *array*. RAID arrays can be created using two techniques. The first is disk mirroring, and the second is disk or data striping.

Disk Mirroring

In *disk mirroring*, two hard drives are combined into an array. When the Mac writes data to the array, it is written to both hard drives identically. Should one of the two hard drives physically fail, the other would continue functioning normally. This provides a level of security for critical files, and it allows the computer to continue functioning without any interruption in the event that one drive in the array fails. It can slow down system performance, however, because all data must be written twice (once to each drive). It also only acts as a safeguard against physical hard drive problems. Any corruption of the directory structures will occur on both hard drives in the array because the directory structures, like all other files stored on the array, are identical for both hard drives.

Disk Striping

Disk striping is a technique that combines two or more hard drives into an array to increase hard drive performance. Disk striping splits all data written to the array into small chunks, or stripes. Each stripe can be written to a single drive the array. This increases overall performance because each drive has to store less data and the physical access times required for each drive to read or write a piece of data are reduced.

If more than two hard drives are combined into a data striping array, one of them can be devoted to error correction. Using error correction in a striped array allows the array to reconstruct lost data should one of the hard drives in the array suffer a physical failure. This isn't as efficient as disk mirroring, because use of the array cannot continue once a drive has failed, but it still provides a similar level of data security. As with disk mirroring, error correction on a striped array only protects against physical drive failure. The array itself behaves as a single hard drive and is therefore still susceptible to directory structure corruption.

Creating an Array

RAID can be implemented in software using some third-party formatting utilities, such as FWB's Hard Disk ToolKit, or it can be implemented at a hardware level. Software RAID arrays rely on the Mac to connect all the drives in an array and on the drivers installed on each hard drive to manage the tasks of disk mirroring or data striping. Hardware RAID arrays use a special device, such as a PCI expansion card or an external case, to connect the drives together to function as a unit and to handle many of the striping and mirroring tasks for the drives in an array. Software-based arrays are less expensive to implement (requiring just the hard drives and the formatting utility) than hardware arrays, which require additional hardware to be purchased. Hardware arrays can give some increased performance, however.

RAID arrays have traditionally been created out of SCSI hard drives only. This makes sense for performance because SCSI tends to outper-

TABLE 5-2

Common RAID
levels

Level	Description
RAID Level 0	Provides data striping only (spreading out blocks of each file across multiple disks) but no redundancy. Improves data read/write speed as a multiple of the number of drives used.
RAID Level 1	Provides disk mirroring only—so that if one disk drive fails, no data is lost and the computer can continue to work normally. This does not increase data read/write speeds.
RAID Levels 3 and 4	Same as Level 0, but also reserves one dedicated disk for error correction data. It provides good performance and some level of fault tolerance.
RAID Level 5	Provides data striping at the byte level and also stripe error correction information. This results in excellent performance and good fault tolerance.

form most other hard drive interfaces. More recently, enclosures for creating arrays out of FireWire hard drives have been developed.

RAID Levels

Because RAID arrays can encompass a number of different levels of performance increase and data security, there are standard levels of RAID. Each level has some advantages. Not all RAID formatting utilities or hardware support all the RAID levels that have been created. Table 5-2 lists the most common RAID levels used today, along with a brief description of each.

RAID Spanning   Another RAID feature is called *spanning*. This allows several disks to be formatted into a single large volume that appears as a single icon on the Mac desktop. This does not provide improvements in speed or reliability, but it is convenient in some situations because it creates a single, very large hard drive out of multiple smaller drives.

Installing a Hard Drive

This section covers the process of installing a replacement internal hard drive (and/or an additional hard drive in the case of Power Macs) in all the Mac models covered in this book with the exception of the iBook. Installing a hard drive in the iBook is extremely challenging even for experienced Mac technicians and is a project better left to Apple or trained professionals.

Replacing a Mac's internal hard drive is usually only done for one of two reasons. Either the internal hard drive has physically failed and can no longer be used or you wish to expand the Mac's internal storage abilities with a larger hard drive. Regardless of the motivation, the process is the same. If you are installing an additional hard drive into a Power Mac computer, you will be doing it to expand the existing storage options.

If you are replacing an existing hard drive, it is important that you make a backup of any files stored on that hard drive prior to replacing it. You will not be able to access the original hard drive once the new one has been installed. You should also have the original software install CDs for any external drives that you are storing the backup on if they are not part of a standard Mac OS installation so that you will be able to access the backups after the new drive is installed and formatted. You will also need a Mac OS CD from which to start up the computer once the new hard drive is installed. If you are using a third-party formatting utility, you will also need the CD for this utility.

After the drive is physically installed, you will need to start up from a CD by inserting the CD into the Mac's CD-ROM drive and holding the C key down until the computer starts up. If you are going to format the hard drive with Apple's Drive Setup, this should be the most recent Mac OS CD you have available or the System Restore CD that came with the computer. If you are using a third-party formatting utility, it should be a bootable CD containing the utility.

Once the computer has started from the CD, use the formatting utility to format the drive. If you started from a Mac OS CD, after the drive is formatted, launch the Mac OS installer and install a copy of the Mac OS onto the drive. If you started from a third-party formatting utility, restart the computer, this time using a Mac OS CD, and then install a copy of the Mac OS on the drive.

Once the Mac OS is installed on the hard drive, restart the computer, using the new hard drive, and then reinstall any software needed to access the external drive on which you stored a backup of your files from the original files. After this is done, copy your files from the backup to the new hard drive.

Power Mac

The Power Mac G3 and G4 computers are generally among the easiest computers to add a hard drive to. There are three versions of the hard drive mounting brackets used in the Power Mac computers covered in this book. The first version was used only on the first models of the Blue and White Power Mac G3. This first version was a single bracket that extended the length of the computer's case. Up to three hard drives could be mounted on this one bracket. This was later replaced by three individual brackets, each of which are easier to handle and are able to hold a single hard drive.

The following steps detail the instructions for installing a hard drive in each of the bracket types. Specific details on cabling for SCSI and IDE drives is covered in greater detail in Chapters 12 and 13, and you should read the chapter referring to the type of drive you are installing before beginning the installation. Once a new hard drive is inserted, you need to use a formatting utility to format the hard drive. If it is a replacement for the original hard drive, you also need to install a copy of the Mac OS, which requires you to start up from a Mac OS CD as described above.

Blue and White G3 Version One Brackets   If you are dealing with one of these first-version brackets, you need to remove the entire bracket to install additional hard drives or to replace any factory installed hard drives. To remove this bracket:

1. Shut down the computer and then open the side door of the Mac.

2. Disconnect the motherboard power cable and the data cable (IDE or SCSI) and power connectors for any installed hard drives.

3. There is a metal retaining plate along the rear of the computer (where the ports panel is when the computer is closed) that secures the entire bracket to the computer. It is held in place with a single screw. Remove the screw and then remove the retaining plate.

4. With the retaining plate removed, slide the entire bracket toward the back of the computer. This releases the tabs underneath the bracket that help hold it in place against the case of the Power Mac.

5. Lift the bracket (along with any attached hard drives) out of the computer.

6. Hard drives are secured to the bracket using screws that are inserted from the underside of the bracket. To remove a hard drive from the bracket, simply remove the screws from the underside of the bracket. To install a hard drive, position it against the upper surface of the bracket and then secure it with screws through the bottom.

7. When reinserting the bracket, make certain that any cables that pass under the central portion of the bracket are lying flat before you replace it.

The process of reinserting the bracket is the reverse of removing it, but make certain the tabs on the underside of the bracket line up with the slot in the Mac's case.

After the bracket is reinserted with the new hard drives, attach a power connector to each hard drive (several will be hanging down in the space above the hard drive bays). These connectors insert in only one direction, but you should be certain that you are inserting it properly because forcing it in backward can damage the Mac's power supply and the hard drive. Attach the appropriate interface cables (IDE or SCSI) to each hard drive.

Version Two Brackets   The second version of Power Mac hard drive brackets are much easier to deal with. In these versions, each of the three drive bays has a separate bracket that can be removed independently of the others. It is also much easier to remove each individual bracket.

To remove these brackets:

1. Each hard drive bracket is held in place by a single mounting screw that is positioned in the center of the front (motherboard) edge of the bracket. This screw can be accessed easily. There are also two tabs on the underside of each bracket. If a drive is mounted in the bracket, remove the power connector and interface cable from the drive so that you can get at the screw (which you need to do before removing the drive anyway).

2. Next, remove the screw and pull the entire bracket (with a hard drive, if one is mounted in it) forward slightly (toward the motherboard of the computer). Then lift out of the computer.

As with the version one brackets, hard drives are mounted to the bracket using screws inserted through mounting holes in the bottom of the bracket. To mount a hard drive, simply position it against the bracket and insert the mounting screws through these holes. Once a hard drive is mounted in the bracket, reinsert the bracket in the computer and secure it again with the screw. Then attach a power connector to the hard drive and attach the appropriate interface cable (IDE or SCSI).

U-Shaped Brackets On the later Power Mac G3 and all Power Mac G4 models, the rearmost bracket has higher sides that extend above the factory-installed hard drive and have curve (U-shaped) edges, as shown in Figure 5-11. These brackets identify Macs that can accept two IDE hard drives in a master/slave configuration and are designed so that you can mount a second IDE hard drive in the same bracket above the factory-installed hard drive.

To install a second hard drive in this bracket:

1. The U-shaped bracket is removed and inserted in the computer using a single screw, just like the other version two brackets. The factory-installed IDE hard drive is mounted in it using screws inserted through the bottom of the bracket, just like the other brackets. However, the U-shaped upper edges of the bracket contain two screw holes on either side, which allow you to mount a second hard drive. To do this, position the hard drive and insert the mounting screws through the holes on each side of the bracket, as shown in Figure 5-12.

2. With a second hard drive mounted in the bracket, reinsert it in the computer and secure it with the screw.

Figure 5-11
The U-shaped bracket used for mounting two IDE hard drives.

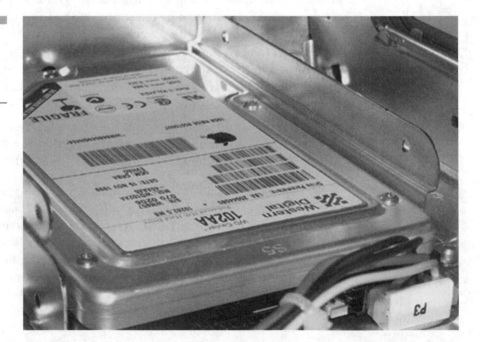

Figure 5-12
A second hard drive
mounted in the
U-shaped bracket.

3. Then attach power connectors to both the lower and upper hard
   drives in the bracket and attach the connectors of the IDE cable to
   each hard drive. You need to remember to set one of the two hard
   drives as a slave drive and the other as a master drive, using the
   jumpers, as mentioned earlier. It is usually easiest to set the new
   hard drive as slave before mounting it in the bracket. Refer to
   Chapter 13 for more information regarding master/slave IDE hard
   drive configurations.

Original iMac

The original iMac uses a single standard IDE hard drive and has only
enough internal space for that single hard drive. The hard drive is
mounted in the motherboard/drive chassis directly beneath the CD-ROM
drive.

To replace the hard drive:

1. Open the iMac and remove the motherboard/drive chassis as
   described in Chapter 1.
2. Set the chassis down, with the drive section pointing toward you.
   The CD-ROM drive is attached to a carrier/mounting frame. This

frame is spring-loaded and is held in the drive section of the motherboard/drive chassis by the force of the spring.

3. To remove the frame and the CD-ROM drive from the chassis, push the CD-ROM backward toward the motherboard until you are able to release the tabs that hold the frame in place (shown in Figure 5-13).

4. Once the tabs are released, lift the front section of the CD-ROM drive out of the chassis and then lift the entire drive out.

5. Disconnect the IDE cable attached to the rear of the CD-ROM drive.

6. The hard drive is mounted in a bracket, similar to the brackets used in the Power Mac computers. This bracket is secured the motherboard/drive chassis by two screws (one on either side). First, remove these two screws. The back of the bracket also has two tabs that are fitted into slots in the bottom of the chassis.

7. To remove the hard drive and bracket, press the bracket back toward the motherboard to release these tabs from the chassis and then lift the bracket and hard drive out of the chassis.

8. Disconnect the IDE cable and power connector from the hard drive.

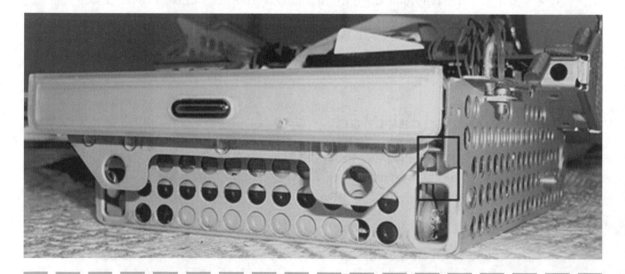

Figure 5-13   There are two spring-release tabs, one on either side of the iMac's CD-ROM drive, which hold it in place in the motherboard/drive chassis.

9. The hard drive is secured to the bracket with four screws. With these screws removed, slide the hard drive out of the bracket and replace it with another hard drive (securing the new drive with the same screws).

10. After the new drive is mounted in the bracket, connect the IDE cable and power connector to it and reinsert the bracket in the chassis.

11. When reinserting the bracket, make certain that you press it in further back than it normally sits and then pull it forward so that the tabs at the back of the bracket fit into the slot of the chassis to secure it.

12. Secure it to the chassis with the two screws. The top of the hard drive bracket contains the spring that secures the CD-ROM drive.

13. When reinserting the CD-ROM, be certain that the tab on the underside of its frame is secured around the center of the spring.

14. Once the CD-ROM drive has been reinserted, start up the iMac from a Mac OS CD or a hard drive formatting Utility CD and format the new hard drive.

15. Install the Mac OS onto it so that it can serve as a startup disk. Then restore any files from the original hard drive.

Slot-Loading iMac

Like the original iMac, the second-generation iMac computers can contain only a single internal IDE hard drive. This hard drive is mounted in a special carrier along with the CD or DVD-ROM drive of the iMac.

To replace the hard drive:

1. Remove the lower casing and EMI shield of the computer, as described in Chapter 1.

2. Remove any installed RAM modules and AirPort card (if installed) because of their close proximity to the carrier and cables for the hard drive and CD/DVD-ROM drive. Also remove the IDE cables attached to both the CD/DVD-ROM drive and the hard drive, as well as the power connector attached to the hard drive.

3. Remove the carrier that holds both the hard drive and the CD/DVD-ROM drive. To do this, remove the four screws that hold the carrier in place, as shown in Figure 5-14.

Figure 5-14 The white circles indicate the recessed positions of the four screws that hold the carrier in place.

4. You can now lift the carrier and the drives out of the computer. To remove the hard drive, remove the mounting screws that secure it to the carrier. Once these screws are removed, slide the drive out of the carrier and replace it.

   Reinserting the carrier is an exact reverse of the process of removing it:

5. With the carrier back in place, replace the RAM modules (and AirPort card if one was installed) and then replace the EMI shield and the lower panel of the iMac.

6. Start up from a Mac OS CD (or a hard drive formatting or utility CD), and use Drive Setup or another formatting utility to format the new hard drive. Then install a copy of the Mac OS.

PowerBook

The PowerBooks covered in this book both use an IDE hard drive specially designed for portable computers. This drive needs to be a 2.5-inch hard drive that is small enough to fit inside the PowerBook's case (the standard IBM hard drive in these Macs is 9.5mm high, though 13mm tall hard drives should also fit in the PowerBook). The process of replacing the hard drive is the same for both PowerBook models covered in this book. Follow these steps:

1. Shut down the PowerBook, and remove the battery and any inserted expansion bay module.

2. Use the keyboard release tabs to remove the keyboard, and flip it onto the PowerBook's built in wrist rests, as described in Chapter 2.

3. Remove the heat sink that covers the processor module (for PowerBooks with FireWire ports, remove both heat sinks).

4. With the heat sinks removed, remove the processor card module as described in Chapter 2 and place it gently on a static-free surface.

5. Disconnect the hard drive cable where it is secured to motherboard (beneath where the processor card was inserted).

6. Pull up on the clear plastic tab that is attached to the hard drive's mounting sled. This releases the sled slightly from the PowerBook's case so that you can lift the sled out. If the plastic tab is missing or comes loose when pulled, use a pair of needle-nose pliers to gently grasp one of the edges of the sled and lift, being very careful not to damage any other components.

7. To remove the hard drive from the mounting sled, remove the four torx screws that secure the hard drive in place in the sled. These screws are located in each of the black plastic/rubber circles on the sled, as shown in Figure 5-15.

8. Once the hard drive is removed from the mounting sled, disconnect the hard drive cable from the connector on the mounting sled and pull it out of the slot, (shown in Figure 5-16) in the bottom of the sled where it is secured.

Figure 5-15
The mounting screws
of the PowerBook's
hard drive.

Figure 5-16
The slot for the hard
drive cable in the
mounting sled.

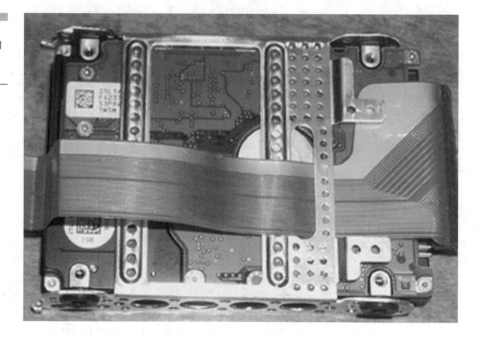

Installing the new hard drive is the reverse of the process of removing the old one:

1. Connect the cable from the mounting sled to the hard drive.
2. Secure the drive with the screws, and reinsert and reconnect the sled in the PowerBook.
3. With the PowerBook reassembled, start up from an alternate disk with a formatting utility and format the new hard drive.
4. Install a copy of the Mac OS onto it.

Hard Drive Damage and Repair Utilities

The physical components of a hard drive are mechanical, and sooner or later, they will fail, making the hard drive useless and rendering any data stored on it unretrievable. Hard drives can also be damaged physically and electronically by improper handling, causing mechanical failure. The eventual failure of any hard drive is inevitable, although most hard drives are rated to last three to five years or longer (though that doesn't always mean they will). The possibility of a drive physically failing at any point is one important reason to maintain a good backup strategy for the files on your hard drive, as discussed in detail in Chapter 39.

However, more commonly, hard drives suffer problems that have nothing to do with the drive's physical components. These problems are the result of damage or corruption of the files that make up a drive's directory structures. Each of the directory structures was discussed earlier in this chapter, as well as the potential problems should that structure be erased or corrupted. Almost all corruption of a hard drive's directory structures and of files on the hard drive occurs when a Mac is restarted or shut down improperly. Computer viruses (addressed in Chapter 40) can also cause hard drive and file corruption, as can an application crashing while it is saving or accessing a file. Another common cause of corruption is disconnecting a hard drive, such as a USB or FireWire drive, without first unmounting the drive, which can also cause an application crash or system freeze.

Hard drive corruption really can't be avoided because there are bound to be times when an application crashes and freezes up, causing you to use the reset button. However, you can minimize the risk of corruption by shutting down the Mac or restarting it properly whenever possible and by not disconnecting drives that are still mounted on the desktop.

When a hard drive becomes corrupted, a number of things can happen. At basic levels of corruption, the Mac may simply become more prone to freezes and crashes, which will create even more corruption. Depending on which directory structures are corrupted, it is possible that existing files will be damaged, deleted, or overwritten with new files. At the worst, the Mac will be unable to access the hard drive at all. If it is the startup disk, the Mac will begin looking for an alternate disk or hard drive to start up from. If it cannot find one, the Mac will display a flashing "?" until you provide an alternate startup disk.

A hard drive repair utility is a special piece of software that is written to look for signs of corruption in a hard drive's directory structures. Hard drive repair utilities can also repair many types of corruption, restoring a corrupted hard drive to normal function. If the corruption is too severe, however, even the best hard drive repair utilities may not be able to repair it, and you will need to reformat the drive and start over.

Disk First Aid

Apple includes the free Disk First Aid repair utility (shown in Figure 5-17) with every Mac OS release. Disk First Aid can diagnose most types of corruption problems and it can repair a number of them that aren't too severe. It is a good idea to run Disk First Aid (and another repair utility if you have one) at least once a month to ensure your hard drive doesn't

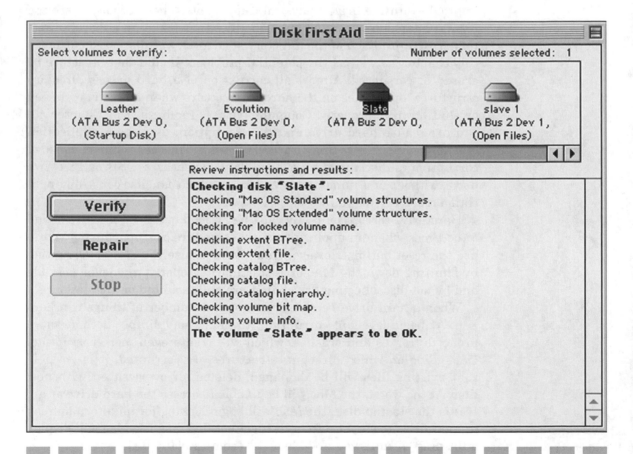

Figure 5-17   The Disk First Aid repair utility.

become seriously corrupted. You should also run Disk First Aid any time your computer has been forcibly restarted (this is done automatically by default in current Mac OS versions).

Disk First Aid is a very simple program to use. When launched, it looks for any type of disk available to the Mac (hard drives or partitions, CDs, floppies, removable-media disks, and so on) and displays them all separately across the top of its window with their names and how they are connected to the Mac. It also identifies which is the current startup disk.

To test a disk for corruption, you simply click on its icon and then click on the Verify button. Disk First Aid will test the drive in question for corruption to each of its directory structures. As is does, it will display its findings. When it's finished, Disk First Aid will tell you one of two things: The disk is OK or the disk needs to be repaired. To repair hard drive corruption with Disk First Aid, click on the disk's icon, and then click on the Repair button. If Disk First Aid is capable of repairing the problem, then it will do so. If not, it will again tell you that it found problems but that it couldn't repair them.

If Disk First Aid does solve the problem it finds successfully, you should click on the icon of the repaired hard drive and then click on the Verify button again to make sure the problem was solved completely. If it did not, you may need to use a more powerful repair utility.

If Disk First Aid tells you that it found problems that it couldn't repair, don't give up hope. Disk First Aid is a good utility, but it is far from being the most powerful hard drive repair utility available for the Mac. Several commercial utilities are available that can repair a large number of problems that Disk First Aid cannot. These utilities can also diagnose some problems that Disk First Aid may miss.

NOTE: *You should always have a current version of Disk First Aid available, and it should be on a CD, alternate hard drive, or other type of disk that you can conveniently access should your internal hard drive develop serious corruption that prevents it from starting up. You should also have at least one (or better yet two) alternate hard drive repair utilities available to handle problems that are beyond the abilities of Disk First Aid.*

Commercial Hard Drive Repair Utilities

A number of commercially produced hard drive repair utilities are on the market, ranging from $50 to just over $100. These utilities ship on bootable CDs, so that you can start up from their CD and launch them in the event of a hard drive problem. Each of them can perform more powerful repairs than Disk First Aid, although to what degree varies. The following is an overview of the primary commercial repair utilities available for the Mac.

Every Mac owner should have at least one of these utilities in addition to Disk First Aid, and they should be run at least once a month to ensure that there is no lingering corruption to a Mac's hard drive. Ideally, users and technicians should have two of these utilities on hand at any given time and they should complement one another, like DiskWarrior and Norton Utilities. It is also important to make sure you update your hard drive repair utilities regularly (most manufacturers make updates available free of charge) to ensure compatibility with the latest Mac OS versions and, in some cases, new disk formats.

NOTE: *As with defragmentation utilities, if you are working with an HFS+ hard drive, make certain you are using a recent utility that supports HFS+ disks. Using older utilities that only support HFS hard drives can result in more damage when used with an HFS+ hard drive.*

Norton Utilities   Norton Utilities for Mac (often abbreviated NUM) is produced by Symantec. It is the longest-running Mac disk repair utility on the market. Norton Utilities includes a hard drive repair utility, a defragmentation utility, and a recovery utility that can recover deleted files and files from accidentally erased hard drives (provided a Low-Level or Zero All Data format wasn't performed on the drive). Although Norton maintained its place as the primary Mac hard drive utility suite for many years, other options are now providing equal and superior repair abilities, though the combination of features provided by Norton continue to make it popular and useful.

TechTool Pro   Micromat's TechTool Pro is actually a suite of Macintosh diagnostic utilities that can test for problems in anything from your hard drive to your processor to your mouse. This excellent combination of additional features makes it a very attractive utility. In addition to basic hard drive corruption repair, it can test the physical components of a hard drive, and it includes a defragmentation utility. TechTool Pro's great strength is in its multifaceted abilities. Although its hard drive tools are adequate, they are not the most spectacular or powerful on the market.

DiskWarrior   Alsoft's DiskWarrior is the most powerful hard drive repair utility I have ever used. It can repair even the most corrupted hard drives. DiskWarrior also lets you test its rebuilt directory structures for a drive before actually rewriting the corrupted structures. This enables you to check and see if important files are fully intact and accessible within the repaired drive before any permanent changes are made to it. DiskWarrior, unfortunately, does not come with any other features beyond repairing drive corruption.

MacMedic   MacMedic from Total Recall is the newest hard drive utility for the Mac. It operates very efficiently and includes a number of safeguards to prevent changes being made to a hard drive until they have been tested, much like DiskWarrior. It also comes with a defragmentation utility, a data recovery utility to recover files even if the hard drive can't be repaired, and a basic utility for backing up files on your Mac on a regular basis. The combination of features makes MacMedic an attractive option for many users.

Troubleshooting Hard Drive Problems

Hard drives tend to either experience catastrophic problems (the inability of a hard drive to be recognized by the Mac, for example) or minor problems, such as sporadic crashes or freezes when accessing the hard drive. As such, it can sometimes be easy to misdiagnose hard drive problems as some other problem. This section addresses situations that are almost always hard drive problems, along with the solutions for dealing with them.

NOTE: *If you experience frequent and unexplained crashes of a Mac, problems immediately at startup, or unexplained slow performance, these can also be symptoms of hard drive problems. If nothing else seems to explain these problems, try running Disk First Aid or another hard drive repair utility to check for hard drive corruption as the culprit. If you're experiencing frequent crashes (whether or not they are hard drive related), you should consider running hard drive repair utilities more often just to be on the safe side.*

TABLE 5-3

Common Hard disk
Errors and Their
Probable Causes.

Symptom/Message	Probable Cause
The Mac displays a flashing question mark at startup or starts up from a disk other than the selected startup drive.	The Mac was unable to locate or access the selected startup drive. This could indicate that the hard drive is corrupted or physically damaged. It can also mean that it is not connected or powered properly. If the flashing question mark appears only briefly and the Mac continues startup without any problems, this is not a sign of hard drive problems. It just means that there is no disk or drive selected in the Startup Disk control panel. The first course of action here is to start up from an alternate disk, such as a Mac OS CD or hard drive repair utility disk or even another hard drive. If the hard drive mounts on the desktop after startup, check it with a hard drive repair utility. If problems are found, repair them. If you can't repair them with any utilities available to you, copy what files you can to another drive as a backup and reformat the hard drive.
The Mac displays a message stating that the disk is unreadable or damaged.	If the Mac displays an error message telling you that the hard drive is unrecognizable or is damaged and asks you if you want to initialize the drive, click on Cancel (clicking on Initialize will reformat the hard drive, erasing any data that may still be there). This indicates that the directory structures on the hard drive and possibly the driver on it are so damaged that the Mac cannot recognize them. Use a hard drive repair utility to scan the disk for corruption and to repair it if possible. If the hard drive isn't recognized by the hard drive repair utility, launch Drive Setup (or the utility used to format that hard drive in the first place, if it was not Drive Setup) and use the Test Disk command to check for bad blocks on the drive. If there are no bad blocks, try using the Update Drive command to replace the driver. After this, attempt to repair the hard drive again with a hard drive repair utility. If this still doesn't help or if bad blocks are found on the hard drive, you need to reformat it. If possible, mount the hard drive using Drive Setup's Mount Volume command, and copy files to a backup before reformatting.
A hard drive doesn't mount and there is no error related to it	If the hard drive doesn't mount on the desktop and there is no error message, this most likely means that the hard drive isn't connected or powered properly. If the drive is an external drive, make sure it is connected properly and that it is powered.

TABLE 5-3

Common Hard disk
Errors and Their
Probable Causes.
(Continued)

Symptom/Message	Probable Cause
A hard drive doesn't mount and there is no error related to it	If the drive is an internal drive, make sure it is connected properly and that it has a power connector attached to it. If an internal drive is connected properly, it is possible that there are too many internal drives for the Mac's power supply to handle. See Chapter 11 for more details on this possibility, as well as solutions. For both internal and external hard drives refer to the chapters that deal specifically with the interface technology of the hard drive (SCSI, IDE, USB, and so on) later in this book for problems and solution specifically related to that technology. Also refer to these chapters for specific cabling rules and other issues to be certain that the hard drive is connected properly. It is also possible that this will be the result when a hard drive's mechanical components have failed. If this is the case, you will need to replace the hard drive. The drive may also be set not to mount automatically. If so, try using drive setup's Mount Disk command to mount.
Disk icon with an X through it at startup.	This means that the Mac cannot find a valid System Folder on any hard drive's or disk available to it. This can indicate damage to a hard drive boot blocks or a corrupted System Folder. Perform a clean install of the Mac OS to solve both problems.
Files disappear from a hard drive.	This can indicate damage to some of the hard drive's directory structures (most likely, to the volume information block), or it can indicate that there are bad blocks on the hard drive. Running a hard drive repair utility will tell you if the problem lies in the directory structures. If not, use Drive Setup (or the appropriate third-party formatting utility, if one was used to format the hard drive) to test the drive for bad blocks. If bad blocks are found, you should back up any files on the hard drive and then perform a low-level format of the hard drive to map those out of the hard drive control circuitry's map so that they aren't used to store data in the future.
File can't be accessed.	This usually indicates bad blocks in the hard drive, though it can also indicate problems with the hard drive's directory structures. Use Drive Setup (or the appropriate third-party formatting utility, if one was used to format the hard drive) to test the drive for bad blocks. If they are found, you will need to perform a low-level format of the hard drive. If not, attempt to use a hard drive repair utility to deal with corruption issues.

NOTE: *Not all error messages indicating trouble accessing a file are signs of hard drive problems. Messages such as "The document untitled cannot be opened because the application that created could not be found. Could not find an application with appropriate translators" almost always just indicate that you don't have an application available to your Mac that can open the file. These messages can also indicate that you need to rebuild the desktop file.*

Resources for Further Study

The following URLs provide additional information on some of the concepts, issues, and products discussed in this chapter:

About.com Focus on Mac Hardware Hard Drive Resources— http://machardware.about.com/msubharddrives.htm

*The Tech Page (jumper and setting information for almost every hard drive ever made)—*http://www.thetechpage.com

La Cie's Hard Drive Encyclopedia— http://www.lacie.com/scripts/support/encyclopedia1.cfm

La Cie:Makers of Silverlining and Hard Drive Devices— http://www.lacie.com

*FWB: Makers of Hard Disk ToolKit—*http://www.fwb.com

Software Architects: Makers of Formatter Five— http://www.softarch.com

CharisMac: Makers of Anubis and Other Utilities— http://www.charismac.com

*Integrated Technologies, Inc. (InTech): Makers of Hard Drive Speedtools—*http://www.intechusa.com

*Symantec: Makers of Norton Utilities—*http://www.symantec.com

Alsoft: Makers of DiskWarrior and Other Utilities— http://www.alsoft.com

Micromat: Makers of TechTool Pro and the freeTechTool— http://www.micromat.com

*Total Recall: Makers of MacMedic—*http://software.totalrecall.com

CHAPTER 6

Macintosh Memory

RAM (random access memory) is one of the cornerstones of any computer, including the Macintosh. RAM is where any data that the processor is working with is stored. This data includes the Mac OS, applications, or open documents.

There are various types of RAM used in the Mac, including *system RAM* where all the data being used by the computer at a given point is located. It is the system RAM that holds any open item on the Mac (application, document, or Mac OS element). System RAM is what most people think of when they hear the terms *RAM* or *memory*, and it is the RAM that you generally upgrade. System RAM is the type of RAM or memory you see displayed in the Finder's About This Computer window.

System RAM is very easy to upgrade, and Apple has designed the current Macs so that any Mac owner can upgrade the RAM without effort. In all cases, the only tools you will need are a screwdriver and an antistatic wrist strap as a precaution against static electricity damaging either the RAM or the computer.

Besides system RAM, there is also *cache RAM* (often referred to just as "cache"). Cache RAM is a special type of very fast RAM that the processor can use to boost performance. It is the RAM in the backside cache that gives such a phenomenal performance boost to G3 and G4 processors.

There is also *video RAM*, or VRAM. VRAM is special memory that is dedicated to the graphics controller of a computer. VRAM is faster than traditional system RAM (though not as fast as cache RAM). Because of the demanding needs of today's graphics and video software and hardware, VRAM allows for increased video display and performance.

RAM vs. ROM

In addition to RAM, there is another type of memory used in the Mac known as ROM (read-only memory). ROM is used to hold permanent instructions that are built into the computer. These are generally very low-level instructions, such as how the processor interacts with the hard drive, how to locate the Mac OS on a hard drive and initiate the startup sequence, how to work with the video controller to display information on a monitor, and so forth. The Macintosh ROM also contains some proprietary data that works as a basic portion of the Mac OS. ROM data is fixed data on the chips soldered onto a Mac's motherboard. ROM can only be read by the processor; it cannot be written to or used to store data the way RAM can be. In addition to the Mac ROM chips on the motherboard, expansion cards, such as video cards or SCSI cards; and other devices, such as hard drives or CD/DVD-ROM drives, also have ROM chips built into them that contain the instructions to control how these devices function. As a rule, when talking about ROM, however, it is assumed that you are talking about the ROM from Apple that allows the Mac to function, which is sometimes also called the *boot ROM*.

There is also a technique used in the current Macs called the *New World ROM architecture*. This is a technique that Apple uses to make the contents of the Mac's ROM chips smaller. This was a desirable goal for several reasons. First, ROM chips are specialized components that are a great deal more expensive to produce than RAM. Second, accessing data stored in ROM is slower than accessing data stored in RAM. Third, once a ROM chip is created, it cannot usually be modified (although this is not always true, as will be discussed in a little bit).

The reason Apple needed to develop the New World ROM technique is that ever since the very first Mac, some of the data that makes up the Mac OS has been coded into ROM. As Macs became more complex, this data grew and so did the size (and therefore the cost) of the ROM used in the Mac. Also, by having Mac OS instruction data in ROM, the Mac was slowed down because ROM is slower than RAM. Lastly, if bugs or conflicts were found in the Mac OS code in ROM after a Mac shipped, there was no way to update that ROM code. The only option was to write patches (which were part of Mac OS updates) that resided on the hard drive and that told the Mac to ignore certain ROM code in favor of instructions now stored in a file on the hard drive.

The New World ROM architecture basically puts much of this code that was traditionally stored in ROM into a file on the hard drive (the Mac OS ROM file in the System Folder). The remaining ROM is used primarily for only the basic instructions that are needed for the processor to access the hard drive, talk to the internal ports and slots, run startup self-tests, and locate the Mac OS on a disk. The remaining contents (that is, the Mac OS ROM file) are loaded into RAM from the hard drive during startup and take up approximately 3 MB of RAM. This results in some performance increase, a cost decrease in producing Mac motherboards, and the ability for Apple to update the Mac OS ROM file as they would any other part of the Mac OS without performance problems.

In addition to this, there is a special kind of ROM that Apple has begun using. This type of updateable ROM or firmware has been used in some parts of the recent Macs. Sometimes called *flashROM*, this ROM can be updated by special utilities in some situations. This allows Apple, or another manufacturer, to update the ROM that controls a given component of the Mac, such as the CD-ROM drive, modem, or even the general ROM.

How RAM Works

RAM holds the data currently available to the processor. This data is essentially nothing but sets of 1s and 0s. Each 1 or 0 is called a *bit*, and data used by the processor is arranged in 8-bit, 16-bit, 32-bit, and so on groups that are known as *bytes*. Each byte of data can represent a single character typed into the keyboard, the color information of a pixel that is part of an image being displayed on-screen, a single basic instruction that is part of a program, or some other small piece of a file, application, or the Mac OS.

Each bit of RAM is actually just a simple transistor/capacitor that can be turned on or off to indicate a 1 or 0. Millions of these tiny transistors are packed into a silicon chip. These chips are then installed on memory modules that can be installed in a computer, such as an iMac. This organization is illustrated in Figure 6-1.

Each byte of data is assigned a specific location in the installed RAM of a Macintosh. This allows the processor (or, rather, the memory controller on the motherboard, which in turn works with the processor) to know where specific segments of data are stored in RAM.

Because there is a limited amount of RAM in a computer, data that is not being used by the processor is stored on some form of mass storage device, such as a hard drive, CD-ROM, or removable-media disk. When that data is needed, it is copied from the mass storage device into a specific location in RAM. It is the amount of RAM that is installed in a com-

Figure 6-1
Each group of bits in a RAM module is addressed as a single unit, much like the rows or columns of a spreadsheet, by the processor and memory controller.

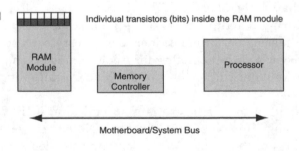

puter that determines how many applications can be running and how many documents can be open at any given time.

Types of RAM

As mentioned earlier, there are three primary types of RAM used in the Mac: system RAM (which is upgradable and relatively inexpensive), cache RAM (which is not upgradable on the current Macs and is very expensive), and video RAM (which can be upgradable on some computers and is moderately expensive). Each of these three types of RAM has different purposes and functions slightly differently, as shown in Table 6-1.

System RAM   System RAM is the basic memory of the computer. It is controlled by the memory controller on the motherboard and can easily be expanded by installing additional memory modules or replacing existing modules with higher-capacity modules.

System RAM in the current Macs is a type of RAM known as SDRAM (synchronous dynamic RAM). The *S* and *D* in SDRAM merit some discussion so you can understand specifically how system RAM works. We'll start with the *D* because DRAM has been around since early computers.

Dynamic RAM means that the information stored in all the tiny transistors that make up the chips on a memory module needs to be continually refreshed. If DRAM isn't refreshed, the information will be lost and the RAM will be useless. The period of time that it takes DRAM to refresh is called the *refresh rate*. Refresh rates occur every few processor clock cycles or instruction sets (depending on the RAM). The majority of RAM used in modern computers is some variety of DRAM.

Synchronous DRAM means that the access speed of the RAM is tied directly to the speed of the motherboard. In the days before SDRAM, the

TABLE 6-1

Types of RAM in
Current Macs

RAM Function	RAM Type	Upgradable	Relative Cost
System RAM	SDRAM	Yes	Low
Video RAM	SGRAM	No*	Moderate
Cache RAM	SRAM	No**	High

*On Power Mac computers, installing a video card besides the factory standard ATI card may allow for additional amounts of video RAM.

**Power Mac models that can accept a processor upgrade may have a different amount of cache on the new processor than was factory-standard.

speed of access between RAM and the motherboard was determined in nanoseconds (ns). This worked fine, with the motherboard supporting specific speeds of RAM, but it meant that there were areas of the processor's clock cycle (the cycle the processor uses every time it performs an instruction) that were unable to be used to access the contents of RAM. By tying the RAM's access speed directly to the speed of the motherboard, this is less often the case. SDRAM often also supports special modes to allow the processor to access some data in RAM even while it is working on other tasks (this is known as *pipelining* and is discussed in Chapter 7).

System RAM in a Mac can be upgraded with memory modules known as DIMMs (for dual inline memory module, see Figure 6-2). This packaging of RAM is discussed later in the chapter. Different Macs use different varieties of SDRAM, primarily differing in the speed of the RAM because of differing motherboard speeds. Specific types of RAM for specific models is also given later.

Cache RAM   The cache is a special form of memory that uses a very high speed type of RAM known as *static RAM*, or SRAM. SRAM functions differently than the DRAM used for system RAM in a Mac. While DRAM needs to be periodically refreshed in order to maintain the data that it holds, SRAM does not need to be refreshed. Because there is no refresh period for SRAM, it is significantly faster than DRAM. SRAM also uses several separate transistors for each bit of data, which means it takes more physical SRAM to achieve an equal amount of capacity when compared to DRAM. This means that SRAM is much faster than DRAM, but it is also much more expensive.

Figure 6-2   A standard DIMM memory module as used in the iMac DV and Power Mac computers.

The cost factor makes using anything more than a modest amount of SRAM in a computer impractical. The performance factor, however, makes even a little SRAM go a long way. This is why SRAM is used for caches.

So just what is a cache? In the most basic sense, a cache is a place where the processor can access data faster than it would be able to if that data was stored someplace else. In the case of an SRAM cache, it is a place where the processor can store data and instructions for access much faster than the system RAM. There are two such places on today's Power PC processors: the L1 and L2 caches.

The L1 cache is SRAM that is built right onto the processor itself to store the most commonly accessed instructions and data. The L2 cache was traditionally stored on the motherboard and accessed through the same memory controller that accessed the system RAM. However, the G3 and G4 processor placed this cache directly on the processor card, which allows it to be accessed much, much faster than if it were on the motherboard. This is called a *backside cache* and is also discussed in Chapter 7. The L2 cache stores data that the processor expects to need in the immediate future. Because this data is copied from system RAM to the cache, or is stored in the cache immediately after it has been worked with, the processor can have access to it much more quickly.

Other types of caches that don't use SRAM include the *disk cache*. This is a section of system RAM that is set aside for commonly accessed pieces of data from a Mac's hard drive. Although accessing the system RAM is slower than accessing the SRAM cache, it is still many times faster than accessing the hard drive. Some hard drives, CD-ROM drives, and removable-media drives have a similar RAM cache built into their control circuitry. This speeds up access of data from the drive but is controlled by the drive itself—not the Mac OS as the disk cache is.

Web browsers also have a type of cache that uses the same principle. This time, accessing the local hard drive is faster than accessing a remote Internet server, so the browser will keep copies of recently accessed Web pages and images on the hard drive and access those local copies rather than download them repeatedly from the remote server to speed up performance. Similarly, other applications can perform similar caching functions.

An important factor in any type of cache is its *hit-to-miss ratio*. Because any cache is working on the principle of storing specific data that is going to be needed in the immediate future, the processor is essentially making educated guesses about what data will be needed and should be stored in the cache. As with any type of guess (even a very well educated one), there are bound to be times when that guess is wrong and a needed piece of data is not stored in the cache, while a piece of data that is not needed is. When the guess is correct, that is called a *hit*. When the guess is wrong, that is called a *miss*. The higher the number of hits to the number of misses, the better the cache functions and the greater the performance boost seen by using the cache. A truly excellent cache should have at least 95 percent hits to 5 percent misses.

Another interesting factor in caches is that doubling the cache size doesn't always double performance. Because the cache is twice the size, one might assume this means it makes the processor (or whatever else the cache is working with) twice as fast. This isn't the case. There are several theories as to why this is. One theory is that the larger the cache, the greater the potential there is for misses, since the processor can store larger and larger amounts of data that might prove extraneous or unneeded. Another theory is that a cache can only be of so much benefit, and all benefits result from a small cache because it stores very commonly used information. However, a large cache simply may not be of much additional benefit because the limit of improved performance has already been reached with that commonly used information already in the cache. Whatever the actual factors may be, the simple truth is that as caches get bigger, the performance increase per kilobyte or megabyte has a tendency to decrease.

Video RAM   Drawing objects on a computer's display requires that an amount of RAM be dedicated to hold the data for each pixel on the screen. The color values for each pixel need to be stored in RAM. When the Macintosh was first introduced with a black-and-white monochrome screen, this was pretty simple because 1 bit could handle each pixel, as there were only two possible values. However, when Macs came out displaying 256 colors, they required 8 bits to handle each pixel. Macs displaying thousands of colors require 16 bits per pixel, and Macs displaying millions of colors require 24 bits for each pixel. To put that into some further perspective, an 800x600 display contains 480,000 individual pixels. Needless to say, that adds up to a noticeable amount of RAM. And as you go to higher monitor resolutions, you have more and more pixels to deal with.

Also, this screen data needs to be updated or refreshed very frequently. Because of this, traditional DRAM is generally considered too slow to be usable for quickly updating the contents of the display. This means that you not only need a fair amount of RAM dedicated to holding all the data on your screen, it also needs to be very fast RAM in order to display things well.

For this reason, video RAM, which holds all the screen data, is a different, faster type of RAM than system RAM. This RAM is dedicated to the video controller and graphics accelerator, which take much of the work of actually controlling the display away from the processor, thus speeding up how fast graphics can be adjusted and displayed on-screen. The type of RAM used for video RAM on the Mac is called *synchronous graphics RAM*, or SGRAM, and it was specially designed for use in video processing and display.

In the current Macs, the video RAM is either soldered directly onto the motherboard along with the graphics controller or it is soldered onto a graphics card (in the case of the Power Mac models). In either case, expanding the video RAM is either impossible or requires replacing the factory-standard video card. The only exception is the original revision A iMac. This iMac shipped with 2 MB of video RAM and can accommodate a special module for video RAM upgrades (the onboard VRAM was maxed out in the revision B and later iMacs). Video RAM and graphics controllers are discussed in detail in Chapter 26.

Parameter RAM   *Parameter RAM*, or PRAM, is a fourth type of memory used in the Mac that is discussed in more detail in various chapters of this book. PRAM is a small amount of RAM that is installed on the Mac's motherboard. It is dedicated to storing certain settings for the Mac that must be maintained even while the Mac is powered down and turned off. PRAM is powered by a small lithium ion battery attached to the motherboard to ensure that the settings are continuously preserved (except in the case of the iBook, where the main battery is used to power the PRAM). The PRAM stores the date and time and settings that need to be accessed at startup before the hard drive is available, such as the startup disk, some network information, and the virtual memory and RAM disk settings.

How the Mac Allocates RAM

To get the most out of your RAM and the applications on your hard drive, it helps to understand how the Mac allocates or uses system RAM. Simplistically, when you launch an application from the hard drive, its code is copied into RAM and run by the processor. Any documents you open or create are also stored in RAM until you quit the application. At this point, the application and any files it had opened or created are removed from RAM, and that RAM can be used for other tasks. This is the basic principle of how mass storage for applications and files works with RAM.

There is also the matter of how much RAM an application actually uses. Obviously, the application will need enough RAM to hold its core code. However, RAM is also needed to hold any open files, to use for any data that may be needed by the application while it is performing certain tasks, or for other support files or data for the application (such as its preferences files or user settings). For all these reasons, the application will need more RAM set aside for it than the application's code itself would fill up. This amount of RAM set aside for an application is sometimes called the application's *memory partition*.

On the Mac, an application's memory partition can be adjusted using the Finder's Get Info command. When you click on an application's icon and use the Get Info command under the Finder's File menu, you can choose to display the memory, file sharing, or general information. When the memory information is displayed (as in Figure 6-3), there is a section of the window entitled Memory Requirements. This contains three items: the suggested size of the memory partition, boxes where you can enter the minimum size, and the preferred size of the memory partition (these will be grayed out and unavailable if the application has already been launched and is in use).

The suggested size is the size memory partition that the developer

Figure 6-3

The Get Info window for the AppleWorks application. Note the suggested, minimum, and preferred size boxes and the menu that can be used to get other types of information concerning this application.

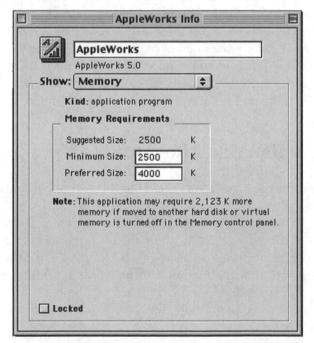

feels is appropriate for the application. This is the amount of RAM that the application should at least have available to perform as the developer intended. Less RAM may work, but it can also reduce performance and cause the application to crash because not enough code or data will fit in the smaller amount of RAM for the application to run properly.

The minimum size is the amount of RAM that must be available in order for the application to be launched. This should be the smallest amount of RAM you feel comfortable launching the application into. Often, by default the minimum size is set lower than the suggested size. It is usually a good idea to set the minimum size to at least the suggested size.

The preferred size is the amount of the RAM that the application will take up if it is available. For example, if you set an application's preferred size to 1024 KB (one megabyte) and there is 4 MB of RAM available when you launch it, the application will still only be allocated 1024 KB of RAM. However, if only 768 KB of RAM is available when you launch the program, then the application will take all of that available RAM because it is less than the preferred size. The preferred size is just what its name implies: the amount of RAM you'd prefer be available for the application (however, you're willing to use less if you have to, provided the minimum size is available).

The actual amount of RAM allocated to an application when it is launched will be at least as big as the minimum size and will not be larger than the preferred size, but depending on the amount of RAM available, it could be anywhere in between, as illustrated in Figure 6-4.

Figure 6-4

In the first illustration there is enough space for the entire preferred size to fit into the available RAM. In the second, however, there is not. In this case, as much of the preferred size as will fit into the free space will be the actual size of the RAM block dedicated to the application when it is launched.

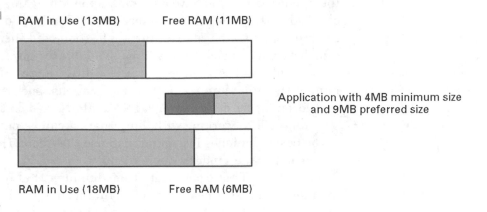

RAM in Use (13MB)   Free RAM (11MB)

Application with 4MB minimum size
and 9MB preferred size

RAM in Use (18MB)   Free RAM (6MB)

How much RAM an application has allocated to it can affect how well the application performs, and one of the easiest ways to speed up a number of applications is to increase their memory partition. In many cases, this allows the application to keep data in RAM that it might otherwise need to read or write to disk. Also, increasing an application's RAM can allow it to have more individual documents open and to work on more tasks concurrently. Several applications will exhibit problems such as crashing when there is not enough RAM allocated to it. This is particularly true of Web browsers and other applications that can be extended by the use of plug-ins. However, setting the memory partition too high can leave an application taking up more RAM than it will use. This isn't a problem in and of itself, but it is a waste of available RAM that might be easily used by other applications.

Determining the best amount of RAM to assign an application's memory partition is sometimes more art and guesswork than science. A good place to start is by assigning the suggested size as the minimum size for the application. Since the suggested size is determined by the developer as allowing the application to run successfully, it is a good value for the lower RAM limit. If an application tends to crash frequently (particularly with Type 2 errors), run slower than seems normal, or regularly displays errors that tasks cannot be completed because of a lack of RAM, you should consider raising this number. Some applications, such as the Eudora e-mail program, will even suggest a minimum size to you when they complain that a task can't be performed because of a lack of RAM. Remember that the minimum size is what must be available to even run the application. If you have a limited amount of RAM, you might want to consider setting the minimum size lower than would otherwise seem a good idea just so you can run the application, and then let the preferred size dictate how much RAM will be available for given tasks.

Determining the preferred size is a little more difficult than determining the minimum size. Some applications, such as Photoshop, suggest formulas for determining a RAM value based on the size of the documents you'll be working with. For others it can be pure guesswork. One of the best techniques I've found is to use the About This Computer item that is under the Finder's Apple menu.

The About This Computer item displays the amount of memory installed in a Mac, the amount of virtual memory in use, and the largest unused block of memory, and it lists the currently running applications (including the Mac OS) and how much RAM they have allocated to them. Next to the applications and the allocated amount of memory is a bar graph that indicates what percentage of that memory they are actually

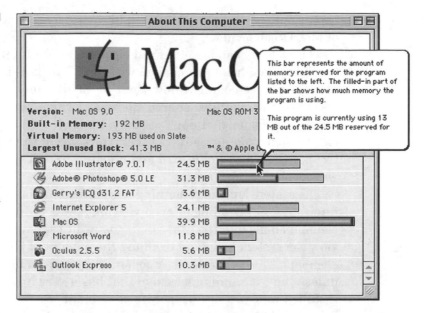

using. By using the Show Balloons command from the Help menu, you
can move the cursor over each of the bar graphs, and a balloon will be
displayed telling you exactly how much RAM the application is actually
using of its allocated block at a given time (as shown in Figure 6-5).

You can use this information to determine the best size for the
Preferred Size box of the memory partition. Set the preferred size higher
than you think will be needed. Launch the application and open as many
documents as you usually work with. Work in each of them as you normally would. Once you've gotten into your usual work habit, switch to
the Finder and use the About This Computer command. Use the balloon
help as described above to determine just how much RAM the application is actually using while you're doing your everyday work with it. You
can then use this value as a guide to set the preferred size to. However,
you'll probably want to add anywhere from 512 KB to 2 MB of additional
space to the setting just to have a buffer in case you find yourself doing
more work than you were at the time you took the measurements.

RAM for the Mac OS   In addition to the memory allocated to currently
running applications, the Mac also assigns RAM to the Mac OS. This is
done as the Mac starts up and is loaded into RAM, before any applications can be launched. The Mac OS partition, normally referred to as the
system heap, is the amount of RAM set aside for the System file, Finder,

extensions, control panels, shared libraries, fonts, and all other manner of Mac OS elements.

The system heap is not a fixed element, and the amount of RAM used for the system heap can change while the Mac is being used. This variability is more common now than in earlier versions of the Mac OS because of things like shared libraries (which are files stored in the Extensions folder that don't actually get loaded into RAM until the Mac or an application needs to use them) or some of the newer styles of control panels, which are loaded and released from RAM in much the same way as applications are.

The system heap is something maintained by the Mac OS. There is no interface for controlling or even viewing how it is divided among Mac OS elements built into the Mac OS. Some utilities, however, do allow you to view the system heap and to adjust the amount of RAM used by Mac OS elements. This generally isn't something you need to be concerned about unless you are running a system that has a very limited amount of RAM installed and you are desperate to eke out every last possible byte of installed RAM (in which case adding more RAM is probably the better solution).

Because the system heap is more dynamic today, you may find that you get error messages from the Finder saying than a task couldn't be performed because there wasn't enough RAM available. This happens when applications have been launched and filled up the available memory. The Finder or Mac OS may at that point need more RAM for the system heap than was originally set when the applications were launched. If this happens, the required RAM won't be available, and the Mac will display an error message in the Finder saying that more RAM is needed and suggesting you quit other applications to make that additional RAM available to the Mac OS.

Memory Fragmentation   When the Mac is started up and run, it begins filling up the installed RAM with data. This begins with the Mac OS and system heap and then continues as you launch applications. When you quit applications, that RAM is then released. However, when you launch and quit applications, RAM can become fragmented. This can lead to situations where the largest blocks of available RAM aren't big enough to allow you to launch an application, even though there is enough total available RAM that you should be able to launch it.

Memory fragmentation is easier to understand by example than explanation. Say you have a Mac with 25 MB of RAM available once the Mac has started up and the Mac OS has been loaded. You launch your Web browser that takes up 15 MB of RAM and do some Web surfing. Then you launch an MP3 player to play some music files, which takes up 3 MB of RAM. Then you launch an e-mail program that takes up 2 MB of RAM. This leaves you a block of 5 MB of available RAM. At this point you decide you want to launch a graphics application that has a minimum size of 18 MB of RAM. So you quit your Web browser because 15 MB plus 5 MB is 20 MB, which is more than the minimum size of your Web browser. But the Mac still claims there isn't enough RAM available, and the About This Computer item displays the largest unused block of RAM as being only 15 MB.

What's happened here is that the 15 MB of RAM released when you quit the Web browser and the 5 MB that was never used are two different blocks of RAM, separated from each other by the RAM being used for the MP3 player and the e-mail program. Both blocks of RAM are available for the Mac to use, but because they aren't contiguous or side-by-side with each other (which would make one single block of free RAM), they cannot be used together. This is why the About This Computer item displays only 15 MB as the largest unused block of RAM. You have more unused RAM than 15 MB, but it is not in a single block and therefore cannot all be used by a single application. However, if you wanted to launch a word processor that needed only 6 MB of RAM, you could do so because that amount of RAM can easily fit inside of the 15 MB block that is available. This example is illustrated in Figure 6-6.

Fragmentation of RAM like this is inevitable when you launch and quit applications one after the other, but it is particularly noticeable when you are dealing with applications that have larger memory foot-

Figure 6-6
Notice how the unshaded areas indicating free RAM remain distinct and separate blocks, even though the total amount of free RAM is larger than both pieces. Because of this separation, the Mac cannot recognize them as a single larger block of free RAM.

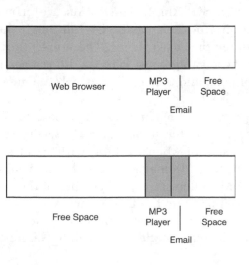

prints. The only way to defragment the RAM is to quit the applications that are between the fragmented blocks.

You can avoid RAM fragmentation by launching applications that you intend to run most or all of the time you're using the Mac first and then launch the applications you expect to use for only a limited amount of time after them. This way, the applications being used constantly won't be fragmenting the RAM of any other applications you may want to run. This won't solve every instance of RAM fragmentation, but it can help alleviate some of the irritation. Installing additional RAM can also help to alleviate the problem because there will be more available RAM in general.

How RAM Is Packaged

When you buy a Mac, it has a set amount of RAM installed in it. You can, if you choose, add more RAM to it. This is because RAM chips come on standard types of modules. As mentioned, the module used in Macs today is known as a DIMM. DIMMs make installing new RAM into a Mac relatively easy and are a standard type of RAM package used in both Mac and non-Mac computers.

DIMMs are basically a piece of circuit board with the memory chips on them and a series of contacts along one edge that are designed to be inserted into the proper socket on a motherboard. There are two principle types of DIMMs in use: standard DIMMs and small outline DIMMs (also called SO-DIMMs). The difference between the two is the physical size of the module and the number of contacts (commonly called *pins*) it has. As you can see in Figure 6-7, a standard DIMM is about twice the physical size of a SO-DIMM. SO-DIMMs are primarily used in laptop computers because of their small size (although the original iMac is a desktop computer that used them). There are other, more subtle differences within these two groups, such as differences in physical capacity, the number of pins, and the speed at which the memory operates.

RAM Damage   DIMM modules can be damaged. The primary cause of damage is from a discharge of static electricity (which is why proper grounding is essential when working with RAM or any other internal computer component). Damage can also be caused by touching the RAM chips on the DIMM themselves, the surface of the card, and the contacts (or pins) that connect into the DIMM slot. When installing DIMMs, you should hold them by the edges to prevent damage. In addition to RAM being damaged during installation, it can be damaged or defective out of the factory.

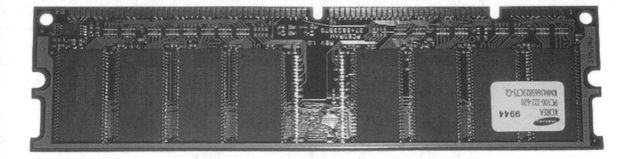

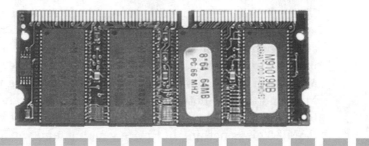

Figure 6-7   Notice the size difference between the standard DIMM (top) and an SO-DIMM (bottom), as well as the difference in the design of the modules.

In most cases when RAM is damaged, the Mac will recognize this when testing the RAM at startup and refuse to continue the startup process. This will either result in a Sad Mac icon or a series of beeps (or possibly the sound of a car crash or series of tones) at startup. This will most likely happen right after new RAM is installed. These symptoms can also occur if a DIMM is not installed properly.

Although it is rare, RAM can incur minor damage that will not be detected by the Mac's startup test. Because only a small number of the millions of microscopic transistors used in the RAM may be affected, symptoms of this damage will appear sporadically or randomly, often as unexplained freezes and crashes that occur when one of the faulty bits of RAM is used to store data. In the case of these crashes, there may be some indication of a memory error, but in many others there may not be.

This is why testing the RAM after installation is a good idea. Utilities such as the RAM diagnostic included in TechTool Pro or Newer's free Gauge PRO utility will write and read data to each bit of RAM to verify that the data is held there properly. TechTool Pro offers a number of very comprehensive RAM-testing options that may be overkill for many situations (and can take long periods of time to complete on a Mac with a moderate or large amount of RAM installed). Testing the RAM immediately after installation alerts you to a problem immediately and spares you the random problems that can be caused by damaged RAM.

Types of SDRAM DIMMs Used in Current Macs

There are three primary types of RAM DIMM modules used in the Macintosh models currently available. This section discusses each Mac and what type of RAM it requires. It is important to note that there is no such thing as "Mac RAM." The RAM modules used in Macintosh computers are industry standards that are also used in a variety of non-Macintosh computers. They do not cost more because they are used in a Mac, and there is nothing special about these modules. This is important to understand because some computer shops will charge extra for "Mac RAM." This is nothing but price gouging, and you should avoid any company that attempts to sell you any special "Mac RAM." Indeed, you can shop for RAM for a Macintosh computer in stores that have no Mac merchandise or knowledge at all if you so choose. You will simply need to know the type of memory that you are purchasing.

Also, when shopping for RAM, be sure to look for a manufacturer that includes a lifetime warranty on their memory modules. Many manufacturers do this at no additional cost. Another way to save money is to buy directly from RAM manufacturers and to shop comparatively between them. Many computer stores and catalog/online resellers tend to inflate the price of RAM two or three times the cost of buying direct from a manufacturer or a company that specializes in selling only RAM. See "Resources for Further Study" at the end of the chapter for Web sites where you can easily find such comparative RAM pricing.

Unlike earlier Macintosh computers and many non-Mac computers, DIMMs in the current Macs do not need to be installed in any specific order or groupings (such as pairs or banks). Nor do all installed modules need to be of the same capacity or from the same manufacturer.

Power Mac G3/G4 RAM

Both the Power Mac G3 and G4 models use the same type of RAM. This is PC-100 SDRAM in a 168-pin, 3.3-volt, 64-bit module. Additionally, the

DIMMs should not be buffered or registered SDRAM and should have a maximum of 16 memory devices per DIMM. Their height should be no higher than 2 inches. This is not only the type of RAM used in the Power Mac computers, it is also the most common type of RAM used in current PC models.

In the case of the Power Mac G3 and G4 models with a PCI graphics slot known by the codename "Yikes," you can install up to 1 GB of RAM. In the Power Mac G4 with an AGP graphics slot known by the codename "Sawtooth," you can install up to 2 GB of RAM, though only 1.5 GB is currently recognized under the Mac OS.

There are four DIMM slots on the G3 and G4, one (or more) of which will have DIMMs installed in it out of the factory. To verify the size of each of the installed DIMMs, you can use the Apple System Profiler. In the Memory Overview, click on the triangle to display the memory details, and then click on the triangle next to Installed Memory to display the capacity of each installed DIMM.

iMac (Slot-Loading) RAM

The iMac models released in the fall of 1999 with a slot-loading CD-ROM or DVD-ROM drive use the same type of RAM as the Power Mac computers (PC-100 SDRAM in a 168-pin, 3.3-volt, 64-bit module. Additionally, the DIMMs should not be buffered or registered SDRAM and should have a maximum of 16 memory devices per DIMM and a height of no more than 2 inches.)

These iMacs have only two DIMM slots and can support up to 512 MB of RAM installed. They will have only one DIMM slot used out of the factory, and this will be filled with either a 64-MB module (iMac and iMac DV models) or a 128-MB module (iMac DV Special Edition). If a second module has already been installed, you can use the Apple System Profiler as described above to ascertain which module is used in which slot.

Original iMac RAM

The original iMac models (revision A though D, Bondi and colored) use SO-DIMMs similar to those used in laptops for memory. The specific type of SO-DIMM is a 100-MHz (10 ns or faster), 3.3-volt, 64-bit, 144-pin SO-DIMM with serial presence detect that is not buffered or registered SDRAM.

The iMac has two SO-DIMM sockets. One is located on the upper section of the processor daughtercard and is empty out of the factory. The other is on the underside of the processor daughtercard and holds the factory-installed RAM. The underside socket requires a low-profile SO-DIMM (still of the above type) when you are installing a module larger than 64 MB. This is because there is a limited amount of space under the daughtercard, and traditional SO-DIMMs over 64 MB will not fit into that space. A low-profile SO-DIMM is specially designed to increase the RAM capacity of the module without increasing its physical size. This allows low-profile modules to fit in the underside slot in capacities larger than 64 MB.

The maximum RAM that the original iMacs can accept is 256 MB, although because low-profile SO-DIMMs were not on the market when the revision A iMac was introduced, Apple's official specs for the revision A iMac reflect 128 MB as the limit, because this is the greatest capacity when using standard-sized SO-DIMMs.

PowerBook G3 RAM

The older PowerBook G3 Series models use the same SO-DIMM RAM modules as the original iMac (100-MHz, 3.3-volt, 64-bit, 144-pin SO-DIMM that is not buffered or registered SDRAM and has serial presence detect). The PowerBook G3 models released in 2000 with FireWire ports must be 125-MHz, 3.3-volt, 64-bit, 144-pin SO-DIMM that is not buffered or registered SDRAM and has serial presence detect. Both types should be PC-100-compliant.

Also, like the original iMac, the PowerBook G3 ships with two DIMM slots, one of which is on the underside of its processor daughtercard. Like the DIMM socket on the underside of the iMac's motherboard, this lower socket requires low-profile SO-DIMMs at sizes greater than 64 MB.

This lower socket also holds the factory-installed RAM for the majority of PowerBook models. This is the case for all models with 64 MB or less installed out of the factory. Greater out-of-the-factory RAM amounts, however, may be installed by a SO-DIMM in both slots. Before buying RAM for a PowerBook G3, you should use the Apple System Profiler as described in the Power Mac RAM section above to determine whether both slots are used for the installed RAM and what-capacity DIMMs are installed in each slot. The maximum amount of RAM supported by the PowerBook G3 is 384 MB for earlier models and 512 MB for 2000 models.

iBook RAM

The iBook also uses SO-DIMM modules, but they are differently sized than those in the PowerBook G3. The SO-DIMMs used in the iBook must be 1.25 inches in size. Aside from the size difference, the iMac SO-DIMMs are of the same type as those used in the earlier PowerBook G3 and original iMac (100-MHz, 3.3-volt, 64-bit, 144-pin SO-DIMM that is not buffered or registered SDRAM with serial presence detect).

The iBook has only a single socket for additional RAM. The factory-installed 32 or 64 MB of RAM is soldered directly onto the motherboard and cannot be removed or upgraded. The iBook can support up to 160 MB of RAM.

Installing RAM

For all but one of the Macintosh models covered in this book, installing RAM is an easy process that nearly anyone can accomplish in short order. The remaining Mac, the original (revision A through D) iMac is a little bit more involved, though still not overly difficult. The following sections discuss how to install RAM into each of the current or recent Macintosh computers.

The Power Mac G3/G4

The current Power Mac computers make installing just about any internal component a painless process. However, installing RAM and PCI cards is particularly easy. The first step, as always, is to make sure you are properly grounded and that the computer is unplugged (for safety's sake).

First, open the side "door" of the Mac, and locate the available DIMM slots to install the RAM into. These are indicated in Figure 6-8. Remove the DIMM you'll be installing from its antistatic bag. Remember to hold the module only by the edges and avoid touching the individual chips, the contacts, and the surface of the card. Make sure the plastic guides on either side of the socket are pushed down. Position the module above the slot you're using. DIMMs install only one way into the appropriate socket. Ensure that the module is properly aligned with the socket by the notches that are located between the contacts, as shown in Figure 6-9.

Figure 6-8   The four DIMM slots of the Power Mac (highlighted here) are located along the side farthest from the case of the computer and toward the front of the machine's case.

There will be two notches at uneven distances along the length of the DIMM.

Press the DIMM into the socket. The side edges of the DIMM will insert into the plastic guides on either side of the socket. Once the DIMM is inserted, raise the plastic guides on either side of the socket to secure the DIMM in the socket. The DIMM should go into the socket easily. The contacts should not be visible at this point. If needed, press gently into the socket until the contacts are no longer visible. Both sides of the DIMM should be evenly inserted. Do not force the DIMM if it seems to have trouble going in. Doing so can risk damage to both the module and the socket. When the DIMM is inserted properly, it should look like the one shown in Figure 6-10.

That's about it for the Power Mac. Close and restart the computer to

Figure 6-9   The notches of the DIMM module and socket allow the DIMM to install in only one direction.

Figure 6-10   A properly installed DIMM module.

ensure that the new memory is being recognized properly. If the Mac refuses to start up, displays a Sad Mac, emits a series of beeps without starting up, plays any other unusual sounds, or begins to start up and then displays a warning that memory is not installed properly, the new RAM is either not installed completely or is damaged. This will prevent

Figure 6-11
The About This
Computer dialog dis-
plays the amount of
installed RAM recog-
nized by the Mac.
This should be equal
to the amount of all
factory and user-tech-
nician-installed RAM.

the Mac from starting up. Double-check that the RAM is installed completely and securely (as shown in Figure 6-11) before assuming it was
damaged (either out of the factory or during the installation).

Assuming the Mac starts up properly, which should be the case in the
vast majority of situations, select the Finder's About This Computer item
under the Apple menu. As shown in Figure 6-11, this will tell you how
much RAM is installed in the Mac. This number should match the total
amount of newly installed RAM, as well as the RAM that was installed
previously.

If this number does not match up properly, double-check that the RAM
is installed correctly. If there still seems to be a problem, run a RAM
diagnostic utility such as Newer's Gauge PRO or the ones included in
TechTool Pro (both are shown in Figure 6-12) to ensure the RAM is functioning properly. If the new RAM is still not properly recognized, remove
it and contact the manufacturer. You can also use the Apple System
Profiler, shown in Figure 6-13, to determine what capacity the DIMM is
being recognized as or if it is being recognized at all.

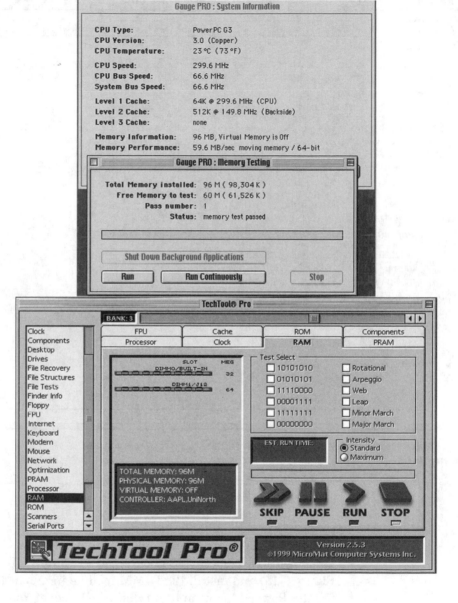

The Slot-Loading iMacs

For the iMacs introduced in the fall of 1999 with a slot-loading CD-ROM
or DVD-ROM drive, installing RAM is also a relatively simple process.
Tip the iMac forward onto its screen, and remove the plastic cover over

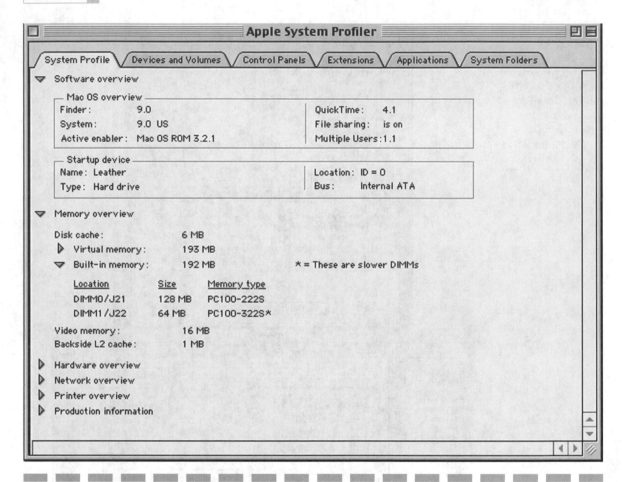

Figure 6-13   The Apple System Profiler can identify the sizes of each DIMM installed, as well as which slot they are installed in.

the RAM and AirPort slots using a coin, as discussed in Chapter 1, and as shown in Figure 6-14. Locate the available DIMM slot (shown in Figure 6-15) and install the DIMM module in much the same fashion as for the Power Mac computers discussed above. You will need to make allowances for the angle at which you will be installing the module, because the socket is on a vertical rather than a flat horizontal surface. The actual DIMM installation is the same, however.

If you are replacing an installed DIMM, remove it in much the same fashion as installing the new one. Push the plastic guides on either side

Figure 6-14   *After tipping the iMac forward onto its screen, use a coin, such as a quarter, to open the slot-loading iMac's RAM/AirPort compartment.*

of the module to release it. In some iMacs, the horizontal angle may cause the module to release very easily and even fly right out of the socket, so it is best to keep a finger on the module as you release the guides. Assuming the DIMM doesn't leap out of the Mac at you, carefully grasp the module by its edges and firmly but gently pull it out of the socket. The module should release and come out easily. Once the module is released, install the replacement module (if you are simply removing but not replacing the RAM, you can just raise the plastic guides on either side of the socket, and you're done).

Once finished, close and secure the plastic cover. Return the iMac to its normal position, and start up to verify the new RAM is installed and recognized properly, as described in the preceding section.

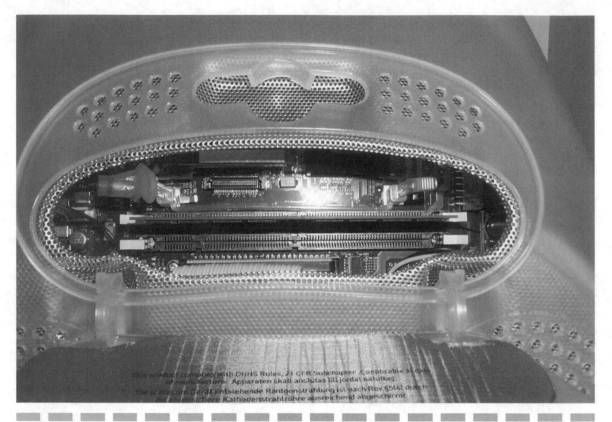

Figure 6-15 Although accessed at a different angle, the DIMM slots of the slot-loading iMac models function the same as those of the Power Macs.

The PowerBook G3

Installing RAM in both the PowerBooks from 1999 and 2000 is extremely similar. First, unplug the PowerBook, and remove the battery. Release the keyboard-locking screw. On the 1999 PowerBooks with a SCSI port, this is on the back of the PowerBook. On the 2000 PowerBooks with FireWire ports, the screw is located in the keyboard tab between the F4 and F5 keys. Next, release and remove the keyboard, using the release tabs at the edge closest to the display, as described in Chapter 2. Once the keyboard is removed, you will need to remove the heat sink that covers both the processor and RAM. The heat sink of the 1999 PowerBooks (shown in Figure 6-16) is larger and held in place by three screws. The

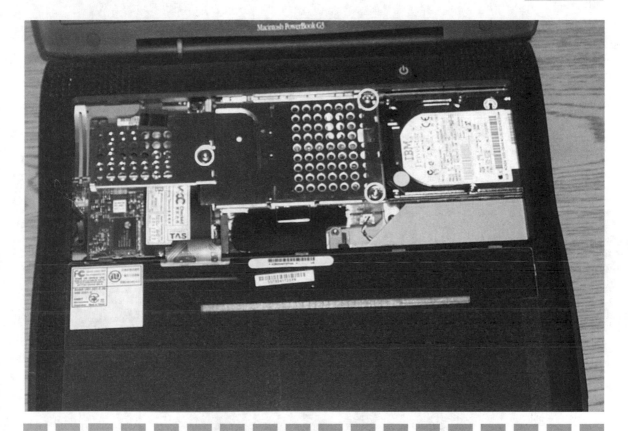

Figure 6-16   Note the three screws that hold the heat sink in place. Also notice the square ferrite bead to the left near the lid. It is important to align this as shown so that the heat sink does not sit on top of it when you are reassembling the PowerBook.

heat sink on the 2000 PowerBooks is smaller, covering just the processor card, and is held in place by two screws. Once the heat sink screws are removed, lift it out of the computer.

If installing into the upper of the PowerBook's two RAM slots, simply install the SO-DIMM module into the available socket. You should begin the insertion of the SO-DIMM at a 30-degree angle, pushing in and down slightly. You should feel a slight snap when the card is properly inserted. At this point, the contacts of the module should be covered by the socket completely, or be just barely visible. You will also be able to tell that the module is inserted completely, because the plastic guides on either side of the socket will be locked into the notches on either side of the module. Figure 6-17 shows a SO-DIMM correctly inserted.

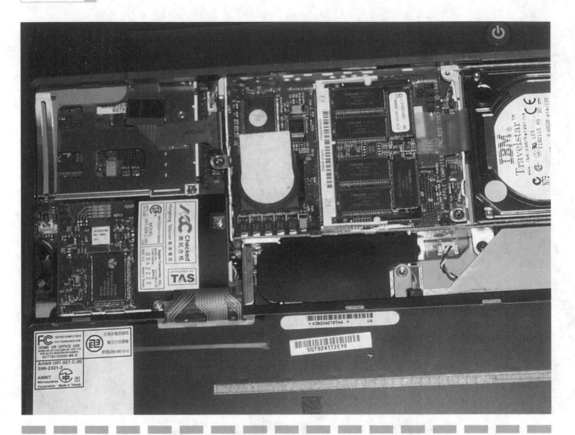

Figure 6-17   The SO-DIMM slot is directly in the center of the daughtercard (in this case, filled with a 256-MB module), which takes up the center of the area beneath the heat sink.

Installing into the lower RAM slot involves removing the processor daughtercard in order to access the underside where the factory-installed RAM is located. This will void an Apple warranty. Carefully remove the daughtercard as described in Chapter 2. When the card is removed, set it on an antistatic surface and turn it over to expose the lower RAM slot. At this point, you will need to remove the factory-installed RAM. To do this, press outward on the guides on either side of the module. The SO-DIMM should release slightly. When it does, grasp the edges of the card and carefully pull up and out until clear of the guides and the socket itself. Then gently lift the existing module and insert the new one. Then reattach the daughtercard.

Once the installation is complete, replace the heat sink and keyboard.

Be certain that the tabs on the keyboard near the wrist rests are properly aligned and inserted fully, since improperly seated keyboards can result in a grinding noise from the CD/DVD-ROM drive. Lock the keyboard screw. It is also important to make sure that the ferrite bead that is part of the keyboard cable on the 1999 PowerBooks with a SCSI port is properly lined up so that it does not rest under the heat sink. If it does rest under the heat sink, you will have trouble securing the keyboard release screw, and the keyboard itself will buckle upwards. Figure 6-16 illustrates the correct alignment of the ferrite bead.

The iBook

Turn the iBook over, and remove the battery as described in Chapter 2. Flip the iBook right side up again, and release the keyboard using the three tabs (shown in Figure 6-18) at the edge closest to the screen/lid. Gently flip the keyboard forward over the wrist rests and trackpad.

Figure 6-18   These three tabs release the iBook's keyboard and allow access to the AirPort card and RAM slots.

Figure 6-19 *The two screws indicated hold the AirPort bracket in place. Once they are removed, simply lift out the bracket.*

Use a screwdriver to remove the metal plate under the AirPort card bracket as described in Chapter 2 and as illustrated in Figure 6-19 (if an AirPort card is installed, remove it first). Set both the two screws and the plate aside. Position the DIMM module at the socket that is now exposed (as shown in Figure 6-20). Gently but firmly install it in much the same manner as the PowerBook's SO-DIMM modules.

At this point you can attach the iBook's power adapter and start it up to ensure the RAM is properly installed and recognized. Reattach the metal plate (and AirPort card if one was installed). Replace the keyboard and secure with the three tabs. Replace the battery, and

Figure 6-20 Once the AirPort bracket is removed, the SO-DIMM slot is visible directly beneath it.

you're done. Verify the RAM was installed and recognized correctly as described earlier.

The Original iMac

The original iMac has two available SO-DIMM sockets. One is located on the upper side of the processor daughtercard and is considered by Apple to be user-installable. The second is located on the underside of the daughtercard. Installing RAM into this socket will void an iMac's warranty. This lower socket is the one that holds the RAM that shipped with the iMac.

In order to install RAM in the original iMac, you will first need to remove the motherboard/drive assembly as described in Chapter 1. Once removed, the motherboard should look as shown in Figure 6-21. For the

Figure 6-21
The iMac's mother-
board/drive assem-
bly. Note the proces-
sor "cage" toward
the top and the
VRAM SO-DIMM slot
(present on revision
A iMac's only) to the
left.

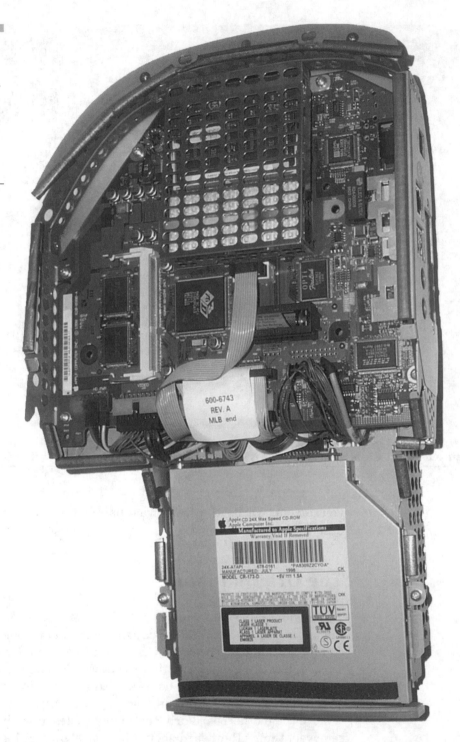

upper RAM slot, you then need only remove the top of the metal "cage" that is over the processor daughtercard. The top of this cage pulls off quite easily.

At this point the DIMM socket is visible (see Figure 6-22). Position the SO-DIMM module and install the same as you would for the PowerBook

Figure 6-22   With the top of the "cage" lifted off, the upper SO-DIMM slot is clearly visible on the early iMacs. Here, a 64-MB SO-DIMM is installed in the slot.

or iBook. Replace the cage, and reassemble the iMac. Start up to ensure the new RAM is recognized properly.

The lower DIMM socket involves removing the daughtercard from the motherboard. To do this you will need to first remove the heat sink that covers the processor. Remove the metal bar that holds the heat sink in place by releasing it from the metal cage. Once the bar is released, lift the heat sink directly up. Be careful not to push to either side before lifting, since the heat sink rests right on top of the processor.

Next, you need to remove the lower section of the metal cage surrounding the daughtercard. The cage is secured to the motherboard by small hooks that insert into holes in the motherboard on all sides, and it is secured to the daughtercard by two tabs on the daughtercard through slits in the cage on the side toward the front of the motherboard/drive assembly. Be careful removing the cage, since it is securely inserted in the motherboard and may need to be worked gently to release. Once the cage is free, set it aside.

Now you remove the daughtercard itself. It is attached via two connectors toward the rear of the daughtercard. Gently pull the daughtercard directly up, using a slight rocking motion if needed. It should release without much effort. Once removed, the motherboard will look as indicated in Figure 6-23. The daughtercard will look as shown in Figure 6-24.

Once the daughtercard is released, turn it over and place it gently on an antistatic surface. Use extreme care, as the card will be lying with the processor side down. The lower SO-DIMM module should be clearly exposed (see Figure 6-25), and you can remove the factory-installed module as described in the section above relating to PowerBook RAM installations.

Once the new SO-DIMM has been installed properly, reattach the daughtercard, then replace the cage and heat sink, using the bar to secure the heat sink in place. Then replace the cover to the cage, and reassemble the iMac. As with all RAM installations, restart to ensure the new RAM is installed properly.

The revision A iMac also shipped with a VRAM socket for accepting additional video RAM. This socket is located on the left side of the motherboard, as illustrated in Figure 6-21. Installing a VRAM SO-DIMM into this socket is basically the same as installing a regular SO-

Figure 6-23   The iMac motherboard after the daughtercard has been removed. Note the daughtercard connectors, which you will need to line up with the card when reassembling the iMac.

Figure 6-24   The upper side of the daughtercard once removed from the motherboard.

DIMM. You will need to use the Apple System Profiler to ensure the additional VRAM is recognized properly (as indicated in Figure 6-26) after restarting.

The Memory Control Panel

The Memory control panel (shown in Figure 6-27) allows you to control three aspects of Macintosh memory management: the disk cache, the virtual memory, and the RAM disk. In this section, we'll look at each of these, as well as some third-party alternatives to the Apple implementations of these features.

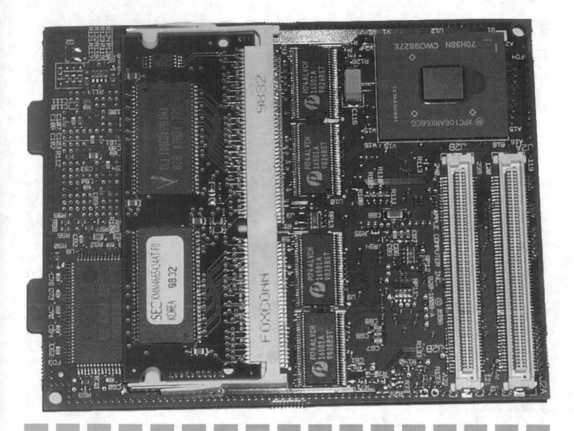

Figure 6-25   The underside of the daughtercard, where the factory-installed 32-MB SO-DIMM is located. Also notice the motherboard connectors that need to be lined up with the corresponding connectors when you are reassembling the iMac.

The Disk Cache

The disk cache was discussed earlier in the chapter in the section on cache RAM. The disk cache is where the processor will store commonly accessed data from the Mac's hard drive. This data is information that the Mac expects to use in the immediate future that can be accessed more quickly in RAM than on the hard drive.

The disk cache is nothing more than a portion of the system RAM that is designated for this cache purpose. By default, the Mac will automatically look at the amount of RAM installed and determine what it believes to be the best disk cache size at startup. This feature can be disabled, and you can set a specific-size disk cache. There are two rea-

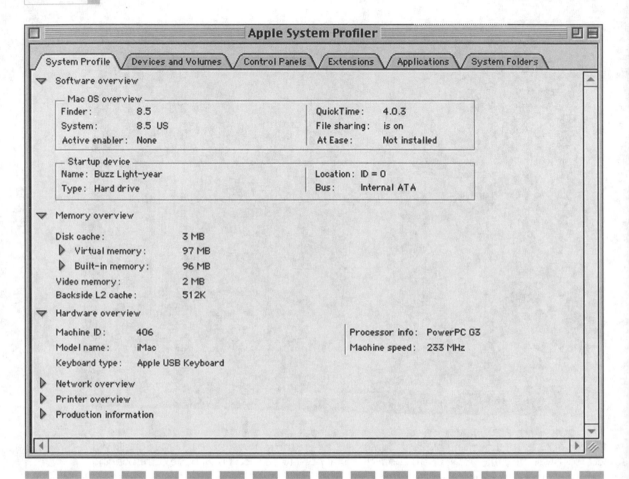

Figure 6-26   Notice the Video Memory item under Memory Overview. In the case of this revision A iMac, no additional VRAM has been installed.

sons you might do this: (1) you want to lower the setting because you have a limited amount of RAM and can't spare any of it from use for running applications, or (2) you have more than enough RAM compared to the applications you expect to run and want to increase the size of the cache to increase performance. As mentioned in the section on cache RAM earlier in this chapter, increasing the size of the disk cache may not provide dramatic performance increases. In fact, if you have more than 64 MB of RAM installed, you aren't likely to see any noticeable increase if you opt to manually increase the cache beyond its automatic size.

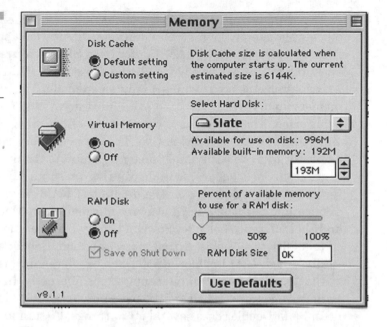

Figure 6-27
The Memory control panel controls three aspects of the Mac's memory usage.

Virtual Memory

Virtual memory is where you take a portion of the hard drive and make the Mac use it as though it were RAM. Doing this can slow down performance considerably, but if you need a little more RAM for certain tasks or applications, it can be worthwhile. If you find yourself using large amounts of virtual memory on a daily basis, however, you should probably install additional RAM, since virtual memory can have a significant impact on performance.

There are various methods for using hard drive space as virtual memory. Apple's method is to map a copy of all the contents and addressing of your physical RAM to the hard drive and to then add to that duplicate map any hard drive space you wish to use as virtual RAM. This has three drawbacks. First, it slows down access even when you aren't using disk space as RAM, because the memory map on the hard drive has to be continually updated. Second, it requires that as much hard drive space as you have installed RAM be used for virtual memory in order to map the contents of actual RAM to the hard drive (which can be a significant use of hard drive space if you have 100 MB or more of physical RAM installed). Third, when you run out of physical RAM, you automatically start using the much slower hard drive.

There are two situations in which Apple's virtual memory can be a benefit beyond simply giving you additional "RAM" for application use. The first is the iBook's Save RAM Contents on Sleep feature. The iBook has a backup feature that will write all the contents of RAM to the hard drive in case problems occur while it is in sleep mode. This works because the memory map already exists on the hard drive when virtual memory is being used. The other, more common benefit is when dealing with software that is not Power PC native. The same memory mapping allows the processor to more easily and efficiently emulate the 680x0 code of earlier Macintosh processors, which results in some minor performance increases and a decrease in the amount of RAM needed to run such an application. See Chapter 7 for more information on Macintosh processors and the difference between Power PC native and earlier 680x0 code.

In addition to Apple's virtual memory option, Connectix manufactures a utility called RAM Doubler. RAM Doubler offers much the same effects as virtual memory, but it implements them differently. Instead of using the hard drive for any and all spillover memory use, as Apple's virtual memory does, RAM Doubler does several other things. First, if an application is not using all the RAM allocated to it, RAM Doubler will reclaim that unused RAM for other applications. Second, RAM Doubler will actually compress the contents of RAM that are not being actively accessed by the processor. Finally, RAM Doubler will create a swap file on the hard drive and swap any data in RAM not being actively used to the hard drive and give the resulting free RAM to processes and applications that are in active use.

RAM Doubler can result in increased performance over Apple's virtual memory setup, but usually only if you are running a number of applications at one time, each of which has only small or moderate RAM requirements. With only one or two applications running, each with large RAM requirements, Apple's virtual memory may actually offer better performance. RAM Doubler also shares the benefit of Apple's virtual memory when dealing with older applications that are not PowerPC native (though not the iBook's Save RAM Contents on Sleep feature).

Although both Apple's virtual memory and RAM Doubler can be good tools, they are not a good substitute for real RAM, and if you find that you need virtual memory of either type on a regular basis, you should buy and install additional RAM. Also, you should be aware of the interaction between the disk cache and virtual memory in terms of performance, because they are very much the opposite of each other. While the disk cache uses RAM as a place to store hard drive data, virtual memory uses the hard drive as a place to store RAM data. This means that turning up the disk cache setting and the virtual memory amount will not result in performance gains, because the advantages of the disk cache are negated by the use of virtual memory.

Another important point for PowerBook and iBook owners is that virtual memory decreases battery life. Accessing the hard drive is one of the biggest drains on portable Mac batteries. Since virtual memory requires accessing the hard drive frequently, if not constantly, this continued access will require more power and drain the battery more quickly.

The RAM Disk

The third feature of the memory control panel is the RAM disk option. A RAM disk is a portion of system RAM set aside to act as though it were a regular disk, such as a small hard drive or removable-media disk attached to the Mac. Because RAM is so much faster than a hard drive, a RAM disk allows files to be copied, updated, or accessed extremely quickly. From the point of view of a user, access to a RAM disk might as well be instantaneous.

Of course, there are two downsides to a RAM disk. First, it uses up RAM. If you don't have excess amounts of RAM installed, using a RAM disk is going to pinch how much system RAM you have for applications and the like. Second, a RAM disk is RAM, which means that the data is lost when the computer is shut down. In deference to the second drawback, Apple has made its RAM disk setup so that the Mac can save the contents of a RAM disk to a special file on the hard drive when the Mac is shut down. However, unexpected shutdowns such as power failures and crashes can wipe out a RAM disk's contents without saving them.

The reason to use a RAM disk is that it is so incredibly fast. Applications launch instantly, and files get saved just as quickly. For programs that use disk space to store temporary or work files, using a RAM disk can boost your performance noticeably if these files are stored on a RAM disk. A good example is the scratch disk settings for Adobe Photoshop or the cache of a Web browser.

In addition to Apple's built-in RAM disk functions of the Memory control panel, there are a number of third-party shareware utilities that you can use for creating a RAM disk. These utilities (two of which are listed at the end of this chapter) offer some interesting and useful advantages over Apple's Memory control panel and are often written as applications rather than as extensions or control panels.

The first advantage is that, being applications, you can create or remove RAM disks without having to restart the Mac to reflect the new

RAM settings. The RAM used for these RAM disks is the memory partition of the applications themselves. This can be a tremendous benefit if you need to use more RAM for running applications than you'd expected. Simply quit the application to put the RAM disk away, and you're done. No need to delete the contents, turn off the RAM disk in the Memory control panel, and restart.

Another very useful feature is that these programs often offer a kind of backup feature that saves the contents of the RAM disks to a file on your hard drive on a periodic basis. While Apple's RAM Disk feature can save the contents of a RAM disk on shutdown, that can result in data loss in the event of a crash or power outage. By periodically saving the contents while the disk is mounted on the desktop, you are less likely to lose data.

Some RAM disk utilities, though not all, also offer the ability to create multiple RAM disks at one time. Apple's RAM Disk feature creates only a single RAM disk. The ability to have multiple such disks allows for organizational benefits, situations where you'd want separate disks for use by separate applications, or where you might want to delete or put away one RAM disk but still have another available.

Resources for Further Study

The following URLs provide additional information on some of the concepts, issues, and products discussed in this chapter.

RamSeeker—Comparative RAM pricing—http://www.ramseeker.com

RAMWatch—http://www.macresource.com/mrp/ramwatch.shtml

Clarkwood Software—Makers of the Rambunctious shareware RAM disk utility—http://www.clarkwoodsoftware.com

Maverick Software—Makers of the AppDisk shareware RAM disk utility—http://members.aol.com/mavsftwre/

Newer Technologies—Produces the Gauge PRO Utility and GURU RAM utilities—http://www.newertech.com

MicroMat—Makers of TechTool Pro—http://www.micromat.com

Processors

The most important component of any computer is the CPU (central processing unit), or processor. The processor is the heart of a computer's ability to perform any action or run instructions. Despite this importance, the processor actually does only three basic things: perform mathematical calculations, compare data values, and manipulate data. Even though this sounds like very little, with the proper instructions these three abilities are what produce all the functions of any computer. This chapter examines the processors used in the current Mac models: the PowerPC G3 and G4 processors.

Terms and Concepts

When talking about or comparing processors, there are several basic terms and concepts you should know. Although this section isn't a complete lexicon to all the terminology used in the world of microprocessor development, it does contain all the relevant information for understanding the basics of the PowerPC processor family, as well as other processors used in personal computing.

Bus

Bus is a term that you'll hear a lot in describing processors. In the most basic sense, a bus is the pathway that is used for data to get from one place to another. Several types of buses are used in a computer, and they can be internal to a processor, extend across the entire motherboard of a computer, or used only between specific components. Wherever data is being moved around or worked with inside a computer, a bus is being used.

You generally need to consider two important factors with regard to bus performance. The first is speed, which determines how quickly information can be transmitted along the bus. Like processor clock speeds, the bus speed is measured in megahertz (MHz). The faster the speed of a bus is, the faster data can be transmitted along it.

The second factor in bus performance is width, which determines how much data can be sent along the bus in a single block. Buses come in widths of 8 bit, 16 bit, 32 bit, and 64 bit. The wider the bus, the more information can be transmitted along it at a given time. This means that a 16-bit bus can transmit twice as much data as an 8-bit bus. Therefore, a 16-bit bus can outperform an 8-bit bus when transmitting 16-bit or larger blocks of data, even if they are running at the same speed or even if the 8-bit bus is running at a somewhat faster speed. You can think of the width of a bus as you would a pipe. The wider the pipe, the more water can flow through at one time, so a bucketful of water will pass through a wide pipe faster than a narrow one, even if the water is being poured at the same speed through both pipes. See Figure 7-1.

The System Bus   The *system bus*, shown in Figure 7-2, is the central pipeline for data that connects all the internal components of a Mac. This includes the drive controllers (for hard drives, CD/DVD-ROM drives, Zip drives, and so on), the boot ROM chips, the RAM, the processor, any ports or expansion slots, and any other internal component. The system bus allows all the components to talk to the processor and to exchange data.

Because its speed controls how fast the various components of the Mac can exchange information, the system bus is one of the key elements of Mac performance. Even if a processor is capable of working very fast, a slow system bus will limit the potential performance because the processor simply can't get data in and out of other parts of the Mac, such as the RAM or hard drive, as fast as it can work with it.

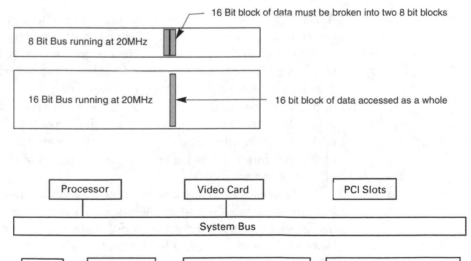

Figure 7-1
Notice how the wider bus allows for the same block of data to be transmitted in one segment, taking half the time.

Figure 7-2
All the components of the Mac connect to the system bus, directly or through various interface technologies (such as USB ports).

In the early days, when Macs used processors running at 25 MHz or so, the system bus and the processor's clock speed were often identical. Today, however, the system bus is usually only about a quarter of the speed of the processor, meaning that the Mac can't always get data to the processor as quickly as the processor can work with it. In some cases, the use of a cache (discussed in an upcoming section) can help to alleviate some of the slowdowns inflicted by a slower system bus.

Internal Data Path/Bus   The processor has its own *internal data path* or bus for transferring information that is currently being processed. This internal bus can be of any width, though it operates at the speed of the processor itself. Like any other bus, the wider it is, the faster the processor can transfer large amounts of data inside itself and the faster it can actually process or manipulate that data. In the early days, processors would have an internal bus that was the same width as the system bus. However, as processors began to develop the ability to receive and organize more than one block of data at a time, internal data paths of larger widths than the system bus began to become common.

Bits and Data Width

A computer stores information, be it data or instructions, as binary data, which is a series of 1s and 0s. Millions of tiny switches known as a *register* hold and work with data inside a processor. Each switch is turned on or off to indicate to the processor whether it represents a 1 or 0. A single 1 or 0 is known as a *bit*. When personal computers were first produced, data was stored in 8-bit segments, known as bytes. Each byte represents a specific piece of data, such as single character typed from the keyboard of a computer. Applications, word-processing documents, image files, or any other data used by a computer are made up of thousands or millions of bytes of data.

Early processors were designed with registers able to work with data only in those 8-bit/1-byte segments, and buses inside the computer were designed to transport data in 8-bit segments. However, it wasn't long before processors began to have registers able to hold and work with 16-bit segments of data. This meant the processor could work with larger blocks of data at a single time. Then 16-bit processors led to 16-bit buses that could transfer the wider segments of data faster. Over time, 32-bit processors and 64-bit processors and buses were developed. Today there are processors (such as the G4) that are capable of handling groups of data as wide as 128 bits.

Data must be a set width such as 8, 16, 32, or 64 bits (and notice those are all multiple of the original 8-bit standard). You can't have a piece of data that is 6 or 7 bits wide. Furthermore, in today's world of processors capable of dealing with, say, 32-bit pieces of data, if a processor receives a piece of data that is only 8 bits, it can only work on that single piece of data at a time. The remaining unused 24 bits of space in the processor's registers are left empty while the processor is working with that 8-bit piece of data. As with many things, technology is currently being integrated into processors to avoid this problem, and we'll discuss that topic later in this chapter.

Clock Speed

Clock speed indicates the speed at which the processor can process information—in other words, how quickly the processor can execute a single processor cycle. In one cycle, a processor performs a single computation, such as adding or comparing bits of data. How fast a process can complete a cycle is determined by the internal data bus of the processor and how the processor is designed.

The speed of a processor is given in megahertz. A speed of 1 megahertz means a processor is capable of completing one million cycles per second. It takes a minimum of two computations or cycles for a processor to complete any instruction, and most actions a processor undertakes require many clock cycles to complete.

Although clock speed is a measure of how fast a processor functions, it is only accurate when comparing the processor to another processor of the same kind and with the same specifications. Real-world performance of a processor is determined by the instructions that are built into the processor, which control how it behaves, as well as by the operating system of the computer. For example, a G4 processor that is also running at 400 MHz will outperform a G3 processor running at 400 MHz because the two processors are built in differing architectures. This is an important concept to understand because clock speed is not the only determining factor of a processor's performance. It tells you how fast the processor performs instructions, but that does not in and of itself tell you how fast the processor will perform in a computer or perform next to a different kind of processor.

Cache

Cache was discussed in Chapter 6 as a special type of RAM. Special types of RAM caches are used in processors, including the L1 and L2 caches. An *L1 cache* is very small but very fast piece of cache RAM that holds the most common instructions sent to the processor. An L1 cache is built into the processor itself, and just about any CPU used today (on a Mac or elsewhere) features an L1 cache. Because it is integrated into the processor and uses a very fast type of memory known as *SRAM* (static RAM), L1 cache is both extremely fast and expensive. Typical processors have an L1 cache of about 32 KB.

An *L2 cache* is a larger cache that is not directly attached to the processor. In processors before the G3, the L2 cache was attached to the motherboard and accessed via the system bus and memory controller, just like other RAM. Although it was a faster type of RAM (static RAM or SRAM) than used for general Mac memory and did offer significant performance advantages, traditional L2 cache RAM was limited in performance by the speed of the system bus.

The G3, however, introduced a new type of L2 cache known as a *backside cache*. This cache is installed either on the processor card or on the motherboard, but it is not connected to the system bus. Instead, it is connected directly to the processor by a special high-speed bus. The backside cache is discussed in greater detail later in this chapter.

Pipelines and Branch Prediction

Pipelining refers to the use of multiple data paths within a processor. Although a processor is only capable of working on one instruction set at a time, modern processors are capable of retrieving additional data for upcoming processes while the processor is busy working on a given piece of information. This saves time and increases performance because the processor doesn't need to wait for one instruction set to be completed before receiving and beginning the processing of the data for the next instruction. Recent processors are also capable of breaking down certain complex computing tasks, such as applying a filter to an image in Photoshop, into several separate smaller tasks and then working on the smaller tasks in parallel in different areas of the processor. This also results in far increased performance over older processors.

Because processors can now retrieve data for upcoming processes, there will be situations where the information produced by the current instruction set determines the data that needs to be used in the next instructions. If this is the case, the processor won't know for certain what data it needs until after it has completed the current instruction set. *Branch prediction* allows the processor to make an educated guess as to what data it will need to retrieve or store when the current instruction set is completed. Branch prediction can therefore work with pipelining to increase performance.

Keep in mind, however, that branch prediction can cause the processor to make incorrect educated guesses about what data will be needed next. Therefore, the branch prediction strategy needs to be a very good one. Otherwise, you will end up actually slowing down performance. In addition, in some older upgrade cards branch prediction has been known to cause problems with some Mac OS elements or software—although this is relatively rare. For this reason, some upgrade cards that support branch prediction allow you to disable the feature.

Registers and Transistors

Registers are the places inside the processor where data is stored while it is being worked on. Like a bus, registers come in widths, such as 8 bit, 16 bit, 32 bit, and so on. The width of the registers inside the processor determine the data width of the processor itself. An 8-bit processor is made up of 8-bit registers, while a 32-bit processor is made up of 32-bit registers.

You can think of registers as cubicles in an office. When data or instructions need to be stored and processed, they are assigned a register just as a temporary employee is assigned a cubicle. When this processing is completed, the bits of data are either moved out of the processor or moved to other registers to be worked with further. Obviously the more registers a processor has, the more work it can do at a given time.

A *transistor* is a like a microscopic switch that can be turned on or off to indicate a single bit of data as either a 1 or a 0. Transistors are the physical places in a processor where information is stored. A transistor can serve as either a register or as a place to store a piece of the processor's instructions. All processors come with an instruction set built directly into them. This instruction set determines how they receive and handle data. Since these instructions need to be stored in the processor itself, they are stored in transistors.

There is no relationship between the number of transistors and processor performance. Transistors that contain instructions for the processor do not serve to speed up the processor in any way. Only an increase in the number of transistors being used as registers will improve performance.

Because transistors require power to function, the more transistors a processor has, the greater its power requirements. The more power required by the processor, the more heat it will generate. These are two important factors in processor development, because heat needs to be dissipated from a processor to keep that heat from causing damage to or destroying the processor. Also, because transistors are a physical part of the processor, the number of transistors a processor has translates into the processor's physical size and therefore cost of production.

CISC and RISC

CISC and RISC are microprocessor designs that determine how quickly instruction sets are decoded and executed. CISC (Complex Instruction Set Computing) processors use a larger number of instruction sets to control what a processor is capable of doing. By adding more instruction sets, you can make the processor capable of accomplishing a wider variety of tasks in various ways. However, each additional instruction set takes up more transistors in the processor itself, making the processor require more power and run hotter.

The RISC (Reduced Instruction Set Computing) architecture has fewer and less complex instruction sets in a processor. Because there are fewer instruction sets, the processor can be smaller and cheaper to produce because fewer transistors are required. This also allows RISC processors to use more of the physical space and transistors in the processor for registers to store and work with data. In addition, the reduced complexity allows more instructions to be handled at once, resulting in faster performance at a given clock speed than a CISC processor. This is one reason why Macs with PowerPC processors of slower clock speeds can outperform Pentium PCs with higher clock speeds. More detailed discussion of differences between PowerPC and Pentium processors is included later in this chapter.

The PowerPC is a RISC-based processor family. The 680x0 processors used in earlier Macs were, like the x86 and Pentium processors used in PCs, CISC based.

680x0 Emulation

When the Mac was originally introduced in 1984, it used the Motorola 68000 processor. Apple continued to base the Macintosh on the 680x0 family of processors until the early 1990s, when Apple, Motorola, and IBM entered into an alliance to create a new architecture of processors. This became the PowerPC.

Because the PowerPC is a different processor architecture than the earlier processors used in the Mac, Apple had to provide backward-compatibility with the software written for the earlier models or face the prospect that all software for the Mac (from any developer) would not function with the Macs based on the PowerPC processor. To provide backward-compatibility, the PowerPC was designed to emulate the code and instructions of the 680x0 processor family. This emulation makes the Mac run applications written for 680x0 processors slower than those written for native PowerPC code and requires additional memory. (Although using virtual memory does reduce the excess RAM requirements.) Over time, applications and the Mac OS itself have migrated to PowerPC native code, and software has been written as "FAT binary" consisting of native code for both processors.

Floating-Point Units

Floating-point units, or FPUs, enable a processor to perform floating-point math computations. In floating-point computations, a decimal point is located in a numeric value. The decimal point is represented to the processor by a segment of the bits in the piece of data the processor is dealing with. Because both the number and the decimal point are made up of the bits in the segment of data, the decimal point is said to "float," hence the term *floating-point*.

Processors used in earlier Macs and those used in a number of non-Mac computers did not have the ability to handle these computations efficiently. As a result, an additional, external coprocessor was developed for many computers to augment the processor by adding floating-point abilities. The PowerPC processors used in current and recent Macs have FPUs integrated into the processor.

There are, however, some rare instances where this built-in FPU is not recognized. This occurs when using older software that is not PowerPC native and is designed to use the FPU of a 680x0 Macintosh. Because the 680x0 emulation of the PowerPC does not include emulation of earlier FPU coprocessors, these older applications will often fail to run because it cannot recognize the FPU built into the PowerPC. The best solution to this is to update to newer software. If that isn't an option, there is an older shareware utility found in many Internet download archives called Software FPU that emulates the FPU coprocessor of early Macs.

Multiprocessing

Multiprocessing refers to using multiple processors in a single computer, distributing the workload among the installed processors. A number of high-end applications are available that can take advantage of multiple processors working together to produce impressive performance. The Mac OS itself is not designed to do so, but because running the Mac OS is not a particularly processor-intensive task, this isn't too great a concern. Applications such as Adobe Photoshop, however, can take advantage of multiple processors for dramatically increased performance.

Multiprocessing ability must be designed into a processor. The G3 processor does not support multiprocessing, although the G4 does. Additionally, a multiprocessing system requires either a special multiple processor upgrade card or a motherboard capable of accommodating additional processors. As of this writing, Apple has made no move to creating multiple processor Macs. There are, however, multiprocessing upgrade cards on the market for some Macintosh computers.

Benchmarks

Benchmarks involve a series of predetermined tests that gauge a computer's performance in specific areas. Special benchmarking software is used to perform these tests and create resulting scores that can be used to compare the performance of a computer against another computer. Although these tests primarily gauge the performance of the processor, the results are also impacted by other factors such as the speed of a hard drive and the speed and width of the Mac's system bus.

Benchmarks are used to compare the performance of different Macintosh models, as well as how well a Mac performs with a processor upgrade card compared to its level of performance before the upgrade was installed. By having a set standard of tests performed on differing Mac models or configurations, you can compare their performance on an empirical level.

Two things are important to remember whenever you look at benchmark scores. The first is that benchmarks do not always reflect real-world performance. A Mac with high benchmark scores may still seem sluggish with certain applications. This is because other factors can affect performance of given applications and tasks. In fact, good product reviews will include real-world tasks such as how long it takes a Mac to start up or how long it takes to perform certain processor-intensive tasks.

Perhaps more important to remember is that benchmark results are fairly accurate guides to performance when comparing computers of the same platform (such as two Macs). However, because differing computer platforms use vastly different processor designs, as well as vastly different operating systems, they are not accurate guides when comparing different platforms (such as a Mac and a Pentium PC). This renders the results of benchmark tests unreliable because each platform's tests are skewed by the differences in the design and functioning of the processor, as well as the way the processor interacts with the other components of the computer.

The G3 and G4 Processors

Macintosh computers currently use G3 and G4 processors. Introduced in 1997, the G3 was a big advance for Macintosh performance for a number of reasons. It was also the first processor ever designed specifically for use in the Macintosh. The G4 was introduced in 1999, and although it was not initially planned for the Mac, it offered some equally significant advances in performance for Macintosh computers, particularly in areas of high-end data manipulation such as digital graphics applications and multimedia content productions.

The "G" in G3 and G4 stands for *generation*, as these processors are the third and fourth generations of the PowerPC processor family, respectively. The previous generations of PowerPC chips include the 601 (first generation) and the 603 and 604 (both second generation) processor families. While the 601 provided a transition from the 680x0 CISC-based processor initially used in the Mac, the 603 and its later variation the 603e served as the workhorse processors of the Mac platform for quite some time. The 604 was developed separately from the 603 and provided quite a respectable performance for its day.

While the 603 was designed with cost and budget in mind, as well as providing good performance returns for the majority of everyday Mac tasks, the 604 was designed with performance rather than cost in mind. This resulted in a more powerful processor featuring more than twice the transistors of the 603 and significantly higher power requirements.

The G3 Processor

The G3 (sometimes also called the PowerPC 750) on the market today is a descendent of the 603e processor, although initial plans for the G3 included variations based on both the 603 and 604. There were, however, several advances made in the core instruction set and other areas of the processor that made the G3 a phenomenally powerful processor when it burst onto the scene in 1997.

The first significant advance was that the G3 has its core instructions optimized to support the functions of the Macintosh hardware and the Mac OS. This provides a significant increase in performance for the Mac because the instructions designed into the processor are specifically tailored to deal with the commands and data associated with the Mac.

The next innovation of the G3, and one of the most powerful features of the processor, was in a new type of cache scheme. As mentioned earlier in the chapter, the L2 cache ability of the G3 allows it to use what is often called a backside cache. This cache exists on an independent data bus. This data bus can run as fast as the processor itself or, more commonly, run at one-half or two-thirds of the processor's clock speed. In the cases of many upgrade cards (or on any G3 Mac with the appropriate utilities), you can actually adjust the speed of this bus to provide increased performance. These utilities are discussed further later in this chapter.

The backside cache allows the processor to store commonly or recently used data in special high-speed memory (see Figure 7-3). In earlier L2 cache designs, this memory was stored on the motherboard and accessed

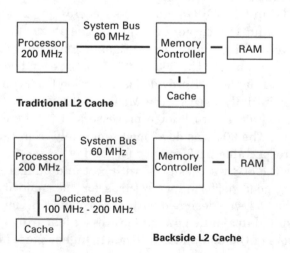

Figure 7-3
The G3/G4 backside cache scheme removes the slower memory controller and system bus from the cache's connection to the processor.

via the same system bus and memory controller as the regular system RAM. Although earlier L2 cache designs did increase performance (sometimes very dramatically), they were still limited to the system bus speed of the computer. This kept the processor from being able to take full advantage of the power and speed of the cache memory.

The independent high-speed bus of the backside cache allows it to be accessed almost instantaneously by the processor, much faster than using the system bus. This ability resulted in extremely dramatic performance increases over earlier processors used in the Mac and made the G3 an instant hit. A wave of G3 upgrade cards for earlier Power Macs created an untapped upgrade market and gave surprising new power to even the very first Power Macs.

The G3 processor is about as small as processor packages go. It also has the advantage of using less power than the majority of processors on the market (including earlier PowerPC processors—in particular, the 604) and likewise producing less heat. This makes it exceptionally good for use in portable computers such as the iBook and PowerBook.

The G3 processor is used in the iMac, iBook, and PowerBook G3 computers and has been used in the Power Mac G3. See Table 7-1 for a comparison of processor specifications.

The G4 Processor

Apple introduced Macs using Motorola's G4 processor (also known as the PowerPC 7400) in the fall of 1999, and upgrade card manufacturers

TABLE 7-1

G3 and earlier PowerPC processor specifications.

Processor	Speed	Size	L2 Cache
603	50 MHz–100 MHz	1.6 million transistors 240 pins	N/A*
603e	100 MHz–300 MHz	2.6 million transistors 240 or 255 pins	N/A*
604	100 MHz–150 MHz	3.6 million transistors 240 pins	N/A*
604e	150 MHz–400 MHz	5.1 or 5.5 million transistors 240 or 255 pins	N/A*
G3	200 MHz–500 MHz	6.35 million transistors 255 pins	512 KB or 1 MB

*Earlier PowerPC processor cache sizes were determined by motherboard design.

began announcing G4 upgrades within a day of Apple's announcement. The G4 processor continues to be an advance in processing power for the Macintosh, adding several new and powerful features.

Larger Backside Cache Capacity   The G4 increased the capacity of the backside cache that the processor could support to a maximum of 2 MB. There is actually some dispute about the advantage to be gained from doubling the potential size of the backside cache. Some benchmark comparisons have shown that there isn't an overly significant performance boost on a G3 Mac when the backside cache is doubled from 512 KB to 1 MB. Assuming the same holds true for a large increase, there will be better performance with a 2-MB cache, but not as great a performance boost as some users might expect from the doubling of the cache capacity.

The G4 supports a wider independent bus to the backside cache, meaning that more data can be transferred between the cache and processor at a given time. This can increase cache performance without increasing the cache size or speed, particularly when large or wide segments of data need to be stored in the cache. In addition, the G4 is a 128-bit processor, capable of working with larger individual data blocks than earlier processors. However, to date, Apple has not even ventured into the possibility of creating such a bus, and the resulting motherboard would be cost-prohibitive to most markets. Therefore, it's likely that Macs will not take advantage of this feature.

Multiprocessing and Enhanced FPU Functions   The G4 also opened up the ability for multiprocessing, allowing Macs with multiple processors, which was impossible with the G3. It is interesting to note, however, that earlier processors such as the 604 also supported multiprocessing. Also, the G4's FPU functions have been improved over the G3, which translates into some gains when performing floating-point calculations.

AltiVec (aka The Velocity Engine)   One of the most impressive components of the G4 is what Apple calls the *Velocity Engine*. This technology, developed for the PowerPC by Motorola, is also frequently referred to by the name Motorola created for it: AltiVec. AltiVec provides for incredible performance increases in applications requiring fast or real-time processing of smaller blocks of data.

Earlier in the chapter you read about how data is handled in groups of 1s and 0s called bits and that these bits can be worked with in groups of

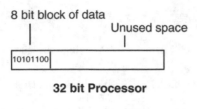

Figure 7-4
When a 32-bit processor deals with an 8-bit piece of data, space that that processor could use for working with more data is wasted.

8, 16, 32, and so on. You also read that if a 32-bit processor was dealing with an 8-bit piece of data, the excess spaces where the processor would store the bits of a large piece of data were left unused. If this appears to be a waste of space, that's because it is. Some registers in the processor are not being used at all, and even though the processor is capable of dealing with larger amounts of data, it is behaving as though it were an 8-bit processor. Obviously, this squanders many of the performance benefits of using a 32-bit processor. See Figure 7-4.

What AltiVec does is to provide a framework in the processor to handle these smaller blocks of data concurrently. AltiVec consists of more than 160 instructions for the processor on how to work with smaller data blocks in a larger register. It also includes a series of 32 registers inside the processor that are 128 bits wide. Each of these 128-bit registers can be filled with either sixteen 8-bit blocks of data, eight 16-bit blocks, or four 32-bit blocks. Because the processor is working on all of these smaller blocks of data at the same time rather than one after the other, they can be processed much faster.

Thus, when dealing with 8-bit data blocks, what would have taken the processor 16 cycles to complete can now be completed in a single cycle. Needless to say, when an application has several smaller pieces of data to deal with, this can result in a very significant increase in performance.

AltiVec is not, however, automatically enabled for all applications. Developers must provide code that tells an application that AltiVec is available and how to take advantage of it. To this end, a number of companies announced plug-ins or updates for their software at the same time that Apple introduced the Power Mac G4.

So what applications is AltiVec specifically well suited for? Digital audio and video production, both of which demand high-end real-time processing of data. Similarly, digital imaging and graphics applications can gain extreme performance boosts from AltiVec, as well as some network software.

Processor	Speed	Size	Cache
G3	200 MHz–500 MHz	6.35 million transistors 255 pins	512 KB or 1 MB
G4	350 MHz–600 MHz	10 million transistors 255 pins	Up to 2 MB

Quite often, AltiVec is compared to Intel's MMX technology, which is designed to accomplish similar acts in Intel's Pentium processors. Although the goal is the same, the methods used and the resulting performance is significantly different. These differences are discussed in the next section of this chapter.

Table 7-2 compares specifications of the G3 and G4 processors.

PowerPC versus Other Processors

The PowerPC processor is vastly different from a number of processors commonly used for personal computers, notably the Pentium family of processors from Intel, as well as the processors of AMD and Cyrix. The two groups are often compared for performance purposes, generally by clock speed. This, however, is extremely deceptive. Comparing the PowerPC and x86 processors (which encompasses the Pentium, AMD, and Cyrix processors) is like comparing apples and oranges (no pun intended). They both function as the heart of a personal computer, but they are based on vastly different strategies and technologies.

PowerPC versus Pentium

The biggest difference that you'll notice immediately is that the PowerPC processors are RISC chips. This means that they have fewer instructions built into the chip, resulting in a less complex architecture and less need for a large amount of transistors inside the chip, which in turn translates into a smaller chip that runs on less power and generates less heat than their competition.

The difference in heat and power are extremely important in generating powerful portable Macintosh computers. If you look at Pentium-based laptops, you'll notice that they rarely have comparable performance to Pentium desktop PCs. This is because not only are the CISC-based Pentium processors larger (making them harder to fit into a laptop), but the faster a processor is, the more heat it will generate and the more power it will consume. In the closed space of a portable computer, heat is an important consideration. Without question, power conservation is a priority for any battery-powered device or computer. The G3 processor, on the other hand, is well suited for laptop computers because it is capable of higher performance while using less power and generating less heat.

An additional comparison between the RISC-based PowerPC and CISC-based Pentium processors is the cost of development. Because RISC-based processors use a reduced number of instructions, there are fewer instructions that need to be developed and then placed into the design of the processor. This savings in design cost is passed on to the consumer when the processor is brought to market. It has been estimated that the Pentium II processor from Intel incurred as much as 10 times the development costs than the G3 did.

Also, because fewer transistors in a PowerPC processor need to be used for the purpose of storing instructions, additional transistors can be devoted to registers where the processor can store and work with data. As discussed at the beginning of this chapter, more registers means better performance.

Like the G3 and G4, the Pentium III processor uses pipelines to break down complex instructions and accomplish multiple processes. However, where the PowerPC processors break data down into four stages for pipelining, the Pentium III needs to break data into 14 separate stages to accomplish the same task.

The L1 cache on the PowerPC processor is twice the size of the similar cache on the Pentium III. The L1 cache is an on-processor cache that stores the most commonly used instructions for the processor and is both the most expensive form of cache memory in a computer per megabyte as well as a significant factor in how fast a processor can perform calculations.

In nearly every benchmark test run to date, the G3 and G4 processors have bested Pentium-equipped machines in virtually every area. These benchmarks are rarely with processors running at the same clock speed. Instead, the Intel processors are often 50 to 75 percent faster than the PowerPC Macs used in the comparisons. Intel's own tests comparing the Pentium III to the G4 indicated that the G4 was twice as fast in performing a number of tasks (primarily those that benefited from the AltiVec instructions) despite a noticeable difference in clock speeds between the two processors.

AltiVec versus MMX   Anyone who turned on a television more than once during the mid- to late 1990s no doubt saw commercials where Intel was hyping the power of its MMX instruction set. MMX soon became a standard part of Pentium processors, and even though most people didn't seem quite clear on what it did, they were caught up in the colorful ads. In order to compare MMX and AltiVec, it's important to understand just what MMX is. (Those clean-suited technicians dancing to disco music in a commercial didn't provide much information.)

In the section on AltiVec, you read about how a processor could be designed to handle several blocks of data that were not as wide as the processor's registers by packing multiple data blocks into a single register and treating it as though it were a single larger block of information. This is the same goal as MMX. The difference is that AltiVec takes the concept further and provides much greater performance increases.

Whereas MMX uses only 8 registers within the processor for performing functions on smaller data pieces, AltiVec uses 32 registers. MMX also forces the processor to share these registers with the floating-point unit of the processor. This means that floating-point and MMX capabilities cannot both be used at the same time, and the processor must move data into and out of the appropriate registers when switching between floating-point and MMX modes. This slows down performance and limits the processor to one of the two tasks. AltiVec's 32 registers are independent of any other processor function.

AltiVec also uses 128-bit registers compared to the 64-bit registers used in MMX. Obviously, the wider registers can hold more data pieces of whatever width is being used. This facilitates faster processing of data because more data can be dealt with at one time.

While MMX produces very powerful performance increases on the Pentium processor family, those increases of themselves still did not rise to the level of PowerPC performance because of the PowerPC's inherently faster RISC-based design. AltiVec, which offers several advantages over the MMX scheme (and consists of approximately three times the number of instructions for dealing with smaller data pieces), shows even more dramatic increases in data-intensive areas of use than MMX does.

Like AltiVec, MMX requires developers to provide support for the technology in their applications in order for it to be used. Given that MMX was developed earlier than AltiVec, there have been a greater number of developers to embrace the MMX instructions than AltiVec. However, because many of the areas where MMX increased performance on Pentium-based machines were not in such need of speed boosts in the first place, this is not great loss to the PowerPC. While MMX is targeted

TABLE 7-3

MMX and AltiVec technology features compared.

MMX	AltiVec
8 registers shared with FPU	32 independent registers
64 bits can be stored per register	28 bits can be stored per register
Under 60 instructions for handling individual data blocks inside each register	Over 160 instructions for handling individual data blocks within each register
Interferes with floating-point calculations when being used	Functions independently of and in conjunction with floating-point operations
Requires switching between floating point and MMX modes	Doesn't require any shift to function with AltiVec or other modes

at a large selection of multimedia applications and has been incorporated into products of many markets, AltiVec is primarily of use for high-end applications such as graphics, audio, and video production markets.

For an overview of MMX versus AltiVec features, see Table 7-3.

PowerPC versus AMD

A comparison that is not made as often concerns the PowerPC processors and the processor family from AMD. AMD is one of Intel's biggest rivals and indeed they made a big splash when they introduced the K7 processor (also known as the Athlon). Although the K7 is also a CISC-based processor, it has several advantages over the Pentium family in performance. The K7 includes twice the L1 instruction cache of the G3 and G4 processors as well as an L2 cache scheme similar to that of the G3 and G4. This gives the K7 a significant leg up over the Pentiums when running against a PowerPC machine. The K7 also has over twice the transistors of the Pentium (which was already higher than the G3 and about equal to the G4), and it also offers enhanced floating-point abilities.

While there is no question that the K7 outclasses its immediate competition and delivers truly impressive performance, there are no hard comparisons that show it outperforming the current PowerPC processors. Much of this is because the K7 continues to be a CISC-based processor like the Pentium. It therefore has many of the same differences from the PowerPC, such as increased number of transistors needed for instructions, for example.

Processor Upgrades

A processor upgrade replaces the processor that came with a Macintosh computer with one that is newer and faster, ultimately allowing the Mac to perform better than with its original processor. Processor upgrades can improve a Mac's performance dramatically. However, because there are several other factors in how fast a Mac performs, they are not a cure-all for a slow Mac. The speed and width of the system bus, the speed of the internal hard drive, the amount of RAM installed, the video chipset and amount of VRAM used on the Mac, and the version of the Mac OS installed all affect how fast a Mac performs.

Even though processor upgrades will not always make an older Mac equal in performance to a brand-new Mac, they can offer significant performance increases. This is particular true if the size of the backside cache installed on the processor module is increased, as well as the processor's clock speed. A larger backside cache can often reduce the impact that other slowdowns of a Mac have on the system's overall performance. If you are on a limited budget or if you have a major investment in your current Mac, a processor upgrade may be a good option to keep your current Mac working for you for a while. On the other hand, if you just want more speed or other features on new Macs, or if you expect to be buying a new Mac within the next six months to a year anyway, you might find a new Mac to be a better solution.

If you are considering a processor upgrade, ask yourself the following questions before deciding whether to upgrade your current Mac or buy a newer model. The answers will help you determine if you will really be satisfied with a processor upgrade card or whether it is really worth the effort and expense of purchasing a new Mac.

- Do you have a major investment in hardware or software specific to your current Mac that you wouldn't be able to easily attach to a newer Mac, such as a large amount of RAM or device-specific expansion cards?

- Are there new features on newer Mac models that you need or want to use, or are you just looking for increased speed?

- Is your desire for increased performance for a specific need (such as the ability to deal with large Photoshop files in a more productive way)?

- What other areas will you need to upgrade besides the processor to get the performance you want (RAM, video card, hard drive, etc.), and will these features be included with a new Mac?

■ Can you afford to buy a new Mac, or do your finances only allow you to purchase a processor upgrade card at this time?

■ Do you plan on keeping the current system for a long time to come, or will you be upgrading to a new Mac in a few months anyway?

Once you consider each of these questions carefully, you will have a clearer picture of what you should do.

How to Compare Processor Upgrades

As mentioned earlier in this chapter, clock speed is not the only factor that determines the performance of a processor. Often other factors such as size of the backside cache and cache-to-processor bus ratio are equally important.

The easiest way to compare upgrade performance is to look at benchmark scores for the cards. Although benchmark-testing software explicitly tests a Mac in only a series of activities to determine a baseline performance against other computers in these areas, benchmark scores do give you a truer sense of how cards compare than just their clock speeds. Likewise, most hardware reviewers will test an upgrade in a number of real-world situations, such as Photoshop filters and actions, boot time, time to access a large file, and so on. This gives you a fairly accurate and good measure of how the card performs.

Cost, stability, and ease of use are also factors. Research the companies and reviews of products. How does the Mac press receive the upgrade cards? Does the company have a proven track record of producing quality upgrades? Are there any noted problems with the stability of the cards? Is the control software for the card easy to use and install? For G4 cards, does the card take full advantage of the AltiVec instruction set, and is it compatible with the AltiVec extensions for whatever software you will be using it with? What type of warranty is included and what are the limitations?

Price is, of course, always a factor, and you should be sure to shop around before buying. Often you can find better deals than you'd expect, and with the ever-growing and competing Mac upgrade market, you can sometimes find extremely good buys on upgrade cards.

Easy Upgrades for Power Macs with ZIF Modules

When Apple introduced Macintosh computers sporting the G3 processor in 1997, they also began using a new method of installing the processor on the Mac motherboard. In previous Macintosh computers, Apple had either installed the processor directly on the motherboard, making removal or replacement virtually impossible, or they installed it directly onto a daughtercard that they then attached to the motherboard. The daughtercard approach enabled third-party processor upgrade cards for the Mac. With the first Power Mac G3 model (a beige minitower or desktop model not covered by this book), Apple began using a ZIF (zero-insertion-force) socket. See Figure 7-5.

ZIF sockets have been around for quite some time on non-Mac computers and motherboards. The socket itself is connected to the motherboard. As shown in Figure 7-5, the socket consists of a grid of holes into which the pins of the processor are inserted and a small lever for securing and releasing the processor module itself. The processor can then be inserted into the socket or removed very easily and does not require the expensive and time-consuming research and development that a daughtercard upgrade would entail. The ZIF socket approach also is transparent across all Macs supporting it, allowing either a ZIF processor module from any upgrade vendor to be installed or one from any other ZIF-equipped Mac. The virtue of upgrading one Mac and then using its original processor to be placed into an even older Mac allows for a nice hand-me-down upgrade possibility, and a market for used ZIF modules has sprung up on Internet classified and auction sites.

The ZIF socket approach was standard on the Power Mac G3 models

Figure 7-5

The ZIF socket and module design allows for easy processor upgrades. The lever to the side secures the module in the socket and, when lifted, allows the module to be easily released.

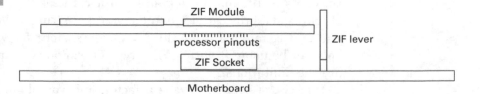

and on the first generation G4 models (known by the Apple codename "Yikes"). Some upgrade manufacturers have even created daughtercards for earlier Macs that consist of nothing more than a ZIF socket, allowing older Macs to be upgraded as easily as any recent Mac with a ZIF socket on the motherboard.

Although G4 ZIF modules are available as upgrades, Apple designed the firmware ROM of the Blue and White G3 so that it cannot accept processors other than the G3. The Mac will refuse to start up if a G4 ZIF unit is installed. This limitation was not initially part of the firmware, but it was enacted in a firmware update for early Power Mac G3 models and on all later G3 models. When this limitation first became public knowledge, there was a great deal of outcry from Mac users who had bought the G3 assuming they would be later able to upgrade to a G4 processor. Apple responded by saying that it had never described the G3 as being upgradable to a G4 and had never expressed an intention to provide G4 upgrades for the Power Mac G3.

Upgrade manufacturers, however, were undeterred in their intentions to provide G4 upgrade cards to owners of the Power Mac G3. Within days of the release of the G4, upgrade makers were shipping upgrade cards with special utilities that would patch or adjust the firmware of the G3 to accept a G4 upgrade module. These utilities need to be installed before the card is, and they must be installed on top of the most recent versions of the Power Mac G3 firmware. As this may not include all Power Mac G3 models, owners should first download the most recent firmware updates from Apple.

One concern about this is how it will affect any future firmware updates from Apple for the G3 and whether or not this might affect warranty coverage. Also, you should realize that this limitation does not affect the earlier beige Power Mac G3 computers, nor does it prevent owners of the Blue and White G3 from using faster G3 ZIF modules.

Both G3 and G4 ZIF modules are available from a large number of manufacturers in a large variety of speeds and backside cache configurations. You can find a list of these manufacturers at the end of this chapter. Figure 7-6 shows a typical G4 processor ZIF module.

Installing a ZIF Processor Upgrade

Installing a ZIF module upgrade is a very simple process. Before doing anything, you should read the manual that comes with the card. The process described and illustrated here is generic to any ZIF card installation; however, there will often be nuances specific to certain cards and manufacturers.

Figure 7-6
This G4 ZIF module is typical of all ZIF modules used in the Mac. (Photo courtesy of Newer Technology)

The first step is to run any installer software that comes with the card. Often these will install software needed for the card to be fully recognized and used by the Mac, or they will install software for controlling features of the card (such as the speed of the backside cache bus). Once you've run the installer, you may want to reboot to make sure the new extensions or control panels have been installed properly. If you are upgrading a Blue and White Power Mac G3 to a G4 card, you will also need to use whatever firmware patch utility the manufacturer provided, as discussed above.

Next, shut down your Mac. Ground yourself with an antistatic wrist strap. As discussed in Chapter 3, this is an important precaution whenever you work with anything inside a computer. Open the Power Mac's case by releasing the side door and swinging it down. Locate the current ZIF module installed. Raise the ZIF lever to release the module from the socket. Holding only by the edges, gently remove the ZIF module from the socket. The module should remove easily. Do not force the module and do not pull it in any direction other than straight up from the socket. Once free, set the module aside, preferably in an antistatic bag or on an antistatic work surface.

Next, remove the new ZIF module from its antistatic packaging. (You should never remove components from their antistatic packing unless you are properly grounded or until you are ready to work with them.) At this point, follow any instructions from the manufacturer regarding setting jumpers on the card for your Mac's motherboard speed or for the backside cache ratio. Some cards are self-configuring; others aren't. Instructions for this process should be included with the card. If they are not, contact the manufacturer before doing anything. You may also need to add a protective rubber "donut" to the processor module around the processor itself, as well as adjust or attach the heat sink. If so, information and any necessary parts should be provided by the manufacturer.

Carefully position the ZIF module over the ZIF socket. Make sure the ZIF lever is in the raised position and ready to accept a processor module. Line up the pins of the card with the holes in the socket, making sure the card is oriented properly. Then, gently set the card into the socket. It should go in easily and without effort. If you encounter any resistance at all, stop and double-check that the ZIF lever is up and that the card is aligned properly. Forcing the card may easily damage both the card and the motherboard of the Mac. Once the module is inserted, lower the ZIF lever to secure it.

Start up the Mac to ensure that the installation was successful and that the card is being recognized as it should be. Double-check both with any utilities that came with the card and the Apple System Profiler to verify the card is being completely recognized at the correct speed, type of processor, and size of backside cache.

Non-ZIF Macs

While the ZIF socket makes upgrading a Power Mac's processor relatively simple, the same cannot be said for other Mac models in Apple's lineup. The original iMac and PowerBook are technically processor-upgradable, while the iBook and later iMac models are definitely not.

The original iMac models and the Powerbook G3 models were not designed with the intention of being processor-upgradable. However, like earlier iMac models, both these computers have used a daughtercard approach to install the processor. The difference is that these daughtercards contain not only the processor, as earlier daughtercard Macs did, but also the SO-DIMM RAM sockets and the ROM chips of the Mac. This makes developing daughtercard upgrades a good deal more difficult and potentially more expensive.

While the RAM being located on the daughtercard presents little problem, since the SO-DIMM RAM modules can easily be removed and placed onto a replacement daughtercard, Apple's decision to place the Mac ROM chips on the card does create major problems. In order to create a new daughtercard for upgrades, manufacturers would need to be

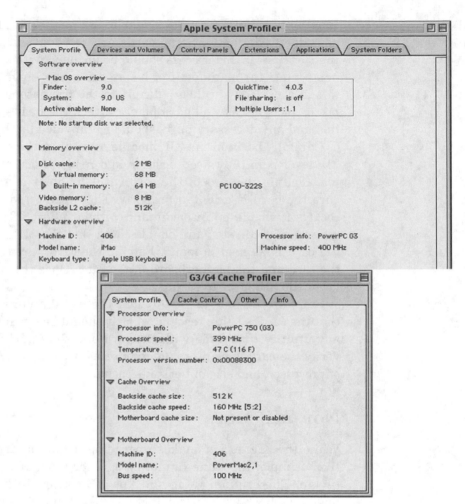

able to replicate the Mac ROM chips. Since Apple will not make the code or the chips available to any other party, upgrade developers cannot create a functional upgrade. Even if upgrade manufacturers could produce the ROM chips themselves, the expense (both in production and development) might make such a proposition too expensive to be practical.

Newer Technology, however, developed a workaround to this problem. Rather than try to create their own daughtercards for the older iMacs, Newer opted to take daughtercards from existing iMacs (shown in Figure 7-8) and remove the soldered on G3 processors from them. Once the processor has been removed. Newer can then solder on a faster replacement processor and sell the daughtercard. These upgrades, called the iMAXpowr, offer owners of the original (revisions A through D) iMacs

Figure 7-8
The processor
daughtercard of the
original iMac (note
the SO-DIMM RAM
socket to the right).

an upgrade possibility, though cost still tends to be a factor, even with the rebate Newer offers for buyers if they return their iMac's original daughtercard.

The second-generation G4 that debuted the AGP graphics slot on the Mac, as well as AirPort on the Power Mac models (Apple codename is "Sawtooth") does not use the standard ZIF socket for its G4 processor. It does use a kind of daughtercard design, however, so it is theoretically processor-upgradable. However, as of this writing, no such upgrades have been announced.

Clock-chipping

Clock-chipping (also called overclocking) is a process by which you can force your computer's processor to run at a faster clock speed than it was designed to. Attempting to clock-chip a Mac will void your warranty or AppleCare coverage and is not for the faint of heart.

When a processor is installed in a computer, that processor has been tested and certified to run properly at a given clock speed. This certified speed is what is stamped on the processor, and the speed that is included in the processor's specifications. It is possible, however, for a processor to

Figure 7-9
The processor
daughtercard of the
AGP graphics card
G4 models with the
heat sink removed.

run at a higher clock speed than what it is certified for. Running the processor at a faster speed like this can present two problems. First, the processor will generate additional heat that the motherboard and heat sink designs of a Mac may not be equipped to safely handle. Second, as you increase the speed at which the processor is running, you increase the chances of the processor (and therefore the Mac) not being stable in performing its functions.

Because the speed of a processor in a Mac is tied in ratio to the speed of the motherboard, clock-chipping requires that you adjust components of the Mac's motherboard in order to force the processor to run faster. Because the processor speed in the Mac is tied to the speed of the system bus for the motherboard by this ratio, making the ratio higher will force the processor to work faster in order to function with the motherboard. The motherboard components that control processor-to-system bus are referred to as PLLs (phase locked loop). These PLLs will be either a series of jumpers on the motherboard (as in the Power Mac models) or a series of components soldered to the motherboard known as resisters (as in the iMac, iBook, and PowerBook computers).

Clock-chipping is often very delicate because the resisters are very tiny, fragile components that you need to solder and unsolder in specific combinations to adjust the system bus to processor ratio. It is not something that should even be attempted by someone who is not expert at soldering small components. It is a warranty-voiding offense because it is so tricky to achieve and because it forces the processor to work harder than it was intended.

As a rule, the performance increases from clock-chipping a Mac and maintaining usable stability and a tolerable amount of heat generation are not significant enough, in my opinion, that they are worth the risk for most people to take. However, it is an extreme form of processor upgrading. The list of resources at the end of this chapter includes sources of additional information on clock-chipping.

Processor and Cache Utilities

Most upgrade manufacturers ship their own utilities for controlling the G3 or G4 processor of their upgrades and its backside cache. These utilities, shown in Figure 7-10, often install as control panels and can also be used to adjust the performance of a factory-installed stock processor. Particularly noteworthy of the abilities imparted by this type of software is the ability to adjust the speed ratio of the bus that connects the processor to the backside cache.

The iMac, for example, uses a standard 2:1 ratio between the speed of the processor and the cache bus. This is not an absolute value, however, and you can gain additional performance by using one of the cache utilities to increase the ratio to something that delivers higher performance,

Figure 7-10

Upgrade makers often use software such as these to control the backside cache of a processor.

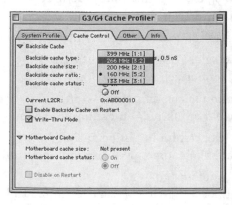

such as the maximum possible value of 1:1, where the cache bus performs at the same speed as the processor.

There is a slight concern that running such a utility might cause some instability of the computer in question, as well as the possibility of increased heat when running the cache speed at a speed other than the standard set by Apple for the computer. In response to the heat concern, these utilities often bundle a processor temperature gauge into the software, allowing you to monitor temperature concerns. You can monitor for signs of instability by simply being aware of whether or not you experience increased application or system crashes after adjusting the cache settings with one of these utilities.

Processor and cache utilities from upgrade manufacturers can often be found by checking the software download and support sections of their websites.

Resources for Further Study

The following URLs provide additional information on some of the concepts, issues, and products discussed in this chapter.

Apple's G4 Processor page—
    http://www.apple.com/powermac/processor.html

Motrola's AltiVec site—http://www.motorola.com/AltiVec/

Accelerate Your Mac—http://www.xlr8yourmac.com/

MacSpeedZone—http://www.macspeedzone.com/

XLR8: Upgrade manufacturer—http://www.xlr8.com/

Newer Technologies: Upgrade manufacturer—
    http://www.newertech.com/

Powerlogix: Upgrade manufacturer—http://www.powerlogix.com/

Sonnet Technologies: Upgrade manufacturer—
    http://www.sonnettech.com/

iMac modification (clock-chipping)—
    http://home.earthlink.net/~nickndan/imac/imacmod1.html

Mystic Room (clock-chipping information)—
    http://www.bekkoame.ne.jp/~t-imai/maine.html

Clock-chipping homepage—
    http://violet.berkeley.edu/%7Eschrier/mhz.html

CHAPTER 8

Expansion Slots

Expansion slots are motherboard components that allow you to easily expand the abilities of a Macintosh by installing expansion cards. Expansion cards can perform a wide variety of functions, including providing support for SCSI devices, providing graphics acceleration and display control, providing additional Ethernet ports, adding older-style Mac serial ports for accommodating legacy devices, and augmenting the audio abilities of the Mac. Assuming a developer can devise a device that meets the standards for a given type of expansion slot, with expansion cards, the hardware-based capabilities of the Mac can be expanded in virtually any manner.

A number of expansion slot techniques have been used in the Mac since it was introduced over 15 years ago. Today, the only Mac models to make much use of expansion slots are the Power Mac computers. The exceptions are the PC Card slots of the PowerBook (which are discussed separately in the next chapter) and the mezzanine slot that was on the motherboard of the original Bondi-Blue-colored iMacs.

Today's Power Mac computers use three types of expansion slots: PCI slots, comm slots, and AGP (Advanced or Accelerated Graphics Port) slots. Each of these three, as well as the mezzanine slot of the original iMac models, are discussed in this chapter.

PCI Slots

PCI (Peripheral Component Interconnect) is a technology that was originally developed by Intel for use in PCs. For non-Mac platforms, they were in many ways revolutionary, offering some of the advantages of plug and play expansion card installation that Mac users had enjoyed for years. With the second generation of PowerPC Macintosh models in the mid-1990s, Apple decided to adopt the PCI technology as a replacement for the platform-specific NuBus slots used in earlier Macs.

PCI slots provide a completely standardized hardware interface that can be used for integrating virtually any kind of technology into the Macintosh. Because the PCI standard is so widely supported throughout the computer industry, PCI slots also mean that developers can easily create expansion cards that, with the appropriate driver software, can function in both Macintosh and non-Mac computers. A typical PCI card is shown in Figure 8-1.

Although PCI slots are industry standard, it is important to understand that there are components of the technology that may need to be

Figure 8-1
A typical PCI card.

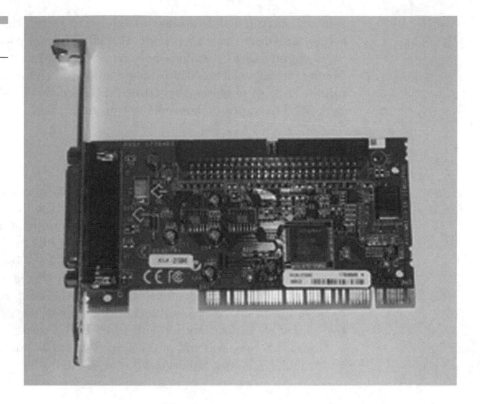

provided in order for PCI cards to function on the Mac (in addition to any other platform). The primary of these requirements is that there must be driver software for the card. As mentioned in other chapters, any piece of hardware that is installed in a Macintosh needs a driver. A driver tells the Macintosh what the card is, what it does, and how to control it. Without Macintosh drivers, the Mac simply will not recognize a PCI card after it has been installed. In almost all cases, the drivers for a PCI card will be installed as extensions and/or control panels, and they should come included with the card.

For cards that need to be recognized and controlled by the Mac at startup, a second component of PCI technology must be present: The cards must support open firmware. This means that the card must provide its control code in ROM (or firmware) on the card itself. This way, the card can be recognized and controlled at startup before extensions (or any part of the Mac OS, for that matter) is loaded. Cards requiring firmware support include video cards (which need to be able to generate a display very early in the startup process) and SCSI cards where the selected startup disk is attached to the card rather than a motherboard connector. Other cards such as additional Ethernet port, serial port, and video capture cards that don't need to be accessed at the beginning of the Mac's startup sequence will function without being open firmware-compliant. This is the reason that several SCSI cards will allow users to connect SCSI hard drives, but not start up from them.

Types of PCI Cards

Although PCI cards can serve many different functions, they generally share the same industry-standard characteristics. Despite these similarities, PCI cards can differ from each other in a number of ways. The most obvious way is in size. There are two standard PCI card sizes: 7-inch and 12-inch, shown in Figure 8-2. While both cards have the same height and thickness, the actual length of the card varies. This is because some uses of PCI cards require more physical circuitry be used, requiring the card to be larger to accommodate it. The PCI slots of the Power Mac G3 and G4 computers support both 7- and 12-inch PCI cards.

Beyond the physical size of the card, PCI cards can be either 32-bit or 64-bit and can run at either 33 MHz or 66 MHz. The Power Mac G3 and

Figure 8-2
The differences between 7-inch and 12-inch PCI cards.

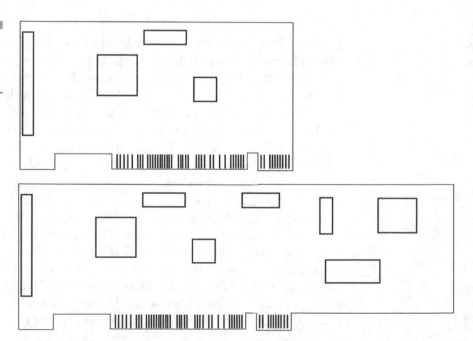

early Power Mac G4 models provide three 64-bit 33-MHz PCI slots and a single 32-bit 66-MHz slot. The faster slot is used for the factory-installed ATI video card. The later Power Mac G4 models provide only the three 64-bit 33-MHz PCI slots (the factory-installed video card uses an AGP slot, discussed later in this chapter).

The 64-bit PCI slots have an additional section for the extra pins needed on the card's connector to provide 64-bit data throughput to the motherboard. A 64-bit PCI slot is compatible with both 64-bit and 32-bit PCI cards. The 32-bit PCI slots are not able to accept 64-bit cards. Figure 8-3 shows the differences between 32-bit and 64-bit PCI cards.

The 66-MHz slot used in the Power Mac G3 and earlier Power Mac G4 is designed differently from a 33-MHz PCI slot. It is designed so that the notch (called a *key*) in the PCI card is in the reverse location of where it is in a 33-MHz card (see Figure 8-4). This means that you cannot install 33-MHz PCI cards into the 66-MHz slot. Similarly, a 66-MHz PCI card would not install into the 33-MHz slots of any of the Power Mac computers.

PCI cards also come with different power requirements. The two primary varieties that you can install into a Power Mac computer are 15W and 25W cards. In the case of 15W cards, you can install up to three cards into the Mac. You cannot install more than two 25W cards, however, because of the higher power requirements. You can mix both 15W and 25W cards, although you can install only one of each if you do so.

Figure 8-3
The differences between 32-bit PCI cards and 64-bit PCI cards.

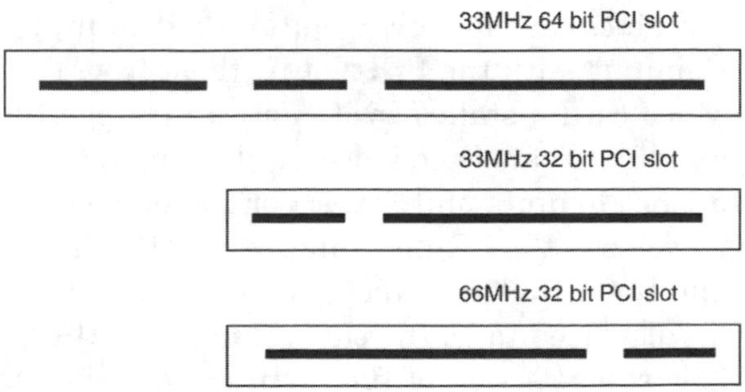

64 bit PCI Slot

32 bit PCI Slot

Figure 8-4
The 66-MHz PCI slot has a different key design than the traditional 33-MHz PCI slot.

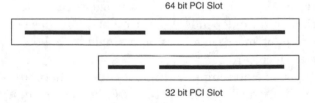

33MHz 64 bit PCI slot

33MHz 32 bit PCI slot

66MHz 32 bit PCI slot

Uses for PCI Cards

The most common uses for PCI cards include the following: SCSI controllers that allow you to attach both internal and external SCSI devices, additional video cards, additional network cards, PC compatibility cards, serial port cards, higher-end audio cards, RAID cards for creating hardware RAID arrays, and cards for capturing, editing, encoding, and exporting video. Many of these types of cards are discussed elsewhere in this book, but the following sections provide a brief overview of some of the more popular types of PCI cards for the Mac.

Video Cards   While the special 66-MHz PCI slot or AGP slot holds a standard ATI Rage 128 graphics card out of the factory in the Power Mac models, many other video cards are on the market as well. There are two reasons you might want to install a second video card into a Power Mac: to run an additional monitor or to add video features not included in the ATI card.

The Mac can support multiple monitors. This can be done using a second (or third or fourth) monitor as an extension of the primary monitor, giving you the additional space for the Mac's desktop and windows. Or it can be done by mirroring the display from the primary monitor to a secondary display (particularly useful for presentations when a projector is attached instead of a second monitor). For each additional monitor you want to attach to the Mac, you obviously need an additional monitor port, and you will need separate video circuitry to control the display of each monitor independent of the others. For these reasons, if you want to use two (or more) monitors on a single Mac, you'll need to install additional video cards.

If you are attaching multiple monitors, there are a couple of things to keep in mind. The monitor that will be your primary monitor should be the one with the highest-quality display, as this is the one that you will probably spend the most time viewing. It is logical to use the highest-power graphics card for this monitor. By default, the Mac numbers monitors beginning with the PCI slot furthest from the hard drive bays that has a video card installed in it. You can change the primary monitor to one connected to another video card by using the Arrange item in the Monitors or Monitors and Sound control panel (though any changes will be lost if you zap the PRAM). Simply drag the Happy Mac icon to the icon that represents that monitor you wish to use as your primary monitor (you will also need to do the same thing with the small icon of the menu bar). This same section of the Monitors or Monitors and Sound control

TABLE 8-1

*Common Features
in Third-Party Video
Cards*

Video capture from analog video sources
Alternate graphics acceleration types (such as the 3Dfx Voodoo chipsets)
Alternate video output types (RCA composite video, S-video, VGA port, older Apple monitor port, digital display port for LCD displays)
Television tuner (to receive and decode antenna/cable TV feeds)
Additional video RAM

panel is also where you can enable video mirroring (which causes both monitors to display the same image). Using multiple monitors is covered in greater detail in Chapter 26 and was also discussed in Chapter 4.

Besides enabling the use of multiple monitors, you might want to install additional PCI video cards in order to use a card that includes features not found in the standard ATI card that ships with the Power Mac. Some of these features, along with the abilities they impart, are listed in Table 8-1. More detail of the types of video cards and video abilities available to the Mac is available in Chapter 26.

If you have multiple video cards installed in a Mac but only one monitor attached, the Mac can still function as if multiple monitors are being used. This can be confusing because if you move the cursor off the edge of the one monitor attached, it may disappear. This happens because the Mac has moved it to one of the nonexistent monitors. You can avoid this by turning on video mirroring if you have multiple video cards but are only using on monitor.

SCSI Cards SCSI cards are probably one of the most common PCI cards you can find for the Mac. Until the iMac was introduced, every Mac since the Mac Plus included a built-in SCSI port (with the exception of the PowerBook Duo models). This meant that many Mac users, particularly professional Mac users, had an investment made in SCSI peripherals. The need to continue to use these devices, combined with the fact that SCSI is a noticeably faster device standard than USB, made SCSI cards for the Power Macs without a built-in SCSI port incredibly popular.

There are a wide variety of SCSI cards on the market, offering support for the various SCSI standards. Almost all them include support for both internal and external SCSI devices. A large number of SCSI cards support using a SCSI drive attached to them as a startup disk, but not all. As discussed earlier, for a drive to be bootable from a PCI card, the card must have the firmware support to be recognized and controlled by the Mac at the beginning of the startup process.

Various SCSI card types and options are discussed along with other areas of SCSI in Chapter 12.

PC Compatibility Cards   Most professional Mac users, as well as many home Mac users, are aware that the Mac needs to be able to work with Windows-based PCs in today's world. One of the surest ways to do that is to be able to run PC software and operating systems right on the Mac, offering the user the options of both platforms. The most popular method of emulating a PC is to use a software product such as Virtual PC. However, there are also hardware options.

These hardware options, called PC compatibility cards, are essentially the major motherboard components of a PC placed onto a PCI card that can be installed into a Power Mac. They include an Intel (or AMD or Cyrix) processor, video circuitry, BIOS, CMOS, and several other components. Some even include PC ports such as the parallel port. They do not, however, include their own hard drives or monitor ports. These are shared with the Mac. As with a software emulator, a disk image file on the Mac's hard drive serves as the PC's hard drive, and the PC monitor is often a window on the Mac's desktop.

PC compatibility cards offer superior performance than software emulators, because there is essentially a PC inside the Mac and it performs as a real PC would. There is no effort on the part of the Mac's processor to emulate the code of a Pentium processor, nor to emulate a PC's video controllers. This advanced performance comes at a price, however. PC compatibility cards are significantly more expensive than software emulators, because you have to pay for the processor and other hardware that is built into the card. For more discussion of both PC emulation options, see Chapter 41.

Serial Port Cards   As with SCSI cards, every Mac computer before the iMac shipped with standard Apple serial ports for connecting external devices such as modems, printers, palmtops, digital cameras, and for LocalTalk networking. When the iMac was introduced without serial ports, many Mac owners had an investment in serial port devices. So, it was not surprising that PCI cards offering additional serial ports became extremely popular when Apple introduced the Blue and White Power Mac G3 without serial ports.

The cards can provide two or more serial ports, but because they are on a PCI card, they may not function with all existing serial port devices. It is important to check with the manufacturer regarding compatibility. Later, comm slot serial port cards (mentioned later in this chapter), which suffer from fewer compatibility issues, were developed. Comm slot cards, however, only offer a single serial port.

Beyond expansion cards, there are also USB-to-serial-port adapters on the market. All of these and other serial port solutions are discussed in detail in Chapter 30.

Network Cards   All currently shipping Macs include a built-in 10/100Base-T or gigabit Ethernet port on their motherboard. This meets the networking requirements of most home users and many professional and educational users. However, for Macs that are being used as network servers (either local network file servers or Internet servers or a combination of the two), there are many instances where additional Ethernet ports may be needed.

If only a single Ethernet port is needed, there are any number of Ethernet cards on the market that can accomplish the task of adding a single Ethernet port. Apple also produces a multiport Ethernet card that includes multiple Ethernet ports and can provide up to four Ethernet connections per card. This card, however, requires Mac OS X Server in order for more than one port to be recognized.

In addition to simply providing more Ethernet ports, Ethernet cards can provide users with different types of Ethernet ports. Although the 10/100Base-T Ethernet port, which uses unshielded twisted pair cabling, is the most common today, there are other variations of network cabling supported under the Ethernet standard. These include 10Base-2, or ThinNet, which uses coaxial cable and connects computers in a daisy-chain fashion rather than through the use of a hub, and 10Base-5, or ThickNet, which uses much larger cabling and requires a special transceiver and "vampire connector" to attach to the cable. Both of these options require different types of Ethernet ports than 10/100Base-T Ethernet. There is also the emergence of the Gigabit Ethernet standard, which is 10 times faster than 100Base-T Ethernet which is only built into the most recent Power Mac G4 models. On older Power Macs, gigabit Ethernet requires a special PCI card that supports both the speed and cabling type of this emerging network standard.

Beyond Ethernet, there are other types of networking that require a PCI card in order to be supported on the Macintosh. The most common of these at the moment are the consumer-oriented products that allow you to network computers through the phone lines installed in your home. These products deliver data at varying speeds (usually around 1 or 2 Mbps) and usually require either a special PCI card or USB adapter. Given USB's limited bandwidth and use for other peripherals, a PCI solution is prefer-

TABLE 8-2

Types of Network
PCI Cards

10/100Base-T Ethernet
10Base-2 coaxial cable Ethernet
10Base-5 ThickNet Ethernet
Gigabit/Fiber-optic Ethernet
Multiple Ethernet standards on a single card
Multiple Ethernet ports on a single card
Token Ring
Home phoneline networking
LocalTalk *

*Some serial port PCI cards offer LocalTalk support.

able if you wish to use one of these products. There is also the older Token Ring networking strategy that has been supplanted by Ethernet in most settings. This also requires a special network card (though the connectors and cabling are virtually identical to Ethernet). Token Ring cards supporting the Mac are, however, becoming increasingly rare.

Table 8-2 shows a list of the networking cards you might need to add to a Power Mac and does not include AirPort wireless networking (which doesn't use a PCI slot) or LocalTalk cabling. Part 4 of this book is devoted to further discussion of Mac networking hardware, software, and protocols.

RAID Arrays   RAID (Rapid Array of Independent Disks) is a method by which multiple hard drives are tied together to function as a single drive. There are multiple ways in which drives can be combined into a RAID array, and arrays can offer both backup and performance benefits. RAID arrays can be created using one of two methods. The first is to purchase a software utility that tells the Mac to treat all the disks as a single drive in the appropriate way. The second is to install a RAID PCI card.

RAID cards offer some advantages in that they are not software, and therefore all the disks will be recognized properly even if a Mac is started up from a disk that doesn't include RAID software. Hardware-based RAID arrays can also offer performance benefits over software-based arrays. To install a hardware-based array, you need to first install a RAID card and then attach the drives in the array to that card. RAID solutions are discussed in Chapters 5 and 39.

MPEG-2 Decoding MPEG-2 is the encoding method used to store DVD movies on a DVD disc. The ability for a computer to decode MPEG-2 data is what allows that computer to play DVD movies. The most recent Power Macs all ship with DVD-ROM drives and support software-based MPEG-2 decoding. The Power Mac G3, early Power Mac G4, and PowerBook G3 models, however, do not support software DVD decoding and require a hardware MPEG-2 decoder. If these models included a DVD-ROM drive when they were manufactured, the MPEG-2 decoder is likely built into the video card that they shipped with. If a DVD-ROM drive is added later, however, that ability is not present. In some cases, if you are buying a DVD-ROM drive for the Mac, the manufacturer will include an MPEG-2 decoder card along with the drive. This will be a PCI card that needs to be installed in order to play DVD movies on the computer. This option may not be available from all manufacturers, however. It is also interesting to note that although the MPEG-2 decoding on the later Power Macs is primarily software-based, it does not function if the factory installed ATI graphics card is removed.

Professional Multimedia Cards In addition to the abilities of the various video cards, a number of other professional-level PCI cards are on the market. These cards include professional-caliber audio cards for recording, playing, and mixing music at higher-quality levels than the built-in audio the Mac offers. They also include cards for encoding audio and/or video into various data formats, such as MPEG-2. These cards offer very high-end multimedia productions abilities and tend to be extremely expensive. Some such cards are discussed in Chapters 27 and 28 of this book.

Installing a PCI Card

PCI cards are quite easy to install in the Power Mac computers. Install any software drivers or utilities that came with the card and then shut down the computer. Make sure that you are properly grounded before beginning. The first step is to open the side of the computer as described in Chapter 1. Once the computer is open, the PCI slots are easy to find. They are located toward the rear of the computer relatively close to the hard drive bays, as indicated in Figure 8-5.

If the PCI card you are installing will provide ports for external devices, you will need to remove the metal covering behind the slot you

Figure 8-5
The location of the
Power Mac's PCI
slots.

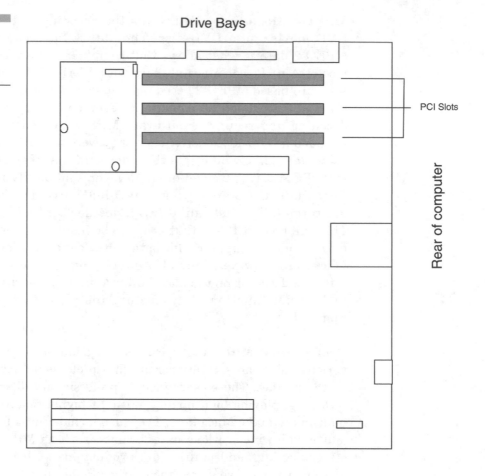

Drive Bays

PCI Slots

Rear of computer

are installing the card into. These metal covers are held in place by a single screw as shown in Figure 8-6. Once the screw is removed, you can slide the cover out. It is a good idea to keep the removed covers in case you decide to remove the PCI card later in the life of the Mac, as they can be replaced to keep dust and debris out of the computer.

Remove the card from its antistatic bag, holding only by the edges (as indicated in Figure 8-7). Position it above the PCI slot you are installing it into. Make sure that the card is lined up properly. For 32-bit PCI cards, only the first two sections of the slot will be installed (see Figure 8-3). Once the card is positioned, press it firmly into the slot. Avoid using a rocking motion, and press straight down until the card is seated securely.

Figure 8-6
The metal covers on the back of the Power Mac, which need to be removed for a PCI card providing external ports, are held on by a single screw.

The gold contacts of the card should not be visible. Figure 8-8 shows correctly and incorrectly inserted PCI cards.

If the card provides ports for external devices, you should secure it to the back of the case. Such cards include a metal bracket with a hole for a screw that will be in the position against the surface of the case that the metal cover was. Secure this with the same screw that was used to secure the metal cover before you removed it.

At this point the card is installed. Restart the Mac and use whatever utilities accompanied the card (or the Apple System Profiler) to ensure that the card is installed and recognized correctly.

Figure 8-7
Avoid damage to PCI cards by holding them by the edges and not touching the components of the card.

The Need for More PCI Slots

For the past few years, Apple has shipped Macs with three PCI slots. However, prior to this, Apple produced Macs that offered up to six PCI slots. These Macs were often intended for high-end uses in such fields as graphic design and desktop publishing, as well as some server markets. Following the transition to only three PCI slot models, several high-end professionals have complained that three PCI slots are not enough for them to install as many expansion cards as they have a need for.

If you need more than three PCI slots, your only option is to purchase a PCI expansion chassis. These devices, which look almost like a second computer, run a cable from one of the internal PCI slots of a Mac to an external case (chassis), which contains additional PCI slots. Once the chassis is connected to the Mac, any PCI cards installed in it are treated as though they were installed in the Mac itself.

PCI expansion chassis tend to be rather expensive devices and are somewhat clunky to use considering they are external devices. They also may not deliver as much performance as individual PCI slots in the Mac itself would because they divide only the bandwidth of a single PCI slot among however many slots are actually in the chassis. If you must use an expansion chassis, it is best to place higher-end and more frequently used PCI cards in the Mac itself rather than the chassis. In addition to

Figure 8-8   Top: Incompletely inserted PCI Card. Bottom: Correctly inserted PCI card.

providing additional PCI slots, some expansion chassis also include internal bays for additional hard drives.

PowerBooks and PCI Slots

Although PowerBooks do not feature PCI slots, a company called Magma makes a special device that enables PCI cards to be connected to a PowerBook. The Magma PowerBook expansion chassis looks and functions like a PCI expansion chassis for a desktop Power Mac. It connects to the PowerBook's PC Card Slot (which functions similar to a PCI slot, as discussed in the next chapter). This PowerBook expansion chassis allows you to connect PCI cards to the PowerBook (albeit externally). This can be useful for some multimedia production professionals needing to add very specific PCI card features to a portable computer. However, the additional cost makes using such a device prohibitive to most users.

AGP Slots

With the later Power Mac G4 models, Apple replaced the 66-MHz PCI slot that holds the Power Mac's video card with an AGP slot. The Advanced or Accelerated Graphics Port (AGP) slot was specifically designed for video card use and offers several advantages over a PCI slot for video purposes.

Like the PCI slot technology, Intel designed the AGP slot for use in PC hardware but it was adopted by Apple for the Power Mac. The AGP slot standard was actually based on the 66-MHz PCI slot, which never gained as much industry support as the standard 33-MHz PCI slot. In addition to being a 66-MHz slot, the AGP standard also offered some unique advantages of its own.

The most interesting advance of AGP technology is its ability to use the system RAM in addition to the video RAM on the video card for graphics processing. The advantage to this is that as displays get larger and complex tasks such as 3D rendering become commonplace, more and more memory is required to process these functions. VRAM, as discussed in Chapter 6, is noticeably more expensive than system RAM. Several tasks of a video card require the extreme speed that VRAM offers, but not all. For tasks where system RAM is adequate, using VRAM is overkill. Beyond being overkill, this can slow down video performance because tasks that require the speed of VRAM have to wait until other tasks (which do not require such speed) are completed and moved out of the VRAM on the video card. Additionally, there are several areas in graphics rendering where an application will render visual data, such as a 3D texture map, in system RAM, and then that data will have to be copied to the VRAM so it can be displayed. By allowing the video card access to system RAM, AGP allows for increased performance in such tasks.

Beyond the direct RAM access, AGP also offers increased performance by allowing the video card to transfer data with the processor at multiple points during the processor's clock cycle. This technique is essentially

Figure 8-9
The differences
between AGP and
PCI cards.

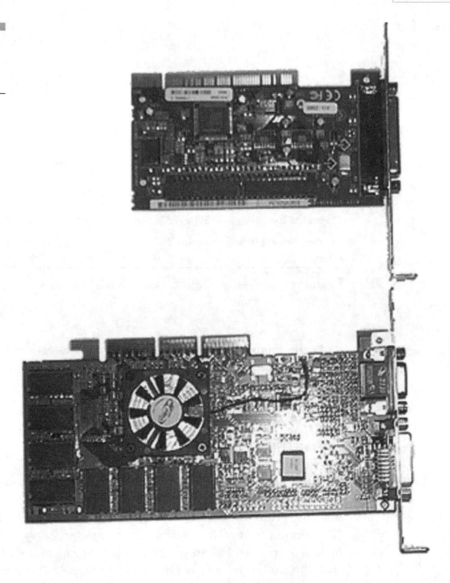

the same as pipelining (discussed in the previous chapter), which allows the processor to access new segments of data even while it is busy working with other data and instructions. The pipelining technique used by AGP allows a video card to transfer twice as much data with the processor in a given period of time as PCI does. This is referred to as the *AGP 2X mode* and is not only supported by the Power Macs with an AGP slot, but also on the slot-loading iMac, iBook, and PowerBook Fireware models, which have their video circuitry soldered directly the motherboard. Table 8-3 compares the AGP and PCI standards for use of video cards.

TABLE 8-3

PCI and AGP
Comparison

PCI	AGP
33 MHz*	66 MHz
32 bit or 64 bit	32 bit only
Access processor once per clock cycle	Accesses processor twice per cycle
Must copy certain graphic data from system RAM	Has direct access to system RAM
Can only use VRAM for graphics acceleration	Can use system RAM for graphic tasks
Can be used for many types of devices	Dedicated only to video cards
Three slots included on AGP Power Mac models	Only one slot per computer
Backward-compatible with earlier PCI video cards	Specialized design accepts only AGP cards

*66-MHz PCI cards are not included in this comparison because they are not included in Power Mac computers with an AGP slot.

At the moment, there are not as large a selection of AGP video cards on the market as PCI video cards, but that will probably change quickly as developers begin to take advantage of the technological advances that AGP affords.

Installing an AGP Card

Installing an AGP card is essentially the same as installing a PCI card. Install any driver software for the replacement AGP card. Shut down the Mac and ground yourself properly. Open the Mac and locate the AGP slot. It is located toward the rear of the computer in about the middle of the motherboard, just before the PCI slots (see Figure 8-10). You'll also notice that the slot is not as close to the rear edge of the computer as the PCI slots are and that it is smaller and differently colored than the PCI slots.

The first step is to remove the existing AGP card. You need to remove the screw that secures the card's metal bracket and ports to the case of the Power Mac (the same as you would to remove a PCI slot's metal cover). Set the screw aside. Grasp the AGP card by the edges and pull directly up without any rocking motion. Once the card is free, set it on a static-free surface or, to be safer, into an antistatic bag.

Remove the new AGP card from its antistatic bag. Position it over the slot, and press down firmly without rocking it back and forth. Once the

Figure 8-10
The location of the
AGP slot.

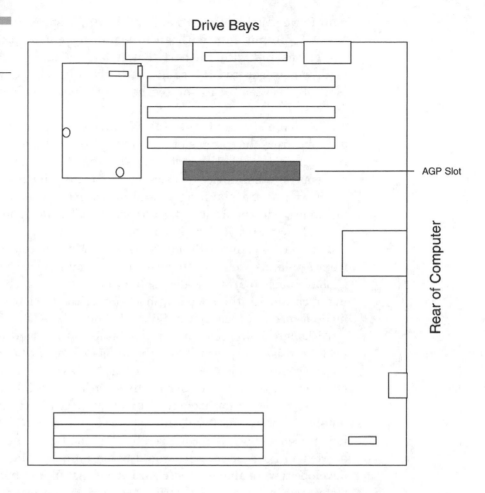

Drive Bays

AGP Slot

Rear of Computer

card is securely seated, you should see nothing of the card's contacts. Secure the metal bracket to case of the Power Mac with the screw you removed when taking out the old AGP card. Then close the Mac and start up to make sure the new AGP card is recognized properly.

Comm Slots

The comm slot of the Power Macintosh computers is designed to hold an internal modem card. In the majority of cases, an internal modem is installed in the comm slot as a standard feature on the Power Mac G4 models. This feature can, however, be omitted when ordering a custom-built Power Mac configuration from the Apple store. Similarly, the Power Mac G3 did not ship with an internal modem installed as standard equipment. Likewise, the early Power Mac G4 units with a PCI graphics card, which featured the same motherboard architecture as the Power Mac G3, also tended to ship without an internal modem as a standard feature.

The comm slot used on the Power Mac G3 and early G4 computers is different from the comm slot used in the later G4 models that include an AGP graphics card. Although both slots function in much the same way, modems (or other devices) designed for one machine are not usable in the other. If you are planning to add an internal modem to one of these machines, you should look for a modem that is designed for the specific model Power Mac you are installing into.

Internal modem cards for the Power Mac computers are available from Apple, as well as other third-party manufacturers, most notably Global Village (currently a subsidiary of Boca Research). When purchasing such a card, the specifications and prices tend to be similar. Apple modems are the ones that are installed out of the factory.

Although the comm slot is intended for an internal modem, it can be used for other purposes. The only other type of card currently available for the comm slot is a serial port card. As described in more in detail in Chapter 30, the Mac no longer ships with the serial ports, which were traditionally used for attaching a wide variety of external devices, most notably printers and LocalTalk networks. The comm slot, even though it is not a serial port, is recognized by the Mac OS in the same manner as a "Modem Port" serial port would be on an older Mac. Because of this, developers were able to create cards that install into both types of comm slots used in the various Power Mac models and provide a single serial port that is recognized by the Mac OS as a traditional serial port would be, resulting in much fewer compatibility concerns (which are discussed in Chapter 30). Obviously, installing a serial port card into the comm slot prevents you from also installing an internal modem in the computer.

Installing either an internal modem card or a serial port card into either variation of the Power Mac motherboard is a relatively straight-forward process.

Installing Comm Slot Cards

Because the Power Mac G3 and early G4 models used a different motherboard and comm slot design from the later Power Mac G4 computers, there will be two sets of instructions here. These instructions are accurate for installing both modem and serial port cards into the comm slot. The first step in either case is to install any drivers or software that comes with the card. Then you need to ground yourself and open the Power Mac.

For the G3 and early G4 models (those with a PCI graphics card known by the codename "Yikes"), locate the metal plate with the telephone picture on the back of the computer. This is where the modem's phone jack (or a serial port) will go. Remove the plate. It is secured with a single Phillips head screw.

Now take either the modem or serial port card out of its antistatic bag. Take the actual port (either the phone jack or serial port, depending on which you're installing) and place it on the inside of the case so that the port itself is pointing outward and is situated in the space where the metal plate was. You'll notice there are two tabs on one side of the port (opposite the hole for the screw). These will insert into the case and help to secure the port. Secure the port in place of the metal plate using the same screw that secured the plate. This will be easiest if you use the fingers of one hand to hold the port in place and the other hand to insert the screw.

Now, you need to insert the actual card into the comm slot. The card may or may not be connected to the port you just attached to the computer's case already. If it is not, connect the cable from the port to the card. Locate the comm slot on the motherboard. It is located toward the rear of the computer and the edge of the motherboard that is farthest away from the drive bays as indicated in Figure 8-11. It is also marked "Modem." Line the card up with the connectors. Although it may not be obvious at first glance, the plastic of the card's connector is molded in such a way that it will install only in one direction. Press the card into the slot. It should go in without much force, and if it seems to resist, stop and double-check that the connector is properly aligned with the slot.

The comm slot of the Power Mac G4 computers which feature an AGP graphics slot (and are sometimes referred to as "Sawtooth" for their Apple codename) is both of a different type and in a different location than on the earlier Power Mac computers. As you can see in Figure 8-12, it is located on the opposite corner of the motherboard, toward the front of the Mac's case and right next to the forwardmost hard drive bay. The opening at the back of the Power Mac's case is also in a slightly different location, as also indicated in Figure 8-12.

As with the earlier Power Macs, once you've opened the Mac's case, you'll need to attach the proper port to the case. Again, the port is held in place with a single screw. There may be a metal box containing a phone jack already in place against the back of the case. If this is so, you can

Figure 8-11
The location of the actual modem phone jack (or serial port) and the comm slot.

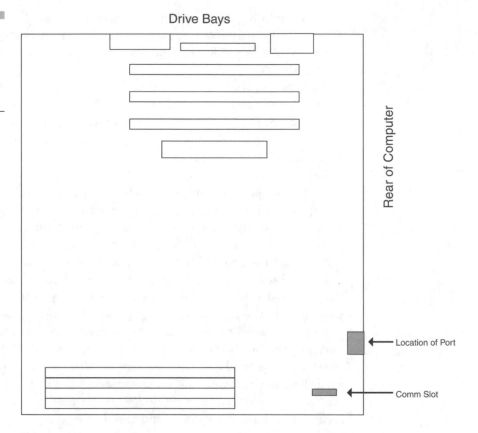

Drive Bays

Rear of Computer

← Location of Port

← Comm Slot

leave it unless you're installing a serial port card. If not, you need to attach the appropriate port, removing a metal plate and securing it with the screw.

The next step is to actually install the card. Locate the comm slot and remove the card from its antistatic bag. Position the connector of the card over the connector on the motherboard. The card will fit only in one direction, with the bulk of the card facing away from the drive bays. There will be two screw holes in the card and on the motherboard, which should remove any confusion about how the card is properly oriented. Press the card's connector onto the connector on the motherboard. It should snap down securely and will be held by a slight metal tab on the edge of the card toward the back of the Mac and right next to the connector. Once the card is in place, you need to secure it to the motherboard with the two screws.

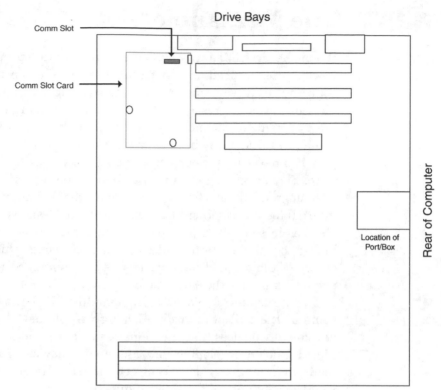

Figure 8-12

The location of the modem phone jack and comm slot in the AGP card G4 models.

Next, you need to run the cable from the port to the comm slot card. With the Apple factory-installed modem, this cable runs under the motherboard. For third-party cards installed later, the cable is generally run between the video card (and any PCI cards) and the motherboard and then under the hard drive cables, going around the edge of the motherboard. You should check the instructions that come with the card to be certain, however. It is better to actually remove the video card and any PCI cards before running the cable underneath them. Doing so will make the process easier and make you less likely to accidentally damage the cards or motherboard while trying to snake the cable between them. Once the cable has been run around the motherboard, you'll want to attach it to the appropriate connector on the card.

Once the card is installed with either type of Power Mac, close the computer. Restart and verify that the card is installed properly (either with utilities included with the card or with the Apple System Profiler).

The Mezzanine Slot

When the first iMac was announced in the late spring of 1998, a lot of news stories focused on a slot that was included on the iMac's motherboard but that was conspicuously not mentioned in any of Apple's technical or developer resources for the new computer. The slot, located on the underside of the motherboard, became known as the *mezzanine slot* (it has less frequently been called the perch slot).

It has never been clear what Apple's intentions for the mezzanine slot were. Some arguments claim that it was there in case Apple decided to offer upgrade options for the iMac, and others claim it was only used for internal testing. Another idea was that it was designed to allow additional abilities in some of Apple's early iMac demo models (two of which were known to include external video output even though this was not a feature of any of the original iMac models). Apple remained very close-mouthed about this slot for the entire time it remained on iMac motherboards.

The mezzanine slot is, actually, a modified PCI slot, and it conforms to some of the PCI standards. Although Apple asked developers not to develop any devices that would make use of the slot, a number of companies did begin developing mezzanine card devices. At this point, Apple made installing any device into the mezzanine slot an act that would void the warranty of the iMac in question.

In a move that made further development of mezzanine cards extremely impractical for developers, Apple removed the slot from the motherboards of the revision C and later iMacs (along with the infrared port that was a standard feature on the revision A and B iMacs). Without a slot to develop products for on later iMac models, the cost returns available to developers became rather limited. Apple responded to complaints by saying they had never intended for the mezzanine slot to be used for iMac expansion products and that they had discouraged companies from developing such products.

Only two types of mezzanine cards ever made it to market: SCSI cards and video cards. Formac, a German company, developed a SCSI card known as the iProRAID that supports all SCSI standards up to and including Ultra Wide SCSI. The card met with moderate success, although it was not available to U.S. markets for some time. Eventually, the iProRAID was sold in the United States, primarily through OEM distributors. The card offered iMac owners the ability to attach and use any of their existing SCSI devices. The Formac card also functioned at full SCSI levels for data transfer and bandwidth performance and worked very reliably with all types of SCSI devices. This contrasted greatly with the SCSI-USB adapters that were the only other option for iMac owners (and weren't even on the market when the iProRAID was introduced) because of the limited bandwidth and performance of USB, as well as the compatibility issues with several SCSI devices. Formac later introduced the iProRAID TV, a card that combines the original iProRAID card with a TV tuner card. This allows owners of the revision A and B iMacs to add SCSI support, video capture, and the ability to decode a television signal.

The iMac GameWizard video card for the mezzanine slot enjoyed a notably shorter life span than Formac's SCSI card. The iMac GameWizard was designed by Micro Conversions and offered 8 MB of video RAM over the maximum 6 MB of the first-generation iMacs. The card also offered Voodoo 2 graphics acceleration, which several 3D games on the market could take advantage of to offer performance superior to that of the ATI graphics chipsets used in the iMac. Because of the threat of voided warranties, Micro Conversions offered its own warranty coverage that extended not only to their card, but anything covered by the voided Apple warranty as well. Sadly, Micro Conversions was forced to go out of business shortly after the release of the iMac GameWizard card. The card itself may still be available from companies dealing in Mac parts, and there have been various companies interested in producing and selling the card themselves in the time since Micro Conversions closed its doors.

Installing a card into the iMac's mezzanine slot involves removing the motherboard as described in Chapter 1. The slot is located more or less in the center of the underside of the motherboard, just to the "front" of the modem card. When installing a mezzanine slot device, note that you need to remove the metal plate the iMac's ports area that is below the ports and covers an empty space that can be used for the ports of whatever card is being installed.

Troubleshooting Expansion Cards

Following are common problems with expansion cards, along with their solutions.

Devices Attached to Card Do Not Mount or Function Properly

If this problem occurs, ensure that the device in question is powered and connected properly. For SCSI devices, ensure that all SCSI rules are followed as described in Chapter 12.

Also ensure that the drivers for all devices attached to the card are installed and configured properly. Likewise, ensure that the drivers for the card are installed properly.

Finally, check to be certain the card is installed properly.

Card is Not Recognized by Utility Software of the Apple System Profiler

Certain devices may not be recognized directly by the Apple System Profiler (comm slot serial port cards, for example). Double-check with other utilities if possible. Also check to be sure that the card is installed properly. If the card appears to be installed properly, try installing it into an alternate slot to determine if the card or slot it was initially installed into is damaged.

Card Is Recognized by the Apple System Profiler but Not by Utility Software Included with the Card

If this is the case, check to be sure that all driver software included with the card is installed properly. Check with the manufacturer for known issues with the utility and/or updates. Also check to be sure that card is fully installed.

Computer Fails to Enter or Wake from Sleep Mode Following PCI Card Installation

This problem is known to occur with some cards not supporting the current being turned off to the PCI cards during sleep mode in AGP Power Mac G4 computers running Mac OS 8.6. Updating to Mac OS 9 alleviates the problem.

PC Cards and PowerBook Expansion Bays

PC Card slots and expansion bays are technologies that are used on PowerBook computers and not on any other Macs (although PC laptops also use PC Cards). Both of these technologies allow PowerBooks to be easily expanded with various types of devices, while at the same time remaining extremely portable.

The PC Card slot allows the PowerBook to accept special expansion cards called PC Cards or PCMCIA cards. These cards are about the size of a thick credit card, and they offer a number of different functions, many of which are similar to the functions that PCI cards can serve on desktop Macs.

The PowerBook expansion bay is a slot in the side of a PowerBook with a special connector. It can accept a number of different types of drives. These drives are treated like internal drives and are accessed with the same level of performance that a true internal drive would offer. They also offer the convenience of operating from the PowerBook's power source (battery or AC adapter) and being as portable as an internal drive.

This chapter looks at how both PC Cards and PowerBook expansion bays function, the benefits they provide, how to use them, and how to solve common problems with these technologies.

How PC Cards Work

PC Cards (such as the one shown in Figure 9-1) are a special type of expansion card designed for notebook computers (both PowerBooks and PC laptops). In many ways they are a portable version of the PCI cards used in the Power Mac computers. PC Cards themselves are credit-card-sized

Figure 9-1
A typical PC Card.
(Photo Courtesy of
Newer Technology)

devices that are inserted into a special slot (called the PC Card slot) that is built into the side of a PowerBook. Like PCI cards, PC Cards can serve a wide range of functions. The most common include providing access to various types of networks, additional modems, and adding SCSI, FireWire, or USB ports to a PowerBook (specific types of PC Cards are discussed later in this section).

PC Cards were originally developed in the early 1990s. At that time, laptop computers were beginning to become serious tools, and there were no easy expansion options for adding devices such as Ethernet cards or modems to a laptop. These were functions that could easily be performed with an internal expansion card on a desktop computer. Laptop computers, both Mac and PC, tended to have model-specific proprietary designs that prevented them from sharing any kind of device, let alone accepting industry-standard expansion cards.

At that time the Personal Computer Memory Card International Association (PCMCIA) began to create a standard for memory cards, such as those commonly used in palmtop and handheld computers. The standard was adopted, and it became used by some laptop manufacturers. Shortly thereafter, the PCMCIA standards were revised to support not only memory cards but also other devices such as device interface cards and networking cards. Thus, PCMCIA cards, which later became known simply as PC Cards, became an industry standard for laptop computer expansion devices, much as PCI cards became a standard for desktop computers. Apple introduced PC Card slots on the PowerBook 5300 and 190 models in the mid-1990s. All later PowerBooks, save the PowerBook 2300, have included at least one PC Card slot.

From a user perspective, PC Cards are simply inserted into a PowerBook's PC Card slot and then recognized by the Mac for whatever function they serve (to provide a modem, FireWire ports, wireless networking, a hard drive, and so on). When you look deeper at how a PC Card works, however, you can see that there is more going on than most users would expect.

On a hardware level, a PC Card is an expansion card that connects using a special 68-pin interface. This interface connects the card to the PC Card slot's circuitry, which is in turn connected to the PowerBook's motherboard. Controlling the interaction of the PC Card and the PC Card slot are what is known as *Card and Socket Services*. These comprise both ROM code that is built into the PowerBook and a part of the Mac OS. The Card and Socket Services are what detect a PC Card and what actually control the PC Card. They act as a sort of relay between the higher functions of the Mac OS and the basic hardware of the PC Card slot.

The PC Card slot can provide any number of different functions. Because PC Cards can be ejected and replaced by a completely different type of card at any time, they present a dilemma to the PowerBook that PCI cards and other expansion cards that are only inserted or removed when the Mac is shut down do not. The Mac must constantly track what functions the PC Card slot is providing at any given time. It must then relay those functions to any open applications in real time. To help keep the Mac aware of what services are available through the PC Card slot, PC Cards use a self-identifying feature. Each PC Card has a unique ID number that tells the PowerBook not only what the card does but also who made it and specifically what type of card it is. This information, known as *attribute memory,* is stored in the PowerBook's RAM whenever a PC Card is inserted. For this reason, PC Cards tend to cause the Mac to use more RAM for the Mac OS when they are being used.

Types of PC Cards

PC Cards and PC Card slots come in various types, each defined by different sections of the PCMCIA standard. This standard defines the primary types of PC Cards, the basic hardware of their interface, and most basic levels of the software needed to interact with them. This section looks at the primary types of PC Cards defined in the original PCMCIA standard, as well as the primary specifications of the newer CardBus standard and the Zoom Video standard.

PC Card Sizes   There are three basic types of PC Cards—Type 1, Type 2, and Type 3—included in the PCMCIA standard. These three types describe the thickness of the card. Although this technically doesn't limit what a PC Card can be used for, the size does limit how much circuitry or mechanical functions can be included in a PC Card. Table 9-1 lists the sizes of each type of PC Card. Figure 9-2 illustrates the dimensions of a PC Card.

By far the most common size of PC Card is the Type 2 PC Card. This is because Type 1 cards tend to be too thin to be able to be used for providing services beyond acting as memory cards for digital cameras, PDAs

TABLE 9-1	Type 1	3.3 millimeters
PC Card Sizes	Type 2	5 millimeters
	Type 3	10.5 millimeters

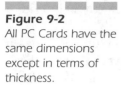

Figure 9-2
All PC Cards have the same dimensions except in terms of thickness.

54 mm

85.6 mm

or palmtop computers, and similar functions. Type 2 cards provide enough space for developers to create interface cards that can be used to provide additional features to a PowerBook, such as SCSI or FireWire ports. Type 3 cards are generally used for devices like PC Card hard drives, which require not only circuitry but also mechanical components that take up additional space.

No matter which of the three PC Card sizes you are dealing with, they all have the same length (just over 8½ centimeters) and width (just under 5½ centimeters), as shown in Figure 9-2. They also all share the same 68-pin connectors, which allow them to be inserted into any PC Card slot, provided the slot supports that type (size) of card.

The current PowerBooks (those covered by this book) include a single PC Card slot that can accept both Type 1 and Type 2 PC Cards. The slot is not big enough, however, to accept Type 3 PC Cards. Earlier PowerBook models included a bay of two PC Card slots. These slots could accept one or two PC Cards if they were either Type 1 or Type 2. The bay could also accept a single Type 3 PC Card if only that one PC Card was inserted.

The CardBus Standard   The CardBus standard is a cross-platform PC Card standard developed in the mid-1990s. It extends the abilities and performance of the initial PCMCIA standard. CardBus PC Cards are 32-bit devices, compared to the original PCMCIA standard, which supported only 16-bit devices. This allows for greater bandwidth and therefore greater performance and data transfer rates between the computer and the PC Card. From a physical perspective, CardBus cards are identical to earlier PCMCIA cards, using the same 68-pin connectors and coming in the same Type 1, Type 2, and Type 3 sizes (though Type 3 CardBus PC Cards are extremely rare).

CardBus PC Cards can only be recognized by a computer if it has a CardBus-compliant PC Card slot. The PowerBooks covered by this book feature a CardBus-compliant PC Card, though many earlier PowerBook models did not. CardBus-compliant PC Card slots, such as those in the current PowerBooks, are backward-compatible, enabling them to recognize both CardBus and non-CardBus PC Cards

Some CardBus PC Cards may simply be referred to as "CardBus cards." They may also be referred to as "Type 4 PC Cards," which is somewhat of a misnomer, since they are only available in the same three sizes as non-CardBus PC Cards. Most SCSI, USB, and FireWire PC Cards are CardBus devices. Network and modem PC Cards, however, are usually not CardBus.

Zoomed Video Cards   The Zoomed Video standard was developed and introduced on the PowerBook 3400 in 1997. This standard was for PC Cards that provide video input abilities for PowerBooks and link the PC Card slot directly into the PowerBook's video circuitry. Zoomed Video provides extremely high-quality video because it bypasses much of the slower sections of the Mac's system bus and sends video directly into the video circuitry. This enables the PowerBook to display video of higher resolutions at full-screen and full-motion quality from Zoomed Video PC Card devices. The primary Zoomed Video products have been developed by iR and include both video capture cards and digital video cameras specifically designed for PowerBook users. In earlier PowerBooks, which included two PC Card slots, the Zoomed Video circuitry was built into the lower PC Card slot only. Today's PowerBooks include only a single PC Card slot, which can accept Zoomed Video devices. Zoomed Video quality is impressive, but not as impressive as digital video imported via FireWire.

Inserting and Using a PC Card

Inserting a PC Card is an effortless procedure, and since PC Cards are hot swappable, you do not need to put a PowerBook to sleep or shut it down to insert them. You simply line the PC Card up with the PC Card slot, making certain that the end with pin connectors is pointing inward and that the primary label side is pointing up. Then you just slide the card into the slot until you feel a click. At this point only the very edge of

Figure 9-3
A PC Card Icon on the Mac's Desktop.

the card will be visible, and none of the card should be protruding from the edge of the PowerBook. If the card resists being inserted at all, particularly when it has been mostly inserted, do not force it. Instead, pull it out and make sure it is lined up properly. Also make certain that you are not using a PC Card of a type that is too big for the slot (the current PowerBooks cannot accept a Type 3 PC Card, for example). If the card is lined up correctly and is the right size, check to see if there are any foreign objects (or even another PC Card) in the slot preventing you from inserting the card properly.

Once a PC Card is inserted, an icon for it should appear on the desktop, such as shown in Figure 9-3. This will occur for PC Cards that function as hard drives as well as for PC Cards that function as modems, network cards, or other devices that normally would not have an icon associated with them. If the PC Card requires driver software that is not installed, the PowerBook will most likely display an error message saying that the software needed for the PC Card to be used is not installed and asking if you want to eject the card. If driver software is needed, it should be included with the PC Card, and you can install it at this point or before you insert the card for the first time. You will then need to restart the PowerBook for the driver software to be loaded as part of the Mac OS.

Once the PC Card is inserted and recognized (with the appropriate drivers installed, if needed), you can begin using it. How you use the card depends on what type of card it is. If it is a hard drive, you can simply format and use it as you would any other hard drive. If it is a network card, you access it through the TCP/IP or AppleTalk control panels. Similarly, a modem is accessed through the Modem control panel or from within a communications program. SCSI or FireWire cards, on the other hand, are used in the same manner as a built-in SCSI or FireWire port, so their function should be essentially transparent; just attach devices to the PC Card's port, and they should be available to the Mac. As with other expansion cards, you may also access the PC Card using utilities that were included with it. The documentation accompanying a specific card will include additional and specific information on how to use the card.

Ejecting PC Cards   Earlier PowerBook models used PC Card slots that auto-ejected a PC Card when the PC Card's icon was dragged to the Trash. The current PowerBooks, however, use a manual eject PC Card slot. To eject a PC Card on today's PowerBooks, first drag the icon of the card to the Trash or click on its icon and use the Put Away command from the Finder's Special menu. This causes the Mac to stop accessing the card and any devices attached to it. If the Mac gives you an error saying it cannot put the card away because it contains items that are in use, check to see if the Mac OS or an individual application is accessing the card or an attached device.

Once the Mac has put the card away, its icon disappears from the desktop. At this point, you can manually eject the card safely. Press the eject button next to the PC Card slot once to extend the button, as shown in Figure 9-4. Once the button has extended, press it a second time to eject the card. You can then remove the card. After removing the card, press the eject button a third time so that it will lock into the side of the PowerBook and not be extended. The button could easily break off if left extended.

Remember not to manually eject any PC Card without first putting it away, unless the PowerBook is completely shut down or in sleep mode. Ejecting a PC Card while the Mac is actively using it can cause the Mac to crash, damage the card and/or PC Card slot, and corrupt files stored on the PowerBook's internal hard drive and drives attached via the PC Card.

Figure 9-4
The manual eject button of today's PowerBook PC Card slots.

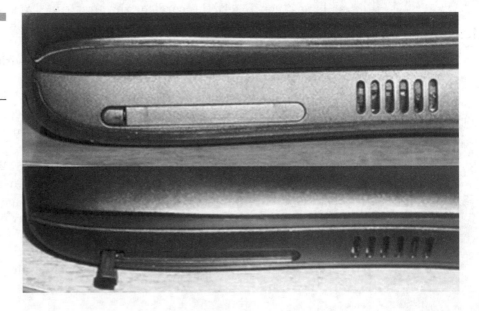

Dongles   If you look at a Type 2 PC Card, you can easily see that it is extremely thin—only half a centimeter. If you look at any type of ports used by a computer, whether a FireWire, SCSI, Ethernet port, or the phone jack of a modem, it's obvious that all of them are larger than the thickness of a PC Card. So, how do you attach devices that use a port that is wider than the PC Card itself? The answer is you use a special adapter that converts a very narrow connector on the outside edge of the PC Card to a traditionally shaped and sized port of whatever type is needed by the PC Card in question. These adapters are traditionally referred to as *dongles*.

Dongles come in all sorts, just as PC Cards do. They are included with a PC Card so that the card can make whatever ports it needs readily available to users. Dongles are device-specific, meaning that each PC Card out there is uniquely designed and requires a dongle that is designed for that card specifically. Typically, the only way to get additional or replacement dongles is from the device's manufacturer.

While dongles are a necessary feature when dealing with PC Cards, because the dongles are often very small, short pieces of cable, they can also be a major annoyance. They are very easy to misplace or lose, especially when you are using your PowerBook on the road. For this reason, you should always take care to make certain where you keep your dongles and to keep them in a pouch or compartment of your laptop bag or carrying case that is zippered or sealed shut so the dongles will not slip out and get lost. You may even want to order a second dongle from your PC Card's manufacturer ahead of time, just to be prepared if you lose the original.

Uses for PC Cards

PC Cards can be used to provide a very wide range of functions. Since the hardware of the cards is based on cross-platform industry standards, cards can easily be developed that will function both with PowerBooks and with PC notebook computers. A Macintosh driver for the card is often needed, however (although most PC Card modems will function in a PowerBook without such driver software). The following are the more common uses for PC Cards used on the Macintosh platform.

SCSI Cards   The most recent PowerBook models include built-in FireWire ports, whereas earlier models included a built-in SCSI port. Many longtime Mac owners have an investment in SCSI devices. A SCSI PC Card provides users of the current PowerBooks with a SCSI controller that can be used to access these devices. SCSI PC Cards are available in the various SCSI types—SCSI-2, Fast, Wide, Ultra, LVD, and so on—which are described in detail in Chapter 12.

FireWire Cards   As just mentioned, while the current PowerBooks include built-in FireWire ports, earlier PowerBooks included a built-in SCSI port instead. For the PowerBook G3 computers released in 1999 or earlier, it is possible to add FireWire ports by means of a FireWire PC Card. There are several such cards on the market, and they usually provide two full-performance FireWire ports. These cards provide many of the benefits of built-in FireWire ports, though they do not support starting up from FireWire drives or FireWire Target Disk Mode. Additional information on these cards and issues relating to them are included in Chapter 14.

Network Cards   Although not commonly used today, since Apple includes a 10/100Base-T Ethernet port on all current and recent PowerBook models, PC Cards can be used to provide an Ethernet port. This can be used on today's PowerBooks if you wish to add a second Ethernet port or as a temporary replacement should the PowerBook's internal Ethernet port be damaged (which would most likely require a motherboard replacement in order to repair).

In addition, PC Cards can be used for other networking types, such as some home phone line networking kits. They can also be used to add wireless networking abilities for PowerBooks released in 1999 or earlier which lack the ability to accept an AirPort card from Apple. Such wireless networking cards are available from Lucent, Farallon, and other manufacturers and are compatible with Apple's AirPort wireless networking. These cards are different from the Apple AirPort card, which is installed internally on the iBook and current PowerBooks. Even though the AirPort card looks very much like a Type 2 PC Card, it is not a PC Card and cannot be installed in a PC Card slot.

Modems   PC Card modems were quite common on PowerBooks for some time before Apple began including a built-in 56-Kbps modem with all PowerBooks. PC Card modems can still be used with the current PowerBooks and may be useful in some situations. As with an Ethernet PC Card, a PC Card modem can be used as a temporary replacement for a damaged internal modem. It can also be used if you wish to have access to two modems at one time. One interesting use of this option is FCR's LinkUPPP software, which allows you to use two separate modem connections to an Internet provider as a single connection with double the bandwidth of a single modem connection. Finally, the PowerBook's internal modem does not support connections through a cellular phone. There are several PC Card modems that do support cellular connections, and these can be used with the PowerBook. If you wish to establish a connection through a cell phone, you may need a PC Card modem that can make such connections. The modem also needs to work with your specific model cell phone, and you need an appropriate cable for your cell phone (which can be acquired from the modem's manufacturer). Keep in mind that a cellular phone connection will not be as a fast or stable as a traditional landline phone connection.

ISDN Cards   ISDN (Integrated Services Digital Network) lines can provide higher-speed connections for either networks or Internet access than traditional modems. Typically, ISDN lines require either a router, which shares access to the ISDN line with an entire network and is rather expensive, or a terminal adapter (more commonly called an ISDN modem), which connects a single computer to the ISDN line. Terminal adapters are generally devices that attach to a Macintosh's serial port or USB port. However, there are PC Cards that act as ISDN terminal adapters and provide a single PowerBook with a connection to an ISDN line. ISDN is discussed in much greater detail in Chapter 35.

Video Cards   Video cards have not been one of the common uses of a PC Card slot, but there have been various types of video PC Cards available for PowerBooks. As you might expect, the most popular of these have been those cards designed for video capture and make use of the Zoomed Video standard to provide high-quality video input for video capture, editing, videoconferencing, and other purposes. Beyond these, there have been a couple of short-lived video output cards, though these have been discontinued. These cards have allowed the PowerBook to drive multiple external displays, as well as adding more powerful video processing circuitry than was built into the PowerBooks of the time.

Hard Drives   There are some companies that provide PC Card hard drives. These hard drives come in two types. The first is the kind where the drive is actually in the card itself. These are often Type 3 PC Cards, which would prevent them from being used with the current PowerBooks. PC Card hard drives like these are the smallest hard drives on the market, significantly smaller than even a PowerBook's internal hard drive. This limits their potential storage capacity, and it also makes them significantly more expensive than other hard drives.

The other, more common kind of PC Card hard drive includes a full-sized external hard drive that is connected by a PC Card interface. These hard drives usually use a Type 2 PC Card, meaning they can be used with the current PowerBooks, as well as with older models. They can feature hard drives of any capacities. In fact, you can buy the cases for these PC Card hard drives and install an internal IDE (Integrated Drive Electronics) hard drive of your choice into them.

Digital Camera Memory Cards   Two types of memory cards—CompactFlash and SmartMedia cards—are commonly used in digital cameras. In the camera, these cards store whatever images you take. They can be removed from a camera and replaced with additional cards to expand the camera's storage. When transferring images to the Mac, these cameras usually use a rather slow USB interface. PC Cards are available that serve as adapters for inserting both types of digital camera memory cards directly in a PowerBook's PC Card slot. When such cards are inserted, they behave as though they are small hard drives, allowing much faster and easier transfer of the stored images to the PowerBook's hard drive.

USB Cards   Although the PowerBooks covered by this book have included two built-in USB ports, earlier PowerBooks did not include USB. For these PowerBooks, adding USB ports via a PC Card is an option. Adding a USB card to today's PowerBooks can also be a temporary option if the PowerBook's built-in USB ports are damaged.

Multifunction PC Cards   Some PC Cards provide more than one function. These cards tend to be interface cards or network cards. Most commonly, they are cards that combine both a modem and Ethernet port into a single PC Card. It is, however, possible that a PC Card could be developed that added both USB and FireWire ports or ISDN and Ethernet ports, though none have been at this time. With today's PowerBooks having only a single PC Card slot, multifunction cards can serve a useful purpose in allowing user expansion.

How Expansion Bays Work

The expansion bay has been a staple feature on most PowerBooks for several years now. The bay uses a special connector that is unique to PowerBooks in general and often unique and specific to a certain PowerBook model or series of models. The expansion bay's connector is built into the PowerBook's motherboard and functions similar to an IDE interface, which allows it to deliver performance equivalent to the standard IDE data transfer rates (up to 16.6 MB/second).

The expansion bay was originally designed for use as a CD-ROM drive interface on the PowerBooks 5300 and 190 (which were functionally the same except for the processors included in them), which were the first PowerBooks to ship with an internal CD-ROM drive. In future PowerBooks, Apple used the expansion bay as a method to provide both CD-ROM and floppy drives using a single internal device (although Apple eventually stopped shipping floppy drive expansion bay modules). Third-party manufacturers also began providing other devices that conformed to the bay's standard interface, and today a number of expansion bay drives are available (most produced by VST Technologies). Additionally, Apple has designed the expansion bays of the current PowerBooks so that they can act as a second battery bay, allowing the use of two batteries at once.

Expansion Bays Compared to Other Interface Methods

The expansion bay provides an easy and convenient way to expand a PowerBook with various types of drives, such as hard drives or Zip drives. While the bay delivers good performance (commonly 16.6-MB/second data transfers), it does not provide the same degrees of performance that some of the faster interface technologies available do, notably FireWire and higher-end SCSI types. This is an issue if you are looking for a high-performance hard drive for quick data transfers. However, for most removable-media drives, such as the Zip drive, performance is comparable to even the faster drive interfaces (see Chapter 18 for removable-media drive performance comparisons).

Expansion bay drives also offer advanced portability compared to any external drives and are easier to use on the road. This is because expansion bay drives are internal to the PowerBook, which relieves the user of any cabling concerns or the effort or carrying any additional items besides the PowerBook (and any additional expansion bay modules he or she may want to use). Expansion bay drives also rely on the PowerBook's power, whether battery or AC adapter. This can be especially useful in situations where a power outlet is not available but where the contents of a Zip disk or hard drive need to be accessed.

Expansion bay drives do, however, tend to cost more than the same

TABLE 9-2

Data Transfer Rates
of Expansion Bays
and Other
Interfaces

Expansion bay	16.6 MB per second
IDE	16.6 MB, 33 MB, or 66 MB per second*
SCSI	5 MB–160 MB per second*
FireWire	50 MB per second
USB	1.5 MB per second

*The data transfer rates of IDE and SCSI will vary depending on the type of IDE or SCSI used (see Chapters 12 and 13 for more information).

type of drive does when using a different interface. This cost difference must be balanced against the ease of use and portability offered by the expansion bay. PowerBook owners may also want to consider that there is no guarantee they will be able to migrate an expansion bay device to a newer PowerBook in the future. This is because future PowerBooks could very well use a different expansion bay interface than the current PowerBook models do. Apple has changed the expansion bay design several times when releasing new PowerBook models, making it impossible to use the same module with a newer PowerBook.

Swapping or Installing Expansion Bay Modules

The expansion bay of the current PowerBooks is hot swappable, which means you can install and remove drives and other modules while the PowerBook is turned on and active. This is easier than dealing with some other device interfaces, like SCSI, that require you to shut down the computer in order to add or remove devices. This contrasts with earlier PowerBooks, which required the PowerBook to either be shut down completely or be in sleep mode in order to swap expansion bay modules.

To remove a current expansion bay device and replace it with another device, use the release latch at the front of the PowerBook to release the current expansion bay module, as shown in Figure 9-5. The module will slide out of the side of the PowerBook partly when the release latch is pulled. When this occurs, just pull the module out of the PowerBook. To insert a new drive or device, simply line it up with the expansion bay and push it into the PowerBook. It should slide in very easily and give a slight click when it is inserted completely and securely. Do not force a module into the expansion bay, as this can damage to both the module and the expansion bay.

Figure 9-5
The release latch at
the front of the
PowerBook ejects an
expansion bay
device.

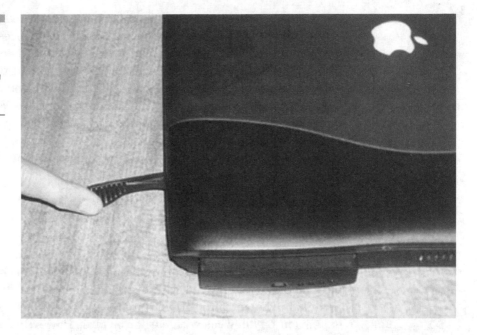

Before removing a module that is a drive of any type, be sure that the Mac is not accessing any files or applications that are on a disk in that drive. For CD/DVD-ROM drives and removable-media drives, simply eject any disks that are in the drive prior to removing it. For expansion bay hard drives, select the drive's icon and either drag it to the Trash or use the Put Away command in the Finder's Special menu. This will cause the Mac to unmount the drive and remove the icon from the desktop. Unmounting the drive ensures that the Mac is not accessing it at all.

Some type of module should always be inserted in the PowerBook's expansion bay. If one is not, the entire expansion bay is left open to the environment and presents an easy way for dust, dirt, and other foreign objects to get into not only the expansion bay but also other internal areas of the PowerBook. This can lead to severe damage. If you do not want to use an expansion bay module of any type at all, then use the expansion bay weight saver module. This is a lightweight plastic module the size of a second battery that Apple ships with all PowerBooks. The weight saver module serves no function at all other than to fill the expansion bay and protect the PowerBook. It is also lighter than any expansion bay device, thereby making the PowerBook lighter.

When installing an expansion bay drive for the first time, you should first run any installer software that came with the drive. This ensures that the driver software needed for the drive to be recognized and function properly is installed. Some expansion bay drives or devices may not require additional driver software (you can check the device's documentation to be certain). When installing software, you need to use the CD/DVD-ROM expansion bay drive. After the software is installed, you need to restart the Mac so that the driver software is loaded as part of the Mac OS. If you wish to use the drive immediately, remove the CD/DVD-ROM module and insert the new drive at that point. Once the driver software has been installed, you can insert the drive at any time without restarting the Mac.

Types of Expansion Bays

Various PowerBook models have shipped with expansion bays for several years now. Some models have used the same expansion bay design, making expansion bay modules interchangeable between them. Most individual models have shipped with expansion bays that are specific to their model, however. This prevents these PowerBooks from exchanging expansion bay devices with earlier or later PowerBooks.

The PowerBook models covered by this book use the same case design and therefore the same expansion bay architecture. This means that you can interchange expansion bay devices among them. You cannot, however, use the expansion bay devices of any earlier PowerBooks with them. Likewise, there is the possibility that today's expansion bay devices will not be able to be migrated to whatever PowerBook models Apple releases in the future.

Common Expansion Bay Modules

A variety of devices use the PowerBook expansion bay as a device interface. The most common of these is the Apple-made CD-ROM or DVD-ROM drive that shipped with the PowerBook. Third-party hardware manufacturers have also created expansion bay drives of various types. These drives deliver performance comparable to that of internal drives of the same type in the desktop Power Mac computers.

CD-ROM/DVD-ROM Drives   PowerBooks ship with either a CD-ROM or a DVD-ROM expansion bay drive module. The current PowerBooks all include a DVD-ROM module rather than a CD-ROM module. Although the drive modules are interchangeable, keep in mind that the last PowerBooks to ship with a CD-ROM drive (the 333-MHz PowerBook G3 models with a bronze keyboard, originally released in May of 1999) still do not include the ability to play DVD movies. As described in detail in Chapter 17, DVD movies require the ability to decode MPEG-2 video content. This ability is not included in these PowerBooks. They will, however, be able to read DVD-ROM disks if a DVD-ROM module is inserted in them.

Hard Drives   Next to the default CD-ROM/DVD-ROM drive modules, expansion bay hard drives are the most common type of expansion bay modules. Expansion bay hard drives install like any other expansion bay modules and are formatted or partitioned the same as any other type of hard drive. Expansion bay hard drives are available in a wide range of capacities and offer respectable performance (16 MB per second). The performance is not, however, as great as that of the internal hard drive's of the current PowerBook models.

Often expansion bay hard drives form a very convenient method for augmenting a PowerBook's internal storage. They provide the ability to easily add several gigabytes of storage space without replacing the internal hard drive and also offer the ease of an internal solution, which is much better than an external solution would be when traveling. Expansion bay hard drives can also offer a useful backup solution when on the road and, because expansion bay hard drives are bootable, an emergency startup solution should your internal hard drive fail (presuming that a copy of the Mac OS is installed on the expansion bay hard drive).

Zip Drives   Expansion bay Zip drives are an increasingly popular use of the expansion bay. Expansion bay Zip drives come in both the original 100-MB Zip and newer 250-MB Zip drive varieties. These drives deliver much better performance than external USB Zip drives do, making them an attractive alternative for PowerBook users. Expansion bay Zip drives can be used as an on-the-road backup solution, as well as provide users access to files and applications stored on Zip disks.

SuperDisk Drives   The SuperDisk drive has gained a fair measure of popularity on the Mac in the past couple of years. This is because it allows Mac users to access older floppy disks, as well as the 120-MB capacity SuperDisks. Currently, the expansion bay SuperDisk drives are the only internal or expansion bay solution for accessing floppies on the PowerBook (though several external USB floppy drives are also available). This makes them useful for people who find themselves in environments where they must store or retrieve data on floppies as a regular part of their activities. Using SuperDisks, the drives can also be an on-the-road backup solution for PowerBook users. For more information on both SuperDisk and Zip drives in general, see Chapter 18.

Additional Batteries The current PowerBook's expansion bay contains the same power connectors as its battery bay. This means that you can insert a battery into either side of the PowerBook or, more conveniently, into both bays at one time. This allows you to double the usable battery life of the PowerBook, a handy feature for any PowerBook user on the go. It also allows you to carry both batteries in the PowerBook and to use the power stored in both batteries without having to swap individual batteries. When two batteries are installed in the PowerBook, both batteries are displayed in the Control Strip's battery item. For more information on using two batteries in the PowerBook, see the next chapter.

The Weight Saver Module As mentioned, the weight saver module is a special expansion bay module that is included with every PowerBook. This module is basically an empty plastic box. Its purpose is to fill the expansion bay so that the internals of the PowerBook are protected when a user does not wish to use any expansion bay modules. It also offers the advantage of being hollow and very lightweight, which means the PowerBook will be lighter than if an actual expansion bay drive were inserted. If you don't wish to use any expansion bay devices, you should use the weight saver module to protect the expansion bay and the PowerBook from foreign objects, dirt, dust, or dampness.

Troubleshooting PC Card Devices

Following are some common PC Card problems along with their solutions.

The Mac Displays an Error Message Saying the Drivers for a PC Card Device Aren't Installed

This error message means that the Mac couldn't find any extensions or control panels installed that are needed for it to recognize the PC Card that was just inserted. Reinstall the software that came with the PC

Card. You will also see this message if you start up from an alternate startup disk or start up with extensions off.

The Mac Refuses to Eject a PC Card

Before ejecting a PC Card manually, you should use the Finder's Put Away command or drag the card's icon to the trash to put the card away. If the Mac refuses to put the card away, the card or a device attached to it is still being actively used by the Mac OS or a running application. Most likely, this occurs if you are using a SCSI, FireWire, or USB card and have a hard drive or removable-media drive attached to it, because a file or application on the drive is still open.

To remedy this situation, close any open files or quit running applications. This should allow you to put the card away safely before ejecting it.

The Mac Doesn't Recognize a PC Card When It Is Inserted

If the Mac doesn't recognize that a PC Card has been inserted at all, try restarting the Mac. If this doesn't help, it is probable that either the PC Card or the PC Card slot is damaged or that the card was not inserted properly. Try reinserting the card or inserting another card to determine if the card or the slot is damaged.

The Mac Doesn't Recognize Devices Attached to a PC Card

If the Mac doesn't recognize devices attached to a PC Card, check to be certain that the drive or other devices are powered and connected properly. Assuming this is the case, ensure that any drivers needed for the devices and for the PC Card are installed correctly. If this doesn't help, try using the drives or devices with another Mac to make sure they are functioning properly. If they are, there may be a problem with the PC Card you are using, and you should refer to the manufacturer's tech support or documentation for further information or resources.

Troubleshooting Expansion Bay Devices

Following are common expansion bay problems, along with their solutions.

The Mac Doesn't Recognize an Expansion Bay Drive

If the Mac won't recognize an expansion bay device, first make sure the drive is correctly and fully inserted. Assuming that it is, try restarting the Mac, as it is possible, although rather unlikely, that some drives may not be recognized properly after being inserted while the Mac is running.

If the drive is inserted properly, make certain that any driver software needed for the drive has been installed correctly. If you have started up from a drive other than your internal hard drive or have started up with extensions off, then the driver software likely has not been loaded at startup. If in doubt, reinstall the driver software that came with the drive.

If the problem does not appear to be with the driver software, the drive or the expansion bay itself may be damaged. Try using another expansion bay module, such as the CD/DVD-ROM drive that came with the computer, to determine if the expansion bay is functioning correctly. If the problem appears to be with the drive, refer to the documentation or tech support from the manufacturer.

The Mac Freezes or Crashes When a Drive Is Removed

This problem will likely occur only if a file or application that is stored on an expansion bay hard drive or on a disk inserted in a removable-media device was open while the expansion bay drive was removed. Restarting the Mac should solve the problem. After you restart, you should also run a disk repair utility such as Disk First Aid, Norton Disk Doctor, or TechTool Pro to be certain that no corruption was caused to either the disk that was in the expansion bay or the PowerBook's internal hard drive. If corruption has occurred as a result of removing the expansion bay drive while the Mac was accessing it, use the utility to repair such corruption as described in Chapter 5. For this reason, you should always eject any removable-media disks and unmount a hard drive as described in this chapter before removing an expansion bay drive.

The Mac Doesn't Recognize a Second Battery in the Expansion Bay

If the Mac doesn't recognized a second battery, check to be certain that the battery is inserted properly. Assuming that it is, wait a moment to see if the Mac does recognize the battery. If not, try removing and then reinserting the battery. The battery will not be shown in the menu bar clock's battery indicator, only in the Control Strip's battery module. If the battery is completely discharged, the display in the control strip module will be the same as if there is no battery in the expansion bay (you can use the Control Strip's expansion bay module's pop-up menu to determine if batteries are recognized in both bays).

If the battery is inserted properly and not recognized, it is possible that the PowerBook's Power Manager is corrupted. Refer to the next chapter for instructions on how to reset the Power Manager. If the battery is still not recognized, try shutting down the Mac and inserting the battery into the primary battery bay to determine if the battery is damaged.

The Mac Recognizes Some but Not All Disks Inserted into an Expansion Bay Removable-Media Drive

This problem most likely means that the individual disks are not formatted properly or have been corrupted. If the disks are formatted using a PC format, then the Mac will need to have the File Exchange control panel installed at startup in order to recognize PC disks.

Resources for Further Study

About.com Focus on Mac Hardware PowerBook Products—
http://machardware.about.com/msubpbproducts.htm

VST Technologies: Manufactures Expansion Bay Drives—
http://www.vsttech.com

*Mac Components Engineered—*http://www.powerbook1.com

Batteries

Batteries are an important part of the Mac. This is particularly obvious with PowerBooks and iBooks, as these Macs use rechargeable batteries as a power source when they are being used away from an electrical outlet. However, even desktop Macs rely on a small rechargeable battery to maintain various settings and information while the Mac is powered down and even unplugged. Several other peripherals, such as digital cameras and palmtop devices, which can be used with the Mac also, rely on rechargeable batteries to power them when away from the user's desk. This chapter looks at the types of rechargeable batteries and how they work in general. It also looks at the batteries used in portable and desktop Macs specifically.

How Rechargeable Batteries Function

Batteries contain two different metal components known as *electrodes* that are immersed in or contained within a chemical known as an *electrolyte*, as shown in Figure 10-1. When the battery is placed in an electrical circuit, each electrode provides a connection between the battery and the circuit. When the battery is inserted and the device turned on, the electrical circuit is completed. Once the circuit is completed, a chemical reaction takes place in between the electrolyte and the electrodes. This reaction results in an electrical current that flows through the circuit. This in turn powers the devices that the battery is used in. The more electrical current required by a device, the faster the chemical reaction within the battery will occur and the more quickly the available electrolyte will be used up, rendering the battery powerless.

In most batteries, once the electrolyte has been used, the battery is useless because the chemical reaction that provided current from the battery cannot be reversed. However, when certain metals are used in

Figure 10-1
Basic battery components.

Negative Electrode
Electrolyte Chemical
Positive Electrode

Figure 10-2
Using and recharging a rechargeable battery.

Battery When Powering a Deivce
(using up electrons in electrolyte chemical)

Electron Flow

Negative Electrode
Electrolye Chemical
Positive Electrode

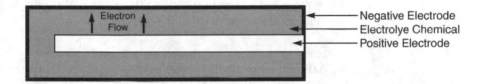

Battery When Recharging
(electron flow reversed, restoring battery charge)

Electron Flow

Negative Electrode
Electrolye Chemical
Positive Electrode

the electrodes and a certain electrolyte chemical is used, it is possible to reverse the chemical reaction. Applying an external power source to the battery does this. As this external current is applied, the chemical reaction essentially reverses itself, returning the battery to its original state. This allows the battery to be recharged again and again, functioning as a renewable power source for electronic devices. Figure 10-2 illustrates how a rechargable battery functions.

Types of Rechargeable Batteries

Over the years, various types of rechargeable batteries have been used in Macintosh computers, as well as for battery-powered peripherals (most notably digital cameras and camcorders). These types of batteries can be broken down into three primary groups based on the types of chemicals the batteries use to hold a charge: nickel/cadmium (NiCD), nickel metal hydride (NiMH), and lithium-ion, each one of which offered advances in rechargeable battery technology. Although all these types of batteries have been used for PowerBooks and other portable devices, they are not interchangeable.

NiCD   NiCD batteries are one of the oldest forms of rechargeable batteries. Of all the types of rechargeable batteries on the market, NiCDs deliver the least amount of battery life per charge. They also hold smaller charges than any other rechargeable battery type. NiCD batteries will lose a charge if left to sit on the shelf without being used for an extended period of time (usually about one quarter to one half the charge will dissipate during a month of inactivity). For these reasons, NiCD batteries have not been used for PowerBooks in several years (only the PowerBook 100 series computers used them, with the exception of the PowerBook 190, which used a NiMH battery) and have been phased out of most non-Mac laptops as well. Other devices, such as digital cameras, some palmtops, and personal electronic devices, still commonly use NiCD batteries because they are inexpensive to produce, function well enough for devices with small power requirements, and can be made in virtually any needed physical shape or size.

NiMH   NiMH batteries offer some significant improvements over NiCD batteries, even though their chemical and physical compositions are very similar. As a rule, NiMH batteries can store 40 percent more electrical power than similarly sized NiCD batteries. They can also provide longer average battery life per charge. Both of these result in better battery performance than NiCD, which has enabled Apple to include more powerful features on PowerBooks with NiMH batteries. Unfortunately, NiMH batteries cannot hold a charge as long as NiCD batteries and will often begin losing a charge within a week if not used. This reduces their effectiveness for most portable devices, such as digital cameras, which aren't used or charged on a daily basis.

Lithium-Ion   Lithium-ion batteries (sometimes called "lion" batteries) are the most powerful rechargeable battery types currently available. They store up to 30 percent more power than similarly sized NiMH batteries, and they can maintain a charge for several months without being used, which makes them ideal for situations where battery backups or power is required but may not need to be available at all times or where equipment is only used occasionally. Lithium-ion batteries are used in the current and recent PowerBooks models (from the PowerBook 3400 on) and the iBook. They are also used to power the PRAM chip in desktop Macs (see later in this chapter).

The Memory Effect

NiCD batteries and to a lesser extent NiMH batteries can suffer from a condition known as the *memory effect*. This occurs when the battery is regularly recharged after it has lost only part of its charge. The battery begins to "remember" at what point it is usually treated as being discharged. When the battery is recharged in the future, it will not fully recharge. Instead, it will only recharge equivalently to what its usual discharge point is. If the battery is actually discharged at more than that point, it will not accept a full charge, but it will report to a battery indicator that it is fully charged. For example, say you have a battery in your PowerBook and you always plug the PowerBook into an outlet and begin recharging the battery once the battery is half drained. Over time, the battery will no longer recharge anymore than halfway, but it will appear on the PowerBook's battery indicators to have a full charge.

Fortunately, the memory effect can be overcome relatively easily. Simply discharge the battery completely (sometimes called a *deep discharge*) before you begin charging it. This will cause the battery to recharge to its full capacity. Many external battery chargers perform this function on their own, in a process known as *battery conditioning*. Apple also includes a battery reconditioning utility that performs a deep discharge automatically with PowerBooks that use batteries susceptible to the memory effect.

Even better than being able to recover from the memory effect is the fact that lithium-ion batteries do not suffer from the memory effect at all, as NiCD and NiMH batteries do. This keeps the condition from being a concern for owners of the current portable Macs altogether (including all models covered in the book), though owners of earlier PowerBooks and of other battery-powered peripherals, such as digital cameras and palmtops, should still be aware of the memory effect.

PowerBook and iBook Batteries

There are two primary uses of rechargeable batteries on the Mac. One is the PRAM battery (discussed later in this chapter), and the other are the batteries used to power portable Macs, such as the PowerBook and iBook. This section looks at the batteries of the current PowerBooks and the iBook, including how portable Macs manage battery power and how to conserve battery power (a must for any Mac user on the road).

How Portable Macs Manage Battery Life

Managing battery life means two things in relation to portable Macs. The first is in conserving battery power so that the Mac runs for as long as possible on battery power. This management is controlled by various user-adjustable settings, most controlled in the Energy Saver control panel. Users can augment these abilities by being aware of what functions and features use the most battery power and by using them as seldom as possible. (We'll discuss how to extend battery life shortly.)

The second feature is controlled by the Mac's internal circuitry and includes such things as charging a battery, regulating the flow of power from the battery through the Mac, and displaying the amount of battery power currently available to the user. These features are collectively a part of the Mac's Power Manager and are, for the most part, outside of user control and concern. The exception is when there are problems with the Power Manager's settings as described in the next section.

Resetting the Power Manager The Power Manager is the component of a portable Mac's firmware or ROM that controls how the computer interacts with the battery. Its settings information is stored with the PRAM data. If you find that a PowerBook or iBook computer is not charging its battery correctly, is refusing to acknowledge that an AC adapter has been connected, crashes when an AC adapter is connected or disconnected, does not recognize a battery, or suffers from an unexplained short battery life, then the Power Manager's settings may have become corrupted. A common cause of Power Manager corruption is connecting a portable Mac's AC adapter to the Mac before plugging the adapter into a wall outlet.

Like the PRAM, the Power Manager's settings can be erased if they have become corrupted. When the Power Manager is reset in this fashion, it will revert to the default methods of interacting with the battery and AC adapter. Because the Power Manager's settings are stored on the PRAM chip, zapping the PRAM will reset the Power Manager. (For instructions on how to do this, see "Zapping the PRAM" later in the chapter.) If you wish, you can reset the Power Manager alone without zapping the PRAM. The process of resetting the Power Manager alone varies depending on the PowerBook model. For the iBook and for the PowerBooks covered by this book, follow these instructions.

For the iBook: Shut down the computer and use a straightened-out paper clip to press the Reset button, located just below the display and above the Power button (see Figure 10-3). Wait at least five seconds

Figure 10-3
The iBook's Reset
button.

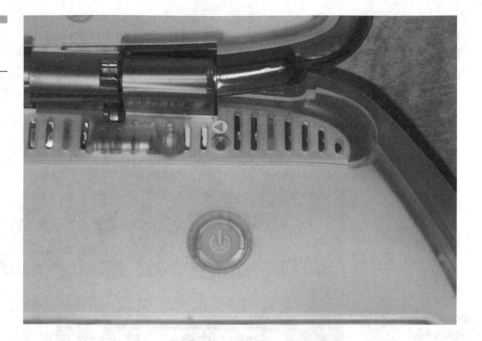

while the Power Manager is actually reset, and then turn the iBook on by pressing the Power button. The brief five-second wait period is important because this is when the iBook and current PowerBooks actually reset the Power Manager. Starting up the computer before at least five seconds have passed can cause further corruption to occur. After resetting the Power Manager, some contents of the PRAM data may need to be reentered (in particular, the date and time settings). This is because the iBook uses the primary battery (which relies on the Power Manager to supply any power) to power the PRAM chip.

For the PowerBooks covered by this book (both models with bronze keyboards): Shut down the computer and press the Reset button, located between the external video (VGA) port and the internal modem's phone jack on the back panel of the PowerBook, as shown in Figure 10-4. As with the iBook, you should now wait a minimum of five seconds before powering on the computer using the Power button. The earlier PowerBook models with built-in SCSI ports will be ready to continue use immediately after the Power Manager has been reset. The newer PowerBooks with built-in FireWire ports, however, may need to have some PRAM data reentered, as with the iBook.

For instructions on resetting the Power Manager on earlier PowerBooks, refer the PowerBook's manual, Apple's Support website, or

Figure 10-4
The current
PowerBook's Reset
button.

Figure 10-4
The current
PowerBook's Reset
button.

Figure 10-5
The Mac's battery
indicators.

one of the URLs in the "Resources for Further Study" section at the end of this chapter.

The Battery Indicators   PowerBooks and iBooks display two primary battery indicators. One is part of the clock in the menu bar, and the other is an item in the control strip. Both of these battery indicators display an approximation of the charge remaining in a PowerBook or iBook's battery, much the same way a gas gauge in a car gives you an approximation of how much fuel is left in the gas tank.

The indicator in the control strip is more detailed than the one in the menu bar and includes a more specific gauge of how much battery power is remaining. It also includes an indicator that resembles a car's speedometer, shown in Figure 10-5. This indicator tells you how much battery power the computer is using at a given time (all the way to the left meaning none, and all the way to the right meaning as much as you could possibly be using at one time). If you are working on adjusting the

PowerBook or iBook to conserve as much battery power as possible, this indicator can help you determine how much power your current settings are using at a given time. Lastly, the control strip item includes an indicator much like a clock that gives you the computer's best estimate as to how long your current battery (or batteries if you're using a PowerBook with two batteries at once) will last. This estimate has never been terribly accurate on any portable Mac and is more of an educated guess. You can use this to approximate how soon you will need to change batteries or find a power outlet, but take the amount of time it tells you with a large grain of salt.

Extending Battery Life

No matter how long Apple claims a PowerBook or iBook battery will last, it will not last that long under most conditions. Even if you do manage to coax the battery to last as long as Apple rates the battery, it may just not seem like long enough if you're on the road with no power outlet in sight when the battery indicator starts to get low. For that reason, extending the life of a battery as much as possible is important. This section looks at the various methods you can use to conserve battery power and prolong battery life.

Access the Hard Drive as Little as Possible The hard drive is the single greatest user of battery power on a portable Mac. The more the hard drive gets accessed, the quicker you'll run out of battery power. Try to avoid accessing the hard drive as much as possible. Beyond just opening and saving files, the Mac accesses the hard drive more than you may be aware of. Every time a dialog box having anything to do with saved files is presented, the Mac must access all drives attached to it (including, of course, its internal hard drive). Applications access the hard drive at a number of points, most notably when you adjust preferences or settings or access special features such as a word processor's spell checker, which require additional files on the hard drive be accessed. Some applications access the hard drive more than others do, though most Microsoft applications seem to access the hard drive more than similar applications by other companies.

Turn Off Virtual Memory Virtual memory uses the Mac's hard drive as RAM. This allows you to have the effect of more RAM if you absolutely need it, albeit with much slower performance than real RAM. Because virtual memory is using the hard drive as RAM, it is almost constantly accessing your hard drive and draining your battery life all the while. Virtual memory can reduce your battery life by more than a third. If you absolutely must use virtual memory, use as little hard drive space for RAM as possible.

Turn Off AppleTalk, AirPort, and Other Communications Utilities When AppleTalk is active, the Mac is constantly accessing its Ethernet port (or printer port on earlier Macs, AirPort card if one is installed, or even an infrared port if the Mac has one) to see if there is any AppleTalk network traffic that it needs to work with. This reduces your battery life. Similarly, if you have an AirPort card installed and AirPort is turned on, the Mac will be constantly sending out radio signals, looking for an AirPort base station to connect to. Several other communications programs, most notably AOL, CompuServe, and ZTerm, will continue accessing the Mac's modem even when there is no active connection, which drains battery life. For this reason, quit any such software when it is not being used.

Turn Down Screen Brightness The backlight that illuminates a portable Mac's LCD display is probably the second biggest draw on battery power that these computers have to deal with. Reducing the brightness of the LCD display can go a long way to conserving battery life. Obviously, you'll want to find a level that conserves battery power but doesn't cause you to squint because the screen is too dark to read.

Avoid Using Expansion Bay Drives Expansion bay drives, including the standard CD-ROM/DVD-ROM drive as well as third-party hard drives and removable-media drives, drain a lot of battery power as well. When accessed constantly (such as when playing a DVD movie or audio CD), they can approach the internal hard drive in terms of battery usage. If you are using the CD-ROM or DVD-ROM module or a removable-media drive, do not insert a disc except when you need to access it. Remove discs when you finish working with them. If there is no disc in the drive, the Mac will not query the drive for information on the disc as it would if the disc was inserted. For hard drive modules, treat them as you would the internal hard drive.

Eject Unused PC Cards Like expansion bay drives, PC Cards require a fair amount of battery power to function, even when they are not being actively used. Most PC Cards support a power-saving rest mode, which will reduce their effect on the battery but not completely eliminate it. If you aren't using a PC Card and it is feasible to eject the card, do so.

 Use the Energy Saver Control Panel   The Energy Saver control panel allows you to control how quickly the Mac's hard drive spins down, the screen dims, and the Mac enters sleep mode. The sooner the Mac does any of these items, the less battery power it will use. Set each of these features for as much battery power conservation as you can without impeding your normal work style. Remember, you can set each of the three independently of the others by clicking the Show Details button, allowing you to specify settings that are more tailored to your particular usage habits.

You can also click the Energy Saver's advanced Settings button to control some additional features that can help you get better battery life. The two important options here are Processor Cycling and Turn Off the Built-in Display Instead of Dimming It. Processor cycling allows the Mac to slow down how fast the processor runs when on battery power and when you are not using the Mac to perform processor-intensive tasks. This can slightly impact performance, but it can also be a big help in extending battery life. Turn Built-in Display off Instead of Dimming It does exactly what it sounds like and can help you conserve power by having the display completely off when you haven't typed or touched the trackpad in a while.

Avoid Using External Devices   USB and FireWire devices drain battery power. This is especially true for devices that draw their power from the Mac's USB or FireWire ports. If you are running on battery power, avoid using any external devices, as any external device will affect your battery life to one degree or another.

Put the Computer in Sleep Mode Whenever You Aren't Using It
The simplest thing is probably the one done the least. When you aren't using the computer for even a couple of minutes, put it into sleep mode. Five minutes spent talking to the person sitting next to you or a flight attendant on an airplane trip while your PowerBook is on and awake is five minutes of battery life that could have been saved and used for performing work. Whenever you aren't actually working on the computer, put it to sleep.

Using Multiple Batteries

The recent PowerBooks have included the ability to use two batteries at once, placing one in the PowerBook's battery bay and one in the expansion bay. This allows you to have increased battery life without needing to remove and swap batteries in a single bay. It also allows you to conveniently carry two batteries inside the PowerBook rather than having to carry an additional battery as well as the PowerBook itself.

Using two batteries at once is very simple. Insert the battery into the PowerBook's battery bay as you normally would. Then, remove any devices or drives in the PowerBook's expansion bay. Insert the second battery into the expansion bay until it clicks securely. The PowerBook can now use both batteries with equal ease.

When a PowerBook is using multiple batteries, the battery level indicator in the control strip will show the level of both batteries. The indicator in the menu bar will display the amount of battery charge remaining from the combined power of both batteries. When working with two batteries, the PowerBook may or may not attempt to discharge them evenly, occasionally alternating which battery it is drawing power from. When connected to an AC adapter, the PowerBook may alternate between the two batteries when charging them.

Switching Batteries

Swapping batteries on the PowerBook computers is relatively easy. For earlier models, simply put the PowerBook to sleep, eject the battery from the battery bay, and slip in a new one. Wake the PowerBook, and you're ready to get back to work without almost any delay. The current PowerBooks with built-in FireWire ports lack a PRAM battery that will preserve the contents of RAM while no battery is inserted. This means swapping batteries will require you to shut down the PowerBook, but the process is essentially the same: Shut down the PowerBook, eject the battery, insert the new battery, and start up. If you have a battery inserted in the expansion bay, you can safely swap the other battery while the computer is being actively used.

The iBook was not designed for use with more than one battery. Rather, it was designed to use a single battery until that battery could be recharged and the iBook powered from its AC adapter. It is possible, however, to swap the iBook's battery if you have a second battery available. First, shut down the iBook. Then flip the iBook over and use a quarter, or other coin, to release the two "screws" that hold the battery cover in place. Pull on the clear plastic tab to release the battery. Insert the new battery. Replace the plastic battery cover, making sure that the clear plastic tab of the battery is underneath the cover. Secure the

Figure 10-6

Removing the iBook's battery.

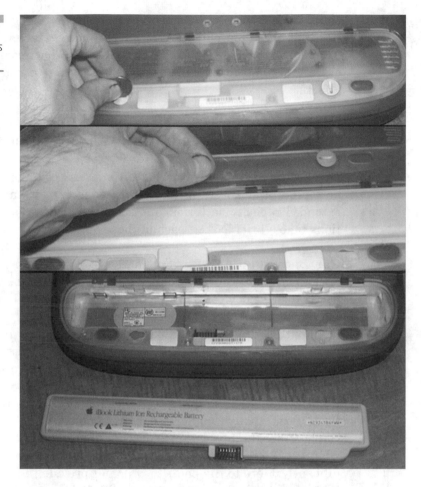

"screws" of the battery cover with a coin. Flip the iBook over and restart. Figure 10-6 illustrates this process.

External Battery Chargers

While the battery of a PowerBook or iBook will charge whenever the computer's AC adapter is plugged in, you can also purchase external battery chargers. These are particularly useful if you have multiple batteries that you want to charge at one time, as you might while on a trip to be sure your spare batteries are all fully charged before you need to use them. Even though the current and recent PowerBooks can use their expansion bay as a second battery bay, they will only charge one battery at a time. If you want to charge two or more batteries at once, you will want to purchase an external charger. Also, for older PowerBooks that used NiCD or NiMH batteries, external chargers often condition batteries when charging to remove the memory effect.

Additional External Power Sources

Beyond the AC adapter, there are some less common power sources for portable Macs. These include power adapters for car batteries, special extended capacity batteries, and solar power devices. The following sections take a brief look at each of these options.

Car Battery Adapters   For many years, various portable electronic devices have used special adapters so that they can be powered by a car's battery. These devices use an adapter that connects to the car's cigarette lighter. PowerBooks have been no exception, and over the years companies that make PowerBook batteries have made car battery adapters as well. Similarly, some general electronics manufacturers have created adapters that plug into a car's cigarette lighter and provide a traditional power outlet interface, which can be used to power just about any electrical device. Both solutions can work to provide power to an iBook or PowerBook, though the former is preferable.

There are, however, some concerns that you should note about these adapters. First, they will drain the car's battery, sometimes rather significantly. More to the point they do not provide the same level of power that a building's electrical outlet would. This means that a PowerBook or iBook may be able to draw enough power to operate, but it will not be able to charge its own battery from a car's cigarette lighter.

Most important to remember about these adapters, however, is that the current they provide is potentially unstable. While the current is usually not unstable enough to damage the computer, there are times when it can—in particular, when the car is running or being started. When you turn the ignition of a car, it requires a good deal of current to start the car. If you have a PowerBook or iBook attached to the car's cigarette lighter at that time, this will cause a major surge in the electrical current and will more than likely seriously damage the computer. Similar surges can occur while the car is running, though they are less likely. If you need to use your PowerBook or iBook with the power from a car battery, do so only while the car is not running. This will be more likely to discharge the car's battery, but it will be safer for your computer.

Extended Capacity External Batteries   The size of a PowerBook or iBook battery limits how much of an electrical charge it is capable of holding. Simply put, larger batteries can hold a larger amount of power. However, batteries for laptops are often kept small so they can fit in the laptop and so that they don't make the computer too heavy to be easily carried. Apple's Mac Portable, which predated the PowerBook line, is a perfect example of the inverse relationship between battery life and size/weight. It used a battery similar to a car battery that could power the computer for about 10 hours. But that battery was one of the things that made the Mac Portable the heaviest laptop in history, as heavy as the desktop Macs of the time, in fact.

All this comes down to the practical fact that an internal battery for a PowerBook or iBook cannot provide a large amount of power simply because of its size. External batteries, however, can hold a larger charge and can be carried separately from the PowerBook or iBook when that longer charge is not needed. Some external batteries are available that can hold 7 or 8 hours of battery life and weigh somewhere between 2 and 5 pounds (depending on the battery). While these batteries aren't something you need for everyday use, they can be a useful addition if you are going on a long trip or will be using the computer in a location where electrical outlets are simply not available, such as on a camping or hiking trip.

Solar Power Adapters   Solar power was a big buzzword a number of years ago, but aside from solar-powered calculators, solar energy never really made much impact in the world of portable electronics. Part of this is because many devices require more power than an inch or two of photo-electric cells can generate. Even so, that did not stop some solar power enthusiasts from developing products or encouraging their use. Keep It Simple Solar is the most well known of these companies, and they have created a number of solar power collectors for use with various laptops (including some PowerBooks). While even a foot or two of photo-electric cells won't generate enough energy to power a PowerBook or iBook on their own, they can be used to recharge a battery, albeit more slowly than an electrical outlet would. They can also be used to provide some power to the PowerBook or iBook, which results in the computer needing less battery power and extending battery life by a noticeable degree.

*Good
Page*

The PRAM Battery

The Parameter RAM (PRAM), sometimes also called Nonvolatile RAM (NVRAM), is a special piece of RAM that the Mac uses to store certain information and settings while the Mac itself is shut down. The currently selected startup disk, AppleTalk and other network information, the screen resolution and color depth, the amount of RAM being used for a disk cache, the size and location of virtual memory, the time zone and location of a Mac, and the Mac's real-time clock are some of the information that is stored in the PRAM. All of this is information that the Mac needs at the beginning of the startup process and that must be maintained in between startups and shutdowns in order for the Mac to deliver a stable and consistent experience to a user.

As with the Mac's system RAM, the PRAM needs to be refreshed regularly with an electrical charge in order for this information to be securely stored. This has to be done while the Mac is shut down and even when the Mac is not plugged into any power source or outlet. In order to provide constant power to the PRAM chip, a small lithium-ion battery is installed on the motherboard of the Mac. This battery, known as the PRAM battery, does nothing but provide power to the PRAM chip when the Mac is shut down. While the Mac is running, the PRAM battery recharges itself from the Mac's power supply.

Zapping the PRAM

As with other files or storage mediums, the information stored in the Mac's PRAM chip can become corrupted. If this occurs, the Mac will behave erratically, perhaps crashing, refusing the startup, refusing access to certain peripherals, and other strange behavior. When this occurs, the solution is to erase the contents of the PRAM chip and reset all the settings stored there by hand, using the various control panels with which the information was originally entered. Erasing, or "zapping" as it is more commonly called, the PRAM data can be accomplished in a couple of different ways, with varying degrees of effectiveness.

The most common method of zapping the PRAM is to use the startup key combination Apple has built into every Mac for this purpose. This involves pressing the Mac's Power key and then immediately holding down the command, option, P, and R keys simultaneously. The Mac's screen will light up briefly, and then the startup chime will repeat. Continue holding the keys down until the startup chime has repeated about five times to ensure that the Mac has zapped the PRAM (different Mac models have required different numbers of startup chime repetitions, but five should cover just about every Mac). Now, let the Mac start up. You should notice that a number of settings controlled by the PRAM have reset to their default settings. If not, then the PRAM was not fully zapped. If the problems you're experiencing are due to corruption of the PRAM data, they should be solved now, and you can reset all the settings controlled by the PRAM including the startup disk, memory, date and time, AppleTalk, keyboard, mouse, monitors, sound, and trackpad (if you're using a portable Mac) control panels.

The other method of zapping the PRAM is to use a utility designed for that function. The most common such utility is MicroMat's TechTool (shown in Figure 10-7), which allows you to zap the PRAM from within its application (without needing to stretch your fingers across the keyboard at startup). TechTool also offers two real advantages. The first is that it is more complete at erasing PRAM data than the keystroke method from Apple. TechTool will completely erase the contents of the PRAM chip at once, whereas Apple's method may leave areas of the PRAM data, particularly relating to an internal video card's settings, intact. TechTool also offers the option of recording your PRAM settings in a file on your hard drive before it zaps the PRAM. This allows you to restore the settings from that file using the TechTool application, without

Figure 10-7
TechTool's easier interface for zapping the PRAM.

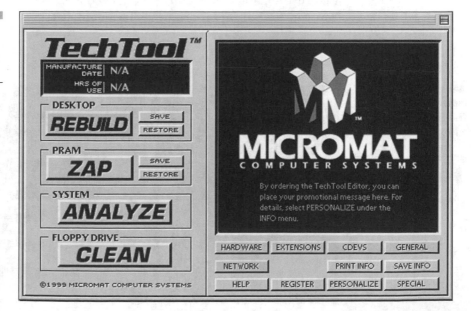

needing to reset them each manually. TechTool also offers the ability to completely rebuild the Mac's desktop file and scan the System file for signs of damage or corruption. Best of all, it is a free utility.

Replacing the PRAM Battery

Like all batteries, the PRAM battery has a limited life span. Over time, the ability of the PRAM battery to hold and maintain a charge slowly degrades. Eventually, usually three to five years after a Mac was built (or a new battery installed), the battery will reach a point where it is no longer able to power the PRAM chip reliably and will need to be replaced.

The sign that a Mac's PRAM battery is beginning to fail is that various settings are no longer maintained through shutdowns. Although any of the settings maintained by the PRAM will revert to the standard defaults when this begins to occur, the most obvious sign is the real-time clock. When a Mac's PRAM battery fails (or when the PRAM is zapped), the clock and date will reset to a date somewhere in the first half of the 1900s (such as 1904). If this happens repeatedly, it is a sure sign that the PRAM battery needs to be replaced.

Replacing the Mac's PRAM battery is generally an easy process. You simply need to access the Mac's motherboard, as described in Chapters 1 and 2. The battery is located on the Mac's motherboard, as shown in Figure 10-8, and can usually be removed and replaced without difficulty. You can find an appropriate replacement battery in most computer or

Figure 10-8
The PRAM battery on a Mac's motherboard.

electronics stores. Just remember to bring the old battery with you to be certain you buy the correct type to replace it with.

The PRAM Battery and PowerBook Sleep

One of the other features of the PRAM battery in many PowerBook models was to power the entire contents of RAM in the time it took a user to remove a nearly discharged battery and insert a fresh battery to power the computer. This allowed PowerBook users on the road to easily swap their batteries without needing to take the time to shut down and then start up the computer. All that was required was putting the PowerBook into sleep mode, which used a very minimal amount of battery power to maintain the contents of RAM. While the PowerBook was in sleep mode, the PRAM battery could power the PowerBook's system RAM for a brief period (usually just a couple of minutes) during which the user could switch the batteries of the computer.

PRAM without the PRAM Battery

When Apple introduced the iBook (and the PowerBooks released in 2000), they introduced a new approach to powering the Mac's PRAM. Since the iBook already used a lithium-ion battery to power the computer, Apple removed the second lithium-ion battery used to power the PRAM chip. As a result, the iBook's rechargeable battery is used to both power the computer when away from an electrical outlet and to power the PRAM chip when the computer is shut down.

Save RAM Contents on Sleep?   When the iBook introduced a Mac that relied on the same battery for a power source as it did for powering the PRAM battery, it also introduced a Mac that has more potential for losing the contents of the PRAM settings (and one that cannot store its RAM contents through a battery swap when in sleep mode). To alleviate potential problems this might cause, Apple introduced a new feature on the iBook, and subsequently on the PowerBooks with built-in FireWire ports, that allows the computer to save the entire contents of RAM (and PRAM) to a file on the Mac's hard drive. This invisible file can then restore this information automatically in the event that the iBook or PowerBook's battery is removed or completely discharged. This feature, shown in Figure 10-9, requires that the iBook or PowerBook in question

Figure 10-9
The Save RAM
Contents on Sleep
option.

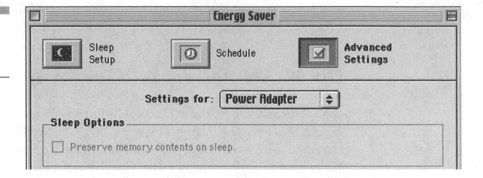

have virtual memory turned on and is activated by a checkbox in the Energy Saver control panel.

Unfortunately, Apple discovered after shipping these computers that this feature presented a separate problem having to do with the Mac's hard drive. In some situations where the RAM contents are stored when the Mac goes to sleep, trying to access them at startup after a problem may actually corrupt the computer's hard drive, resulting in a loss of possibly all data stored on it. For this reason, Apple has been advising users to disable the Save RAM Contents on Sleep feature and has even made an extension available for download that prevents the feature from being available at all.

Battery Failure

No matter what type of rechargeable battery you are working with, there will ultimately come a time when it can no longer be recharged and will no longer be able to hold a charge. This is inevitable, since various chemical side effects occur over time as the battery is recharged again and again. These chemical changes can take one of two forms: They can include a buildup of conductive compounds on the electrodes of a battery, or they can be the result of a loss of the electrolyte chemical in the battery. A battery can lose some of its electrolytes by evaporation because of high temperature or high current charging (something that several rapid-charging battery chargers use to recharge a battery more quickly than normal).

When a battery has begun to fail, the first symptom is that it will no longer hold a charge as long as it should. A charge may completely dissipate from a battery if it hasn't been used in a few days. Also, a battery

TABLE 10-1

Expected Life Spans of Battery Types

Type	Recharge Cycles	Expected Life Span
NiCD	500	2 to 4 years
NiMH	700	5 years
Lithium-ion	1200	5 to 7 years

Note: Recharge cycles and battery life spans are not the same for all batteries, and actual performance may vary depending on both the individual batteries and the treatment of individual batteries over their lifetime.

will fail to recharge fully or provide power to a computer as long as normal. These can, however, be symptoms of other battery problems, such as the memory effect or corrupted Power Manager settings in a PowerBook or iBook computer. Exhaust all other possibilities before assuming that a battery has failed. Once a battery has failed, there is no solution except replacing it with a new battery. Table 10-1 lists the expected number of recharge cycles and life span of the three types of rechargeable batteries.

Disposing of Batteries

The chemicals used as electrolytes in batteries are often highly corrosive and poisonous. For this reason, it is important to dispose of failed batteries safely and correctly. Do not simply throw them out with the trash, as the chemicals can be dangerous and toxic to the environment and can pose a significant health risk if they seep into the groundwater. For PowerBook and iBook batteries that are physically intact, contact the nearest Apple Authorized Service Center. Apple can and does recycle some types of the batteries that it produces. If not, the service center can either dispose of it safely or give you instructions regarding disposal. For a battery that has been damaged, broken, punctured, or that has ruptured, contact your town or city's hazardous waste disposal department immediately and follow their instructions and regulations for disposing of the battery safely.

Resources for Further Study

About.com Mac Support Battery Resources—
http://macsupport.about.com/msub24.htm

Macintosh Logic Board Battery Information Page—
http://www.academ.com/info/macintosh/

VST Technologies: Manufactures Replacement PowerBook/iBook
Batteries and Related Products—http://www.vsttech.com

CHAPTER 11

Power Supplies

A Mac's power supply is an essential component that performs a number of important functions. First and foremost, the power supply provides the electrical power that every internal component of the Mac needs to operate. It does this by converting the alternating current (and sometimes unsteady flow of electricity) from a building's wall outlet into the steady, constant direct current that all the internal components of a Mac can use to function properly and without damage. The power supply also grounds the Mac's internal components from electrical discharges that can occur inside the Mac. This chapter looks at how the power supply functions to power the Mac and how it interacts with a building's electrical wiring.

Before reading this chapter you should be aware that there is always the risk of electrical discharge if you open the power supply of a computer that could injure (or possibly even kill) you. Although this chapter discusses the internal components of the power supply, it does so for the purpose of helping you understand how power supplies function. If a power supply fails, you should replace it rather than trying to repair it, because repairing a faulty power supply is dangerous—not to mention more trouble than it's worth, most of the time.

Electricity Coming into the Power Supply

In the most basic sense, electricity is the movement of charged particles (electrons) through a substance. Although electrons can flow through any substance, those that permit electrons and electrical energy to flow freely are called *conductors*. Metal is one of the best conductors, and therefore, metallic wire makes an excellent way for electricity to flow into a building, through the power outlets, and into electrically powered devices, such as a computer.

Electricity can be made available for powering devices in two ways: direct current (DC) or alternating current (AC). Computers require DC power to run. The electricity supplied to a building by its power company provides AC power. Much of what the Mac's power supply does is to convert the AC current into DC current for the internal components of the computer.

Getting Power to the Outlet

Alternating current provides an efficient way to move electricity over great distances, which is why power companies use it to provide electricity to their customers. When you look at a power outlet (such as the one in Figure 11-1), you generally see three holes: two rectangular (the left one slightly larger than the right) and a round one beneath them. The smaller rectangle hole is the "hot" and the larger rectangle is the "neutral." These two holes connect an outlet to the power company delivering the electricity.

The round hole is the ground wire of the outlet. The ground wire of an outlet leads directly into the ground, as shown in Figure 11-2, and it is the route an electrical discharge will follow in the case of a short circuit or similar discharge. It prevents the discharged electricity from searching for another place to flow and protects both people and devices from

Figure 11-1
A standard North American power outlet.

Figure 11-2
The ground wire dis-
charges excess elec-
tricity into the earth.

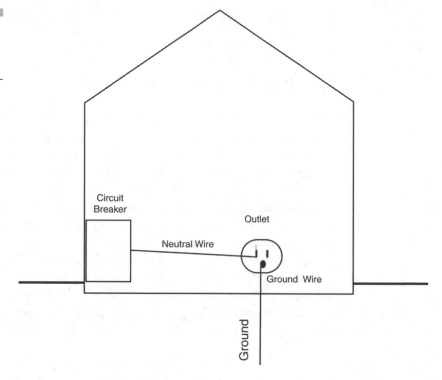

being that other place. This is important because an electrical flow can cause damage to devices, start fires, or severely injure and even kill people. The ground wire acts as a safeguard for both equipment and people. It also makes sure that all attached equipment has the same electrical potential of zero volts. This means that an accidental discharge inside equipment is less likely to result in serious damage. The ground also provides an excellent way to secure yourself from static electrical discharges when repairing or upgrading a Mac.

Grounding is extremely important in preventing damage from a short circuit or other electrical discharge that can occur when you are dealing with any electrical components (including those inside a Mac). You should always use outlets that provide a ground wire with a Mac and not older power outlets that contain only the hot and neutral wires.

Grounding and Static Electricity

In Chapter 3, you read about the importance of using an antistatic wrist strap to prevent static electricity from damaging internal components when you are upgrading or repairing a Macintosh. Based on the principles discussed in the previous section, you can see why grounding is important.

Static electricity is electrical energy that has built up a charge but that is stationary, or static. However, like any electrical energy, static electricity won't stay stationary for very long. The electrical charge will follow the path of least resistance to an area or object where there is a lesser electrical charge. This happens with static electricity, as well as with the energy discharged from a short circuit. And the principle of grounding is also the same: You must give the electrical energy someplace to go where it won't do any harm.

The ground wire of an electrical outlet is also why the more expensive antistatic wrist straps that have a power cord connector at the end are better choices than those that use an alligator clip. Those with a power connector ground you and the equipment you're working on against electrical discharges in the same way that the ground wire of an outlet grounds a Mac that is operating far better than an alligator clip can in many situations. Although both wrist straps work, the more well grounded you are, the safer the computer you're working with will be. Figure 11-3 shows both types of wrist straps.

It's easy to overlook the danger of static electricity to internal components of a computer. Table 11-1 will give you an idea of just how real a danger static electricity can be.

How the Power Supply Converts AC to DC

The basic function of the Mac's power supply is to convert the AC current from your power outlet into DC current to power all of the internal components of the Mac. The power supply also works to balance out any variations in current from the outlet such as power spikes or dips so that the Mac receives a constant stream of DC power at an appropriate voltage for each of its internal components.

The power supply actually consists of three separate sections that perform three different, but equally important, functions in providing your Mac with the proper electrical current to run. These sections are the switching network, the transformer, and the voltage regulator. In the following pages we'll look at how each of these actually function. Figure 11-4 illustrates the parts of a power supply.

Figure 11-3

Antistatic wrist straps such as these ground you while you are working inside a computer.

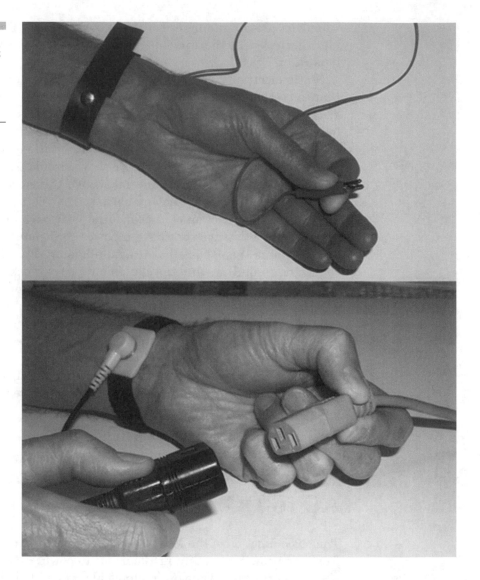

TABLE 11-1

Common Static Electrical Voltages (Approximate).

Action	Voltage
Voltage required to damage processors and sensitive components	10 volts
Voltage required to damage ROM and PRAM chips	1000 volts
Voltage required for human awareness of static discharge	3000 volts
Voltage built up by walking across carpet	1500 to 25,000 volts
Voltage built up from handling a plastic bag	1200 to 20,000 volts

Figure 11-4
Electricity flows
through the sections
of a power supply as
shown in this dia-
gram.

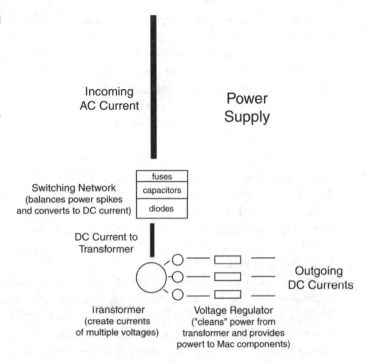

Incoming
AC Current

Power
Supply

Switching Network
(balances power spikes
and converts to DC current)

| fuses |
| capacitors |
| diodes |

DC Current to
Transformer

Outgoing
DC Currents

Transformer
(create currents
of multiple voltages)

Voltage Regulator
("cleans" power from
transformer and provides
powert to Mac components)

The Switching Network

The switching network performs two important functions for your Mac.
First, it converts the AC current coming into the computer into a DC current. Second, it works to balance out power spikes and sags in the current it is receiving.

AC power arrives at the power supply in a wave of constantly adjusting voltages. These changes can vary significantly from cycle to cycle of
the alternating current and can include severe spikes in power, as well
as equally severe drops (called *sags*) in the current. The actual frequency,
or time between alternating cycles, can also vary. These variations are
not significant enough that they will affect the majority of household
devices such as a toaster or lamp or even a dishwasher. The delicate components inside your Mac, however, can be damaged or have their operation disrupted by such occurrences. The switching network uses fuses
and capacitors to filter out these fluctuations in power so that there is a
constant and steady stream of power continuing through the power supply and into the Mac.

A *fuse* is a small piece of wire that is designed to burn out or melt if
the current passing through it goes above a certain level. Fuses prevent

too strong a current or power spike from being transmitted to the rest of the power supply, because they simply break the connection that electricity flows through if the flow becomes too strong. In essence, the fuses in a Mac's power supply act exactly like the circuit breaker in a house or building (in fact, many older buildings still use fuses to accomplish the same function as a circuit breaker).

A *capacitor* is a like a battery. It builds up a charge from excess current and releases that charge when the current moving through the capacitor drops below a certain level. The result is an even flow of power even when the actual power coming into the computer may rise above or drop below a given level. A power supply generally contains at least two capacitors, and although not common, it is possible for a capacitor to burn out, resulting in the power supply no longer functioning.

While the fuses and capacitors in the switching network ensure an even flow of power, the remaining segment of the switching network acts to convert the sine wave of the AC current into the particular square wave specific to DC current. This is accomplished using a series of devices called *diodes*. Diodes act as one-way street signs to electrical power, and when used in pairs or groups of four, diodes perform a process called *rectification*, which converts a constant AC current into DC current. The switching network uses several pairs or groups of diodes known as *rectifiers* and a transistor to create a stream of square-wave DC power.

The Transformer

Once the DC power current leaves the switching network, it goes through the transformer. The *transformer* takes the single current of power coming out of the switching network and separates it into multiple currents of separate voltages. This is important because different parts of the Mac, such as parts of the motherboard and internal drives, require different levels of power. It is the transformer's job to supply the separate voltages from the single incoming current.

The transformer is actually nothing more than coils of wire wrapped very tightly. Power is passed from one coil to another by induction, and one coil will be larger than the other, thus reducing the current as it is passed on (which is known as a *step-down transformer*). The coil that connects to the power coming in from the switching network is called the *primary*, and the coil or coils that lead out to the voltage regulator (and then out of the power supply into the Mac) are known as the *secondaries*.

While there is a single primary, there will be secondaries for each voltage that the power supply needs to produce.

The Voltage Regulator

The final section of the power supply, the *voltage regulator*, takes the individual streams of power coming from the transformer and converts each one into clean, flat-line DC currents without any fluctuations in power or voltage. The regulator uses diodes and capacitors (that function the same as those in the switching network) as well as coils to accomplish its function. The coils in the regulator section works to filter out any minor alternating current that might be remaining in the circuit. Although the coil has no impact on DC current, it will not allow any alternation in the current passing through it.

Once the electrical current emerges from the regulator, it is a clean, constant DC current in the variety of voltages required to power the internal components of the Mac. This resulting voltage is then split off into the individual connectors that attach to the motherboard, drives, and any other internal devices that require separate power.

Power out from the Power Supply

Coming out of the power supply are the connectors that attach to the motherboard and to the internal drives. Power connectors for internal drives such as hard drives, CD-ROM drives, or removable-media drives almost always use the industry-standard power connector that is known as a *molex connector*. By contrast, the power connectors that attach to a Mac's motherboard are often specific to the Mac platform and/or to a specific Mac model.

The power connector from the motherboard is fairly straightforward in how it attaches and will only insert in the proper orientation. If it seems as though the connector won't fit, make sure you are orienting the connector properly and do not force it. Always take care when attaching the motherboard connector, because an improper attachment can cause severe damage to a computer. Figure 11-5 shows the motherboard connectors from a Power Mac G4 and an iMac.

You will find that the molex connectors, such as the one in Figure 11-6, used for internal drives also attach only in a given direction. The

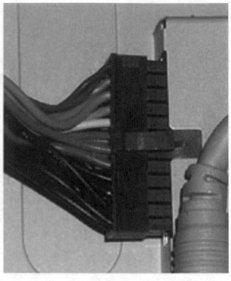

Figure 11-5 The motherboard power connectors on a Mac will look similar to the Power Mac (left) or iMac (right) connectors shown here.

notches at the top of the connector ensure this. Always line up the connector properly. Again, don't force the connector. A molex connector can be forced to attach in the wrong orientation, and doing so will likely damage the device the connector is meant to power. Also, as one colleague of mine says, it's next to impossible to disconnect an improperly inserted molex connector.

You will find that there are a finite number of molex connectors coming out of your power supply. If you install additional internal drives and discover the need for more connectors, you can purchase a molex splitter or a Y connector that will attach to one of the molex connectors coming out of your power supply and provide you with two molex connectors.

Keep in mind that there is a limit to the amount of power that the power supply can provide. Adding too many internal devices can overtax

Figure 11-6
A standard molex power connector.

the power supply and prevent the Mac from starting up and running (removing the excess devices will resolve the problem).

In addition to the motherboard and molex connectors, you may find smaller power connectors known as *mini* or *submini connectors*, as seen in Figure 11-7. These connectors provide power to devices not requiring a great deal of power, such as the internal cooling fan, internal speakers, or LEDs in a Mac's case. Mini and submini connectors are usually easy to attach backwards or upside down. It is extremely important to note the way these are connected before you disconnect them. The colors of the wires attached to the connectors will be different for each wire (red and black in the case of a submini and, generally, red, black, and yellow for a mini). As with any other power connection, improper attachment can result in damage to the components.

Protection from Power Surges and Outages

As discussed earlier in this chapter, the alternating current from a power outlet fluctuates and can spike. The fuses and capacitors in the switching network of the power supply exist to protect a Macintosh from such surges. But keep in mind that these components are not designed to deal with massive or abnormal power surges. They have limits, and if they

Figure 11-7
A mini power connector.

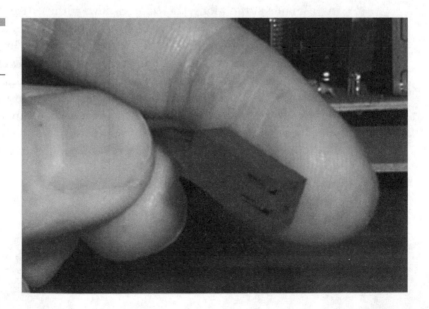

are pushed beyond them, you may find yourself replacing a power supply at best and an entire Mac at worst.

The fuses in the power supply exist to protect the computer from too much power. But when these fuses burn out, which is the way they protect the computer, you will usually find yourself replacing the power supply. It is possible to replace the fuses, but the general attitude with most power supply problems is that it is easier and safer to replace than repair. It is also possible that the fuses alone will not be enough to protect the Mac's components or that the surge may be powerful enough to spike through the computer before or while the fuses are burning out.

Likewise, the capacitors have a limit to how much power they are designed to handle and how much of a charge they can hold. Like a fuse, a capacitor can be burned out to the point where it will no longer function to hold a charge. Again, replacing the individual capacitor is a possibility, but the general practice is to simply replace the entire power supply.

Simply put, you don't want to trust the existence of a Mac to safeguards that are, in all honesty, relatively weak. The power supply's purpose is to adjust and regulate power for the Mac. It isn't to protect the Mac from power surges. That is the job of a surge protector or uninterruptable power supply.

Although power spikes and surges can occur at any time, there are times when they are more likely to occur. The two most notable of these are during a thunderstorm and after an outage. In a storm, lightning may strike a power line or station or even the building a Mac is in, causing a major surge along the related power lines. If possible, it is a good idea to shut down and unplug Macs and peripherals at these times. If a power outage occurs due to an overloaded circuit breaker, unplug the equipment where the outage has occurred before power is reapplied.

It is a good habit to run hardware diagnostic utilities for such things as hard drives, RAM, processors, and other internal components following a power outage or a power surge even if there appears to be no obvious damage. Since some damage can elude the Mac's self-tests at startup, a diagnostic will alert you to any hidden damage caused by the electrical problems immediately.

Surge Protectors

Surge protectors, such as the one in Figure 11-8, are quite common devices, and you can find them in any store selling computers, office sup-

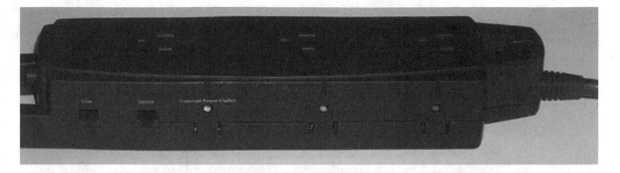

Figure 11-8   A typical surge protector with phone line protection.

plies, or other electrical and home entertainment devices. Often surge protectors have built-in power strips that provide additional power outlets as well as surge protection. Many will also indicate the quality and safety of the power line of the outlet they're plugged into, which is a nice feature. You can even find translucent surge protectors in colors designed to coordinate with the various iMac colors (not that this is a particular priority in choosing a surge protector).

Surge protectors often come with phone jacks these days for protecting against power surges coming through your phone line. I've heard a couple of interesting reports that more power surge damage to computer motherboards are caused by a power surge from the phone line traveling through the modem into the computer. This makes sense for two reasons. First, most people don't think of their phone line as transmitting electrical current, which it does. Second, there are no fuses or capacitors inside the modem to protect a computer from a power surge coming through the phone line, as there are in the power supply. For these reasons and risks, it is a good idea to consider a surge protector that also includes phone line protection if you plan on using a modem with your Mac.

Uninterruptible Power Supplies

An uninterruptible power supply, or UPS, goes beyond providing protection against power surges (though it does provide that protection as well). A UPS is basically a big battery, designed to store up power on its own. In the event of a power outage, the UPS immediately switches to its battery supply of power and powers the devices attached to it for as long as possible. This prevents the computers from suffering a hard shutdown because of the power outage. Some uninterruptible power supplies include software that allows the Mac to be aware that there is a power outage and to safely shut itself down before the available power supply runs out. This is excellent for computers that are left unattended.

Two kinds of uninterruptible power supplies are on the market that you may want to be aware of. The first is the *standby UPS*. A *standby UPS* (also called an SPS—standby power supply) charges its battery but doesn't engage the battery as a replacement for the AC power from the outlet until the current falls below a certain level (generally 80 to 90 volts). This is a significant dip from the standard voltage of an AC outlet (110 to 120 volts), but it should be safe enough to provide continuous power to your computer.

An *online UPS* is the second uninterruptible power supply available. An online UPS maintains the battery in the AC circuit. The battery is always active, being constantly recharged, and it is used whenever there is a sag in the power from the outlet, no matter how small. There are two advantages to this approach. First, it is always online and functioning. This means there is no possibility that the battery won't kick in in time to save your machine in the event of an outage. Second, an online UPS acts much like a giant external capacitor, effectively isolating your Mac from the building's power line. This is because the battery is constantly being recharged and kicking in extra power for any dip in the outlet's current. So, you have a "power conditioning" effect that provides a very smooth and steady stream of power to your Mac at all times. This can lead to a moderately increased life span of the capacitors inside the Mac's power supply.

Obviously, an online UPS has performance and benefit advantages over a standby UPS. Cost, however, is not one of them. An online UPS is noticeably more expensive and is being overtaken in the market by the standby UPS because of the cost difference. The majority of uninterruptible power supplies on the market today are SPS models. Remember that both versions of the UPS provide protection against both power surges and power outages.

iBook and PowerBook Power Supplies

The power supplies of the iBook and PowerBook are somewhat different from those of a desktop Mac. Although all the requisite functions and sections of the power supply are present, they are generally present in the external AC adapter (shown in Figure 11-9), which consists of a bricklike section in the middle where the power cord from the outlet is attached. The internal power connectors will also differ on portable Macs from their desktop counterparts. Often, the power connectors of the AC adapter plugs directly into the motherboard or a special section of the portable Mac's power management circuitry. The standard molex and motherboard power connectors are not used simply because of space considerations. The internal components and connectors of the iBook and PowerBook are discussed and illustrated in more detail in Chapter 2.

The battery of a portable Mac, discussed in more detail in Chapter 10, can also act like an uninterruptible power supply, as it automatically kicks in if the AC adapter is removed or if the outlet loses power. Also worth noting at this point is that portable Macs can be powered from a DC current such as a car battery. This requires the use of a special DC adapter, and you can find such devices that plug into the cigarette lighter of a car to provide power on the go. If you use such a device, it is extremely important that you do not leave the Mac plugged into the car's battery while starting the car. When a car is started, a power surge occurs that is transmitted through the cigarette lighter and the DC adapter. This surge can severely damage a portable Mac, since there is little power conditioning in the DC adapter and none in the Mac itself.

Power Outside the United States

Although this primarily relates to owners of portable Macs traveling to other parts of the globe, it is also relevant to desktop Mac owners. As anyone who's traveled abroad knows, power outlets and standard voltages are not the same in every country. In almost any case, your Mac should be able to handle the current from a foreign power outlet, as the actual voltage doesn't differ by a particularly great degree.

When going abroad, however, you need to bring an adapter for the appropriate power outlets. There are kits, such as the one shown in Figure 11-10, for such things in many airport gift shops, as well as in electronics stores. Most of the time these kits contain multiple adapters for various parts of the world. These adapters simply attach to the plug of an AC power cord and then plug into the wall outlet. You may also want to bring a surge protector with you to provide additional "native-style" outlets for other equipment, as well as for protection purposes.

If you plan to be gone long or are worried about the differences in voltage, consider bringing an online UPS to act as a power conditioner. It is always a good idea to check with the hotel or other accommodations

Figure 11-9
The AC adapter used for the current iBook and PowerBook models.

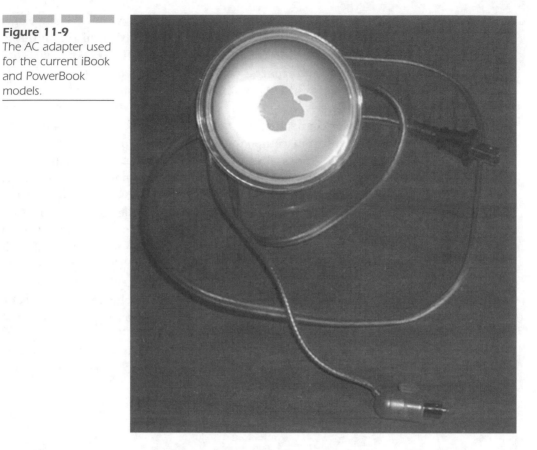

Figure 11-10
Travel kits like this one allow you to use portable Macs and other electrical devices in countries with differing power systems.

you'll be staying at and ask about the voltage from their power outlets and the safety of using your equipment with them. You can then reference this against the safe operating environments of your specific Mac, which can be found in the computer's documentation, as well as in its online help.

Replacing versus Repairing Power Supplies

In almost any situation, you will probably not want to try repairing a damaged power supply. The power supply is a component made of so many integrated subcomponents that diagnosing a problem within it and replacing the subcomponents that are damaged is simply not worth the time or effort.

If the Mac shows absolutely no signs of life when you press the power button, chances are, there are problems with the power supply. Before assuming that this is the case, however, double-check that there is power going into the Mac. Everyone I know has heard stories of a person that called tech support complaining his or her computer wouldn't start up only to discover there was a power outage or it wasn't plugged in. Check the power by plugging other devices into the same outlet and by plugging the Mac into a different outlet. Likewise, be sure that the surge protector or UPS being used with the Mac is turned on, plugged in, and functioning properly.

Assuming there is power coming into the Mac, double-check to see if there are any other possible problems. For example, if you pressed the power button on the keyboard, try pressing the power button on the Mac itself. Or try pressing the Mac's reset button. If there are still no signs of life, then you should suspect the power supply as being the cause.

It's important to remember that the power supply might not be damaged. It may simply be that there are too many devices for it to properly power all of them. This is often the case if you've recently installed a new drive and later discover problems in getting a Mac to turn on and start up.

Problems with a power supply can occur without causing the Mac to be unable to start up. If you notice that the Mac has trouble starting up cold but that it has no problems restarting, this could be a symptom of power supply problems (and also of PRAM battery problems, which are discussed in Chapter 10). Power supplies can also be at fault in random crashes and freezes when the power output drops enough to prevent some internal components from functioning. This occurs when the power supply "wears out slowly," partially losing function of its internal diodes and capacitors.

Testing the Power Supply

Once you suspect problems with the Mac's power supply, you'll want an easy way to test it. The simplest way to do this is to use a multimeter. A *multimeter*, such as the one shown in Figure 11-11, is a tool designed to measure the voltage passing through an electrical circuit and can be found in most electronics shops.

Attach the red lead (positive) of the multimeter to one of the red wires of the motherboard power connector. Attach the black lead (negative) to the corresponding black wire. Read the voltage that is displayed. It should be between 10.8 and 13 volts. If it is less than this, there are prob-

Figure 11-11
A typical multimeter.

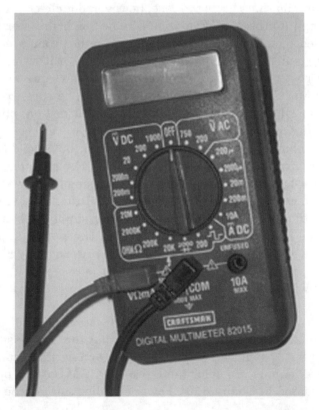

lems with the power supply and it is not adequately supplying power for the Mac's internal components. If the voltage is less than 10 volts, then the Mac will most likely be incapable of even beginning the startup sequence.

This gives you a quick and easy way to ensure that the power supply is functioning. Since every power connector has wires running to it, each one is susceptible to damage. If there is a specific device that appears not to be getting power, you can test the power connectors of every device in the same way.

If the power supply appears to be functioning but the Mac still won't start up properly or if one of the individual drives or internal components won't power up or function, the problem may likely be that you have too many internal drives installed for the power supply to handle. You can verify this by testing the motherboard power connector as described above with no internal devices connected. If there appears to be no problem, add one internal drive and test again. Then add another and another until you find which one is drawing too much power for the power supply to adequately power the Mac and all the internal drives.

Caution!   *Opening or working with a Mac's power supply voids a Mac's warranty. This precaution is there for a very good reason. Electricity can injure and kill you if you are not careful. It can also damage and destroy components of the Mac and cause damage to other property as well. This is particularly true of electricity from a power outlet. Always make sure that a Mac is unplugged before working with it, and never go near the power supply without double- or triple-checking to be sure that the Mac is completely unplugged and unpowered.*

Resources for Further Study

The following URLs provide additional information on some of the concepts, issues, and products discussed in this chapter:

Design Electronics: Using a Multimeter—
    http://www.doctronics.co.uk/meter.htm

About.com: Power Protection Resources—
    http://peripherals.about.com/msub_power.htm

SCSI

SCSI (Small Computer System Interface) has long been a part of the Macintosh. The SCSI standard was created during the early 1980s as a standard method for attaching hard drives and similar devices to computers. Apple adopted SCSI as a feature on the Mac with the Mac Plus in 1985. For years, the internal hard drives and CD-ROM drives of all Macs were attached using an internal SCSI connector on the motherboard. Even after Apple migrated to IDE (Integrated Device Electronics) as the typical interface for internal drives, Macs continued to ship with a SCSI port for external drives and other devices up through the beige Power Mac G3. The iMac was the first Mac to ship without support for SCSI in over 10 years when it was released in 1998.

Although the iMac set the stage for Macintosh computers to ship from Apple without built-in SCSI support, it didn't end the use of SCSI on the platform. Any of the Blue and White Power Mac G3 or Power Mac G4 computers can have the ability for external and/or internal SCSI devices added by means of a PCI card. The PowerBook computers continued shipping with SCSI ports built in until February of 2000, and later models can accept SCSI by way of a PC Card. Even the very first iMacs (revisions A and B), with their mezzanine slot, have the option of accepting a specially designed SCSI card. And for Macs without the ability to accept SCSI device directly, there are a number of adapters that allow for SCSI devices to be attached by both USB and FireWire. This chapter looks at the various applications and rules associated with SCSI, as well as what to do when SCSI problems arise.

Figure 12-1 shows the symbol that indicates the SCSI standard.

Figure 12-1
The SCSI symbol.

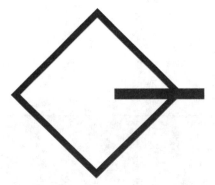

How SCSI Works

SCSI is both a physical standard for hardware such as cabling, termination, and port types and a standard of instructions that allow the computer to interact with any SCSI devices attached to it. SCSI involves a series of rules that must be followed when attaching devices, and unlike USB and FireWire, and it is not self-configuring. This means that you need to understand how to configure individual devices before you can attach them by using SCSI and that you risk damage to the device or the computer if you do not follow these rules.

Also, unlike USB and FireWire, SCSI is *not* hot-pluggable. Do not attempt to connect, disconnect, or adjust the settings of any device in a SCSI chain while the Mac is running. This can cause serious damage to the devices in the chain and to the Mac itself.

SCSI acts in a chain fashion, where one device is attached to the computer, then another device is attached to the first, then the next device in the chain is attached to the second one, and so on for all the SCSI devices you're using. SCSI chains can include both internal and external devices. Some SCSI cards support multiple SCSI channels or buses. Each of these channels can support its own SCSI chain independent of the others.

SCSI chains must follow some basic rules with respect to device identification and termination. These are probably the most important things to understand about SCSI and where most SCSI-device-related problems stem from.

SCSI IDs

A SCSI chain can support up to seven devices. (Wide SCSI, however, discussed later in this chapter, supports up to 15 devices per chain.) Each of these devices needs to have a unique SCSI ID number assigned to it. You must make sure that no two devices in a SCSI chain have the same ID. Otherwise, the Mac won't start up or run as it should, and in the worse case, it can cause some serious damage and data loss.

The SCSI controller (a PCI card in the current Power Macs, a PC Card in the current PowerBooks, or a built-in SCSI port on earlier Macs) also needs a unique SCSI ID number. The numbers used in assigning SCSI IDs range from 0 to 7. In almost all situations, the SCSI controller is assigned SCSI ID 7. Although some cards allow this to be changed, it is always best to leave this be simply because it is such an accepted standard.

The primary internal hard drive attached to a SCSI controller is traditionally assigned SCSI ID 0. This is an accepted practice that is good to follow. In Macs where the SCSI controller supports SCSI hard drives being used as startup drives for the Mac, the Mac will by default use the drive at SCSI ID 0 as the startup drive. (You can, however, assign any hard drive as the startup drive in the Startup Disk control panel.) If the Mac has a SCSI CD-ROM drive, it is almost always set to SCSI ID 3.

Any other SCSI ID settings are up to you, for either internal or external devices. However, keep in mind that not all SCSI devices will allow themselves to be set to any of the available SCSI IDs. The original SCSI Zip drive, for example, only allows users to choose between SCSI IDs 5 and 6. You should be aware of what SCSI IDs a device supports before you decide to add it to a SCSI chain. If you find that you need to attach a device that only supports one or two SCSI IDs that you already have used for existing devices in your SCSI chain, you will probably have to change the SCSI IDs of the existing devices to make room for the new device.

It's also a good idea to keep a list or inventory of what SCSI devices are attached to a Mac and what SCSI ID each is set to. This makes knowing which IDs are available for use very easy. However, if you don't keep such a list, you can use a utility such as Adaptec's free SCSI Probe to determine the SCSI IDs of all the devices attached to a Mac.

Setting SCSI IDs   SCSI IDs are set in a variety of different ways depending on the type of SCSI device you are dealing with. Internal SCSI drives, such as hard drives and CD-ROM drives, tend to be set by using jumpers on the drive itself (see Figure 12-2). Often there will be various combinations of jumper settings to indicate the various SCSI ID numbers, and you will need to consult the drive's manual or manufacturer to determine how to set the jumpers to a specific SCSI ID.

External SCSI devices tend to use dip switches and small dials to set SCSI IDs. Devices that use a dial, such as the scanner shown in Figure 12-3, often support the full range of SCSI ID numbers, and you can adjust the SCSI ID of the device by turning the dial with a flat-head screwdriver. Devices that use dip switches may use a single switch with which you can choose from two available SCSI ID numbers, or they may use a series of dip switches that you need to set in a certain order to choose a SCSI ID (see Figure 12-3). With the latter, as with internal devices, you will probably need to consult the manual or manufacturer to determine the correct settings for a specific SCSI ID number.

Figure 12-2
Jumpers like these
are used to set SCSI
IDs on internal
drives.

Remember: The device must be powered down when you are changing its SCSI ID. Never try to change the SCSI ID (or any other part of a SCSI chain) while the Mac is powered and running.

Termination

Whenever you have a wire transmitting electrical signals of any notable speed, the ends of that wire will need to be terminated. If they aren't, then the signal is likely to reach the end of the wire and be reflected back, disrupting any other signals that are being transmitted.

When terminating a SCSI chain, keep in mind that each end of the chain must be terminated, but anything in between those two ends must

■■ ■■ ■■ ■■

Figure 12-3
Dials dip switches are sometimes used to set SCSI IDs on external devices.

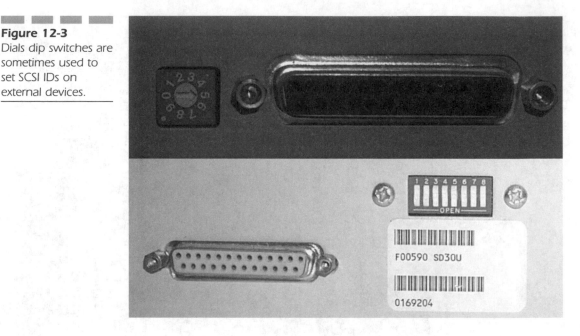

Figure 12-4
A SCSI chain with one internal drive only.

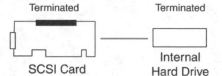

remain unterminated to allow data to pass through. For example, if your SCSI chain consists of a single internal hard drive and the SCSI card it is attached to, then both the drive and card need to be terminated because each one is at the end of the chain, as shown in Figure 12-4. If your SCSI chain consists of two internal hard drives and the SCSI card, then the card and the last hard drive needs to be terminated. It is not necessary to number SCSI devices according to their locations in a SCSI chain, by the way. For example, the chain in Figure 12-5 shows two internal SCSI hard drives and a SCSI card in a chain. The card is terminated, as is the "second" hard drive on the internal SCSI cable, even though that drive's ID is set to SCSI ID 2, while the "middle" hard drive is set to SCSI ID 0.

If you have only external devices, the same rules apply. The SCSI card

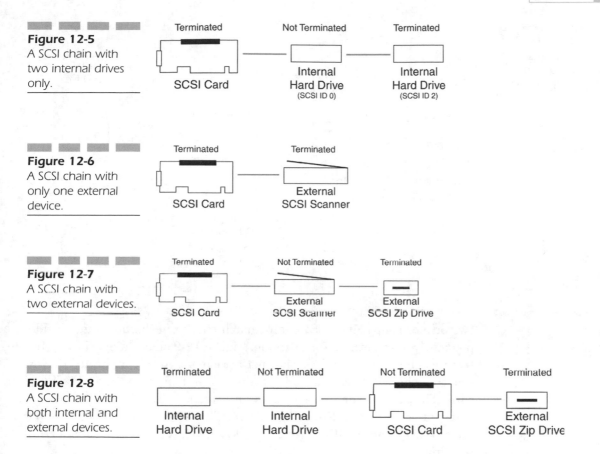

Figure 12-5
A SCSI chain with two internal drives only.

Terminated — SCSI Card
Not Terminated — Internal Hard Drive (SCSI ID 0)
Terminated — Internal Hard Drive (SCSI ID 2)

Figure 12-6
A SCSI chain with only one external device.

Terminated — SCSI Card
Terminated — External SCSI Scanner

Figure 12-7
A SCSI chain with two external devices.

Terminated — SCSI Card
Not Terminated — External SCSI Scanner
Terminated — External SCSI Zip Drive

Figure 12-8
A SCSI chain with both internal and external devices.

Terminated — Internal Hard Drive
Not Terminated — Internal Hard Drive
Not Terminated — SCSI Card
Terminated — External SCSI Zip Drive

is terminated, as is the last device that is physically connected to the chain. As shown in Figure 12-6, if there is only one device (such as scanner), then that device and the card are terminated. If there is the SCSI card, then the scanner, and then a Zip drive, the card and Zip drive are terminated but the scanner is not, as shown in Figure 12-7.

If you have both internal and external SCSI devices in a single chain, as shown in Figure 12-8, then the card is not terminated. The endmost device inside the computer is terminated, as is the endmost external device, but nothing in between. Most SCSI cards use separate SCSI channels for internal and external devices, meaning internal and external devices are part of separate SCSI chains. Cards that use a single channel for both internal and external devices often terminate or unterminate themselves automatically.

If you are using a SCSI card that has multiple channels to support

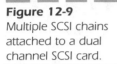

Figure 12-9
Multiple SCSI chains
attached to a dual
channel SCSI card.

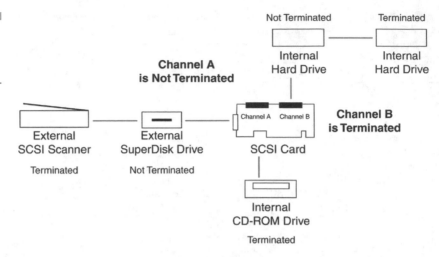

two or more separate SCSI chains, each chain will be terminated independently of the other. For example, Figure 12-9 shows a SCSI card that has two channels. The first channel attaches two internal hard drives. For this chain, the endmost hard drive is terminated, as is the SCSI card. The second channel contains an internal CD-ROM drive plus an external scanner and SuperDisk drive. This channel of the card is not terminated, whereas the internal CD-ROM drive and the scanner are terminated.

It is extremely important to follow these rules for correctly terminating a SCSI chain. If a chain is improperly terminated, any number of problems can occur, from random freezes and crashes, to devices simply not being recognized, and finally to serious damage to data on a SCSI hard drive or other device in the chain.

There are only two possible exceptions to these rules, and these apply to very long and short SCSI chains. If a SCSI chain contains only a single device and contains less than 18 inches of cable, you can probably get away without terminating it. This isn't good practice, but it will usually work. More importantly, if a SCSI chain is more than 10 feet (which is pushing the limits of most types of SCSI), you may need to terminate it a third time in the middle of the chain at or near the 10-foot mark. This should only be done if the chain is more than 10 feet and only if you are experiencing SCSI related problems. Some older SCSI-scanners may require a pass-through terminator regardless of their place in a chain; if so, this should be mentioned in the documentation.

How to Set Termination

Once you know which devices in a SCSI chain need to be terminated, you're faced with the question of how to terminate them. Today, most devices offer terminators built into them that can be activated or deactivated as needed. In many cases, these internal termination features are similar to setting SCSI IDs. Internal drives invariably use jumpers to set termination, while external devices tend to use dip switches or sliders. Instructions for setting termination manually with jumpers or switches should accompany the device in question.

Some devices are self-terminating, or auto-terminating (also known as *active termination*). This means that they can sense whether or not they are at the end of a SCSI chain and turn termination on or off appropriately. Some devices can self-terminate only when used with a SCSI card that will tell them whether or not to turn termination on or off. For the most part, self-terminating devices are easier to use because they do the work for you. External self terminating devices also usually include an LED to indicate whether or not they have activated their termination features. If the device should get confused and not self-terminate properly, you can usually turn the feature off and set the termination of the device manually. You should also check the device's manual to be certain of any known problems with a self-terminating SCSI device.

Some devices don't support built-in termination at all. These tend to be older SCSI devices. In this case, you should either put the device in the middle of the SCSI chain or attach an external terminator to it (if it is an external device). As shown in Figure 12-10, an external terminator is a small device that will attach to the second SCSI port of an external device and provide termination. You can usually find them in any computer store.

With a few exceptions, external terminators are generic across all devices. The exceptions are the Macintosh IIfx and the Apple LaserWriter IIf, IIg, and LaserWriter Pro 630 printers. These require special 200-ohm terminators that are not used for any other SCSI device. These terminators are usually black in color to differentiate them from other terminators, which tend to be gray.

Some older internal drives include terminating resistors built into them to provide termination to the drive but don't allow you to disable them. This means that the drive will always be terminated. If you run across such a hard drive, you can either use it at the end of a chain (which needs to be terminated) or remove the terminating resistor with

Figure 12-10
An external SCSI
terminator.

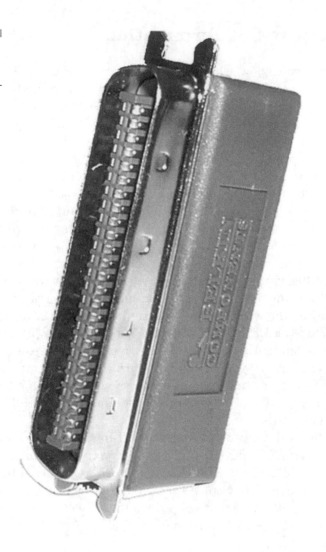

a pair of needle-nose pliers (if possible). Be sure to check the drive's manual or with the manufacturer to be certain that you can't disable termination before removing the resistors.

Types of SCSI

Although *SCSI* tends to be a generic and commonplace term for Mac users, it actually encompasses several different standards beyond the original SCSI standard developed during the early 1980s. The original SCSI standard has become known as SCSI-1. Around 1990, an updated standard was officially created known as SCSI-2. SCSI-2 includes additional instructions as part of the SCSI standard, as well as support for SCSI to operate at increased speeds and an increased data width. Although these are features of the SCSI-2 standard, most manufacturers list these types of SCSI as Fast SCSI and Wide SCSI, respectively, and use the term *SCSI-2* to refer to the additional instructions used for communicating with SCSI devices.

Fast SCSI is defined as adhering to the SCSI-2 instruction set but also allowing for communication as fast as 10 MB/second (double the speed supported by SCSI-1). Wide SCSI is defined as adhering to the SCSI-2 instruction set and making the data width of the SCSI bus 16 bits instead of the original 8-bit standard. Wide SCSI can also include a data width of 32 bits, though this is much less common, and Wide SCSI usually refers to a 16-bit data width.

Wide SCSI also increases the number of devices that can be connected to a SCSI chain, doubling it to a total of 16 possible devices (one of which remains the SCSI card, which continues to be assigned the SCSI ID 7).

Fast and Wide SCSI can be combined to produce Fast/Wide SCSI. Fast/Wide SCSI offers both speed and bandwidth advantages, making it faster than any earlier SCSI type (capable of transmitting 20 MB/second) and still allowing it to accept 15 devices per chain.

A third SCSI standard, called SCSI-3 or, more commonly, Ultra SCSI, was also developed. There are several variations of Ultra SCSI. Ultra SCSI defines a 20-MHz SCSI bus, capable of transferring data at 20 MB/second. Ultra Wide SCSI is the same as Ultra SCSI, but with a 16-bit bus, meaning it is capable of twice the transfer rates (40 MB/second) and up to 16 devices.

Ultra2 SCSI uses a 40-MHz bus, giving it a transfer rate of 40 MB/second. As with Ultra SCSI, there is a wide version of Ultra2 SCSI that allows for a 16-bit bus and transfer rates as high as 80 MB/second.

Ultra3 SCSI, which uses a speed of 80 MHz, delivers transfer rates as high as 80 MB/second. As with the earlier SCSI types, Ultra3 Wide SCSI, also called Ultra 160, is a wide variation that delivers rates up to 160 MB/second.

Table 12-1 compares the various types of SCSI, and Table 12-2 lists their uses.

TABLE 12-1

Comparison of SCSI types.

Type of SCSI	Max. Transfer Rate	Number of Devices*	Max. Cable Length
SCSI-1	5 MB/second	7	6 meters
Fast SCSI	10 MB/second	7	3 meters
Wide SCSI	10 MB/second	15	1.5 meters
Fast/Wide SCSI	20 MB/second	15	1.5 meters
Ultra SCSI	20 MB/second	7	1.5 meters
Ultra Wide SCSI	40 MB/second	15	1.5 meters
Ultra2 SCSI	40 MB/second	7	1.5 meters
Ultra2 Wide SCSI	80 MB/second	15	1.5 meters
Ultra3 SCSI	80 MB/second	7	1.5 meters
Ultra3 Wide SCSI	160 MB/second	15	1.5 meters
LVD SCSI	Varies**	Varies**	12 meters

*Number of devices excluding the SCSI card itself, which is almost always defined as SCSI ID 7.

**LVD SCSI is available in each existing SCSI type, deferring to the SCSI type's transfer rates and device limitations.

TABLE 12-2

Common uses for various types of SCSI.

Type of SCSI	Common Peripherals Used
SCSI-1	Zip drives, low-end scanners.
Fast SCSI	Zip drives, mid-range scanners, laser printers.
Ultra SCSI	Jaz drives, CD-R/RW drives, high-end scanners.
Ultra2 SCSI	Faster hard drives, Jaz drives, CD-R/RW drives.
Ultra3 SCSI	RAID arrays, high-end hard drives.

Differential SCSI

The traditional SCSI standards discussed in the preceding section have all been single-ended, meaning that one wire in each SCSI cable was used to transmit one bit of data. By using only a single wire per bit of data, it is possible for noise to creep into the signal along the SCSI wires. The computer has no way to determine what is noise and what is data. This noise is what restricts SCSI chains to a specific cable length. As the cables get longer, there is more chance for noise to get into the data.

Differential SCSI was defined as an optional part of the SCSI-2 standard. It allows for a SCSI cable to use two wires for each bit of data. The second wire contains the opposite information of the first. This allows the computer and any SCSI devices to determine what is data and what is noise in the signal sent along a SCSI cable. Differential SCSI allows for much longer SCSI chains and increased SCSI performance.

There was only one problem with the technology. Differential SCSI and traditional single-ended SCSI are incompatible. You cannot mix Differential SCSI devices with traditional SCSI devices without risking serious damage to the devices in the SCSI chain and to the computer. For this reason, Differential SCSI has been extremely rare.

However, a newer form of Differential SCSI known as Low-Voltage Differential SCSI, or more commonly, LVD SCSI, offers some compatibility. LVD SCSI uses less power than the original Differential SCSI, (also called High-Voltage Differential SCSI). LVD SCSI devices are also able to sense what types of SCSI devices are in a SCSI chain with them. If the rest of the chain is made up of LVD SCSI devices, a device will act as and provide the advantages of LVD SCSI. If there is even one "traditional" single-ended SCSI device, the LVD SCSI devices will behave as though they were single-ended devices, ensuring safe compatibility but giving up the advantages of LVD SCSI. This process is accomplished automatically without user intervention.

LVD SCSI devices require an LVD SCSI card and can support a maximum cable length of up to 12 meters. LVD SCSI is compatible with each of the various other SCSI types, but it is most commonly found in Ultra2 and Ultra3 SCSI.

SCSI Cabling

In addition to the various changes in speed and data width between SCSI types, there are changes in SCSI cables. Currently a number of types of SCSI cables are in use. The primary differentiation concerns those for internal devices versus those used for external devices.

Internal SCSI devices use either a 50-pin (for narrow SCSI devices) or a 68-pin (for wide SCSI devices) ribbon cable. Because internal SCSI drives do not have two SCSI ports for daisy chaining devices as external SCSI devices do, internal SCSI cables usually include multiple connectors so that you can connect multiple drives in a chain. If you are only using a single device, you will generally use the two end connectors (one attached to the drive and the other to the SCSI card).

External cabling falls into the following categories: 50-pin Centronics, 50-pin standard, 50-pin high-density, 68-pin high-density, and DB 25-pin. The types of cabling you'll use for external devices will depend on the type of SCSI you're using and the type of connector used by a particular device. Table 12-3 describes the types of cables commonly used for the various SCSI types. Figure 12-11 shows various external cables.

With all the different types of cables used for connecting SCSI devices, there is an obvious need for adapters that will allow you to connect SCSI devices that use different types of cables. These adapters can be found in just about any computer store.

When mixing external "narrow" SCSI and wide SCSI types attached to a wide SCSI card, you will most commonly be looking for an adapter that converts from the wide SCSI 68-pin cable to a 50-pin cable. You should look for adapters that support high data byte termination. As illustrated in Figure 12-12, the 68-pin cable of a wide SCSI connector

TABLE 12-3

Types of SCSI cables.

SCSI Type	Cables Traditionally Used
SCSI-1	25-pin DB and 50-pin Centronics
SCSI-2, Fast SCSI	50-pin high-density, 50-pin standard, 50-pin Centronics
Wide SCSI	68-pin high-density
Ultra SCSI	50-pin high-density, 50-pin standard, 50-pin Centronics
Ultra Wide SCSI	68-pin high-density

Figure 12-11
Typical external SCSI cable connectors.

Figure 12-12
External high data byte termination.

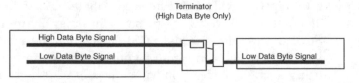

Terminator
(High Data Byte Only)

High Data Byte Signal

Low Data Byte Signal   Low Data Byte Signal

68 Pin Wide SCSI Cable   Adapter   50 Pin Narrow SCSI Cable

includes both high data byte and low data byte signals, while a narrow SCSI cable has only a single (low) data byte signal. High data byte termination in an adapter will terminate the high data byte signal but will allow the low data byte signal to pass through. All narrow SCSI devices should be placed on the opposite side of an adapter from any wide SCSI devices.

In the case of narrow internal SCSI drives attached to a wide SCSI card, you will need individual adapters for each device, rather than using a single wide-to-narrow adapter as you would for external devices. For internal adapters, if the last device in the chain is a narrow device, you will want to use an adapter that supports high byte termination. If the last device is a wide SCSI device, however, you will want to use adapters that block the high data byte but do not terminate it for any narrow drives in the chain. This is illustrated in Figure 12-13.

It is also important when buying SCSI cables to make sure you buy high-quality cables. SCSI cables should be double-shielded in order to prevent noise from easily entering the signals being sent along the cable. Low-quality cables tend not to be properly shielded and can lead to erratic SCSI behavior because noise will enter the SCSI signal. Some SCSI devices may ship with lower-quality cables. If you experience erratic behavior from a perfectly configured SCSI chain, low-quality or damaged SCSI cables may be the problem.

Also, there is a practical limit of how long the entire cabling for a SCSI chain can be. This varies depending on the SCSI type, but even when dealing with SCSI types that support longer chains, it is a good idea to keep the individual cables and therefore the total cable length as short as possible. The limits of SCSI chain lengths are included in Table 12-1.

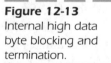

Figure 12-13
Internal high data byte blocking and termination.

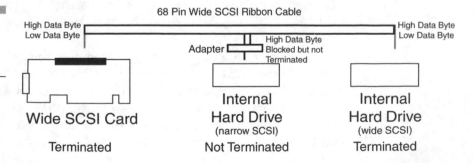

Compatibility Between SCSI Types

In theory, all SCSI types are compatible with each other. The exception is High-Voltage Differential SCSI devices, which are only compatible with other High-Voltage Differential devices. Although older SCSI devices can be supported on newer and faster types of SCSI chains, this does not mean that they will perform with the speed that devices designed for that faster type of SCSI would. For example, an old SCSI-1 hard drive should be usable on an Ultra SCSI chain, but it will still only deliver 5-MB/second data transfer rates at best, whereas an actual Ultra SCSI hard drive would deliver four times that performance.

Also important to understand is that a SCSI chain may only be as fast as the slowest SCSI device in it. So, if you are using older SCSI types in a chain with newer, faster SCSI devices, you probably will not get all the performance benefits. For this reason, if you have a SCSI card that supports multiple SCSI channels, you should consider placing all the older SCSI-type devices on a separate channel from your newer, high-performance devices.

When mixing SCSI types, the question of how long the chain can be may come up. For example, SCSI-1 supports 6 meters, while Fast SCSI supports only 3. Although some might say that you can use a cable length somewhere between the two, you should consider the maximum length of a mixed chain to be the maximum length of the SCSI type that allows for the shortest chain.

The SCSI Manager

The SCSI Manager is a part of the Mac OS that controls how the Mac communicates with a SCSI port and devices attached to that port. When you do something that requires the Mac to communicate with a SCSI device, the driver software for that device sends commands to the SCSI Manager, which sends the appropriate signals to the device(s) in the SCSI chain. Every Mac since the Mac Plus has contained the SCSI Manager.

The original SCSI Manager supported only the SCSI-1 standard and used only the SCSI-1 instruction set. It wasn't until SCSI Manager 4.3 was developed in 1993 that support for the SCSI-2 standard was added. SCSI Manager 4.3 provided much improved SCSI performance, as well as the ability to take advantage of the various parts of the SCSI-2 standard. However, in order for a SCSI device to take advantage of SCSI

Manager 4.3, the driver software for the device needs to support SCSI Manager 4.3. If the driver doesn't support SCSI Manager 4.3, then the SCSI Manager needs to translate the older-style commands, which can cause SCSI performance to degrade by as much as 50 percent.

Virtually all current SCSI devices include drivers that support SCSI Manager 4.3. Older devices or device drivers, however, may not. A device manufacturer or a device manual should be able to tell you for certain. If the driver does not support SCSI Manager 4.3, check to see if there is an updated driver available that does. If you must use both devices that don't support SCSI Manager 4.3, try to keep them in a separate SCSI chain from devices that do. A SCSI chain tends to be only as fast as the slowest device in the chain, and even one pre-4.3 device can slow down every other SCSI device in the chain considerably. Additionally, some SCSI cards require device drivers to be SCSI Manager 4.3-compliant, or the attached devices simply will not function. You can check with the manufacturer of a card to determine if this is the case.

SCSI Cards and Devices

If you want to add SCSI devices to the current or recent Power Mac computers or the current PowerBook computers, the first thing you'll need to do is add a SCSI card. In the case of the Power Macs, these are 7-inch PCI cards that offer internal and/or external SCSI ports (see Figure 12-14). Various SCSI cards offer support for the different types of SCSI and may contain multiple SCSI channels, allowing you to have more than one SCSI chain attached to the card.

SCSI cards may or may not allow you to use an attached SCSI drive as a startup drive for the Mac. In order to support starting up from attached SCSI devices, the card must have open firmware-compliant ROM. This type of ROM on the card allows the Mac to recognize and use the card before the Mac OS is loaded, rather than having to wait for a piece of driver software to be loaded during the startup process. Several SCSI cards on the market support starting up from attached drives, but you should look to see this explicitly mentioned in a card's specifications rather than assume a card supports it.

SCSI cards that support multiple channels (i.e., multiple SCSI chains) can be an excellent choice if you expect to attach a large number of SCSI devices. They are also a good choice if you have devices of a slower SCSI type, and many devices of a faster SCSI type, because you can separate

Figure 12-14
A basic SCSI PCI card.

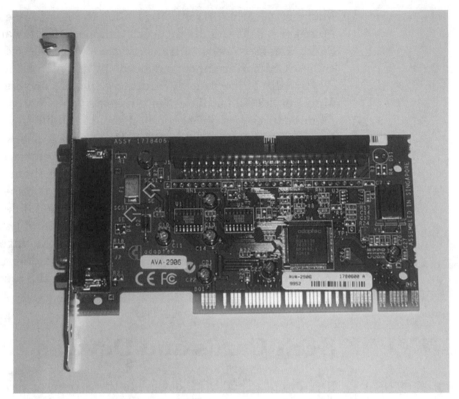

the slower devices from the faster ones by using a separate SCSI chain. This prevents your higher-performance devices from being slowed down by the slower devices. Cards supporting multiple channels will have multiple sets of SCSI connectors, and the card's manual should tell you which connectors are associated with which channels.

When choosing a SCSI card, consider what types of SCSI you need or are likely to need in the future. Most inexpensive cards today support Fast SCSI, which is good for Zip drives, scanners, and similar low-end SCSI uses. However, the cost of cards that support Wide SCSI and Ultra SCSI may not be all that much more expensive and will offer you the option of adding more powerful SCSI devices later on.

Also be aware that not all SCSI cards deliver complete compatibility with all of the SCSI devices available. Compatibility issues may be specific to a single Mac model or, more likely, to a specific version of the Mac OS. For this reason it is important to check the specifications and information available regarding a SCSI card before buying. If there are known incompatibilities, the card's manufacturer should make this information available, generally through their Web site. You can also contact the manufacturer or Macintosh news sources for additional information on the performance and compatibility of a given SCSI card.

Installing a PCI SCSI card is the same as installing any other PCI card. You first install the drivers, then you shut down the computer and install the PCI card as described in Chapter 8. Once the card is installed, restart the Mac and use either the Apple System Profiler, Adaptec's free SCSI Probe utility, or software included with the card to verify that the card is installed and recognized properly. At this point, you may need to use a utility included with the card to define the SCSI ID of the card, whether the card is terminated, how the card will work with self-terminating devices, or other options related to the card.

Assuming the card is recognized and functioning properly, you can now shut down the Mac and attach any internal or external SCSI devices you wish to use. Remember to be certain that each device has a unique SCSI ID and that the chain(s) is terminated properly, as described earlier in the chapter.

SCSI PC Cards

For owners of the most recent PowerBooks, which shipped with FireWire ports built in and no SCSI port, you can add SCSI through a PC Card. To do so, install the driver software for the card and then simply insert the PC Card into the PC Card slot of the PowerBook (PC Cards are discussed in Chapter 9). When the card is inserted, an icon for it should appear on the desktop. Once the card is recognized, you can shut down the PowerBook and attach any external SCSI devices you wish.

Internal SCSI Devices

Internal SCSI devices are all drives of some sort. The majority of the time, they are hard drives. Installing an internal SCSI hard drive is the same as installing any other internal hard drive; however, you will use a 50 or 68-pin ribbon cable and attach the cable to the SCSI card rather than to a connector on the motherboard. It is also important to make sure that the hard drive has a unique SCSI ID. If it will be the primary hard drive of the Mac, you should set the SCSI ID to 0. Some internal hard drives are self-terminating, though others are not. Check with the manufacturer to determine whether the particular hard drive you are installing is self-terminating. If it is not, you should be able to switch termination on or off using jumpers on the hard drive. The manual for the hard drive should include information on how to set the jumpers for both termination and SCSI ID. If the hard drive does not allow termination to be adjusted (either it provides no termination or has terminating resistors that cannot be turned off), you will need to place it appropriately in the SCSI chain.

In addition to attaching the internal drive and setting termination, you will also need to insert the power connector for the new drive and secure it to the inside of the computer with a mounting bracket. There should be ample power connectors inside the computer, and these install in only one direction. If you need additional power connectors, you can purchase a "Y" splitter for the internal power cables for a couple of dollars in most computer and electronic stores. See Chapter 11 for more information on powering internal devices in the Mac.

The manufacturer of the hard drive may provide the mounting kit for an internal hard drive, or you may need to purchase one separately if the drive does not fit securely in the brackets inside the Mac. If you do require such a kit (usually, you won't), you will need a mounting kit where the screw holes on the bracket line up with the screw holes in the case of the Power Mac. This is discussed more in Chapter 5.

Once the drive is installed, you start up the Mac (from a Mac OS CD if the new hard drive is the only hard drive installed in the Mac). If the Mac crashes or fails to start up, there is most likely a problem with the SCSI chain. If the Mac starts up normally, you can use SCSI Probe (or a similar utility) to make certain the new drive is recognized. If it is recognized by SCSI Probe, you can then use a formatting utility (if it's a hard drive) to format it for use. The computer may recognize the drive and ask you if you want to initialize it during startup, or if the drive has already been formatted for use with the Mac, it may simply appear as an icon on the desktop. If the device is not recognized by SCSI Probe, it is most likely not installed properly. Shut down the Mac and ensure that you have connected the drive properly and that it is powered.

External SCSI Devices

Over the years many external peripherals for the Mac have used a SCSI interface. These have included external hard drives, CD-ROM drives, removable-media drives (such as the Zip or Jaz disk), scanners, tape drives, and some digital cameras and laser printers, to name the most common. Installing any of these devices is generally the same because they all operate using the SCSI interface and command set.

The first step is to install driver software for the new device. Then you assign each device a unique SCSI ID, attach the device to the chain, and terminate both ends of the chain. Next, you start up the Mac. If you encounter problems at startup, it is very likely that there is a problem with the way the SCSI chain is configured. Make sure all devices are powered, that each has a unique SCSI ID, and that the chain is properly terminated. If startup is successful, use SCSI Probe or the Apple System Profile to ensure all devices are recognized. Assuming they are, you should be able to use the devices. You can also use a utility included with the new device to verify it is working correctly.

Some external SCSI devices are designed to function properly only when they occupy a specific place in a SCSI chain. Most commonly, these devices need to be the last device in a chain. A few devices will not function while other external SCSI devices are part of a SCSI chain. Usually, a device with such requirements will mention this as part of the device's documentation. Similarly, some devices simply do not like working with each other or being situated in specific places relative to each other in a SCSI chain. Such problems are often called "SCSI Voodoo," and there is no real way to be certain when this will occur other than trial and error. For this reason, troubleshooting SCSI problems often involves changing the order of devices in a chain.

Older PowerBook SCSI

Older PowerBooks included SCSI as a standard feature. These PowerBooks include a unique square, 30-pin SCSI port (shown in Figure 12-15) that requires a special adapter in order to connect to actual SCSI devices. These adapters are relatively low cost and can be found at any Mac shop. The SCSI port of the PowerBook supports only external devices and follows the SCSI-2 standard.

Another feature of older PowerBook SCSI is *Target Disk mode* (formerly called SCSI Disk mode). Target Disk mode allows the PowerBook to be attached to another Mac and act as though it were a SCSI hard drive. The PowerBook's hard drive shows up just like any other external hard drive would on the other Mac's desktop, and you can copy, move, delete, or work with files on the PowerBook's hard drive exactly

Figure 12-15
SCSI port on older
PowerBook models.

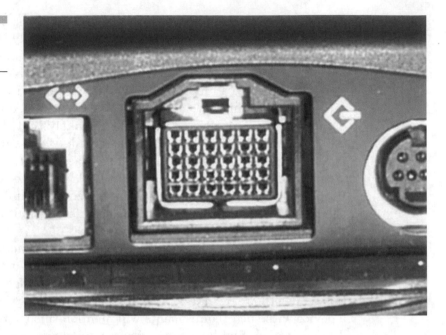

as though the PowerBook were nothing but that hard drive. This is an excellent way or transferring files extremely quickly between the two computers.

To use Target Disk mode, you need a special PowerBook SCSI adapter. Unlike the standard PowerBook SCSI adapter, which has 29 pins, the Target Disk mode adapter has 30 and uses all of the connections in the PowerBook's SCSI port. Some PowerBook SCSI adapters have a built-in switch and can function as both types of adapters, depending on how the switch is set. When you turn the PowerBook on with this adapter attached (you should always turn the PowerBook off when connecting either the standard SCSI adapter or the Target Disk mode adapter), the screen will display just the diamond-shaped SCSI logo and a number. This number indicates what SCSI ID the PowerBook is assigned when it is in Target Disk mode as an external SCSI device (this SCSI ID can be changed in the PowerBook control panel).

You must make certain you are using the appropriate adapter when using Target Disk mode. Otherwise, the PowerBook's SCSI controller and the SCSI card of the other Mac will both be set recognized as SCSI devices set to ID 7, and you can cause serious problems and damage to both computers. Before connecting the PowerBook to the desktop Mac via SCSI, make certain that the PowerBook has started up into Target

Disk mode by displaying the SCSI logo onscreen. If it displays the Mac startup sequence or desktop, it has not started up in Target Disk mode and should not be connected to a desktop Mac. Also note that some of the early PowerBook 100 series computers do not support Target Disk mode.

SCSI Utilities

SCSI utilities are software that can be used to view information about a SCSI chain, to mount drives that are attached via SCSI, and to reset the SCSI port. The most well known and widely used SCSI utility is Adaptec's free SCSI Probe, shown in Figure 12-16.

Utilities such as SCSI Probe can help you diagnose problems with a

Figure 12-16
SCSI Probe utility.

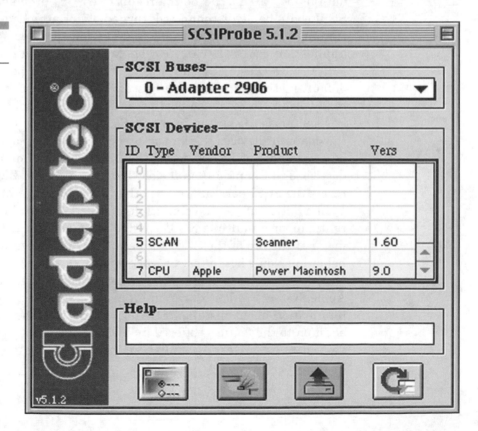

SCSI chain. When launched, SCSI Probe will query the SCSI chain and display all the devices it recognizes. If the chain is not terminated properly, SCSI Probe should display an alert telling you so. In addition to scanning the attached SCSI chains for devices, SCSI Probe can also be used to mount hard drives (and some removable media disks) and to reset the SCSI port.

SCSI Probe is useful in troubleshooting to ensure that a newly installed SCSI card is being recognized, as well as to make sure that all the devices attached to a SCSI chain are recognized by the Mac.

In addition, SCSI Probe can be used to mount hard drives if for some reason they weren't mounted when the Mac started up. This may be because of a problem with the drive and its SCSI connection, or it may be because the drive was formatted such that it would not be mounted at startup. Although SCSI Probe can only mount SCSI drives, similar utilities are available for mounting non-SCSI hard drives.

Another useful feature is SCSI Probe's ability to reset the SCSI port. Occasionally, the SCSI port may become confused and stop transmitting data properly. This can be the result of a SCSI problem, a device in the SCSI chain being disconnected, turned off, or attached while the Mac is running (all of which can cause other serious problems), or a Mac OS or application crash. It can also be caused by corruption of the Mac's PRAM data. Resetting the SCSI port causes the port to revert to its default instructions and settings and should cause it to function normally again. To reset the port using SCSI Probe, hold down the Option key and press the button in the SCSI Probe window that is used to scan the chain for devices. If the port needs to be reset repeatedly, this may be a symptom of PRAM corruption, and you should zap the PRAM as described in Chapter 10 and elsewhere in this book. Zapping the PRAM resets the SCSI port, as well as other settings of the Mac.

In addition, if you have multiple SCSI cards installed or a SCSI card that supports multiple SCSI channels/chains, you can use the pop-up menu at the top of the SCSI Probe window to choose which SCSI channel or bus you wish to test or work with.

Although it does not offer the SCSI-related abilities of SCSI Probe, the Apple System Profiler, shown in Figure 12-17, can also be used to display information about installed SCSI cards and attached SCSI devices. In addition to the features offered by SCSI Probe, most manufacturers will ship utilities for testing and changing the settings of their individual SCSI cards.

Figure 12-17
SCSI information
displayed by the
Apple System Profiler.

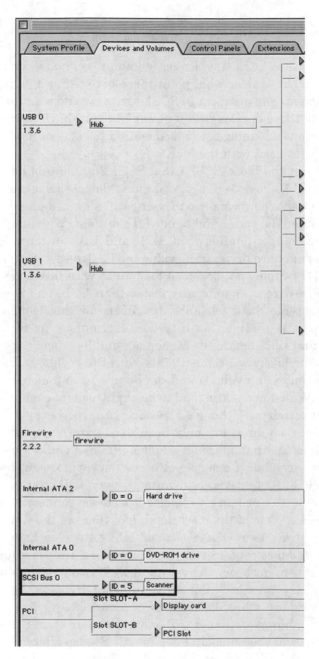

Reasons for Using SCSI

Given that SCSI is no longer a default technology on the Mac, some people might wonder what point there is to using it. Obviously, people with an existing investment in SCSI devices would want to be able to continue using those devices with a newer Macintosh. However, SCSI has several inherent advantages when compared to some of the other interface technologies used with the Mac.

Even the basic SCSI-1 and SCSI-2 standards have more bandwidth than USB does. While a good many devices have migrated to USB with acceptable performance, they are still slow compared to SCSI. When you consider the speed and bandwidth of Fast, Wide, and Ultra SCSI, there is no competition between SCSI and USB in terms of performance for external hard drives, removable-media drives, scanners, or other devices. USB is simply not designed to operate with faster devices.

FireWire is significantly faster than USB, and it is potentially faster than some SCSI variants. However, for the moment, FireWire is not nearly as common an interface technology as SCSI. SCSI has been around since before the Macintosh and has done a remarkable job maintaining backward-compatibility with the earlier SCSI types. This means that many individuals and companies have major investments in SCSI. FireWire devices also tend to be slightly more expensive than their SCSI counterparts. Although FireWire can, in theory, be used for internal devices, so far it has only been used externally. FireWire is a hot new technology that offers several benefits and can complement SCSI in various ways, but it has not yet become a replacement for SCSI.

SCSI offers several advantages over IDE, which, as mentioned, has become the primary technology used for connecting internal drives on the Mac. One of the most notable of these is the limitation that you can only attach two IDE drives to an IDE controller. Even though the current Power Macs contain two IDE controllers, that is a limit of four devices. SCSI can, in theory, deliver up to 15 internal devices per chain. Granted, there is a practical limit of five internal drives in the cases of the current Power Macs (three hard drives, a removable-media drive, and a CD/DVD drive); however, that is still one drive more than IDE can accommodate.

Beyond the number of devices, SCSI also offers a performance benefit over IDE. SCSI offers increased bandwidth and it requires less processor work to access data because much of the work involved in accessing SCSI devices is handled by the SCSI controller chips on the SCSI card and not the processor itself. SCSI can also access system RAM directly under the control of the SCSI controller without needing to work through the

TABLE 12-4

SCSI performance
compared to IDE
performance.

IDE Type*	Transfer Rate	SCSI Type	Transfer Rate**
Ultra ATA/66	66 MB/second	Ultra3 SCSI	80 or 160 MB/second
		Ultra2 SCSI	40 or 80 MB/second
Ultra ATA/33	33 MB/second	Ultra2 SCSI	40 or 80 MB/second
		Ultra SCSI	20 or 40MB/second

*This table includes only the fastest and more recent IDE variations. See the next chapter for additional IDE types and standards.

**Rates listed are narrow and wide variations of the given SCSI type.

processor, further increasing performance compared to IDE (recent IDE standards also support such direct memory access modes, however). In general, SCSI can be considered capable of delivering more than twice the data transfer performance of IDE. However, when you compare the faster IDE transfer speeds and those granted by various types of SCSI (as in Table 12-4), you can see that SCSI can deliver substantially higher performance. This increased performance has made SCSI the interface of choice for multimedia and graphics arts work for years, because when you are dealing with large files, the seemingly slight differences in access time can be noticeably magnified.

SCSI is also preferable if you wish to create RAID arrays. Because RAID arrays require that multiple drives be tied together to act as a single drive (usually for increased performance and extremely fast drive access), you will almost always be using more than two hard drives. This eliminates the use of IDE drives unless you are using RAID to make identical copies of a single drive or a more expensive IDE PCI card. Not only is SCSI required for RAID, but if you are using RAID for performance benefits, you will want to use the fastest technologies available.

Beyond comparisons with other technologies, SCSI is simply a tried-and-true method of attaching devices to the Macintosh. It has been around for years and is firmly entrenched in the computer industry, while newer interfaces such as USB and FireWire are still finding their place. Despite not being a self-configuring technology, SCSI is relatively simple and easy to work with.

SCSI Adapters for non-SCSI Macs

While the Power Mac and PowerBook computers feature slots that can accept SCSI cards, this is not true for other Macs such as the iBook and most iMacs. (*Note*: the revision A and B iMac's mezzanine slot can accept an Ultra Wide SCSI card manufactured by Formac.) Since these Macs feature no internal expansion slots, the only option for SCSI devices is specially designed adapter products.

There are adapters on the market that attach to either the USB or FireWire port of a Mac computer and include a SCSI connector that allows you to attach SCSI devices. These products tend to have compatibility issues with some SCSI devices, and manufacturers should be able to provide you with a list of SCSI devices tested to successfully work with the adapter. Generally, these adapters seem to work best with SCSI hard drive and some types of removable-media drivers. Other SCSI devices, such as scanners, tend not to work as easily or as well with these adapters.

Aside from the compatibility concerns, USB adapters are limited by the bandwidth of USB, which is even lower than the original SCSI-1 standard. The result will be that SCSI devices will have significantly lower performance rates when used with a USB adapter.

Note: Because both USB and FireWire are hot-pluggable, you will be able to reconfigure a SCSI chain attached to one of these adapters without needing to shut down the Mac while doing so.

Termination may also be an issue with these adapters. The adapter itself may not support termination at all. This means that the first SCSI device and the last SCSI device in the chain will need to be terminated but may require special terminators that supply their own power for termination. Check with the adapter's manufacturer for details.

Troubleshooting SCSI Chains and Connections

Following are common problems you might encounter while working with SCSI connections, along with their solutions.

A SCSI Drive Is Attached, But the Drive Does Not Mount

If the drive is a CD/DVD drive or removable-media drive, make certain that a disk is inserted in the drive. If a disk is inserted and still does not mount or if the drive is a hard drive, use a utility such as SCSI

Probe to check the SCSI chain and determine if the drive is being recognized at all.

If the drive is recognized at the appropriate SCSI ID, attempt to mount the drive or the disk inserted in it with the SCSI utility (SCSI Probe supports this feature as do several shareware titles such as Mt. Everything). If the utility fails to mount the drive or disk, verify that any driver software needed for the drive is installed. If the drive is a hard drive, use a drive utility to ensure that the drive is functioning properly and to be certain that the drive has been formatted for use with the Mac.

If the drive is not recognized by SCSI Probe, first check to ensure that it is plugged in and turned on. Check to be certain that the outlet, power strip, or UPS that the drive (if external) is plugged into is actually delivering power. If the drive is powered properly, make sure that the SCSI cables leading from the computer to the drive are attached securely, and check to be certain that the chain is terminated properly. If the drive in question supports internal or automated termination, make certain it is turned off if the drive is in the middle of the chain or on if it is at the end of the chain.

No SCSI Devices Are Recognized at All

Follow the steps outlined in the previous section for a single drive not being recognized. If none of those yields any help, it is possible that the SCSI card is not installed properly or that the port(s) on the card are damaged. TechTool Pro includes a utility that allows you test the chips that control the SCSI port to ensure they are working properly.

This symptom can also mean that the SCSI port needs to be reset. Sometimes, the SCSI port can stop transferring data correctly. The port can be reset by using a SCSI utility or by zapping the Mac's PRAM.

Devices Work Normally at First But Then Cause Erratic Crashes

As always, check the SCSI chain to make sure all devices are connected, have unique SCSI IDs, and are properly terminated. Then try resetting the SCSI port. If this doesn't help, try to determine if specific devices are involved in the crashes. If this is the case, check with the manufacturer for any known problems and for updated driver software. Also, try changing the SCSI ID the device is set to and its location in the SCSI chain.

If none of this helps, check the total cable length of your SCSI chain to be certain that it is not too long for the type of SCSI you are using. Damaged or low-quality SCSI cables can also lead to this kind of problem.

Devices Don't Function with a Specific SCSI ID

Sometimes devices will experience problems when they are set to certain SCSI ID numbers. There have been reports of earlier PCI Macs where various devices failed to function when set to SCSI ID 5, for example. If a problem can be traced back to a specific device in a SCSI chain, try assigning a different SCSI ID to that device.

Multiple Icons for the Same SCSI Drive Appear Across the Desktop

This indicates that the SCSI chain is not terminated properly (generally, that one end is not terminated at all) and the signal on the chain is being reflected back from the end of the chain. Check for proper termination of the entire SCSI chain.

The Icon for a SCSI Drive Appears on the Desktop, but the Mac Crashes When the Drive Is Accessed

This can indicate a termination problem or a SCSI ID conflict. Verify that the SCSI chain is functioning properly. It can also indicate that the drive is corrupted or otherwise damaged. If there appears to be no SCSI-related problem, use a disk utility to test the drive.

The Mac Does Not Start Up or Crashes During the Startup Process

This can (but does not always) mean there is a problem with the SCSI chain. First, disconnect the SCSI chain from the Mac and attempt to start up. If the Mac still crashes, then it is doubtful that the problem is

SCSI-related. Consider other possible problems such as extension conflicts.

If removing the SCSI chain clears up the problem, then the problem is almost certainly SCSI-related. Most likely, this indicates problems with two devices both being set to the same SCSI ID or an improperly terminated SCSI chain. Since two drives sharing a single SCSI ID can lead to data loss, check to be certain each drive has a unique ID first. If this is not the problem, verify that the SCSI chain is terminated properly. Also check to be certain all devices are connected and powered properly.

If this doesn't help, try disconnecting all devices and reconnecting them one at a time. This will allow you to determine if a specific device is causing the problem. If you find that a specific device is causing problems, try rearranging the order of the devices in the SCSI chain. Some devices will only function if they are in a specific place in the SCSI chain (such as the first or last device).

If this doesn't help, check all the SCSI cables to be certain none are damaged. Also be certain that you are using the appropriate type of SCSI cable and that the entire cable length of cables for the chain do not exceed what is allowed for in the type of SCSI you are using.

If this all fails to help, check the individual devices for signs of damage. In addition, if a single device is causing problems check it for damage or contact the manufacturer to ensure that there is no known problems with the device and any other hardware or software you may be using.

Finally, if none of this helped, check to be certain that the SCSI card you are using is installed and functioning correctly.

IDE

IDE (Integrated Drive Electronics) replaced SCSI as the primary means for attaching internal hard drives to the Mac in the mid-1990s and is currently the default technology for all internal drives on the Macintosh. IDE enjoys broader industry usage than SCSI and is less expensive both in terms of motherboard design and in the cost of actual drives. Unlike SCSI, IDE is designed to support only internal drives and not external drives or other types of devices.

Many users find the various terms referring to IDE drives confusing. The actual name for the standard is ATA, which dates back to when the standard was first created and was officially named the Common Access Method AT Interface. (ATA actually stands for AT attachment; AT for Advanced Technology, refers to a type of PC motherboard.) To further confuse the matter, within a year of the standard's official adoption, a newer IDE version called Enhanced IDE (or EIDE) was created. Even more recently, newer IDE standards known as Ultra ATA have been adopted, which offer significant improvements in performance over the earlier IDE versions.

Beyond IDE, ATA, and EIDE, you will probably find the term ATAPI, which stands for AT Attachment Packet Interface. The original IDE specifications were limited to connecting only hard drives. Other internal drive types, such as Zip drives or CD-ROM drives, were not included. The ATAPI standard was developed later to enable internal drives besides hard drives to be connected to a computer using the IDE interface. For the majority of purposes, these terms all refer to IDE devices. The specific types of IDE that they represent are discussed in this chapter.

Not all IDE drives will work in Macintosh computers. Mac requirements for IDE drives are listed in Table 13-1. Current IDE drives tend to support all these requirements, but you should check before buying an IDE drive.

TABLE 13-1

IDE Drive Requirements for Macintosh Use

Must support Logical Block Allocation

Must support the Identify command

Must support PIO Mode 2 or higher

Must have Write Caching enabled

How IDE Works

Although IDE and SCSI achieve similar results and functions from an end-user perspective, the two technologies differ in some significant ways. SCSI requires not only the interface of a SCSI port but also specially designed chips that control all the activity of the devices attached to the SCSI port without the processor's direct intervention. IDE, on the other hand, is more direct, with the IDE controllers (or connectors) being controlled by the processor itself. IDE also places much more of the control technology for a drive in the circuitry on the drive itself. These differences mean that IDE is both simpler and less expensive to implement than SCSI. It also means that it does not, as a rule, perform as well SCSI does.

IDE is also less flexible than SCSI. Indeed, of all the technologies used to connect drives (internal or external) to the Mac, IDE is probably the least flexible. It supports only two devices per controller at best (compared to SCSI's 7 or 15 devices, FireWire's 63, and USB's over 100 possible devices), and each of those devices must be internal.

IDE involves a relatively few basic components. These include the IDE controllers, which are included on the motherboard of all current and recent Macs, the IDE drive itself, and the ribbon cable used to connect the two. There is no concern about termination, as there is with SCSI chains. In addition, because there can be only two devices per controller, there can be only two identification settings for any IDE devices.

IDE Controllers

IDE controllers are currently built into the Mac's motherboard and are the connectors to which IDE cables are attached. Despite what the term *controller* might imply, IDE controllers actually do very little controlling. An IDE controller is mostly just a connector with enough buffer circuitry to keep the flow of data between the drives and the processor at an appropriate rate for the processor to deal with. Most of the control is actually handled by the drive's internal circuitry and the Mac's processor.

As discussed later in this chapter, there are variations on the IDE standard, primarily in terms of data throughput that is supported. The IDE controllers are of a certain type and are restricted to the data throughput of that type. For example, the original iMac uses a type of

IDE controllers called Ultra ATA, which supports data transfer rates up to 33 MB per second. Since the iMac's release, an IDE variation called Ultra ATA/66, which supports transfer rates of 66 MB per second, has become common (and it is used on newer, high-end Macs, such as the Power Mac G4). Since the original iMac's IDE controllers don't support this type of Ultra ATA/66, such a drive would be limited to the 33-MB-per-second speed of the original iMac's controller.

Each Macintosh computer has two IDE controllers (such as the one in Figure 13-1). One controller is designated for connecting internal hard drives, while the other is designated for connecting the internal CD or DVD-ROM drive and any internal removable-media drives, such as a Zip or tape drive. The hard drive controller is also known as the *primary IDE controller*, as it is the one that Mac will look for first for a valid startup disk if it cannot start up from the drive chosen in the Startup Disk control panel (or if no drive has been selected in the Startup Disk control panel).

These designations are mostly for convenience. In fact, there is no rule that says that a hard drive couldn't be attached to the controller designated for the CD-ROM drive or vice versa. However, unless you want to have three hard drives installed in your Power Mac, it is probably better for organizational purposes to use the controllers as they are designated. Beyond the convenience of proximity to the actual drive bays the con-

Figure 13-1   A typical IDE controller located on a Mac's motherboard.

trollers are intended for, there is another reason that you may want to attach CD-ROM and removable-media drives to a separate IDE controller than you use for your internal hard drives: CD-ROM drives and removable-media drives are slower drives than hard drives.

IDE Cables

An IDE cable is a 40-pin ribbon cable that looks very similar to internal SCSI cables. IDE cables usually have three connectors: one for the controller and two for internal drives. If you are only connecting a single internal drive to a controller, then you do not need to worry about the second connector. Figure 13-2 shows a typical IDE cable.

It makes no difference which drive is attached to which connector on the IDE cable. For the sake of convenience, you will probably use the middle connector for the drive closest to the IDE controller. If only one drive is attached to the cable, it is customary to use the end connector for the drive, although this is not required.

Some Macintosh models will come with cables that are different from the standard ribbon cable with two connectors. Some of the Blue and

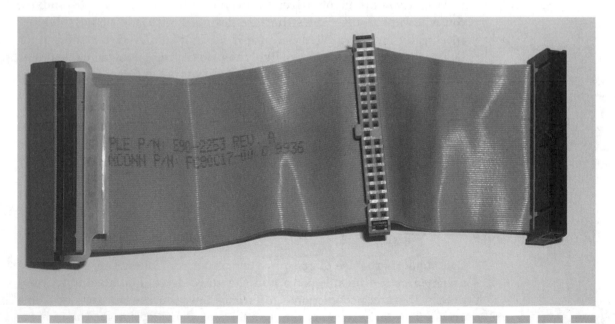

Figure 13-2   A typical IDE cable with connectors for the motherboard and two drives.

White G3 models, for example, will use a ribbon cable with only one connector for the internal hard drive because they do not officially support more than one drive on the primary (hard drive) IDE controller. Similarly, the iMacs use cables that are very short and support only a connector for one drive because they have do not have space internally for more than one hard drive and CD/DVD-ROM drive. In the case of the original iMac, the cable was also gathered up out of the standard ribbon shape just beyond the connectors to fit between the motherboard and drive areas.

Although IDE cabling does not have as stringent a set length limit as the various SCSI types do, it is a good idea to keep the length of an IDE cable as short as possible. This is because, as with SCSI cables, signal noise can become mixed in with the data be transmitted along an IDE cable. The chances of this happening are, however, lower with IDE simply because the cables are limited in length to begin with compared to SCSI. As with SCSI, you will want to make sure you use cables that are well shielded—again, to keep noise out of the data stream. These concerns are greater for the faster types of IDE, where there is the greater potential for signal noise to disrupt data transmission. Higher-quality shielded cables can also lead to an increase in performance of IDE drives. IDE cables should ideally be kept to a length of 18 inches or shorter.

Also, if you are using drives that conform to the Ultra ATA standard, you will want to use cables that are designed with additional shielding specifically for Ultra ATA, because it is significantly faster than other IDE types and therefore more likely to benefit from shielded cables. (For more on Ultra ATA, see the section on IDE types later in this chapter.) This is true both in terms of performance and, more importantly, in terms of accuracy of transmitted data.

IDE ribbon cables often have a small gap or hole in the cable at a specific point. This gap is precisely 1 millimeter by 4 millimeters and is located along 67th wire of the cable. (See Figure 13-3.) This is perfectly normal and should not alarm you if you see it.

Master and Slave Drives

IDE supports the use of up to two drives per controller. These drives are assigned as the master drive and the slave drive. For Macintosh computers, there is no functional difference between the master and slave drives. The designation is simply a form of identification for the individual drives, analogous to a SCSI ID number. If a drive is the only drive

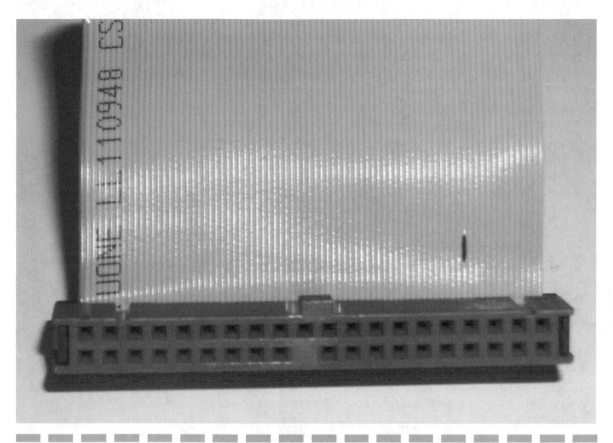

Figure 13-3   This small gap is normal on IDE ribbon cables.

attached to an IDE controller on the motherboard, it will need to be assigned as the master drive. If there are two drives, one must be assigned as the master drive and the other as the slave drive in order for both drives to be recognized by the Mac. Therefore, if you are adding a second drive to an IDE controller that already has a drive attached to it, the second drive will generally be designated as the slave drive. If you assign both drives attached to an IDE controller as master or slave, the Mac will either refuse to start up or will start up and only recognize one of the two drives.

Adjusting jumpers on the drive (as indicated in Figure 13-4) before it is installed designates whether a drive is a master or slave drive. Hard drives are almost always designated as a master drive out of the box and will need to be changed if they are to be used with another hard drive.

Figure 13-4 *Jumpers such as these are used to determine if a drive is designated as master or slave on an IDE controller.*

CD-ROM, DVD-ROM, and removable-media drives (such as an internal Zip or SuperDisk drive) may be assigned as either master or slave out of the box, and you should check the manual to see which is the default setting. A drive's manual should include instructions about which jumpers need to be set to designate the drive as either a master or slave drive. Many hard drives also include the appropriate jumper settings right on the drive itself. If neither the drive nor the manual include jumper information, you should contact the drive's manufacturer.

If no drive is selected in the Startup Disk control panel or the selected drive is not available, the Mac will look for a viable startup drive. When checking IDE channels for a viable drive, the Mac will first look to the drive designated as the master drive. The order is as follows: primary (hard drive) IDE controller master drive, primary IDE controller slave drive, secondary (CD-ROM/removable-media) IDE controller master drive, and finally, secondary IDE controller slave drive. For this reason, you should make your primary hard drive the master drive of the primary IDE controller.

If you are running Mac OS X Server, you must install it onto a hard drive (or a partition of a hard drive) that is designated as a master IDE device. Mac OS X Server will not install onto or run from an IDE drive that is designated as a slave drive on the IDE controller.

Also important to note is that although the IDE standard includes the ability for controllers to support two drives, not all Macintosh models have honored this part of the standard. Many of the earlier Mac models that used IDE drives supported only a single drive per IDE controller. Apple didn't begin supporting two drivers per controller until the later revisions of the beige Power Mac G3 were introduced in 1998.

The Blue and White Power Mac G3, however, is a potential exception. The first revision motherboards for the Power Mac G3 supported master and slave configurations on the secondary IDE controller that is used for a CD-ROM and Zip drive (or other removable-media drive). The primary IDE controller, however, supported only a single IDE drive—at least, that's the story officially. Unofficially, some enthusiastic Mac users willing to experiment found that you could indeed attach a second hard drive to the primary IDE controller, although you needed to replace the standard IDE ribbon cable that had only one IDE connector. However, these earlier Power Mac G3 models did not always accept a slave drive and were known to have some problems when using a slave hard drive on the primary IDE controller. These problems included data corruption errors on the slave drive, as well as problems in using hard drives at higher IDE performance modes (see later in this chapter for information on IDE modes and types). In some cases, there were no problems with an IDE slave drive on the revision 1 motherboard Power Mac G3 models until they were updated to Mac OS 9 or had their firmware upgraded using the update from Apple. Given that there seems to be little way to predict whether or not problems will occur, I suggest erring on the side of caution and following Apple's official guidelines regarding support for slave drives on these Power Mac G3 models.

The Blue and White G3 models with a revision 2 motherboard feature an updated IDE control chip and are able to accept slave drives on both channels without any problems (as are all the Power Mac G4 models). You can generally identify the motherboard revision by the type of hard drive mounting bracket used for the primary, factory-installed IDE drive or by the included IDE cable. Power Macs with Apple support for master and slave drive configurations will include an IDE cable with two connectors. The drive bracket will have a U-shaped top edge (as shown in Figure 13-5) if the Mac is designed to support both master and slave

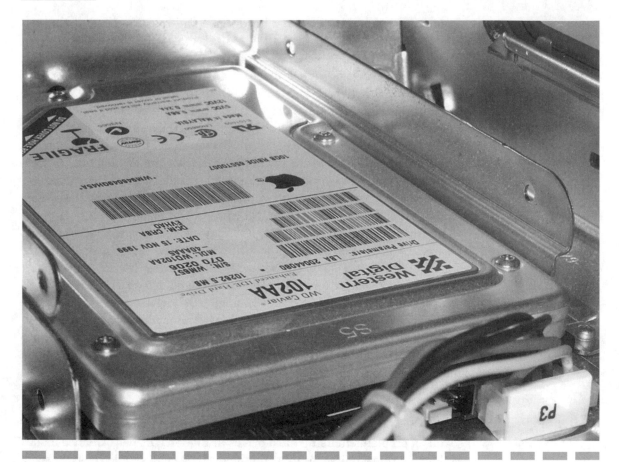

Figure 13-5 Blue and White Power Macintosh computers with a U-shaped mounting bracket such as this officially support slave hard drives on the primary (hard drive) IDE controller.

drives on the primary IDE controller. This U-shaped bracket also supports mounting of two hard drives in a single drive bay.

External IDE Drives

As stated earlier, IDE was designed as a technology for attaching internal drives, not external devices. There are, however, a couple of exceptions to this rule. The most common are devices that adapt the IDE interface and command set to function as another interface technology. When the Mac first began the transition from SCSI internal hard drives to IDE, such adapters were used to convert internal IDE drives for use with SCSI-based

Macs. More recently, technologies have focused on FireWire and USB adapters. In addition, iDrives uses a technique that is quite literally an external IDE drive with no adaptation to another interface technology.

iDrives

IDE was designed as a technology for connecting internal drives. Unlike SCSI, there is no type of cabling or connector designed to allow IDE devices to be used outside of a computer. Aside from the connector cable, IDE devices use the Molex-style power connectors of any internal drive, making external use impossible without a power supply.

Following the iMac's introduction in 1998, which had no support for any external hard drives except USB ones that offered only extremely slow data transfer rates compared to SCSI and IDE, a company called iDrives created a type of external IDE drive for the iMac. Since the iMac's IDE controllers support master and slave configurations, it is possible to support a second hard drive.

This technique used a case similar to the ones designed for external SCSI drives, which had a small power supply and an internal IDE cable that led to an IDE connector in the case. The company also devised an IDE connector faceplate that could be attached to the inside of the ports' compartment, using the area just below the ports (which was covered by a removable metal plate in the revision A and B iMacs). The iMac's original internal IDE cable for the hard drive was replaced with one that supported two connectors, and one connector was attached to the back of the newly added connector faceplate (the other was attached to the internal hard drive). A very sturdy and well-shielded IDE cable was then connected between the connector's faceplate in the iMac's ports compartment and the one on the outside of the external drive. The result was the world's first external IDE drive. iDrives has produced both fully manufactured drives, as well as kits for users who want to place their own IDE drives in the external case.

Adapted IDE Drives

Special external cases are available that adapt an IDE drive to function as an external drive using another interface. The most common external cases of this type convert the IDE drive to use a FireWire or USB interface. As with the iDrives technique, a separate power supply is installed in the external case and used to power the hard drive.

A special adapter is also built into the case. When the IDE drive is installed in the case, the IDE ribbon cable is attached to the adapter on the inside of the case. The adapter then acts to convert the pinouts and signals of the IDE drive to the connection type being used externally to attach the drive to the Mac. A device driver to be installed on the internal hard drive of the Mac using the adapted drive is also included.

Adapting an IDE drive in this way provides a low-cost alternative to producing an external drive dedicated to the newer interface technology that is actually being used to attach it to the Mac. It also provides users with a way to continue to use an IDE drive that they have replaced in their computer for the moderate cost of buying the external case/adapter. This is particularly useful for iMac owners, who need to replace their internal hard drive when upgrading because there is no room inside the iMac's design for a second hard drive.

It is important to note that some of these external case/adapter kits do seem to have compatibility problems with some brands and types of IDE hard drives. If you plan on using such an adapter/case, check with the manufacturer to see if there are any known incompatibilities and buy from a company that offers a good return policy.

In addition to do-it-yourself adapter kits, several companies will simply install IDE drives in these cases and sell them as a way to move excess inventory of IDE drives to users who want USB or FireWire hard drives. When buying a USB or FireWire hard drive, you may want to be wary if it includes IDE in the specs or description, as some of these drives from smaller companies have been known to have compatibility issues.

Types of IDE

The original standard for IDE drives was limited only to hard drives and to relatively low performance. The standard was also limited to hard drives of 520-MB or smaller capacities. Over the years, several advances in IDE technology have spawned variations on the original IDE standard. These variations are reflected primarily in terms of performance, but other issues are involved as well.

IDE, EIDE, and ATAPI

IDE, EIDE, and ATAPI were mentioned at the beginning of this chapter. Each one can be considered to be an IDE technology, and all are often simply called IDE. There are, however, some differences between them that you may want to be aware of, primarily because of some of the advances made in the creation of the EIDE standard.

When it was first created, IDE had one major drawback. Hard drives using an IDE interface were limited to 520-MB capacities. This limitation existed because of the way that non-Mac computers (where IDE was originally developed to be used) reacted to the number of sectors, platters, and cylinders inside of a hard drive. Based on the standards used in such computers and therefore the IDE standard, a hard drive would not be able to have more sectors inside it than could account for 520 MB of data.

To overcome this limitation, the Enhanced IDE (EIDE) standard was created. EIDE used a technique known as *logical block allocation* that allowed drives to be made larger than 520 MB and still use an IDE interface. Logical block allocation, or LBA, allowed a kind of fake or pseudo geometry that supported more sectors and therefore more drive space to be reported to the non-Mac computers of the time.

This is relevant because Macintosh computers using IDE drives require a drive that supports logical block allocation. As you might remember from Chapter 5, when a hard drive is formatted to work with the Mac, allocation blocks are created, and each block will hold a portion of the data that composes a file. This allocation size is determined by the total capacity of the hard drive and the Mac formatting utility used. It is not dependent on the geometry of the drive, and the number of sectors on the drive does not determine the size and number of allocation blocks. Because this style of formatting is similar to logical block allocation, it requires a drive that supports this. In practical terms, a Mac requires the use of an EIDE drive.

Of course, this is pretty much a moot point unless you are dealing with older drives. Almost any hard drive on the market today is well over the 520-MB size limit to begin with and is therefore EIDE and supports LBA. If you are buying a used hard drive or salvaging components from an older PC, however, you will want to be aware of this concern.

In addition to logical block allocation and the ability to allow for larger hard drives, EIDE also opened the way for faster IDE data transfer modes than had been previously supported by the standard.

ATAPI was added to IDE later on. ATAPI stands for ATA Packet Interface and, as mentioned at the beginning of the chapter, is the technology that allows for drives besides hard drives to be connected using IDE. Because much of the control circuitry for IDE drives is placed directly on the drive itself, creating a similar standard for non-hard drive devices, such as CD-ROM drives, required a standard set of commands be created for transferring data packets that was not so device-dependent. ATAPI has become a standard feature of IDE controllers.

PIO Modes

IDE drives were initially designed to transfer data from the hard drive into RAM by working through the processor. This is slower than SCSI, which can directly access system RAM. In order for IDE drives to communicate data to RAM through the processor, a series of instructions for how the processor talked to the drive had to be created. These instructions are known as *programmable input/output*, more commonly, PIO.

The original IDE standard's PIO instructions limited the drive to data transfer rates of 3.3 MB per second. This was slower than even the most basic SCSI standards and was speed-bumped several times to allow for faster data transfer. Including the original PIO instructions, there have been five PIO modes, each defining progressively higher performance. These modes are listed along with the maximum transfer rates they support in Table 13-2.

Different drives have supported the various PIO modes over the years. In order for an IDE hard drive to be used with the Macintosh, it must support PIO Mode 2 or higher. Modes 0 and 1 are simply considered too slow. Again, this eliminates only older hard drives. In fact, almost any hard drive that supports logical block allocation, as described in the previous section, will support at least PIO Mode 3. However, you should be aware of this limitation if you ever come across used hard drives that you want to use.

TABLE 13-2

PIO modes.

PIO Mode	Max. Transfer Rate
0	3.3 MB/second
1	5.2 MB/second
2	8.3 MB/second
3	11.1 MB/second
4	16.6 MB/second

Direct Memory Access

Working through the processor for all hard drive (or other internal drive) access slows down the entire computer because the processor needs to use precious clock cycles controlling access to the hard drive that could be used to run applications. This was one of the biggest advantages of SCSI in the early days of IDE, because the SCSI controller did the work of communicating with the hard drive and transferring data into RAM. Direct Memory Access, or DMA, is a technique that allows IDE drives to access RAM directly, as SCSI drives can, without needing to work through the processor.

DMA modes do not translate to increased drive performance and higher data transfer rates. In fact, if you look at the various DMA modes specified in Table 13-3, you'll notice that the maximum transfer rates of DMA modes are actually the same as those offered through PIO modes. What DMA does offer is less drain on the processor, since fewer clock cycles are needed in transferring data between the drive and RAM. While this doesn't readily improve drive performance, it can boost overall system performance, though there is no real measure of how great that performance boost is. Estimates run from as a little as 1 or 2 percent increases in overall performance to as high as 20 percent.

Ultra ATA

Ultra ATA, which is sometimes called Ultra DMA, was a significant leap forward in IDE performance. Developed in 1997, it gave IDE technology its closest performance to SCSI. Ultra ATA was initially crafted to allow

TABLE 13-3

DMA modes.

DMA Mode		Max. Transfer Rate
Single Word	0	2.1 MB/second
Single Word	1	4.2 MB/second
Single Word	2	8.3 MB/second
Double Word	0	4.2 MB/second
Double Word	1	13.3 MB/second
Double Word	2	16.6 MB/second
Ultra ATA/33		33 MB/second
Ultra ATA/66		66 MB/second

drives to have data transfer rates of up to 33 MB per second—double what IDE had previously supported. More recently, however, Ultra ATA has again been advanced to support rates as high as 66 MB per second. The first of these advances is referred to as Ultra ATA/33 (sometimes simply called Ultra ATA) and the second as Ultra ATA/66.

Ultra ATA requires an IDE controller that supports the Ultra ATA standard, as well as a driver for the drive that also supports Ultra ATA, in order to deliver its potential performance. Ultra ATA drives will function on older IDE controllers or without such device drives, but they will do so without the performance benefits. Similarly, Ultra ATA controllers support older IDE drives.

Beyond requiring the controller support Ultra ATA, the controller must also support the specific Ultra ATA speed variant. For example, an Ultra ATA/66 drive requires an Ultra ATA/66 controller to deliver 66-MB per second performance. Table 13-4 lists the types of IDE that are supported on the Macs covered by this book.

Despite the performance advantages of Ultra ATA and the fact that some current Mac models ship with Ultra ATA drives, Apple does not officially support the use of this standard on the current Mac models. This is because Ultra ATA performance requires a device driver that supports the Ultra ATA command set and transfer rates. Apple's hard drive formatting utilities do not install a driver that is fully compatible with all of the faster Ultra ATA transfer modes. Third-party formatting utilities, such as FWB's Hard Disk ToolKit, do support Ultra ATA and can enable these features on Ultra ATA hard drives that have been installed in the Mac.

If you are using Ultra ATA, you should be aware that the higher-performance modes can actually perform too high for the Mac's built-in IDE

TABLE 13-4

Recent Macs and the IDE types they support.

Mac Model	IDE Types
Original iMac	All non-Ultra ATA types
Power Mac G3 (Blue and White)	Ultra ATA/33
PowerBooks (SCSI - 1999)	All non-Ultra ATA types
iBook	Ultra ATA/33
iMac (Slot-loading and DV)	Ultra ATA/33
Power Mac G4 (PCI graphics card)	Ultra ATA/33
Power Mac G4 (AGP graphics card)	Ultra ATA/66
PowerBook G3 (FireWire—2000)	Ultra ATA/66

controllers to handle. This is particularly true when dealing with early models such as the Blue and White Power Mac G3 (the same ones that do not support master/slave configurations, as described earlier in this chapter). The problem can manifest as an inability to open applications or files or perform other disk-access-related activities. Some hard drives seem more prone to this problem than others. Also, corruption of existing data has been known to occur on such drives.

One way to determine if a drive is experiencing this data-corruption problem is to copy a relatively large self-mounting disk image file to the drive. These are generally used by Apple for distributing software updates and have an .smi file extension. Because these disk images automatically verify their own data before mounting themselves, they will alert you if that data has become corrupted. Figure 13-6 shows the icon of a self-mounting disk image and the verifying data dialog that is displayed when one if mounted. If the file is corrupted on a drive that is newly installed or formatted to provide Ultra ATA performance, then the drive is experiencing corruption as a result of the Ultra ATA mode being used.

Reducing the performance of the hard drive in question to either a lower Ultra ATA or a more traditional IDE transfer mode may correct the

Figure 13-6
Because a self-mounting image file such as this one verifies its data when mounting, it can be used to test for hard drive data-corruption problems.

Open Transport 2.6 Update.smi

problem. This can be accomplished by using the same formatting utility that you used to enable the higher-performance modes.

If you are using both Ultra ATA drives and older IDE drive types, you will want to keep them on separate controllers. Ultra ATA drives will be slowed down significantly if they are placed on the same controller as an older IDE drive. This is because only one of the two drives on an IDE controller can transfer data with the processor at a given time. Since there are several times when the Mac must query both drives on an IDE channel, the slower drive will cause both drives to be slowed down.

Installing an IDE Drive

Installing an IDE drive is a very simple process that is covered in greater detail in other sections of this book where specific drive types are discussed (Chapter 5, for example, covers installation of both SCSI and IDE hard drives in the various Macintosh computers). However, a brief overview of the process is presented here for convenience.

First, if you are installing a CD-ROM, DVD-ROM, tape, or removable-media drive, install any drivers that came with the device. Then shut down the computer. Next, determine which IDE controller you will be using. Set the jumpers on the device to either master or slave drive designations, depending on whether the drive will be used alone or with another drive on the same IDE controller. Once the jumpers are set, mount the drive in the appropriate bay. If this is a hard drive, use the appropriate mounting brackets. For CD/DVD-ROM drives or removable-media drives, you should also mount the drive in the appropriate internal brackets, which should already be attached to the computer's case.

Once the drive is securely mounted in the drive bay, attach the 40-pin IDE ribbon cable's connector to the drive's connector. As discussed earlier, IDE cables traditionally have two connectors for drives, and it makes no difference which connector is used with which drive. Attach the power connector. There should be plenty of power connectors in the case of a Power Mac for additional drives (if not, a "Y" splitter power cable, as described in Chapter 11, can be used). Make certain that you insert both the ribbon cable and power connectors in the appropriate orientation. These should install easily only in one direction, but use caution because they could be forced in upside down.

Now restart the Mac. If the drive installed was a hard drive, it may be recognized and formatted when the Mac starts up, or the Mac may say the disk is unrecognizable and ask if you want to initialize it. If neither occurs, you will most likely need a formatting utility such as Apple's Drive Setup (which can format several, though not all, IDE hard drives) or a third-party formatting utility such as FWB's Hard Disk ToolKit. If you wish to take full advantage of an Ultra ATA drive, you will want to use a third-party tool as described earlier. It is a good idea to run a formatting tool to test the drive and use formatting and/or partitioning options even if the Mac recognizes and formats the drive at startup.

If the drive is a CD/DVD-ROM, tape, or removable-media drive, you can verify that it is recognized by using the Apple System Profiler or utilities that may have come with the drive. Assuming the drive is recognized, you should be able to use it as described in the manual that came with it.

IDE Advantages

There are two big advantages to using IDE drives in the current Macs. The first is cost. IDE drives are noticeably less expensive than similarly rated SCSI drives. Considering the performance of Ultra ATA drives, there isn't a particularly great advantage to buying a low-end or mid-range SCSI drive for many uses compared to an IDE drive. The exceptions are high-end uses such server machines, desktop publishing and graphic arts work, and professional multimedia production.

The other big advantage, which is also cost-related, is that Macs ship with support for IDE drives out of the factory. SCSI drives require users to purchase an additional PCI card or PC Card in order to use them. Granted, SCSI has several other uses and advantages, but if you are looking solely for a larger hard drive, a second hard drive, or other internal drive, IDE could very well be a better option. Similarly, there is no SCSI option for internal drives on the PowerBook computers and no SCSI option at all for the iBook and most iMac computers (the revision A and B iMacs are the only exception because of their mezzanine slot, described in Chapter 8, and internal SCSI drives are not an option for them).

IDE also offers the benefit of being simpler than SCSI in that there are no ID or termination issues. Although this is only a small advantage, it is one that relatively inexperienced Mac owners will appreciate.

Even at its slowest, IDE is still faster than USB. It is also an internal technology, however, which does separate its uses from those of USB. On the other hand, IDE is generally slower than FireWire. In practice, FireWire is also an external feature. However, an internal FireWire connector is included in the recent Power Mac models, which means FireWire could eventually give IDE a run for its money as an internal drive technology. Certainly, FireWire is as easy to configure (if not easier) and can support up to 63 devices.

IDE Expansion Cards

For Macs with PCI slots, it is also possible to add additional IDE controllers via a PCI card. The advantages include supporting newer and faster IDE types and providing controllers for additional IDE drives. A growing number of IDE expansion cards are on the market, and their most common use is to support the faster Ultra ATA/66 standard on Power Macs that have IDE controllers that are incapable of providing such support.

Interestingly enough, the Mac recognizes IDE drives that are attached to an IDE controller card as SCSI devices. One of the advantages of this unusual feature is that IDE drives attached to an IDE PCI card can be combined to create a software-based RAID-1 disk mirror. RAID-1, as discussed in Chapters 5 and 39, mirrors all drive contents to two hard drives, creating a complete backup in case one of the drives should suffer a hardware failure and be rendered unusable.

Troubleshooting IDE Drives

Following are a couple of common problems and their solutions.

A CD/DVD-ROM or Removable-Media Drive Does Not Mount Any Disks or Cartridges

First check to be certain that the driver software for the drive is installed. With third-party CD/DVD-ROM drives, you will usually need a third-party driver such as FWB's CD ToolKit installed.

If the driver software is installed, use the Apple System Profiler to determine if the drive is being recognized by the computer. If not, check to be sure the drive is connected properly to both the IDE ribbon cable and the power connector. Also, check to make sure that the drive's jumpers are set properly (master if it is the only drive on the cable/controller, slave if another device is set to master, or master if another device is set to slave).

A Hard Drive Is Installed but Not Recognized at Startup

Use the Apple System Profiler to see if the drive is recognized at all. If the drive is recognized but not mounted, it may be formatted to not mount at startup. Try using a hard drive mounting utility to mount the drive (and to test for problems with the drive itself and not the IDE interface). The drive may also not yet be formatted, in which case you'll need to use a formatting utility as described in Chapter 5.

If the drive is not recognized at all, double-check to be certain that it is connected and powered properly and that the jumpers are set appropriately (master if it is the only drive on the cable/controller, slave if another device is set to master, or master if another device is set to slave).

FireWire

FireWire (also known as iLink and IEEE 1394) is a technology designed by Apple that has been embraced as an industry standard on both Mac and non-Mac computer platforms, as well as other home electronics devices. FireWire combines the ease of being hot pluggable and self-configuring, which makes USB so simple to use, with data transfer performance better than that of most SCSI types. FireWire devices and ports are identified by the logo in Figure 14-10.

How FireWire Works

FireWire is a high-speed digital interface capable of transfer rates as high as 50 MB/second. This makes it one of the fastest interface technologies currently available. FireWire devices can be attached to the Mac in a daisy-chain fashion, with one device plugged into the device before it (like external SCSI devices), or hubs can be used to attach multiple devices to the Mac, and each device can support its own chain. Unlike SCSI, FireWire is completely self-configuring and self-terminating, making it far easier to use. When attaching a device, you simply add it to the chain; you do not need to be concerned with setting any ID numbers for the device or worrying about whether the chain needs to be terminated at any point.

FireWire supports up to 63 devices connected to the computer. These devices can be both internal and external, although as of this writing there are only external FireWire devices on the market. The Power Mac G4 models with an AGP graphics card (known by the codename "Sawtooth") contain an internal FireWire port near the edge of the case, as indicated in Figure 14-2.

FireWire is also hot pluggable. This means that you do not need to shut down the Mac when adding or removing devices. You do not even need to put the Mac into sleep mode. Simply attach the device, and

Figure 14-1
The FireWire logo identifies FireWire ports, cables, and devices.

Figure 14-2
The AGP graphics card G4s have an internal FireWire port.

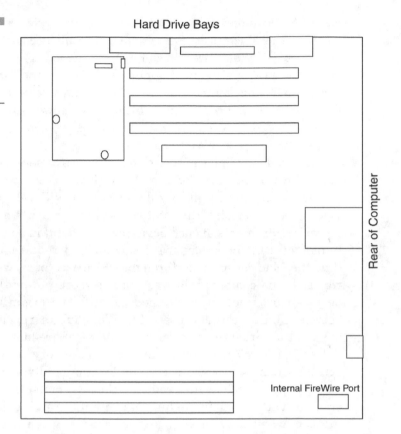

assuming driver software for it is installed, it will be recognized and available for use at that time.

FireWire Bus Power

FireWire is a powered bus. This means that devices can receive the power that they require in order to operate directly from the Mac's FireWire ports without needing an external power supply. FireWire provides a higher level of power than USB does. Many FireWire hard drives, as well as other devices, will rely entirely on the FireWire bus power. These devices provide the ability of easy transport and sharing between multiple computers, because you do not need to carry cables or bricklike power supplies with the device.

However, it is possible to attach too many devices that require power to a single FireWire port. If the Mac displays a message saying there is not enough power for a device to function, it is because there are too many FireWire devices connected drawing their power from the FireWire ports on the Macintosh. This problem can also occur without any error messages where a device will simply not function. You can sometimes alleviate this problem by moving devices between the Mac's two FireWire ports or by using devices that have their own power supplies. Additionally, FireWire hubs and repeaters with their own power supplies (independent of the Mac's power supply) can alleviate this problem, as they can also provide power to the FireWire bus.

You can determine whether or not a device or series of devices is capable of functioning solely on the Mac's FireWire bus power by adding the power requirements of any devices that will rely on FireWire bus together to determine the total power requirements of the devices. The power requirements of each device can be found in the device's specifications. You can then compare this combined requirement to the power that the Mac can provide through a FireWire port, which is at best 15 watts. If the combined devices require more power than the FireWire port can provide, you will need to shift the organization of devices between multiple ports, use a FireWire hub or repeater, or use fewer devices that draw their power from the FireWire bus.

Several FireWire devices include the ability to operate using the FireWire bus as a power source and to optionally work with their own power supply. Such devices combine the ease of using FireWire as a powered bus with the ability to function without draining that bus in order to function when many devices are attached or when used with a portable Mac running on battery power. A few FireWire devices can also function with rechargeable batteries of their own, making them extremely attractive to portable Mac owners. Some of these actually use the same type of rechargeable battery as a PowerBook, which provides a useful crossover of battery use and ease of finding additional batteries for the device.

FireWire Ports, Cables, and Chains

FireWire uses a six-pin connector and a relatively thin cable. The six-pin connector is used on the FireWire ports of the Mac, as well as the ports of most FireWire peripherals. The connector, shown in Figure 14-3, is shaped like a rectangle with one of the narrow sides rounded instead of flat. The rounded edge makes it impossible to insert a FireWire cable in any orientation other than the correct one. Some FireWire connectors lock into the FireWire port. If you are using such a connector, do not try to forcibly disconnect it. Squeeze gently on the sides of the connector to release it before pulling it out of the port.

Figure 14-3
FireWire ports on any Mac or peripheral resemble these from the Power Mac G4.

As discussed later in this chapter, FireWire can be used to attach digital video devices, such as camcorders, to the Mac. When FireWire is being used to attach a digital video device, the connector on the digital video device will use a different four-pin interface. To use these devices with a FireWire-equipped Mac, you will need to use a special six-pin to four-pin FireWire adapter cable. These adapters are included by Apple with FireWire-equipped Macs. The four-pin connector on the cable and digital video devices is more fragile than the six-pin connector used for the Mac and other peripherals. You should take care to ensure that you have properly lined up the cable and that you do not force the connector in order to avoid damage to the cable or to the device.

FireWire supports cable lengths up to 14 feet between individual devices. As with SCSI and IDE, the reason for a cable length restriction is that electrical noise can become mixed in with the data being transmitted along a cable. The longer the cable, the more chance for noise to get mixed in with the signal, rendering the cable unusable for data transmission.

FireWire devices can be connected in a daisy chain, as SCSI devices can be. To facilitate this, FireWire devices have two ports (which are functionally identical). You connect one port of a device to the computer and the next device to the second port on the first device and so on to form a chain of FireWire devices. FireWire chains are limited to no more than 17 devices or, more accurately, 16 segments of cable between the last device in the chain and host computer. Should you wish to use more than 17 FireWire devices on one of your Mac's FireWire ports, you will need to use a device such as a FireWire hub to create a "tree" of FireWire devices. Figure 14-4 shows an example of a FireWire chain and a FireWire tree.

FireWire Hubs and Tree Configurations   FireWire hubs connect to the FireWire port of a Mac and provide additional ports, much like USB or Ethernet hubs do. Since FireWire devices are designed to be daisy chained with one device being connected to the device before it, FireWire hubs are not a necessary piece of hardware unless you wish to have more than 17 devices connected to a given FireWire port on the Mac. If you wish to connect more devices than can be put into a single FireWire chain, you will need to use a hub to design a tree arrangement of multiple FireWire chains. To create a tree of FireWire devices, attach a FireWire hub to either the Mac's FireWire port or to the FireWire port of a device that is attached to the Mac. Then attach individual FireWire devices or chains of FireWire devices to each port of the FireWire hub. Each of these chains will become a branch of the tree. You are still limited to a chain of FireWire devices containing no more than 17 devices. Also make sure that the cables from one branch of a tree do not connect to any other point in the tree, as this will create a loop (illustrated in Figure 14-5) that will prevent FireWire devices from being recognized.

Using a hub to create a FireWire tree can also help you organize devices more efficiently Since you can attach a separate chain to each port of a FireWire hub, you can group FireWire devices according to use. You could have all your hard drives in a chain on one branch of the tree, all your digital video devices on another branch, and your scanners and similar devices on yet a third branch. Each chain will be kept smaller and easier to configure or diagnose problems with.

FireWire hubs can be bought as stand-alone devices, but some other

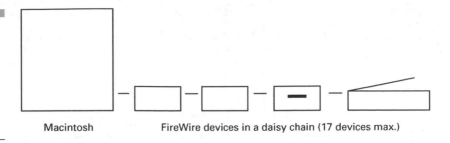

Figure 14-4
FireWire devices can
be attached in
a chain of up to 17
devices or, by using
a FireWire hub,
a tree with multiple
chains/branches.

Macintosh

FireWire devices in a daisy chain (17 devices max.)

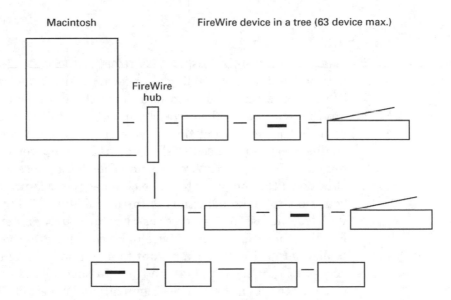

Macintosh

FireWire device in a tree (63 device max.)

FireWire
hub

FireWire devices may have more than two FireWire ports and therefore can function as a hub. Such devices can include hard drives, printers, and repeaters, among others.

One further important advantage of using a FireWire hub is that it provides an independent power supply for any devices that use FireWire bus power to function. This helps ensure that all FireWire devices or chains attached to a FireWire hub will have enough power to function and will not drain power from the Mac's FireWire ports.

Figure 14-5
If a cable from one branch of a FireWire tree is connected to a device in another branch of the tree, as shown, the devices in the tree will not be recognized properly.

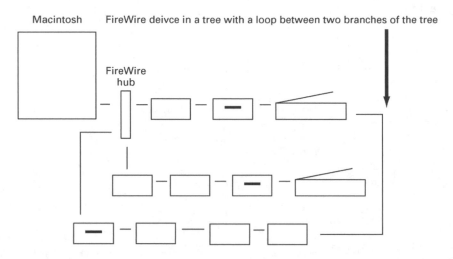

FIREWIRE HUBS WHEN USING LESS THAN 17 DEVICES. FireWire hubs can also be helpful when dealing with fewer than 17 devices in other ways. When devices are connected in a daisy chain, disconnecting one device anywhere in the middle of the chain will disconnect all the devices in the chain attached beyond that device. This is not a concern with SCSI chains because you need to shut down the computer in order to disconnect any devices. FireWire, on the other hand, does not require you to shut down the computer to make changes to a chain. This means that if you want to make adjustments in the middle of a FireWire chain, you will lose access to any devices that are further down the chain. A FireWire hub allows each device to be connected to the hub rather than to another device. When you want to disconnect a single device, you lose access to that device alone and not to several that might have been attached to it in a chain. This organizational aspect of FireWire hubs can also be helpful if devices need to be placed in different physical locations.

FireWire Repeaters FireWire repeaters are devices that extend the usable cable length of a chain of FireWire devices. A repeater is a device that is plugged into the middle of a FireWire chain. It receives the transmitted data from the devices on one side of it. Once the repeater has received the data, it uses its own electrical power to rebroadcast that signal to the devices on the other side of it. The result is a stronger, clearer signal that is free of any noise. Since the signal is essentially re-created at a repeater, it can travel further along a chain of devices without being degraded. This allows you to extend the length of cabling used in a FireWire chain.

A FireWire repeater will extend the FireWire chain by 15 feet. Many powered FireWire devices include a built-in repeater that allows for 15 feet of cable between each FireWire device without restrictions on the overall length of the entire FireWire chain. You can use multiple repeaters in between FireWire devices to extend the length of cabling between individual devices to as much as 236 feet.

FireWire Performance

FireWire's specifications include three standard data transfer rates: 100 Mbps, 200 Mbps, and 400 Mbps. Note that these speeds are megabit per second and not megabytes per second. A speed of 400 Mbps is equal to 50 MB/second (200 Mbps is equal to 25 MB/second, and 100 Mbps is equal to 12.5 MB/second). Although the Mac's FireWire ports support all three transfer rates, individual devices may only support the slower 100-Mbps or 200-Mbps rates. While these devices will perform slower than other devices that support the full 400 Mbps, they will not slow down other devices that are capable of faster transfer rates, provided that they are placed "downstream" or further toward the end of a chain than higher-performance devices.

FireWire also supports *isynchronous data transfer*. Isynchronous transfer means that if a device requires a specific amount of bandwidth on the FireWire bus, that amount of bandwidth can be reserved for the functioning of that device. This ensures that the device will always be able to transfer data at the speed that it requires. This is one of the features that makes FireWire so ideally suited for dealing with digital video because it ensures that the digital video stream will always transfer at the rate needed in order for the video to be received, captured, or displayed, without errors, jerkiness, or other problems.

FireWire and PowerBooks

The most recent PowerBook models (those released in February of 2000) include two built-in FireWire ports, shown in Figure 14-6. This allows FireWire to function almost exactly as it would on a desktop Mac. Any earlier PowerBook models did not include FireWire ports (instead, they included SCSI ports). For some earlier PowerBooks, it is possible to add FireWire by means of a PC Card.

TABLE 14-1

FireWire performance compared to other interface options.

Interface	Speed
FireWire	50 MB/second
Ultra3 Wide SCSI	160 MB/second
Ultra2 Wide SCSI	80 MB/second
Ultra3 SCSI	80 MB/second
Ultra2 SCSI	40 MB/second
Ultra Wide SCSI	40 MB/second
Ultra SCSI	20 MB/second
Fast and Wide SCSI	20 MB/second
Fast or Wide SCSI	10 MB/second
SCSI-1	5 MB/second
Ultra ATA/66 (IDE)	66 MB/second
Ultra ATA/33 (IDE)	33 MB/second
IDE	16.6 MB/second*
USB	1.5 MB/second

*16.6 MB/second is the highest-possible transfer rate for IDE drives that are not Ultra-ATA. There are also lower performance IDE modes (see Chapter 13 for details).

Figure 14-6
The FireWire ports on the PowerBook models from February 2000.

FireWire PC Cards

Any PowerBook that supports a CardBus-compliant PC Card slot (this includes the PowerBook G3 models with a SCSI port and bronze keyboard that are covered by this book, as well as the earlier PowerBook G3

Series models that are not covered in this book) can make use of one of several FireWire PC Cards on the market. A number of FireWire PC Cards are available, and these cards all function similarly and offer roughly comparable performance. Figure 14-7 shows one such card from Newer Technologies.

FireWire PC Cards install as easily as any PC Card and provide one or two FireWire ports. The ports on these cards can be used for accessing FireWire drives and devices, as well as digital video devices, as easily as a built-in FireWire port. While these ports will function as normal FireWire ports, they do not provide power to the FireWire bus. This means that any devices that rely on the FireWire bus power to operate will not function unless a powered device such as a hub or repeater is attached to the FireWire chain.

You will also want to be aware of some other issues when using FireWire PC Cards. One is that you should use the Energy Saver control panel to set the PowerBook so that it will not go to sleep automatically. You can do this by moving the slider labeled "Put computer to sleep whenever it's inactive for" to Never (the far right of the window). This is because the PowerBook can lose a video image if it goes to sleep while importing digital video through the FireWire PC Card. If the PowerBook goes to sleep while importing video and you do lose the video image, closing and reopening the log/capture window of the application you are using to import the video stream may resolve the problem.

Another issue to be aware of is that you should not try ejecting the FireWire PC Card while any application that works with digital video streams is running. Ejecting the card by using the Finder's Put Away command or by dragging the card's icon to the Trash while such applications are running, regardless of whether or not they are actually trans-

Figure 14-7
The FireWire 2 Go PC Card provides FireWire ports to earlier PowerBooks. (Photo courtesy of Newer Technologies)

ferring digital video through the card, will most likely cause the Mac to freeze and require a forced restart.

FireWire and Battery Power

FireWire devices that draw power from the FireWire bus are supported on the PowerBook models with built-in FireWire ports. However, these PowerBooks provide enough power to support only a single such device. This is because of the demand on battery power that such devices make. Even the one device that can be powered by the PowerBooks' FireWire ports can significantly impact battery life and performance. You should avoid using any FireWire devices that draw power from the FireWire bus with a PowerBook running on battery power.

If you must use FireWire devices that draw power from the PowerBook's FireWire ports while running on battery power, try to do all tasks requiring the device at one time and to disconnect the device as soon as you are done with these tasks. This will help minimize the time you have the device attached and draining power. Whenever the device is not needed, it should be disconnected.

FireWire Target Disk Mode

As mentioned in the earlier chapter regarding SCSI, PowerBooks with SCSI ports included a feature known as Target Disk Mode that allowed the PowerBook to be attached to another Mac as though it were an external SCSI device. This caused the PowerBook's internal hard drive to be mounted on the other Mac's desktop as an external SCSI hard drive that could be used for easy and fast data transfers between the computers. When Apple transitioned from a built-in SCSI port to built-in FireWire ports on the PowerBook, they transitioned Target Disk Mode to function over FireWire instead of SCSI.

FireWire Target Disk Mode functions in much the same way as SCSI Target Disk Mode. The PowerBook is started up in a special manner and is then attached to another Mac that supports FireWire. Its internal hard drive is then recognized as an external FireWire hard drive. This makes for easy and extremely fast transfers of files between the two computers. FireWire Target Disk Mode is actually easier to use than SCSI. It does not require any special adapter cables. Also, because FireWire is self-configuring and hot pluggable, you do not need to shut down the other Mac or be concerned about any ID issues as you do with SCSI Target Disk Mode.

In order to use FireWire Target Disk Mode, the PowerBook must be one of the models released in February 2000 with built-in FireWire ports. Earlier models with FireWire ports on a PC Card will not work. Also, several non-Apple hard drive formatting utilities seem to have compatibility issues and may prevent FireWire Target Disk Mode from functioning if they are used to format the PowerBook's hard drive. The other Mac to which the PowerBook will be connected must have Mac OS 8.6 or higher installed, as well as version 2.3 or higher of the FireWire Enabler and FireWire Support extensions. Mac OS 9.0.4 is recommended. The PowerBook must also be the only FireWire device attached to the other Mac.

In order to establish the connection and use FireWire Target Disk Mode, first, shut down the PowerBook. Then use a FireWire cable to attach it to the other Mac's FireWire port (it should be the only FireWire device attached). Press the PowerBook's Power Key, and then immediately hold down the T key on the keyboard. The PowerBook screen should then display a FireWire logo instead of the Macintosh startup sequence, and the hard drive should mount as an external FireWire drive on the other Mac's desktop. At this point you can use it as you would any such hard drive and transfer files at FireWire speed.

When you are finished transferring files, drag the PowerBook's hard drive icon to the Trash or select it and use the Finder's Put Away command to unmount the drive. Then, simply press the PowerBook's Power button to shut it off. Once the PowerBook is turned off, disconnect the FireWire cable. You can then restart the PowerBook normally for regular use.

Connecting and Disconnecting a FireWire Device

Adding a FireWire device to a Mac is a very easy process. The first step is to install any drivers or other software that came with the device. The next step is to restart the Mac so that any extensions or control panels installed for the device are loaded as part of the Mac OS at startup.

Once the Mac has been restarted, you plug the FireWire device into a wall outlet, surge protector, or power strip if it requires its own power supply. Devices that draw power from the FireWire bus obviously don't need to be plugged in. You then attach the device to either the FireWire port on your Mac or hub or to the second FireWire port on the last device in a FireWire chain. The device should now be recognized by the Mac and available for use.

When you are done using the device, you can simply disconnect it. However, be certain that the Mac is not actively using the device before disconnecting it, as disconnecting a device while the Mac is actively accessing it can cause damage or corruption to files stored on the device (if it is a drive of some sort) or on the Mac's internal hard drive. Several background processes or applications may be communicating with the device without you realizing it. For FireWire hard drives, use the Finder's Put Away command (or drag the drive's icon to the Trash) to unmount the drive before disconnecting it. If any applications are still accessing the drive or if any files on the drive are still open, the Mac will refuse to put the drive away. Similarly, with removable-media drives, eject any disks in the drive before disconnecting it. For other devices, check to see if any currently running applications (including the Finder) are performing any tasks that might involve the device before disconnecting it. If in doubt, quit the application before disconnecting the device (you can always relaunch the application after the device has been disconnected).

Typical Uses for FireWire

FireWire can be used for several different types of high-speed devices that require high data transfer rates, most commonly hard drives. It can also be used for directly transferring digital video streams from digital video devices such as digital camcorders. The following sections look at the common nondigital video uses for the FireWire interface. Digital video and FireWire is discussed later in this chapter, as well as in Chapter 27.

Hard Drives

Aside from digital video purposes (discussed later in this chapter), the most common use of the FireWire interface is for hard drives. This makes sense given the incredible performance FireWire can potentially deliver for data transfer. FireWire hard drives are available from quite a large number of manufacturers and function much like any other hard drive. When the drive is first used, it may need to be formatted. This generally requires the use of a third-party formatting utility (typically included with the drive). You can partition the drive or use any other formatting options that are supported by the utility you are using to format it.

When a FireWire hard drive is attached to the Mac, it will mount and its icon will appear on the desktop immediately (if the drive is partitioned, icons will appear for each partition). You work with the drive as you would any other drive. When disconnecting a FireWire hard drive without shutting the Mac down, you should unmount it first by either dragging its icon to the Trash or using the Finder's Put Away command (a partitioned drive should have all of its partitions unmounted before being disconnected).

Some hard drives offer both a USB and FireWire interface. These drives are good if you are in a situation where you need to share data with computers that have FireWire ports as well as those that only include USB ports (such as the original iMac or the iBook). When being used as USB devices, they will, of course, be subject to the much slower data transfer rates of any USB device.

Bootable FireWire Drives   Some FireWire drives can be used as a startup drive. In order to function as a startup device, the FireWire drive will need to be designed so that it supports being accessed by the Mac in the very beginning of the startup process. This means that the code to recognize and control the drive must be stored in ROM on the drive rather than as an extension that is loaded during the start up process. If a drive is bootable (meaning you can start up from it), this will be included in the drive's specifications.

In order to function as a startup drive for a Mac, the Mac must also be designed with support for starting up from a FireWire drive. This requires that the code to access FireWire devices be present in the boot ROM on the Mac's motherboard. If the needed ROM code isn't available, the drive would require a device driver that would be loaded as an extension much later in the startup process (which is described in Chapter 37). FireWire booting is a relatively new feature for the Mac and, so far, is only an option for the PowerBook models introduced in February 2000 with built-in FireWire ports and more recent Mac models with a boot ROM version 3.22f1 or newer. If you are using a desktop Mac, you can use the Apple System Profiler to locate which boot ROM version is built into the G4's motherboard (as shown in Figure 14-8) and determine if it supports starting up from FireWire drives.

In order for a FireWire hard drive to function as a startup drive, you will first need to install any drivers that were included with it onto your

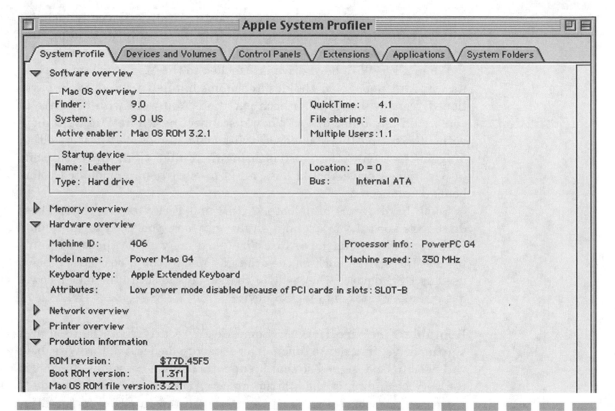

Figure 14-8 The Production Overview section of the Apple System Profiler displays a Mac's boot ROM version. In the case of this G4, it is not new enough to support FireWire booting.

Mac's internal hard drive and connect the FireWire drive. Once the FireWire hard drive's icon is available on the Mac's desktop, you will need to install a copy of the Mac OS onto the drive. Once this is complete, you should be able to start up from it by using the Startup Disk control panel to select it as your start up device.

FireWire RAID   Chapter 5 introduced the concept of RAID (redundant array of independent disks) where multiple hard drives could be tied together to function as a single drive. As discussed there, RAID arrays can be used to provide much increased data transfer rates by storing data in segments across multiple drives in a process known as *striping*. When an array is striped, pieces of data are simultaneously stored on each drive in the array. Because each drive needs to do only a fraction of the process of storing and accessing data, the performance of the array acting as a single hard drive is far higher than an individual drive could afford.

FireWire hard drives can be combined into RAID arrays. Unlike SCSI-based RAID arrays, FireWire arrays are currently limited to only external drives. These drives can be tied together using a special external FireWire case that includes connections for all the drives in the array. This case is then connected to the FireWire port of the Mac, and the drives attached to it are tied into a single array using your RAID method of choice. The first FireWire RAID solution developed by VST is extremely portable and can be powered by a traditional PowerBook battery. FireWire arrays are also more easily configured and involve less hardware-based setup issues than SCSI or IDE arrays. These arrays can then be attached externally to any FireWire Mac, where they will function as a single very fast drive.

Adapted FireWire Drives   There are some special external FireWire cases on the market that can adapt an internal IDE hard drive to function as an external hard drive using a FireWire interface. These cases include an independent power supply that accepts a standard power cord and provides a single internal molex power connector that is used to power the drive. The case also includes a built-in IDE-to-FireWire interface adapter. On the inside of the case, this adapter has a standard IDE interface to which the IDE ribbon cable is attached. Externally, the adapter uses a standard FireWire cable interface.

These FireWire adapter cases allow you to continue to use an IDE drive if you upgrade the internal drive in your Mac. This is a good method for owners of the iMac DV models, which support FireWire but lack the internal space for more than one hard drive. It is also an option if you are already using the maximum number of internal IDE drives in a Power Mac model and wish to make use of your earlier hard drives.

Because many IDE drives do not support data transfer rates as high as FireWire, the drive may continue to operate at only the performance level of IDE and not FireWire. If you want a hard drive that offers the performance advantages of FireWire, you should choose an actual FireWire drive. Additionally, some FireWire/IDE drive adapter kits do have compatibility issues with a number of IDE drive types, and you should check with the manufacturer of the FireWire adapter/case regarding the specific IDE drive model that you plan to use in the case before buying it.

While the cost benefit over buying a new FireWire hard drive is good if you already have an IDE drive that you want to continue to use, it is not as cost-effective when looking to purchase a new external hard drive. This is because using an adapter with a new IDE hard drive will add about $100 to the cost of the IDE hard drive. This brings the cost near that of an actual FireWire hard drive. Given the potential lower performance and compatibility concerns, a true FireWire drive is a better choice for the price.

Recordable CD/DVD Drives

Drives used for recording custom CD-ROM and DVD-ROM disks have traditionally been connected using SCSI because SCSI supports faster transfer rates. However, FireWire affords equal transfer rates to many SCSI types, as well as an easier-to-use interface. Several companies have begun to offer recordable/rewritable CD drives (CD-RW) and recordable/rewritable DVD drives (DVD-RAM) using a FireWire interface.

One of the advantages beyond simple performance of using these interfaces for recordable CD and DVD drives is FireWire's support for isynchronous data transfers. One of the potential pitfalls of both of these types of drives has been that they require that the data be consistently transferred from the Mac to the device at a constant speed. This is because these devices record data by using a laser to melt (or burn) the data in specific patterns on the disk. The laser is continuously moving, and if the data is not being transmitted in a constant stream equal to the speed that the laser is moving, the disk will not be burned properly and will be useless. Isynchronous data transfer can help to ensure that there is consistent bandwidth for the data to be streamed at a constant rate regardless of any other activity on the FireWire bus.

See Chapters 16 and 17 for additional information on the process of creating a CD-ROM using CD-RW and DVD-ROM using DVD-RAM technologies, respectively.

FireWire Scanners

With Apple's transition away from SCSI in favor of USB and FireWire, scanners have transitioned to both of these new technologies. While consumer and mid-range scanners are available in USB models, FireWire is used for more high-end, professional scanners. FireWire offers significant performance boosts over USB for scanners because it has literally over 30 times the bandwidth for the scanner to transmit data through. This is primarily an issue for scanners that function at resolutions of 1200 dpi and higher.

Removable-Media Drives

While USB is the interface of choice for most consumer-oriented removable-media drives such as the Zip and SuperDisk drives, almost any removable-media drive is slowed down by the limited performance available through the USB interface. As a result, many higher-end removable-media drives such as the magneto-optical, Orb, tape, and Jaz drives are not suited for use with USB because they are designed to rapidly transfer and store much larger quantities of data. These drives, which initially used faster SCSI interfaces, are much better suited to using a FireWire interface.

FireWire allows these drives to realize their full potential and still retain an easy-to-use interface that is hot pluggable and self-configuring. Although higher-end drives benefit the most from FireWire as an interface over USB, just about any removable-media drive will provide faster performance over FireWire than USB, and there are FireWire Zip drives on the market.

If you wish to use one of the more powerful removable-media drive types (which are discussed and compared in detail in Chapter 18), you will want to consider FireWire as an option. The primary alternative is SCSI, which also offers good performance but does so at the added cost of a SCSI card and with the added hassles of device ID and termination concerns.

Printers

Most consumer and mid-range printers today use USB ports to connect to a Mac. High-end and specialty printers being used to print extremely large or complex documents easily benefit from a FireWire interface. This is because these printers receive larger amounts of data than can be quickly or conveniently transferred over USB. FireWire enables the data to be transmitted to the printer at a much faster rate, much as older laser printer models used a SCSI interface because it was faster than serial ports.

Digital Cameras

The recent digital camera models on the market tend to offer resolutions of more than three million pixels, and in the near future, those resolutions will likely double or even triple. This provides incredibly true-life image quality that is almost indistinguishable from a traditional photo when printed, even at high magnification. As powerful as these image qualities are, the sheer number of pixels makes these files increasingly large.

As digital cameras offer higher and higher resolutions, it takes longer and longer to transfer the stored images to a computer. USB is currently the interface of choice for consumer and professional digital cameras, but even with today's digital cameras, it can be a very slow way to transfer even a moderate amount of high-quality images. With future digital cameras offering the ability to store larger file collections and higher-quality images, FireWire will almost certainly replace USB for high-end digital cameras. Some digital video editing applications (such as Edit DV by Digital Origen) supporting FireWire are even beginning to support capturing images directly from a digital still camera.

FireWire SCSI Adapters

When Apple began shipping Macs with built-in FireWire ports, they stopped shipping Macs with built-in SCSI ports. As a result, several companies have made adapters for connecting SCSI devices to the current Macs. While USB-SCSI adapters are more common, there are also companies that produce FireWire-SCSI adapters.

FireWire adapters offer one distinct advantage over USB adapters: sheer speed. USB is slow, and that slowness prevents SCSI devices being used with an adapter from delivering even a fraction of the performance they may be capable of. FireWire is as fast as all but the very fastest SCSI types, and it easily allows for performance equal to what would be delivered with a native SCSI port.

As with USB adapters, you should be aware that FireWire-SCSI adapters tend to suffer from compatibility issues with various devices and are most compatible with hard drives. There may also be issues with termination, as these adapters do not provide internal termination or terminating power for a SCSI chain. You will most likely need to terminate both the first and last SCSI devices attached to the adapter.

If you are using a Power Mac or PowerBook computer with FireWire ports, it is best to consider an actual SCSI PCI card (or PC Card for PowerBooks). This card will inexpensively provide native SCSI support with fewer compatibility concerns. Owners of the iMac DV computer models, which do not offer any other SCSI options, should be the only Mac owners who seriously consider using a FireWire adapter. If you do choose a FireWire adapter, be sure to check for compatibility with the specific SCSI devices you will be using before purchasing.

FireWire and Digital Video

FireWire's power as a peripheral interface technology is impressive because of its ease of use and its incredible data transfer speeds. However, FireWire also offers another powerful advantage: the ability to directly transfer digital video data from a digital video device.

What Is Digital Video?

Digital video (also called simply DV) is a video format developed during the mid-1990s. As its name implies, DV stores audio and video digitally. This contrasts with the analog video devices that have been extremely common in home electronics markets, such as the VHS-style VCR and camcorder.

Analog video devices work by recording both video and audio signals as electrical signals that are recorded as waves. The high and low points of these waves determine the values of light and dark, coloring, sharpness, and sounds. These waves can be distorted by electromagnetic interference during or after recording, and the accuracy of these waves will degrade over time. DV, on the other hand, records data as combinations of discrete 1s and 0s in the same manner that audio CDs and computer audio/video files such as QuickTime movies are recorded. As a result, digital video provides much more accurate rendering of objects, colors, movement, contrast, and sound that is not affected by interference. Digital video also stores additional data for each frame, which allows the recording to include higher-quality renderings of recorded video.

DV also allows for perfect copying of a digital video recording. When you make a copy of an analog video recording, you lose a generation of quality in the recording. This is because the copy you make records the video in waves as the original copy did. However, just as the initial recording allowed for inaccuracies and interference in the wave recording, the second recording allows these discrepancies to occur again. And this is on top of any such inaccuracies in the original recording. If you make a third-generation copy (a copy of the copy), the quality degrades further. Since digital video is a precise series of 1s and 0s, there is no loss of quality anymore than there would be in copying a word-processing file, because each 1 and 0 is copied to be exactly the same as the original.

The fact that digital video can be copied just like any other data or file by a computer means that it can be directly copied to a Mac's hard drive with no loss of quality in the conversion process from digital video tape to a file that you can work with in a video editing application. The same holds true for exporting a digital video file from the Mac's hard drive to a digital video device. In both directions, the copy is exact.

Digital video devices use a different type of videocassette tape to record video. This tape is not compatible with the analog tapes used in VHS, Super VHS, or Hi 8 video devices (all of which are analog devices). This is because digital video is stored differently on the cassette than analog video is. To convert digital videotape to analog, you can use the analog-style audio/video outputs of the digital video device (either S-Video or composite video) to attach the digital device to an analog device. To convert from analog to digital, you will need a special conversion deck.

Connecting a Digital Video Device with FireWire

Digital camcorders, and other digital video devices, use a FireWire port (though it may be referred to as an iLink or 1394 port) to connect to each other for dubbing or copying digital videocassettes. This same FireWire port can be used to attach the camcorder to a Macintosh computer that supports FireWire and can be used to import digital video into the Mac or to export digital video from a video-editing program on the Mac to a digital videocassette in the camcorder.

Not all digital camcorders and devices are fully compatible with Mac DV tools. Table 14-2 lists those that are compatible or partially compatible (along with detail and solutions regarding devices that are not fully compatible) at the time of this writing. You can check Apple's website for updated lists of compatible digital video camcorders and other devices.

To connect a digital video device to the Mac, you will need to use a six-pin to four-pin FireWire cable. These cables are included with all

TABLE 14-2

Digital video devices currently supported for Mac FireWire use.

Sony Digital Camcorders

DCR-PC1
DCR-PC100
DCR-TR7000
DCR-TRV103
DCR-TRV110
DCR-TRV310
DCR-TRV310e
DCR-TRV510
DCR-TRV7
DCR-TRV8
DCR-TRV9
DCR-TRV9e
DCR-TRV10
DCR-TRV900
DCR-TRV900e
GR-D300

Sony DV/Analog Converters*

DVMC-DA1
DVMC-MS1 AV

Canon Digital Camcorders**

Elura
Optura
Vistura
XL1
ZR

Panasonic Digital Camcorders***

AG-EZ20
AG-EZ30
PV-DV710
PV-DV-910

Sharp Digital Camcorders***

VL-PD3

*Sony digital-to-analog video converter decks do not support computer application-based control of the video device. You will need to use the controls on the analog video device rather than the onscreen controls of a digital video editing application on the Mac to select a video segment to capture.

**Canon digital camcorders do not offer complete compatibility with the Mac digital video application controls. There is an issue that may prevent the camcorder from being able to pause in video playback while using the rewind and fast-forward controls within a digital video editing application. If you experience this issue, use the Stop button to completely stop the video from rewinding or fast-forwarding.

***Panasonic and Sharp Digital Camcorders have known issues when exporting from a digital video editing application to tape via FireWire. The issue manifests as the camcorder's LCD screen flashing "Check DV Input" and then going into REC/Pause mode and not recording video. If this occurs, stop the camcorder and cancel the export-to-tape process on the Mac. You can work around this problem by adding a few seconds of solid black frames to the beginning of a movie project. When exporting to tape, watch the camcorder's LCD screen for signs of the black frames being sent from the Mac. At this point use the Still button on the camcorder's VTR controls to begin recording the movie being exported by the Mac. Alternatively, you can attempt increasing the wait time in the Export dialog box of the video editing application (this is the time that the Mac will wait for the digital video device to begin recording when exporting a movie project).

FireWire-equipped Macs and can be purchased from any computer store.

First, turn off the digital video device. Next, plug the six-pin end of the cable into the Mac's FireWire port. Plug the four-pin end into the four-pin FireWire port on the digital video device. The four-pin connector is more fragile than the six-pin connector is, and you should take care not to force the cable into the port. Also, make certain that the connector on the cable and the port are aligned properly, as inserting the cable backwards is possible and will damage both the device and the cable.

Finally, turn on the digital video device. If the device is a camcorder, set the power switch to VTR mode. Also, if you are using a camcorder with a power supply, make sure the power adapter is set to VTR or Camera mode to supply power to the camcorder rather than to charge the battery. If the power adapter is set to Charge, you may not be able to power the camcorder while the battery is charging (refer to the camcorder's manual for additional information).

The DV device should now be available to video editing applications that support working with digital video devices. You can use the Apple System Profiler's Devices and Volumes tab to see if the Mac is recognizing the video device as being attached to the FireWire bus.

Capturing and Exporting Video over FireWire

There are several video-editing applications that support working with the DV video format for both importing and exporting. The most common and simplest of these tools is the iMovie software that Apple bundles with all iMac DV computers. Additional titles include Apple's Final Cut Pro, Adobe's Premiere and After Effects, and Radius's Edit DV.

Each of these tools allows you to capture digital video from a digital video device over FireWire. Although the process is similar in each application, there will be differences in the interface that you should take into account. The documentation that comes with your application of choice should include instructions on how to import and export video using FireWire. The following sections include a brief overview of the video import, and export functions of the free iMovie application to give you an idea of how the process works. These are only intended as an introduction. Refer to the documentation for your specific video-editing application for details and further information. Chapter 27 of this book also includes additional information regarding working with video on the Mac.

Capturing or Importing Video   Once your digital video device is attached via FireWire and powered, you can import video from it into an application such as iMovie very easily. To do this in iMovie, click on the Camera Mode button in the iMovie display (see Figure 14-9).

Once iMovie is in camera mode, you can use the onscreen controls (see Figure 14-10) to view the contents of the tape (or other digital recording medium) in the digital video device. These controls include the traditional videotape play, pause, stop, rewind, and fast-forward functions. The contents of the tape will be displayed in the application's display area.

If you are using an analog-to-digital video converter deck, you will not be able to use iMovie's onscreen controls. This is because FireWire does not support controlling of an analog video device, such as you would have attached to this type of converter. You will instead need to use the controls built into the analog video device to select the appropriate sections of video that you want to import into iMovie.

Once you have located the segment of video that you wish to capture, simply press the Import button in the iMovie display. Press the same button to stop capturing video when you have finished importing the segment that you wish to capture and edit. You can also press the spacebar to start and stop importing video.

iMovie will store captured video clips in the shelf section of the display.

Figure 14-9
These buttons let you switch between capturing video from a FireWire device and editing video in iMovie.

Figure 14-10
These buttons control the playback and importing of an external DV device in iMovie.

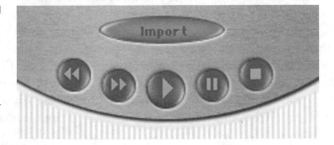

When this section becomes full, you will need to move these segments into a movie track with iMovie's clip viewer (this applies only to iMovie versions 1.X, and not to iMovie 2). You can also specify that iMovie store clips in a movie track rather than the shelf when capturing them.

When capturing digital video, it is important that you capture it to a device that can support the sustained data transfer rates at which digital video operates. This rate must be at least 3.6 MB/second. Virtually all hard drives are capable of such transfer rates, but many removable-media drives and all USB drives are inadequate for digital video work, as are network drives and servers. Also when capturing video, you should disable virtual memory (unless you have 64 MB or RAM or less), disable file sharing, and quit any background applications that you do not need to have running. This will allow the Mac to perform better when importing and working with video clips.

Once you have imported the video clips that you wish to work with, you can simply work with them in whatever manner your video-editing program of choice supports. You can save the work to your hard drive, and you can export it back to a digital video device or to a permanent file once you're finished.

Exporting Video to Tape   Exporting a completed project to a digital video device is also very easy over FireWire. First, make certain that the digital video device is connected and powered properly. Also, make certain that there is a tape available for it to record video onto and that you are not recording over any existing video (including the source video that you captured and edited on the Mac).

In the iMovie application, select Export Movie from the File menu. This will provide you with a pop-up menu that allows you to designate how you want to export the movie. To export to a digital video device, you would choose Camera. You can also export to other file formats such as a QuickTime movie.

At this point you will have the option of setting the Add and Wait values for the export process. Most users will be able to simply use the default values. If you are working with a camera that has issues regarding not receiving video during export, you may want to increase the wait times above their defaults.

Finally, press the Export button, and the movie will be exported to the digital video device. You can then switch back to camera mode in iMovie and preview the movie, or you can attach the digital video device to another video source (such as a television or monitor) and verify that the video was exported correctly. At this point if you want to transfer the video to an analog video source such as a VHS, Super VHS, or Hi 8 tape, you can do so use the analog video connectors on your digital video device in the same manner as you would make a copy of any other videotape.

Troubleshooting FireWire

Following are some problems you may encounter with FireWire, along with their solutions.

The Mac Displays an Error Message Saying It Doesn't Recognize a FireWire Device

This message means that the Mac was unable to find driver software for the device. This can mean that the driver software was never loaded, that it has been disabled with the Extensions Manager, that the Mac was started with extensions turned off, or that the Mac was started from an alternate startup disk (such as a Mac OS CD or a different hard drive) that did not contain the driver software for the device. It could also be a symptom that the driver software files have been damaged, though this is rather unlikely.

Assuming you have not started up with extensions off or from an alternate startup disk, check to be sure that the drivers are installed. If they aren't or if you aren't sure whether they are or not or you believe they have become corrupted, reinstall them from the CD-ROM that accompanied the device.

A FireWire Device Suddenly Powers Down

Disconnect the device immediately. This occurs when the FireWire bus experiences a power overload and can result in damage if the device is not disconnected quickly. You can try using the device in another location of a FireWire chain or tree, but it is best to avoid using it in the same configuration or with the same devices in operation.

A FireWire Device Is Not Recognized in a Specific Application

If the device is recognized by the Mac (such as in the Apple System Profiler) or by other applications, try quitting the application that is not recognizing the device and relaunching it. Assuming there is not a conflict that prevents the application from working with the device in question, this should make the application recognize the device. If this does not help, it is possible that the application and the device may not be able to function with each other. Check with the manufacturer of the device and the developer of the application for additional information and updates to the device's driver software or to the application.

A FireWire Device Is Not Recognized At All

First, make sure the device is plugged in and powered (if it uses its own power supply). If the device uses FireWire bus power and there are other devices also using the FireWire bus power, there may be insufficient power to support all the devices. Try removing one (or more) of the other devices to see if this is the case.

Check to be certain that all cables in the chain that the device is in are connected and that all the devices are turned on. If you have a tree arrangement of FireWire devices, make sure that all devices are connected and powered properly and that none of the cables loop back into another branch of the tree. Also make sure that each chain contains no more than 16 separate segments of FireWire cabling and that no point in the chain uses a cable longer than 15 feet.

Make certain that any drivers for the device are installed properly. You can also try restarting the Mac, as this will cause all device drivers to be reinitialized and loaded during the startup sequence.

A FireWire Hard Drive Is Attached, But Its Icon Will Not Show Up on the Desktop

Use the Apple System Profiler to ensure the drive is being recognized as a FireWire device attached to the Mac. Also check to be certain that you've installed any needed drivers on your startup hard drive for the FireWire hard drive in question. Assuming these things check out, run a hard-drive utility to attempt to mount the drive and to test the drive for any problems as described in Chapter 5. If the drive has never been used, it is possible that it will need to be formatted. It may also be formatted such that it doesn't mount automatically or that it is password-protected.

If you have the Apple Network Assistant extension installed, check to see if the version number is lower than 3.5. Earlier versions of this extension were known to conflict with some FireWire hard drives. You can resolve this conflict by upgrading to version 3.5 or higher of this extension or by disabling the Apple Network extension with the Extensions Manager.

The Mac Freezes or Crashes When a Specific FireWire Device Is Attached

This usually signals a problem with driver software of the device rather than with the device itself. It most likely indicates an extension conflict between the device's driver and either another extension or control panel or an application that is running at the time the device is attached. See Chapter 38 for information on how to isolate and resolve an extension conflict.

A Digital Video Device Is Not Recognized while Transmitting Digital Video

Check to be certain that the device is connected properly and that you are using the appropriate cables. Make certain that you are using a video-editing application that supports working with DV devices and that you are using the appropriate mode of the application for working DV hardware.

Try turning the DV device off and then back on again while it is connected to the Mac. If this doesn't help, try turning the device off, disconnecting it, reconnecting it, and then turning it on.

A FireWire Device Performs Slowly

The device in question may only support one of the slower transfer rates included in the FireWire standard. Check the device's specifications to see if this is the case. If this is not the case, then check to see if one of the devices between the device in question and the Mac is a device that supports only one of the slower transfer rates. If this is the case with one (or more) device, move that device to the end of the FireWire chain, as it is slowing down data transfer for any device beyond it in the chain. Also check to see if there are any applications or processes, such as file sharing, that may be slowing the Mac as a whole down.

Resources for Further Study

The following URLs provide additional information on some of the concepts, issues, and products discussed in this chapter:

Apple's FireWire home page—http://www.apple.com/firewire

Apple's FireWire Developer Information—
http://developer.apple.com/hardware/FireWire/index.html

FireWire Watch—http://www.michael-amorose.com/firewire

About.com Mac Hardware FireWire Resources—
http://machardware.about.com/msubfirewire.htm

USB

Universal serial bus, or USB, took the Mac world by storm when Apple announced in 1998 that the iMac would use USB as the sole method for connecting any external drives or other peripherals. At the time, USB was just beginning to emerge as an industry-standard technology—one with incredible platform-independent hardware design and several advances over earlier technologies.

USB is a relatively slow serial technology. USB channels are capable of transmitting up to only 1.5 MB of data per second. Each USB cable can carry power as well as data. This allows many devices to be powered directly through the USB cable rather than requiring the use of an external power supply. Although a Mac only comes with one or two USB ports, additional ports can be provided through the use of devices known as *hubs*, allowing up to 127 individual devices to be attached to each individual USB channel.

Working with USB

USB is a technology that is revolutionary in many ways, particularly in that it's completely hot pluggable. With SCSI devices (or virtually any earlier interface technology), you need to shut down the Mac before adding or removing devices. USB doesn't require you to shut down the computer or put it into sleep mode to add or remove devices. You simply plug them in or unplug them.

USB is also a very versatile technology. Like SCSI, it can be used for hard drives, removable-media drives, and scanners. In addition, USB is designed to support much more low-bandwidth devices like keyboards, mice, joysticks, and other input devices. It even accommodates devices that traditionally used serial ports such as printers, modems, and digital cameras. This is not to say that USB is the perfect interface for all the devices it supports. Indeed, it is actually very slow compared to other interfaces and this is very noticeable with any type of external drive, such as a hard drive or Zip drive.

USB actually operates at two levels of performance. One is intended for devices that need minimal bandwidth to transmit data, such as keyboards and mice. The other is designed for the majority of USB devices that communicate much larger amounts of data. The lower performance level operates at a speed of 1.5 Mbps, while the higher operates at 12 Mbps (or 1.5 MB/second), which is about one quarter the speed of the original SCSI standard.

USB can support up to 127 devices per channel. In practice, most people will not use 127 devices with their USB Mac. (In fact, the most devices I've heard of was in a test of USB at Comdex a few years ago when about 100 devices were connected to a single non-Mac USB computer). One important consideration is that having that many devices all trying to use USB's limited bandwidth at one time would result in each device transmitting data extremely slowly. In practice, most users will probably attach and use less than half a dozen USB devices at a time.

USB Ports

USB ports come in two varieties: type A and type B, both of which are shown in Figure 15-1. These two types of ports are functionally the same. Type A USB ports are narrow and rectangular in shape. These are the types of ports built into a Macintosh computer. Type B connectors are square-shaped and tend to be used as the connector on most (though not all) USB devices, such as printers or Zip drives. USB cables are available with a type A connector at both ends or with a type A Connector at one end and a type B connector at the other end. USB hubs use type A connectors for attaching devices and type B connectors for the USB cable that leads from the hub to the computer.

USB connectors will install in only one direction into a USB port and are usually completely standard and interchangeable, though some companies do create nonstandard USB cables for their devices. USB cables tend to come in lengths of 6 feet or less. As with SCSI and IDE cables, this is because signal noise can get into the data being transmitted along a USB cable. The use of USB hubs, however, extends the usable length of cabling between a USB device and the host computer that it is attached to.

Figure 15-1
Typical connectors. The type A connector is the flat one on the left, while the type B is the boxier one on the right.

USB Bus Power

USB is a powered bus, which means that devices that do not require a large amount of electrical current to operate can draw power directly from the USB port. Such devices need to be connected directly to the computer or to a powered hub. If the Mac displays a message saying that there is not enough power to use a device, it is because the device is either plugged into an unpowered hub or because there are too many devices currently drawing power from the USB port or hub that the device is attached to.

Devices that draw power from the USB bus can be divided into devices like keyboards and mice, which require a very small (almost negligible) amount of power, and devices such as digital video cameras (like the Logitech QuickCam), some external drives, or modems, which require a good deal more power to function.

Some devices can operate on power from the USB bus or can operate off their own power supply. These devices are generally aimed at owners of portable computers who can use the device with a battery-powered Mac, such as the iBook, while on the road or away from an outlet by using the USB port to power the device. However, they can also use the device at their desk, with the device powered by the wall outlet.

PowerBook and iBook owners should be aware that a USB device that drains power from the USB port of their computer may significantly impact how quickly the Mac's battery power becomes used up. For this reason, these devices should be used as sparingly as possible when running on battery power and should be disconnected when they are not being used.

Multiple USB Channels

While the early USB Macs had two USB ports built into the computer, they had only a single channel. This means that the combined throughput from both ports is still limited to the 12 Mbps. One way to look at this is to imagine that the Mac has only a single USB port, but it has a two-port hub built into it. The Power Mac G4 computers with an AGP graphics card, the slot-loading iMac and iMac DV models, and the PowerBooks announced in February of 2000 with onboard FireWire ports (and any more recent Macs) all have two separate USB channels, one for each port.

Although this doesn't technically double the performance of USB on these machines, if you divide high-performance USB devices between the two ports, you can get the effect of doubling the USB bandwidth available. If you have a computer that supports independent USB channels for each port, I highly recommend that you look at the higher-performance USB device you use and try to distribute them as evenly as possible between the two ports. If you typically use your laser printer, scanner, QuickCam, and Zip drive, space the devices out two to each port and try to put the ones used most commonly on separate ports from each other. This way, you are less likely to see one device saturating a USB channel and slowing down performance on that channel for all the other devices.

Having multiple USB channels also doubles the number of devices you can connect to the Mac. In theory, you could attach 127 devices to each port of such a Mac, allowing for a total of 254 devices. In practice, this is probably just a point of trivia, as I cannot imagine anyone having 254 USB devices attached to a single computer (just the sheer number of individual cables that would be involved is a little frightening to me, actually).

USB Hubs

A *USB hub* is a device that connects to one USB port (such as one on a Macintosh computer) and then provides additional ports. USB hubs can be dedicated devices, meaning they do nothing but provide more USB ports, or they can be embedded in another device, such as a keyboard or monitor. Dedicated or stand-alone hubs come in any number of varieties, but most provide four or seven USB ports from the one port that they attach to. The Apple USB keyboard is an example of a hub embedded in another device, providing not only the keyboard, but two additional USB ports as well (one of which is usually used for a USB mouse).

Hubs perform two important functions. First, they provide you with additional ports. If you run out of USB ports, you can simply add a hub (or multiple hubs) and gain as many more as you need. Since hubs can be plugged into other hubs, there is no end to the number of USB ports you can provide by adding additional hubs. This makes the theoretical limit of 127 USB devices per USB channel possible.

Second, hubs can act as repeaters. As you'll remember from Chapter 12 on SCSI, after a certain cable length is exceeded, electrical signals used to transmit data begin to degrade because signal noise becomes mixed in with the data being transmitted along the cable. A USB hub will actually act to negate this by receiving the signal from a USB device attached to it and rebroadcasting it along the cable to the computer. This

Figure 15-2
This diagram shows
how USB hubs can
be used to connect
additional USB
devices and even
more USB hubs to
a computer.

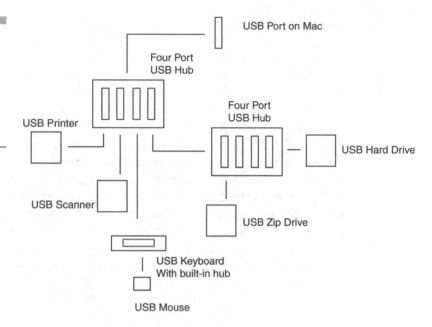

allows for greater distance between USB devices and their host computer
than other technologies, because you can employ hubs as a method of
extending USB cable lengths.

Hubs can come in powered and unpowered variations, although powered hubs are far more common. A powered hub uses its own power supply. This allows it to provide power to any USB devices attached to it
(much as the USB ports of the computer do). The powered hub also
allows the hub to act as a repeater and to avoid draining power from the
USB port of the computer. Unpowered hubs do not provide their own
power supply. As a result, devices attached to an unpowered hub must
have their own power supplies and cannot operate by drawing power
from the USB bus.

Some hubs, such as the IceView and BusView hubs from Interex, also
offer the ability to monitor the level of activity within a USB channel,
showing you how much of the limited bandwidth is being used. This
allows you to determine which devices you're using impose the most
drain on the USB channel. If you are using a Mac with multiple USB
channels (see the previous section), you can use such hubs to optimize
the spacing of high-end devices between the two channels for better overall performance.

Installing a USB hub is extremely simple and basic. You just plug the
"upstream" cable into the hub and then into the USB port of the Mac (or

another hub), plug in the hub's power supply (assuming it's a powered hub), and then attach devices to it. That's all there is to it. Although you can use any number of hubs to provide additional ports, it is usually less confusing and more cost-effective to use one or two hubs with a large number of ports than several hubs with three or four ports each.

Figure 15-2 illustrates the use of USB hubs.

USB Devices and the Apple System Profiler

The Apple System Profiler displays information about any piece of hardware attached to the Mac. In the case of USB devices and hubs, these are displayed in a format much like a tree. The hubs are listed as individual devices, and then the devices attached to them are listed as branches off of the hub. If one hub is plugged into another hub, then that branch divides again into still more branches. Knowing which hub a device is attached to can help you find the device in the "tree" of USB devices and branches attached to a Mac if you are looking to verify the device is recognized and functional.

Figure 15-3 shows an example of how the Apple System Profiler will display devices and how they are connected. Notice how each hub, including the one built into the Apple USB keyboard, is displayed with branches leading to individual devices or other hubs.

Installing a USB Device

Installing a USB device is probably the simplest thing you can do with the Macintosh when it comes to adding new hardware. You simple insert the CD-ROM included with the device and run the installer program to install the needed driver software and whatever utilities or software may have been included with the device. In some cases, the driver software may be built into the Mac OS, such as the Iomega USB Zip drive. In some other cases, the software may be downloaded from the manufacturer's website rather than included with the device (particularly devices initially designed for PCs).

Once the drivers are installed, you restart the Mac to ensure that they are loaded as part of the Mac OS. Some drivers may not require this, but most driver software is written as an extension (or occasionally as a control panel) that the Mac OS will not have available until after you have restarted. At that point, you simply plug the device into power outlet, if

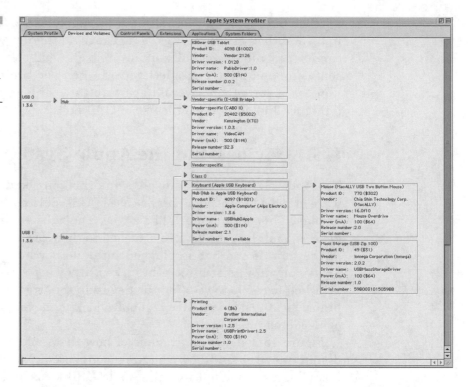

it requires its own power supply, and then attach the USB cable from the device to the USB port on the Mac or to a hub that is connected to the Mac.

The device should now be recognized by the Mac and available to whatever applications or utilities will be used with the device. In the case of a USB hard drive, the drive's icon should appear on the Mac's desktop. Removable-media drives should function normally when a disk or cartridge is inserted. Other devices such as printers, cameras, or scanners should function once the appropriate settings are made in any utilities, control panels, or applications that they are to be used with (the Chooser is used to select a USB printer, for example).

Resetting USB Drivers

Occasionally, it may be necessary to reset the drivers of a USB device. These times are when the device has stopped functioning or being recognized or when the device has begun to behave erratically. Resetting the drivers causes the device to be recognized as though it had not been in use before.

To reset the drivers of a USB device, simply unplug the device from the USB port it is attached to. Wait about 10 seconds for the Mac to realize that the device has been disconnected. Then plug it back in again. The Mac should now reinitialize its connection with the device.

Resetting the drivers of a USB device in this fashion can solve a majority of USB device problems. However, you should not disconnect a USB device while the Mac is actively accessing it. For example, don't disconnect a USB printer while the Mac is printing to it or a USB camera while your videoconferencing software is receiving image data from it. This can cause the application or process of the Mac OS involved to become confused and to crash or hang.

Typical Uses for USB

USB is an incredibly diverse technology that can be used to connect a greater variety of devices than any previous device interface. As you look through this section, you will see that virtually every type of device has been made available in a USB format. This does not mean that USB is the optimal connection method for all of these devices. Indeed, the limited bandwidth and transfer rates of USB make a relatively poor choice for several devices when compared to SCSI or FireWire. However, for several other devices, such as printers, modems, and keyboards, USB is more than adequate.

Printers

Printers are probably the most common type of device connected by USB outside of the Mac's keyboard and mouse. Traditionally, printers were connected to the Mac by way of the Macintosh serial ports. When Apple made the transition to USB, printers were just beginning to support the USB standard. USB is very well suited to most printing needs. It offers increased data transmission performance compared to the Mac's earlier serial ports and is very easy to configure for printing use. Printers will probably use USB as the interface of choice for quite some time to come, both in low-cost ink-jet and laser models, as well as some of the higher-end printer types.

Many early (and some current) printers supported USB on the Mac by way of an adapter. Usually, this adapter converted the printer's parallel port (meant for use on PC computers) to a USB port that could be used with the Mac (parallel port adapters are discussed in further detail later in this section). In the time since USB's first debut, many printers have begun offering USB as a standard option, and today it is rare to find a new printer that doesn't include a USB port.

Hard Drives

USB hard drives appeared on the market shortly after the iMac's release. While they provide good methods for backing up data and even an acceptable method for transferring file collections between USB-equipped computers, USB hard drives are slow. USB hard drives are best suited for storing basic documents or files that you don't use regularly so that your internal hard drive space can be put to better use (such as holding applications and multimedia content that you are working with) or for use as backup drives. Applications usually run slowly when launched from a USB hard drive and multimedia files may not play smoothly from a USB hard drive.

USB hard drives function much the same as any other hard drive. You can format them with a formatting utility, partition them, password-protect them, and so on. The difference is that they are external and they may or may not require a driver installed on the Mac in order to be recognized. They also may or may not be able to function as startup disks in an emergency (see the next topic, "Bootable USB Drives").

When working with USB hard drives, you can disconnect the drive while the Mac is running. However, you should still unmount the hard drive before doing so. You can do this by dragging the hard drive's icon to the Trash or by clicking on it and then using the Put Away command from the Finder's File Menu. When you unmount the drive before disconnecting it, the Mac will know that it is no longer available to access. Any open files, particularly the invisible files used by the Mac for storing data on a drive, will be closed and put away. If you don't unmount it first, you may find the Mac repeatedly asking you to insert (meaning reconnect) the drive, and you might even cause corruption to the drive's directory structures.

Bootable USB Drives   USB drives can be used as startup devices only on certain Macintosh models, because the code to access the USB drive must be present in the boot ROM on the Mac's motherboard. If the needed ROM code isn't available, the drive would require a device driver that would be loaded as an extension much later in the startup process

TABLE 15-1

Macs that Support Starting Up from USB Drives.

iBook
iMac (slot-loading and DV models)
Power Mac G4 (models with AGP Graphics card only)
PowerBook G3 (models with built-in FireWire ports)
Power Mac G4 cube

(which is described in Chapter 37). Early USB-enabled Macs did not include the ability to start up from USB drives. Table 15-1 lists which Macs can start up from USB drives.

In addition to the support being built into the motherboard of a Mac, the drive itself needs to support being used as a startup device. This requires the drive to be made such that it can be accessed very early in the startup process, as well as requiring that it is a drive type that can reasonably be used for storing a copy of the Mac OS (such as a hard drive). If a USB hard drive can be used as a startup drive, this is often included in the drive's specifications or manual. To start up from the drive, you will also need to install a copy of the Mac OS on the drive.

USB hard drives should not be used as startup drives except for emergency situations because USB is too slow to allow the computer to be truly useful or functional. However, as an emergency disk, USB hard drives have the advantage that you can install any diagnostic utilities you like on a single bootable drive, as well as a customized copy of the Mac OS. You can even use a single USB hard drive as an emergency disk for an office or computer lab full of Macs, provided they support booting from a USB drive.

Removable-Media Drives

USB removable-media drives were released shortly after the iMac. Removable-media drives suffer from the same USB performance limitations, but the lower performance is not as noticeable as in the case of hard drives. This is because removable-media drives tend to be slower drives to begin with. In fact, some of the USB floppy drives on the market are faster than many standard internal floppy drives.

The most popular removable-media drives using a USB interface include the Zip drive, SuperDisk drive, and a variety of USB floppy drives. The Zip drive was primarily a migration from the original SCSI

Zip model, and it does suffer a moderate performance decrease in the move to USB, as one might expect. The floppy drive (and SuperDisk drive for its ability to read and write floppies) became popular because there was no other floppy option for the iMac or any other later Mac model.

Although higher-end removable-media drives, such as the Iomega Jaz drive or the Orb drive (which store larger amounts of data and traditionally offer better performance) will be slowed down considerably by using USB, many drives operate well on USB without an intolerable hit to their performance. For drives such as the Zip or SuperDisk, USB does provide an adequate connection method. This is especially true when using the drive primarily for backup and archival purposes.

Recordable CD Drives

USB CD-RW drives became popular in 1999 when Adaptec offered support for USB in the popular Toast CD authoring utility. Since recordable CD drives at that time tended to be limited to writing CDs at about 4x recording speed (about 0.61 MB/second), the limitation of USB's bandwidth did not adversely affect performance. However, it does require much of the available USB bandwidth to be devoted to the CD-RW drive rather than any other devices to write a disk at such speeds. Table 15-2 lists the various recording speeds, their data transfer rates, and whether or not they are suitable for USB connections.

Since that time, CD recording speeds have increased, making USB less attractive for this function than some other technologies. It is, how-

TABLE 15-2

CD Recording Speeds and Usability with USB.

Speed	Data Transfer	USB Possible?
1x	0.15 MB/second	Yes
2x	0.30 MB/second	Yes
4x	0.61 MB/second	Yes
6x	0.92 MB/second	Yes*
8x	1.20 MB/second	Possibly*
10x	1.50 MB/second	No
16x	2.4 MB/second	No

*These speeds are theoretically possible for USB CD-RW drives, but they would require best-case scenarios to achieve and no other USB devices in use while recording.

ever, still adequate for many people, as 4x speed does allow a completely full CD to be burned in about 20 minutes. The advantage here over SCSI or FireWire is primarily in cost, though. FireWire CD-RW drives tend to be, on average, at least $100 more expensive than their USB counterparts. SCSI models tend to be around the same price as USB (and sometimes lower), though you then have to factor in the cost of the SCSI card, which is not an option for iMac or iBook owners.

Scanners

Scanners are another class of device that was traditionally relegated to SCSI connections. Scanners made the move to USB relatively quickly, and a wide variety of USB scanners are on the market today. While USB scanners are slower than SCSI models, they usually offer performance that is suitable to most consumer needs. Higher-end users such as graphic artists and desktop publishing firms will probably want to consider a SCSI or FireWire alternative. Not only is this because of USB's performance limitations, it is also because higher-end scanners with greater resolutions, output quality, and additional features tend to be offered in SCSI and, more recently, FireWire models rather than USB models, which tend to dominate the consumer space.

Digital Video

A number of digital video USB devices have been released. These include desktop video cameras like the QuickCam, as well as video capture and TV tuner devices, which can be used to capture or view analog video from sources such as a VCR. A number of these devices have provided impressive video quality, given the limitations of USB performance, although it is not nearly as impressive as the digital video abilities offered by FireWire. USB video solutions are good for personal entertainment, videoconferencing, and similar activities. It should be noted that some USB video drivers have a tendency to interact negatively with each other but without any negative effects to other areas of the Mac OS.

Input Devices

Keyboards, mice, trackballs, trackpads, graphics tablets, joysticks, and gamepads are all input devices, and all use USB as an interface on the recent and current Macs. These devices use only a small fraction of the USB bandwidth and suffer no performance issues by being used with USB. In fact, because USB is hot pluggable, it is often a better option for input devices, which you can plug and unplug quite easily.

Modems

Most recent and current Macs have shipped with internal modems. The primary exceptions were several standard configurations of the Blue and White Power Macintosh G3. Although internal modem cards were available for these computers from both Apple and third parties, external modems were also a popular alternative for them. Since these Macs lack a serial port, which was the traditional method for attaching external modems, these computers were among the first that used USB modems. USB modems can also be useful if you use one of the comm slot serial port cards that replace your internal modem card with a serial port card. Using these devices require you to use an external modem. Such serial port cards are discussed in Chapter 30.

One advantage of USB modems is the situation where you would want to attach multiple modems to a single computer. Situations such as running a local bulletin board service, using an AppleTalk Remote Access server, or providing Internet access through dial-up connections require multiple modems if you want to accept more than one connection at a time. USB's self-configuring abilities and the fact that it provides as many ports for modems (or other devices) as you need easily lends itself to multiple modem configurations.

ISDN

USB can also serve for ISDN terminal adapters (also known as ISDN modems). ISDN terminal adapters work to connect a computer to an ISDN line, which can be used for fast Internet access or connections to other networks. ISDN lines require a special router or terminal adapter in order to be connected to an individual computer or network. While ISDN routers connect a line to an entire network by Ethernet, a terminal adapter connects it to only one computer. Like modems, terminal adapters have traditionally connected through serial ports. USB terminal adapters offer the same benefits over their serial counterparts as USB modems do over serial port modems.

Networking

USB can also be used for networking. Presently, USB is used as an interface method for the relatively new home phone line networking kits. These kits, discussed in detail in Chapter 32, allow you to connect computers using the wiring that connects the phone jacks in your house rather than installing Ethernet cables or opting for Apple's AirPort wireless networking. These kits provide only limited performance, which tends to be about 1 Mbps (one-tenth the speed of Ethernet of 10 Base-T Ethernet and one-twelfth the potential of USB).

Palmtop Docking

Probably the most recent use for USB is to sync data with a palmtop or handheld computer. These devices, such as the Palm series of devices from 3Com, were originally designed to use a serial port to transfer information with a desktop computer. Today, only some palmtops support connection by USB, but that number is expected to grow. Because of the relatively small amount of data being transmitted (almost always less than 20 MB and usually about 2 MB), USB is more than adequate for this function.

For devices that don't support syncing to a USB port, there are adapters that can serve as well. Some of these adapters are specifically designed for palmtop USB transfers, such as the Keyspan USB PDA Adapter. Others are more traditional serial-port-to-USB adapter products. When buying such an adapter, you should check for compatibility with the palmtop device in question (the next section of this chapter and Chapter 30 include information on such adapters and serial ports).

USB Adapters

When the iMac was introduced with USB as its only option for connecting any peripherals or devices, it began Apple's migration away from three different types of ports that had been traditionally included on every Mac model. These included SCSI, the traditional Mac serial ports used for printers and other devices, and ADB ports, which had been used for connecting keyboards, mice, and other input devices. Needless to say, Mac users buying the iMac tended to have investments in hardware using at least one of these three interface technologies. As a result, adapter products began to become available as soon as manufacturers could develop them.

It is important to understand that an adapter is never as good as having the actual port on the Mac would be. Adapters tend to have varying degrees of compatibility with devices, and they are all limited to the performance abilities of USB. If at all possible, the better options are to migrate to USB versions of a device or to install a solution that offers an actual port of the type you would be using an adapter for. A SCSI card provides a far better option of using a SCSI device on the Mac than a USB adapter, for example. Similarly, actual serial ports tend to provide better performance and far less compatibility concerns than a USB adapter. Use adapters only when there are no other solutions, and be sure to check with the manufacturer about compatibility with the specific devices that you will be using the adapter for before buying it.

USB-SCSI Adapters

USB-SCSI adapters were designed to allow Mac users to use their older external hard drives, removable-media drives, and scanners with the iMac. These adapters provide support for narrow SCSI devices only and provide support for up to seven devices.

As mentioned in Chapter 12, these adapters tend to have compatibility issues with a number of devices. They are most compatible with external SCSI hard drives. Removable-media drives also tend to offer fewer compatibility problems than other devices. Other devices, including scanners, tape drives, and recordable CD (CD-R and CD-RW) drives, tend to have a higher number of compatibility problems. Some adapters will not support anything but external hard drives and a few removable-media drives.

Before buying, check with the manufacturer to see if the device has been successfully or unsuccessfully tested with the device you plan to use. Ask about specific device models rather than just types of devices. For example, if you want to use your Microtek ScanMaker E6 SCSI scanner with an adapter, ask about that specific model rather than just asking if the adapter in question supports scanners. If a device has not been tested, it may or may not work. If similar devices have been successfully tested, then that's a sign your device may work, but not a guarantee that your device will work as well.

Even if all the SCSI devices you want to use with an adapter are compatible with the adapter you choose, remember that you will still be dealing with the limited performance of USB (which is less than one-third the speed of the slowest SCSI standard). Your devices may work, but they will work more slowly than they did on a Mac with a real SCSI port.

Also remember that the rules of SCSI ID numbers and SCSI termination still apply to the devices you're using with the adapter. Regarding termination, these adapters rarely supply termination or termination power. You will probably need to use a pass-through terminator at the very beginning of the SCSI chain, in order to terminate that end. Or you will need to use a device that supports internal termination at the beginning of the chain, as well as the end of the chain.

One advantage the USB-SCSI adapters have over actual SCSI ports is that, because USB is hot pluggable, you can usually make adjustments to your SCSI chain without restarting the Macintosh the chain is attached to. You should still consider turning all the devices off before removing or adding one, however.

USB-Serial Port Adapters

USB serial port adapters were probably the first adapters developed for the iMac. The adapters tend to give two serial ports per USB port and also tend to suffer from limitations. As discussed in Chapter 30, many serial port devices look for serial ports named "Modem port" and "Printer port" by the Mac OS. Since USB adapters are neither of these ports, they tend to have trouble working with devices that look for these specifically identified ports. For this reason, it is even more important to check with an adapter's manufacturer regarding compatibility of specific devices before buying the adapter. Chapter 30 has additional information on USB-serial port compatibility, as well as other serial port solutions that are available for today's Mac models.

USB-Parallel Port Adapters

The parallel port is a common port on non-Mac computers. No Mac has ever shipped with a parallel port. However, a very wide range of printers and other devices were designed to be used with a PC's parallel port. Because so many devices used a parallel port, many companies developed adapters that convert this port to USB. This allowed companies making printers that support both the Mac and PC to provide a single adapter for migrating the printer to USB on both platforms. It also allowed companies that had not previously offered Mac support to develop Mac drivers and open their existing products to the Mac market without incurring much in the way of development costs.

USB-parallel port adapters are almost always used for attaching printers. As mentioned earlier in this chapter, many printer manufacturers supplied such adapters for their printers when the iMac began the USB transition on the Mac. These adapters tended to be company-specific and were sold by printer manufacturers intended for use with their printers specifically. Some generic USB-parallel port adapters are also available. I suggest that you stick with company-specific adapters, since they will have been tested for compatibility with the printers in question.

Another reason for this suggestion involves the next point about such adapters: The driver software for the printer must also support a USB-parallel port adapter. Many companies selling adapters specific to their printers will include drivers for this type of use with the adapter kit. Some printers may simply not function properly when a USB adapter is used with the printer. As a general rule, you should check with the manufacturer before assuming.

The exception to this advice about using manufacturer-specific adapters is PowerPrint USB. PowerPrint is a product made by Infowave that has been around since before USB was implemented on the Mac. PowerPrint was designed to allow Macs to print to non-Mac printers. Originally this was done with a Mac-serial-port-to-PC-parallel-port adapter. For USB Macs, Infowave developed a USB to parallel port adapter. In both cases, Infowave also ships a collection of special drivers for any printers they support with PowerPrint. The number of printers that they support is constantly growing and is extremely impressive. If the printer you want or need to use is not available with Mac support (in a USB or non-USB model), check with Infowave to see if they support it. If they do, you can use their adapter kit. However, if the printer's manufacturer supplies their own adapter and drive, then that is generally a better option.

USB-ADB Adapters

The ADB port on older Macs was rarely used for attaching anything but input devices. Since USB keyboards, mice, and other input devices are quite common and inexpensive, it is generally easier to simply migrate to USB and replace them than to use an adapter. However, there is a USB-ADB adapter for people who have an attachment to or need for a specific device. The adapter is called the iMate and it seems to have few compatibility issues. This is probably because there is very little data being transmitted.

Multiport USB Docks

Several companies have created USB docking devices, which combine more than one of the more common USB adapter types into a single product. The specific adapters included in these docks vary, but SCSI and serial ports are common in most docks. The docks are also usually a USB hub, providing additional USB ports as well as adapters to older types of ports. The iDock 2 from CompuCable includes a floppy drive as well as adapters.

As a rule, these docks tend to be less expensive than buying separate adapters for each of the ports they include. You should, however, remember that USB docks are essentially a group of several different USB adapters. Those adapters are as likely to have compatibility issues with specific devices as any stand-alone adapter would. In fact, because they have so many separate adapters bundled into one product, some of the adapters included may have more compatibility problems than a similar stand-alone adapter. Check for compatibility listings for each type of adapter before buying a dock and make sure that it provides compatibility with each type of device on each type of port that you expect to be using with it.

Some of these docks, such as the iDOCK and iDOCK 2, are designed to also serve as swivel stands for the iMac. While this is a nice touch, it does not mean that these docks can only be used with the iMac, they can easily be used with any other USB Mac.

Advantages and Disadvantages of USB

USB's biggest advantages are that it is extremely easy to use and, on a hardware level, it is completely cross-platform. Because USB is completely self-configuring, there is little more involved in attaching a USB device than plugging it into the USB port and installing a driver for it. There is no setting of IDs, no cabling restrictions, and no termination concerns. Anyone who has spent time dealing with SCSI chains and SCSI problems can easily appreciate the simplicity of USB.

USB enjoys the advantage of being platform-transparent on a hardware level. This means that the same USB device can be used on a Macintosh or a Windows-based PC with no changes at all, provided that there is a device driver written for both platforms. This has made USB development for the Mac particularly attractive to manufacturers, because there is very little additional effort in developing a product for both platforms. It is also useful to consumers if they are in mixed-platform environments and want to share the same devices between their Mac and non-Mac USB computers.

USB's biggest disadvantage is speed. No matter how you look at it, USB is a slow interface technology, because it has a very limited bandwidth compared to just about any other technology used today for attaching peripherals or drives of any sort. While USB is fine for devices such as keyboards, mice, cameras such as the QuickCam, syncing small amounts of data with a palmtop, and other low-drain functions, it is limiting for most other uses. Hard drive performance is extremely slow when compared to even SCSI-1 or one of the slower IDE variations. Scanner performance is passable but is also slow by comparison.

Troubleshooting USB

Following are some common USB problems and their solutions.

The Mac Displays an Error that a USB Device Is Not Recognized

This message means that the Mac wasn't able to find any driver software with a specific USB device attached to it. You will see it if you have attached a USB device before installing the drivers for it, if the drivers are disabled using the Extensions Manager or a similar utility, if the Mac is started with extensions off, or if you start up the Mac from a CD or other disk besides the internal hard drive (where the drivers are installed).

The solution to this problem is to make sure all the driver software for a device is correctly installed. The easiest way to do this is to run the installer program again and reinstall the drivers for the device. If the Mac is running Mac OS 9 or higher, the Mac will ask if you want it to look for drivers for the device over the Internet (which requires that an Internet connection be available). Although this is a nice feature, it doesn't guarantee it will find appropriate drivers or the most recent drivers (more often than not it will not, be able to find such drivers).

The Mac Displays an Error Message Saying that a Device Cannot Be Used because There Isn't Enough Power Available

This occurs with devices that draw power from the USB bus rather than using their own power supplies. It will be displayed if you are attaching such a device to an unpowered hub or if you have attached too many devices that draw power from the USB bus to a single-powered hub or to the USB ports built into the Mac. The solution is to attach the device in question to a powered hub or directly to the Mac.

If you get this message after attaching the device to a powered hub or to the Mac, you can either remove another device attached to the Mac or hub that draws power from the USB bus. This will make more power available to the device that generated the message. Or you can add another powered hub for the device (and for other devices), which will ensure there is power available for all your USB devices.

A USB Device Is Attached to the Mac but Not Recognized at All

If the Mac doesn't appear to respond to a USB device's presence at all, first double-check that the device is securely connected, turned on, and plugged into a viable power outlet (if it requires its own power supply). If the device is attached via a USB hub, make sure that the hub is connected to the Mac correctly and plugged in (if it is a powered hub).

Try putting the Mac to sleep and then waking it or restarting. Both these actions cause the Mac to examine the USB channels for any connected devices. If this doesn't help, use the Apple System Profiler to determine if the device is being recognized at a hardware level. If so, then the problem lies with the drivers, the Mac OS, or the applications you are trying to use the device with. If not, then the problem is likely with the USB cables between the device and the Mac or with the device itself.

Assuming the device is connected properly, make sure that the drivers for the device are installed. If you aren't certain, run the installer software again just to be sure that they are. If none of this seems to help at all, it is possible that the device itself is damaged to the point that it isn't capable of being recognized. Contact the manufacturer for additional instructions.

The Mac Recognizes a USB Device at a Hardware Level and by Some Applications but Not by Other Applications

Some applications may simply not be designed to talk to USB devices in general or to a specific type of device. If the Mac and other applications are recognizing the device properly, this is probably the case. Contact the software's developer to find out if there are any known compatibility issues with the device you are trying to access and to see if there is an updated version that offers compatibility.

Less likely, it is possible that the device's drivers are conflicting with the application you are trying to use. Again, check with the software's developer as well as the device's manufacturer for any known compatibility issues and updates to either the application of the device's driver software.

A USB Hard Drive Is Attached but the Drive's Icon Doesn't Appear on the Desktop

In this situation, use the Apple System Profiler to ensure the drive is being recognized as a USB device attached to the Mac. Also check to be certain that you've installed any needed drivers on your startup hard drive needed for the USB hard drive in question. Assuming these things check out, run a hard drive utility to attempt to mount the drive and to test the drive for any problems, as described in Chapter 5. If the drive has never been used, it is possible that it will need to be formatted. It may also be formatted such that it doesn't mount automatically or that it is password-protected.

A USB Device Was Working but Has Suddenly Stopped Working or Started Working Sporadically

This problem could mean that the device has become unplugged from either the USB port or the wall outlet (assuming it uses its own power supply). It can also mean that a hub between the device and the Mac has become unplugged.

More commonly, it means that the Mac has gotten confused in how it is interacting with the device and that the USB drivers for the device need to be reset. Try simply unplugging the device, waiting a few seconds, and then reconnecting it. This should clear up most such problems. If not, try restarting the computer.

If the device continues to function erratically, it is possible that the preferences files for its drivers have become corrupted. You can solve this by locating the file(s) associated with the device in the Preferences folder inside the System Folder and dragging them to the Trash and then restarting. If this doesn't help, try reinstalling the driver software.

A USB Device Performs Well at Some Times but Very Slowly at Others

This problem is most likely because other devices are using the limited bandwidth of the USB channel at the same time. Try to be aware of what other devices may be transmitting data at the time when the device in question seems sluggish. If you have a Mac with separate USB channels for each USB port, try spacing out the higher-bandwidth devices between the two ports.

It is also possible that other processes of the Mac that affect performance, such as various applications, the use of virtual memory, file sharing, and so forth, may be slowing the entire Mac down, as well as the USB device in question.

The Mac Freezes or Crashes When a Specific USB Device Is Attached

More likely than not this is a result of the device's driver software and not the device itself. Device drivers are almost always written as extensions, and extensions can conflict with other extensions or with applications to cause crashes. Since a USB device's driver may not be activated until the device is attached, the conflict may not be noticed until then. Treat this as you would any other extension conflict. Extension conflicts and how to resolve them are covered in Chapter 38.

Resources for Further Study

The following URLs provide additional information on some of the concepts, issues, and products discussed in this chapter:

MacInTouch USB Information and Peripheral Guide—
   http://www.macintouch.com/imacusb.html

Peripherals.Net USB Product Guide—http://www.peripherals.net

Apple's USB Technology Training Site—
   http://www.info.apple.com/info.apple.com/te/training/usbpub/index.
   html

*About.com Mac USB Product Support and Information Resource
   List*—http://macsupport.about.com/msub42.htm

About.com Mac Hardware USB Information Resource List—
   http://machardware.about.com/msubusb.htm

CD-ROM, CD-R, and CD-RW Drives

CD-ROMs have become a ubiquitous part of computers today. They are the almost exclusive way for developers to distribute software. Any piece of software you buy today, from the latest version of the Mac OS to Microsoft Office, from Tomb Raider or other games to the driver software for your new printer, you will find on CD-ROM. Yet CDs have even gone beyond just installing software. With the emergence of recordable and rewritable CD technology, CDs have become a convenient way to store data. They can be used to manage your backups, to archive older files and projects that you want to keep safe but don't have hard drive space for, and to share files with other computer users. And, of course, audio CDs, which were the first consumer product to use a compact disc, are still the most common way to buy and play music (or record your own), whether in a computer's CD-ROM drive or in a traditional home stereo.

This chapter looks at how CDs store information, how CD-ROM drives retrieve that information, and the various kinds of CD drives available for the Mac. It also looks at the various CD standards in use today, as well as the hardware and technology that allow you to create audio or data CDs.

How CD-ROMs Store Data

CD-ROMs consist of multiple layers of material (shown in Figure 16-1) that allow the discs to store data and be read by a computer's CD-ROM drive. These layers include a polycarbonate substrate, a silvered coating that covers the substrate, and a scratch-resistant protective layer. An optional fourth layer of a silk-screened label may also be applied to professionally created CD-ROMs.

The first layer is a polycarbonate substrate. This substrate contains the actual information that is stored on the disc. Information is stored in

Figure 16-1
The primary layers of a CD-ROM disc.

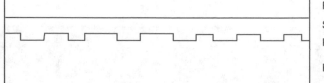

Protective Laquer

Silver Reflective Layer

Pits and Lands

Polycarbonate Substrate

Physical Layers of a CD-ROM

the substrate layer in the form of depressions in the layer known as *pits* and areas where the layer is not depressed known as *lands*. The alternation between pits and lands allows data in specific patterns to be translated into binary data that the computer can use. Pits and lands do not immediately represent the 1s and 0s of binary data as the magnetic fluctuations used to store data on a hard drive or other magnetic medium do. The computer must translate the sequences of pits and lands through a specific pattern into binary data.

Pits and lands are marked in a CD-ROM in a continuous spiral that extends from the beginning to the end of the disc. This contrasts starkly with the way hard drives and other magnetic media divide a disk up into separate tracks, which are concentric circles, with each circle being subdivided into sectors to use when storing or retrieving data, almost like a circular grid. The spiral track of a CD is divided into individual sections, analogous to the allocation blocks and sectors of a hard drive.

On top of the substrate layer where data is stored is a reflective layer. This layer is applied evenly across the disc, coating the pits and lands evenly. The process by which this layer is applied is known as *silvering*. The silvering layer is what makes a CD reflective. The reflective layer is also the key to how the CD-ROM drive reads the data on CD discs.

The CD-ROM drive includes a laser, which emits a concentrated beam of light. This light passes through a lens and is focused on a specific point in the spiral track of the CD-ROM disc. When the beam of light strikes a land on the CD-ROM, the reflective coating of the disc bounces the laser light directly back toward a photocell detector located next to the laser. When the beam strikes a pit on the CD-ROM, the reflected light is scattered and strikes the photocell with far less intensity than if it had hit a land. This allows the drive to distinguish the lands from the pits. The transitions between the two kinds of reflections are then translated by the computer into binary data.

The protective layer of the CD is a layer of strong, clear plastic lacquer. This layer is sturdy and scratch-resistant. It serves to protect the layers beneath it from damage. The most common such damage the lacquer protects against is scratches, but they aren't the only thing it protects against. If the reflective layer of the CD-ROM disc were exposed to the oxygen in the air, it would begin to oxidize or tarnish. If this happened, the disc would become useless.

The CD-ROM drive consists of several components, including the laser/photocell detector, which acts similarly to the read/write heads of a hard drive or floppy drive. This optical drive head is mounted on two guide rails that allow it to slide back and forth so that it can access any point on the disc. Above these rails is an exposed section in the frame of the drive, so that it can access the CD.

The spindle motor assembly of a CD-ROM drive keeps the drive spinning at a constant speed. It is essential that a CD spins at this constant speed in order for the disc to be read properly, just as with a hard drive's internal disks (platters). The optical head is mounted on a part of the drive known as the *sled*. The sled allows the drive's optical head to move to any point on the CD-ROM's surface in a smooth motion.

Various models of CD-ROM drives are capable of reading the data on the disc at different speeds. These speeds are measured in relation to the speed used for an audio CD, which is 150 KB/second. This was the original speed used for CD-ROM drives as well as audio CDs. However, while an audio CD player must play at this speed in order for the audio content stored on it to be converted into sound properly, a CD-ROM can transfer at much faster speeds. Each speed that a CD-ROM drive can transfer data at is measured as a multiple of the original audio CD speed. This is why you will see CD-ROM drives sold as 8X or 24X. This means that the drive can read CD-ROMs at 8 times or 24 times the speed of the original CD standard. Table 16-1 lists the common speeds used by CD-ROM drives and the corresponding data transfer rates.

TABLE 16-1

CD-ROM Speeds and Their Data Transfer Rates

Speed	Transfer Rate
1X	150 KB/second
2X	300 KB/second
4X	600 KB/second
6X	900 KB/second
8X	1.2 MB/second
10X	1.5 MB/second
12X	1.8 MB/second
14X	2.1 MB/second
16X	2.4 MB/second
18X	2.7 MB/second
20X	3.0 MB/second
24X	3.6 MB/second
32X	4.8 MB/second
36X	5.1 MB/second

Keep in mind that faster CD-ROM drives are still capable of reading CD-ROM discs at all of the slower speeds. This is important because some CD-ROM types are designed to be read only at slower speeds. Audio CDs, of course, can only be read at 1X speed. In addition, although drives today are capable of reading disks at 24X or higher, that doesn't mean they will always do so. Some discs are incapable of being read that fast, and most applications that continually access CD-ROM content, such as multimedia games or presentations, are designed to do so only at a slower speeds. Most multimedia content on CD-ROM, however, requires at least 4X speed to display properly without jerkiness or distortion.

CD-ROM Drivers and Extensions

Like any other device, a CD-ROM drive requires that driver software be installed on the Mac in order for it to be recognized and used. Apple provides a driver extension as part of the Mac OS that will function as a device driver for any of the Apple factory-installed CD-ROM drives in a Mac. This driver recognizes a few third-party CD-ROM drive as well. Depending on the specific version of the Mac OS installed, this extension may be named Apple CD/DVD Extension, Apple CD/DVD Driver, Apple CD-ROM, AppleCD, or Apple CD/DVD.

Several third-party CD-ROM drives, particularly SCSI models, are not supported by Apple's CD-ROM driver extension. In these cases, the drive should ship with an alternate third-party CD-ROM driver if they are intended for use with the Mac. If not, you can purchase one separately from the drive. The most common non-Apple driver is FWB's CD-ROM Toolkit. This control panel supports many CD-ROM drives from most manufacturers (both internal and external models).

If you are considering a drive that is not designed for use with the Mac, check to be sure that you can find a Macintosh CD-ROM driver that will support it before buying. In the case of internal IDE drives, Apple's driver will likely recognize the drive, even though it isn't officially supported. Unfortunately, there will be some cases where trial and error is the only way to be certain whether a CD-ROM drive will be supported on the Mac with Apple or third-party drivers.

Beyond needing a driver for the CD-ROM drive itself, there are a number of other CD-ROM-related extensions that are part of the Mac OS. These include the Audio CD Access, Foreign File Access, ISO 9660 File Access, High Sierra File Access, Apple Photo Access, and UDF Volume

Access extensions. Each of these extensions allows the Mac to access CDs that use a different file format than the traditional HFS format used for Mac discs and CD-ROMs. Without these extensions, the Mac will not be able to recognize some forms of CDs and will display an error message saying the disc is unrecognizable when inserted.

CD-ROM Formats

Like any other disc used with the Mac, CD-ROMs need to be formatted in such a way that the computer can recognize them and read the data stored on them. Also, like other types of discs, there are varying types of formats depending on which platform the CD-ROM is intended to be used. However, whereas most disc types can be boiled down to a "Mac format" and a "PC format," there are more than two basic CD-ROM formats in use, some of which are specialized for specific uses. This section looks at the most common formats used for CD-ROM discs. The Mac can read all of these formats, provided the appropriate extensions are installed, as mentioned in the previous section.

HFS

HFS (also known as Mac OS Standard format) is the standard format Macs use when formatting smaller hard drives, lower-capacity removable-media drives (such as Zip disks and SuperDisks), and floppies. This

TABLE 16-2

Common CD Formats and Their Uses

Format	Macintosh Use
HFS	Files, folders, applications, startup CD-ROMs
ISO 9660	Files and folders, data intended for use on a PC
High Sierra	Files and folders, data intended for use on a PC
Hybrid	Files, folders, applications, data intended for Macs and PCs
UDF	Recordable CDs recorded incrementally
Audio CD	Music or other audio content, playable in audio CD Players
Enhanced CD	Audio CD with data content (files, folders, applications, etc.)
Video CD	MPEG video content
Kodak Photo CD	Image archives

is the typical format used on CD-ROMs that contain files and applications and are designed specifically to be used with the Mac. Because the format is the same that you would use for a hard drive, the Mac simply treats the CD-ROM as any other type of disk with the exception that it is read-only.

ISO 9660

ISO 9660 is the most common CD format used on Windows-based PCs. It is a format that was ratified by the International Standards Organization (ISO) and is pretty much the industry standard for non-Mac computers. Macs are capable of reading ISO 9660 CD-ROMs, provided the File Exchange or PC Exchange control panel and Foreign File Access and ISO 9660 extensions are installed properly. While the disc and any files will be available to the Mac, any applications that are included on the CD-ROM will most likely not run because they will be written to be used with non-Mac computers.

High Sierra

The High Sierra format is another format used for CD-ROMs on non-Mac computers. It predates the ISO 9660 standard and was initially developed in the mid-1980s. Replaced by ISO 9660, High Sierra CD-ROMs are fairly uncommon today, though older software and games may still be found on them. Macs are capable of reading High Sierra CD-ROMs, provided the File Exchange control panel and the High Sierra File Access extension are installed. In fact, some multi-CD games that were available for both the Mac and PC shipped with High Sierra discs containing some of the data.

Hybrid CDs

Hybrid CDs are CD-ROMs that use both the ISO 9660 and HFS formats. When the CD-ROM is inserted into a drive attached to a Mac, the CD will be recognized as an HFS format CD-ROM and treated as though it were exclusively that format. When inserted in a Windows-based PC, the CD-ROM would be recognized as an ISO 9660 CD and any HFS format would be ignored.

Hybrid CDs are often used by developers who want to distribute a product to both Mac and PC computer users. The one CD can contain the files and applications needed for each platform. Also, since only the native format for the computer reading the CD is recognized, only the files specific to that computer will be displayed to the user.

Hybrid CDs can also contain a segment of the CD where data can be accessed by either platform computer as needed. This is useful for game developers because they can create separate sections of the CD for the Mac and Windows versions of a game application. However, any video or image files used by the game (which would be platform-transparent, unlike the application itself) need only be written to the CD once.

UDF

UDF (Universal Data Format) is a new format being used for CD creation. Specifically, it is oriented to users with recordable CD drives because it allows for easier incremental methods of recording data to recordable CD media than traditional CD formats like HFS and ISO 9660. The Mac can read CD-ROMs created in this format, provided the UDF Volume Access extension is installed. UDF is discussed in more detail in the "Creating CD-R/CD-RW Discs" section later in the chapter.

Audio CD

Audio CDs are the CDs you buy in a record store. They contain tracks of music (or other digital audio content) and can be played in the CD players in a home stereo, portable CD player, and some car stereos. Provided the Audio CD Access and Foreign File Access extensions are installed on your Mac, audio CDs will be recognized by the Mac and you will be able to play the CD and listen to the audio content through your Mac's speakers.

Audio CDs are, essentially, a data CD-ROM with a specific disc format (sometimes called Redbook format) and specific file format. Each track on an audio CD is an audio file that has been recorded on the CD under the audio CD format. If you double-click on an audio CD icon in the Finder, a window will open displaying the disc's contents: a series of individual audio files, one for each track.

Playing Audio CDs on the Mac   The Mac can play audio CDs as long as the Audio CD Access and Foreign File Access extensions arc installed. Apple provides two methods for playing audio CDs on the Mac: the AppleAudio CD Player application and the CD strip item in the Mac's control strip. The AppleAudio CD Player provides a simple interface that

Figure 16-2

The AppleAudio CD Player and the CD control stip module both allow you to play audio CDs on the Mac.

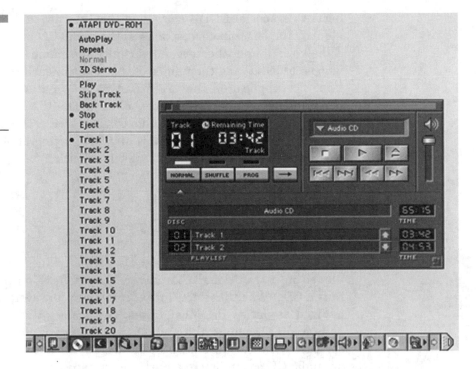

resembles a traditional stereo CD player's faceplate and controls. The CD strip item in the control strip provides a menu that allows you to play, stop, pause, or select an individual track of the CD. Both of these are shown in Figure 16-2.

There are also a number of additional applications that you can use that provide alternate interfaces to playing CDs. The FWB CD-ROM Toolkit third-party CD-ROM driver includes its own CD-playing application, for example, and there are several shareware applications. Some shareware options also offer the ability to play other audio file types such as the popular MP3 audio files.

CDDB The CDDB, or CD Database, is a nonprofit project to make all the information about the tracks contained on various audio CDs easily accessible over the Internet. CDDB applications for the Mac include stand-alone CD player applications, such as the shareware NetCD, as well as applications that simply connect to a CDDB server and query for information when a CD is inserted but do not play the CD themselves.

When used, a CDDB application looks at the lengths of individual tracks and other identifying information about an audio CD. It then connects to a special CDDB server on the Internet and asks the server to identify the CD that corresponds to the audio CD inserted in the Mac. If a match is found, the server transmits the name of the CD, the artist who recorded it, and the names of the songs in each track to the application. The application then records this information in the CD Remote Programs file in the Preferences folder inside the System Folder. From that point on, whenever that audio CD is inserted, the title of the CD and of each track will be displayed in any CD playing application instead of the generic "Audio CD 1" and "Track 1," "Track 2," and so forth being displayed, as shown in Figure 16-3.

Enhanced Audio CDs

Enhanced audio CDs are audio CDs with an added data content. When played in a traditional CD player, they behave as perfectly ordinary music CDs. When inserted into a computer, however, they are also recognized as data CDs. Most times, two icons will be displayed for an enhanced CD, one for the audio CD and one for the data content (as is the case with the CD shown in Figure 16-4). In a way, you can think of an audio CD as similar to a partitioned hard drive.

The data content of an enhanced CD can be anything, but it is usually additional content relating to the recording artist whose music is on the audio portion of the CD. Small multimedia clips in a self-playing application, lyric sheets, commentary from the artist, or links to the artist's website are some of the things you can expect to find on the data portion of an enhanced CD.

Enhanced CDs can cause problems if you want to use the CD as an audio CD and play the music tracks using the AppleAudio CD Player (or a similar application). The Mac will almost always recognize the audio content and allow you to play the audio tracks as it would a normal audio CD. However, when you perform an action that requires the Mac to query the drives attached to it, such as using an open/save dialog box, the Mac will look to the enhanced CD as a data CD. This will cause it to stop playing the audio content and "forget" that the audio content is there. This means that you will then have to start playing the CD from the beginning again.

Also, when ejecting enhanced CDs, it is important to drag the icons of the audio and data segments of the CD to the Trash. If you drag only one to the Trash to eject it, you may cause the Mac to freeze or hang when it queries the drive at some later point.

Figure 16-3
CDDB information allows artist, disc, and song names to be included in CD-playing applications.

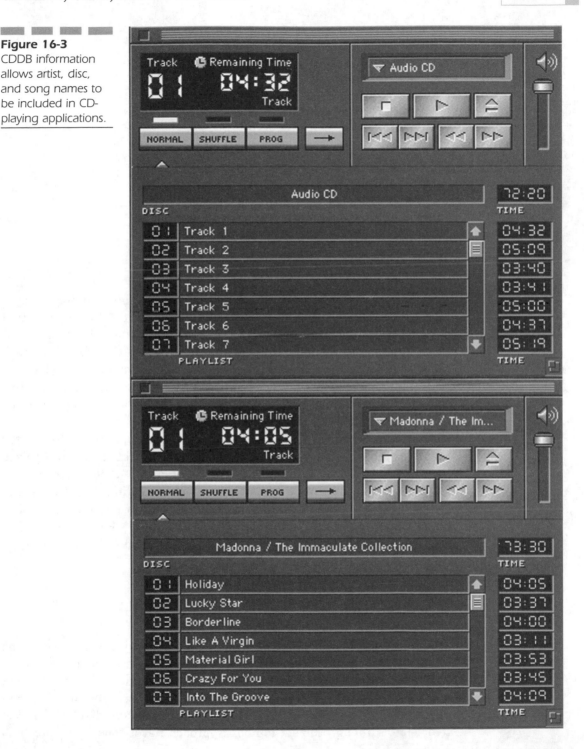

Figure 16-4
This Enhanced audio CD displays both of these icons when inserted into a Mac's CD-ROM drive.

Video CDs

Video CDs, sometimes referred to as VCDs, are a home entertainment technology that never really caught on in the United States, but that have been extremely popular in Asia. They are a special format of CD that contains an MPEG-1 encoded video file. Video CDs function much like DVD movies, only it generally takes at least two or more video CDs to contain a single movie. Video CD players can be found that attach to a television set. When a video CD is inserted in the player and played, the video contained on it is displayed on the television.

Although the video CD format never became popular in the United States as a home entertainment option, it is a format that is recognized by the Mac. If a video CD is inserted into a Mac's CD-ROM drive, an icon for it will appear on the Mac's desktop. Double-clicking on the CD's icon will reveal an MPEG-1 video file. All recent versions of Apple's QuickTime include the ability to decode and play MPEG-1 video files. This means that you can open the file on a video CD and play with Apple's QuickTime Player application.

Kodak Photo CDs

The Kodak Photo CD was a technology developed by Kodak back in the late 1980s. It was initially designed to function as a home electronics device that was attached to a television set. When users had traditional camera film developed, they could have the pictures placed on special photo CDs that could then be put in the set-top box and displayed on the television. Although the set-top box approach never took off as much as expected, the Kodak Photo CD format can be read by computer CD-ROM drives as well. These photo CDs are still an option when having film developed at Kodak photo shops, and the CDs can be read by the Mac as long as the Apple Photo Access extension is installed. The developed photos can then be opened by an appropriate image application on the Mac.

Types of CD-ROM Drives

CD-ROM drives come in internal and external models, though internal models are by far the most common, as just about every computer today includes either an internal CD-ROM drive or a DVD-ROM drive capable of reading CD-ROMs. Still, there are situations where an additional CD-ROM drive may be desired or needed, and external models are available as well.

Essentially, CD-ROM drives are all the same or very similar. They all use the same laser technology, and they all feature the same basic design. In fact, the drive engine, which contains the major components of the drive, is identical in many drives from different companies. This is because only a few manufacturers produce drive engines for CD-ROM drives. These engines are then sold to individual developers who use the drive engines in their CD-ROM drives and sell the finished product under their own name. Similarly, the CD-ROM drives Apple uses in the current and recent Macs are all OEM drives produced by other companies for Apple.

The biggest difference you're likely to see among CD-ROM drives is the speed at which they are capable of reading CD-ROMs. As discussed earlier, all CD-ROM speeds are a multiple of the initial speed (150 KB/second) used by audio CDs. Beyond speed, the biggest differences you'll find are the interface methods, which are discussed in the next section.

CD-ROM Interfaces

Like any other drive, CD-ROM drives can be connected to the Mac through one of the common device interfaces, including IDE, SCSI, FireWire, and USB. If you are replacing the CD-ROM drive of a Mac, you will most likely opt for an IDE model, as this is what Apple ships in all Macs, save the PowerBook models. SCSI internal drives are also an

Speed	Interface Methods Capable of Speed
1X	IDE, SCSI, USB, FireWire, expansion bay
2X	IDE, SCSI, USB, FireWire, expansion bay
4X	IDE, SCSI, USB, FireWire, expansion bay
6X	IDE, SCSI, FireWire, expansion bay
8X	IDE, SCSI, FireWire, expansion bay
10X	IDE, SCSI, FireWire, expansion bay
12X	IDE, SCSI, FireWire, expansion bay
14X	IDE, SCSI, FireWire, expansion bay
16X	IDE, SCSI, FireWire, expansion bay
18X	IDE, SCSI, FireWire, expansion bay
20X	IDE, SCSI, FireWire, expansion bay
24X	IDE, SCSI, FireWire, expansion bay

option for the Power Mac computers, though not one worth considering if you do not already have a SCSI card installed.

Table 16-3 shows the various CD-ROM speeds and their corresponding interfaces.

IDE (ATAPI)   The internal CD-ROM drives of the Power Mac computers and the original iMac models are standard IDE CD-ROM drives. These can generally be replaced by any other internal IDE CD-ROM drive if you choose to do so. Short of a CD-ROM drive failure, however, there should be no real need to replace the drive. Generally, the drives used in the Mac are close to the fastest on the market (and faster drives probably won't offer really noticeable real-world performance improvements anyway).

You could replace them with an internal CD-R or CD-RW drive if you wanted an internal solution for creating your own CDs. It is also possible to replace them with an IDE DVD-ROM drive. However, as discussed in the next chapter, DVD-ROM drives also need a special MPEG-2 decoding card if you want to use the drive to view DVD movies. The current Power Mac models use an internal DVD-ROM drive instead of a CD-ROM drive already.

The second-generation, slot-loading iMacs also use an IDE CD-ROM drive (some of the iMac DV and all iMac DV Special Edition models use an IDE DVD-ROM drive instead). This drive can be replaced with another IDE model, but because of the iMac's case design, it must be a slot-loading CD-ROM drive. Slot-loading CD-ROM drives are rare, unlike the traditional tray-loading CD-ROM drives. Most likely, replacing a slot-loading iMac CD-ROM drive will require ordering a replacement drive from Apple, which can be done only by Apple Authorized Service Centers.

The iBook also uses an IDE CD-ROM drive, but it is a special thin model designed for portable use in general and the iBook's design in particular. It can be replaced, but like the slot-loading iMac models, a replacement drive will probably need to be ordered from Apple directly, which can be done only by Apple Authorized Service Centers.

SCSI For several years, internal CD-ROM drives on the Mac were of the SCSI variety. However, IDE has been the interface of choice for quite some time and is the only option at present unless you choose to add a SCSI card with internal SCSI connectors. SCSI also offers support for external CD-ROM drives. Again, this requires that a SCSI card be added to the Mac.

External SCSI CD-ROM drives offer an advantage of performance over the other principal option, which is USB (FireWire drives also offer such a performance advantage, though they are only beginning to become readily available). There are also special CD-ROM towers that contain multiple CD-ROM drives, enabling you to access several CD-ROMs at once. These are particularly useful if you are running a file server and need to provide several of your users with access to the different CD-ROMs at one time. When accessing multiple CD-ROMs at once, USB's performance limitations become very obvious.

USB USB CD-ROM drives offer a solution if you want to add a second CD-ROM drive to a Mac. They can also be used as an emergency solution should the internal CD-ROM drive of a Mac suffer damage that prevents it from being used. This is only a stopgap measure to allow the Mac to use CD-ROMs and should not be used as a permanent solution. Rather, the internal CD-ROM drive should be replaced, as it offers better performance and the ability to start up from Mac OS or utility CD in an emergency.

USB CD-ROM drives can also appeal to PowerBook owners who wish to use a CD-ROM drive at the same time that they are using an expansion bay drive besides the CD-ROM or DVD-ROM drive that came with the computer. If a PowerBook user has an expansion bay hard drive installed that he or she needs to use for critical files or applications but also needs to access the contents of a CD-ROM, a USB solution is an option that may be easier than constantly putting the PowerBook to sleep and swapping the two drives.

Expansion Bay PowerBook CD-ROM or DVD-ROM drives install into the PowerBook's expansion bay. They are easily removable modules that can be replaced by a second battery or another type of expansion bay drive, such as a hard drive or Zip drive. The expansion bay itself is a modified IDE device and delivers equivalent performance to an internal IDE CD-ROM drive. To replace a damaged expansion bay CD-ROM drive, you need to request a replacement drive from Apple, either directly or through an Apple Authorized Service Center.

CD-ROM versus DVD-ROM Drives

CD-ROM drives have been replaced in most of the current Macs by DVD-ROM drives. DVD-ROM drives are completely backward-compatible when reading any type of CD-ROM and function perfectly fine as CD-ROM drive replacements. As the name implies, they are also capable of reading DVD-ROM disks (see the next chapter). Currently, only the iBook and some slot-loading iMac models feature a CD-ROM drive. The Power Mac G3, original iMac, one option of the 1999 PowerBook models, and some of the early Power Mac G4 models with a PCI graphics card did ship with CD-ROM drive instead of a DVD-ROM drive as well.

Installing or Replacing a CD-ROM Drive

For the most part, you will probably not need to install or replace the CD-ROM drives of a Mac. If you do find yourself having to do so, the following sections describe the process for both the internal drives of current and recent Macs as well as external models.

External CD-ROM Drives   External CD-ROM drives are fairly uncommon today, and all the current Macs ship with internal CD-ROM or DVD-ROM drives. Installing an external CD-ROM drive means using a SCSI or USB CD-ROM drive. The installation process is the same as it would be for any other external device using these interface technologies. For the most part, this is the simple process of installing the driver software for the new drive, restarting the Mac, and attaching the drive. For SCSI models, you also need to be sure to follow all the rules described in Chapter 12 regarding unique SCSI ID numbers for each device and SCSI chain termination.

PowerBook Expansion Bay CD-ROM Drives   For years now, PowerBooks have used expansion bay modules for CD-ROM drives.

Installing or removing these CD-ROM drives (or DVD-ROM drives on the most recent PowerBooks) is quite simple. Just remove the drive or battery that is in the expansion bay, and insert the CD-ROM drive (or other drive) into the bay. Wake the PowerBook from sleep mode, and you're done.

Power Mac Internal CD-ROM Drives   The CD-ROM drive of the Power Mac computers (a DVD-ROM or DVD-RAM drive in some models, including the current models) is mounted in a drive carrier that is shared with the internal Zip drive (or other removable-media drive), if one is installed. This carrier, shown in Figure 16-5, must be removed as a unit when replacing either the CD-ROM drive or when replacing or installing a Zip drive (or other removable-media drive).

The first step in removing the carrier that holds the CD-ROM and Zip drives is to open the Mac and remove the cables attached to the back of these drives. This includes the IDE ribbon cable and the individual

Figure 16-5   The carrier unit containing the CD-ROM drive and an optional Zip drive.

power connectors for each drive, assuming both a CD-ROM and Zip drive are installed. You may also need to remove the CD audio cable that may be attached to the back of the CD-ROM drive.

Next, you need to remove the faceplate on the front of the Mac that covers both drives. There are two tabs on the inside of the Mac's case that secure this faceplate. As shown in Figure 16-6, these tabs are located right next to the carrier itself. Once these tabs are released, the faceplate can be disconnected from the computer.

Figure 16-6 The plastic tabs indicated here must be released to remove the faceplate covering the CD-ROM and Zip drive.

Once you have removed the faceplate, you will notice that there are two screws located behind where it was. These screws, shown in Figure 16-7, are located just below the CD-ROM drive. You need to remove these screws in order to remove the carrier for the CD-ROM drive and Zip drive.

Once the screws are removed, you can remove the carrier from the computer. Do this by pushing it forward through the front of the computer (where the faceplate was removed), as shown in Figure 16-8. There

Figure 16-7   These two screws secure the carrier to the Mac's case.

Figure 16-8   The carrier is removed through the front of the Mac.

is an electromagnetic interference (EMI) gasket on the underside of the
carrier that may make pushing the drive out somewhat difficult.

Once the carrier is free of the computer, you can remove and replace
the CD-ROM drive. First, remove the EMI gasket that is attached to the
back of the CD-ROM drive. The gasket is attached by an metal tab on
each side of the drive (shown in Figure 16-9). These tabs are easily
released. Then you need to remove the mounting screws that hold the
drive in place in the carrier. These are indicated in Figure 16-10. Use
these same screws to secure the replacement drive and then replace the
EMI gasket.

Before installing the CD-ROM drive, you should set the jumpers on it
to the appropriate master or slave setting for the IDE channel. As
explained in Chapter 13, if there is no other drive on the channel, the
CD-ROM should be set as the master drive. If there is also a Zip drive (or
other removable-media drive), one of the two will need to be set as master and one as slave. Traditionally, the CD-ROM is set as the master
device, though both drives will still function if the CD-ROM is set as

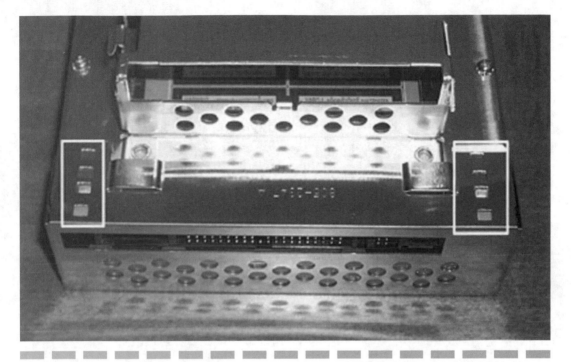

Figure 16-9   The tabs indicated here are used to release the EMI gasket from the CD-ROM drive.

slave and the Zip drive is set as master. CD-ROM drives usually ship from manufacturers with the jumpers set to the master position.

When you are reinserting the carrier, the process is essentially the reverse of removing it. You should ensure that the tab on the drive shelf that the carrier sits on inside the computer is positioned so that it extends into the hole on the base of the carrier. The tab is shown in Figure 16-11.

Original iMac CD-ROM Drives   Open the iMac and remove the motherboard/drive chassis as described in Chapter 1. Set the chassis down, with the drive section pointing toward you. The CD-ROM drive is attached to a carrier/mounting frame. This frame is spring-loaded and is held in the drive section of the motherboard/drive chassis by the force of the spring. To remove the frame and the CD-ROM drive from the chassis, push the CD-ROM backward toward the motherboard until you are able to release the tabs that holds the frame in place (shown in Figure 16-12).

Figure 16-10
The mounting screws used to secure a CD-ROM drive to the carrier.

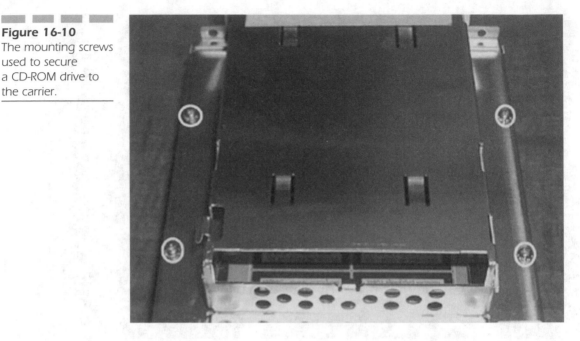

Figure 16-11
This tab needs to be lined up with the appropriate section of the carrier unit.

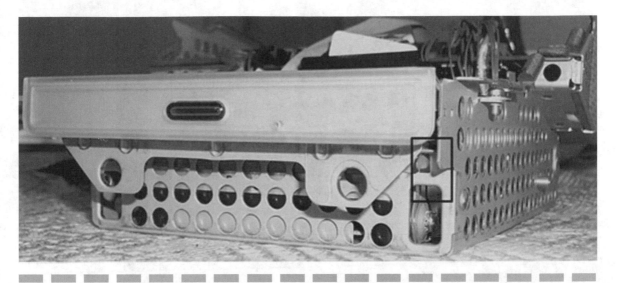

Figure 16-12 *There are two spring-release tabs, one on either side of the iMac's CD-ROM drive, which hold it in place in the motherboard/drive chassis.*

Once the tab is released, you should be able to lift the front section of the CD-ROM drive out of the chassis and then lift the entire drive and mounting frame out. At this point, disconnect the IDE cable attached to the rear of the CD-ROM drive. The CD-ROM drive and frame are now free of the motherboard/drive chassis.

Apple ships the iMac CD-ROM drives with the spring-loaded carrier/frame attached as a single unit. Replacement drives from Apple will come already assembled for installation (with the exception of the bezel/faceplate for the drive tray's door). When dealing with a non-Apple drive, you can remove the drive from the frame and replace it with an alternate drive by removing the screws indicated in Figure 16-13

The bezel/faceplate at the front of the CD-ROM drive can also be removed from the Apple CD-ROM drive and attached to an alternate drive. To remove the bezel from the CD-ROM drive, you will first need to use a paper clip to open the tray of the CD-ROM drive, as you would when forcibly ejecting a CD. On the underside of the drive's tray, centered just behind the bezel is a micro-screw. You need to remove this screw in order to release the bezel/faceplate. Once the screw is removed, you need to release three tabs that hold the bezel in place against the CD-ROM tray.

Once you have replaced the CD-ROM drive in the carrier/frame (or used a replacement CD-ROM drive from Apple, with its own car-

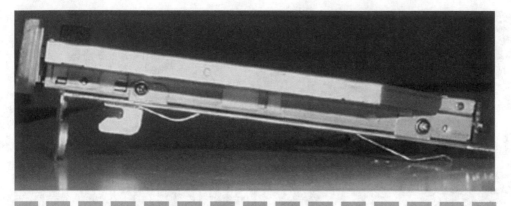

Figure 16-13   These mounting screws (two on each side) attach the drive to the frame.

rier/frame attached) and the bezel, you are ready to reinsert the drive into the motherboard/drive chassis. This is very much the reverse of removing the drive; however, you need to be certain that the spring catch on the underside of the carrier/frame is hooked onto the spring, which is now resting on top of the hard drive (as shown in Figure 16-14). You also need to be sure that the two tabs at the front of the carrier (which you released when removing the drive) are inserted into the appropriate slots in the chassis.

Second-Generation iMac CD-ROM Drives   The internal drives of the second-generation iMacs require a slot-loading CD-ROM drive. This type of drive is rather difficult to find, which will present problems if you wish to replace it. Also, some iMac DV and all iMac DV Special Edition computers use a DVD-ROM drive instead of a CD-ROM drive.

To replace the drive, first remove the lower casing of the computer as described in Chapter 1. Once you have done this, you need to remove the carrier that holds both the hard drive and the CD-ROM drive. To do this, you must remove the four screws that hold the carrier in place, as indicated in Figure 16-15. You also need to remove the IDE cables attached to both the CD-ROM drive and the hard drive, as well as the power cable attached to the hard drive.

You can now lift the carrier and the drives out of the computer. To remove the CD-ROM drive, remove the mounting screws that secure it to

Figure 16-14   *This spring needs to attach to the hook on the back of the CD-ROM's frame.*

the carrier, as indicated in Figure 16-16. Once these screws are removed, slide the drive out of the carrier and replace it. Reinserting the carriers is an exact reverse of the process of removing it.

Recordable and Rewritable CD Technologies

Professionally made CD-ROMs, such as those that you buy in a computer store, are produced by a process known as *pressing,* where a mold is made of all the pits and lands of the CD-ROM. This mold is then pressed into the polycarbonate substrate of the new CD-ROM, creating the

Figure 16-15 The white circles indicate the recessed positions of the four screws that hold the carrier in place.

actual pits and lands of the CD-ROM. The silvering process then adds the reflective layer to the CD-ROM, and then the protective lacquer and label are applied. Needless to say, the equipment needed to press CDs in this way is expensive and far beyond the resources of small businesses or individuals.

Two alternate technologies, known as CD-recordable (CD-R) and CD-rewritable (CD-RW) allow for individual users to create their own CD-ROMs. CD-R and CD-RW discs are read in the same way as CD-ROMs, but they are structurally different from CD-ROMs, which is notable in that they have a bluish color compared to the silver of a pressed CD. The following sections of this chapter look at how CD-R and CD-RW technology functions, as well as at the hardware and software needed to create your own CD-ROMs using these technologies.

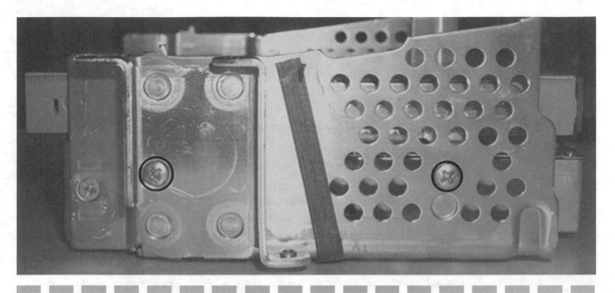

Figure 16-16 These mounting screws (two on each side) hold the CD-ROM drive in place in the carrier.

How CD-R and CD-RW Drives Store Data

CD-R and CD-RW discs store data in the same way as professionally pressed CD-ROM discs do, using pits and lands. The difference exists in the materials used to create the disc and in the way the pits and lands are created on the disc. While the pits and lands in a pressed CD-ROM are created from a mold being pressed into the polycarbonate substrate layer of the disc, CD-R and CD-RW discs are created using a laser and a layer of dye. This approach works because of how the disc is constructed.

A CD-R disk still contains a substrate layer made of the same material as a pressed CD-ROM. This layer contains a single spiral track that is preformed in the disc when it is constructed. It is along this track that the pits and lands of the CD will be created. The substrate layer is then covered with a greenish-blue translucent layer that is, in turn, backed by a reflective gold layer. When the CD-R or CD-RW drive records data on a CD-R disc, the heat of the laser adjusts the dye in the greenish-blue layer to create areas that are more or less reflective. Although not created in the same manner as the more or less reflective areas that are the pits and lands of a pressed CD-ROM, the pits and lands of a CD-R disc achieve the same result. When the disc is read, the lands reflect the light beam from the laser directly onto the photocell detector of the optical

Figure 16-17
The physical layers
of a CD-R disc. Note:
The pits and lands
are generated by
dye coloring, not
depressions in the
substrate's surface.

Protective Laquer
Reflective Layer
Dye Layer (pits and lands)

Polycarbonate Substrate

Physical Layers of a CD-R Disk

drive head. Meanwhile, the pits do not reflect the laser light with nearly the same level of intensity as when the light beam strikes a land. This allows CD-R discs to be compatible with the vast majority of CD-ROM drives. Figure 16-17 illustrates the layers of a CD-R or CD-RW disc.

CD-RW allows for the disc to be erased and reused. This contrasts to CD-R, where once a disc is created (or burned) in a CD-R drive, it is permanent. CD-RW discs use a metallic alloy layer instead of the dye layer used by CD-R discs. The laser of a CD-RW drive can heat the alloy to make it less reflective, thus creating a pit. This alloy, when heated sufficiently by the same laser that was used to write data to the disc in the first place can be restored to its initial state, thereby allowing the disc to be erased and then reused. The downside to this process is that the metallic alloy is not as reflective as the dye coating used in a CD-R disc, which can cause compatibility issues with traditional CD-R and CD-ROM drives reading the created discs. See the next section for more details.

CD-RW drives are much more recent than CD-R drives, and they can write data to both CD-R and CD-RW discs. Because reusing a CD-RW disc involves erasing the original contents of disc, the process is usually slower than writing a CD-R disc is.

Compatibility Concerns with CD-R and CD-RW Discs Although CD-R and CD-RW discs are functionally the same as pressed CD-ROMs, there have been some compatibility issues with these discs. This is because they are not as fully reflective as pressed CD-ROMs. In the case of CD-R discs, it is because the blank CD-R discs created by various companies do not all use the same types of dye. Each company tends to use its own dye formula for CD-R discs. Some of these formulas are compatible with all existing CD-ROM drives and audio CD players, while others are not. As a rule, compatibility is less an issue with modern CD-ROM drives and audio devices than with older devices, and most name-brand CD-R disks do not, in my experience, pose compatibility problems.

More to the point is the compatibility of CD-RW discs. CD-RW discs are less reflective than either CD-ROM or CD-R discs. This means that they are open to more compatibility problems. They are also a much more recent technology, having only come of age in 1998 and later. If an audio CD is created using them, it will not be read by most audio CD players. There are also some potential compatibility issues with CD-ROM drives more than two years old being able to read CD-RW discs.

A solution developed by Hewlett-Packard and Philips, who create various computer peripherals, including CD-ROM drive engines, was to formulate a new CD-ROM standard. This standard, known as Multiread, calls for CD-ROM drives that are designed to read a very wide range of CD media, including all the varieties of CD-R discs and CD-RW discs. This standard should help to ensure that any modern CD-ROM drives will not suffer any compatibility problems at all with CD-R and CD-RW discs.

Comparing CD-R and CD-RW Drives

There are several things to consider when choosing a CD-R or CD-RW drive. As with any peripheral, a company's reputation and the quality of their product lines as a whole is one of them. Beyond this, when choosing CD-R or CD-RW drives, you should look primarily at the reliability of the drives and at the speeds at which they are capable of recording. You should also look at the size of a drive's cache.

CD-R and CD-RW recording speeds are given in the same increments as CD-ROM speeds (refer to Table 16-1 for a list of these speeds). CD-R drives will list the speeds the drive is capable of as something like 4X/16X. The first speed is the drive's write speed, or the speed at which it records data to a CD-R disc. The second speed is how fast it is capable of reading discs as a CD-ROM drive. CD-RW discs have their speeds given like 4X/2X/16X. The first speed is, again, the write or recording speed of the drive. The second speed is the rewrite speed. This is the speed at which the drive will erase and then record a CD-RW disc. The third speed is the read speed when the drive is functioning as a CD-ROM drive.

Cache A CD-R or CD-RW drive will come with a relatively small amount of RAM built into it. This RAM cache is designed to ensure that the drive receives a constant flow of data. The cache receives data from the Mac until it is filled. The drive then takes the data from the cache and records it to the CD. The cache functions as a buffer. If the Mac's hard drive or the interface with the CD-R/CD-RW drive is momentarily slowed down so that it cannot transfer data to the drive at the speed the drive is writing to a disc, there will be some data stored in the cache for the drive to access. This keeps the drive from being affected by the momentary slowdown and keeps the flow of data to the CD constant. The bigger the cache, the larger the safety margin and the less likely for CDs to not be written correctly. CD authoring utilities also allow you to set a cache in the Mac's RAM that augments the built-in cache of a CD-R or CD-RW drive in case of a hard drive slowdown.

CD-R and CD-RW Interfaces

As with CD-ROM drives, or any other peripheral, there are various options for connecting a CD-R or CD-RW drive to the Macintosh. The most common methods are to use external SCSI or USB connections. However, internal IDE models are available, and FireWire models are beginning to become available as well.

IDE (ATAPI)   IDE CD-R or CD-RW drives are all internal drives. A number of such drives are on the market, and they can be used with a desktop Macintosh (such as the Power Mac or iMac), provided that your CD authoring software of choice supports the drive model in question. However, using these drives on the current Mac models does present one problem. None of the current Macs includes more than one 5.25-inch drive bay that can be used to install a CD drive of any type. The one drive bay that desktop Macs (both the iMac and Power Mac models) do offer is already in use by the computer's internal CD-ROM or DVD-ROM drive.

It is possible to remove the internal CD-ROM or DVD-ROM drive of the Power Mac computers and the original iMac and replace it with a CD-R or CD-RW drive. The slot-loading iMacs and iMac DV computers would require a slot-loading CD-R or CD-RW drive because of its case design, and such devices are not currently available. The process for doing so would be the same as described earlier in this chapter for replacing an internal CD-ROM drive on these computers.

Before you decide to replace the internal CD-ROM or DVD-ROM drive of a Mac with a CD-R or CD-RW drive, you should consider a few factors. While the replacement drive will be able to read CD-ROMs as easily as the original drive, it will likely not support as high a speed when reading them. Also, you will probably not be able to use the drive to start up from a Mac OS or utility CD-ROM. This can present severe problems in an emergency situation, such as a hard drive failure or System file corruption. If the Mac in question uses a DVD-ROM drive, you will lose the ability to read DVD-ROM discs, as well as DVD movie discs. Although DVD-ROMs are not yet a standard in the way CD-ROMs are, I would not opt for losing the ability to read them in the future.

SCSI   SCSI CD-R and CD-RW drives are available in both internal and external models. Both of these types require the Mac to be equipped with a SCSI card, and an internal solution presents the same issues as described in the last section relating to IDE models. External models, however, function quite well with few limitations.

The higher data transfer performance available to SCSI devices, as well as SCSI's firm entrenchment in the computer marketplace, means that there are a large number of CD-R and CD-RW drives that use a SCSI interface. The performance advantages of the faster SCSI types also means that SCSI drives can offer very good performance in a CD-R or CD-RW drive.

SCSI has also served well as a CD-R/CD-RW interface method for several years and is well supported by virtually all CD authoring utilities. This means that you are less likely to run into any bugs, issues, or compatibility concerns with a SCSI CD-R or CD-RW drive than you are with newer technologies such as USB and FireWire. Some CD authoring utilities, such as Adaptec's DirectCD (see the "UDF CDs" section later in the chapter) are currently only supporting SCSI drive options.

USB   USB has become one of the most common methods for attaching CD-R and CD-RW drives because of its simplicity and its existence as the default interface technology on all the current and recent Macs. Indeed, for some Mac models, such as the original iMac and the iBook, USB is the only option for adding a recordable CD solution (short of repacing the internal CD-ROM drive).

As with other types of devices, USB's performance limitations do affect how well it works with CD-R/CD-RW drives. Most notably, USB limits these drives to recording data at 4X speed at best. Slightly higher speeds may be supported on a drive, but 4X is the practical limit, considering that the USB channel must deal with additional devices transferring data as well as the CD-R/CD-RW drive.

USB CD-R/CD-RW drives have gotten a good deal of support from CD authoring software developers and are supported by most CD authoring utilities. This combined with USB's ease of use does make these drives attractive and easy to use, even though some utilities may not support USB drives and there are the obvious performance limitations.

FireWire FireWire is the latest technology to be used for CD-R and CD-RW drives. It combines performance equal to that of SCSI with the ease of interface that has made USB so popular. It also is supported on the majority of current Mac models. FireWire's performance is its biggest asset when being used for recordable CD drives, but also important is FireWire isynchronous transfer abilities. Isynchronous transfer allows FireWire to ensure that a set amount of bandwidth is continually available between an application running on the Mac and a FireWire device. This ability means that a FireWire CD-R/CD-RW drive will be assured that enough bandwidth is available to continually transfer data from the Mac to the drive, even at very high transfer rates and with other high-performance FireWire devices being used at the same time.

The problem with FireWire as an interface method for CD-R and CD-RW drives is that CD authoring software is still catching up to the performance abilities offered by the faster hardware interface. Many don't offer all their features when working at higher recording speeds over FireWire. If you want to consider a FireWire drive, you should check to see what CD authoring software is available and how fully it supports the FireWire drives you're considering. These issues will probably be resolved in the near future, as developers work to meet the demands for high-performance FireWire CD authoring.

Creating CD-R/CD-RW Discs

To store data on a CD-R or CD-RW disc, you will need to use special CD authoring software. The most popular such software is Adaptec's Toast. Generally, your CD-R or CD-RW drive should include authoring software that includes support for that type of drive. If you aren't satisfied with the utility included with your drive, you can purchase an alternate utility. You should, however, be certain that the alternate utility you choose includes support for your specific CD-R or CD-RW drive model. You can check with the utility's developer for this information.

This section describes how to create either a data CD containing files or an audio CD using the Toast software. It is intended to give you an overview of the process and does not cover all details and may not be relevant when using a different CD authoring utility. Be sure to check the manual and documentation that comes with the utility of your choice.

When you launch Toast, you are presented with a window such as the one pictured in Figure 16-18. From the pop-up menu in the window, you can determine which type of disc you want to create. The options in this

Figure 16-18   The standard window for preparing to create a new CD in Toast.

menu will vary depending on what version of Toast you're using, but you will always have the options Files and Folders (a basic Mac data CD) and Audio CD. You may also have options for video CDs, ISO 9600 (PC data CDs), enhanced audio CDs, and hybrid (Mac/PC data) CDs. The lower section of the window displays the recordable CD drive that Toast has recognized as being connected to the Mac. If no drive is recognized but the drive is connected, you can use the Search button to make Toast look for drives. If you are using a USB or FireWire drive that has been connected after startup, you may need to restart the Mac before Toast will recognize the drive.

To create a data CD, select the CD format that you wish to use from the menu. If the disc is going to be used on Macs only, you can use the default Files and Folder or Mac Files and Folders setting. Then simply drag the files and folder you want to include on the CD onto Toast's window. Toast will add any folder or file dragged to its window to the contents of the CD. You can click on the Data button if you want to organize how the files and folders will be appear on the CD of if you want to remove any items from the CD before you create it. As you drag the items into Toast's window, Toast will begin creating a disc image file on your hard drive, containing the files that you are adding to the CD (up to 650 MB). This disc image is then copied to a CD as it is burned.

If you want to create an audio CD, for each audio track to be recorded on the CD, you need to create an AIFF sound file. Several audio utilities (commercial, shareware, and freeware) allow you to record AIFF files or convert other sound files, including the popular MP3 format, into AIFF files. Toast also ships with a utility called the Toast Audio Extractor that creates AIFF files from the tracks of an existing audio CD. Recent versions of Toast and other utilities have begun to include the ability to convert from other audio file formats (such as MP3) while burning a disc. This requires a very fast processor and may not function properly at very fast recording speeds.

Once you have AIFF files for each track on the audio CD you wish to create, choose the Audio CD option from the pop-up menu of the Toast window. Then drag all the AIFF files into the Toast window. You can then click the Audio button to arrange the order of the individual tracks on the audio CD.

Once you've arranged the files and folders of a data CD-ROM or the audio tracks of an audio CD using Toast, you can use the Save command to save a copy of the disc image of the CD to your hard drive for later use. At this point, you're ready to actually create your CD.

To create, or burn, the CD, you click the Write CD button in the Toast window. This brings up the dialog box shown in Figure 16-19. Here you are presented with various options about how to create the CD. These include the speed that the CD will be written at (speeds not supported by

Figure 16-19
The dialog presented by Toast when you are ready to actually burn a CD.

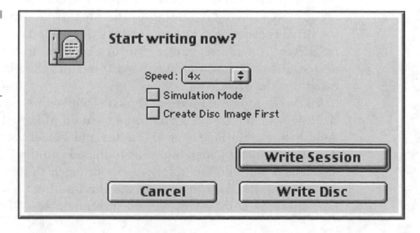

the drive will be grayed out and unavailable), whether the disc should be written as a single session disc or as a complete disc at once (see the next section), and the option to use simulation mode.

Simulation mode does not actually create the CD. Rather, it goes through all the motions and acts of creating the CD to ensure that the settings used by Toast and the drive will allow you to burn the CD in question without any problems. If you are attempting to use the highest speed available to a drive, particularly a USB drive, or if you have modified the Toast settings from their defaults, you may want to try using simulation mode to be certain that the disc will be created properly and without errors.

Single Session versus Multisession   Each time you record data to a CD-R or CD-RW disc, you are opening what is known as a *session*. A session is a section of the CD where data is stored. Each session contains lead-in and lead-out information before and after the session. This lead-in and lead-out information allows the CD to be read. Commercially pressed CD-ROMs have a single session that contains all the data on the CD-ROM. Single-session CDs are written all at one time, and thus the method of writing a single-session disc is sometimes called disc-at-once.

The first generations of recordable CD drives only supported recording single-session discs. The problem with writing a single-session CD-ROM is that once the CD-ROM is created, you cannot go back and add data to it later. This means that if you only use 100 MB of a CD-R disc for a backup of files, you can't add any more files to the disc later on, and you've essentially wasted 550 MB of storage space.

As you might guess, a multisession CD-ROM contains more than one session. Each session contains its own lead-in and lead-out sections, as well as the data of the session. Each session is recognized as a separate CD-ROM from the other sessions on the disc. Also, be aware that the lead-in and lead-out spaces for each session on a disc use up disc space as well, meaning that each session will generally use up 13 MB of storage space in addition to the size of the data being stored in it.

When you write data to a CD-R or CD-RW disk, Toast (or your authoring utility of choice) lets you determine whether you want to write the entire disc at once or whether you want to write a single session. Writing a single session allows you to add more sessions to the disc later on. When you write a session, you will also be given the choice to close the disc or not. Closing the disc means that the lead-out information for the session you're writing is created in such a way that it will not support additional sessions being added after. Once a disc is closed in this way, no more data can be added to it. Audio CDs intended to be played in audio CD players should be single-session discs, as audio CD players do not support multiple-session CDs.

UDF CDs   One of the problems or complaints people often have with using CD-R and CD-RW discs is that you cannot treat the disc as you would a hard drive or other removable-media drive. In other words, you cannot simply drag files to the disc's icon and have them copied to it. Instead, you need to use special CD-ROM authoring software to prepare an image file of the disc, and then you need to use that software to burn the disc, either entirely or in part. Another similar problem is that if you create multisession CD-ROMs, you effectively waste disc space between each session (not to mention that each session shows up as a separate CD-ROM icon when the CD is inserted into a Mac's CD-ROM drive).

Adaptec has made an attempt to make this easier by using the UDF file format and a technique known as *packet writing* to create CD-ROMs. In short, this approach allows a CD-R or CD-RW disc to be mounted on the Mac's desktop the same as any other disc. Users can then drag individual files or folders to the disc as they would to a hard drive. The disc will also be accessible through the Open and Save dialogs of various applications. The result is that storing data to a recordable CD becomes like storing data to any other type of disk.

To create UDF CD-ROMs, you need to install Adaptec's DirectCD. As of this writing, DirectCD does not function with a large number of CD-R or CD-RW drives. It does not support any USB of FireWire drives, though Adaptec does plan to add such support. To read a UDF CD-ROM, a Mac must have the UDF Volume Access extension installed (this is part of the standard Mac OS installation). The UDF CD is readable by a supported CD-R or CD-RW drive while it is being added to. It is not readable by a standard CD-ROM drive until after the disc has been closed (meaning no additional data can be added to it). Once the disc is closed, it can be read by any Mac with the UDF Volume Access extension installed.

UDF CD-ROMs are cross-platform and can be created on both Mac and Windows-based computers using the DirectCD software. To be read on a Windows PC, however, a UDF reader utility must be installed.

Adaptec's DirectCD is not a perfect solution for all CD-ROM creation needs, though it does serve in many instances. It is limited to creating only UDF CD-ROMs, meaning that traditional Mac HFS CDs, audio CDs, or any other format is not supported under it. It makes a good complement to other CD-ROM authoring tools, such as Adaptec's Toast, but it should not be used as a replacement for them in all situations. If you plan to create CD-ROMs to share data with other computer users or as backups, you should avoid using DirectCD for these purposes.

Also, be aware that although DirectCD gives you the same convenience of being able to store data on a CD-R or CD-RW disc as you would on your hard drive, these discs do not record data as quickly as a hard drive or even many types of removable-media drives. This means that UDF format CDs are not suitable for all the everyday functions of a Mac, such as updating word-processing files as you work on them or modifying image files from the CD in Photoshop.

Emergency Startup and Installation CD-ROMs

Every Mac ships with two CD-ROMs that can be used to start up the Mac in an emergency: the System Install and System Restore CDs. The System Restore CD contains a hard disk image file with all the contents that the particular Mac's hard drive contained when it left the factory. It can be used to start up the Mac in emergency, to reformat the Mac's internal hard drive, and to restore the hard drive to the state it was in when the Mac was first purchased. It can also be used to restore all the items that were initially on the Mac's hard drive without erasing anything that has been added later. The System Install CD contains a standard installer for the version of the Mac OS that shipped with the computer.

Beyond these two emergency CD-ROMs, every version of the Mac OS that is sold on CD-ROM is sold on a CD that can be used as a startup disk to boot the Mac in an emergency. Several utility and diagnostic software packages, such as Norton Utilities for Mac, TechTool Pro, and Disk Warrior, also ship on bootable CDs that can be used as a startup disk in emergencies.

Starting Up from a Mac OS or Utility CD

Starting up from a bootable CD-ROM is a very easy process. Insert the disc into the Mac's CD-ROM or DVD-ROM drive. Press the Mac's power button, and then immediately hold down the C key on the keyboard. This will cause the Mac to look to its internal CD-ROM or DVD-ROM drive for a valid startup disk. Assuming one is there, it will start up from that CD-ROM instead of the internal hard drive or other disk.

You can tell that the Mac has started up from the CD-ROM in one of several ways. First, while the startup process occurs, you will hear the CD being accessed instead of the internal hard drive (the startup process will also take longer because the CD-ROM drive is slower than a hard drive).

Second, Apple's bootable CD-ROMs will display a desktop pattern containing a repeated CD theme. Non-Apple bootable CD-ROMs, such as those used by third-party drive utility manufacturers, will often use a startup screen displaying their company logo to let you know that you are starting up from the CD. Third, the CD-ROM's icon will be displayed in the upper right-hand corner of the desktop where the internal hard drive's icon (or the disc being used as a startup disk) is usually displayed.

Once you have started up from a CD-ROM, you can then run whatever utilities or tools you need to run, provided they are included on the CD-ROM. When starting from Apple's bootable CDs, however, you will not have access to many of the extensions and control panels that are part of the Mac OS. Similarly, you will not have access to any third-party extensions or to your Preferences for specific applications—nor will the CD contain drivers for any non-Apple hardware (drives, PCI cards, and so on.).

Emergency CDs and Non-Apple CD-ROM Drives   It may be impossible to start up a Mac using a Mac OS or utility CD-ROM if you are using a third-party CD-ROM drive. This is true regardless of whether the CD-ROM drive is internal or external. The reason is that startup CDs for the Mac need to be supported by the Apple CD-ROM driver extensions. Startup CDs have these extensions as driver software burned into the very first portions of the drive so that when loaded, they are what the Mac sees immediately when it queries the drive during the startup process.

If you are using a third-party drive with your Mac, test the drive when you first get it to be certain whether you will be able to start up from a CD-ROM. If not, either return it and use a drive that will allow you to start up from a CD-ROM or purchase some other type of drive for your computer that you can install a System Folder and utilities on to start up from in case of emergencies. Be sure to include the drivers for your CD-ROM drive in the System Folder you create on this emergency drive. Remember, however, that not all external drives are bootable and that some SCSI cards do not allow any drive connected to them to be used as a startup device.

Creating Your Own Emergency CD

If you have a CD-R or CD-RW drive, then you can create your own bootable CD-ROMs. This is particularly useful if there are a series of specific utilities that you wish to have available to you when starting up from a CD. It can also be helpful if, as some Mac network administrators do, you wish to include all the software regularly used on a given Mac so that you can start up from the CD, reformat the hard drive, and reinstall all your software on the Mac in question in one or two quick and easy steps. This allows you to get a problem Mac back up and running very quickly.

The process of creating a bootable CD-ROM varies slightly depending on the version of Toast (or other CD authoring utility) you are using. In the current version of Toast, you can create a bootable CD-ROM simply by dragging a copy of your Mac's System Folder into the Toast window when creating a Files and Folders CD. In versions of Toast earlier than 4.0, creating a bootable CD-ROM required first creating a hard drive partition that included a viable System Folder and then creating a CD-ROM that was a mirror of the partition. Regardless of the utility or version you use, you need to make either a single-session CD-ROM or make the first session bootable. Multisession CD-ROMs are not bootable if any session besides the first one contains the System Folder.

In addition to the System Folder, you should include any utilities you commonly use when you cannot start up from a Mac's internal hard drive. These would include your disk repair utilities of choice, such as Norton Utilities or Disk Warrior; your hard drive formatting utility of choice, such as Apple's Drive setup or FWB's Hard Disk Toolkit; any additional diagnostic utilities, such as TechTool Pro, Newer's Gauge PRO, or SCSI Probe; your antivirus utility of choice, such as Virex or Norton AntiVirus; and any utilities specific to your Mac's hardware, such as those included with processor upgrades or PCI cards.

The System Folder you use should also not be a generic Mac OS install System Folder. It should contain any extensions, control panels, or other items that are associated with your hardware and can include software you usually work with and consider a part of your usual Mac experience. As much as possible, you should be certain before using a System Folder for an emergency CD that there are no extension conflicts in it.

Caring for CD-ROM, CD-R, and CD-RW Discs and Drives

CD-ROM, CD-R, and CD-RW discs are generally quite resilient. They are, in fact, the most stable media available today on which to store data and have an expected life span of close to a century or longer. However, it is possible to damage any type of CD media to the point where it can no longer be read by a CD-ROM drive. The following tips should ensure that your CD-ROM, CD-R, and CD-RW discs last a long time, probably much longer than your computer.

■ *Don't bend the disc.*   The polycarbonate material that all CDs are made of is resilient, but it isn't meant to withstand deliberate abuse, and with enough force you can break a CD in two. You can also cause part of the disc to crack, which makes the disc useless.

■ *Avoid exposing the disc to excess heat.*   The polycarbonate and lacquer that CDs are made of are types of plastic. Like any plastic, they will melt if enough heat is applied. Don't leave CDs near a heater or in direct sunlight, such as the dashboard of a car. CD-R and CD-RW discs are even more easily damaged by heat than pressed CD-ROMs.

■ *Avoid scratching either side of the disc.*   A scratch on the underside of the disc will not damage the pits or lands of the disc, but it can keep the laser from being able to read the disc correctly. If a scratch occurs on the underside of the disc, it is possible to polish it out, and some record stores offer this service for both audio CDs and CD-ROMs. What most people don't realize is that scratching the top of the CD is equally dangerous, because this is the side that is closest to the substrate layer where the pits and lands are. A scratch to that side can damage the pits and lands themselves, making the disc useless without any hope of repair.

■ *Don't write on the surface of a CD.*   This applies to CD-ROM, CD-R, and CD-RW discs. Writing on the upper surface of the disc with a ballpoint pen can scratch the pits and lands. Writing directly on the CD with a felt-tip pen may expose the disc's protective layers to a chemical in the ink of the pen that can break down the lacquer of the protective layer and damage the disc. If you need to write on a CD-R or CD-RW disc, use a felt tip on a label on the disc. Most recordable discs have a label that is applied to the upper surface of disc so you can safely write on it with a felt-tip pen only. Some CD-R manufacturers even sell felt-tip pens with ink specifically designed so that it will not harm their CDs.

■ *Do not add labels onto the disc unless they are specifically designed for use in labeling CD-ROMs.*   Labels pose two possible problems. First, there may be a detrimental chemical in the glue of the label that could damage the disc. Second, the label may unbalance the weight of the CD, which can keep it from spinning properly in the drive, making it difficult or impossible to read reliably. If a label is applied to a CD, don't try to remove, as you may pull off some of the disc's outer layers. You may also unbalance the disc and allow any remaining glue to come into contact with the mechanisms of a CD-ROM drive, which could damage the drive.

■ *Do not use chemical cleaners on the disc.* Many cleaners are solvents, which can dissolve the various layers of a CD. If the CD becomes clouded and unreadable as a result of debris or fingerprints, use a clean cloth to gently buff the disc clean, or use one of the CD cleaning kits you can find in both computer stores and record stores.

Troubleshooting CD-ROM, CD-R, and CD-RW Drives

Following are several common problems with CD drives, along with possible solutions.

The Disc Is Unreadable by This Macintosh Dialog

This problem indicates that the Mac is unable to read or understand the format used by the CD in question. If the CD is not a traditional Mac (HFS) format, make sure the File Exchange or PC Exchange control panel is installed in the Control Panels folder and that you haven't started with extensions off. Also, make certain that extensions listed earlier in this chapter that relate to various CD formats are installed.

It is also possible that the disc is scratched to the point that the Mac can no longer read it or that there are fingerprints, condensation, or other similar impediments preventing the laser from reading the disc properly. You can try cleaning the disc with a water-moistened soft cloth.

If the CD is a CD-R or CD-RW, the CD-ROM drive may be an older model that is not able to read the disc you are using. The disc may also have been created with errors. Try using it in a different CD-ROM drive or in the CD-R or CD-RW drive that created it.

A CD Is Inserted, but the Mac Makes No Response at All

If you insert a CD and the Mac doesn't respond by either mounting the CD's icon on the desktop or by displaying an error message, check to make sure the drive is connected properly and that it is powered. Also, make sure that driver software for the CD-ROM drive is installed (whether Apple's drivers or a third-party option). You can use the Apple System Profiler to tell if the drive is being recognized properly by the Mac as well.

If the drive appears to be working properly and works with other CDs, check to be sure that the CD that isn't recognized is not damaged or dirty and that you are inserting it properly.

The Mac Refuses to Eject a CD

As a rule, to eject a disc, you use Finder commands or drag a disc's icon to the Trash. However, some drives may require that you manually eject the disc once you have performed these actions. If so, this should be described in the drive's manual.

If the drive is designed to auto-eject the disc and doesn't, there may be problems with the drive. However, like traditional Mac floppy drives, almost all of today's drives include an emergency eject hole that can be triggered with a straightened-out paper clip. This can also be a solution if the Mac freezes or crashes and you need to eject a disc. It should not be done, however, while the Mac is running normally and the disc's icon is displayed on the desktop.

If the Mac displays a dialog saying the disc cannot be ejected because it contains items that are in use, you probably have a file on the disc open in some application or an application on the disc is still running.

The Mac Ejects a CD and Then Constantly Asks for It to Be Inserted

This symptom means that some application of Mac OS element is looking for something on the CD, possible a recently accessed file or the desktop file. Try reinserting and ejecting the CD again. If this doesn't solve the problem, try quitting all open applications while the CD is inserted and then ejecting it. If this still doesn't happen, restart the Mac and eject the CD before or during the startup sequence.

Audio from a CD Is Not Played through the Mac's Speakers

If this situation is occurring, first check to be certain the speakers are working properly and that the sound is not turned down. Assuming there is a real problem besides the obvious one, it is most likely that some CD related extensions (see earlier in this chapter) are not installed or the CD-ROM drive's audio cable has become disconnected. Refer to the "Installing or Replacing a CD-ROM Drive" section earlier in this chapter to locate the cable and reconnect it. *Note:* Not all Mac CD-ROM drives will use an audio cable.

After Installing a CD-ROM, CD-R, or CD-RW Drive, the Drive Is Not Recognized

In this case, make certain that all driver software is installed, that the drive is attached properly by whatever interface it uses, and that it is powered properly. For USB and FireWire drives, even though the interface is hot pluggable, you may need to restart for the drivers to be active. This is particularly true with some CD authoring software, which will not recognize a drive if it wasn't connected at startup.

Only the First Session of a Multisession CD-R or CD-RW Disc Is Recognized

This situation can occur if with older versions of Apple's CD-ROM drive and older versions of third-party CD-ROM drives. Update to the most recent driver version available.

DVD

While CD-ROM drives have been a staple feature on computers for several years, they are slowly being replaced by an evolving technology known as DVD (digital versatile disc). Like CD-ROMs, DVD discs are a 5.25-inch disc that contains a layer of a polycarbonate substrate onto which pits and lands are pressed or burned to store data (refer to the previous chapter for more detail on using pits and lands to record data). They also have a similar reflective layer and a protective lacquer layer. DVD discs, however, are capable of storing much larger amounts of data per disc. DVDs can be used to store data in a read-only format known as DVD-ROM (analogous to CD-ROM discs), as well as in a number of recordable and rewritable formats. DVD discs are also used for the DVD movies that are becoming extremely popular for home entertainment. Many of the Macintosh computers with DVD-ROM drives are able to play DVD movies onscreen. This chapter looks at how DVD technology works, the types of DVD discs currently in use, and the technology involved in playing DVD movies on the Mac.

How DVDs Store Data

On a very basic level, DVD discs store data in the same way CD-ROMs do. They use a similar optical head that projects a beam of laser light to the disc. This light is then reflected off the pits and lands of the disc back to a photocell detector mounted in the head (see Chapter 16 for details of how data is stored on a CD-ROM). Based on the intensity of the light when it is reflected back to the head, the drive can determine whether the light struck a pit or a land.

DVD technology, however, includes several advances over how a CD-ROM drive works. The first and most notable advance is in the laser itself. The laser used in a DVD drive is a visible-red laser rather than the infrared laser used in CD-ROM drives. This means that the beam of light emitted by the laser is much finer and can be aimed more precisely. The result is that the pits and lands on a DVD disc can be smaller than those on a CD-ROM; therefore, more pits and lands can fit on the disc. Since the pits and lands represent the data stored on the disc, this makes DVD discs capable of holding more data.

Beyond simply being able to store more data on the same surface area of a disc, DVD technology also provides the ability to read discs that have multiple layers, as shown in Figure 17-1. The layer of a DVD disc that contains data was designed to be semitransparent. This allows the laser

Figure 17-1

The physical layers of
a DVD disc

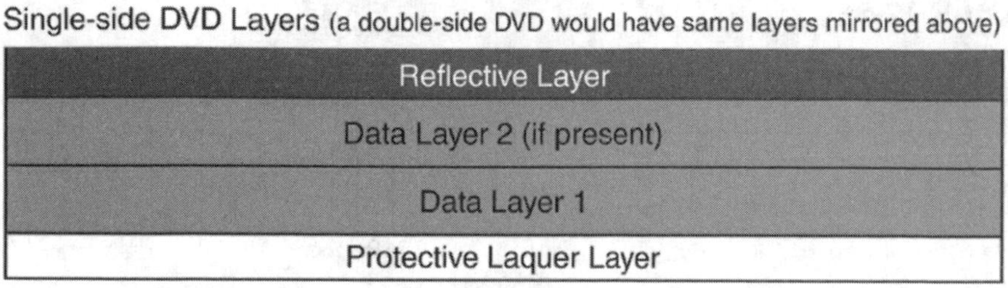

Single-side DVD Layers (a double-side DVD would have same layers mirrored above)

| Reflective Layer |
| Data Layer 2 (if present) |
| Data Layer 1 |
| Protective Laquer Layer |

TABLE 17-1

DVD-ROM disc
layers and storage
capacity.

Layers	Sides	Capacity
1	1	4.7 GB
2	1	8.5 GB
1	2	9.4 GB
2	2	17 GB

to essentially look past the first layer of the disc and to read the data in a layer beyond it. Therefore, you can have two layers of data on a single-sided DVD disc, doubling the already impressive capacity of the disc. It is also possible to store data on both sides of a DVD and to read both sides without needing to physically turn the disc over. So, if you used a DVD disc that was double sided, storing data on both the top and bottom layers of each side of the disc, you could theoretically quadruple the available data storage capacity. With current DVD technology, a single-sided, one-layer DVD disc can store up to 4.7 GB of data. A double-sided, double-layered DVD disc can store up to 17 GB. Table 17-1 shows the storage capacities of different types of DVDs.

Beyond storage space, DVD discs store data in a method that makes reading the disc more efficient. As you may remember from the previous chapter, CD-ROMs record data on a disc in a single spiral track that extends from the edge of the disc to the center of the disc. This is very different from the way data is stored on a hard drive or other media. DVD discs do not use that spiral track approach. Instead, they format a disc like a hard drive does, with the surface of the disc being broken up into discrete tracks and sectors. This allows the Mac to more readily locate where a specific segment of data is stored on the disc and to access that data more quickly.

Because the laser of a DVD drive can determine the type of disc it is dealing with and adjust the beam of light to match that of the disc

TABLE 17-2

DVD-ROM speeds.

Speed	Transfer Rate
1x	1 MB/second
2x	2 MB/second
4x	4 MB/second
6x	6 MB/second

inserted in the drive, DVD-ROM drives are complete backward-compatible with all existing CD-ROM formats. Thus, for practical purposes, the optical head of a DVD drive will behave exactly as though it were a CD-ROM drive when a CD is inserted. When a DVD disc is inserted, it will behave as a DVD-ROM drive.

Like CD-ROM drives, DVD drives come in a variety of speeds. These speeds are based on the original DVD specification, with a 1x DVD-ROM drive being able to read data at a rate of 1 MB per second. DVD speeds are not the same as CD-ROM speeds. This is important to note if you are comparing the specifications of DVD and CD-ROM drives or are looking at the drive speed requirements of a CD-ROM game or other software. A 1x DVD drive is roughly equivalent to a 7x CD-ROM drive. Most Macs currently feature a 4x DVD-ROM drive, which is comparable to a 30x CD-ROM drive. Table 17-2 shows various DVD-ROM speeds.

DVD Formats

Several DVD formats are currently in use. Each format is usable for different purposes and may require different hardware. Some DVD formats use discs that will be the standard 5.25-inch disc that looks very much like a CD-ROM, while others will use a cartridge of the same size when storing data. The following sections look at each of the DVD formats and the hardware needed to use them.

DVD-ROM

DVD-ROM is the basic DVD format for computer data and is analogous to CD-ROMs. DVD-ROMs, as mentioned earlier, can potentially store up to 17 GB of data on a single read-only disc. DVD-ROMs can be used to store large file collections and to distribute software. Currently, very few software companies are distributing software on DVD-ROM discs rather than CD-ROMs.

However, some game developers have begun shipping their titles on DVD-ROM, though CD-ROM versions are still available as well to support a much wider audience. It is expected that for the time being most software will continue to be distributed on CD-ROM or be available in both CD-ROM and DVD-ROM packages. The transition between the two will probably occur much as the transition in distribution between floppy disks and CD-ROMs did during the last decade.

In particular, DVD-ROMs offer great potential to game developers who have in the past had to ship a game on multiple CD-ROMs, requiring the user to change CD-ROM discs at various points in the game. The game data can now be contained on a single DVD-ROM disc and will not require the user to stop playing the game at any point to change the disc. This allows for a much smoother gaming experience.

DVD-Video

DVD-Video is the format that DVD movies use. DVD-Video discs, like audio CDs, are actually a DVD-ROM using a specific format that can be recognized by DVD players that you can attach to your television, as well as computers with a DVD-ROM drive. The DVD-Video format allows for three separate components to be included on a DVD. These include an MPEG-2 video component, an audio component (usually uncompressed digital audio or Dolby Digital audio), and a data component. The data component allows additional features, such as production notes, subtitles, or other extra information and segments to be included in a DVD movie. The format also allows for multiple audio tracks; users can then select the one that they wish to listen to (such as choosing from multiple language offerings).

The majority of DVD-ROM drives can read DVD-Video format discs. This means that a DVD-ROM drive has the potential ability to play DVD movies. In addition to a DVD-ROM drive, the computer you are using must also support a method for decoding the MPEG-2 video content and the audio content stored in Dolby Digital (AC-3) format in order to play a DVD-Video disc's contents. You also need an application that will allow you to interact with the DVD in the same manner as a DVD player would. MPEG-2 decoding, DVD audio, and playing DVD movies on the Mac is discussed later in this chapter.

DVD-Hybrid   DVD-Hybrid discs are much like enhanced audio CDs. They are discs that include traditional DVD-Video content as well as traditional data content. When a DVD-Hybrid disc is inserted into a set-top DVD player, it will behave as a traditional DVD movie. When it is inserted into your Mac, it will provide both the DVD movie content so that you can watch the movie on your computer as well as data content.

The data content of a DVD-Hybrid disc may contain additional, separate material, or it may contain interactive multimedia content, such as a game, that relies on the MPEG-2 video or audio material that is part of the DVD movie itself. This approach provides users with a completely unique experience without requiring a large amount of excess data. As with enhanced audio CDs, you may find two icons presented by the Mac when a DVD-Hybrid disc is inserted, one for the movie content and one for the data content. Alternatively, there may be a single icon that contains both the video and data content.

DIVX   DIVX is a format for DVD movies that has never been embraced by consumers as much as the creators of the format would have liked. DIVX is used for special DVD movies that you can buy for about $5. From the time you first put the movie in your DVD player, you have two days to watch it. After that, you need to pay an additional fee to continue watching it indefinitely. If you don't pay the fee, after two days, the disc becomes more or less useless. DIVX requires special DVD players in order to be used. These players are all set-top boxes designed to be used with a television. DIVX is not supported as a format that DVD-ROM drives can recognize and play.

DVD-R

DVD-R is a recordable DVD technology. Analogous to CD-R technology, DVD-R discs can be recorded only once and cannot be erased. DVD-R discs can be read by most DVD-ROM drives once they have been recorded and can store either 3.95 GB or 4.7 GB of data per disc. DVD-R discs can be used to record in either DVD-ROM or DVD-Video format, allowing you to create DVD movies of your own, provided that you have the appropriate hardware and utilities to encode the video, audio, and data content properly. DVD-Video content created on a DVD-R can be read by most home entertainment DVD players, as well as computers with DVD-ROM drives.

DVD-R drives are primarily available for the Mac using a SCSI interface. They are not the most popular of DVD recordable formats, however, and DVD-R drives are more limited than the other principle recordable DVD drive, DVD-RAM. DVD-R discs function extremely similar to CD-R discs in how they store data, using a laser to heat a special dye layer on the disc to change the reflectivity of the dye in patterns of pits and lands to store information.

As with CD-R, you will also need to use special DVD authoring software in order to record DVD-R discs. The most commonly DVD authoring utility is Adaptec's Toast DVD. Toast DVD is an extension of the Toast utility used for creating CD-R and CD-RW discs. It features much the same interface and approach as the original Toast product.

DVD-RAM

DVD-RAM is the most popular recordable or rewritable DVD format. DVD-RAM drives use a special DVD cartridges rather than DVD discs. These cartridges are the same size as a DVD-ROM disc and contain a 5.25-inch disc inside of the plastic cartridge, shown in Figure 17-2. In the more recent DVD-RAM discs (called Type 2), the actual disc can be removed from the plastic cartridge. The disc can then be inserted into a DVD-ROM drive and read as any other DVD-ROM disc. This requires a DVD-ROM drive that supports reading DVD-RAM discs, which not all do. Table 17-3 lists which recent Mac models include a factory-installed DVD-ROM drive with support for DVD-RAM discs and which do not. Most DVD-ROM drives support reading only single-layered DVD-RAM discs, though you can check the specifications of more recent drives (spring of 2000 or later) to see if it will support double-layered DVD-RAM discs.

DVD-RAM stores data differently than DVD-R, DVD-RW (discussed in the next section) CD-R, or CD-RW. DVD-RAM discs contain a crystalline compound on their surfaces. This compound is heated by a laser during recording (much like the dyes in CD-R and CD-RW discs). When the compound is heated, the crystal layer is melted. Once the laser stops heating the compound, it cools very quickly. It cools so quickly, in fact, that the compound hardens again without recrystallizing. This leaves a mark (or pit) in the DVD-RAM media. When data is erased, the laser again heats the disc, this time targeting the individual pits made during recording. This time, however, the laser doesn't heat the compound as high and it doesn't stop completely. Rather, it allows the compound to cool more slowly, which causes the material to recrystallize into its original state, erasing the pit. This crystalline compound is more sensitive to damage

Figure 17-2
A DVD-RAM
cartridge.

TABLE 17-3

Mac model DVD-ROM drive and DVD-RAM disc compatibility.

Mac Model	Recognizes DVD-RAM Discs
Power Mac G3	No
PowerBook G3 (1999)	No
Power Mac G4 (PCI graphics)	No
Power Mac G4 (AGP graphics)	Yes
iMac DV/ iMac DV Special Edition	Yes
PowerBook G3 (2000)	Yes

from outside than the pits and lands of other DVD or CD media, which is why most DVD-RAM discs come in a protective cartridge.

DVD-RAM discs have a distinct advantage over other recordable DVD and CD formats in that they can be formatted and used much like a hard drive or removable-media drive. They require only that a DVD-RAM drive be installed and that the Apple CD/DVD Driver, Foreign File Access, and UDF Volume Access extensions be installed on a Mac; they do not require any special authoring utilities. DVD-RAM discs can be formatted in both the HFS and HFS+ (aka Mac OS Standard and Mac OS Extended, respectively) file formats, as well as the UDF file format described in the previous chapter. Formatting for use with PCs is also possible. However, DVD-RAM discs must be formatted in a PC format the first time they are formatted. After that, if they are reformatted for the PC Mac. Format will no longer be an option. DVD-RAM discs cannot, however, be used as a startup drive for the Mac (despite the fact that Apple erroneously reported they could be in some Help and Read Me documents for Mac OS 9).

DVD-RAM drives are available in both internal IDE and SCSI models, as well as external SCSI and FireWire models. Installing an internal IDE or SCSI DVD-RAM drive is identical to the process of installing an internal DVD-ROM drive, as described later in this chapter. The one difference to note is that a DVD-RAM drive may not be as tall as a DVD-ROM drive, and you should take this into account when securing the drive with mounting screws.

Two different methods are used for loading DVD-RAM discs into a DVD-RAM drive: the traditional tray design used for CD-ROM and DVD-ROM drives and a newer slotted-tray design. The difference is mainly cosmetic, and you can easily insert DVD-RAM, DVD-ROM, and the various types of CDs into drives with either tray type.

Like DVD-ROM drives, DVD-RAM drives can read CD-ROM discs. This includes all CD formats and types including CD-R and CD-RW discs. DVD-RAM drives cannot, however, record data to a CD-R or CD-RW disc. DVD-RAM discs are available in both single- and double-layer variations. The single-layer DVD-RAM discs can store 2.6 GB of data per disc, while double-layer DVD-RAM discs can store up to 5.2 GB per disc.

DVD-RW

DVD-RW is another rewritable DVD format that was created without the approval of the DVD Commission. DVD-RW is very much like CD-RW using DVD discs instead of CDs. DVD-RW drives can read DVD-ROM discs as well as the various CD types, but they cannot read DVD-RAM discs. More recent DVD-ROM drives can read DVD-RW discs, but earlier DVD-ROM drives and DVD-RAM drives cannot. DVD-RW discs can store up to 2.8 GB of data. DVD-RW has yet to become as popular as DVD-R or DVD-RAM. Table 17-4 compares the various technologies.

Viewing DVD Movies

Watching DVD movies on a Mac requires more than just a DVD-ROM drive. It requires an MPEG-2 video decoding solution. MPEG-2 is a specific video compression and encoding format that is used to store digital video content. It is currently used in the DVD-Video format, as well as in digital television broadcasting. MPEG-2 allows for data to be compressed without losing any of the substantial and impressive video quality offered by digital video.

In order to play MPEG-2 video, a computer requires the technology to decode the video. MPEG-2 is both a powerful and complex encoding format, and it requires equally powerful technology to decode. For the first

TABLE 17-4

Comparison of recordable DVD technologies.

Drive/Disc Type	Capacity	Rewritable?	Industry Usage
DVD-R	3.95 GB or 4.7 GB	No	Moderate to low
DVD-RAM	2.6 GB or 5.2 GB	Yes	Moderate to high
DVD-RW	2.8 GB	Yes	Low

couple of years that MPEG-2 and DVD movies existed, MPEG-2 decoding required a special MPEG-2 decoder card. More recently, Macs have become powerful and fast enough that special software can accomplish the decoding without the need for such dedicated hardware.

Whichever MPEG-2 decoding method a given Mac uses, it will also need a piece of software that actually plays the DVD movie. This software needs to be able to recognize the decoded video and audio, as well as to interact with the DVD to control such functions as play, stop, fast-forward, and so on. It also needs to provide an interface for the user to access a DVD movie's various menus and specific options, such as scene selection, language, sound track, and subtitle choices, along with optional information that may be included. For Macs that ship with DVD movie capabilities, this software is the Apple DVD Player (though which version a Mac uses will depend on whether or not it supports software- or hardware-based MPEG-2 decoding). For third-party DVD movie solutions, a player application should also be included with the drive and MPEG-2 decoder card kit. Table 17-5 lists the decoding methods on various Mac models.

Hardware MPEG-2 Decoding

MPEG-2 decoding is accomplished with a hardware solution in all but the most recent Macs. This hardware solution can be by means of an expansion card that installs into a PCI slot on the Mac, circuitry built onto the Mac's motherboard, or even a PC Card for a PowerBook's PC Card slot.

Hardware MPEG-2 decoding offers an advantage in that it doesn't rely on the Mac's processor to do the actual work of decoding the video infor-

TABLE 17-5

Mac models using hardware and software MPEG-2 decoding.

Mac Model	Decoding Method
Power Mac G3	Hardware
PowerBook G3 (1999)	Hardware
Power Mac G4 (PCI graphics)	Hardware
Power Mac G4 (AGP graphics)	Software
iMac DV	Software
iMac DV Special Edition	Software
PowerBook G3 (2000)	Software

mation for a DVD-Video disc. Instead, all the decoding work is done by the circuitry included in the MPEG-2 hardware. This allows Macs with processors that are too slow to decode the video content quickly enough to allow full-screen, full-motion video to be able to play DVD movies. Also, by freeing the processor of the decoding work, a DVD movie is more likely to play smoothly in situations where virtual memory is being used or where multiple applications are being run along with the DVD player application.

The Macs with Apple-installed MPEG-2 decoding hardware require a different version of the Apple DVD Player application than those that use a software-based MPEG-2 decoding solution. These Macs use an earlier version (1.x) of the Apple DVD Player application, while Macs with software-based decoding use a later version (2.x).

Built-in Decoding Hardware   The PowerBook G3 models with a bronze keyboard from 1999 that included a built-in SCSI port came in two models: a low-end 333-MHz model and a high-end 400-MHz model. The high-end model also included MPEG-2 decoding circuitry as a built-in feature on the motherboard. When the DVD-ROM expansion bay drive was inserted, these PowerBooks could play DVD movies.

Optional Decoding Hardware   It is possible to add DVD-ROM drives and MPEG-2 decoder cards to Power Macs that did not initially ship with them. Some third-party companies have created special kits for owners of Macs who didn't choose this as an option on the Blue and White Power Mac G3 and for earlier Macs that didn't offer DVD abilities.

These third-party solutions often include a SCSI or IDE DVD-ROM drive plus a PCI card that handles the MPEG-2 decoding. Because their hardware is unsupported by the Apple DVD Player application, they also ship with their own DVD player application for viewing DVD moves. "Installing DVD Hardware" later in this chapter provides an overview of how to install a kit containing a DVD-ROM drive and an MPEG-2 decoder card.

MPEG-2 Encoding Hardware   In order to create DVD-Video formats, a DVD disc requires an MPEG-2 video component. If you are interested in creating your own DVD-Video disc, you will need to be able to encode video footage into MPEG-2. For most Macs, this requires a special MPEG-2 encoding card, which can take existing video files (of various formats) and apply the MPEG-2 compression and encoding standards to them in order to create MPEG-2 video data. These cards are available for the Mac and can be installed into a PCI slot of the current and recent Power Mac computers. Combined with a DVD-R drive and a DVD authoring utility, you can then create your own DVD movies or create the content needed for a professional DVD production facility to create professionally pressed DVD-Video discs. More for the professional video artist than for the home hobbyist, these cards can often cost upwards of $1500.

Software MPEG-2 Decoding

The most recent Macs include processors that are fast enough to perform software-based MPEG-2 decoding. As a rule, this requires a 400-MHz G3 processor or a 350-MHz G4 processor. Apple also seems to have designed its software-based MPEG-2 decoding solutions so that it references parts of the ATI Rage 128 graphics chipset, which is included on all the current Macs (either built onto the motherboard, or, as in the Power Mac G3/G4, on a graphics card). If owners of the Power Mac G3 or G4 replace their ATI graphics card with another company's card, they may find themselves unable to play DVD movies.

DVD Movie Audio Tracks

The audio tracks of a DVD-Video disc can be in any one of several audio formats, although at least one audio track must be either PCM Audio or Dolby Digital audio. Both of these are supported on all DVD video playback devices, including Macintosh computers with the ability to play DVD movies. The following sections give an overview of the various audio formats that may be used on a DVD-Video disc. Although many of these formats provide the ability for five or more individual audio channels, because the current Macs do not support multichannel digital audio output, they will automatically decode the audio signals and mix them to be appropriate to two-channel Dolby Pro Logic Surround Sound or two traditional stereo speakers. This allows the resulting audio to be compatible with a vast array of stereo speaker types with high-quality playback. It also allows the audio to be produced at high quality from the built-in surround sound speakers of the iMac DV and PowerBook computers.

Linear PCM   This is one of the two basic audio formats included in the DVD-Video standard. It can contain up to eight individual audio channels, although because it is an uncompressed audio format, only five or fewer audio channels are generally used. PCM provides audio streams that are at the least just above CD quality and that can deliver qualities twice that of CDs.

Dolby Digital   This is the other basic format included in the DVD-Video standard. Dolby Digital, also known as AC-3 because it is the third generation of this particular digital audio compression technology, typically provides 5.1 channels of audio. These channels include left, center, right, surround left, and surround right. The *.1* defines a separate audio channel used for low-frequency effects (LFE) audio, which is delivered to a subwoofer. Not all of these potential audio channels are required to be used in Dolby Digital audio, however.

MPEG-2 Audio   MPEG-2 is an audio encoding based on the same MPEG-2 standard used for encoding video on a DVD-Video disc. It supports all the same 5.1 audio channels as Dolby Digital audio, as well as two additional channels: center-left and center-right. If the audio device being used with MPEG-2 audio doesn't support all the potential channels, the sound is delivered as standard stereo.

Digital Theater Sound   Digital Theater Sound, or DTS, is a digital audio format traditionally used for sound in movie theaters. It supports multiple audio channels, generally using the same 5.1 channels as Dolby Digital audio, but it also supports a much higher data rate. This means that there are less likely to be any distortions or other sound artifacts caused by the audio compression scheme used to deliver the audio track of a DVD-Video disc. DTS is relatively new to DVD movie use, though several movies have been released with DTS audio tracks. The downside of DTS is that more space on a DVD-Video disc is required to store the DTS audio track than other formats, which means less additional content can be included with the movie.

Region Codes

Beyond decoding the MPEG-2 video stream, there are some things you should be aware of with regard to DVD movies. One of these is DVD region codes. *Region codes* are special sequences of information that are encoded into a DVD-Video disc. These codes are designed so that a DVD movie can be played only in certain parts (or regions) of the world.

Region codes are found on most commercial DVD movies and are designed to keep DVDs intended for sale in one part of the world, such as the United States, from being sold in other areas, such as Asia, where the movie hasn't been released in theaters yet. DVD players and DVD-ROM drives have a region code built into them that corresponds to the area of the world that they are intended to be used in. If the region code for a DVD-Video disc doesn't match that of the DVD player or DVD-ROM drive it is inserted into, it won't play.

On the Macintosh, region codes are controlled by the Apple DVD Player application. The region code is automatically set to the region code of the first DVD movie that is played on the Mac. The region code can be reset up to four times after it has been set initially. The option to reset the region code of the DVD-ROM drive will be presented if a Mac user inserts a DVD movie with a different region code on it. You should only change the region code of your Mac if you actually move to another part of the world. Once the region code of a Mac has been changed for the fourth time, it is permanently set and cannot be changed.

Aspect Ratios

When playing commercial DVD movies on the Mac, you might also want to be aware of the aspect ratios of the displayed video. The *aspect ratio* is the relationship of the video image's width to its height. DVD movies use either an aspect ratio of 4-to-3 or 16-to-9. The standard ratio of NTSC (National Television Standards Committee), the display used for televisions in the United States, is 4-to-3, while the ratio used for many widescreen movies is 16-to-9. A 16-to-9 ratio is, in fact, often described as *widescreen* or *letterbox* format. The 16-to-9 ratio is the standard format used for shooting movies today. When you view a DVD movie or even a home video that uses 4-to-3 ratio, some of the image has been cropped in order for it to display in the NTSC visual field.

When playing a 16-to-9 ratio movie, you will notice black bars at the top and bottom of your Mac's screen or the DVD movie window. Because most Mac monitors and displays use a 4-to-3-sized screen, this is necessary to present the video. Some DVD-Video discs include both a 4-to-3 and 16-to-9 version of the video content, allowing you to select which you wish to view. You can also check before buying a movie to see what aspect ratio it uses and whether it includes both ratios.

DVD Playback and Screen Resolutions

Because the DVD movie is actually presented in a specially formatted window, a DVD movie can be played when a monitor is set to any resolution that is available to a Mac in the Monitors or Monitors and Sound control panel. This window, which is sized at 720×480 pixels, is drawn independently of the Mac's desktop and application windows, so the resolution of the Mac's display is irrelevant to the DVD playback. Similarly, the number of colors that the monitor is set to display will have no effect on the level of color seen in the DVD movie's playback.

As with anything else the Mac might display, however, DVD video display still requires video RAM. When the Apple DVD player is in use, the available VRAM will be split between the Mac's normal processes and the displayed DVD movie. If your Mac's display is set too high, there may not be enough VRAM available for the movie to be displayed properly. This may make the movie appear as though you were watching it through venetian blinds. If this happens, either reduce the screen resolution or reduce the color depth of the Mac's display. Both acts will reduce the amount of VRAM needed to draw the Mac's display and make more VRAM available for DVD playback.

Using a PowerBook to Play DVD Movies on a TV

PowerBooks include an S-Video out port, shown in Figure 17-3, for presenting video from the PowerBook on a television or other video device with S-Video support. If you want to use a PowerBook that supports playing DVD movies to present a movie on a television, first attach the television to the PowerBook using the built-in S-Video port. Then use the Monitors control panel's Arrange button, shown in Figure 17-4, to choose the television screen as your primary monitor. Finally, simply insert the DVD movie and use the Apple DVD Player application to play the movie as you would on the PowerBook's internal display.

For convenience, Table 17-6 lists the keyboard shortcuts that correspond to the various buttons in the Apple DVD Player, such as Play, Stop, and so forth.

The Apple DVD Player Application

The Apple DVD Player application is designed to be very simple to use and to mimic the controls of a set-top DVD player. If the DVD AutoLauncher extension is installed, the Apple DVD Player will launch automatically when a DVD-Video disc is inserted into the Mac's DVD-ROM drive.

Once the program has launched, you can control movie playback using the controller window—a small, round window, shown in Figure 17-5, that can be moved around the screen by dragging the Apple logo in its upper

Figure 17-3
The S-Video port on
a PowerBook.

section or any other part of the controller that does not act as a button. The controller is fairly intuitive with the traditional Play/Stop, Pause, Rewind, and Fast-Forward buttons. The volume control is included as a series of buttons. Simply press the button indicating how high you wish the volume to be relative to the Mac's speaker/system volume (which can be adjusted using the control strip's sound module or an external speaker's controls if you want to play the movie louder). The DVD Menu button brings up the DVD menu in the main viewer window where the DVD movie played (the same as on a set-top DVD player). Keyboard shortcuts are also assigned to these buttons, as listed in Table 17-6.

In addition to these features, pressing the bottom section of the controller where the DVD logo is located will display buttons for choosing an alternate audio track, subtitles, and different camera angles, if these features are supported on the inserted DVD movie. Also displayed in this area are the Slow Motion and Single Frame Forward buttons.

Figure 17-4
Use the Arrange item in the Monitors control panel to designate a TV as the primary display.

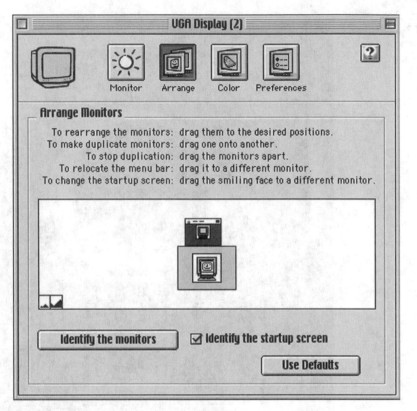

TABLE 17-6

Apple DVD player keyboard commands.

Command	Keystroke
Play	<Space>
Pause	<Space>
Stop	Command-Period
Fast-Forward	Command-Right arrow
Rewind	Command-Left arrow
Skip to Next Chapter	Right arrow
Skip to Previous Chapter	Left arrow
Return to DVD Menu	Escape
Volume Up	Command-Up arrow
Volume Down	Command-Down arrow
Mute	Command-M
Eject DVD	Command-E

Figure 17-5
The Apple DVD
Player controller
window.

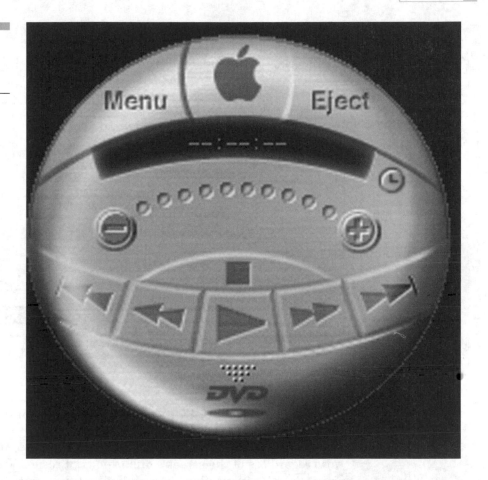

Additional options for the Apple DVD Player application that one would find on a traditional set-top DVD player can be accessed by selecting the Preferences item in the Edit menu. The Preferences dialog box, shown in Figure 17-6, allows you to set the default language for audio tracks and subtitles (for situations where a movie includes alternate languages), the type of output audio that the DVD's audio content will be mixed to, and parental controls. Parental controls allow you to specify movie ratings (G, PG, PG-13, R, or NC-17) that can be played on the Mac, assuming that all DVD movies inserted support the parental controls features. This feature is also password-protected so that children cannot change it without their parent's knowledge.

The Video menu allows you to control the size of the window in which the DVD movie is displayed. Normal Size is the standard resolution/size of the window (720×480 pixels), Half Size and Smallest Size are one half

Figure 17-6
The Apple DVD
Player Preference
dialog box.

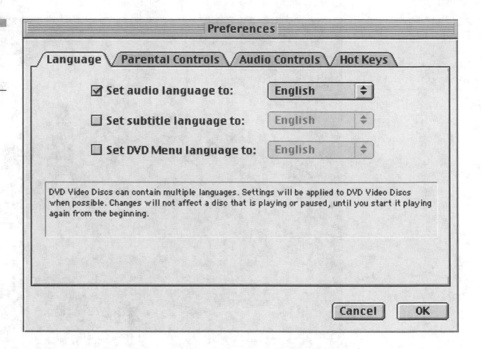

(360×240) or one quarter (180×120) of that size, respectively. Fill Screen makes the window fill the Mac's display, regardless of its resolution (though the DVD movie will be displayed with the appropriate aspect ratio regardless of the screen's dimensions). Present Video Onscreen will cause the Mac to display the movie full screen without the menu bar, desktop, or window being shown. When Present Video Onscreen is selected, the controller window will disappear after 10 seconds when no keyboard or mouse activity has taken place.

Installing DVD Hardware

DVD hardware can range from a DVD-ROM drive to a DVD-RAM or DVD-R drive to the MPEG-2 decoder hardware needed to play movies on all but the most recent Mac models. This section looks at how to install or replace the most common pieces of DVD hardware, including the factory-installed DVD-ROM drives of the Power Mac and the iMac DV and iMac DV Special Edition computers.

Power Mac Internal DVD-ROM/DVD-RAM Drives

The internal DVD-ROM or DVD-RAM drive of the Power Mac computers is mounted in a drive carrier that is shared with the internal Zip drive (or other removable-media drive), if one is installed. This carrier, shown in Figure 17-7, must be removed as a unit when replacing the CD/DVD-ROM drive or when replacing or installing a Zip drive (or other removable-media drive).

The first step in removing the carrier that holds the CD/DVD-ROM and Zip drives is to open the side door of the Mac and remove the cables attached to the back of these drives, including the IDE ribbon cable and the individual power connectors for each drive (assuming both a CD/DVD-ROM and Zip drive are installed). You may also need to remove any cables connecting the DVD drive to an MPEG-2 decoder card.

Next, you will need to remove the faceplate on the front of the Mac that covers both drives. Two tabs on the inside of the Mac's case secure this faceplate. As shown in Figure 17-8, these tabs are located right next to the carrier itself. Once these tabs are released, the faceplate can be disconnected from the computer.

Once you have removed the faceplate, you will notice that there are two screws located behind where it was. These screws, shown in Figure 17-9,

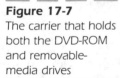

Figure 17-7
The carrier that holds both the DVD-ROM and removable-media drives

are located just below the CD/DVD-ROM drive. You will need to remove these screws in order to remove the carrier for the CD/DVD-ROM drive and Zip drive.

Once the screws are removed, you can remove the carrier from the computer. Do this by pushing it forward through the front of the computer (where the faceplate was removed. There is an electromagnetic interference (EMI) gasket on the underside of the carrier that may make pushing the drive out somewhat difficult. See Figure 17-10.

Once the carrier is free of the computer, you can remove and replace the CD or DVD-ROM drive. First, remove the EMI gasket that is attached to the back of the drive as shown in Figure 17-11. This should disengage relatively easily. Then you will need to remove the mounting screws, shown

Figure 17-9
These screws secure the carrier to the case.

in Figure 17-12, that hold the drive in place in the carrier. Use these same screws to secure the replacement drive, and then replace the EMI gasket.

If you are installing a DVD-RAM drive, you may notice that it is not as tall as the DVD-ROM or CD-ROM drives typically used in the Power Mac computers. This is normal, but you should be aware of the fact and adjust the positioning of the mounting screws appropriately so that the drive is seated securely.

Before installing the DVD-ROM drive, you will want to set the jumpers on it to the appropriate master or slave setting for the IDE channel. As explained in Chapter 13, if there is no other drive on the channel, the DVD-ROM should be set as the master drive. If there is also a Zip drive (or other removable-media drive), one of the two will need to be set as master and one as slave. Traditionally, the DVD-ROM is set as the master device, though both drives will still function if the DVD-ROM is set as slave and the Zip drive is set as master.

Figure 17-10
The carrier is pushed out through the front of the Mac.

Figure 17-11
These tabs secure the EMI gasket to the DVD-ROM drive.

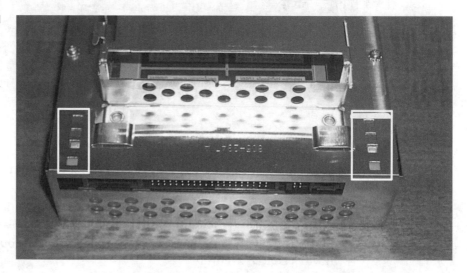

When reinserting the carrier, the process is essentially the reverse of removing it. You will want to ensure that the tab on the bottom of the carrier's shelf is positioned so that it extends into the slot on the carrier itself, as shown in Figure 17-13.

If you are using an internal SCSI DVD-ROM or DVD-RAM drive (which is unlikely, as most internal DVD drives are IDE), the process is

Figure 17-12
The mounting screws for a DVD-ROM drive.

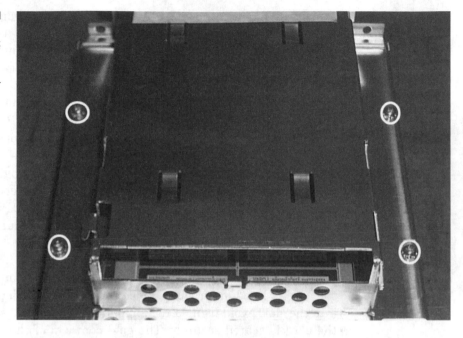

Figure 17-13
The tab of the carrier shelf.

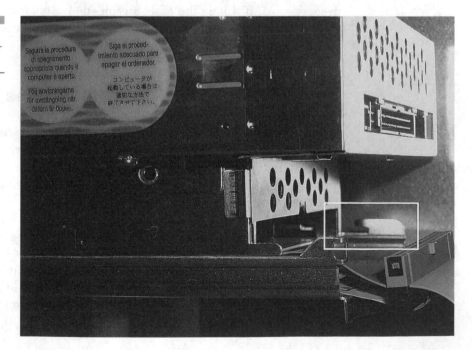

the same. You will, however, want to use the appropriate SCSI ribbon cable instead of the IDE cable (which will attach to your Mac's SCSI card). You should also make sure the drive is assigned a unique SCSI ID and the chain is terminated properly.

Installing an MPEG-2 Decoder Card   While the computer is open, locate an available PCI slot. Since the majority of MPEG-2 decoder cards will include video and audio outputs for external devices, you will need to remove the metal covering behind the slot you are installing the card into. These metal covers are held in place by a single screw. Once the screw is removed, you can slide the cover off. It is a good idea to keep the removed covers in case you decide to remove the MPEG-2 card later in the life of the Mac, as they can be replaced to keep dust and debris out of the computer.

Remove the card from its antistatic bag, holding it only by the edges. Position it above the PCI slot you are installing it into. Make sure that the card is lined up properly. Once the card is positioned, press it firmly into the slot. Avoid using a rocking motion, and press straight down until the card is seated securely. The gold contacts of the card should not be visible. Secure this with the same screw that was used to secure the metal cover before you removed it.

You may also need to connect the DVD-ROM drive to the MPEG-2 decoder card. If this is the case, any needed cables will be included with the card/drive kit. You should follow the specific instructions for any such connections that are included with your kit.

PowerBook Expansion Bay Drives

PowerBook DVD-ROM drives install into the PowerBook's expansion bay. They are easily removable modules that can be replaced by a second battery or another type of expansion bay drive such as a hard drive or Zip drive. The expansion bay itself is a modified IDE device and delivers equivalent performance to an internal IDE DVD-ROM drive. Installing or removing the DVD-ROM drives on the most recent PowerBooks is quite simple. Just remove the drive or battery that is in the expansion bay, and insert the DVD-ROM drive (or other drive) into the bay.

The PowerBook models covered in this book use either software-based MPEG-2 decoding (the 2000 PowerBooks with built-in FireWire ports) or will have the MPEG-2 decoding hardware built into the motherboard if playing DVD video is an option (only the 400-MHz models of the 1999 PowerBooks with a built-in SCSI port). This being the case, you have no need to be concerned with installing MPEG-2 decoding hardware for these computers. Earlier PowerBooks, which are not covered by this book, provided MPEG-2 decoding through a PC Card.

iMac DV and DV Special Edition

The internal drives of the iMac DV and iMac DV Special Edition require a slot-loading DVD-ROM drive. This type of drive is rather difficult to find, which will present problems if you wish to replace it. As a rule, you would most likely need to order replacement drives from Apple, which is something that only Apple Authorized Service Centers have the ability to do.

To replace the drive, first remove the lower casing of the computer as described in Chapter 1. Once you have done this, remove the carrier that holds both the hard drive and the DVD-ROM drive. To do this, remove the four screws that hold the carrier in place, as indicated in Figure 17-14. You also need to remove the IDE cables attached to both the DVD-ROM drive and the hard drive, as well as the power cable

Figure 17-14
The locations of the screws that hold the carrier in place.

Figure 17-15
The mounting screws
(two on each side)
for the DVD-ROM
drive.

attached to the hard drive. This is done most easily and safely if any install RAM modules are removed first.

You can now lift the carrier and the drives out of the computer. To remove the DVD-ROM drive, you will want to remove the mounting screws that secure it to the carrier, as indicated in Figure 17-15. Once these screws are removed, you can slide the drive out of the carrier and replace it. Reinserting the carriers is an exact reverse of the process of removing it.

External DVD-ROM/DVD-RAM/DVD-R Drives

DVD-ROM, DVD-RAM, and DVD-R drives are also available in external models. These models primarily use a SCSI interface, although FireWire drives are becoming fairly common as well. USB models have been created; however, they have not gained much popularity because USB's small bandwidth severely limits the possible performance of such drives and makes them unusable for playing DVD-Video discs.

Connecting a FireWire drive is easy, as you might expect. Simply install the drivers for the drive, restart the Mac so that these drivers are loaded as part of the Mac OS at startup, and then connect the drive to your FireWire chain or tree. At this point, the Mac should recognize the drive and allow you to access any DVD discs in it or to record data to them if it is a DVD-RAM or DVD-R drive.

Connecting a SCSI model requires your Mac to have a SCSI card/port installed and is the same basic process that you would follow for attaching any SCSI device. Install the software for the drive, shut down the Mac, and add the drive to your SCSI chain. Remember to follow the appropriate rules for unique SCSI IDs and termination in your SCSI chain when adding a DVD-ROM, DVD-RAM, or DVD-R drive.

If you are installing a DVD-ROM and MPEG-2 decoding kit that uses an external DVD-ROM or DVD-RAM drive, you may also need to connect the drive to the ports of the MPEG-2 decoder card or to external speakers or other hardware. The instructions that come with the kit can provide details on this if it is required.

Troubleshooting DVD-ROM Drives and DVD Movie Playback

Following are common problems and their solutions:

The Disc Unreadable by This Macintosh Error Message Appears

This message indicates that the Mac is unable to read or understand the format used by the DVD in question. If the DVD is not in a traditional Mac format (HFS or HFS+), make sure the File Exchange or PC Exchange control panel is installed in the Control Panels folder and that you haven't started with extensions off. Also, make certain that DVD related extensions, particularly device drivers, are installed. Another possibility is that the disc is scratched to the point that the Mac can no longer read it or that there are fingerprints, condensation, or other similar impediments preventing the laser from reading the disc properly.

If the DVD is a DVD-R, DVD-RW, or DVD-RAM disc, the DVD-ROM drive may be an older model that is not able to read the disc you are using (refer to the earlier sections of this chapter for which DVD drives support which DVD disc types). The disc may also have been created with errors. Try using it in a different DVD-ROM drive or in the DVD-R or DVD-RW drive that created it to ascertain if it was created correctly. Also remember that some formats, such as DIVX, are not supported by Mac DVD drives (see earlier in the chapter for details).

A DVD Is Inserted but the Mac Makes No Response at All

If you insert a DVD and the Mac doesn't respond by either mounting the DVD's icon on the desktop or by displaying an error message, check to make sure the drive is connected properly and that it is powered. Also, make sure that driver software for the DVD-ROM drive is installed (whether one of Apple's drivers or a third-party option). You can use the Apple System Profiler to tell if the drive is being recognized properly by the Mac as well.

If the drive appears to be working properly and works with other DVDs, check to be sure that the DVD that isn't recognized is not damaged or dirty and that you are inserting it properly.

The Mac Refuses to Eject a DVD

When the Apple DVD Player is running, the Mac will not eject a DVD disc. Quit the Apple DVD Player application and then attempt to eject the disc.

If the Mac displays a dialog saying the disc cannot be ejected because it contains items that are in use, you probably have a file on the disc open in some application or an application on the disc is still running. If, on the other hand, the drive is designed to auto-eject the disc and doesn't, there may be problems with the drive. However, like traditional Mac CD-ROM drives, most all of today's DVD-ROM drives include an emergency eject hole that can be triggered with a straightened-out paper clip. This can also be a solution if the Mac freezes or crashes and you need to eject a disc. It should not be done, however, while the Mac is running normally and the disc's icon is displayed on the desktop. The iMac DV models are the exception to this rule, as they do not have an emergency eject hole.

The Mac Ejects a DVD and Then Constantly Asks for It to Be Inserted

This problem means that some application of the Mac OS element is looking for something on the DVD, possible a recently accessed file or the desktop file. Try reinserting and ejecting the DVD again. If this doesn't solve the problem, try quitting all open applications while the DVD is inserted and then ejecting it. If this still doesn't happen, restart the Mac and eject the DVD before or during the startup sequence.

A DVD-RAM Disc is Not Recognized by a DVD-ROM Drive

Not all DVD-ROM drives can read DVD-RAM discs. Table 17-3 lists which Macs with Apple factory-installed DVD-ROM drives can read DVD-RAM discs (for non-Apple drives, check with the manufacturer). Even some DVD-ROM drives that can read DVD-RAM discs cannot read double-layer DVD-RAM discs.

If you are using a Mac and DVD-ROM drive that should support DVD-RAM discs and a single-layer DVD-RAM disc, check to be certain that the Foreign File Access and UDF Volume Access extensions are installed properly and that the File Exchange or PC Exchange control panel is installed. Also make sure the DVD-RAM disc is not damaged and is formatted properly.

DVD Video Playback Results in a Picture that Resembles Watching the Movie through Venetian Blinds

This problem means that there is not enough VRAM available for the Mac OS and the Apple DVD Player. Quit the Apple DVD Player and reduce either the screen resolution and/or color depth in the Monitors or Monitors and Sound control panel. This should make more VRAM available for DVD playback. Relaunch the Apple DVD Player.

DVD Movie Audio Playback Does Not Match DVD Movie Video Playback

Audio that is out of sync with video is a known issue for Macs that rely on software-based MPEG-2 decoding. Apple has released a number of software updates to compensate for the problem. Ensure that you have the latest version of the Apple DVD Player, the latest version of QuickTime, and the Mac OS 9 Audio Update (the latest version of the Sound Manager extension). These can be downloaded from Apple's website.

Additionally, turn off virtual memory, and file sharing, and quit any other applications that may be running while you are playing the DVD movie.

Apple DVD Player Cannot Open because the Required Hardware Was Not Found Error Message Appears

This message indicates that you are trying to use a version of the Apple DVD Player designed for hardware-based MPEG-2 decoding but the Mac was unable to find the MPEG-2 decoding hardware. If you are using a Mac that supports software-based MPEG-2 decoding (see Table 17-5), update to a more recent version of the Apple DVD Player application.

If you are using a Mac that requires hardware-based MPEG-2 decoding, double-check to ensure that your DVD-ROM drive and decoder card are installed properly. You can do this with the Apple System Profiler.

If the drive and card are installed and recognized, make certain the following extensions are installed: Apple CD/DVD Driver, ATI Driver Update, ATI MPP Manager, ATI Resource Manager, DVD Decoder Library, DVD Region Manager, QuickTime, QuickTime Power Plug, UDF Volume Access, and Video Startup.

If this fails to help, make sure that Speakable Items (Apple's speech recognition software) is turned off. If Speakable Items is already turned off and nothing else has alleviated the problem, you can also try deleting the Apple DVD Player preferences file (inside the Preferences folder in the System Folder).

Apple DVD Player Cannot Open Because the Apple CD/DVD Extension Is Not Installed or the DVD-ROM Module Could Not Be Found Error Message Appears

This error might be displayed if the driver extension for the Apple DVD-ROM drive is not installed (in which case no CD or DVD would be recognized by the Mac). It can also occur when file servers are set to mount automatically at startup. If this dialog appears and servers that require a password are set to mount at startup, use either the Chooser or the

Network Browser to access the servers in question and deselect the checkbox next to the hard drive(s) of the server.

Video from a DVD Movie Stutters during Playback

To address this problem, disable virtual memory, file sharing, and do not run any applications besides the Apple DVD Player while playing the movie. This should resolve most causes of DVD movie stuttering. You can also try cleaning the DVD disc with a soft, dry cloth if it appears dirty.

DVD Video Appears Blocky or Pixilated

This can occur if there is not enough VRAM for the movie to display properly. Try reducing the screen resolution of the Mac to make more VRAM available. Also, quit any other applications that may be running. If this doesn't help, try displaying the movie in a window rather than full-screen.

Apple DVD Player Has Stopped Because the Disc May Be Dirty or Scratched Error Message Appears

Obviously, this can indicate that a DVD disc needs to be cleaned because dust, other debris, or scratches are preventing it from being read. This error can, however, be incorrectly displayed with a number of DVD movies on Mac with hardware-based MPEG-2 decoding that are running version 1.0 or 1.1 of the Apple DVD Player. Updating to version 1.3 resolves the problem with these movies.

This error will also be displayed if the Apple DVD Player is launched and there is not a DVD-Video disc in the DVD-ROM drive.

Resources for Further Study

Apple's DVD Home Page—http://www.apple.com/dvd

About.com Mac Hardware CD/DVD Resources—
http://machardware.about.com/msubcddvd.htm

About.com Mac Support DVD Resources—
http://macsupport.about.com/msub66.htm

Removable-
Media Drives

Removable-media drives store data on disks or cartridges that can be easily removed from the computer and replaced with another disk or cartridge. The media (the disk or cartridge) can then be stored, used in another computer with the same type of drive, or used in the same computer at a later time. Removable-media drives can be used to share large collections of data between computers, to store backups, or to augment the storage abilities of a computer with a limited-capacity hard drive.

Several types of removable-media drives are on the market today, and most of them are cross-platform (though the file format of the disk inserted into the drive does vary from platform to platform, just as hard drives do).

How Removable-Media Drives Work

From a user's perspective, a removable-media drive works by the user inserting a disk or cartridge into the drive. An icon for this disk or cartridge then shows up on the Mac's desktop, as a hard drive or floppy disk icon would. You can then copy, move, and delete files from the disk exactly as you would the Mac's internal hard drive. The disk can also be used to open or save files from within applications. When you're done working with the disk, you can eject it by dragging its icon to the Trash or selecting the icon and using the Finder's Put Away or Eject Disk commands. Removable-media disks will behave somewhat slower than a hard drive by varying degrees, because the media cannot usually be accessed as quickly as the data on a hard drive.

Although all removable-media drives accomplish similar tasks and from a user perspective function the same way, the actual mechanics of how they work and how they store data can vary widely. The differences affect how much data these drives are capable of storing, as well as how fast they are capable of storing, and retrieving data. They also affect the reliability of the media as a method of storing data for long periods of time. There are three primary types of removable-media drives: super floppy drives, removable hard drives, and magneto-optical drives.

Super Floppy Drives

The most common removable-media drives are super floppy types. These include the extremely popular Zip drive and the SuperDisk drive. These drives are exactly what the name implies: big floppy drives. The media used are extremely similar in design, construction, and data storage technique to a floppy disk. They use a flexible mylar disk that is coated with a magnetic substance. This disk is then placed inside a hard-plastic casing to protect it. When the disk is inserted into the drive, a movable section of the casing is retracted. This allows the drive heads, which are built into the drive itself rather than the disk, to access the flexible magnetic disk inside the case.

Super floppy media are the most common removable media on the market, as well as the least expensive type of drive. They also offer the least capacity per disk, are the slowest in transferring data, and are the most easily affected by electromagnetic fields. In addition, the disks are the smallest and most physically fragile removable media on the market.

Removable Hard Drives

Removable hard drives use cartridges rather than disks to store data. These cartridges often include much of the same mechanisms that a hard drive would, such as actuator arms, drive heads, and hard platters (disks) on which data is stored. However, the control circuitry that allows the drive to locate data on the platters and to communicate with the Mac, as well as the power source and motor for the drive, are stored in the drive itself rather than in the cartridge

Because the cartridge functions very similarly to a hard drive, it can offer performance that is faster than some other types of removable media. It is also capable of storing larger amounts of data on a given cartridge than super-floppy-type media. This allows for higher integrity of the stored data because the magnetic properties of the cartridge are stronger than those of a disk-based technology (though not as high as those used in magneto-optical drives).

Removable hard drives and media are more expensive than some of the other removable-media drives on the market. This is because the cartridges are actually small, removable hard drives, which are more expensive to produce than something that is essentially a large-capacity floppy disk. However, while the cartridges themselves are more expensive, they also store more information per cartridge, giving them a lower cost per megabyte of storage space. The Castlewood Orb drive is an excellent example of a removable hard drive, providing 2.2 GB of storage space per cartridge, with data transfer rates over 12 MB per second. The Iomega Jaz drive is another good example, storing either 1 GB or 2 GB per cartridge, with transfer rates over 7 MB per second.

Magneto-Optical Drives

Both cartridge and super floppy removable drives store data solely by adjusting the arrangement of magnetic material on the disk/cartridge using a powerful electromagnet in the read/write heads of the device to designate patterns of information. This works well, but it also poses the possibility that a strong enough electrical or magnetic field can erase some or all of the data stored on the media.

Magneto-optical drives (also called MO drives) store data using a magnetic dye stored inside of a plastic disk. To read or write data, the drive uses a laser, much like a CD-ROM drive. When the drive writes data, the laser heats up the metallic dye, adjusting its magnetic particles. When reading data, the same laser is used, but this time it reflects off the dye that was adjusted during the write process

Because they use a laser to store information in the magnetic dye of the disk, magneto-optical disks offer a far greater degree of stability than other removable-media technologies. They cannot be easily disrupted by magnetic fields as other methods can be because they require the heat generated by the laser in the drive to adjust the magnetic fields of the dye inside the disk. This makes them an excellent alternative if you want to use removable media that is stable and unlikely to be affected by the passage of time. Unfortunately, every spot on the disk where a bit of data is stored requires the laser to heat up the dye in order to store that information. This means that magneto-optical drives take longer to store and retrieve data than some purely magnetic media technologies.

Table 18-1 shows a comparison of the different drive types.

TABLE 18-1

Removable Drive Type Comparisons.

Aspect	Removable Hard Drive	Super Floppy	MO Drive
Data integrity	Moderate	Low	High
Performance	High	Low	Moderate
Average cost/MB	Low	High	Moderate
Drive cost	Moderate	Low	Low
Size of user base	Moderate	High	Low

Internal versus External Drives

Removable-media drives come in both internal and external models. Internal models are available for only the Power Mac G3/G4 models. PowerBook computers can accept expansion bay models of removable-media drives, though these are designed specifically for a given PowerBook model and behave more as external drives even though they are internal to the PowerBook's case. iMac and iBook computers do not have the internal drive space to accommodate internal removable-media drives of any kind.

There are advantages and disadvantages to choosing internal and external drive models. On the one hand, internal drives are, of course, internal, which means there is one less power cord, one less cable, and one less device taking up space on your desk. In addition to taking up less desk space, an internal drive is easier to transfer if you move the computer, to another location because you need only move the computer, not the computer plus the external drive. They also tend to cost an average of $20 to $40 less than the same drive in an external model, because they do not require an external case or power supply.

On the other hand, because they are internal, they are more involved to install and can only be used with one computer. Also, internal removable-media drives may not be able to be migrated to a new computer at some point in the future, and only one internal removable-media drive can be installed at any given time. They also increase the drain on the Mac's power supply.

Removable-Media Drive Interfaces

Internal and external removable-media drives can use any of several different device interfaces, including USB, SCSI, FireWire, IDE, and the expansion bay technology of the PowerBook computers (and most drives are available in models using each of these interface technologies). Each interface offers differing advantages and limitations. Also, not all drives are available in models supporting all of the available interfaces, and not all Macs support all of the possible interfaces. The Iomega Jaz drive, for example, is not available in USB models, and the iBook supports only USB as an interface.

When choosing a removable-media drive, you should consider which interface method you wish to use. If the drive is to be used with multiple Macs, however, you should use an interface that all the Macs in question have available to them. You would not choose a FireWire drive if you want to share a drive with both a Power Mac and an iBook.

You should also consider the performance of the interface. If you will be transferring moderate or large collections of data on a regular basis or you expect that you will be working with files directly from the removable-media disk rather than just copying them to your hard drive, you should choose one of the faster interface options in order to be more productive (and to save your patience).

USB

USB (universal serial bus) is probably the most common interface used for less-expensive removable-media drives today. USB is included on all the recent Macs (as well as most Windows-based PCs), meaning a drive using USB as its interface will function on any current Mac model. USB is also very easy to use; you simply attach the drive to a USB port on the Mac or hub, and you're ready to go.

Unfortunately, USB is very slow. You can use USB drives for backups and for storing files that you don't use regularly, but if you try to run an application or open a large file from a USB drive, you'll find that the performance limitations of the USB interface make it slow to run no matter what you're working with.

It is a credit to removable drive manufacturers that there have been some very impressive strides made in providing higher data transfer rates for USB drives. Some are very impressive, considering that USB can only deliver 1.5 MB/second of usable bandwidth in the best of circumstances. For example, the most recent Zip and SuperDisk drive can play moderately sized QuickTime movie clips from a removable disk without the video being jerky or distorted. But even with these efforts, there is simply a practical limit to how much they can accomplish.

USB is a good choice if you will be using the smaller-capacity removable-media drives such as the Zip and SuperDisk drives, because you will not be transferring large file collections at a single time. It is also good for storing small documents, archiving material you don't expect to use all the time, or performing moderately sized backups. It is not good if you are looking to truly augment or replace space that is being filled up on your hard drive.

SCSI

SCSI is the oldest technology used for attaching removable-media drives to the Mac. It has been, and continues to be, used for every removable-media drive option. SCSI offers excellent performance for removable-media drives of any type. It allows the full performance abilities of the drive to be utilized, and it can be used for both external and internal drives, although most internal drives today use the IDE interface instead.

Unfortunately, SCSI is not an option for most of the recent Macintosh models. The iMac and iBook models do not have any option for attaching SCSI drives. The Power Mac models can use SCSI, but you need to add a SCSI card to them. The most recent PowerBook models with FireWire ports built in can accept a SCSI PC Card, which allows them to attach SCSI devices, but at the added cost of the SCSI card. The older PowerBooks did include a built-in SCSI port, which makes them the easiest candidate of any Mac covered by this book to use a SCSI-based removable-media drive.

SCSI is also the only option for several drives, particularly if you have older models of a current removable-media technology, such as the Jaz drive. This is also true if you have an investment in any of the discontinued removable-media drive technologies, such as the SyQuest line of drives that were discontinued when SyQuest went bankrupt in 1998.

FireWire

FireWire is the newest interface and has yet to become popular with the majority of removable-media drive developers. There are, however, several FireWire removable-media options on the market, including Zip, MO, and Orb drives. FireWire offerings are all external, and they offer the performance advantages of SCSI with the ease of use of USB. All in all, FireWire is an excellent combination and probably the best option you can find for most Macs at the moment (provided you are using the drive with a Mac that has FireWire ports).

FireWire is particularly attractive in a drive that stores large amounts of data per disk, such as the Orb, which stores 2.2 GB per cartridge. Many people use these higher-capacity removable cartridges as separate additional hard drives (albeit low-performance ones). This often means using the drive to run applications or to open and work with large file collections. When using any external drive like this, you want to get the best performance possible, and right now, FireWire is the only technology built into most Macs that offers this performance for many types of drives.

FireWire also works well if you are using a drive for regular large backups. When regularly making copies of a 10-GB (or larger) hard drive, or of large file collections, speed and ease of use are extremely important. FireWire offers both, particularly if you are using a single drive to back up data from multiple Macs, such as in a small office or lab setting.

IDE (ATAPI)

IDE removable-media drives are only an option for internal drives and can only be installed in the Power Mac computers because they are the only models that have an internal drive bay for removable-media drives. The drive bay and IDE channel is officially supported only for Zip drives installed in the factory by Apple. Despite this, any 3.5-inch internal removable-media drive that includes Macintosh drivers and supports the IDE/ATAPI standard should work fine in these Macs.

As discussed earlier in this chapter, there are benefits to using an internal drive instead of an external model. While it is possible to connect an internal drive using a SCSI card with support for internal SCSI devices, IDE is a more practical choice for a few different reasons. IDE will give you performance comparable to the majority of internal SCSI drive options.

One reason IDE is a better option is simplicity. Apple designed the drive bay to be used with an IDE drive. The second connector of the IDE cable used for the Power Mac's CD/DVD-ROM drive is already located at the back of the removable-media drive bay. Similarly, IDE is an easier interface technology to deal with, since there is no concern about individual device settings or termination as there is in a SCSI chain.

Using IDE is also a less expensive solution. IDE drives tend to be moderately less expensive than their SCSI counterparts. Since SCSI doesn't offer a large enough performance advantage for most removable-media drives, there is less reason to spend the extra money to choose a SCSI drive if you don't have to. Also, the Power Mac comes with an IDE connector designed for this drive bay. If you choose a SCSI drive instead, you will need to purchase a SCSI card that supports internal drives, which will be another added expense.

PowerBook Expansion Bays

The expansion bay drives of the PowerBook computers can be used to provide any type of drive that a developer cares to create for them. The most common use for these bays is the CD/DVD-ROM drive included with the computer. Probably the next most common use is expansion bay hard drives. However, some removable-media drives for these expansion bays are available (most made by VST Technologies). These are predominantly Zip and SuperDisk drives.

PowerBook expansion bay drives offer the ease of use of an internal drive. This is even more pertinent to PowerBook users on the road because you don't need to deal with carrying an external drive or cables with you if you expect to work with removable-media disks. Similarly, since the drive is internal, it is one less thing to carry around or have to explain to the guard at the airport X-ray machine. You also don't need to worry about finding a place to plug the drive into while you're using it away from the home or office, because an expansion bay drive is powered directly by the PowerBook's battery.

PowerBook expansion bay drives also offer a speed advantage. The expansion bay is an internal IDE device, meaning it is capable of data transfer rates much higher than external drives using a USB interface. This speed advantage can be quite noticeable.

Table 18-2 compares performance rates of different removable-media interfaces.

TABLE 18-2

Typical Performance of Removable-Media Interfaces.

Interface	Average Transfer Rate	Reasonably Supported Drives
USB	1.5 MB/second	Zip, SuperDisk
SCSI	5 MB/second–160 MB/second	Zip, SuperDisk, Jaz, Orb, MO, legacy drive types
FireWire	Up to 50 MB/second	Jaz, Orb, MO
IDE	16.6 MB/second	Zip, SuperDisk, MO
Expansion bays	16.6 MB/second	Zip, SuperDisk

Installing a Removable-Media Drive

With the exception of an internal model for the Power Mac computers, installing a removable-media drive is a fairly simple procedure. The following sections give you instructions on how to install a removable-media drive with each type of interface.

Installing a USB, FireWire, or SCSI Removable-Media Drive

As a rule, installing an external removable-media drive is an extremely simple procedure. First, you install any drivers or other software included with the drive on your Mac's internal hard drive. Then you restart the computer so that the drivers are loaded during the Mac's startup sequence and attach the drive. If the drive is a USB or FireWire drive, this simply means attaching the drive to an available port, either on the Mac, on a hub, or in a chain of devices.

If you are connecting a SCSI drive, you need to assign a SCSI ID that is unique in your SCSI chain. You also need to be certain that the chain is properly terminated once the new drive is added. As Chapter 12 details, the last device in a SCSI chain needs to be terminated. Many removable-media drives include the option for internal termination if they are placed at the end of the chain.

Installing a PowerBook Expansion Bay Removable-Media Drive

The PowerBook expansion bay is, for all practical purposes, an internal drive. However, for installation purposes, it resembles an external drive. This is because the installation process is much like installing a USB or FireWire drive. You install the driver software, shut down the PowerBook, remove the current drive in the expansion bay, and slide in the removable-media drive you want to use. Start up the computer, and the drive is available to use. Once the driver software is installed and loaded with the Mac OS at startup, you can insert or remove a drive in the expansion bay whenever you have the need to use it.

Installing an Internal Removable-Media Drive

The only current Macs that support an internal removable-media drive are the Power Mac models. These computers come with a 3.5-inch drive bay directly below the CD/DVD-ROM drive that can support an internal Zip, SuperDisk, or other internal IDE drive that fits the 3.5-inch form factor. In addition to the drive itself, you may also need to purchase a bevel or faceplate for the front of the computer that matches the appropriate drive opening.

As always, the first step in installing any new drive is to install whatever driver and utility software came with the drive. You also need to use the drive's jumpers to set it as either the master or slave drive on the IDE channel. Apple sets the factory-installed internal CD/DVD-ROM drive of these Macs as the master drive, so you should opt to make the removable-media drive a slave drive. Instructions for setting the drive as master or slave should be included with the drive.

Once that is done, you should shut down the computer and open the side door. As you can see in Figure 18-1, the drive bay for a removable-media drive is located directly beneath the bay for the CD/DVD-ROM drive. The IDE connector you will use is shared on the same cable as the CD/DVD-ROM drive and should hang from the cable directly behind the

Figure 18-1
This carrier contains both the CD/DVD-ROM drive and the bay for the removable-media drive.

drive bay. A standard molex power connector should also hang in this position.

To install a drive into the drive bay, you first need to remove the carrier unit that holds both the CD/DVD-ROM drive and the removable-media drive. To accomplish this, remove the faceplate from the front of the Mac. This is done by releasing the two tabs on the inside of the Mac's case that secure this faceplate. As shown in Figure 18-2, these tabs are located right next to the carrier itself. Once these tabs are released, the faceplate can be disconnected from the computer.

There are two screws behind where the faceplate on the front panel of the Mac was. These screws, shown in Figure 18-3, are located just below the CD-ROM drive. You need to remove these screws in order to remove the carrier for the CD-ROM drive and removable-media drive bays.

Next, you need to disconnect the cables from the internal CD/DVD-ROM drive. This includes the IDE ribbon cable, the power cable, and the CD/DVD audio cable (if there is one). These cables are shown in Figure 18-4. If there is an existing internal removable-media drive, you also need to disconnect the IDE cable and power cable from it.

Once the screws and cables are removed, you are free to remove the carrier from the computer. Do this by pushing it forward through the

Figure 18-2
These tabs hold the faceplate over the CD/DVD-ROM drive and removable-media drive bays.

Figure 18-3
These screws need to
be removed in order
to remove the carrier
containing the
CD/DVD-ROM drive
and the removable-
media drive bay.

Figure 18-4
The cables on the
back of the
CD/DVD-ROM
drive.

front of the computer (where the faceplate was removed), as shown in Figure 18-5. There is an electromagnetic interference (EMI) gasket on the underside of the carrier that may make pushing the drive out somewhat difficult.

Once the carrier is free of the computer, you can remove an existing removable-media drive and replace it or install a new drive if none was present. To do this, you need to use the mounting screws that hold the drive in place in the carrier. There are holes on both sides of the carrier for the mounting screws, as shown in Figure 18-6. Once the new drive is secured to the carrier, you can reinsert the carrier.

Reinserting the carrier is essentially the reverse of removing it. You should ensure that the hole on the bottom of the carrier unit is positioned so that it extends into the tab of the drive shelf that the carrier sits on inside the computer (see Figure 18-7). Once the carrier is secured in the Mac, reattach the cables for the CD/DVD-ROM drive. Attach the second IDE connector to the back of the new removable-media drive, and attach one of the power connectors inside the Mac to the drive as well.

SCSI Internal Drives   Although IDE internal removable-media drives are, by far, more common than SCSI models, you may find SCSI internal drives on the market or you may have one from an earlier Mac. Provided the drive fits the size specifications for the drive bay in the Power Mac G3/G4, you can use it in one of the current Power Macs. You will, how-

Figure 18-5
The carrier must be pushed out the front of the Mac's case.

Figure 18-6
The holes for the
mounting screws of
a removable-media
drive (use the upper
or lower holes
depending on the
size of the drive).

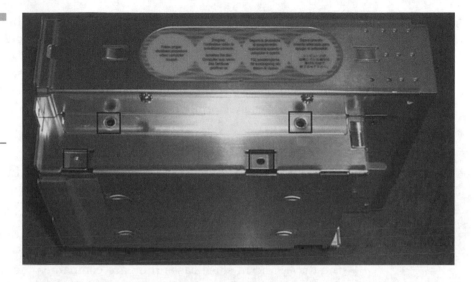

ever, also need to have a SCSI card that supports internal SCSI devices installed in the computer.

Installing a SCSI removable-media drive is very much the same as installing an IDE drive. You still mount the drive in the bay in the same manner, and you still use the same power connector for the drive. The difference is that you need to set the device's SCSI ID and ensure that it

Figure 18-7
This tab must be
inserted properly in
order for the carrier
unit to seat properly
on the shelf inside
the Mac.

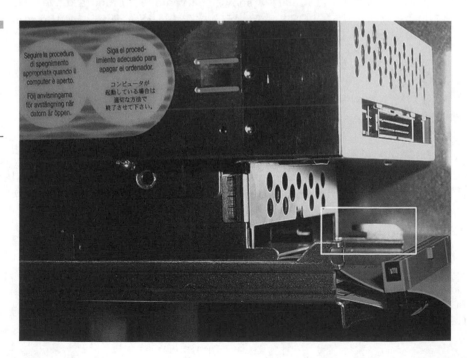

is terminated properly as part of the SCSI chain that it is attached to (see Chapter 12 for more information). Also, you would ignore concerns about setting the device as a master or slave drive, as this is used only when dealing with IDE drives. Finally, you would use a 50-pin SCSI ribbon cable instead of the 40-pin IDE ribbon cable to connect the drive to the internal connector of your SCSI card.

Common Removable-Media Drive Types

Several different types of removable-media drives are produced by various manufacturers. In some cases the manufacturers are the creators of the drive, and in some cases they are companies that have licensed the drive technology from the drive's creator. Each type of drive has its own inherent strengths and weaknesses, and each one is suited for different types of use. Each drive also enjoys a different level of market share (the percentage of computer owners or businesses that use the drive). The market share of a drive can be an important consideration if you plan to use removable-media disks to share files with other computer users.

Table 18-3 shows the removable-media driver software bundled with Mac OS 8.6 and higher. Table 18-4 compares the capacities and costs per megabyte of various removable-media drive types. Tables 18-5 compares the performance of removable-media drives.

Zip Drives

The Zip drive (shown in Figure 18-8) is the most popular removable-media drive on the market today. It was developed by Iomega in the early 1990s and uses 3.5-inch disks that are very similar to floppy disks, although about twice as thick. The original Zip drive used disks (known as Zip disks) capable of storing 100 MB of data. In 1998, Iomega intro-

TABLE 18-3

Removable-Media Driver Software Bundled with Mac OS 8.6 or Higher.

USB Zip Drive
USB SuperDisk Drive

TABLE 18-4

Capacities and
Relative Costs of
Current
Removable-Media
Drive Types.

Drive	Disk Capacity	Average Cost of Storage per MB
Zip	100 MB	$0.10
	250 MB	$0.07
SuperDisk	120 MB	$0.09
	1.44 MB (floppy)	$0.20
MO	128 MB	$0.07
	230 MB	$0.05
	540 MB	$0.05
	640 MB	$0.05
	1.3 GB	$0.04
	2.3 GB	$0.03
Orb	2.2 GB	$0.02
Jaz	1 GB	$0.10
	2 GB	$0.05

Note: Costs are at time of writing, based on prices from multiple sources. Prices of removable media are subject to change.

duced an updated version of the Zip drive capable of using Zip disks that could store 250 MB per disk. These drives are backwards-compatible with the earlier 100-MB Zip disks, but the 250-MB disks can only be used in the newer Zip 250 drives. Several companies have licensed the Zip drive design from Iomega and produced Zip drives of their own, primarily as PowerBook expansion bay drives and drives with a USB or FireWire interface. Currently, the Zip drive is available in models supporting all five interface options for removable-media drives.

Because of its extreme popularity, the Zip drive is probably the removable-media drive most used to share files among multiple computers. This is because the original 100-MB Zip disk has been around for several years and has been adopted by both individual users and companies as a method for sharing moderately large collections of files. If you are looking for a removable-media technology that will be used to share files with other computer users, the Zip drive (shown in Figure 18-8) is probably the best choice.

TABLE 18-5

Performance of
Current
Removable-Media
Drive Types.

Drive	Average Sustained Data Transfer Rate
Zip 100 MB	
USB	1.2 MB/second
SCSI	1.4 MB/second
IDE	1.4 MB/second
FireWire	2.4 MB/second
PowerBook Expansion Bay	1.4 MB/second
Zip 250 MB	
USB	1.2 MB/second
SCSI	2.4 MB/second
IDE	2.4 MB/second
FireWire	2.4 MB/second
PowerBook Expansion Bay	2.4 MB/second
SuperDisk	
USB	0.7 MB/second
SCSI	1.1 MB/second
IDE	1.1 MB/second
PowerBook Expansion Bay	0.67 MB/second
MO	
USB	1.5 MB/second
SCSI	3.9 MB/second
IDE	3.9 MB/second
FireWire	3.9 MB/second
Orb	
USB	1 MB/second
SCSI	12.2 MB/second
IDE	12.2 MB/second
FireWire	12.2 MB/second

TABLE 18-5

Performance of
Current
Removable-Media
Drive Types.

Drive	Average Sustained Data Transfer Rate
Jaz 1 GB	
SCSI	5.4 MB/second
Jaz 2 GB	
SCSI	7.4 MB/second

Figure 18-8

A USB Zip drive from
Iomega.

SuperDisk Drives

The SuperDisk was developed as a replacement for the floppy drive. It uses disks that are the same size and shape as a floppy known as SuperDisks. SuperDisks can store up to 120 MB of data per disk. The SuperDisk drive can also read and write traditional 1.44-MB floppy disks, making it useful as both a removable-media drive and as a floppy drive replacement. The SuperDisk is most commonly found using a USB interface; however, internal and external SCSI models are also available, as well as internal IDE, FireWire, and PowerBook expansion bay varieties.

The SuperDisk existed in relative obscurity on the Mac platform until the iMac was released without an internal floppy drive. The iMac's release gave the SuperDisk a fair measure of popularity because of its ability to read existing floppy disks, as well as for storing large backups or archived data.

Magneto-Optical Drives

Magneto-optical drives were discussed as a technology type at the beginning of this chapter. Although all magneto-optical drives use this technology to store data, the MO drive standard is fairly open, and several variations are available. MO drives are available from several manufacturers.

The primary division of MO drive types is in the size of the cartridges used. There are both 5.25-inch and 3.5-inch magneto-optical drives. Each of these drive types use separate-sized cartridges that are not compatible with each other. The 5.25-inch cartridge MO drives use cartridges that come in a variety of different capacities, including 128 MB, 230 MB, 540 MB, 640 MB, 1.3 GB, and 2.3 GB (640 MB is the most common capacity). Each of these capacities was added as the standard, and technology used in the MO drives progressed, resulting in several separate cartridge capacities. Because not all drives support all cartridge capacities, when choosing an MO drive, you should check which cartridge types it is compatible with. The 3.5-inch variety of MO drive is less common and also comes in differing capacity cartridges, including 128 MB, 230 MB, 650 MB, and 1.2 GB. Again, not all drives support all cartridge capacities.

Magneto-optical drives are available in internal and external SCSI, as well as in internal IDE, external USB, and external FireWire models. These drives deliver good performance, but they are not at the high end of the performance spectrum. This has also kept them from becoming a popular removable-media drive choice. The big advantage to MO drives is that they offer a very high degree of data integrity and work well as a secure backup method or for archiving data. However, their place in these areas is becoming usurped by the cheaper and ever easier to deal with recordable and rewritable CD and DVD technologies (see the last two chapters for information on these options).

Orb Drives

The Orb drive by Castlewood is the newest removable-media drive type). It is a removable hard drive that can store up to 2.2 GB of data per cartridge. The Orb drive currently comes in internal IDE, internal and external SCSI, and external USB and FireWire models. Despite being a relative newcomer, the Orb does deliver near-hard-drive levels of performance, making it the fastest removable-media drive on the market. This coupled with its low per-megabyte cost and large-capacity cartridges makes a very attractive option for many uses.

Jaz Drives

The Jaz drive was developed by Iomega as a kind of big brother to the Zip drive, although, unlike the Zip disk, it is a removable hard drive technology rather than a super floppy. The original Jaz drive used disks that could store up to 1 GB of data. A later generation of the drive offers disks that can store up to 2 GB. The 2-GB Jaz drive is backward-compatible with the earlier version; it can read and write 1-GB Jaz disks as well as the 2-GB disks.

Both the 1-GB and 2-GB versions of the Jaz drive are currently available, and you can find good values on the 1-GB model. The downside is that Iomega has taken much longer to develop Jaz drives with an interface besides the external SCSI or internal IDE models. This has resulted in people considering alternate removable-media options that do support Apple's current built-in interface technologies instead of the Jaz.

SyQuest Drives

SyQuest was Iomega's biggest competitor and one of the top removable-media drive producers for several years. During that time, SyQuest manufactured a number of removable-media drive types before going out of business in the fall of 1998. Although SyQuest drives are no longer manufactured, a number of them are still in use, and they can be used with some of the current Mac computers. Because virtually all of the SyQuest drives use a SCSI interface, they require a Mac, such as the Power Mac or PowerBook models, that can support a SCSI card or has a built-in SCSI port.

The following sections take a brief look at each of the SyQuest drive types. Note that each drive used its own proprietary cartridge design and that the cartridges are not compatible across the various drive types. Also, even though the drives themselves may still be in service today, finding new cartridges for them is becoming very difficult (if not impossible). If you are using these drives today, it is probably a good idea to consider upgrading to one of the current removable-media types discussed in the previous sections.

SyQuest 44-MB, 88-MB, 200-MB Drives   These were SyQuest's earliest drives. The initial drive used cartridges that were capable of storing 44 MB of data per cartridge. A later advance in the drive resulted in a drive that could store 88 MB of data per cartridge. This was followed by a further advance, which resulted in 200-MB cartridges. The 88-MB and 200-MB drives were backward-compatible with the earlier cartridges. These were the most common of SyQuest's offerings.

EZ Flyer Drives   SyQuest's EZ Flyer line offered improved performance over its initial drive products. It was a cartridge drive that initially debuted using cartridges that could store 135 MB of data. This was later superseded with a version of the drive that used 230-MB cartridges but was backward-compatible with the earlier 135-MB cartridges.

SyJet Drives   Where SyQuest's earlier offerings had been competitors to Iomega's Zip drive, the SyJet was competition for the Jaz drive. It was a removable hard drive that could store 1.5 GB of data per cartridge. The slightly larger disk size and slightly faster access times made it a fair competitor to the Jaz. It was the last drive SyQuest released with support for the Macintosh platform.

Other Removable-Media Drive Types

The preceding sections looked at the most common types of removable-media drives on the market for the Mac. In addition to these, there have been some other drive types that either never gained significant popularity or user bases or became outdated and obsolete. These include the now-defunct Bernoulli cartridge drive that was Iomega's initial product back in the late 1980s, as well the Iomega's current Clik drive, which stores 44 MB of data on a small disk that is roughly half the size of the PC Cards used in the PowerBook. For the most part, these drives are simply not something that many Mac users or technicians will deal with on a regular basis.

Uses for Removable-Media Drives

There are a variety of uses for removable-media drives; however, the most common are backing up data, sharing files and applications between multiple computers, and acting as a hard drive extension for storing files or archiving older data. Some types of removable-media drives are better suited to some of these tasks, while other drives are better suited to others. Let's look at each use individually.

Backups

Removable-media drives are often used for storing backups of data, both of specific files or projects and for complete system backups. When using removable-media for backups, it is important to consider the type of removable media that is appropriate for the type of backup you are performing. For example, a complete system backup would not be appropriate to Zip disks (or other super floppy technology drives), because these disks are most susceptible to damage or degradation by exposure to magnetic fields or time. By the same token, a high-capacity magneto-optical disk might not be appropriate to backing up a small collection of files for current projects, because it will take longer to copy the data to the drive than it would some other media and the majority of the disk might not be used. Chapter 39 includes detailed advice on choosing a backup method and strategy.

Sharing Files

Removable media are commonly used to transfer collections of files from one computer to another, often between two computers in a single home or between an office and several clients. This technology gives you the power to store large collections of data on a single, portable disk. The disk can then be used by any other computer user with the same type of drive—assuming that the disk is formatted in a method the other computer can read. PC computers cannot readily read Mac-formatted disks, for example (although Macs have no problem reading PC-formatted disks).

When using removable media as a method for sharing files with other computer users, you should choose the same type of drive that anyone you intend to share files with uses or is likely to use. For this purpose, it is best to stick with the more popular drive types. Probably the safest option is the Zip drive because it has a large segment of the removable-media market for both professional and home users.

Supplementing Small Hard Drives and Archiving Data

When removable-media drives first came on the scene, they were marketed as a solution for people who were quickly filling their hard drives to capacity. Removable-media drives can be used as an extension of the hard drive, storing infrequently used or archived data off the hard drive and thus freeing space while still making the data available when it is needed. For faster removable-media drive types, it is possible to use individual cartridges as though they were each a low-cost, independent hard drive, storing applications and current files on the removable cartridges just as you would your internal hard drive. Given the increasingly low costs of hard drives today, this use of removable-media technology is probably one of the less common.

If you intend to use a removable-media drive as though it were an additional hard drive and perform everyday actions with the drive rather than simply archiving or storing data, you should choose a media that delivers both large capacity per cartridge and performance as close to actual hard drive transfer speeds as possible. Similarly, you should use one that uses a higher-speed interface, such as FireWire or SCSI. This is simple logic because in order to function as a hard drive supplement or extension to this degree, the drive needs to offer performance that is comparable to an actual hard drive. You can use Table 18-5, which appeared earlier in the chapter, to compare removable-drive transfer rates with hard drive performance.

In most cases, however, you should also consider buying a large-capacity hard drive simply because it may be more cost-effective. A typical 20-GB internal Ultra-ATA hard drive today costs around $200. This provides a large amount of storage space for most users, as well as very good performance for most uses. Compare that with the cost of a higher-end removable-media drive such as the Orb, which is the least-expensive high-end removable option and also runs around $200. Although the initial prices are the same, you would need to purchase about eight Orb disks to equal the capacity of the hard drive (one disk is included with the drive). At about $20 per disk, this adds up to $160 more for the same amount of usable storage space, and that isn't taking into account any other factors, such as the ease of use of having all the files on a single hard drive instead of on several cartridges.

Removable-Media versus Other Storage Devices

Removable-media drives are excellent for the purposes of sharing files, backing up data, and acting as an archive for data that is not used every day. However, there are additional options for several of the functions of a removable-media drive that you should also consider, depending upon the drive's intended use.

Hard Drives

Hard drives are good for mass storage. As capable as removable-media drives are for many purposes, because of performance concerns, cost concerns, and organizational and ease-of-use concerns, they are not really suited to be hard drive replacements.

A hard drive still offers the highest performance of any drive used in a computer. Granted, some removable-media drives offer performance equal to most low-end and some mid-range hard drives, but they may still suffer from slower interfaces that render them less powerful. The Ultra-ATA hard drives currently used in the Mac do offer excellent performance, and the higher-end SCSI hard drives (not to mention RAID solutions) make hard drives, on average, more than a cut above removable-media drives. If you are dealing with large graphics files or with large file collections of any type, running applications, doing multimedia work, or performing any type of drive-intensive task on a daily or even weekly basis, a good and fast internal hard drive is your only real option for decent performance.

In addition, hard drives are simply cheaper per megabyte than even the best removable media. These days, even 30- to 40-GB hard drives can be found for a few hundred dollars. None of the removable media on the market can match the per-megabyte costs that today's hard drives offer.

Hard drives are also easier to use, and most hard drives offer much more room compared to any removable-media disk. No file is too big to fit on most hard drives. If you have large collections of files and applications, you can keep them all on a single hard drive. You don't have to wonder about which removable disk they're on and hunt for a specific disk to find a file.

However, a downside is that internal hard drives are far from being portable. Even external hard drives are not as portable as a removable-media disk is. Hard drives don't make good options for sharing files with other computers, particularly computers located in another office, building, or city. Removable disks or cartridges are highly portable, and you can hand them to another user or mail them relatively easily and inexpensively.

Hard drives are also not as good for backups as removable media. This is because a hard drive is a fixed size, and when your backups become larger than the hard drive you're backing up to, you either need a larger hard drive or a different backup medium. Hard drives are also not viable for creating multiple copies of a backup, and they do not serve at all if you plan to create an off-site backup (which is always a good idea in case of a disaster in your home or office).

CD/DVD Drives

Removable-media drives are generally much easier to use than CD or DVD drives. For one thing, the drives can read and write to removable media, whereas the CD/DVD drives installed on most computers are read-only.

While there are recordable and rewritable CD and DVD drives on the market, they have several limitations when compared to removable-media drives. The most common is ease of use limitations. Recordable CD/DVD drives require you to use specific software to record a disk. You cannot, as a rule, just drag files from your hard drive to the CD/DVD disk as you can with a removable-media disk. Instead, you need to use a piece of software to create an image of the disk before you can record it. CD/DVD drives tend to record data at slower speeds than most removable media, although it probably won't be long before CD/DVD technology reaches recording speeds equal to some removable-media drives.

On the other hand, CD/DVD disks offer three very big advantages compared to removable-media disks. The first is that they are significantly less expensive. An average 100-MB Zip disk costs $10 or more. A CD-R disk for recording a custom CD costs less than two dollars and can hold 650 MB of data. That's quite a difference in cost per megabyte.

Second, CD/DVD disks are much more reliable. They do not degrade over time. Nor can strong electrical or magnetic fields that can accidentally erase data from a removable-media disk affect them. Even the best removable-media disks have expected life spans of less than a decade. CD and DVD disks, on the other hand, can last the better part of a century without losing their contents.

Third, virtually any computer, including every Mac on the market, has either a CD-ROM or DVD-ROM drive. Each of these computers can read a CD-ROM, even one that is custom-made using a CD-R or CD-RW drive. This means that once the disk is created, you don't need any special hardware to read it. This is great if you expect to be sharing files, since the other person or computer won't need to have the same type of removable-media drive.

Tape Drives

Tape drives are good for one thing—backing up data. In this area they outclass many removable drives simply because they offer a much higher megabyte-per-dollar ratio than any removable-media solution. However, you won't use tape drives to supplement a hard drive, and you won't use them to share files with someone in the next office. You'll use them for backups, if you use them at all.

While tape drives are wonderful for backups, most home users and many small offices won't bother using them. Not only do you need a specific drive for backing up files, you'll also need software that supports the tape drive, not to mention the tapes themselves. While this is fine for corporate environments where lots of files are being backed up, most people probably won't use the tape drive to its full potential to gain any cost advantage—particularly when a removable-media drive can also provide the advantages of sharing file collections, archiving older data, being readily available without cluttering their hard drives, and offering a way to back up their Macs.

Troubleshooting Removable-Media Drives

Following are a few common problems with removable-media drives, along with possible solutions.

The Disk Unreadable by This Macintosh Dialog Box Appears

This message indicates that the Mac is unable to read or understand the format used by the floppy (or other type of disk) in question. If the disk is a PC-formatted disk, make sure the File Exchange or PC Exchange control panel is installed in the Control Panels folder and that you haven't started with extensions off.

The disk itself may have degraded over time or been damaged by exposure to a magnetic field that has rendered it unusable. Depending on the severity of the problem, some disk utilities described in Chapter 5 might be able to retrieve some of the data, but this is not particularly likely.

If the disk has never been used, it may simply need to be formatted, and this dialog allows you to format it.

The Drive Refuses to Eject a Disk

As a rule, to eject a disk, you use Finder commands or drag the disk's icon to the Trash. However, some drives may require that you manually eject the disk once you have performed these actions. If so, this should be described in the drive's manual.

If the drive is designed to auto-eject the disk or cartridge and it doesn't, there may be problems with the drive. However, like traditional Mac floppy drives, almost all of today's drives include an emergency eject hole that can be triggered with a straightened-out paperclip. This can also be a solution if the Mac freezes or crashes and you need to eject a disk. It should not be done, however, while the Mac is running normally and the disk's icon is displayed on the desktop.

If the Mac displays a dialog saying the disk cannot be ejected because it contains items that are in use, you probably have a file on the disk open in some application or you haven't quit an application on the disk.

The Mac Ejects a Disk and Then Constantly Asks for It to Be Inserted

In this situation, some application of Mac OS element is looking for something on the disk, possible a recently accessed file or the desktop file. Try reinserting and ejecting the disk again. If this doesn't solve the problem, try quitting all open applications while the disk is inserted and then ejecting it. If this still doesn't work, restart the Mac and eject the floppy before or during the startup sequence.

The Mac Doesn't Recognize the Drive

If the Mac displays a dialog box saying that the drivers for a USB or FireWire device are unknown, this indicates that the drivers needed for that device to function are not installed. Without the drivers the Mac can't access the drive. Similarly, SCSI and IDE drives won't be recognized without drivers, although there will be no convenient dialog to inform you of this.

If no dialog appears and the Mac simply doesn't acknowledge the drive when you insert a disk, the drive may not be connected and powered properly. Check to be sure that the drive is connected and cabled properly according to whatever interface method it uses.

Resources for Further Study

The following URLs provide additional information on some of the concepts, issues, and products discussed in this chapter.

Iomega—http://www.iomega.com

Imation—http://www.imation.com

SuperDisk HomePage—http://www.superdisk.com

Castlewood Systems—http://www.castlewood.com

VST: Makers of Expansion Bay and FireWire Drives—http://www.vst-tech.com

Proline: Makers of IDE Drive Faceplates and Bezels—http://www.pro-line.com

About.com Mac Hardware Removable-Media Drive Resources—http://machardware.about.com/msubdrives.htm

Tape Drives

Tape drives are special drives that use magnetic tape to store data. Because data stored on a tape cannot be as easily accessed as data on a disk, tape drives are not optimal for daily use. However, they are excellent as a backup solution for a number of reasons. First, tape is very cheap and it can store a lot of data. It is feasible to have a separate tape for every day of the week, plus complete, redundant backups for each month. Second, automating tape backups is extremely simple. Since the entire contents of your hard drive can fit into a single tape, no work is required from the user to estimate the size of files to be backed up or to change media in the middle of the backup. Third, tape drives are very fast, allowing data to be written and retrieved at up to 6 MB/second (although they are not so fast when you need to access a specific segment of data on the tape).

How Tape Drives Work

All computer tape drives use magnetic tape that is very similar to the tape in an audio cassette player or a VCR. This tape is a plastic film that is coated with metal particles that can be magnetized. The tape moves from one spool to another across magnetic read/write heads, and the data is recorded in a linear stream along the tape (sequential access). This means that in order to retrieve a specific piece of data from a tape, the drive must first wind the tape until the region where that data is stored is underneath the heads. This is in contrast to the nearly instantaneous random access to data provided by disk technology such as hard drives, CDs, Zip disks, floppy disks, and so on.

One result of this linear data format is that tapes cannot be mounted on the Macintosh desktop as a volume. Instead, special backup software must be used to write and retrieve data from tape. The backup program Retrospect by Dantz Development Corporation is by far the most popular backup software for the Macintosh. However, this backup software reveals both the primary strength and the primary weakness of tape as a backup solution. The benefit of Retrospect is that it provides a completely automated, hands-off backup solution. The downside is that your data is essentially invisible; it is locked inside tapes until you need to retrieve something—at which point you will find out if those backups really worked properly. Therefore, I highly recommend that you test your backups periodically by retrieving the occasional document.

Unlike audio cassette tapes and VCR tapes, which store analog data, computer tapes store information in a digital format. As with digital video tapes, as discussed in other chapters, there is no loss of signal quality with repeated copying and erasing and minimal degradation with age (digital tapes have an estimated life span of 30 years).

Most tape drives use a single-speed motor to move the tape from one reel to the other, which means that data must be written to the tape at a constant speed. However, computer hard drives do not retrieve data at a constant speed because of variable file sizes, data fragmentation, and other tasks interfering with the flow of data through the system bus. Therefore, all tape drives must include a cache of RAM to serve as a buffer, smoothing out the flow of data from the computer to the writing heads, the same as a recordable CD drive. In general, the larger the buffer the better. A recent innovation in tape drive design has been the development of variable-speed motors that allow the tape to slow down when data is not being delivered fast enough from the computer and to speed up when data arrives faster.

Most tape drive systems make use of some form of data compression algorithm to allow more data to be stored on each tape. The data compression can either be done by the backup software or the compression algorithms can be built directly into the tape drive's hardware. Hardware compression is generally considered superior, since it does not tax the computer's processor and often permits higher data transfer rates. Most tape drive vendors advertise that compression allows the amount of data that can be stored on each tape to be doubled. This is an unrealistic estimate. In fact, different types of data can be compressed to different degrees. Ordinary text files from word-processing software can compress more than 50 percent, but drive-hogging applications (such as Adobe and Microsoft products) generally compress 25 percent or less. Many large files such as QuickTime videos and audio MP3 files are already compressed and are not reduced in size at all by the compression algorithms used by tape backup systems. Keep this in mind when looking at the specifications of tape drives.

Tape Formats

There are many different incompatible standards for computer tape drives. These different formats use different styles of tapes and cartridges and provide various storage capacities and data-writing speeds. All of these various tape formats are very stable, making it unlikely that your backups will be corrupted or erased by the passage of time or by strong magnetic fields. This is an advantage that all tape formats have over other magnetic removable-media, such as Zip, SuperDisk, or Jaz drives (recordable CD/DVD drives or magneto-optical drives do offer superior data security, however).

The most important parameter that will determine your choice of tape drive technology is the amount of data that you plan to back up. If your computer hard drive is only 4 GB, then it is not necessary to buy a drive that uses 50-GB tapes. On the other hand, if you have huge amounts of digital data being generated each day, then the fastest, largest-capacity tape drives are essential.

Another important consideration is that each of these different tape drive formats is patented and controlled by a single company or a small group of companies. If you buy a drive that is made by only one manufacturer and that company discontinues the product or goes out of business, then you may find yourself in trouble should you need to access your backups. If your drive should fail, then how will you read all of those tapes created in a now obsolete format? It is generally a wise idea to stick with industry-standard formats that are supported by many manufacturers and to buy tape drives (and other computer devices) from companies with a history of good customer support.

Travan (QIC)

Travan tape (also known as QIC) is at the low end of the price/performance curve. The Quarter-Inch-tape Cartridge (QIC) was first developed in 1972 by the 3M company. QIC tape uses a linear read/write head similar to those found in audio cassette recorders. The head contains a single write head flanked on either side by a read head, which allows the drive to verify data immediately after it is written. Data is written onto the tape in parallel tracks that run along the length of the tape. The tape moves past the read/write heads at 100 to 125 inches per second. Once the end of the tape is reached, the tape reverses direction and the head goes to the next track. Some error-correction data is included in the data blocks and a directory of files is written onto a special track on the tape. It is possible to include multiple read/write heads which write to parallel tracks as the tape moves, thus increasing the data throughput rate.

There have been a bewildering number of different QIC/Travan standards since 1972, involving different widths and lengths of tape, different numbers of tracks on the tape, as well as different storage capacities and read/write speeds. The most recent generation of Travan products uses a standard called NS20 (also known as TR-5 and QIC-3220) which

Figure 19-1
Travan NS-20
cartridge. Photo
courtesy of Imation.

has a 10 GB-native (20 GB compressed) capacity and writes data at 1 to 2 MB/second (see Figure 19-1). The TR-5 tape is 0.315 inches wide, and it contains 108 parallel tracks. TR-5 tapes cost about $37 per 10 GB tape.

ADR

OnStream, Inc., a spinoff of the Philips Corporation, has developed a new tape drive technology called ADR (Advanced Digital Recording). ADR tape drives use a set of eight read/write heads that write simultaneously in parallel tracks that run the entire length of the tape. The drive writes data at up to 2 MB/second. ADR drives also incorporate a true continuously variable-speed motor that allows the drive to write data at any speed from 0.5 to 2 MB/second. This greatly reduces the need for data buffering within the drive and also prevents stop-and-start operation that is common for other tape drives when data flow from the computer drops below the drive's write speed.

Figure 19-2 shows an OnStream USB drive, along with a 30-GB ADR disk.

DAT

DAT (digital audio tape) was originally developed for the professional audio recording industry as a method for storing CD-quality digital recordings on high-capacity, inexpensive 4mm tape. In 1998, Sony and Hewlett-Packard created the DDS (Digital Data Storage) standard for storing computer data on 4mm DAT tape. There have been several versions of the DDS standard since then, up to the current DDS-4 format (see Table 19-1), but fortunately, current drives are backward-compatible with all previous DDS formats. Figure 19-3 shows a DAT drive and a DDS-3 tape.

Figure 19-2
OnStream USB drive and 30-GB ADR media. Photo courtesy of OnStream.

TABLE 19-1

DDS Standards.

Standard	Capacity	Max. Write Speed
DDS	2 GB	55 KB/sec
DDS-1	2 GB	0.55 KB/sec
DDS-2	4 GB	0.55 KB/sec
DDS-3	12 GB	1.1 MB/sec
DDS-4	20 GB	2.4 MB/sec

Figure 19-3
DAT tape drive and
DDS-3 tape. Photo
courtesy of Sony.

DAT drives use a "helical scan" method of recording data onto the tape, which is quite different than the linear method used by QIC drives. Data is written in parallel diagonal lines across the tape by a set of two read heads and two write heads (the data is read as soon as it is written in order to verify it). Each diagonal track is approximately 32 mm long and contains 128 KB of data. The two write heads actually write using different magnetic polarities at different angles in tracks that overlap. This helical scan method is inherently slow, and it subjects the tape to substantial physical wear, but it has the advantage of packing data onto the tape at very high density.

DAT drives are about twice as expensive as Travan drives, but the tapes have much larger capacity. DDS-2 media costs about $9 per tape (4 GB), while DDS-4 media costs about $40 per tape (20 GB), giving a cost of data storage of only $2 per GB. Compare that to Zip disks at about $150 per GB.

8mm (AIT and Mammoth)

The 8mm tape technology was originally designed for the video industry. Many high-quality analog consumer video recorders (camcorders) use 8mm tape, but these are rapidly being replaced by digital video offerings.

Eight millimeter tape drives use a helical scan technology that is very similar to DAT drives. However, there are two incompatible 8mm tape formats. The Exabyte Corporation uses a standard called Mammoth, while Seagate and Sony have a standard called AIT, for Advanced Intelligent Tape. Both of these types of tape drives use a capstan and pinch roller to move the tape across a spinning drum that contains the read/write heads.

Mammoth supports a maximum of 25 GB per tape and write speeds up to 6 MB/second. AIT supports up to 50 GB of data per tape and write speeds of up to 12 MB/second. AIT drives cost from $1500 for 20-GB/1.5 MB/sec to over $4000 for 50-GB/6 MB/second. AIT media costs about $80 per 25-GB AIT tape or $120 per 50-GB AIT-II tape.

DLT

DLT was originally developed by the Digital Equipment Corporation (DEC) in the late 1980s, but it was licensed for broader applications by Quantum Corporation (a popular manufacturer of hard drives) in 1994. DLT is the most popular technology for data storage for high-performance computers. According to a Quantum press release: "With more than 1.4 million DLTtape drives and more than 40 million DLTtape media cartridges shipped to date, DLTtape technology is the de facto standard for backing up and archiving business-critical data for mid-range servers and high-end workstations. DLTtape is used on approximately 90 percent of the mid-range servers." While somewhat self-aggrandizing, this seems to state the case accurately—the majority of companies who utterly depend on tape backups use DLT. DLT drives are frequently incorporated into large "jukeboxes" for ultra-high-capacity data storage and automated rotation of tapes.

DLTtape is ½ inch wide, which is 60 percent wider than 8mm tape. DLT drives record data in pairs of parallel tracks that extend the entire length of the tape. When data is recorded, the first set of tracks is recorded on the whole length of the tape. When the end of the tape is reached, the heads are repositioned to record a new set of tracks, and the tape is again recorded on its whole length, this time in the opposite direction. The process continues, back and forth, until the tape is full.

DLT drives use technology similar to an old reel-to-reel tape recorder for pulling and guiding the tape past the read/write heads which minimizes friction and wear on the tape. Because of decreased wear on the tape and heads, DLTtapes can be rewritten up to 1 million times and the drive heads are rated to last far longer than those of 8mm helical scan devices. DLT drives currently support up to 40 GB per tape and data write speeds up to 6 MB/second.

TABLE 19-2

Tape Formats
Compared.

	Travan (QIC)	ADR	DAT	8mm (AIT)	DLT
Capacity	10 GB	15 GB	20 GB	50 GB	40
Speed (MB/sec)	0.8-1.5	2	2.4	6	6
Drive cost	$500	$700	$1150	$3800	$4400
Tape cost (per GB)	$4.50	$3	$2	$2.40	$2.25

Table 19-2 shows how the formats we've discussed compare on several key factors.

Drive Interfaces

Tape drives are predominantly available in SCSI models. This offers excellent performance, but it limits the number of current Macs with which they can be used. FireWire and USB models for the Mac are in development by a number of companies at the time of this writing (with expectations of release ranging from the fall to the end of 2000). Internal IDE models are also available, though these can only be used with the Power Mac computers.

Care and Maintenance of Tape Drives and Magnetic Tape

Tape drives are more prone to mechanical failure than most other computer components, since they have many moving parts that are subject to considerable wear during normal operation. In particular, the read/write heads come into physical contact with the tape as it streams along at many inches per second. Head-cleaning media is available for all types of tape drives. In many cases, the backup software recommends when it is time to use the head-cleaning tape, however you should be sure to adhere closely to the manufacturer's recommendations for head cleaning and not rely on the software to inform you when to clean the drive's heads. In general, it is wise to obtain the longest-possible manufacturer's warranty on a tape drive.

The tapes themselves are quite sturdy, but the normal precautions that apply to any magnetic medium should be taken. Keep them away from magnets, strong electrical or magnetic fields, dust, and extreme heat. Many people store backup tapes in a fire safe, since those tapes contain the crucial data that will allow them to reconstruct computer systems in the event of some catastrophe. It is also a good idea to keep some backup tapes in another physical location from the computer. See Chapter 39 for more information on developing a backup strategy and storing your backups.

Backup Software

As mentioned earlier, tape drives are sequential-access devices, the tapes themselves are not mounted on the Macintosh desktop. As a result, you must use specialized backup software to interact with the tape drive. For the Macintosh, the vast majority of tape drive owners use the Retrospect program from Dantz Development Corporation. Figure 19-4 shows Retrospect's main menu. In fact, virtually all tape drives come with a bundled OEM (original equipment manufacturer) version of Retrospect.

The first thing to keep in mind when using Retrospect is that your data is being written onto tapes, but the catalogs of what files are on each tape are kept on your hard drive. While it is possible to extract data

Figure 19-4
Retrospect startup menu, showing the four main buttons.

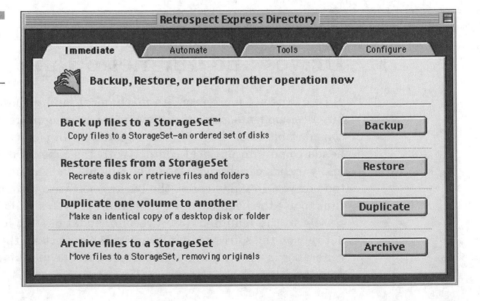

from a tape without these catalogs (as in the case of a complete hard drive crash), it is important to keep these catalog files in a safe location. Without them, it can be very difficult to determine what version of a specific file was written to tape on what day.

The next consideration is that Retrospect can make two different kinds of backups: complete and incremental. A *complete* backup is simply a snapshot of the contents of your hard drive (or some selected subset of its folders) at a specific point in time. If you make a complete backup every night, then you will be copying over and over again many files such as the Mac's System Folder and your application programs that do not change at all from day to day. This is a waste of tape, but it would be a good idea to make a complete backup at least once in a while as an archive of your system, and to make new complete backups when you install a new version of the Mac OS or finish a huge project.

An *incremental* backup (called a "normal" backup in Retrospect), copies your entire hard drive the first time a backup is made, and then in all subsequent backups, it only copies new files and files that have been changed. This means that a single backup tape that is only slightly larger than your hard drive can be used to make nightly backups for weeks (or even months if you don't create lots of new files). There is also the significant advantage that files that have changed from day to day are copied to new sections of the tape, so that you can recover the file as it was saved on any particular day. If you made backups by just repeatedly copying a folder of documents to a Zip disk or other media, then old versions of files will be overwritten and lost. Once a tape is filled, you can choose to just continue adding incremental data to a new tape, or you can start fresh with a complete backup followed by incremental additions. See Chapter 39 for more information on developing and implementing a backup strategy.

Resources for Further Study

The following URLs provide additional information on some of the concepts, issues, and products discussed in this chapter.

Quantum Corporation DLT technology site—http://DLTtape.com

The PC Technology Guide: Tape Backup—
http://www.pctechguide.com/15tape.htm

*Retrospect Software from Dantz Development Co. (includes
a downloadable free trial version)*—http://www.dantz.com/

Life without Floppies?

For over two decades, the floppy drive was a standard computer component, either in the original 5.25-inch variety or the 3.5-inch variety that became a standard in the mid-1980s. The floppy drive was a component that existed on virtually any type of personal computer ever made and was used for backup purposes, transferring data between two computers, software installations, and as a convenient way to carry files between various locations.

Apple made news in 1998 when it announced that the iMac would be the first desktop Mac to ever ship without a built-in floppy drive and the first Mac (portable or desktop) to ship without an Apple-designed option for adding a floppy drive to the computer. This decision continues to be a point often used by critics of the Mac platform. Like the iMac, subsequent Mac models have also shipped without floppy drives.

Just how important the floppy drive actually was in 1998 when Apple decided to discontinue it as a standard feature on the Mac or how important it is today is a matter of debate and personal opinion. Both sides of the issue will be looked at in this chapter.

Whether you feel the floppy is an outdated piece of equipment or you feel that the floppy is still an important tool for many computer users, no one can question that the floppy drive enjoyed a standard function and use that few other pieces of computer hardware ever have. Indeed, many long-time computer users agree that there will probably never again be a single type of drive for sharing and backing up files that has the staying and standardization power of the floppy. Thus, the floppy is an important part of computer history and still a technology that is used in some situations today.

How Floppy Drives Work

In earlier chapters, the concepts involved in storing data on magnetic mediums such as a hard drive were discussed. Floppy drives work in much the same way; however, rather than placing the actual magnetic material on a hard platter as a hard drive does, the floppy drive uses a flexible mylar-based disk (hence, the term *floppy disk*). This disk is then surrounded by a hard plastic case that protects the disk itself, as well as the data stored on it, from damage.

The plastic case of a floppy disk has a movable panel in it that is retracted, or slid over to one side, by the drive when the disk is inserted. This panel, which covers both the upper and lower faces of the disk, allows the drive to actually access the magnetic-coated mylar disk inside the casing. This panel is made of either plastic or metal and is at the edge of the disk that is inserted into the drive first. You can actually push the panel aside yourself and see the disk, though this exposes the disk to potential damage.

The casing of the disk also has a special tab or notch at one of the corners opposite the retracting panel. This notch allows the disk to be locked so that data can be read from the floppy but not written to it. This notch allows you to secure a floppy against accidentally deleting or replacing files on it. The notch often has a movable plastic piece inside it that lets you easily switch between locked and unlocked. Figure 20-1 shows a typical floppy disk, where you can see each of these features.

The read and write heads of the floppy drive work along the same principles as those of a hard drive, except that they are not a physical part of the disk as is the case in a hard drive (see Figure 20-2 for an illustration of how the floppy drive's read/write heads function). Floppy drive heads access both the upper and lower surfaces of the disk, giving the drive the ability to record data on both faces; such disks are said to be *double-sided*. In the very early Macs (the original Mac 128K and the Mac 512K), only a single side of the floppy could be used to store data. Such

Figure 20-1
An average floppy disk.

Figure 20-2
The heads of the
floppy drive do not
come into contact
with either the disk
casing or the mag-
netic disk itself.

Floppy Casing
Magnetic Disk

Read/Write Heads

drives and formats are extremely rare today, and unless you are dealing
with very old Macs, you're unlikely to need to worry about this.

Because the drive heads are not part of the floppy disk and are used to
read floppy after floppy over their life span, over time they can develop a
coating of debris (dust particles, skin oils, and such) that will prevent them
from properly reading or writing a floppy disk. This is similar to what can
happen to the recording heads of a VCR or an audio cassette player. The
solution is much the same: Use a specially designed floppy disk to clean
the heads. In addition, you can use a floppy-cleaning software utility, such
as MicroMat's TechTool to ensure that the entire head is cleaned thoroughly. Alternatively, you can use a can of compressed air to spray debris
from the entire floppy drive. Compressed air will often remove debris that
has built up inside the drive that is not specifically on the drive heads.

Obviously, the limit of only two surfaces on which to store data makes
a floppy more limited than a hard drive. However, data is stored the
same way in terms of tracks and sectors of the disk. How a floppy disk is
formatted will determine the number of individual sectors on the disk
and thus the amount of data the disk can store. Early Macintosh floppy
drives used a format that only supported 800 KB of diskspace. Although
beginning in 1988, Macs used floppy drives capable of a higher-density
format that allowed users to format the disk at 1.44 MB of space known
as high-density disks, they were backward-compatible with the earlier
drive standard. It is important to note that the current floppy drive
options for the Mac very rarely support that earlier standard and will
read/write only 1.44-MB formats.

Floppy Formats

Chapter 5 described the two primary file systems used for Mac drives
(Mac OS Standard or HFS and Mac OS Extended or HFS+). Floppies
only support the Mac OS Standard format (they also support the MS-

DOS file format used by Windows-based computers). The obvious reason is that because a floppy has so little data capacity, there is no practical gain from or reason to attempt to make use of the Mac OS Extended format. Mac floppy drives also support the use of the FAT (file allocation table) file system used to format floppies for use under DOS and Windows, as well as the ProDOS format, which was used to format floppy disks on Apple II computers. This ability is imparted by the File Exchange control panel (Mac OS 8.5 or later) or by the PC Exchange control panel (Mac OS 8.1 or earlier). If these control panels are not present, alternate platform floppy disks will not be recognized.

In order to format a floppy under the Mac OS, you first insert the floppy. If it is not formatted or uses a format not recognized by the Mac, you will be told the disk is unreadable and are asked to initialize (format) it. If the disk is readable, the Mac will display its icon on the desktop. To reformat the disk, select the Erase Disk command from the Finder's Special menu. Then the Erase Disk dialog (shown in Figure 20-3) appears, and you will be asked to name the disk and choose a file format to use. The Mac can format and read/write to floppies in both the traditional Macintosh format, as well as the format used for Windows- and DOS-based computers.

Floppy Care and Concerns

The floppy disk does not have as high a degree of stability as does a hard drive or some removable media. The magnetic components of the floppy are more easily affected by outside influences and by the passage of time. This makes floppy disks far more susceptible to damage from magnets and electromagnetic fields.

Figure 20-3
The Finder's Erase Disk command allows you to reformat floppies for use on both Mac and PC computer platforms.

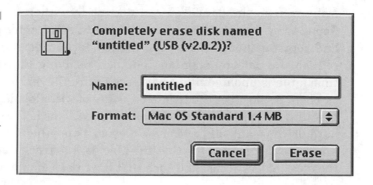

A floppy disk can be affected by refrigerator magnets, the magnetic heads of a VCR, the electromagnetic field of stereo speakers, unshielded monitors and televisions, motors of various kinds, and even telephone ringers, as well as many other things. Any of these can cause the magnetically arranged particles of the floppy disk to be pulled out of their arrangement and thus damage the data that is stored on the disk. It is a good practice to store floppy disks away from any electrical or mechanical devices because most put out some degree of electromagnetic field. Likewise, it is good to store floppies in a nonconductive container, such as the plastic floppy storage cases commonly found in office supply stores.

Floppy disks are also very susceptible to damage just by the passing of time. Once data is written to a floppy, it begins to degrade as the magnetic particles slowly lose the coerciveness that allows them to retain that data. This occurs with all magnetic media (even videotapes, which is why you'll notice images are a little grainy or fuzzy on something you taped 10 years ago). This degradation affects floppies more than it does other magnetic media simply because the floppy's magnetic layer is not as coercive as that of a hard drive or other removable media. Although it usually takes at least a couple of years for this effect to cause problems, it can be exacerbated by the presence of strong magnetic fields. Likewise, the older a floppy is, the more susceptible it is to damage by magnetic fields.

Floppies are also physically very fragile. The plastic casing is not particularly hard or durable, and the mylar disk inside is extremely flimsy. You should always take care when dealing with and storing floppies to avoid physically damaging the disk. Never write on the disk itself or its label with a ballpoint pen.

This physical fragility, coupled with lack of data stability, makes floppies a poor choice for storing important data. However, if you intend to store data for long periods of time on a floppy, it is a good idea to periodically refresh the data. You can do this by either copying it to another floppy or by copying the contents to a hard drive, reformatting the floppy, and copying them back to the freshly formatted floppy. You can even refresh the data by opening and then resaving the specific files. Each time a file is updated and saved, the entire file on the disk is refreshed.

There is one other concern to be aware of with floppies, particularly floppies that are regularly copied to or updated. This is the desktop file. Like a hard drive or any other Mac disk, every floppy has an invisible database known as the *desktop file* that the Mac uses to track information about all the files, folders, icons, and such that have been stored on that floppy. Over time, as more files are updated or added or deleted or otherwise accessed and adjusted, the desktop file grows. While this generally isn't a problem from a perspective of the desktop file's size on a hard drive (which has a much greater storage capacity than a floppy), it is a concern in the limited 1.44 MB of a floppy. The desktop file on a floppy can get as big as 200 KB or larger. To alleviate this, you can rebuild the desktop file of a floppy just as you can a hard drive. Simply hold the Command and Option keys down when you insert the floppy, and the Mac will ask if you want to rebuild its desktop file (the same as with a hard drive). You can also simply copy the data off the floppy, reformat it, and copy the data back.

You can see how bloated a floppy's desktop file has become by selecting the floppy's icon and choosing the Finder's Get Info command from the File menu. As shown in Figure 20-4, this will display both the floppy's total capacity, the amount of space used, and the amount available. If the space used and the space available don't add up to something pretty close to the total capacity, the desktop file is probably taking up most of that missing space. Some bad sectors of the disk that have been

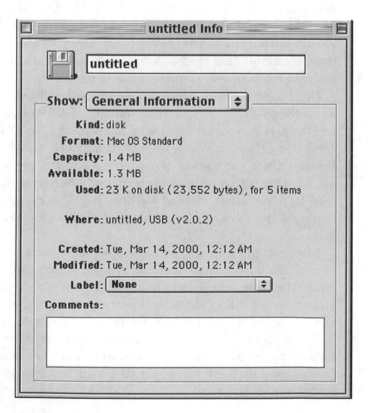

Figure 20-4
The Get Info command displays how much of a floppy is available to store data, as well as how much is being used for files.

mapped out when the disk is formatted can also account for missing space on a floppy.

Is the Floppy Drive Still an Important Peripheral?

The floppy drive was a standard fixture across computer platforms for quite some time. Although the heyday of the floppy seems to be over, many people still feel that the floppy drive is an important peripheral. On the other hand, a large (and growing) percentage of Mac users are acknowledging that they don't really need a floppy drive. In order to accurately assess the value of a floppy drive (or any other peripheral), you need to look at two factors: how frequently the drive is used and what it is used for.

The first question is something that varies depending on the individual. Personally, I can remember the last Mac I owned that came with floppy drive. It was a PowerBook 1400 with removable drive bay modules for the CD-ROM and floppy drives. In the nearly two years that I owned that PowerBook, I can only remember inserting the floppy module a few times, certainly less than a dozen. Obviously, I was not even then someone who had a massive need for the floppy drive.

On the other hand, I have spoken to several people who do routinely use a floppy drive. The most prominent of these tend to be people who use floppies as a convenient way to transport small files between their computer (Mac- or Windows-based) at work and their Mac at home. Because these computers are separate and the people in question may not have access to either the Internet or other removable media at work, they lack any other method for bringing files home to work on. So, for them a floppy drive is something that gets used frequently and regularly.

Interestingly enough, some people seem to feel a sort of nostalgia toward the floppy drive, wanting it even if they don't use it that much. When the iMac was first announced, I remember polling Mac users for an article regarding the announcement of a Mac with no floppy drive. One of the questions I found myself asking people was "When was the last time you used your floppy drive?" The results were rather inconsistent in that most of the people who went weeks or months without using their floppy drive were people who still felt it was a needed piece of equipment on the Mac.

Uses for the Floppy Drive

The other question, which could be viewed as more important than how often the drive is used, is what that drive is used for. Even a rarely used but important piece of hardware can be considered a need for a computer user. For example, many users who own Macs solely for Internet access use their printer as infrequently as most people use a floppy drive. That doesn't mean the printer isn't important to these users if they want to print out an e-mail or have occasion to type a letter or résumé on their computer.

The primary uses for the floppy drive have historically been as follows: backing up files, transferring files between computers or users, installing software, and serving as an emergency startup or utility disk. Let's look at each of these uses separately and consider both the advantages of the floppy and the disadvantages of it for each one of these uses. Keep in mind, however, that there is no real right or wrong answer to whether a given person needs a floppy drive. It can be a matter of personal preference, business contacts, and existing file storage or hardware.

Backing Up Files   For many years, a primary function of the floppy was for backup. The drive came free with the computer, the disks weren't all that expensive, and it was a low-cost, no-additional-hardware way to back up everything on the computer. Whether you performed the backups of files by hand, copying each file to a floppy or with an automated utility that simply asked you to insert disks while it copied everything onto the floppies, the process was pretty simple.

The simple fact that the drive and methods for performing a backup came with the computer meant many consumers simply used the floppy drive as a backup method because of convenience. And, it was a convenient solution for many people, for many years. Even today, floppy drives can serve as a low-cost solution for backing up text documents, e-mails, and other small files. Indeed, there are only two real drawbacks to using floppies for backup: size and reliability.

Size is the bigger concern, so let's look at it first. In 1990, Macs typically shipped with hard drives ranging from about 40 MB to 120 MB. The standard floppy disk could store 1.44 MB of data. This meant you could back up your entire hard drive's contents on anywhere from 30 to 100 floppies. You'd want to be careful to number or label them properly, but that wasn't too big a problem and you could still get that number of disks fairly cheap (especially compared to the pricey removable-media drives of the day).

Today, Macs are shipping standard hard drives of 10 GB or bigger. I shudder to even think how many floppies it would take to back up an iMac DV's hard drive—much less any larger drives. Floppies simply aren't feasible for full backups of a hard drive at this point. Even if they were, the effort and cost probably wouldn't be worth doing so because of removable-media disks and CD-R disks costing so little these days. There just wouldn't be the cost advantage to using them for large amounts of data.

Of course, not everyone would want floppies to serve as whole backup solutions. That raises the point that it isn't just hard drives that are growing in size. Many applications and commonly used document types are also larger. Most applications, not counting their support files, are well over 1.44 MB today. And common file types such as QuickTime, audio, and even many graphics files easily go over the 1.44-MB limit of a floppy or can take up most of the space on a floppy with a single file.

Word-processing and text documents, along with smaller image files, are about what you might conceivably use a floppy to hold these days. And even then, backing up anything more than a handful of files becomes unwieldy with floppies, particularly compared to other backup mediums. For quick backups of small files, however, a floppy drive might still be an acceptable alternative, particularly if you want to back something up but don't have a Zip, Jaz, Orb, or CD-R disk available.

Beyond the concern of available space when using floppies as a backup, there is the concern of their reliability. When choosing a backup medium, you need to think about how long the backups will last. Floppies are probably the least reliable method of storing files and the most susceptible to damage from magnetic or electrical fields. While all magnetic mediums (including hard drives, Zip, and Jaz disks, and even digital tape) are potentially at risk from damage by such electromagnetic fields and the passing of time, most have a higher degree of magnetic coerciveness and are more well shielded or secure than the average floppy disk. Given the importance of reliability to a backup, floppies are not only the smallest but also the weakest method of backups on the market today.

Transferring Files between Computers   One of the most common uses of floppies has been sharing files between users and computers. In this, the fact that the floppy was such a standard worked well for it. Since virtually every computer had a floppy drive, saving files to a floppy ensured that those files could be accessed from a different computer.

There were cross-platform issues, such as a Windows- or DOS-based PC being able to recognize a Mac-formatted floppy or vice versa. However, when Apple introduced the ability of the Mac to read, write, and format disks that were used for either platform as part of the standard Mac OS in System 7.5, this became a very small concern. The same approach allowed Macs to share files with Apple II computers as well.

Today the use of sharing files between computers by floppy is still a viable option. It is still an option for PCs as well as earlier Macs (and Apple II computers, though these are extremely rare to see in use anymore). The issue of size is still a concern, though. As with backing up files, many files will either take up the majority of space on a floppy or simply not fit on a floppy. Also, most users today have access to a network in a corporate or school environment or to the Internet, both of which can make file sharing more efficient by not requiring a floppy be used as an intermediate step in transferring data. This does not, however, negate the fact that floppies can be an excellent and portable way to share word-processing and text documents (or other small files or applications) with other users of any platform. In fact, in some situations where privacy is an issue, the floppy might be a preferred option over using the Internet or a network.

Installing Software Before CD-ROM drives became ubiquitous components of a computer, software was routinely distributed on floppies. This was because the floppy drive was the only standardized drive that developers could use for getting data onto the computers of their customers. The transition from floppy to CD-ROM for software distribution had much to do with the fact that the software products were getting too big to fit on individual floppies. Many installers began to consist of multiple floppies, sometimes ranging to over a dozen. Not only was this confusing when an installer needed to request disks (sometimes out of their numerical sequence), but it was slow. CD-ROM drives, even at their slowest, were an inherently faster drive type than floppies.

Although for many years, developers sold software in both floppy and CD-ROM distributions to allow for compatibility with earlier customers, that period served mainly as a transition to today's time of CD-ROM-based distributions. Virtually every computer for at least five years has come with a CD-ROM or DVD-ROM drive as standard equipment. The only Mac not to do so in this period was the subnotebook PowerBook 2400. Because of this, there was no real reason for developers to continue with the expense and effort of developing installations for both floppies and CD-ROMs, after a certain point. Even Apple stopped developing floppy-based versions of the Mac OS in 1997 with Mac OS 8 (which would have required somewhere around 100 individual floppies).

Although floppy-based installers are not available today, there are probably a good many Mac users with copies of floppy-based software installers. If the software was never updated to a CD-ROM installation and is no longer available, floppy installation on future computers may be required (although alternatives discussed later in this chapter will likely suffice for continued use of such software).

Emergency Startup or Utility Floppies   One of the nice features of the floppy was the ability to have a drive you could start up from in an emergency, such as hard drive damage or corruption of the drive's directory structures or the System file. Every version of the Mac OS released on floppies contained a Disk Tools disk, which you could start up from. The Disk Tools disk included copies of Disk First Aid and Drive Setup (or Apple's now-retired Apple HD SC Setup disk-formatting utility) for checking, repairing, and if needed, reformatting your Mac's hard drive. The first floppy of the Installer could also be started up from, although it didn't contain any version of the Finder and launched directly into the Installer application.

Today, the Mac OS is far too large to fit on a single floppy, making emergency floppies impractical. Mac OS and System Restore CDs themselves are bootable disks that you can start up from in an emergency. The CDs contain all the required utilities to check and repair hard drives that the old Disk Tools disks had. Several companies making disk formatting and repair utilities also distribute their software on bootable CDs in case of emergency. The only real need for anything besides such a CD is in the case that you have a non-Apple CD-ROM or DVD-ROM drive that the Mac cannot boot from. This concern should apply mainly to Power Mac owners who have replaced their internal CD/DVD drive with a third-party vendor's drive.

Today's Mac OS CDs allow you to start up the computer, but limit you to a specific set of tools. Since they may not contain the driver software for things like Jaz drives, USB floppy drives, or other external drives, you can find yourself without the ability to access the tools you prefer or need to work with, such as a specific hard drive utility or formatter. Even bootable CDs from utility manufacturers only come with that manufacturer's tools on them. Since you can't eject the active startup disk (such as a CD-ROM), you may find yourself cut off from your preferred tools.

The easiest solutions to this is to create your own emergency startup CD with a CD-R or CD-RW drive (see Chapter 16) or to have a backup hard drive in place that you can either replace the existing hard drive with or install alongside it. Keep in mind the USB and FireWire drives may require drivers on the active startup disk in order to be used. Fortunately, today several USB hard drives and some USB removable-media drives are bootable (though not all Macs can boot from USB devices), meaning you could start up from an external USB drive in an emergency and not worry about access to your favorite emergency tools. This is something to be aware of when choosing a USB drive and is discussed along with other USB information in Chapter 15.

Floppy Drive Alternatives

Although no drive has been developed since the floppy that offers the same industrywide standard for use on every computer yet is easy and convenient to use, there are several other options out there that can fulfill each of the four uses of the floppy drive that were discussed in the previous section. In particular, there are four areas to look at for floppy drive replacements. These include recordable CD or DVD technology, removable-media drives, network or Internet storage, and floppy disk images.

CD and DVD Technology

While no convenient, easy-to-use drive for writing data to a disk has come along that matches the floppy as a standard fixture on every computer, that isn't true for drives that only read data from a disk. The CD-ROM drive has been a fixture on computers for several years now, and no recent Macintosh computer has shipped without a CD-ROM or DVD-ROM drive. The difference is that neither CD-ROM nor DVD-ROM drives allow you to store data. The various recordable drives of both CD and DVD technology do allow you to create your own CD or DVD disks, but recordable drives are not standard on the Mac and therefore involve an extra cost to purchase and use.

Another big difference between recordable CD-ROMs is that you will need a special utility, such as Adaptec's Toast, to create a CD-ROM. This is not as simple or straightforward as a floppy, where you can simply drag onto the floppy's icon to copy them. For more information on this process, see Chapter 16.

On the other hand, CD-ROMs burned with an appropriate utility will be completely standard disks recognized by any computer that uses the file system the disk was burned in. Likewise, CD-R and CD-RW disks can be burned so that they are bootable disks that can be used to start up a Mac in an emergency. In this way, CDs can function with all the advantages of the industrywide standard that the floppy drive enjoyed. They are also much more reliable, and CD-ROMs can be expected to survive for decades with their data fully intact.

Removable Media

The floppy drive actually is a removable-media drive, albeit one that enjoyed completely standard use across the computer industry and one that holds very little data by today's standards. The construction and functioning of floppy disks is not all that different from the construction and functioning of Iomega's Zip disks or Imation's SuperDisks (SuperDisks are discussed later in this chapter because of their extreme similarities to floppies). Removable-media drives, as a whole, are for practical purposes very much like large-capacity floppy disks. This is true regardless of whether their construction and physical functioning is similar to or different from floppies.

Like floppies, you use removable-media drives by popping a disk into the drive. When its icon shows up on the desktop, you copy, open, save, move, and delete files from it in the same manner you do your hard drive. You eject the disk either by dragging it to the Trash or by using the Eject Disk or Put Away commands (from the Finder's Special and File menus, respectively).

The big difference is that none of today's removable media have ever become a fully adopted standard drive for the Mac like the floppy drive was. The closest example is the Zip drive, which is a factory-optional feature on the Power Macs (or can be later installed as well) from Apple and which is commonly available as PowerBook expansion bay modules and external USB drives for many Macs. Many companies that accept large files or groups of files from contractors or clients, such as graphics design houses or service bureaus, use and accept Zip disk submissions. Despite the wide use of the Zip drive, however, not every Mac user has a Zip drive and not everyone agrees that the Zip drive is the best removable-media drive out there. It is pretty doubtful that the Zip, or any other removable-media drive, will ever gain enough of a market to be considered a replacement for the floppy.

Removable media also have some other distinctions from floppies. Not all removable-media drives are bootable. Some internal IDE models are, as are some SCSI and USB models, but it is best not to assume without checking first. And it is also a good idea to try starting up from the drive once you've bought it, regardless of what the specs say, to be certain you can boot from it, rather than waiting for a crisis to hit to find out.

Removable-media drives also often require driver software to function, where built-in floppy drive access has always been built into the Mac's ROM. In some cases, such as the Zip and SuperDisk, these drivers are bundled with the Mac OS. In other cases, particularly drives that are newer or not as widely adopted such as the Orb drive, these drivers may not be part of the standard Mac OS. The advantage of the drivers being part of the Mac OS is that they are likely part of the drivers included on a Mac OS CD, meaning you will probably (though not certainly) have access to the drive if you boot from a CD in an emergency. The other concern, regardless of whether the drivers are part of a standard Mac OS release, is that if you start up with extensions off, you will probably not have access to the drive because driver software is almost always written as either an extension or control panel.

Network and Internet

While not a total replacement for floppy drives, local networks and the Internet do facilitate a number of the functions that were historically the domain of floppy disks—sharing files, for example. You can easily attach files to e-mails, put them on an FTP server, or store them on the Internet by some other means. If you use Apple's iDisk technology, you can drop them in your Public folder, and other people can access them (actually anyone will be able to access them).

Sharing files over a local network gives you the ability to share any file or folder on your hard drive with other computers and users on the network. This is often more convenient than copying a file to a floppy, bringing it to the other computer, and copying it to the other computer's hard drive. You can simply access the original file much as you would access the file on the receiving computer's hard drive. You can even open it, make changes, and save them without the effort of copying the updated file back to its original location by floppy.

I suspect in many ways the ability of the Internet to share files with friends by just attaching them to e-mails is actually gaining more all-around popularity than using floppies. However, the Internet does pose the question of security. In theory, your e-mail can be read by other parties between the time you send it and when the recipient receives it. So, if there is something extremely confidential or personal, e-mail might not be the best alternative. On the other hand, Aladdin System's DropStuff does allow you to compress and encrypt files with a password at the same time. Mac OS 9 also offers encryption abilities.

FTP server access requires that you have access to an FTP server. Other options, such as the iMac Floppy site, which basically gives you 3 MB of free Internet storage, or Apple's iDisk technology, which gives you 20 MB on a virtual disk that appears right on your desktop and integrates it into other Apple Internet services known as iTools, make some alternatives for moderate storage or file transfer. The iDisk is an excellent option because it behaves exactly as a Macintosh disk does (albeit slowed down by the access to a remote Internet server).

Floppy Disk Images

Disk images are special files that when opened cause a "virtual disk" to appear on your desktop. Although the actual files on this disk are located right on the same drive as the disk image file, the disk behaves for all intents and purposes as though it were an actual disk. Disk images created using Apple's free Disk Copy utility even have a floppy-style icon to them. A disk image file and mounted disk image are shown in Figure 20-5.

Disk images can be useful for software that requires a floppy. In many cases, this will be an older application or installer that is designed to look for components on a floppy instead of in another folder. For example, say you had an installer program for an old application and you want to keep a copy of the installer around so you could reinstall the application

Figure 20-5
A disk image file will mount as a disk when opened.

floppy1.img

floppy1

if needed or install it on a future Mac. If the installer was on multiple floppies, it would likely be designed at various points to look for the other installation floppies. If you don't have these and only have their contents in folders, you will eventually get to a point where the installer won't continue and will just keep asking you to insert a specific disk.

If you use Apple's Disk Copy (or a similar third-party utility like ShrinkWrap), you can make a disk image of the original floppies. You do this by inserting each floppy and using the Create Image from Disk command to select the disk you want to create an image of. Then you simply save the disk image and perform the command with each subsequent floppy. When needed, you then double-click on the disk images or open them from within Disk Copy, and you have, for most intents and purposes, the original floppies on your desktop.

You can also create empty disk images and then drag files to them and save them. You can actually create disk images of any size, not just the standard 1.44-MB floppy size. These disk images will also function just like floppies and can provide a convenient way of sending files to someone by e-mail so that all the files are neatly organized in a virtual floppy disk. The other person will need a copy of Disk Copy or similar utility to actually mount and access the images, however. This shouldn't present much trouble, since Disk Copy accompanies every Mac OS installation.

Floppy Drive Options

Sometimes the alternatives aren't worth the effort or may simply not be practical. For these cases, there are options for actually adding a floppy drive to the current Mac models. These generally consist of USB options that were introduced following the iMac's announcement, but there are also internal options for the Power Mac computers.

USB Floppy Drives

The most common floppy drives on the market for Macs today are of the USB variety. A number of companies announced their intention to develop USB floppy drives within weeks of the iMac's announcement in May of 1998. The USB models tend to have a price tag of around $100, or maybe a little less.

As one might expect, the installation process for USB floppy drives is extremely basic. This is true of the majority of USB devices. One simply installs the driver software that ships with the drive and then only needs to restart the Mac and attach the drive.

Although there are various options to choose from, the average USB floppy drives tend have very similar specs. Each uses a typical USB interface, supports both Mac- and PC-formatted floppies (actually, this is more a feature of the Mac OS than the drive), and each is limited to using only 1.44-MB floppies. Earlier 800-KB Mac and 720-KB PC floppy formats are not readable using these drives. Since Macs have shipped with the 1.44-MB floppy drive for nearly a decade, this should not pose much of a concern.

The differences between Mac USB floppy drives tend to be in slight variations of price, access speeds, physical design, and the need for an external power supply. Although all USB floppy drives tend to have similar pricing, comparative shopping between models can sometimes get you a better buy from one manufacturer or another. In addition, access speeds of most USB floppy drives are actually above those of traditional internal floppy drives. These access speeds can vary from model to model and are something worth looking at when comparing two equally priced floppy options.

Each USB floppy manufacturer has applied their own design to their drives; however, most tend to be similar to the Ariston iFloppy shown in Figure 20-6. Although design usually follows performance as a consideration, you may want to consider the look of the drive as a factor; some of these drives are designed to complement other product lines from a company. For example, all of USB products from Newer Technology are of the same size and physical dimensions. This makes them easily stackable and can result in increased desk space if you are using several of their products.

Figure 20-6

Ariston's iFloppy is a typical USB floppy drive. (Photo courtesy of Ariston Technologies)

Lastly, since USB allows developers to create products that draw their power from the USB bus rather than from their own power supply, some USB floppy options don't require separate power sources. This can be a useful feature in terms of attaching a drive or sharing it between several computers.

The SuperDisk

Imation's SuperDisk was discussed in Chapter 18 because it is a removable-media drive. The SuperDisk stores data on disks that hold 120 MB of data but are of the same physical dimensions as a floppy disk (as shown in Figure 20-7). SuperDisk drives are also capable of reading and writing to both traditional 1.44-MB floppy disks and the 120-MB SuperDisks. In many ways, this makes the SuperDisk an excellent floppy option, because you also get the benefits of a larger-capacity removable-media drive for backup or other storage purposes. The SuperDisk drives are, like USB floppy drives, unable to deal with 800-KB Mac or 720-KB DOS floppies.

The interesting thing about the SuperDisk is that it seems to have

Figure 20-7   The floppy and SuperDisk look similar despite varying widely in their storage capacities.

been designed as a kind of next-generation floppy. The device was first introduced into the Windows- or DOS-based PC computer markets and was designed as an actual replacement for the traditional floppy drive. Installation tended to use the same controllers as the floppy drive, and the SuperDisk was designed to serve as a completely backward-compatible replacement for the floppy drive. Although it never truly took off as a next-generation floppy in terms of becoming a standard product or fixture on computers, the SuperDisk did establish itself as a floppy option with the ability to use the larger-capacity SuperDisks.

The SuperDisk is available in USB models (one of which is shown in Figure 20-8), but it is also available in PowerBook expansion bay models and SCSI models. The PowerBook expansion bay model gives you much the same feel or access that a traditional floppy drive would. SCSI models offer increased performance over USB because of USB's limited bandwidth.

The USB SuperDisk drives also tend to offer another benefit over the traditional USB floppy drives: performance. When used with the 120-MB SuperDisks, these drives need to be faster than a floppy drive, so they can be competitive with other removable-media drives. This performance

Figure 20-8
Imation's USB SuperDisk Drive can read and write standard floppy disks as well as much higher capacity SuperDisks.

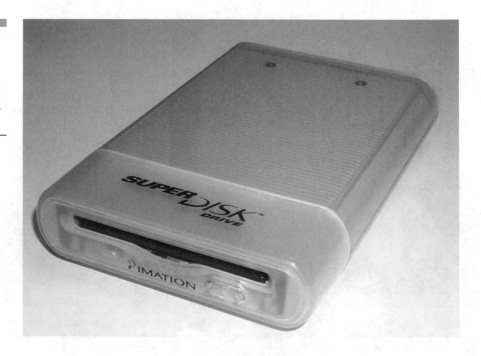

is not, however, limited strictly to SuperDisks, and floppy performance tends to be higher with a SuperDisk solution than other floppy solutions.

The Imation USB SuperDisk drive model also benefits over other options because, like the Iomega USB Zip drive, its drivers are bundled with standard installations of the Mac OS. This means that the drive tends to be more readily accessed on additional Mac computers, without the need to install drivers for it on each machine.

The SuperDisk options are more expensive than the USB floppy drives on the market. It is up to the individual to determine if the benefits of using the drive as a higher-capacity removable-media drive is worth the added expense. If you don't expect to need to access Zip or other removable-media disk types, then the advantage might very well be worth the cost. This is particularly true considering that the cost of buying both a USB floppy drive and a separate removable-media solution is noticeably higher than the cost of a SuperDisk drive, which serves both purposes. Chapter 18 compares the SuperDisk with the Zip and other removable-media drive types.

Troubleshooting Floppy Drive Problems

Because most floppy drive solutions on the market are, strictly speaking, either USB devices or SCSI devices, troubleshooting the majority of problems follows the same patterns as any other USB or SCSI device. The following symptoms and solutions are problems specific to floppy drives of any variety.

Disk Unreadable By This Macintosh Dialog

This problem indicates that the Mac is unable to read or understand the format used by the floppy (or other type of disk) in question. If the disk is a PC-formatted disk, make sure the File Exchange or PC Exchange control panel is installed in the Control Panels folder and that you haven't started with extensions off. If the disk is Mac disk of the earlier 800-KB Mac or 720-KB PC floppy formats, your USB or SuperDisk solution will not be able to read it, and therefore, the Mac will not recognize it.

The disk itself may have degraded over time or may have been damaged by exposure to a magnetic field that has rendered it unusable. Depending on the severity of such a problem, some disk utilities described in Chapter 5 might be able to retrieve some of the data, but this is not particularly likely.

Another possibility is that the drive or drive heads may need cleaning. This can be accomplished as described earlier in the chapter with special head-cleaning floppy disks, MicroMat's TechTool, compressed air sprayed into the drive, or any combination of the three.

Finally, if the disk has never been used, it may simply need to be formatted, this dialog will allow you to format it.

The Drive Refuses to Eject a Disk

As a rule, disks are ejected by using Finder commands or by dragging the disk's icon to the Trash. However, some floppy drives may require that you manually eject the disk once you have performed these actions. If so, this should be described in the drive's manual.

If the drive is designed to auto-eject the floppy and doesn't, there may be problems with the drive. However, like traditional Mac floppy drives, almost all of today's floppy solutions include an emergency eject hole that can be triggered with a straightened-out paper clip. This can also be a solution if the Mac freezes or crashes, and you need to eject a disk. It should not be done, however, while the Mac is running normally and the disk's icon is displayed on the desktop.

If the Mac displays a dialog saying the disk cannot be ejected because it contains items that are in use, you probably have a file on the disk open in some application or you haven't quit an application on the disk.

The Mac Ejects a Disk and Then Constantly Asks for It to Be Inserted

Some application or Mac OS element is looking for something on the disk, possible a recently accessed file or the desktop file. Try reinserting and ejecting the disk again. If this doesn't solve the problem, try quitting all open applications while the disk is inserted and then ejecting it. If this still doesn't happen, restart the Mac and eject the floppy before or during the startup sequence.

The Mac Doesn't Recognize the Drive

If the Mac displays a dialog box saying that the drivers for a USB device are unknown, this indicates that the drivers needed for that device to function are not installed. Without the drivers for a USB floppy or SuperDisk drive installed, the Mac will not be able to access the drive. Similarly, SCSI SuperDisk drives will not be recognized without drivers, although there will be no convenient dialog to inform you.

If there is no such dialog, but the Mac simply doesn't acknowledge the drive when you insert a disk, the drive may not be connected properly or there may be some other USB problem. Check the section on troubleshooting USB at the end of Chapter 15 for additional information.

Individual Disks Are Not Recognized

If the drive is connected properly, but a disk is still not acknowledged by the Mac at all, check to be sure that there is no obstruction in the drive blocking the drive heads. A somewhat common problem of this type is the labels peeling off of a floppy and getting stuck inside the drive.

Another possibility is that the drive heads may be dirty. In this case, try using the solutions described in "Disk Unreadable By This Macintosh Dialog" above to clean them.

Available Floppy Disk Space Is Smaller than It Should Be

Check to be sure that the desktop file on the floppy has not grown overly large, as described earlier in the chapter.

Resources for Further Study

The following URLs provide additional information on some of the concepts, issues, and products discussed in this chapter:

Ariston Technologies—Makers of the iFloppy USB Floppy Drive— http://www.ariston.com

Newer Technology—Makers of the uDrive USB Floppy Drive—http://www.newertech.com

VST Technologies—USB Floppy and Power Expansion Bay SuperDisk Drive Manufacturer—http://www.vsttech.com

iDrives—Makers of the iDrive iFloppy-USB floppy drive—http://www.idrives.com

CompuCable—Makers of USB docks (some containing floppy drives)—http://www.compucable.com

Imation—Makers of SuperDisk drives and disks—http://www.superdisk.com

Winstation—Makers of SCSI and USB SuperDisk drives for the Mac—http://www.winstation.com

MicroMat—Makers of TechTool PRO—http://www.micromat.com

iMac Floppy—Internet storage site—http://www.imacfloppy.com

Apple iTools site—Register or Access the iDisk—http://itools.mac.com

CHAPTER 21

Keyboards

Keyboards are, from any user's perspective, one of the most essential peripherals attached to a computer. The keyboard allows you to control the computer, selecting settings or inputting data, and it provides one of the most fundamental interfaces you and your Mac will ever use. This chapter looks at how keyboards actually function, the types of keyboards available for the Mac, and what to do when you have problems with your Mac's keyboard.

How Keyboards Work

Although anyone using a computer today knows how to use a keyboard to type, most people don't understand how a keyboard actually functions. On a basic level, a keyboard is a large collection of individual switches, one switch for each key. When each key is pressed, the switch is momentarily turned on for that key, and the appropriate signal for that key is sent from the keyboard to the Mac.

Two types of key switches are used in keyboards: mechanical and membrane. Each has its own distinct feel, and each has advantages. Both types have been commonly used by Apple and other keyboard manufacturers.

Mechanical switches contain two electrical contacts. A plastic bar separates these two contacts. This bar is attached to a spring at the base of the switch and to the underside of the key cap. When the key is pressed, the bar is slid down. This allows the two metal contacts to touch, causing an electrical signal to pass between them, which means that the switch is turned on. When the key is released, the spring forces the bar (and the key cap) upward. This breaks the contact and turns the switch off again. Figure 21-1 illustrates a mechanical keyboard switch

Membrane switches also use a plastic bar, but this bar is attached to a rubber base rather than a spring. The inside of the rubber base contains a metal compound. Beneath the base are two metal contacts. When the key is pressed, the rubber base collapses. The metal compound inside the base then touches both metal contacts at once, allowing an electrical sig-

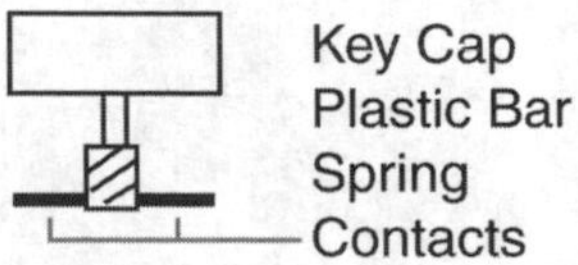

Figure 21-1
Mechanical keyboard switch.

Key Cap
Plastic Bar
Spring
Contacts

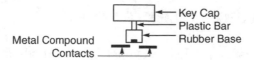

Figure 21-2
Membrane keyboard switch.

nal to flow between them and turning the switch on. When the key is released, the rubber base returns to its initial position, and the metal compound loses touch with the contacts beneath it, turning the switch off. Figure 21-2 illustrates a membrane keyboard switch.

Because they function differently, mechanical switch and membrane switch keyboards have different strengths and different feels. Mechanical switches are more rugged and generally have a longer rated life span than membrane switches (sometimes as much as five times as long). However, the rubber membranes used in membrane keyboards give them more resistance to the effects of dust, dirt, spills, and other foreign matter than mechanical switches.

Mechanical switch keyboards tend to feel more firm and provide a better tactile feedback or responding click when typed on. They are also the more expensive of the two keyboard types. Membrane keyboards are less expensive and have a more yielding or "mushy" feel to them. The type of keyboard feel can be very important in choosing a comfortable keyboard and is very much a matter of personal preference. Some people prefer the feel of membrane keyboards, while others prefer the feel of mechanical keyboards. The keyboards used in the current PowerBooks and the iBook are examples of membrane keyboards.

Whatever type they are, all keyboards transmit information to the Mac in the same way. Each keyswitch produces a specific electronic key code that is generated by the keyboard's internal circuitry. Contrary to popular misconception, each key on the keyboard is not individually identified and coded to a specific character. Rather, the series of switches in a keyboard are recognized as a series of rows and columns. Each key has a corresponding location in the rows and columns and is identified by its location in the grid of keys. The key code sent to the Mac from the keyboard is based on this grid location rather than an actual character or key on the keyboard. This allows the keyboard to be used for recognizing different keyboard layouts easily. Various keyboard layouts and how to switch between them are discussed later in this chapter.

Keyboard Interface

Over the years, Apple has provided four methods of connecting a keyboard to the Mac. The first was only used on the first three Mac models and is not a concern to anyone using an even moderately old Mac today. The second method was via the ADB port, which was included on virtually every Mac until the iMac. The iMac, as well as later Macs, removed the ADB port in favor of USB. The final keyboard interface is the built-in keyboards used in the PowerBook and iBook computers. In this section, we'll look at the three main interfaces: ADB, USB, and built-in keyboards.

ADB

ADB was the keyboard interface of the Mac from the Mac SE in 1987 through the iMac's release in 1998. ADB, which stands for Apple Desktop Bus, was a technology used on both the Mac and on some later Apple II computers. It supported the connection of keyboards, as well as pointing devices, such as mice and trackballs. ADB was a powered bus, meaning that devices requiring a small amount of power could draw that power from the bus. However, ADB provided nowhere near the power that USB or FireWire are capable of. An ADB port and the ADB logo are shown in Figure 21-3.

Figure 21-3
An ADB port and the logo for ADB ports and devices.

The only recent Mac that has included an ADB port is the Blue and White Power Mac G3. Even there, the ADB port was not designed to attach a keyboard so much as it was designed to attach graphics tablets and similar input devices in which users might have an investment. It also did not offer the degree of performance benefits that earlier ADB-equipped Macs did.

ADB is not a hot-pluggable technology, and Apple has always advised that a Mac should be turned off before connecting or disconnecting ADB devices such as keyboards. In practice, most users have noticed that the Mac does not crash or experience any major problems when ADB devices are added or removed while the Mac is running. However, Apple reports that there is a small risk of causing an electrical short along the entire ADB interface, potentially damaging the keyboard, mouse, any other ADB devices, and the Mac. Given this caution, it is a good idea not to hot-plug ADB devices.

USB

USB keyboards are now the standard on all desktop Macs. Apple's standard USB keyboard includes a built-in two-port USB hub. Many non-Apple USB keyboards also include built-in hubs. The function of the hub in the keyboard is generally accepted as a convenient way to attach a mouse, or other pointing device, to the computer. It can, however, be used for attaching any USB device that doesn't draw a significant amount of power from the USB bus.

Of the current technologies used on the Mac, USB is the logical choice for a keyboard interface. It is included on all Macs and can easily provide the minimal amount of power that a keyboard requires in order to function. USB also provides two different data transfer speeds along its bus, one of which is designed for very low-performance devices such as keyboards and pointing devices. This makes USB ideal for use as a keyboard interface.

USB is also cross-platform. This means that a USB keyboard designed for a non-Mac computer will function without any problems when attached to a Mac. This gives Mac users a broader range of keyboard choices. Keep in mind, however, that USB keyboards that are not Mac-specific, include different keys. There is no Command key on a PC's keyboard; conversely, there is no Alt key on a Mac keyboard. Although the key assignments are generally translated without much trouble, some of the translation places keys in areas of the keyboard different from a Mac-specific keyboard.

For most practical purposes, USB keyboards function exactly the same as ADB keyboards. The one exception is that you cannot force the Mac to restart from a severe crash using the keyboard. For most ADB Macs, pressing the Command, Control, and power keys on the keyboard will force the Mac to restart if it has frozen. However, the code for this forced restart cannot be hard-wired into USB devices as it could be with ADB or built-in keyboards. This means that a physical reset button on the Mac has to be used instead. Similarly, the power key on USB keyboards may not start up the Mac if the keyboard is attached to a hub rather than a USB port on the Mac itself.

Built-in Keyboards

Both the iBook and PowerBook models include a built-in keyboard. This keyboard is not part of the computer's case and can be removed if needed. It is held in place by tabs at the lower and upper edges of the keyboard. To remove the keyboard, the tabs at the upper edge of the keyboard (shown in Figure 21-4) can be released. The keyboard is connected to the computer's motherboard by means of a narrow orange ribbon cable.

Normal maintenance of the PowerBook and iBook computers will not involve disconnecting the ribbon cable that attaches the keyboard. Most tasks, such as RAM and AirPort card installations, should take place with the keyboard removed to allow access to the internal components, but with the cable still connected. The keyboard itself should rest on the portable Mac's built-in wrist rests during such work.

You may need to entirely disconnect the keyboard for other types of repairs or upgrades. Replacing the hard drive of an iBook, for example,

Figure 21-4   The location of the iBook and PowerBook keyboard release tabs.

would require you to disassemble the case of the computer, which is done much more easily with the keyboard disconnected from the motherboard. Disconnecting the keyboard from either the PowerBook or iBook is fairly simple. Remove it as you would to access the RAM or AirPort slots, and then follow the orange ribbon cable to where it connects to the motherboard (shown in Figure 21-5). The ribbon cable is attached to the motherboard by a connector that can be removed by gently pulling either directly up or to the right of the computer (assuming that you are facing the LCD screen). Reconnecting the keyboard is an equally easy reverse of the process.

Replacing a portable Mac's internal keyboard involves disconnecting the ribbon cable where it connects to the Mac's motherboard. A replacement keyboard can then be attached. Replacement keyboards are often specific to a portable Mac's model and are proprietary designs that must be obtained from Apple. As a rule, only Apple Authorized Service Centers will be able to obtain replacement keyboards from Apple for PowerBook and iBook computers.

The PowerBook and iBook can both function with an external USB keyboard as well. Simply plug the USB keyboard into the USB port of these Macs, and you can begin using it as easily as the built-in keyboard. This is particularly useful if you are using a PowerBook and an external display, since it delivers the same feel as a desktop Mac would.

Figure 21-5
Internal keyboard
connector on a
PowerBook's mother-
board.

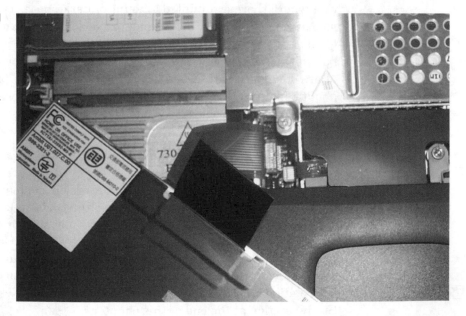

Third-Party Keyboards

Several companies produce replacement keyboards, both USB and ADB, for the Mac. These companies give Mac users a choice besides the standard Apple keyboards. Apple's original USB keyboard is physically smaller than most keyboards and uses half-size function and arrow keys. Some users find this to be uncomfortable to use or difficult to get accustomed to. By contrast, third-party keyboards often use more traditional keyboard sizes and key arrangements.

Third-party keyboards almost always have lower prices than an Apple-made keyboard, sometimes by a significant difference. This provides users with an excellent low-cost alternative. Additionally, some keyboards have special features, such as those with built-in pointing devices, those intended for disabled users, and those with an ergonomic design to help avoid repetitive stress injury.

Keyboards with Built-in Pointing Devices

Several third-party keyboards include a built-in pointing device, such as a trackball or a trackpad. This is usually placed to the right of the keyboard itself, between the text keyboard and the numeric keypad, or in the center of the keyboard between two wrist rests. Keyboards such as these are available in both USB and ADB models and provide an excellent solution where there is a limited amount of desk space. These keyboards can also serve if you prefer a trackpad or trackball instead of a mouse.

In addition, keyboards are available that combine a trackpad or trackball onto an ergonomic keyboard. This is both convenient in the method of any keyboard with a built-in pointing device and for users concerned about repetitive stress injuries, because both of these types of pointing devices produce less strain on the wrist than a mouse.

Specialty Keyboards

Beyond the common replacement keyboards on the market and ergonomic keyboards (discussed in the next section), specialty keyboards are available that are designed for those users with physical or developmental disabilities. Several companies deal specifically in such keyboards and can provide models to accommodate users who are able to type with only one hand or even those needing to type with their feet. You can find additional information on these keyboards by referring to the "Resources for Further Study" section at the end of this chapter.

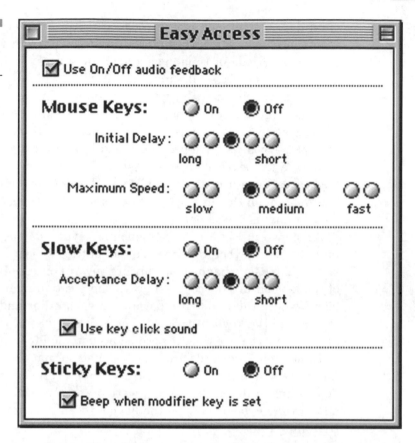

Figure 21-6
The Easy Access control panel.

Apple also provides a control panel called Easy Access (shown in Figure 21-6) for adjusting the keyboard for use by users with disabilities. Easy Access can allow you to set keystrokes to be registered especially slowly, as well as allowing key combinations (such as Command-S for Save) to be typed one key at a time. It also allows you to control the Mac's pointer using the keyboard rather than a mouse or other pointing device. Easy Access is included with all Mac OS releases, but it is not installed as part of a standard installation.

Ergonomic Keyboards and Repetitive Stress Injuries

Repetitive stress injury, or RSI, is a range of medical conditions brought about by consistently repeating the same motion with a specific part of the body. The most commonly known RSI condition is carpal tunnel syndrome, in which repetitive motions of the wrists and hands cause calcium deposits to form in the wrist, which pinch nerves and can cause severe problems with the hands. Typing on a traditional keyboard for extended periods of time over a span of several years is probably the greatest cause of carpal tunnel syndrome. A slightly less common RSI condition associated with typing is tendonitis in the wrists and elbows.

With ergonomics in mind (an applied science that designs and arranges workspaces and tools for optimum comfort, efficiency, and safety), keyboards have been designed in shapes that are far less likely to induce the level of repetitive strain on the wrists. These ergonomic keyboards have a distinctly different shape than most traditional keyboards, though the arrangement or relative locations of keys on the keyboard remains the same.

As shown in Figure 21-7, ergonomic keyboards have a split down the middle of the keyboard, with each half of the keyboard placed at an angle so that the user's hands point inward toward one another and the center of the keyboard. This contrasts with the positioning of a traditional keyboard where the hands are parallel to each other and point toward the top edge of the keyboard. Some people find this split jarring at first, and most people require time to become accustomed to ergonomic keyboards.

Ergonomic keyboards are also designed so that the angle at which the hands rest against the keyboard is more relaxed. This angle varies depending on the keyboard in question and may differ at varying points on a given keyboard, giving the keyboard an appearance similar to gently rolling hills.

While very experienced touch typists often have no problem switching to an ergonomic keyboard, the same cannot be said of everyone. Novice

Figure 21-7
A USB ergonomic keyboard. (Courtesy of Adesso)

or relatively new typists often have trouble migrating to an ergonomic keyboard because they still have a tendency to glance down at the keyboard on occasion, looking for keys. In addition, the shape of the keyboard is often too visually jarring for such users. Some people find the sloping design of many ergonomic keyboards to be uncomfortable as well.

A few ergonomic keyboard makers have gotten around the worst of these problems by making keyboards where the slope of the keyboard and, occasionally, the angle of the keyboard split can be adjusted to a user's preference. Several years ago, Apple provided a keyboard that could be adjusted to nearly any degree of slope and keyboard-split angle, from that of a traditional keyboard to the most extreme of ergonomic designs. Sadly, that model ADB keyboard was discontinued quite some time ago and never replaced.

Even nonergonomic keyboards today tend to offer adjustable feet that can be used to adjust the height and angle of the keyboard to more comfortable positions. This may help reduce repetitive stress injuries.

Wrist Rests   Most ergonomic keyboards include built-in wrist rests. In these keyboards, the wrist rest is an extension of the keyboard's frame that the user's wrists and the base of the hands rest on while typing. Like the other design factors of an ergonomic keyboard, a wrist rest helps to avoid repetitive stress. The wrist rest supports the wrists so that the hands do not need to be held at an angle over the keyboard. This keeps the wrist straight, thereby reducing the stress that would otherwise occur.

Although wrist rests are a built-in part of many ergonomic keyboards, they are not limited to use in ergonomic keyboards. The cases of all PowerBook and iBook computers extend beyond the keyboard, offering wrist rests as a part of the case design (as well as providing a location for the machine's trackpad). Also, a vast number of plastic, foam, fabric, and even gel-filled wrist rests are on the market that can be used with any keyboard, as shown in Figure 21-8. At least a few of these wrist rests can be found in a typical office supply or computer store.

Independent wrist rests can be a good option for users wanting to avoid repetitive strain, for those just beginning to suffer RSI problems, and for those who need ergonomic support for their wrist and hands but are uncomfortable typing on a fully ergonomic keyboard.

Posture and Repetitive Stress   While the design of a keyboard can impact the stress it has on a user's hands and wrists, posture when typing can also be a significant factor in repetitive strain. Good posture may

Figure 21-8
Typical wrist rest.

Figure 21-9
Proper arm angle for
typing.

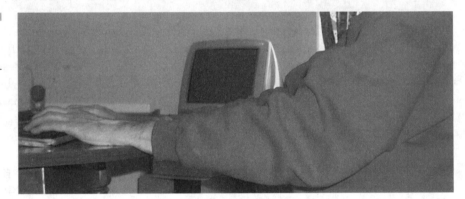

even have as much impact on reducing repetitive strain as an ergonomic keyboard. The following tips can help you maintain good posture with even the worst keyboards.

Keep your arms and shoulders relaxed while typing. The angle between your upper arms and forearms at the elbow should be slightly beyond the perpendicular shape of a right angle, as shown in Figure 21-9. The angle should never be less than a right angle.

As shown in Figure 21-10, your hands should form a more or less straight line and not be angled at the wrists. This is especially important, as a bend or twist at the wrist is one of the things that will induce strain on the wrist muscles and tendons.

Following are additional tips on sound ergonomic practices:

Figure 21-10
Proper hand positioning for typing.

- Avoid rolling or placing your thumbs underneath your other fingers of the palm of your hands. This is an unnatural position that can pull on the tendons that link your thumbs to your wrists.

- Avoid pressing hard on the keys. This will keep your fingers from having to exert excess force and save the tendons and muscles running along the back of your hands some strain. It can also extend the life of your keyboard.

- Take breaks and change your hand positions as often as possible. The longer your hands are in a typing position without breaks, the tighter the muscles in your hands and wrists are apt to become. Working without breaks can also cause your fingers to cramp up.

- A good chair can also impact your posture and comfort while typing. Optimally, a chair should be adjustable to meet your height needs. It also should offer support for your lower back. Adjust the chair's height so that your thighs are parallel to the floor when sitting and your feet are flat. The chair should encourage your back to be straight and your shoulders relaxed without being hunched forward. The chair and/or desk should not encourage your arms to be at an angle other than described earlier. If it does, consider raising or lowering the chair and/or the keyboard (such as with a keyboard drawer) as needed.

■ The computer's mouse or trackball should be at the same height and positioning as the keyboard. There should be little effort involved in moving your hand from the keyboard to the mouse.

Most importantly, if you experience any degree of chronic pain while typing or any pain centered in the wrists, hands, or elbows, seek medical attention. The longer a repetitive stress condition goes without appropriate treatment, the worse it will become. RSI conditions can become quite serious if left untreated. If treated early, they can also be resolved quickly and easily in many cases.

The Keyboard Control Panel

The Keyboard control panel, shown in Figure 21-11, allows you to adjust a number of settings with regard to how the Mac responds to your typing on the keyboard. These include the selected keyboard layout and the key repeat and delay rates, as well as the controls for programming function keys (assuming the Mac and Mac OS in question supports programmable function keys).

Keyboard Layouts

A keyboard layout tells the Mac which keys produce which characters on the screen. There are several keyboard layouts included with the Mac OS, many of which are designed for use with different languages or to conform to the standard keyboards of different countries. You can use the list of layouts in the main body of the Keyboard control panel's window to select which layout(s) you want to use.

If you want to be able to switch between multiple layouts very quickly, select the checkboxes next to the layouts you plan to switch between. When you close the Keyboard control panel, you'll notice that a new item has appeared in the menu bar between the clock and the application menu. This item, shown in Figure 21-12, will look like a small flag and represents the currently active keyboard layout. The menu that is provided by this item allows you to easily switch between any of the layouts that you selected in the Keyboard control panel. If you have selected multiple key-

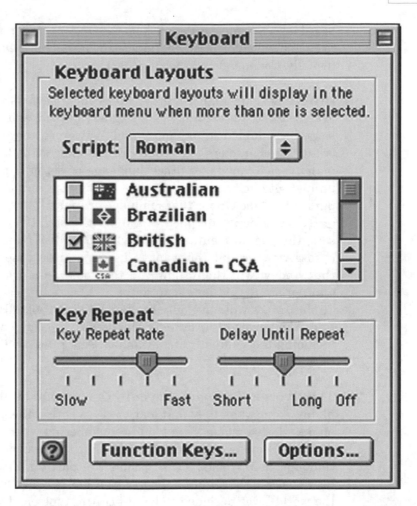

Figure 21-11
The Keyboard control panel.

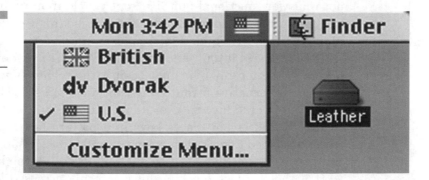

Figure 21-12
Keyboard layout menu.

board layouts, you can also click on the Options button in the control panel to enable switching between the selected layouts using a keyboard shortcut (usually, Command and the spacebar).

Different Language Scripts   Many languages use the same basic set of characters, but not all. While English, French, and Spanish all use the same basic alphabet, Japanese and Arabic use very different alphabets or sets of characters. The Mac can function with the character sets of many varied languages. Each language or set of languages that uses a unique set of characters will have a language script that is installed as part of the Mac OS for that language or region.

If your Mac is equipped to handle the scripts of multiple language sets, the pop-up menu in the Keyboard control panel will allow you to choose which script you want to use at a given time. The main body of the window will then allow you to choose from the keyboard layouts appropriate to that language script.

Most Macs will have only the Roman script installed. This script contains the keyboard layouts for the majority of languages and countries, including the United States, Canada, Australia, and virtually all countries in Europe.

The Dvorak Keyboard Layout   One thing that almost anyone complains about when they first learn to type is that the placement of letters on a keyboard makes typing and remembering where letters are located difficult. Some people even grumble that this was done intentionally to confound new typists. Those people are partly right. The current keyboard used in the United States (variations of which are used throughout the world), was designed to be difficult to type on. This is because back when typewriters were first being produced, typing too quickly would jam the machine. So the inventors of the time designed a keyboard layout that was functional but also kept people from typing fast enough to cause jamming. Unfortunately, that keyboard became a standard on almost all typewriters and later on computers.

This keyboard layout, known as the QWERTY layout (for the first six letters in the top row), has not been without challenges over the years. Only one alternative layout truly continues to be used to this day. It is called the Dvorak layout, after its inventor.

The Dvorak layout places keys in a pattern (shown in Figure 21-13) that is designed to make typing easier and reduce typing stress. The keys are spaced so that the most used letters are all in the home (center) row so that there is less reaching for commonly accessed keys. In addition,

Figure 21-13
The QWERTY (above)
and Dvorak keyboard
layouts.

Figure 21-13
The QWERTY (above) and Dvorak keyboard layouts.

commonly used keys are spaced relatively evenly between the two sides of the keyboard so that any wrist strain will be equal for both hands.

Apple includes a Dvorak keyboard layout in the keyboard control panel. So, if you are a fan of the Dvorak layout, you can easily switch between it and the more conventional keyboard layouts. The downside is that you will need to either ignore the letters on the keyboard or change the layout of the keycaps to match the Dvorak layout. You can change the keycap letters by using a transparent plastic overlay for the keyboard, by using letter stickers that can be placed on the keys themselves, or by physically removing the keycaps and replacing them in the alternate layout (which I do not suggest you do). Of the three options, the first is the most practical.

Figure 21-13 shows a comparison of QWERTY and Dvorak keyboard layouts.

The Key Caps Desk Accessory   The Key Caps desk accessory is a small application installed in the Apple menu. When launched, it will display a schematic of the Mac's keyboard. The characters assigned to each key in the active keyboard layout will be displayed on the keys in this schematic. When you press a key on the keyboard, the corresponding letter or character will be typed and the image of that key in the display will be highlighted. Also, if you hold down the Shift, Option, Control, or Command keys, all of which can act as modifier keys, the keyboard schematic will display what characters the keys will produce while these keys are held down.

The Key Caps desk accessory, shown in Figure 21-14, can be useful in determining some problems with keyboard. For example, if an unusual

Figure 21-14
The Key Caps desk
accessory

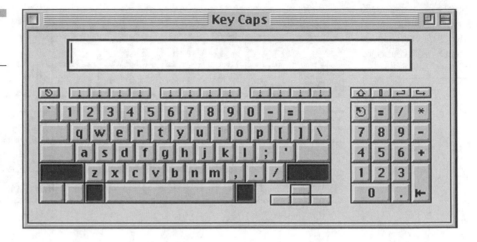

keyboard layout has been selected, you can verify the characters in the Key Caps window. It can also be used to determine if a modifier key has become stuck, causing several other keys to type unusual characters.

Beyond troubleshooting, Key Caps can be a temporary solution if a single key on the keyboard becomes damaged. Say, for example, your keyboard's "Q" key is broken and you need to prepare a document before you can get hold of a replacement keyboard. Open the Key Caps desk accessory, then click on the "Q" key in the Key Caps window. This will cause the "Q" character to be typed in the text box at the top of the window (the same as typing the letter would). You can then use the Copy and Paste commands to place that "Q" in your document where needed. It isn't even close to a perfect solution, but it can serve in an emergency.

Key Repeat and Delay Rates

At the bottom of the Keyboard control panel are two sliders labeled Key Repeat Rate and Delay Until Repeat. These sliders control how the Mac responds when a key is pressed or held down. The Key Repeat Rate determines how quickly the Mac will repeatedly type a character when a given key is held down. The Delay Until Repeat determines how long the Mac will wait before it begins repeatedly typing a character when the key is held down. If the Delay Until Repeat slider is moved to the "off" position, then the Mac will not repeatedly type any characters no matter how long a key is held down.

Programmable Function Keys

The keyboards of the PowerBook and iBook include special uses for many of the function keys above the keyboard. The first two function keys control the screen brightness of the computer; the second two control the volume of the internal speakers. The fifth function key acts as the Num Lock key, and the sixth works as an easily accessible Mute button. To use any of these keys as function keys, users must also hold down the "Fn" (function) key located to the left of the control key at the bottom of the keyboard.

The remaining function keys (F7 though F12) can be programmed to open any document, application, or folder on the Mac. This is done by pressing the Function Keys button in the Keyboard control panel and then pressing on the onscreen buttons displayed for each key in the resulting window (see Figure 21-15). This allows you to select what item you want to assign each key.

If an item is assigned to one of these keys, pressing the key will open the corresponding item. To use the key as a function key, you would hold

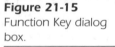

Figure 21-15
Function Key dialog box.

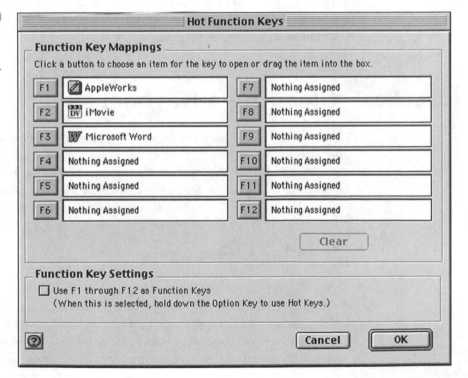

down the Fn key while pressing it. Keys with nothing assigned to them will act as function keys whether the Fn key is held down or not.

The Function Keys dialog also offers you the option of reversing the use of the Fn key. When this checkbox is checked, the function will act as function keys when pressed normally. They will then act for whatever built-in features or user-defined items are assigned to them when the Fn key is held down.

In Mac OS 9, Apple added the programmable function keys feature to desktop Macs as well as portable Macs. The process of programming these keys is done in the same way. The difference is that on desktop Macs, all 12 function keys can be programmed. Also, since desktop Macs lack an Fn key, the Option key is used in its place to access the assigned items of programmed function keys.

Other Uses for the Fn Key   The Fn key of the PowerBook and iBook also functions with keys other than the function keys. When held down, it causes the arrow keys to behave as Page Up, Page Down, Home, and End keys. It also causes several letter keys to the right of the keyboard to function as a numeric keypad would on a full-sized external keyboard. This allows the smaller keyboard of a portable Mac to offer all the same keys as a full-sized external keyboard without needing to be larger than would be appropriate for a laptop.

Cleaning a Keyboard

In addition to be the primary input device of a computer, the keyboard is also the component most likely to become dirty and dusty, endure spills of various kinds, and suffer from wear and tear due to constant use. Cleaning a keyboard doesn't just keep it looking nice and clean; it can also help prolong its usable life span and prevent problems.

Regular Cleanings

The biggest threat posed to keyboards is the sort of thing to which they are exposed every day. Dust, pet hair, smoke, pollen, other airborne particles, and even skin oils can build up on and around the key caps and eventually work their way into the keyboard. The buildup of this debris can then accumulate, preventing keys from making contact (in which case the key will not be recognized when pressed) or causing the key to stick (in which case it will remain depressed after being struck). Regular cleaning of the keyboard can go a long way to preventing this from happening.

For general cleanings, just cleaning the external portions of the keyboard should be enough to prevent problems. Such cleaning should be performed about every three months to be fully effective. In the home or other environments where there may be more exposure to foreign matter, you may want to clean the keyboard more often.

A regular cleaning of the keyboard can be accomplished very quickly and easily. Disconnect the keyboard and turn it upside down. Run a soft-bristled brush along the surfaces of the keys and in between the keys to dislodge any material that may be accumulating there. Next, take a can of compressed air (available in any electronics and most office supply stores), and place the long thin nozzle between the rows of keys. Blow any accumulated dust out with the compressed air. You may want to use the compressed air outside or away from furniture, as it will have a tendency to blow the accumulated dust from the keyboard in all directions.

You can also purchase special "static-safe" vacuum cleaners to use instead of the compressed air. These vacuum cleaners are specially designed for cleaning electronic components and will not build up a static charge as most ordinary vacuums will. Do not use a vacuum cleaner that is not static-safe, as the bristles of its attachments may build up an electrostatic charge that could damage your keyboard.

More Thorough Cleanings

Regular cleanings of the keyboard should go a long way to preventing problems and prolonging the life span of your keyboard. However, sometimes a more thorough cleaning is needed if dust and grime has gotten into the keyboard severely enough to cause a key to stick or not make proper contact when pressed. In these cases, you can clean the keyboard more deeply by removing individual key caps from keys exhibiting problems.

To remove the key caps, take a paper clip and bend it into a "U" shape. Bend the ends of the "U" inward so that they form small tabs. Slip the tabs under the key cap in question and gently pull upward. The key cap should release. (See Figure 21-16.) If it doesn't, do not force it, as this may damage the keyboard. Try removing adjacent key caps and then removing the stubborn one. Note that the spacebar is attached differently than other key caps in many cases, using a wire threaded along its

Figure 21-16
Removing a key cap
with a paper clip
bent into a "U"
shape.

length. You should only remove the spacebar if it is unresponsive and you have no other option but to try cleaning under it.

Once the key caps of any problem keys have been removed, tip the keyboard upside down and tap gently on its back. This should help dislodge any really stuck-on debris. Use a brush to remove as much debris as possible from the inside of the keyboard. Then take a can of compressed air and blow out any remaining dust or dirt.

After the keyboard has been cleaned, you can apply a small amount of electronics-grade contact cleaner to the key contacts (most electronics stores should carry this). Work the key to distribute the contact cleaner evenly. Give the cleaner a few minutes to dry completely, and then reattach the key caps.

Test the keyboard to ensure that cleaning the keyboard solved any problems. If not, the keyboard may be damaged or too worn from use or debris to function. If this is the case, it should be replaced.

Spills and Foreign Objects

While everyday dust and dirt poses an eventual threat to a keyboard if it isn't cleaned, foreign objects and spills pose an even greater and much more immediate threat. Should an object such as a staple or a paperclip fall into the keyboard, you will want to deal with it immediately. The same holds true for any liquid spilled on a keyboard.

Objects such as a staple or paperclip can easily jam a key if given the opportunity to get under a key cap. If they are metal, objects can also short out an individual key. If a metal object manages to work its way down to the keyboard's circuitry, it can do even more serious damage to the keyboard and possibly to the Mac itself. As soon as you've noticed that an object has fallen into the keyboard, immediate disconnect the keyboard (if it is not a USB keyboard, shut the Mac down first). If you can easily remove the object, do so. Otherwise, remove the key caps from keys near the object. Use needle-nose pliers or tweezers if necessary to remove the object.

Spills of any liquid are the biggest threat to a keyboard, and they need to be dealt with quickly and safely. As with a foreign object, disconnect the keyboard as soon as the spill has occurred. This will prevent any short that might be caused by the liquid from affecting the Mac itself.

The most common way spills are dealt with is to simply let the keyboard dry and begin using it again. This has two inherent problems. First, liquids such as soda or juice will become sticky once they dry, making the keyboard stick. Even liquids without sugar, such as tap water, can cause a keyboard to become tacky if it mixes with any dust or dirt.

The second problem is that many liquids, including most tap water, have trace minerals that are corrosive. These minerals can easily damage the contacts of the keyboard if left to dry for an extended period of time. The result will be that the keyboard will never be as responsive as it was before the spill, if it is functional at all.

To truly prevent a spill from damaging a keyboard, you should disassemble the keyboard (if possible) and remove the circuit board inside it. Rinse the circuit board in demineralized water as soon after the spill as possible. Clean the housing and keys of the keyboard separately. Allow both sections of the keyboard to dry completely on their own. Do not use a hair drier or other heating element to try and accelerate the drying process. Usually, it is a good idea to give the keyboard a full 24 hours to ensure it has dried completely.

If you can't disassemble the keyboard, you can thoroughly rinse the entire assembly in demineralized water, though I don't suggest this unless disassembling it is impossible. If you do raise the entire assembly, you should add additional drying time and perform the steps outlined in the preceding section, "More Thorough Cleaning," afterwards.

Once the keyboard is dry, you may want to apply a small amount of electronics-grade contact cleaner to the key switch of each key. Allow this to dry, and then reassemble the keyboard. Assuming the circuitry wasn't damaged in the initial spill, the keyboard should continue to work fine. If it experiences problems, you should replace it.

Troubleshooting Keyboards

Following are a few common problems and their solutions.

A Key Isn't Recognized when Typed

This symptom means that debris or dirt is preventing the key switch inside the keyboard from making contact properly. Clean beneath the individual key caps for affected keys as described earlier in this chapter. If this does not solve the problem, the keyboard is most likely damaged or worn out and should be replaced.

A Key Doesn't Release after It Is Pressed

This symptom means the key has become stuck. Again, the solution is to clean beneath the affected key caps as described earlier in this chapter.

The Mac Responds to Keystroke Extremely Slowly

Most likely this means that the Easy Access control panel is installed and is causing the Mac to recognize slow keystrokes. Disable Easy Access with the Extensions Manger.

The Mac Types a Letter Multiple Times When I Press a Key While Typing

Assuming that the key is releasing after you've pressed it and isn't sticking, this is caused by the Key Repeat Rate slider in the keyboard control panel being set too high for your typing style. Adjust the slider until it is more comfortable for your typing.

No Matter How Long I Hold Down a Key, the Mac Will Not Repeat the Character Onscreen

The Delay Until Repeat Slider in the Keyboard control panel is set to "Off." You can adjust the slider to turn this feature back on so that the delay before key repeats are comfortable for your typing style.

The Built-in Pointing Device of a Third-Party Keyboard Doesn't Work

Software drivers for the keyboard are probably not installed. Reinstall any software that came with the keyboard.

Strange Characters Not Matching Any Keys Are Displayed Whenever I Type

Open the Keyboard control panel and determine which keyboard layouts are being used. Chances are, you have inadvertently selected a foreign keyboard layout. Select only the layout appropriate to your country.

If the correct layout is being used, open the Key Caps desk accessory. Check to see if the Shift, Control, Option, or Command keys are highlighted in the display. If so, this indicates that the key which is highlighted is stuck. Clean under that particular key cap as described earlier in this chapter.

Resources for Further Study

The following URLs provide additional information on some of the concepts, issues, and products discussed in this chapter:

About.com Mac Hardware Keyboard and Pointing Devices Resources—http://machardware.about.com/msubmice-keyboard.htm

KeyAlt.com: Alternatives for Disabled Users—http://www.keyalt.com

22

Mice and Trackballs

When the Mac was introduced in 1984, it became the first commonly used computer to use a mouse as an input device. Since then, the mouse has become an integral part of computing, and no desktop computer today is sold without a mouse. In fact, the mouse (or a similar pointing device) is such an integral part of the Mac user experience that without a mouse, the ability to use the Mac is so severely limited you could consider it impossible. Still, the mouse is a device whose importance is often overlooked. This chapter looks at the mouse and the alternate pointing device most closely related to it, the trackball.

How Mice Function

A mouse is one of the simplest computer peripherals used today. It includes just a few basic components, including mechanical switches that are used in the mouse buttons, a hard rubber ball, a pair of mechanical or opto-mechanical sensors, and a circuit board designed to translate the information derived from the mechanical sensors or switches.

When the mouse is moved along a flat surface, the ball inside the mouse rolls. As the ball rolls, it turns rollers that are inside the mouse's case. Sensors that are connected to the rollers register this movement as a series of pulses. The faster the mouse is moved, the more pulses are generated. The circuit board inside the mouse is attached to the sensors and reads the amount and direction of the pulses as well as which sensor is generating them. This information is then sent along the mouse cable to the Mac, which translates the pulses into the actual movement of the mouse and moves the cursor on the screen appropriately. Figure 22-1 shows the components of the mouse.

In conventional mouse design, there are two types of sensors used: mechanical or opto-mechanical. These sensors work similarly. In a mouse with purely mechanical sensors, as the roller is moved by the mouse's ball, metal contacts on the roller would touch metal contacts in the mouse case (the sensors). When the contacts touched, an electrical contact was made and a pulse generated.

Opto-mechanical sensors are an advancement on the original mechanical sensors. In a mouse with opto-mechanical sensors, the rollers do not have electrical contacts. Rather, they have narrow slots. The sensors for the mouse shine a narrow beam of light from one side of the roller to the other. As the mouse ball moves the rollers, the slots allow light to pass, causing a pulse. When the slotted area of the roller moves across the sen-

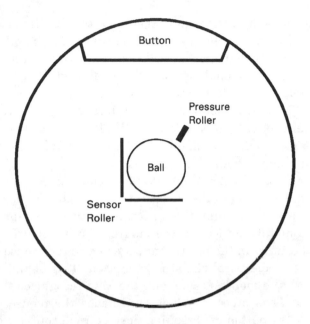

Figure 22-1
The mouse tracks movement by means of the mouse ball and the sensor rollers shown here.

sor, it blocks the light, ending a pulse. An opto-mechanical mouse should not be confused with the more recent optical mouse designs, which are covered later in this chapter and do not use a mouse ball at all.

Because both mechanical and opto-mechanical mice function the same way, they present one basic problem. As the mouse is used, it is rolled over various surfaces; dust, pet hair, skin oils, and other debris will be picked up by the rubber ball and pulled into the mouse. This debris will eventually collect on the rollers. As the rollers become coated with debris, the sensors (whether mechanical or opto-mechanical) will eventually have trouble generating pulses properly when the mouse is moved. This will result in jumpy or jerky behavior of the cursor on the screen, eventually leading to the cursor not registering mouse movement accurately or at all. This is an eventual effect of use for any mouse and is inevitable. Cleaning the mouse regularly, as described in the "Mouse Cleaning and Maintenance" section of this chapter, can help prolong the life of the mouse. Eventually, however, the debris will cause severe enough problems that continued cleaning may not help solve mouse problems and the mouse will need to be replaced. This is especially true if a mouse has not been cleaned properly over its life. Mice that use opto-mechanical sensors handle debris somewhat better than purely mechanical sensors, but the resulting mouse problems will eventually occur to both types of conventional mice.

In addition to the two rollers that work with the sensors to determine the movement of the mouse, there is a third roller that is not connected to a sensor. This roller is much narrower than the other two, and it may have a larger diameter as well. The third roller is a pressure roller and is attached to a small spring. It presses slightly against the mouse ball and helps ensure that the ball is held in proper orientation to the two sensor rollers. In addition to its difference in size, you can identify the pressure roller by its positioning. While the sensor rollers are positioned at a right angle to each other, the pressure roller is positioned at a different angle to both of them.

The mouse button (or buttons on some mice) is a basic mechanical switch. Underneath the surface of the button is a plastic bar that is held up by a spring. When the button is pressed, the spring is forced down where metal contacts on the mouse's circuit board are connected by a metal contact in the plastic bar attached to the mouse button. When this occurs, an electrical signal is generated. This signal is sent to the Mac through the mouse's cable, and the Mac recognizes that the mouse button has been pressed. When you release the mouse button, the spring pushes the button up, breaking the electrical contact. The signal that the button has been pressed is no longer sent to the Mac, which responds by acknowledging that you have released the mouse button. Figure 22-2 shows the construction of the mouse button.

Apple's Round USB Mouse

Apple's round USB mouse, shown in Figure 22-3, is probably the most unmouselike computer mouse ever created. It is completely round and about half the size of most mice. This mouse was included with both iMac and Power Mac computers (color-coordinated with the computer in question) and can be connected to any USB port on a Macintosh computer (including the PowerBook and iBook) or to a USB hub, such as the one built into the Mac's USB keyboard. Apple recently replaced the round mouse with a more traditionally-shaped optical mouse.

Apple's USB mouse includes only a single mouse button and is a very

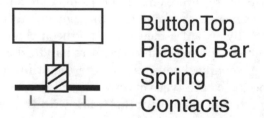

Figure 22-2
The components of
the mouse button.

ButtonTop
Plastic Bar
Spring
Contacts

Figure 22-3
Apple's round USB
mouse.

basic tool, despite its unusual shape and coloring. For traditional Mac use, Apple's mouse is quite adequate. With its smaller size, it is particularly well designed for the smaller hands of children. Adults, however, often complain that the mouse is too small and that its round shape allows it to become easily turned around in the user's hand. Responding to the second complaint, Apple released a newer version of the USB mouse not quite a year after its debut on the iMac. The second-generation mouse features a ridge in the mouse button, which is supposed to help users keep the mouse oriented properly. The new optical mouse responds to both complaints.

Some versions of Apple's round USB mice can be locked so that the retaining ring, which keeps the mouse ball inside the mouse, can't be removed. This feature may be useful for libraries, schools, or other places where Macs are used by a large number of people. To lock the mouse, you use a straightened out paper clip. First, remove the retaining ring. Insert the end of the paper clip into the small hole in the retaining ring as shown in Figure 22-4. With the paper clip inserted, press down through the hole and turn the ring clockwise to secure it. The mouse should now be locked, and you shouldn't be able to turn it counterclockwise to release the ring. To unlock the mouse, again insert the paper clip into the hole and press down on it. This time, turn the ring counterclockwise. The mouse should unlock, and the ring be released.

Figure 22-4
This hole, present on some of Apple's USB mice, allows you to lock the mouse shut.

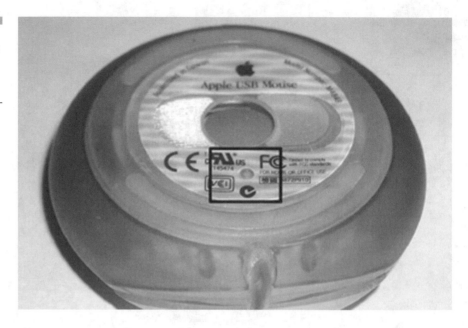

Figure 22-4
This hole, present on some of Apple's USB mice, allows you to lock the mouse shut.

Round Mouse Adapters   In response to complaints from users that Apple's round mouse was too great a departure from the traditional mouse shape, a few companies created round mouse adapters. These adapters are basically a plastic shell in the shape of a more traditional mouse. The forward end of the shell includes a round opening for Apple's USB mouse. The shell can be snapped onto the mouse, giving it the shape and feel of a more traditional mouse design, usually at a lower cost than buying a replacement mouse. The round mouse adapters are available in all of the common iMac colors. Figure 22-5 shows one such adapter.

Third-Party Mouse Options

A number of third-party USB mice are available for the Mac. In fact, after the complaints of many users about Apple's round USB mouse, providing more traditionally shaped alternative mouse options has become a fairly good-sized industry. The primary feature of these mice is that they have a more traditional shape and size, but many also offer some additional features, such as multiple mouse buttons, scrolling wheels, and an ergonomic design. In addition, a recent development is the fully optical mouse, which uses a completely new mouse construction. Each of these is discussed in the following sections.

Figure 22-5
The iCatch, one of
the round mouse
adapters on the mar-
ket. (Photo courtesy
of MacSense)

Although many USB mice are designed specifically for the Mac as replacements for the Apple USB mouse, there are also several USB mice on the market designed for use with Windows-based PCs. These mice will function on the Mac because USB and mouse construction are cross-platform. Any special features or additional buttons require a Macintosh driver (either developed specifically for the mouse or a universal Mac mouse driver, such as the shareware USB Overdrive) to function. Mice that use an interface other than USB, such as the PC serial or PS/2 ports, will not function on the Mac at all.

Multibutton Mice   Several mice for the Mac currently on the market have more than one button. In fact, most other computing platforms use two or three button mice by default. On the Mac these multibutton mice are usually designed so the extra buttons can be programmed to specific functions, usually a modifier key. For example, when you mouse-click in the Finder (and several other applications) while holding down the Control key, a contextual menu pops up, offering you various options for whatever item you clicked on. If you program the right button of a two-button mouse to be the equivalent of pressing the Control key and the mouse button, you can access contextual menus without using the keyboard.

The ability to program a multibutton mouse relies on the driver for the mouse. Often manufacturers will include a number of programmable options. How limited these options are depends on the manufacturer and the driver used. If no special driver is used or the additional button(s) are

Figure 22-6
A typical multibutton mouse.

not programmed to any specific function, pressing any of the buttons will function as a standard mouse click. Some mouse drivers allow button functions to be set on an application-by-application basis. Figure 22-6 shows a typical two-button Mac mouse.

Scrolling Mice   The scrolling mouse is a specially designed mouse that allows the user to scroll up or down through the contents of a window without having to move the cursor to the scroll bar on the right-hand side of the window. Instead, the user simply moves a small wheel that is set in the center of the mouse (usually between two mouse buttons, as shown in Figure 22-7). Moving the wheel away from the palm of the hand makes the active window scroll up, while moving it toward the palm makes it scroll down. Scrolling mice allow users to read a long text document or an entire webpage without having to break their concentration away from what they are reading to scroll down or even to use the Page Up and Page Down keys on the keyboard. The scrolling wheel in a scrolling mouse functions much the same as the rollers inside of the mouse. The difference is that instead of a ball moving the roller, the user's finger moves the wheel.

Ergonomic Mice   In the last chapter, you read about ergonomic keyboards and how they are designed to reduce repetitive strain on a user's hands and wrists, thereby reducing the chances of developing or aggra-

Figure 22-7
A mouse with a
scrolling wheel.

vating repetitive stress injuries. Keyboards are not the only input devices that can contribute to repetitive stress injury (RSI) conditions. The shape of a mouse and the way that the user's hand and wrist are held while using the mouse can also contribute to RSI conditions. To help alleviate this, several manufacturers have released ergonomically designed mice. These mice tend to be larger than traditional mice and have a greater slope in their shape (see Figure 22-8).

Also on the market are ergonomic mouse pads, which include a built-in wrist rest at the bottom edge of the mouse pad to support the user's wrist in the same way that wrist rests for a keyboard do. Similarly, you can avoid some RSI conditions with any mouse by placing it even with the keyboard and making certain that there is support for the wrist and that the wrist and arm are held as straight as possible while using the mouse.

Ergonomic concerns when using mice is also one of the factors that has contributed to the development of alternate pointing devices, such as trackballs and trackpads. Both of these tend to provide better hand and wrist support than a mouse. (We'll look at trackballs later in the chapter and trackpads in the next.)

Optical Mice

A fairly new entry into the mouse market is the fully optical mouse. Unlike traditional mice, an optical mouse contains no mouse ball and no

Figure 22-8
Some of the varia-
tions in shape used
in ergonomic mice.

Figure 22-9
Whereas a traditional
mouse has a ball, an
optical mouse has a
laser sensor.

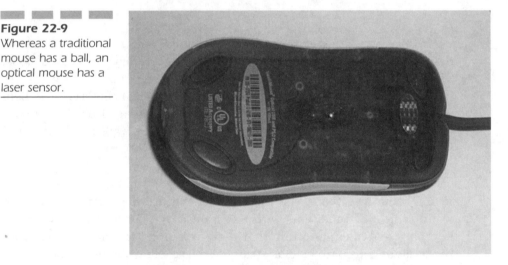

rollers. Instead, it relies on an optical sensor built into the bottom surface of the mouse, as illustrated in Figure 22-9. This sensor uses a beam
of laser light to continuously scan or take pictures of the surface beneath
the mouse at a rate of over 1000 scans (or pictures) per second. A special,
dedicated processor built into the mouse itself then compares each scan
to the next. The processor translates the differences in the scans into
movement and sends the mouse movement information via the mouse
cable to the Mac in the same way a traditional mouse sends pulses from

the movement of its rollers. The Mac reads this information the same way it would read the signals from a traditional mouse and responds by moving the cursor on the screen accordingly.

Optical mice offer a big advantage over traditional mice in that they do not need to be cleaned and are far less likely to ever wear out. The optical sensor of the mouse is recessed (sometimes under a clear plastic cover), and there are no mechanical components (except the buttons and scrolling wheel, if present). This means that there is no way for dust or dirt to get into the mouse. Also, because an optical mouse has no ball to roll, it can be used on a wider variety of surfaces than a traditional mouse and rarely requires a special surface such as a mouse pad for comfortable use.

Like traditional mice, optical mice come in a variety of styles and features. They do tend to have a higher price than traditional mice, though you should consider the longer life span of the mouse when looking at prices between a traditional and optical mouse. Apple's new standard mouse (see Figure 22-10) is an optical mouse.

Choosing a Replacement Mouse

Whether you're replacing Apple's USB mouse because you find it uncomfortable, because you want a mouse with more features, or because the mouse has reached the end of its life span (at least at two or three years if properly maintained) and simply needs to be replaced, you will find a plethora of options, with prices ranging from $15 to over $80. In addition to the wide range of prices are an equally wide range of sizes, shapes, features, and even colors. So, how do you choose?

First, consider your needs in a mouse. Do you experience repetitive stress problems that might warrant an ergonomically designed mouse? Will you take advantage of the ability to program one or two extra mouse buttons? Are you left-handed? (Some mice are designed for right-handed use only.) Ask yourself questions like these to narrow down the features that you either want or need in a mouse.

Next, consider your budget. How much are you really willing to spend on a mouse? Some mice are expensive, but that expense can come with powerful features or with a longer life span. After determining a price range, look at the mice available in that range that have the features you want. If possible, go to computer store and actually handle the mice. Finding out just what a mouse is going to feel like can be important, particularly with more expensive or more radically designed mice. Remember that you'll be handling this mouse for hours every day.

One consideration that many people overlook when choosing a mouse is the length of the mouse's cable. Look at this and remember that the shorter the cable, the smaller the range of motion you'll have with a mouse and the closer it will need to be to the USB port. This is a particular concern when choosing a mouse to use with an iBook very few mice include cables long enough to reach from the USB port on the left of the iBook to the table/desk space on the right of the iBook where most users would place the mouse. If you do choose a mouse with a cable that is too short, a USB extension cable can be an option for extending its length.

Also check for reviews of mice in Macintosh magazines or websites. Mice reviews don't get as much attention as upgrade card or drive reviews, but they can be valuable in determining if a mouse is solidly constructed, logically designed, and works well. They can also tell you if a mouse's driver software enables the level of programmability and features that you may want.

You may also want to consider alternative pointing devices. While the mouse was the first pointing device used on the Mac and is still the most common, several other options are available. These include trackballs (discussed later in this chapter), trackpads, and graphics tablets (both of which are looked at in the next chapter). You may find that one of these alternative pointing devices is more to your liking or is more comfortable for you. This may be particularly true if you suffer from chronic RSI conditions.

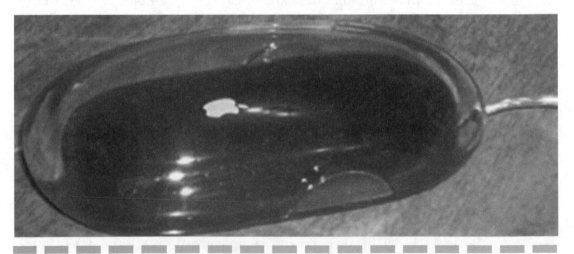

Figure 22-10   Apple's new standard, optical mouse.

Mouse Pads: Needed or Not?

Go into almost any store, even some supermarkets, and you'll probably see a rack of mouse pads. The mouse pad is usually a piece of foam or rubber with a coating of a synthetic fabric on it. The purpose of the mouse pad is to provide an even and consistent surface to run a mouse over. This surface offers enough resistance to the movement of the mouse to make using it easier and more comfortable than the smooth polished surface of a desk (and it keeps the mouse from leaving streaks or scratches on a desk's surface).

Mouse pads have been around for quite a while and became increasingly popular when companies began putting photos, cartoons, company logos, and just about any other image or design you can think of on them. This transformed a mouse pad from a bland single-colored utilitarian tool that often resembled a piece of an office cubicle into something that could express the user's personality, like a personalized coffee mug or a bumper sticker.

There are various opinions as to whether a mouse pad is necessary. My own opinion is that they may or may not be. On the one hand, many desks have surfaces that aren't conducive to comfortable mouse use. In this case, a mouse pad is extremely important. If your mouse moves well on your desk, however, then a mouse pad probably isn't needed. Some mouse pads offer built-in wrist rests, which are good for people who suffer from RSIs and can be used even if a mouse pad isn't really needed. If you're not sure whether your desk really needs a mouse pad, just try using the mouse without one. If the result is uncomfortable at all, run down to the nearest store and pick up a mouse pad with your favorite design.

Keep in mind that a mouse pad with a fabric surface will collect dust, hair, and skin oils more than the hard surface of a desk will. As the mouse is moved over the pad, that dust, hair, and skin oil will be picked up by the mouse ball and work its way into the mouse. For this reason, it is a good idea to buy a new mouse pad every few months.

Mouse Drivers

Like any other piece of hardware, a mouse needs driver software to control it. Apple has built a basic mouse driver into the Mac OS. This driver supports the basic Apple USB mouse and third-party USB mice, as well as many other types of pointing devices. It does not support any special features or more than one mouse button, however. This driver is primarily designed so that in any situation, a Mac user can continue using the Mac without any special software to use the mouse (which is needed for just about any function of the Mac OS). Apple's Mouse control panel allows users to interact with the mouse driver and adjust some very basic options of how the mouse behaves. Third-party mice may require additional driver software, specifically for additional mouse buttons or other features.

Apple's Mouse Control Panel   While Apple's mouse driver is built into the Mac OS, Apple also includes a control panel that allows users to refine the behavior of the mouse. This behavior controls how the Mac interprets the movement pulses generated by the mouse's rollers and how the Mac responds to the clicking of the mouse button. The Mouse control panel's window is shown in Figure 22-11 and contains two primary items: Mouse Tracking and Double-Click Speed. Portable Macs, such as the PowerBook and iBook, may include a third section called Mouse Tracks.

The Mouse Tracking section controls how the Mac responds to mouse movement. Essentially, it designates how quickly the cursor moves compared to the speed of the mouse's physical movement. When the slider is set to Very Slow, you can move the mouse as fast as possible across the entire area of your mouse pad, and the cursor will move about an inch

Figure 22-11
Apple's Mouse
Control Panel.

and a half on the screen. When the slider is set to Fast, you can move the mouse an inch on the mouse pad, and the cursor will move across the entire screen. You can use this slider to determine how responsive you want the cursor to be to your mouse movement.

The Double-Click Speed slider controls how quickly the Mac expects you to click on the mouse button to generate a double click (such as you would use for opening a file or folder). When the slider is all the way to the right, you must click the mouse button twice in extremely rapid succession to generate a double-click. Otherwise, the Mac responds to the clicks as two separate mouse events. When the slider is positioned all the way to the left, you must wait a moment or two between separate mouse clicks, or the Mac will interpret two separate clicks as a double click. If you have a very fast or slow mouse finger, you can use this slider to make the Mac respond appropriately to you. Most users, however, are quite fine using the default setting, which is the middle of the slider.

The Mouse Tracks section of the control panel is not included on all Macs. It dates back to the time when PowerBooks used lower-quality, passive matrix LCD screens. When using these screens, the cursor often had a tendency to disappear if moved too quickly or to be very hard to see when in its text-insertion "I-beam" form. The Mouse Tracks slider allows you to turn on a tracking or ghosting effect, where slightly faded ghost images of the cursor follow it around when it is in its pointer form. On the LCD screens of older PowerBooks (and possibly on some current Mac displays), this could make locating the cursor easier. Selecting the Thick I-beam checkbox makes the text-insertion form of the cursor twice as thick as it normally is. This makes locating the I-beam cursor easier in a large text document.

Drivers for Specific Third-Party Mice Most third-party USB mice include special features, such as multiple buttons or a scrolling wheel. While Apple's built-in mouse driver will recognize such mice when they are connected to the Mac, it will not enable these features, which are often designed specifically for a given mouse. For this reason, most third-party USB mice require a mouse driver. The exception is third-party mice that have only a single button and are the same basic type of mouse as the Apple USB mouse but in a more conventional and less round shape.

The drivers used for various third-party mice are usually designed by the manufacturer and allow features such as additional buttons to be programmed. Such drivers are usually (though not always) written as control panels. The control panel provides an interface for users to assign modifier keys or specific keystrokes to a mouse button. This interface varies

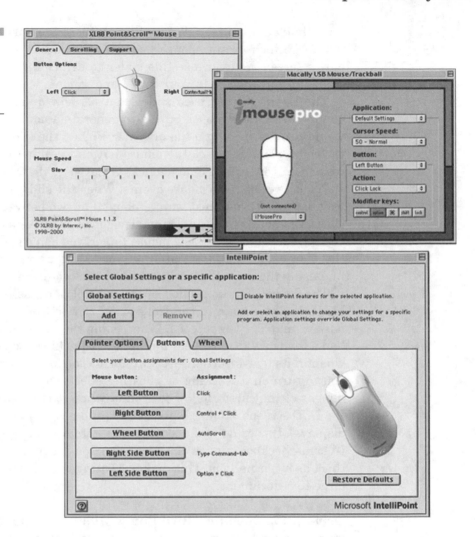

Figure 22-12
Third-party mouse drivers have varying interfaces such as these.

from mouse to mouse and may require users to select from a predefined list of programming options, or it may allow users to choose any modifier keys or keystrokes they wish. Several mouse drivers will even allow users to assign mouse button functions on an application-by-application basis. Figure 22-12 shows some third-party mouse control panel interfaces.

USB Overdrive, the Universal Mouse Driver One of the problems with using third-party mice is that each mouse needs its own driver software. Often these drivers conflict with each other, and users are advised to disable the extensions or control panels for one mouse when installing the software for another. This presents a problem if you want to quickly and easily switch between different mice. And for some mice not designed for Mac use, there are no drivers to enable additional buttons or other features. For these situations, having a single universal mouse driver would be useful, one that was capable of being used for all kinds of USB mice and enabling any possible features or buttons that they might have.

Although the idea of a universal mouse driver might seem far off or unlikely, thanks to a man named Alessandro Levi Montalcini, it is something that actually exists. Montalcini is the creator and developer of a piece of shareware called USB Overdrive. USB Overdrive is a combination of a control panel (see Figure 22-13) and various extensions that functions as a universal USB mouse driver (and a universal USB joystick driver as well) for any USB mouse out there. Amazingly, the shareware fee for USB Overdrive is a scant $20.

USB Overdrive is designed to enable and configure a mouse (or a mouselike pointing device) with up to five buttons and a scrolling wheel. The assignments of individual buttons can be made on a per application basis and can include anything from a simple mouse click to a full-fledged macro and just about anything in between. It also allows users to define a mouse's tracking speed on a per application basis—something very useful to graphic designers who would like very fine mouse movement and control in Photoshop or Illustrator but want much quicker mouse movement in the Finder or a web browser.

Figure 22-13
The USB Overdrive
control panel.

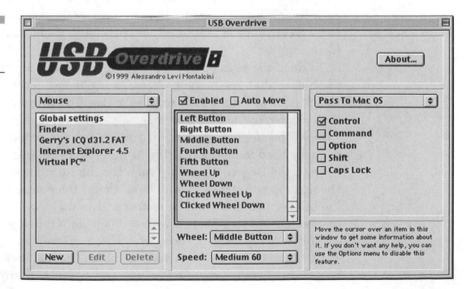

Using Multiple Mice/Pointing Devices

Because USB supports such a wide variety of devices and can recognize over 100 devices simultaneously, it is possible to attach more than one mouse or a mouse and other pointing devices at once. The Mac will recognize and accept input from each of them. However, if you do have more than one pointing device attached, you should only use one of them at a time. If you try to use two mice at the same time, the Mac will not know which one to pay attention to and will try to make sense of the signals coming from both mice simultaneously. While this probably won't do any harm to the Mac, it will result in the cursor moving extremely erratically (usually not in the direction being indicated by either mouse).

Mouse Cleaning and Maintenance

The mouse may be the simplest peripheral out there for the Mac in terms of electronics and construction, but it is also (with the exception of optical mice) the one that needs the most attention with regard to maintenance and cleaning. You should clean your mouse often, at least once a month, to keep it in good working condition. If, when using the mouse, you find that the cursor seems to be jumping a lot or not moving reliably, clean the mouse as soon as is feasible. Fortunately, cleaning the mouse is a relatively easy process. In most cases, you should disconnect the mouse from the computer before cleaning it, because (1) it prevents any feedback from reaching and possibly damaging the computer and (2) it gives you a freer range of motion, since the mouse cable will not be tethered to the computer.

To clean the mouse, first remove the retaining ring on the underside of the mouse that keeps the ball inside the mouse, shown in Figure 22-14. This is done by rotating the ring clockwise. The ring will usually have grips that you can use to turn it more easily. Once rotated about half a turn, the ring will release and come off. If you are using a round Apple USB mouse, you may need to unlock the ring as described earlier in this chapter.

Once the ring is off, simply turn the mouse right side up, and the ball should drop out of it (keep one hand under the mouse to catch the ball). If the ball seems stuck, give the mouse a little shake to free the ball. Once the ball is free, you can clean it with a damp cloth or warm water. Use a lint-free towel to dry the ball thoroughly before reinserting it into the mouse.

Once the ball is cleaned, you can clean the inside of the mouse. First, use a can of compressed air (which you can get in any electronics store

Figure 22-14

Figure 22-14
The retaining ring
must be removed to
clean a mouse's ball
and rollers.

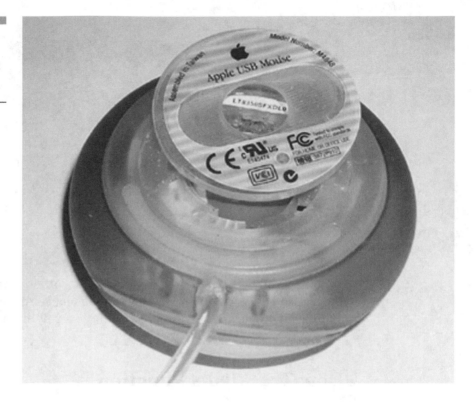

and most office supply stores) to blow out any accumulated dust inside the mouse. You may want to do this outdoors, as the dust will spray out of the mouse in multiple directions.

Next, clean off the three rollers. The rollers inside a mouse are not supposed to look like they have little rubber bands in the middle of them. Figure 22-15 shows what dirty mouse rollers look like and how they should look after cleaning. This is the accumulated dust and dirt, which builds up in little bands around the center of each roller. Use a cotton swab dipped in (but not dripping with) rubbing (isopropyl) alcohol to clean off the rollers. If the accumulated dirt is extremely stubborn, you can try picking a bit of it off with a toothpick or tweezers, but do so very carefully and gently to avoid damaging the rollers.

If you used rubbing alcohol to clean the rollers, give it a few minutes to dry thoroughly. Also give the mouse ball a few minutes to be sure it is completely dry. Then, reassemble the mouse and test it to see if it functions properly. If not, the mouse may be damaged and may need to be replaced.

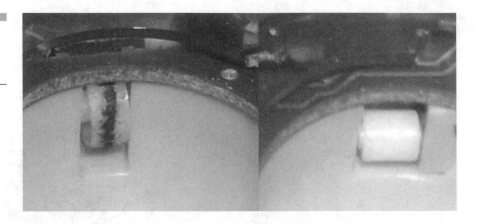

Figure 22-15
Left: Dirty mouse
rollers. Right: Clean
mouse rollers.

You should not use any cleaning materials other than warm water for the mouse ball and rubbing alcohol for the mouse rollers. Other cleaning agents may contain solvents that can severely damage or destroy a mouse.

How Trackballs Function

The trackball, as in Figure 22-16, is a very close cousin to the mouse with regard to construction and function. A trackball is, in essence, an upside-down mouse. The circuit board, rollers, and sensors that are used in a mouse to generate the signals that tell the Mac which way to move the pointer are virtually identical to those used in a trackball. The difference is that while a mouse is moved around on a flat surface, with the ball being rolled as a result of the movement of the mouse's case, a trackball is stationary, with the user moving the ball itself with his or her fingers.

The ball is situated on the intersection of a series of rails or tracks. These tracks hold the ball suspended and just touching the rollers enough to turn them when the ball is moved by the user. Figure 22-17 shows a diagram of trackball construction. Without being suspended slightly by these tracks, the ball would rest directly on the rollers, or between the rollers, and its weight might make moving the rollers difficult or impossible. The rollers are, of course, connected to sensors of the same type used in a mouse. The button or buttons of a trackball are mounted on the outside of the case. Where exactly the buttons are located depends on the design of the trackball in question. Usually they are mounted someplace within easy reach of the user's thumb or fingers.

Figure 22-16
A typical trackball.

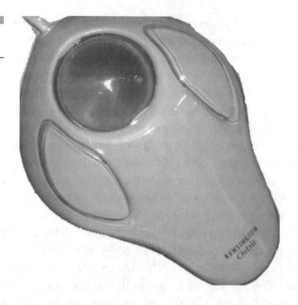

Figure 22-17
Trackball construction
is very similar to
mouse construction.

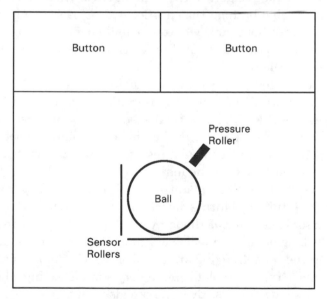

Why Use a Trackball?

Trackballs are not nearly as popular as mice; however, they do have some
advantages. One big advantage is that they are stationary devices that
do not require much additional desk space to use. A mouse, on the other
hand, may require an area of over a square foot in order to traverse the

entire display of a screen. Trackballs are also self-contained devices, which means they can be (and have been) incorporated into laptop computers and keyboards that have built-in pointing devices. In addition, hand positioning on a trackball is relatively stationary and more ergonomically sound than a mouse. This makes them popular with users who suffer from RSIs that may be aggravated by mouse use.

Trackballs come in any manner of shapes and sizes, from the marble-sized trackballs that served as the built-in pointing devices for older PowerBook models (circa 1993 and earlier) to the softball-sized trackballs that are available from a number of manufacturers. Each size of trackball offers the user different advantages and may be designed for different fingering when in use. Some trackballs are slightly larger than a marble and are designed to be moved by the user's thumb, while the two or three buttons available are located on a hand-shaped pedestal/case under which the index and middle fingers rest. Other trackballs are the size of a baseball and are designed to be moved by the three middle fingers of the hand at once. These may have up to four programmable buttons that are located at each corner of a square-shaped case, with the primary button usually being assigned to where the user's thumb is positioned. Still other trackballs fill the range between these two extremes.

You'll notice that most trackballs have at least two buttons and may have upwards of four. This is a further advantage of trackball design. Because the entire trackball assembly doesn't rest under the hand as a mouse does, it isn't as limited in the amount of space that can be made available for buttons. As a result, several trackballs offer more programmable buttons that the majority of mice could.

One common complaint with trackballs is that they are probably the least intuitive pointing devices on the market. With a mouse, moving the cursor feels much as though you are physically moving it with your hand. Clicking on an icon feels very much like physically tapping it, and clicking and then dragging an item feels much like physically dragging something. Graphics tablets offer a very similar feeling when used as pointing or drawing devices. Even trackpads tend to have a similar intuitive feel because you are moving your finger across the pad.

Trackballs are different. You feel more as though you are moving a ball and not touching an item onscreen. The trackball requires that you continually reposition your hand or fingers to keep the ball moving. And for some trackballs, clicking a button may very well involve releasing the ball entirely. This can make trackball use seem uncomfortable and clumsy, at least at first, to many users.

Multibutton Trackballs   With the exception of trackballs that are built into the case of older PowerBooks, most trackballs you buy will have at least two buttons. Others have four or more buttons, each one of them programmable. While being able to program all of these buttons is very nice, keep in mind that with more than two buttons, remembering which item is assigned to which button may prove difficult, especially if someone should accidentally (or deliberately, as a joke) turn the trackball around. Also, not all the buttons will be as comfortable or easy to access as the primary buttons.

Trackball Maintenance

As with its close cousin the mouse, maintenance for a trackball consists primarily of cleaning out dirt and dust that has worked its way inside the case underneath the ball. In some ways, trackballs are less prone to dust and dirt problems than a mouse because they are not rolled over a dust-collecting surface such as a desk or mouse pad. On other hand, they do easily pick up any oil or dirt that may be on a user's fingers and hands. Again, regular cleanings are important to keep a trackball functioning at its best. Avoid using the trackball when your hands are dirty or covered with salt, sugar, or similar material from snack foods (the orange residue from eating Chee-tos comes immediately to mind).

As with a mouse, before cleaning you should disconnect the trackball from the computer, if possible. If the trackball is built into the keyboard, then disconnect the keyboard. If the trackball is in an older PowerBook, you should disconnect the PowerBook's AC adapter and remove the battery.

The trackball uses a retaining ring to hold it in place, just as a mouse does. The difference is that the ring is on the top of the case rather than on the underside. You may need to apply more downward pressure to get the retaining ring of a trackball to release than you would with the ring of a mouse. Also, there will probably not be any grips on the ring to help you release it. Once the ring is released, tilt the trackball case (or keyboard or PowerBook) to one side to release the ball itself.

From this point on, cleaning a trackball is essentially the same process as cleaning a mouse. Gently clean the ball in warm water and dry with a lint-free towel. Blow out the entire enclosure using a can of compressed air. Clean the three rollers inside the trackball. Let dry and then reassemble. Refer to the earlier section on mouse cleaning for more details.

Troubleshooting Mice and Trackballs

Following are some common problems with mice and trackballs, along with their solutions.

The Mouse or Trackball Jumps or Responds Erratically

If this occurs, the rollers of the mouse or trackball most likely need to be cleaned as described in the previous section and earlier in the chapter. It is also possible, though less likely, that the mouse or trackball's cable is damaged or loose. This behavior can also occur if the Mac is performing one or more extremely processor-intensive tasks, though this is fairly rare on today's Macs. If this is the case, the erratic behavior will end when the task is completed.

The Mouse or Trackball Doesn't Respond at All

In this case, first, be certain that the Mac hasn't frozen completely by trying to switch applications or enter data using the keyboard. If the Mac has frozen, you will need to force it to restart. Assuming the Mac hasn't frozen, check to be certain that the mouse or trackball is plugged into the Mac. If it is plugged into a USB hub, check to be sure that the hub is powered (if the hub uses its own power supply) and connected to the Mac. Also check to see if the cable of the mouse or trackball is broken or damaged at any point.

If the mouse or trackball is plugged in properly, try cleaning it as described earlier in this chapter. If this does not solve the problem, the mouse or trackball is most likely damaged severely and should be replaced.

The Mouse or Trackball Moves Too Slowly or Too Quickly

If this is the case, the mouse's movement can be adjusted in the Mouse control panel as described earlier in this chapter. Several third-party mice and trackballs can also have their tracking speeds adjusted using the control panels that are installed with them as driver software.

The Scrolling Wheel of a Scrolling Mouse Isn't Recognized, or Additional Buttons of a Multibutton Mouse Aren't Recognized

Additional features such as programmable buttons and scrolling wheels require that the driver software for a mouse or trackball be installed and configured properly. If it is not, the scrolling wheel and additional buttons will simply be treated as basic mouse clicks from a one-button mouse by the Mac. Use the control panel installed as part of the mouse driver to program additional buttons and to configure a scrolling wheel. The documentation that accompanied the mouse or trackball should include specific information on what options are available and how to configure them.

If adjusting the settings of the control panel doesn't help, reinstall the driver software as you did when first installing the mouse or trackball. Also, be certain that there are no drivers for other third-party mouse or trackball installed, since mouse drivers have a tendency to conflict with each other, rendering the additional features inaccessible. If you wish to use multiple types of third-party mice, consider using a universal driver, such as USB Overdrive.

Resource for Further Study

The following URLs provide additional information on some of the concepts, issues, and products discussed in this chapter:

USB Overdrive Homepage—http://www.usboverdrive.com

About.com Mac Hardware Keyboard and Pointing Devices Resources— http://machardware.about.com/msubmice-keyboard.htm

About.com Computer Peripherals Mouse Resources— http://peripherals.about.com/msub_mouse.htm

About.com Computer Peripherals Input Devices Resources— http://peripherals.about.com/msub_track.htm

23

Graphics Tablets and Trackpads

Along with mice and trackballs, discussed in the last chapter, trackpads and graphics tablets make up the major types of pointing devices commonly used with Macintosh computers. Although trackpads and graphics tablets may seem very different when you first see them, these two device categories are extremely similar in the type of technology used and how they function. This chapter looks at how the hardware of these devices work, as well as how to get the most performance out of a trackpad or graphics tablet.

How Graphics Tablets Work

From a user's perspective, using a graphics tablet, such as the one shown in Figure 23-1, is much like using a pen to draw or write on a piece of paper. This is one of the benefits of a graphics tablet for professional artists and designers migrating from use of drawing or painting tools in the physical world to graphics and illustrating applications for creating or modifying digital artwork. Essentially, a graphics tablet is a large flat surface (the tablet) on which the user moves a special pen, often called a stylus. As the user moves the stylus over the tablet, the cursor on the Mac's screen moves accordingly. Position the tip of the stylus on the upper right-hand corner of the tablet, and the Mac moves the cursor to the upper right-hand corner of the screen. Move the stylus in a circle in

Figure 23-1
A typical graphics tablet.

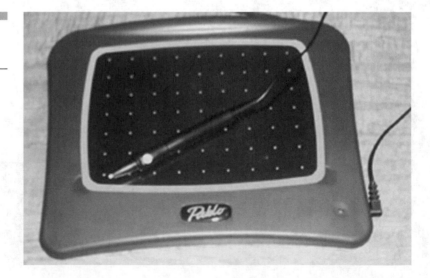

the middle of the tablet, and the Mac moves the cursor in a circle in the middle of the screen.

Graphics tablets offer digital artists and graphic designers a more life-like feel to the projects they are working on in programs like Adobe Illustrator. And most tablets go beyond simply moving the pointer according to where the stylus is placed. Most can also sense the pressure of the stylus against the surface of the tablet and the angle at which the stylus is held in relation to the tablet. This allows a graphics program that can accept such data to respond accordingly, making a line darker on-screen when pressure is applied to the stylus, as a pencil would produce a darker line on paper when pressed harder. Similarly, brushes in a graphics program can react differently in relation to the angle of the stylus the same way holding a brush at varying angles against a physical canvas would create lines of varying widths or shapes.

Beyond their graphics use, tablets can be used as a general pointing device in place of a mouse. In this respect, they can be useful for users that experience pains from repetitive stress injury induced from using a mouse as their pointing device. Tablets can also be easier to get used to than some of the other pointing device options, such as a trackball, because they are more intuitive to users in that they function like drawing on a piece of paper.

Digitizing Hardware

At the heart of a graphics tablet is the digitizing hardware. This is the hardware built into the tablet that determines where a stylus is in relation to the physical surface area of the tablet. It is also the hardware that determines how much pressure is being exerted by the user on the stylus and the angle at which the stylus is striking the tablet.

Digitizing hardware basically divides the surface area of the tablet up into rows and columns, much like the grid lines of a map. Each row is numbered, providing an X-coordinate for each point on the tablet. Each column is also numbered, providing an Y-coordinate for each point on the tablet. The tablet is designed to allow it to detect when the stylus is positioned in a particular row or column. The circuit board built into the tablet tracks at what coordinates on the of "map" of the tablet's surface the stylus is located. As the coordinates of the stylus's position change, the coordinates are sent to the Mac. The drivers for the tablet installed on the Mac translate this coordinate data into cursor movement on the Mac's screen, and the Mac moves the cursor accordingly.

Tablets often also include a button either on the tablet itself or on the stylus. This button functions like a mouse button when pressed. In addition to the button, many tablets that can sense the degree of pressure being exerted on the stylus will respond to a certain amount of pressure as though it were a mouse click. These tablets usually allow the user to determine how much pressure is needed through a control panel interface.

While all digitizing hardware functions like this, there have been three primary types of digitizing hardware used in various graphics tablets over the years. Each type has led to progressively more accurate technology and introduced new features into the graphics tablet industry (such as pressure and angle sensitivity). The following is a brief overview of these three types of technology.

Resistive Digitizers   Resistive digitizers are found only in older graphics tablets. Resistive digitizers place a conductive film over a protective covering (such as glass). The tablet will then place the top edge at a slightly different voltage than the bottom edge. The stylus carries a voltage back to a converter that reads the voltage and determines how far up or down the tablet the stylus is placed, providing an X-coordinate. The same process is performed with the left and right edges of the tablet, which provides a Y-coordinate for the stylus's location. This is called a *single-layer resistive digitizer* and requires the stylus be connected or tethered to the tablet by a cable through which it transmits the voltage at its position. There is also a similar technique known as a *double-layer resistance digitizer*. It functions essentially the same, with a gradient of voltage between the upper and lower left and right edges determining the location of the stylus. However, the stylus itself isn't used to transmit the voltage levels at its location. Instead, a second conductive surface is overlaid with the first one. The stylus then presses the surfaces against each other when it contacts the tablet. The second conductive layer then transmits the voltage levels to the converter instead of the stylus. This allows for a stylus that doesn't need to be connected or tethered to the tablet. In fact, a stylus isn't really needed because any object capable of pushing the two layers together at a specific point will work, even a finger.

Resistive digitizers are crude by today's standards because they don't offer any ability to determine stylus pressure or angle. They are also limited in how many individual rows and columns they can divide a tablet's surface into, meaning that movement on-screen is less precise than with other digitizers.

Capacitive Digitizers   Capacitive digitizers, sometimes also called electrostatic digitizers, mark the second generation of digitizer technology and are still used today. Capacitive digitizer tablets contain a protective layer (generally glass) bonded to a conductive film. The hardware of the tablet generates a low-power, high-frequency electrical signal that is transmitted through the tip of the tablet's stylus (which must be tethered to the tablet by a cable). When the stylus is placed on or near the surface of the tablet, the conductive film in the tablet picks up the signal being transmitted from the tip of the stylus. The strength of the signal picked up by the conductive film is dependent on the position of the pen, which allows the circuitry of the tablet to determine X- and Y-coordinates for the stylus based on the relative strength of the signal to each edge of the tablet. The signal strength from the stylus is also dependent on how close the tip of the stylus is to any area of the conductive film. This means that if the tip is pressed closer to the film, the signal received will be slightly stronger than if it is just resting on the surface of the tablet. This allows the digitizer to determine the pressure of the stylus against the tablet.

Finally, as the angle of the stylus's tip to the conductive film changes, so does the pattern of the signals received by the film. Using the changes generated in these patterns, the tablet can also extrapolate changes in the positioning of the stylus's tip. This allows it to accurately respond to changes in the angle of the stylus, giving a capacitive digitizing tablet all the abilities used by graphic artists in a modern graphics tablet.

Electromagnetic Digitizers   Electromagnetic or RF digitizing graphics tablets are the most powerful tablets currently available. Electromagnetic tablets consist of five-layer PC boards. Four layers of PC board are devoted to detecting stylus position and motion (two to each direction, horizontal or vertical). Each of these layers has an intricate pattern of sensing coils etched into it, with actual design and pattern varying between tablet models and manufacturers. These sensor boards are designed to actively pick up a low-power, high-frequency electromagnetic signal generated by the stylus. The fifth board layer is used to absorb any excess signal and prevent it interfering with the circuitry of the tablet or nearby devices. When the signal from the stylus is detected, the sensor board layers actively scan the tablet's entire sensing surface for the signal from the stylus and the strength of the signal.

This allows for greater accuracy and tracking performance than any other kind of tablet. Also, because the stylus's signal is so low power and is generated in the stylus itself, it can be powered using a battery and does not need to be tethered to the tablet by a cable (as capacitive tablets require). Because there are multiple layers of sensor board, the tablet can also interpret the pressure of the stylus tip and the angle of the stylus with very good accuracy.

Graphics Tablet Resolution

The number of individual rows and columns a graphics tablet uses to detect the position of a stylus determines how accurate the movement of the cursor on the Mac's screen will be when the stylus is moved. The more rows and columns in the tablet, particularly in each square inch of surface area, the more accurate the movement of the cursor will be. The measure of how many rows and columns are built into the tablet can be referred to as the tablet's *resolution*.

In many ways, a tablet's resolution will be described similarly to that of a monitor, being a set number of lines wide by a set number of lines or sensing points high. Or, sometimes resolution may be expressed as with a printer, giving you the number of lines per inch. By looking at the resolution of the tablet, you can determine how accurate it is compared to other tablets.

The resolution of a graphics tablet is important because, unlike any other pointing device for the Mac, a graphics tablet has a finite movement area. Each point on the tablet corresponds to a point on the screen. With a mouse, trackball, and even a trackpad this isn't the case. If you run out of mousing surface, you just pick the mouse up and set it down more in the middle of your mouse pad and continue moving the mouse in the direction you were moving it when you ran out of space. If you're using a trackpad and your finger gets to the edge of the trackpad, you just pick up your finger and put it down elsewhere on the trackpad and continue moving it in the direction you were.

Since a graphics tablet maps the entire area of the Mac's screen onto its surface, the resolution of the tablet is important in determining the precision of the cursor's movement on-screen. If you place the stylus in between the lines of a tablet's sensing grid, the Mac will either need to estimate the location of the stylus or use the location of the nearest sensing point. This is usually fine for using a tablet as a mouse because even the cheapest tablets have enough resolution to emulate a mouse. For very fine, one- or two-pixel movement in a graphics application, however, estimating the location of a stylus just may not be good enough. Look at the resolution of a tablet when considering them for professional graphics work and consider just how accurate your work tends to be. If you aren't sure based on the resolution of a tablet whether it will be accurate enough, go to a computer store and try using it. Or, if trying it out isn't an option, read reviews of the tablets you're considering (and buy from a store or catalog with a good return policy, just in case).

Graphics Tablet Interfaces

Graphics tablets have been around for several years and have come in a variety of interfaces for use with the Mac. The primary three have been the ADB and serial ports of older Macs and the USB ports of today's Macintosh models.

ADB ADB was the primary interface for input devices on virtually all Macs before the iMac. The earlier graphics tablets used ADB as their interface because it was a standard for devices such as mice or track-balls. Unfortunately, once graphics tablets began including higher resolutions and features like pressure sensitivity or detection of the stylus's angle, there was too much data to be transferred to the Mac through the very limited ADB interface. As a result, only older and feature-limited tablets have used ADB as an interface.

In the unlikely event that you need to use one of these tablets today, you may be able to use them by purchasing an ADB-to-USB adapter. However, it would probably be a better choice to opt for a new low-end USB tablet, as you will not need to spend much more money and you will enjoy better performance, accuracy, and features. If you are using the Blue and White Power Mac G3, you can connect an ADB tablet directly, because these computers do include an ADB port (making them the only Macs covered by this book that do).

Serial Port Following the need for an interface that provided better data throughput than the ADB port, graphics tablet manufacturers began using the Mac's serial port. The serial port offered much greater through-put than the ADB port, which made it an optimal choice. A large majority of tablets have used the serial port as an interface, and some are still being produced today. As a rule, most graphics tablets that use a serial port interface will function with a serial-port-to-USB adapter or with the serial port cards on the market for current Macs (see Chapter 30 for details about such products). You should check with the manufacturer of the adapter/card to see if compatibility for your specific graphics tablet has been verified, however.

USB   Most graphics tablets today use a USB interface. This enables them to be used with all of the current Macs without problems. If it is at all possible, you should opt to use a USB tablet because of USB's native support on the current Macs. USB also provides enough data throughput that it is unlikely there will be a need in the foreseeable future for tablet manufacturers to stop using the USB interface. USB's cross-platform standardization also makes developing new tablets and features easier and less expensive for manufacturers, because the same hardware can be used with Mac and Windows-based computers.

Graphics Tablet Software

Like any piece of hardware, a graphics tablet needs driver software for the Mac to be able to recognize and use it properly. However, unlike many pieces of hardware, graphics tablets often also need special software for all of their features to be fully enabled in a graphics application. Because of the software needed for the Mac to interact fully with a tablet, you need to buy a tablet that explicitly supports the Mac platform. This is another respect in which tablets are different from mice or other input devices, where the Mac OS includes built-in generic drivers that will recognize the device even if it isn't designed specifically for the Mac.

Control Panels and Drivers   At the basic level, a tablet requires driver software that tells the Mac how to interpret the information it gathers from the placement, angle, and pressure of the stylus. The generic mouse drivers built into the Mac OS may or may not provide enough support for the tablet to be used for basic mouse use. The tablet should come with whatever driver software it needs, and this should be installed prior to connecting the tablet.

Some tablets include a control panel that allows the user to configure some global options. These options determine how the tablet performs in any and all applications. One common such feature is whether or not the Mac will respond to pressure of the stylus against the tablet as the click of a mouse button and, if so, how much pressure is required to qualify as a mouse click. Some tablets may be able to be configured on an application-by-application basis. Figure 23-2 shows the control panel for the consumer-level Pablo graphics tablet.

Plug-ins   Many graphics applications can make special use of the stylus pressure and angle information transmitted by a graphics tablet. More pressure can mean for a line to be drawn darker or a blur to be

Figure 23-2
The control panel interface for the consumer Pablo graphics tablet.

applied more opaquely. The angle of the stylus can determine which brush the program uses to draw a line. For this to be accomplished, the graphics program needs to have some way of understanding the information transmitted by the tablet and to know how to respond to that information. Since it would be unwieldy, if not impossible, for the developers of graphics applications to include instructions on how to deal with each and every possible tablet on the market, many tablet manufacturers use plug-ins to accomplish this task.

A plug-in is a file that is stored in a special folder for the graphics application. When the application is launched, it reads each plug-in file in the folder and adds the features that are coded into the plug-in files to the application's abilities. This allows developers to create any manner of plug-ins that extend an application to recognize additional hardware (such as a tablet), recognize additional graphics file formats, and add brushes or effects to the application's pallet of features.

Plug-ins are often written to be specific to a given application. Other applications may copy the plug-in architecture of a popular graphics program, such as Photoshop, which allows them to recognize and use plug-ins intended for use with the original program. A graphics tablet will usually ship with plug-ins for one or two popular graphics applications to make use of additional features. These plug-ins may be updated from time to time, and you can check the manufacturer's website periodically to see what new features have been added to the plug-in or what bugs have been fixed in an update.

Graphics Tablet Maintenance

As a rule, the only real maintenance for a graphics tablet you need to perform is to clean any dust, dirt, or other debris off of it. This can be accomplished using a soft, damp cloth. Do not use any detergents or soaps, as these may contain solvents or other chemicals that can damage the tablet. Make sure the tablet is unplugged from the computer before cleaning. If the tablet uses a battery as a power source or if the stylus requires a battery, remove this before cleaning as well. Once clean, allow the tablet to dry thoroughly before using it again.

If the tablet or stylus uses a battery, you may also want to check the charge of the battery on a periodic basis. The amount of electricity used by a tablet or stylus, however, is small enough that this usually isn't needed. However, you should always keep a second battery on hand in case the battery does begin to wear out and need replacing.

How Trackpads Work

PowerBook and iBook users will be most familiar with the trackpad, as it is the primary pointing device for these computers. The trackpad is a square pad, usually with a button under it. When you place your finger on the pad and move it, the cursor on the screen moves in the same direction. The faster you move your finger, the faster the cursor moves. If your finger runs off the edge of the trackpad, you simply put it back on the trackpad and continue moving it in the direction your were moving it, just as you pick up a mouse if you were about to run off the edge of your mousepad.

Capacitive Digitizing Trackpads

The trackpads used in the PowerBooks and the iBook use a variation on the capacitive digitizing technology described earlier in this chapter. The trackpad consists of two layers of electrodes. One layer is placed in horizontal rows, and the other is placed in vertical columns along the surface of the trackpad. Special circuitry mounted to these grids of electrodes measures the mutual capacitance between each electrode and the one next to it. When your finger comes close enough to two electrodes in the trackpad, it changes the mutual capacitance between them. The circuits built into the trackpad detect this change and track the changes that are caused by your finger as it moves across the trackpad. This information is then sent to the Mac's motherboard, where the Mac processes it in much the same way it would the information provided by a mouse or other input device.

Why a Trackpad Doesn't Work When Wet   Anyone who's used a trackpad for any length of time will have noticed that if you touch it while your fingers are damp (with water or sweat), the cursor won't track properly. Instead, it will jump back around a bit but stay in about the same place. This is because the water affects the change in capacitance generated by your fingers between the electrodes in the trackpad. The trackpad senses your fingers and their motion, but the water interferes with the process and keeps your finger movements from tracking properly.

The easiest solution is not to use a trackpad while your fingers are damp or wet or to dry them if they become damp. Another solution that some PowerBook users have espoused in placing a single-ply paper towel evenly across the trackpad. This absorbs dampness and is often thin enough to still transmit the motion of your fingers to the trackpad.

Using Two Fingers with a Trackpad   Like using a trackpad when your hands are damp, placing two fingers on the trackpad will cause it to not track properly. This is because the trackpad will be trying to track both fingers simultaneously. As a result, the cursor will jump between positions on-screen relative to the locations of each of your fingers on the trackpad. Obviously, this means you should only use one finger to operate the trackpad.

There is a use for two fingers on the trackpad, however. If you need to move the cursor from one side of the screen to the other, you can place one finger on one edge of the trackpad, hold it there, place a second finger at the opposite edge, and then release the first finger. This will cause the cursor to jump from its initial position to one that is almost on the opposite edge of the screen.

Tapping the Trackpad   All PowerBooks (and the iBook) that have used built-in trackpads have included a feature known as the tappable trackpad (the only exception was the first PowerBook to use a trackpad in the early 1990s, the PowerBook 520/540). This feature is enabled in the Trackpad control panel, and when it is enabled, you can tap the trackpad to generate a mouse click rather than pressing the trackpad's button. The feature also extends to allowing you to tap the trackpad once and then move your finger to drag items or menus without needing to press and hold the trackpad's button. This can be a nice feature or an annoying one depending on individual preference, though most users tend to find it helpful. It can also be a helpful feature if the trackpad's button becomes damaged and cannot be used to click on items reliably.

The Errant Thumb The trackpad of PowerBook and iBook computers is positioned between the two built-in wrist rests. This is a logical, fairly ergonomic, and generally good placement for it. It does present one problem that new users may face. When you rest your fingers over the keyboard, your thumb may rest over the trackpad. If your thumb gets close enough to the trackpad, it will be sensed (even if it isn't in physical contact with the trackpad), and the Mac will respond by moving the cursor or initiating a mouse click, the same as if you'd moved your index finger on the trackpad. This is something that one just needs to get in the habit of avoiding, and some PowerBook models (and the iBook, in particular) seem more prone to this issue than others.

Trackpad Software Elements

Like any other piece of hardware, a trackpad requires driver software in order to be recognized and controlled by the Mac. The mouse drivers built into the Mac OS will recognize input from a trackpad even if no other drivers are installed. Specific features of a trackpad, either external or built in, will require additional driver software or control panels in order to be available. This is true for the tappable trackpad functions of Apple's trackpads in the PowerBook and iBook, as well as any features that are included with an external trackpad or a trackpad that is built into a third-party keyboard.

The Trackpad Control Panel For portable Macs with built-in trackpads, the additional driver is the Trackpad control panel, shown in Figure 23-3. This control panel enables the tappable trackpad feature as well as mirroring the tracking speed and double-click speed options of the Mouse control pad (discussed in the previous chapter). When the values in the Tracking Speed and Double-Click speed sections of the Trackpad control panel do not match those of the Mouse control panel, then the Mac will rely on the values entered in the Trackpad control panel when accepting input from the trackpad only. When accepting input from an external mouse, the Mac will rely on the values entered in the Mouse control panel.

Figure 23-3
Apple's Trackpad
control panel.

Other Drivers   External trackpads and trackpads that are built into a third-party keyboard will require their own driver extensions or control panels in order to enable any features beyond basic use. This includes the use of a tappable trackpad feature (if included with the device), programming of any additional buttons (external trackpads may have as many as four buttons), or any other features. You can refer to the documentation included with a third-party trackpad for information on how to control any additional features that it offers.

Trackpad Interfaces

Although the trackpad is the staple pointing device of a portable Mac, trackpads can be used with desktop Macs as well. As mentioned in Chapter 21, some keyboards come with a trackpad built into them for ease of use and ergonomic concerns (trackpads are more ergonomically sound than a mouse). Even if you don't use one of these keyboards, you can find external trackpads in many computer stores that can be used with the Mac. The most common of these are the Cirque GlidePoint devices. The following paragraphs discuss the interfaces for trackpads on portable and desktop Macs.

Portable Mac Built-in Trackpads   The built-in trackpad of a portable Mac is something that you should only rarely, if ever, have to deal with. It is built right into the case of the Mac, and its control circuitry is mounted right on the underside of the wrist rest casing. The trackpad connects to the motherboard of a portable Mac using a narrow, orange ribbon cable. This ribbon cable can be detached by pulling the plastic surrounding its connection upward slightly (it is designed to do this, but the plastic will not release from the motherboard). While the plastic is pulled upward, the ribbon cable inside the connector can be lifted out. Replacing the trackpad usually involves replacing the entire plastic casing and will require parts from Apple (meaning only Apple Authorized Service Centers can order them). The only reason you should ever have to disconnect a built-in trackpad is when performing work on the iBook that requires removing the white plastic case of the unit.

Keyboards with Trackpads   Trackpads that are built into a keyboard are treated as part of that keyboard. There is no interface concern beyond the connection of the keyboard itself. The trackpad will be recognized by the keyboard's drivers and will generally not have any independent interface for controlling it.

ADB   Like mice and keyboards, external trackpads that predate the iMac will come in only ADB models. These models require an ADB-to-USB adapter in order to be used with the current Macintosh computers. The exception is the Blue and White Power Mac G3, which does feature a built-in ADB port for connecting such legacy devices. Generally, by this point, you will not see any new trackpads being produced that use the ADB interface.

USB   USB is the only current interface for using external trackpads with the Mac. Trackpads will function as any other USB pointing device. Simply plug the trackpad into a USB port on the Mac or a hub, and it should be recognized and ready to use, provided any needed driver software is installed.

Trackpad Maintenance

Trackpads are extremely easy to maintain. In fact, the only real issue is to keep them clean. Cleaning a trackpad can be accomplished with a damp cloth when needed to remove and dirt or debris that has built up on the trackpad's surface. Don't use any cleaning agents, such as soap or detergents, because these may contain solvents or other corrosive chemicals that might damage the electrodes in the trackpad. Once wiped clean, if needed, use a soft paper towel or tissue to absorb any remaining water before using the trackpad.

Resources for Further Study

The following URLs provide additional information on some of the concepts, issues, and products discussed in this chapter:

Wacom: Manufacturer of Graphics Tablets—http://www.wacom.com

CalComp: Manufacturer of Graphics Tablets—
http://www.gtcocalcomp.com

Cirque: Maker of GlidePoint Trackpads—http://www.glidepoint.com

About.com Desktop Publishing Input Devices—
http://desktoppub.about.com/compute/desktoppub/msubhwinput.htm

CHAPTER 24

Joysticks and Gamepads

As the Macintosh has moved more and more into the consumer space, gaming has become a more important part of the Mac. One of the most important parts of gaming is the input device used to control the game environment. This chapter looks at the two most common such devices: joysticks and gamepads.

How Joysticks Work

From a user's perspective, a joystick functions very simply and intuitively. You press the stick forward, right, left, or back. Depending on the game you're playing, a character on the screen will move up, right, left, or

Figure 24-1

A typical joystick and gamepad.

down in response to your movements, or the scene will shift as though you were moving forward, right, left, or backward. Pressing the button or buttons of the joystick will cause your character to shoot a weapon, pick up an object, jump, or perform some other action. Although the actual actions varies from game to game, the general use of a joystick is something almost anyone who has played a video game or two, whether on a computer, in an arcade, or on a set-top box like a Nintendo or PlayStation, has experienced.

Typical Joystick Design

A joystick is a very simple device essentially made up of two analog electromechanical sensors. These sensors, known as *potentiometers,* are mounted in the base of the joystick. A stick runs from the base up through the top of the case. When you move this stick forward, one of the two sensors detects how far the stick has been moved. When you move the stick backward, the same sensor detects the motion. When you move the stick to the right or left, the other sensor detects the motion. If you move the stick forward and right, both sensors detect the motion (each in the direction it is designed to register). Figure 24-2 shows the basic components of a joystick.

The detection of these sensors gives the joystick's control board X and Y coordinates for your motion. Because the sensors used in the joystick are analog sensors, they do not detect movement in discrete digital signals. Circuitry built into the joystick is designed to convert the analog signal from the sensors into digital data for the computer. This digital data is then sent down the joystick's cable to the Mac.

Joysticks often have at least one or two buttons as well. These buttons

Figure 24-2
A joystick's primary components: two sensors and the control stick.

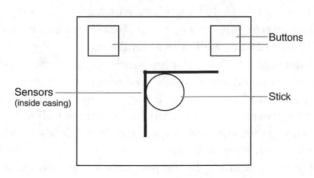

Joystick Construction

Figure 24-3
The parts of
a joystick's button.

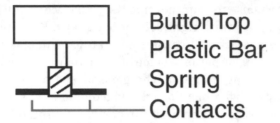

ButtonTop
Plastic Bar
Spring
Contacts

are simple mechanical switches, much like the button on a mouse. As you can see in Figure 24-3, underneath the surface of the button is a plastic bar that is held up by a spring. When the button is pressed, the spring is forced down where metal contacts on the joystick's circuit board are connected by a metal contact in the plastic bar attached to the button. When this occurs, an electrical signal is generated. This signal is sent to the Mac through the joystick cable, along with the data from the two sensors. The Mac responds accordingly by recognizing that the button has been pressed. When you release the button, the spring pushes it back up, breaking the electrical contact. When this happens, the signal that the button is being pressed is no longer sent to the Mac, which responds accordingly.

Some joysticks today are designed to actually send feedback to the user from a game being played. This is called *forced feedback* and often takes the form of shudders or shimmies. This requires that a joystick include the needed motors to generate these effects, as well as that its circuit board be designed to recognize the code to generate them.

Joystick Maintenance

Generally, there is very little maintenance that needs to be performed with a joystick. Only two things can happen to a joystick to end its useful life span: general wear and dust or dirt. The first of these cannot really be avoided, while the second can.

Unfortunately, joysticks are prone to daily wear and tear. As a joystick is used repeatedly, the inside surfaces of the sensors wear down. This is inevitable, and short of not using the joystick, there is little that can be done to prevent it. Eventually, as joysticks suffer increasing wear, they will simply become less responsive. Various joysticks have different life spans. When a joystick becomes too unresponsive to be usable, it's time to replace it (and maybe get one with some new features in the process).

One possible, if very unlikely, concern is the joystick not wearing evenly. This can sometimes occur when the joystick is habitually moved in a single direction. The surfaces of the sensors won't wear evenly, which will result in one direction of movement being less responsive than the others. This is a fairly rare circumstance, however, because most games require a user to move the joystick in every direction pretty much evenly.

Dust may be an issue for some joysticks more than for others. Some joysticks place a rubberized covering over the area at the base of the stick, which keeps dust and other debris from getting into the joystick. Other joysticks do not include such a covering and are prone to dust collecting inside the joystick. As the dust collects inside, it can build up between the stick itself and the sensors. If this happens, the joystick becomes less responsive. You can clean a joystick using a can of compressed air and some electronics-grade contact cleaner.

To clean a joystick, you usually need to disassemble the button casing. This varies between models, but it almost always involves removing the screws that hold the case together. Always disconnect the joystick from the computer before attempting to disassemble it. There should be some narrow holes surrounding the sensors of the joystick. Spray compressed air into these holes to remove any built-up dirt and dust. You may want to do this outside, as dust tends to fly out in all directions. Once the area is as free of dust as possible, spray in some of the contact cleaner. Move the joystick through its complete range of motion and then reassemble. Give the contact cleaner about 10 minutes to dry before connecting and using the joystick.

How Gamepads Work

Although gamepads haven't been around nearly as long as joysticks (which started with the earliest arcade games at least 20 years ago), they have become extremely popular over the past 10 or so years. This is primarily because of their extremely common use in set-top video game devices. Gamepads are usually held in both hands, with a cross-shaped directional control under one thumb and a series of buttons under the other. Pressing the directional control forward, backward, or to each side causes a game to respond in the same fashion as moving a joystick would.

Typical Gamepad Design

Gamepad design is actually a good deal simpler than joystick design. The buttons under one thumb are just mechanical switches that function the same as the buttons on a joystick do. The directional controller is also nothing more than a series of mechanical switches, one button or switch dedicated to each direction for which you can move the controller. Since the mechanical switches in a gamepad generate distinct digital data, there is no need for an analog-to-digital a converter and no need for any other sensors. All you need is a circuit board capable of recognizing when each button is pressed and transmitting that data to the Mac.

Gamepad Maintenance

Because gamepads are little more than a series of mechanical switch buttons and a piece of circuit board, there is little maintenance you can or need to do. Dust cannot easily work its way into most gamepads, and there are no other mechanical parts to deal. Simply use them to play whatever games you want to play.

Connecting a Joystick or Gamepad

A joystick or gamepad connects to the Mac using a standard interface, such as ADB or USB. This is a contrast to the non-Mac computer world because PCs use a special port specifically designed for connecting joysticks or gamepads. The Mac's approach of using standard Mac input ports offers an advantage and a disadvantage.

The advantage is that Macs don't need to have a special expansion card installed or a special port built into them in order for you to use a joystick. You simply attach the joystick or gamepad right to one of the Mac's existing ports. As a rule, this means that you don't have to worry about whether your Mac will have a joystick port that can accept a joystick or gamepad you might want to use.

The disadvantage of this approach is that the Mac uses a different type of port for joysticks and gamepad connection than PCs do. This means that joystick or gamepad developers need to redesign the interface of their joystick or gamepad in order for it to be used on a Macintosh (in addition to developing a Mac driver for it). This means that fewer joysticks and gamepads—particularly inexpensive, low-end models—are out there for Mac users. On the other hand, it means that the developers producing the products are a bit more committed to Mac development and may produce better products.

This issue is slowly beginning to change, however, as more and more PC manufacturers embrace the potential of USB. USB is a standard port on both PCs and Macs today, and many consumer-oriented PCs are shipping with USB ports instead of some of the more traditional PC ports, such as the joystick port. This is slowly leading PC joystick and gamepad creators to invest in developing USB products. Since USB devices are cross-platform, requiring only a Macintosh driver for use on the Mac, these joysticks and gamepads could easily be used with Macs. Even if the manufacturer never writes a Mac driver, a universal driver like USB Overdrive can be used.

Standard Mac Interfaces

Two interfaces have served for connecting joysticks and gamepads to the Mac: ADB (Apple Desktop Bus) and USB. Obviously, the current Macs require USB joysticks and gamepads by default. Additionally, there are adapter products for using non-Mac joysticks and gamepads with the Macintosh.

ADB   ADB served as the joystick/gamepad interface for Macs for several years. Because the input from a joystick or gamepad is very similar to that of a mouse or other pointing device, ADB provided adequate data throughput for them. As Apple has moved away from ADB for connecting input devices, Mac gaming hardware has shifted as well. Although you may still find ADB joysticks or gamepads being produced, they are becoming somewhat rare because only older Macs can use them.

If you do have an existing ADB joystick or gamepad that you want to use with a current Mac, an ADB-to-USB adapter (such as Griffin's iMate) will probably serve to allow you to do so. Unless you are dealing with a very specialized or expensive joystick/gamepad, however, it probably would be easier, and maybe even cheaper, to invest in a USB model instead of using an adapter. It is also possible, though not at all supported or certain, that such an adapter, being extremely simple in design, would allow you to connect a USB joystick or gamepad to an older ADB Mac.

USB   USB is the interface of choice for all kinds of devices on the current Macintosh computers, so it is no surprise that joysticks and gamepads use this as their interface today. USB is hot pluggable, allowing you to connect or disconnect a joystick/gamepad whenever you want to, whereas ADB devices should only be plugged or unplugged while the Mac is shut down. USB is also cross-platform, which may appeal to manufacturers when developing joysticks or gamepads for the Mac, particularly as USB gains a stronger foothold in the PC world.

Adapter Products

In addition to ADB and USB joysticks and gamepads, adapters are on the market for using joysticks and gamepads that rely on a different interface with the Mac. These adapters may or may not give performance equal to an actual USB or ADB joystick/gamepad, but they generally function fairly well. And these adapters don't just limit you to using joysticks and gamepads intended for PCs. There are also adapter products that allow you to use the gamepads and joysticks from set-top video game systems such as Nintendo, Nintendo 64, PlayStation, and Sega Genesis.

For PC Joysticks and Gamepads   Using a PC-joystick-port-to-USB adapter, you may be able to use a PC joystick with one of the current Macs. Although such products exist, some of them are only intended for use with PCs that lack a joystick port but include USB. These may or may not enable a PC joystick to be used with the Mac. There are some Mac-specific adapter products, however, including some older PC-joystick-port-to-ADB adapters.

For Other Joysticks and Gamepads   More powerful than an adapter for the PC joystick port is a multipurpose adapter that allows you to take joysticks or gamepads designed to be used with a wide variety of video gaming systems, including PC joysticks, gamepads from PlayStation and Sega Genesis, and even older set-top gaming devices, such as the old Atari systems from the 1980s. Although not the most publicized products, these devices have been on the market for some time in both ADB and USB variations. This allows you an extremely broad range of joystick and gamepad choices and should certainly satisfy any preference out there. Some adapters allow the use of virtually any joystick or gamepad, while others are limited only to devices from a specific gaming system.

How Games Interact with Joysticks and Gamepads

A game interacts with the data it receives from a joystick or gamepad somewhat differently than other applications interact with pointing devices. In fact, there are a series of software layers that are involved in the recognition and assimilation of data from a gamepad or joystick to the game itself. These layers include the device drivers, Apple's Game Sprockets, and the game application itself. The next sections look at each of these three layers and the roles they play in a game's interaction with a joystick or gamepad.

Device Drivers

The device drivers are the extensions and control panels that tell the Mac how to recognize a joystick or gamepad. Device drivers control the Mac's ability to receive any data from the joystick or gamepad at all. For some early joysticks, drivers were written as little more than adjusted mouse drivers, which allowed the Mac OS to interpret movement and button click but didn't really offer the best interaction between the Mac and the joystick. As time has gone by and gamepads and joysticks have become more feature/button-filled and complex, so have the drivers that control them. Today, device drivers are designed to interact with each function or button of a joystick or gamepad in a much more sophisticated manner than simply as an extended mouse driver.

Device drivers are also often written so that the information received from the device is sent directly to a game or to a specific portion of the Mac OS, such as Apple's Game Sprockets. This allows game developers to interact with a joystick or gamepad more easily than if they had to treat the device as an extended mouse or keyboard sequence.

USB Overdrive   You were first introduced to the shareware USB Overdrive in Chapter 22 because it can function as a universal mouse driver. This means it can be used to enable and control just about every feature or button on any USB mouse in existence. This can come in handy if there is no Mac driver for a mouse or if the Mac driver isn't particularly well written.

In addition to serving as a universal mouse driver, USB Overdrive can function as a universal gamepad/joystick driver. When being used as such, it can recognize and interact with just about any USB joystick or gamepad on the market.

There are two reasons you might want to use USB Overdrive for such a purpose. The first is a situation where you are using a USB joystick that doesn't include Mac support and you need a device driver for it. This can happen, but it isn't particularly common because most non-Mac joysticks and gamepads are designed to be used with a PC's joystick port (which the Mac doesn't have) and not a USB port. The number of USB joysticks for PCs is rising, however, and this may change in the not-so-distant future. Similarly, joysticks or gamepads designed for set-top video game boxes, such as Nintendo 64 or PlayStation, use proprietary interfaces and not USB.

The second, and more likely, situation is where a device driver for a joystick or gamepad exists but does not support Apple's Game Sprockets. Since many games now require the Game Sprocket layer in terms of joystick/gamepad interaction, you will probably need a driver that supports Game Sprockets. In these cases, USB Overdrive can be the only solution to using a gamepad or joystick with newer games because it does support Game Sprockets. Figure 24-4 shows the USB Overdrive window when used for configuring joystick control.

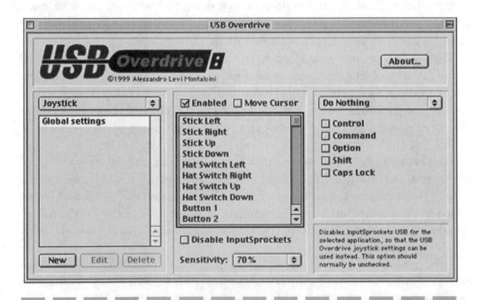

Figure 24-4   USB Overdrive can function as a universal joystick driver.

Game Sprockets

In 1997, Apple made a renewed commitment to improve the state of computer gaming on the Macintosh platform. This commitment has been renewed several times since and has borne a good deal of fruit in terms of new games being developed for the Mac. Part of that initial commitment was the creation of Game Sprockets.

Game Sprockets are special Mac OS components created by Apple to help simplify the development of games on the Mac. These sprockets are written as shared libraries, which are stored in the Extensions folder within the System Folder. Table 24-1 lists the entire line of Game Sprockets currently used by Apple; however, for the purposes of this discussion, we are interested in the InputSprocket.

The InputSprocket is designed to accept data input from the joystick or gamepad. It then processes this data into a standard format. Game developers can then design games knowing that input data from a joystick or gamepad will always follow that standard format. They won't need to design games to interact with the device driver itself, and they won't need to design games to take into account a vast array of differing input types from various pieces of gaming hardware. Some games and joysticks/gamepads may install additional InputSprockets of their own into the Mac's Extensions folder.

As a result, the InputSprocket sits between the device driver and the game, giving the developers of both an easy and common reference point with which to design their products and making both of their jobs easier. Most new games and most new gaming hardware for the Mac support and require the InputSprocket to function. This also means that

	Sprocket Name	Function
TABLE 24-1 Primary Game Sprockets.	NetSprocket	Provides standard routines for initiating games between players over the Internet or local networks.
	InputSprocket	Provides standard routines for recognizing game input from joysticks or gamepads. Includes easier driver interface development.
	DrawSprocket	Provides an easier method for rendering visual game elements. Also offers the abilities to buffer images in RAM before they are needed and to integrate with other display and multimedia technologies on the Mac.
	SoundSprocket	Provides easier access to traditional sound effects, as well as access to new sound technologies, such as 3D audio playback.

Figure 24-5
Some of Apple's
Game Sprockets

DrawSprocketLib

InputSprocket USB

InputSprocket Thrustmaster

InputSprocket MacALLY

SoundSprocketLib

you don't need to worry about your joystick being supported by a new game, or vice versa. As long as both support Apple's Game Sprockets, they should work together without any problems. Figure 24-5 shows the icons of some of the Game Sprockets you may find in your Mac's Extensions folder.

The Game Itself

The game itself receives input data from the InputSprocket, which in turn receives it from the device driver, which originally receive it from the device itself. At each level, the information is provided in a form that the next level can understand. Once the data has been received by the game, the game responds accordingly. This can mean firing missiles at some enemy in the game's scenario or moving in one direction or whatever the game is designed to do.

Resources for Further Study

The following URLs provide additional information on some of the concepts, issues, and products discussed in this chapter:

The Mac Gomers Ledge—http://www.macledge.com

USB Overdrive Homepage—http://www.usboverdrive.com

Mac Ally—http://www.macally.com

CHAPTER 25

Digital Imaging

Digital imaging is the process of taking a picture, such as a photograph or drawing, and creating a computer file of it. Digital imaging can be accomplished in a variety of ways. The most common method is to use a scanner to digitize an existing image. Also increasingly popular is the use of digital cameras, which create an image file immediately when a photograph is taken rather than using film as traditional cameras do. This chapter examines the most common digital imaging methods today.

Scanners

Scanners are probably the most common method for creating digital images, as well as the most versatile. A scanner enables users to take an existing still image, such as a photograph, drawing, or even a page of text, and create a computer graphics file of the image that can be edited with an image program like Photoshop, put on a web page, sent as an e-mail attachment, or used in any other way that you would use an image file. Scanners of various types have been around for several years now, and many models offering very good quality are now priced low enough for most consumers to purchase. The next few sections look at how scanners function, the types of scanners, and how to determine the quality and limitations of a scanner.

How Scanners Work

Let's start with how a grayscale scanner works. When you use a scanner to digitally render an existing still image, the scanner passes a light over the image. Immediately after the light source has passed over an area of the image's surface, the scanner passes a charge-coupled device, or CCD, over the same area. A CCD is a collection of light-sensitive circuits. The light that the scanner passes over this section of the image is reflected back to the CCD. Areas where the image is white or lightly shaded reflect more light back at the CCD than areas that are dark or black (true black reflects no light at all). The CCD then creates a data representation of each tiny piece of the image as a being lighter or darker than the areas next to it. The computer can then use this data to re-create the original image's shades of light and dark.

Color Scanners   Now that we've covered a grayscale scanner, the question becomes how a color scanner creates a scan of a colored image.

Well, the process is essentially the same, except that the scanner performs the scanning process three times for each piece of an image it scans. Each time, the scan is done for each of the three primary colors of light (red, green, and blue). This is accomplished by either shining each of three colors of light on the image in succession instead of using white light or, more commonly, by applying a filter of each of the three colors over the scanner's CCD in succession. On most scanners, the readings for all three colors are made with a single pass of the scanner head, with each color light or filter being applied in very quick succession. In some scanners, however, three separate passes are made, one for each color.

The effect is the same; each color of light is scanned separately. Data for the areas of the image reflecting red-tinted light, green-tinted light, and blue-tinted light is recorded. The data from these scans is then fed through in the same manner as the data for a grayscale scan. The scanner software allows the computer to map all three scans together into a single color scan by overlaying the three sets of scan data one on top of the other. Where the three primary colors of light blend together with different degrees of shading, individual hues of colors made by mixing the primary colors are generated.

Types of Scanners

For the most part, all scanners function the same way, as described above, but different scanners are designed for different tasks, and as a result, scanners come in varied shapes and sizes. The next few paragraphs discuss the common types of scanners on the market today.

Flatbed Scanners Flatbed scanners (such as the one shown in Figure 25-1) are what most people think of when they here the term *scanner*. Flatbed scanners have a large glass surface, usually 8.5 by 11 or 14 inches (the sizes of standard letter and legal-sized paper, respectively) onto which documents to be scanned are placed. The scanner head is located beneath the glass surface and is moved along beneath the document being scanned by a stepping motor. Flatbed scanners often resemble the top half of a photocopy machine.

Flatbeds are the most common scanners on the market today, and there are flatbed models aimed at both the consumer and professional markets. Of all the scanners, flatbeds tend to be the most versatile, being able to scan any type of medium or surface, provided the image will fit fully on the scanning surface (if not, you can take multiple scans of a larger image and then piece them together in a graphics application

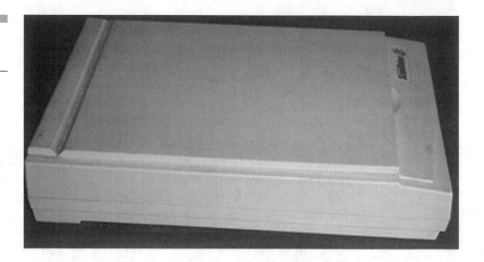

afterward). Flatbeds also tend to offer greater color depths and image resolutions than most other types of scanners.

When you unpack a flatbed scanner for the first time, you will need to remove a special piece of plastic or metal called the *shipping pin*. The shipping pin is used to keep the scanner head and stepping motor from moving or shifting while the scanner is being transported (which could damage the scanner's internal components and break or scratch the glass scanning surface). Different models will use different types of pins, and they will be located in different parts of the scanner. You can refer to the scanner's manual for instructions on the removing the shipping pin. You should save the shipping pin once the scanner has been unpacked. It is an important precaution against damage to the scanner's sensitive scanning head and surface when moving or shipping the scanner. If you ever need to move the scanner from on office or building to another, reinsert the shipping pin first to avoid the risk of serious damage to the scanner.

Sheet-fed Scanners   Sheet-fed scanners are not nearly so common today as flatbed scanners. Sheet-fed scanners are narrow devices that resemble the intake or tractor portion of a fax machine. Measuring about 9 inches long, sheet-fed scanners are only 1 or 2 inches wide. A narrow slot and a motor allow a piece of paper to pass into the scanner from one side, under the scanner head, and out the other side.

Sheet-fed scanners are usually grayscale only (though there are a couple of color models out there) and do not offer the higher resolutions that flatbed scanners do. As a trade-off, sheet-fed scanners take up far less desk space and tend to have lower price tags. While not useful for scanning art or photographs for graphics work, sheet-fed scanners can be useful for making a record of documents, faxing a document (when combined with fax software on the Mac), and Optical Character Recognition (or OCR, a process that converts a scanned image of a page of text into an actual text document; OCR is discussed further in the "Scanner Software" section later in this chapter).

Handheld Scanners   A handheld scanner is a device roughly the size of a large index card with a roller and other scanner components in a case that is laid on top of a picture or page and slowly rolled across the image to be scanned. While the user moves the handheld scanner along the image, the light and CCD sensors transmit data to the computer, which translates that data into an image. Handheld scanners enjoyed a period of immense popularity in the consumer market a couple of years ago because they offered low-cost solutions compared to the higher-priced flatbed scanners of the day. Handheld scanners were also almost exclusively grayscale and usually did not deliver image quality near what was offered by flatbed models. The increasingly lower costs of flatbed scanners over the past few years has led to handheld scanners becoming increasingly rare, as they no longer offer any real cost benefit.

Photo Scanners   Photo scanners are special consumer-oriented scanners that are designed to scan only one thing: home photos. Photo scanners can generally only scan an area of at most 4 by 6 inches (the size of a large standard photo). Photo scanners are designed to be easy to use, one- or two-button machines that most home users who don't want to deal with complicated scanning software will find attractive. Despite the limits on size, photo scanners usually produce rather good-quality images and are good for consumers who just want to get their family photos onto a website or attached to e-mail messages.

Slide Scanners   Slide scanners are specially designed for scanning the images on 35mm slides. Slides offer professional photographers some different options than traditional prints do, including the ability for presentation use, a smaller form factor for shipping or storage, and sometimes higher quality. Slide scanners function by placing the slide in a special slot where light is projected through it onto a CCD sensor array that allows the image to be captured.

Drum Scanners   Drum scanners are specialized high-performance professional scanners, often used only for generating scans of sufficient color and image quality to be used in glossy print publications like magazines and coffee-table books. Drum scanners function somewhat differently than most other scanners in that the document to be scanned is placed on a drum and then passed mere millimeters from a high-intensity light source and extremely powerful CCD sensor array. This allows the scanner to acquire far more accurate color and image data than other, more traditional, and consumer-oriented scanners are capable of capturing. The result is images that are as true to life as digital-imaging technology can achieve.

Scanner Interfaces

As with many other peripherals, scanners can be connected to the Mac through a variety of means. USB is currently the most common for Mac users because it is an interface built into all current Macs and is very easy to use. FireWire is also emerging in higher-end scanners (over 1200 dpi quality) that can make use of the additional bandwidth available from FireWire. SCSI scanners are also still quite popular.

When connecting a scanner to a Mac, you will follow the same procedures and rules that you would with any other device using that interface. SCSI scanners need to adhere to all rules of device ID numbers and termination, for example. You can use a utility included with the scanner or the Apple System Profiler to ensure that the scanner is connected and recognized properly.

SCSI   SCSI was the first interface used for most scanners. It provides an interface with plenty of bandwidth, and until the iMac was released, it was an interface that every Mac offered. SCSI still tends to be common for scanners because it does offer better performance as an interface than does USB. Attaching a SCSI scanner is essentially the same as attaching any other SCSI device. SCSI scanners need to be added to a chain of SCSI devices following all the rules and other considerations described in Chapter 12. The only real difference is that a scanner is not a drive, so no icon, or other Finder-level indication, will appear when a SCSI scanner is attached. Most SCSI-USB or SCSI-FireWire adapters do not support scanners. If you plan to use a SCSI scanner, you should do so on a Mac with an actual SCSI port/card.

Some SCSI scanners have unusual compatibility issues. Most SCSI scanners require that the scanner be the final device in the SCSI chain. Also, many older SCSI scanners have problems with some SCSI PCI cards. If you are using an older SCSI scanner, you may want to check with the manufacturer for any compatibility concerns before purchasing a SCSI card.

USB   USB scanners began to emerge when Apple began converting Macs to use USB as a default interface technology. Today, there is a wide array of USB scanners on the market, most of which offer the quality comparable to SCSI models. The actual scanning process may be slower as a result of USB's more limited data transfer speeds, however. Some recent USB scanners also offer the advantage of using the USB bus as a power source rather than requiring their own power supply. If you are looking at scanners for most home computing uses today, a USB model will probably be the simplest and least expensive choice.

FireWire   FireWire is beginning to edge into the scanner arena for some scanners with higher resolutions. These are primarily models aimed at professional markets. FireWire offers increased performance over USB, though for scanners under 1200 dpi resolutions, their additional performance doesn't really translate into practical time savings. At this time, there are still only a few FireWire scanners, however, as SCSI still tends to dominate professional models and USB the consumer space.

Serial Port   A few early scanners, most of them low-quality sheet-fed and handheld models, used the Mac's serial port as an interface. Only lower-quality scanners used a serial port interface because the Mac's serial ports have much lower data transfer rates than other interface technologies. These serial port scanners tend not to have gained much place in the scanner market, but they are out there. As mentioned in Chapter 30, serial port scanners can usually be used with current Macs by using some of the serial port cards and USB-serial port adapters on the market.

Scanner Specifications and Image Quality

When you look at a scanner, you'll notice that the specifications note several different values that are designed to tell you the quality of the images generated by the scanner. There are two important values that you'll want to look at: the scanner's resolution, which determines how much image data is recorded by the scanner for creating a digital rendering of your original image, and the scanner's color depth, which determines the amount of color data the scanner is capable of recording from your original image.

Resolution   Resolution is the trickier concept when you are dealing with scanner specs, so let's tackle it first. When you look at a scanner's spec sheet, you'll see something like "600×600 dpi (dots per inch) resolution." That means that in every square inch of the surface area of a scanned image, the scanner will record image data for 600 individual dots in a row and that there will be 600 rows of dots. Each individual dot represents one microscopic piece of the image. The more dots that are recorded, the more actual image data, and the sharper and clearer the digital image your Mac renders.

SCANNER RESOLUTION COMPARED TO SCREEN RESOLUTION   As you probably know (or remember from Chapter 4), computer monitors are rated in resolutions like 640 pixels by 480 pixels. This is a fixed number of pixels, but it is not a fixed physical size. Scanners, on the other hand, record both a number of pixels and a fixed physical size for the image. This means that if you scan a 4-inch image, it will probably not display as being 4 inches big on screen. The size of the picture onscreen will be determined by how many pixels were recorded in the scan, regardless of how these pixels translate to a physical size.

When you print the scanned image file, however, it will probably be the same size as the original image. This is because many types of graphics files, including the very common JPEG type, include information about an image's print size in the file's data. This means the file contains information on how big the original image was. This image data is then read when the file is printed. If the image is scaled up or down after it has been scanned, the print size should be scaled the same as the onscreen size. I say *should*, because some low-end graphics programs might not do this properly. Similarly, not all graphics programs and printer drivers will read the print image size data in a file when they print it (though these are rare), which will result in the print size being different than the original image. Also, remember that some file types, such as GIF, don't support including data on an image's print size in the file.

An oddity of this is that the size of a physically smaller scanned image—say, a 2-inch image scanned at 300x300 resolution—will look larger on screen than a physically larger image scanned at a lower quality, say, a 3-inch image scanned at 200x200. On screen, the 3-inch image will take up 200 pixels in length and width, which is less screen space than the 300 pixels taken up by the smaller image. When printed, the 2-inch image will once again be smaller. It will also be sharper because there is more data there being included in the smaller size.

SCANNER RESOLUTION COMPARED TO PRINTER RESOLUTION   Unlike monitors, printers measure resolution in the same manner as scanners, where the size of an image is measured in physical units (inches or centimeters) and pixels represent the amount of dots that can be packed into a given physical inch. Pixels are not themselves an absolute value, as they are on screen. So, you'd think that scanner resolution being in dots (pixels) per inch and printer resolution also being measured in dots per inch, they'd be the same values. Unfortunately, computing isn't always that simple.

In actuality, scanned resolutions are more closely related to the number of lines per inch that a printer is capable of printing. This means that you need to compare a scanner's dots per inch to your printer's lines per inch (which you can find in your printer's specifications). As a rule, 1 line per inch of a printer is equivalent to 1 dot per inch of a scanner.

Color Depth   *Color depth* refers to the amount of color data that can be gathered by a scanner when it scans an image. If it gathers 1 bit of data, then you can have two color values (black and white) for each dot in an image. If it gathers 8 bits, then 256 colors are available for each dot. For 16 bits of color data, each dot in an image can use any one of over 16 thousand colors. If a scanner can gather 24 bits of color data, each dot can be one of millions of colors. If this sounds like the same color depths as your Mac's video is capable of displaying, that's because it is. Scanners, however, are actually capable of recording color data at anywhere up to 48 bits, well beyond billions of individual colors.

So, how much color depth do you need? Unless you're doing very advanced and professional color separation work, 24-bit color will suffice (after all, human beings can't distinguish higher color depth than that anyway). 24-bit color depth is pretty much the standard for consumer-oriented scanners. Scanners with greater color depths can pick up very gradual color transitions that lie at the very edge of human perception, which makes them very useful for professional print work and situations where the images will be digitally manipulated.

Scanner Software

While a scanner's hardware reads the light and dark areas of an image and converts that information into data, a Mac still needs software that can control how the scanner collects image information, interprets that data, and creates an image out of it. This is the function of the scanner driver and scanning utility software, both of which are included with a scanner. While the scanner driver controls the Mac's interaction with the hardware of the scanner, it is the utility software that allows the Mac to interpret data from a scanner. Scanner utilities are a vital part of the scanning process.

There are two primary types of scanner utilities: dedicated scanning applications and graphics application plug-ins. Additionally, there is a third category of scanner-related software, mentioned earlier, of which you should be aware. This is Optical Character Recognition (or OCR) software. OCR is a process that allows the Mac to translate an image of text, such as a scanned page from a book, into an actual text document. The following paragraphs look at each of these three types of scanning utilities.

Dedicated Scanning Software   As you might expect from the name, dedicated scanning applications are programs (such as the one pictured in Figure 25-2) that ship with a scanner and do nothing but receive data from a scanner and render an image. If you just want to create a JPEG file from a family photo but don't want to edit the image in a program like Photoshop, you can use a dedicated scanning application. When the scanner scans the image, the application will render the data into an image file and save it to your hard drive. You can then put the image on a website or edit it with a graphics program at a later date.

Figure 25-2
The dedicated scanning utility included with Microtek's scanners.

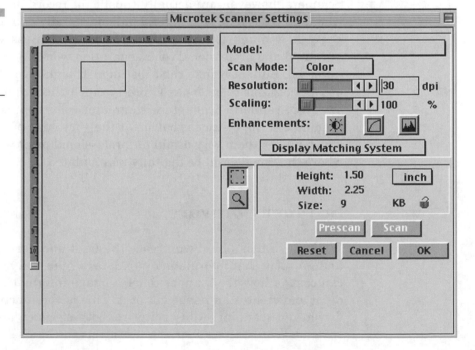

Scanner Plug-ins and TWAIN Many graphics applications use a plug-in architecture. Plug-ins are mini programs that extend the ability of the graphics application much like Extensions provide new abilities for the Mac OS. Often plug-ins are used to add new image editing features such as applying shadows, blurs, or other effects to an image. Another common use of plug-ins is to allow an application to support additional image formats than it would out of the box. Plug-ins can also be written that allow graphics programs to directly import data from a scanner, without using a dedicated scanning program. This helps save you a step because you don't need to scan an image with one program, save it, and then open it with a graphics application like Photoshop to edit it.

Adobe's Photoshop is one of the most popular and powerful image-editing applications on the market. It pioneered the plug-in architecture for graphics programs. Several other commercial and shareware applications make use of the same plug-in architecture as Photoshop, meaning that they can use plug-ins written for Photoshop. Most scanners will ship with a Photoshop-compatible plug-in that allows you to scan directly into Photoshop or another application that uses the Photoshop plug-in architecture (some scanners even ship with a low-end graphics application that supports Photoshop plug-ins).

In addition to scanner-specific plug-ins, there is a standard plug-in type known as TWAIN (which stands for "technology without an important name," believe it or not). A TWAIN plug-in uses a standard set of techniques for rendering data from a scanner into an image. This allows the same plug-in to work with many different scanners, provided the scanners themselves conform to the TWAIN standard (which you can find out by reading a scanner's specs). A TWAIN plug-in is included with Photoshop and can be used if a scanner does not come with a plug-in of its own, but does support TWAIN.

Optical Character Recognition OCR brings the power of a scanner beyond simply scanning images. With an OCR application, such as OmniPage or TextBridge, you can take a piece of paper that contains nothing but text, scan it, and convert the text that you scanned into a word-processing document rather than an image file. This allows companies or individuals to create computer records and electronic versions of existing documents without having to retype each and every word of a document. This is a powerful technology, particularly for companies that have a great deal of records from before the computer era that they wish to convert into an electronic format.

OCR works by the Mac looking at each black area in a black-and-white image as though it were an individual character (a letter, number, punctuation mark, and so on) and trying to determine which character each black mark looks the most like. Doing this, it creates text based on how it recognizes each letter in a document. This works fairly well on the whole, but any document created by OCR will need to be proofread to be certain that each character was recognized properly (personally, I've never used OCR to create a document that didn't have at least some minor errors). Usually, it is easier and faster to fix these errors than it would've been to retype the entire document from scratch.

There are a number of things you can do to decrease the possibilities of inaccuracies when using OCR to scan a document. One is to make sure that the page and the scanner's surface have no specks of dust or smudges. Use the highest-quality original documents as possible (documents that are photocopies, particularly second- or third-generation photocopies, tend not to scan as well as originals). If possible, don't use documents that have images in them. OCR software is also usually designed to recognize specific fonts. If possible, scan documents using those fonts or use an OCR application that supports the fonts used in the documents you wish to scan.

Digital Cameras

When you hear the term *digital camera*, you immediately think of the digital equivalent to point-and-click 35mm cameras. While these digital still cameras are the most easily recognized as digital cameras, they technically aren't the only type of digital cameras today. Desktop cameras, like Logitech's QuickCam, are also digital cameras, albeit ones that have followed a much different path in terms of design, function, and application. Technically, you could also call a digital camcorder a digital camera, though I would prefer to consider those as video devices more than imaging devices. In this section, we'll look primarily at the more traditional still image cameras first and then briefly discuss the desktop cameras as imaging devices.

How Digital Cameras Work

From a user's point of view, a digital camera works much the same as a traditional film camera. You click the button, a flash may go off, and the photo is taken. The counter indicating how many pictures are left for you to take even goes down by one photo (although here it's due to how much memory or storage is left rather than how much film is left). One difference is that you get to see how your picture turned out right away because almost all digital cameras come with a built-in LCD screen for previewing and, if you choose, deleting pictures stored in the camera's memory. Another difference is that you can usually use that LCD screen instead of a viewfinder, giving you a larger and clearer view of the photo you're about to take.

While the user's experience shifts very little when moving to a digital camera from a film camera, the same cannot be said of the technology used in a digital camera. Technologically, digital cameras resemble scanners far more than they do traditional film cameras. Earlier in this chapter, you read about how scanners use a CCD sensor array to accurately determine contrast and color data of an image. Digital cameras use a very similar CCD sensor array. When the camera's photo button is clicked, the aperture of the camera opens, exposing an image to the CCD. The CCD captures that image in the same manner as the CCD sensor array in a scanner does, with each one of thousands or millions of light-sensitive sensors responding to a different tiny bit of the image. The camera processes the data from each circuit in the CCD and converts that data into a single picture, which is stored as a graphics file in whatever memory storage method the camera uses. These graphics files, usually JPEG files, can then be transferred to a computer to be printed, modified with a graphics application like Photoshop, attached to e-mails, put on web pages, or simply stored for later viewing and use. Some photo printers can also accept data directly from a digital camera (or a camera's memory card) for printing without needing to use a computer at all.

Pixels and Digital Camera Resolution   While scanners and printers measure resolution based on dots per inch, digital cameras measure resolution more like a computer monitor. The resolution of a digital camera is usually given in megapixels, or millions of pixels. This is the total number of pixels that the digital camera includes in each image it takes (the number of pixels wide the image is multiplied by the number of pixel high, so 1000 pixels times 1000 pixels wide equals one million pixels, or one megapixel). As with a computer monitor, this number of pixels bears no relation to any physical measurement. A camera that takes photos that are a thousand pixels wide takes pictures that will display at a thousand pixels wide on a monitor. On a relatively large monitor, say, one set to display at 1024x768, that image will fit completely on the screen.

On a smaller monitor, say, 640x480, you will need to scroll across a window or scale the image down in order to see it all.

How many inches an image from a digital camera will be on a printed page depends on the graphics software used to print the image and how it converts onscreen size values to print. It may also depend on the printer driver and the printer's resolution. There is no set built-in size information with the image itself, however. Therefore, digital camera resolutions are absolute size values of themselves and are not related to the amount of dots or pixels per inch as are printer resolutions and scanner resolutions.

Interpolated Resolution   Some digital cameras advertise an interpolated resolution. An *interpolated resolution* is where the camera's CCD array is capable of a low or moderate resolution, but the camera's circuitry is designed to interpolate the data to create a higher-resolution image. When the camera interpolates the data, it takes the color and contrast values of two pixels in the image and computes what the value halfway between them would be. It then inserts another pixel halfway between the two original pixels with data that is exactly halfway between them. Of course, this data isn't from the actual image. It is something that the camera made up to create a larger image that conforms to the existing contrast and color information of the actual image.

So, is a digital camera that offers an actual resolution of 2.5 megapixels and an interpolated resolution of 3.3 megapixels as good as a real 3.3 megapixel camera? Of course not. The interpolated data creates an image of the same size, but since the interpolated data is not real image data, it doesn't give you any additional image detail. Instead, it gives you an image that will be smoother than if you took a picture from a 2.5-megapixel camera and scaled up to be a 3.3-megapixel image, but it will not be as sharp or detailed as an image produced from an actual 3.3-megapixel camera.

Image Compression and Quality Options   Most image file formats support compression of an image when it is stored. This is because image files, left uncompressed, can be quite large. By compressing the image, the file simply won't take up as much memory. The issue when compressing an image is that some quality is going to be lost the more the image is compressed. This is why an image format needs to offer a high-quality compression scheme or algorithm, one that makes the file smaller but retains as much quality as possible. Probably the best, and most common, compression scheme in use today is the one that is part of the JPEG file standard. JPEG has become the de facto image file type for the web and e-mail because it allows for high-quality images with a good compression scheme that retains that quality even when a file is made fairly small.

Most digital cameras store images as JPEG files. This means that they can take advantage of the JPEG standard's powerful compression features. When taking images with a digital camera where you have a limited amount of memory/storage available to the camera, compressing the images as they are created allows you to take more photos at one time. Most digital cameras offer three levels of JPEG compression, usually labeled as good, better, and best, with good being the most compressed image and best being the least compressed.

The good, better, and best options tend to refer to image quality, as a compressed image will generally be a little less sharp than an uncompressed image and may have slight distortions in the image. In most cameras and for most uses, the differences will usually not be particularly great. Some people may not even notice any real difference at all. For high-end desktop publishing or graphics work, however, some differences may be seen.

Digital Camera Speeds   One thing you might find when perusing a digital camera's specs or manual is a reference to how fast the camera can take pictures. This is because it takes some time, usually somewhere between a fraction of a second and several seconds, for the camera's circuitry to render an image based on the data received from the CCD sensor array. Even once the image is created, it takes the camera some additional time to turn that image into an appropriate image file and to store that file on whatever type of memory the camera uses. The design of the camera, the resolution of the image, the compression applied to the image file, and the type of memory storage used are all factors in determining how fast a camera can take an image and be ready to take the next image after it.

Some cameras include a burst mode. *Burst mode* is a special mode that allows the camera to take images faster than normal. This can be good if you expect to take several shots in a minute or are trying to get as many photos of a high-action scene as possible. To take pictures faster in burst mode, the camera usually ends up decreasing the image quality or size so that it doesn't need as much time to render the image and store the file.

What the Specs of a Digital Camera Mean

When you look at digital cameras, you will see a wide array of different specifications. These relate to a variety of aspects of how the camera performs, the size or quality of the images it delivers, how many images it can store, and how it can transfer those images to a computer. The following paragraphs look at some of the common specs you'll find when comparing digital cameras and what these specs actually mean.

CCD Sensor Size   This is the physical size of the CCD sensor array. The larger the size of the array, the more light-sensitive circuits are built into it. As you might guess, more circuits in the CCD results in the ability to distinguish more individual bits of an image. This means that you get a higher resolution and better-quality image with a larger CCD. Although CCD size may be included in a camera's specs, also look at the available resolutions to get a more accurate guide of the camera's image quality. If two cameras claim to have the same resolution options but vastly different CCD sizes, the one with the smaller CCD likely uses interpolation to get larger images, which will be of lower quality.

Color Depth   As mentioned, color depth is how many individual colors can be assigned to each pixel of an image. Obviously, the greater the color depth (more colors), the truer the resulting image will be to the actual scene. Color depth for digital cameras is expressed the same way as color depth for a monitor or a scanner is (16 bit being thousands of colors and 24 bit being millions of colors). Most digital cameras today use 24-bit color and deliver very true coloring in their images. Some low-end cameras, however, may still use 16-bit coloring. Cameras supporting higher than 24-bit color are in development, though these will probably be reserved for extremely high-end professional photography when they become available. As mentioned in the scanner section of this chapter, 24-bit color is the typical limit of Mac displays and also beyond the limit of the human eye's ability to distinguish individual color variations. Grayscale cameras are usually 8-bit and are very rare, as are cameras that support grayscale modes of photography.

Resolutions   The resolution of the camera is expressed in the total number of pixels the camera is capable of producing in an image. In most recent cameras, the number is expressed as megapixels, such as 2.1 megapixels. Camera resolution may also be presented in the same manner as monitor resolutions, illustrating the number of pixels an image is in width and height (1280x960, for example). Some cameras include the ability to take photos at varying resolutions and will list all the resolutions that they support. Cameras may list their resolutions as the interpolated value or as the noninterpolated, depending on how honest the manufacturer is when providing the specs. Check to be certain which value is being presented before buying.

Zoom: Optical and/or Digital Like many traditional film cameras, digital cameras often offer a zoom feature that allows you take close-up shots easily. When looking at the zoom, be sure to note whether it is an optical zoom or a digital zoom. *Optical zoom* is the same type of zoom used in traditional cameras, where a lens is used to achieve close-up images. The optics of an optical zoom on a digital camera may be built into the camera's lens assembly or may attach to a camera.

Digital zoom is a feature not found on traditional film cameras (it is sometimes found on digital camcorders and other video devices as well as digital still cameras). A *digital zoom* enlarges a portion of the image you are photographing, much the same as the image size function of Photoshop or another graphics program does. The remainder of the image is cropped out of the photo so only the enlarged section is left. This allows a digital camera to achieve more zoom factors than an optical zoom. It is also cheaper to build a digital zoom feature into a camera than an optical zoom. However, digital zooms never have the same quality as an optical zoom, because you aren't actually getting any new image data for the section you are zooming in on as you do with an optical zoom; you're simply making the pixels in a small image bigger. The edges of these pixels will become blurred (or if the zoom is high enough, blocky) to varying degrees as a result.

ISO Speed Equivalent ISO speeds are the standard speeds for 35mm film used in traditional photography. The ISO Speed Equivalent specification for a camera tells you what film speed a digital camera's photos will be equivalent to. A digital camera the ISO Speed Equivalent to 400 speed film would render the same results as using that 400 speed film in various lighting conditions or action shots.

Viewfinder Type There are three types of viewfinders that are used in digital cameras: LCD (liquid crystal display) screens, optical viewfinders, and reflex viewfinders. Nearly all digital cameras include an LCD screen that functions as a viewfinder, as well as to preview and delete images or control some of the settings of a camera. Using the LCD screen drains a fair amount of battery power, however, and a number of cameras also include a more traditional viewfinder (reflex or optical) that can be used instead of the LCD. Also, the LCD may not react fast enough or may be blurry if the camera is moved quickly.

A reflex viewfinder is the better (and more expensive) choice in a viewfinder because when you look at the viewfinder, a prism or mirror is reflecting the image from the camera's lens to your eye. This means you're seeing exactly what the camera will see when you take a picture. An optical viewfinder shows you the image in front of the camera, but it is not the same image that would be seen through the lens of the camera because the viewfinder is mounted to one side and (usually) just above the lens assembly. For mid-range shots, this makes little difference, but for close-ups and when using an optical zoom feature, the view through an optical viewfinder can be notably different from that of the lens.

Base Storage   Base storage is the amount of memory that comes with the camera for storing images. This can be memory that is built into the camera itself or a removable memory card that is included with the camera. Most cameras today will use a memory card of one type or another for storing images. This card can be swapped with additional cards during use. In the case of a memory card, the base memory refers to the standard capacity card included with a given digital camera model.

Additional Storage Options/Capacity   This specification refers to what type of memory storage a camera uses. Most cameras support only one of the various storage types currently on the market and cannot be changed to use a different type. The next section of this chapter looks at the various types of devices currently used for digital camera memory.

Image Capacity   A digital camera's specs may list the amount of images its base memory can hold under the description "image capacity." This will usually be more than one number, as digital cameras can often store files in multiple file types and with varying amounts of compression applied to the images when they are stored as graphics files. Generally, *the highest-quality frames value*, which tells you how many images can be stored if all are at the maximum quality/least compression available to the camera, and the *maximum image value*, which is the largest number of images with the greatest amount of compression applied to each, are given in a camera's specs. Remember that if you choose to use additional memory cards or cards of different capacities than the base memory, you will find different amounts of images can be stored on them than what is included in the camera's specifications.

Supported File Formats   There are dozens of different file formats that can be used by a computer to store digital images. The most widely used format today is the JPEG format. Most digital cameras will support storing images as JPEG files. The JPEG format offers varying levels of compression to reduce file size, and digital cameras will usually support two or three levels of compression. Some cameras support additional file formats such as the uncompressed TIFF format or the bitmap image (BMP) format that is commonly used on Windows-based PCs. A few digital cameras will use proprietary file formats, which will require special software from their manufacturer to open and convert to more commonly used image file formats.

Interfaces   A digital camera's interface is the method by which it is connected to a computer to transfer image files to the computer's hard drive. USB is establishing itself as the primary method for digital cameras to interface with the Mac. In addition to USB, FireWire will likely become a popular interface over the next year or two because of its vastly increased speed when transferring files (though only a few cameras currently support FireWire connections). Some cameras may support only PC serial ports, which limits them from being used with the Mac.

In addition to the camera's built-in interface, cameras that use CompactFlash or SmartMedia cards to store data (see next section) are able to use card readers to transfer data from the memory card to the Mac without needing to use the camera itself. Such card readers are available in USB, FireWire, and SCSI, models PC Card slot adapters (for PowerBooks) are also available. For digital cameras without support for the Mac or those that use a slow interface, such as USB, using an external card reader may be an attractive option for transferring images.

Storing Data from a Digital Camera

A digital camera needs to be able to store image files from the time you take a photo until you transfer the files to the computer. This requires some form of data storage. The following paragraphs look at the most commonly used storage methods for digital cameras. These include built-in memory, CompactFlash and SmartMedia memory cards, and the built-in floppy drive units and memory sticks used in Sony's digital cameras.

Built-in Memory   When digital cameras first appeared on the market, they came with a finite amount of memory built into the camera where image files could be stored. This memory could either be traditional DRAM, which needed battery power constantly to keep data refreshed (as described in Chapter 6) or it could be flash RAM. Flash RAM is technically not RAM at all because it stores information chemically rather than electrically as most computer memory does. This allows the data to be stored without needing to have an electrical current constantly applied. Very few cameras use actual DRAM to store image files anymore.

Built-in memory is not used on most cameras today because it has one primary problem. It is finite and cannot be expanded. This means if you have a camera with only 2 MB of RAM that can store 24 images, you will never be able to expand it and store more than 24 images in the camera. You will have to either delete images when the built-in memory becomes full or you will need to transfer the stored images to a computer before taking more (which may not be convenient or even possible at the time). With other storage options—memory cards, for example—you can fill up the available memory and then simply take out one memory card and replace it with another. This allows you to continue taking pictures and seems very much like changing the rolls of film in a traditional camera. The ability to buy and use larger memory cards also allows you to expand how many pictures you can store in the camera at one time, which cannot be done with built-in memory.

CompactFlash Cards CompactFlash cards are the most common memory cards on the market for digital cameras. A camera must be designed for the CompactFlash card to use one as its storage device. CompactFlash cards (and SmartMedia cards, discussed in the next section) store data using a special chemical reaction and can have images stored on and erased from them hundreds or even thousands of times. This chemical method also allows the memory on the card to be non-volatile, meaning it will retain its contents even when no power is being applied to the card (as a hard drive will).

CompactFlash cards use an interface that is based on the traditional IDE interface used for hard drives (and other internal drives). This places much of the control and access circuitry directly on the card itself. As a result, CompactFlash cards tend to be more expensive memory cards than the SmartMedia cards that are their main competition in the digital camera memory card market. However, that extra cost needs to be balanced against the two advantages it affords.

First, CompactFlash cards tend to have slightly faster access speeds than SmartMedia cards. For practical purposes, this speed only has a negligible impact on actual camera performance. Second, CompactFlash cards can be attached directly to a computer using an adapter that is significantly cheaper than a similar adapter would be for a SmartMedia card, where more control circuitry must be built into the adapter itself because it is not contained on the card.

Physically, CompactFlash cards are about half the size of a standard Type 2 PC Card, measuring 3.6 centimeters long by 4.3 centimeters wide and 0.33 centimeters thick. They are available in capacities ranging from 4 MB through 128 MB. They can be inserted into a PowerBook's PC Card slot with the use of a low-cost PC Card frame/adapter (or a desktop Mac's Card reader, such as the USB and SCSI models available from various companies). Once connected in such a manner, the CompactFlash card is treated by the Mac as a disk and mounted on the desktop where files can be copied to the hard drive or opened in a graphics application.

SmartMedia Cards SmartMedia cards are the second primary type of memory cards for digital cameras. Currently, they are less commonly used than CompactFlash cards, and their use by manufacturers in new camera models seems to be diminishing. SmartMedia cards are functionally similar to CompactFlash cards, though they do not use the standard IDE architecture that is designed into CompactFlash cards. Physically, SmartMedia cards are smaller than CompactFlash cards and appear to be more fragile, measuring 4.5 centimeters long by 3.7 centimeters wide and only 0.08 centimeters thick.

SmartMedia cards are available in two separate voltages: 3.3 volt and 5 volt. These voltages are not compatible with each other, and individual cameras and adapters will use only one of the two voltages. Currently, the 3.3 volt variation is more common in the marketplace.

The SmartMedia standard initially supported cards ranging in capacity only from 2 MB through 8 MB, though a later addition to the standard introduced 16-MB and 32-MB capacity SmartMedia cards in 1998. These cards are not backward-compatible with earlier cameras and card adapters, however. The standard has now been advanced to support cards with capacities as high as 128 MB.

SmartMedia cards have slightly lower pricing than CompactFlash cards, though the adapters needed to place SmartMedia cards into a PC Card slot or desktop Card readers are up to four times as expensive as those used for CompactFlash cards. Because SmartMedia cards are much thinner than CompactFlash cards, it was possible for an adapter known as the FlashPath adapter to be developed that allows SmartMedia cards to be inserted into a standard floppy drive. Although the FlashPath adapters generally don't ship with Macintosh driver software, Fuji has designed a Macintosh utility for using the adapter. The FlashPath adapter is still limited to floppy drive access speeds, however.

Floppy Disks and Memory Sticks   Back in 1997, Sony unveiled their Mavica line of digital cameras. The Mavicas took a new approach to storing image files on a digital camera. Where other cameras use either a cable connection to transfer data from the camera's memory to a computer or use a memory card that requires a special adapter to be used with a computer, Sony's Mavica cameras store data on the one type of media that virtually every computer can accommodate (or could before the iMac was released): a floppy disk. Users simply insert a blank floppy into the camera, take pictures, and then insert the filled floppy into a computer to access the image files of their photos. No need for special adapters or cables to transfer images. Floppies are also a low-cost media compared to memory cards, and you can easily carry a number of floppies with you, almost like rolls of film for a traditional camera.

Unfortunately, floppies have some drawbacks as well. They are slower than either internal memory or a memory card. Sony has narrowed this drawback a bit by using special 4x floppy drives in their cameras, which are noticeably faster than a traditional floppy drive would be. Floppies also require more battery power to write image files to than a memory card or internal memory, meaning users may need to carry more batteries with them when taking photos. Floppies are also magnetic media, making the image files stored on them susceptible to damage from strong magnetic or electrical fields, an issue not shared with other digital camera storage options. Finally, floppies have a very limited storage capacity of 1.44 MB. This means that after only a relatively few pictures, you'll need to replace one floppy with another. This issue is becoming an even greater one as cameras come out with higher and higher resolutions, meaning larger and larger image files.

In addition to using floppy disks as a storage method, Sony has developed their own proprietary storage device known as the memory stick. The memory stick is very similar to a SmartMedia card in terms of function and size. Memory sticks deliver comparable performance to other digital camera memory types and are available in capacities up 64 MB. Memory sticks are used as an optional storage device on many Sony cameras (although Sony has also begun using them as storage for audio and video recording devices). A special memory stick adapter is needed to transfer the images directly from the memory stick to a computer. A number of such adapters are available including PC Card adapters and floppy disk adapters, similar to those available for SmartMedia cards. Alternatively, data can be transferred by using a cable attached to the camera as with other cameras.

Desktop Cameras

Technically, digital cameras also encompass a series of devices known as desktop cameras or tethered cameras. These cameras, such as the QuickCam, are not designed to be used away from the computer. They have no built-in storage options, no autofocus abilities, no shutter button, and no viewfinder, and they are little more than the lens/CCD assembly of a digital camera attached to a cable (such as a USB cable) that is connected to the computer. To take a picture with a desktop camera, you need to use software on the computer that can take a still photo or capture video from the camera (usually included with the camera). Like other digital cameras, desktop cameras have varying levels of resolution, usually given in the width and height of the image the camera generates (320×240 is a common resolution, for example).

Although desktop cameras are digital imaging devices, and you can use them to take digital photos, this tends not to be their primary function. Far more often, desktop cameras are used for videoconferencing, where a video stream is transmitted to another user in real time over the Internet. This can be done with two users exchanging their own real-time video images or with a group of people all seeing each other. There are a number of applications available for videoconferencing, and most are cross-platform (CUseeMe, iVisit, and ICU II being the most popular). Desktop cameras can also be used to record video clips that can be stored on your Mac's hard drive and edited.

Another growing use of desktop video cameras is to create webcams. A webcam is a website with a self-updating picture from some remote location. A site that displays a new picture of Times Square in New York City every minute for people to watch is an example of a webcam. Personal webcams of individual homes and offices are becoming a growing fascination on the Internet. These can be set up easily enough using a desktop camera attached to a Macintosh and one of several utilities that will take a still image from that camera and upload it to an Internet server at predefined intervals. Special HTML code, JavaScripts, or Java applets can then be used to make the image on the web page refresh at the same predefined interval.

Photo Conversion Services

If you don't want to go to the expense of buying a digital camera or the effort of using a scanner, but you still want to be able to have digital images of your photographs, there is another option. Today, most places that develop film from traditional cameras will offer the option of having your photos provided to you electronically as well as in the form of traditional prints. Some of these services will put your photos on floppy disks, though these are becoming rare. Most commonly, you will either be able to have your photos placed on a special Photo CD using the format pioneered by Kodak (mentioned in Chapter 16 as a CD-ROM format), or, growing in popularity, you will be able to have your photos e-mailed to you or placed on a special website where you use a name and password to retrieve them. Usually, these services cost a few dollars more when developing your film and are available as options if you provide the negatives of your pictures at some later date.

If you want to have images other than photos converted to a digital format, many graphics houses and printing/copy shops will offer scanning services to you for all kinds of images and documents. The prices will often vary depending on the company and level of service you are using. If you find yourself using the services of such a company on a regular basis, however, you might want to consider the cost and time involved compared to purchasing a scanner and performing the process yourself.

Troubleshooting Common Scanner Issues

Following are a few common problems with scanners, along with possible solutions.

The Scanner Software Says It Can't Find the Scanner

This means that one of two things have likely happened. Either the scanner's driver extensions (or possibly a control panel) are not installed properly and the Mac doesn't have the ability to interact with the scanner as a result, the scanner is not connected properly, or the power is not turned on.

First check the obvious things to make sure all the cables attaching the scanner are connected properly. If it is a SCSI model, be sure that all SCSI rules about device ID numbers, termination, and appropriate cable length are followed (see Chapter 12 for details). If it is a USB model, make sure that any hub the scanner is connected to is attached and powered (if it is a powered hub). Also check to be certain that the scanner is turned on and that it is plugged in.

If the scanner appears to be connected properly, use the Apple System Profiler or, for SCSI models, Adaptec's SCSIProbe to make sure the Mac is recognizing the scanner. If it is, you probably have a problem with the driver or scanner utility software not being installed properly. Reinstall it from the original source CD-ROMs.

Images Aren't as Clear as They Should Be

This situation can indicate a number of possible problems. First, check to be certain that you are using scanning utilities appropriate to your scanner. If your scanner can scan at varying resolutions, it may be scanning at a lower resolution than you intended. Check with your scanner's manual for details on choosing an appropriate resolution. This can also indicate a problem with the CCD sensor or the scanner head, though this is unlikely.

Images Are a Different Size Onscreen or Printed than They Should Be

As described earlier in this chapter, screen size of an image is not truly related to the physical size of the image when scanned. Scanning at different degrees of resolution will result in variations in how large an image appears on-screen.

If an image prints at a vastly different size than it was scanned, the most likely cause is that the application used to print the image does not support using the print-size data stored when the image was scanned. Try printing in another application. Some graphics applications may also modify this data when they edit an image. Similarly, some file formats simply don't support recording the print size of an image when it is scanned or saved.

The Mac Won't Start Up with a Scanner Attached

This should only occur with SCSI scanner and indicates a problem with the SCSI chain, rather than the scanner itself. Refer to Chapter 12 for information on solving SCSI chain problems.

Resources for Further Study

The following URLs provide additional information on some of the concepts, issues, and products discussed in this chapter.

About.com: Mac Hardware Digital Camera Resources— http://machardware.about.com/msubcamera.htm

About.com: Mac Support Scanner Resources— http://macsupport.about.com/msub35.htm

*About.com: Computer Peripherals Scanner Resources—*http://peripherals.about.com/msub_scanners.htm

CHAPTER 26

Video Cards/Chipsets and Graphics Acceleration

To display information on a monitor or LCD display, the Mac requires special circuitry devoted to processing video data. This video circuitry can be built onto an expansion card that is installed in the Mac (as in the Power Mac G3/G4), or it can be built directly into the Mac's motherboard (as in the iMac, iBook, and PowerBook computers). Video circuitry is dedicated first to displaying data on-screen, but it can also provide other functions.

A function almost all video cards today provide is graphics acceleration. Graphics acceleration uses special hardware circuitry to help the Mac draw and render complex images (particularly 3D images) on-screen more quickly. Often it is the graphics acceleration features that differentiate different types of video circuitry more than it is their ability to display information on-screen. Other features can also be contained in video circuitry, including hardware to speed up access to compressed or encoded video data, the ability to capture analog video, the ability to display television signals, and the ability to provide video output to varying types of displays.

This chapter examines how video circuitry is used to perform each of these functions on a Mac. It also looks at the video circuitry used in the Macs covered by this book and options for extending the video abilities built into these Macs.

How Video Cards/Chipsets Send Data to a Mac's Display

The first function of a Mac's video circuitry is to allow the Mac to send data to a display. Functions such as graphics acceleration, DVD movie decoding, and video input or TV tuning are all secondary to allowing the Mac to transmit data to the monitor or display. The Mac requires circuitry devoted to transmitting data to the display.

At this most basic level, the Mac sends the information of what needs to be displayed on-screen to the video circuitry in individual frames, one frame at a time. A frame for computer display is very much like a frame in a movie. It is a single still image. When one frame is replaced by another and then another very quickly, it appears as though the image being displayed is moving. Each frame is stored in the Mac's video RAM (VRAM) until it is actually displayed on the screen. As each frame is displayed, it is sent to the monitor by the connections built into the video circuitry and is displayed on-screen. The process of sending frames to the screen occurs so fast that users are often unaware it is even happening.

The video circuitry also communicates with the display attached to it. This allows the Mac to be aware of what screen resolutions and refresh rates are supported by the display. This information is important because it determines how large each individual frame sent to the monitor can be, as well as how often the Mac needs to send individual frames to the display. The refresh rate of the monitor determines how quickly individual frames are sent from the Mac's video circuitry. Since the monitor can only paint one frame at a time while it is refreshing the screen, the refresh rate is the same as the number of frames displayed per second. So a monitor with a refresh rate of 75 Hz displays 75 frames from the video card each second.

Digital-to-Analog Video Conversion

When the Mac's processor sends data to the video circuitry to be displayed on-screen, it is sending digital representations of what the image on the screen should look like. Most monitors today are analog video devices (the exception being some recent LCD displays). This means that they can only function when dealing with a consistent signal much like a waveform and not with the strict on-or-off digital signals that the Mac uses to work with data. Because of this, the video circuitry of the Mac needs to convert the digital signal it receives from the Mac's processor into a series of analog signals that can be understood and displayed by the monitor. To do this, the video circuitry uses three digital-to-analog converters, one for each of the three primary colors of light used in a monitor (red, blue, and green). The electrical waveform signal generated by each of these converters is sent through the monitor port and along a separate wire in the cable to monitor, which then displays the image on-screen.

Timing the Signal Properly   The video circuitry of the Mac is outputting each individual frame as an analog electrical waveform of three different colors. As the crests of these waveforms rise and fall, the monitor displays greater or less amounts of each color as the image is drawn on the screen. For each frame to be displayed properly, the signal being sent must be timed perfectly with the part of the screen being drawn at any given moment. This is why communication between the monitor and the video circuitry is so important. Most monitors are designed to sync with the timing chip built into a Mac's video circuitry so that the timing is perfect. This process usually uses special sync signals, though some monitors have used a specific color signal (often green) instead of using a separate sync signal.

Video RAM

Video RAM was discussed in Chapter 6 as one of the three types of RAM that are used in Macintosh computers. The VRAM is where the Mac's video circuitry stores each frame before sending it to the monitor to be displayed. If the video circuitry supports any type of graphics acceleration, the VRAM will also be used to store data being used by video circuitry to increase the processing of graphics data.

The amount of VRAM installed in a Mac determines the screen resolutions that can be displayed from that Mac, as well as the color depths that are available at each resolution. This is because each pixel in each frame on-screen needs to have a specific amount of VRAM dedicated to holding the color data that it displays. At a color depth of 256 colors, each pixel requires 1 byte (or 8 bits) of data. On a screen displaying 800x600, there are 480,000 pixels in each frame being displayed on-screen. That means each individual frame requires nearly half a megabyte (480 KB) of VRAM. As you move to higher resolutions and color depths, each frame requires more and more VRAM.

The situation becomes even more complicated because of two other issues. The first is that the Mac needs to constantly store new frames in the VRAM (while sending existing frames out to the display). It also needs to refresh the data stored in the VRAM, just like any other RAM, as discussed in Chapter 6. This means that not only do you need to have enough VRAM to store all of your frames at once, but the VRAM needs to be fast enough to continually refresh the data it is storing and to refresh the frames it contains and the individual frame being displayed on-screen at any given time. This is why VRAM is often a special type of RAM known as SGRAM (synchronous graphics RAM) that is both much faster and more expensive than traditional RAM.

Types of Video/Monitor Ports

A video card or the video circuitry built into a Mac can use a number of different types of ports to send data to a monitor or other type of display. While the current Macs tend to support primarily the computer industry-standard VGA port, this is not the only type of port that some video cards and/or Mac models have featured.

Traditional Apple Monitors   For many years, Apple used a proprietary monitor interface. This interface used a 15-pin DB connector, shown in Figure 26-1. The pins were arranged in two specific rows, making the connector longer than the one used for VGA and SVGA monitors used with PCs. Although Apple abandoned this connector in favor of the industry-standard VGA connector with the Blue and White Power Mac G3, any older Macs and several current Mac video cards still use this interface. Additionally, all Apple monitors before the iMac-like Studio Displays introduced along with the Blue G3 used the same interface. If you wish to use one of these older monitors with a current Mac, you will need to use an adapter such as the one shown in Figure 26-2 (one is included with the PowerBook computers and one was included with the Power Mac G3; others can be purchased from various companies). Similarly, if you have an older Mac or are installing a video card with the older connectors and wish to use a VGA or SVGA monitor with it, you will need an adapter.

Figure 26-1
The older Apple monitor port.

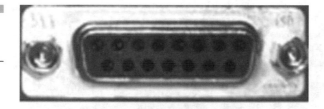

Figure 26-2
An Apple-to-VGA adapter.

VGA-Style Ports All the current Macs that support video-out (the Power Mac, PowerBook, and iMac DV models) use an industry-standard VGA monitor port, as shown in Figure 26-3. The big advantage of using this type of port is that it is used in virtually any monitor currently made and will allow you to connect an extremely wide variety of monitors to the Mac with no effort at all.

S-Video S-video is a technology used for high-quality connections of home entertainment devices, such as televisions, VCRs, and DVD players. The PowerBook computers and some video cards for the Power Mac include an S-video out port. This allows you to directly connect the computer to a television, VCR, or other device, such as some projectors, and to use the TV (or other device) as an external monitor. Because of the scan rate and resolution limitations of most home entertainment equipment, you may not get overly powerful video. Even so, this does provide you a method of outputting video directly to home electronics and can be useful if you need to record the actions on your Mac's screen to videotape. Figure 26-4 shows the S-video port on the PowerBook.

Digital Ports CRT monitors are analog devices and need to receive analog data from a video port as described earlier in this section. It is the

Figure 26-3
The VGA monitor port used on today's Macs.

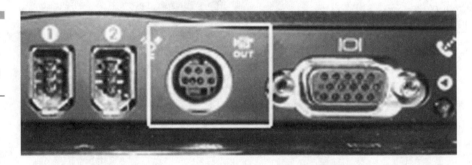

Figure 26-4
The S-Video port on today's PowerBooks (also found on some video cards).

signal that determines how the electron guns in the monitor fires for each pixel. LCD screens, however, function differently (as discussed in Chapter 4). Rather than using an electron gun to paint the screen, LCD screens are huge collections of individual on and off switches, with one switch indicating the status and color of each pixel on the screen. This is very much like the digital way in which the Mac handles data. As a result, it is possible for LCD screens to directly accept digital data for a faster and smoother display than can be achieved when working with a digital-to-analog converter. The most recent desktop LCD screens (including those from Apple) use a special digital port for receiving data directly from the video circuitry rather than using the VGA-style connector. These LCD displays require a separate type of video port (often a DVI port). The video cards used in many Power Mac G4 computers include a digital video out port, though other Macs and other video cards have yet to include such a port. In several cases, manufacturers of digital LCD displays also produce adapters for using their new displays with traditional VGA-style ports.

Apple's ADC Monitor Port Apple recently unveiled a new proprietary monitor port. This port combines the standard video output features of earlier ports with a USB channel and a power supply connection. The purpose of this port is to allow a display to use only a single cable. This cable provides power to the display from the computer, the video signal, and data, and a connection for USB ports that may be built into a monitor (many monitors, including all of Apple's current displays, include a built-in USB hub).

The new monitor port is included on some of the latest Macintosh models and is used on Apples newest displays. As of this writing, the technology is extremely new and the port has yet to be adopted by any other monitors or video card manufacturers. The Macs supporting the new port also tend to include a standard VGA port as well. It is likely that an adapter will be produced to convert between the port and a VGA or digital standard port for using monitors that rely solely on the ADC port with older Macs.

Multiple Video Cards

For Power Macintosh computers, or other Macs where it is possible to install an expansion card, it is possible to install more than one set of video circuitry. When you do this, each set of video circuitry will be recognized separately by the Mac. Each one will be sent separate data to display, meaning that you can use multiple monitors, each displaying different pieces of data. Each display will be treated independently by the Mac, and each will be limited to the abilities of the video card it is using.

Configuring Multiple Monitors   When you have multiple video cards installed in a Mac, you need to configure how the Mac OS uses them. This includes determining which video card's monitor will be the primary display (the one containing the menu bar and displaying the startup process). You also need to tell the Mac where the monitors are in relation to each other (i.e., is one "above" the other or are they side by side, and which is on the left or right). You do this using the Arrange item in the Monitors control panel (shown in Figure 26-5) once you have attached monitors to each video card that is installed.

Figure 26-5
The Arrange feature in the Monitors control panel.

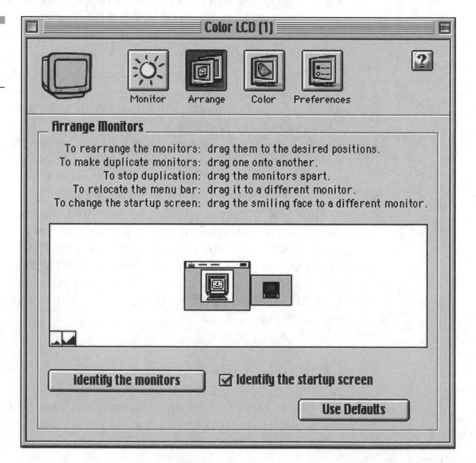

By default, the primary display will be the monitor that is connected to the Power Mac's primary video card (the one installed in the AGP slot or 66-MHz PCI slot). This monitor will be identified as monitor number 1 by the Mac and will be the one that displays the menu bar and startup process. Additional monitors will be numbered 2, 3, or 4, depending on which PCI slot the video card to which they are connected is attached. To identify which monitor is assigned which number, press the Identify button in the Arrange item. Each monitor will display a large number that corresponds with its identification.

To arrange the monitors in orientation to one another, simply drag the icons for each monitor around in the Arrange item (each icon will display the identification number of the monitor it represents). If the icon for monitor 2 is positioned above the icon for monitor 1, then moving the cursor above the top edge of monitor 1 will cause the cursor to appear on the bottom edge of monitor 2 (the same is true of dragging an icon or window). If the icon for monitor 2 is to the left of the icon for monitor 1, then moving the cursor beyond the left edge of the screen on monitor 1 will cause the cursor to appear on the right edge of monitor 2, and vice versa.

If you want to move the menu bar from one monitor to another, simply drag the tiny menu bar that is on the icon of the primary monitor in the Arrange item to the icon of one of the other monitors. Similarly, if you want to change which monitor displays the startup process, simply drag the tiny Happy Mac that is on the icon of the primary monitor to another monitor's icon.

When you make changes to the Arrange item of the Monitors control panel, they take effect immediately. You do not need to close the control panel or restart. Also, this information is stored in the Mac's PRAM, so all monitors will be appropriately recognized at startup. However, your multiple monitor settings will be lost along with your Mac's date and time settings (and other PRAM data) if you need to zap the contents of the PRAM.

How 2D Graphics Acceleration Works

The Mac uses certain routines to draw images on-screen. These routines are part of a language known as QuickDraw. QuickDraw allows developers to insert a simple set of instructions into a program to draw a window or a pop-up menu or any other typical Mac OS interface item on-screen without needing to describe each and every pixel that makes up the window, menu, and so on. This is because QuickDraw has the specifications for these elements built into it. It also has other specifications for various items that the Mac regularly needs to create on-screen built into it. Because these drawing routines and objects are so universally used in the Mac OS and in Mac applications, video circuitry can be designed that includes the instructions for drawing these devices in hardware. This means that the process of actually drawing the item performs much faster because the Mac doesn't have to repeatedly perform the basic computations relating to drawing the item.

For example, the items in a Mac's menu are always displayed at the same font size and usually using one of a very limited selection of fonts. Each time it needs to draw a new letter in the menu bar, the Mac can tell the video card the exact instructions for how to draw that letter, which means that the video circuitry needs to go through the process of following those instructions. However, if the video card includes the knowledge of how that letter is supposed to look, then the Mac can just say "draw the letter M" without needing to describe what the letter M looks like and how to draw it.

Beyond QuickDraw Acceleration

Almost all video cards of chipsets for the Mac include QuickDraw acceleration to make drawing common Mac OS elements faster and more efficient. Some video cards also include acceleration hardware for other kinds of 2D graphics acceleration. These cards usually include special hardware that follows the routines used in Adobe's Photoshop or other powerful and widely used graphics applications. This allows certain actions performed within Photoshop to be accelerated, which can significantly speed up the performance of manipulating image data in the application.

How 3D Graphics Acceleration Works

This section is divided into two areas: an explanation of how Macs process, render, and display 3D images and a discussion of how video cards or chipsets can act as hardware accelerators to those tasks. Understanding a number of the tasks involved in rendering 3D objects or scenes on-screen is important to truly understanding the benefit of good hardware 3D graphics acceleration and the importance of a number of features involved in video cards that offer such functions.

How the Mac Displays 3D Information

The most commonly discussed type of graphics acceleration is 3D graphics acceleration. When the Mac is being used to display three-dimensional scenes, such as in a 3D CAD (computer-aided design) application, a 3D modeling application, or a 3D game, there are many demands being placed on the Mac in order to accurately draw the image on-screen. This is because the Mac's screen is a flat, two-dimensional surface, and drawing three-dimensional objects or scenes requires that the Mac add the dimension of depth to its display by computing the appropriate angles, textures, and shadows that would be displayed in a three-dimensional scene or on a three-dimensional object.

The World Is Wires and Textures A three-dimensional scene or object being displayed on the Mac's screen is actually a series of wire frames that represent each object. These frames, such as the one shown in Figure 26-6, define all of the objects in a 3D scene or virtual world. As the apparent angle of view for the person looking at the Mac changes, the

Figure 26-6 *The same scene in the wire frames the Mac uses to map 3D objects and rendered with a series of texture maps.*

geometry of the wire frame objects being displayed also needs to change. This is one of the things that make 3D rendering so complex. Just shifting the wire frames of the virtual world to reflect each and every change in position is computationally taxing.

When you render a 3D scene or play a 3D game, you don't see wire frames. Instead, you see objects, each with a different surface texture and/or color, because the Mac maps a texture over each object. This texture map needs to only be placed on specific individual objects, but the texture needs to be adjusted for each of the angles and positions that are part of each object. This is because very few surfaces in a virtual world or 3D scene are perfectly flat or perpendicular to each other.

Texture mapping requires an immense amount of computing effort. The Mac needs to be able to apply each texture to each varied surface of each object in a scene. It also needs to constantly update those textures if the perspective of the scene and thus the wire frames of the objects themselves change. This is what makes 3D rendering so complex.

Polygon Drawing   Polygon drawing is an approach to simplifying 3D rendering. Polygon rendering uses a set colored polygon rather than a texture to cover the surface of a wire-frame object. Because each shape is much simpler than a complete texture for covering an object, it requires less computing power to apply a surface to the objects in a world. But because there will be variations where the edges of each polygon touches the next polygon on the surface of an object, there will be some definition and pattern to an object's surface (though not as much or as realistic as using texture mapping).

Maintaining Perspective   In addition to drawing the individual wire-frame objects and applying surfaces to them (either with texture mapping or polygon drawing), the Mac needs to be able to maintain perspective in a 3D scene. To maintain perspective, the Mac needs to have some way of defining which objects should be displayed in front of others. This can be done by adding another value to all the pixels on-screen, which tells the Mac not only where a pixel is on the two-dimensional screen and what color it maintains, but also how much depth it is supposed to have. This is known as the *z-buffer,* and it works in concert with the traditional display techniques for drawing data on the screen. Unfortunately, the z-buffer requires a lot of memory because you need to add varying degrees of depth to each pixel on-screen. The more levels of the depth, the more excess memory is needed. Often, the z-buffer easily takes up as much VRAM as is needed for simply managing the resolution and color depth of the Mac's screen all by itself.

There are a couple of other ways of maintaining perspective that don't require as much VRAM but do make the Mac work harder. The first is to calculate which objects or points are "further away" from the user and then to draw those on-screen first. As the other objects and points are drawn, they will be drawn on top of the existing objects and will therefore cover them. Of course, this means that the Mac has to do a lot of excess work in drawing every object again and again for each frame.

A variation on this technique is to determine which objects will be hidden behind other objects before the Mac draws anything and to eliminate them from the frame being drawn completely. This keeps the Mac from having to redraw each point and object, but it means the Mac does need to work harder beforehand to determine which objects will be hidden.

Lighting and Shading   Yet another factor in rendering a 3D scene or virtual world is the lighting and shading. In the real world, light sources illuminate some objects more than others, and any object in the path of a light source will cast a shadow on the objects and surfaces behind it. A large surface is illuminated more on the areas that are closest to the light source and shade gradually darker as you move away from those areas. Some surfaces also reflect light more than others.

All of this needs to be taken into consideration when rendering a 3D scene. Many 3D rendering applications give you the ability to place light sources and determine the types of light that each source generates. Many games vary the light sources and types when moving from one scene to another.

The ability to shade textures and adjust brightness for different textures is an integral part of 3D rendering, and it requires that the Mac make additional calculations for objects when rendering their surface textures based on the location of the light source relative to an object's surface. It also requires that the Mac calculate the shapes, sizes, and positions of shadows generated by objects. This shadow needs to then be rendered as an object unto itself or as light variations on other objects and surfaces. Table 26-1 lists the basic process of rendering a 3D scene.

Accelerating 3D Rendering

Video circuitry that includes 3D acceleration features actually includes one or more dedicated processors. These processors are designed to take over much of the work of rendering 3D objects and scenes by performing a number of the rendering functions for the Mac's processor. This allows the Mac to perform other needed functions rather than performing all

TABLE 26-1

The General Steps
of Rendering a 3D
Scene.

1. Compare the position of each wire-frame intersection (vertex).

2. Cut off edges of objects at boundaries (such as the edge of window or positioned behind other objects).

3. Eliminate surfaces that are hidden behind other objects or outside the user's perspective.

4. Translate 3D locations to 2D positions for display.

5. Map textures or polygons to object surfaces.

6. Incorporate resulting image into a display frame.

7. Send frame to VRAM for transmission to monitor.

the calculations involved in rendering a 3D scene. Since the processors used in 3D acceleration circuitry are designed and dedicated to performing specific functions relating to 3D rendering, they are often able to perform some of these functions more efficiently and more quickly than the Mac's processor. Not all video chipsets can perform each and every 3D rendering function. In many cases, the actual rendering functions are split between the dedicated processors in the video circuitry and the Mac's processor.

The ATI Rage 128 video chipset, which is the basis for all current Macs, save the iBook, is designed to perform most of the important functions of 3D rendering on its own, without much additional effort from the Mac's processor. This includes the drawing of basic wire-frame shapes, maintaining the z-buffer for proper perspective in 3D scenes, mapping textures to objects and filtering texture maps as needed, and shading objects as appropriate to light sources and texture types. The Rage 128 chipset then takes the 3D images and coordinates them with other video to be displayed and sends them to the screen.

Also, because the chipset supports the AGP standard, it can exchange data with the Mac's processor and system RAM at rates far in excess of previous video cards and chipsets. This improves rendering speed even further. AGP, originally mentioned in Chapter 8, also allows the video card to store data, such as texture maps, directly in the Mac's system RAM if the VRAM is too limited or is needed for other functions.

Types of 3D Graphics Acceleration

Beyond the hardware abilities of a video card or video chipset, the Mac needs to know how to interact with the available 3D acceleration hardware. Not only does this mean that the Mac OS needs to be aware of the hardware, it also means that the application doing the 3D rendering needs to use a specific set of instructions to communicate with the hardware. There are three primary types of 3D acceleration that have been supported under the Mac OS: the original QuickDraw 3D RAVE acceleration, the newer industry-standard OpenGL, and the device-specific Voodoo acceleration developed by 3Dfx Inc.

QuickDraw 3D RAVE Apple created a standard set of 3D rendering routines as part of the Mac OS. Known as QuickDraw 3D, these were extensions of the original QuickDraw standard and did essentially the same thing as QuickDraw did for 2D data being displayed on-screen. QuickDraw 3D gave developers of Mac 3D applications and games a series of predefined standards for drawing objects so they wouldn't have to reinvent the wheel each time they wanted to draw a common object or shape on-screen.

To facilitate accelerating the 3D rendering process, Apple developed a technology known as QuickDraw 3D RAVE. QuickDraw 3D RAVE was a special extension to the QuickDraw 3D routines that interacted with whatever acceleration hardware was installed, provided it supported QuickDraw 3D RAVE acceleration. QuickDraw 3D RAVE would intercept the requests being made of the QuickDraw 3D routines. If the video chipset or card of the Mac was capable of accelerating any of the tasks involved in rendering the requested material, QuickDraw 3D RAVE would send those tasks to the video hardware rather than to the processor.

QuickDraw 3D RAVE offered an advantage in that it kept the developers of software from needing to worry about what hardware would do what work. They simply had to write software to use the QuickDraw 3D routines. If there was hardware to accelerate every part of the process, RAVE would invoke it. If there was no graphics acceleration hardware at all, the Mac's processor would deal with every QuickDraw 3D request. If only some aspects of the process could be accelerated, then those that could would be accelerated.

The only real problem with QuickDraw 3D RAVE is that it is very Mac-centric. Although the QuickDraw 3D routines can be placed over the native 3D routines of Windows, they aren't by default. QuickDraw 3D is, at its heart, a Mac technology. This meant that developers often needed to develop software separately for the Mac and PC, gaming software in particular. This added cost and effort to developers for the Mac, which is for many products a smaller market. Similarly, video cards supporting graphics acceleration needed to be designed to support RAVE, either in their hardware or at least in their driver software. Otherwise, RAVE would not be able to separate out QuickDraw 3D requests to them.

OpenGL   OpenGL is a standard set of 3D rendering routines that functions much like QuickDraw 3D and includes hardware support in much the same way as QuickDraw 3D RAVE. There is one fundamental difference, however. OpenGL is a widely accepted computer industry standard. The OpenGL routines were originally designed to be used with UNIX-based Silicon Graphics Workstations (often powerhouses of 3D design and rendering for advanced professional uses). OpenGL has also been added to the Windows operating systems as a built-in feature of Windows NT/2000 and an optional feature for Windows 95/98. This means that it is far more established than QuickDraw 3D as a series of 3D rendering routines and libraries. It is also somewhat more advanced.

Apple added OpenGL support to the Mac as part of a renewed commitment to Macintosh game development in 1998. The OpenGL libraries (stored in the Extensions folder) are now a standard part of every Mac OS installation. As a result, developers using OpenGL do not need to do the same degree of redeveloping their applications and games for use on the Mac that they needed to do during the QuickDraw 3D era.

Like QuickDraw 3D RAVE, OpenGL provides a layer where 3D rendering requests can be passed to hardware accelerators instead of the Mac's processor. As with RAVE, what tasks are passed to hardware acceleration depend on the hardware installed and what it can support. Also, as with RAVE, the video chipset and/or driver software for it must include support for OpenGL in order for OpenGL to be able to send appropriate tasks to the video hardware.

Voodoo   Both QuickDraw 3D RAVE and OpenGL provide developers with the ability to simply write applications that make requests to a software layer of the Mac OS. This layer than forwards these requests to the appropriate graphics acceleration hardware as indicated by the available hardware. In both cases, the developer creates software that talks to a component of the Mac OS and not directly to the video circuitry. Voodoo technology is a graphics technique that works the opposite of this, where an application (usually a game) deals directly with the video hardware.

Voodoo acceleration (sometimes called 3Dfx or Glide acceleration) was developed by 3Dfx Inc., and it includes a specific set of hardware. This hardware is defined for any Voodoo card, and a card adhering to one of the Voodoo standards (at this writing there have been five either proposed or produced) needs to provide the same acceleration components as another card adhering to the same standard. Some features such as the type of monitor port, amount of VRAM on the card, and support for other types of acceleration may vary from one card to another, but the Voodoo chipset itself needs to be the same.

The reason the Voodoo chipset on the card needs to be the same is that Voodoo acceleration works because a 3D game is designed to interact with specific hardware, looking to the video card to perform specific types of graphics acceleration and ignoring the processor or the 3D rendering abilities of the Mac OS. That a game developer can do this and reliably know exactly what results (both in terms of output and rendering speed) the hardware will produce allows the developer to incorporate very device-specific commands into the game. This results in much faster 3D rendering of specific game elements. And these elements are almost always rendered very crisply and realistically, often more so than OpenGL and almost always more so than RAVE.

Voodoo is extremely powerful for 3D gaming, where specific routines can be used for rendering 3D objects and the same primitive objects and textures are repeatedly used. However, for other 3D graphics applications, such as 3D modeling or drawing programs, Voodoo is rather limited in that the wide variety of tasks that can be handled by various other video chipsets and/or the Mac's processor cannot be sorted by a layer of the Mac's screen drawing technology such as in OpenGL or QuickDraw 3D RAVE.

Also, applications or games need to be written specifically for Voodoo video cards in order for the 3D acceleration functions of a Voodoo card to kick in. The Mac OS can't determine the card can perform a task and send it to a Voodoo chipset using OpenGL or RAVE. This means that, unless you're specifically interested in running Voodoo-enabled games, you're probably better off considering some of the other 3D acceleration options on the market.

There have been five generations of the Voodoo technology to date, and each generation introduces more powerful 3D acceleration. You can add a number of Voodoo-enabled video cards to the Mac, including some cards that do not ship with specific Macintosh support. If you choose a Voodoo card that doesn't include Mac-specific drivers, there are generic Mac drivers that can be downloaded from 3Dfx. These drivers may not provide total support for other features of the card, but they usually allow the card to function in combination with the basic video drivers that are part of the Mac OS.

Because adding Voodoo cards to the Mac requires an expansion slot, only the Power Mac computers are designed to accept such a card (although a mezzanine slot Voodoo2 card was created for the original iMacs). Voodoo cards are available in both PCI and AGP variations, though the AGP versions will give better performance. If you plan to replace a Power Mac G4's stock AGP video card with a Voodoo card, be aware that you will lose the ability to play DVD movies because (as discussed next in this chapter and in Chapter 17) the Mac relies on circuitry included in the ATI Rage 128 video chipset to decode DVD movies for playback.

Video Compression Acceleration

In addition to accelerating the Mac's ability to draw or render objects on-screen, some video cards or chipsets include dedicated hardware designed to help the Mac deal with various types of digital video compression. A compressed video stream, such as an MPEG encoded file or the MPEG-2 encoding used for DVD movies, often requires a good amount of processing power for the Mac to be able to decode and display the video data in real time without any signs of choppiness. As newer, more powerful compression and encoding techniques are created, they allow for greater and greater compression, meaning multimedia files take up significantly less space. However, that compression requires the processor to work harder to decompress the data.

Video compression acceleration isn't generally a feature of a video card or chipset. Most of the time, decompression of video is either relegated completely to the Mac's processor, and the instructions for decompressing the data are given in software, or a dedicated expansion card is used that is separate from the video card. Some compression schemes, however, are too complex for the Mac to deal with entirely by the processor using software-based instructions, and yet only a limited amount of hardware decompression technology may be needed. In these cases, smaller amount of decompression hardware can easily be placed on a video card.

MPEG-2, the scheme used for DVD movies, is the principle example of a compression scheme that the processor in some Macs is capable of handling but is still too complex to rely exclusively on the processor and software-only instructions. The use of a video card that can accelerate the MPEG-2 decompression (but does not handle the decompression on its own) is how the current Macs allow DVD movie playback. A 400-MHz G3 or G4 processor is fast enough to do much of the work of decompressing MPEG-2 video, but it still needs some help to accelerate the process. The ATI Rage 128 video chipset or card used in the current Macs includes MPEG-2 acceleration hardware, enabling the current Macs to play DVD movies without requiring a separate decoder card. However, because the Mac relies on the acceleration hardware on the card/chipset, it cannot decode MPEG-2 if the card was to be replaced with a different video card.

Video Cards/Chipsets Used in the Current Macs

This section lists each of the Mac models covered by this book and includes an overview of the video card or chipset that is the standard setup for that Mac. It also includes some information on the additional video options available to each Macintosh computer.

The Power Mac G4 (AGP Video Card Models)

All but the earliest Power Mac G4 models use an AGP (Advanced Graphics Port) slot for the primary video card. As described in Chapter 8, AGP offers a number of advantages for boosting video performance—particularly 3D graphics acceleration—over PCI slots. AGP enables the video card to communicate more often and more quickly with the Mac's processor. It also gives the video card's dedicated graphics coprocessors direct access to the Mac's system RAM in addition to the card's video RAM. This means that the video card has more flexibility in dealing with 3D rendering data that requires large amounts of RAM, such as the z-buffer for maintaining perspective between 3D objects and for more advanced and detailed texture maps for 3D objects.

RAGE 128 AGP Card   The AGP video card that is included with the Power Mac G4 is an ATI Rage 128 card. This card includes 16 MB of VRAM (which cannot be upgraded). The Rage 128 chipset is considered by many to be more than a consumer-level 3D graphics chipset, easily surpassing the performance of similar chipsets used in many PCs. It includes support for both QuickDraw 3D RAVE acceleration and OpenGL 3D acceleration, as well as some 2D acceleration. It does not include support for any Voodoo acceleration (the card is positioned opposite many Voodoo cards, in fact). The stock ATI card also includes hardware for aiding in the decompression of MPEG-2 video for DVD movie playback on the Mac.

Other Video Card Options   A growing number of AGP video cards are on the market, several of which include Mac support and drivers, including some cards from ATI. These cards come with their own sets of features and VRAM amounts (some of which can have additional VRAM modules installed later for better performance). These cards take advantage of the same benefits of using AGP technology as the ATI card (though it is important to choose a 2X AGP card for maximum performance benefits). Keep in mind that should you replace the stock ATI card, the Mac will lose the ability to play DVD movies. Adding an alternate ATI card may prevent this problem, but cards from other manufacturers most likely will not.

Using Both AGP and PCI Video Cards   It is possible to install additional PCI video cards into the Power Mac G4 in addition to the primary video card installed in the AGP slot. As described earlier in this chapter, installing multiple video cards allows the Mac to send data to multiple monitors, each relying on the video capabilities of the card to which it is connected. When installing PCI video cards in addition to an AGP card, be aware that the PCI cards will not have performance equal to an AGP card when working with higher-end video tasks such as 3D rendering. This is because PCI slots do not have the data throughput or processor and system RAM access abilities that the AGP slot does. If the monitors you wish to use will be of varying size or quality, it is generally better to attach the higher-quality monitor to the AGP graphics card and use it as the primary monitor. When identifying monitors, the Mac identifies the AGP monitor as the primary monitor (with menu bar and startup process) by default. It will then identify monitors attached to PCI slots sequentially, beginning with the video card installed in the slot that is closest to the AGP slot.

The Power Mac G3 (and Early G4 Models)

The early Power Mac G4 and the Blue and White Power Mac G3 computers feature a 66-MHz PCI slot as the primary video card slot. The differences between a 66-MHz PCI slot and the more traditional 33-MHz PCI slots (which make up the other three PCI slots in the Power Mac) are discussed in detail in Chapter 8. The 66-MHz slot gives better performance than most traditional video cards; however, it lacks the major benefits of an AGP slot.

Rage 128 PCI (66-MHz Card)   The stock video card of these Power Macs is also an ATI Rage 128 card. This card has much the same graphics acceleration functions of the card included on the AGP Power Mac G4 computers. It is not, however, relied upon for DVD playback, as these Macs require an independent MPEG-2 decoder card.

Other Video Card Options As with the Power Mac G4, the G3 can use alternate video cards in place of the original Rage 128 card. However, the use of a 66-MHz PCI slot for video cards has never gained the level of popularity that the AGP or slower 33-MHz PCI slots have. This means that finding a replacement for the primary video card may prove difficult. There are, however, a wide variety of video cards that can be installed in the three traditional PCI slots available to the Power Mac G3 (this also allows the use of multiple monitors).

The PowerBook G3

The two PowerBook models covered by this book have both shipped with ATI video chipsets and 8 MB of VRAM, which is not upgradable. Both PowerBooks have also shipped with video output capabilities.

The PowerBook with FireWire Ports The most recent PowerBooks, with FireWire ports, contain the ATI Rage 128 Mobility chipset. This chipset is comparable to the Rage 128 chipset used in the Power Mac computers and in the iMac DV models (see later in the chapter). It supports the use of AGP technology for faster and more frequent access to the PowerBook's processor and direct access the system RAM, even though the chipset is built into the motherboard and is not using an AGP slot. As with the Power Mac G4 computers, the Rage 128 Mobility chipset's hardware is used in the decoding of MPEG-2 video for DVD movie playback.

The PowerBooks with a SCSI Port The earlier PowerBook computers covered by this book, which feature a SCSI port rather than a FireWire port, include the ATI Rage LT Pro chipset built into their motherboards. This chipset is not as advanced as the Rage 128, and it does not include AGP standard support for faster processor or system RAM access. For models that include DVD support, the video chipset is not used for MPEG-2 decoding. Separate MPED-2 decoding hardware is included on the motherboards of such models (as described in Chapter 17).

Multiple Monitor Support The PowerBook computers come with both a built-in LCD display and the ability to use an external monitor. The external monitor can be a traditional monitor attached to the PowerBook's VGA-style video out port or a home electronics device (such as a TV) attached to the PowerBook's S-video port. When using an external monitor with the PowerBook, you can use it as either a mirror of the

PowerBook's internal screen or as a completely independent monitor. You control the use of an external monitor through the Monitors control panel, just as you would on a desktop Mac with multiple video cards installed. In effect, the PowerBook behaves as though it has a separate video card driving both external monitor and built-in LCD display. However, it is only the one set of video circuitry in the PowerBook doing the work for both displays.

PC Card Video Cards   There have been one or two attempts at creating video cards for the PowerBook using the PC Card slot. The most well-known of these was the ixMicro Road Rocket card, which is no longer being produced but can be bought from companies dealing in Mac parts or from Mac users wishing to sell the card. PC Card video cards like the Road Rocket include the functions of a traditional video card, allowing the PowerBook to drive additional external displays as well as adding its own VRAM and other video circuitry to enable the PowerBook to take advantage of graphics acceleration and other features.

The Original iMac

The original iMac relied on either the ATI Rage II (revision A iMacs) or Rage Pro (revision B and later iMacs) video chipset. The chipset was built into the motherboard and cannot be replaced. Although passable for many consumer uses, the Rage II chipset in the revision A iMacs is considered pretty out-of-date for even consumer-level 3D acceleration today. The Rage Pro chipset is also beginning to show its age at this writing. The revision B and later iMacs include 6 MB of VRAM on the motherboard, which is not upgradable.

Upgrade the VRAM on Revision A iMacs   The very first models (revision A) of the original iMacs shipped with only 2 MB of VRAM, which could be expanded using a special VRAM SO-DIMM memory module. As described in Chapter 6, this upgrade is only relevant to revision A iMacs because all later original iMacs ship with a full 6 MB of VRAM. The revision A iMacs are the only recent Macintosh computer that can have its VRAM upgraded.

Mezzanine Slot Video Card   As mentioned in Chapter 8, the revision A and B (233-MHz) models of the original iMac shipped with a special connector on the underside of the motherboard referred to as a *mezzanine* slot. The mezzanine slot was removed from later iMacs, and Apple discouraged developers from creating products that installed into the slot. Despite Apple's discouragement, Micro Conversions did develop a video card that installed into the mezzanine slot. The Game Wizard was a Voodoo 2 video card with 8 MB of RAM. It did not provide external monitor support, but it did offer Voodoo-based 3D graphics acceleration to owners of the iMac. It also provided a warranty covering the entire iMac, because installing a card into the mezzanine slot voids the machine's Apple warranty. The Game Wizard may be available from some Mac parts resellers, but it is not being produced today because Micro Conversions went out of business shortly after introducing the card.

Although not truly a video card, the iProRAID TV is a mezzanine slot card that is still produced by Formac. The card does not provide monitor or graphics acceleration support, but it does provide video capture and TV tuning abilities to the iMac when installed, as well as support for external Ultra Wide SCSI devices. TV tuning and video capture are discussed more in the next chapter.

iMac Video Out Products   There have been two products designed specifically to add video output abilities to the original iMac. These include the iPort from Griffin Technology and the iPresenter from Power R. The iPort gives users a traditional Apple monitor port and also provides a serial port for the iMac and can only be used with revision A and B iMac models. The iPresenter provides external monitor ports for both a traditional Apple monitor and a monitor using a VGA-style connector. It can be used with all of the original iMac models (revisions A through D).

Both the iPort and the iPresenter are limited to mirroring the iMac's internal display on an external monitor. The iPort does support the use of additional resolutions and refresh rates beyond those of the iMac's built-in monitor, but when alternate resolutions or refresh rates are selected, the iMac's internal monitor is deactivated and data is only displayed on the external monitor.

The Slot-Loading iMac/iMac DV

The slot-loading iMac and iMac DV models use the ATI Rage 128 VR chipset. This is virtually the same chipset on which the video card in the Power Mac computer is based, except that it is built into the motherboard. This makes the current iMacs good contenders for many video and 3D graphics tasks, though it does limit them from using Voodoo acceleration options. Although the video chipset in these iMacs is not on an AGP card, it still uses the AGP standard to allow the graphics hardware access to the Mac's processor more quickly and frequently and to access the system RAM directly for increased 3D performance. These iMacs ship with 8 MB of VRAM, which is not upgradable. As with the Power Mac G4, the video chipset is relied upon for DVD video playback.

The iBook

The iBook uses the ATI Rage Mobility chipset. Although this video chipset is not as powerful as the Rage 128 chipsets used in the current iMacs and Power Macs, it is more powerful than the video capabilities of many non-Mac laptop computers, where 3D acceleration is not usually considered a priority. The iBook only ships with 4 MB of VRAM (not upgradable). However, the Rage Mobility chipset does adhere to the AGP standard, giving the video hardware direct access to the iBook's system RAM and more frequent access to the iBook's processor for graphics acceleration functions.

Other Video Hardware

In addition to the functions so far described in this chapter, some video cards add other features to the Mac. The most common of these abilities is video capture and video output with TV-style connectors. This section discusses some of these varying technologies, though several are covered in more detail in the next chapter.

Video Cards with RCA Composite Analog or S-Video Output

Some video cards are designed to allow you the use of televisions or other home entertainment devices for display. Such videocards often include an S-video port and/or the traditional RCA composite video connectors (for devices not supporting S-video). Because the resolutions and refresh rates used by a television are inferior to those of a computer monitor, using such items as a display will result in much lower quality. However, they may be passable for presentations, classroom settings, and as a method for transferring video projects to analog videotape using a VCR. This approach can also be used to record to tape actions performed on the Mac for use in training videos. Most such cards include video capture abilities from similar analog video sources as well.

Video Cards with Video Input Abilities

Although video input and capture is the topic of the next chapter of this book, these abilities merit some mention here. A number of video cards integrate analog video capture and input into their offerings. These cards allow you to attach analog video devices, such as VCRs, to them in order to view a video stream on your Mac or to capture incoming video to a file for later editing or playback. These cards traditionally come with RCA composite video (accepting both video and audio input) or S-video input jacks or both. The driver extensions for the card also often include a video digitizer so that any applications supporting video or still image capture can accept input from the card as a video source.

TV Tuning Many video cards allow a computer to accept a video stream from a VCR or television using RCA composite or S-video connections. This allows you to view an incoming video signal. The signal from a cable TV wire or a TV antenna, however, is not a straight video signal. It contains many different video signals and requires a tuning device to select and display one of those signals. This tuning ability is built into all television sets and virtually all VCRs. It is not, however, built into a computer, nor is it always built into a video card that supports video input. To enable TV tuning, additional circuitry is needed, as well as control software (to choose a specific channel and display the incoming program). Some video cards include TV tuner circuitry; others include a special add-on component that can be purchased separately to add TV tuning abilities.

External Scan Converters

A scan converter is an external device that is designed to use a TV or other device as a display source rather than a computer monitor. Scan converter's traditionally attach to a computer's VGA monitor port and then provide either S-video or RCA composite video connections for a TV or similar projection device. Scan converters tend to provide even lower video quality than using a video card with support for RCA or S-video devices. However, this may be adequate for some presentations. It is a good idea to ask for a demonstration before opting for a scan converter.

USB Video Devices

USB is a very versatile technology. Several USB devices are available that allow the Mac to accept and capture video from an analog video source, usually RCA composite video. Some USB devices even include TV tuners. These products are discussed in more detail in the next chapter.

Less commonplace are USB devices that allow you to attach an external monitor to the Mac. These devices, such as AVerMedia's USBPresenter attach to a Mac's USB port and can support an external TV as a display, mirroring the contents of the primary monitor or internal display, and usually can only support very limited resolutions and refresh rates. Such products can function with any Mac but are probably best suited to use with the iBook, which lacks any video output abilities.

Resources for Further Study

The following URLs provide additional information on some of the concepts, issues, and products discussed in this chapter.

About.com Focus on Mac Hardware Video Card Resources— http://machardwarea.btou.com/msubvideocards.htm

*Accelerate Your Mac—*http://www.xlr8yourmac.com

*The MacGamer's Ledge—*http://www.macledge.com

*Mac 3dfx.com—*http://www.mac3dfx.com

*Apple's OpenGL Page—*http://www.apple.com/opengl

*3dfx—*http://www.3dfx.com

*ATI—*http://www.atitech.com

*Formac—*http://www.formac.com

*Village Tronic—*http://www.villagetronic.com/

CHAPTER 27

Video Capture, Digital Video, and TV Tuning

Video is an ever-growing part of the Mac's abilities. The ability to transfer video from a digital camcorder to the Mac over FireWire and Apple's iMovie application has made video work on the Mac extremely simple. And the ability to stream video content over the Internet has made video a practical application for Internet developers.

But even with video becoming an easily accessible part of the Mac experience, there are still issues that elude many people. These include how to work with video from analog (non-digital) camcorders and VCRs, how to store and edit video beyond using iMovie, and other various uses for digital video. In addition, there's the question of whether you can actually use your Mac to watch TV. This chapter looks at each of these issues and provides an overview of video work on the Mac.

How the Mac Works with Video

Before you can begin working with video on your Mac, you need to have an understanding of how the Mac processes and stores video data. This includes an understanding of the differences between digital video and analog video (which was touched upon in Chapter 14), the primary standards for broadcast video, the formats in which video files can be stored, and how codecs can be used to compress video data for storage on a Mac. This first section of the chapter looks at these underpinnings of Mac video.

Analog Video versus Digital Video

Video can be transmitted or stored on a video device in digital or analog form. When stored in digital form, video content is stored much like a computer file, with all the information of the video stored as discrete bits of data (each bit corresponding to a 1 or 0/ on or off value that determines a portion of an image or sound). Analog video is transmitted as a series of analog waveforms. The crests and troughs of the wave correspond to the color, sharpness, and level of light and dark in parts of the image, as well as the sound track that is part of the video stream.

Analog video has traditionally been used for both broadcast and video storage purposes. However, analog video has some downsides, particularly in terms of storage and archiving. As mentioned in Chapter 14, analog video signals are often stored on magnetic media, where the magnetically archived waveform can become distorted or degraded over time and can also be disrupted by magnetic or electrical interference. Because digital video is stored as discrete values rather than undulating waves, this degradation or disruption does not affect the quality of the signal because the on/off value of each bit of data remains the same even if the relative strength of that bit is weakened.

Analog video also poses a problem for copying existing video. The waveforms in the copy will contain various distortions from the original waveform. As copies are made of copies, each one will have successively lower levels of accuracy to the original. Because digital video uses discrete signals and not shifting wave patterns, each copy is equally identical to the original and successive generations do not lose quality compared to the original.

Computers require discrete data in order to work with any type of information, including video. For this reason, computers can only work with digital video data and not analog video signals. Any analog video to be worked with on a computer must first be converted into digital form. This is the function of analog video capture cards or devices.

Digital video devices use a different type of videocassette tape to record video. This tape is not compatible with the analog tapes used in VHS, Super VHS, or Hi 8 video devices (all of which are analog devices). To convert digital videotape to analog, you can use the analog-style audio/video outputs of the digital video device (either S-Video or composite video) to attach the digital device to the analog device. To convert from analog to digital, you will usually need a special conversion deck.

NTSC or PAL Video

There are two primary standards for broadcast video today. NTSC (for National Television Standards Committee) is the video standard that is used in the United States and other parts of North America. PAL (for Phase Alternating Line) is the standard used in Europe and other parts of the world. The two formats differ in terms of the screen aspect ratios, in the number of individual frames of video displayed per second, and in other ways. Table 27-1 lists the differences between the two formats.

NTSC and PAL formats are not compatible with each other. This means that a TV set designed for use in the United States will not be able to display broadcasts in England and that a videotape recorded in France will not be able to play properly in a VCR intended for use in the United States. These differences may or may not be a concern for you when capturing and editing video on your Mac. Most video capture

TABLE 27-1

NTSC and PAL
Video Compared.

NTSC	PAL
30 frames per second	25 frames per second
575 scan line resolution	625 scan line resolution
Overscanned video	Normal scanned video
DV picture size: 720x480	DV picture size: 720x576

devices can handle both NTSC and PAL video, though you may want to check the specifications before buying a device. Most video software will simply scale a video window appropriately to match the incoming video ratio. However, when exporting video back to videotape, you should check to be certain you are exporting to the appropriate video format for the tape because of the differences in the two formats.

QuickTime and Other Multimedia Formats

A number of file formats and related technology are available for use in recording video files. QuickTime is the native multimedia format of the Mac OS. QuickTime is a series or extensions that enable the Mac to recognize a wide variety of video file formats (as well as sound and graphics formats). Most Macintosh video applications are designed to use the QuickTime architecture to open and save files in any one of several different file formats.

The default video file format for the Mac is the QuickTime Movie (.mov) format. Other common video file formats include the AVI format, which is often used on Windows-based PCs, and the MPEG (.mpg) file format. QuickTime Movie is the best file format to use if you plan on sharing a file with other Mac users. If you expect to share it with PC users, you may want to consider using the AVI format.

QuickTime on PCs   QuickTime is a cross-platform technology, and Apple does produce a QuickTime version for Windows that includes many of the same technologies and features as QuickTime for the Mac OS. However, QuickTime for Windows is not always installed on a PC by default. Even if you are sharing a QuickTime movie with a Windows user that has QuickTime installed on his or her PC, you may need to save a QuickTime movie differently. When saving a QuickTime movie that you expect to share with PC users, make certain to check the Make Movie

Playable on Non-Apple Computers checkbox in the Save dialog. Macs use different methods for storing files than PCs, and checking this box ensures that the movie file is stored such that it will function properly on both platforms (this situation is discussed more in Chapter 41).

Codecs and Compression Technology

Raw digital video data takes up a lot of disk space (one minute of digital full-screen video usually takes up 216 MB, though differences in the frame rate may cause some variations in size). To keep even small video clips from taking up an entire hard drive, technology is used to compress and encode video data when you are storing it as a file. There are a number of different techniques used to compress and encode video files, each with its own advantages in terms of how much it can compress data (the compression ratio) and in terms of the video playback quality in the resulting file.

For a compressed video file to be opened and played on the Mac (or another computer), the same compression technology used when saving the file is needed on the computer playing the file. Compression technologies are added to a computer using special software components known as *codecs* (compressor/decompressor). On the Mac, codecs are stored as extensions that are loaded as part of the Mac OS during the startup process. The QuickTime extension set includes a wide variety of codecs for the most common video technologies used today. This means that any application that is QuickTime-aware (including any modern video editing application for the Mac) will be able to use these codecs when opening or saving video files.

Some file formats may be more limited in what codecs can be applied to them. This is particularly true of the AVI and MPEG file formats. MPEG is itself a compression standard and generally cannot be compressed using other techniques. AVI files can use varying codecs, but the specific codecs available differ from what can be used with QuickTime movie files.

Keep in mind that the more you compress a file, the lower the quality will be when the file is played back. Some codecs are better at compressing files while retaining quality, but there will always be some degree of quality loss. This is usually more noticeable if a movie has a larger picture size (such as 640×480).

Also, you should avoid applying a codec until you actually save a file to disk. Some video-editing applications offer the option to apply codecs while recording (and some do this without giving you any option). This will usually result in lower-quality video to start with because the Mac will be compressing the file as it is recording the digitized video. Only if you have very limited disk space should you apply a codec during recording. If you do need to apply a codec while recording, set it to the lowest compression ratio available, as this will result in the highest-possible-quality recording.

Playback and Editing Software

Applications designed to let you work with and edit video or just play back existing video files on the Mac vary from the simple and free utilities included with most Macs like iMovie and Apple's QuickTime Player to the expensive and feature packed applications like Final Cut Pro and Adobe After Effects, which can provide all of the functions of a professional editing suite. The following paragraphs contain an overview of the more common video editing and playback applications for the Mac. Additional information on these products can be found through the websites of their manufacturers, which are included in the "Resources for Further Study" section at the end of this chapter.

iMovie   iMovie, shown in Figure 27-1, is a very simple consumer-oriented video-editing application that Apple designed to accompany the iMac DV. Apple later released iMovie as a free download for all Mac users. It allows video capture from a digital video source, such as a DV camcorder, and can export video to a digital video device. It doesn't support working with analog video or most video file formats, though it does support exporting completed projects to QuickTime video file formats. iMovie is an excellent choice for consumers wanting to dabble in digital video editing for home movie projects or for students wanting to learn some basics about video work before moving on to a more expensive professional tool.

QuickTime Player Pro   Apple's QuickTime Player (shown in Figure 27-2) comes with every version of QuickTime (and every Mac OS release). The QuickTime Player can open and display just about any video file format in use today. In its unregistered state, the QuickTime Player only allows you to play video files. If you pay the $30 fee to upgrade your Mac's QuickTime version to QuickTime Player Pro, a number of additional features are made available to you in the QuickTime Player application.

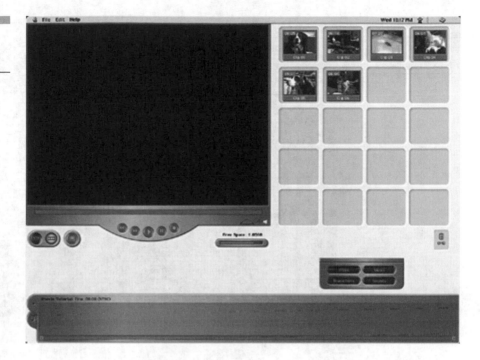

Figure 27-1
The iMovie application.

When registered, the QuickTime Player Pro allows you to open video files, to make changes and save them, to export into a wide variety of video file formats, to enable or delete video or audio tracks, and to change the compression level or codec used in a file. QuickTime Player Pro also lets you copy and paste segments of video or still frames from one file to another and to delete selected portions of a movie. This is very basic editing compared to other applications, but it may be helpful because of the QuickTime Player's basic and easy-to-use interface.

Another powerful use of the registered QuickTime Player Pro for iMovie users is the ability to convert existing video files into the DV format. iMovie cannot import from any video file format other than the DV format, meaning you cannot directly add existing video files to an iMovie project. Using QuickTime Player Pro, you can convert an existing file into the DV format and then import it into iMovie. This is also useful for saving DV clips in compressed formats on your hard drive for later use, because uncompressed DV takes up much more disk space than most video file formats.

Figure 27-2
Apple's QuickTime
Player.

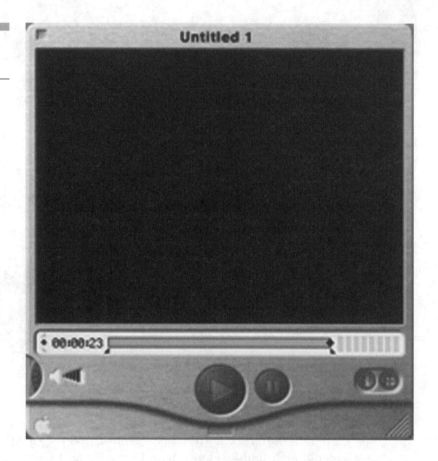

Strata VideoShop   VideoShop is a consumer video-editing application by Strata that allows for some additional abilities beyond iMovie, including the ability to work with both analog and digital video. VideoShop also allows you to open various file formats directly within the application.

Avid   Avid makes a number of video tools for the Mac, ranging from the consumer level with Avid Cinema to several high-end production packages. Most of Avid's products also include video capture and exporting hardware.

Final Cut Pro   Final Cut Pro, shown in Figure 27-3, is Apple's high-end video editing application. It includes virtually all the video-editing features of a professional production studio, including a number special-effects and track-editing features.

Figure 27-3
The Final Cut Pro
application.

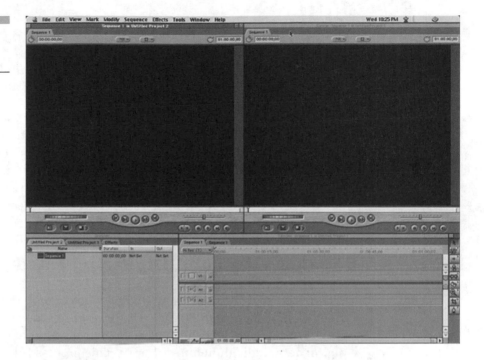

Adobe Premier   Adobe Premier is Adobe's professional video editing application. It allows you to perform several higher-end video-editing tasks on the Mac. It can capture and work with both digital and analog video devices, as well as with the various video file formats available through QuickTime.

Adobe After Effects   After Effects is an advanced video package from Adobe that allows you to have an incredible level of control over video production. It also enables you to add a number of animations and other special effects to a video production beyond the original video content. These abilities include integration with Adobe's graphics utilities (Illustrator and Photoshop). After Effects also supports a plug-in architecture that allows third parties to develop special-effects plug-ins to extend the program's abilities (much like Photoshop). Several companies produce plug-ins for After Effects.

EditDV   Digital Origin's EditDV is a video-editing application designed for working with digital video devices. EditDV offers many professional-level editing features and can be used to produce broadcast-quality video projects.

Capturing Video

The first step in working with digital video on the Mac is to import or capture the video from its source (a videotape, TV signal, and so on). Capturing video requires the use of both hardware and software. The hardware must provide a way for your Mac to access the video signal and record the video data to the hard drive. The specific hardware needed and the process of importing it into an application is noticeably different depending on whether you are capturing video from an analog or a digital video source. This section examines the hardware and software process involved in capturing from both types of video sources.

Analog Video and Digitizing Hardware

When you are working with an analog video signal, the process is somewhat more complicated because the Mac needs to convert the incoming data from a constantly shifting analog waveform into discrete packets of digital data (individual bits of 1 or 0). This process is known as *digitizing* and is very important because the Mac's processor can only work with discrete digital data. Digitizing incoming video requires additional hardware that can convert the analog waveform into digital data properly. This hardware is not a built-in part of the Mac and will need to be added, either by means of an expansion card or an external device (usually a USB device).

Video Capture Cards   Until recently, the most common way to digitize video from an external video source was to install a video input or capture expansion card in the Mac. Video capture cards can be independent PCI cards (there are also a couple of PC Card video capture devices for the PowerBook), or the ability to capture video can be an additional feature on a video card that also supports external monitors or graphics acceleration.

Video capture cards will provide either RCA composite video connectors or S-Video connectors. To use the card, you generally just connect your incoming video source, such as a VCR, to the connectors on the back of the card the same way you would connect the video device to a TV. Once the device is connected, you can launch a video-editing application that supports analog video and use it to capture video from your source.

USB Video Capture Devices   USB video capture devices are a recent invention in the computer industry. They began showing up a while after the original iMac was released and have gained a fair measure of popularity for use with Macs that don't support expansion cards for analog video input. Many of these devices simply connect to a USB port and then have RCA or S-Video connections on the other side of a small box or cable. These devices usually only capture video over USB and use the Mac's audio line-in port for capturing audio along with the video.

USB video capture devices are generally functional, but they are subject to the bandwidth limitations of the USB interface. Although most manufacturers have used compression technology to provide very good video quality despite these limitations, USB is fairly limited. This means that the resolution of the captured video is usually limited to 640×480 pixels at best. Video may also be a bit choppy at higher resolutions, though this depends on the device being used, as different manufacturers have provided varying quality devices. Even in the best situations, however, USB devices simply won't be able to provide the video capture performance of a PCI card or PC Card designed for video capture.

Using Editing Software to Capture Analog Video

Once you have the hardware needed to allow your Mac to receive and digitize an analog video stream, you need a software application that allows you to record the incoming video to a file. Many utilities that allow you to edit video provide the ability to capture analog video (the exceptions are iMovie, which only works with digital video, and QuickTime Player Pro, which only works with existing video files or data). In fact, most analog video capture devices come with one utility or another for capturing and editing video.

The actual interface for capturing video varies from application to application, but the process is similar regardless of the application. First, connect the video source. Second, select the video source you wish the application to use. If you have multiple video devices attached to a Mac or drivers for multiple video devices installed, you need to instruct the Mac which one to use. This is done in a dialog such as the one shown in Figure 27-4.

You should now be ready to capture video. Use the *capture* command (which may be called *record* or *import* in some applications) of your video-editing application. A dialog box will be displayed that shows the

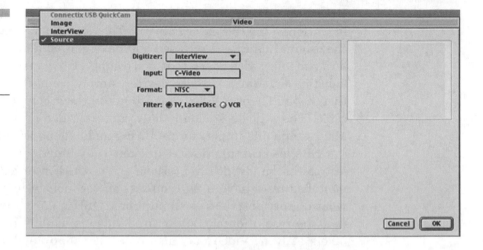

Figure 27-4
A typical dialog for
selecting a video
input device and
digitizer.

incoming video signal and includes buttons for beginning, pausing, and stopping the recording process. The actual look of this dialog can vary widely between video-editing applications. Use the Record or Pause buttons to record the segment of video that you wish to capture. Once the video is captured, it may be stored in RAM, in a temporary file for the application, or you may be asked to enter the permanent filename before you begin recording. This will depend on the application you are using.

Once the video is captured, you can simply save it to a file (choosing the compression options and file type that you wish to use), or you can begin editing it immediately using the application. If you choose to begin editing immediately, you should still save the file in case of application crash or system freeze during the editing process. As to the actual process and controls involved in editing your video, refer to the documentation that accompanied your editing software for details.

Getting Better-Quality Recordings

When you are recording and digitizing an incoming analog video signal, there are some things you can do to improve video quality. One of the most important of these is to make sure the Mac is devoting as much processing power as possible to recording the video. This means turning off AppleTalk or other networking uses, quitting any applications that may be running, turning off virtual memory, and running with a minimal set of extensions.

Another important step is to make sure you are using the fastest hard drive possible. For most users, this will be the internal hard drive. If you have a choice of hard drives, choose the one with the fastest access rates. As a rule, most SCSI hard drives are faster than IDE drives. Most IDE drives are slightly faster than FireWire drives. And anything is faster than USB, which is not at all suitable for dealing with video. If you have a RAID array (see Chapter 5), this is usually ideal for video recording because it gives you speeds faster than any individual hard drive. (*Note*: RAID 1 disk mirroring is the exception, as this is actually slower than individual drives because it is solely a backup medium.) Defragmenting a hard drive can also speed its performance and provide better video quality when recording.

Make sure you have as much RAM as possible installed. Devote as much of that installed RAM as you can to the video-editing application. All the video data will pass through RAM, and excess RAM can act as a buffer when a hard drive needs to slow down during the recording process. If you are lucky enough to afford over 500 MB of free RAM in your Mac, consider using a RAM disk as the drive to which you record video. This will guarantee very high quality recordings. As soon as the video clip is recorded, copy it to a hard drive (just in case of an application crash or Mac OS freeze-up).

As mentioned in "Codecs and Compression Technology," earlier in the chapter, do not apply any compression during the recording process. This will give you higher-quality, uncompressed video data that can be compressed when the file is saved to a permanent file. This may not be an option with some USB devices, because they generally need to compress data to transmit reasonably sized video over the limited bandwidth of a USB channel.

Use at least 16-bit color. The higher the color depth you set the recording and your Mac's display to while recording, the better the quality of the resulting video. You should always record at 16-bit color (thousands of colors) or higher. A 24-bit color (millions of color) setting is a better choice if your video card will support it at your chosen screen resolution.

Set the frame rate of the recording to 30 frames per second. The frame rate determines how many individual images will be displayed one after the other to form the moving picture of the video recording. The more frames per second, the more fluid and realistic the movement in the video file. The standard for NTSC video broadcast is 30 frames per second and is an excellent choice (though if you're recording from a PAL source video, it may not provide more quality than recording at 25 frames per second, which is the PAL standard). Motion pictures are shot at 24 frames per second, so that should be the minimum you use in any case. Higher frame rates will result in larger files, however, because there is more data to be recorded.

Record video at the largest resolution or window size possible. Even if you don't expect to display video at anything larger than 320×240, recording it at 640×480 will result in a higher-quality original. You can always reduce the resolution later if you must, but you will be reducing the size with a higher-quality original. This is better than starting with a low-quality original and possibly deciding that you want to expand it, which would make the resulting image blocky.

Digital Video and FireWire

When working with digital video from a digital video device, the process is pretty simple because the video is already in a discrete data format that the Mac can simply copy using a FireWire connection. You merely need to transfer the video from the digital videocassette in your DV device to the Mac's hard drive. As described in Chapter 14, this will vary from application to application, but it generally follows the same procedures. You should be certain that you are using a digital video device that is fully supported for use on the Mac and with the video-editing software that you will be using. Table 27-2 lists the DV devices known to be compatible with the Mac at this writing. You will need to use a six-pin to four-pin FireWire cable. These cables are included with all FireWire-equipped Macs and can be purchased from any computer store.

Connecting the DV Device   First, turn off the digital video device. Next, plug the six-pin end of the cable into the Mac's FireWire port. Plug the four-pin end into the four-pin FireWire port on the digital video device. The four-pin connector is more fragile than the six-pin connector is, and you should take care not to force the cable into the port. Also, make certain that the connector on the cable and the port are aligned properly, as inserting the cable backwards is possible and will damage both the device and the cable.

Finally, turn on the digital video device. If the device is a camcorder, set the power switch to VTR mode. Also, if you are using a camcorder with a power supply, make sure the power adapter is set to VTR or Camera mode to supply power to the camcorder rather than to charge the battery. If the power adapter is set to Charge, you may not be able to power the camcorder while the battery is charging (refer to the camcorder's manual for additional information).

TABLE 27-2

Digital Video
Devices Currently
Supported for Mac
FireWire Use

Sony Digital Camcorders	
DCR-PC1	DCR-TRV7
DCR-PC100	DCR-TRV8
DCR-TR7000	DCR-TRV9
DCR-TRV103	DCR-TRV9e
DCR-TRV110	DCR-TRV10
DCR-TRV310	DCR-TRV900
DCR-TRV310e	DCR-TRV900e
DCR-TRV510	GR-D300

Sony DV/Analog Converters*	
DVMC-DA1	DVMC-MS1 AV

Canon Digital Camcorders**	
Elura	XL1
Optura	ZR
Vistura	

Panasonic Digital Camcorders***	
AG-EZ20	PV-DV710
AG-EZ30	PV-DV-910

Sharp Digital Camcorders***	
VL-PD3	

*Sony Digital to Analog video converter decks do not support computer-application-based control of the video device. You will need to use the controls on the analog video device rather than the on-screen controls of a digital video editing application on the Mac to select a video segment to capture.

**Canon digital camcorders do not offer complete compatibility with the Mac digital video application controls. There is an issue that may prevent the camcorder from being able to pause in video playback while using the rewind and fast-forward controls within a digital-video-editing application. If you experience this issue, use the stop button to completely stop the video from rewinding or fast-forwarding.

***Panasonic and Sharp digital camcorders have known issues when exporting from a digital video editing application to tape via FireWire. The issue manifests as the camcorder's LCD screen flashing "Check DV Input" and then going into REC/Pause mode and not recording video. If this occurs, stop the camcorder and cancel the export-to-tape process on the Mac. You can work around this problem by adding a few seconds of solid black frames to the beginning of a movie project. When exporting to tape, watch the camcorder's LCD screen for signs of the black frames being sent from the Mac. At this point use the Still button on the camcorder's VTR controls to begin recording the movie being exported by the Mac. Alternatively, you can attempt increasing the wait time in the export dialog box of the video-editing application (this is the time that the Mac will wait for the digital video device to begin recording when exporting a movie project).

The DV device should now be available to video-editing applications that support working with digital video devices. You can use the Apple System Profiler's Devices and Volumes tab to see if the Mac is recognizing the video device as being attached to the FireWire bus. Once the DV device is connected to your Mac, you should be able to interact with it to copy video for editing from within a DV/FireWire-aware video-editing software.

Capturing Video with iMovie   The following describes the process of capturing video for editing using the iMovie application. This process varies slightly from application to application, but this will give you an overview of the steps involved. First, connect the DV device as described, and then instruct iMovie to capture video material by clicking on the new Camera Mode button in the iMovie display (shown in Figure 27-5).

Once iMovie is in Camera mode, you can use the on-screen controls (see Figure 27-6) to control the camcorder and view the contents of the tape (or other digital recording medium) in the digital video device. These controls include the traditional videotape play, pause, stop,

Figure 27-5
These buttons let you switch between capturing video from a FireWire device and editing video in iMovie.

Figure 27-6
These buttons will control the playback and importing of an external DV device in iMovie.

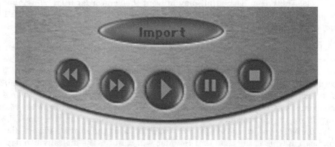

rewind, and fast-forward functions. The contents of the tape will be displayed in the application's display area.

If you are using an analog-to-digital video converter deck, you will not be able to use iMovie's on-screen controls. This is because FireWire does not support controlling of an analog video device, such as you would have attached to this type of converter. You will instead need to use the controls built into the analog video device to select the appropriate sections of video that you want to import into iMovie.

Once you have located the segment of video that you wish to capture, simply press the Import button in the iMovie display. Press the same button to stop capturing video when you have finished importing the segment that you wish to record or edit. You can also press the spacebar to start and stop importing video.

iMovie stores captured video clips in the shelf section of the display. When this section becomes full, you need to move these segments into a movie track with iMovie's clip viewer. You can also specify that iMovie store clips in a movie track rather than the shelf when capturing them.

When capturing digital video, it is important that you capture it to a device that can support the sustained data transfer rates at which digital video operates. This rate must be at least 3.6 MB/second. Virtually all hard drives are capable of such transfer rates, but many removable-media drives (such as Zip or magneto-optical drives) and all USB drives are inadequate for digital video work, as are network drives and servers. Also when capturing video, you should disable virtual memory (unless you have 64 MB of RAM or less), disable file sharing, and quit any background applications that you do not need to have running. This allows the Mac to perform better when importing and working with video clips.

Once you have imported the video clips you wish to work with, you can simply work with them in whatever manner your video-editing program of choice supports. You can save the work to your hard drive, and you can export it back to a digital video device or to a permanent file once you're finished.

Exporting Video

Once you've edited a video project on the Mac, you may want to export it back to an external video device. This is most easily done to a digital video camera (or other DV device), as the Mac can transfer the video data very easily as though it were making a copy of the digital video file on an external drive. The DV tape can then be copied to analog devices such as a traditional VHS VCR tape. It is also possible to export directly to analog video devices; however, this is usually more involved, and you will suffer a degree of quality loss in the process.

In addition to exporting video back to tape (or other external devices), there are a growing number of ways that you can use or distribute video from your Mac. This section looks at some of these uses.

To Digital Video Devices

Exporting digital video to a DV device is much simpler than exporting to an analog device. For consumer uses, it may be simplest to export a video project to a DV device first and then to make analog video copies from the DV tape. The process will vary from one application to the next, but the process will generally be as follows:

First, use the application's Export command. This will provide you with a pop-up menu or dialog that allows you to designate how you want to export the movie. To export to a digital video device, you would choose "Camera" or something similar indicating the external DV device. At this point you will have the option of setting the Add and Wait values for the export process. Most users will be able to simply use the default values. If you are working with a camera that has issues regarding not receiving video during export, you may want to increase the wait times above their defaults. Once this is done, press the button that actually indicates to the Mac to export the video (usually labeled Export or OK). The video will then be copied to the device.

Once the video has been exported, you should watch the exported recording to ensure that it was transferred properly. Assuming that it has been, you can make copies of the video or transfer the video to an analog video source such as a VHS, Super VHS, or Hi 8 tape. You can do so using the analog video connectors on your digital video device in the same manner as you would make a copy of any other videotape.

When using the iMovie application, you need to convert your existing project to a DV file (if it is stored as another format) so that you can open it in iMovie. This is because iMovie does not support any other file formats. Other applications may be able to open a non-DV video file, but they will still force you to convert the file before transferring it to an external tape.

When exporting digital video, make certain that the format (NTSC or PAL) that you are using for the actual video file is the same as the video format of the device to which you are exporting. A PAL signal will not be able to record properly on an NTSC digital camcorder and vice versa. This shouldn't pose problems for most users, but if you are working with video types of varying countries, it is something to be aware of.

To Analog Video Devices

Most professional-level expansion cards for video capture and editing also include the needed hardware to export video to an analog device for recording. The specific features will vary from card to card, as will the way they are implemented. Consumer-oriented video capture devices and cards are a different story. Often consumer-level cards are designed to get the video into your Mac, but not back out.

The easiest solution for consumer-level devices is to export the video to a DV device. However, if one is not available, you will need to find an alternative. That alternative is usually to use a scan converter or a video card that supports S-Video or RCA composite video output. This enables you to output the entire contents of your Mac's display to a VCR for recording. The only trouble with this is that you need to have video that is capable of filling the display for recording. This can usually be done at 640×480 resolution, and many applications include a full-screen playback mode. Simply attach the Mac to the analog video device using whatever method is available (the preceding chapter covers scan converters and video output in more detail), put the video into full-screen mode, and play. Then record on your analog video device.

As with digital video devices, you should be certain that you are using the same video format for your video project as the video device to which you are transferring the project.

Using Video in Other Ways

In addition to exporting video to an external device, such as a camcorder or VCR, there are a number of additional uses for video that has been captured and edited on the Mac. The following is an overview of some of the common uses for both consumer and professional markets. This is by no means an exhaustive list, but it can give you some idea of the uses for digital video files.

Interactive Multimedia Projects   Video data can be integrated into an interactive package in a number of ways. This can be a video-enhanced website, a game featuring actual video content, a multimedia presentation, or a self-contained application utilizing a video component. A number of products are available for creating such interactive devices. One of the primary companies producing such products is Macromedia. Macromedia Director, for example, can be used to create interactive presentations within self-contained applications. Such applications are a growing trend in the new uses for video that have been opened up by the computer industry.

MPEG-2 Encoding for DVD Production   Creating your own DVD movies is one potential use for video data edited on the Mac. This use is limited to professional production markets, however. As you read in Chapter 17, DVD video disks (the format used for DVD movies) require both the audio and video tracks stored on the disk to be encoded in certain formats. The video track needs to be encoded using the MPEG-2 standard. MPEG-2 encoding can be done on the Mac; however, it requires either a special expansion card standard or a special encoding utility designed to perform the compression and encoding associated with the MPEG-2. MPEG-2 encoding technology generally costs more than consumer or small business markets are able to afford, although this is likely to change in the future.

Video CDs   Video CD is a CD format that includes an MPEG-1 encoded video file on a CD-ROM disk. As mentioned in Chapter 16, set-top video CD players have been popular as a home entertainment medium in some parts of the world. Additionally, most computers are capable of playing video CDs. Video CDs aren't capable of storing as much video data as a DVD, but they can be a method for distributing video files. Toast, along with other CD authoring utilities, allows you to create video CDs by selecting the Video CD format and placing an MPEG (.mpg) movie file on the CD.

Streaming over the Internet   Streaming audio and video files are becoming a popular part of many websites. Streaming video means that the person downloading the video file can watch the file as it is downloaded and does not need to wait for the download to be completed. You can make your own video files available to others over the Internet using streaming technology. You can create two primary types of streaming video with your Mac: QuickTime and RealVideo.

QUICKTIME In QuickTime version 4.0, Apple introduced the ability to stream video data online. This is done with a special server known as the QuickTime Streaming Server (versions are currently available for Mac OS X Server and Linux). When QuickTime movies are streamed, they can be viewed using the QuickTime Player application, or they can be embedded in a web page. When storing QuickTime movies, most applications will give you the option of optimizing the file for streaming over the Internet. This should be chosen if you wish to stream the file. Even if you don't have access to the QuickTime Streaming Server, you can still embed a QuickTime movie in a web page. When a portion of the movie has been downloaded, it will begin playing while the remaining portion downloads.

REALVIDEO RealVideo is another streaming format that was developed by Real Inc. RealVideo functions similar to QuickTime streaming but must be viewed from within the RealPlayer (shown in Figure 27-7) application (which can be downloaded from Real's website). To create RealVideo content, you need to use the RealProducer application, which you can get free at Real's site. RealProducer allows you to record video directly in its application or to import it from an existing file. The resulting RealVideo file can then be placed on an Internet server that is run-

Figure 27-7
The RealPlayer
application.

ning the RealServer application (which is not available for the Mac OS) and streamed similar to the methods used in the QuickTime Streaming Server. RealVideo can also be streamed from any traditional web server, but with fewer features and lower streaming quality.

Distributing Using Computer Media   The easiest way to share video data with other computer users is to just place a copy of your video file on a removable-media disk or a recordable CD or DVD disk. When distributing video files using computer media, you should choose media that can support reasonably fast access speeds in order for the video to play directly from the media without jerkiness. You also need to choose media that is appropriate for the file size of the video file that you are distributing.

TV Tuning

TV tuning refers to the ability to watch a TV signal or transmission on the Mac. Although this ability seems to go hand in hand with watching, recording, or editing video from an external source, technologically, the two tasks are rather different. The ability to accept and digitize an analog video signal only requires a very basic level of hardware, one that converts the incoming analog wave signal into digital data. Since you are working with a single, predefined video stream, the video capture device need only convert that incoming signal.

When you are working with a television transmission, however, you are not dealing with a single, predefined analog signal. Instead, you are dealing with many individual signals being transmitted all together, usually using radio frequencies or some similar technique to broadcast multiple video signals all at once. This means you need another level of technology to be able to differentiate one signal from the rest. Once you have selected that one signal, you still need to convert it from its analog waveform into digital data before it can be processed by the Mac and displayed onscreen. You then need another level of software that can interact with your new hardware to determine which incoming signal (or TV channel) you want to select for processing and display.

Obviously, the hardware involved is related to traditional video capture hardware because you still need to translate the incoming analog signal into digital data. However, additional hardware is needed on top of that. Because the two are related, it follows that a card or device that supports TV tuning will also support video capture. Also, because the two are related, it is possible (as some manufacturers have done) to make a video card that doesn't have TV tuning abilities itself but can have an optional TV tuning device added to it at a later date.

A number of TV tuning products are available for the Mac. Several are PCI cards that can only function in the Power Mac G3 or G4 computers (or earlier Power Macs). A growing number are USB devices that function much the same as USB video capture devices. These devices can be used with any of the current Macs. TV tuning devices usually have a coaxial cable connection, similar to those used for connecting cable lines or TV antennas. This may be in addition to S-Video or RCA composite inputs, or it may be the only input option, depending on the device.

TV Tuning from a VCR

While it is possible to build TV tuning abilities into a hardware device to be used with the Mac, there is also a relatively simple workaround to use a traditional video capture device for viewing TV signals on the Mac. Almost all VCRs can function as TV tuners, so you can select a given channel to record. Most VCRs also include either S-Video or RCA composite video outputs, which can connect the VCR to a video capture device for the Mac. This means that you can attach a VCR to the Mac, simply use the VCR as your TV tuner, and watch the TV signal through a video-editing application. Although this isn't as elegant a solution as a true TV tuner, if you are going to be using the VCR as a source for capturing video anyway, it might be worth the effort to simply leave it connected all the time and save a little money on a video capture device. Of course, this only functions with analog video capture devices and not with FireWire and digital video.

Resources for Further Study

The following URLs provide additional information on some of the concepts, issues, and products discussed in this chapter:

About.com Desktop Video—http://desktopvideo.about.com

ATI—http://www.atitech.com

Pinnacle Systems—http://www.pinnaclesys.com

Digital Origin: Produces Video Editing Software and Hardware— http://www.digitalorigin.com/

*AVer Media—*http://www.avermedia.com/

XLR8: Makers of the InterView USB Capture Device— http://www.xlr8.com

Aurora Design: Makers of High-end Video Capture Cards— http://www.auroravideosys.com/

Eskape Labs: Makers of the MyTV line of USB TV Tuners— http://www.eskapelabs.com/

*Formac—*http://www.formac.com

iRez: Maker of USB and PC Card Video Capture Devices— http://www.irez.com

*Adobe: Producers of Video-Editing Software—*http://www.adobe.com

*MacroMedia—*http://www.macromedia.com

*Strata—*http://www.strata.com

Avid: Producers of Video-Editing Software and Hardware— http://www.avid.com/

CHAPTER 28

Audio In/Out, Sound, and MIDI

From the very first model, Apple has built audio hardware and capabilities into every Macintosh computer. This includes at least one speaker and the integrated audio circuitry and hardware on the Mac's motherboard to allow the Mac to produce audio playback. Therefore, for most users, there is no need to add audio hardware to a Mac. Typically, users will only want to add more powerful speakers and perhaps a microphone to the Mac.

The exception is professionals wanting to do high-end audio work on the Mac, such as recording their own professional audio content and mixing audio tracks for professional-quality CD recordings or radio broadcast. The Mac can very easily accomplish these tasks and is often the computing platform of choice for professional musicians and audio engineers. These tasks do require more powerful audio hardware than is built into the Mac, however.

This chapter examines how the Mac actually records audio and produces sounds using its internal hardware and speakers. It also includes an overview of how to use the recording abilities built into the Mac, as well as some discussion of the additional consumer- and professional-level audio hardware available to Mac users.

How Computer Audio Works

Before we get into discussing the audio functions built into the Mac, how to record audio, and so forth, you should have a basic understanding of how a computer works with audio and sound. This is important in judging the quality for your own sound-recording needs.

Recording

When a sound is generated, such as somebody playing a guitar, speaking, or clapping, the sound itself is actually a wave of vibrations. The molecules in the air (or water or other material) carry these vibrations. When sound waves reach a human ear, the ear and the brain translate those waves into auditory information.

When you record a sound on your Mac, several things need to happen. First, the sound needs to be converted from a wave of vibration into an electrical signal. A microphone easily accomplishes this. The microphone converts the waves into an analog electrical signal that is modulated in a waveform much like the original sound waves.

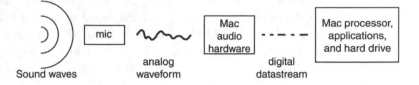

Figure 28-1
Sound waves are converted to electrical signals by the mic and then to digital data by the Mac's circuitry.

Once the mic produces an analog electrical signal, the Mac needs to be able to convert this signal into digital data. This process is accomplished by the hardware built into the Mac, which turns the continuous, varying analog waveform into discreet digital data packets (patterns of individual 1 or 0/on or off bits of information). This stream of digital data can be worked with by the Mac's processor and other components. Figure 28-1 illustrates the recording process.

Once the sound is converted into digital data, the Mac can record that data into a file that is stored on the hard drive. This is accomplished using a sound-recording application that reads the incoming sound data and stores it in a specific file format that it, and other applications, can later access and play. The program can also apply compression algorithms to the data as it is saved to the hard drive, if they are supported by the chosen file format. This keeps audio files from becoming exceedingly large and unwieldy, which can easily happen for even short uncompressed sound clips.

Factors Affecting Recording Quality

A number of factors can affect the quality of recording, including the type of microphone used, the volume at which the source audio is being produced (i.e., how loud someone is speaking), the proximity of the mic to the audio source, ambient background noise levels, and so forth. These are all environmental factors in the recording and would apply to using a tape recorder or even to a live broadcast. Beyond these typical recording concerns, there are some specific factors in recording quality relating to how a computer records audio that you should be aware of and understand. These factors include the sampling rate of the recording, the bit or sample size of the recording, the compression level and scheme used when saving the audio file, and whether the file is being recorded for mono or stereo playback. In addition to affecting the quality of the recording, each of these also affects the size of the resulting file.

Sampling Rates   When the Mac records a sound, it converts the analog form of the sound wave into discrete digital data. This process is often referred to as *sampling* (and less often as *digitizing*). When sampling, the conversion process works by periodically checking the voltage of the analog electrical signal coming from the microphone (which is directly created by the sound waves striking the mic). Each time the voltage is checked, or sampled, a discrete digital value is recorded for that level of the voltage. This creates the digital data stream for the processor and Mac to work with when recording a sound file.

The trick is that each sample you take of the analog signal is only a single point of the signal. As you can see in Figure 28-2, the signal may increase or decrease between one point and the next. If the points are not recorded closely enough to each other, the Mac won't be able to accurately capture all the changes in the analog signal. This means that when the signal is re-created for playing back the recording, it will be missing varying pieces of data, and the recording won't be faithful to the original and may sound distorted or choppy.

The only solution to capturing digital audio that is accurate and faithful to the original sound is to sample the analog signal extremely frequently. The higher the sampling rate, the truer the sound. There is a recording principle, known as *Nyquist's Sampling Theorem,* that is considered a standard when it comes to determining the sampling rate you need. This theorem says that you should use a sampling rate that is at

Figure 28-2

In the first digital capture, the samples are not close enough to mimic the original sound data. In the second, the more frequent samples allow the sound data to be captured more faithfully.

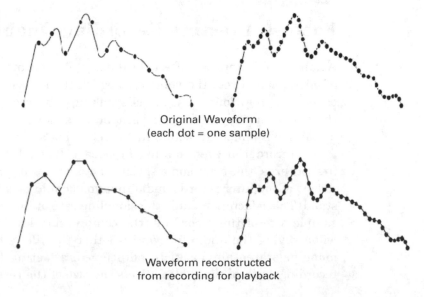

Original Waveform
(each dot = one sample)

Waveform reconstructed
from recording for playback

least twice as fast as the highest frequency contained in the sound you're recording.

Following this rule, the lowest sampling rate that should ever be considered is 11 kHz, because this is twice the frequency at which human speech tends to carry. This is the first most common level of sampling in digital audio and may be referred to by some sound programs as *speech quality*. The next-highest sampling rate commonly used is 22 kHz, which is twice the frequency of most musical instruments and is usually referred to as *music quality*. The highest sampling rate commonly used 44 kHz, which is the highest sampling rate that human ears are capable of distinguishing. Anything higher will simply not result in our ability to detect higher audio clarity or accuracy (much as the human eye is limited to distinguishing only thousands of individual colors).

Audio CDs are recorded at 44 kHz. Thus, this is often referred to as *CD-quality recording*. Some audio programs will sample at rates below 8 kHz and refer to this as *phone quality*. This level of quality should rarely, if ever, be used today because of its very low level of accuracy.

At this point, you may be wondering, why not just use CD quality as a default sampling rate, since it delivers the truest playback? There is a very good answer: hard drive space. As your sampling rate increases, you are actually recording more and more data. This means you end up with bigger and bigger files. A sound that would generate a 25-MB file when sampled at speech quality (11 kHz) will generate a 100-MB file when sampled at CD quality (44 kHz). When you are recording larger sound files, particularly if you are only recording them for personal use, this can be a big difference in terms of drive space. It can also make a difference if you are planning to place these files on a website for others to listen to or if you plan on sharing or storing them using a removable-media disk.

Sample (Bit) Size   The sampling rate tells the Mac how often to sample an incoming audio signal. It doesn't tell the Mac how much data to actually gather from each sample. That is the realm of the sample, or bit, size of a recording. Sample size is the audio equivalent of color depth on a monitor.

If each sample recorded from the sound were represented by one bit of data, there would be two possible values: sound and no sound. With 4 bits of data for each sample, there would be 16 possible different levels of pitch or tone. This allows the Mac to differentiate the sample from each other sample, but it will result in a very low quality, "computer-sounding" recording. At 8 bits, there can be 256 individual levels of tone or pitch for each sample. This allows for a passable recording, particularly for human speech, where there are a limited number of tones being used. For music, however, the recording will still lose some quality because you are limited to 256 individual tones (not much when you consider the powerful range of most instruments, including the human vocal cords when singing). Audio that is 8 bits is much like 256-color resolution on a display where the colors will be shown and you can see the image clearly, but the gradations from one color to the next will be very visible.

A recording at 16 bits gives your Mac the ability to distinguish tens of thousands of individual tones in each sample of a recording. This is passable for reproducing the majority of sounds and music, and it is also the limit of the audio hardware built into the Mac. It is possible to go to even higher levels of accuracy by using 24-bit and higher audio recording hardware. Such hardware is only used for professional music recording and broadcast. For virtually any consumer use (and even some uses that step out of the consumer range), 16-bit audio is accurate enough.

Only 8-bit and 16-bit sampling sizes are commonly used by most recording software. For recording spoken words, 8-bit audio can often be enough. However, for anything where you want the truest quality, 16-bit audio is a much better choice. Obviously, 16 bits of data per sample results in sound files that contain twice the amount of data than you would have with 8-bit sampling. This results in files that can be twice as large.

Stereo verses Mono　　When you record a sound file, you are often given the option of choosing between stereo and mono sound (this option is sometimes called *channel depth*). When stereo is chosen, two audio channels are created in the file. Each channel is dedicated to one of the two stereo speakers when the sound file is played. If you choose mono, only one channel is created, and the resulting sound file is only played from one of two speakers. Usually stereo is the preferred choice because most computers today use stereo speakers. As you might guess, two audio channels take up twice the amount of disk space than one channel does.

Table 28-1 compares file size requirements for various sample rates sizes, and channel depths.

Compression　　Compression schemes allow sound data to be compressed as it is recorded. Given that sound files left uncompressed can easily take up tens or hundreds of megabytes for a few minutes of audio, compression is definitely an important consideration. A huge variety of audio compression schemes are available. Some are tied to specific file formats (such as the scheme used in MP3 files), while others may be available to several file formats. Compression of an audio file when it is

TABLE 28-1

*Uncompressed
Audio Recording
File Size
Requirements*

Sample Rate	Sample Size	Channel Depth	Disk Space/Second	1-Minute Recording
11 kHz	8 bit	Mono	11 KB	660 KB
11 kHz	16 bit	Mono	22 KB	1.3 MB
11 kHz	8 bit	Stereo	22 KB	1.3 MB
11 kHz	16 bit	Stereo	44 KB	2.6 MB
22 kHz	8 bit	Mono	22 KB	1.3 MB
22 kHz	16 bit	Mono	44 KB	2.6 MB
22 kHz	8 bit	Stereo	44 KB	2.6 MB
22 kHz	16 bit	Stereo	88 KB	5.2 MB
44 kHz	8 bit	Mono	44 KB	2.6 MB
44 kHz	16 bit	Mono	88 KB	5.2 MB
44 kHz	8 bit	Stereo	88 KB	5.2 MB
44 kHz	16 bit	Stereo	176 KB	10.4 MB

stored and decompression of it as it is played requires something known as a *codec*. As discussed in the previous chapter, a codec is a software component that tells the Mac how to compress and decompress data in a given way. Apple's QuickTime extension set includes a wide variety of audio codecs. This allows you to choose from a variety of audio compression schemes when saving a file.

Different codecs use different compression schemes. Some schemes allow for greater levels of data compression but result in poorer playback because of that high level of compression. Others focus more on preserving the integrity of the sound at the expense of a greater file size. And some compression schemes manage to combine high levels of compression with relatively high audio quality. Choosing the right compression method can be difficult. As a rule, if you are recording with a QuickTime-aware application, choosing the default compression method for your chosen file format is a good idea.

In addition to allowing you to choose from a wide variety of separate compression schemes, each codec usually supports two or more levels of compression. Obviously, higher compression rates (such as 6 to 1) result in sacrificing some of the audio clarity and quality while saving disk space. The actual values will vary depending on the compression scheme being used.

Playback

Playback of a sound is essentially the reverse of the recording process. The Mac's processor reads the data in the sound file. The sound hardware built into the Mac's motherboard is used to create an analog electrical signal from the digital data stream from the processor. If sampled at a high rate and bit size, this signal should be a near-identical replica of the original analog signal from which the sound file was recorded. The signal is then passed to the speaker or speakers of the Mac (built-in or external). If the sound was recorded in stereo and there are two or more speakers attached, the individual channels are sent to each speaker. The speakers then translate the analog electrical signal into the appropriate physical, vibrational sound waves. The resulting waves should be very close to the original sound waves, and when those waves reach your ears, you hear the sound. Figure 28-3 illustrates the audio playback process.

The quality of the playback of a sound is limited to the quality of the speakers. Some inexpensive speakers may be incapable of providing stereo sound, or they may not be able to produce any sound without a degree of signal noise or other audio artifacts. However, with more powerful speakers and a signal amplifier, if needed, the Mac can produce truly excellent sound playback and output.

MIDI

MIDI (pronounced "middy") is an audio technology that works on a significantly different premise than traditional audio recording. MIDI, an acronym for "musical instrument digital interface," allows you to attach an electronic instrument, such as a synthesizer or electric piano, to a computer using a special interface. When connected, you can play music on the instrument, and the computer will record the data from the instrument as a series of commands. These commands can then be stored in a file. The

Figure 28-3
The Mac translates digital sound files into an analog electrical signal from which the speakers can create a sound.

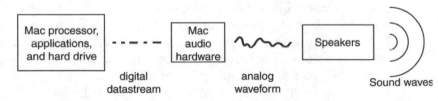

Mac can later issue them to a MIDI instrument, and that instrument will play the same notes for the same length of time, much like an old-fashioned player piano. In addition, musical notation (sheet music) can be generated by the commands from the MIDI instrument, or the file can be read by a software synthesizer that will create a playback from the Mac's speakers. Such a synthesizer is built into Apple's QuickTime technology. Regardless of how a MIDI file is used, you should note that the file itself is nothing more than a series of instructions for generating music and it is not a recording of that music.

On a hardware level, MIDI is simply a specially designed interface between the Mac and the electronic instrument. This hardware is called a *MIDI interface* and usually looks like a small box with connector cables for both the instrument and for the Mac (usually a serial port cable or, more recently, a USB cable).

MIDI supports the use of many different instrument types, just as most synthesizers can produce the sound of many different instruments. There are 128 standard MIDI numbers, each number devoted to a specific instrument. These instruments are grouped into 16 categories, or channels. If you have a synthesizer capable of playing multiple instruments at one time (or if you hook several electronic instruments up to a single MIDI interface), you can play back multiple channels at once, each one defining the playback of a different instrument. This means that you can record individual instrument tracks separately and then layer them into a single playback movement, like a string quartet or even an entire orchestra. Table 28-2 lists the MIDI instrument numbers and the instruments assigned to them.

Remember, however, that each synthesizer or other MIDI instrument will produce sound differently. Thus, a MIDI recording may sound different depending on what MIDI instruments or software synthesizers are being used.

MIDI software packages allow you to record MIDI input to a standard. MID file type that can be accessed and used on any computing platform supporting MIDI and with any MIDI device. These can also be converted to other sound file types when you are using the software-based MIDI synthesizer that is built into Apple's QuickTime. As mentioned, beyond simply recording MIDI data, MIDI applications also allow you to combine MIDI tracks, can notate a recorded composition into sheet music (a useful feature when composing music), and can send MIDI commands back to an instrument or a series of instruments for playback. Table 28-3 lists the makers of MIDI interface hardware and software packages for the Mac.

TABLE 28-2

MIDI Instruments

Channel	Number	Instrument
0—Piano	1	Acoustic grand piano
	2	Bright acoustic piano
	3	Grand piano
	4	Honky-tonk piano
	5	Electric piano 1
	6	Electric piano 2
	7	Harpsichord
	8	Clavi
1—Chromatic percussion	9	Celesta
	10	Glockenspiel
	11	Music box
	12	Vibraphone
	13	Marimba
	14	Xylophone
	15	Tubular bells
	16	Dulcimer
2—Organ	17	Drawbar organ
	18	Percussive organ
	19	Rock organ
	20	Church organ
	21	Reed organ
	22	Accordion
	23	Harmonica
	24	Tango accordion
3—Guitar	25	Acoustic guitar (nylon)
	26	Acoustic guitar (steel)
	27	Electric guitar (jazz)
	28	Electric guitar (clean)
	29	Electric guitar (muted)
	30	Overdrive guitar
	31	Distortion guitar
	32	Guitar harmonics

TABLE 28-2

MIDI Instruments
(Continued)

Channel	Number	Instrument
4—Bass	33	Acoustic bass
	34	Electric bass (finger)
	35	Electric bass (pick)
	36	Fretless bass
	37	Slap bass 1
	38	Slap bass 2
	39	Synth base 1
	40	Synth base 2
5—String	41	Violin
	42	Viola
	43	Cello
	44	Contrabass
	45	Tremolo strings
	46	Pizzicato strings
	47	Orchestral harp
	48	Timpani
6—Ensemble	49	String ensemble 1
	50	String ensemble 2
	51	Synth strings 1
	52	Synth strings 2
	53	Choir aahs
	54	Voice oohs
	55	Synth voice
	56	Orchestra hit
7—Brass	57	Trumpet
	58	Trombone
	59	Tuba
	60	Muted trumpet
	61	French horn
	62	Brass section
	63	Synth brass 1
	64	Synth brass 2

TABLE 28-2

MIDI Instruments
(Continued)

Channel	Number	Instrument
8—Reed	65	Soprano sax
	66	Alto sax
	67	Tenor sax
	68	Baritone sax
	69	Oboe
	70	English horn
	71	Bassoon
	72	Clarinet
9—Pipe	73	Piccolo
	74	Flute
	75	Recorder
	76	Pan flute
	77	Blown bottle
	78	Shakuhachi
	79	Whistle
	80	Ocarina
11—Synth Lead	81	Lead 1 (square)
	82	Lead 2 (sawtooth)
	83	Lead 3 (calliope)
	84	Lead 4 (cliff)
	85	Lead 5 (charang)
	86	Lead 6 (voice)
	87	Lead 7 (fifths)
	88	Lead 8 (bass and lead)
12—Synth pad	89	Pad 1 (New Age)
	90	Pad 2 (warm)
	91	Pad 3 (polysynth)
	92	Pad 4 (choir)
	93	Pad 5 (boweed)
	94	Pad 6 (metallic)
	95	Pad 7 (halo)
	96	Pad 8 (sweep)

TABLE 28-2

MIDI Instruments
(Continued)

Channel	Number	Instrument
13—Synth effects	97	FX 1 (rain)
	98	FX 2 (soundtrack)
	99	FX 3 (crystal)
	100	FX 4 (atmosphere)
	101	FX 5 (brightness)
	102	FX 6 (goblins)
	103	FX 7 (echoes)
	104	FX 8 (sci-fi)
14—Ethnic	105	Sitar
	106	Banjo
	107	Shamisen
	108	Koto
	109	Kalimba
	110	Bagpipe
	111	Fiddle
	112	Shanai
15—Percussive	113	Tinkle bell
	114	Agogo
	115	Steel drums
	116	Woodblock
	117	Taiko drum
	118	Melodic tom
	119	Synth drum
	120	Reverse cymbal
16—Sound effects	121	Guitar fret noise
	122	Breath noise
	123	Seashore
	124	Bird tweet
	125	Telephone ring
	126	Helicopter
	127	Applause
	128	Gunshot

TABLE 28-3

Makers of Mac MIDI Tools

Mark of the Unicorn

Opcode

Coda Music Technologies

TABLE 28-4

Current Macs and Their Audio Hardware

Audio Hardware	iMac	Power Mac (G3/G4)	PowerBook	iBook
Built-in mic	Yes	No	Yes	No
Audio line-in	Yes	Yes	Yes	No
Built-in speakers	Stereo*	Mono	Stereo	Mono
Audio line-out	Yes**	Yes	Yes	Yes
CD-ROM input	Yes	Yes	Yes	Yes
USB audio support	Yes	Yes	Yes	Yes

*The iMac models ship with internal speakers capable of supporting Dolby Digital surround sound.

**The iMac models ship with a single line-out jack plus two headphone jacks.

The Audio Abilities Built Into the Mac

The current Macintosh computers all come with audio abilities built into them. The iMac and PowerBook models have pretty much all the basic hardware most users will need. The Power Mac G3/G4 models have most abilities, with the exception of a built-in microphone. The iBook offers no audio recording abilities built in or any audio input abilities, save a CD-ROM drive (USB devices can make up for this lack, however). Table 28-4 lists the Macs covered by this book and the audio capabilities they ship with. The sections that follow examine these built-in abilities.

Audio Line-In

A line-in audio port, shown in Figure 28-4, allows the Mac to accept audio input from external devices. This can include external microphones, as well as other devices, such as analog tape recorders. With the exception of the iBook, all currently shipping Macs include an audio line-in port. This port takes the form of a standard audio mini-plug.

Figure 28-4
The Mac's audio line-in mini-plug and the symbols used to distinguish it from a line-out mini-plug.

Microphones

The iMac and PowerBook computers ship with a built-in microphone. These microphones are functional and work for many purposes. Unfortunately, they are not well suited for all uses. They tend to easily pick up hard-drive sounds and other noise from the Mac and are not good for accurately capturing sounds. If you are planning on doing any serious audio recording or if you plan to use a mic for speech recognition functions, I suggest using an external mic for these machines. For the Power Mac and iBook computers, an external mic is needed because there is no built-in microphone. In addition, the iBook requires a USB mic because it lacks a line-in audio port.

CD-ROM

The CD-ROM drive (or DVD-ROM drive) of a Mac can be selected as an audio input source. When this is done, the Mac records audio from any audio CD that is inserted in the CD-ROM drive and played. This allows you to create digital audio captures of specific sounds or track segments on your audio CDs.

Built-in Speakers

Every shipping Mac includes at least one basic internal speaker. The iMac and PowerBook computers include built-in stereo speakers. The Power Mac ships with a single speaker that is passable for producing sound, but not one that anyone would consider more than functional.

Audio Line-Out

All current Macs ship with an audio line-out. This line-out takes the form of a standard mini-plug. Although this is acceptable for many uses and is perfect for attaching headphones, the mini-plug does introduce a certain level of signal noise into the audio output. This isn't a concern for most home users; however, it is if you are an audio professional converting your audio data to another form for professional use. Also, some high-end speakers use standard RCA audio connectors. These speakers can be attached to the Mac's mini-plug using an adapter that can be found in most home electronics stores. The iMac models actually include three line-out mini-plugs: one in the ports compartment intended for external speaker use and two on the front of the iMac intended for headphone use. The line-out mini-plug is identical to the line-in mini-plug, but will be distinguished by the symbol in Figure 28-5.

Figure 28-5
The Mac's line-out mini-plug and the symbol used to identify it.

MIDI

MIDI includes both hardware and software components of the Mac. At the hardware level, there is no built-in support for MIDI devices. To use MIDI instruments with the Mac, you need to purchase a MIDI interface box. This small piece of hardware features a MIDI cable that connects to the instrument (or multiple instruments) and a cable that connects to the Mac using either a serial port or USB interface. The software needed to accept MIDI input data and to send commands to a MIDI instrument is also needed (and is usually included with the MIDI interface).

Beyond the use of actual MIDI hardware and software, Apple's QuickTime technology does offer software support for MIDI as a multimedia file format. QuickTime has always supported the ability to open MIDI files and to play them using the software-based synthesizer that is built into the QuickTime architecture. With the recent releases of QuickTime, Apple has included some of the most powerful musical device synthesizers available in the standard QuickTime MIDI synthesizer. This gives the Mac built-in support for playing MIDI files with a very impressive result in terms of quality. In fact, the quality may surpass some physical synthesizers on the market.

USB Audio Devices

There has been a gradual shift by makers of computer audio hardware to USB devices. This shift has been more intended for users of Windows-based PCs, which do not include audio circuitry on the motherboard. Because such computers require an expansion card to support any device but ship with USB as a built-in feature, many manufacturers are creating USB microphones and other hardware for computers that don't include audio hardware capable of traditional connections. Although all Macs can use USB audio hardware, the only one particularly needing such hardware is the iBook because it ships without audio line-in support.

Speakers USB speakers are not something that will likely appeal to the majority of Mac users simply because the speakers are more limited in terms of features, performance, and choices of models than traditional speakers. They also tend to have higher prices because of the development costs involved. However, the use of USB speakers is supported under Mac OS 9 and higher without the need for additional driver software.

Microphones   USB microphones are primarily aimed at users of the iBook because the iBook is the first Mac portable in several years to ship without a built-in mic. It is also the first Mac (portable or desktop) in many years to ship without line-in audio support. USB microphones can be used with the iBook (or any other Mac). Although several companies have promised Mac-specific USB mics for the iBook, none have been released as of this writing. However, USB mic models intended for PC use will function with any Mac running Mac OS 9 or higher, because Apple has built support for USB audio input into Mac OS 9. This means that no additional software or drivers need to be installed for the Mac to recognize and use USB microphones. Simply plug the microphone into a USB port, and the Mac should recognize it in the Sound control panel or within specific audio applications.

MIDI   MIDI hardware has traditionally been attached to the Mac using a serial port interface. However, following the iMac's shift to USB in 1998, the major Mac-MIDI manufacturers (Opcode and Mark of the Unicorn) have developed USB MIDI interface hardware. This hardware functions much the same as serial port devices, acting as an adapter between your MIDI instrument and your Mac. Some serial-port-to-USB adapters and serial port expansion cards also support connecting earlier serial port MIDI hardware to the current Macs (see Chapter 30 for more information on serial port solutions for today's Macs).

Recording Audio

This section looks at your various options when recording and working with digital audio on the Mac. It includes an overview of audio file formats, as well as a discussion about the types of recording and sound editing software available for the Mac.

Audio File Formats

A wide variety of file types can be used to save digital sound data, each with differing levels of quality and compression options. They are also designed with different types of use in mind. Most audio recording applications allow you to record sounds as a few of these different file types. Likewise, many applications allow you to convert between various audio file formats. QuickTime Pro actually lets you convert files between almost any audio file format. The following paragraphs list the common audio file formats available today and provide some information about each one.

System Sounds   System sounds are the native sound format for the Mac. They are the type of sound file used for each of the Mac's alert sounds (any System Sound file dragged into the System file inside the Mac's System Folder will be available as an alert sound). When not used as alert sounds, they are files that the Mac can play without any need for special applications or system extensions. Simply double-click on them in the Finder, and the Mac will play them.

AIFF   Audio Interchange File Format, or AIFF, is the file format used for recording audio tracks on a CD. The format was developed by Apple some years ago and supports the highest sampling rates and sizes, resulting in very good quality playback. Originally, the AIFF format did not support compression of sound data in a file. This ability was later added to the format and is sometimes referred to as the AIFC format.

AU (also known as the μlaw format)   This is the native audio format for Sun workstation computers. AU files are limited to lower sampling rates, which limits the quality of audio recorded in this format. However, because of the small sizes of AU files, they have had some popularity for downloadable sound files on the Internet.

WAV   WAV files are the Windows equivalent of Mac System Sounds. This means that the file format is quite common in the computer world today. If you want a file to be easily playable on a PC, the WAV format is probably the best one you can use.

QuickTime Movie   Apple's QuickTime movie (.mov) file format can be used to save video clips. It can also be used to simply save an audio track for an audio-only file. This can be done by converting an existing audio file into a QuickTime movie or by deleting the video track of an existing QuickTime movie. When used in concert with Apple's QuickTime Streaming Server (see Chapter 42), you can stream audio-only QuickTime movie files over the Internet.

MPEG   The MPEG (Moving Picture Experts Group) file format was mentioned in earlier chapters. Like QuickTime movies, MPEG files are traditionally video files. However, it is possible to store MPEG files that are audio-only. This provides high-quality sounds with a fairly good compression scheme and is often used for storing the audio tracks of many CD-ROM based games.

Note: MPEG files and compression should not be confused with the MPEG-2 video encoding used for DVD video (see Chapter 17) or the MPEG-1 layer 3 format, commonly referred to as MP3.

MP3   MP3 has become quite popular in the past couple of years and very controversial in the past year. MP3 stands for MPEG-1 layer 3, meaning it uses a compression scheme similar to that of the MPEG video file format. MP3 files deliver near-CD quality but are able to compress the audio considerably, usually resulting in files that are one-tenth the size of an equivalent uncompressed AIFF file. This makes MP3 an ideal format for transferring songs with other users over the Internet. MP3 files can also be stored on a special portable MP3 player that can be carried with you much like a Walkman so you can listen to your favorite MP3 files without needing your Mac to play them.

MIDI   MIDI files are really not sound files at all. Rather, they are files that contain commands for MIDI instrument devices. These files can be produced by some applications and by using a MIDI keyboard or other instrument with the Mac. They can be played back to a MIDI instrument or using the built-in MIDI synthesizer of the Mac's QuickTime. QuickTime can also convert MIDI files into other sound file formats. When this is done, the audio produced will be what would be played by QuickTime's built-in software MIDI synthesizer.

MOD   MOD files are special short audio files, usually computer-generated audio compositions. These files are designed to loop well and are really only used as the file format for background music in Mac games. Because today's games ship on CD-ROMs, where a more robust audio track can be stored on the CD, MOD files tend to be only used in older games and shareware games. Usually, MOD files are embedded directly into the game itself. Some software utilities can be used to extract MOD files from a game and store them on a hard drive. A few games allow you to import MOD files into the game so you can create your own sound track for the game.

Real Audio   If you've been online at all over the past few years, you've probably come across sites that offer streaming audio or video files using the Real Audio or Real Video format, respectively, and the RealPlayer application. Real Audio is the format used for streaming audio files using this technology. You can record Real Audio files using Real's RealProducer application (or you can record in a different format and convert using RealProducer). These files will then need to be stored on a web server or RealServer for playback. The RealServer offers more powerful streaming abilities, but it is not available for Mac computers.

Recording Using the Software Included with the Mac

Apple includes some very basic audio software with the Mac that can be used to record or work with digital audio files. These are, however, not the best tools for recording digital audio available, and if you are looking to record audio for personal use, you can find any number of shareware audio applications for recording sounds. Additionally, there are many commercial- and professional-caliber audio tools available for the Mac. The tools included with the Mac will give you an idea of how other tools work, however.

The Sound Control Panel   Apple's Sound control panel is one of the basic interfaces for audio work on the Mac. In some Mac OS releases, this is bundled with the Monitors control panel into a single Monitors and Sound control panel (though the functionality is essentially the same as with separate control panels). The Sound control panel includes four primary functions that you can choose to work with: Alert Sounds, Input, Output, and Speaker Setup.

The Alert Sounds section, shown in Figure 28-6, is fairly straightfor-

Figure 28-6
The Sound control panel's Alert Sounds section.

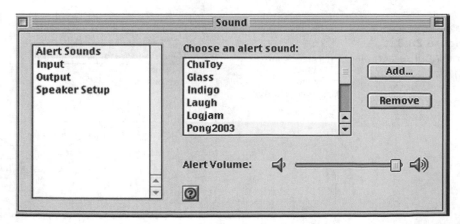

ward. It allows you to choose any System Sound file currently in your Mac's System file to be played whenever the Mac needs your attention, such as when an alert or dialog box is displayed. This section also lets you specify the volume of alert sound playback and record new alert sounds. Pressing the Add button brings up a very basic audio dialog with Record, Play, Stop, and Pause buttons. These buttons are used to record your new alert sound. When recording an alert sound with this dialog (shown in Figure 28-7), you are limited to sounds of only five seconds. Once the sound is recorded, you can press the Save button in this dialog, and you will be asked to enter a name for the sound.

The Input feature, shown in Figure 28-8, lets you choose from the available sound input devices. This generally includes built-in mics, external mics, the line-in port, and the CD/DVD-ROM drive. The choices will vary depending on what hardware is available to the Mac. This item sets the default audio input for the Mac. Any Mac OS elements that accept audio input (speech recognition and recording alert sounds in the

Figure 28-7
The recording dialog for adding new alert sounds (other basic sound-recording applications may also use this same dialog).

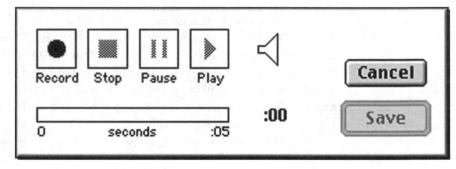

Figure 28-8
The Input section of the Sound control panel allows you to choose from various input sources.

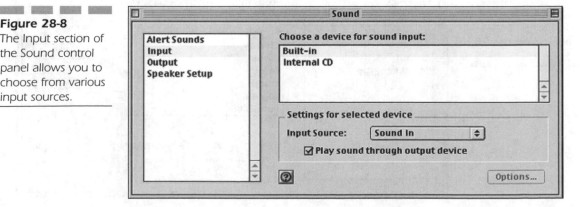

Sound control panel, for example) will use the chosen device. Many audio applications will also use the device chosen here, although some may offer a similar dialog for choosing what audio input to use for just that application. You also have the option of determining if the sound from the chosen input source will be played through the Mac's speakers.

Output lets you choose what hardware (if multiple choices are present) will be used to play any sounds generated by the Mac (alert sounds, game noises, audio CDs, and so on.). This also allows you to designate the volume of sound output or to mute the Mac's audio (this can also be accomplished using the control strip and, on portable Macs, the hot keys of the function keys). For external speakers with their own volume controls, you can adjust the volume in the Mac OS and/or use the volume control of the speakers themselves.

Speaker Setup is available only to Macs with stereo speakers and provides a Mac OS-level interface for balancing the sound for both speakers of the Mac. This is particularly useful for Macs with built-in stereo speakers, as they have no built-in balance controls. It will also function for external speakers, overriding or compensating for any balance controls built into the speakers themselves.

SimpleSound   SimpleSound, shown in Figure 28-9, is a very basic sound-recording application that Apple includes with all Macs. As its name suggests, it is the audio equivalent to Apple's bare-bones text editor, SimpleText. SimpleSound can be used to record new alert sounds in the exact same fashion as the Sound control panel, without the five-sec-

Figure 28-9
The SimpleSound
application.

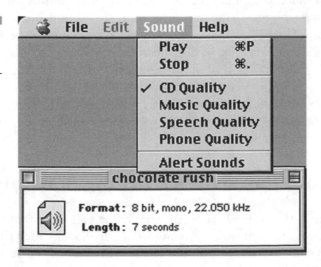

ond time limit. It can be used to record sound files of any size (limited only by the amount of disk space available) and at varying sampling rates and sizes. Unfortunately, SimpleSound does not give you much choice in terms of sampling rate or sizes. It uses predefined rates, sizes, and channel depths for each of its four possible levels of quality (phone, speech, music, and CD), as well as predefined compression schemes and levels. If you need to record audio quickly, SimpleSound does work, but if you want any real control over the recording process, you should use a more powerful recording utility.

QuickTime Apple's QuickTime is the basis behind most audio and video work on the Mac. It includes a wide array of codecs, an amazing software-based MIDI synthesizer, and the ability to open or translate virtually any graphics, video, or audio file format currently used. Out of the box, Apple's QuickTime Player application is limited to just opening and playing files. However, if you pay the $30 to register and upgrade the tool to QuickTime Player Pro, you get a pretty formidable tool for converting among the available sound formats.

While not being a recording application in and of itself, QuickTime Player Pro does allow you to change the sampling rate and size as well as the channel depth and compression used in a recording when converting the file to another format, as you can see in Figure 28-10. This can be a particularly useful ability, but whatever file you do create will be limited to the quality of the original recording. The QuickTime Player also gives you the ability to extract audio tracks from existing QuickTime movies and copy, cut, and paste audio files together.

Combine the basic recording features of SimpleSound with some of the more advanced conversion, compression, and basic editing features of QuickTime Player Pro and you get a passable setup for recording basic audio and working with it for either saving your own audio files or creating audio files that you can share with others. You can even convert it for streaming over the Internet. If you do combine these two tools, however, you should remember to record audio in SimpleSound using the CD-quality option, which is uncompressed stereo sound sampled at 44 kHz and 16 bits.

More Powerful Recording Software

While the Mac ships with very basic software tools that allow you to record and edit audio, no one would really consider them to be anything beyond just the extremely basic functions of audio work. This section

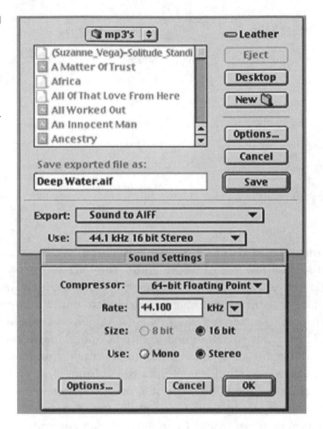

Figure 28-10
The Export dialog of QuickTime Player Pro allows you to select a number of sound quality options.

contains an overview of some of the more powerful Macintosh recording and editing tools out there for audio content. These tools are broken up into three fairly well defined areas: basic recording software (suitable for recording and editing personal sound files), commercial audio editing software (powerful enough to add some additional features and effects but still suited for consumers or hobbyists), and professional audio mixing software (aimed at music or broadcast industry professionals for creating pro-level audio output).

Basic Recording Software   A number of tools are available that allow you to directly record audio on the Mac into a number of different file formats, with varying degrees of compression. These may offer some basic noise reduction features, microphone gain control, and other functions. However, the real use for these tools is simply recording sound files for personal use. As a result, such tools are often shareware or freeware and will serve many home users as perfectly good tools

TABLE 28-5

Commercial Audio Editing Software Packages

Software Title	Manufacturer
Musicshop	Opcode
Vision DSP	Opcode
Micrologic AV	eMagic
SoundEdit 16	Macromedia
SoundDesigner II	Digidesign
Audiodesk	Mark of the Unicorn
Performer	Mark of the Unicorn

Commercial Audio Editing Software   While shareware or freeware tools can allow you to record audio, they are really only a relatively small step above the abilities of SimpleSound and QuickTime Pro combined. If you really want to be able to work with sound on your Mac, you'll want to invest in a commercial application such as those listed in Table 28-5.

These tools are designed to offer professional-level editing effects and the ability to work with more than one track of audio at a time. This allows you to add sound effects, adjust the volume of an audio track, accurately edit the sound, add fade-in and fade-out features, and similar functions. It also allows you to overlay one audio track on top of another and combine the two or more tracks (usually recorded separately) into a single sound file. These tools can yield professional-sounding results and can be great tools if you want to learn more about mixing your own audio compositions or want to provide something like your own Internet-based radio station.

Professional Audio Mixing Software   The third level of audio software is designed for and aimed exclusively at professional recording studios or broadcast sites, such as radio stations. It includes the ability to mix multiple audio tracks (sometimes a dozen or more) and to apply any needed effects or adjustments in real time. In fact, at this level of software (and the appropriate level of additional audio hardware), you can have a virtual mixing board and recording studio running completely in software on the Mac. Such tools are listed in Table 28-6 and function for audio content producers like Photoshop and Quark XPress do for graphics artists and desktop publishing markets. In fact, much like Photoshop, some of these tools even use a plug-in architecture to enable even greater audio abilities and effects to be added to the application's already impressive array of features.

TABLE 28-6

Professional Audio
Mixing Software

Package Name	Manufacturer
Digital Performer	Mark of the Unicorn
StudioVision Pro	Opcode
ProTools	DigiDesign*
Deck II	Macromedia
Logic Audio Series	dMagic

*ProTools includes software tools as well as DigiDesign's line of
high-end audio hardware.

Additional Audio Hardware

Even with the Mac's built-in audio abilities, there will be times when
those abilities need to be expanded. For most users this will primarily
consist of adding better speakers and a higher-quality microphone.
However, users interested in the abilities of more professional audio production and the types of tools listed in Table 28-6 will want to go further
and consider adding more elaborate input and output hardware, as well
as audio cards capable of sample sizes greater than the standard 16-bit
audio of the Mac. This section looks at some of the additional audio hardware that can be added to the Mac.

Speakers

There are any number of speakers on the market intended for use with
computers. They range from very simple and low-cost models (say, $20) to
full-fledged audio powerhouses costing hundreds of dollars. In addition to
speaker systems specifically designed for computer use, there is an
almost dizzying array of speakers out there for home stereo and theater
systems. As a rule, any speaker that features a standard mini-plug (or
can be attached to such a mini-plug with an adapter) can be used with the
Mac. This can give you an amazing range of options for any Mac.

Also, don't just assume that because the iMac has built-in surround
sound speakers that they are the best option. Although the speakers
built into the iMac are the best speakers used by Apple in the current or
recent Macs, they do suffer from some limitations. One such limitation is
that they are placed very close together and therefore can't generate the

sound quality of speakers placed at a distance from each other. This is an annoying limitation given the iMac's support for stereo surround sound.

Going into detail about all the speakers available is beyond the scope of this chapter. If you want to consider other speaker options, I suggest going to your local home electronics store and checking out what is available in your price range. If you do opt for external speakers, remember that you will have the choice of the speakers' own volume controls or the volume controls built into the Mac OS (or both). The same is true of balance controls. However, bass and treble controls are a different story, and I suggest choosing speakers that include such controls on them, as adjusting these features is not an ability built into the Mac OS (though some applications designed for playing audio CDs and MP3 files do support this). You can also use a standard stereo amplifier and/or equalizer with external speakers to enhance the audio signal from the Mac.

Microphones

Whether you are recording audio for playback later, to edit and create your own audio CD, to use with a telephony package to create a speakerphone setup on your Mac (see Chapter 31), to broadcast your voice to another person or group over the Internet, or to use with one of the speech recognition products (such as Apple's PlainTalk, which is included with the Mac OS) or dictation software packages (such as IBM's ViaVoice), you'll need a microphone. As discussed earlier in the chapter, the iMac and PowerBook computers ship with a built-in microphone, but this may not be powerful or clear enough for your needs.

For any Mac, save the iBook, you can purchase a large number of mics that support the standard mini-plug connection of the Mac's line-in audio port. Some microphones have had compatibility problems with the Mac, particularly with Apple's PlainTalk speech recognition software (some mics are produced specially for PlainTalk use). You may want to check for Mac compatibility with a mic when using it for speech recognition functions. Otherwise, you should buy from a company that has a good return policy.

A range of microphones are available, from $5 models that serve for just recording your voice at a basic level of quality to expensive freestanding or headset models that offer extraordinary clarity. Which one you choose depends on your needs. Often, if you look in many computer stores, microphones are organized by function as much as by price, and this can help you determine a model appropriate to your needs. Also, some speech recognition packages or other audio editing tools include a mic as a standard feature along with the software.

Audio Cards

The Mac's built-in audio circuitry and hardware is good for consumers, but recording professionals will find it very limited both in terms of the supported sampling size of the hardware and in terms of the available interface for connecting audio equipment. For this reason, a number of more powerful audio expansion cards are available for Power Mac computers. These are PCI cards that can add a wide variety of additional features and better-quality sound support to the Mac. To a much smaller extent, there are some PC Cards that can be used for similar purposes on the PowerBook computers. The following paragraphs look at some of the features these cards can offer.

RCA-Style Connectors   While the mini-plug used by the Mac's line-in and line-out ports is functional, it is far from being professional quality. It can introduce a certain level of signal noise into any recording being passed through it. By contrast, RCA-style connectors provide a much clearer signal both when connecting audio devices for dubbing or recording purposes and when connecting higher-end speakers.

Multiple Connections   The Mac includes only a single built-in audio input. Most professional audio cards include multiple audio inputs or channels (sometimes as many as a dozen). This is particularly important if you intend to mix or remix audio tracks on your Mac. Even if you are not using all the available channels at once, having multiple inputs allows you to leave several different audio devices connected to the Mac at one time and eliminates the effort of needing to remove one device in order to record from another.

Improved Digital Signal Processors   The Mac's built-in sampling circuitry is adequate for home and school uses. But most professional use requires a higher of sampling rate and/or size. To achieve this, you need to use a digital signal processor (DSP) that is more powerful. In addition to offering higher sampling sizes, an improved DSP will often offer clearer and sharper recordings by improving other factors of the sound-digitizing process. Virtually all audio cards offer improved digital processing over the built-in offerings of the Mac.

Noise Reduction   Audio cards often include hardware that is designed to suppress any signal noise in the recording. This is usually signal noise generated in the analog electrical signal from the microphone (or analog playback device), but it can also include the ability to suppress unwanted background noise. Noise reduction features result in cleaner audio where only the desired audio source is recorded and preserved without any other artifacts of the recording process.

Digital Audio Digital audio recording at high sampling rates and sizes offers advantages over traditional analog recording, where sound data is stored by magnetic patterns corresponding to the analog waveform of a sound (as happens with conventional audio cassette recorders). Digital audio functions very much like digital video, as discussed in the last chapter. The magnetic patterns used in analog sound recordings are prone to degradation and distortion over time or as a result of the medium being exposed to electrical or magnetic fields. This is not the case with digital audio because the data is stored as discrete values rather than waveforms that can be distorted. For these reasons, it is preferable to record audio digitally. For the purpose of recording digital audio, professionals use a special kind of digital tape rather than the analog audio cassettes most people use for personal recording.

All professional recording equipment used today records data digitally from the start, usually using digital audio tape (DAT) technology. This preserves the highest recording quality right from the beginning of the recording process. However, the audio hardware built into the Mac is designed to work only with analog audio devices. To record from a DAT source to the Mac's hard drive, the DAT source recording would need to be converted to analog form by the digital playback device and then back to digital form by the Mac's audio hardware. This could introduce distortions or signal noise into the recording being made by the Mac.

Many devices that use DAT technology, however, have special connectors for copying a recording as digital data rather than an analog signal, much as FireWire provides when transferring or copying digital video. Many audio cards include these special connectors for attaching such digital recording/playback devices to the Mac. This allows the Mac to copy the original sound data in much the same manner that it copies digital video over FireWire, without any risk of distortion or degradation from the original sound recording.

Troubleshooting Audio Problems

Following are some common audio problems, along with possible solutions.

There Is No Sound

If there is no sound at all, first, check to be certain that the volume is turned up and that the Mac's sound output is not muted. This can be done using the Sound control panel or the Sound control strip module (or the hot keys on a PowerBook or iBook's keyboard). If you are using external speakers, check to be certain that the volume control on the speaker is not turned down.

If you are using external speakers, make certain that they are turned on and plugged into an electrical outlet. Also check to be sure that they are plugged into the Mac's line-out audio port completely. If a speaker is only connected partway, you may not get any sound from it. Also be certain that any connection between the two speakers is secure.

If you are using the Mac's internal speakers, make certain there is nothing connected to the audio line-out port. If you have recently performed any repairs or upgrades inside the Mac's case, it is possible that you may have disconnected the internal speaker's cable from the motherboard. This is not particularly likely on most Mac models, but you may wish to check. The internal speaker cable is a narrow red and black cable, such as is shown in Figure 28-11.

If there still doesn't appear to be any explanation for a lack of sound output, try zapping the PRAM (perimeter RAM) as corruption of the PRAM might be responsible for problems with the Mac's audio, though

Figure 28-11
A typical speaker cable that connects a Mac's internal speakers to the motherboard.

this is pretty unlikely. If that fails to help, it is likely that the speaker(s) or cabling is damaged. For external speakers, this can be confirmed by connecting the speaker to another audio device.

Sounds Being Recorded Are Not Played through the Mac's Speakers

This usually applies to CD-ROM or other line-in audio recording. When recording from a microphone, you would not want sound played through the speakers, because it would generate a peculiar audio feedback "howl" if the mic is within range of the speaker. You can select whether or not sound will be played during recording in the Sound control panel.

Resources for Further Study

The following URLs provide additional information on some of the concepts, issues, and products discussed in this chapter:

Pure-Mac Audio Software—http://pure-mac/audio.html

Mark of the Unicorn—http://www.motu.com

Opcode—http://www.opcode.com

EMagic—http://www.emagic.de

Macromedia—http://www.macromedia.com

Digidesign—http://www.digidesign.com

MIDI Manufacturer's Association—http://www.midi.org

About.com Industrial Music Gear—
http://industrialmusic.about.com/msubgear_manuf.htm

About.com Computer Peripherals Audio Equipment (not Mac-specific)—
http://peripherals.about.com/msub_speaker.htm

CHAPTER 29

Printers

Aside from the keyboard and mouse, printers are probably the most commonly used computer peripheral. Two primary types of printers are used today: laser printers and ink-jet printers. This chapter examines both of these types of printers and how they function. An understanding of these printers can help you troubleshoot several problems. A detailed explanation of how to repair most printer hardware failures is beyond the scope of this book, however. This chapter also discusses how the Mac interacts with printers and how to use printers directly connected to the Mac or shared over a network.

How Laser Printers Work

Laser printers have become the standard for producing high-quality grayscale printouts. Laser printers have the advantage of offering very accurate image and text quality and the ability to print faster than ink-jets or many other types of printers. Documents printed on a laser printer also offer two advances over most ink-jet-printed documents: The printed text or images will never fade, and it will not smudge or run if the paper gets wet. Laser printers are also more expensive than ink-jet printers. However, the toner cartridge of a laser printer will usually be enough for 10 times (or more) the number of print jobs that an ink-jet printer's ink cartridge will provide. This leads to cost savings per printed page compared to the more expensive initial purchase cost.

This section looks at how laser printers actually produce printed documents. The process is more involved than most people realize and relies on the fact that some chemical compounds are photoconductive. A photoconductive compound conducts electricity only when it is exposed to light. Laser printers use a laser to draw an image of light that can then be charged by a photosensitive compound.

One of the primary components of a laser printer is a photosensitive drum. This drum is a metal cylinder that is coated with a photoconductive compound. The metal in the cylinder is connected to the printer's power supply in order to ground in the inner parts of the drum. This is important for the photoconductive compound to function as is needed for printing. The photosensitive drum (and several other components involved in reactions between the drum and paper) is usually a built-in part of the toner cartridge, though some laser printers have a separate drum. Having the drum built into the toner cartridge increases the toner cartridge cost, but it also makes replacing the drum easy, should it be damaged.

When you print an image using a laser printer, the photosensitive drum is the first part of the printer to be activated. The first thing that happens is that the drum is cleansed. This cleaning involves a rubber cleaning blade that scrapes any residual toner from a previous print job off of the drum's photosensitive surface. Toner particles scraped off are redeposited back in the toner supply of the cartridge in many printers, although some may deposit it in a debris storage section of the toner cartridge.

It also involves the drum's surface being electrically cleaned. This is accomplished by bombarding the surface of the drum with light of a specific wavelength. These wavelengths of light will cause any electrical charge held in the photosensitive surface of the drum to be drained through the grounding connection to the printer's power supply. One or more devices known as *erase lamps* are designed to do this. Electrically cleaning the surface of the drum with erase lamps is important because it creates a neutral charge across the entire surface of the drum. Figure 29-1 illustrates the cleaning of the drum.

Once the surface of the drum is given a completely uniform, neutral charge, the printer applies a completely even negative charge to the drum. This step prepares the drum to have an image drawn on it by the laser. A wire called the *primary corona* is located very close to the drum's

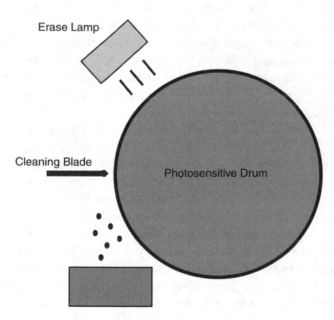

Figure 29-1
Cleaning the photosensitive drum.

Figure 29-2
Charging the drum
after cleaning.

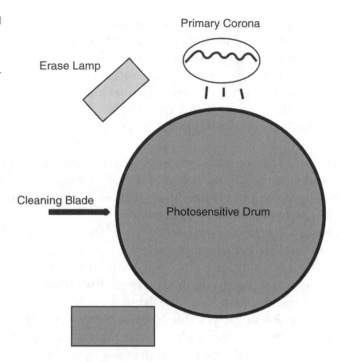

surface but doesn't actually touch it. When the primary corona is supplied with enough electrical current, it creates a negative electrical field that applies a uniform negative charge to the photosensitive drum's surface. This is illustrated in Figure 29-2.

With the drum's surface negatively charged, the printer's laser draws an image on the drum's photosensitive surface. Because of the photosensitive nature of drum, wherever the laser touches the surface, a positive electrical charge is generated. This allows the laser to draw the contents of a page onto the drum's surface.

The toner in a laser printer is a very fine powder of particles made of iron bonded to plastic. When the printer receives a print job, these particles are all given a negative charge by a component known as the *toner cylinder*. Because the toner particles have a negative charge, they are attracted to the areas on the surface of the photosensitive drum that are positively charged by the laser, but not to the surface areas that still maintain a negative charge from the primary corona. As the drum is rotated over the toner particles, they are pulled onto the drum's surface where there is a positive charge. This is illustrated in Figure 29-3.

Once the image is drawn on the photosensitive drum by the laser and the toner has been pulled over the image, the toner needs to be trans-

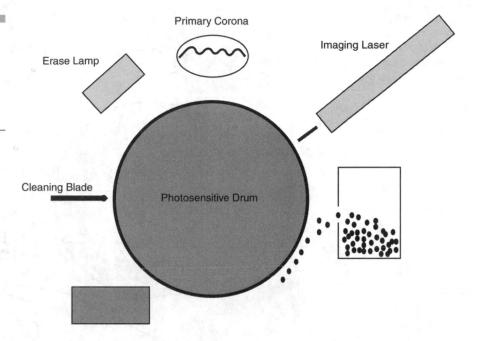

ferred to the paper. For the toner particles to be transferred to the paper, the surface of the paper needs to have a more powerful positive charge than the surface of the drum where the toners are being held because of the electrical charge generated by the laser. The *transfer corona*, which operates the same way that the primary corona operates to charge the drum, only applying a positive charge instead of a negative one, applies a uniform charge to the paper. As the paper is moved along next to the drum by rollers, the toner particles move from the drum's surface to the paper, but they maintain their existing positions, preserving the image.

Once the toner particles have been transferred to the paper, a static eliminator removes the electrical charge from both the paper and the particles. A fusing assembly consisting of two rollers then bonds the toner particles to the paper's surface. One of these rollers is a heat roller, which melts the plastic material in the toner particles. The other is a pressure roller, which presses the toner particles against the page, bonding the toner to the paper itself. Because the toner is melted or bonded right into the paper, it will not fade and it will not run as ink might. This final step in the process is shown in Figure 29-4.

Because the fusing assembly uses heat to melt the plastic in the toner particles and bond them to the paper, a laser printer cannot be used to print images on mediums that contain plastic, such as overhead trans-

Figure 29-4
The toner particles
are transferred to the
paper, any remaining
charge is removed,
and the toner is
bonded to the paper.

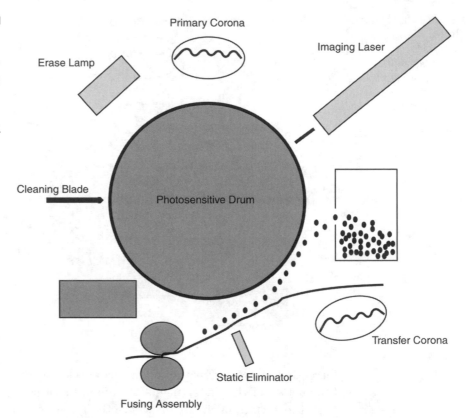

Figure 29-4
The toner particles are transferred to the paper, any remaining charge is removed, and the toner is bonded to the paper.

parencies or some types of photo paper. Some manufacturers have made special materials of these sorts approved for laser printer use because they can withstand the high heat. Do not use anything besides paper or these specially designed mediums in a laser printer. Also, when using such specially designed mediums, make certain that they are approved for use in your printer, as your printer may use higher temperatures than other printers. If you use nonapproved materials, you could seriously damage your printer and void its warranty.

Laser Printer Maintenance

Laser printer maintenance varies depending on the manufacturer and model of the laser printer you are dealing with. Consult the printer's manual for specific information. As a rule, there are two tasks involved in maintaining laser printers: cleaning and periodically replacing certain components.

Cleaning   The toner particles used by a laser printer are very small and very fine. The toner itself is a powder of these particles. Although the aim of a laser printer is to bond these particles to the paper and to either recycle particles that remain on the photosensitive drum into the toner supply or to safely store them inside the toner cartridge, a small amount of toner particles will get out of the cartridge and into the printer itself. Also, paper fed into the printer may have some powder or dander on it. Both excess toner and paper dander should be cleaned out of a laser printer periodically. This can be done with a can of compressed air when you change the toner cartridge (although you may want to do it outdoors, since the toner will get sprayed out of the printer like chimney ash when you do it).

You may also want to clean the rubber rollers that feed the paper through the printer. These can build up excess toner, paper dander, or other dusts on them over time. This can eventually cause them to skip and jam paper. You can clean them off with a cloth or cotton swab that is slightly damp.

Beyond this general overview of cleaning, you should consult your printer's manual for additional instructions and specific cleaning requirements.

Replacing Components   Some parts of a laser printer do need to be periodically replaced. Most printer manufacturers try to bundle as many of these components as possible into the same unit that contains the toner cartridge and photosensitive drum. However, certain components simply can't be incorporated that way. The specific components needing periodic replacement vary from printer to printer, as will the times at which they need to be replaced. As a rule, the fusing assembly on most laser printers needs to be replaced periodically. Other components often needing to be replaced include the transfer corona, paper guides/rollers, the thermal fuse used to keep the printer from overheating, and the ozone filter. Some manufacturers even sell kits with all such parts, along with any needed tools. Refer to the manual that came with your printer for details.

How Ink-Jet Printers Work

Ink-jet printers are generally one-third or less the cost of laser printers. This makes them extremely popular in the consumer and education markets. Ink-jet printers also offer the ability to print images in color for that low price, whereas color laser printers are often 10 times the price of a similarly equipped grayscale laser printer.

Compared to the complex process involved in printing a page on a laser printer, ink-jet printers function with almost boring simplicity. These printers have a print head where ink cartridges are installed. This print head is built onto a traverse assembly that allows it to move back and forth along the width of the paper path, as illustrated in Figure 29-5.

The print head itself consists of a large number of tiny nozzles or jets that ink is sprayed out of as the print head moves across the paper. The ink is sprayed or ejected through the jets in the print head by heating the ink with tiny electrical resistors at one end of the jet. These resistors actually boil the ink to create a tiny air bubble, which pushes a droplet of ink through the jet and onto the paper at a specific point. These points are such that when the paper absorbs the droplets, they form the image or text that was sent to the printer from the Mac. A paper feed mechanism moves the paper through the printer as the traverse assembly completes each passage of the print head over the width of the paper.

The ink stored in an ink-jet printer's ink cartridges has a tendency to dry out if it is not used frequently. This can happen fairly quickly. To extend the time it takes for an ink cartridge to dry out, ink-jet printers move the print head to a special area designed to keep the ink from drying out. This area is often called the park, cleaning, or maintenance posi-

Figure 29-5

The print head and traverse assembly are the main components of an ink-jet printer.

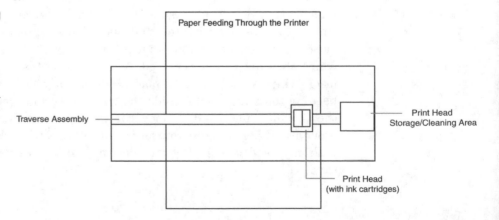

Paper Feeding Through the Printer

Traverse Assembly

Print Head
Storage/Cleaning Area

Print Head
(with ink cartridges)

tion. This helps keep a cartridge from going bad by drying out, but it isn't a complete solution. An ink cartridge left in the printer for months or even weeks (depending on the printer and quality of the cartridge) will become unusable.

Ink-Jet Printer Maintenance

Ink-jet printers don't require much maintenance to keep them running smoothly. You may want to occasionally blow some compressed air through the printer's paper intake to ensure that no dust is building up in there. Similarly, you can use compressed air to blow any dust out of the printer entirely. This does not need to be done as often for ink-jet printers as laser printers because there are no toner particles getting loose in an ink-jet printer as there can be with a laser printer.

You should also make certain that you shut the printer down properly, by pressing the button or switch on the printer and not by using a surge protector's switch to turn the printer off along with other devices. This is because ink-jet printers go through a special routine of parking the print head that is essential to keeping the ink in the printer's cartridges from drying out.

Cleaning the Print Head   The one real task you need to do periodically with an ink-jet printer is to clean the print head. Occasionally, ink can build up in the jets of the print head that actually perform the printing process. When this happens, the printed page may have white lines or smudges on it. Usually, cleaning the print head alleviates this. The printer actually cleans the print head on its own. You simply need to tell it to do so by using an option in the Print dialog box. The name of the option and how to access it varies depending on your printer driver, but all ink-jets include such a feature. Figure 29-6 shows the print head cleaning option in various printer Print dialogs. When selected, the printer cleans the jets of the print head before printing a page.

Printer Resolutions, Languages, and Other Specs

A number of different specifications differentiate the abilities of printers on the market today, both laser and ink-jet. This section contains an overview of these specifications and what they mean. Specifically, it looks

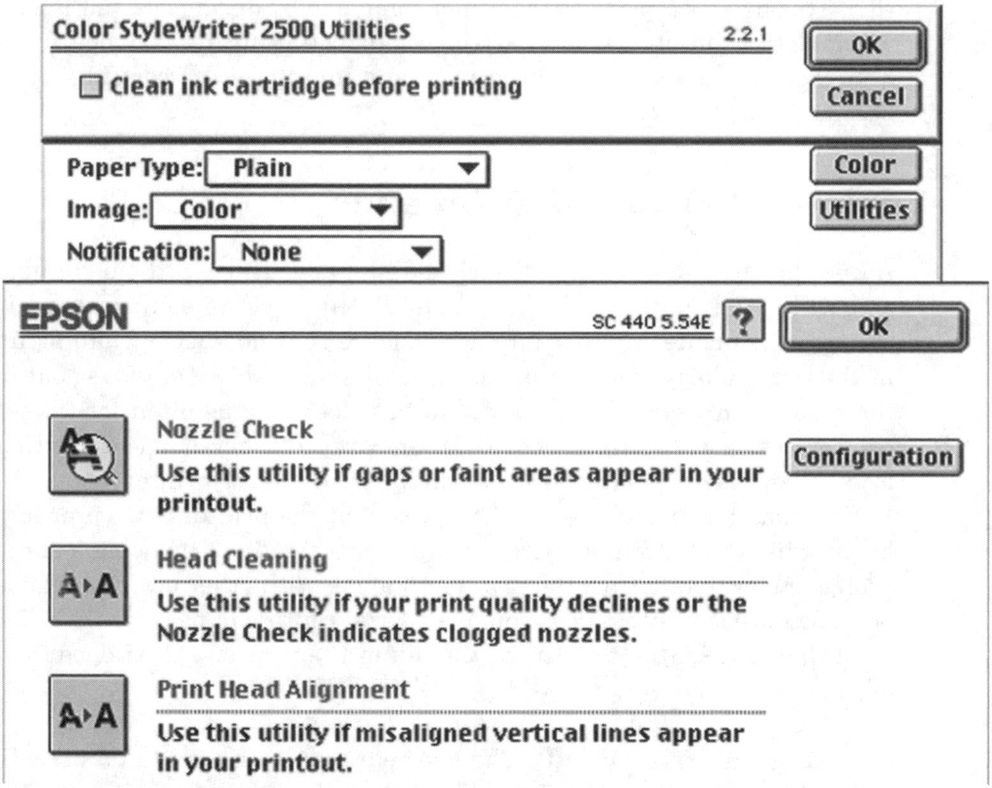

Figure 29-6 The options for cleaning the print head will appear similar to these, but they will vary depending on the printer being used.

at printer resolution, speed, control languages, and the memory needs of laser printers.

Resolution

Chapter 4 introduced you to the way that monitors measure resolution, and Chapter 25 introduced you to how scanners measure resolution as dots per inch. This is the same way that printers measure resolution—as dots or pixels per inch. Printer resolution is often given as, for instance, 300×300, meaning the printer is capable of printing 300 dots per horizontal inch and 300 dots per vertical inch. As the resolution of a printer increases, the size of the individual dots produced by the printer decreases. As each dot becomes smaller and more individual dots are placed together, the text or image printed becomes smoother and more accurate to the actual shape, rather than looking jagged or blocky.

Most midrange printers today print at 600 dpi resolution or higher. This gives a good level of accuracy for consumer uses and is more than adequate for printing text and other documents for business use. The lowest resolution currently used, 300 dpi, provides accurate printing of text documents for routine uses. For professional-level graphics or text output, however, you should use a higher-resolution printer that supports at least 1200 dpi. To give you a comparison, the resolution used in professional typesetting (such as for books and magazines) is typically as high as 5000 dpi.

Lines per Inch In addition to dots per inch, printers often include lines per inch in their resolution specs. Lines per inch (lpi) is the measurement used when printing halftone (grayscale) images. Because a printer only prints in black and white, not true shades of gray, the printer needs to approximate the individual shades of gray by individual black and white dots. The higher the lines per inch resolution, the better the printer is capable of accomplishing this process. The better halftone print quality, the more realistic black-and-white photographs will appear when printed.

Resolution Enhancement Technology (RET) Resolution enhancement technology is a technique incorporated into some printers to allow them to offer smooth output, particularly for curves. RET places smaller dots in certain areas, such as the end of a curve. The smaller dots result in the curve being smoother because they fill in what would have been a hard-edged gap between one line of the print job and the next.

Speed

A printer's speed tells you how fast the printer prints each page. Printer speed is measured in the number of pages the printer is capable of printing in a minute. The faster the printer's speed, the less time you have to wait for a print job to be completed. If you are printing a long document (say, 20 to 100 pages), printer speed becomes an important consideration.

The printer speed listed in a printer's specs will be an average speed.

Several factors actually influence the speed of the printer, including the complexity of the images or text being printed and how long it takes for the printer to image the data coming from the Mac, the percentage of the page that is covered by text or images, and how long the printer needs to warm up if it has just been powered on or if it has been in a rest or sleep mode.

The printer speed you need will vary depending on what you are printing and the environment you are printing in. A busy office where a printer is shared between a dozen computers needs a faster printer than a single home user, for example. Also, if you are printing long text documents or large image files, you will want a faster printer than if you are just printing the occasional two-page e-mail or letter to grandma.

Printer Quality Modes

Related to both printer resolution and speed is the use of varying print modes. When you use the Print command, you'll notice that almost all printers will offer you a choice of three qualities. These will usually be labeled something like "Good," "Better," and "Best" or "Faster," "Normal," and "Best." These qualities refer to the three levels at which the printer can print. The lowest of the three will print your document as fast as the printer is capable of, but it will do so at the expense of some quality (usually at a lower resolution, though sometimes just with less ink, resulting in a lighter image). The highest-quality mode, on the other hand, will print the image at the highest resolution and deepest intensity that the printer can manage, but it will take a good deal longer to complete each page. The middle mode is a balance between both quality and speed. You can check your printer's manual for details on what each level of quality means in terms of print resolution or intensity and resulting speed.

QuickDraw, PostScript, and Other Languages

The Mac needs to use a language to send data to a printer. This language defines the characteristics and shapes of whatever images or text are contained within the print job and tells the printer what sort of output it needs to produce. Obviously, both the Mac and printer needs to be able to use the same language, usually called a page description language (PDL), for the Mac to be able to send print jobs to a printer.

There are three commonly used page description languages that you should be aware of: QuickDraw, PostScript, and PCL. The next few paragraphs include information about each of these, PostScript being the one that requires the most detail and explanation.

QuickDraw   QuickDraw is the Mac's native printing and screen drawing language. It has existed since the very first Mac and is the built-in series of routines that is used to describe to the Mac what text or images look like. Because QuickDraw is the Mac's native language for drawing data to the Mac's screen, it takes very little effort for the Mac to convert data on-screen for output to a direct-connect printer. The Mac itself sends the image data to the printer directly, and the printer merely reproduces the image data on a page. These means that QuickDraw printers don't need to be very advanced because they receive the data already processed and ready to print from the Mac.

QuickDraw has some limitations, however. It is only supported on Macintosh computers. Other computers will not use QuickDraw for print jobs. This limits the effective use or market share of QuickDraw. QuickDraw is also designed for displaying information on-screen and is not as readily scalable as other languages. This means that your printouts may not be as smooth as with more advanced PDLs, because the output will usually be at the on-screen resolution (72 dpi) unless you print with an application that can send higher-resolution data to the printer driver. Similarly, QuickDraw includes no built-in routines for describing fonts to the printer. This means that fonts will have a tendency to look blockier. Apple solved this problem by creating TrueType fonts, which scale well both on-screen and in print, but it is not nearly as polished as using a more advanced language.

QuickDraw also requires the Mac to steadily send data to the printer, because the printer needs to receive the print data itself rather than a file containing a description of the page, as more advanced languages allow. This will slow the Mac down in performing other tasks while you are printing because it is constantly processing the print job and feeding it, bit by bit, to the printer.

On the plus side, QuickDraw printers don't need to be able to store font information or to convert a page description into an actual page image for printing. The Mac is doing this for them. This means that less elaborate hardware needs to be built into the printer, making QuickDraw printers less expensive. For most consumer and business uses, QuickDraw printers produce acceptable results. For desktop publishing and graphics work, however, a PostScript printer should be used.

PostScript   PostScript was created by Adobe and is a much more robust PDL than QuickDraw. PostScript is scalable, meaning it will automatically scale your print job from whatever your screen resolution is to whatever the printer is capable of. This can be literally up to resolutions that are beyond what many printers are capable of producing. This makes PostScript output extremely smooth. PostScript also supports the use of font definitions. PostScript fonts are font files that tell the printer exactly what each letter (or other character) of a font is supposed to look like at any point size and resolution. This means that PostScript fonts will always look smooth and professional and will almost never include blocking or jagged edges. This is extremely important in desktop publishing work. PostScript also supports printer controls, meaning that a PostScript print job not only contains a description for the printer of what a page is supposed to look like, but it also includes the commands for the printer to adjust margins, page breaks, text pages, and other functions. This means that the Mac doesn't have to continually feed specific line-by-line instructions to the printer. It just sends a PostScript file containing the print job. The printer then interprets all the data contained in the print job itself and performs the printing without the Mac's intervention (though it will alert the Mac if there is a problem with the print job). This makes PostScript excellent for networked printers where there is no need for the Mac to continually send instructions and data to the printer.

Because the printer needs to process a PostScript print job and then forward it to the print mechanisms, PostScript printers require a processor. This is the same kind of processor that a computer needs (in fact, some Macs and Apple LaserWriter printers used the exact same processors). The printer also requires RAM to store the print job and memory to store its collection of PostScript fonts.

Since PostScript is not the default screen drawing language of the Mac, the Mac needs to convert a document into PostScript when printing to a PostScript printer. This conversion is done by the printer driver (usually the LaserWriter 8 printer driver from Apple). When doing this, the Print dialog box contains a number of additional features that allow you to control how the Mac converts the document to PostScript for printing. This includes information on what fonts are used and how they are converted, color matching, and how the printer should alert you if there is a problem. You can even save a print job as a PostScript file on your hard drive.

ADOBE TYPE MANAGER   Adobe Type Manager (ATM), shown in Figure 29-7, is a control panel for dealing with PostScript fonts on the

Figure 29-7
The Adobe Type
Manager control
panel.

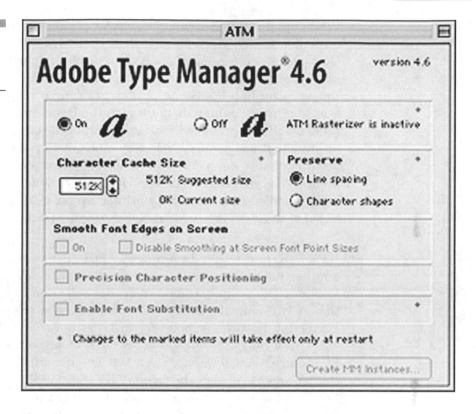

Mac. One of the advantages of ATM is that it allows the Mac to display
PostScript fonts on-screen, a feature that is not a standard part of the
Mac OS because of the Mac's use of QuickDraw as a screen description
language. Additionally, ATM improves the look of PostScript fonts when
they are printed to a QuickDraw printer. Normally, PostScript fonts sent
to a QuickDraw printer would look jagged or blocky. If you deal with
PostScript fonts and printers, you should install ATM on your Mac. It is
usually included free with the current Mac OS releases or with the Adobe
Acrobat Viewer (used for viewing PDF files on the Mac) and can be downloaded from Adobe's Website (www.adobe.com). For advanced features,
you can also purchase the commercial Adobe Type Manager Deluxe.

STYLESCRIPT PostScript printers are by nature of the additional hardware
they require more expensive than QuickDraw printers. Also, PostScript is
primarily used for laser printers and not ink-jet printers. Since color laser
printers tend to be out of the price range of most consumers and small
businesses, there is no easily provided option for including the clarity of

PostScript printing with affordable color printers. InfoWave has provided a solution to this dilemma with the StyleScript utility. StyleScript gives QuickDraw printers all the advantages of PostScript but without any additional hardware costs. StyleScript actually uses your Mac in place of the processor in a PostScript printer, grabbing print jobs before they are sent to printer, running them through the PostScript language, and then sending the post-processed PostScript output to your printer. The result is printing that has quality levels very much like PostScript. Keep in mind, however, that it slows down the printing process and other tasks on your Mac because your Mac needs to perform all of the PostScript routines normally handled by a PostScript printer's processor, as well as the traditional printing actions associated with a QuickDraw printer.

HP's PCL and Other Languages   PCL (Printer Control Language) is another page description language that was developed by Hewlett-Packard. The primary information that you need to know about PCL is that it is commonly used on PC printers as a cheaper alternative to PostScript. However, support for PCL has never been built into the Mac OS. This means that Macs aren't capable of outputting to printers using PCL. Since you will want to use a Mac-specific printer in most situations, this isn't an issue. Also, the printers HP sells for Mac use do accept either PostScript or QuickDraw print jobs. The only time you may run afoul of PCL is if your Mac is connected to a mixed Mac and PC network. In this situation, you need to be aware of what printers on the network use only PCL and avoid using them. Many printers (including several models from HP) support both PCL and PostScript. When PostScript is enabled on such printers, Macs can print to them.

Laser Printer Memory

Unlike ink-jet printers, laser printers need RAM installed in them just as a computer does. This is because a laser printer needs to be able to create an image of what it is printing before the page can be passed through. The Mac can't simply send a line or two of print data to the printer at once because most of the laser printer's components move too quickly for the printer to receive data that slowly. So the laser printer has memory installed in it where an image of what is to be printed is stored. This memory needs to be enough to store the entire contents of a page. Since higher printer resolutions mean more detail in an image and therefore more data, higher-end printers require more RAM than low-

TABLE 29-1

*Laser Printer
Resolution Memory
Requirements.*

Resolution	RAM*
300×300	2 MB**
600×600	4 MB
600×1200	8 MB
1200×1200	12 MB

*Requirements may vary depending on network use and the number of PostScript fonts installed on a PostScript printer.
**Some low-end laser printers use a built-in compression scheme to operate 300x300 laser printers with only 1 MB of RAM.

end printers. Table 29-1 lists the general RAM requirements for printers based on their resolutions.

Laser printers that support PostScript also need to be able store fonts in their memory, as well as any image data sent to the printer as part of a document. This adds to the amount of RAM needed by PostScript laser printers. The more fonts a printer has installed, the more RAM it needs.

For network laser printers, there is yet another need for RAM: storing incoming print jobs. Unlike a non-network printer, which receives print jobs a page at a time, network printers often get an entire print job at once and need to store the entire print job in memory. They then transfer one page to the printer's processor for translation into image data and then back into RAM before sending it to the printer's mechanisms for actual printing. This can require a printer to have a lot of RAM if it will be getting several print jobs at once or extremely long print jobs.

Some laser printers augment internal RAM by actually having their own internal hard drives. This gives the printer a place to store long print jobs or a large number of smaller print jobs until it can get to them. Since a hard drive is a lot cheaper per megabyte than RAM, it is a good cost-saving concept. Some printers will even store PostScript fonts on a hard drive, reserving RAM for only those fonts currently being used in a document or those that are commonly used and for the current print job.

Power-Saving Modes

Like monitors and Macs themselves, some printers include a sleep or power conservation mode. These are mostly laser printers, as the components used in a laser printer often require a good deal of electricity to operate. Similarly, many laser printer components generate a lot of heat, and a sleep mode allows these components to cool off so that the printer is not damaged by continuous heat emanating from these components. How much of an idle period is required before a printer enters sleep mode will vary depending on the printer.

Usually it takes the printer less time to warm up and be ready to print when waking from a sleep mode than it does when first powered on. Again, this depends on the individual printer and the rest mode it uses. Some printers have two or more rest modes, each one using progressively less electricity and generating less heat. This allows the printer to take advantage of some form of power conservation but also be readied very quickly for printing if it is likely to be used.

Connecting and Using a Printer

This section covers the process of connecting a printer to the Mac using a direct connection (as opposed to a network connection, which is discussed later). It also covers the basic process of installing printer software and selecting a printer for use.

Printer Interfaces

There are three primary methods for directly connecting a printer to a computer: the traditional Mac serial port, the USB port, and the PC parallel port, shown in Figure 29-8. Only the USB port is supported on the current Macs, and it is the most common printer type used with the Mac today. However, a wide variety of adapter products make it possible to use the other printer types with today's Mac as well.

Figure 29-8
Left to right: A Mac serial port, a PC parallel port, and a USB port.

Serial Port   The Mac serial port was used to connect printers to Macintosh computers for many years before the iMac began Apple's removal of the serial port from Macs. The Mac serial port is unique to Macintosh computers, so it required that printers be manufactured specifically for the Mac. This meant that there tended to be a much more limited choice of printers for Mac users during the serial port era than there is today. In fact, the most common printers used by Mac users at that time were made by Apple.

Many longtime Mac users may have an existing investment in serial port printers. This is particularly true of Apple's well-built LaserWriter line of laser printers, many of which continue to be quite usable even though they are well over 10 years old. Such users may be able to use their earlier printers with USB Macs through a serial-port-to-USB adapter or with a serial port expansion card. The next chapter discusses the serial port and the solutions for using serial port printers and other devices with the current Macs. For serial port printers that support LocalTalk network printing, an Ethernet-to-LocalTalk bridge can be used to enable the printer to function with today's Macs (see "Network Printing" later in the chapter for more details).

USB   USB is currently the default option for Mac printing. Since USB is a cross-platform technology, printers developed for USB can be used on the Mac or the PC (device drivers simply need to be provided for the Mac). Almost all printers today include a USB port for easy connection and use. The only real concern about a USB printer is that printing jobs can completely saturate the USB channel and slow down the performance of other USB devices.

PC Parallel Port   The parallel port is a standard port on PCs that is almost always used for printer connections. Although the parallel port has never been built into any Mac, there are a number of adapter products designed to attach PC parallel port printers to the Mac. The most common such product is InfoWave's PowerPrint, which is designed to allow printers without Mac support to be used with the Mac by including a parallel-port-to-USB adapter and generic drivers for thousands of parallel port printers.

Additionally, a number of printer manufacturers today produce their own parallel-port-to-USB adapters. These adapters are designed to allow their existing products to be used with USB Macs. This approach allows companies to quickly and easily add Macintosh support to their printers by just adding the adapter and a Mac driver. It was especially common immediately following the iMac's release, when companies were still developing USB printers but wanted to offer immediate support for the iMac.

SCSI   Some high-end laser printers print at such high resolutions that sending print data to them through the Mac's serial port or a PC parallel port was too slow to enable the printer to function as well as it could. As a result, printer manufacturers have used other interface methods for such printers. One such method was to attach a printer via SCSI. This allowed the printer to have much more data throughput available for print jobs. For such printers, a SCSI card would be needed for use with today's Macs, though a USB- or FireWire-to-SCSI adapter might suffice (check compatibility lists with individual manufacturers). SCSI printers should be attached the same as any other SCSI device, following the same rules for cabling, ID number, and termination discussed in Chapter 12.

Printer Drivers

Like any other device, a printer needs driver software for the Mac to communicate with it. Printer drivers are almost always written as extensions. Before using a printer, you need to install its driver software. Apple does include a number of printer drivers preinstalled with the Mac OS; however, many of these are for older Apple printers. Some printer manufacturers use a single driver for multiple printers in a product line. Often this means that the printers are very similar in design (though they may support different printing speeds or resolutions) and probably also use the same type of ink cartridges.

Each printer driver is responsible for the Print dialog box that is displayed when you use an application's Print command. This means that this dialog box will vary from printer to printer, though it will generally look somewhat similar to those shown in Figure 29-9. The printer drivers are also responsible for generating the Page Setup dialog. The Page Setup dialog is accessed in each individual application and used to set such things as the page orientation (portrait, which is the standard way text documents are printed, or landscape, where the page printed is wider than it is long), the paper size (legal, letter, or other sizes supported by the printer), and any scaling of the print job's size as it is sent to the printer.

Once the printer drivers are installed and the Mac is restarted so they are loaded along with the Mac OS, your Mac should be able to access the printer. To do so, you need to select the printer as the one you wish to print with in the Chooser.

Figure 29-9
Print dialog boxes for various printers. Each printer driver will provide a variation to the basic Print dialog.

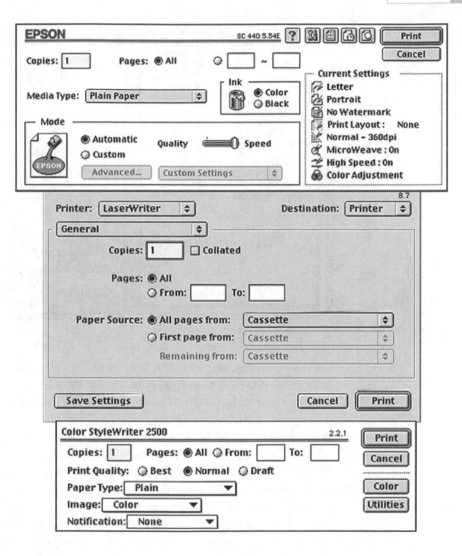

The Chooser

The Chooser is the Macintosh utility for selecting which printer you want the Mac to use when printing documents. The Chooser is probably one of the oldest Mac OS elements and has remained relatively unchanged over its entire existence. As you can see in Figure 29-10, the Chooser's window is primarily divided into two sections. On the left is a list of icons for all printer drivers installed on the Mac plus an AppleShare icon (some other utilities, such as KeyServer from Sassafras

Figure 29-10
The Chooser.

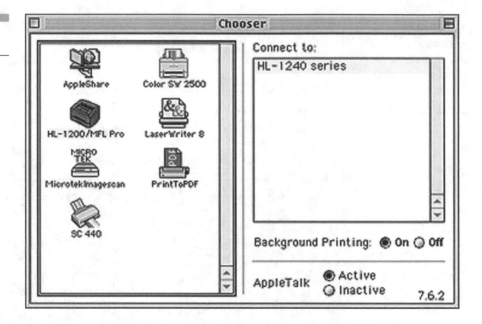

Software or scanner drivers, may also install icons in the Chooser). To select a printer for use, first click on its icon in this list.

The right side of the Chooser's windows contains those options for determining where the printer is connected and how it will function. The primary section of this portion of the Chooser is the Connect To box, which lists the available ports where the printer could be connected (USB, Printer, or Modem serial ports, or SCSI). If the printer driver supports multiple ports for the printer you've selected, you need to choose the port that the printer is connected to by clicking on the appropriate port. If the printer is a network printer, you will see a list of network printer names or addresses listed here (network printing is discussed later in this chapter).

Once you've selected the printer and the port, you may have the option of adjusting other features for the printer. If the printer supports adjusting any other features, there will be a button or buttons beneath the Connect To pane of the window. The one option that will almost always be available is the Background Printing option. Background printing means that, on non-PostScript printers, the Mac will send data to the printer as a background task, allowing you to continue working while the Mac is sending the data to the printer. With background printing turned off, you need to wait for the print job to be completed before you can do anything else on the Mac.

The Chooser and AppleShare   In additional to icons for any installed printer drivers, the Chooser always contains an AppleShare icon. This is because, for many years, the Chooser was also the method used to log in to file servers on an AppleTalk network. Although this ability has been included in the more intuitive Network Browser utility in recent Mac OS releases, the Chooser still maintains the ability to establish connections to an AppleTalk server. If you want to use the Chooser for this purpose, click on the AppleShare icon. The right side of the window will now contain a list of available file servers. If your AppleTalk network consists of multiple zones, individual zones will be listed beneath the Printer icon pane. Clicking on a zone causes the servers available in that zone to be listed on the right side of the Chooser window.

When you've decided which file server you want to log in to, click on its name in the list and then click on the OK button. You will be asked for a username and password to log in to the server (some servers may support Guest access without a username and password). You will then be shown the list of hard drives or shared folders on the server that you can access. Select the ones you want to access and then click on the OK button to mount these drives/folders on your Mac's desktop. Refer to Chapter 32 for more information on Mac networks and file servers.

Desktop Printing

Although the Chooser has been a venerable way for selecting a printer, it has grown somewhat limited. You can only have one printer selected at a time, and you need to go through the complete process of opening the Chooser to switch to a different printer. One solution has become extremely popular in recent years, particularly with PostScript printers. This solution is desktop printing.

Desktop printing places an icon for the printer right on the Mac's desktop, as shown in Figure 29-11. If you to have easy access to several printers, you can create icons for multiple printers. That way, when you want to print a document to a specific printer, you simply drag its icon to the icon of the printer that you want to print. The print job will then be sent through appropriate driver software to that printer. This is a good solution in network environments where users have access to several printers over a network.

Setting Up Desktop Printing for PostScript Printers   The primary use of desktop printing today is with PostScript printers. Apple

Figure 29-11
A Desktop Printer
icon.

Figure 29-12
The Desktop Printer
utility's first dialog.

includes a special utility called the Desktop Printer utility, shown in
Figure 29-12, with the Mac OS (located in the LaserWriter Software
folder in the Apple Extras folder placed on a hard drive following a Mac
OS installation) that makes it easy to set up PostScript printers as desktop printers.

The Desktop Printer utility allows you to choose a PostScript printer driver from those installed on the Mac for a desktop printer using a pop-up menu (as a rule, you can use Apple's LaserWriter 8 printer driver for any PostScript printer). It also provides a list of the various printer connection types for you to identify how the printer is connected to the Mac. The available options for this are listed in the utility's primary window and include AppleTalk (for printers shared over an AppleTalk network), LPR (Line Printer Remote; used for connecting to a printer shared using the TCP/IP network protocol), No Printer Connection (this generates the print jobs for a printer but stores them rather than sending them to a printer), USB (for directly connected USB printers), and Translator (this creates PostScript files of print jobs, which can be saved for later use or for sharing with other platforms or PostScript-aware applications).

Once you've chosen a printer driver and connection method, you can click on the OK button to continue the Desktop Printer setup. In the second window, shown in Figure 29-13, you can choose a PostScript Printer Definition file for the printer, as well as the location of the printer. PostScript Printer Definition (PPD) files tell the printer driver exactly what the characteristics of a specific printer are. This includes informa-

Figure 29-13
The second window of the Desktop Printer utility.

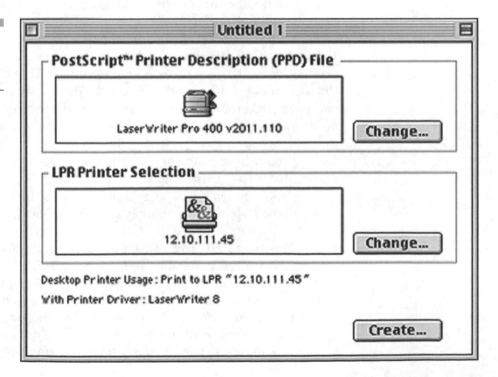

tion about page sizes supported, the printer's memory, and the number and location of paper trays available to the printer. PPDs are stored in the Printer Definitions folder inside the Extensions folder. A PPD is needed for any PostScript printer used with the Mac. Apple includes PPDs for all of its LaserWriter printers with the Mac OS. Any other PPDs should be provided with a software installer from the printer manufacturer. To select a PPD, click on the Change button in the upper section of the window. The Auto Setup feature will have the Mac look for the printer and attempt to choose the correct PPD on its own.

The lower section of this second window lets you enter information about where the printer is located. When the window first opens, this usually says "<<unspecified>>". You can use the Change button here to select the printer's location. The exact dialog generated by the Change button depends on what connection method you chose earlier. AppleTalk will ask you to locate the printer in your AppleTalk network. LPR will ask you to enter the IP address of the printer. Once you have entered the information, click on the Create button. A standard Save dialog box will appear. You can enter any name you want for the printer and, contrary to the implication of the name Desktop Printer, you can store the printer anywhere on your hard drive, not just on the desktop. You can change the setup of a desktop printer by clicking on its icon and selecting Change Setup from the Printing menu.

Using Desktop Printing for Other Printers   Many non-PostScript printers can also be set up as desktop printers. This is done through the Chooser, however. Choose the printer for use as usual, making sure that you have background printing turned on. If the printer supports being used as a desktop printer, a Setup button may be included in the Chooser that allows you to specify settings for the printer, such as desktop printing. Or the printer may simply generate a Desktop Printer icon automatically. If the printer doesn't automatically generate a Desktop Printer icon and there is no Setup button in the Chooser when it is selected, then the printer probably doesn't support desktop printing.

Using Desktop Printing   When printing using desktop printers, you can use the Print command in an application's File menu to print a currently opened document to the default printer. Doing this, the process is exactly the same as when if you had chosen the printer within the Chooser. You can also print a document by dragging its icon onto the desktop printer you want to use for printing the document (this is good if you don't want to use the currently selected default printer).

When you drag a document's icon onto a desktop printer, the document will be opened (if it isn't already open). The Print dialog box is automatically displayed and you can change whatever options you choose, just as when using the Print command to send a job to the default printer. The job is then sent to the printer you dragged the document's icon onto.

You can change the default printer easily using the desktop printer icons as well. Simply click on the printer you want to be the default printer. A Printing menu will appear in the Finder's menu bar. Choose the Set Default Printer from the Printing menu. The selected printer is now the default printer that will be sent print jobs that are created using the Print command in any application's File menu. Its desktop icon will also have the darkened border, indicating that it is the current default printer.

When using desktop printing, you can also check the status of any print jobs by double-clicking on a printer's icon. This brings up a window (shown in Figure 29-14) that lists any current print jobs being sent or waiting to be sent to that printer and includes the name of each document being printed, the number of pages, the number of copies of the document being printed, and the time for each print job. There are also four buttons at the top of the window that allow you to do the following (respectively, left to right) to any print jobs selected in the list: pause or hold the selected job(s), resume printing the selected job(s) (if one has been paused), set the print time for the selected job(s), and cancel or trash the selected job(s).

Figure 29-14
A desktop printer's window.

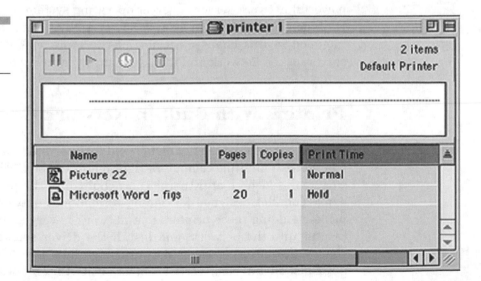

Network Printing

Network printing allows a single printer (or a group of separate printers) to be shared with any computer that is on a network. This approach is particularly common in offices or other situations where many computers are used and giving each one its own printer would be absurdly expensive. It is also attractive in homes where you might want to share one printer among two or more computers.

There are two ways that a printer can be shared over a network. The first is to offer direct network support in the printer. In this approach, the printer has the needed abilities to function as a network device itself (just as a computer does) and includes a port for one or more network cabling schemes. The printer can simply be attached to the network as you would attach a computer.

The second approach is to have a computer act as a printer server. This is used for printers that don't offer network support. To share a printer in this way, you attach the printer to one Mac on the network as you would for normal printing. You install or enable a piece of software on the Mac, which allows it to accept print jobs from other Macs on the network. When the Mac receives these print jobs, it then sends them on to the printer attached to it. To the printer, it looks like the computer it is attached to is sending the print jobs and not a computer somewhere else on the network.

A third approach, used for large-scale networks, is to use a network connect printer and a special high-power print server running on a special computer on the network. This is an option only if you are running a powerful network server or server operating system, such as AppleShare IP, Mac OS X Server, Windows NT, or UNIX. Details on this are not included in this chapter because of the requirement of a high-power server on the network and the issues involved in running such a server.

Printers with Built-in Network Connections

Several printers, especially higher-end laser printers, are designed to be shared with multiple computers right out of the box. They include a network port, such as an Ethernet port, built into the printer or a special expansion slot designed for adding an optional network module to the printer. Adding these printers to a network is very simple; just plug the printer into the network, and install the driver software on each Mac that will be printing to the network. Installing the driver software will often also install some sort of control utility that allows you to configure the printer on your network by giving it a network name and/or address and to add a password to the printer. Password-protecting the printer allows you to control who has access to it. Most printers also offer you the ability to keep a log of printer activity.

LocalTalk   LocalTalk was Apple's original network cabling system. It connected networked Macs and other network devices, like printers, using the standard Mac serial port. LocalTalk network printers are becoming much less common today because today's Macs don't ship with a LocalTalk serial port—or any serial port. Printers capable of LocalTalk networking simply attach to LocalTalk cable, much like another Mac on the network. Once attached, the printer is available to the network. For more information on LocalTalk serial ports, see the next chapter. See Chapter 32 for details on LocalTalk network cabling.

LocalTalk printers can be used with today's Macs or with an Ethernet-based network, provided that a LocalTalk-to-Ethernet bridge is used. As discussed in both the next chapter and in Chapter 32, a LocalTalk-to-Ethernet bridge is a special device with both a LocalTalk and an Ethernet port capable of joining the two different networks (or simply connecting a LocalTalk printer to an Ethernet Mac or network), or it can be a special control panel from Apple installed on a Mac that has both serial ports and Ethernet ports, allowing the Mac to serve the same purpose as a hardware device would. Apple provides two separate control panels for bridging LocalTalk and Ethernet using a Mac. The first is the LocalTalk Bridge control panel, which is designed for bridging two separate networks of Macs. The second is the LaserWriter Bridge control panel, which is designed for adding a LocalTalk-based LaserWriter printer to an Ethernet network.

Ethernet   Ethernet is a far more common type of network cabling than LocalTalk. It is included on all the current Macs and can be used with both Macs and other computing platforms to create mixed networks. Ethernet capable printers simply plug into an Ethernet hub. There is no other real concern about using an Ethernet printer.

Sharing a Non-Network Printer

Printers without built-in network support can be shared over a network by using the Mac they are connected to as a print server. Alternatively, there are several hardware products designed to adapt a non-network printer for network connection. The following paragraphs give an overview of some of these types of solutions.

Using Apple's PrinterShare Apple made the ability to share their non-network printers part of the Mac OS, using the PrinterShare extension. A few third-party printers can also take advantage of this feature if their drivers are designed to support it. Printers shared through the PrinterShare feature are shared over an AppleTalk network only.

To share a printer using PrinterShare, open the Chooser on the Mac that the printer is connected to. Select the printer as you normally would, and then click on the Setup button that appears on the left side of the window (if the printer supports Apple's PrinterShare). The dialog box this produces allows you to enable sharing of that printer. It will also give you the option of entering a password so that you can restrict access to the printer, as well as the option of keeping a log of print jobs sent to it. Once you are finished, close the Chooser to start sharing the printer.

Other Macs on the network can now print to the shared printer, provided that they have the driver software for the printer installed. Simply use the Chooser on each Mac to select the printer. When the icon for the appropriate printer is selected, the Connect To section of the Chooser's window lists the printer with a little network icon and the name of the Mac to which it is connected. Select that name to choose the printer. With the printer selected (and the password provided, if needed), simply use the Print command as normal to send print jobs to the printer.

Using Apple's USB Printer Sharing PrinterShare was originally designed for Apple-branded printers, although some third-party manufacturers also took advantage of it. More recently, Apple has provided a newer way of sharing non-network printers—USB printers, to be specific. The Apple USB Printer Sharing is a control panel, shown in Figure 29-15, that Apple developed to support the sharing of just about any USB printer, and it does not require manufacturers to write the driver with specific support for it. The USB Printer Sharing feature shares printers using the TCP/IP networking protocol instead of AppleTalk, however. Also, the printer's drivers must be installed on the Mac sharing it and any Macs printing to it.

USB Printer Sharing functions much like the Mac's File Sharing control panel. When installed, users can use the Start/Stop tab to turn on sharing of attached printers. The My Printers tab allows users to designate which printers currently connected to the Mac will be shared (simply check the checkbox next to each printer to share it). The Network Printers tab allows users to choose a shared USB printer on the network to send print jobs. The Options button available in all three tabs allows you to control the logging of printer jobs sent to a shared USB printer.

To add a printer or printers to the list of shared USB printers avail-

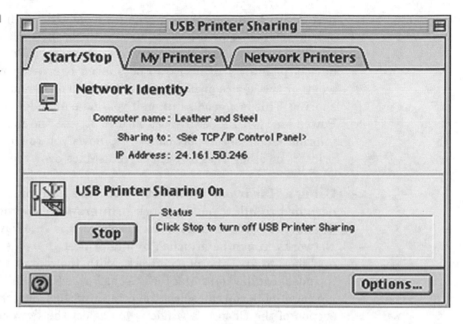

Figure 29-15
The USB Printer
Sharing control panel.

able to a Mac, click on the Add button. Navigate to the server through the available network neighborhoods, much as you would to choose a file server in the Network Browser utility. Unless a specific network neighborhood is created in the TCP/IP control panel of the Mac sharing the printer, the printer will be located under the neighborhood Local Services. If this neighborhood is not listed or you need to access another neighborhood that isn't listed, click on the Add Neighborhood button and type the name of the neighborhood. Once you have reached the neighborhood where the printer is located, it should be listed. Click on it and then click on the Open button to select it. The printer should now be listed (as well as the name of the Mac it is connected to). To make the printer available to the Mac, use the checkbox next to its name.

Once you have selected a shared USB printer or printers for use, simply select the printer in the Chooser much as you would a printer connected to the Mac you are using. In the Connect To section of the Chooser's window, the name of the printer along with the name of the Mac it is connected to will be listed instead of a specific port. Select that name to choose the printer, and then close the Chooser. Use the print commands as normal to send print jobs to the shared USB printer.

Using PortShare Pro   Apple's PrinterShare works for many serial port printers and some SCSI laser printers that don't have network support. USB Printer Sharing works for most USB printers. Sharing other older serial port printers requires a different tool, however—namely, PortShare Pro by Stalker software. PortShare Pro allows any serial device, primarily printers, to be shared over a network regardless of whether the device or its driver software is designed to support network sharing. This is a good solution if you have an older serial port Mac (or a Power Mac with a serial port card in it, see the next chapter for more information on serial port cards). It allows you to share older serial port printers or other devices with current Macs over your network.

Using a Hardware Adapters   There are also some hardware adapters designed to allow non-network printers to be connected to networks directly. The most robust of these solutions is InfoWave's PowerPrint for Networks. It can be attached to any printer that has a PC parallel port and then to an Ethernet network. With the driver and utility software included installed on a Mac (or PCs, as PowerPrint for Networks is a cross-platform tool), you can select the printer in the Chooser. In the Connect To section of the Chooser's window, you select the PowerPrint for Networks device, which is usually listed by its serial number (Infowave includes a tool to rename it, however). You then print as normal. Farallon makes a similar tool for serial-port printers called the Print SL.

Troubleshooting Printer Problems

Following are several common printer problems, along with their solutions.

Nothing Happens When You Try to Print

There are a couple of reasons that this could happen. First and foremost, make certain the printer is turned on and connected properly. If you are using a network printer, make certain that you are connected to the network with the printer. Also be certain that the printer isn't processing print jobs from other Macs on the network before yours.

If the printer has just been turned on, it may need to warm up before printing. This is particularly true of laser printers. If the printer needs to warm up, wait for it to warm up and see if it processes the print job. If not, try printing again after it has warmed up.

You may not have selected the printer properly. Use the Chooser to select the printer you want to use. If you are using desktop printing, make the printer you wish to use is the default printer (and if that doesn't help select it in the Chooser).

Assuming you have selected the printer properly, you may not have the driver software for the printer installed completely. Many printer drivers consist of multiple extensions. Make certain that the driver software is installed properly. Reinstall from the original CD that came with the printer if needed.

Also check to be certain that the printer is not displaying any error light or messages, such as those indicating it is out of paper, toner, or ink, and those indicating a paper jam or other problems.

Some laser printers support both PostScript and PCL page descriptions. If you are using such a printer, make certain that it is set to accept PostScript and not PCL.

When dealing with a network printer, make certain that the problem is a printer problem and not a network issue. You can do this by attempting to log in to file servers on the same network segment as the printer. If the problem is network-related, treat it as such (see Chapter 32 for Mac network issues). Also make certain that the network protocol (AppleTalk or TCP/IP) needed for the printer is enabled.

You Get a Message Saying the Printer Cannot Be Found

Various printer drivers may word this message slightly differently, but a "printer cannot be found" message means that the Mac cannot detect the printer you have requested to send your print job to. Refer to the instructions in the preceding section for troubleshooting steps in this situation.

Port In Use and Other Serial Port Issues

If you are using a serial port printer, make certain that the serial port card or USB adapter you are using supports the printer and the printer drivers you are using (you should do this before buying the card or adapter). Assuming it does, make certain that AppleTalk or another device driver is not actively using the serial port at the same time (usually you will receive a "port in use" error message of one sort or another if this is the case).

You can change AppleTalk port use in the AppleTalk control panel, or you can disable AppleTalk completely in the Chooser. For other devices, check the control panel associated with the device to see if it can be disabled or adjusted to use another serial port (if you have multiple serial ports). If it cannot be, disable the device's extensions and/or control panels with the Extensions Manager and restart.

Also be certain that the software controlling your serial port card or USB adapter product is properly configured. Some serial port solutions for today's Macs require that a printer be connected to a specific port. You can check the documentation for your product for details.

Gibberish Pages Get Printed

If your printer continually prints pages of unintelligible characters, this tends to indicate print jobs in the printer queue have become corrupted. Stop printing (if possible), and open the folder containing the printer queue (usually the Desktop Printer icon itself or a folder created by the printer driver in the System Folder). Delete any items in that folder and restart the Mac. Attempt to print again.

This can also mean that the printer's preferences files have become corrupted. If so, delete the preferences files associated with the printer (or with printing in general) and restart the Mac. You may want to avoid deleting the Printing Prefs folder, as this contains a selection of watermarks that can be applied by certain printer drivers.

The Mac Crashes or Freezes When You Try to Print

This problem usually indicates either an extension conflict involving your printer driver (see Chapter 38 for information on dealing with extension conflicts) or corruption of one of the printer-related files in the System Folder. Follow the instructions given for gibberish pages getting printed. If this doesn't help, try reinstalling your printer drivers and, if that doesn't help, the entire Mac OS.

Pages Have Odd White Lines in Them or Are Smudged

White lines sometimes occur with ink-jet printers. This can mean that your print head needs to be cleaned (as described earlier in this chapter) or that you are running out of ink. Smudges can also be related to a print head that needs cleaning, or they can mean that the ink is not dried before you pick the document up.

Smudges or lines in a page from a laser printer indicate that the photosensitive drum isn't being cleaned properly in between print jobs. Replacing the drum and/or related maintenance components usually solves this problem.

PostScript Errors

There are various PostScript-related error messages that you may get when printing to a PostScript printer. Most of these errors are caused by similar issues. First, is the case of a Mac or printer not having enough RAM available to process a PostScript print job. Second, a document may have too many fonts in it to be processed properly. Third, one of the fonts installed on the Mac may be corrupted (font utilities such as ATM Deluxe and FontAgent can be used to inspect fonts for corruption).

A Time-Out Error Message Is Displayed

This situation often occurs with PostScript printers. Time-out messages tend to occur when there are several print jobs in a printer queue. Try waiting until some print jobs have been completed before printing additional documents to the same printer.

Resources for Further Study

The following URLs provide additional information on some of the concepts, issues, and products discussed in this chapter:

About.com Mac Hardware Printing Resources—
http://machardware.about.com/msubprinter.htm

About.com Mac Support Printing Resources—
http://macsupport.about.com/msub32.htm

Infowave—http://www.infowave.com

HP—http://www.hp.com

Epson—http://www.epson.com

LexMark—http://www.lexmark.com

Alps Electric—http://www.alpsusa.com
Tektronix—http://www.tek.com
GCC—http://www.gcctech.com

Serial Ports

Serial ports were a standard feature from the very first Mac introduced in 1984 up until Apple introduced the iMac in 1998. With the iMac, Apple began a shift away from its own port technologies (including serial ports), favoring industry-standard technologies such as USB instead. This move has made it easier and more cost-effective for other companies to develop Macintosh peripherals. However, it has also presented many long-time Mac users with a problem in using older Mac devices with their newer Macs and Mac networks. This chapter discusses the original Mac serial ports and their uses, as well as the ways in which devices that use serial port interfaces can be used with today's Mac models.

What Are Serial Ports?

The original Mac shipped with two small, round (miniDIN) connectors with eight pins for attaching printers and modems. This continued to be the primary use for these ports for many years, and it was common to find two such ports on every desktop Mac. These ports were designed primarily for connecting a modem and a printer, and each was named for its purpose. Although each port was named "modem port" or "printer port" by the Mac, a printer or modem could actually be connected to either one. The technical details of the serial port are that it is an eight-pin miniDIN connector capable of transmitting 230 Kbps. Two serial ports from a Power Mac 7200 are shown in Figure 30-1.

There was also a variant of the serial port known as the GeoPort. The GeoPort featured a ninth pin and allowed GeoPort devices to draw power directly from the Mac through the extra pin. This ability, used almost exclusively for modems, meant the device did not require a separate power supply. While GeoPorts were compatible with all other serial port devices, GeoPort devices were not compatible with other serial ports. None of the current serial port solutions for the Mac support GeoPort devices.

In the case of earlier Macs with internal modems, the modem serial port was actually disconnected. Although the port was still there, it was covered up. This was because the internal modem of the Mac was still assigned, by the Mac OS, to the modem serial port. Because of this, the Mac would treat the internal modem the same as it would treat an external modem using the modem port. When the internal modem of such a Mac was removed, however, the modem serial port became usable.

The printer serial port also became the port traditionally used for

Figure 30-1

*Macintosh serial
ports.*

Apple's own network cabling, known as LocalTalk. LocalTalk allowed
users to connect two Macs to share files with just a simple serial port
cable like the one used for attaching printers. LocalTalk was also
expanded on by Farallon to use devices called PhoneNET connectors for
network cabling. PhoneNET connectors consist of a serial port connector
and one or two standard RJ11 phone jacks. By attaching regular phone
cables into the phone jacks of two PhoneNET connectors, you can network multiple Macs using plain old phone cable (which was significantly
cheaper per foot than serial port cables and a fraction of the cost of other
networking cables, such as those used for Ethernet). Since each of the
connectors had two phone jacks (PhoneNET connectors with only a single jack do exist but are rare), you could create a network of as many
devices as you wished. Figure 30-2 shows a PhoneNET connector.

The excellent feature of LocalTalk being built into serial ports on the
Mac was that multiple Macs (and other network devices, such as printers that supported LocalTalk) could be connected without the need to
purchase Ethernet cards or hubs. The cost comparison between

Figure 30-2
PhoneNET
Connector for
LocalTalk
networking.

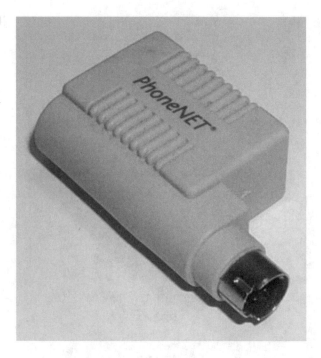

LocalTalk and Ethernet networking models in the late 1980s and early 1990s was quite significant, particularly for home users who just wanted an easy way to share files and printers, and who didn't need to worry that LocalTalk was very slow compared to some Ethernet standards. LocalTalk and Ethernet networking styles are discussed in detail in Chapter 32.

Beyond just connecting printers, modems, and LocalTalk networks, a number of other serial port devices were developed for the Mac during the serial port era. These devices included digital cameras, palmtop computers, and graphics tablets, to name a few (these are discussed in the next section, and Table 30-1 includes a more complete list.).

Serial ports and LocalTalk networking were not just limited to the Mac. Apple's other popular product line of the 1980s, the Apple II computers, used the same miniDIN ports for printers and modems as the Mac. This made it easy to buy one device, such as a printer, for a home or school that used both Macs and Apple II computers and share it with both computers. Similarly, LocalTalk, when implemented on both machines, allowed users to share files across two different types of computers.

PowerBooks traditionally offered only a single serial port. This port was identified to the Mac as the modem/printer port. The idea behind this concept seemed to both be an effort to save space and an acknowledgment that many PowerBook owners would take advantage of internal or PC Card modem options rather than use an external modem that required a power supply. This port also served for LocalTalk networking purposes.

Non-Apple computers such as today's Windows-based PCs also use serial ports, but they are not the same types of serial port that is used on the Mac. A PC's serial port is either a 25-pin or 9-pin DB connector secured with thumbscrews, and it would not be mistaken for a Mac serial port when seen in person (as you can see in Figure 30-3). When talking about serial port devices or USB to serial port adapters, it is important to make sure that you are discussing Mac serial ports and not PC serial ports. However, some ports on a PC, especially those used for keyboards and mice, do rather closely resemble a Mac's serial port; you should therefore note that these are very different types of ports on two completely different computer platforms.

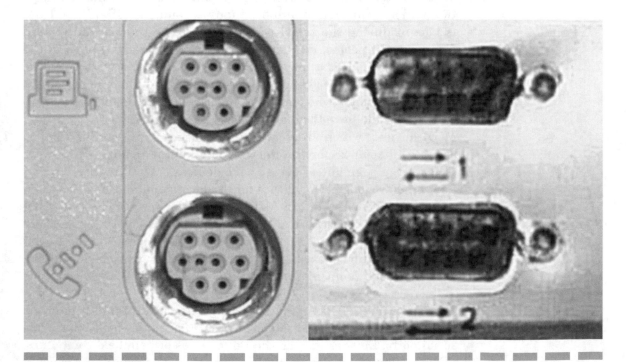

Figure 30-3   *Macintosh serial ports (left) look vastly different from the serial ports of PCs (right).*

Serial Port Devices Still Being Used

Even two years after Apple began the migration away from Mac serial ports with the iMac, there are many serial port devices still in use today (although very few, if any, are being actively produced by manufacturers). The majority of these tend to be printers. Many of Apple's LaserWriter printers are still going strong more than a decade after being introduced, and a large number of users see no reason to replace them.

Furthermore, it's not only Apple printers still being used. For over a decade, any printer that offered Mac support (and given Apple's big boom in the late 1980s and 1990s in the desktop publishing field, there were plenty) needed to do so with a Macintosh-style serial port. In many cases, these printers are not low-cost inkjets (though they certainly make up a sizable percentage of the printers in question), but specialty printers, such as wide-format printers, solid dye printers, impact printers, high-end or color laser printers, and so forth. Many of these are not easy to find and are quite expensive, and another reason for their continued use is the cost and difficulty involved in replacing them with USB models.

In addition to printers, there are many consumers with digital cameras bought during the serial port's reign of use that are still going strong. To many people, if a device is still working well, why go to the expense of replacing it a few years after you bought it? Although this doesn't always fit the professional market for digital cameras, it does fit with many consumers who just want an easy way to take photos at family gatherings and have them available to their computer.

MIDI devices, which are used for generating and recording digital music (see Chapter 28 for more details and information on MIDI) were another large segment of serial port devices. MIDI keyboards and sequencers have long been a device for producing digital compositions on the Mac. QuickTime's built-in MIDI synthesizer for playback of MIDI files is a testament to the use of MIDI music on the Mac. However, there were no MIDI devices using USB when the iMac debuted, and even today, a large portion of existing MIDI hardware still uses the Mac serial port, even though companies have started shipping USB MIDI solutions over the past two years.

A large variety of PDAs (personal digital assistants) and palmtop computers that had included support for the Mac platform also made use of serial ports. Devices such as the Palm series of handheld computers, the Psion palmtops, and even Apple's own (but now terminated) Newton line all used a Mac's serial port as a method for syncing data and files with the Mac. In fact, it wasn't until late 1999 that any PDAs offered out-of-the-box USB support for exchanging information. Many older palm-tops that are still in use, such as Newton and early Psion devices, still offer no alternative to serial port connections.

LocalTalk is also a serial port use, if not a device, still common for many people. Because many consumer Macs of the early and mid-1990s shipped without Ethernet ports or industry-standard expansion slots, there are a number of Macs still in use where the primary means of networking is LocalTalk. LocalTalk is also still cheaper than Ethernet from a cabling perspective. Many people who have upgraded to new Macs still have uses for their older computers. This means that they will still have the earlier Macs they've been using LocalTalk to network. Similarly, several printers from Apple shipped with built-in LocalTalk networking abilities, and users of these printers may want to simply be able to plug their new iMac into their existing Mac/printer setup.

Table 30-1 lists several serial port devices still commonly in use.

Adding Serial Ports to the Power Mac

The Power Macintosh G3 and G4 both offer the ability to readily accommodate serial ports without much effort. Both of these machines have three available PCI slots, into which PCI cards that add serial ports can be installed. Additionally, the internal comm or modem slot in the Power Mac G3 and the Power Mac G4 models can be used for specially designed serial port cards.

Even before Apple introduced the iMac without serial ports, there were PCI expansion cards from a few manufacturers that were used to add additional serial ports to Power Mac computers. Although all desktop Macs up through 1998 had shipped with two serial ports, there were many professional uses where two serial ports were simply not enough. These uses included, among other things, providing dial-up Internet or other online service connections where several modems needed to be supported by a single Mac; digital music composition using MIDI and non-MIDI solutions; providing access to multiple printers from a Mac without having to reach behind to plug and unplug printers; and using several serial port devices such as a modem, printer, digital camera, and graphics tablet at once.

Although these cards were available prior to the Power Mac G3's pre-

TABLE 30-1

*Common Serial
Port Devices Still
in Use*

Apple StyleWriter printers

Apple LaserWriter printers

Newton palmtops

eMate computers (Newton-based)

Palm PDAs

Psion Series palmtops

Graphics tablets

Epson Stylus printers

HP DeskJet and DeskWriter printers

HP LaserJet printers

Label printers

Uninteruptable power supply interfaces

Digital cameras (AGFA, Apple, Fuji, Canon, Casio, Kodak, Epson, Olympus, Nikon,
Minolta, Ricoh, Sanyo, Toshiba, and Sony manufacturers)

QuickCam (serial port and grayscale versions)

Sharp PDAs

Modems

ISDN terminal adapters

LocalTalk network devices

MIDI hardware

Scanners (Visioneer, HP, and ACCLE manufacturers)

Color calibrators

Scientific measurement and lab equipment

Plotting and cutting hardware

Barcode scanners

mier without serial ports in January of 1999, they were not well-known products. When the news came out that Power Macs were shipping without serial ports but with PCI slots, companies were quick to test their cards to ensure compatibility with the blue and white Power Macs. The cards worked well for many (though not all) devices, and for the month or so following the G3's introduction, suppliers couldn't keep up with demand for the serial port PCI cards.

Serial port PCI cards can offer any number of serial ports. The most common variants offer either two or four ports. Keyspan, the most well-known creator of serial port PCI cards, and MegaWolf, a lesser-known company, not only produced cards with more ports than traditional Macs had offered, they also produced cards that offered faster serial ports. In early 1999, Keyspan announced it was developing a serial port card capable of transferring data as fast as 1 Mbps. Although these speeds are not actually realized with all traditional serial port devices, the potential throughput for any number of devices is very impressive. Figure 30-4 displays one of Keyspan's four-port serial cards.

The comm slot serial port cards came later (such as the ones shown in Figure 30-5), after developers had time to look at the design of the G3 and find a better way to implement serial ports on it. These cards install into the slot designed for an internal modem card. They provide a single serial port instead of the multiple ports that the PCI solutions offer and also offer some notable advantages.

In order to understand the advantages of the comm slot cards over the PCI slot versions, you need to understand how the Mac identifies serial ports. The Mac OS Communication Toolbox has always offered built-in recognition for the two ports named "printer port" and "modem port." Many device drivers are designed to look for one of these two ports through the Communications Toolbox.

PCI serial port cards (along with the USB-to-serial-port adapters discussed later in this chapter) are not designed to be identified as "printer port" or "modem port." If they were, then they wouldn't be able to function properly in a Mac that has a printer port and modem port built into

Figure 30-4

A typical four-port serial port PCI card. (Photo courtesy of Keyspan)

Figure 30-5

The Stealth comm slot serial port cards for the Power Mac G4 with AGP Graphics card (left) and the earlier G4 and Power Mac G3 models (right).

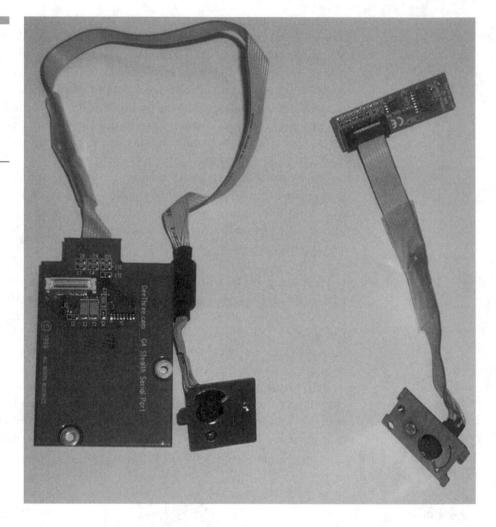

it or in a Mac that uses an internal modem (because an internal modem is always designated as the modem port). Even though the drivers for these cards are set up to identify the ports on the card to the Mac OS Communications Toolbox, many drivers for serial port devices are written to accept only devices on the printer port and modem port as actually being connected to the Mac. This means that a number of devices will not be fully compatible with a serial port PCI card. This is true of the current PCI Macs as well as older Macs that had built-in serial ports.

The comm slot cards, however, don't suffer from this problem. As described earlier in this chapter, if a Mac has an internal modem, that modem is automatically assigned to the modem port. Since the internal comm slot of the Power Mac is designed for an internal modem, it carries over this Mac OS Communications Toolbox assignment and is recognized as modem port. With this understanding, developers created a card that installed into the comm slot to provide a serial port that would be recognized by device drivers designed to accept the modem port as a viable serial port for their device to be attached to. The result is that the comm slot cards have a greater range of compatibility with serial port devices than the PCI slot cards do.

Of course, there is a downside to the comm slot cards. First, they can only provide a single serial port, because there is only one designated port for the comm slot. Second, they eliminate the ability to use an internal modem with the Power Mac. You can use an external serial port modem (which would be self-defeating, since it would use up the single serial port), or you can use one of the USB modems on the market.

With either type of card, it is a good idea to check the manufacturer's compatibility list. These lists, which contain all the serial port products that have been tested to successfully function with the card (as well as devices known not to work with the card) are often available from the manufacturer's Web site, and an abbreviated list is usually included on the box. If in doubt, it is always wise to contact the company before buying the card. Table 30-2 lists several common serial port devices and printer types, as well as which types of cards they are known to be compatible with. Keep in mind that this is a general list accurate at the time of this writing. Additional devices may have since been certified compatible by a given manufacturer. Also, it is worth pointing out that Keyspan has made efforts to make its serial port PCI cards recognized by the Communications Toolbox and does offer some advanced compatibility over other PCI cards.

Installing Serial Port Cards in the Power Mac

Installation of both the PCI and comm slot serial port cards is an easy process that includes only a few basic steps, which are described in this section. As always, remember to read the manual and Read Me files that come with a specific card for any device-specific information or instructions.

The first step, as with any device, is to install any driver or control software needed for the card. This is done from the installer software that accompanies the card on CD-ROM. Once the software is installed, you're ready to actually install the card.

TABLE 30-2

Common Serial
Port Devices and
Printers and
Known
Compatibility with
Serial Port Cards

Note: "Some PCI slot"
indicates compatibil-
ity with some PCI
cards on the market,
but not all. (Check
with individual card
manufacturers.)

Device	Type of Card Compatible With
Apple ImageWriter printers	comm slot, some PCI slot*
Apple StyleWriter printers	comm slot, some PCI slot**
Apple LaserWriter printers	comm slot, some PCI slot**
Epson Stylus printers	comm slot, some PCI slot
HP DeskJet printers	comm slot, some PCI slot
HP DeskWriter printers	comm slot, some PCI slot
HP LaserJet printers	comm slot possibly
NEC printers	comm slot possibly
CoStar label writer	comm slot, PCI slot
Seiko label printer	comm slot, some PCI slot
Wacom graphics tablets	comm slot, PCI slot
Digital cameras	comm slot, some PCI slot
QuickCam (serial port model)	comm slot
Palm devices	comm slot, some PCI slot
Psion Series palmtops	comm slot, some PCI slot
Newton computers	comm slot
External modems	comm slot, PCI slot
ISDN terminal adapters (modems)	comm slot, PCI slot
LocalTalk networking	comm slot
ACCLE scanner	comm slot, some PCI slot
Visioneer Paperport scanner	comm slot, PCI slot
MIDI devices	comm slot, some PCI slot***
La Cie color calibrator	comm slot, PCI slot
Bar code scanners	comm slot****

*ImageWriter driver known to be incompatible with recent Mac OS versions but is compatible with serial port cards as listed.

**Apple printers function only in serial port mode on PCI slot cards; LocalTalk models or setups will work only with comm slot cards.

***MIDI support on PCI slot cards seems to vary both between card manufacturers and some types of MIDI devices. Check for specific devices in advance.

****Bar code scanners are supported by comm slot cards; no definitive data was available regarding the use of such a device with PCI slot cards as of this writing.

For PCI cards, the process is similar to installing any PCI card. Shut down the Mac, and make certain that you are properly grounded, as described in Chapter 3. Release the side "door" of the Power Mac, and lower so that the motherboard is lying flat.

Locate an available PCI slot. Which of the three available slots you choose is up to you. Remove the cover from the back of the Mac's case that is behind the slot you have chosen. This is where the back of the card with the actual ports will be.

Remove the card from its antistatic bag, and position it over the PCI slot you've chosen. You may need to angle the card slightly so the actual ports on the back end of the card don't catch on the case of the Mac while you're installing it. If so, angle them so they protrude out of the area where the cover you removed was. Remember to hold the card only by the edges to avoid damaging it. Press the card into the slot. Avoid any rocking motion, and press straight downward. Once the card is installed, the contacts of the card should not be visible, and it should be seated securely in the slot.

That's about it. Restart the Mac and ensure that the card and its ports are recognized. You can do this with a utility that may be included with the card or by checking the Chooser to see if the ports are recognized for use with printers.

For comm slot cards, the process is a little different. Once you've installed the software, shut down the Mac and ground yourself. Open the Mac's side "door." Locate the comm slot. It is a smaller slot than the PCI slots. Chapters 1 and 8 illustrate where the comm slot is located on both Power Mac G3 and G4 computers. Remove the cover on the back of the case that covers the space for the actual modem's phone jack (or in this case, the serial port).

Position the card's connectors above the comm slot, and press down until it is seated securely. Again, you shouldn't be able to see the contacts when it is fully installed. Next, you need to attach the serial port itself to the back of the Mac's case where the space for the port is. This is done with the securing screw that you needed to remove in order to remove the cover that was over the space.

If the Power Mac shipped with an internal modem, you will need to remove the internal modem card before beginning the installation of the comm slot serial port card. Additional instructions for dealing with comm slots and comm slot cards is included in Chapter 8.

Serial Port Cards for the Original iMac

There are two options for serial ports on the original iMac models. One is limited to only the revision A and B iMacs, while the other will function with all four revisions of the original iMacs.

iMac Infrared Serial Port Cards

The revision A and B (Bondi Blue-colored) iMacs can have an actual serial port installed by a special card or adapter. This is because these iMacs featured an infrared port on the front of them (in the blue plastic around the left speaker, to be exact) for communicating with other infrared-equipped Macs such as some PowerBook models. Because the Mac recognizes this infrared port as a port for transferring data, it can be adapted to function as a serial port. Unfortunately, the infrared feature wasn't a big hit, and Apple removed it from any later iMac models when the five-colored iMacs were introduced in January of 1999.

Again, there are some compatibility issues to be aware of when devices install a serial port via the iMac's infrared port connector, though they tend to be far less extensive than when using a USB-to-serial-port adapter. The primary product in this category, the iPort from Griffin Technologies, also installs a video out port for these early iMacs.

Installing the iPort involves removing the iMac motherboard/drive assembly as described in Chapter 1. It also involves removing the panel covering the unused port space beneath the other ports so that you can run the monitor and serial port connections to this opening.

More importantly, installing the iPort involves disconnecting the original iMac video cable from below the motherboard (which will be replaced by the iPort connector). After this, you likewise remove the infrared port connector (labeled "Ir-DA") from the motherboard. This is where the iPort's serial port connection will be made.

iMac Internal Modem Serial Port Cards

Similar to the comm slot cards of the Power Mac models, there are cards on the market from GeeThree known as the Stealth Serial Port card. They can be used in all the original iMac models (revisions A through D, Bondi and colored) to add a single serial port at the expense of the iMac's internal modem. Installing these cards offers the same compatibility advantages for the iMac that the comm slot port cards do for the Power Macs. It is treated as a modem port, so that it is correctly recognized by a broader array of device drivers than other solutions.

Installation of these cards involves physically removing the iMac's internal modem card. This means that an external modem (USB or serial) will need to be used instead. This installation is about the same in complexity as the infrared card installation, and it likewise involves removing the iMac's motherboard from its internal case in order to access the internal modem slot. As such, both installations will void the iMac's warranty.

Installation of the Stealth Serial Port card in an iMac requires removing the motherboard/drive assembly, as described in Chapter 1. It then requires the removal of the motherboard from the assembly case or chassis. Once the motherboard has been removed, you can locate the internal modem card on the underside of the motherboard (as illustrated in Figure 30-6).

Once the internal modem card is located, it must be removed. This is similar to removing such a card from the Power Mac. Remove the card at the connector, and remove the actual phone jack located along with the rest of the iMac's ports. Once this has been completed, insert the serial port card in the modem connector, and attach the actual serial port where the modem's phone jack was. Then reassemble and replace the motherboard in the chassis, reassemble the iMac, and restart to ensure the card is properly recognized.

Figure 30-6
The approximate location of the internal modem card/slot on the original iMac's motherboard. (Note: only revision A and B iMacs will have the mezzanine slot connector on the motherboard.)

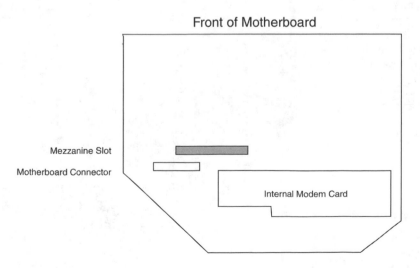

Front of Motherboard

Mezzanine Slot

Motherboard Connector

Internal Modem Card

Although this process may sound simple, it is actually rather involved, and GeeThree recommends against user installation.

USB-to-Serial-Port Adapters

The most common serial port solution seen on the market today is that of a USB adapter. These devices (such as the one shown in Figure 30-7) attach to a USB port and give you access to a variety of serial port devices via anywhere from one to four serial ports. Of all the serial port solutions on the market, these generally tend to be the ones with the least degree of compatibility with existing serial port devices. Table 30-3 lists the general compatibility of known devices. Again, this information in not product-specific, and you should check with a manufacturer's compatibility list for updates if you need to use a specific device not listed here.

Serial Port Devices by Network

For situations where an older Mac with a built-in serial port is available, sharing devices attached to that Mac's port by network might be a viable option. This solution can be implemented in one of three ways. First, the

Figure 30-7
The Keyspan USB serial adapter provides two serial ports from a USB port and is similar to other adapters on the market. (Photo courtesy of Keyspan)

TABLE 30-3

General Compatibility of Serial Port Devices with USB Adapters

Note: This list is not manufacturer-specific. Where Yes is indicated, devices may not be supported by all USB serial port adapters. Check with individual company compatibility lists.

Device	General Compatible Yes/No
Apple ImageWriter printers	Yes
Apple StyleWriter printers	Yes
Apple LaserWriter printers	Yes*
Epson Stylus printers	Yes
HP DeskJet printers	Yes
HP DeskWriter printers	Yes
HP LaserJet printers	No
NEC printers	No
CoStar label writer	Yes
Seiko label printer	Yes
Wacom graphics tablets	Yes
Digital cameras	Yes
QuickCam (serial port model)	No
Palm devices	Yes**
Psion Series palmtops	Yes
Newton computers	Yes
External modems	Yes
ISDN terminal adapters (modems)	Yes
LocalTalk networking	No
ACCLE scanner	Yes
Visioneer Paperport scanner	Yes
MIDI devices	No
La Cie Color calibrator	Yes
Bar code scanners	No

*Not All LaserWriter printers are supported by USB serial port adapters; check with manufacturers regarding specific models.
**Palm devices are supported under some USB adapters, as well as adapters specifically designed for PDA devices.

device may be designed to be shared through the Mac OS File Sharing abilities. Second, the device may be designed to attach directly to a LocalTalk network, which can be bridged with Ethernet. Third, the device may be supported by serial-port-sharing software.

In the first scenario, the device itself is not a network device but comes with software that is designed to allow the Mac that the device is attached to the ability to act as a server, sharing the device. Several printers from Apple, for example, use Apple's Printer Share extension. When installed and activated, this will enable the Mac attached to the printer to act as a printer server, receiving print jobs from other Macs on an AppleTalk network. The Mac will then pass those jobs on to the printer as though it was printing them. Some third-party printers include similar software.

In the second scenario, the device can be connected directly to a LocalTalk network and accessed by Macs on that network directly. Although LocalTalk is no longer a direct option for Macs, there are two ways to create a mixed LocalTalk and Ethernet network. These methods include using either a bridge device (such as Asanté's AsantéTalk, Farralon's EtherMac adapters, and Dayna's EtherPrint) or a host Mac with both LocalTalk and Ethernet ports and the free LocalTalk Bridge control panel from Apple.

In the case of bridge devices or adapters, one simply plugs the LocalTalk and Ethernet cables into the device. Once this is done, both network printers and Macs on the network are accessible in both directions between the LocalTalk and Ethernet sections of the network.

Using a host Mac and the LocalTalk Bridge control panel functions much the same way. You attach the host Mac to the Ethernet network by using its built-in Ethernet port (or the port on an Ethernet card), and you use the Mac's serial port to attach it to the LocalTalk network. You can then use the LocalTalk Bridge control panel to enable the Mac to act as a gateway between the two networks, bridging them into a single network much as a separate bridge device would.

In both cases, this creates a mixed network and can be done even if the printer or other serial/LocalTalk device is the only LocalTalk device on the network. Bridging LocalTalk and Ethernet to create a mixed network is discussed more in Chapter 32.

A similar device to a LocalTalk/Ethernet bridge specifically designed for non-LocalTalk serial StyleWriter Printers was developed by Farallon and is known as the iPrint SL. The iPrint SL works to connect a serial printer to the Ethernet port of a Macintosh. The iPrint SL is only compatible with Apple StyleWriter printers that did not ship with LocalTalk abilities.

The final scenario involves serial devices that are not designed to be networked either directly (as in the second option) or indirectly (as in the first option). There is a software product called PortShare produced by Stalker Software, however, that allows any device attached to a given serial port to be shared. PortShare can be an excellent solution to sharing non-network serial printers. InfoWave also makes a similar product called PowerPrint for Networks aimed at allowing printers of any type to be shared in this manner.

Resources for Further Study

The following URLs provide additional information on some of the concepts, issues, and products discussed in this chapter.

Ariston Technologies—Manufactures USB Serial Port Adapter—http://www.ariston.com

Belkin—Manufactures USB serial port adapter—http://www.belkin.com

CompuCable—Manufactures USB serial port adapter and USB docks—http://www.compucable.com

Entrega—Manufactures USB serial port adapter—http://www.entrega.com

Inside Out Networks—Manufactures the Edgeport USB serial port adapters—http://www.ionetworks.com

Momentum—Manufactures uConnect USB serial port adapter—http://www.usbconnect.com

Keyspan—Manufactures USB serial port adapter, USB PDA connector, and serial port PCI cards—http://www.keysan.com

GeeThree.com—Manufactures the Stealth Serial Port cards for Power Mac G3/G4 and Original iMac modem slots—http://www.geethree.com

Farallon—Manufactures the iPrint SL StyleWriter Ethernet adapter—http://www.farallon.com

Griffin Technology—Manufactures the iPort and gPort (G3/G4 comm slot serial port card)—http://www.griffintechnology.com

Stalker Software—Makers of PortShare—http://www.stalker.com

CHAPTER 31

Modems

One of the oldest ways to get computers to communicate with each other is with a modem. Modems allow computers to communicate over ordinary phone lines. The primary use of modems today is for dial-up Internet access or other online services like America Online. This chapter looks at how modems communicate data, the various modem standards, and the types of modems on the market. It also includes information on how to use a modem to the best of its ability and some of the nontraditional modem features you may find yourself using today.

How Modems Work

Modems function by converting the digital data stream being sent from a computer into an analog waveform that can be transmitted as a sound over a phone line. But modems do a good deal more than this simple conversion. They also need to handle such functions as handling error correction, performing data compression, and negotiating a connection rate with another modem. The first section of this chapter looks at the principles behind modem function and the factors that determine how two modems communicate with each other.

Modulation and Demodulation

The primary function of a modem is to modulate and demodulate data signals. (*Modem* is actually short for "modulate/demodulate.") This is because the data being sent from or received by a computer must be a digital signal, which is a discrete pattern of on and off (or 1 and 0) electrical signals. However, when that data is sent over a phone line using audible signals, it needs to be sent in an analog form, much like a wave. The modem converts between these analog and digital signals, receiving an analog wave and converting it to discrete digital bits for incoming data to the computer and receiving a discrete digital signal from the computer and converting into a waveform that can be transmitted along a phone line for outgoing data from a computer.

Modem Speeds

When you are discussing modems today, one of the main topics is modem speed. Modem speed is the amount of data the modem is capable of transmitting over a phone line each second. Modem speeds are usually given in the number of kilobits per second, such as 28.8 Kbps. The current crop of modems all boast that they are 56-Kbps modems, as this is the fastest speed available to modems with today's technology.

Baud versus Bits Per Second   Back in the 1980s, modem speeds were measured not in bits per second as they are today but by something called *baud rate*. A *baud* is a single change in the signal being transmitted by the modem over the phone line, and the baud rate is the number of times a signal changes in a second. At the time, 1 baud equaled 1 bit of data, so a 300-baud modem was capable of transmitting data at 300 bps.

What happened in the late 1980s that changed this naming convention was the development of modems that could split up a single baud such that one single change could actually carry more than one bit of data. The result was that a 600-baud modem could convey more than 600 bits of data per second. It's important to remember that baud and bps are not the same thing, though most modern software and hardware will probably not use the term *baud* today. If you are working with a text-based bulletin board system (BBS) or other older dial-up services or you find yourself dealing with older hardware, however, you should be aware of the difference.

Even though today's modems don't measure their speeds in terms of baud, the baud rate of a connection can determine the actual transfer speed. A modem connection of 28.8 Kbps, for example, requires a baud rate of 2400. Similarly, phone lines are sometimes rated based on the maximum baud rate they can support. This is why some older phone lines that are only capable of 1200 baud will not support connections faster than somewhere around 20 Kbps. If you suspect you can only establish slow connections because of older phone lines, you may wish to ask the phone company about the baud rate supported on the phone lines in your neighborhood (most phone companies guarantee rates of 2400 baud on their lines, which is sufficient for today's high-speed modem connections).

Modem Speed versus Connection Speed   Just because a modem can support connections as high as its listed speed doesn't mean you'll always get speeds that fast. In fact, you'll never actually get a 56-Kbps modem connection even with two top-of-the-line 56-Kbps modems. This is because, even though 56-Kbps modems can support such speeds, phone companies in the United States are not permitted to allow data transfer faster than 53.3 Kpbs. Aside from this restriction on 56-Kbps communication, there are a number of other factors that will affect the speeds at which your modem actually connects. The rest of this section looks at the issues that will affect your connection speed.

Error Correction   Phone lines transmit data from one modem to another in the form of audible signals. This means that if the phone line or phone connection experiences any noise, there's a probability that the modem receiving the data transmission won't get quite the same information as the transmitting modem sent. To ensure that the data being received by one modem is the same as the data transmitted by the other modem, modems include the ability for error correction in their design.

Error correction can be accomplished through the use of parity bits or synchronous communications checksum. When a modem uses parity bits to identify errors in a data transmission, it adds an additional bit of data (a 1 or 0/on or off segment of data) to each series of 8 bits (1 byte). This additional bit of data will be either a 1 or 0 added to the byte, depending on how many 1s and 0s are in the byte of data. If the parity bit conforms to the bits in the data, then the modem will know that the data has been received properly.

Unfortunately, parity bits are a cumbersome and inefficient method to verify data as it is received. More common today is the use of synchronous communications, where the modems sync using a standard protocol. This protocol will send data in special packets. A series of signals is sent before the actual data in each packet. The actual data of the packet is then followed by another series of special signals. The signals at the end of the packet will be determined based on running the actual data bits in the packet through a special algorithm. If the signals at the end of the packet don't match the data bits received when they are run through the same algorithm in reverse, then the modem knows that it didn't receive the packet correctly and will ask the sending modem to resend that packet. If the ending signals do match the data packet, the receiving modem acknowledges that it successfully received the complete packet, and the sending modem begins sending the next packet.

Error correction allows modems to use faster data transmission rates because the modems can constantly check the data coming in for discrepancies relatively easily. This has been one of the factors that allowed the development of modems that communicated faster than 9600 bps. Almost any modem today uses a good and standard error detection scheme. In fact, most modems support several schemes so that they are virtually guaranteed to have at least one error detection method in common with any other modem they may connect with.

Data Compression   Error correction and the ability to transmit multiple bits in a single baud cycle were two big factors in allowing modems to transmit data at faster speeds. Another important factor is the ability to compress data in the modem itself. Although data compression doesn't allow modems to actually connect and exchange data faster, certain segments of data can be compressed so that they are smaller when transmitted and thus can be transmitted faster than if they were transmitted without being compressed first. As with all modem communication, data compression requires that both modems in a connection support the same compression standard.

Unlike other modem factors, data compression's advantages will vary depending on what is being transmitted. This is because certain types of data are more inherently compressible than others. Text data, for example, is very simple and basic, and most compression algorithms can compress text documents quite a bit more than any other type of data or file. Files that have already been compressed with a program like DropStuff, on the other hand, probably won't benefit at all from a modem with compression abilities, because DropStuff has already compressed the data so much that the modem won't be able to compress it much further (if it can compress the file anymore at all).

Line Quality   The abilities of a modem (and the modem it is dialing into) are important factors in how much data the modem will be able to communicate per second. Another factor, however, is the quality of the phone lines you're dialing and connecting over. This includes both the phone company's cables that run along telephone polls (or underground), as well as the physical wiring inside your home or office and the actual phone cord running from your phone jack to the modem. If any of those phone lines are of low quality, data will not be able to be transmitted very fast. This is because the phone lines will impart signal noise into the data stream being transmitted. This will disrupt higher-speed signals and it will introduce errors into the data, which will need to be compensated for by the error-detection features of the modem (and will require portions of data to be re-sent).

When buying phone cables, don't skimp. If you find one phone jack in your house seems particularly slow, try using another. If none is particularly good for modem connections, chances are that the phone lines in your neighborhood are not the best. You can try asking the phone company to upgrade them (though there's no guarantee that they will). If you find that you cannot connect any faster than 19.2 Kbps, chances are that the lines in your neighborhood are only rated at 1200 baud. When calling the phone company, mention that you suspect the phone lines are limited to 1200 baud. This will sometimes get more attention because phone companies often guarantee lines capable of 2400 baud.

Flow Control   When a Mac communicates with a modem connected to it, both the Mac and the modem exchange information with each other. Since only one of them can be "talking" at a time, you need some method for signaling the end of data transmission between the Mac and modem. A good analogy is an old CB radio, where users had to hold a button to speak, but while they were holding the button, they wouldn't be able to here anyone talking on the other end. So, CB users got into the habit of saying "over" whenever they were finished speaking, to let the other person know he or she could press the button to speak without missing anything.

Flow control (sometimes also called handshaking) is the modem equivalent of the CB radio users saying "over" when they were finished speaking. It operates in one of two ways: via hardware or software. In hardware flow control, some of the wires in the modem's cable not used for transmitting data are used to transmit a signal that is the computer equivalent of saying "over." These wires are labeled as CTS (clear to send) and RTS (ready to send). When the Mac has finished sending data to the modem, it transmits a signal on the CTS wire so the modem knows it is time to transmit data to the Mac. Because the wires are labeled CTS and RTS, you may find hardware flow control called CTS flow control or RTS/CTS flow control. It may also be called hardware handshaking. If you are using an older serial port modem with a Mac, you will need to use a special modem cable called a hardware handshaking cable in order to use CTS flow control with that modem.

Software-based flow control predates the use of CTS flow control and is not nearly as efficient. This means Macs using software-based flow control with a modem will not achieve as high a connection speed as if they were using CTS flow control. Software flow control works by either the Mac or the modem sending a special character before or after sending data. This character (XON for beginning to send data and XOFF for having finished sending data) works in much the same way as the CTS and RTS wires do. However, it is less reliable and is therefore rarely used today. The internal modems of the current Macs will use hardware flow control by default, and unless you are dealing with a very old modem (or low-quality modem cable), you should not have any reason to use software-based flow control.

Port Speeds   While the speed capabilities of a modem, the modem you are dialing into, and the quality of your phone lines all determine how fast your modem can communicate data to another modem (and then to another computer), the speed of the port on your Mac can limit how fast your modem can communicate data with the Mac itself. This isn't a particular concern with the current Macs, as the internal modem slot/port can transmit data at a rate of at least 230 Kbps, much higher than the current modem standards are capable of transmitting. Nor is it usually a concern with USB modems because USB is capable of communicating data at 1200 Kbps. If you have a large number of high-bandwidth devices using the same USB channel as a USB modem, however, this could potentially become an issue. On older Macs, however, the serial port or internal modem slot speeds are more limited and simply may not support transmitting data as fast as a modem is capable of sending it.

Modem Standards

Despite all the different features available to modems in terms of how they work with data, compress data, handle error correction, as well as the various speeds at which they are capable of transferring data, two modems still need to support exactly the same sets of these features and the same speed over a given series of phone lines in order to exchange data. With all the possible variations in speed, features, and phone line quality, it makes it almost amazing that two modems can reach identical sets of features at one time.

The reason that two modems can establish such a communication is because modems are designed to support specific communications standards. Each of these standards includes specific information about what features are used and how they are used (which algorithms are used for error correction or data compression, for example) as well as what transfer speeds are supported.

There have been a large number of modem standards over the past two decades that modems have been used. Most of these standards have been created by the members of the International Telecommunications Union (ITU), although some have been adopted by other organizations or by groups of individual modem manufacturers. Table 31-1 lists some of the more common modem standards and the speeds and features they support.

As a rule, users will not need to be concerned with the standards their

TABLE 31-1

*Common Modem
Standards.*

Standard	Speeds Supported	Notes
Bell 103	300 bps	
v.21	300 bps	
Bell 212A	1200 bps	
v.22	1200 bps	
v.22bis	2400 bps	
v.29	9600 bps	
v.32	9600 bps	
v.32bis	14.4 Kbps	
v.terbo	19.2 Kbps	U.S. Robotics Proprietary Standard
v.34	28.8 Kbps	
v.34bis	33.6 Kbps	
X2	56 Kbps	U.S. Robotics Proprietary Standard*
56KFlex	56 Kbps	Rockwell Proprietary Standard*
v.90	56 Kbps	

*These proprietary standards were superseded by the v.90 standard. Many modems using these standards were flash upgradable to the v.90 standard when it was adopted.

modem is using because this will be determined automatically when the modem initiates communication with another modem (this process is called *negotiation* and is described in "Modem Negotiation," coming up). The only exception is when choosing a modem when a new modem standard is released that affords faster connections (like the v.90 56-Kbps standard).

Flash Upgradable Modems   The standards supported by a modem are built into the modem's firmware when the modem is created. This means that most modems cannot be upgraded to support newer standards when they are released. Newer modems, however, store this information in an upgradable type of memory sometimes called flash RAM. This allows modem manufacturers to issue updates to the modem's firmware when new standards and features are released, maintaining a user's investment in the modem. For this reason, it is always a good idea to buy a flash upgradable modem, particularly if there is any news of a new modem standard being developed when you buy your modem.

Modem Negotiation When two modems communicate over a phone line, the first thing they do is negotiate for a common speed and standard. This is an important first step in establishing a connection that can be used to reliably transmit data. Modem negotiation begins when the receiving modem first detects the ring of the calling modem. When the receiving modem detects the ring, it answers and then waits to see if the incoming call is a modem or a person. When the call is answered, the calling modem emits a carrier signal (the infamous screech sound) to identify itself as a modem. The receiving modem responds by emitting another carrier signal so that the calling modem knows that another modem has answered the call.

Once both modems have emitted their carrier signals to identify themselves as modems, the calling modem broadcasts a series of signals indicating all the various standards that it supports. Following this, the receiving modem responds by broadcasting all the standards that it supports. Then the modems continue to exchange standards until they determine which standard they both support that will provide the optimal quality over their current connection.

Once the modems have determined a common standard to use for communications, they go through all the possible speeds for that standard. They transmit data at the speeds supported by the standard until they determine the highest speed that they can support over their connection with reliable transmission quality. Once the speed is negotiated, both modems report to the computers they are connected to that they have successfully connected and inform the computers of the speed of the connection. The modems continue to negotiate adjustments in data compression and error correction as long as the connection is maintained in response to changes in the connection and the data being transmitted.

Modem Scripts

A *modem script*, sometimes also called a configuration or initialization string, is a series of basic commands that the Mac uses to communicate with a modem. Generally, a modem script contains a couple of very basic commands, such as the attention (AT) command that causes a modem to enter attention mode and initializes the modem for use in dialing a phone number and establishing a connection.

Because each modem is different and supports different standards, features, and basic commands, each modem may have a separate modem script. Although modem scripts generally follow the same basic structure, some modems require very specific commands to activate some of their features or even function at all. Apple includes a wide array of modem scripts for the most commonly used modems with every Mac OS release. Additionally, Mac-specific modems and other communications software (such as CompuServe) may install additional modem scripts on a Mac. Modem scripts are stored in the Modem Scripts folder inside the Extensions folder (within the Mac's System Folder).

When you configure a Mac for Internet access or you configure other communications software like America Online or CompuServe, you need to select the appropriate modem script for your modem. This is usually done from a menu of the installed scripts, such as the one shown in Figure 31-1. If a script for your specific modem is not installed, you can try using a script for a similar modem from the same manufacturer or using a generic Hayes-compatible modem script (Hayes was the first company to pioneer the AT command set on which modem scripts are based, and most modems conform to standard Hayes command scripts). You can also create a custom modem script for your modem using the Modem Script Generator tool that can be found at Apple's support website. This can be useful if you cannot find a script for your modem and/or if the installed scripts deliver low or unreliable performance.

Figure 31-1

A menu, such as this one from America Online's software, is often used to select a modem script.

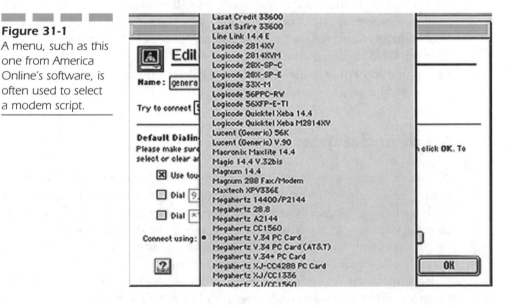

Apple Internal v.90 and v.34 Modem Scripts   The internal modem built into the current Macs supports many modem standards including the v.90 56-Kbps standard. However, there are times when the standard modem script enabling the v.90 standard features of the internal modem may result in problems establishing a reliable connection at slower speeds, such as 33.6-Kbps. This is a particular concern if you are dialing another modem that doesn't support 56-Kbps connections or are limited to slower speeds because of the quality of your local phone lines. For these situations, Apple has included a modem script for the internal modem that limits it to the features and standards of the earlier v.34 modem standard. This modem script is installed by default with Mac OS 9 and higher. It can also be downloaded from Apple's support website and used with earlier Mac OS versions. You can choose this modem script, which is labeled Apple Internal 56K Modem (v.34), the same way that you would choose any other modem script. Unless you experience connection problems, however, you should use the standard v.90 script that is selected by default and labeled Apple Internal Modem (v.90).

AT Commands   The AT command set is a series of modem commands originally created by Hayes in the 1980s as a standard set of modem commands. It is the command set on which modem scripts are based. Over the years it has been expanded and altered by various modem manufacturers. As a result, not all modems support all the commands in the AT command set, which is one reason why individual modems need individual modem scripts.

It is rather unlikely that you will need to use the AT command set yourself today. Usually, your communications software or the Mac OS Internet elements will handle using any commands for you. The only real reason you might need to use AT commands directly is if you are using a terminal emulator. A terminal emulator establishes text-based connections directly with another computer over a modem. Many terminal emulators do not access the modem scripts installed on a Mac and may ask for an initialization string to activate the modem. This string is a series of AT commands that function like a modem script. AT commands can also be used within the terminal emulator to dial the modem, to hang up a modem, or to perform other tasks while the connection is active (although most terminal emulators let you perform such functions using menu items). In case you find yourself needing to work with AT commands or if you are simply curious, Table 31-2 includes some common AT

TABLE 31-2

Common AT Commands.

Command	Modifiers*	Use
AT	none	"Attention" used as the beginning of a command or command string.
D	T	Dials using Touch-Tone dialing (followed by phone number).
	P	Dials using pulse dialing (followed by phone number).
H	none	Hangs up the modem.
Z	none	Resets the modem.
&F	0 or 1	Instructs the modem to use its standard factory settings.
A	none	Answers incoming call(s).
L	none	Redials last phone number (must be placed immediately after the D command).
M	0	Modem speaker off.
	1	Modem speaker on during connection establishment.
	2	Modem speaker always on.
	3	Modem speaker on only when receiving a call.
&K	0	Disables flow control.
	1	Enables hardware flow control.
	2	Enables software flow control.

*Some AT commands need a modifier directly after the command to determine how the command is used.

commands.

Types of Modems

There are two basic types of modems: internal and external. An internal modem is an expansion card attached to a special connector on the Mac's motherboard. It provides a phone jack (RJ11) connector along with the Mac's other ports into which a phone line can be plugged. An external modem, on the other hand, needs to be attached to one of the Mac's existing interface ports (such as a USB or serial port) and includes two phone jacks: one for the incoming phone line and an outgoing phone jack where an actual phone can be attached.

Internal All the Macs covered by this book ship with an internal v.90 modem already installed, with two exceptions. The exceptions are the Blue Power Mac G3 and the early Power Mac G4 models with a PCI graphics card (sometimes referred to as "Yikes" because of their Apple code name), which did not ship with an internal modem unless one was chosen as a built-to-order option. For these models, an internal modem can be purchased from Apple or from Global Village. Both modems offer v.90 standards and are similarly priced. Alternatively, an external modem can be used instead.

The internal modem in the current Macs will serve the needs of the majority of Mac users and will rarely require the need for using an external modem with these machines. However, as discussed in the previous chapter, it is possible to install a special serial port card in the Power Mac G3 and G4 models, as well as the original iMac models, into the special comm slot on the Mac's motherboard where the internal modem is installed. In these cases, an external modem is needed as a replacement. If the internal modem card of the Mac is damaged, replacing it with a new internal modem or with an external modem is needed. Instructions for removing and installing an internal modem are included later in this chapter.

Apple has made strides to use universal motherboard components across their product lines. This includes the internal modem. The Power Mac G4 (AGP graphics card models), iMac DV, iBook, and PowerBook (both models covered in this book) all share the same type of internal modem card and comm slot design. The difference between these Macs is primarily where the comm slot is located on the motherboard and the length of cable that leads from the comm slot to the phone jack built into the case of the Mac.

External Serial Port Modems Until the iMac was introduced as the first Mac without serial ports, an external serial port modem was the most common type of modem used with the Mac. Today's Macs can use a serial port modem if they have a serial port card installed (see the previous chapter for information on serial port cards). External serial port modems are essentially cross-platform devices, meaning that a modem does not have to be Macintosh-specific. A Mac modem cable, which converts the 25-pin PC serial port on an external modem to a Mac-style serial port is needed, however. This cable should also support hardware handshaking.

External serial port modems require their own power supply (with the exception of Mac-specific GeoPort modem, which used an extra pin to draw power directly from the Mac and required a GeoPort-style serial port). They also offer a series of LED indicators on the modem that can be used to determine modem activity and connection status. External modems also tend to have both incoming and outgoing phone jacks, allowing users to plug the phone line into the modem's incoming jack and then to plug a phone (or answering machine) into the modem's outgoing jack.

External USB Modems   External USB modems became popular with Mac users when the Blue Power Mac G3 premiered without an internal modem or serial ports. Partly this was because Apple was behind schedule in shipping internal modem cards for the new Power Mac G3 and users were anxious for any type of modem they could find.

External USB modems offer many of the same design and features of an external serial port modem, though they almost always draw power from the USB bus and therefore don't require an independent power supply. USB modems do require a Mac-specific USB driver for the Mac to recognize and communicate with the modem.

Most USB modems on the market are top-of-the-line v.90 models and can be used as a replacement for an internal modem or in addition to one. One nice feature about USB for modem use is that there is no limitation on how many USB modems you can attach to a Mac (as there was with serial port modems). This can be useful if you are running a dial-up server on your Mac for such things as Internet access, an AppleTalk Remote Access server, remote connections to an intranet, or a bulletin board service. Of course, if you have enough incoming connections to a single Mac, you will see performance from that Mac decrease.

PC Card Modems   PC Card modems were briefly discussed in Chapter 9. Although the current PowerBook models include an internal modem, several earlier models did not. Since they did include a PC Card slot, a PC Card modem was a common choice for adding a modem, as it behaved much like an internal modem. As with serial port modems, PC Card modems are cross-platform devices, and you don't need to purchase a Mac-specific model, although Mac-specific models may include Macintosh drivers that enable additional features, such as cellular phone connections and fax abilities.

PC Card modems can be used as a replacement for a PowerBook's internal modem or to augment the abilities of a PowerBook's internal modem. There are two ways you might wish to augment a PowerBook with a PC Card modem. The first is to make connections using a cellular phone. Many cell phones can support dial-up connections being made through them but require a modem that supports such connections. Several PC Card modems do support cellular connections, while the PowerBook's internal modem does not. The second instance is where you want to use two modems at once, either to access to separate dial-up services or to use both modems to establish a single Internet connection (see "Accessing the Internet" later in this chapter).

Connecting and Using a Modem

Almost every Mac user reading this book has probably used a modem at one point or another, whether to connect to America Online or to dial up an Internet service provider (ISP). With the current Macs, this is an easy process that involves no need to connect hardware. You simply plug the phone cable into the phone jack of the built-in modem and launch the Internet Setup Assistant or the AOL software, and the Mac uses its internal modem to perform the connection to the ISP or online service without much need for user intervention or concern. The following sections look at how to attach an external modem or replace the existing internal modem of a Mac if it is damaged (or install one in the Power Mac models that shipped without an internal modem). Following that, we'll look at how to manually configure your Mac to establish a dial-up Internet connection and how the modem can be used to access other online services.

Attaching an External Modem

Attaching an external modem is almost never a difficult procedure. The next few paragraphs include a brief overview of the process of attaching the various types of external modems to the Mac.

USB USB modems act pretty much like any other USB device. Install the driver software that comes with the modem on the Mac. Restart the computer so the drivers are loaded as part of the Mac OS at startup, and attach the modem to a USB port on the Mac or a hub. With the modem connected to the Mac, simply attach a phone cable to the incoming line phone jack on the modem. If you wish to connect a phone to the same line, do so using the outgoing-line phone jack on the modem. If the modem doesn't draw its power directly from the USB bus, plug in the included AC adapter. The last step is to open the Modem control panel and select the USB port and an appropriate modem script (see "Modem Scripts" earlier in this chapter for more information). If you use America Online or other communications software, you also need to follow the appropriate steps to choose your new modem in that application.

Serial Port   Serial port modems are almost as easy to install as USB modems. If the modem is Mac-specific and comes with driver software, run the installer program on the included CD-ROM. Shut down the Mac. Next, connect the modem cable to the Mac's serial port and the port on the modem (assuming the cable is not built into the modem). Next, plug in the modem's power adapter and the phone line the same as you would for a USB modem. Start up the Mac, and the modem should be ready to go. Choose the appropriate modem script and the appropriate serial port in the Modem control panel and/or whatever online service software (such as America Online) you use. You should now be ready to go.

PC Card Modems   PC Card modems install like any PC Card device. Install any driver software for a Mac-specific modem and restart the Mac. Then, simply insert the modem PC Card into the PowerBook's PC Card slot. An icon for the modem should appear on the desktop, indicating that it is recognized by the Mac. Choose the modem in the Modem control panel of whatever other communications software you use, choose an appropriate modem script, and you should be ready to go. When you are ready to use the modem, you will probably need to attach the appropriate dongle with a phone jack to the outside edge of the PC Card. Refer to Chapter 9 for more information regarding PC Cards and dongles.

Installing or Replacing an Internal Modem

As a rule, you shouldn't have any need to install an internal modem in any Mac, save the Blue and White Power Mac G3 models and some of the early Power Mac G4 models. Installing a modem into these computers is a relatively easy process and is considered by Apple to be a user-installable process. Installing an internal modem into any other Mac, including the Power Mac G4 (models with an AGP graphics card), the iMacs, the iBook, and the PowerBook should only be needed if the internal modem fails.

Replacing the internal modem of any iMac or the iBook is extremely challenging and will void the computer's warranty. It is also not considered user-installable in that Apple does not make replacement modems available to individual users (only Apple Authorized Service Centers can order them). As such, the only modem installation instructions included here are for the Power Mac computers.

The Power Mac G3 and G4 (PCI Graphics Card)   First, shut down the computer, make sure you are properly grounded, and open the side door of the Mac. Locate the metal plate with the telephone picture on the back panel of the computer. It is positioned as indicated in Figure 31-2. This is where the modem's phone jack will go. Remove the plate. It is secured with a single Phillips head screw.

Now take the modem port card out of its antistatic bag. Take the actual phone jack and place it on the inside of the case, so that the port

Figure 31-2

The location of the internal modem or comm slot and phone jack on the Power Mac G3 and early G4 models.

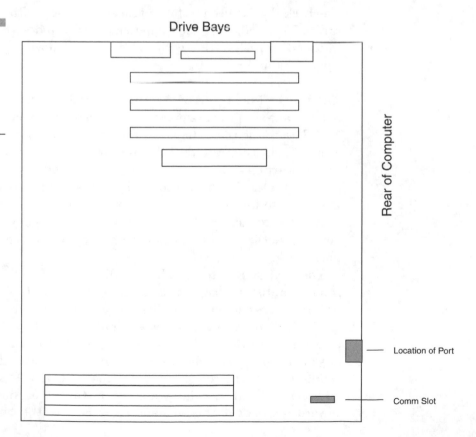

itself is pointing outward and is situated in the space where the metal plate was. You'll notice there are two tabs on one side of the port (opposite the hole for the screw). These will insert into the case and help to secure the port. Secure the port in place of the metal plate using the same screw that secured the plate. This will be easiest if you use the fingers of one hand to hold the port in place and the other hand to insert the screw.

Now you need to insert the actual card into the comm slot. The card may or may not be connected to the port you just attached to the computer's case already. If it is not, connect the cable from the port to the card. Locate the comm slot on the motherboard. It is located toward the rear of the computer and the edge of the motherboard that is farthest away from the drive bays, as indicated in Figure 31-2. It is also marked "Modem." Line the card up with the connectors. Although it may not be obvious at first glance, the plastic of the card's connector is molded so that it will install only in one direction. Press the card into the slot. It should go in without much force, and if it seems to resist, stop and double-check that the connector is properly aligned with the slot. Once the card is installed, close the computer. Restart and verify that the card is installed properly (either with utilities included with the card or with the Apple System Profiler).

The Power Mac G4 (AGP Graphics Card)   First, shut down the computer, make sure you are properly grounded, and open the side door of the Mac. Locate the comm (modem) slot. As you can see in Figure 31-3, the comm slot is located toward the front of the Mac's case and right next to the forwardmost hard drive bay. If you need to remove an existing modem, the card is held in place by two screws. It is also secured by a metal tab to the edge of the card toward the back of the Mac and right next to the connector. Once the screws are removed, you can lift the card out gently. Disconnect the cable running from the modem card to the phone jack.

The next step is to actually install a modem card. Remove the card from its antistatic bag. Position the connector of the card over the connector on the motherboard. The card will fit only in one direction, with the bulk of the card facing away from the drive bays. There will be two screw holes in the card and on the motherboard, which should remove any confusion about how the card is properly oriented. Press the card's connector onto the connector on the motherboard. It should snap down securely and will be held by a slight metal tab on the edge of the card toward the back of the Mac and right next to the connector. Once the

Figure 31-3
The location of the
comm slot on the
Power Mac G4.

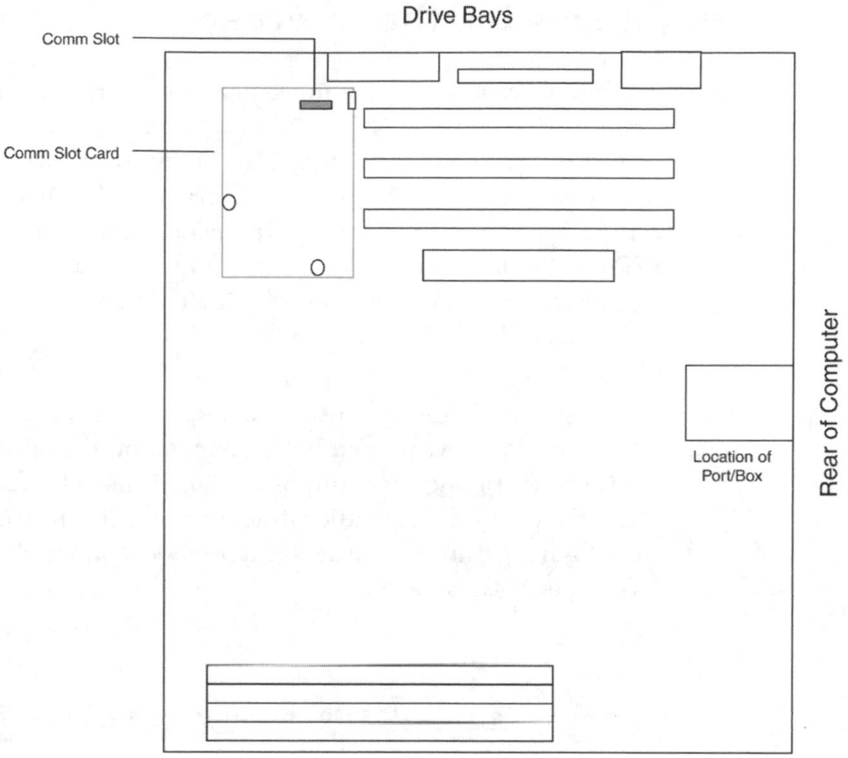

card is in place, you need to secure it to the motherboard with the two screws.

Next, you may need to run the cable from the port to the comm slot card. With the Apple factory-installed modem, this cable runs under the motherboard. For third-party cards installed later, the cable is generally run between the video card (and any PCI cards) and the motherboard and then under the hard drive cables, going around the edge of the motherboard. You should check the instructions that come with the card to be certain, however. It is better to actually remove the video card and any PCI cards before running the cable underneath them. Doing so will make the process easier and make you less likely to accidentally damage the cards or motherboard while trying to snake the cable between them. Once the cable has been run around the motherboard, you should attach it to the appropriate connector on the card.

Once the card is installed, close the computer. Restart and verify that the card is installed properly (either with utilities included with the card or with the Apple System Profiler).

Accessing the Internet

The most common use of modems today is to establish a dial-up Internet connection with an ISP. This requires not just the hardware of the modem and the modem script to communicate with it, but also the software that enables the Mac to interact with other computers using the TCP/IP protocol on which the Internet is based and a protocol called PPP (Point-to-Point Protocol) that is used to actually establish the connection between your Mac and your ISP. This software is part of the Open Transport Mac OS components.

Using the Internet Setup Assistant Apple's ads have proclaimed that new Mac owners can have their computers on the Internet within 10 minutes of taking them out of the box. This is largely because Apple provides an easy utility called the Internet Setup Assistant, which makes configuring Internet access extremely simple. Figure 31-4 shows the Internet Setup Assistant.

Figure 31-4
Apple's Internet Setup Assistant.

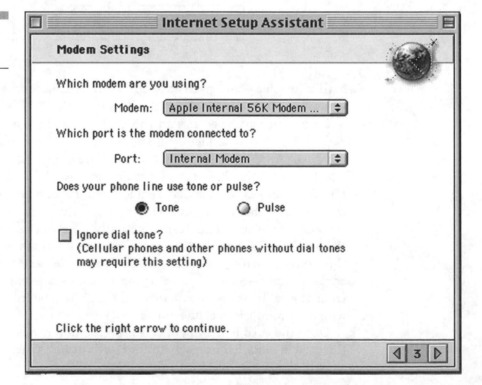

When launched, the Internet Setup Assistant asks a Mac user each of the various pieces of information needed by the various Internet-related control panels. First, it asks the user to choose a modem for the connection (the Apple internal modem is chosen by default). Then it asks for the phone number to dial into an ISP, the user's ID and password with the Internet provider, the user's e-mail information, and various other information such as the ISP's domain name servers. When finished, the Setup Assistant enters all the information in the appropriate control panels and enables Internet access.

The Modem, Remote Access, and TCP/IP Control Panels   Rather than using the Internet Setup Assistant, users can enter all the dial-up Internet account information using the three control panels that control such access. The first of these control panels is the Modem control panel. The Modem control panel identifies the modem that the Mac will use to communicate and allows the user to choose an appropriate modem script.

As you can see in Figure 31-5, there are only a few options in the Modem control panel. The first is the Connect Via item at the top of the control panel. If multiple modems are installed on a Mac, this allows a user to choose a modem based on the port it is connected to. The next item is the Modem menu. This pop-up menu contains a list of all the modem scripts installed on the Mac and can be used to select a script appropriate to the modem being used. The sound radio buttons allow you to indicate whether or not you want the sound of the modem dialing and connecting to be transmitted through the Mac's speakers. The dialing radio buttons allow you to indicate whether you are using a Touch-Tone

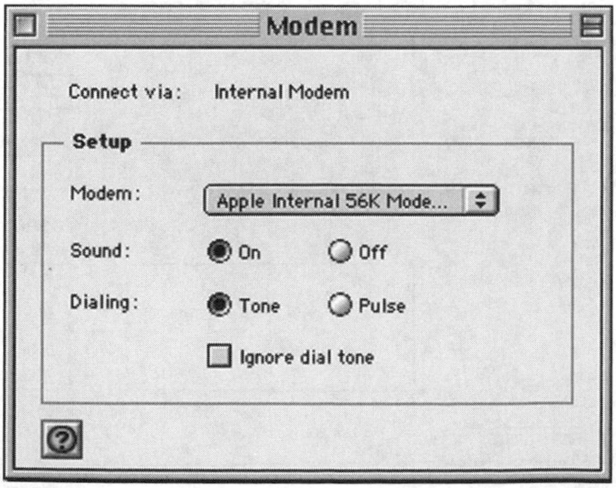

Figure 31-5
The Modem control panel.

![Modem control panel window. Connect via: Internal Modem. Setup — Modem: Apple Internal 56K Mode... ; Sound: ● On ○ Off ; Dialing: ● Tone ○ Pulse ; ☐ Ignore dial tone]

or pulse dialed phone line (all but the oldest phone lines should use tone dialing). Finally, the Ignore dialog checkbox tells the Mac whether or not to listen for a dial tone. Some office phone systems (or cellular phones) will not provide a standard dial tone when the phone is picked up. If you use such a phone setup, you will need to check this box; otherwise, the Mac will report an error that it cannot dial the phone because it doesn't recognize a dial tone. If you do not use such a phone, leave this box unchecked so that the Mac will alert you if it tries to dial but cannot get a dial tone on the phone line.

TCP/IP   The TCP/IP control panel, shown in Figure 31-6, allows a Mac user to designate how the Mac receives information on its Internet connection (or another network connection using the TCP/IP protocols that the Internet is based on). Receiving TCP/IP information and communicating via TCP/IP protocols can be done using a dial-up connection, an Ethernet connection, a wireless AirPort connection (if an AirPort card is installed), and a number of other connection methods. To select a connection method for a Mac, use the Connect Via pop-up menu in the TCP/IP control panel. For dial-up connections to an ISP, you would choose PPP from this menu, since PPP is the primary protocol used by ISPs to support a dial-up connection (users of America Online, however,

Figure 31-6
The TCP/IP control panel.

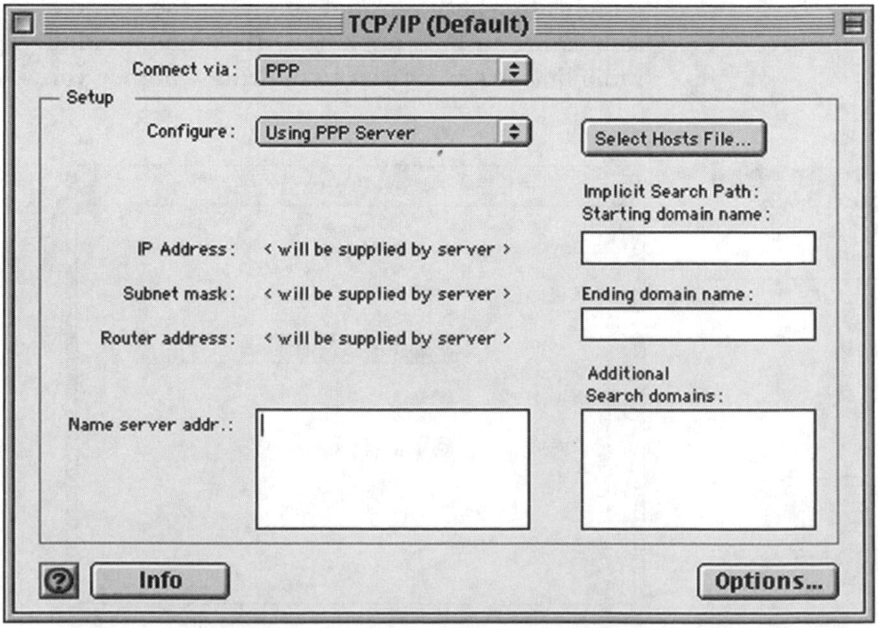

would choose AOL Link or AOL Link Enhanced from this menu, because America Online doesn't use traditional dial-up Internet connections).

In addition to choosing the method by which the Mac will establish a TCP/IP connection, the TCP/IP control panel allows you to designate how the Mac receives TCP/IP information that it needs to communicate with the Internet. This includes an IP address (a unique identity that every computer connected to the Internet requires), a router address, a subnet mask, and domain name server addresses. Various methods can be used to send this information to the Mac, and one is selected with the Configure pop-up menu. For almost all dial-up connections, this information is provided by selecting the PPP server option. Your individual ISP will tell you if a different method is used, though this is extremely rare. The only piece of information you may have to enter manually for a dial-up connection is the domain name server addresses for your ISP, which are entered into the Name Server Addr: box. These addresses will be groups of four individual numbers such as 20.45.65.1. Your ISP should tell you what addresses to use. If you need to enter multiple server addresses, press Return between each of them.

REMOTE ACCESS The Remote Access control panel, shown in Figure 31-7, actually handles dialing the modem and establishing a connection. It can be used to establish a connection to your ISP using the PPP protocol as

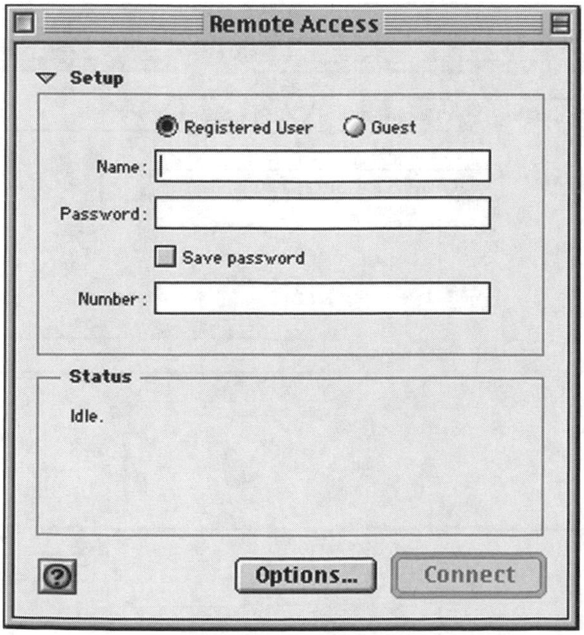

Figure 31-7
The Remote Access control panel's main display.

well as establishing a dial-up AppleTalk connection to a remote AppleTalk network or server (see "Using Other Online Services" later in this chapter for how to use Remote Access for AppleTalk connections). By default, Remote Access is set up to be used for connections to an ISP.

For most connections, Remote Access is very simple to configure. Simply enter your username and password for your Internet account in the Name and Password text boxes, and then enter your ISP's dial-up phone number in the Number text box. If you don't want the Mac to store your Internet account's password, uncheck the Save Password checkbox (you will then be asked for it whenever you connect). If you don't want the Mac to store your username, select the Guest radio button instead of the Registered User button. The Connect button at the bottom of the window dials the modem and establishes a connection to your ISP. Once connected, the Connect button becomes a Disconnect button, which terminates the connection. The status area of the window displays your connection speed, as well as the amount of data being transferred to or from your computer through the connection. You can also connect/disconnect and view status using the Remote Access control strip module.

The Options button of the Remote Access window brings up a dialog box that allows you to configure various additional functions for your dial-up connections. It is divided into three tabs: Redialing, Connection, and Protocol. The Redialing tab, shown in Figure 31-8, allows you to acti-

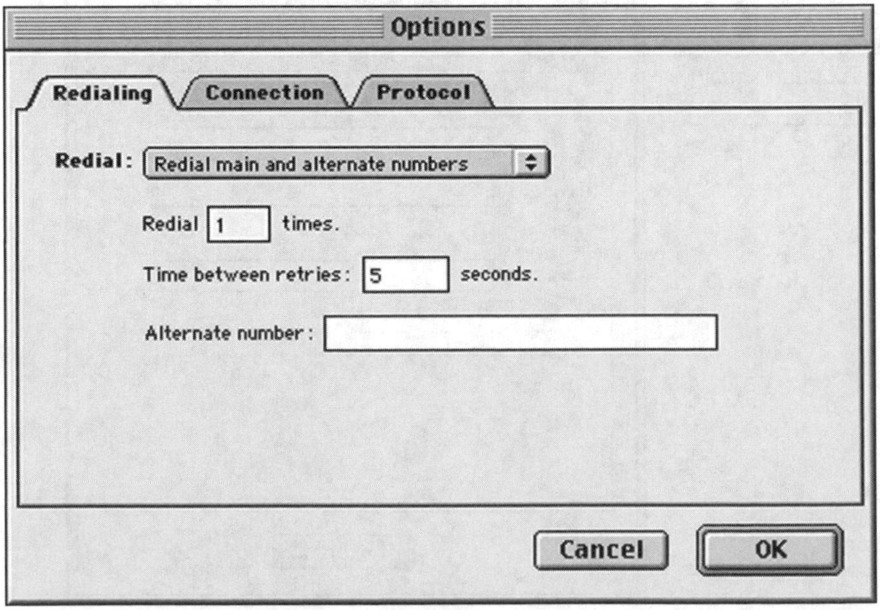

Figure 31-8
The Redialing tab of the Remote Access Options dialog.

vate automatic redialing. When activated, this causes the Mac to redial your ISP if it receives a busy signal or has some other type of failure when it tries to connect. Redialing is chosen from a pop-up menu that includes Redialing Off (the default setting), Redial Main Number Only, and Redial Main and Alternate Numbers. Both redialing items are functionally the same, except Redial Main and Alternate Numbers allows you to enter a second dial-up phone number, which can be used if your ISP provides multiple modem pools and dial-up numbers in your area (it contains a text box for entering your alternate dial-up phone number). Both items include boxes where you can enter the number of times for the Mac to attempt to redial a number and how many seconds the Mac should wait between dialing attempts.

The Connection tab, shown in Figure 31-9, contains several checkboxes. The first is Use Verbose Logging, which causes the Mac to keep a detailed log of any dial-up connections (a feature not needed by most users). The second is Launch Status Application When Connecting, which launches an application that displays the status of your connection, much like the status section of Remote Access's main window. The Flash Icon in the Menu Bar feature causes the Apple menu to alternate with a telephone pole image whenever you have an active dial-up connection. With the Prompt Every X Minutes to Maintain option, the Mac

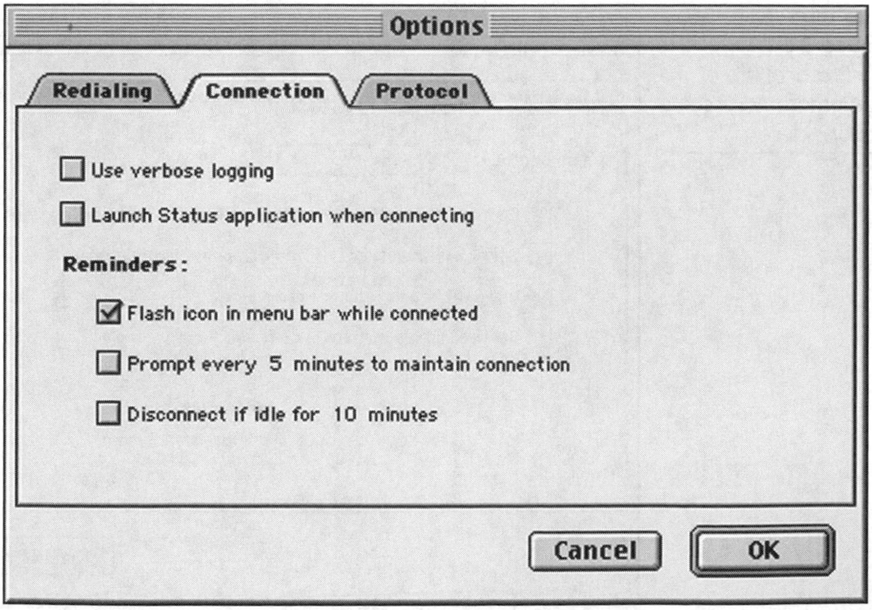

Figure 31-9
The Connection tab of the Remote Access Options dialog.

asks you if you want to continue using your connection at a set interval (where X is a text box that you can enter any interval you want into). This is a nice feature if you pay by the minute for Internet access and want to be reminded how much time/money you're using, but it can also get very annoying. The last item, Disconnect If Idle for X Minutes, lets you tell the Mac to terminate the dial-up connection and hang up the modem if you haven't actually used the Internet connection (i.e., checked e-mail or visited a Web page) for a specified amount of time (where X is a text box to enter the time limit). This is good if you're likely to forget to use the Remote Access control panel or control strip module to disconnect when you're done using the Internet.

The Protocol tab, shown in Figure 31-10, allows you to set a few different functions. The first is to determine whether you will be using Remote Access to establish a PPP (Internet) connection or an AppleTalk Remote Access Protocol (ARAP) connection to an AppleTalk network or server that supports dial-up connections. When ARAP is chosen, there are no other options in this tab. When PPP is chosen, there are four checkboxes. With the first checkbox, the Mac automatically uses Remote Access to establish an Internet connection when you launch any Internet application (such as Internet Explorer). The second checkbox tells the Mac to use a modem's built-in error correction and data compression fea-

Figure 31-10
The Protocol tab of the Remote Access Options dialog.

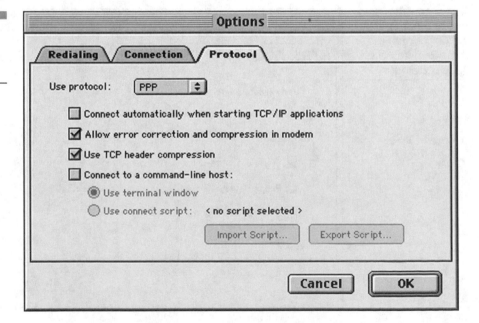

tures. If left unchecked, the Mac performs these functions using software-based commands, which, as described at the beginning of this chapter, is much slower than using the abilities built into a modem. Use TCP Header Compression tells the Mac to use the Internet-style TCP compression scheme. The final checkbox, Connect to a Command-line Host, should only be used with ISPs that require a PPP login script or other text-based command instructions. These are extremely rare, and most users will never need to use these features. Your ISP will tell you if you do need to use them and provide instructions on how to do so.

Replacing Remote Access with Another Dialing Method   Apple's Remote Access control panel is the default method for initiating a PPP connection to your ISP, but it isn't the only one. In fact, several alternatives served many Mac users for years before Apple bundled Internet setup and access software into the Mac as a default option. The principle alternative to the Remote Access control panel is the venerable FreePPP, a freeware PPP control panel and extension set.

FreePPP can be downloaded from a number of shareware archives on the Internet and must be manually installed by users. It uses a different interface for setting up communications than Remote Access and needs to be configured manually because it isn't supported by Apple's Internet Setup Assistant. Proponents of FreePPP claim that it provides better-speed connections, particularly on lower-quality phone lines, and that it is a more stable option that is less prone to crashing or unexpectedly dropping a connection to the ISP. Your experiences may vary using FreePPP. Personally, I usually opt for the convenience of using Apple's Remote Access.

Doubling Your Connection with Two Modems   FCR makes a utility called LinkUPPP. The purpose of LinkUPPP is to enable a feature called Multilink. Multilink was initially designed for Windows NT computers and allows a computer to use two separate modems to dial into an Internet provider (or some other type of computer network). Once both modems have dialed in and connected, the computer will treat the two separate connections as a single connection with performance equivalent to the transfer speeds of both modems combined. Needless to say, this has the potential to double your Internet performance and can be an excellent feature if you want better performance but live (or work) someplace where higher-speed connections such as ISDN, cable modems, or DSL are not available. LinkUPPP requires two modems (preferably of the same performance standard) and an ISP that supports Multilink connections.

Using Other Online Services

Internet access may be the most common use of modems today, but it isn't the only use. A number of other dial-up services are out there, most notably America Online (AOL). Beyond online communities like AOL, there are still some dial-up bulletin board services that use a simple terminal emulator program. There is also the ability to dial into an AppleTalk network that uses AppleTalk Remote Access. While these may not be used by everybody, they are still services that it is good to know about on at least a very minimal level.

AOL, CompuServe, and Similar Services   AOL is probably the most famous (or infamous) online service out there. They provide an online community and experience all their own via a graphical application that users use to visit various aspects of the AOL service and to communicate with other users. Despite the fact that many longtime Internet users speak of AOL with varying degrees of derision, AOL is still the largest single Internet provider and the largest non-Internet online service. This means that they have plenty of users. CompuServe, which is now owned by AOL, also uses a similar independent graphical application to permit users to log on to the service and access its features. Both AOL and CompuServe have Internet access integrated into their services (both as part of their application and with the ability to use separate Internet applications through the connection). Less commonly, there are smaller services that will use a graphical application to provide access to a dial-up community independent of the Internet. In fact, a number of server/client packages are available that allow anyone to set up his or her own, unique graphical online service (TeleFinder and First Class are the most well known).

Using an online service that includes its own graphical application for dial-up access means that you need to configure that application to work with your modem. As a rule, this is fairly easy. One of the steps AOL's software goes through when setting up an account is asking the user to choose a type of modem, the modem port, the modem script, and similar features. Actually, the process is extremely similar to setting up a computer using Apple's Internet Setup Assistant.

Text-based BBSs   Before America Online or CompuServe ever existed and back in the days before *Internet* was a word that the average person had heard, there were more basic online communities and services. These were services with a few phone lines that you could dial from your computer called a bulletin board service, or BBS. You didn't connect with a graphical application. Instead, you used a program called a terminal emulator. A terminal emulator is a program that does nothing but send text back and forth between your computer and a remote computer. When you connect to a BBS, you enter a username and password, and then you just enter text commands into a prompt and receive text displays back.

You can send messages to other users, post messages on bulletin boards, sometimes use real-time chat features, and maybe even access a file archive (using one of the earliest file transfer methods, presuming both your terminal emulator and the service supported the same one). Pretty primitive by today's standards, but 10 to 15 years ago, it was the height of technology. When the Internet became popular, you could even access it using text-based applications on the BBS's server through your terminal emulator (some BBSs and ISPs still support this today).

While most people don't use BBSs today, and some people don't even know what they are, some do still exist. Usually they are free services, and if your town or city has any kind of local computing newspaper or magazine, you may find some listed in it. To access a text-based BBS, you need a terminal emulator. Several of these applications are still out there, and you can find them in any shareware archive on the Internet. The most common is ZTerm. To use one, you'll need to either select your modem from those listed by the application (if any are) or enter a modem script or command string by hand. Usually, terminal emulators are set up to use a basic AT command string for the features they need to use. You then use whatever dialing method, usually a menu item, the application supports to enter the BBS's phone number and connect.

AppleTalk Remote Access Servers   AppleTalk networks can be accessed via a modem connection, provided that a Mac on the network is running AppleTalk Remote Access Server. If one of the Macs is, you can dial into the network from a remote location. Once connected to a network remotely, you can access any file servers; mount drives on your Mac's desktop; save, copy, and create files; and even print to networked printers. The slowness of the dial-up connection, however, will make everything, even opening a folder and waiting for icons to be displayed, a slower process than you would have if you were connected to the network by Ethernet, AirPort, or LocalTalk.

Dialing into an AppleTalk network with a Remote Access Server running is handled by the Remote Access control panel. As you read in the earlier section on setting up dial-up Internet access, pressing the

Options button in the Remote Access control panel brings up a dialog with three tabs. One of those tabs is labeled Protocol. The Use Protocol menu in this tab contains two options: PPP and ARAP. ARAP stands for AppleTalk Remote Access Protocol. When this menu is set to ARAP, Remote Access will be set up to dial into an AppleTalk Remote Access Server instead of an ISP's PPP server. You can then use Remote Access's Connect button to dial up the server and connect much as you would to dial an ISP. Once connected, you can access AppleTalk resources on the network in the same manner you would normally. See the next chapter for details about AppleTalk networks.

Other Modem Features

The modem's first use was allowing two computers in remote locations to exchange information, and this remains its primary use. However, several other tasks can be performed with a modem, either using features built into the modem or software installed on the Mac. This section looks at some of the common and interesting additional features and uses available with modems today.

Remote Controlling Another Mac

Yes, you can operate a Mac by remote control. This can be a useful feature if you need to adjust the settings of a Mac that is running a server (such as a web server or AppleTalk file server) that is not in the same location as you and your Mac. To do this, you need a utility called Timbuktu by Netopia (a demo is included on the CD with their look). Timbuktu includes two modules: one must be installed on the Mac being remote controlled and the other on the one doing the remote controlling. Once it is running on a Mac, you can dial that Mac up, and its desktop and menu bar will be displayed in a window on the computer you are dialing from (Timbuktu supports dialing from Windows and Mac computers).

You then simply move items, launch applications, and adjust application settings in the Timbuktu window as you would if you were sitting at the Mac you have dialed into (albeit with some lag because of the speed of the dial-up connection). An interesting use for this ability that I have seen some tech support people do is to use Timbuktu to remote-control a troublesome Mac in order to diagnose and resolve a problem from a remote location. This can be excellent if you are dealing with a new user or a difficult problem and cannot actually sit down in front of the Mac that is having trouble.

Faxing

Fax machines act almost like long-range copy machines. You pass a document into one fax machine, where it is scanned and a data representation is created (in much the same way as a scanner creates a digital image of a document). The fax machine then dials another fax machine over a phone line. When the second fax machine answers, the two negotiate a common speed (much as two modems do). Then the first machine transmits the data representation of the document to the second machine, which prints out a copy of the document.

Since fax machines operate using the same phone lines and audible frequency ranges of a modem, there is no reason that a computer can't send a document over a phone line to a fax machine to be printed. In fact, almost any Mac with the appropriate software and a modem that supports the same communication standards as a fax machine can do this. Not only that, but they can accept calls from a fax machine, receive a document, and save it as a file on the hard drive. This file can then be viewed or printed by the Mac's user.

The two components involved in allowing a Mac to offer faxing abilities are the modem and the needed fax software. Most modems today come with faxing abilities built into them (including the internal modems included in the current Mac models). Of course, you should check a modem's specifications to be certain before buying, however. A modem that comes with fax capabilities will also come with fax software (you can buy fax software separately as well). Which fax software is included depends on the modem. Apple includes the FAXstf software with each Mac that has an internal modem. Various fax utilities include different interface and some different features, but all tend to work very similarly.

For sending faxes, most fax utilities install an extension that allows you to select faxing in the Chooser, exactly as you would a printer. Simply choose this fax option instead of a printer, and when you are ready to fax something, follow the same steps you would to print it. Instead of sending the data for a page to a printer, the Mac sends it to your fax utility, which then asks you to input the destination fax number and similar information before dialing the remote fax machine and sending the fax. In some fax utilities, including FAXstf, which is bundled with the Mac, you can access the fax option without needing to select the fax item in the Chooser by holding down the Option key when you click on the File menu. You'll notice that the Print item has changed to Fax.

This ability can also be helpful for PowerBook/iBook users on the road if they need to print something but don't have access to a printer. If in a hotel, send a fax to yourself using the hotel's fax machine. If you aren't staying at a hotel, most copy and printing shops allow you to send faxes to their fax machines for a fee.

Voice Mail, Speakerphone, and Other Telephony Features

Usually, modems just use your phone line to send data to another modem and another computer. However, because your phone line plugs into the modem, you can use it for a variety of other phone-related tasks. These include setting up a voice mail system for your home or office, using your computer as a speakerphone to call other people, turning your Mac into a Caller ID box, and even setting up more sophisticated features like fax-on-demand service (where a caller calls your computer, enters their fax number, and is faxed a document automatically) or auto-forwarding calls to a specific number or extension. All of these features fall into a category known as *telephony*.

Some modems come with hardware built into them to handle various telephony tasks out of the box. When the modem's software drivers are installed, so are the needed applications or control panels to enable and control the hardware-based telephony services. These modems tend to be more expensive by varying degrees than conventional modems.

Beyond using special modems to enable telephony services, there are a number of software packages that will work with whatever modem you have installed to offer telephony features. These software packages require more resources from your Mac (RAM, processor time, speakers and/or microphones, and such) in order to operate. They may also present more problems in terms of crashing or conflicting with other applications you may be running at a given time.

Whether or not you want to use your Mac for telephony services is up to you and your specific needs. However, remember that if you rely on your Mac for these functions and your Mac crashes or freezes, these services will cease to be available. In some cases, it may simply be a more logical option, particularly for home users, to just buy an answering machine, a speakerphone telephone, and a Caller ID box for your phone

TABLE 31-3

*Major Mac
Telephony
Software Packages.*

Title	Manufacturer	Features
Phone Pro	Bing Software	Network- and pager-integrated voice mail, phone menu navigation, fax-back, and call routing
PhoneMaker	MicroMat	Office voice mail, voice-response, fax-on demand
MacComCenter	Smith Micro	Voice mail, Caller ID, paging

line. Small offices, however, can benefit greatly from the professional quality and array of services offered by some telephony solutions, such a sophisticated voice mail and phone menu features. Table 31-3 lists a few of the more full featured and popular Mac telephony software packages.

Portable Mac Modems and Cell Phones

Today it seems almost everyone owns a cell phone. One thing many portable Mac owners wonder about is whether they can attach their Mac to their cell phone and access the Internet (or another online service). The answer to this question is yes, but with some provisions.

First, you'll need a modem that supports cellular phone-based connections. This is because cell phones don't work the same as a traditional "land-line" phones do. The most obvious difference is that they don't have a dial tone. Dialing a cell phone involves entering the number and then pressing a Send button (which many cell phones now label Talk or OK). These differences mean that a modem has to function somewhat differently when it is communicating through a cell phone. The internal modem of the PowerBook and the iBook do not support cellular phone connections at all. A number of PC Card modems that can be used with PowerBooks, however, do support such connections. There are also several USB modems (or special adapter devices) that allow modem communication over a cell phone.

The second thing you'll need is a cell phone that supports data transmission. Because cell phones function differently than traditional phones, some of them are not designed to cope with data transmission. You should check your cell phone's manual to see if it supports data transmission. Going hand in hand with this is the need for a data cable that connects a cellular-capable modem to a cell phone. Since cell phones don't have a traditional phone jack, you need a special cable that will support both your modem and your cell phone. Cellular-capable modems usually come with a cell phone cable, but you may need to contact the modem's manufacturer for a cable that matches your phone (assuming they make one that supports your phone).

Once you have the modem and the cell phone, you need software that supports making a cell phone connection. This is the reason you should buy a Mac-specific cellular-capable modem, as it should include any dialing software you may need. Some online services, such as America Online, support cellular connections directly in their applications without the need for such software.

Even once you have the modem, phone, and software, don't expect that you're going to get terrific connection speeds. Cell phones rely on radio transmissions with connection quality that is not as strong as a traditional phone at the best of times. And that connection quality will vary as you move from place to place. At the very best, cell phones tend to offer connection speeds of 14.4 Kbps or lower (most of the time, speeds are slower than 9600 bps). Needless to say, these connections are passable for checking e-mail or uploading small text files, but they are not going to be high enough for real web surfing.

Protecting Your Modem and Mac from Power Surges

A power surge from an electrical outlet can be transmitted to the Mac's internal circuitry and cause serious damage to many of the Mac's internal components. The same is true of a phone line. Phone lines do carry a small electrical current, needed for a phone to function without an external power source of its own and to provide the electrical signals that a phone line uses to transmit voices or other sounds. Just like an electrical line from your power company, a phone line can experience surges in power. These surges are less common and, usually, less powerful than those experienced from an electrical outlet.

As you read in Chapter 11, the Mac's power supply includes components to help filter out minor surges. A modem doesn't have such components, which makes it more susceptible to even minor power fluctuations. In the event of a surge from your phone line, your modem can easily be damaged or destroyed. Worse, the modem can transmit that power surge into your Mac (this is particularly true of internal modems) and damage your motherboard or other internal components.

Before you rush to unplug your phone line from your modem and swear never to use it again, there is a simple solution to this danger. You can use a surge protector for your incoming phone line, much the same as you should be using with the incoming AC power cable for your Mac. Most surge protectors today even have phone jacks built into them to offer surge protection on your phone line.

Beyond the danger posed by a traditional phone line, there is an even greater threat of power surges wreaking havoc on your Mac through its modem: plugging your modem into a digital phone line. Digital phone lines such as PBX (Private Branch Exchange) or voice ISDN lines are often used in office buildings and other institutions that have their own internal phone system, including some hotels. Digital phone lines don't transmit data in the same analog method as traditional phone lines. Rather, they transmit signals in discrete data packets. To do this, they have much more electrical power running through them than traditional phone lines. So much power, in fact, that often just plugging a modem into a digital phone line can destroy it and damage the motherboard and internal components of a computer attached to it.

There are two ways to avoid having your modem and your Mac fried by a digital phone line. The first is to simply avoid using a digital phone line. Whenever and wherever you plug your modem in, find out first if it is a digital or PBX phone line. If there is any doubt, don't use it. The second solution is to buy a digital phone line adapter. These adapters act almost like a second modem, converting the digital phone line to analog signals your modem can understand and reducing the electrical power on the line to a safe level at the same time.

Troubleshooting Common Modem and Connection Problems

Following are common modem problems and their solutions.

The Modem Doesn't Appear to Be Recognized by the Mac

If the modem is external, make sure that all its physical connections are secure and that it is plugged in and turned on. Also make certain that the Modem control panel or other communications software is set to use the proper port to which the modem is connected. Presuming the modem is connected, check any LED indicator lights on it that might indicate the modem has failed its built-in self-tests (in this case, the modem will need to be replaced). Also be certain that the modem gives an indication that it is functioning at all, such as an LED indicating power.

For internal modems, make sure that Internal Modem is chosen at the modem port in the Modem control panel or other communications software. If this isn't an option or doesn't help, use the Apple System Profiler to determine if the Mac is recognizing the modem as even being installed. If not, you will generally need to replace it.

Also be certain that any driver software needed for the modem to be used is installed (this is particularly true of USB modems and third-party internal modems).

The Mac Displays an Error Message Saying the Serial or Communications Port Is in Use When You Try to Use the Modem

This problem is less common in today's Macs without serial ports, but it may still happen. This means that some of the Mac OS or some application is trying to use either the modem or the port the modem is connected to. It can occur if fax software on the Mac is set to receive incoming calls, for example. It can also happen if one application is either using a modem connection or has finished using the modem but not released its claim on the modem.

The first thing to do is to make sure the modem is not being used for an Internet connection or other type of connection to another modem. If it is, disconnect that connection and then try again.

If no other applications are actively using the modem, check to see if your fax software, telephony tools, or some other communication software is waiting for incoming calls. If so, this may be the source of the problem. Try setting the application to not receive incoming calls (this process will vary depending on the application) or quitting it.

If one application has recently used the modem and has not released its claim on the modem's resource, you may need to reset the modem. For external modems, you can do this by turning the modem off and then on again. For internal modems, you can try unplugging the phone line from the modem's phone jack. If this doesn't help, try restarting the Mac.

The Mac Dials the Modem but Fails to Connect

This problem can be caused by any number of reasons, most commonly because the Mac got a busy signal or no answer. It can also indicate a problem with your phone lines, the individual connection, or the other modem. Most times the problem can be solved simply by dialing again.

If this happens repeatedly, it may indicate that you are using the wrong modem script. Check with the modem's manufacturer for another script, try choosing a different script, or try using Apple's Modem Script Generator. Also try using a different phone jack in your home or different phone cables between the phone jack and your Mac.

The problem can also indicate that your ISP or other online service is having difficulties and you are unable to connect because of those problems.

The Modem Drops a Connection

Several things can cause the modem to hang up a connection unexpectedly. Probably the most common is picking up another phone on the same line in your home or office. Another common cause is Call Waiting, which can usually be disabled for individual calls by appending *70 to the beginning of the phone number you are dialing.

Other problems that can cause a modem to drop a connection include a very noisy phone line, a problem with the other modem (such as an ISP's PPP server going down unexpectedly), limits on connection time being imposed (such as the disconnect after an idle period feature of Remote Access), or problems with your modem configuration.

There isn't much you can do about noisy lines other than trying to avoid using them. You can check with your ISP to see if they are experiencing problems. You can also check and/or change the idle connection limits in the Remote Access control panel.

If the problem is with your modem configuration, it will likely be in one of two areas: flow control or the modem script. If the problem is flow control, it is usually because hardware flow control is not enabled. If the problem is with your modem script, try using another script, checking with the modem manufacturer for newer scripts, or using the Apple Modem Script Generator to create a special script for your modem.

Resources for Further Study

The following URLs provide additional information on some of the concepts, issues, and products discussed in this chapter:

About.com Mac Hardware Modem Resources—
http://machardware.about.com/msubmodem.htm

About.com Mac Support Modem Resources—
http://macsupport.about.com/msub38.htm

Konnexx: Manufactures Digital Phone Line Adapters—
http://www.konnexx.com

CHAPTER 32

Mac
Networking

A computer network allows you to connect multiple computers (and other network devices, such as some printers) together to exchange information. Networks allow users of computers to access files without needing to physically copy them to removable media to transfer them from one computer to another. A network also allows computers to share printers and (as described in Chapter 34) an Internet connection.

This chapter looks at how to create a network of Macintosh computers. It also looks at how to configure the Macs on the network to share files with each other and to access files on a remote Mac.

Network Cabling

Your first decision when planning a network is the type of cabling that you will use to connect all the Macs and other network devices in the network. This involves determining the speed of data transmission through the network as well as the actual type of cable and other network hardware (such as hubs, bridges, transceivers, and terminators) that may be needed in order to connect all the devices using your chosen cabling method. Each cabling method will also have its own topology or method to connect the cables or devices to each other.

Two primary types of network cabling are used with the Mac: LocalTalk and Ethernet. Ethernet is the most common, since LocalTalk has been abandoned as a built-in technology on the Mac in favor of Ethernet. There are also several types of Ethernet and a few more obscure network cabling technologies. Each of these types of cabling is discussed in this section.

10/100Base-T Ethernet

Although there are multiple types of Ethernet cabling, the most common today are 10Base-T (which transmits data at 10 MB or about 1.25 MB per second maximum) and 100Base-T Ethernet (which transmits data at 100 MB or about 12.5 MB per second maximum). Both 10Base-T and 100Base-T Ethernet use the same type of physical cabling (unshielded twisted pair, or UTP, network cables) and both traditionally use a hub to connect each device in the network. The differences in the two are at the level of the hardware of the Ethernet port on the Mac (or on an expansion card installed in the Mac) and the type of hub being used.

All of the Macs covered in this book include an Ethernet port, such as the one shown in Figure 32-1) that can function for either 10Base-T or 100Base-T. If the hub a Mac is connected to is a 10Base-T network (i.e., other devices are transmitting data at 10 MB per second through the UTP network cable), the Mac's Ethernet port will behave as a 10Base-T port. If the network is a 100Base-T network, then the Mac's Ethernet port will act as a 100Base-T port and transmit data at the faster rates.

Using a Hub   10Base-T and 100Base-T Ethernet connect devices to each other through the use of hubs like the one in Figure 32-2 (switches and routers can also be used in some network situations, as described

Figure 32-1
The RJ45-style port used for both 10Base-T and 100Base-T Ethernet.

Figure 32-2
A typical Ethernet hub.

later in this section). Hubs are devices that have multiple Ethernet ports—anywhere from 4 to 50 or more. An Ethernet cable is run from each computer to a port on the hub. This is called a *star topology* and allows each computer to have an independent connection to the network. This makes tracing a broken cable very easy because it will affect only one computer.

Hubs also act as repeaters, rebroadcasting the data from one computer to all the other computers on the network. This means that, aside from the length limit between individual computers and the hub, there is no limit on how far apart each device or computer on the network can be from the other computers or devices. Because data is rebroadcast to all computers in a network, hubs do make it possible for any computer to observe or intercept network traffic being sent through the hub.

Using Multiple Hubs   Ethernet hubs can be connected to each other, allowing you to create larger networks than might be feasible with only a single hub. For example, computers for a network might be strung across multiple floors of a building, where running all the cables to a single hub would be impractical. Or you may have two computer labs at opposite ends of a school, where using a single hub for all the computers is virtually impossible.

When connecting a hub to another hub, you use a special port on the hub called an *uplink port*. This port is designed to let the hub communicate with another hub rather than with a separate device. The uplink port is also used when connecting a hub to a router to combine multiple local networks into a wide area network (the use of routers to combine multiple networks is discussed later in this chapter).

Combining 100Base-T and 10Base-T Ethernet   Although 10Base-T and 100Base-T Ethernet use the same types of cables, they cannot be readily combined into a single network. This is because they transmit data at differing speeds and using differing techniques. They also require different hubs (a 10Base-T hub versus a 100Base-T hub). Despite this initial incompatibility, it is possible to combine both in a network by using a device called a *managed hub*. A managed hub allows you to control how data is transmitted between the computers, whereas most hubs simply rebroadcast signals to any computer or device connected to the hub. Because of this ability, managed hubs can support both 100Base-T and 10Base-T Ethernet connections, albeit using separate types of ports for each. Similarly, other devices such as network bridges or routers (discussed later) can be used to bridge 10Base-T and 100Base-T networks together.

Using a Crossover Cable   Although not terribly overpriced, Ethernet hubs can be expensive if you only want to network two Macs to transfer files. For this reason, there is a special type of Ethernet cable called a *crossover cable*. A crossover cable has some of the pairs of wires reversed as to the way they are located in traditional UTP cable. This makes it possible for two (and only two) computers to exchange data via Ethernet without needing to use a hub. When using a crossover cable to connect two individual Macs, you plug each end of the cable into each Mac's Ethernet port. You then start up the two Macs and configure file sharing or other network tasks as you normally would when using Ethernet.

One concern when using older Macs is that the Mac may not initialize its Ethernet port at startup if it doesn't detect another Ethernet device. This is not a problem normally, since a hub is another Ethernet device. However, when using a crossover cable, the only other device is the other Mac. For this reason, if you are networking a current or recent Mac with an older Mac using a crossover cable, you should turn on the more recent Mac first.

Types of UTP Cable   Both 10Base-T and 100Base-T Ethernet rely on UTP cable. This is a special type of cable that resembles traditional phone cables, only with more individual wires inside each cable and a large (RJ45) connector on the end. There are a series of categories of UTP cable. Currently, there are five categories, with each category number delivering greater performance. Category 5 UTP cable (often referred to as Cat 5 network cable) is the highest UTP cable available and delivers the best performance. 100Base-T Ethernet requires the use of Cat 5 cable. 10Base-T Ethernet can function with Cat 3 or Cat 4 cable, however, it is advisable to purchase Cat 5 cable for both types of Ethernet because it does deliver clearer signals and thus better performance. This is particularly important for cable lengths of more than a few feet. Cat 5 cable is generally the only type of UTP cable that is commonly stocked by many computer stores today anyway.

Other Ethernet Types

Although 10/100Base-T Ethernet is the most common form of Ethernet used today, the Ethernet standard for data transmission can be applied to a variety of cable/wire types (in fact, the UTP cable used today is a relatively recent adoption for Ethernet). There are three other types of Ethernet that have been used in the past or are expected to be used in the future. These include the antiquated 10Base-5 standard, the more recent 10Base-2 standard, and the emerging Gigabit Ethernet. To add support for these standards to the Mac, you need to use an Ethernet expansion card that supports the appropriate connections. Alternatively, you can use a bridge to combine networks based on one of these Ethernet types with a 10Base-T or 100Base-T network or device or an adapter known as a transceiver to use the current Macs with earlier Ethernet networks.

10Base5   10Base5 Ethernet, often referred to as ThickNet, was one of the earliest cabling forms of Ethernet to be widely used. ThickNet uses a very thick (½ inch) cable to carry data at a rate of 10 MB per second. Special connectors known as vampire connectors are used to attach a device to the ThickNet cable by actually being pressed through the cable's casing like a spike until they come in contact with the wire running through the cable. These vampire connectors can only be attached to a cable at specific points every 2.5 meters of cable length (these points are usually marked on the cable). The vampire connector is then attached to a transceiver that actually deals with transmitting and receiving data along the cable. This transceiver is a device that is external to the computer. The transceiver is then attached to a special port on the computer itself.

The cable used in ThickNet does not connect to a hub, as 10Base-T and 100Base-T Ethernet do. Instead, it uses a *bus topology*, as indicated in Figure 32-3, where any computers or devices connected to the network are simply connected to a length of cable. The cable is terminated at both ends, much like a SCSI chain, to keep signal noise from being reflected along the length of the cable. If the cable is broken at any point (not likely because of the thickness of it), the entire network will likely go down. Also, because it is a bus topology, ThickNet has a limit of how long you can make the cable serving a segment of the network and how many devices can be used on that length of cable. These limits are 500 meters per segments and 100 devices, respectively.

Figure 32-3
A bus topology connects all devices to a single cable. This is unlike a start topology, where each device has its own cable running to a central hub.

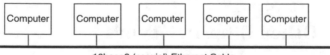

10base2 (coaxial) Ethernet Cable

The sheer size and thickness of the cable makes ThickNet very unwieldy and is one reason it is no longer used on any scale. The additional cost of a transceiver is another reason that ThickNet is not used much. For the most part, modern Ethernet cards do not include support for ThickNet.

10Base2   10Base2 Ethernet was developed as a replacement for ThickNet and is often referred to as ThinNet (because it uses much smaller cables than ThickNet), coax Ethernet (because it uses coaxial cables to transmit data), or BNC (because the connectors that connect devices to the cable are called BNC—for bayonet-Neill-Concelman—connectors). ThinNet uses coaxial cable that is extremely similar to the cable used to connector cable TV services or TV antennas to a television or VCR to transmit data at 10 MB per second. ThinNet requires a special type of coaxial cable, called RG-58 or radio-grade cable (this is sometimes also called 802.3 cable, as that is the official designation of the 10Base2 Ethernet standard), to ensure good performance of data transmission.

Like ThickNet, ThinNet is a bus topology, where a series of computers are connected to a length of cable without the use of a hub. ThinNet often uses transceivers, though they are different from the ones used with ThickNet. The ThinNet transceivers are basically T-shaped devices with three cable connectors—one for the incoming cable, one for the connector on the back of the Mac, and one for the outgoing cable. Each Mac or ThinNet device on a network will require a transceiver because you cannot just connect the end of a ThinNet cable to the BNC connector on a computer or other device. If a computer or device is at the end of the BNC cable, you still need to use a transceiver, but you also need to place a terminator where the outgoing cable would be placed to prevent the signal from being reflected at the end of the cable segment. As with ThickNet, ThinNet has a cable length limit per network segment. This limit is 185 meters. There is also a limit of 30 devices per network segment. Multiple network segments can be joined using a special device called a repeater, however.

ThinNet is much more manageable than ThickNet, and several Ethernet cards still support BNC connectors for using ThinNet networks. ThinNet is not as easy to work with as 10Base-T Ethernet because it relies on a bus topology. However, ThinNet is still used in many academic and institutional settings where an existing network was originally put into place several years ago.

Gigabit Ethernet   Whereas ThickNet and ThinNet represent past iterations of Ethernet, Gigabit Ethernet represents the future of Ethernet. As its name implies, Gigabit Ethernet is designed for data transmission rates as high as 1 gigabit (about 128 MB) per second. Gigabit Ethernet is just now beginning to be commonly used in larger institutions and corporations, and it will be quite a while before most homes or small businesses will have reason to use Gigabit Ethernet (or the money, as implementing Gigabit Ethernet is still expensive). The latest versions of the Power Mac G4 now ship with an Ethernet port that supports Gigabit Ethernet.

LocalTalk

Ethernet was not the first network cabling used in the Mac. Originally, Apple designed their own cabling scheme called LocalTalk that used the serial port built into every Mac until the iMac. LocalTalk was mentioned in Chapter 30, because it is the Mac serial port that serves as the connector for LocalTalk cables.

LocalTalk served as a low-cost networking option for small- to medium-sized Mac networks for years. There was no additional hardware needed beyond the cables and connectors themselves. Although LocalTalk was relatively slow compared to most Ethernet variations, at only 230 kilobits per second at best (1/40 the potential of 10Base-T Ethernet), its much lower cost made it attractive to many home users who didn't need all the bandwidth and performance provided by Ethernet. LocalTalk is limited to only 32 computers or other network devices. It is also has a total cable length limitation of 1800 feet for the entire network.

Another disadvantage of LocalTalk is that it doesn't support the TCP/IP network protocol (discussed later in this chapter). Rather, LocalTalk is limited to AppleTalk networking. However, it is possible with the right additional utilities to disguise TCP/IP data as AppleTalk so that it can be transmitted over LocalTalk.

LocalTalk Cables and Transceivers   Originally, LocalTalk consisted of special LocalTalk cables. These cables resembled serial port cable but had only three pins for transmitting information. LocalTalk cables were plugged into devices known as LocalTalk transceivers. The transceiver was then plugged into a Mac's serial port. Each transceiver provided ports for two LocalTalk cables, which allowed users to connect multiple devices together without needing a hub or similar device. If only one port on a transceiver was being used, a terminating resistor needed to be inserted in the unused port to prevent electrical signals from being reflected back from the unused port (much like the termination at the end of a SCSI chain).

PhoneNet Connectors   LocalTalk cables and transceivers performed adequately, but they were a little high priced for many users. Additionally, the cables were bulky and inflexible, making them less attractive to use for networks spanning more than one room. Farallon introduced an alternative that eventually took over almost the entire LocalTalk cabling market called PhoneNet connectors, such as the one shown in Figure 32-4.

As mentioned in Chapter 30, PhoneNET connectors plug into a Mac's serial port like a LocalTalk transceiver. Instead of using connectors for LocalTalk cables, however, PhoneNET connectors include standard RJ11 phone jacks. Using standard phone cable (the kind you'd use to connect a phone to the jack in the wall), PhoneNET connectors could be joined together to provide a LocalTalk network. Phone cable is far cheaper and much more manageable than LocalTalk cables.

Like LocalTalk transceivers, PhoneNET connectors usually have two phone jacks for connecting multiple computers or devices into a LocalTalk network. PhoneNET connectors also require that a terminator be placed in an unused phone jack (one is usually included with the connector). Although uncommon, there are also some PhoneNET connectors that include only one phone jack for connecting a single device. Figure 32-5 illustrates how multiple computers or other LocalTalk devices can be networked using either LocalTalk cables and transceivers or PhoneNET connectors and phone cable.

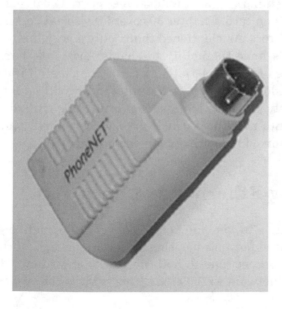

Figure 32-4
A PhoneNET connector.

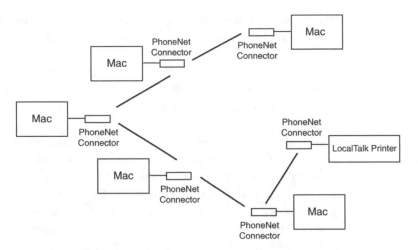

Figure 32-5
LocalTalk devices are connected in a modified bus topology because each connection can support two devices, forming a chain.

Using a Serial Printer Cable to Connect Two Macs   A standard Mac serial cable (such as those used for serial port printers) can serve to connect two Macs using LocalTalk. Simply attach the cable to a serial port on each Mac. The two Macs can then be networked with LocalTalk communication passing through the serial cable as it would over LocalTalk cabling.

LocalTalk on Today's Macs   Today's Macs don't ship with a serial port, which makes them unable to support LocalTalk without the use of an expansion card. Chapter 30 covers the serial port expansion cards and USB adapters. As mentioned there, only a very limited selection of serial port cards have the ability to enable LocalTalk communication. These are limited to those serial port cards that install in the comm (internal modem) slot on a current Macintosh. Beyond adding such a card, the only way to integrate today's Macs into a LocalTalk network or LocalTalk devices into an Ethernet network (which today's Macs can access) is to create a mixed network of both cable types.

Mixing Ethernet and LocalTalk

It is possible to combine LocalTalk- and Ethernet-based networks into a single mixed network by using a network bridge. A bridge is a device that contains connections to both networks and allows data to flow across from one network to the other. This bridges the two networks into a single network much as a physical bridge combines the roads on either side of a river into a single roadway for travel.

There are two types of LocalTalk/Ethernet bridges: hardware and software.

Using a Hardware Bridge   Hardware bridges are devices that are dedicated to doing nothing but acting as a bridge. These devices include the EtherMac, Etherwave, and iPrint devices from Farallon, the AsantéTalk from Asanté, and the Sonic Systems' microPrint. These devices all have an Ethernet port and a LocalTalk port. To use them, you simply plug a cable from each network into the appropriate port on the bridge. The bridge then transfers network data and requests between the two networks.

Using a Mac as a Software Bridge   A software bridge is a Mac running Apple's LocalTalk Bridge control panel (which can be downloaded free from Apple's Support site) that has both Ethernet and LocalTalk ports. Since a Mac with Ethernet and LocalTalk ports can be connected to both types of networks, it can perform the same function as a hardware bridge, passing network traffic from one network to another.

Other Network "Cabling" Types

Ethernet and LocalTalk make up the two primary types of Mac network cabling used in the past and today, but they are not the only network cabling options available. Apple's AirPort wireless networking technology can be considered another type of network cabling, even though there are no cables. So can the infrared network option built into some Macs. Also growing in popularity are the kits that allow you to network Macs using the phone lines in your house.

Infrared Networking   Infrared, or IR, networking is a form of wireless networking where data is transmitted as beams of infrared light (which is outside the spectrum discernible by human vision), much like those used by a television or VCR remote control. Several Macs have supported IR networking, almost all of them PowerBook models (the revision A and B iMacs also supported IR networking). IR network connection speeds will vary depending on the IR ports of the Macs being used but will be no faster than 4 MB per second.

Although IR networking isn't used much, it is still available to Macs

Figure 32-6
Right: The IR port on
the first iMacs
(revisions A and B
only). Left: The IR port
on a PowerBook.

that shipped with an IR port. To use IR networking, both Macs being networked need to have an IR port. You select the IR port for network use the same as you would Ethernet or LocalTalk, point the IR ports of the two Macs at each other, and then connect and share files in the same manner as using any other network cabling type, as discussed later in this chapter. You also need to be certain that nothing blocks the line of sight between the two IR ports, or the network connection will be lost. Figure 32-6 shows the IR ports on a revision A iMac and a PowerBook.

AirPort and Radio-Based Wireless Networking   While infrared networking was technically wireless, it still had some distinct limitations (a maximum distance of a few feet between the computers exchanging data and the requirement of an uninterrupted line of sight, for example). Far better is the current use of radio-frequency-based wireless networking. For Macintosh computers, wireless networking today is enabled by Apple's AirPort wireless networking technology. AirPort can provide transfer speeds as high as 11 MB per second, making it equivalent to 10Base-T Ethernet. The next chapter of this book focuses on setting up and maintaining AirPort networks.

Home Phoneline Networking   Go to the network section of most computer stores today and you'll find kits for networking computers using the phone lines built into a house. These kits are primarily aimed at PC users, but some also allow you to network Macs in this manner. These kits use the phone cables within your home to transmit data between computers. You install a special device on your Mac (usually a PCI card or USB device) and then connect the device to one of the phone jacks in your house. This is done for all the Macs (or PCs) you want to network.

These kits work because most homes have phone cables with four separate wires in them. Only two of these four wires are used for a standard phone line (though if you have two phone lines, you will be using all four wires). If you are only using two of these four wires for a standard phone line, then you can use one of the sets of wires to transmit data. The important consideration is that the wires being used must be closed and not in use by the phone company (which may pose problems if you live in an apartment). The kits themselves usually use a proprietary network style all their own.

Once all the Macs you wish to network are connected, and assuming there are no problems with the phone lines in your home, your Macs will have access to the kit as a type of network cabling. Phone line network kits are usually limited to data transfer rates of 1 to 2 MB per second at best. They are also usually not interchangeable, meaning you'll need to use the same type of kit for every Mac in the house.

Combining Different Networks

It is possible to join two or more networks into a larger network. There are two ways to do this. The first way is to join the two using a bridge, which is often the tool for combining networks of different types (LocalTalk and Ethernet, for example). The second way is to use a router. This is done when you want to maintain some separation between the networks, but still have users on network be able to interact with devices on another network.

Bridges   As mentioned, you can combine varying types of networks, such as LocalTalk and Ethernet into a single network using a bridge. When this is done, the two networks that are joined behave as a single network, with data being passed through both segments as though there was little or no difference between the two. In addition to LocalTalk/Ethernet bridges, there are bridges for combining multiple types of Ethernet (this includes some special hubs, usually referred to as managed hubs), and Apple's AirPort Base Station can function as a wireless/Ethernet bridge combining wireless and Ethernet networks.

Routers   While bridges make one big network out of different types of networks, there are times when you will want to join networks together for transferring data between them but keep the two (or more) individual networks as separate networks. This is the task of a router. A router is a device that can be connected to multiple networks. The networks joined by a router remain independent networks. Traffic between devices in each separate network is not shared with the other joined networks unless access to a specific device on another network is requested. This keeps the traffic in one network from slowing down the performance of another network. Each individual network is referred to as a local area network (LAN) while the entire combination of LANs is referred to as a wide area network (WAN).

Using a router to join networks is generally only done in corporate or institutional networks where each department primarily shares files or devices with only other users in that department but might have reason to access data in another department occasionally. For example, in a company the advertising office and the accounting department aren't likely to share files very often. So, there is no logical reason for access to the accounting department's shared spreadsheets to be slowed down by traffic generated by the advertising department members sharing large image files intended for ad brochures with each other. Still, there might be an occasion where the advertising department needs to check something in a budget file stored in the accounting department.

Besides restricting network traffic, routers also allow administrators to organize file servers and shared printers for users. In a company with 20 servers and 30 shared printers, finding the server or printers intended specifically for the press office would be time-consuming if all the servers and printers were in one list. However, if the press office has a separate network from every other department, then their servers and printers would be listed separately from everyone else's. And if someone in the press office needed to access a server in the human resources department, he or she could look at the servers specific to human resources rather than the list of all the company's servers.

Network Protocols

Once you've decided on the cabling your network will use and installed the physical cables and other hardware such as hubs, routers, and bridges as needed to connect all the Macs in the network, you need to make it possible for the Macs to exchange data over the network. You do this by selecting a network protocol. A *network protocol* is a language that computers use to transmit data to each other over a network (whether a small two-Mac network or the entire Internet). The network protocol gives each computer on the network a unique identity so that other computers can recognize it to send data to it or recognize where data sent from it originated. The network protocol also determines how data is split up into small packets of information and how those packets are moved from one computer to another.

There are a number of different network protocols that are used in computers today, but only two that most Mac users or administrators will need to use regularly. These are AppleTalk, the original Mac networking protocol, and TCP/IP, the protocol used by the Internet. Historically, AppleTalk has been the primary protocol used by Mac networks. However, there has been a distinct shift to using TCP/IP on the Mac in recent years. This section discusses both of these protocols, their advantages, and how to implement each of them.

AppleTalk

AppleTalk is Apple's own networking protocol. It has been a part of every Mac OS release, allowing any Mac ever made to access an AppleTalk network for file and printer sharing. For the most part, AppleTalk is a very simple protocol to work with. This is because when the Mac starts up or AppleTalk is turned on, the Mac will assign itself a network address, checks to see if that address is already in use by another Mac on the network, and chooses a different address if it is. Although a user can manually enter an AppleTalk network address, this is usually not something that needs to be done. Most Mac users simply need to turn on AppleTalk and are ready to go. In addition to defining each Mac or other device on a network, an AppleTalk address defines each individual network. When a router is used to join multiple AppleTalk networks, the AppleTalk address defines each separate network as a zone that is distinct from the others.

Beyond its simplicity, AppleTalk offers two other advantages. First, it is not a universal network protocol used by almost every computer. This and the inherent design of the AppleTalk protocol make it a much more secure network protocol than TCP/IP. This is particularly important if you are using the same network cabling for your Internet connection as you are for your local network and file sharing (as is the case in many offices that rely on an office building's high-speed Internet connection or in homes using a cable modem).

Second, AppleTalk is a separate network protocol from TCP/IP, allowing you to exist on two separate networks at once (provided each uses separate cabling). This is important for home users with dial-up Internet connections. If your home network uses AppleTalk, you can maintain your AppleTalk connection and use a dial-up Internet connection (which is a TCP/IP network connection) at the same time. If you use TCP/IP for your home network, you need to switch between your home network settings and your ISP's dial-up access settings, because the Mac can only support one TCP/IP configuration at a time.

AppleTalk Zones   Earlier in the chapter, you read about routers being used to join separate local networks into a wide area network. When using AppleTalk, each individual LAN is referred to as an AppleTalk zone. When accessing AppleTalk servers or printers, users are allowed access to various zones in the network (unless the administrator password protects a zone), but by default, only the machines in their zone are displayed unless they choose to access another zone.

The AppleTalk Control Panel   The AppleTalk control panel has three user modes: basic, advanced, and administration. Figure 32-7 shows the advanced mode of the AppleTalk control panel. For most use, the basic mode will suffice. The AppleTalk control panel has two main sections: the Connect Via pop-up menu and the Setup section. The Connect Via menu allows you to specify which port or cabling method the Mac should use to access an AppleTalk network. For today's Macs, the options will usually be Ethernet Built-in (which uses the Mac's built-in Ethernet port), AirPort (if an AirPort card is installed), or Remote Only (which is used to define a dial-up connection using AppleTalk Remote Access). Other

Figure 32-7
The AppleTalk control panel.

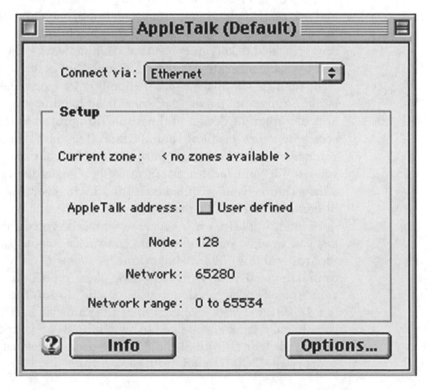

options may include an infrared port, an alternate wireless network card, a home phone line networking device, or a serial port (if a serial port card is installed that supports LocalTalk). Simply choose the method your Mac will use to connect to an AppleTalk network.

The Setup section will vary depending on which user mode is used in the AppleTalk control panel (you can switch between user modes using the User Mode command in the Edit menu). It will always include the Current Zone item, which specifies which AppleTalk zone the computer resides in if the network has more than one zone. In the advanced and administrator modes, the Setup section also displays the AppleTalk address that the Mac has chosen and the AppleTalk node it is using. It also allows you to specify a specific network number and node if you choose. The administrator mode allows you to lock each AppleTalk item with a password so that no user can change the settings.

Enabling AppleTalk   Once you have chosen the appropriate connection method in the AppleTalk control panel's Connect Via menu, you may need to make AppleTalk active. You can do this in three ways. First is the Options button in the AppleTalk control panel, second is the AppleTalk radio buttons in the Chooser, and third is with the AppleTalk control strip module. Each of these options is shown in Figure 32-8. Once AppleTalk is active, you can begin sharing files over your physical network using AppleTalk or log in to AppleTalk file servers as described later in this chapter.

TCP/IP

TCP/IP is a network protocol originally developed for UNIX machines that has become used by virtually every modern computer platform. It is the protocol on which the Internet is based. As a result, TCP/IP is cross-platform. Macintosh file sharing and related network functions (printer sharing, program linking, and such) can be performed over TCP/IP. This offers two major advantages. First, TCP/IP is an inherently faster protocol than AppleTalk, meaning data is transferred between computers on a network faster when using TCP/IP. Second, you can log in to Mac file servers over the Internet as easily as you would one on your local network.

Although TCP/IP itself is cross-platform, file sharing over it is not. Out of the box, Macintosh computers cannot access Windows file servers over TCP/IP and PCs cannot access Macintosh file servers over TCP/IP. There are utilities enabling the two to share files via TCP/IP (see Chapter 41). Network printers that use the TCP/IP protocol, however,

Figure 32-8
AppleTalk can be turned on and off by (top to bottom) the AppleTalk control panel's Options button, the Chooser, or the AppleTalk control strip module.

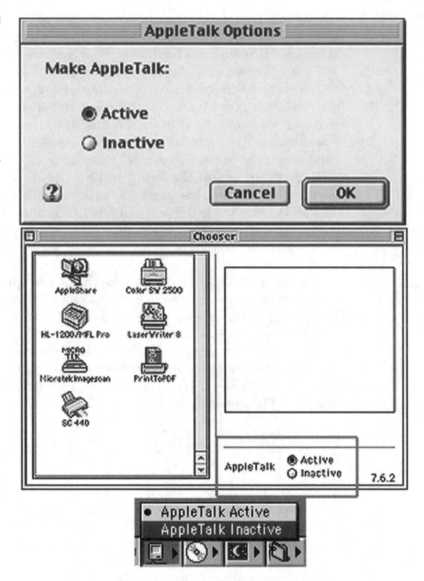

Figure 32-8
AppleTalk can be turned on and off by (top to bottom) the AppleTalk control panel's Options button, the Chooser, or the AppleTalk control strip module.

are often accessible by both Macs and PCs, provided both platforms use the same page description language as the printer.

TCP/IP is a slightly more complicated protocol to use for networking than AppleTalk. You need to make sure each computer on a TCP/IP network has a unique IP address and is configured to access any routers or domain name servers that your network is using. These individual issues are discussed in the following sections.

IP Addresses   Every computer on a TCP/IP network requires a unique IP address, much like every computer on an AppleTalk network requires a network address. IP addresses are four numbers (each ranging from 0 to 255) separated by periods, such as 192.168.1.56. On a closed network, you can use whatever IP addresses you wish to assign to a computer or other device. However, if your network is going to be connected to the Internet, you are limited to what IP addresses you can use. This is because the Internet is one giant TCP/IP network, and no two computers on the Internet can have the same IP addresses. If your network is connected to the Internet, you can either use a series of IP addresses provided by the Internet service provider that is providing your network its Internet connection for each Mac (which can get expensive, since you are paying for each address) or you can assign your Macs to use on one of the series of private network IP addresses (which begin with 192.168. or 10.0). These addresses are ignored by the Internet at large, which means you can use these for your internal network. However, Macs using private IP addresses will not be able to access the Internet (at least not without an Internet router, which enables a network to share one Internet connection and is discussed in Chapter 34).

Assigning and Distributing IP Addresses   Unlike AppleTalk addresses, where a Mac can randomly pick an address on its own, TCP/IP requires that each Mac be assigned an IP address. There are a series of methods for assigning IP addresses. The simplest is to manually assign each Mac a static IP address. In this case, an administrator will personally give each computer a specific IP address. This is the simplest per Mac, but it can easily get confusing if you have a network of hundreds or thousands of computers and other network devices.

More commonly, a special server can be run on one of the computers on the network. This server will be given a series of IP addresses that can be assigned to each computer as it starts up or makes contact with the network. When using such a server, the administrator needs only to tell the server what addresses to share, and then Macs will be provided with the address automatically. The most common of these server types is a DHCP (Dynamic Host Configuration Protocol). There are also two less common servers that can provide IP addresses dynamically: Boot-P and RARP. For dial-up connections, a PPP server often performs the same function, as well as establishing the modem connection with the computer.

If no IP address is assigned to the Mac and the Mac is unable to locate a server to request an IP address from, it will automatically assign itself an address beginning with 169.254. These addresses cannot be used for transferring data, however.

The TCP/IP Control Panel   The TCP/IP control panel, shown in Figure 32-9, allows you to adjust the TCP/IP network settings on a Mac. The control panel contains three user modes—basic, advanced, and administrator—though the primary settings are available in all of these modes. The primary settings for TCP/IP include the Connect Via pop-up menu, the configure menu, and the name server address box.

The Connect Via menu is where you tell the Mac which network connection you want to use to establish a TCP/IP connection. This serves the same purpose as the Connect Via menu in the AppleTalk control panel, though it may contain more options. In addition to the built-in ports available for network choices, TCP/IP's Connect Via menu will include PPP, which is used for dial-up Internet connections, and AppleTalk (MacIP). AppleTalk allows you to use TCP/IP communication over a LocalTalk network by disguising TCP/IP data packets as AppleTalk packets (LocalTalk does not support the TCP/IP protocol), provided your network has a server, router, or bridge that supports converting the packets back into traditional TCP/IP data using the MacIP protocol.

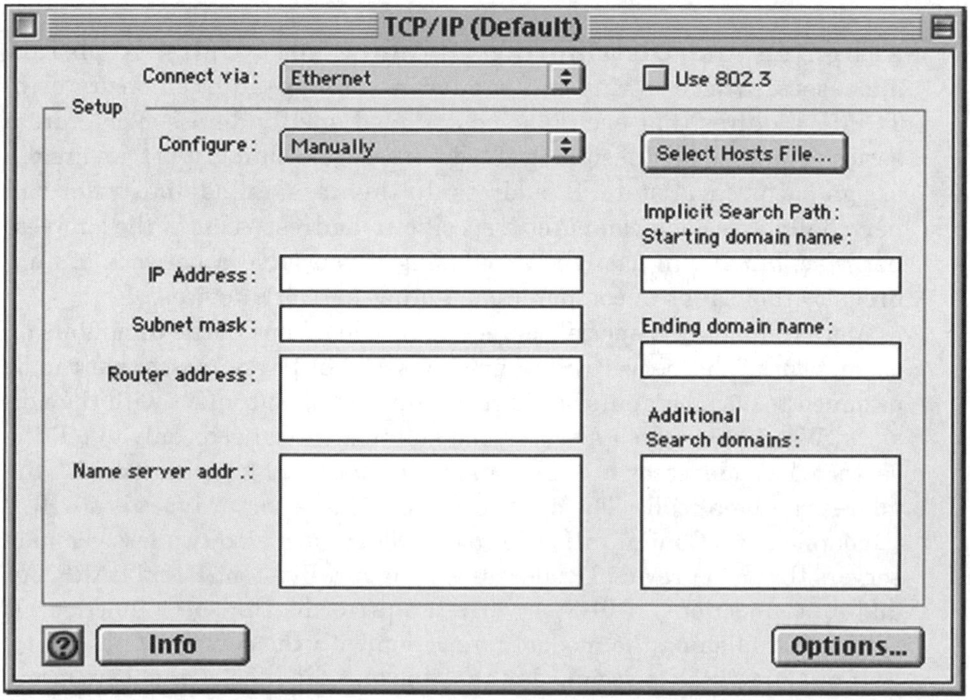

Figure 32-9   The TCP/IP control panel.

The Configure menu lets you tell the Mac if it should use a server to obtain its IP address and related information or that the information will be manually entered. If you choose to configure the Mac's IP address manually, you will also see a series of text boxes beneath the menu for entering the Mac's IP address, the subnet mask number for the Mac, and the IP address of the router the Mac will use to communicate with other networks or the Internet. The subnet mask indicates what class of IP address your Mac is using. If you are using one of the ranges of private IP addresses, this will be 255.255.255.0. If you are using a public IP address provided by an ISP, the ISP should tell you the appropriate subnet mask for your IP address. The Router Address is the IP address assigned for the router on your network or the router of your ISP (if you have a closed network with no router, this field can be left empty).

The Name Server Address box is where you should enter the IP address of the domain name servers that your Mac will use. Domain name servers convert IP addresses into actual domain names (17.254.3.183 into www.apple.com, for example). Domain names are easier to remember than IP addresses of specific machines on a TCP/IP network. If your network will function as an intranet with domain name servers, or if the Mac will access the Internet (either directly or through your network), you should enter the IP address of the domain name servers to use here (press Return between individual addresses if entering multiple servers).

If you will be switching a Mac between multiple TCP/IP configurations (such as a PowerBook between home dial-up Internet access and an office network or an iMac with multiple dial-up Internet accounts), you can create multiple configuration files. This allows you to store a configuration and switch between stored configurations without needing to change the individual items in the TCP/IP control panel each time. You do this by using the Configurations command under the File menu.

Once you have configured the TCP/IP control panel in a Mac on your network, you can begin sharing files or accessing Mac file servers over TCP/IP, as described in the next sections.

Setting Up and Using File Sharing on a Mac

Once you have the physical network in place and have configured AppleTalk, TCP/IP, or both for your network, you need to enable file sharing on the individual Macs that will be acting as file servers. This section describes how to configure file sharing and how to create individual user accounts. It also describes how to share specific folders or disks on a Mac with network users. This is followed by a description of how to log in to a Mac and access shared resources.

The File Sharing Control Panel

The File Sharing control panel is the interface you use to allow other Mac users to log in to your Mac over a network and access shared files. It contains three separate tabs: Start/Stop, Activity Monitor, and Users and Groups. Figure 32-10 shows all three of these tabs.

The Mac's Identity   The Mac's Identity refers to the name the Mac has as a file server on your network. You can give the Mac any name that you want, provided no other Mac is already using that name. You are given the option of choosing a name for your Mac when you run the Mac OS Setup Assistant after first starting a new Mac or installing the Mac OS. The Mac's name is displayed in the Computer Name box in the Start/Stop tab of the File Sharing control panel. You can change it anytime you like (though you should keep one consistent name so other people on the network can recognize your Mac).

Associated with the Mac's name is the owner name. This is the username of the person who "owns" or controls access to that Mac. The owner name can be a person's actual name, or it can be any username you wish to use. The owner password is the password that is associated with the owner username. To log in to the Mac over the network and have access to the owner's privileges, you need to use this username and password.

File Sharing and Program Linking   The Start or Stop File Sharing button does exactly what its name implies: It either initiates file sharing, allowing people to log in to the Mac through a network and access shared files, or it deactivates file sharing so that users cannot log in to the Mac (and allows you to disconnect all users already connected).

Program linking is a function where users logged in to a Mac over the network can launch applications from that Mac. This allows them to run an application without first copying it to or installing it on the Mac on which they are working. Program linking is enabled or disabled with the appropriate button on in the Start/Stop tab of the File Sharing control panel. Program linking can make it easier for users to use the same application, but it will also slow down network performance because any Mac running

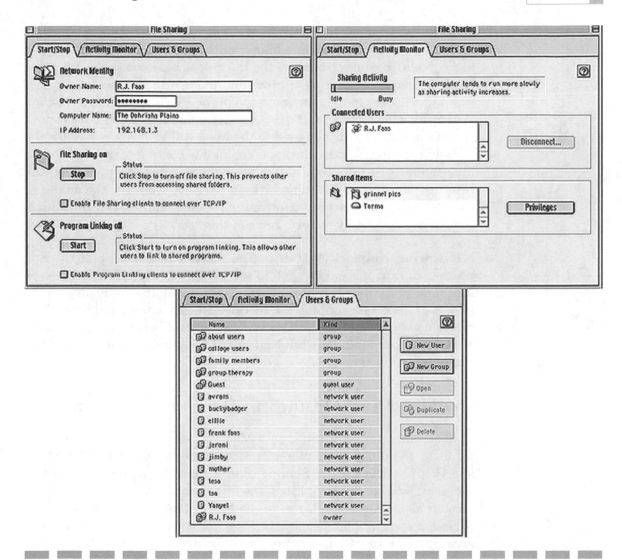

Figure 32-10 The three tabs of the File Sharing control panel.

an application from a remote Mac will constantly be transmitting data with that remote Mac. This will also decrease the performance of the linked application compared to its performance when running on a Mac's local hard drive.

Sharing over TCP/IP Until recently, Macs have only been able to share files using the AppleTalk protocol. However, Mac OS 9 has added the built-in ability to share files using the TCP/IP protocol. This enables faster file sharing because TCP/IP is a faster protocol than AppleTalk. It also allows users to log in to a Mac over the Internet, provided the Mac has a public IP address, because the Internet is based on the TCP/IP protocol. To enable file sharing or program linking over TCP/IP, use the relevant checkboxes in the Start/Stop tab of the File Sharing control panel. When file sharing over TCP/IP is enabled, the Mac's IP address (and domain name, if one is assigned to the Mac) will be displayed below the checkbox. Be aware that when you enable file sharing over TCP/IP on a Mac connected to the Internet, it becomes possible for anyone on the Internet to access your Mac and its shared files (following the advice in the "Network Security" section later in this chapter can minimize, though not completely remove, some of this risk)

Monitoring Network Activity   The Activity Monitor tab of the File Sharing control panel allows you to see what users are connected to your Mac (and to forcibly disconnect them if you wish). It also displays what folders or disks on your Mac are currently being shared, and to see how much network activity (accessing or copying files) is going on with respect to your Mac. This tab contains three sections (each devoted to one of these functions).

Creating and Managing Users and Groups

To allow other users to log in to your Mac, you need to create user accounts for them. Creating and editing user accounts is the function of the Users and Groups tab of the File Sharing control panel. When you first use this tab, there will be two users listed, the owner name and Guest. The Guest account allows anyone to log in to the Mac without needing to provide a password and shouldn't be used, because there is no control over who can access the Mac (the Guest account's access is disabled by default).

Users   To create a new user, press the New User button. A window like the one in Figure 32-11 will open for you to enter information about the new user. There are three areas of information you can enter about users: their identity (username and password, and if the user is allowed to change that password on their own), their sharing information (whether they are allowed to log in to a Mac, what groups they belong to, and whether or not they can access programs shared from the Mac), and Remote Access (which allows them to dial into the computer using a modem). You choose which of these three you want to enter or change using the Show pop-up menu at the top of the window.

Figure 32-11
The User window
lets you enter or
adjust information for
each user account
on the Mac.

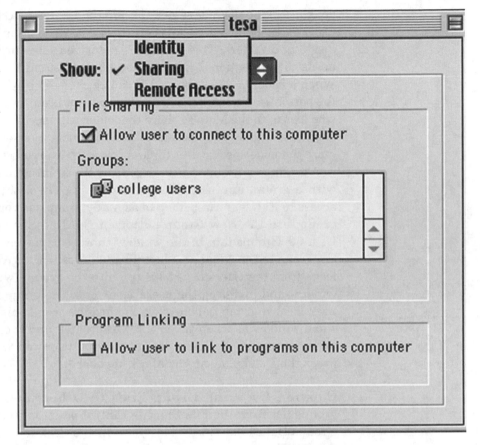

Figure 32-11
The User window
lets you enter or
adjust information for
each user account
on the Mac.

When you've entered all this information (only the username and password are needed at first), close the window, and the user's account will be created. Once you've created a user, you can change the user's settings later by selecting the user's icon and clicking on the Open button (or double-clicking the icon). You can select a user's icon and use the Delete button if you want to erase his or her account.

Be careful when selecting an existing user's icon. If you click on just the user's name, it will become highlighted (much like an icon's name in the Finder), and you will be able to type a different username in its place. This will not delete the user's account, but it will change the username of the account to whatever you type (thus making it impossible for the user to log in with his or her original username).

Groups By default, only one account has complete access to all the files on a Mac's hard drive: the owner account (this ability can be disabled by double-clicking the Mac owner's icon in the Users and Groups list). All other users must be given permission to access various hard drives (or other disks) and folders. This process is described later in the chapter, but it needs to be mentioned here for you to understand the concept of groups. When a folder or disk is shared, it can be accessed by the owner of the Mac, the person who created the folder, by a user or group of users, or by any user who logs in to the Mac. To share the folder with specific multiple users, you need to create a group because it isn't possible to share a folder with any more than one specific user (unless you want everyone to have access to it).

A group is a group of user accounts. When an item is set to be shared with a group, any user whose account is part of that group will have access to it. Users can belong to as many groups as you want. To create a group, use the New Group button in the File Sharing control panel's Users & Groups tab. In the window that is displayed, enter the name of the group in the Name text box. To add users to the group, just drag their icons from the Users & Groups tab into the group's window (or close the window and just drag the users' icons onto the group icon). To remove a user from a group double-click the group's icon. This will bring up the same window as when the group was created and it contains a list of all users in the group. Select the icon of the user you wish to remove and press the Delete key on the Mac's keyboard.

Copying User and Group Files to Other Macs   The users and groups list from the File Sharing control panel is stored in the Users & Groups Data File. This file is stored in the Preferences folder within the System Folder. You can make a copy of this file. Copying the Users & Groups Data File can be done for two reasons. First is to create a backup of the file. In case the original file becomes corrupted, the Mac's hard drive becomes damaged beyond repair, or the Mac requires a clean install of the Mac OS, you can use the backup to restore user and group settings without needing to reenter all the information manually.

The other reason to copy this file is to use the same user and groups settings on another Mac. If you have multiple Macs in a network that the same users will be accessing over the network, it makes sense to use a single username and password for each user on all of the Macs. Similarly, you may want the same groups of users to be able to access shared items on various Macs. Copying the Users & Groups Data File from one Mac and using the same file on every Mac allows you to do this without needing to enter the same settings manually on every Mac in the network. Just remember to update the copy on all Macs regularly to account for password changes by individual users, changes in what users are in what groups, and to add new users to all Macs.

Choosing Which Items to Share

Once you've enabled file sharing on your Mac and you've created user accounts for whoever will be logging in to the Mac to access files on it, you need to actually choose individual items to be shared. Only the Mac's owner account has the ability to access every folder, file, and hard drive on a Mac. When choosing to share items on your Mac, you can enable sharing of either a folder or a disk. You cannot share individual files.

Sharing a Folder or Disk   To share a hard drive (or other disk) or folder with other users, you need to select the drive or folder icon in the Finder and use the Finder's Get Info command. Use the Get Info window's Show pop-up menu to select Sharing. The result will be like the window shown in Figure 32-12. To allow the folder or drive to be shared, check the Share This Item and Its Contents checkbox. The disk or folder can now be shared with other users.

Once you've allowed a folder to be shared, you need to indicate which users will be allowed to access the folder or disk. You do this using the User/Group pop-up menu. This menu contains every user and group that has been created in the Mac's File Sharing control panel. From that menu, you can choose either an individual user or a group of users to allow access to the folder/disk. This is where using groups becomes valuable, because you can only choose one item from this menu, meaning you cannot choose two separate users.

You can also share an item with everyone who has access to the Mac. This item is directly below the User/Group menu. To give everyone access to an item, you simply adjust the access privileges associated with the Everyone item.

Choosing Access Privileges   In addition to choosing who will have access to a shared item, you need to determine what level of access they will have. The Privilege pop-up menus allow you to choose access privileges for a shared item. There are four access levels you can choose from for a shared item. Read and Write allows users to be able to open files in the shared folder or on the shared disk and make changes to it (or to move and delete files) Read Only allows users to open files in the shared item but not to make any changes (nor can they move or delete files). Write Only allows people to store files in a shared folder but not to be able to see or open any files that are already there. This is also referred to as "drop box" because it functions like a drop box, enabling users to drop off files (say, reports for a supervisor) without being able to look at whatever is in the folder (say the reports of their coworkers). The final access level is None, where users cannot even open the shared item.

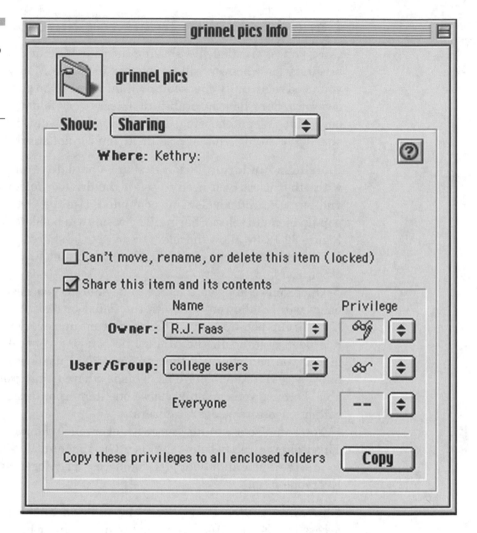

You can choose access levels for the folder's owner, for the User or Group that is allowed access to the file, and for Everyone. By default, the folder's owner has Read and Write access to the folder. The user/group and Everyone items are set to None by default.

You can also lock folders (though not disks) so that they cannot be deleted, moved, or renamed from a remote computer or the Mac that they are on. This can add some additional security, though individual items within those folders can still be changed, moved, or deleted. You can lock individual files as well, using the Finder's Get Info command.

For each access level, there is a different icon that will be displayed when the folder or disk is accessed over the network. Figure 32-13 shows each of these folders and what access level they are associated with.

Figure 32-13
Folder icons associated with shared items. Clockwise from upper left: A normal folder (one that you have Read or Read and Write access to), a folder that is being shared, a folder that is shared with users accessing it, a folder is locked, a folder you do not have access to, and a folder you have Write Only access to.

The Mac's Owner and the Folder's Owner Are Different   The user that is the owner of a shared item and the user that is the owner of the Mac are not necessarily the same user. If a user besides the owner is granted Read and Write access to a shared folder or disk and creates a folder, the user will be considered the owner of the folder. This means that the owner that created the folder will have Read and Write access to it, as well as the ability to set access levels for the folder. That user will also be listed as the folder's owner in the sharing section of the Get Info window. Of course, the Mac's owner will also have full Read and Write access to the folder, as well as the ability to change any sharing attributes (including the ability to change the owner of the file).

Take Care When Making Changes to a Folder's Sharing Attributes
When changing the sharing attributes of a shared folder, you should take care to be certain that anyone who needs to has access to the folder. However, there is one thing you should be particularly aware of. There is a button beneath the sharing information of the Get Info window that says Copy These Privileges to All Enclosed Files and Folders. When pressed, this button will give any folders within the shared item the exact same access privileges and sharing settings. It will erase any existing sharing settings and access privileges on those folders and replace them with the sharing information of the parent folder. Take care when doing this, particularly if you have several different sharing setups on various enclosed folders (including folders within those folders), as once you copy the privileges, you cannot undo it except by changing each enclosed folder by hand.

Allowing Dial-up Connections

Beginning with Mac OS 9, Apple included the ability for dial-up network connections for file sharing and related tasks to be made to any Mac. Prior to this, users needed to purchase separate software (the AppleTalk Remote Access Server) from Apple to allow for remote connections. To enable dial-up connections, you need to use the Remote Access control panel.

With the Remote Access control panel open, choose Answering from the Remote Access menu. This brings up the dialog shown in Figure 32-14. To enable incoming dial-up connections, check the Answer Calls checkbox. The Maximum Connection Time checkbox enables you to limit the length of time anyone can remain connected to the Mac over a dial-up connection. The Allow Access To radio buttons give you the choice of allowing users to connect solely to the Mac they have dialed into or allowing them access to the entire network through that Mac.

Figure 32-14
The Answering dialog in the Remote Access control panel.

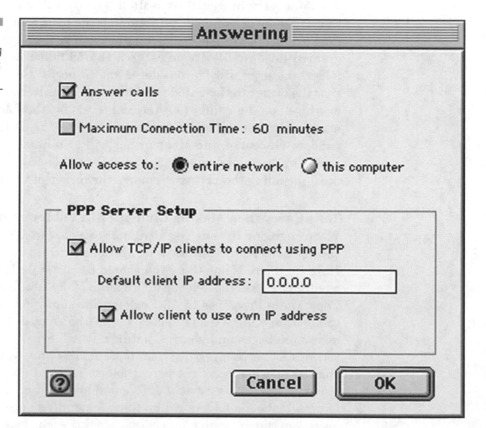

NOTE: *if your Mac is part of a larger network (such as an academic or corporate network), you should ask your network administrator before allowing your Mac to accept dial-up connections to access the entire network, as this can pose a significant security risk.*

The PPP Server Setup section of the dialog allows you to enable TCP/IP dial-up connections, as well as AppleTalk connections. This is important if your network uses the TCP/IP protocol for file sharing or if you want to allow users to connect to the Internet through the dial-up connection to your Mac (essentially turning the Mac into a small ISP). The Allow TCP/IP Clients to Connect Using PPP checkbox enables TCP/IP-based dial-up connections. When this is checked, you need to assign an IP address to the dial-up computer. This can be any IP address that is free on your network. You can also allow the connecting computer to use its own IP address if one has been manually assigned to it by checking the Allow Client to Use Own IP Address checkbox. This is useful if the connecting computer is a PowerBook or iBook that has a manual IP address assigned to it when it is connected to the network directly.

Logging in to a Mac File Server and Locating Shared Resources

Once you have a Mac set up to share files, you need to log in to that Mac in order to access those shared folders and disks. There are varying ways that you can accomplish this, though the most convenient tends to be using the Network Browser.

Using the Network Browser   The Network Browser application, shown in Figure 32-15, is located in the Apple menu and is one of the easier ways to connect to network servers and to specific disks and folders on a server. When launched, the Network Browser displays any network neighborhoods that it finds. It will, by default include AppleTalk as one entry. If there are computers sharing files over TCP/IP, a neighborhood named Local Services will be displayed. If the network is using TCP/IP for file sharing and providing domain name services, you may also see neighborhoods for specific domain names.

You can navigate through each neighborhood by either double-clicking its icon (which will display each of the servers or zones in the neighborhood replacing the display of available neighborhoods) or by clicking on

Figure 32-15
The Network
Browser.

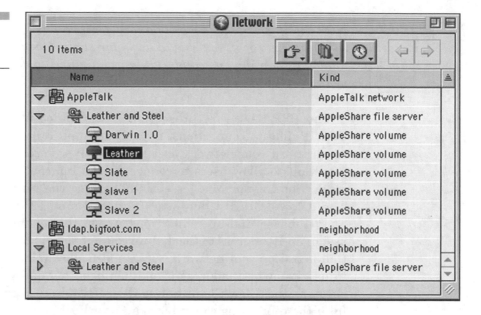

the triangle next to the neighborhood name (which will display the servers in that neighborhood, as well as the other neighborhoods). To access a specific server, perform one of the same actions with the icon indicating the server. At this point, you will be asked to log in to the server. Once you provide a valid username and password for the server, shared disks and folders that you have access to will be displayed. To mount one of those disks or folders on your desktop, simply double-click on it. The folder or disk will appear on your Mac's desktop and open.

The Network Browser also lets you enter a specific IP address for a file server (either using the four-number IP address or a domain name). This can be either a local network IP address or even a remote Internet address. To access this function, select the Connect to Server item from the Shortcuts menu (see Figure 32-16). The resulting dialog will ask for the server's address. Enter the IP address or domain name. When entering a domain name, do so using the following URL format: afp://my.file-server.net. When using a domain name, you can also add slashes to access a specific folder (as you can with a webpage). For instance, afp://my.filserver.net/HardDrive1/documents would access the documents folder at the root level of the hard drive named HardDrive1. The *afp* stands for Apple File Protocol, and it indicates a Mac file server as http:// indicates a web address or ftp:// indicates an FTP server address.

Figure 32-16
Selecting the
Connect to Server
feature in the
Network Browser.

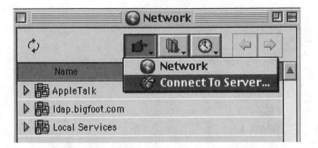

Figure 32-17
Using the Chooser to
select a file server.

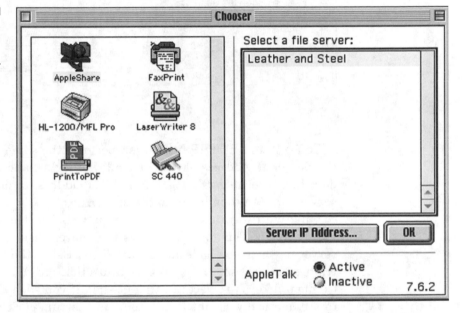

Using the Chooser   For many years, the Chooser (shown in
Figure 32-17) was the default method for accessing file servers and
mounting shared disks or folders on a Mac's desktop (as well as choosing
a printer). Although this function of the Chooser has been replaced with
the more versatile Network Browser application, it is still available. To
access a file server using the AppleTalk protocol, click on the AppleShare
icon in the Chooser window (in the same section as various printer driver
icons). Available file servers will be listed in the right-hand pane of the
window. Select a server and click on OK to log in to it. If your AppleTalk
network contains multiple zones, the individual zones will be listed in a
box beneath the printer driver icons. To select a server in one of those
zones, click on the zone and then select from the listed servers.

Figure 32-18
This dialog allows
you to mount shared
disks and folders
once you have
logged in to a server
using the Chooser.

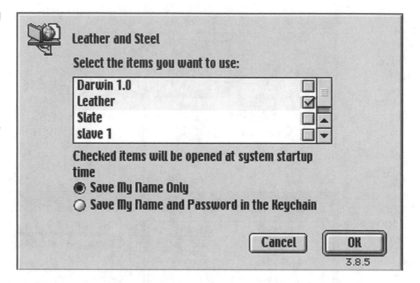

To log in to a TCP/IP file server, perform the same steps, but click on the Server IP Address button in the lower right-hand section of the window. In the resulting dialog, enter the IP address or domain name of the server. You can then log in to the server.

Once you log in to a server, you will see the dialog shown in Figure 32-18. This dialog displays the shared disks and folders on that server to which you have access privileges. Select the disks or folders you wish to mount on the desktop, and click on OK (hold the Shift or Command keys to select multiple items). If you wish the Mac to attempt to automatically mount these items at startup, click on the checkboxes next to them (be aware that this will cause the Mac to attempt to connect to the appropriate server and ask a user for an appropriate password whenever it is restarted). The items should now appear on the Mac's desktop for you to access.

From a Remote Location   Chapter 31 introduced the Remote Access control panel and its ability to establish dial-up connections. To log in to a Mac through a dial-up connection, you use the Remote Access control panel as described in that chapter to establish the connection. If you plan to connect using AppleTalk, you should configure the Protocol tab the Remote Access Options dialog to use ARAP (AppleTalk Remote Access Protocol) instead of PPP (used when establishing a TCP/IP connection). You will also need to choose Remote Access in the Connect Via menu of the AppleTalk control panel. The remaining steps (entering dial-up phone number, modem choice, and such) is the same as using Remote Access to establish an Internet connection. If you plan to establish a TCP/IP connection, use Remote Access in the same manner as you would to dial into an ISP. To dial into a Mac for network access, the Mac you are dialing into will also need to be set to accept incoming connections, as described earlier in this chapter.

Disconnecting from a File Server   Unless you explicitly disconnect from a file server, your Mac will usually remain connected indefinitely (unless the owner of the server disconnects you or the Mac shuts down, enters sleep mode, or is disconnected from the network). To disconnect from a file server, you only need to unmount any shared items from your Mac's desktop. To do this, simply drag the icons for any shared items to the Trash or select them and use the Finder's Put Away command (under the Special menu).

Aliases of Shared Items   You can create aliases of shared items to make accessing them quicker and easier. Do this in the same manner you would create aliases of a local file or folder. When you double-click on the alias in the future, the Mac will access the server the original item is located on and ask you to log in. After doing this, the shared folder or disk will mount on your Mac, and the item will open.

If the Remember Recently Used Items feature in the Apple Menu Options control panel is enabled, the Mac will store aliases of your recently accessed shared disks and folders in the Recent Servers submenu of the Apple menu.

AppleShare IP and Mac OS X Server

For networks with more than a dozen users, the file sharing abilities built into the Mac OS are generally not powerful enough to run a full network. For larger networks, you should use a more industrial-strength file/print server. Apple produces two such products to consider: AppleShare IP and Mac OS X Server.

AppleShare IP   AppleShare IP is software that is installed on top of an existing Mac OS release. It has highly advanced file server management abilities using both AppleTalk and TCP/IP. It also enables much faster network file sharing, the ability to create more users and groups, and the ability for 500 users to access a server at one time. AppleShare IP also offers advanced printer server abilities beyond those of the traditional Mac OS.

One ideal advantage of using AppleShareIP is that it allows you to create one (or a few) dedicated file server for a network that all users can access more easily and quickly than they can access individual Macs on the network. This allows for more streamlined network traffic, as well as a better user experience. It also saves you from needing to manage the user and sharing settings on many Macs simultaneously.

Beyond just file sharing, AppleShare IP includes a suite of Internet servers. This includes a powerful mail server, a web server, and an FTP server. It also offers the ability for remote administration from any Internet connected computer. Also included is support for multiple dial-up user connection. In addition, AppleShare IP offers several advanced security features that can be extremely important in a large network, particularly if that network is also connected to the Internet.

Mac OS X Server   Mac OS X Server is a special operating system that uses the UNIX underpinning of Mac OS X to provide very powerful file and Internet server functions. This gives Mac OS X Server the advantages offered by AppleShare IP plus several others. Mac OS X Server is more stable and extremely unlikely to suffer crashes or other network outages. It also enables some additional features such as NetBooting of client Macs, QuickTime Streaming, and the ability to use multiport Ethernet cards—items that cannot be done in the traditional Mac OS. Additional information on Mac OS X and Mac OS X Server can be found in Chapter 42.

NETBOOTING   NetBooting is a function introduced on the original iMac (all the Macs covered by this book support NetBooting) and enabled with Mac OS X Server. NetBooting allows a Mac to use a disk image file on a Mac OS X Server computer as a startup disk instead of its local hard drive. To enable NetBooting on a Mac, open the Startup Disk control panel and select the Network Disk icon. NetBooting requires that at least one Mac on the network is running Mac OS X Server and has NetBooting enabled and a startup disk image configured for the Macs that will be using it as a startup disk. If no NetBoot server is available, a Mac set to NetBoot will hang for up to 15 minutes at startup while it continually tries to locate a NetBoot server.

NetBooting can be useful in computer lab situations where an administrator wants to maintain control of what Mac OS release is available to all Macs and prevent users from adjusting the System Folder of a Mac. It also allows administrators to perform one update to the Mac OS version (the disk image) and have all Macs on the network be updated as a result. Any applications stored on the disk image can be updated just as easily.

Intranets

An intranet is a concept that has become popular in a number of corporate and institutional network settings. An intranet is essentially a private Internet. Running on a TCP/IP network that isn't connected to the Internet (or that is connected to the Internet only through an Internet router), an intranet runs web, news, and e-mail servers that can only be accessed from within the intranet and not from the Internet at large.

Intranets provide an easy way to disseminate information within a corporation, because managers can make web pages or e-mails available to employees that are still confidential to the company. They also allow employees to collaborate on projects and discuss business events by using news servers to provide company-only newsgroups or e-mail servers to provide communication and mailing lists for the company. Intranets can even be used with videoconferencing protocols intended for the Internet to allow employees in different offices to communicate face-to-face in real time for presentations or other collaborative efforts.

Setting up an intranet is relatively simple. The first task is to create a TCP/IP network for your office or company. Once the TCP/IP network is in place, you simply need to run Internet server applications (web server, FTP server, e-mail server, and so on) on computers that are part of the network. Each computer within the network will then be able to access these servers using conventional Internet applications, such as the Internet Explorer web browser or the Eudora e-mail program. Most intranets also provide domain name services for easy access to computers on the intranet. Chapter 34 contains some additional information on running such servers on the Mac.

Network Security

Whenever you open a Mac to outside users, you face the issue of security. If users can access the files and folders on your Mac, they can delete crucial data, corrupt your Mac's hard drive, change important files, or infect your computer with a virus. All of these are occurrences that can happen when a Mac is connected to a network. You need to take steps to secure your Mac and network from such threats, whether it is a small home network or a large company network.

Users and Groups Privileges

One of the best ways to secure an individual Mac on a network is to use the access privileges involved in file sharing wisely. Following are a few tips:

- *Don't give anyone any more access to your Mac than he or she needs.* Certainly, don't give anyone unrestricted access to your primary hard drive and don't give anyone access to your Mac's System Folder.
- *Don't enable the Guest user account.* This is the biggest security hole that can exist because it means anyone at all can log in to your Mac and do whatever he or she wants without you knowing about it. Never set the Guest user to be able to log in to a Mac.
- *Don't give the Everyone group any more than Read privileges.* This will limit what users can actually change files or move them.
- *Lock important items.* The lock checkbox is present in Get Info window of files and applications. Use it to secure important documents or files that you don't need to update frequently (since you can't update a locked item).

Passwords

Be careful when assigning passwords. Don't assign or allow users to choose passwords that are easy to guess. Use passwords that are at least six characters and that are not actual dictionary words. Combining letters and numbers is another good tactic for creating passwords.

The Owner User Account

Don't use the owner account to log in to your Mac unless you have a need. This account gives you complete access to your Mac and presents a big security risk if someone should see your owner username and password. Where feasible, create and use a regular user account when accessing your own Mac over a network.

Rotate your owner password regularly, since this is the password, that allows complete access to your Mac. As with user passwords, make it as difficult to guess as possible.

Always make sure you unmount your Mac's drives to disconnect from it before you stop using a Mac from which you logged in as owner. If you don't, that Mac will still be connected to your Mac using the owner account. Anyone who sits down at it before it has been disconnected will still be logged into your Mac with full access to everything on your Mac.

Who Can Physically Access Your Network?

Certain cabling setups make it easier for other people to access your Mac or network. If your office or apartment building is wired for Ethernet and provides shared Internet access over those Ethernet cables, then any Mac plugged into that network will be visible to any other. This is also true of cable modems, where a single cable line services several individual homes, thus sharing a physical connection (although a number of cable lines will not support AppleTalk data communication).

If you physically share network cabling with other users, you have to rely on your username and password choices to keep them from accessing your shared files. If possible, use network cables that do not interact with networks outside your own. If not, consider using AppleTalk instead of TCP/IP for file sharing, as AppleTalk is more secure and not as readily observed as TCP/IP.

If you do have to share physical network cables or your Mac network is connected to the Internet, see "Securing Your Mac/Network from the Internet" in Chapter 34 for additional security information and tips.

Troubleshooting Network Issues

Network troubleshooting usually involves checking three separate types of issues: Hardware, software, and configuration problems. Unlike the troubleshooting section in most of the chapters in this book, this section is devoted to looking at each overall type of problem rather than to specific symptoms and their solutions.

Configuration Issues

Configuration issues are one of the most common causes of network trouble, especially when that trouble affects only a single Mac. Configuration issues are simply cases where a Mac isn't set up properly to access the network. To alleviate them, make certain that the AppleTalk and TCP/IP control panels have the correct information for your network. Make certain that AppleTalk is active if you are using AppleTalk. Also be sure that the appropriate IP address and related information is entered if you are using TCP/IP, and verify that all of your network settings are correct.

If the problem involves one user or a group of users accessing shared folders or other resources on a specific Mac, make sure that file sharing is configured properly on that Mac. Ensure that usernames and passwords are entered properly and that file sharing is turned on. If all this seems to be in order, you probably have a hardware- or software-related issue. Hardware issues usually (though not always) affect more than one Mac on a network, while software issues are usually limited to a single Mac.

Hardware Issues

Network hardware issues tend to manifest with one Mac, a group of Macs, or every Mac being unable to access a network. Hardware issues tend to be the result of cabling problems, though a damaged Ethernet port, improperly installed network card, or damaged hubs (or transceivers, bridges, or routers) can also cause hardware networking problems. To help you with many hardware/cabling issues, you should have a map or sketch of your network indicating which cables go to which Macs and which cables are inserted into which ports on a hub (using various-colored cables can also help).

If you suspect a hardware problem, the first thing to check is the network cabling. Cabling problems are much easier to isolate on 10Base-T and 100Base-T Ethernet networks than on LocalTalk or ThickNet/ThinNet Ethernet networks. Because 10/100Base-T Ethernet uses a hub, you will usually only be dealing with a single Mac experiencing trouble when there is a cabling problem. You can easily isolate the cable leading to that Mac and check it for signs of damage and to be certain it is connected properly. You can also easily identify the cable at the hub and try using a different port to see if the port the Mac was connected to is damaged.

With LocalTalk (or ThinNet/ThickNet Ethernet), isolating a cabling problem is much more difficult because often the entire network will go down in response to one broken connection. Sometimes, only Macs on one side of the break will go down, which can help you guess where the break is. In either case, you will probably need to go from one Mac to another, following the cable along the network and looking for places where it is disconnected, damaged, or loose. You should also make certain that any unused ports on LocalTalk transceivers or PhoneNET connectors are terminated. For ThinNet, you must ensure that both ends of the network cable are terminated as well. Also, be certain that there are no areas where the cabling of one of these networks loops back and connects to itself, as this will cause problems with the network.

Assuming the cabling is not broken, worn, bent, caught in an unusual position, or in any other way obstructed and that all cables are inserted properly, make certain that any hubs, bridges, or routers in the network are all powered and connected properly. For routers and managed hubs, you will also need to check that the device is configured properly (see its documentation).

Also make certain that you are following any cable length restrictions. This varies depending on the network type and is discussed earlier in the chapter. Be certain that no individual segment of cable is too long. Also be sure that you are not exceeding the total cable length for a network type (this does not apply to 10/100Base-T Ethernet). Some network types are limited to a certain number of network devices. Make sure you are not using too many devices for your network.

If the problem is not solved by any of the above, but you still suspect a hardware issue, make certain that any network expansion cards in the affected Mac(s) are installed properly. If such a card is installed properly or you are dealing with a built-in Ethernet port on a Mac, you can try placing another Mac at that network segment (or using that Mac elsewhere on the network) to verify that the Mac's network port isn't damaged.

Software Issues

If the problem is not hardware-related, it may be a software issue. First, make certain any extensions or control panels needed for the network protocol you wish to use are installed and enabled. This consists of the Open Transport set of extensions, shared libraries, and control panels that are part of the Mac OS. The specific items involved vary from one Mac OS release to another. If in doubt, you can reinstall the Mac OS to be certain.

In addition to Open Transport, you need to be certain that the drivers for any network hardware are installed. This includes the drivers for any network cards, including the Ethernet extensions that are included with the Mac OS built-in Ethernet ports. Reinstalling driver software or the Mac OS should ensure that these are installed.

Certain preference files associated with Mac networking can become corrupted. These can include the following Preferences files (in the Preferences folder inside the System Folder): AirPort Prefs, AppleShare

Prep, AppleTalk Preferences, File Sharing CP prefs, the contents of the File Sharing folder inside the Preferences folder, Infrared Prefs, Network Browser Preferences, the contents of the Open Transport Preferences folder inside the Preferences folder, the contents of the Remote Access Preferences folder inside the Preferences folder, ShareWay IP Prefs, SLP Preferences, TCP/IP Preferences, Users & Groups CP Prefs, the Users & Groups Data File, and the contents of the Web Sharing Folder inside the Preferences folder.

Resources for Further Study

The following URLs provide additional information on some of the concepts, issues, and products discussed in this chapter:

About.com Mac Hardware Networking Resources— http://machardware.about.com/msubnetwork.htm

Three Macs and a Printer—http://threemacs.com

Apple's AppleShare IP Site—http://www.apple.com/appleshareip

Farallon—http://www.farallon.com

Asanté—http://www.asante.com

Sonic Systems—http://www.sonicsys.com

CHAPTER 33

AirPort Wireless Networking

When Apple introduced the iBook in July of 1999, they also announced a new type of Mac network, the AirPort network. AirPort is a wireless networking technology that has since been integrated into each of Apple's product lines. It allows you to share files, to access network servers and printers, and to surf the Internet, all without any physical connection or cable between your computer and any other computer or device on the network. This chapter looks at how AirPort functions, how to plan and set up an AirPort network and integrate AirPort into an existing wired network, and how to install an AirPort card in each of the current Macintosh computers.

An Introduction to How AirPort Works

Traditional networks use wires or cables to connect the various computers in the network. This provides a physical connection for data to flow between the computers of the network. AirPort is a network strategy that transmits data without using any cables. Instead, AirPort-equipped computers use a radio transceiver to transmit and receive information using radio signals of a specific frequency range (2.4 GHz).

Apple developed AirPort with Lucent Technologies, a big name in computer network development. AirPort is based on an existing wireless networking protocol called 802.11. Because it is based on an existing protocol, AirPort is compatible with other wireless networking technologies (see "Non-Apple Wireless Products and AirPort" later in this chapter for more information on using AirPort with other wireless products). Apple and Lucent did, however, extend 802.11's typical performance from 1 to 2 Mb/second to 11 Mb/second (about the performance of typical 10Base-T Ethernet). This was an important achievement because it enables AirPort to offer performance that is usable for a variety of tasks (although moving large file collections is still better suited to wired 100Base-T Ethernet or via the use of removable-media drives). AirPort's development of 11 Mbps wireless networking using the 802.11 protocol spurred other network product developers to increase the performance of their products (both Mac and PC based) to be competitive.

Base Stations and Access Points

An access point is wireless networking talk for a device that acts as a bridge between the wireless computers in a network, as well as a bridge between wireless and a traditional cabled Ethernet network. An access point controls the interaction of wireless connections for multiple computers. It is roughly analogous to an Ethernet hub in that it receives requests for information and forwards those requests to the appropriate file server, network printer, or Internet address.

Apple calls the access points it produces for use in AirPort networks *Base Stations*. AirPort Base Stations can be independent hardware devices, such as the one shown in Figure 33-1, or they can be a software

Figure 33-1   Apple's AirPort Base Station.

utility run on a computer that is equipped with an AirPort card. It is important to realize that you do not need a stand-alone hardware base station to create an AirPort network (although using one will provide better performance).

To avoid interference with other wireless devices or with other Base Stations, each Base Station can be set to use one of 14 separate channels. Each channel broadcasts and receives at a slightly different frequency, much like the channels of a CB radio. AirPort-equipped computers will display each Base Station as a separate AirPort network that you can access.

Apple recommends that no more than 10 AirPort-equipped computers access a single Base Station at one time. This is not a hard-and-fast limitation, and Base Stations will support more than 10 simultaneous connections. Wireless network performance will degrade as more AirPort equipped computers connect to a single Base Station, however.

Hardware Base Stations Apple's hardware Base Station is shaped like an oversized and rounded Hershey's Kiss candy. It includes an Ethernet port for connecting it to a terrestrial or wired Ethernet network (or to a cable modem, DSL line, or ISDN router), as well as a built-in modem, which can be used to establish Internet connections that can be shared with any computers connected to the Base Station. The Base Station also includes a hardware router, meaning that it can share an Internet connection, both with Macs connected wirelessly and with Macs on a terrestrial network that is attached to the Base Station.

Software Base Stations A software Base Station is an AirPort-equipped computer that performs the functions of a Base Station. This feature is present only in version 1.1 or higher of the AirPort software. When a computer is set to be a software Base Station, it performs all of the functions of a hardware Base Station. To function as a software Base Station, the computer must remain on and must not enter sleep mode. If the computer is shut down or goes into sleep mode, the software Base Station feature will be deactivated and any computers accessing the network through the software Base Station will be disconnected.

AirPort Cards and Antennas

AirPort-equipped computers consist of two important components: a built-in antenna and an AirPort card. The antenna is used to send and receive AirPort radio signals, as you would expect. AirPort antennas are

Figure 33-2
Apple's AirPort card.

built into the case design of all AirPort-capable Macs, and you should never have a situation where you have to worry about dealing with the antenna itself.

The AirPort card, shown in Figure 33-2, is a piece of hardware that resembles a Type 2 PC Card in size, shape, and connectors (AirPort cards cannot, however, be used as PC Cards, nor can PC Cards be installed in an AirPort socket). The AirPort card contains the required circuitry for the Mac to be able to communicate with an AirPort network. This includes the ability to receive and send AirPort signals through the built-in antenna, as well as the ability for the Mac to identify itself to a Base Station, transmit data using the 802.11 wireless networking protocol, and support data encryption when talking to a Base Station. There is a single design for AirPort cards, and the cards can be used in any Mac that is designed to accept an AirPort card (AirPort card installation instructions for the current Macs are given at the end of this chapter).

Like every Ethernet card made, each AirPort card and Base Station includes a unique MAC address. This address defines the card or Base Station from every other network card or other network device of any type anywhere else in the world. This allows each computer with an AirPort card to be identified from every other computer with an AirPort card and is the basis of how a Base Station recognizes each computer that it is communicating with. The ability to recognize specific cards/computers can allow for increased security in AirPort networks, because you can set up a Base Station to only accept connections from computers with a specific MAC address (or AirPort ID number, as Apple refers to the MAC address of an AirPort card).

Computer to Computer Mode

In addition to an AirPort network managed by a hardware or software Base Station, you can also transfer data directly between two or more AirPort-equipped Macs without using a Base Station. This mode is called Computer to Computer and is the wireless equivalent of networking two Macs with an Ethernet crossover cable to share files without using a hub. Computer to Computer mode allows any AirPort-equipped computers within range of each other to connect to each other and exchange files. However, Apple recommends using this feature to share files between only two computers at a time.

Internet Access through AirPort

Apple's base stations are designed to function as routers, allowing a single Internet connection to be shared with any computers connected to the AirPort network (see the next chapter for more information on routers). This feature can be extended to computers that are connected to a terrestrial network as well. For Macs that use a cable modem or DSL line for Internet access, the device can be plugged into the base station's Ethernet port. Hardware base stations also include a built-in 56 Kbps modem. This modem can be dialed and controlled from any computer connected to the base station. Setting up a base station for Internet access is described later in this chapter.

Non-Apple Wireless Products and AirPort

Because AirPort is based on the 802.11 computer networking standard, several other wireless networking products that are based on the same standards are compatible with AirPort. This is particularly helpful if you want to include earlier Macs that cannot accept AirPort cards into an AirPort network. Older PowerBooks, in particular, can be integrated into an AirPort network using PC Cards from both Farallon and Lucent. Older desktop Macs can also be integrated into AirPort networks using Ethernet-to-wireless converters that are based on the 802.11 standard.

Although many 802.11 wireless networking devices can integrate into AirPort networks, some may have compatibility concerns with AirPort. You should check with the manufacturer of such products before purchasing to see if AirPort compatibility has been determined with a product and what special issues or concerns there may be when using it with AirPort. Also, not all 802.11-based products will deliver 11 Mb/second data transfer rates. A number of older products will only support 1 to 3 Mb/second. Likewise, the range of non-AirPort wireless networking devices may be different (larger or smaller) than AirPort, and you should check before purchasing. The "Resources for Further Study" section at the end of this chapter includes website addresses where you can find references about Mac-compatible 802.11 wireless networking products.

AirPort can be used for cross-platform networking because 802.11 is a platform-transparent standard. However, this only means that PCs with 802.11 wireless networking hardware will be able to transmit data through an AirPort network or use shared Internet access. It does not mean that PCs will be able to share files or printers with Macs on the network (because these are platform-specific tasks). See Chapter 41 for more information on cross-platform file and printer sharing.

AirPort and Travel

The radio frequencies used by AirPort connections are perfectly harmless. However, there are situations in which those frequencies may pose a problem. This is when the same frequencies are being used for other forms of communication. In such situations, using AirPort could cause interference with other devices. If you find yourself in one of these situations, you should turn off the AirPort card in your Mac (either using the AirPort utility or the AirPort control strip module). Even if you are not connected to an AirPort network, the Mac is still sending out signals from its built-in AirPort antenna whenever the AirPort card is on, so that it will be aware of any AirPort network or communication that might be present.

The most common such situation is when you are on an airplane. This is because there is a possibility that the radio signals being sent out by your computer's AirPort card could interfere with some of the frequencies used by the plane's instruments. The same is true for cellular phones, which are also required to be turned off when you are on a plane. While most flights will allow laptop use while in flight because a computer in and of itself poses no such problems, AirPort cards can pose problems and should be turned off before boarding a plane.

Another situation is if you happen to be using your AirPort-equipped computer in a hospital or medical clinic. There are several different types of medical equipment, particularly those used in intensive care units, that can be affected by strong radio signals such as those generated by AirPort devices or by a cellular phone. A Mac sending out AirPort signals near this equipment can cause it to malfunction, with potentially catastrophic results. When in a hospital or clinic or near any medical equipment that carries a warning about cellular phone use, play it safe and turn your AirPort card off.

Some countries also have communications regulations regarding various radio frequencies, including those used by AirPort. As a result, not all countries permit civilians or visitors to use those radio frequencies. While Apple has made efforts to have AirPort communication allowed in many of the countries where Macs are sold, you should check regarding the regulations of countries you intend to visit to be certain. If in doubt, play it safe and turn off your AirPort card. Table 33-1 lists the countries where Apple has secured regulatory certifications for AirPort use.

In various countries or areas, the use of individual AirPort channels may be restricted from civilian or nongovernmental use. Table 33-2 lists the channels that are available in the United States, Japan, France, and the remainder of Europe. It is important that you use only those channels permitted by law in the country that you are establishing an AirPort network in. If in doubt about which channels are permitted, check with an Apple representative for the country you wish to use AirPort in. By default, only the AirPort channels allowed in a county where the computer is intended for sale will be available to you.

TABLE 33-1 Apple Regulatory Certification for AirPort in Effect.	United States
	Australia
	Canada
	Denmark
	Finland
	France
	Germany
	Netherlands
	Norway
	Sweden
	Switzerland
	United Kingdom

TABLE 33-2

Permitted AirPort Channels.

Country	Channels Permitted
United States	1-11
Japan	14
France	10-13
Most of Europe	1-13

Creating an AirPort Network

This section looks at the process of placing and configuring Base Stations (both stand-alone hardware Base Stations and Macs acting as software Base Stations) to create an AirPort network.

Placing Base Stations

When creating an AirPort network, it is important to consider where to place the Base Station(s) that will be used for the network. In a home network consisting of a single Base Station, the optimal place is centered within the home so that it is equidistant from all locations where AirPort communication is likely to take place. In a home or small office environment where an existing Ethernet network will be bridged with the AirPort network, the Base Station should also be placed within easy cable reach of the Ethernet hub into which the rest of the computers on the network are connected. In addition, the Base Station should be placed away from radio interference sources, such as microwave ovens and other radio-based communications devices that use the same frequency spectrum as AirPort (such as a number of cordless phones).

You can set up the Base Station and try accessing it from various points to determine the strength and stability of the AirPort signal. The AirPort Admin Utility includes a feature for helping you determine the optimal placement of Base Stations. This feature is designed for you to be able to carry an AirPort-equipped computer around the area where it will be used to test for AirPort signal strength. You can then use this information to help determine where to move a Base Station for better performance. To access this feature, launch the AirPort Admin Utility and connect to the Base Station you wish to determine the signal strength of (see the upcoming section on setting up a hardware Base Station for details on doing this). Once connected, choose the Optimize Placement button from the bottom of the configuration window. A window with a time-delayed graph of signal strength and signal noise will be displayed, as will a bar graph indicating signal strength, as shown in Figure 33-3. Carry the portable Mac around the network site and move the Base Station until you are able to get the best-possible signal strength for each location where you expect to work with the computer.

Remember that although AirPort has a range of 150 feet indoors, this may be limited by some factors, including the materials used in a building's construction. Soft materials, such as wood, glass, and plaster, will

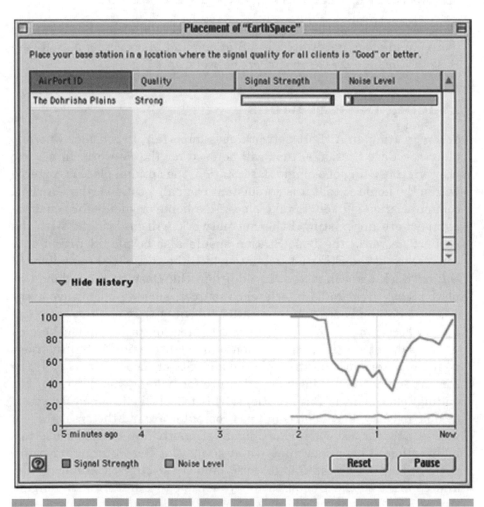

Figure 33-3   The AirPort Admin Utility's Optimize Placement window.

absorb some of the AirPort signals, which weakens signal strength. Hard construction materials, such as concrete and metal, on the other hand, will reflect AirPort signals. Reflected signals create signal noise, which reduces signal quality. Both soft and hard materials will reduce AirPort performance. Outdoors, where there are few materials to absorb or reflect AirPort signals, AirPort's range may be noticeably larger than 150 feet.

If you are creating a network that will span more than one floor, remember that AirPort uses radio signals that transmit in all three dimensions. This means that a single Base Station can easily service more than one floor. Hardware Base Stations come with the appropriate brackets to allow them to be mounted on a wall, as well as set on a flat surface. Also, remember that there is more material to absorb or reflect AirPort signal between floors than there is in the walls between rooms, so it is unlikely you will be able to connect from more than one (or maybe two) floors above the base station.

Placing Multiple Base Stations If you are creating a network that will use more than one Base Station, you should consider placing the Base Stations such that there is no gap in network coverage anyplace within your network site. To do this, you should ensure that the effective communication zone for each Base Station slightly overlaps the zone for the next (remember that this applies to placing stations vertically on different floors, as well as horizontally in different rooms of a single floor). The Base Stations will also need a physical network connection between them to provide continuous access to shared resources.

Choosing Base Station Channels When Base Stations overlap, they will need to be set to use different channels for their signal transmissions. If two Base Stations are set to use the same channel in the same physical area, their signals will interfere with each other and network performance will grind to a near standstill, if it is usable at all. Not only does each Base Station in a given area need to use a separate channel, but each must use a channel that is five channels away from the others. This is because each AirPort channel's frequencies bleed off slightly into the surrounding channels, as shown in Figure 33-4.

This signal bleed-off will cause interference for other Base Stations if they are set to use a neighboring channel. Again, this will degrade network performance (though not as totally as if the overlapping Base Stations were using the same channel). Also, remember that you need to

Figure 33-4
AirPort channel
frequencies bleed off
into neighboring
channels.

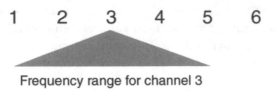

Frequency range for channel 3

abide by the restrictions of what channels are allowed by the country that you are setting up the network in (listed in Table 33-2).

Before you start worrying that you will only be able to use two or three Base Stations in a network, remember that you can reuse the same channels as many times as you need to in a network. You just cannot have the same channels being used by Base Stations that are placed within range of each other. Setting AirPort channels is a function of the AirPort Admin Utility and is described in the next section.

Setting Up a Hardware Base Station

Once you have determined the placement of the Base Station(s) that will be used to create your network, you need to actually set them up to create the network. For basic setup, the AirPort Setup Assistant allows you to configure the Base Station. However, for advanced setup options and configuration choices not offered by the AirPort Setup Assistant, you need to use the AirPort Admin Utility. The following sections look at the use of both utilities.

Using the AirPort Setup Assistant   The AirPort Setup Assistant allows users to enter the basic settings for a Base Station without any real effort, as shown in Figure 33-5. However, it does not allow the user to have any real control over the configuration of the Base Station. The user will really only be able to control the choice of network and Base Station names and passwords. Internet or TCP/IP information for the Base Station is simply copied from the settings being used by the Mac from which the Setup Assistant is being run (if the Mac has not been configured for Internet access, the AirPort Setup Assistant will launch Apple's Internet Setup Assistant to perform such configuration). If multiple TCP/IP or Internet configurations are stored on a Mac, the user can choose which one is copied to the Base Station (though the one currently in use will be the default choice).

The first real step in configuring a Base Station using the AirPort

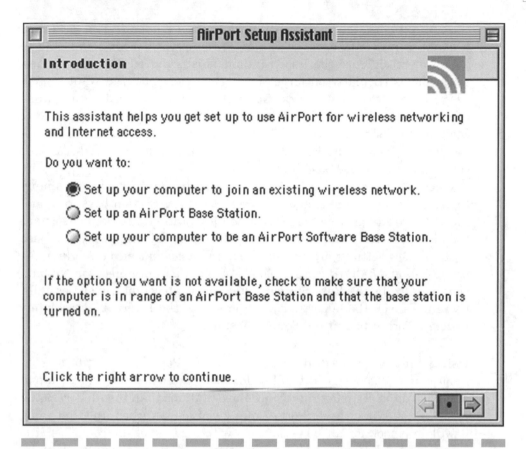

Figure 33-5   The AirPort Setup Assistant can be used for Simple Base Station setup.

Setup Assistant is to connect to the Base Station. If the Base Station has been configured previously, the user may be asked to enter password for both the network created by the Base Station and for the Base Station itself. Following this, the user chooses which TCP/IP settings to copy to the Base Station. Next, the user is asked to provide a name for the network created by the Base Station and a password for the network. A network password is not required, but it is strongly recommended, as without a password, anyone with a computer equipped with AirPort (or a compatible 802.11 wireless technology) will be able to access the network and no encryption for wireless connections will be available without a network password.

The user is then given the ability to assign a separate password to the Base Station or to use the same password for network access and Base

Station configuration. A separate Base Station password is a good idea because it prevents users of the AirPort network from being able to adjust or reconfigure the Base Station. This is a good idea on any network, but particularly on larger networks where you will want to give users access to the network, but not control over individual Base Stations. It is also a good idea in a network consisting of multiple Base Stations to assign a different password to each Base Station. Unlike a network password, the Base Station password is mandatory because it controls access to the Base Station itself.

Once the Base Station password is set, the Setup Assistant simply copies the network name and password, the Base Station password, and the TCP/IP settings from the Mac to the Base Station. The Setup Assistant then issues a Restart command to the Base Station. On restart, the Base Station's new settings are active. The Setup Assistant also configures the AppleTalk and TCP/IP control panels of the Mac to connect via the network created by the Base Station. After this is all completed successfully, users are given the opportunity to connect to the Internet immediately using AirPort or to quit the Setup Assistant.

Using the AirPort Admin Utility The AirPort Admin Utility, as its name implies, is designed to allow for more extensive configuration and administration of AirPort hardware Base Stations than the AirPort Setup Assistant is. When the AirPort Admin Utility is launched, the first thing it will do is look for all Base Stations within range of the computer it is being run on. It displays all Base Stations it finds in a window both by name and by the IP address assigned to each Base Station. Unlike the Setup Assistant, the AirPort Admin Utility can also be run from a computer that is not AirPort-equipped but is connected to the same terrestrial network as a Base Station. To configure a Base Station in this manner, the administrator will need to click the Other button in the Admin Utility's list window and enter the IP address of the Base Station he or she wishes to configure, as well as the Base Station's password. Once a Base Station has been chosen to configure, a separate window opens to allow you to adjust the settings of the Base Station. This window includes the AirPort, Internet, Network, and Access Control tabs that contain all the administration features available for a hardware Base Station.

THE AIRPORT TAB The first tab, AirPort (see Figure 33-6), allows you to configure many of the basic options for the Base Station. These include the name and password of the Base Station itself in the top section of the window, as well as the optional fields for an administrator contact's

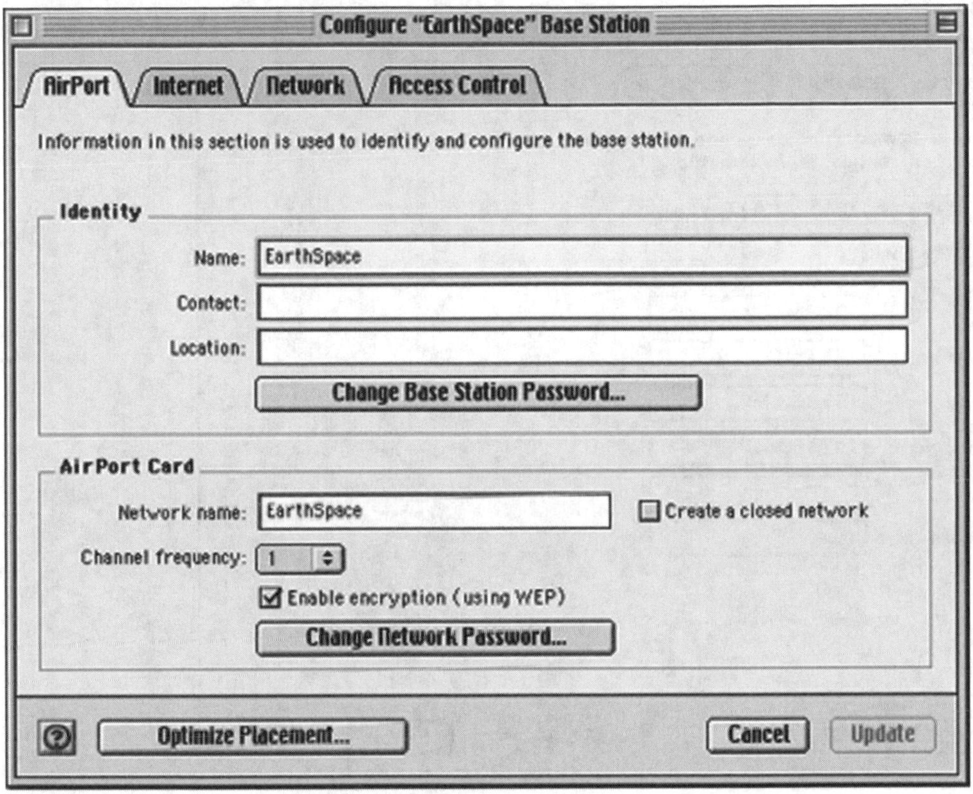

Figure 33-6   The AirPort Admin Utility's AirPort tab.

name and location (phone number, e-mail address, fax number, physical address, or whatever contact information you want to enter). The bottom section of the window includes the name of the network that is generated by the Base Station and the option to change the password for that network. This area also allows the administrator to set which AirPort channel the Base Station communicates on and the ability to turn encryption of AirPort communications through the Base Station on or off (encryption and AirPort security is further discussed in the "Securing an AirPort Network" section later in this chapter).

THE INTERNET TAB   The Internet tab (see Figure 33-7) allows the administrator to control the TCP/IP settings of the Base Station and is similar to the TCP/IP control panel of the Mac. When set to connect to the Internet using a modem, it also includes fields for the information

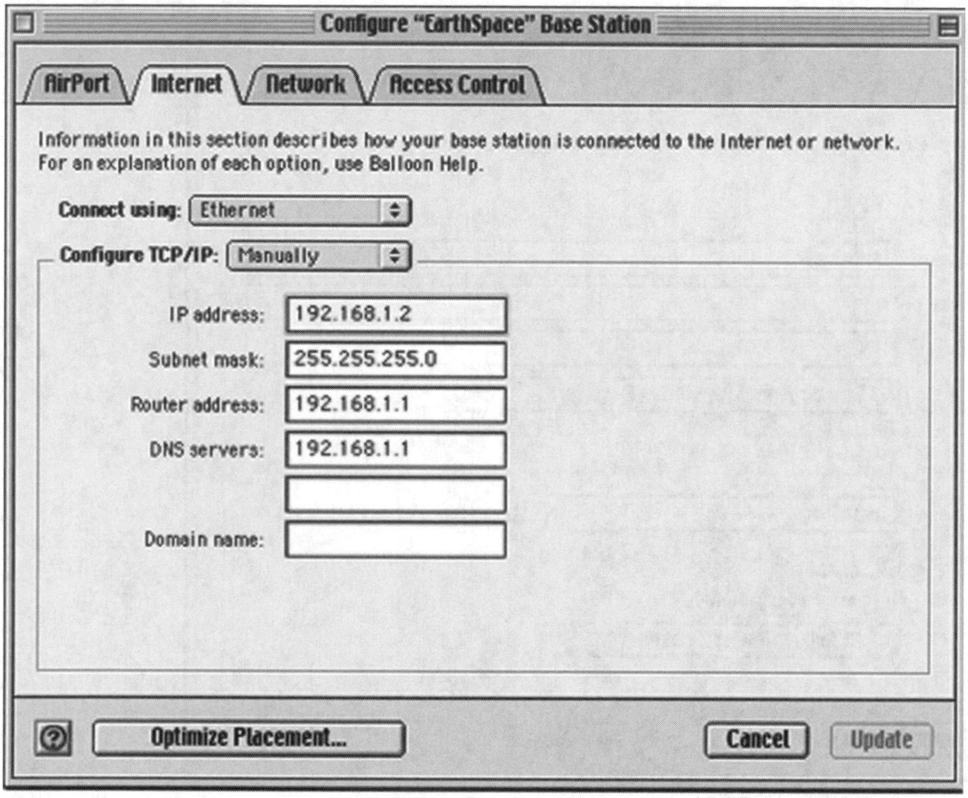

Figure 33-7   The AirPort Admin Utility's Internet tab.

located in the Mac's PPP control panel, including the Internet service provider's dial-up number and alternate number, the username and password of the customer, and the options for disconnecting after a specified idle period, using a login script (if required by an ISP), ignoring the dial tone (needed for some phone systems), and the use of pulse dialing for older phone systems. Most users familiar with Internet connections and TCP/IP should have no trouble understanding the Internet tab.

The Network Tab   The Network tab (see Figure 33-8) is, without a doubt, the most complicated tab in the AirPort Admin Utility's window for novice administrators. This tab determines how the Base Station's built-in DHCP server functions. The primary option here is Distribute IP Addresses. When this is checked, the Base Station's DHCP server will provide IP addresses to any computer connected by AirPort, as well as

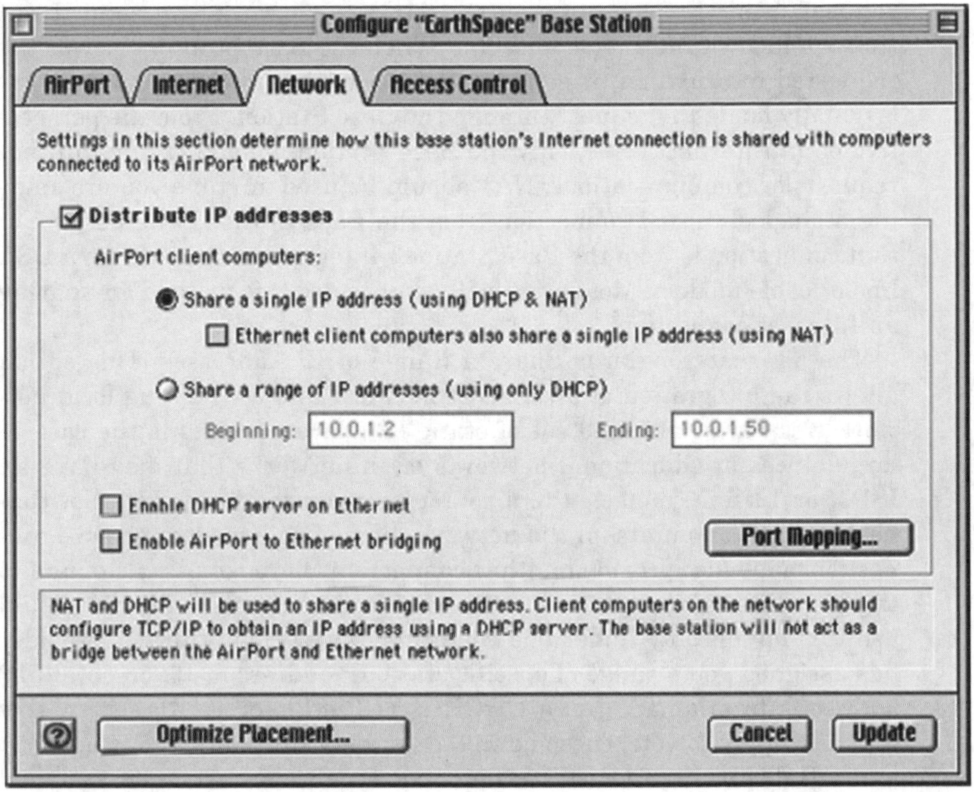

Figure 33-8   The AirPort Admin Utility's Network tab.

any other TCP/IP information needed for these computers to communicate with the network or the Internet.

The subfeatures of this the Distribute IP Addresses option are Share a Single IP Address (using DHCP and NAT) and Share a Range of IP Addresses (using only DHCP). Let's look at what each of these means. The first and default option is to share a single IP address. This is when the Base Station functions as an Internet router. It holds the only Internet connection used by any computer accessing the Internet through the AirPort network. It provides IP addresses that are internal to the AirPort network and do not extend to the Internet at large (much like the IP addresses of a private intranet) to each computer that connects to the AirPort network using the DHCP protocol. When each of these computers requests something from the Internet, the Base Station uses a technique called NAT (network address translation) to take that request from the computer on the AirPort network and send it out through its own Internet connection. When the Base Station receives the requested information, it sends that information to the computer that originally made the request through the Base Station. From the perspective of an Internet server, only the Base Station is making any Internet requests or communications. NAT should be used anytime you are sharing a single Internet connection from the Base Station, whether or not that connection is from the Base Station's internal modem or from a DSL line or cable modem. Most users will want to use this method for sharing an Internet connection

The alternate option is Share a Range of IP Addresses. This option allows the integration of an AirPort network into an existing local network with an established set of static IP addresses This is the case in large offices or educational networks or in networks that may have an ISDN or T1 line connected to a router providing multiple Internet connections for computers on the network. Some cable modem or DSL connections may also provide multiple connections for business customers in this way. Even if your network supports multiple connections, you should use this option only under one condition: when your Internet provider has assigned you a range of specific static IP addresses. If you obtain IP addresses from an ISP via a DHCP, Boot-P, PPP, or RARP server, this does not apply to you. These addresses are not internal to your network and are directly connected to the Internet. If you have been assigned multiple addresses like this, the DHCP server built into the Base Station can manage them for you, assigning them to computers connected via AirPort as needed. This can save you the hassle of manually configuring computers to a single static IP address when the computers in question may enter or leave your network at any given moment. It also allows those IP addresses (each of which is costing you money to use) to be used efficiently, rather than having each one used for only a small amount of time while a specific user is present at the network site. If you use this option, you will enter the range of IP address assigned by your Internet provider or network administrator in the appropriate fields. This option is probably the one that the least amount of people will use, but it is also the only way to use AirPort in any large-scale academic, corporate, or institutional setting.

When the Base Station is set to distribute IP addresses, either acting as a router and sharing a single Internet connection or simply acting as a DHCP server for a range of IP addresses from an Internet Service Provider, it can also be set to provide IP addresses to computers that are connected to a terrestrial Ethernet network, as well as to AirPort connected computers. This is an excellent option for home and small office users who want to share an Internet connection with both their AirPort-equipped and non-AirPort-capable computers. This option is set using the Also Provide IP Addresses on Ethernet checkbox.

If your network already has a DHCP server that handles the distribution of IP addresses to all computers, you can disable the Distribute IP Addresses feature completely. When this is done, the Base Station will serve no TCP/IP functions and will do nothing but act as a bridge between your wireless AirPort network computers and your existing Ethernet network. The computers using the AirPort network will continue to receive their IP addresses and TCP/IP information directly from your network's DHCP server. Similarly, you would uncheck the Distribute IP Addresses option if you want complete control over your network; you can manually assign IP addresses to each AirPort computer (though this is not something I suggest doing because of the additional work involved and because it isn't as efficient as using a DHCP server).

The last feature offered by the Network tab of the AirPort Admin Utility's window is the Port Mapping button. Port mapping allows you to run a server, whether a web server, an FTP server, or an AppleShare IP server, on one of the computers connected to the network by AirPort without turning off the Base Station's ability to share an Internet connection. Ordinarily, running such a server would require that the server be assigned its own static IP address. To assign it an individual address and still use AirPort, you would need to turn off the Base Station's Distribute IP Addresses abilities. This would mean no other computers could share the Base Station's Internet connection and that they would all need to be manually assigned an IP address as well. Port mapping gets around this by assigning ports of the IP address of the Base Station to specific computers connected to the Base Station.

For example, if you're running a web server off of an iMac DV connected by AirPort through a Base Station. Rather than assigning all the computers using that Base Station static IP address, you can set the web server to use the IP address of the Base Station. Since the default port of any web server is port 80, you can map any requests to that port of the Base Station's IP address to be sent to the IP address of the iMac DV. You still have to assign the iMac DV in question a manual IP address, but not all other computers using the Base Station are so restricted.

THE ACCESS CONTROL TAB   The final tab of the AirPort Admin Utility is the Access Control tab (see Figure 33-9). This tab allows you to restrict access to the Base Station to only certain computers. This is done by list-

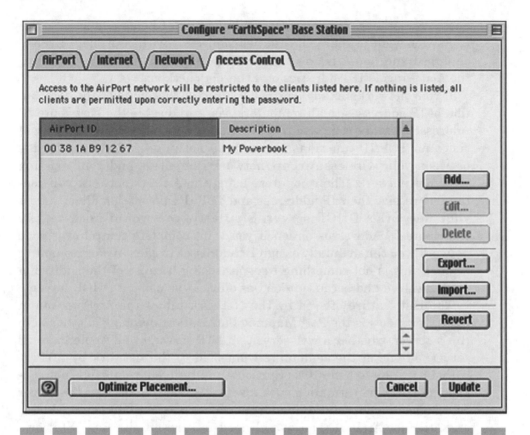

Figure 33-9   The AirPort Admin Utility's Access Control tab.

ing the MAC address/AirPort ID number of a computer's AirPort card. Only those computers that have one of the listed AirPort cards installed will be able to connect to the Base Station. This offers you the highest-possible level of AirPort network security. This tab is fairly easy to understand. The Add, Edit, and Delete buttons along the side of the window allow you to enter new AirPort Card ID numbers in the list, edit existing entries, and delete entries, respectively. When using the Add and Edit fields, you will be asked to include both the AirPort ID number of the card, as well as a description to help you remember which Mac goes with which card's ID number (such as Mr. Smith's iBook or Mom's PowerBook). The next two buttons, Export and Import, allow you to save access control lists as files on a disk and to retrieve those list files and enter them into the same or a different Base Station without having to retype the entire list. This also offers you a backup function for the access control lists. The Revert button will revert the access control list to the last updated changes (much like the revert function in Photoshop or Microsoft Word does with documents).

OTHER AIRPORT ADMIN UTILITY FEATURES The final section of the AirPort Admin Utility is consistently displayed along the bottom of the configuration window, regardless of which tab you're using. This includes the Optimize Placement, Cancel, and Update buttons. Optimize Placement brings up the dialog described in the "Placing Base Stations" section earlier in the chapter allows you to move an AirPort-equipped computer and/or a Base Station around a room or building and displays a graph of the signal strength. This is used to help you determine the best placement for Base Stations making up a network in a specific building.

The cancel button closes the configuration window for a Base Station without sending any changes you've made in the AirPort Admin Utility to the Base Station. Update sends the changes to the Base Station and updates the Base Station to reflect all of the changes you've made. Once the changes in configuration have been sent to the Base Station, the AirPort Admin Utility then issues the Base Station restart command. This causes the Base Station to restart immediately so that the changes you have made will be effective (much like restarting a Mac after installing new extensions).

Allowing Active Roaming Active roaming is a feature designed for AirPort networks that consist of multiple Base Stations. It allows all Base Stations in a network to behave as a single AirPort network rather than as individual AirPort networks unto themselves (each with separate names and passwords). An administrator enables active roaming by setting up all Base Stations with the same network name and password. Active roaming also requires that all the Base Stations be connected to each other by a terrestrial Ethernet network.

When active roaming is enabled, the individual Base Stations will communicate with each other (which is why active roaming requires a physical network connection between the Base Stations being used). When a user leaves the range of one Base Station, his or her connection will automatically be transferred to the Base Station whose range he or she has just entered. This allows users in a large AirPort network environment, such as an entire office building or college campus, to maintain a single connection while at the network site, regardless of their location relative to individual Base Stations.

All Base Stations must also be on the same TCP/IP subnet to enable active roaming. This means that the first three sections of the IP addresses assigned to each Base Station must be the same, with only the final section being used to determine each Base Station from the next. One approach to simplify subnet use for large-scale networks when using AirPort is to use a separate subnet for all Base Stations. This would be a subnet separate from the subnet(s) used for other devices or computers on the network (if you use this approach, you should keep one Mac on the AirPort subnet in case you need to reset one of the Base Stations, as described later in this chapter).

Also, if you are using the single AirPort network created by all the Base Stations for shared Internet access or to distribute IP addresses to AirPort-connected computers, you should set only one of the Base Stations to distribute IP addresses to the entire network. You should disable the Distribute IP Addresses feature for all remaining Base Stations by using the AirPort Admin Utility. You may also need to have a range of actual IP addresses assigned to you for computers connected to an active roaming network using both Active Roaming and network address translation (NAT) to share a single Internet connection.

Base Station LED Indicators   Apple's hardware Base Stations include three LED indicator lights. These lights allow you to determine the status of the Base Station. The lights will glow or flash either green or amber to indicate the Base Station's status. Table 33-3 describes the functions of each of the lights.

Sharing Internet Access   Sharing Internet access through AirPort is generally a relatively simple process. This is particularly true if you will be sharing access in a small home network. The following paragraphs discuss setting up shared Internet access in specific situations.

TABLE 33-3

Hardware Base Station LED Indicators.

Light or Combination	Meaning When Green	Meaning Amber
Center	Powered and operating	Awaiting reset
Left	AirPort data communication in progress	
Right	Ethernet or modem data communication in progress	Modem dialing
All three		Starting up

WHEN THERE IS NO EXISTING NETWORK If you are creating an AirPort network where no network previously existed, such as in a home, or where a network did not previously include shared Internet access, the process involved in setting up a Base Station to share an Internet connection is extremely basic and can usually be performed using just the AirPort Setup Assistant. Simply have your Internet settings (whether they use a dial-up modem connection, cable modem, or DSL line) already configured on the Mac on which you are running the AirPort Setup Assistant. When the AirPort Setup Assistant asks if you wish to configure the Base Station for shared Internet Access, simply say OK. The current Internet settings for your Mac will be copied to the Base Station.

WHEN YOU ALREADY HAVE SHARED INTERNET ACCESS If your existing network already has a method for shared Internet access, such as a software-based router (routers are discussed in more detail in the next chapter) or full LAN connection, then you may face some more complicated issues. For home or small office uses where a software or hardware router is being used, you may opt to use the Base Station instead of such a router product. Simply remove the router and proceed to use the Base Station instead.

WHEN YOU ARE USING A DIAL-UP CONNECTION If your Internet connection is a dial-up modem connection and you use the Base Station for Internet access, you need to use the AirPort application to dial your Internet service provider using the Base Station's modem. Similarly, you use the AirPort application to hang up the modem connection when you are done with the connection. This can be accessed from any Mac that is connected to the Base Station's network.

WHEN YOU HAVE A LARGER NETWORK If you have a moderate or large network, using the Base Station to share the Internet connection may not be the best situation for all computers on the network. If this is the case, you can configure the Base Station to share whatever Internet connection you are using for your LAN with only Macs connected via AirPort. Do this by manually assigning an IP address to the Base Station. Then turn on the Base Station's Distribute IP Address feature in the AirPort Admin Utility's network pane, but do not check the Also Provide IP Addresses on Ethernet option. This allows the Base Station to have an Internet connection through your LAN, as an individual computer would, and to share that connection with only those Macs connected to the network via AirPort. For AirPort-equipped Macs to use the Internet connection shared by a Base Station, it will need to have TCP/IP set as follows: The Connect Via menu needs to be set to AirPort, and the Configure menu needs to be set to Using DHCP Server.

AirPort Versions   As of this writing, Apple has released two revisions to the AirPort software (the current version is 1.2). When new versions are released, an updater utility can be downloaded from Apple's website. This utility allows you to update both the AirPort software on AirPort-equipped Macs to take advantage of new features or refinements and to update the firmware of existing hardware Base Stations so that they can provide newer features and more stable performance. You can check Apple's website to see if such updates have been released on a periodic basis. The updater applications will include instructions for how to update earlier Base Stations.

NOTE: *When you download AirPort updates, you must install them consistently across your network so that all AirPort-equipped computers and Base Stations are running the same version of the AirPort software. Running an AirPort network with multiple versions of AirPort present can lead to poor performance and unexpected network behavior.*

If You Forget a Base Station Password   If you forget or lose the password to a Base Station, you can reset the Base Station to its default password (public) for a period of five minutes. Do this by using a straightened-out paper clip to press the reset button that is located in the bottom of the Base Station (see Figure 33-10).

NOTE: *When doing this, you must only press the reset button for one second. If you continue pressing the reset button for five seconds, you will begin the process of completely resetting the Base Station to its factory specifications (see next section).*

During the five minutes that the Base Station's password is reset to "public," connect to the Base Station and use the AirPort Admin Utility to change the password. If you do not do this within five minutes, the Base Station will resume using the previously entered password and you will need to start the process over again.

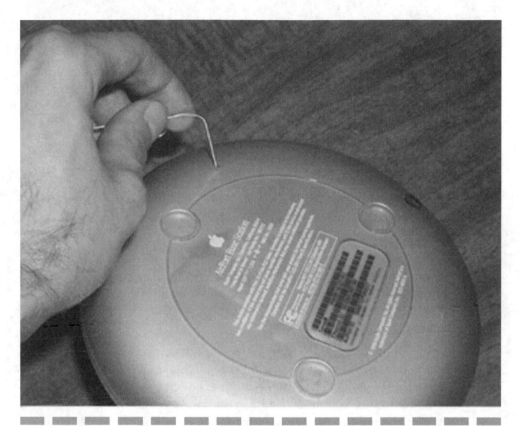

Figure 33-10   Pressing a Base Station's reset button.

Resetting a Base Station   If needed, a hardware Base Station can be reset to its factory default settings. This can be done if you are experiencing repeated problems with a Base Station, if you plan to give or sell the Base Station to someone else, or if you have any other need to restore the Base Station to its initial state and to remove any and all settings that have been stored in the Base Station. Because all settings and information will be lost during a reset, you should only reset the Base Station as a last resort.

To reset the Base Station, you need the AirPort CD-ROM that came with the Base Station and a straightened-out paper clip. If the Base Station has been updated to a newer version of the AirPort software than it originally came with, you should use the updater's files when resetting the Base Station, rather than the ones that were included on the CD-ROM that came with the Base Station.

To reset the Base Station, follow these steps:

1. First, connect to the Base Station from a computer that is on the same Ethernet network as the Base Station (if the Base Station is not part of an Ethernet network, connect a computer to it using an Ethernet hub or crossover cable). Resetting a Base Station requires an Ethernet connection and cannot be done by a computer connected via AirPort. On a large network with multiple subnets, the computer you connect from should be on the same subnet as the Base Station.

2. Next, change the TCP/IP and AppleTalk settings for the Mac connected to the Base Station to connect via Ethernet (if this is not already selected).

3. In the TCP/IP control panel, set the Configure menu to Manually. Manually configure TCP/IP as follows: In the IP Address field, enter "192.42.249.14," and in the Subnet Mask field enter "255.255.255.0." Close the TCP/IP (and AppleTalk if you needed to change it) control panel.

4. Now disconnect the Base Station's power adapter and reconnect it. As the Base Station powers up, all three lights on it will glow amber. When this happens, insert the straightened-out paper clip into the reset hole in the bottom of the Base Station (see Figure 33-10). Continue using the paper clip to press the reset button inside the hole until only the center light is glowing amber (the light to the right may or may not flash green). At this point, launch the AirPort Admin Utility.

5. Choose the Base Station you want to reset from the list in the AirPort Admin Utility's window. The Base Station will have its AirPort ID/MAC address number listed as its name and it will be using the default IP address of 192.42.249.13.

6. After you've selected the Base Station, select Open Configuration File from the File menu. In the Open dialog box, select the Base Station Software file on the AirPort CD-ROM.

7. Once you have selected this file, choose the Upload Software item from the File menu. The AirPort Admin Utility should then reset the Base Station and inform you when the reset is complete.

8. At this point, use the AirPort Setup Assistant or the AirPort Admin Utility to configure the Base Station as needed.

Setting Up a Software Base Station

A software Base Station can be created using either the AirPort Setup Assistant or the AirPort Utility. Using either one, the process is fairly simple, though the AirPort Utility does allow you to control some of the advanced functions. When a Mac is being used as a software Base Station, it can share its Internet connection as easily as a hardware Base Station can. Simply establish the connection (dial-up modem or otherwise) as you normally would when using the Mac as a software Base Station. If a Mac acting as a software Base Station is shut down or enters sleep mode, the software Base Station feature will become inactive and any computer connected to the AirPort network through the software Base Station will be disconnected.

Using the AirPort Setup Assistant   The AirPort Setup Assistant makes it extremely simple to turn an AirPort-equipped Mac into a software Base Station. Simply choose the Setup Your Computer to Be an AirPort Software Base Station radio button from the Setup Assistant's main window, and click on the right arrow button at the bottom of the window. The Setup Assistant will then go through a process similar to when you are setting up a hardware Base Station, after which it will turn on the software Base Station function with the network name and password you choose. It will also turn on sharing of the Mac's Internet connection to any AirPort-equipped Macs that connect to the software Base Station.

Using the AirPort Utility   Using the AirPort Utility, it is also fairly easy to configure an AirPort-equipped Mac to act as a software Base Station. Simply launch the AirPort application and click on the Software Base Station button. This will display the window shown in Figure 33-11, which contains the Start/Stop, Network, and Access Control tabs. As you can see, this window bears a striking resemblance to the AirPort Admin Utility's window for configuring a hardware Base Station. In fact, the Network and Access Control tabs function exactly the same as these tabs do in the AirPort Admin Utility's window (refer to the earlier "Using the AirPort Admin Utility" section for details on these functions).

The remaining tab, Start/Stop, allows you to turn on the Software Base Station feature and make the Mac into a software Base Station. It also allows you to enter the network name created by the software Base Station and to choose the AirPort channel that the software Base Station

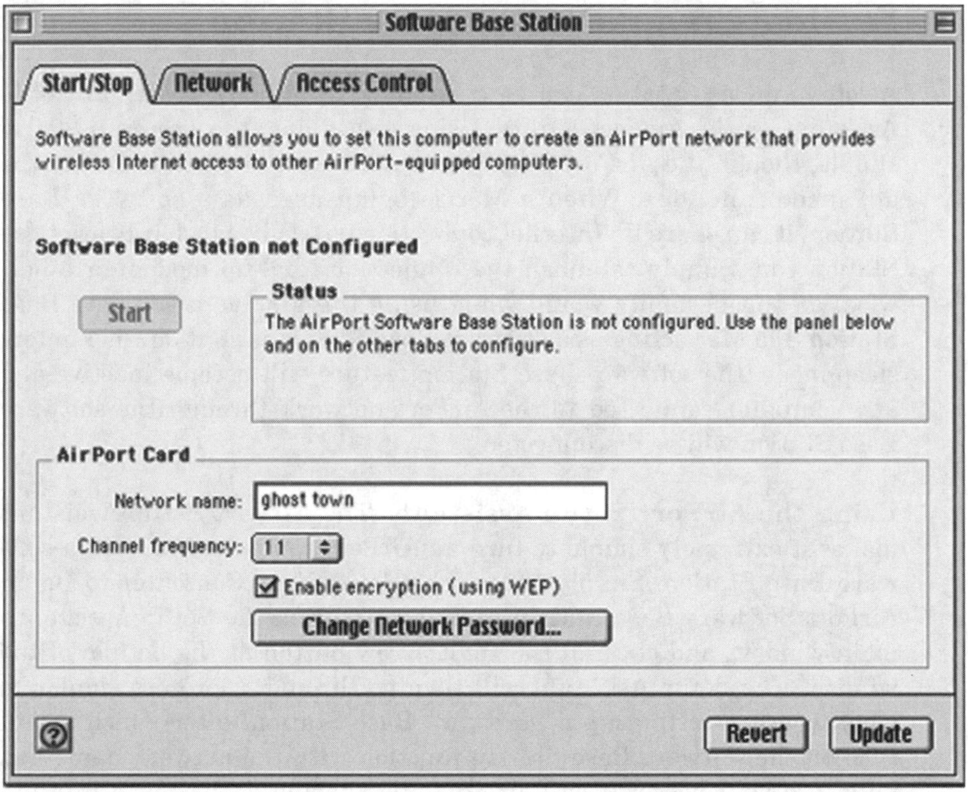

Figure 33-11   The Configuration window for a software Base Station.

will use for all its AirPort communications and to create or change the network password. The Enable Encryption checkbox turns the encryption function on or off for the Base Station. This should be left checked unless you are using third-party 802.11 wireless products that don't support encryption.

Connecting to an AirPort Network

Connecting to an AirPort network is a very simple procedure. Once an AirPort network is configured, you simply need to make sure your Mac's AirPort card is turned on and then select the AirPort network that you wish to connect to. This can be done through a number of methods. Whichever method you use, you will be asked to supply the network password to access the network when you establish the connection. You may also be asked for this password when waking the Mac from sleep mode. The network password is entered when setting up the Base Station. If you did not enter a password, that the Base Station may be continuing to use Apple's default password, which is "public." If someone else set up the Base Station for you or you are connecting to a larger-scale business or institutional network, ask the person who set up the Base Station or your network administrator for the network password.

If you wish to use AppleTalk file sharing over AirPort, you need to be certain that the AppleTalk control panel is set to Connect Via AirPort. Similar to accessing the Internet connection of a Base Station (or TCP/IP-based file sharing), you must set the TCP/IP control panel to Connect Via AirPort. This is automatically set by default if you use the AirPort Setup Assistant to establish your connection.

Using the AirPort Setup Assistant   The AirPort Setup Assistant is a good tool for users using AirPort for the first time on their Macintosh computers. After selecting the Setup Your Computer to Join an Existing Wireless Network radio button from the Setup Assistant's window, the user is presented with available AirPort networks to choose from (if only one network is available, this is skipped). The user then is asked to enter the network's password. Following that, the Setup Assistant connects the Mac to the chosen AirPort network and also configures both TCP/IP and AppleTalk to connect via AirPort without the user needing to change either control panel's settings by hand. Once a user is familiar with using AirPort, he or she will probably find connecting to or choosing networks through the Control Strip module or the AirPort Utility easier and more convenient.

Using the AirPort Utility   The AirPort application (by default installed in the Apple menu) allows you to select from all AirPort networks that are within range of your AirPort-equipped Mac. This list is presented as a pop-up menu in the AirPort Network section of the application's window, as shown in Figure 33-12. Select a network name from the list to join that network. Just below the pop-up menu is a bar graph indicating the signal strength of the connection with the chosen network or Base Station. Below this indicator is the Base Station ID, which is the MAC address/AirPort ID number of the Base Station.

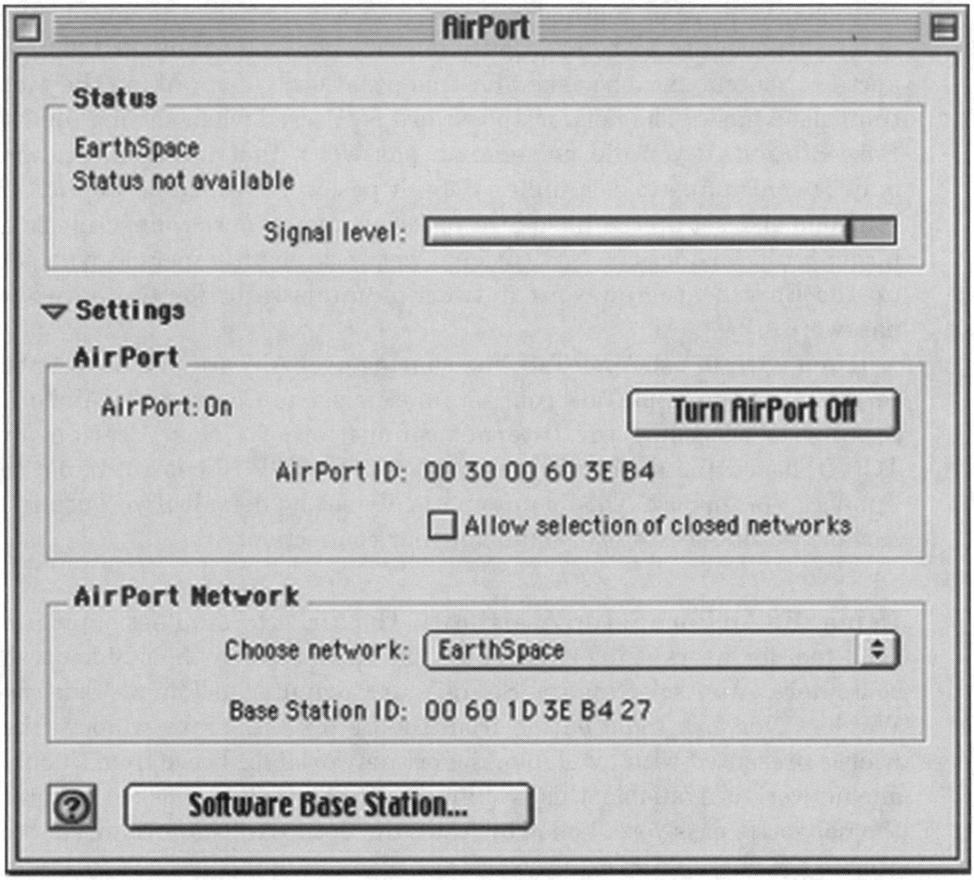

Figure 33-12 Connecting to a network using the AirPort Utility.

Using the AirPort Control Strip Item The AirPort Control Strip module, shown in Figure 33-13, provides a menu that, when clicked, includes the names of all AirPort networks within range of the Mac. To join one of the networks listed, simply select it from the menu. In addition to the available networks, the control strip module allows you turn the Mac's AirPort card on or off and to select computer to computer mode.

Connecting to a Closed Network One of the features of the 802.11 wireless networking protocol (which AirPort is based on) is the ability for network administrators to create closed networks. These are wireless networks with an added security feature that prevents them from being

Figure 33-13
The AirPort control
strip module.

listed in the AirPort application's Select Network menu or in the AirPort Control Strip (or similar utilities for non-AirPort 802.11 networking products). To access a closed network, you must know the network's name.

To access a closed network, you first need to obtain the network's name and password from your network administrator. You can then access the network by launching the AirPort application and checking the Allow Selection of Closed Networks checkbox. This adds an item entitled Other to the Choose Network pop-up menu. Selecting this item brings up a dialog box asking the user to enter the name and password of the closed network, as shown in Figure 33-14.

Connecting by Computer to Computer

To establish a computer-to-computer connection, first open the AirPort utility. Select Computer to Computer from the Choose Network pop-up menu. You can also choose Computer to Computer Mode from the menu of the AirPort control strip module. Once Computer to Computer Mode is chosen, you can establish a connection to another AirPort-equipped Mac that is also in computer-to-computer mode using the Network Browser

Enter the name of the AirPort network to join and the optional password.

Name:

Password:

Cancel   OK

application as you would for accessing any other Mac over a network. The Mac that is sharing files must have File Sharing turned on. Both Macs also must have AppleTalk (or TCP/IP) turned on and set to AirPort.

Apple suggests that computer-to-computer mode be used only by two AirPort computers at once, although multiple computers can be used at one time. Also, Computer to Computer mode does not include any built-in security or encryption features beyond the Mac OS File Sharing privileges. If you are using computer-to-computer mode and have a guest account active for file sharing, someone may be able to connect to your computer without any authentication.

Securing an AirPort Network

When using a Base Station (whether hardware or software), AirPort supports the Wired Equivalent Privacy (or WEP) security features of the 802.11 wireless networking standard. WEP requires that anyone connecting to a wireless network identify himself or herself with a password. Once a connection is established, all communications between an AirPort-equipped computer and the Base Station are secured with 40-bit encryption. This makes it very unlikely that someone would be able to eavesdrop on the communication taking place between a user's computer and the Base Station. It also ensures that someone without the network password will not be able to access the network. WEP requires that a network password be set when a Base Station is configured.

On top of the basic WEP security functions, you also have the same security options that a wired network has for individual computers and servers by using the Mac OS File Sharing feature to create individual users and groups. These access privileges are controlled on each computer or file server exactly as they would be when you are administering a traditional wired network. These privileges can help prevent users from accessing servers and files that you don't want them to have access to.

Beyond these two security options, AirPort administrators can establish a third level of security by restricting access to an AirPort network to specific computers. The AirPort Admin Utility's Access control tab allows you to restrict access to a Base Station by specifying the MAC address (also referred to as the AirPort ID) numbers of specific AirPort cards. This prevents any computer that does not have the specified AirPort cards installed from accessing the network at all.

Adding AirPort to a Terrestrial Network

Adding AirPort abilities to an existing network is a fairly simple procedure. Attach the Base Station that you wish to add to the network using the Base Station's Ethernet port. If the network already has a DHCP server being used to configure the TCP/IP settings of computers on it, you can turn off the DHCP functions of the Base Station as described in the "Using the AirPort Admin Utility" section earlier in the chapter. When set this way, the Base Station will function as nothing but a bridge between the wireless AirPort-equipped Macs and the terrestrial wired network.

If the existing network uses manually configured TCP/IP settings, you can assign an IP address to the Base Station manually. With a manual IP address, you can then enable the Base Station's DHCP services but only enable them for computers connected by AirPort. This allows you to maintain your existing network without needing to manually configure all of the AirPort-equipped Macs that you may offer service to (alternatively, you can assign IP addresses manually to each AirPort-equipped Mac, if you so choose).

For AppleTalk connections, you do not need to be concerned with any special settings when using AirPort or a Base Station. Simply add the Base Station to your network, and configure all AirPort-equipped Macs to Connect Via AirPort in the AppleTalk control panel. These Macs will then have access to any AppleTalk servers on the network.

Network printers connected to an existing Ethernet network can also be accessed by AirPort-equipped Macs. Users of these Macs will see no difference in accessing the printers over AirPort than in accessing them through an Ethernet connection. This is because the Base Station will function as a wireless bridge for all network traffic, allowing print jobs to be directed to a network printer chosen using the Chooser or Desktop Printer Utility on the AirPort-equipped Mac.

Installing an AirPort Card

Unless you custom-order a Mac with an AirPort card installed from the Apple store, you need to buy the AirPort card separately and install it yourself. Installing an AirPort card in the current Macs is an extremely easy process and can be accomplished by just about anyone. The following sections describe the process of installing an AirPort card in each of the current Macs. As with all hardware installations, make certain that the computer is shut down, unplugged, and that you are properly grounded. You should also remove the internal batteries from portable Macs, such as the iBook and PowerBook, during installation.

When you purchase an AirPort card, it will most likely come with an AirPort card adapter attached to the card itself, as shown in Figure 33-15.

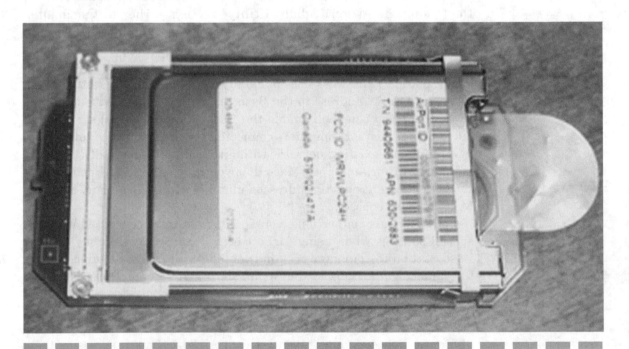

Figure 33-15   The AirPort Card adapter attached to an AirPort card.

This adapter is only used when you are installing the AirPort card into a slot-loading iMac computer. For Power Mac, PowerBook, and iBook installations, you need to remove the adapter from the card. Do this by removing the metal clip that holds the card against the adapter. With the clip removed, simply pull the card from the adapter's connector. You can save the clip and adapter if you expect to ever install the card in an iMac.

Before installing an AirPort card, make sure that the most recent version of Apple's AirPort software is installed on the computer. You can generally be assured of this by running the installer program on the CD-ROM included with the AirPort card. It is possible, however, that a recent Mac OS update includes a newer version of the AirPort software. To be certain which version is newer (the one included with the card or the one installed on your Mac), launch the AirPort application installed on your hard drive and select About AirPort from the Apple menu. This will display the version of the AirPort software installed. The CD-ROM included with the AirPort card will include its version number right on the label.

The Power Mac G4

NOTE: *This applies to Power Mac G4 computers with an AGP graphics card only. The earlier G4 computers with a PCI graphics card cannot accept an AirPort card.*

To install an AirPort card:

1. Open the side door of the computer.
2. With the side of the computer laying flat in front of you, locate the AirPort card guide and insertion socket, as shown in Figure 33-16.
3. Insert the card through the guide with the side of the card that contains the card's ID number and bar codes facing up (the side with the AirPort logo should be facing down).
4. Press the card into the connector until it is secure.
5. Next, locate the antenna cable. This should be located somewhere near the card guide and may be tucked under the guide.
6. Attach the round end of the antenna cable into the small round hole in the edge of the card that protrudes from the guide/connector, as shown in Figure 33-17.

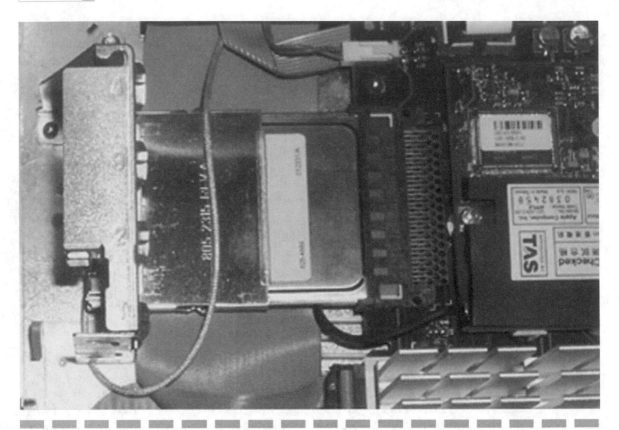

Figure 33-16   The AirPort card inserted through the guide into the insertion socket inside a Power Mac G4.

7. Once the antenna cable is connected, the card is installed. You can now close up the computer and restart.

The AirPort Setup Assistant should launch on restart. If it does not, you can launch it or the any of the other AirPort utilities to set up or join an AirPort network as described earlier in this chapter.

The iMac

NOTE: *This applies to slot-loading iMacs only. Older iMacs cannot accept an AirPort card.*

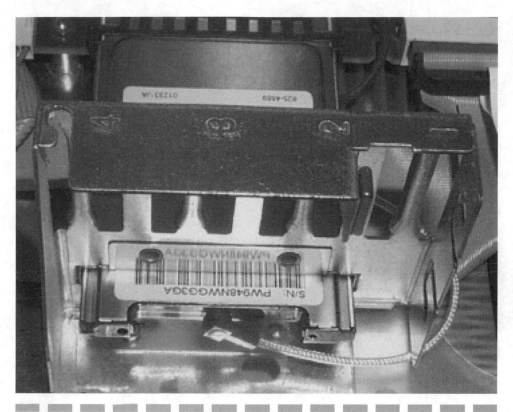

Figure 33-17   The AirPort antenna cable connected to the AirPort card.

To install an AirPort card:

1. Place the iMac forward on its built-in display. The AirPort card will be installed in the same compartment as the iMac's RAM and can be installed without disassembling the iMac at all.

2. Locate the access panel that covers the RAM and AirPort sockets. It has a large plastic "screw" at the top and is shown in Figure 33-18.

3. Use a coin to turn the oversized "screw" and release the access panel. The panel will drop forward but not come off completely.

4. Inside the panel, locate the two RAM sockets (one or both of which will have a DIMM module installed). Above these is the bracket into which the AirPort card is installed.

5. Attached to one side of the bracket is the AirPort antenna cable, shown in Figure 33-19. Remove it from the bracket. There may be a protective cap over the end of the cable. If so, remove it.

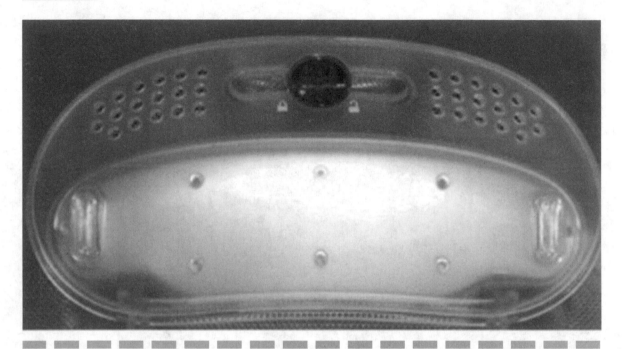

Figure 33-18   This "screw" secures the compartment where the iMac's RAM and AirPort card are installed.

6. Attach the cable to the round hole at the edge of the AirPort card that is not secured in the AirPort card adapter, shown in Figure 33-17.

7. Next, line the AirPort card adapter up with the bracket. The side of the adapter with the AirPort card and metal clip should be facing down, and the antenna cable connection should be to the left, as shown in Figure 33-20. Slide the adapter (with the card) into the bracket until it is seated securely.

8. Close the access panel and secure it using the oversized plastic "screw."

9. Restart the iMac and set up your AirPort network connections using the one or all of the AirPort software as describer earlier.

The iBook

To install an AirPort card:

1. With the iBook shut down and battery removed, release the keyboard tabs at the top edge of the keyboard as described in Chapter 2.

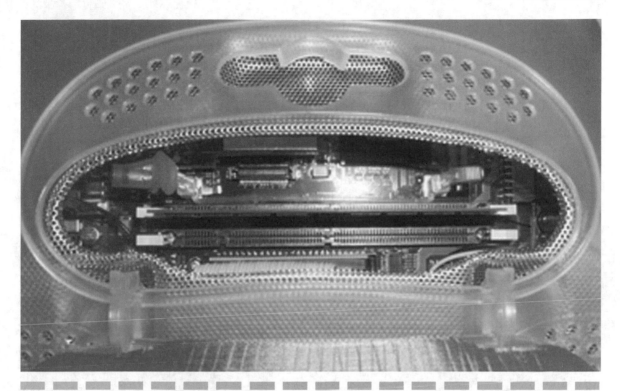

Figure 33-19   The compartment for the iMac's RAM and AirPort card.

Figure 33-20   Inserting the AirPort card and AirPort card adapter into the iMac.

2. Flip the keyboard up onto the iBook's built-in wrist rests.

3. In the center of the iBook beneath the keyboard, locate the metal bracket, shown in Figure 33-21, that will secure the AirPort card. Also locate the AirPort antenna cable, which is tucked under the bracket.

4. Flip the bracket up and release the antenna cable. Attach the end of the cable to the round hole in the edge of the AirPort card opposite the card's connectors, as shown in Figure 33-17.

5. Next, slide the card underneath the metal bracket. The side of the card with the serial number, AirPort ID number, and bar codes should be facing up and the side with the AirPort logo should be

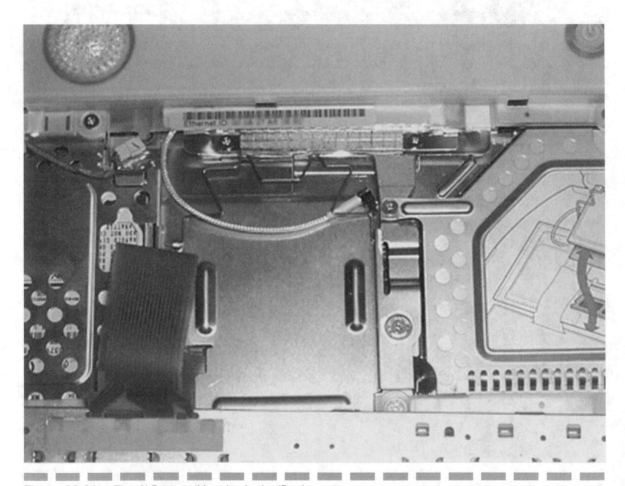

Figure 33-21   The AirPort card bracket in the iBook.

facing down. The edge with the card's connectors should be facing the iBook's trackpad. Push the card straight forward toward the trackpad until it is secure in the connector.

6. Once the card is securely inserted, flip the metal bracket down. The edges of the metal bracket should fit behind the AirPort card, securing it in place, as shown in Figure 33-22. The bracket should not rest on top of the AirPort card.

7. Replace the keyboard and reinstall the battery.

Figure 33-22 The AirPort card inserted in the iBook and secured with the metal bracket.

8. Restart the iBook and use the AirPort Setup Assistant or the other AirPort utilities to establish your wireless network settings.

The PowerBook (FireWire)

NOTE: *This applies to only PowerBooks with built-in FireWire ports released in 2000. Earlier PowerBooks will need to use a third-party wireless PC Card such as Farallon's SkyLINE or Lucent's WaveLAN products to connect to an AirPort network.*

1. Unplug the PowerBook and remove one or both batteries.
2. Remove the PowerBook's keyboard and flip it up over the PowerBook's wrist rests, as described in Chapter 2.
3. Remove the two screws indicated in Figure 33-23 that hold the first heat sink in place. Then remove this first heat sink (there is no need to remove the lower L-shaped heat sink that covers the first processor and the modem card).

Figure 33-23   These screws hold the heat sink in place.

4. With the heat sink removed, locate the AirPort antenna cable. It should be located to the left of the processor module and may be tucked under a narrow ribbon cable. Attach the end of the antenna cable to the hole in the edge of the AirPort card opposite the edge with the card's connectors, as shown in Figure 33-17. With the antenna cable attached, align the card for insertion. The side of the card with the AirPort ID and serial numbers should be facing up. The edge of the card with the connectors should face the left side of the PowerBook, away from the processor module.

5. Press the card into the AirPort socket. The socket is located underneath the lip of the case on the left side of the PowerBook, directly above the PC Card slot. Tuck the side of the card under this lip of the case as well as the lip of the back edge of the case (between the keyboard opening and the display). When the card is inserted completely, as shown in Figure 33-24, and is secure beneath the edges of the case, you are ready to replace the heat sink and keyboard. When completely inserted, the card should appear as shown in Figure 33-24.

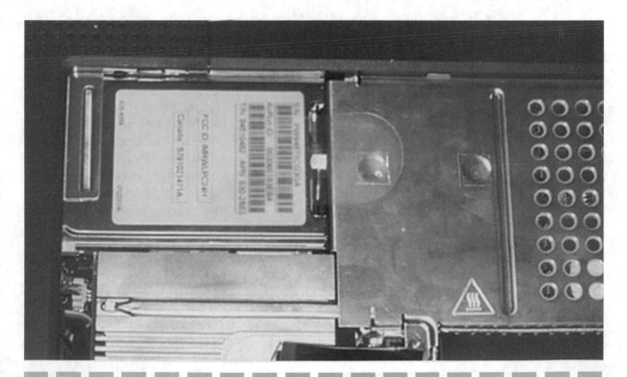

Figure 33-24   The AirPort card properly inserted in the PowerBook.

6. When replacing the heat sink, make sure that the clear plastic tabs attached to the AirPort card and the hard drive (which is to the right of the processor module, opposite the AirPort card) are not caught under the heat sink. The clear plastic tab attached to the processor module, however, should be tucked under the heat sink.

7. With the heat sink replaced and secured with the two screws, reattach the keyboard. Once the keyboard is reattached, replace the battery and AC adapter and restart the PowerBook. Use the AirPort Setup Assistant or other software to establish or join an AirPort network.

Troubleshooting AirPort

Following are common AirPort problems, along with their solutions.

The Mac Doesn't List Any AirPort Networks

Check to be certain that the Mac's AirPort card is turned on. Make sure you are within range of a Base Station (hardware or software) that is turned on and properly configured. Also make certain that AirPort is chosen in the Connect Via menu in both the AppleTalk and TCP/IP control panels.

If this doesn't help, there may be problems with your computer or the Base Station. Try accessing the Base Station using the AirPort Setup Assistant or AirPort Admin Utility. If the Mac is still unable to see the Base Station, try restarting the Base Station by unplugging it and plugging it back in. If this doesn't solve the problem, try restarting the Mac. If this doesn't help, ensure that the Mac's AirPort card is installed correctly. If the AirPort card is installed correctly, try reinstalling the AirPort software on the Mac and/or resetting the Base Station to its initial default settings as described earlier in this chapter.

AirPort Network Performance Is Very Slow

You may be too far from the Base Station for good performance. Check the AirPort signal strength indicator in the AirPort control strip module or in the AirPort utility. If signal strength is very low, move closer to the Base Station. This should increase performance. If you are within range of multiple Base Stations, check to be certain that each is using a separate AirPort channel that is at least five channels away from the others.

Also, if there are a number of users accessing the Base Station simultaneously, performance will degrade because of the increased traffic.

Unable to Connect to an AirPort Network

If the Mac displays an AirPort network but is unable to connect to the network, ensure that you are using the correct password to access the network.

Loss of Connection

If you lose your AirPort network connection, it may be due to a number of factors. First, ensure that you are still within range of the Base Station. Leaving a Base Station's range will, obviously, cause you to lose your connection. Also, make certain that you are not near any objects that might be generating interference.

Loss of connection can also occur if you are accessing a software Base Station and the computer running the software Base Station is shut down or goes into sleep mode, or experiences a crash or freeze up. If you are using a software Base Station, ensure that it is set not to enter sleep mode by using the Energy Saver control panel.

Finally, if you move out of range of one Base Station and into the range of another Base Station where active roaming is not enabled between Base Stations in a network, you may briefly lose connection as the Mac switches to the new Base Station. You may need to select the new Base Station using either the AirPort application or the AirPort Control Strip. You will also likely need to provide the network password for the new Base Station.

Required AirPort Software Is Not Installed Error

If the Mac displays an error saying that the required AirPort software is not installed when you launch any of the AirPort utilities or when you try to connect to an AirPort network, it is likely that one or more of the AirPort extensions have become disabled or deleted. Reinstall the AirPort software from your Mac OS CD or the CD-ROM that came with your AirPort card.

If this error persists, it may indicate that the Mac's AirPort card is not installed properly. Check to be certain that the AirPort card is installed correctly as described earlier in this chapter.

Base Station Modem Is Unable to Access the Internet

Check to be certain that the access settings being used by the Base Station are correct.

NOTE: *Online services such as AOL and CompuServe, which are not true Internet service providers, are not supported by AirPort and cannot be accessed or shared by a Base Station.*

Assuming the Internet connections are correct, try redialing. It is possible that a problem may be an isolated case, such as you ISP's modem not responding quickly enough, that will be solved by making another access attempt. If the problem persists, check with your ISP to be certain that they are not experiencing any technical problems. If they are not, try dialing using the Mac's internal modem to verify that the problem is with the Base Station. If the Mac connects with no problem, run the AirPort Setup Assistant again to copy the settings from your Mac to the Base Station a second time. If the Mac is unable to dial your ISP successfully, contact your ISP to verify your settings are correct.

Base Station Is Unable to Access a Cable Modem or DSL Connection

Chapter 36 describes known issues when Macs and Base Stations are being used to access a cable modem or DSL connection because of a problem with the provider's DHCP server. Refer to that chapter for additional information.

Resources for Further Study

The following URLs provide additional information on some of the concepts, issues, and products discussed in the chapter:

About.com Mac Hardware AirPort Resources—
    http://machardware.about.com/msubairport.htm

Apple's AirPort Support Page—
    http://www.info.apple.com/support/pages.taf?product=airport

*Apple's General AirPort Site—*http://www.apple.com/airport

CHAPTER 34

Mac Networks and the Internet

This chapter looks at some of the ways that the Internet can be important in your Mac network setup. Two primary areas are covered: running web servers and FTP servers on the Macintosh and sharing Internet access among a network of Macs. Later, we'll discuss how to prevent your network from intrusion through your Internet connections and services.

Running Web and FTP Servers on the Mac

Providing Internet services, including web and FTP services, means you have a computer running as a server. This server receives requests for information using the TCP/IP protocols on which the Internet is based. The server evaluates the request and returns the requested information. The computer that requested the information is often called a *client*.

There are several different kinds of Internet servers that can be run on the Mac, though we will only look at web servers and FTP servers. You can offer Internet services to the Internet at large or to your own local intranet (intranets are discussed as a network component in Chapter 32). The software and setup process is virtually identical for both Internet and intranet servers.

When a Mac is referred to as a server, that means the Mac is running a software package (also called a server) that allows it to receive and respond to requests for a given type of Internet service. A web server application, such as WebSTAR, gives your Mac the ability to receive requests for web pages from a computer with a web browser and to transmit the requested pages to that computer. Each type of Internet service works somewhat differently, but all are handled by a server application responding to requests from a client computer. You can run multiple Internet servers on a given Mac, but it is best to run only one server package for each type of service you want to offer (one web server, one FTP server, and so on).

Each Internet server uses what is called a *port*. A port is like a channel to which the server will listen for requests from clients. Each server listens to a single port, and each type of Internet service has a default port number assigned to it. For example, the default port of a web server is port 80. You can choose to assign nonstandard ports to a server, meaning it will listen for requests on whatever port you assign to it. This can be good if you are running multiple servers of the same type on a single machine (web servers running on ports 80 and 81, for example). An example of why you might want to do this would be in order to maintain separate servers for a company's Internet web site and a separate server for their intranet site. When you assign a different port to a server, users attempting to access it will need to know the nonstandard port number and include it in the URL. This is done by placing a colon after the server's address followed by the port number (www.myserver.com:81 or 192.0.0.1:220). In web, FTP, and similar addresses, where a URL continues with a path to a specific document after the initial server address, the remaining portion of the URL is placed after the port number (www.myserver.com:81/myfiles/mypage.html).

A number of server applications are available for Mac users to run web servers. These applications can run the gamut from simple, freeware titles to commercial software costing hundreds of dollars with extremely powerful features and flexibility. For simplicity, I'll use only one or two examples for web and FTP servers to give you an understanding of the concepts and setup of these services.

Almost all servers produce log files. These files contain lists of all the activities the server has performed. All file requests, transfers, attempts by unauthorized users to access files, and so forth are logged. Some servers allow you to specify which types of events you want included in server logs, which can make reviewing the logs easier. Server logs allow you to search for specific information and problems (though given the size of some of these logs, it may seem like finding a needle in a haystack to do so).

It is important to understand that running an Internet web server on your Mac does present risks. It exposes your Mac to anyone on the Internet. Even with the best security measures available, it is possible to hack into any such server. If someone does gain access to your Mac through a server running on it, that person can do serious damage to files that are stored on it, as well as gain access to any personal information you keep on that computer. For this reason, you should consider other alternatives, such as free or commercial web hosting, before deciding to use your Mac as an Internet web server. FTP servers also pose these risks, though they may be slightly less likely if you limit the number of users, do not allow anonymous or guest logins, and limit what folders users have access to. If you are using your Mac as a server solely on a local or corporate intranet, you are still at some risk, but only from users of your intranet.

Web Servers

The most popular type of Internet service is the Web, which makes it an excellent place to start our discussion of servers you can run on the Mac. The Web functions by using a protocol known as *Hypertext Transfer Protocol* (the well-known *http* of an Internet address) to send and receive data between a server and client (a web browser such as Netscape or Internet Explorer). A web server can serve just about any kind of file over HTTP, from basic HTML documents (or web pages) and simple image files to Java applets and applications, QuickTime movies, and just about anything else. In general, HTTP operates in one direction between the client and server, sending files to the client in response to requests for them. Requests are generated when someone clicks on a link, loads a page with images or other files embedded in it, or types in the address of a given Web page or file. Data from forms, scripts, or applets can, however, be sent back to the server for processing.

A very basic web server is actually part of the standard Mac OS. Apple's Personal Web Sharing control panel enables users to set a folder for web pages and to make those pages available without installing any other software. Although Personal Web Sharing is effective, it is extremely basic and doesn't offer any advanced features, settings, or controls. In the following sections, we'll look at Apple's Personal Web Sharing, as well as three other web server packages.

Once set up and running, web servers generally don't need any intervention to function. They receive file requests and respond to them. There isn't even much to see while they're running—just a window indicating activity and, perhaps, the ability to change settings.

While there are any number of features to be found in web server packages, there are two—CGI scripts and server-side includes—that you should be familiar with regardless of your intention to use them. These features are discussed in the following sections relating to specific web server packages. They are also commonly used in web page design and allow you to provide more interactive and dynamic websites.

CGI (common gateway interface) scripts are small programs that you can store on your Mac that take information submitted from a user, process it, and return a given action. CGI scripts can be used for a wide variety of purposes. One common use is to receive form data from a web page and process it in some way. Other common uses for CGI scripts include operating a site search feature, operating a page counter, providing current (self-updating) information like stock quotes or weather forecasts, and directing users to specific pages based on the time of day or the type of web browser they are using. When used effectively, there are many ways that CGI scripts can be used to create a powerful interactive and dynamic website.

CGI scripts can be written in any scripting or programming language that is supported by a specific web server. Common languages include AppleScript, Perl, and Frontier. A wide number of scripts are also freely available on the Internet. CGI scripts are run on the Mac running the server. Therefore, they can potentially be a security issue, and you should never allow someone you don't know or trust to upload or install a CGI script on your server, as they can be used for malicious purposes, such as interacting with files elsewhere on your Mac. CGI scripts are often stored in a folder known as the *cgi-bin* and often are restricted to interact only with items inside that folder for security reasons.

Server-side include (also called SSI) is a technology supported by many web servers that allows you to insert special HTML comment tags in a document. HTML comment tags appear as <!---> tags and of themselves have no meaning to the HTML language. When the page is served to a user with a SSI comment tag, however, that comment tag refers to a specific function or file, which is inserted into the HTML code at the time it is sent to the user by the server. This allows you to have separate material that is not "hard-coded" into a web page. For example, the server could support a tag that would insert today's date into a page or insert the last web page a user visited.

Another common and powerful use of SSI is to have a comment tag reference an external HTML document. Say, for example, you have a standard masthead for every web page on your server. By using SSI, you can simply insert a single tag at the beginning of every page rather than the complete code for the masthead. This not only saves you entering the code on every page, it also makes updating the masthead extremely easy. Simply change the document that the SSI tags point to, and every page that it's used on is updated in one shot.

Personal Web Sharing   Apple's Personal Web Sharing feature is about as basic as you can get for providing web services from the Mac. Because it is so basic, it is also extremely easy to set up and operate. You simply open the Web Sharing control panel (see Figure 34-1), select which folder will contain your web pages (by default, a folder named Web Pages is created during the Mac OS installation), and choose which page should function as the home or index page (the page that is returned if a user enters the server address with no path to a specific web page). With these settings selected, you just decide whether to give all visitors to

Figure 34-1
Apple Web Sharing
control panel.

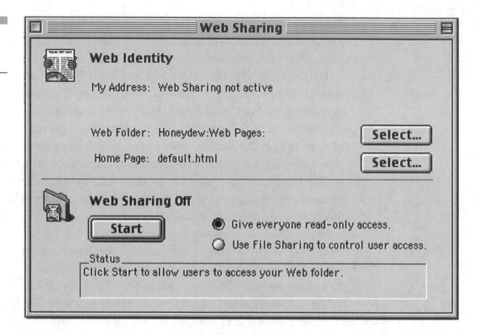

your server read-only access (meaning they can receive web pages but not actually make changes to any files on your Mac) or whether to allow access to be controlled by your File Sharing Users and Groups settings. Then click on the start button in the control panel, and you're done.

The Mac reads its IP address from the TCP/IP configuration of Open Transport and begins serving any web pages that are requested of it. By default, no logs are generated, users are restricted to reading only items in the selected web pages folder, and everything works very simply.

By selecting the Preferences item from the Edit menu, you can make some adjustments, such as enabling a server log (always a good idea), allowing users Write access so they can make adjustments to files on your Mac (not such a good idea with a public server) and allowing aliases inside the web pages folder to transmit the original files stored outside the folder if requested by a web browser. You can also create some basic filtering and processing scripts for the web server and how much RAM you want the Mac to allow the built-in web server to use.

Although Personal Web Sharing is completely functional, there are no specific security features, and no frills or advanced features. I would say the best or only good use of Personal Web Sharing would be in an intranet environment where some individuals have the need to share a small amount of data with others in the company, but not so much that a complete web server package is needed or desired.

NetPresenz   NetPresenz is a shareware server produced by Stairways Software that combines a basic web server, FTP server, and a server for the Gopher protocol (which is a pre-Web protocol that is rarely, if ever, used on the Internet today). NetPresenz is somewhat more sophisticated than Apple's Personal Web Sharing, including support for both CGI scripts (using the Frontier scripting language) and server-side includes. In addition, it also comes with the added convenience of a built-in FTP server (see the following section for more information on its FTP server functions).

NetPresenz uses separate setup and server applications. The setup application, shown in Figure 34-2, allows you to define the very basic features of the web server element of NetPresenz, such as whether or not web serving is enabled, the port number assigned to the web server, whether CGI access is enabled, and what folder (or directory) web pages and related files are being stored in for the server to make available. Setting up NetPresenz as a web server is a very simple process. Simply configure the basic web server settings and then launch the NetPresenz application. When the application is in the foreground, the log window will be displayed.

NetPresenz makes a very good basic web server, being both functional and simple. Although not as feature-filled as other options, it is extremely simple and easy to set up, making it a good choice for users new to providing Internet service. It does lack any real security measures, however, and should therefore be used with caution and with other security measures (discussed later in this chapter).

Figure 34-2
The NetPresenz
Setup application's
web server dialog.

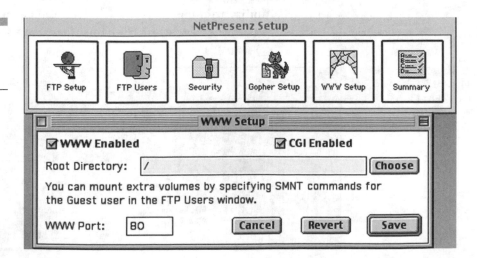

Quid Pro Quo   Quid Pro Quo is a freeware web server from Social Engineering that has several useful features, including support for CGI scripts written in multiple languages and server-side includes. It also incorporates a plug-in architecture, allowing third parties to develop plug-ins for the server that can extend its functionality in a variety of ways. Quid Pro Quo is also very configurable, allowing administrators to adapt it specifically to their needs and the Mac on which they are running it.

Unlike NetPresenz, Quid Pro Quo's settings and configuration are controlled directly from within the server application itself. When first run, a very easy to use configuration wizard runs (as you can see in Figure 34-3), allowing you to easily and conveniently set the majority of Quid Pro Quo's features. The wizard does not, however, extend to all of Quid Pro Quo's settings options, so most users will want to look through the Global Settings and Server Settings items in the application's Control menu, shown in Figure 34-4.

When looking at the available options, you can easily see the advantages to using Quid Pro Quo over a web server with fewer features. You can specify exactly what is reported in server logs (which can help in reading or analyzing them later), set a cache for frequently requested files, and determine how much processor time the Quid Pro Quo application will use in relation to other processes being run on the Mac. Additionally, one can specify port numbers for the server, restrict access to or from specified domains and IP addresses, set a maximum number of connections, create custom file not found (error 404) web page designs and similar server responses, and control password-required access and similar security features. The extreme versatility of Quid Pro Quo, as well as the ability to implement security functions (in conjunction with or independent of the Mac's File Sharing Users and Groups), make it a

Figure 34-3
Quid Pro Quo's setup wizard.

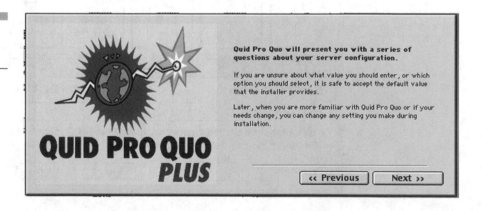

Quid Pro Quo will present you with a series of questions about your server configuration.

If you are unsure about what value you should enter, or which option you should select, it is safe to accept the default value that the installer provides.

Later, when you are more familiar with Quid Pro Quo or if your needs change, you can change any setting you make during installation.

QUID PRO QUO PLUS

<< Previous   Next >>

Figure 34-4
The Quid Pro Quo
Settings dialogs.

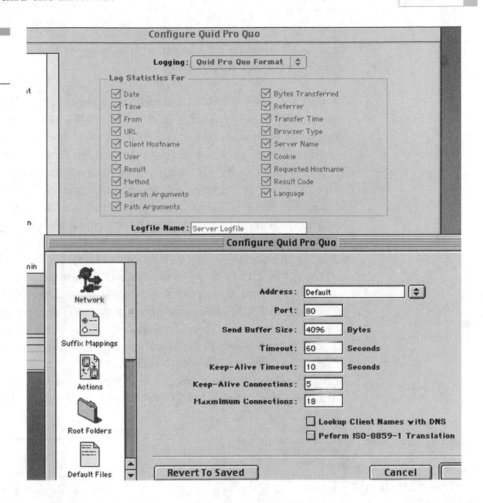

reliable and attractive web server. The fact that this powerful a server is available as freeware is equally attractive.

Quid Pro Quo also includes an option for remote administration, allowing the administrator to log in to a special, predetermined URL to control and adjust server configurations and actions. The Remote Administration feature presents a web-based interface to all the configuration features available from within the Quid Pro Quo application, as well as access to server status information.

Advanced commercial versions of Quid Pro Quo are also available that enable additional features. Some of these features include the use of Secure Sockets Layer protocol for encrypting and safely transmitting secure information over the Internet (such as credit card numbers for an online store's ordering page), a special fast graphics server, and the ability to run multiple "virtual servers" with separate domain name addresses on a single Mac, as well as other features. See the end of this chapter for sources of further information.

WebSTAR WebSTAR is a commercial server suite that includes a web server, FTP server, and e-mail server in a single package. Because WebSTAR is so feature-packed that its user manual is over 300 pages in length, I'll only give a brief overview of its features and abilities. Like NetPresenz, WebSTAR uses a separate application called WebSTAR Admin, shown in Figure 34-5, to control settings for all server elements. Unlike NetPresenz, the admin application can be used for remote administration of a server by entering the appropriate domain name/IP address of the server and administration password (this is needed even if you are running the server on the same Mac as the Admin application).

Even more than Quid Pro Quo, WebSTAR is extremely configurable. It supports CGI scripts written in several languages, SSI, and third-party plug-ins, and it includes security functions, allowing you to restrict access to the server. WebSTAR also includes the ability for virtual hosting of multiple servers with independent domain name addresses on a single Mac, Secure Sockets Layer protection for establishing encrypted and secure connections over the Internet, the ability to integrate with database applications being run on the Mac using the lasso tools, and

Figure 34-5
The WebSTAR Admin application, showing web server options.

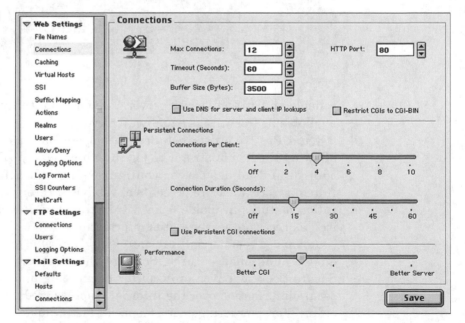

several other features. Since the WebSTAR suite includes an integrated e-mail element, it also includes the ability to run a web mail feature, allowing users to log into the e-mail server through a web interface to send, receive, and view e-mail in their account (similar to the well-known Hotmail and similar services).

FTP Servers

The FTP (File Transfer Protocol) service predates the web. It is used for, as its name implies, transferring files between a client machine and a server. Unlike web services, where the transfer of files is primarily from the server to the client, FTP allows users to upload files to the server as well as retrieve files. Probably the most common uses for FTP on the Internet today are software archives and the method by which users of a web server update their web pages.

An FTP server works much like file sharing. A user logs in (or you can allow anonymous connections) and is given access to a folder or set of folders on your hard drive. Depending on what permissions are set for them, they can download files from or upload files to those folders. Which folders users are given access to is up to you as the administrator of the server. Keep in mind that you don't want people having access to any sensitive files or to your System Folder. Also, it's a good idea to limit who can upload files to people you trust.

You might want to run an FTP server if you wanted to make files on your hard drive readily available to other computer users over the Internet. This can be done in a publicly available archive or by giving usernames and passwords to people you want to allow access to these files. One advantage of using FTP for sharing files in this way is that it is cross-platform, meaning users of any computer platform will be able to access your shared files. As discussed in Chapter 41, using an FTP server can provide a free way to share files between Macs and PCs on a local network.

NetPresenz   NetPresenz was discussed in the preceding section on web servers because it includes a relatively basic web server element. What NetPresenz is much more well known for, and commonly used for, is its FTP server functions. The FTP server functions built into NetPresenz uses the File Sharing Users and Groups settings to determine who may connect to the Mac via FTP. NetPresenz reads these settings and then allows you to define what folders and files each user or group may access, as well as what type of access they are granted (read-only, write-only, or read-write). You can also assign a login message to be displayed to each user when they connect to the FTP server. Additionally, you can assign the port number used by the FTP server and set the maximum number of users that can log in at any given time.

The NetPresenz FTP server, like its web server element, is very simple to set up and use (especially if you're familiar with assigning Users and Groups privileges). Once configured, you simply launch the NetPresenz application, and users can log in to the server to upload and download files.

It's important to remember when assigning user privileges in NetPresenz that users could theoretically access any file on the Macintosh on which NetPresenz is running, if granted enough access. Keep this in mind when setting up your NetPresenz server.

WebSTAR   The FTP element of WebSTAR offers the security features of the entire WebSTAR suite, which is a useful feature that doesn't require separate firewall (a firewall is a good idea for NetPresenz). User settings are handled independent of the Users and Groups settings for the Mac's File Sharing, but it is done through a typical interface within the WebSTAR Admin application, as shown in Figure 34-6. You select the

Figure 34-6
The WebSTAR Admin application's FTP settings.

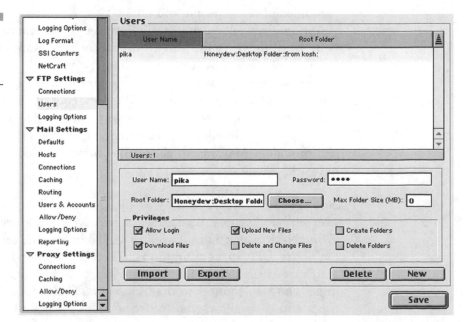

Users option and can then create a user, set a password, a default folder to limit the user to, and access privileges (which are more specific than NetPresenz and offer create, delete, and change files/folders, as well as read/download and write/upload privileges). WebSTAR also allows you to set general login and logout messages.

Domain Name Service

Every computer in a TCP/IP network, whether an intranet or the Internet, requires a unique IP address. This was discussed in Chapter 32 on how to set up an intranet. However, remembering the IP address of even a few sites or servers easily gets confusing. That's where Domain Name Service (DNS) steps in. DNS allows you to assign domain names to IP addresses. Instead of seeing something like *205.180.175.30*, you see something like *www.apple.com*.

DNS servers are servers that handle the translation of IP address into domain names. Each server regularly broadcasts its new DNS information to other servers and also receives new information from other servers, allowing for smooth translation across an intranet containing multiple DNS servers or across the Internet. DNS can be used either for a closed intranet or for the Internet. When dealing with the Internet, it's important to remember that domain names need to be registered with InterNIC. The domain name registration procedures exist so that only one entity on the Internet can define what IP address a specific domain name points to.

A variety of freeware, shareware, and commercial domain name servers are available for the Mac platform. In the coming sections, we'll look at two of these. Once your chosen DNS server is installed and running, your next step will be to configure any client Macs that will be using the server to retrieve DNS information to use that server. This is done by entering the IP address of your DNS server in the Name server Addr. box of the TCP/IP control panel and restarting the client machine.

QuickDNS Pro QuickDNS Pro is a commercial DNS server by Men and Mice that is fully featured and can serve as the DNS server for an intranet, for a local network with Internet access or services, or even for a full-blown Mac-based Internet service provider. As powerful as QuickDNS Pro, it is also easy for users new to DNS to use and it includes a Domain Setup Assistant that takes almost all the hassle and confusion out of setting up DNS service for a domain. QuickDNS Pro consists of both the actual server application, which has no real interface, and an administration application for configuring and maintaining the server.

QuickDNS Pro also incorporates the ability to create and maintain virtual domains. A *virtual domain* is a domain name that does not have an independent IP address and points instead to an existing domain, allowing a web server or other Internet service to provide services under multiple, independent domain names. This function is also included with some commercial web server packages, such as WebSTAR and the commercial variations of Quid Pro Quo.

MacDNS   MacDNS is a free DNS from Apple. MacDNS is not as full featured as a commercial DNS server such as QuickDNS Pro. It requires a parent server when being used for Internet DNS service. This means that it will speed up DNS service through your network by acting as a local DNS server, but it will not be able to function as a stand-alone DNS server and will rely on your Internet provider's DNS server. It is functional for intranet use, however. MacDNS is also a bit more hands-on in terms of setup. You need to set the relevant information into domain entries manually, rather than using a setup assistant.

Sharing Internet Access with the Network

If you have a network of Macs, whether a couple of individual iMacs in a home or an entire computer lab in a school, one of the things you will probably want to do is provide them all with shared access to the Internet at the same time. To accomplish this task, you'll need something called a *router*.

In Chapter 32, you read about creating a Mac network using the same TCP/IP protocol that the Internet is based on. This includes assigning an IP address to each computer on the network. The Internet works the same way, with every computer attached to it assigned an IP address. It is through the IP address that data finds its way from the computer where it originated to the computer that is its destination.

A router acts as a doorway, using its Internet connection and the IP address assigned to it and its local network address (IP or AppleTalk) with the rest of your network to transfer information between computers on your network and the Internet at large. Since the router actually receives all the incoming Internet connections before passing them on to the computers in your network, it uses a technique known as *multihom-*

ing to maintain both an IP address for its Internet connection and a separate address for its local network connection. Because it maintains addresses for both connections (or networks), it can transfer information between your network and the Internet.

Routers can be individual hardware devices, separate from any computer on the network, or they can be a computer (Mac or PC) on the network running a special software tool. Since the TCP/IP protocol is platform-transparent, it makes no difference what types of computers in the network are accessing the Internet through the router. Likewise, the platform of the router (if it is a computer on the network and not a separate device) is irrelevant to the computers accessing the Internet through it.

Hardware Routers

Routers come as both separate hardware devices and software packages. Hardware routers are physical pieces of hardware that perform this function of maintaining both an Internet and local network identity and transferring data between the two connections. Apple's AirPort Base Station is an example of a hardware router, though one that is specifically designed to be used with the AirPort wireless networking strategy.

Most routers look similar to an Ethernet hub. Some can even function as an Ethernet hub as well as a router. You plug the Ethernet cable for each Mac into the router (or an Ethernet cable connecting to a hub), configure it, and then attach your Internet connection to it. This works well with things like cable modems, DSL (Digital Subscriber Line) modems, and other high-speed Internet solutions that directly link to an Ethernet port or cable. Some routers come with modems built into them to facilitate their use with dial-up Internet connections (again, the AirPort Base Station is an example of this).

Configuring a router is different for each router on the market, though many use a web-style interface for easy setup and configuration. Routers are also cross-platform tools, meaning they will function with Macs and PCs. Because each computer is connected to the router through its own Ethernet cable, the router doesn't need to deal with AppleTalk-style addressing or file transfer for individual computers.

Hardware routers are more expensive than their software counterparts. The advantages of hardware routers are that they are separate components not susceptible to crashes or other problems that can take down a Macintosh using a software router, package. However, many hardware routers don't offer some of the additional features that you'll find on software routers, such as a built-in firewalls, logging abilities, DHCP server functions, or content screening.

Software Routers

Software routers are software packages that you install on an individual computer. This computer then performs the routing functions for your network once the network and Internet connections are in place. There are two big companies providing software routers for the Mac platform, Vicomsoft and Sustainable Softworks, and we will look at both of their offerings in the following sections.

Before we start talking about individual router software, we should discuss some of the features involved in these packages. Although software routers practice multihoming as hardware routers do, they often include a number of additional features that can increase their benefit to your network (with or without being used for integrating Internet access). Note that these features are in addition to the actual router functions used for sharing Internet access.

DHCP   DHCP (Dynamic Host Configuration Protocol) is one of these features. As you remember from Chapter 32, when you set up a TCP/IP network, you need to assign an IP address and related TCP/IP information to each computer on the network. DHCP allows a software component called a *DHCP server* to assign this information for you. When a Mac on the network is configured to use a DHCP server for its TCP/IP information (this option is chosen from the Configure menu in the TCP/IP control panel), it contacts the DHCP server on the network at startup. The server assigns an IP address (and related TCP/IP information) to the Mac, usually based on the hardware address coded into the Mac's Ethernet port. The Mac will then use this IP address until it is either shut down or forced to give up the IP address for some other reason (such as a change in the TCP/IP settings). Needless to say, DHCP simplifies a large portion of network administration and setup. Like most Internet protocols, DHCP is cross-platform and can be used in mixed networks. There are, however, known problems between some non-Mac DHCP servers and the Mac's Open Transport networking. These issues are discussed in Chapter 36.

Firewalls   Firewalls are discussed later in this chapter and are a common security feature integrated into software router packages that can be used to significantly reduce the risk of someone on the Internet gaining access to your network through your router software.

Remote access   Remote access support is a way of giving users the ability to dial into your network and share the network Internet connection, as well as access to the network itself for either file sharing or for intranet uses.

Content Filtering   Content filtering is another feature. As you might guess, content filtering allows you to block sites that contain certain content from being accessed from your network through a shared Internet connection. This can be excellent in an educational setting, where you don't want students to have access to adult or other material.

Security Concerns

In addition to features, there is a security concern that you should be aware of before using a software router. When a router is used, the entire network essentially becomes part of the Internet. This makes it possible for someone outside your network to monitor your network traffic. It is also possible that someone outside your network could gain access to your shared files and printers, including critical data or Mac OS components of each Mac on the network.

One way to reduce this risk is to use a Macintosh with two Ethernet ports. This can be accomplished by installing an Ethernet PCI card into a Power Mac, as that will provide a second port to the built-in port. You then attach the Internet connection to one port and the local network connection to the other port. This way there is no possible exchange between local network traffic and the Internet. Also, any intrusion will be limited to only a single computer serving as the router.

If you cannot use a Mac with two Ethernet ports, follow every possible security precaution available and avoid running an intranet or TCP/IP file sharing over the network. TCP/IP is an extremely common network architecture that can be more easily read or accessed from computers external to your network than AppleTalk.

Major Mac Software Router Packages

The next sections discuss the features of the major software router products. Because these products ship with such robust and complete documentation, these descriptions will not go into detail on how to configure the majority of features.

IPNetRouter   IPNetRouter from Sustainable Softworks includes the multihoming abilities that enable you to share Internet access among your network and a DHCP server to auto-configure the IP addresses of your network. IPNetRouter is industrial-strength in its ability to handle large numbers of individual computers. Although there is no "true" built-in firewall, IPNetRouter does allow you to create a firewall by specially configuring some of its components. While it isn't as feature packed as its primary competition (Vicomsoft's Internet Gateway), it does make up for that with a noticeably lower price tag for a site license of the software.

Vicom Internet Gateway   Vicomsoft's Internet Gateway is the most full-featured Mac network/Internet integration package on the market. Its features boast a built-in firewall, content filtering, DHCP server, remote access, a TCP locator that displays a list of all the Internet/intranet servers running on a local network, built-in DNS services, and virtual hosting abilities for web servers being run from the Mac network it is installed on.

Another interesting feature included with Internet Gateway is the Web Headers feature, which displays messages to all network users in a frame placed above any web page they visit. This makes a great way to ensure users receive important messages. The web header frame content can include any web elements such as graphics, text, HTML documents, and even multimedia.

The sheer number of features offered by Internet Gateway make it attractive to network administrators because so many features that Mac Internet integration and services are likely to use are included in a single package. The cost of all those additional features in Internet Gateway does make itself known in the price tag, however, and the competing IPNetRouter as well as Vicomsoft's SurfDoubler may make better alternatives for users where cost is a factor.

Vicomsoft SurfDoubler   Vicomsoft also produces a product called SurfDoubler, which is aimed more at home users wanting to share an Internet connection. SurfDoubler provides the router functions and the firewall, DNS, and DHCP server abilities of Internet Gateway, as well as optional content filtering (for an additional cost). It does not include many of network-specific features such as web headers, remote access, and local server locator functions.

Securing Your Mac/Network from the Internet

The Mac is arguably the most secure networking and Internet platform available today. Whether you're talking about file sharing via AppleTalk or TCP/IP, the Mac OS File Sharing model offers some native security features not found in other platforms. Likewise, Mac-based web servers tend, as a rule, to be more secure than their UNIX- or Windows NT-based counterparts.

The Mac remains so secure for networking for several reasons, including the fact that the Mac strictly separates applications from the Mac OS itself, preventing applications from being able to easily modify the System file or other critical Mac OS elements. Another reason is the inherent strengths of the Open Transport networking elements built into the Mac OS. Still another is that Mac users can create customized names for disks and directories on their computers rather than being forced to use the same names as every other computer (for example, every Windows computer has a primary hard drive named C and the same folders for storing critical files). Most developers take advantage of the Mac's innate security when developing products, so that they are equally secure. This means that the Mac is far less vulnerable out of the box than comparable platforms. It does not, however, mean that infiltration into a Mac based server or network is impossible.

Whenever you open your network or a Mac on it to the Internet, there is the possibility that someone out there will be able to break into your network or into the Mac from which you are providing Internet services. This is inevitable, but there are a number of ways you can prevent people from gaining such access and limit their abilities should they gain access. The following areas describe some of the steps you can take to make your network more secure.

Use a Firewall

A firewall sounds like something a wizard in a fantasy story might set up, but it's really something far less spectacular. A *firewall* is a network utility that restricts where data can come from or go to on the Internet through your network. Firewalls can be used to block specific servers from sending data to any Mac on your network, and you can block your users from sending data and requests to those servers. Or you can block whole networks of servers based on the components of their IP addresses. You can also selectively block access to specific types of Internet services (such as Usenet newsgroups) and specific Internet ports. This helps you control exactly what type of data is accessible to your network, as well as who can access what.

By limiting access to only types of Internet services that are unlikely to allow intrusion, you can limit what someone can do to your Mac server or network. By limiting access to only servers on the Internet that you know to be reasonably safe or excluding areas you know to be unsafe, you can gain some measure of control over who can access your Mac. Both of these tactics help you take an important step toward making your Mac or network more secure.

Firewalls can also be used to log any incoming or outgoing connections between your network and the Internet. This allows you to tell who is accessing what on the Internet and what computers outside your network are trying to gain access (or have gained access) to your server or network.

Firewalls come as individual utilities that you can install on one or all Macs in your network, as well as parts of Internet-related software. For example, the WebSTAR suite includes a built-in firewall, as does Internet Gateway. Figure 34-7 shows the Netbarrier firewall, which is an independent firewall utility.

Use Users and Groups Options

Most Internet software allows you to set limits on who can access files on your Mac using the Users and Groups feature of the Mac's File Sharing setup. Use these abilities to control who can access your Mac and what they can access. Limit any users to only what they truly need access to. The fewer people who have access to large areas of your Mac, the better. Don't give anyone complete access unless they're the administrator of the network, and always leave the guest account's access disabled.

Don't Use Administrative Accounts Every Day

If you're the administrator of any server, don't log in using your administrator or owner account unless you absolutely need to. Create a normal, limited user account for yourself to use for routine daily tasks. For example, if you administer an e-mail server, don't log in using the postmaster account all the time. Set up the server to forward any postmaster mes-

Figure 34-7
Netbarrier firewall
utility.

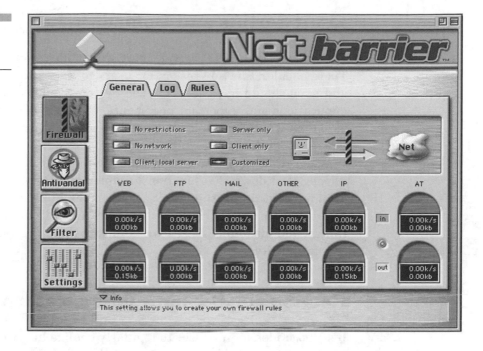

sages to your personal account. This keeps people from being able to watch your access, learn your password, and infiltrate your Mac. The same principle holds for file sharing access, FTP, and other uses. Unless you're actually modifying server settings, you shouldn't have a real need to log in using your administrative or owner account, and doing so for just day-to-day routine usage is a bad habit.

Don't Use a Guest Account

A guest account allows anyone to connect to your Mac or part of your network without having to provide a password or identify themselves to you. This lets anyone in, and it keeps you from being able to track where they came from or who they are. It is not a good practice at all. This goes for all types of servers, including FTP servers, which allow for anonymous FTP connections.

The only component anyone should be able to access without identifying themselves and providing a password for authorization on an Internet serving Mac is your web server to request web pages. In addition, they should only be allowed to read files from your Mac. Never allow a guest to have Write access privileges.

Limit Scripts and Uploads

When running an FTP server, limit what folders users have access to. There shouldn't be any reason for users to access the entire hard drive, and none should have access to the System Folder or the folders where applications and important documents are stored. One useful technique is to limit users to a separate hard drive or partition than the Mac actually starts up from and stores important files on.

When running a web server, limit CGI access. If you don't need CGI scripts, shut down CGI functions completely. Always restrict CGI use to a folder containing the scripts, and never allow CGI access to your entire hard drive. Scripts can be written to do all sorts of insidious things, and disabling CGI uses or limiting them is an important step in server security.

Rotate Your Owner/Administrator Password

It's a good idea for any user to regularly change his or her passwords for whatever accounts they have (e-mail, dial-up Internet access, file sharing, even chat rooms), but it is especially important for accounts that control functions of a Mac server or network. Change your ownership passwords at least every three months; more frequently may be better, so long as you aren't likely to forget the passwords. Avoid picking obvious passwords or reusing the same ones. If you suspect someone has seen your password, change it immediately.

Similarly, don't use the same password for all your accounts. The old saying about not keeping your eggs in one basket has a high-tech meaning here, but it still applies. Keep a separate administrator password for each server you control, and keep that different from your typical day-to-day account passwords. This way, if someone does manage to gain access to one password, it isn't particularly likely that they'll be able to break into all of your systems and servers.

Use Difficult to Guess Passwords

When assigning user passwords (and when choosing an administrator password), use difficult-to-guess phrases. Combine both numbers and letters (this prevents hackers from using software that will simply try every word in the dictionary). Also use punctuation marks and shift between capital and lowercase letters. On the Mac OS and in most servers for the Mac, passwords are case-sensitive. Using combinations like this can greatly increase security. Another thing to remember is the length of passwords. Longer passwords are less likely to be guessed. You should always use passwords that are at least six characters long.

Don't Allow Users to Change Their Passwords

This tip is a bit controversial to some people. Allowing users to change their own passwords at will causes two problems. First, it allows them to change their password and then forget what it was. Second and more important, if someone oversees a user's password or if a user forgets to log out of a server, then anyone can change the password and lock the user out while they gain access to anything they want.

On the other hand, allowing users to change their own passwords will give them a sense of privacy. It will also allow them to pick passwords they're more likely to remember, and save you some headaches from listening to users complain.

Like rotating your administrator passwords, make sure users change their passwords regularly. Again, this keeps someone from having prolonged access to your files if he or she manages to get ahold of someone's password.

Change All Passwords in the Event of Problems

In the event that someone does gain access to your Mac or network, or even if you only suspect someone might have, immediately change not only the owner/administrator passwords, but change all passwords of any kind for every user. This prevents whoever might have gained access from keeping that access for long.

Read Server Logs

Your server logs can easily be long, seemingly unending lists of text. However, they can also contain a record of every single access made to your server. Learn to read through them, and learn what usage patterns are familiar to your server so you can spot a pattern that might mean trouble.

Notice when the server has refused access to something. That can indicate someone trying to gain access that they shouldn't have. If you notice the same IP address showing up more than a couple of times as being refused in a server log, you may want to add that address (and related addresses) to the areas that your firewall restricts access to/from completely.

Server logs can become exceedingly large files for active servers, and there are some tools that will analyze logs for you. You can also limit what is recorded in the logs of many servers. This can cut down on your log review time, but it can also block out signs of trouble. Choose which information to exclude from logs or from log analysis tools carefully, and reconsider such settings regularly.

Regularly Reconsider Your Access Settings

On a regular basis, take a look at the settings you have for who can access what on your Mac or network. If someone no longer requires the level of access they have, consider restricting their access a little. If someone is no longer regularly using your servers at all, consider suspending their access completely.

Resources for Further Study

The following URLs provide additional information on some of the concepts, issues, and products discussed in this chapter.

Frontier Scripting Language/Environment—
  http://frontier.userland.com/

*StarNine: Makers of WebSTAR—*http://www.starnine.com

Stairways Software's NetPresenz
  —http://wallaby.seagull.net/netpresenz/

Social Engineering: Makers of Quid Pro Quo—
  http://www.socialeng.com/

Server Side Includes Resource from About.com—
  http://html.about.com/compute/html/msubssi.htm

*MacPerl Scripting Environment—*http://www.ptf.com/macperl/

Sources of Ready-Made CGI Scripts—
  http://html.about.com/compute/html/msubcgiscripts.htm

Download of FTPShare—
ftp://ftp.deltanet.com/pub/macintosh_files/ftp-share.hqx

Eudora Internet Mail Server HomePage—
http://www.eudora.com/eims/

Stalker Internet Mail Server HomePage—
http://www.stalker.com/SIMS/

Stairways Software's Rumor Mill—
http://wallaby.seagull.net/rumormill/

Men and Mice: Makers of QuickDNS Pro—
http://www.menandmice.com/

Apple Software Updates (where you can find MacDNS)—
http://asu.info.apple.com/

Vicomsoft: Makers of Internet Gateway and SurfDoubler—
http://www.vicomtech.com/

Sustainable Softworks: Makers of IPNetRouter—
http://www.sustworks.com

Macsense: Makers of Hardware Routers and Other Products—
http://www.macsensetech.com/

Ramp Networks: Makers of WebRamp Hardware Routers—
http://www.rampnet.com/

*Linksys: Makers of Hardware Routers—*http://www.linksys.com

Open Door Networks: Makers of the DoorStop Personal Firewall—
http://www.opendoor.com/

*Intego: Makers of the Netbarrier Firewall—*http://www.intego.com/

Active Concepts: Makers of the FunnelWeb Log Analysis Tool—
http://www.activeconcepts.com/

*Summary.Net: Makers of Commercial and Freeware Log Analysis
Tools—*http://www.summary.net/

CHAPTER 35

ISDN

ISDN, which stands for Integrated Services Digital Network, is a technology that relies on copper wires similar to those used for traditional phone lines to transmit data digitally. This enables faster and clearer transmission of data along those wires. ISDN was originally conceived in the 1960s as a new standard for telephone lines that would enable greater clarity and additional features, such as videoconferencing phones. Although initially created nearly three decades ago, it wasn't until the late 1980s and early 1990s that ISDN began to see extensive use. This is because ISDN allows for greater throughput of data than a traditional phone line when used for Internet connections. ISDN is also used for some digital phone systems in corporate or institutional settings. Today, ISDN has been surpassed in popularity by faster and much cheaper DSL (Digital Subscriber Line) and cable modem Internet connections; however, it is still the best option for people who do not have access to DSL or cable.

How ISDN Works

ISDN usually consists of three communications channels per ISDN line. Two of these are called B channels (short for "bearer channels") and can each transmit data up to 64 Kbps. The third channel is known as a D channel (for "delta channel") and is used for controlling the two B channels in an ISDN line. The D channel handles such functions as initiating an ISDN connection and terminating that connection, as well as regulating the flow of data being sent over the B channels.

Each of the two B channels in an ISDN line can be used for either data transmission or for voice communication. These channels can be combined to create a single Internet connection with a capacity of 128 Kpbs or they can be used independently to provide data access, used with a digital phone line or fax machine, or used with a converter to provide access to traditional analog telephone devices (phones, modems, answering machines, and so on.).

ISDN Wiring

ISDN wiring sends communications digitally, as opposed to the analog signaling used on traditional telephone lines. Although much of a phone company's internal network uses digital signaling, the telephone lines that actually run into your house or office are probably still traditional analog lines. For you to receive ISDN service, these lines must be converted to digital ISDN lines.

Does this mean you need to rewire all the phone jacks in your house? Probably not. ISDN lines still use the same type of copper wires that are already installed in your home. Usually, if you qualify for ISDN service, your phone company can convert your existing lines to use ISDN. If you have multiple phone lines, one line can be converted to ISDN while the other can maintain analog phone service.

ISDN versus Analog Service for Phone and Fax   ISDN can be used to provide digital phone service, as well as digital fax service. This requires special phones or fax machines that support ISDN's digital connection. Connecting a traditional analog device such as a phone, fax, or modem to an ISDN line directly will damage the device and may damage the ISDN line. Some ISDN hardware comes with connectors built in that allow you to safely connect traditional analog devices, and you can also purchase such adapters separately. In fact, as mentioned in Chapter 31, having such an adapter for your portable Mac's internal modem is a good precaution if you use a dial-up connection on the road, because it avoids risk to your modem and computer.

Even with ISDN phones (or similar devices) or hardware that allows you to connect your analog phones or devices to an ISDN, you should be aware of another issue: ISDN requires an independent power source, whereas analog phones draw power directly from the phone line. This means that if you rely on an ISDN line for phone service and the power goes out, so does your phone service (some ISDN hardware allows you to install a battery backup in case of power failure). Even if you have an adapter for your analog phone devices, you will still lose service during a power failure. For this reason, many people opt to have an analog phone line in addition to an ISDN line.

Multilink   Each ISDN line typically consists of two separate B channels. Each channel is capable of transmitting data at 64 Kbps. Combined, this would enable performance of 128 Kbps. However, each ISDN channel needs to be dialed and connected separately to an ISP from the other. A technology known as Multilink allows both connections to be made at once. When Multilink is used to establish a connection, the two ISDN B channels behave as a single channel. For this reason, it is important to choose an ISP that supports Multilink ISDN protocols, which most do.

Using Multiple Devices   ISDN is designed to support the use of multiple devices on a single ISDN line. This is because the D channel can allocate the B channels of an ISDN to function independently of each other for different functions. For example, you can be using both B channels together for your Internet connection. If you then decide to place a phone call using the ISDN line, one of the two channels will be removed from use of the computer and transferred to the phone. When you finish your call, the line can then be given back to the computer for Internet use, or it can be transferred to another device, such as an ISDN fax machine.

A single ISDN line can support being connected to up to eight pieces of ISDN hardware at one time. Most people do not use more than three or four ISDN device on a single line, and most home users will use an ISDN line for Internet access and, perhaps, phone service.

64-Kpbs versus 56-Kbps Connections   ISDN lines were designed so that each B channel in an ISDN line would be capable of 64-Kpbs connections. Unfortunately, there are some areas where the existing telephone network is not sufficiently powerful to actually enable transmission that fast over its switching network or internal ISDN lines. In these areas, which are diminishing as time goes by, individual B channels in an ISDN line will be limited to 56-Kbps speeds until the telephone company can upgrade its internal network to support the full performance of ISDN.

Dial-up versus Dedicated ISDN   As a rule, ISDN service is considered a dial-up service. This means that the connection is not active 24 hours a day. Instead, you need to initiate the connection by telling your computer to dial up your ISP over your ISDN line. The Mac then establishes the connection similar to how it would establish a modem dial-up connection (the process takes about one-tenth the time, however). You can, however, request a dedicated ISDN connection, though this will be more expensive. A dedicated connection means that your ISDN hardware will be connected to your ISP 24 hours a day, 7 days a week. With its extremely fast connect time, having a dial-up ISDN connection can feel like having a permanent connection, however.

The most common reason for using a dedicated connection is if you are using an ISDN router to maintain a constant connection for all the computers in your local network. It is generally a feature reserved for offices and other institutional uses. A dedicated connection is also needed if you plan to run an Internet server (such as described in the last chapter) from your computer or local network, because you will need a constant connection. As a rule, however, consumer ISDN lines do not support the bandwidth needed by most Internet services today.

Primary Rate Interface   Primary Rate Interface, or PRI, is a special type of ISDN connection. Instead of having the traditional two B channels carrying data, PRI uses 23 B channels (each capable of 64 Kbps) and a more powerful D channel for control. The 23 B channels can be tied together to enable much, much faster Internet connections than a traditional ISDN line (sometimes referred to as a BRI, for Basic Rate Interface, line) is capable of delivering. Outside the United States, PRI connections use 30 B channels rather than 23.

Similar to a PRI line of 23 B channels, it is possible to tie other numbers of B channels together to provide higher-level Internet access. This may be attractive for an office located outside the range of other high-speed connectivity options. Most home users will find the ability to combine or aggregate ISDN lines like this to be cost-prohibitive, both in terms of setup cost and in terms of monthly fees. This is particularly true in light of competing technologies aimed at the consumer space like cable modems and DSL connections (see the next chapter for details).

ISDN Protocols

ISDN is a type of network connection. Like any other network connection, use of ISDN requires certain standard protocols for the devices using the ISDN line to communicate with each other. Your phone company will require your ISDN hardware to use the same protocols for sending data that is used for their ISDN lines. This means that you should check with them before buying ISDN hardware to be sure the hardware supports their protocols. The same holds true for Internet providers offering ISDN service, as they will also use specific protocols for establishing your ISDN connection to the Internet.

ISDN Hardware

There are several pieces of hardware that you need to install in order to use an ISDN line for Internet access or for other purposes. The piece of hardware that is always needed is a network terminator, which connects to the ISDN line coming out of your phone jack. Beyond the network terminator, you need a device to actually connect to the computer or local network. There are two such devices that you can consider to accomplish this: a terminal adapter or an ISDN router. A terminal adapter is preferred if you only have a single computer that you want to use with the ISDN line. A router is preferred if you want to share the ISDN line between an entire network of computers.

Network Terminator

The ISDN line that comes out of your phone jack generally uses a U-type connection that looks like a standard RJ11 phone cable. Most ISDN hardware requires an S/T-type connection that uses the RJ45 connector (the same connector as 10Base-T or 100Base-T Ethernet). To convert from the U-type connection to the S/T connection, you need a device known as a *network terminator,* or NT-1. An NT-1 is needed whether you're planning to attach a computer to the ISDN line or other digital phone equipment. Most NT-1s include connectors for multiple ISDN devices. This is useful if you are planning to attach a phone, fax, or other ISDN device to the line in addition to your computer. As stated earlier, you can connect up to eight devices to an ISDN line, and most NT-1s will support up to eight devices. Generally speaking, though, you will probably only need to connect one or two devices (such as the device that connects to your computer and a phone). An NT-1 can usually be purchased from your phone company.

Additional Features   Some NT-1s come with additional features besides simply converting the U connection of your ISDN line into the S/T connection your other ISDN hardware uses. There are two primary additional features that you may want to consider when buying an NT-1. The first is support for analog devices. If you are planning to use your ISDN line for phone service as well as for Internet access, an NT-1 with analog device ports allow you to connect your existing phones, fax machines, answering machines, and an analog modem. This means that you won't have to go out and spend the money to buy ISDN phones and such to use with the ISDN line. If you are maintaining an existing analog phone line in addition to your ISDN line, this ability may be of less importance to you.

The other useful feature is a battery backup. ISDN devices require a power source in order to operate. These means if your electricity goes out, so does your ISDN-based phone service. A battery backup will provide power to your NT-1 and allow you to use a phone attached to it even if your power goes out. Although the battery will have a limited life span, it can be useful, if not crucial, to have in an emergency, particularly if you have opted to replace your existing analog phone service with ISDN completely. If you are replacing your analog phone service with ISDN completely, I strongly suggest buying an NT-1 with a battery backup for emergencies.

Built-In NT-1s   Some pieces of ISDN hardware, terminal adapters (see the next section) in particular, come with what is called an *integrated NT-1*. This means that the device connects directly to the U-type connector at your ISDN phone jack and does not require an NT-1 to convert between U- and S/T-type connections. These devices can simplify use of ISDN lines, but some of them do not provide any additional S/T ports, meaning you will not be able to attach any other ISDN hardware. If you do opt for a device with an integrated NT1, look for one that supports additional ISDN and/or analog devices.

Terminal Adapter

A terminal adapter (also called a TA) is a device that connects non-ISDN hardware to an ISDN line. For most practical purposes, the only use of a terminal adapter is to connect a computer to an ISDN line. A terminal adapter is the hardware that is used to connect a single computer to the ISDN line. It communicates with the Mac using the same standard commands that a modem uses and looks like a modem to the Mac. In fact, you choose to use a terminal adapter for Internet connection by using the Modem control panel and selecting an appropriate modem script, just as you would choose a specific modem. With the appropriate script selected, the Remote Access control panel will handle establishing your connection the same as it would with a traditional analog modem.

Many terminal adapters include analog ports that allow you to connect analog phone devices, such as traditional telephones, fax machines, and even an analog modem. This allows you to use one of an ISDN line's B channels for traditional communication without needing to buy ISDN phone equipment. This is also important if you buy a terminal adapter that has a built-in NT-1, as there may not be any additional S/T connections available for additional ISDN devices to be connected.

Internal versus External TAs   Terminal adapters come in both internal and external models, though the external type tend to be much more common for the Mac. External TAs are available using traditional serial port connections (you will need a hardware handshaking serial port cable as you would for a modem) and USB models. Because the current Macs don't include serial ports, a USB model is preferable. Internal TAs can come in the form of PCI cards for desktop Power Mac computers or PC Cards for PowerBooks. An external, USB TA is probably the optimal choice for most Mac users at this point, because it will support all the Macs currently on the market, whereas PCI-card or PC Card models will only support Power Mac and PowerBook computers, respectively.

ISDN Modems   You've probably heard the term *ISDN modem* before, and you may be wondering why I haven't mentioned it yet. The reason is that there is technically no such thing as an ISDN modem. An ISDN modem refers to a terminal adapter with an NT-1 built into it. It physically resembles a modem, is an all-in-one box for using ISDN, and communicates with the Mac the same way a modem does (like any terminal adapter). So, marketing people have taken to calling terminal adapters with built-in NT-1s ISDN modems. The name is actually inaccurate because it doesn't perform the functions (modulating and demodulating a signal between analog and digital data) that a true modem does.

Router

While a terminal adapter is designed to connect directly to a single computer, an ISDN router is designed to connect to a network of computers. Routers are the ISDN hardware needed if you want to share an ISDN line's connection with a group of computers. An ISDN router will usually connect directly to your NT-1. Sometimes they may come with an integrated NT-1 and connect directly to the U-type connection at your ISDN phone jack. Less commonly, you will find a router that comes with a PC serial port and is designed to be connected to a terminal adapter that is, in turn, connected to the ISDN line. Once the router is connected to the ISDN line, you simply run an Ethernet cable from it into the hub that serves to connect the Macs in your network. Or, if the router has multiple Ethernet ports, you plug the Ethernet cables from each Mac into it, as you would an Ethernet hub.

What About Software Routers?   In the last chapter you read about routers—that is, products designed to share any type of Internet connection. You may be wondering if you could use such a router to share an ISDN connection between computers. The answer is yes. In fact, an ISDN router is nothing more than a hardware router specifically designed to connect to the Internet via ISDN rather than a network connection.

Since a hardware ISDN router is more expensive than a terminal adapter and a software router product, you can conceivably install an ISDN line, connect a terminal adapter to one Mac on your network, and then run a software router on that Mac to share the ISDN connection with other Macs that you have. Performance may be slightly less than using an actual ISDN router, because you must work through a single Mac for all connections and you face the problems of that Mac crashing and taking down the whole Internet connection. However, the process is possible. Keep in mind, though, that some phone companies or ISPs may have policies against such use.

Choosing and Installing ISDN

The remaining bulk of this chapter is dedicated to describing the process of choosing an ISDN line, having it installed, and setting up the needed hardware. This process is an overview not specific to any particular hardware but is helpful for users wanting to fully understand the process of setting up and using ISDN with their Macs.

ISDN versus Other Options

A few years ago, ISDN was *the* method for high-speed Internet access for most people. The only real alternative was a dedicated or leased T1 line, which was cost-prohibitive for most people and was almost unheard of outside of urban centers. However, times have changed a bit, and ISDN no longer looks as attractive as it once did. This is particularly true when you look at some of the alternatives.

Traditional Modems Back in the mid-1990s, the fastest modems were limited to 14.4-Kbps or 28.8-Kbps connections. Compare to that a single-channel ISDN line's 64-Kbps speed, and the power of ISDN seems incredible. However, today's modems can connect at speeds over 50 Kbps. That doesn't present much difference between the best modems and an ISDN line.

True, there are still some advantages to ISDN. ISDN connections occur much faster, and a dual-channel ISDN line can provide access speeds as high as 128 Kbps (maybe more if your terminal adapter and your ISP both support the same compression schemes). There's also the fact that ISDN is more stable and will provide a consistent access speed where a modem may not. The question is whether or not this is worth all the setup and ongoing costs involved in using an ISDN connection.

Cable Modems   Traditional modems may still be slower than ISDN, but cable modems aren't. In fact, cable modems frequently achieve connections that are well over 10 times the speed of ISDN. Even the slowest cable modems on the market are rated to be more than three times as fast as a dual-channel ISDN line. And cable modem connections are dedicated, meaning they are active as soon as you turn a Mac on. There are also fewer hardware considerations and generally much smaller setup and service fees than ISDN. You are often charged a flat monthly rate for cable modem access that includes rental of any needed hardware. Finally, cable modems tend to be more readily available outside urban centers than any other high-speed Internet access. Of course, this has to be balanced against the fact that you are at the mercy of one ISP (your cable company). See the next chapter for more information on cable modem technology.

DSL Connections   Like cable modems, DSL (Digital Subscriber Line) connections are faster than ISDN, and they are dedicated connections that are available whenever your Mac is turned on. DSL uses your existing phone line, rather than needing a special new line installed as ISDN does. It presents no need for migrating your existing phones or fax machines to digital versions or using a converter. And, like ISDN, you can choose from multiple ISPs when using DSL. Also, DSL is almost always charged at a flat rate depending on the amount of bandwidth you choose. Unfortunately, like ISDN, DSL requires you to live relatively close to your phone company's switching station. You can find out more about DSL in the next chapter.

Leased/Dedicated Lines   If you really want dedicated, high-speed Internet connections, particularly connections suited to running a web or other Internet server, you should consider leasing a dedicated TI line from an ISP. These lines afford you with a direct Internet connection and usually provide a good amount of bandwidth. They also usually provide a static IP address or range of IP addresses to use for whatever Internet devices or service you plan on operating. You usually end up paying a flat monthly rate as well. Dedicated lines are rare outside of urban areas, however, and may involve a fair amount of expense in terms of setup and installation, as the line must be installed into your home or office.

Contacting Your Phone Company

Once you've made the decision to go with an ISDN connection, you begin the process by contacting your phone company. When contacting your phone company, there are several items you should find out: whether you can get ISDN service, what kind of switching protocols your company uses, the costs involved in receiving ISDN service from them, whether they provide their own ISP services for their ISDN lines, and so forth.

Are You Eligible for ISDN? The first question you need to ask when you contact your phone company about getting ISDN service is whether or not you can even get ISDN service. Because ISDN uses digital signaling, there is an effective length on how far you can be from the local phone company office or switching station. This length is 18,000 feet of phone cable. Your phone company may be able to tell you as soon as you call up if you can get ISDN service, or they may need to perform a test called a *loop qualification* to determine if the signal into your home or office over the existing lines is strong enough to support ISDN. If they need to perform a loop qualification, they may need to send a technician to your home or office to perform the test, or they may be able to do it completely from their office.

If you are too far away to receive ISDN service on your existing lines, your phone company may be able to use a signal amplifier or repeater to boost the signal strength to enable ISDN service for you. They may also be able to connect you to a different switching station for ISDN service. Some phone companies will also offer to install any needed lines or hardware into their network in order to provide you ISDN service, but usually at increased costs to you that may make ISDN setup too costly to consider.

Considering the Costs Once you know that you can get ISDN installed, you should consider the costs. There will be initial setup costs from your phone company to convert an existing phone line or install a new one to provide ISDN service. ISDN service often costs more per month than traditional phone service. Each phone company handles billing differently, and you should check out what options they offer. Remember that these are only the costs involved in operating the ISDN lines for connections. The ISP you choose to connect with through the ISDN lines will also charge you either a flat or per-minute rate for Internet access.

Getting ISDN Installed It takes at least a few days for the phone company to install an ISDN line and involves a technician coming and adjusting the phone lines coming into your home or office. You need to be there when the technician comes. In situations where the phone company needs to install phone cabling or other hardware outside your house, it takes considerably longer to install ISDN service. If you are converting an existing analog phone line to ISDN, the phone company usually deactivates the line 24 to 48 hours before ISDN service is installed and enabled. This means you will probably be without phone service temporarily.

Choosing an ISP

When you sign up for ISDN service from your phone company, the ISDN line is installed and set up in your home or office. This provides you the physical connection, but it doesn't provide you the actual Internet service. For that you still need to find an Internet service provider. Beyond simply picking an ISP at random, you will need to find one that supports ISDN. Optimally, you should make sure your ISP uses the same kind of ISDN hardware that you do. This way, any data compression scheme supported by your ISDN hardware will also be supported by their hardware, resulting in better effective data transfer rates than the 128 Kbps that is ISDN's maximum throughput.

Use Your Phone Company's ISP If your phone company offers ISDN service, chances are, they also operate their own ISP. If they do, then they may seem the best choice for your ISDN Internet access. This can be a good situation because you don't have to go hunting for an ISP that supports ISDN and you have a single place to call when something isn't working right. You may also be able to get a discounted rate on ISDN service by using your phone company's ISP through a package deal for both ISDN lines and Internet access. However, you also should realize that your phone company's ISP is not the only option.

Find Another ISP Several Internet service providers at the national, regional, and local levels offer ISDN Internet service. Table 35-1 lists

TABLE 35-1

National Level ISPs Offering ISDN Service.

Provider	Homepage Location
GTE	http://www.gte.net
PSI	http://www.psi.net
Sprint	http://www.sprintlink.net
UUNET	http://www.uunet.com
EarthLink	http://www.earthlink.net

some of the national level ISPs that support ISDN connections. If you are looking at a national ISP, make certain they offer ISDN access numbers that are local calls for you so you don't end up paying long-distance charges. In addition to the ISPs listed in Table 35-1, there are often many local and regional ISPs that provide ISDN Internet service. Check with the ISPs in your area to see which ones offer ISDN.

When comparing ISPs, look at what setup costs they require, what their rates are, and whether or not they charge a monthly flat rate regardless of how much time you spend connected or if they charge by the minute/hour. Usually, it is best to choose a provider that charges a single flat rate. With the ease and speed that ISDN connections can be established, having a flat rate connection can be like having a virtually constant connection.

Making the Connection

Once you've made an appointment to have your ISDN line installed and you've signed up for ISDN Internet service from an ISP, your next step is actually making the connection. There are several components of ISDN hardware that you need to configure to make the equipment work with your new ISDN line. This section includes a brief overview of the process of setting up a terminal adapter once the technician actually installs the ISDN line, though the specifics will vary depending on what hardware you're using. Using a router is somewhat more involved, though several steps are similar. If you wish to set up a router, you will also likely want a dedicated connection. Your phone company and ISP can provide details about configuring a router to work with their ISDN services for such a connection.

Installing the ISDN Line This step is completed when a technician from your phone company comes to install, activate, and test your new ISDN line. In most cases, this involves very little internal wiring in your home because ISDN uses the same copper wires used for traditional phone service. The only time you need to have additional wiring installed is if your existing phone lines are old and deteriorating or if you already have multiple phone lines coming into your home (in which case, you may want to consider converting one of these to ISDN).

The technician will install the line into the house to a phone jack, referred to as the *demarcation point* (or demarc). This point defines where the phone company's responsibility for the line ends and your responsibility begins. Anything outside of your house that leads into the demarcation point is their responsibility to service and maintain. Anything from the demarcation point inward is your responsibility. Some phone companies will take care of maintaining lines inside the demarcation point for an extra monthly fee.

The technician will usually be willing to install an ISDN phone jack at whatever location you will actually be connecting ISDN equipment. This should be the room or office where your Mac is located (or where your Ethernet hub is located if you will be using a router to connect a network of Macs). If the technician only checks the line at the demarcation point, you should request he or she check it at the actual ISDN phone jack that you will be plugging your hardware into. Once the technician confirms that the line is functioning properly, the installation is usually complete, though the ISDN equipment and possibly the ISDN line itself will still need to be configured at this point.

Information You Need from The Phone Company Before the technician leaves, you need to ask for the following information about your new ISDN line: Circuit identification code, service profile identifiers for each B channel (often called SPIDs), and the phone numbers for each B channel in your new ISDN line. You will need this information to configure your ISDN hardware. You should already have asked about what type of ISDN switching protocol the phone company uses and have bought an NT-1 (or terminal adapter with integrated NT-1) that supports this protocol.

Installing the NT-1 Once the ISDN line is installed, you can install your NT-1 if you are planning on using multiple ISDN devices with your connection or have opted for a terminal adapter or router that does not include an integrated NT-1. To install the NT-1, plug the RJ connector cable from the NT-1 into the phone jack of the ISDN line. Plug the NT-1's

Figure 35-1
The NT-1 is placed as
an intermediary
between your ISDN
device and ISDN
phone jack.

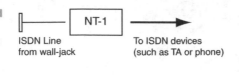

Figure 35-1
The NT-1 is placed as
an intermediary
between your ISDN
device and ISDN
phone jack.

power supply into your wall outlet. Figure 35-1 shows the placement of the NT-1 in your ISDN connection.

Once connected to the ISDN line and powered, the NT-1 should be operational and will have at least three LED lights to indicate that it is functioning properly. These lights will include an indicator to let you know that the NT-1 is receiving power and is turned on, an indicator to tell you that the U connector is active and attached, and an indicator to tell you that the S/T interface is functioning. There may be additional LED indicator lights for other functions as well. Assuming the ISDN line and NT-1 are functioning properly, all three of the indicators mentioned should indicate power and functionality. If not, try connecting the NT-1 again to see if this resolves the issue. If not, refer to the NT-1's manual for additional help. If this does not seem to solve the issue, contact the phone company, as there may be trouble with the ISDN line. You can refer to the NT-1's manual for additional information on LED indicators and how to use the NT-1.

Installing a TA　To install an internal TA that is a PCI card, follow the instructions in Chapter 8 for installing a PCI card into a Power Mac computer. To install an internal TA that is a PC Card into a PowerBook, see Chapter 9.

To install an external TA that uses a serial port or USB interface, install any driver or utility software for the TA, plug in the TA's power supply (this may not be needed for a USB TA that draws power from the USB bus), connect the TA to a serial port or USB port, and restart the computer. If you are using a serial port TA, make sure you are using a high-speed serial cable that supports hardware handshaking, the same as those described for use with serial port modems in Chapter 31. Figure 35-2 shows the placement of the TA in your ISDN hardware.

If the TA has an integrated NT-1 or a U interface (which refer to the same thing), then it can be connected directly to your ISDN line without using an NT-1. Connect it directly to the RJ11 interface coming out of your ISDN phone jack. If the TA does not have an integrated NT-1, you need to use the RJ45 S/T connector cable to attach it to one of the ports

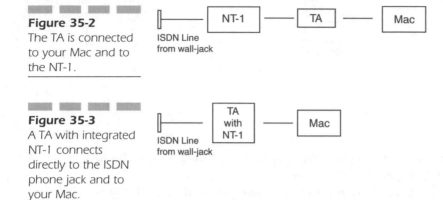

Figure 35-2
The TA is connected to your Mac and to the NT-1.

Figure 35-3
A TA with integrated NT-1 connects directly to the ISDN phone jack and to your Mac.

on your NT-1. Once the TA is connected, you are ready to configure it. Figure 35-3 shows the placement of a TA with integrated NT-1 in your ISDN equipment.

Configuring a TA   Terminal adapters can be configured through a wide variety of interfaces. Some use a utility application that runs on the Mac, some need to be configured using AT commands entered from a terminal emulator program (see Chapter 31 for more information on both AT commands and terminal emulators), and some are configured using a keypad on the front of the TA. Refer to the manual of your specific TA to find configuration information.

The information that needs to be entered when you are configuring a TA includes the phone numbers assigned to each B channel of the ISDN line, the ISDN switch protocol used by your phone company, and the SPIDs for each channel (the SPID for each channel will be the channel's phone number with some additional numbers before and after it). All of this should have been provided to you from your phone company before or during installation.

You may also be asked to enter additional information, such as the type of calls that will be placed using the TA, the data rate of those calls, and the B channel protocol to be used. In addition, you may be asked to choose between hardware and software flow control (as with a modem, you should opt for hardware flow control). The TA should come with instructions for entering all of this information, all of which should be provided by the phone company and/or your ISP.

Once the TA is configured, it should attempt to initialize with your phone company's ISDN network. The TA will usually indicate that it has successfully initialized its connection via an LED indicator light (external TAs only). Some do so by flashing an alert or dialog box on the Mac's display. The TA's manual will include information indicating how the TA will signal a successful (or unsuccessful) initialization. If the TA does not initialize its connection successfully, check to be sure it is connected and powered properly. Try powering it off and then back on, as this may be necessary right after configuring the device. If this doesn't help, ensure that you entered all the needed configuration information properly. If this doesn't help, there is likely a problem with either your TA or your ISDN line. Contact your phone company and/or TA manufacturer's tech support department for additional information.

Configuring Your Mac and Making an ISDN Internet Connection
Once your terminal adapter is connected and configured as described above, you are ready to actually try out your ISDN line and make a connection to your ISP. To establish the connection, you can pretty much follow the same steps described in Chapter 31 for configuring a modem connection. Just make certain you choose the modem script appropriate to your terminal adapter and that you choose the appropriate port (internal, USB, or serial port) to which the TA is connected. As you can see in Figure 35-4, most terminal adapters will have two scripts, one for PPP connections and one for Multilink PPP connections. The difference

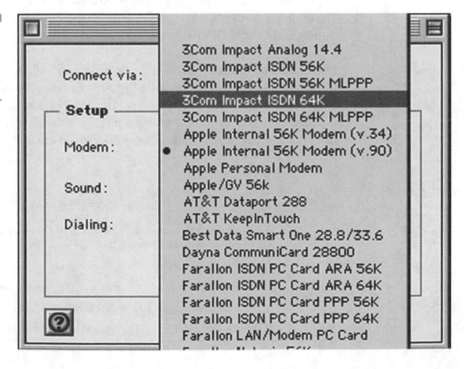

Figure 35-4
Choosing a script for a terminal adapter in the Modem control panel.

between the two will be that the Multilink scripts will end in MLPPP. You may also need to check the Ignore Dial Tone checkbox.

Once you have chosen the appropriate modem script, simply enter the rest of the information for dial-up phone number (your ISP should provide a phone number for placing ISDN calls for connections), username and password, and so forth. You can perform these steps using the Internet Setup Assistant application or using the Remote Access control panel, as described in Chapter 31.

Once the connection information has been entered, simply open the Remote Access control panel and click on the Connect button to initiate the call. Or you can use the Remote Access control strip module. Unlike a modem, there will be no sound of a phone dialing or connecting. The Remote Access window's status section should indicate if you are connected, however. Once connected, try launching your web browser and accessing a website to verify that the connection is completely successful.

Placing a Voice Call   You may also want to place a voice call to completely test your ISDN line, assuming you are going to use the line for voice as well as data service. To do this, connect your ISDN phone to the NT-1 or your analog phone to an analog port on your TA or NT-1 (if one is provided). Then dial the phone as normal to try and place a voice call. If you have ordered other ISDN features or devices, test them as is appropriate for each device as well.

ISDN Cause Codes   To help determine why individual ISDN data calls fail to complete, some terminal adapters may display an ISDN cause code. This cause code will be returned by the ISDN network to the device after a failed call attempt and can be equivalent to a busy signal. Table 35-2 lists the most common ISDN cause codes and their meanings.

TABLE 35-2

Common ISDN
Cause Codes.

Code	Meaning
16	This generally means that the call was dialed correctly, but some other issue occurred like an invalid password or the use of the wrong B channel protocol.
17	This is the ISDN equivalent of a busy signal.
18	This means that there is no response at the number you have dialed.
34, 44	These indicate that both your ISDN B channels are currently in use.
100	This is displayed if the SPID number(s) you entered into your TA are incorrect.

CHAPTER **36**

Cable Modem
and DSL Issues

Even the best modems on the market deliver Internet connections of limited speeds. While ISDN lines do offer better performance than traditional modem connections, they are more expensive to install and maintain, involving costs that must be paid to both a phone company and an Internet service provider. ISDN also requires special hardware—a terminal adapter or router—which must be purchased at the user's expense. In addition, ISDN service is not available in all areas.

Two new technologies have sought to make higher-performance Internet available to a wide segment of consumers, particularly home users: cable modems and DSL (Digital Subscriber Line). These technologies both deliver performance much faster than a traditional modem connection and often much faster than an ISDN line. Unfortunately, there have been some Mac-specific problems with these services that have existed over the past couple of years. This chapter looks at how these technologies function, as well as at the problems that Mac users should be aware of when using them.

How Cable Modems Work

Cable modems allow you to receive high-speed Internet access through the same cabling that provides the cable television feed to your house, as shown in Figure 36-1. These lines generally have a good deal of excess bandwidth that is not used for transmitting cable TV to consumers. This excess bandwidth in the cable network can support two-way data transmission, such as the TCP/IP communications used to access the Internet. Assuming a cable company supports data access over the cable lines that run through your neighborhood, very little is needed to provide cable modem access other than attaching the cable modem to one of the coaxial cables that comes in through the wall of your house.

The name *cable modem* is actually a misnomer. In fact, the device is

Figure 36-1
The cable line used for both cable TV and data.

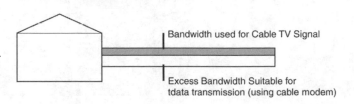

Cable Line Servicing a Home

Bandwidth used for Cable TV Signal

Excess Bandwidth Suitable for
tdata transmission (using cable modem)

not really a modem at all. Instead, it is a network bridge that connects your computer (or your local network) to the cable company's Internet servers and routers. As a bridge, it converts the standard 10Base-T Ethernet connection used in most networks to the coaxial cable connection that comes into your house and connects to the cable television line that services your neighborhood.

A number of different cable modems are in use today, produced by several companies. Most of them function in the same way but will vary in terms of what kind of data throughput (or connection speed) they are capable of delivering, as well as whether or not they will support simultaneous Internet access for multiple computers in a single location. The modem you use will generally be determined by your cable company, who will essentially lease it to you. Often, they will choose a cable modem model because it is compatible with their infrastructure. Cable modems themselves are completely platform-transparent devices. A typical cable modem is shown in Figure 36-2.

Figure 36-2
A typical cable modem.

The cable modem itself is one of the factors that determines just how fast your Internet connection will be. This is because various cable modems are designed to support transmitting data at different speeds. Most cable modems today will transmit 512 Kbps (10 times what a traditional dial-up modem can offer under the best circumstances). Some older models may be limited to 384 Kbps, and some newer models offer transfer rates as high as 3000 Kbps (60 times faster than a traditional modem). Your cable modem provider can tell you the maximum throughput of your particular cable modem, and this information should be included in the manual included with the modem itself.

The cable modem is not, however, the only element that will determine your actual data transfer speed. Another important factor is the number of subscribers in your neighborhood. Your cable modem connection runs through the cable line that services your entire neighborhood, as shown in Figure 36-3. This means that anyone else in your neighborhood that is also a subscriber to the company's cable modem service will be sharing that same connection. The more people there are sharing the cable line for Internet access, the less bandwidth that is available for each person. Get enough people using the same line, and eventually the transfer rates for each person are going to be reduced. Some cable modem companies will offer a guaranteed minimum transfer rate (usually this is comparable to the performance of an ISDN line), but others may not. You should check on this before signing up for cable modem service. Also be aware that your neighborhood, at least in terms of the cable company, may be bigger than you think. The cable line that defines your neighborhood may also service hundreds or thousands of other homes.

The shared nature of a cable line can also introduce a security risk to your home computers and network. In theory, someone with the right software tools might be able read network traffic that is being sent to

Figure 36-3
A cable modem connection is shared with several homes.

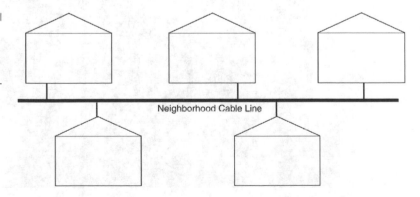

Neighborhood Cable Line

and from your computer(s). This means that someone might be able to detect the data that you are transmitting. This potential concern is addressed differently by different cable modem providers, and you may wish to ask about it before signing up for service. It is also possible that other users whose connection shares the same neighborhood cable line as yours could make a network connection to your computer or network. To prevent this, you can take the same network precautions discussed in Chapter 34 relating to having an individual Mac or network connected to the Internet. Additionally, you can gain some protection by disabling the File Sharing over TCP/IP option of Mac OS 9 and higher.

Even assuming you have the maximum possible bandwidth and transfer rates afforded by your cable modem and your neighborhood's cable line, you may still not get high transfer rates with every website or e-mail server or FTP connection. This is simply because the servers you are connecting to may not be able to transmit data as fast as your high-speed connection is capable of receiving it. Or, one of the Internet servers your communications need to pass through between your computer and the server you're requesting data from may not be able to transmit the data as quickly as your connection allows. This is an inherent weakness of the Internet: your communication can be hampered by the performance of the servers it must travel through. In fact, it is very rare for data to be transmitted from a single remote Internet server to your computer at even half the speed that cable modem connections are capable of providing.

As you can expect from the description of a cable modem, you will need a computer that supports 10Base-T Ethernet to use a cable modem service. If the cable modem supports multiple computers, you might also be able to connect an Ethernet hub to allow multiple computers to connect to it. All of the Macs covered in this book include a built-in 10/100Base-T Ethernet port as a standard feature. Some older Macs, however, will require an Ethernet card (or a 10Base-T transceiver if the Mac uses an older-style Mac Ethernet port known as an AAUI port). An Ethernet-to-LocalTalk adapter may or may not function for older Macs that cannot accept an Ethernet card.

A cable modem provider may provide the needed TCP/IP configuration to your computer(s) in one of two primary methods. The first is to manually assign you an IP address, as well as a router address, subnet mask, and DNS server address—all of which are entered into the TCP/IP control panel. Far more likely, your Mac will obtain this information from a DHCP server at startup, in which case you will set the TCP/IP control panel as shown in Figure 36-4. The use of DHCP servers is explored further later in this chapter for both cable modems and DSL connections.

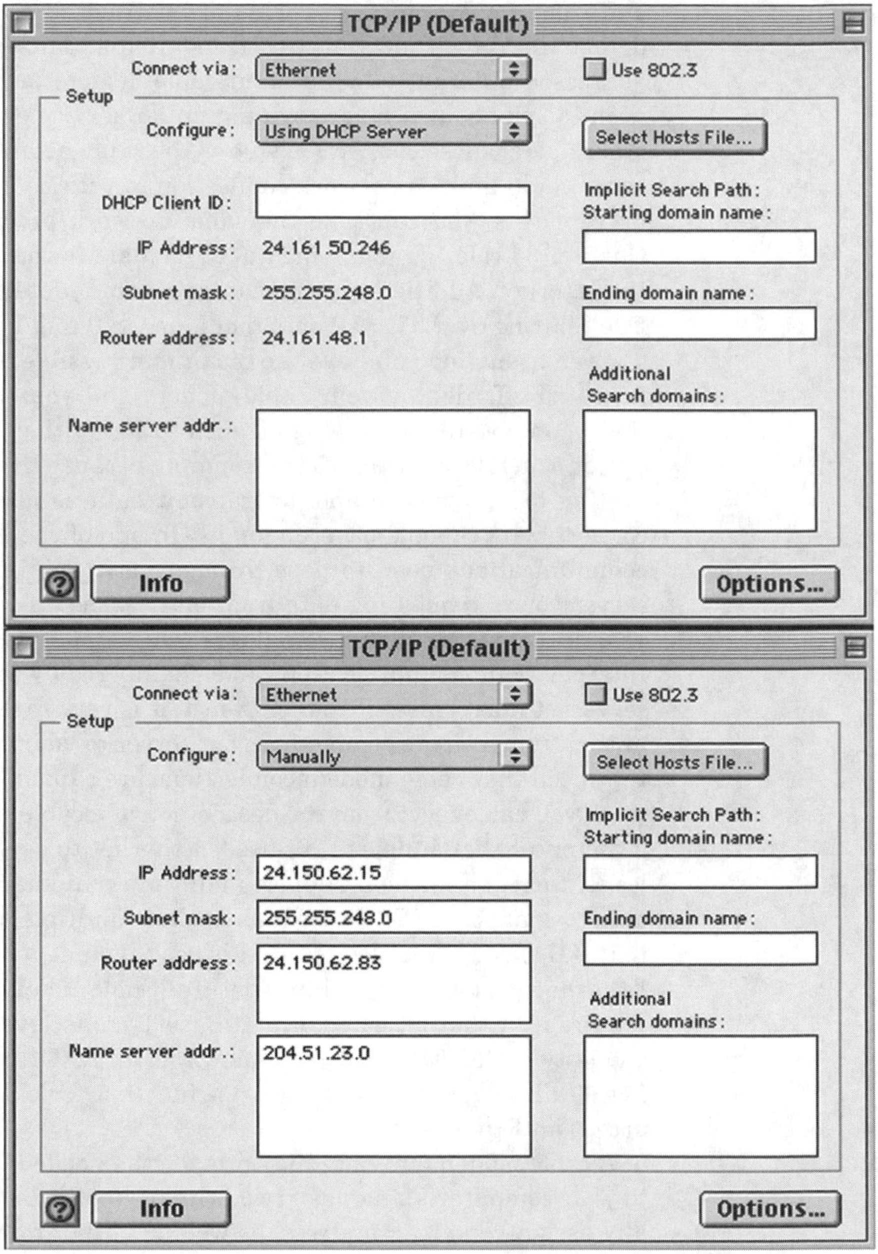

■■■ ■■■ ■■■ ■■

Figure 36-4
DHCP versus manual
TCP/IP settings.

Asynchronous Cable Modems

Some cable modems are *asynchronous*. This means that they support higher data transfer rates when data is being sent from an Internet server to your computer (downloading) than they do when you are sending data or requests to a remote Internet server (uploading). The principle here is that most users spend more time downloading information, files, web pages, and so on from the Internet than they do uploading material. Following that belief, the only outgoing data most consumers are likely to transmit are requests for files or web pages. Since such requests are small and take little bandwidth or data to transmit, there is no need to provide as much uploading bandwidth or performance.

So, if you have an asynchronous cable modem connection, you may commonly see download speeds of say 1000 Kbps but will only see upload speeds of 150 Kbps. Those upload speeds are still faster than any dial-up modem connection, but not nearly as fast as your download performance. If you are in the position of performing massive uploads of data on a regular basis, you might want to request that you not receive asynchronous connections (although, depending on your cable modem provider, you may not have a choice). Otherwise, you will likely not notice much difference with an asynchronous cable modem.

Telco-Return Cable Modems   Telco-return is an offshoot of asynchronous cable modem technology. Telco-return cable modems use your cable TV line for only incoming or downloading data. Any outgoing connections, such as uploads, outgoing e-mail messages, or file requests, are sent using a separate connection. This separate connection uses your traditional phone line and is essentially a dial-up modem connection made from the Telco-return cable modem. Telco-return modems can deliver superior web-surfing speeds to traditional modems, but they remove two of the big advantages of cable modem technology: freeing your phone line and having your Internet connection always available when your computer is turned on.

How to Share a Cable Modem Connection

Cable modems are versatile tools. While they were originally conceived for connecting a single computer to the Internet at high speeds using cable lines, they can often be used to connect a small home network. In fact, several cable modem providers include this ability at no extra charge, because many cable modem models have the ability to support multiple computers directly. Even if a cable modem or provider doesn't offer support for multiple computers, it may be possible to share the connection using a router as you would a dial-up modem or other connection (see Chapter 34).

Direct Support for Multiple Computers   Several cable modems have the ability to provide access to multiple computers from a single cable modem. These cable modems have the needed circuitry and software built into them to recognize individual computers and their Internet requests, and they function much like simple routers. If your specific cable modem supports this feature, you will find that you can simply plug the cable modem into a 10Base-T Ethernet hub along with Ethernet cables for each of the Macs in your home. You can then configure each Mac to work with the cable modem as though it was the only Mac being connected (usually by choosing Connect Via Ethernet and Use DHCP Server in the TCP/IP control panel). Each Mac will then receive its own IP address and related information from the cable modem provider, and the cable modem will process its Internet requests and transfer separate from the other computers on the network.

Although the basic process for using cable modems that support multiple computers is the same regardless of the modem, there are some differences in how the cable modem needs to be connected to an Ethernet hub in order to function. Most cable modems can simply be connected to an Ethernet hub using standard category 5 Ethernet cable and should be plugged into the hub's Uplink port (the port that would be used to connect this hub to another hub if you were creating a larger network). Some cable modems, however, will work fine when connected to any traditional port on the hub rather than the Uplink port. And in some rarer circumstances, cable modems have been known to require an Ethernet crossover cable (the cable traditionally used to connect only two computers by Ethernet without using a hub) to connect to a traditional port on the hub. These are the primary methods of attaching a cable modem that supports multiple computers to a hub. You can check your cable modem's manual or consult your cable modem provider for additional specifics or details if these methods do not work.

Using a Router   If a cable modem does not include support for multiple computers connecting to a provider through it, then the cable modem will be designed so that it can only register a single computer through the connection. This means that directly connecting multiple computers to the cable modem service is not an option. However, using a router may be an option. Likewise, a router is an option if your Macs are connected using a networking method besides 10Base-T Ethernet, such as LocalTalk, one of the home phone line networking kits available, or Apple's AirPort (the AirPort Base Station is a router itself, however, so an additional router should not be needed).

Routers were discussed in greater detail in Chapter 34. As mentioned in that chapter, a router is a tool (either a specially designed piece of hardware or a utility application running on a Macintosh) that has connections both to the Internet and to a local network of computers. The router can then transfer Internet requests between the network and the Internet. Routers can be used with some cable modems that support only a single connection to share that connection between a number of computers in a home or small office network. Some cable modem providers have a policy of not allowing individual consumers to share their connection via a router. Although such rules are rare, and it is unlikely that a provider would be aware that consumers are using a router unless a technician notices it on a service call, it is best to verify the policy in advance. If such a policy is in place, it is best to comply with it, because if you are caught violating it, you will probably be banned from receiving cable modem service from that company. Ideally, you should also encourage the company to consider changing its policy and to shop around for another high-speed Internet access company (cable or DSL) that does not have such a policy.

How DSL Connections Work

Digital Subscriber Line is a technology that uses the same phone lines that are already installed in your home to provide high-speed Internet access. Prior to the development of DSL, the use of these phone lines was limited to voice transmission and data transmission using the same audible frequencies as voice transmission, such as the characteristic screech of fax machines and traditional modem communication. These uses rely on a very limited spectrum of frequencies (0 kHz to 4 kHz) and ignore a much larger selection of higher-audio frequencies (100 kHz to 2.2 MHz) that can be used to transmit data (as illustrated in Figure 36-5). DSL technology uses those higher frequencies to transmit data. Since these frequencies are much higher than the frequencies used for transmitting audible information, such as your voice or data from a fax machine, the

Figure 36-5
DSL versus voice
frequencies.

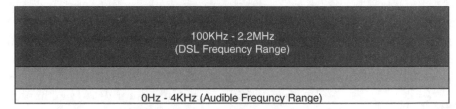

Frequency rage of Most Telephone Lines
(0Hz - 2.2MHz)

100KHz - 2.2MHz
(DSL Frequency Range)

0Hz - 4KHz (Audible Frequncy Range)

phone line can be used for both traditional functions (i.e., talking on the phone or sending a fax) at the same time it is being used to transmit data via DSL.

In order to use a phone line for DSL, a special device known as a splitter is installed where the phone line enters your house. The splitter separates the voice frequencies of the phone line from the higher frequencies used for the DSL data transmission. The line for voice frequencies goes to your telephone jacks (where you can plug in your phone, answering machine, fax machine, and such). The other line goes into a DSL modem.

A DSL modem (sometimes called a terminal unit-remote) is similar to a cable modem in that it connects to your computer or network via a 10Base-T Ethernet port. Unlike a cable modem, a DSL modem is also similar to an actual modem, because it does need to translate data for communication via audio frequencies (albeit higher frequencies than those used by a traditional modem). Figure 36-6 shows the basic wiring for a DSL connection.

Unlike a cable modem, the DSL modem connects to your phone line, which in turn connects directly to the phone company. The line is not shared with anyone else in your neighborhood. This means that you should

Figure 36-6
Splitting of phone
line for phone jacks
and DSL modem.

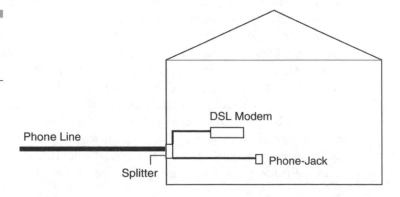

always get the same level of bandwidth and the same transfer rates, unlike a cable modem connection, where your connection is shared and performance is related to how many people are sharing the same cable line.

This freedom comes at a price, however. The higher frequencies that DSL uses to transmit data suffer signal degradation far more quickly and easily than those used for voice transmission of traditional phone and fax calls. This results in a limit to how far away from a local phone company office your house can be and still receive DSL service. That limit is about 3 miles of phone cable, which may be less than 3 physical miles depending on how the cable travels between your house and the company's switching station. You will need to check with your phone company to see if you are within the DSL connection range, as well as to see if the phone line running to your home is of sufficient quality to permit DSL service. Some phone companies offer special phone services that either use the same frequencies as DSL or frequencies close enough that DSL service isn't possible on the same phone lines. Again, you'll need to check with your phone company to see if you qualify for DSL service. Figure 36-7 illustrates these issues.

Figure 36-7

Each home has its own DSL connection if it is close enough to the telco office.

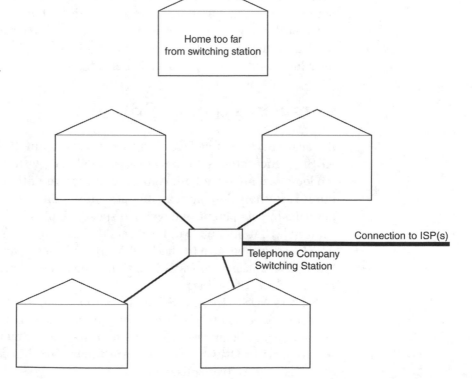

Home too far
from switching station

Connection to ISP(s)

Telephone Company
Switching Station

Beyond having phone lines that support DSL, you'll need an Internet provider that supports DSL in general and the DSL lines owned by your phone company in particular. In some cases, the phone company itself provides such Internet access, but in others, you will need to work with a separate Internet service provider. Sometimes, you may have the option of choosing between the phone company's Internet services and those of another ISP.

DSL lines are capable of data transfer rates as high as 7 Mbps. However, companies providing DSL service will often charge you based on how much bandwidth you wish to use. Low-end DSL service, such as 384 Kbps, may run you about $50 per month, while more high-end service, such as 1.5 Mbps, will run about three times that, depending on the provider. For cost reasons, most consumers will probably opt for lower-performance DSL options. Also, as with cable modems, you will be limited to the performance of whatever Internet servers you are connecting to, so choosing more expensive options may not return much higher performance in real-world usage.

As with cable modems, DSL service providers primarily use DHCP servers to deliver IP addresses and related TCP/IP information to a user's computer. Less often, static or manual IP addresses are assigned (again, in the same manner as with a cable modem). Even less commonly a protocol known as PPPoE is used. This is a variation on the PPP protocol used for dial-up Internet connections that was designed to support user login and passwords over Ethernet.

Common Types of DSL

Several variations of DSL are in existence, but the most common is ADSL, which stands for *asymmetric DSL*. As with asynchronous cable modems, asymmetric DSL connections receive data at a different maximum rate than they are capable of sending data. ADSL service is often described by its potential download speeds. Upload speeds tend to be less than half that of download for most ADSL services. When signing up for ADSL service, be sure to check what upload speeds are included. In most low-end situations, you will find that upload performance is comparable to that of an ISDN line.

Next to ADSL, there is SDSL, or *symmetric DSL*. As you can guess, in this service, upload speeds are the same as download speeds. SDSL is often aimed at businesses rather than consumers and will cost more than ADSL service. Other variations are fairly rare but include options for even faster data transmission.

How to Share a DSL Connection

Unlike cable modems, DSL connections are not designed to be shared with multiple computers. For this reason, it isn't possible to simply connect multiple computers and a DSL modem to an Ethernet hub and allow each computer to connect on its own. It is, however, possible to use a router, as described in Chapter 34, to share the connection between a small network of computers

DHCP Servers and the Mac OS

Every computer connected to the Internet needs a unique IP address. This means that any Mac connected via a cable modem or DSL line needs to be assigned an IP address by the cable modem or DSL provider. As you may remember from earlier chapters, DHCP is a protocol that allows a network administrator to simplify the assigning of IP addresses by giving a server a pool of IP addresses. The server then assigns an IP address from this pool to computers when they connect (usually when they are first turned on). Given the sheer number of subscribers that cable modem and DSL providers have, a DHCP server allows administrators of these services to allow a DHCP server to handle providing IP addresses to hundreds or thousands of computers with very little effort.

Beyond simply keeping the network administrators from having to manually assign every computer of every subscriber an IP address, DHCP also simplifies problems when the provider experiences an equipment failure. For example, if a provider experiences a failure of one of their routers, a backup router will often be activated. This may cause some IP addresses to be removed from the pool available for client computers. It may also require other TCP/IP information to be changed to support the backup router. A DHCP server immediately transmits this new information to computers as they connect (or are restarted). Were IP addresses assigned manually, the cable modem or DSL provider would need to call every subscriber to their service and give them the new information to enter manually in order for their connection to function properly. Needless to say, this would prove an incredibly daunting task and would use resources that the provider should be using to fix the original router that went down in the first place.

So, DHCP seems like the ideal method for providing TCP/IP information and IP addresses to users of cable modem and DSL connections. Unfortunately, very few things are perfect in the computer world, particularly when those things need to work with several different computing platforms (Mac, Windows, Linux, and other UNIX variations are the three most common platforms that are supported by DHCP servers, and this doesn't count the variations within each of these platforms).

Each platform has a networking element built into its operating system that manages TCP/IP communication (Open Transport for the current Mac OS), and this includes a component that handles how the operating system interacts with a DHCP server known as the DHCP client. Because DHCP is an industry standard protocol, both DHCP servers, such as those used by cable modem and DSL providers, as well as the DHCP clients built into various operating systems need to be designed according to certain specifications. In theory, this ensures that all DHCP servers will be able to reliably support all DHCP clients. In practice, this is usually the case as well—but not always.

In 1998, some advances were made to the industry standards on which DHCP is based. Several companies that produced DHCP servers began upgrading their servers to take advantage of the new advancements. At the same time, companies that designed operating systems developed newer DHCP clients as part of their networking architectures, including Apple, who updated the Open Transport software of the Mac OS. Difficulties were expected for users who still had older versions of Open Transport installed when the new DHCP servers began to be used, but everyone assumed updating to the newest versions of Open Transport would solve them.

Unfortunately, the updates Apple made and the updates made by some DHCP server developers didn't always match up as they were expected to. Although Apple and the other companies involved each claimed they had developed their products according to the DHCP standards, the results tended to be unreliable for many users. Particularly affected by these problems were users of Time Warner's Road Runner service, the biggest cable modem provider. Other cable modem providers and DSL providers, however, reported the same problems, as did several companies using the DHCP servers to manage their corporate networks and intranets.

The problems manifested themselves primarily in the inability of a Mac to obtain an IP address at startup. The Mac would then either assign itself a default IP address beginning with 169.254. (such as 169.254.200.1) or simply display that an IP address was unavailable or that one would be supplied by the server (although it never was). Figure 36-8 shows the various possible results in the TCP/IP control panel when a Mac isn't able to receive an IP address. The result is that the Mac would be unable to establish an Internet connection, leaving users cut off from the high-speed Internet for which they were, on average, paying at least twice as much as a traditional ISP.

In fairness to both Apple and DHCP developers, efforts were made to figure out the problem, and both parties, as well as individual cable modem and DSL service providers, attempted to provide workarounds to the issue. Unfortunately, it wasn't until over a year later, when Apple released Open Transport 2.6, that the problems seemed to be fully addressed and resolved.

Figure 36-8

The possible displays in the TCP/IP control panel if the Mac cannot obtain an IP address from a DHCP server.

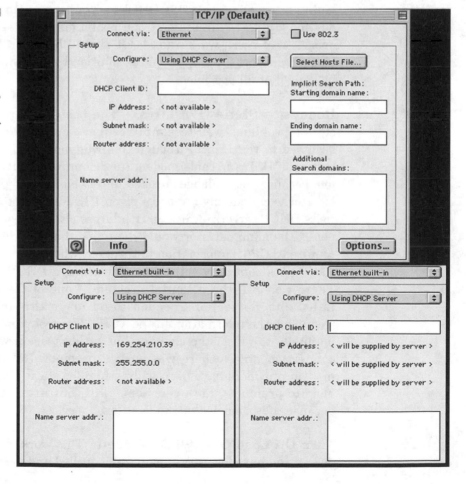

Open Transport 2.6, Apple's Solution

Although it took well over a year, Apple finally released a version of Open Transport that addressed many of the underlying causes for DHCP server connection failures with the Mac. The best solution for any Mac user experiencing problems with a DHCP server is to download Open Transport 2.6 (or higher) from Apple's support site and install it. The basic requirement is Mac OS 9, although it will function with Mac OS 8.6 on the iMac DV and Power Mac G4 computers with an AGP graphics card.

Earlier Workarounds

Before Apple released Open Transport 2.6, Mac users and companies providing Internet access using DHCP servers developed a number of methods for trying to circumvent the problems. This section includes an overview of these workarounds. It should be noted that upgrading to Open Transport 2.6 is a far better solution than any of these and should be done if at all possible.

Request a Static IP Address   The best workaround to the DHCP server problems was to simply request a permanent IP address be assigned to your Mac. Although this was more of a hassle for administrators of DSL and cable modem service providers, it did solve the problem because you no longer needed to rely on a DHCP server. The administrator would simply remove a given IP address from the pool allocated to its DHCP servers (or use an IP address already reserved outside of the pool). The administrator would then give that IP address and the other required TCP/IP information to the user, who could manually enter it in the TCP/IP control panel rather than using a DHCP server to obtain it. There was still the potential problem if one of the provider's routers failed and connections needed to be made through another router (requiring the information in the TCP/IP control panel of the user's Mac manually to reflect the change), but at least users would be assured a connection unless there was such a problem. Not all DSL and cable modem providers have been willing to offer static IP addresses to users despite problems, however. Some will, but at an additional charge, because they consider this to be a "pro" service.

Turn Off Load Only When Needed   This workaround is a good idea even if you have Open Transport 2.6 installed and even if you have never experienced any DHCP server problems, because it can increase performance somewhat and cut down on the potential for connection problems. By default, Open Transport allows the Mac to only load TCP/IP network information when the Mac is actually using a TCP/IP connection. When a period of time has passed without TCP/IP communications occurring, the Mac will give up its IP address and unload all TCP/IP information. Needless to say, if you're having trouble getting an IP address in the first place, you don't want to give one up once you have it.

The Load TCP/IP Only When Needed feature can be disabled relatively easily. Open the TCP/IP control panel. Click on the Options button. If the Options button isn't displayed, the control panel is displaying the Basic user mode, and you will need to switch to either the Advanced or Administrator modes by selecting User Mode from the Edit menu. When you click on the Options button, a dialog is displayed (shown in Figure 36-9) that contains two radio buttons for making TCP/IP active or inactive (active is needed for any Internet connection to function) and a checkbox labeled Load Only When Needed. Unchecking the checkbox will keep the Mac from releasing its IP address and TCP/IP information.

Use a Boot-P Server The Mac can also use protocols other than DHCP to dynamically obtain an IP address and other relevant TCP/IP information at startup. These are not widely used protocols, but some cable modem and DSL providers do support one of them—the Boot-P server. If you experience problems obtaining an IP address from a DHCP server, you can try using a Boot-P server instead (it is selected by the same menu in the TCP/IP control panel as a DHCP server is, as shown

Figure 36-9
The TCP/IP Options
dialog box.

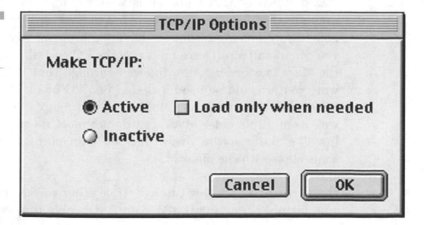

Figure 36-10
Selecting a Boot-P
Server instead of
a DHCP server.

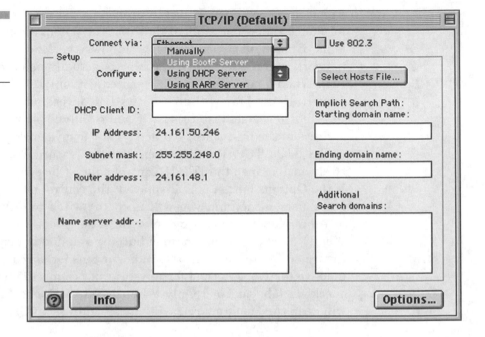

in Figure 36-10). If you do use a Boot-P server, you will probably find that the Mac hangs for as long as a minute before launching the Finder at startup. This is because the Mac is attempting to request an IP address from the Boot-P server at this time and is one reason a DHCP server is preferable to a Boot-P server under most conditions. If you cannot obtain an IP address from a Boot-P server, it is likely that your provider does not support the use of this protocol.

Use a Router Other platforms were not affected by the same DHCP issues as the Mac was. If you have a Windows- or Linux-based PC in your home as well as Macs that are having a problem with the DHCP server, you can install a software router on the PC and then manually configure the Macs to connect to the Internet through that PC. Similarly, a hardware router could be used if there is no PC available to use. For situations where you have one Mac capable of using Open Transport 2.6 as well as multiple older Macs that do not meet its requirements, you can install a router on the Mac with Open Transport 2.6 to share its reliable connection with the older Macs.

Restart until You Get Lucky If no other workaround is available to you, simply restarting the Mac until it is able to receive an IP address and connection is the only option. This could take many attempts and is very frustrating. Once you have an IP address and connection, do not shut the Mac down unless you absolutely have to (such as in response to a crash or software installation). Also, make certain that you have turned off the Load TCP/IP Only When Needed feature, as described earlier.

AirPort Base Stations and DHCP Servers

While most people have assumed that Open Transport 2.6 meant an end to DHCP issues with the Mac, it seems that some users will not be so lucky. The software built into the hardware AirPort Base Stations seems to suffer from the same problems when working with DHCP servers as earlier versions of Open Transport's DHCP client did. Since the Base Station can function as a router for sharing an Internet connection, it can be plugged into a DSL line or cable modem, obtaining an IP address for itself and then sharing its connection with both a terrestrial (Ethernet) network and a wireless network. If the Base Station does experience the same problems as earlier Open Transport versions, however, it may not be able to obtain an IP address and will therefore be unable to establish a connection that can be shared by other Macs. This presents a dilemma for Mac users wishing to use AirPort to deliver wireless Internet access.

Workarounds for Base Stations Each of the workarounds described earlier in this chapter for the DHCP server problems can be adapted to work with hardware Base Stations. Since the AirPort Setup Assistant utility will copy a Macintosh's TCP/IP information to the Base Station, simply set up the Mac as though it were the computer having problems with the DHCP server, using each of the workarounds described. The obvious exception is restarting in hopes of getting lucky. In this case, you'll want to repeatedly restart the Base Station and then use the AirPort Admin Utility to determine if it has successfully obtained an IP address.

A very good workaround for a hardware Base Station is to use a router on a desktop Mac that has been updated to Open Transport 2.6 (or a PC). Use the router software to assign an IP address manually to the Base Station. The Base Station will then treat this as its active IP address and allow Macs wirelessly to connect to the router of the desktop Mac through it. The router running on the desktop Mac will then transfer the requests through the Internet.

Possibly a better option is to use a recent desktop Mac that can accept an AirPort card (the slot-loading iMacs or the Power Mac G4 models with an AGP graphics card) as a software Base Station. Because these Macs can (and should) be upgraded to Open Transport 2.6, it is very unlikely that they will experience problems obtaining an IP address from a DHCP server. With an AirPort card installed and acting as a software Base Station, they can then share that connection with other AirPort-equipped Macs.

Resources for Further Study

About.com Mac Hardware High-Speed Internet Resources—
  http://machardware.about.com/msubcable-dsl.htm

Cable Modem. Net—http://www.cable-modem.net/

DSL Digest—http://www.DSLDigest.com/

DSL Reports—http://www.dslreports.com/

DSL Center—http://www.dslcenter.com/

CHAPTER 37

Mac OS Startup

When you turn on a Mac, you're greeted by the smiling Mac icon, followed by the "Welcome to Mac OS" splash screen (or a custom-designed startup screen if you've installed one in your System folder). The march of extension and control panel icons is next, followed by the appearance of the desktop and the Finder. While all this is what the average user sees, there's actually a good deal of activity occurring during the startup process that you don't see. This chapter looks at what is actually going on inside the Mac during that time and the various ways in which the component pieces of the Mac OS work together to make the Mac and its various abilities function. Later on, we'll also take a look at what happens when something goes wrong during startup.

The Startup Process

When you first press the power button on a Mac (or on its keyboard), a signal is sent that causes the power supply to send power to the motherboard and other internal components. This causes the Mac's internal fan (if one is present) to start and also initiates the startup commands stored in the Mac's ROM (read-only memory). One of the first commands the ROM sends is to play the Mac's startup chime. The ROM also sends a signal to each of the individual components inside the Mac, including the processor, hard drive and CD ROM controllers, any expansion slots inside the computer, the video card (or video chipset if built into the motherboard), and the internal ports. This signal triggers the self-test process to ensure that all the components needed for the Mac to function are working properly.

Assuming the basic components all pass their self-tests, the Mac begins testing the installed RAM. All sections of the installed RAM must function properly in order for the startup process to continue. The startup process will be halted if the RAM is damaged or if any module is not installed fully or correctly.

It is possible for some minor damage to the RAM to escape detection at this point. If this happens, the Mac will start up normally, but it may behave erratically. If this does happen, it will almost always be right after a new RAM module is installed and should therefore be easy to diagnose. (RAM problems and installation are discussed in detail in Chapter 6.)

Once the internal components and RAM are verified to be working correctly, the Mac then accesses the parameter RAM, or PRAM. From the settings stored in PRAM, the Mac knows which drive is designated as the current startup disk. The Mac then attempts to locate the selected startup disk in order to begin loading the Mac OS into RAM. If the selected startup disk is not found, the Mac will then search for another disk that is bootable and load the Mac OS off of that disk. If the Mac cannot find a bootable disk, the startup process will halt and a flashing question mark icon will be displayed.

If the selected startup disk is a network disk, the Mac will attempt to connect to another Mac running Mac OS X Server that is equipped to allow it to net-boot from that disk (or disk image). If the Mac cannot locate such a server or if the server is unable to allow the Mac to net-boot, the Mac will then begin searching for a bootable disk that is directly attached to it.

Once the Mac has located a bootable disk, it will proceed to look for an active System Folder (the presence of an active System Folder is a primary requirement for a disk to be bootable). An active System Folder (also called a "blessed" System Folder) is the System Folder designated by the Mac from which to load the Mac OS. There can be only one active System Folder on a disk. However, there can be any number of inactive System Folders on a given disk (the active one will be the only one to have the "System Folder icon"). Figure 37-1 shows both active and inac-

Figure 37-1
An active (left) and inactive (right) System Folders.

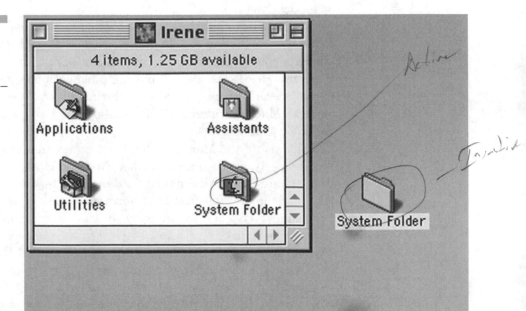

tive System Folders. If you have multiple System Folders on a disk, you can use a utility such as the shareware System Picker to manually designate one as active, or blessed. If not, you can "un-bless" a System Folder by removing the System file from it and renaming it. It is generally not a good idea to have multiple System Folders on a single disk.

Not as extensive on the pc!

When the Mac locates the active System Folder, the first item it will load into RAM is the Mac OS ROM file. This file contains most of the basic commands needed for the Mac to interact with hardware and the lower levels of the operating system. The file is so named because it contains 3 MB of code that, until the iMac's introduction, had been stored in the Mac's ROM on the motherboard. The Mac OS ROM file contains the most basic sections of the Mac OS, forming the foundation of the operating system and allowing the Mac to fully access and utilize both its internal components and low-level commands that are part of the Mac OS Toolbox.

What's the benefit of this code being on a ROM chip on the system board?

It is at this point that the Mac displays the smiling Mac icon onscreen and begins to load the operating system into RAM. The Mac begins loading the operating system by loading the System file, which contains most of the operating system's commands and libraries. At this point, the "Welcome to Mac OS" splash screen will appear on the screen, unless you have installed your own custom startup screen. (A custom startup screen is an image file stored as the name "Startup Screen" in the System Folder in a startup screen format that can be produced by several graphics applications.)

Also loaded at this time are any Macintosh model-specific enablers and/or System Resources. In some cases, a new Macintosh is released before its specific hardware elements can be incorporated into the Mac OS. In this case, an enabler file is included with any needed instructions for that specific Mac to function with the current Mac OS version. With the next Mac OS revision, an enabler will most likely no longer be needed by that computer.

At this point, the Mac may display a notice that it had not been shut down properly, and it may run Disk First Aid in order to verify that the internal hard drive(s) did not suffer damage. This feature, obviously, only kicks in if the Mac was not shut down or restarted using the commands in the Finder's Special menu or by the dialog box displayed by pressing the power button.

When the Mac is turned on, a flag is set in RAM that will be deactivated when the shut down or restart commands are used. When the shut down commands are used, the Mac is able to safely terminate all hard drive access and park the drive. If the Mac is not shut down properly, there is the possibility of damage to the drive's directory structures and of corruption to any open files (including documents and any preferences files or open applications). If these commands are not used, the flag will not be deactivated, and the Mac will know that it was not shut down properly the next time it starts up. You can disable the automatic notice and launch of the Disk First Aid feature in the General Controls control panel.

Once the System file has been loaded, the Mac begins loading other contents of the System Folder, beginning with the contents of the Extensions folder (like the Control Panels folder loaded after it, the contents of the Extensions folder are loaded alphabetically). After the contents of the Extensions folder are loaded, the Mac proceeds to load the contents of the Control Panels folder. A list of common extensions and control panels and what functions they serve is included in Appendix A.

If an extension or control panel references other files within the System Folder, those related items may also be loaded at this point (an example being the ColorSync extension referencing a ColorSync profile), or they may be loaded when the item's abilities are actually used (such as the Contextual Menu extension referencing the Contextual Menu Items folder).

When all of the items in the Control Panels folder have been loaded, the Mac accesses other System Folder items such as the contents of the Fonts folder. Although the actual contents of other folders inside the System Folder may not be loaded into RAM, the Mac will note descriptions of various items, such as which fonts are available to the computer.

Once the Mac has finished loading, where appropriate, the contents of the System Folder, it then displays the Mac desktop and menu bar. At this point, the operating system itself has completed loading. The Finder then launches. The Finder, which is the interface Mac users almost always use to access files and applications, is technically not a part of the Mac's operating system. The Finder is actually an application that is automatically loaded after the operating system. The launch of the Finder is so integrated into the Mac user experience that most people don't recognize it as a separate element from the Mac OS itself. Once the Finder has launched, the Mac launches any items in the Startup Items folder and, if the Launcher control panel is installed, the Launcher.

There are two situations in which the Finder is not launched immediately following the loading of the operating system. One of these is when the Multiple Users feature introduced in Mac OS 9 is being used. In this case, the Mac instead launches an application called Login, which allows you to select your user name and password, and then it launches the

Finder. The other is when using At Ease, an older multiple-user interface for the Mac that bears a resemblance to the "panels" option of the Mac OS 9 and later Multiple Users feature. In both cases, the automatic launch of the Finder is stopped by an extension loaded during startup. Figure 37-2 illustrates the entire startup process.

Startup Key Combinations

There are several instances where you may need to interrupt the startup process on a Mac or when you may need to invoke one of several different features available in the startup process. This section looks at the various key combinations that can be used at startup to accomplish various troubleshooting and maintenance tasks.

Start with Extensions Off

One of the most well-known startup options is to start the Mac without loading any extensions or control panels, and without launching the contents of the Startup Items folder. This is done by holding the Shift key down at startup until the "Welcome to Mac OS" splash screen appears (which will now include the line "Extensions Off").

The primary reason to start with extensions off is to determine if a problem you are experiencing is caused by an extension conflict. Some other uses can include installing certain software, needing to start up quickly (albeit with limited functionality of the Macintosh), or needing to start up solely to adjust various settings on the Mac.

Startup from a CD-ROM

Holding the C key down immediately at startup will cause the Mac to ignore any other bootable disks and attempt to start up from a CD-ROM in its internal drive. This is useful if the System file on your current startup disk is corrupted, if you are reformatting your internal hard drive, or if you are installing an update to the Mac OS (see Figure 37-3).

Generally, you will want to start up from a Mac OS CD or a System Restore CD provided from Apple (hard drive utilities and some backup utilities also often come on a bootable CD in the event that you need to reformat, reboot, restore, or perform other tasks to a drive). However, if

Figure 37-2
The startup process.

 Power button pressed

 Power applied to motherboard
and internal components

 Internal component self-test initiated

 Installed RAM tested

 PRAM data tested

 System Folder on startup disk located

 Mac OS ROM file loaded—Happy Mac displayed

 System file/basic Mac OS elements loaded

 Extensions loaded

 Control panels loaded

 Finder launched/Desktop displayed

 Contents of Startup Items folder launched

 Launcher displayed if installed

Figure 37-3

Mac OS, Software Restore, and other bootable CDs.

you have a CD-R or CD-RW drive, you can create your own CD-ROMs that are bootable. This is discussed in detail in Chapter 16. Figure 37-3 shows a variety of bootable CDs.

Startup from a Network Disk

Similar to starting from a CD, holding down the N key at startup will force the Mac to look for a network disk to start up from rather than any local disk that might be available or selected as the current startup disk. This requires that there is a server on your network that is running Mac OS X Server and is configured to allow net-booting. Mac OS X Server and the ability to start up from a network disk is discussed in detail in Chapter 42.

Startup from any Disk Besides the Current Startup Disk

If you need to start up from a disk besides the one currently selected in the Startup Disk control panel, you can hold the Command-Option-Control-Delete keys down at startup. This will force the Mac to ignore the currently selected startup disk, search for the first bootable disk it finds, and start up from that disk. This can be useful if you are unable to boot from your currently selected startup disk but don't have a Mac OS CD to start up from.

Startup from a Specific Disk or Partition

On Macs introduced during or after the fall of 1999, you can hold the Option key at startup to select a specific disk or hard drive partition to start up from. This feature, called the Startup Manager and shown in Figure 37-4, forces the Mac to locate all bootable disks available and display them in a graphical environment. Not only are individual disks listed, individual hard drive partitions are listed as separate disks. The only downside to the Startup Manager is that all disks may be displayed without names and using generic icons. If you have a large number of disks or partitions available, determining which is which may prove difficult.

The currently selected startup disk will be highlighted, and you can choose which disk you wish to start up from and then continue the startup process. In order to select a disk, either click on its icon or cycle through all the available disks with the keyboard arrow keys. Once you've selected a disk, click on the straight arrow icon or press the Return key to start up from that disk.

There are more uses to the Startup Manager than just being able to start from an alternate disk in an emergency. It allows you to have multiple Mac OS configurations on separate drive partitions and to switch between them on the fly at startup. This could be useful if you occasionally use an older application that isn't compatible with the current Mac OS version, because when you need to use it, you could simply boot into a Mac OS version that is compatible with that application.

Figure 37-4
The Startup
Manager.

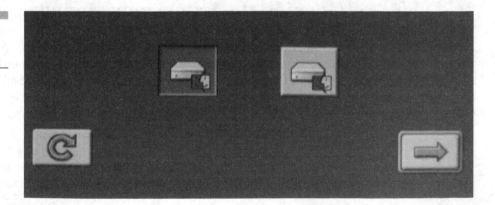

The Startup Manager can also be helpful to users of portable Macs. If you are on the road and suffer a problem (such as System Folder corruption) that prevents you from using your Mac but is software- rather than hardware-based, you can boot using a second partition. This allows you to continue working without having to worry about whether or not you remembered to bring a Mac OS CD with you.

Startup without Virtual Memory

Pressing the Command key at startup will cause the Mac to start up without virtual memory. If you usually use virtual memory and for some reason need to start up your Mac without using virtual memory (perhaps to create a CD, do some digital video work, or perform some other task where the presence of virtual memory would impact performance), this action can let you disable it without needing to completely start the Mac, turn virtual memory off in the Memory control panel, and then restart. Also, it allows you to leave virtual memory on by default.

Startup without Launching Items in the Startup Items Folder

If you want to allow your Mac to start up with the full load of extensions and control panels but without launching anything you might have in your Startup Items folder, you can hold the Shift key down after the extensions and control panels have begun loading but before the desktop is displayed. This will prevent the Mac from launching anything in your Startup Items folder.

Opening the Extensions Manager at Startup

If you want to open the Extensions Manager control panel to enable or disable certain extensions and control panels without waiting for the Mac to completely start up, you can hold the spacebar down at startup. The Extensions Manager will open before any extensions are loaded. This works because the EM extension, which enables the Extensions Manager, is generally the first extension to load.

If you are trying to troubleshoot an extension conflict that is preventing you from starting up the Mac, this can spare you the time of continually starting up with extensions off solely to access the Extensions Manager to

Why would you have "sets" of extensions???

test for which extensions are causing the problem. It can also be used to switch extension sets without waiting for the Mac to finish starting up.

Rebuilding the Desktop

Holding the Command and Option keys down at startup will cause the Mac to ask if you want to rebuild the desktop file of your hard drive(s). Rebuilding the desktop is both a troubleshooting and maintenance task in which the Mac updates its database of several pieces of information relating to files, icons, document/application associations, and aliases. The desktop file itself is discussed in other chapters, and the task of rebuilding is discussed in more detail in Chapter 39.

Zapping the PRAM

As discussed in Chapters 6 and 10, the PRAM (or parameter RAM) is a special area where the Mac stores settings that would ordinarily be lost when it is shut down (such as date and time information). Occasionally, the PRAM can become corrupted and cause problems. Holding the Command-Option-P-R keys down immediately at startup will cause the Mac to repeat the startup chime and erase the PRAM data. You may need to hold the keys down through multiple repeats of the startup chime in order to erase all the PRAM data. Zapping the PRAM is described in more detail in Chapters 10 and 39.

3 times

or what else! could you do?

Accessing the Open Firmware Settings

Pressing Command-Option-O-F will open the Open Firmware menu. The Firmware is the name given to the software built into the Mac that allows for basic control of the internal components. The Open Firmware settings screen allows you to adjust settings as to how the Mac recognizes internal hardware and how it boots into the Mac OS.

As a rule, there is little or no reason to access this screen, and it is exceedingly easy to damage the computer by doing so. It can, however, be used if you are running the Linux operating system on your Mac and wish to designate Linux as your primary operating system. (Linux is discussed briefly in Chapter 41.)

If you should access the Open Firmware settings screen, typing `bye` or `mac-boot` should cause the startup process to continue normally.

Troubleshooting the Startup Process

There are several obvious instances in the startup process where something can go wrong. The component self-tests, the RAM tests, locating a
selected startup disk, being unable to load various parts of the Mac OS,
and extension conflicts are some examples. In several cases, it isn't so
much what errors or symptoms are displayed but when they are displayed that indicates just what is actually the problem. The following
section lists various startup problems, what the common causes are, and
how to solve them. For the sake of convenience, these are listed in the
order in which they can occur following the startup process.

There Is No Startup Chime, Light, or Sign of Power

This occurrence essentially means the Mac isn't getting any power or that
it didn't acknowledge that the power button was pressed. First, check the
obvious things and make sure everything is plugged in and connected
properly. If the Mac is plugged into a power strip or uniterruptable power
supply, make sure that the strip or UPS is plugged in and turned on. Also
make sure that the electrical outlet you are using is providing power.

If you pressed the power button on an external keyboard, try pressing
the power button on the Mac itself. If this doesn't help, it may indicate a
problem with the Mac's power supply. See Chapter 11 for more information on power supplies.

If you are using a PowerBook or iBook on battery power, the battery
may simply be severely discharged and unable to power the machine. Try
attaching an AC adapter. If you know the battery is charged, there may
be a problem with the Power Manager or with the battery itself. See
Chapter 10 for more information on PowerBook and iBook battery issues.

There Is No Startup Chime, but the Mac Starts Up

This occurrence likely means that the volume on the Mac is completely
turned down or muted. When the Mac finishes starting up, try adjusting
the volume. It could also mean that there is a problem with the speakers

or audio abilities of the Mac. See Chapter 28 for information on speakers and audio.

There Is a Startup Chime but No Fan

Assuming the Mac has a fan, shut it down as soon as it is safe to do so. If your Mac is designed to need a fan and it isn't working, the heat will build up quickly inside the case and could damage several internal components. If you're not sure if your Mac should have a fan, shut it down to be safe and then consult Chapter 1 or 2 to be certain. Check to make certain the fan is installed and connected properly. If so, then there may be a problem with the fan requiring it to be replaced.

There Is a Startup Chime and Fan but No Light on the Display

Check to be certain the monitor is attached properly (if it is an external display). Also check to be certain that the screen brightness is not turned down. If the brightness is not turned down and the display seems to be attached properly or is an internal display, there are likely problems with either the display itself, with its connection to the Mac, or with the video circuitry controlling it. Consult Chapters 4 and 26 for additional information.

Instead of a Startup Chime, There's a Sound of a Car Crash or Odd-Sounding Chimes and/or the Sad Mac Icon is Displayed

The Sad Mac icon (shown in Figure 37-5) and so-called "chimes of death" (which include a car crash sound, glass breaking, or a series of musical notes similar to the "Twilight Zone" theme) can indicate serious problems for a Mac, particularly if they occur instead of the startup chime. This generally indicates that one of the internal components failed its startup self-test. The Sad Mac should be accompanied by a hex code. The hex code can help determine which component is at fault, though it may not be particularly specific. Although most of the hex code isn't helpful, the last four digits of the first line can help you deduce what component is at

Figure 37-5
The Sad Mac icon.

TABLE 37-1

Sad Mac Code
Explanations

Refer to the last four
digits/characters of
the top line of the
Sad Mac error code.

Code	Meaning
0001	Problem with the Mac's ROM chip
0002	Problem testing first block of RAM
0003, 0004, or 0005	Problem testing RAM
000B	Problem testing SCSI controller
000E	Problem with data bus or RAM
Other codes	Generally refer to motherboard or motherboard component problems

fault. Consult Table 37-1 for a guide to generalized meanings of the Sad
Mac hex code.

If there is no sad Mac icon, but you hear such a chime or the sound of
a car crash, this likely indicates a problem with the Mac's RAM. Double-
check to ensure that the RAM is installed properly. Try removing indi-

vidual RAM modules to test if one is faulty. Also see Chapter 6 for more information on RAM.

If instead of a series of chimes you hear a single beep, this indicates that there is no RAM installed in the computer. Similarly, two or three beeps indicates that the RAM is either bad or of the wrong type. Four or five beeps indicate a problem with the Mac's ROM.

Following the Smiling Mac Icon, There's a Flashing Question Mark Alternating with a Folder Being Displayed

This occurrence means that the Mac has passed all the internal component self-tests, but it cannot locate a bootable disk to start up from. This could indicate problems with the Mac reading an internal hard drive (such as when the drive's directory structure has become corrupted), that the hard drive is physically damaged, or that it is not installed properly. It can also indicate that the System Folder on the hard drive has been deleted or de-blessed.

Start up from an external drive or CD and determine if the hard drive is being recognized. If it is, then check to be sure that the primary System Folder components are in place (the Mac OS ROM and System files and the Finder in the System Folder itself). If they are, try dragging them out of the System Folder and dragging them back in. This should re-bless the System Folder. If this doesn't help, perform a clean install of the Mac OS.

If the Mac displays a message saying that the hard drive cannot be recognized and asking you to initialize it, the drive has become damaged or corrupted. Do not initialize it. Use a disk repair utility to attempt to repair the disk, if possible. If the Mac does not appear to recognize the disk at all, it is likely not installed properly or it is physically damaged. For both of these situations, refer to Chapter 5 for more information.

The Mac Begins to Start Up but then Displays an Error Message Saying the RAM Is Not Installed Properly

This obviously means that either the RAM is damaged or not installed completely or correctly. Check to be sure that all modules are seated properly. If all RAM appears to be installed correctly, one of the modules is most likely damaged. Remove the modules one at a time to determine which one it is. See Chapter 6 for additional information on installing and replacing RAM.

Following the Smiling Mac Icon, There's a Flashing Question Mark, but It Disappears and the Mac Proceeds to Start Up

You have no disk selected in the Startup Disk control panel, or the disk you have selected isn't available. When the Mac starts up, open the Startup Disk control panel and select the appropriate disk.

There Is a Startup Chime and/or Smiling Mac Icon, but It Is Followed by the Sad Mac

If the Sad Mac is displayed at this point, it is rarely due to a hardware problem and is usually due to corruption in the System Folder, almost always in the System file. Start up from an alternate disk to ensure that the problem is software-based and then perform a clean install of the Mac OS.

The Mac Freezes or Displays an Error Message while Loading the Extensions and Control Panels

- This occurrence generally signifies an extension conflict, but it can also indicate a SCSI problem or corruption within the System Folder or PRAM. Restart with extensions off to verify if an extension conflict is the case. If it is an extension conflict, the Mac should start up normally. If so, proceed to diagnose which extension(s) are causing the conflict. For more information on extension conflicts, see Chapter 38.
- If the problem persists even when starting with extensions off, and you have SCSI devices attached to the Mac, check to be sure that each SCSI device has a unique SCSI ID and that the chain is terminated properly. For additional information on dealing with SCSI problems, see Chapter 12.

If the problem is neither an extension conflict nor a SCSI problem, there may be corruption somewhere within the System Folder or the PRAM. First attempt zapping the PRAM. If this fails to help, attempt to start up from an alternate disk to determine that the problem is software-based. Assuming you can successfully start from an alternate disk, consider deleting System and Finder Preferences and other similar preferences files, and use a disk utility to verify the selected startup disk is functioning properly. If this fails to solve the problem, perform a clean install of the Mac OS.

If this problem occurs when starting up from a Mac OS CD, check to be sure that AppleTalk is active, and/or try starting with extensions off.

The Mac Completes the Startup Process but Hangs for a Long Period before Launching the Finder

If you are using a DHCP or BootP server to obtain information in the TCP/IP control panel, such as for a corporate network, cable modem, or DSL (Digital Subscriber Line) provider, refer to Chapter 36. There are known issues between the Mac OS and these types of servers, which are discussed in detail in that chapter. If you do not use one of the services, verify that the TCP/IP control panel is not configured to use either type of server.

If the problem occurs even when the TCP/IP control panel is not using this type of server, try disabling any startup items and the Launcher. If that fails to help, try deleting the Finder Preferences file. If that fails as well, you may have a corrupted font. Try removing all fonts from the Fonts folder and restarting, or test the fonts with a utility such as Font Agent.

The Finder Crashes upon Launch

If the crash is associated with Error 41, this means the Finder has become corrupted. Reinstall the Mac OS.

If the crash does not occur with Error 41, this can indicate an extension conflict. Try restarting with extensions off to determine if there is an extension conflict. If there is, troubleshoot the conflict using the Extensions Manager. (See Chapter 38 for more information on extension conflicts.)

If this is not the problem, then it is likely that the directory structures on either the internal hard drive or other type of disk are damaged or corrupted. Use a disk repair utility to test each disk inserted when the problem occurs to determine if one (or more) of them is damaged and to repair them, if possible. Chapter 5 includes additional information on disk damage and repair utilities.

Also try rebuilding the desktop and zapping the PRAM. If this does not help, start up from an external disk and delete the Finder preferences file (which may have become corrupted). If that fails to yield any results, suspect a corrupted font and troubleshoot as described above.

If all else fails, perform a clean install of the Mac OS.

REVIEW: Steps to try to recover a failed system. [handwritten margin note]

Resources for Further Study

The following URLs provide additional information on some of the concepts, issues, and products discussed in this chapter:

Apple's Mac OS site—http://www.apple.com/macos

Apple's QuickTime site—http://www.apple.com/quicktime

Apple's ColorSync site—http://www.apple.com/colorsync/

AppleScript resources—http://www.apple.com/applescript/

Official Sherlock homepage—http://www.apple.com/sherlock/

CHAPTER 38

Freezes, Force Quits, and Crashes

Most of the chapters in this book have dealt with specific pieces of hardware that are physical components of the Mac or specific software elements and processes that are part of the Macintosh operating system. Each of these chapters has covered errors and problems specific to those components or Mac OS elements. This chapter deals with a more generalized problem or threat: application crashes and Mac OS freezes.

Abnormal end/event

[Application crashes or system freezes are unhappy events that probably every Mac user has experienced. Crashes are the events when you get an error saying that an application has unexpectedly quit or generated a system error. Freezes are what happens when the Mac simply locks up and won't do anything.]

Crashes and freezes can happen for a number of reasons, and sometimes they can happen for no apparent reason at all. If an application crashes once and then never again or your Mac freezes up a single time and then doesn't do it again for weeks or months, there probably isn't a systemic or reoccurring problem. However, if crashes or freezes occur often or consistently, then it indicates that there is a specific underlying cause that needs to be addressed. This chapter is devoted to helping you diagnose that underlying cause, as well as helping you know what actions to take when an application crashes or your Mac freezes.

There are two things you should understand before we go any further. An application can crash or a Mac freeze at any time. When you are working in any application, save your work as often as you can remember to do so (some applications even have autosave features, in case you forget to keep pressing the Command-S key combination to save your work). This is the only way to avoid losing massive amounts of time and effort in a document or project should the application you're using crash or should the Mac freeze while you're working.

Also, crashes and freeze can occur for any one of several reasons. Because the causes can be varied and can involve multiple facets of the Macintosh, it is impossible to cover every trouble spot that could be responsible for a freeze or crash in this chapter. That being said, I can and will give you as much general information about dealing with crashes and freezes as possible and be specific where appropriate. However, the cause of each crash or freeze is different, and you will need to diagnose them yourself. [The greatest tool you have in doing this is to be aware of what the Mac is doing when a crash or a freeze happens or what it was doing beforehand.]

Application Crashes

Crashes can happen to any application, including the Finder. When an application crashes, it means that the application has tried to make the Mac do something that it doesn't understand or simply can't do. This can cause the Mac to throw up its virtual hands in confusion and ask to be restarted, or it can cause the application to spontaneously and ungracefully quit without warning.

Types of Crashes

Applications will crash in one of three ways: with a bomb dialog that leaves you no choice but to restart the Mac, with a message that the application has crashed but without directly affecting other applications, or inexplicably without any message or dialog at all. Generally, the type of crash can indicate the severity of the problem (i.e., a bomb dialog usually indicates a more severe problem with the application).

Bomb Dialog Crashes The most severe application crash occurs when you see a dialog box with a bomb icon telling you that the application has crashed and that the Mac needs to be restarted. Often when you see this, you have no choice but to click on the Restart button in the dialog box (and sometimes that doesn't have any effect, and you need to use the Mac's reset button). Bomb dialog crashes are the worst way an application can crash, because it means that the application has actually done something that has confused the Mac's processor so badly that the Mac can't get beyond it. Generally, the only option is to restart. Figure 38-1 shows a typical bomb message.

However, there is one possible hope. The Mac OS contains a built-in miniature program debugger that is ordinarily only used for developers debugging code as they write programs. Accessing this debugger jumps past many levels of the Mac OS and can sometimes get you back to the Finder when an application crashes with a bomb dialog.

Figure 38-1
A typical bomb message asking the user to restart.

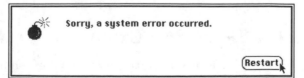

Figure 38-2
The mini-debugger
that can sometimes
save you from
a severe crash or
freeze.

```
> G FINDER
```

You invoke this debugger by holding the Command key and pressing the power button on a Mac's keyboard or by pressing a desktop Mac's programmer's button (usually located next to the reset button). This action brings up a command-line dialog, shown in Figure 38-2, in the middle of the Mac's screen. Typing G Finder or G0 and then pressing Return may get you back to the Finder. If not, typing ES and pressing Return may work. If this still does not work, you can also try typing the following: SM0A9F4 <Return> PCFA700 <Return> G <Return> (those are all zeros, by the way, and not the letter "O". If any of these does get you back to the Finder, immediately save any work in other applications and restart the computer, because something else will almost certainly crash at some point if you try to keep working.

"Unexpectedly Quit" Crashes   Most crashes occur where the application disappears from use and the Finder displays an error saying something like "The application Internet Explorer has unexpectedly quit because a Type 3 error occurred. You should save your work in other applications and restart the computer." When this happens it means the application tried to make the Mac do something it couldn't understand or do. However, the Mac wasn't so confused that it lost the ability to do anything.

Crashes without Any Messages   Sometimes an application will just disappear. One minute it will be running and the next it won't—no error message, no sign of trouble, just a disappearing application. This type of crash is the kind that is the least likely to be noticed immediately. However, it can lead to other applications crashing or erratic behavior of the Mac. When you notice this has happened, you should treat it as any other crash and restart.

What to Do after a Crash

Regardless of how an application crashes, you should restart the Mac afterward. Even if an application doesn't bring down the entire Mac when it crashes, it will probably leave bits of corrupted code in the

Mac's RAM. If another application is launched into that same memory space, it will likely crash as a result. Also, because the Mac OS doesn't isolate the memory spaces used by separate applications, this corrupted code can then affect other running programs, causing them to crash or potentially causing the Mac to freeze up completely. However, a crash that doesn't take down the Mac does offer you the opportunity to save any files that you may be working with in other applications before restarting.

finally!

NOTE: *Mac OS X will offer <u>protected memory</u>, which will prevent the crash of one application from affecting any others.*

While you are waiting for the Mac to restart, you might want to mentally review what was happening when the application crashed. This can help you determine what actions (either yours or the computer's) were responsible for the crash. After you restart, you should run a hard drive repair utility just to be sure that there wasn't any hard drive corruption caused by the crash.

General Reasons for Crashes

Applications can crash for a number of different reasons. Often they may crash with a cryptic error message. Unfortunately, these error messages are designed for programmers who can use them to debug their software more than for technicians or general users. Table 38-1 includes some of the meanings of the more common error codes, but with a few exceptions (noted in the table), knowing what these mean probably won't help you diagnose the specific cause of a crash. Rather, they provide an observation about what was happening when the application crashed.

More useful is knowing the general reasons that applications crash, as well as steps that can be done to deal with each of these causes. I've listed these in order of the how likely they are to be the source of a problem, so you can use the following paragraphs like a checklist.

Not Enough RAM   As discussed in Chapter 6, every application needs sufficient RAM in order to run. If the application doesn't have enough RAM, it will behave erratically or crash. Increasing the amount of RAM each application has to use can eliminate not only crashes, but also slow

TABLE 38-1

Common Error
Codes Associated
with Application
Crashes.

Positive Error Codes (these usually cause crashes)

ID=01: Bus Error (also known as Type 1 error)
A problem with RAM; the computer tried to access memory that doesn't exist.

ID=02: Address Error
A problem with RAM.

ID=03: Illegal Instruction
A program gave an instruction to the processor that it doesn't understand.

ID=08: Trace Mode Error
The Mac has tried and failed to activate a built-in programmer's debugger.

ID=09 and ID=10: Line 1010 and Line 1111 Trap
A program has given an instruction that the computer doesn't understand.

ID=11: Miscellaneous Hardware Exception
An error in PowerPC-specific code. These were extremely common in System 8.0 and 8.1 with versions 2 and 3 of Netscape Navigator. They have become very rare in System 8.6 and above.

ID=12: Unimplemented Core Routine
An improper instruction (a bug) in a program.

ID=13: Uninstalled Interrupt
A program does not know how to deal with input from a keyboard or other device.

ID=15: Segment Loader Error
A problem using old 680×0 program code on a Power Mac.

ID=17-24: Package Load Error
Errors in some complex functions built into the operating system (such as creating a dialog box) because of a corrupted System file, reinstall the System.

ID=25: Memory Full Error
You have run out of free RAM (or the computer thinks it has).

ID=26: Bad Program Launch
The code for an application is damaged; reinstall that program.

ID=27: File System Corrupted
There is damage to the directory map that tracks the locations of files on your drives. Use Disk First Aid or another hard drive repair utility.

ID=28: Stack Ran into Heap
You have run out of free RAM.

TABLE 38-1

Common Error
Codes Associated
with Application
Crashes.
(Continued)

Negative Error Codes (These Generally Don't Cause Crashes)

-1 to -8: General system errors.

-31 to -61: File system errors.

-33: Directory is full.

-34: Disk is full.

-35: No such disk.

-37: Illegal filename.

-38: File not open.

-39: Corrupted file.

-41: File is too big to fit into available memory.

-42: Too many files open.

-43: File not found.

-44 to -46: Disk is locked (you can't write to a locked disk).

-47: File is busy.

-49: File is already open.

-60: Disk directory error (bad master directory block).

-64 to -66: Font problems.

-64 to -90: Disk, serial port, PRAM, and clock errors.

-87 & -88: PRAM error.

-91 to -99: AppleTalk errors.

-108 to -117: Memory allocation errors (RAM errors).

-108: Ran out of memory in heap.

-120 to -127: HFS errors.

-123: Not an HFS volume.

-124: Server volume has been disconnected.

-126 to -128: Menu problems.

-130 to -132: HFS FileID errors.

-189: Attempted to write past end of file.

-200 to -232: Sound Manager problems.

-207: Insufficient memory available.

-208: File is corrupt or unusable.

-223: Invalid compression type.

-230: Input device hardware failure.

Figure 38-3
An application's
memory allocations
can be adjusted in
the program's Get
Info dialog box.
Here, Netscape
Navigator's allocation
is being adjusted.

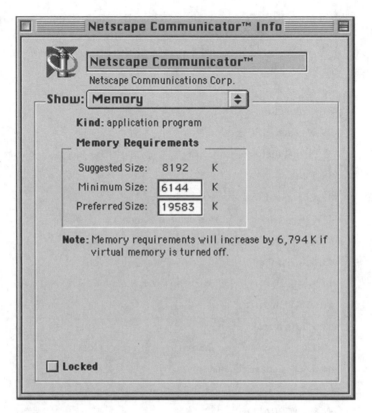

performance and other problems with many application. Figure 38-3 shows Netscape Navigator's Get Info dialog box in which the memory allocation can be adjusted. Refer to Chapter 6 for additional information on setting application RAM sizes.

Memory Fragmentation and Needing a Restart If a Mac has been running without being restarted for an extended period of time, its RAM will become fragmented as various applications are launched and quit and as documents are continually opened and closed. When the RAM becomes fragmented enough, it may cause an application to crash. Restarting the Mac will solve the problem. If you are running several applications on a Mac for more than six hours, this memory fragmentation is something you should be aware of.

Loss of a Peripheral If you suddenly disconnect a peripheral (a digital camera, scanner, hard drive, and so on), this can cause an application to crash, or the entire Mac to freeze. This is particularly likely if an application is actively accessing the device when it is disconnected. You can avoid this by not removing peripherals while an application is actively using them. Also, remember that some types of devices (such as SCSI devices) shouldn't be added or removed unless the Mac is shut down first.

Corruption　Corruption of data can easily cause crashes because the instructions for the Mac no longer make sense as they should. Although the code of an application itself can become corrupted, this is rare. More often, the code of other files that the application relies upon become corrupted, resulting in a crash.

PREFERENCES FILES　Preferences files are special files that applications use to store current settings, registration information, and other information. Because preferences files are continually updated (whenever you adjust the settings of any application and sometimes just by launching it and performing certain tasks), they can easily become corrupted. If the preferences files for an application have become corrupted, you should resolve the situation by opening the Preferences folder inside the System Folder, locating the preferences files for the application that is crashing, and dragging them to another location, such as the Trash or the Desktop.

After you remove them from the Preferences folder and launch the application, it will function as it did when it was first installed (and create new preferences files). For this reason, you may want to try launching the application after removing the preferences file(s) but before deleting them.

If the application no longer crashes, then the preferences were corrupted and should be deleted (and your settings and registration information reentered manually). If the application continues to crash, however, then the preferences files were not the problem at all, and you can move them back into the Preferences folder.

CACHE, TEMPORARY, AND HISTORY FILES　A large number of applications today use cache files or history files. The most common such programs are web browsers, though many graphics and other editing tools also create such files. Using these files allows the computer to more quickly perform common functions or access recently used files and data (such as images on a web page). They can also be used to allow you to backtrack through the actions of an application and make a file revert to a specific point in your work with it.

These files can become corrupted as much as any file, thereby causing problems. Most applications purge cache or temporary files when they quit. However, this probably won't happen when the application crashes, which can lead to further crashes when it is launched again. Deleting the corrupted files will remove the corruption and can be done by either manually locating the files on your hard drive and dragging them to the trash or by using a Clear Cache command, if available, in the application. Using a Clear Cache command is generally faster and easier (this is particularly true of web browsers).

If you cannot find a Clear Cache command in the application, then try locating the files on your hard drive. Most applications will store cache or history files in a specific folder (usually in the same folder as the application itself or in the Preferences folder inside the System Folder). Some may store them in the same folder as the file they pertain to. Cache files tend to have names that end with strange combinations of numbers and icons that indicate the application they belong to, which can help make distinguishing them a little bit easier. Some shareware utilities actually specialize in locating and deleting cache, temporary, and history files automatically.

PRAM, THE DESKTOP FILE, AND HARD DRIVE CORRUPTION The Desktop file tracks information about individual files and folders. If it becomes corrupted, the Mac may experience general troubles between files and applications, particularly when it relates to documents and their associated applications or applications needed to access specific files. Desktop file corruption can also lead to general problems and erratic behavior, as discussed elsewhere in this book. Rebuilding the desktop file can solve a number of problems without requiring much effort, which is why it is often a good thing to try whenever a Mac is experiencing crashes or other problems.

The PRAM doesn't store application-specific settings, but it does store various general settings and information for a Mac. If the PRAM becomes corrupted, it can lead to crashes whenever an application or the Mac OS needs to access or change those settings (such as when an application accesses a network device or changes the resolution of the monitor).

Corruption of the directory structures on a hard drive can lead to severe disk problems. It can also lead to frequent crashes when applications attempt to access parts of the hard drive affected by the corruption. Using a hard drive repair utility, such as described in Chapter 5, can tell you if crashes are due to hard drive corruption. Using a hard drive repair utility at this point can almost always enable you to repair the corruption before it becomes severe enough to cause serious problems.

All three of these types of corruption can affect any application and often will cause crashes in multiple applications, rather than a single application. If you are experiencing frequent crashes that cannot be easily isolated to a single cause, one of these three is probably to blame.

SUPPORT FILES Many applications today have external support files or plug-ins that they rely on. Examples of such support files are the dictionary files for many word-processing applications or the plug-ins of a web browser. These support files can be corrupted, leading to crashes when the application needs to access them. Unfortunately, spotting corruption in these files can be difficult because you may not be certain when the application is accessing its support files. Being aware of what the application was doing when it crashed can be very helpful. Knowing that Word was about to access its grammar check function, for example, tells you that the problem likely lies with those files. The only way you can resolve corruption of an applications support files is to reinstall the application or the plug-ins (or similar add-on files) that are causing the problem.

THE APPLICATION ITSELF An application is a file on a Mac's hard drive, which means that it can become corrupted just like any other file. Corruption of an application isn't particularly common, although it can happen. Therefore, you will probably want to consider all other causes before assuming this is the problem. When an application becomes corrupted, it will usually refuse to launch or will crash immediately after being launched. The only solution for a corrupted application is to reinstall it.

Conflicts Sometimes pieces of software don't interact well with each other. This can happen for a number of reasons, but often it has to do with one or more extensions or control panels. Extensions and control panels extend the ability of the basic Mac OS, adding new code and therefore additional functionality. However, if an application doesn't react well to the code added by an extension or if the extension modifies the resources available to applications, this can cause the application to crash (sometimes it takes combinations of extensions to trigger a problem or multiple extensions and no applications at all). This is known as an *extension conflict*. Extension conflicts can be difficult to diagnose and solve. For this reason, there is a separate section devoted to them later in this chapter.

It is also possible, though far less common, that two applications are conflicting with each other. This can happen when both applications are trying to access the same piece of hardware, locations in RAM, or Mac OS resources. Application conflicts tend to be a bit more obvious than extension conflicts because they involve two or more specific applications rather than an extension or control panel that is running as part of the Mac OS. Again, this is a situation where observing what you were doing when the crash occurred can pay off because you will be able to tell what applications were running alongside each other when the crash occurred. The solution to an application conflict is to simply not run the applications involved at the same time or to check for updated versions of one or both of them.

Bugs or Badly Written Software Sometimes software just isn't written as well as it could be. When this happens, certain actions or tasks will cause the application to do something it shouldn't and result in a crash because the Mac doesn't know how else to handle the situation. The application acting or reacting in a way it shouldn't is often called a *bug*. Some applications, especially shareware and freeware applications, will include a list of known bugs. This lets you know about things that can cause the application to crash. It also tells you that the developer is aware of these problems and is probably working on fixing them so that the next version of the application won't have them.

If an application crashes and you can find no other explanation for its crashing, then it probably is a bug. This is particularly true if you've just installed the application or if you're trying to do something new with it. If the application begins crashing while performing tasks you've been doing for a while without a problem, then one of the other causes mentioned here is far more likely.

If you suspect that there is a bug in an application, you can check for an updated version. Chances are, other people have noted the same bug and the developer has been working to fix it. If there is no updated version and there is no list of known bugs with the application (or the problem you've uncovered isn't on it), consider contacting the developer and letting them know about the problem. They may be able to advise you on dealing with it or give you an idea when a new version of the application will be out that may solve it. If nothing else, you'll be making them aware of the situation so that they can decide what (if anything) to do about it. Aside from that, there's not much you can do about bugs other than avoiding using the application or not performing the tasks that provoke a crash.

Freezes and Hangs

Sometimes a Mac will freeze up, preventing you from doing anything at all. This can occur where the cursor responds to mouse movement, but not to mouse clicks of keyboard input (called a hang or hang-up) or the

Mac can completely freeze up to the point where the cursor comes to a complete stop on the screen. Freezes and hangs are more severe than most crashes (with the possible exception of bomb dialog crashes), and they can leave you unable to save any work in progress.

When a freeze or hang-up occurs, it is usually because some piece of software or hardware has made the Mac try to do something that it can't do. Or the culprit has done something that the Mac doesn't know how to handle or can't handle. The result is the Mac either loses all functionality or it enters a state where it is constantly repeating nonsensical instructions and can't get out of the loop.

What to Do When the Mac Freezes or Hangs

The first step you want to do when the Mac freeze or hangs is to figure out what happened. This can help you diagnose any problems and deal with them. The second step is to try and regain control of the Mac (which may or may not be possible) so you can try to save any work in progress and restart the Mac. When a freeze or crash happens, follow the steps outlined in here.

Wait to See If It Is Really Frozen   Just because the Mac hangs, it doesn't always mean that it's frozen up completely. If the cursor still responds to mouse movement, then the Mac may be hung up completely or it may just be working on some task that is so complicated that there isn't enough processor time available for anything else to happen. If the menu bar clock continues ticking, then the Mac is almost certainly just busy working on something (though some tasks can be so complex that even the clock stops while the Mac deals with them). This is a particularly important step if you have asked the Mac to do something complex, such as applying a Photoshop filter or action to a large file.

Try to Cancel the Current Process   If the Mac does appear to be hung up and you find yourself staring at the stopwatch or the small turning circle that indicate the Mac is working but nothing is actually happening, try to use the Command-Period key combination and/or the Escape key on the keyboard. These key combinations are often used to tell the Mac to cancel whatever it is currently doing. If the Mac is just hung up because of a task (either a complicated one that it should be doing or one that has generated some sort of problem), this can sometimes stop the procedure and let you resume control. If this works, you should restart and treat the situation like a crash, unless you did ask the Mac to perform a complex, time-consuming action.

Try to Force Quit   If you can't cancel the current process, try to force quit the application that is causing the problem. You can do this by using the Command-Option-Escape key combination. This brings up the Force Quit dialog (or it may cause the Mac to completely freeze up). Don't be surprised if the application mentioned in this dialog is not the application you were working in when the Mac got hung up. Often, background applications (and sometimes extensions) cause hangs and freezes, and the one that is actually responsible tends to be the one displayed in the Force Quit dialog. If you can successfully force the application to quit, treat the situation as though it were a severe crash.

Try to Get Back to the Finder   If you can't force quit an application that's causing problems, you might be able to get back to the Finder by using the programmer's debugger. As mentioned in the section on crashes at the beginning of the chapter, the debugger is invoked by holding the Command key and pressing the power button on a Mac's keyboard (or pressing a desktop Mac's programmer's button). This brings up a command-line dialog.

As mentioned, this dialog is usually only used when developers are debugging a program. However, there are some commands that can return you to the Finder after a hang or severe crash. Try using the same commands listed in the section on bomb dialog crashes under "Types of Crashes" at the beginning of the chapter.

If this does work and you can return to the Finder, immediately save your work in any remaining applications, restart the Mac, and treat this like a severe crash. A hang-up severe enough to require using the debugger is second only to a total freeze, and the Mac will crash, hang, or freeze again if you don't restart it.

Use the Reset Button   Using the debugger is your last hope to deal with a hang or freeze gracefully. If it doesn't work or if the Mac has frozen to the point that the cursor won't respond to mouse movement, you have no choice but to force the Mac to restart. Do this using the reset button on desktop Macs or the Command-Control-Power Button key combination on portable Macs. Treat the problem as a severe crash, and run a hard drive repair utility, as forced restarts can often lead to hard drive corruption.

General Reasons for Freezes

Freezes and hangs can occur for all the same reasons as crashes. However, the problems are usually more severe or they involve Mac OS elements, like extensions or control panels, as well as applications. If corruption is the cause, there are more places for corruption to exist. Any of the Mac OS elements or their preferences files can be corrupted in addition to the places listed in the section on crashes. As mentioned earlier in this chapter and elsewhere in the book, observing what the Mac was doing (or trying to do) when it froze can be the most important tool for diagnosing the cause of a freeze or hang.

Hardware problems can also be responsible for freezes. If the Mac overheats, it may freeze up. If an expansion card malfunctions, the Mac may also freeze. If a hard drive fails, the Mac may hang or freeze. Again, being aware of what was happening can help you determine if the problem was hardware- or software-related. If it was hardware-related, try to figure out what piece or pieces of hardware are involved and refer to the appropriate chapter in Parts 1 or 2 of this book.

If the hang or freeze was software-related, consider what actions you were taking when it occurred. Equally important, note what was going on in the background—what other applications were running and what were they doing? Any of these could be responsible for a freeze or hang, and the problem could be due to corruption, conflicts, or bugs. Try to isolate what pieces of software are involved with the freeze or hang and try to diagnose the problem with those pieces of software. If you are able to force quit an application when the Mac gets hung up, what application's name (or Mac OS element's name) was displayed in the Force Quit dialog? This can often indicate the main piece of software that is at fault.

Dealing with Extension Conflicts

Extension conflicts are a common cause of crashes and freezes, and they can also be responsible for extensions or control panels not functioning or not functioning as intended. An extension conflict occurs when one of the extensions or control panels that are designed to extend the abilities of the Mac OS interact with each other or with applications in a negative way. The average Macintosh computer has well over 100 extensions in use at one time (plus one or two dozen control panels). It isn't surprising that with so many items at work modifying the way the Mac OS functions, some will grab for the same system resources or function in ways that interfere with each other.

Extension conflicts usually appear when new extensions, control panels, or applications are installed on a Mac (or when existing elements are updated). Conflicts are also commonly seen when new hardware is added because the extensions or control panels that are functioning as drivers for the new hardware are involved in the conflict.

In many cases, you can determine if a crash or other problematic behavior actually is an extension conflict by restarting the Mac with all extensions turned off. This will cause the Mac to start up without many of the features you're used to, but it will prevent any extension conflict from happening. If the problem disappears when the Mac is started with extensions off, then it is most likely an extension conflict. Keep in mind that you may not be able to run the software that was involved in the problem with extensions off. If this is the case and there is no other explanation for the problem, you can assume that it is due to an extension conflict and deal with it as such.

The following sections outline the steps to take when faced with an extension conflict.

Identify the Conflict

The first thing in dealing with an extension conflict is to identify what extensions or control panels are involved. In some cases this can be obvious, but most of the time it takes a little bit of detective work. The only way to verify that any extension or control panel is involved in a conflict is to use the Extensions Manager control panel, shown in Figure 38-4 (or a third-party alternative like Conflict Catcher or Mac OS Items Manager) to selectively disable extensions and then to restart the Mac and see if the conflict has been resolved.

Start with Recent Additions   The first extensions or control panels to try disabling with the Extensions Manager should be any that were recently added to your system. If you recently added items to the System Folder of your Mac or you have recently run an installer program to add an application or a new piece of hardware (upgrade card, digital camera, scanner, printer, and so on) before noticing the conflict, odds are it is an extension of a control panel associated with this that is the culprit.

A useful habit to help you identify recent additions is to create a custom extensions set for the extensions and control panels you regularly

Figure 38-4
The Extensions
Manager.

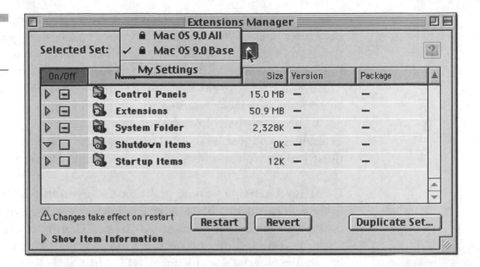

use. You can do this with New Set command in the Extensions Manager's File menu and include the date of the set in its name. Periodically, create new sets as you add or remove extensions from everyday use (again, include the date of each set). When a conflict occurs, you can go back to the past sets until you find the set that doesn't generate the conflict, thus identifying any recently added extensions and allowing you to test each one of them.

Check Extensions Based on the Symptoms If the conflict doesn't seem to involve any new extensions or control panels, you may be able to identify it based on the symptoms. If the problematic behavior occurs when a specific piece of hardware is accessed, this can indicate a conflict involving its driver software. If the behavior occurs with specific applications, it may be due to extensions used by that application. If it involves network access, it's probably because of a conflict involving the Open Transport extensions.

Testing Extensions in Groups In isolating extensions involved in a conflict, it is sometimes easiest to start by dividing the extensions and control panels into larger groups. This can be significantly faster and easier than testing every one of hundreds of items individually until you find the source of the problem.

The easiest way to start testing by groups is to select the Mac OS Base extensions set from the Extensions Manager's Selected Set menu. This includes the basic set of extensions that are part of whatever Mac OS version you have installed. Assuming these extensions and control panels aren't part of the conflict (they very rarely are), you can move on to the Mac OS All set, which contains all the extensions and control panels that were installed with the Mac OS version on your Mac.

Beyond that, you can just enable groups that have perhaps a dozen or so additional extensions. Restart after you enable each group. When you get to a point where the symptoms of the conflict reappear, note which extensions you just enabled. Then begin testing each of those extensions until you figure out which one is responsible for the conflict.

Conflict Utilities Some utilities are available to help you diagnose extension conflicts a little more easily than testing every extension manually. The big name in such utilities is Conflict Catcher, produced by Casady and Greene. Two other shareware titles to keep in mind are Extension Overload and InformINIT. Although all of these tools can help you identify extension conflicts, they won't be able to perform the process completely on their own, and you will need to put in some effort even when using them.

CONFLICT CATCHER Conflict Catcher helps you find extension conflicts in a couple of ways. The first is that it automates the process of disabling and testing groups of extensions. Conflict Catcher will perform all the subdividing into groups for you; you just need to test after each restart to see if the problem is still occurring and tell Conflict Catcher whether it is or not. Conflict Catcher also includes a database of common extension conflicts, so that it can identify what potential problems there are in addition to just testing them (of course, there are so many individual extensions and control panels out there that this database simply can't contain all of them). Conflict Catcher is also designed to look at the interaction of all your extensions. If it sees any signs that indicate a conflict, it can alert you to it.

EXTENSION OVERLOAD AND INFORMINIT Extension Overload and InformINIT don't actually do any testing for you. Instead, they provide you with a database to determine what individual extensions and control panels actually do. When you find yourself trying to troubleshoot a conflict, this can help you figure out which extensions may be involved ahead of time. It can also be useful to help you determine if you actually need some of the extensions and control panels that are installed on your Mac. Extension Overload is the better tool for diagnosing problems because it specifically looks at the extensions and control panels installed on your Mac (both active and disabled) and tells you what each one does. InformINIT, on the other hand, displays every known extension and control panel in a large alphabetized format.

After You Identify the Conflict

Identifying an extension conflict does not, of course, solve the problem. Once you know which extensions or control panels are causing problems, you still need to figure how best to deal with the conflict. Following are a few steps you can take to try to resolve the situation.

Check for Updates   Many times an extension conflict is resolved in a later version of either the extensions, control panels, or applications involved in the conflict. Check with the manufacturers to see if there are updated versions of any of the pieces of software involved in a conflict. If the conflict is widespread, developers will often make an effort to deal with the underlying causes within their software. Even if no update is presently available, asking for one will let the developers know that the conflict exists (and the more people reporting a conflict, the more likely they'll be motivated to fix it).

Use Older Versions   In some cases, an extension conflict may crop up in a new version of an existing extension or application that wasn't an issue in previous versions. If this happens, you may be able to get by if you continue to use an older version. This certainly isn't a great solution, but if the update didn't provide any desperately needed additions, it can be better than nothing.

Change the Loading Order   Sometimes, though not most times, extension conflicts can be alleviated by changing the order in which the offending extensions are loaded into RAM during startup (making the extension in the conflict that normally loads second load first, for example). You can change the order extensions and control panels load in two ways. The first is by changing the filename of an extension. This doesn't affect the extension's functionality in most cases, but because extensions and control panels are loaded in alphabetical order by name, it changes when it loads in relation to other extensions.

The second method is to take extensions that you want to load later and placing them in the Control Panels folder instead of the Extensions folder (or if you want one control panel to load first, placing it in the

Extensions folder). This may sound a bit strange, but the use of these folders is more for housekeeping purposes, and extensions and control panels will load regardless of which folder they are stored in. Keep in mind, however, that it is less confusing to keep items in the folders Apple has designated for them, particularly for installer applications or other support personnel.

Use Multiple Extension Sets   If you can't solve the extension conflict, you can work around it by creating multiple extension sets in the Extensions Manager. Each set can contain one of the offending extensions or control panels (or none of them if the conflict is with an application) and you can switch between them when you need one of them. This isn't ideal by any means, but it sometimes is the only option you have.

More than likely

Replace or Do without the Software Involved   If you don't want to deal with the hassle of multiple extension sets for different tasks because of an extension conflict, you might want to consider replacing one of the extensions, control panels, or applications involved in the conflict with another piece of software that performs the same function. This is easier in some situations—say, where the problem is with a web browser or e-mail program (with several alternative choices)—than it is in others, such as where the problem is between your printer driver and an application you need to use every day like PowerPoint. If you can't replace one of the offending pieces of software, you may want to consider if you can just do without one of them (at least until a new version is released that fixes the conflict).

Resources for Further Study

The following URLs provide additional information on some of the concepts, issues, and products discussed in this chapter:

> *About.com Mac Support Extension Conflict Resources*—
>   http://macsupport.about.com/msub2.htm
>
> *The Complete Conflict Compendium*—http://www.mac-conflicts.com
>
> *Casady and Greene*—http://www.casadyg.com/
>
> *Extension Overload HomePage*—http://www.mir.com.my/~cmteng/
>
> *InformINIT HomePage*—http://www.InformINIT.com/

CHAPTER 39

Regular Mac Maintenance

When you own a car, you perform certain tasks on a regular basis to keep it in good working order, such as changing the oil every three months, getting a tune-up every year or two, and rotating your tires so that they wear evenly. Just like with a car, there are a series of tasks that can help keep a Mac in good working order and increase performance when done regularly. The majority of these tasks are relatively simple and software-based. There are rarely hard-and-fast rules as to how often each of these should performed, so I will include the recommendations that I have found to be the most useful.

Rebuilding the Desktop

The desktop file is an invisible file (or more accurately a pair of files composing a database) that is created on every disk used by the Mac, from a small floppy to the biggest hard drives and everything in between. The Mac uses the desktop file to store information about all the items on the disk. The information stored in the desktop file includes what files or applications aliases point to, any custom icons attached to files, the comments stored in Finder Get Info windows for each item, what applications created which documents, and where on the disk (in terms of folders and subfolders) each item is located. Every time an item is moved, copied, or deleted, the desktop file is updated.

Over time, the desktop file can become corrupted, and this can cause the Mac to behave erratically. The most common symptom of a corrupted desktop file is that applications, files, and folders on a disk have reverted to generic icons (see Figure 39-1). Microsoft Word documents, for exam-

Figure 39-1
Generic (right) and custom (left) icons.

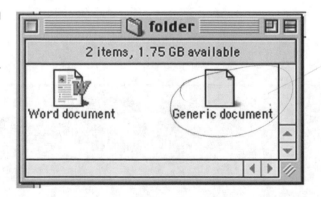

ple, would be displayed with the generic "page with an edge folded over" document icon instead of the "page with a W" icon you're used to seeing. In more severe cases, aliases will refuse to function, and the Mac may be unable to locate files.

Even if the desktop file doesn't become corrupted, without being rebuilt regularly, it can decrease performance. As the desktop file tracks all the changes made to where any file on the disk is stored, it will become larger and larger each time you move a file, delete a file, create a new file, copy a file, and so forth. As the desktop file gets more complex, tracking all the items that have ever been on a disk and every place they have been moved to on that disk, performance can be negatively affected.

When you rebuild the desktop, you're telling the Mac to erase the current desktop file, with all the extraneous information on all of these previous file changes, and create a new one that only contains references to your current files and their current locations. No real information will be lost. The Mac will save any comments you have on files ahead of time, and when the desktop file is re-created, the Mac will re-create all the other information relevant to a file (such as which application created it, where it is currently located on the disk, and so forth).

It is a good idea to rebuild the desktop files on your internal hard drives at least once a month. You can do this easily enough by holding down the Command and Option keys at startup. Once the operating system has loaded, the Mac will ask if you want to rebuild the desktop file on any disks present at that time, as shown in Figure 39-2.

It is possible, though unlikely, that some desktop file corruption will manage to survive the Mac's rebuilding the desktop file. This is because the Mac doesn't completely erase the entire desktop file. It copies certain information, such as directory structures and comments in Get Info windows, before it deletes the desktop file and proceeds to rebuild it. It is a rarity that desktop file corruption will survive Apple's rebuilding the desktop technique. In fact, I have only once or twice run across a case where corruption or damage wasn't removed by rebuilding the desktop using the key combination built into the Mac. Of course, if this should

How often?

Figure 39-2
The Rebuild Desktop dialog box.

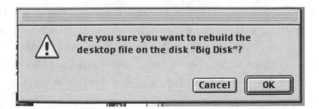

Are you sure you want to rebuild the desktop file on the disk "Big Disk"?

Cancel   OK

happen, future problems could result, or when rebuilding is used for troubleshooting rather than maintenance, you could mistake desktop file corruption for another problem.

Because of this possibility, MicroMat manufactures a freeware tool called TechTool. TechTool deletes the desktop file before shutting down the Mac. Since the complete desktop file has been deleted, the Mac has no choice but to build a new one from scratch as though there had never been a desktop file for the disk. This ensures that there is no possibility of prior corruption continuing to reside in your desktop file. TechTool also includes other abilities, which are discussed later in this chapter.

Another thing to remember is that every disk has a desktop file. The Mac generally only rebuilds desktop files on internal hard drives at startup (the same is true for TechTool). You can also rebuild the desktop file on any removable media disk (such as a Zip, Jaz, or floppy disk) by holding down the Command and Option keys when you insert this disk. This generally doesn't need to be done, but consider it every once in a while if you find you are saving and deleting a lot of files on a specific removable disk or if you are noticing erratic behavior or problems associated with a disk.

Verifying Your System File

Another useful feature TechTool has is that it can analyze your System Folder to ensure there is no sign of corruption to the System file that is the primary component of the Mac OS. Since a corrupted System file disables a Mac completely and requires a clean install of the Mac OS to resolve, anything done to prevent this from happening is excellent medicine.

If TechTool finds trouble with your System file, you'll be able to do a clean install without the inconvenience of having it happen when you're busy working. The only downside to using TechTool to do this is that when Apple updates the Mac OS, it takes MicroMat some time before they release a new version of TechTool capable of analyzing the new Mac OS version for trouble. Although not a standard maintenance activity for the Mac, I suggest verifying your System file with TechTool every so often (doing so at the same time as rebuilding the desktop makes a good schedule for most people). Figure 39-3 shows the TechTool opening screen.

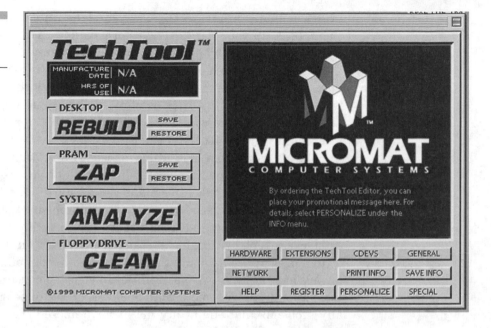

Figure 39-3
TechTool opening
screen.

Checking Your Hard Drive for Problems

As discussed in Chapter 5, hard drives contain a number of special invisible files that the Mac uses to store and retrieve data on the drive. These files can become corrupted or damaged. Most often this is caused by application or system crashes while files on the drive are open and while the drive is being accessed by the Mac. When this happens, the disk may begin to behave erratically (perhaps causing more crashes and then more corruption), or it may not give any immediate signs of trouble. Even though there are no obvious signs of problems, corruption of the directory structures on the drive will almost certainly grow until a serious problem does arise.

The easiest way to prevent problems with your hard drive is to test it with a disk utility on a regular basis. When you test a disk, if problems are found and repaired, run the utility again to verify all problems were resolved. If problems are found again, continue to run the utility (or better still another utility) until you get a clean scan indicating no problems. If you continue to find problems that can't be solved by that disk utility or that continue to appear even if the utility claims to have fixed them, back up your hard drive, reformat, and then restore your files to ensure that you aren't going to run into problems.

It's a good idea to have at least two disk utilities to use when verifying disks. Some utilities may find trouble that other utilities will miss. This is because different utilities examine disks differently. Likewise, there are several instances where one utility is unable to repair problems and a second utility can fix them easily.

I suggest running a disk utility at least every couple of months (more often if the disk is heavily used, almost full, or you experience frequent crashes). Although Disk First Aid is run at startup if a Mac was not shut down properly, this doesn't present a list of problems to the user, and Disk First Aid cannot solve all disk problems. Therefore, don't rely on it to catch everything by running at startup. Also, Disk First Aid is not as powerful a disk utility as many third-party commercial offerings. You should always have at least two disk utilities in your toolbox, and it is a good idea to check a drive with more than one disk utility to be sure you've caught any problems that one utility might have missed. Table 39-1 contains a list of several good Macintosh disk utilities. Disk utilities are also discussed in greater detail in Chapter 5.

Defragmenting Hard Drives

If your drive is heavily used, files on the drive can become fragmented with pieces of the files scattered across the disk. This has a definite impact on system performance. Although Apple's Hierarchical File System (HFS) makes Macs far less prone to severe disk fragmentation than other computing platforms, fragmentation can and does still occur on disks that are close to being full (more than 75 percent of the disk is in use) and/or used frequently for storing and deleting large (20 MB or

TABLE 39-1

Commonly Used
Mac Disk Utilities

(Generally
Considered More
Effective Tools Are
Listed First.)

DiskWarrior
Norton Utilities for Macintosh
TechTool Pro
Mac Medic
Disk First Aid

bigger) files. For drives that are regularly used for such tasks as large-scale multimedia editing, CD/DVD-ROM writing, and similar tasks, it is extremely important to defragment often.

It is a good idea to use a disk utility that includes defragmentation abilities to check for the degree of fragmentation on a given drive and to defragment that drive, if needed, on a periodic basis. The key phrase here is "if needed." A certain amount of drive fragmentation is bound to occur on any drive or disk, and relatively small amounts of fragmentation probably won't cause a noticeable degradation in how fast your Mac performs. If anything more than 10 percent of the files on a drive are fragmented, however, it is a good idea to defragment.

Related to defragmenting a drive is optimizing a drive. Optimizing a drive places related files next to each other on the disk (all extensions together, for example) and places them in the order the Mac will most likely use them (all the startup and System Folder items at the beginning of the disk and so on). This can increase performance because the head of the drive won't need to travel as far to locate files as they are needed.

I point optimization out here because it is often confused with defragmenting a drive, not because the two need to be performed together. In fact, I would suggest that optimization doesn't need to be performed as often as checking for fragmentation does, and you can usually do this about half as often or less frequently. Unless you're extremely conscious of every possible fraction of a second of your Mac's performance, you may not even want to bother with the effort of optimizing your drives. However, since most utilities that do one task do both, there's no reason you can't perform both at the same time. Figure 39-4 shows a fragmented and defragmented, optimized hard drive.

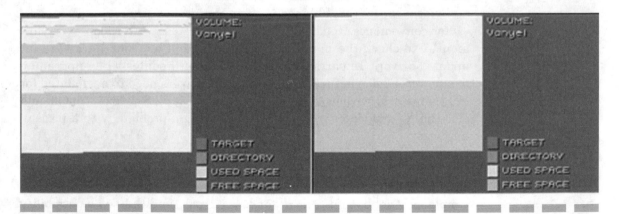

Figure 39-4   *Fragmented, defragmented, and optimized hard drives.*

You should also be aware that defragmenting a hard drive does pose a risk of data loss. Should there be a power outage or drive problem during defragmentation, some files or even the entire contents of the drive may be lost. For this reason, be sure there are no problems with the drive and that you have an accurate backup before defragmenting or optimizing a drive.

[I usually suggest checking for fragmentation every three months for professional use] Home users can check less frequently. For extremely heavy use of a drive, you might want to check for fragmentation more frequently. Fragmentation and optimization of a drive is discussed in detail in Chapter 5.

Updating Drivers

From hard drives and scanners to video cards and recordable CD drives to USB mice, every piece of hardware requires a piece of software known as a *driver* that allows the Mac to be able to communicate with the device. [Drivers are usually stored as extensions in a Mac's System Folder (with the exception of drivers for hard drives, which are stored in the very first sectors of the drive).]

Companies that make computer hardware often update the driver software that controls the hardware. These updates are released to fix bugs, increase performance, offer new features, and add compatibility with the recent version of the Mac OS and other software. It is a good idea to check for updated drivers to all the major components of your Mac on a regular basis (even if you have nothing beyond the hard drive and video chipset that shipped in your Mac).

For convenience, you may want to designate an afternoon every few months to check the manufacturer websites of all your hardware for updated drivers. [In particular, check for driver updates when upgrading to a newer version of the Mac OS, as many drivers need to be updated for full compatibility when Apple releases a new Mac OS version] You should also check for updates if you are experiencing a problem with a piece of hardware.

Also, when checking for updates, check to see why a company updated the driver. In some cases, driver updates may only be made for users with specific hardware configurations or certain software packages. You simply may not benefit from an updated driver, and there is a possibility that an updated driver may conflict with other components of your system. It can be helpful to remember the old adage "if it isn't broken, don't fix it" when looking for driver updates. Also, always keep a copy of your existing drivers just in case there are unexpected problems with the updated drivers.

Checking for Viruses

As discussed in the next chapter, viruses wreak all kinds of havoc to your Mac. They can destroy any and all data, corrupt or delete files, replicate and spread to other drives and computers, and make a Mac user's life miserable. There has been an attitude in the Mac community that viruses were not a serious threat because there tend to be fewer Mac viruses than there are viruses for other platforms. This attitude is extremely dangerous. A number of Mac viruses are out there that can cause serious damage to a Mac or network. And Mac viruses are on the rise as new viruses and virus strains appear more frequently each year.

Two primary tasks regarding viruses should be part of any maintenance schedule. The first is to run a virus protection utility regularly. It's always a good idea to scan files from the Internet before using them and to scan your entire hard drive at least once a month minimum. Weekly or even daily scans of a hard drive are better (particularly if you deal with a lot of files or disks from other computers or networks), and daily scans of the Mac's System Folder are also prudent. Commercial antivirus products also allow you to install a virus protection extension or control panel that can be set to scan files downloaded from the Internet as soon as they are downloaded and to scan removable media disks (such as Zip disks or floppies) as they are inserted. Both of these features are excellent and should be used.

Equally important, make sure to check for updates to your antivirus utility at least once a month. New viruses and virus strains appear all the time, and in order to be effective, your antivirus utility needs to be able to recognize and deal with new viruses. The only way to ensure this will happen is to keep the utility updated with information on new and recent viruses. Any company producing a decent antivirus utility also makes regular updates and updates the software to include information as soon as a new virus hits the scene. The two antivirus packages that provide the most effective protection are Norton AntiVirus and Virex, both of which provide updates every month.

Performing a Clean Install of the Mac OS

Although performing a clean install of the Mac OS is generally regarded as a last resort in terms of resolving operating system problems, it is also a good practice to do this as a maintenance task. Performing a clean install creates a completely new System Folder on your hard drive and de-blesses the existing System Folder (renaming it "Previous System Folder"). In order to perform a clean install, you need to run the Mac OS installer program from a Mac OS CD and select the Clean Install option (see Figure 39-5). You then proceed through the installation as normal. Figure 39-6 shows the results of a clean install.

Figure 39-5
Mac OS Installer with Clean Install selected.

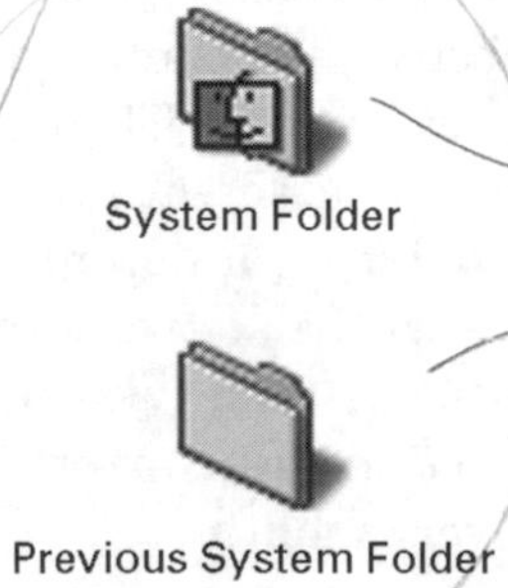

Install Mac OS 9

Select Destination

Choose a disk to install the software on, then click Select.

☑ **Perform Clean Installation**

Installs a completely new System Folder that does not include your third-party extensions, control panels, or fonts. System software and application preferences are reset to their default settings.

Cancel   OK

Options...   Go Back   Select

Figure 39-6
The System Folder and Previous System Folder after a clean install.

System Folder

Previous System Folder

Just creates a new System Folder

The disadvantage of a clean install is that no preferences files, third-party extensions or control panels, or any other items stored in the System Folder are placed in the new System Folder. All you get is the standard System Folder installed on a new Mac. You then need to select the necessary files out of the Previous System Folder and move them into the new System Folder. Where possible, you should reinstall components of the System Folder from their original installers rather than copying them to avoid any chance that anything you copy might be corrupted.

The advantage of performing a clean install as a maintenance task is similar to why you'd want to verify your System file regularly using TechTool. After a while, the System file (and possibly other System Folder contents) can simply become corrupted. This is especially true if the Mac has gone through several Mac OS updates where the existing System Folder has been updated to include new or changed code of the newer versions of the Mac OS.

The good news is that you don't need to perform a clean install very often as a maintenance task. You perform a clean install whenever you perform a major Mac OS update. These updates, such as the Mac OS 9 update, are often shipped on a Mac OS CD and advance the Mac OS version number by 0.2 or greater (for example, Mac OS 8.1 to 8.5 was a major update, while Mac OS 8.5 to 8.6 was not). When you run the installer for such updates for the first time, simply use the Clean Install option. This is particularly good, since there are no changes made to an existing System file as there are when simply updating an existing System Folder. If you don't regularly buy major Mac OS updates, then I'd suggest performing a clean install every 18 months to 2 years.

Not too frequent

Reformatting Your Hard Drive

Reformatting a hard drive removes all the data that is on it, including the files and applications you've stored there, the desktop file, and the directory structure that makes the disk usable to the Mac. Even with defragmenting a disk, rebuilding the desktop, and running disk repair utilities on a regular schedule, it is still a good idea to occasionally reformat a drive simply to remove every hint of corruption or possible troubles.

In addition to removing any corruption of the disk's directory structure (which is what causes the majority of hard drive problems), the drive formatting utility will note any bad sectors on the drive. Bad sectors are areas of the disk that can no longer reliably store information.

These are physical areas on the disk, and storing data to them can cause problems when you later try to retrieve the data. Although bad sectors usually only occur when a disk is created, they can also occur later in the life of a drive. Whenever a disk is formatted, the utility should note bad sectors and map them out of the drive's usable space. That way, no files will ever be stored in those areas.

Periodically reformatting a drive can prolong the usable life of the disk and will definitely eliminate problems that might have been developing over time. It can, however, seem somewhat drastic. Because the other tasks listed here will deal with all but the most persistent of troubles, I don't suggest reformatting a disk as part of general maintenance any more often than every 18 months to 2 years.

Removing Orphaned Preferences

Although there isn't really any problem that will occur if you allow your Preferences folder to grow larger and larger, keeping it smaller will simplify matters if you ever need to copy items out of it (such as following a clean install of the Mac OS or if you regularly make backups of your preferences). As mentioned in Chapter 37, every time an item such as an application, control panel, or even some extensions is used for the first time, a preferences file is created. This file stores information such as your settings for that item, when it was installed, registration data, or other information it may gather from the state your Mac is in or how you use the item. Preferences files remain even after you delete the item that created them.

Although these files rarely cause harm because they aren't accessed unless the application or other item that created them is used again, they do take up disk space (although rarely enough to be concerned about), and they do clutter up the Preferences folder. So, every once in a while, it can be a good idea to go through the Preferences folder and look for files relating to applications or other items you no longer use. However, be aware that there are times that the preferences files and whatever created them may not be obviously linked. Since some preferences files do store serial numbers and registration data, you will want to make sure that the preferences file is actually orphaned before deleting it. If you're not sure what a preferences file is for, you should err on the side of caution and leave it in place in the off chance that it may be associated with something you are still using.

If you find the idea of sorting out your Preferences folder to be a little too daunting or intimidating, you might want to consider the Spring Clean utility by Aladdin Systems. This associates preferences and applications by their invisible creator codes and does almost all the work for you. As I said, this isn't a task that will result in trouble if not done, so doing it whenever you have the time to spare is as good a schedule as any.

Deleting Duplicate Files and Applications

Sometimes you'll find that you have multiple copies of the same application or of a folder or individual documents. One common cause of this is software installers. Often, installer programs for applications and software packages will install a copy of an application or a given file that you already have on your hard drive.

Probably the most common example of this is the SimpleText application. Just about every installer CD comes with a copy of SimpleText so that you can read any ReadMe files and documentation on the CD. A number of times, this extra copy of SimpleText manages to be copied to your hard drive when the installer is run.

Another scenario is when you install a new version of an application, and the original version you had installed isn't deleted in the process. For example, if you use the ICQ messaging software and download a newer version from the Internet, you may find that the software creates a second ICQ folder on your drive for the newer version rather than replacing the earlier version you had been using.

Having duplicate copies of things can confuse the Mac. If you have Photoshop 4.01 and Photoshop 5.5 on your hard drive, for example, and you double-click on a Photoshop file, the Mac will not be certain which version of Photoshop you want to open it with. The result is that you may end up having the file opened with Photoshop 4.01 when you want to be using the features of Photoshop 5.5 to edit the image. For this reason, having only a single copy of each application on your Mac is a good idea.

Additionally, the extra copies of applications and other files will be taking up valuable disk space. I'd suggest doing a quick check for duplicate applications every three or four months. An easy way to do this is to open Sherlock (shown in Figure 39-7) and search for files by kind, setting the kind to "application" so that all the applications installed are displayed. You can check for other files somewhat less frequently. You may

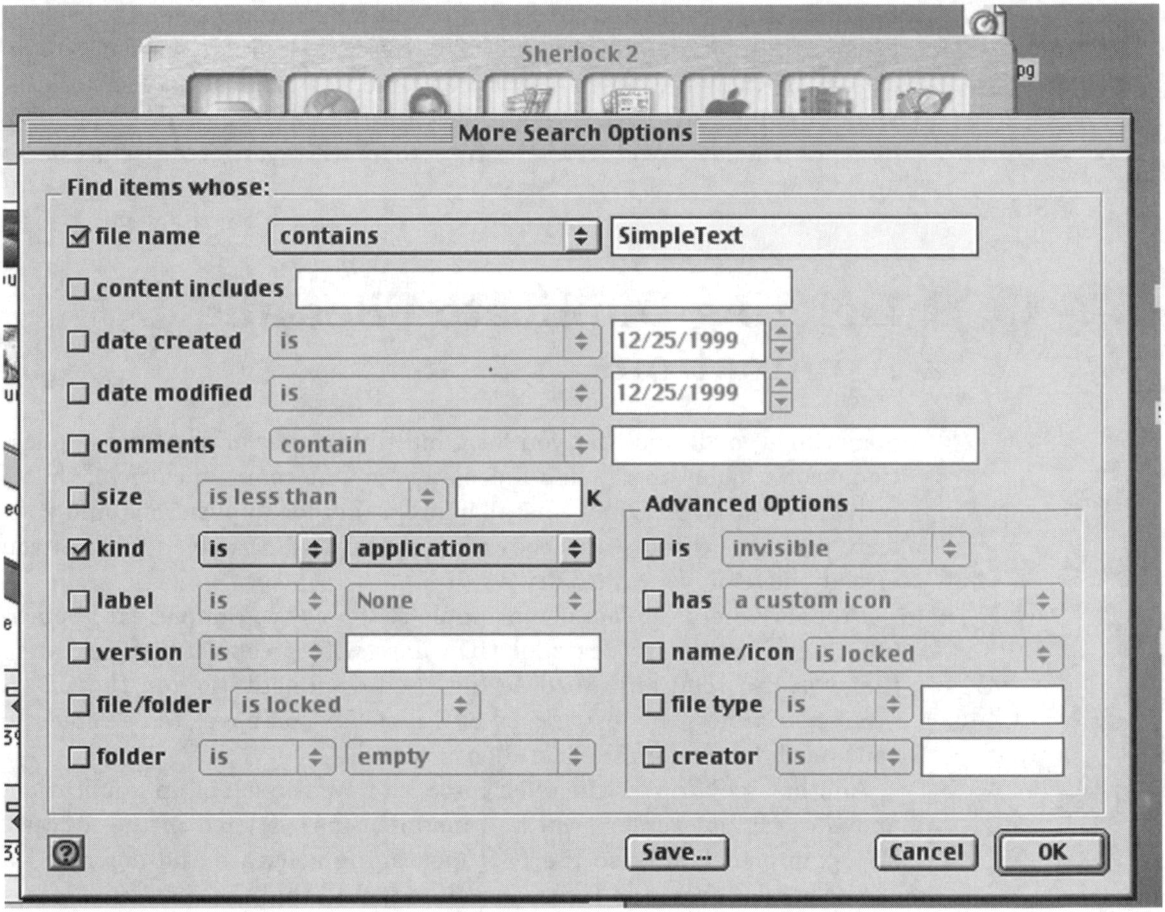

Figure 39-7 Using Sherlock to locate duplicate items.

want to consider using the Spring Clean utility mentioned in the last section to take the labor out of this task as well.

Checking for Unused Extensions and Control Panels

Extensions and control panels, when installed, use up not only disk space but also RAM. Extensions and control panels can also cause conflicts with each other or with applications. For these reasons, if there are extensions and control panels that you don't need, it's a good idea to either disable or delete them.

You can use the Extensions Manager to look through your current extensions and control panels and to disable items. This also gives you an easy way to test and be certain that various items you might consider deleting don't provide an ability or feature you need. Assuming they don't, you can then either leave them disabled or delete them completely. Since it can sometimes be completely baffling to figure out what a given extension does based on its name, Appendix A contains a list of the more common extensions and control panels, along with descriptions of what they actually do and if the majority of users can consider disabling them. Like deleting duplicate files, this is something that can be done every three or four months.

Creating a Backup Strategy

Like it or not, the truth is that even the most well maintained Macs will eventually suffer from a problem that will result in some degree of data loss. These events can be as serious as a complete loss of a hard drive and all its contents or as mild as simply needing to restore a file that was deleted accidentally. No matter how severe or minor the problem is, you'll be extremely glad if you have a backup to restore the data from and extremely frustrated if you don't.

Also consider that a hard drive is a mechanical device that will ultimately stop working. Some studies suggest that the average hard drive will fail within three years of use. However, a hard drive can fail within a month of use or last for 10 years. This inherent uncertainty makes developing a backup strategy essential.

In some ways, choosing a backup strategy for your Mac is like choosing an exercise regimen: To be effective, a backup strategy has to be designed to meet your needs, and it must be performed consistently if it is to be truly effective. For some home Mac users, a backup strategy as basic as copying updated files to a Zip disk every few weeks may be enough. For a graphics design house, backing up client files and work three or four times a day and then performing a complete backup of every file on the Mac or an entire network every afternoon may be appropriate. Be sure to design a strategy that will enable you to recover as completely and quickly as you need, but also one that you have the means, time, and inclination to stick to. A backup strategy that goes undone because you're too busy, too tired, or don't have the appropriate hardware or supplies isn't going to be of any use.

There are several basic areas to consider when planning your backup strategy, each of which will be discussed in this section. These areas are what files to back up, how often to back up files, what medium(s) you are going to store your backups on, where the backups are going to be physically stored, and how you are actually going to perform the backup process.

What to Back Up

shouldn't be a problem if G lost??

[In an ideal world, you'll want to keep a current backup of your entire hard drive.] Having a complete backup makes recovering from an emergency extremely simple because you can just reformat a hard drive and restore everything from the backup to its original state. The problem is, with the average Mac now having over 10 GB of internal hard drive space, backing up everything can not only take a while, it also requires a large amount of space available to hold the backup (an iMac DV with only half its 10-GB hard drive filled would require 50 Zip disks to hold everything, for example). Depending on what medium you use to store your backups and what method you use to actually back up files, you may find keeping current copies of everything to be difficult to achieve.

There are two main types of backups: complete backups and incremental backups. A complete backup is what it sounds like—a complete copy of your entire hard drive(s). An incremental backup is a backup of only those files that changed since the last backup was performed. Complete backups tend to be unwieldy and time-consuming to perform, and because they copy everything, they will involve copying files that may not have been changed in months. An incremental backup, on the other hand, doesn't copy anything but files that have been updated since your last backup. It is therefore a good idea to combine the two approaches and perform a complete backup every once in a while and then perform incremental backups the rest of the time to keep all the files in the backup current.

In addition to incremental and complete backups, you must decide whether you want to back up an entire hard drive. While doing so allows you to easily recover from a crash, it is also time-consuming to make backups of every single file when there may not be such a need. Applications, device drivers, and the Mac OS can be restored from their original installation CDs, for example. User-created documents, e-mails, and preferences files, however, should be backed up so that they can be restored.

If you intend to only back up certain files, it is a good idea to store those files together on your hard drive. Store any current projects in a single folder. Archived material that rarely gets updated should be stored in a different folder. This allows you to easily locate files that are updated. When a current project is finished, move the related files into the "archive" section of your hard drive so that it is easy to tell which projects need to be backed up because of recent changes regularly and which ones don't.

How Often to Back Up

Once you know what files you're going to back up regularly, the next question is how often are you going to make a new copy of your backups. This depends on two main questions: How often does your data get updated and how much time do you have to spend creating the backups. For files that get updated constantly, you'll want to back them up as often as is feasible. For other files, such as applications that don't get updated most of the time, you can afford to back up somewhat less often. Also consider how long it will take you to recover from the loss of files if there is no current backup. When that amount of time is longer than it would take to back up the files regularly, then it is time to back them up more often.

Professional Mac users who depend on their Macs for their income will want to perform incremental backups at least once a day and full or complete backups at least once a week. Home users will want to consider a less strenuous backup strategy but should consider incremental backups of their important files on at least a weekly basis. Also remember that you can have a schedule that consists of multiple types of backups (say, a complete backup every month with incremental backup of files you're working with twice a week).

Suggested Backup Strategies for Different Types of Mac Users

The preceding material is a good start to helping you determine your own backup strategy. In case you feel you need more-specific suggestions of what to back up and how often to perform backups, this section contains discussions of the general types of Mac users and provides an idea of what files and schedules they should consider when creating a backup strategy. These groups are going to be generalized and are meant to be flexible. Read through them and get idea of which group (or groups) you fit into, and then use the suggestions as a guide to determining which files you need to consider backing up.

Client Service Professionals   These are the companies or individuals that earn a living from services they perform for others using the Mac, such as graphic designers or web developers. Ideally, you'll want to keep backups of everything you're working on for a client. You should consider having at least two separate sets of backups on a regular basis: one for the current projects you're working on, which should include all the files relating to those projects, and one for complete system backups. You may also want to have a third for all e-mail and letter correspondence and even a fourth with your preferences and settings files (though these would be caught in your complete backups).

Backing up your current projects is simple enough (often you can just drag files to a Zip, Jaz, or similar removable media disk throughout the project). Complete backups are also obvious, since you're backing up everything. To back up your e-mail files, you'll need to locate the folder where your e-mail program stores both incoming and outgoing messages. You can usually locate this by going into the program preferences settings and looking for the dialog where it offers you a choice of where to store these. In order to back up preferences and settings, you can either back up the entire Preferences folder or you can back up the preferences files relating to specific applications.

In the event of a severe (or even moderate) problem, you can reformat the hard drive, restore the majority of files from your complete backups, and then restore your current projects and correspondence in short order. Aside from the time it takes to physically copy the files, there should be little downtime.

Client service professionals should also create a permanent archive of completed products using optical media such as recordable CDs. Optical media has a projected life span of over a century and presents an excellent and secure method for keeping completed projects that no longer need updating.

Client service professionals should consider making full backups once a day or once every other day. Supplementing the full backups, work on current projects should be updated as often as possible throughout the day. Other backups suggested for this group should be considered once or perhaps twice a day in addition to the full backup.

Small/Home Office Users   Many small and home businesses are run from the Mac, where everything from correspondence and current projects to payroll and hours worked is performed on a single computer or a small network of Macs. For these businesses and individuals, the Mac is an essential tool in their work, but it isn't the sole element in producing their product or service.

Here, complete backups are still useful as often as feasible, though not as total a requirement as the earlier group. Constant backups of current correspondence, e-mails, time sheets, reports, and other documents is, however, essential. Again, a dual backup strategy is a good idea. Make a complete backup regularly but also schedule backups of every document that is essential (correspondence, reports, e-mails, application settings). If you have a severe problem, your complete backups will let you get back in business quickly. Your complete back ups are less frequent, there may be several items in your day-to-day incremental backups to replace as well.

Small/home office users should perform a full backup as often as is feasible (at least consider a weekly complete backup). Supplemental backups of important files should be made daily or even twice a day, if time permits (one strategy is to back up essential files that have been updated before going to lunch and then before the end of the day).

Power Users   Power users are people who may not rely on their Mac for managing a business, but do use it for a wide variety of personal and professional tasks such as scheduling, writing (anything from proposals to novels), managing finances, and so on. As always, a complete backup is a good idea, but in this case isn't necessarily a requirement.

Power users can get by backing up the contents of the Preferences folder and third-party System Folder items, their documents, e-mail files, and applications (all together or in separate incremental backups, depending on how often these files are updated). A good, solid schedule for performing backups is still important. And breaking the backups into separate groups such as applications, documents, e-mail, preferences, and other categories works well. By having these backups organized into groups, you can back them up independently rather than all at one time (for example, perhaps your e-mail and documents every day, but your preferences and other System Folder items every two weeks and other items every month). You can also have backups organized by tasks (applications, documents, and preferences relating to school papers, financial information, personal letters, and such), organizing each of these tasks in separate folders. You can even give each type of task/backup its own disk or disks.

Power users may want to perform daily backup of certain files that are frequently updated (such as those for financial tracking and e-mail/correspondence) and back up the remainder or their files however often they are able or feel the need to. Weekly or biweekly backups of less frequently updated files and folders is a good idea. Backups of the Applications and Preferences folders, along with the System Folder, should be scheduled depending on how often these items are likely to be updated. (For some users this might be every other day, and for others every month or less.)

Basic Home Users   Basic home users are people who just use their Macs for simple tasks such as e-mail, surfing the Web, writing letters or school papers, playing DVD movies and audio CDs, gaming, and similar uses. These are the people who don't get the computer overly involved in their personal or professional lives and who still balance their checkbook by hand and not with Quicken.

Since these users essentially have a computer as a convenience and not a necessity of life, they are the ones who need to be least concerned with massive backup efforts (although even the most basic user should have some backup strategy). For these users I suggest backing up their personal documents and, perhaps, e-mail folders. This will usually take a minimum of effort and disk space. Since they customize their computer experience the least, it would probably take them less time to reinstall software and restore application settings by hand in the event of a problem than it would to perform extensive backups constantly.

Basic home users should back up their files as often as they can. A daily backup strategy is good, but a weekly or biweekly schedule should suffice. The exception is if there are important documents being worked on, in which case these files can be added to a backup immediately without waiting for the next scheduled backup date.

Education and Public-Use Macs   These are Macs that have many users and are used in lab settings such as colleges and elementary schools or that are used in a kiosk display or other situation where large numbers of people will access them but no one will really "own" them. Backups are not a great concern since in these settings anyone saving data should do so to a network or removable media disk rather than on the computer itself.

If these Macs are in a situation where users are expected to save files in a single folder on the hard drive, then the administrator should develop a regular activity for backing up user folders. Preferences and other System Folder items should be left as basic as possible. A reinstall of the generic Mac OS settings should suffice for these machines, although a single source disk with all applications to be installed on them may be a good idea (though this isn't truly a backup).

For education and public-use Macs, a regular backup strategy need only be implemented if users in a lab environment are being asked to store documents in a given folder on the computer. In this case, the administrator should consider performing at least daily backups of these folders.

Backup Mediums

Once you've decided on what files you're going to back up and how often, the next question becomes which type of storage device to use for your backups. While the individual options for this are rather large, they can be narrowed into five basic groups: magnetic removable media, optical media, digital tape, fixed media drives, and network storage. This section looks at each of these groups, along with their advantages and disadvantages.

Magnetic Removable Media   Removable media, discussed in detail in Chapter 18, include such things as Zip, Jaz, magneto-optical, SuperDisk, and floppy drives. These are drives where a disk or cartridge is inserted for use and then removed. They can store files as easily as a hard drive. With the exception of magneto-optical (or MO) disks, all these devices store data in the same basic way as a hard drive does. Since these files are stored magnetically, they are likely to suffer degradation over time (usually in years, not weeks) and can be damaged if exposed to strong electrical or magnetic fields.

The big advantage to using removable media as a backup medium is that the disks are easy to use. You insert them, they show up on the desktop, and then you use them just like a hard drive. The disadvantages are that they tend to be more expensive than some other options and that each disk can only hold a limited amount of data. This means large backups need to be split between disks, and some individual files can be larger than one removable media disk (a hard drive image for SoftWindows or Virtual PC will likely be 500 MB or larger and wouldn't fit on a Zip disk).

Removable media serve well as backup methods for basic homes users and power users. They can function well for some small/home office users and for the incremental backups of client services professionals. They generally are not well suited for complete backups of moderate to large hard drives.

Optical Media   Optical media include recordable and rewritable CDs, as well as the various formats for recordable and rewritable DVDs. There are two big advantages to using optical media for backups: cost and security. Compared to removable media, CD-R and CD-RW deliver an amazing amount of storage space per dollar spent. And optical media do not degrade over time like magnetic media. Unless deliberately scratched or broken, they are not susceptible to data loss by physical damage or exposure to electrical or magnetic fields. The long life span of CD and DVD media make them excellent choices for long-term storage of archived data.

Unfortunately, optical media tend to have the disadvantage of being more difficult to work with. Even rewritable CD and DVD disks usually require special software in order to record data. The DirectCD utility from Adaptec is a step toward making optical media easier to record to and more convenient for backup purposes, but it doesn't make them as convenient as other methods. Optical media, along with their advantages for data storage, are discussed in detail in Chapters 16 and 17.

Digital Tape   Tape drives are discussed in Chapter 19 and are primarily sold for use as backup devices. Tape drives can store an enormous amount of data on a single tape and deliver an amazing cost-per-megabyte return. This makes them extremely popular for backing up large file collections on a single computer or a whole network.

Using digital tape as a backup method does have some notable drawbacks. It is even less convenient than optical media, requiring special software to store and retrieve files. Also, because the tape needs to be rewound and fast-forwarded, it is unwieldy for backing up specific files and then easily restoring them. This detriment does not, however, apply so much when faced with backing up one or multiple large hard drives, which are becoming quite common these days, or extremely large collections of data, making tape a good choice for complete system backups.

Fixed Media Drives   Fixed media refers to drives such as a hard drive, where the physical size and capacity of the drive is fixed and cannot be adjusted by removing one cartridge and inserting another. Backing up an external (or internal) hard drive offers the ease of removable media backups (it appears on the desktop and behaves just like any other drive). With a large hard drive, it also allows you to back up large files and file collections without needing to worry about splitting them up among removable media disks. Also, assuming you do full backups to a hard drive, in an emergency you can actually boot from that drive and continue working, with all your system settings and attributes available to you. The downsides to hard drives as a backup method are that they are not as cost-efficient as other options, they are a fixed size and cannot be made larger if you eventually find your data collection growing, and they are often large and bulky, which makes carrying them or storing them off-site difficult.

In addition to traditional hard drives, fixed media can also include RAID arrays for backup purposes. RAID, which stands for redundant array of independent (formerly inexpensive) disks, is a method for making multiple hard drives function as a single drive. There are two RAID methods that can be used for backup: disk mirroring and disk striping.

Disk mirroring involves taking two hard drives and using them as though they were a single drive. When you save a file to what appears as one hard drive on your desktop, it is actually saved twice—once on each drive. The same is true for moving files, deleting files, and anything else done with items on the drive. If a disk failure should occur to one drive, the other continues to work normally and without any interruption. This allows you to have no downtime at all in accomplishing a project.

Disk striping uses three or more hard drives in what is called a *striped array*. The drives will, again, appear as a single drive. When you save files to this drive, pieces of them will actually be saved on each drive in the array. This makes disk striping noticeably faster than disk mirroring (where each action must be performed twice, once on each drive). When one of the drives fail, the remaining drives are able to reconstruct the missing data. The array is, however, unable to continue as a functional drive at this point.

RAID solutions are continuous and complete backups that don't need conscious effort to maintain. They will serve to protect your data in the case of physical damage to one of the drives in the array, but they will not be a solution against damage to the disk's directory structure or other types of corruption that can occur to either the file system on a drive or to the Mac OS.

RAID setups can be created either by hardware, using a special PCI card to tie the various hard drives together in an array, or by software, which installs special driver software to the same effect. A hardware solution is generally more reliable and less prone to problems created by corruption, extension conflicts, or other software issues. However, RAID cards are more expensive, costing at least two to three times more than a software solution. While being slightly less reliable as a rule, software-based RAID solutions are still functional and cost significantly less (RAID setup is an option in FWB's Hard Disk Toolkit, which sells for less than $150).

Network Backups   In addition to backing up data on physical drives attached to your Mac, you can back up data to a network disk. This disk can be a hard drive partition on a second Mac in the home, a network file server used solely for backups in the office down the hall, or an Internet server clear across the country. The only requirement for network backups is a network connection and disk space to store files on whatever network you're using.

Since network backup options come in such a wide variety of flavors, defining them and their advantages is a bit difficult. As a result, I'll stick to discussing two primary network backup options here: backup to a server on a local area network and backup to an Internet server. Other options are basically extensions of these, and thus the information can be useful to any network backup option.

BACKUP TO A LOCAL AREA NETWORK DISK   Backing up to a local area network can be an excellent solution for offices. Designate a single Mac as a backup server and have every computer in the office back up to it (or, for larger offices, designate a separate Mac for a given number of workstations). Everything is in one, organized location, and there's no concern about lost disks.

The only ways this setup can be problematic is if you don't supply the server with enough disk space to hold all the backed up files and if you don't have a network with adequate speed. If you are working with a 10-mbps network and have a dozen Macs all backing up to a single server at one time, network performance is going to suffer. You can avoid this by staggering when individual workstations perform backups, performing backups when there is little or no other network activity, or by using 100-mb Ethernet.

If you use a network server to back up all your data, don't forget to develop a backup strategy for that server's contents regularly as well. A backup server is still a Mac and can suffer the same faults as any other Mac. Although it isn't likely that the backup server and one of the Macs using it will suffer a failure resulting in data loss at the same time, it is a possibility.

BACKUP TO AN INTERNET SERVER Using an Internet server for backups is more suited to individual use. It became popular when the iMac was introduced without a floppy drive and there were a limited number of USB drives on the market. Although that is no longer the case, Internet backups are still a viable option, particularly with the growing availability of high-speed Internet connections.

In order to back up via the Internet, you will need either an account with a provider that allows you transfer and store a large amount of data by FTP or an account with one of the companies now devoted to Internet-based backup. You will also want to have a high-speed Internet connection if you are going to back up anything larger than a couple of megabytes. The process is pretty basic; you upload (either by FTP or other software such as Apple's iDisk) your files to back up and then download them when you need to restore data.

One advantage of Internet backups is that they are stored in a remote location and often are stored on mirrors in multiple locations. They also don't require any extra hardware. On the downside, they do require a fast connection, aren't suitable for moderate to large backup collections, and you are not in control of the actual data (in theory, someone else could get access to it despite protections taken by the providers).

Where to Store Backups

An often overlooked part of designing a backup strategy is where to store backups. Although the most common needs for having backups are situations such as a hard drive or whole Macintosh is damaged beyond repair, damage to the file system is beyond the help of any disk utility, corruption of the System Folder or other files, or in case a file is accidentally deleted; there are more extreme possibilities where backups could be needed. These include disasters like fires, flooding, or other catastrophic damage that results in not only the loss of a hard drive or computer but also the entire contents of a building. While these incidents are unlikely, they can happen, and you should at least consider the possibility, particularly if you depend on your computer and the data it contains for your livelihood.

The only way to be prepared for disasters that could wipe out not only your computer but also your home or office is to store at least one copy of your backups off-site. This is an advantage of Internet server backups, because the data is stored remotely as soon as it is transmitted (and often mirrored at multiple sites in case of disaster at one site). In a corporate environment, the same can be accomplished with network servers at multiple sites.

If you don't use Internet backups and aren't part of a corporate network, you can still be prepared. On a regular basis make a second copy of your backup and store it elsewhere—either in another office, a friend's house, or even a safety deposit box. Try to choose a location that is not particularly nearby, since a fire can take out more than one building and an earthquake can level whole city blocks. You probably won't need to update this backup copy as often, but do so regularly nonetheless.

Ways to Perform Backups

When you've finally sorted out all the when, what, how, and where considerations of your backup strategy, you're left only with the question of how you actually want to perform the task. You can back up simply by copying files by hand from one disk to another (or using the recording software that came with a CD-R or similar optical drive), though this is the most time-consuming method.

The best option is to purchase one of the backup utilities on the market. These utilities, such as the Retrospect family of products from Dantz, are designed to simplify and automate the backup process. They include an option to create a complete backup and restoration of a hard drive, as well the ability to designate specific files to be backed up. These utilities can also be set to work with just about every kind of backup medium available. Some even ship on a bootable CD, enabling you to start up from that CD to quickly restore a disk completely after you have replaced or reformatted it. There are also a number of shareware backup utilities that can work to make the backup process easier.

Another alternative for users not willing or able to invest in backup software is to use the File Synchronization control panel (see Figure 39-8). Included with standard Mac OS installation on the iBook and PowerBook, this control panel is designed to synchronize selected items on two separate disks or computers. Although the intent of the control panel is for you to quickly be able to make sure that when you work on a document on one computer, it is also updated on the other. This control panel can also be used on any Macintosh as a backup utility (though you may have to use the Mac OS installer to do a custom installation in order to install it).

To use the File Synchronization control panel like this, you'll need to make an initial backup of the files to be backed up with it. Once that is

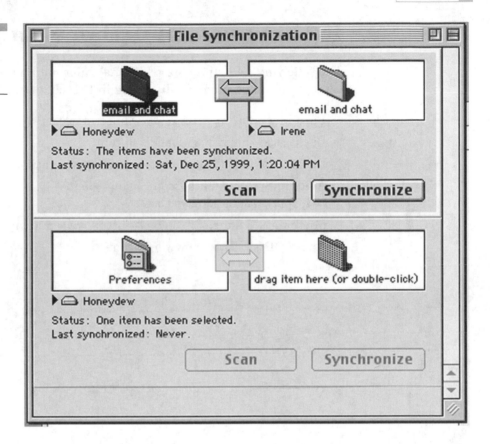

Figure 39-8
The File
Synchronization
control panel.

done, open the control panel, select the folder or file you want to back up, select the backup copy you already made, and set the control panel to only sync the file from the original copy to the backup. You can do this with as many items as you like. One thing to be aware of, however, is that Apple designed this control panel to work with relatively small documents or file collection and that it has been known to crash with moderate or large file collections. An actual backup utility is generally a better option.

Whatever backup strategy you choose, it can't be said often enough to make sure you stick to it. Have a clearly defined plan for handling backups in advance and follow it. After the fact, all the "I meant to get to it" talk in the world isn't going to keep you from having lost the file or files you spent hours or weeks working on, whether they're projects in Photoshop, school papers, or saved games of Quake. The only way to be prepared for potential data loss is to keep good backups.

Resources for Further Study

The following URLs provide additional information on some of the concepts, issues, and products discussed in this chapter.

Pure-Mac: Backup—http://www.pure-mac.com/backup.html

Back Jack—http://www.backjack.com/

Dantz: Makers of Retrospect—http://www.dantz.com/

Aladdin Systems: Makers of Spring Clean—
http://www.aladdinsys.com/

MicroMat: Makers of TechTool—http://www.micromat.com/

Apple's iDisk—http://www.mac.com/

CHAPTER 40

Viruses

The term *computer virus* conjures up images of malicious software that migrates from one computer to another, deleting data, stealing crucial information, sending copies of itself onto other computer networks, and wreaking havoc in general. This is not too inaccurate a picture in a number of cases. This chapter is devoted to explaining what viruses are, how they function, how to prevent your Mac from becoming infected with one, and what to do if you Mac does become infected.

What Is a Virus?

A *virus* is a piece of software that operates on your Mac without your knowledge or consent. As the name implies, computer viruses function much like biological viruses, infecting a healthy system, causing damage, replicating, and then moving on to other systems. There are a variety of functions that a virus can be designed to fulfill and various ways in which a virus can function to infect a computer and to propagate.

Viruses do not need to be independent applications themselves. In fact, a true virus is not an application but rather a piece of code that gets added to an application and then, acting as part of the application it was added to, copies itself into other applications or files. Although, technically, other self-propagating artifacts designed with the same goals as viruses (spreading themselves to computers and disks without the user's knowledge and possibly performing more destructive functions) fall into other classifications like worms and Trojan horses, they are often referred to as viruses.

This first section of this chapter looks at what a virus (or similar piece of code) actually is and how it functions. This includes descriptions of the possible characteristics and intended functions of viruses, as well as descriptions of the various types of viruses that are known to exist. It also includes a brief description of how antivirus software (discussed in later sections of this chapter) works to eliminate viruses and the differences in viruses intended for the Macintosh and those intended for other computing platforms, primarily Windows.

General Intents and Characteristics

The following paragraphs contain an overview of the possible functions of a virus. Some of these are not deliberately harmful (though they may be dangerous anyway), while others are. Not all viruses will include all of these characteristics. However, this gives you an idea of what viruses might be designed to do.

Simply Propagating   By definition, almost all viruses make copies of themselves. This replication is, in fact, the primary function of a virus. Some viruses don't do anything but make copies of themselves. They seem to simply exist for the sake of existing, spreading as far and wide as possible. Even if a virus does nothing else, it can be dangerous because viruses usually write their code into the code of an existing application or other Mac OS element. This can interfere with the original code and cause corruption of important system data or cause unexplained crashes.

Displaying a Message   Some viruses display a message on-screen. This may be in a dialog, on the desktop, in a document, or someplace else. Some virus authors only want to get your attention or spread a message. Others include a message telling you what the virus is going to do to your Mac. Still others just make a claim about what the virus will do when, in fact, it won't do anything. If a message is displayed, try quitting all applications that are running (including the Finder), using the force quit keystroke (Command-Option-Escape) if needed. Immediately after that, launch your antivirus utility. Usually at this point, it is too late to prevent the virus from replicating and possibly too late to prevent it from doing whatever it is designed to do. Avoid shutting down the Mac completely or forcing a restart at this point. If there is no real damage being done, forcing the Mac to shut down might actually cause corruption of the hard drive directory structures.

Destroying Other Viruses   Believe it or not, some viruses are designed to do nothing but destroy other viruses. These viruses replicate and search your hard drive for the code of other viruses. They may even alter some files to prevent the virus they are designed to destroy from being able to take root in your system. This makes them sound like good viruses, but there is no such thing. Even if a virus is designed to destroy other viruses, it is still writing its code into applications and Mac OS elements on your computer. This can interfere with the original code and cause crashes and corruption of the application or Mac OS element in question. And these viruses are still acting without your knowledge or consent. Even these "good viruses" should be avoided.

Self-Destructing   Some viruses self-destruct. That is to say, once they do whatever they were designed to do, they erase their code from whatever applications or Mac OS elements they were written into in the first place. This is sometimes a feature added to viruses that destroy other viruses. It is sometimes also a feature added to viruses that are designed to display a message. Even after a virus self-destructs, however, there can be spaces left in the code it altered when replicating that can cause problems. Again, even a polite self-destructing virus is a bad virus.

Issuing Commands   Beyond the other, more basic functions of viruses is the issuing of commands. Examples of viruses that issue commands include ones that send e-mails to anyone in your e-mail program's address book (such as the Love Bug virus from the spring of 2000). Another example is an older virus that randomly changed the passwords of printers attached to a Mac network. Yet another example is a virus that simply renames files or hard drives without changing, damaging, or infecting the file's contents. Each of these tasks doesn't actually involve the virus adding or deleting code; it just involves it issuing a series of commands to the application or Mac OS element that it is affecting. This means that a virus can be written so that it can take over the computer and perform any tasks that a person sitting at the keyboard might be able to do.

Destroying or Damaging Information   These are the most dangerous and malicious functions of viruses. They are also what most people think of when they think of viruses. Viruses that destroy or corrupt data can be designed to erase the contents of a hard drive or erase specific files. They can also be designed to simply overwrite the data in a file or on a hard drive to the point where it becomes corrupted and unintelligible. At this point, the files in question become completely useless. Although not all viruses will do this, it is best to assume that any virus out there is being designed to completely destroy everything on your hard drive. After all, some are designed to do just that, and even one virus can be enough to accomplish that task.

Triggers   Most viruses immediately replicate and spread to other applications and Mac OS elements as soon as the application or file that contains them is opened. However, they may just sit there and do nothing after that. If they do just sit there, they may be viruses that do nothing but propagate, as mentioned earlier, or they may be waiting for a trigger. A *trigger* is something that causes a virus to do whatever it is designed to do beyond just propagating. Triggers can be anything from a specific command or keystroke to the presence of a certain file or application to a specific state of the Mac OS. Usually, however, triggers are a specific date and time. One of the variants of the SevenDust virus (variant E, if you're curious), for example, tries to delete all files that are not applications on a Mac's startup disk. But it will only do this between 6:00 a.m. and 7:00 a.m. on the sixth and twelfth days of the month (using the date and time as a trigger).

Types of Viruses

There are a number of different types of viruses. Each kind functions differently in terms of how it actually infects a Mac and what it actually is capable of accomplishing. In fact, some of these categories technically aren't viruses because they function differently from the classic understanding of how viruses work. The following is an overview of the major categories of viruses.

Viruses Classic viruses function by adding code to an existing file or application or other Mac OS elements (such as control panels, extensions, preferences, and even the System file itself). This code then uses the application's resources to insert copies of itself into the code of other applications. Usually, opening an infected file or application will transmit viruses. The virus's code is then typically copied to the Mac's System file, where it can be copied into any application that the Mac has access to or to specific applications that the virus is designed to infect. Once an application or Mac OS element is infected, the virus can be designed to do any number of things from the malicious destruction of files to simply sitting there doing nothing at all.

Worms Worms function much the same as viruses but with one major difference: They don't need a host application. Rather, worms simply create copies of themselves on a hard drive, removable-media disk, or network drive. These copies are usually invisible files that are full-fledged applications or other Mac OS elements. Worms can therefore infect a computer and cause damage without needing a specific application to be run, though something does have to launch the worm. This is why most worms exist as Mac OS elements, so that they will be launched as part of the Mac OS. To date, there has been only one known worm that has widely affected Macintosh computers, and this is the 9805 Autostart Worm virus, which is only able to infect computers that have the CD-ROM autoplay feature of QuickTime 2.0 or higher enabled.

Trojan Horses If you remember your ancient history, the original Trojan horse was a gift of a large horse sculpture that actually contained an invading army. In other words, it was something that looked like one thing, while it was, in fact, something completely different. A Trojan horse virus is very similar. Trojan horses look like one thing, such as a game or helpful system extension, but are actually something very different. While the file may look like a game or even an extension promising to boost system performance, it is in fact designed to do something else when run that is usually malicious. Trojan horses can be applications or extensions designed to do damage by themselves, or they can simply serve as a way to get you to allow a more traditional virus to be installed on your Mac.

Macro Viruses Macros are scripts that can be embedded in a document, such as a Word document, that allow you to perform some sort of action directly within the document. The most common use is a document template, where all the needed formatting information is built into a template. This prevents users from having to enter all the formatting for creating a specific type of document (say, a résumé or a fax coversheet). More powerful macros can support commands or languages used in writing software, such as the Visual Basic editing features of Word 98. With the ability to write script commands of such magnitude, it becomes possible to actually embed the code of a virus into a typical document. Most macro viruses are built into Word or Excel documents, though it is possible to create macro viruses for other applications (e-mail programs were used for this year's Microsoft Outlook Love Bug virus, for example). As discussed later, macro viruses are actually the only time that viruses not specifically written to affect the Mac platform typically affect Mac users.

A macro virus only affects the applications that specifically support a given application macro language (the one the virus is written to use). However, this doesn't limit the power of the virus, as it can potentially affect any document or file on your hard drive that can be opened by those applications. All macro viruses to date have used the macro language of the Microsoft Office applications.

HyperCard Viruses HyperCard is a technology that can be used to create a number of interactive elements on the Mac, including games and other "applications." HyperCard works by displaying individual onscreen cards. Each card has commands, visual and text elements and input abilities associated with it. These cards are then combined into stacks, which form programs when run. Users move through a program by moving from one card in the stack to another. The HyperCard application, which runs the stacks, also contains a home stack of primary commands and interfaces. A virus can be written as a HyperCard stack or commands on an individual card. When that stack or card is accessed, the virus can copy itself to other HyperCard stacks, including the home stack. HyperCard viruses usually do not infect files other than HyperCard stacks.

AppleScript Viruses   AppleScript is the Mac OS scripting language. It can be used to record strings of commands into self-running scripts, to create CGI scripts for web servers running on the Mac, to automate various tasks, and to create small applications. The Mac OS and Finder support being scripted using AppleScript, as do many applications. This means that an AppleScript can be written to perform a wide variety of functions, borrowing from multiple applications with or without user input. This can be very useful for automating complex tasks on the Mac. It also opens the possibility of AppleScript being used to create viruses that can use the resources of multiple applications and Mac OS elements to replicate and perform malicious actions. Despite the potential for development of some pretty damaging viruses using AppleScript, only two AppleScript viruses have ever been spread widely enough to be confirmed as virus threats. Nevertheless, you should avoid using any AppleScript if you don't know where it came from.

How Antivirus Software Works

Antivirus software is a special class of software package designed to look for the presence of a virus on your computer. If it finds a virus, it will try to remove it. Antivirus utilities work by looking through the code that makes up a file (a file as defined here could be an application, document, or Mac OS element). It looks for code that is known to be a virus or to be part of a virus. If it finds a piece of code that matches one of the viruses it is designed to search for, it will either alert you or it will try to remove the code. If the code has just been inserted into the file without changing the existing code, the utility will probably be able to remove the virus without trouble. If the virus has deleted or modified bits of the file's code, the file may become corrupted when the virus is removed.

Antivirus software is designed to look for code that is part of known viruses or virus strains (a strain is a group of similar viruses, usually where the varying viruses have derived from a single virus). Commercial antivirus applications use special files known as virus definition updates to add new virus code to an antivirus program's library of what to look for. This means that you can continually add definition updates to your antivirus software to allow it to recognize the latest virus threats. Antivirus developers provide updates on a regular basis (usually once or twice a month), as well as whenever a new virus threat is identified. It is *essential* to regularly obtain these update files (usually from the manufacturer's website) to protect your computer from new viruses.

Viruses on the Mac versus Viruses on Other Platforms

Mac software differs from Windows software, because the operating system and hardware of the computer platforms are fundamentally very different. Applications interact with each other and the operating system differently. Hard drives are formatted using different approaches to store files. The processor families used are based on different technological approaches. This has an important impact on viruses affecting each platform.

Beyond these differences, there's also the difference of market share. There are a lot more PCs out there than Macs. In addition, the attitudes of Mac users tends to be somewhat different than that of PC users, just as the common uses for the Mac tend to be somewhat different from the common uses of the PC. All of these differences, both in terms of the computers themselves and the people who use them, are factors in determining the level of virus threats between the two platforms.

Different Intents and Frequencies   There are a lot more viruses out there for Windows-based PCs than there are for any other platform, the Mac in particular. Probably this is because when someone decides that they want to write a virus, they are thinking about infecting as many computers as possible (this is true whether or not the virus itself is of a malicious nature). This would mean aiming the virus to infect Windows computers simply because there are more of them. It may also be because most virus programmers don't think the Mac is worth the effort of targeting with viruses. Whatever the actual reasons, a lot more viruses and virus strains are attacking Windows computers than Macintoshes. In fact, the number of Mac-specific viruses only number between 100 and 150, compared to the thousands of Windows-specific viruses.

As a rule, the intents of the viruses tend to be different as well. This is a little surprising, but it is something I noticed when reviewing known Mac viruses for this chapter. A fair amount of Mac viruses are not intentionally harmful. Many simply replicate themselves and do no other damage. Some are even written to seek out and eliminate more harmful viruses. Of all the virus caracteristics discussed at the beginning of this chapter, malicious viruses seem to be the least common among Mac viruses. This, of course, doesn't mean they aren't out there. Nor does it mean that viruses that aren't intentionally malicious aren't harmful. As mentioned, even a virus that just makes a copy of itself and that self-destructs can corrupt important files on your Mac or cause crashes that can result in damage. Still, it does shed an interesting light on the different mind-sets of people writing viruses to attack Macs versus those writing viruses to attack PCs.

What PC Viruses Can Affect Macs?   The bigger question is whether or not Mac users need to be worried about Windows or other PC viruses. As a rule, no. Most viruses rely on a specific operating system and/or application. Since the majority of viruses are not written with the Mac OS in mind, they aren't a threat to Macintosh computers. So don't be alarmed if you see a virus scare or alert in the news saying that some new virus is attacking Windows-based PCs. It is virtually impossible that the same virus will be a threat to Mac users (of course, the flip side of this is that Mac viruses rarely get that much press attention and you may not be alerted to them as easily).

The exception to this rule is macro viruses. As mentioned earlier in the chapter, macros are a series of application-specific commands, and in order to provide cross-platform ease, many applications developed for both the Mac and PC will support the same macro structure on both platforms. This means that a macro virus may be able to infect your Mac even if it was designed to infect Windows computers. Chances are, the damage will be more limited, probably just the replication of the virus into new files and possible damage to open files of the application in question (although this is not guaranteed). However, you will still be at some degree of risk.

Also, remember that even if you aren't at risk from a virus, you may still be able to pass it on to others. This is true of macro viruses as well as other forms of PC viruses. If you give someone a disk with an infected application on it, you could pass the virus on. If you make a copy of a Word document that contains a macro virus and give it to a Windows user, you will pass the virus on, and it will do all its possible damage to them.

PC Virus and PC Emulators on the Mac   Even though the Mac itself is not at risk from PC viruses, PC emulators such as SoftWindows and Virtual PC running on the Mac are at risk. PC emulators, which are discussed in more detail in the next chapter, actually emulate the same hardware, hard drive formats, and operating systems of a PC. This means that they can be infected with a PC virus just as easily as any PC can be. If you are planning to run such an emulator, you should consider using antivirus protections for the PC that you are emulating.

Preventing, Detecting, and Dealing with Virus Infections

An ounce of prevention is worth a pound of cure. Anyone who has been the victim of a virus can usually attest to the truth of this adage. Avoiding and preventing virus infections on your Mac is a fairly painless process. It is certainly easier than dealing with losing some or all files on your hard drive because of a malicious virus. This section looks at how to avoid virus infections and what to do if you actually do become the victim of a virus infection.

Avoiding Infected Files

The easiest way to avoid a virus is to avoid any files that might be infected. This is relatively easy. Just be aware of where you're getting files or applications from. Certain sources are much safer and less likely to contain viruses than others are. One approach, if you are dealing with shareware files, is not to download shareware except from sources that check files for infections before making them available (such as America Online's download archives or ZDNet's shareware library). Since these sources check for viruses before allowing files to be publicly available, it is unlikely that you would get a virus from their archives.

Also, don't download any scripts, applications, or similar files from a newsgroup. Newsgroups allow anyone to post any message (with or without file attachments) that they want. There is no way to control what is posted, and once a message is posted, it will usually be available in a newsgroup for months (unlike website or FTP archive sources where a file containing a virus can be deleted once it is reported as infected). Newsgroup postings with files claiming to be commercial applications, in particular, may contain Trojan horse viruses (the claim being to get you to download and open the file). *Note:* Many newsgroups are designed for posting image, sound, or video files. Files of types such as JPEG, TIFF,

GIF, AIFF, AU, MP3, MOV, MPEG, and AVI contain only data and not application or scripting elements. It is generally considered impossible to hide a virus in these types of files. However, Word, Excel, AppleScript, HyperCard, and other documents that include scripting elements can contain viruses.

Be aware of where you get things like HyperCard stacks or AppleScripts. There are a number of sources for trading such things online. While most of these sources are simply there for users to share their work and ideas with others, the nature of scripts means that they could easily contain viruses. Unless you are familiar enough with AppleScript to be able to read through the script and understand exactly what it does before compiling it, only use scripts from a source that is known to be safe (such as a reputable site or Apple).

Also, check Mac news or general virus alert sites regularly. These sites can alert you to a new virus, what it does, and what the sources of infection may be. This can help you be aware of when and where a virus threat exists so that you can avoid it. These sites can also help if your Mac does become infected with a virus because you will be aware of the symptoms of the virus. This will alert you to an infection even if you can't manage to avoid it. A selection of virus alert sites is included at the end of this chapter.

Using Antivirus Tools to Prevent Infection

Even if you make an effort to avoid infected files, there is still the possibility that they could get onto your Mac. You could receive files from a source that is usually reputable that contain an undiscovered Trojan horse, a macro virus attached to a document from a friend or colleague, or a virus on a disk. A couple of years ago, a small number of CD-ROMs containing the CorelDRAW application actually shipped with the Autostart Worm virus on them, for example. For these reasons, you need to make an effort to actively prevent infections even when you are working to avoid infected files in the first place.

Scan New Files Always use your antivirus software to scan any new files or disks (floppy, removable media, or CD-ROM) that you receive, regardless of the source of those files or disks. In particular, this includes applications downloaded from shareware sites, as well as files that have been sent to you as e-mail attachments (particularly Word or Excel documents that can contain macro viruses). Most antivirus utilities can be set to scan files downloaded from the Internet automatically (this feature is illustrated in the Virex utility in Figure 40-1). This is an excellent idea and should always be used. However, this may still not scan all files received as e-mail attachments, so you should be sure just what files are scanned automatically and to manually scan anything else before opening it.

Most antivirus applications can also be set to scan any removable-media disk or CD for viruses as soon as it is inserted (this feature is pictured in Figure 40-2). This is also a good feature to leave enabled. If your antivirus software doesn't support this, you should still manually scan

Figure 40-1
The scan new downloaded files feature of Virex.

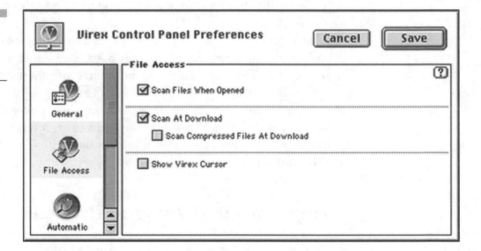

Figure 40-2
The scan disks as they are inserted feature of Virex.

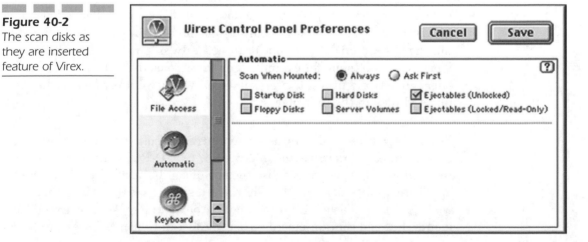

removable-media disks for viruses, particularly if you are unsure of the source or what is contained on the disk.

Startup Extensions Almost all antivirus software offers you the ability to install a protection extension. This extension is usually one of the first loaded during the Mac's startup process. Protection extensions are usually not designed to look for viruses themselves, as scanning a file or hard drive with an antivirus application does. Rather, they are designed to constantly watch for the actions of known viruses. This way, the extension will notice if a virus tries to replicate its code into new applications or to perform more dangerous tasks. This may not prevent an infection, but it will alert you to the presence of a virus, and it will usually stop the virus from spreading from one application to another or from one disk to another.

The only concern with antivirus extensions is that they can mistakenly react to software installers as viruses. Many software installers create new files based on their code (sometimes in the System Folder). A few might even modify the code of existing files. And many move, replace, and/or delete existing files. These functions all look much like the actions of a virus and can set off an antivirus extension. For this reason, many installer programs suggest that you turn off antivirus extensions before installing new software (accomplished most easily by starting up the Mac with extensions off). Usually, there is no harm in doing this, but you might want to scan the installer program for viruses before restarting without your antivirus extension and running the installer and/or scanning your hard drive afterward just to be safe.

Removing/Repairing Infected Files

The possibility of your Mac receiving a virus-infected file or being infected by a virus is the reason to use antivirus software. You should regularly scan your entire hard drives for viruses (as shown in Figure 40-3), in addition to scanning new files as they are downloaded from the Internet, copied from removable-media disks, or acquired as e-mail attachments. If you suspect a virus because of increased crashes or other unexplained erratic behavior of your Mac, run a full scan with an up-to-date antivirus utility immediately. Also, run a full scan whenever you update your antivirus software so that you will catch any new viruses whose definitions are included in the update.

If your antivirus software finds evidence of a virus, either during a scan of a file or your hard drive or as a result of a protection extension that is installed to detect virus activity, it will alert you. Depending on

Figure 40-3
Scanning a Mac's
hard drives with the
Norton AntiVirus
utility.

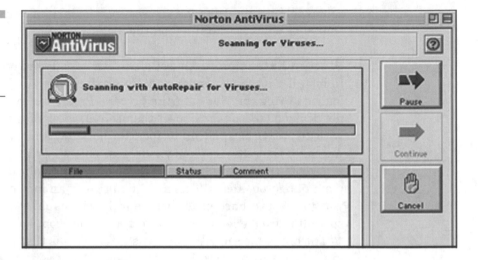

Figure 40-3
Scanning a Mac's hard drives with the Norton AntiVirus utility.

the software and your preferences, it may attempt to remove the virus code as soon as it detects the virus. If it does not do this automatically, use whatever prompts or commands are within the application to attempt to remove the virus code (also called "disinfecting").

The utility will then remove the virus code from the files where it has detected it. Depending on the virus, this may or may not damage the remaining code of the file. If the utility is not able to fully remove the virus code or if removing the virus code is likely to corrupt the file further, the utility will warn you that the file may no longer be functional after it is disinfected. Even after the file has been disinfected, you should probably replace it with a backup or copy the contents into a new file and delete the originally infected file. If the infection was located in Mac OS elements in the System Folder, it is prudent to perform a clean install of the Mac OS (as described in the last chapter) to avoid any remaining corruption.

In the case of worms or Trojan horses, the offending files should be deleted from your hard drive (or removable-media disk). If the virus code is part of a file in a compressed file archive (such as a .zip or .sit archive), the entire archive is usually deleted. This assumes the utility has the ability to scan compressed archives, which most do.

Once the utility has completed its work, it will record any virus detections and the actions it took to remove them in a log file. This log file will be immediately available for you to review (it will be similar to that shown in Figure 40-4) and will be stored as part of the utility's preferences file. At this point, you should run the utility again and scan your hard drive and any recently used removable-media disks to ensure that

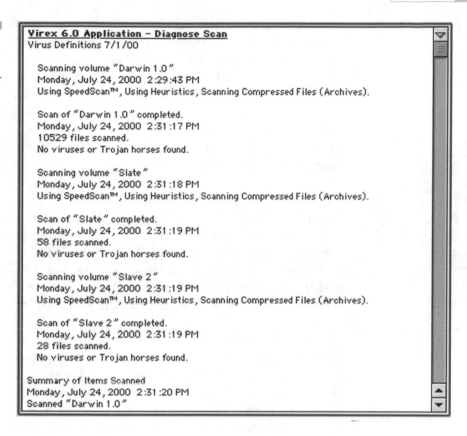

Figure 40-4
An antivirus software log report.

the virus has been completely removed from your system. If you make regular backups of your hard drive, be aware that you may have saved the virus along with one of your backups. For this reason, you should also scan all of your backups for the virus.

If you are scanning a HyperCard stack and a virus had previously been detected but has been removed, there is the possibility that your antivirus software may alert you to the presence of a virus. This is because of the way HyperCard stacks store information. It is advisable to run Vaccine, a special freeware antivirus utility to confirm a virus infection before attempting to remove the virus code, as this can corrupt a HyperCard stack.

Is It a Virus?

Just because your Mac is crashing a lot or behaving strangely in some way doesn't necessarily mean that you've got a virus. There are many possible reasons the Mac starts behaving erratically (most of which have been discussed earlier in this book). If your Mac is experiencing what you think is the work of a virus, run your antivirus software and scan your hard drive and any other drives or disks you routinely use (such as removable-media disks). If the antivirus utility reports that it didn't find a virus, chances are, the problem is the result of some other problem. If you're still skeptical, you can try running a second antivirus utility, but this usually isn't needed if you ran an up-to-date, commercial antivirus utility in the first place. If it isn't a virus, following are some likely candidates for what could be the problem.

An Extension Conflict   Extension conflicts can result in unexplained and unpredictable crashes. They can also generate other forms of erratic behavior across the Mac or within certain applications. If you have recently added software that includes new extensions, updated the Mac OS version on your computer, or updated an application that is now exhibiting problems, chances are, you have an extension conflict. Diagnose and resolve it as discussed in Chapter 38.

Other New Software   New software installed on your Mac can cause problems if the software is buggy. If you have just installed a new application and begin experiencing problems, the software may present problems running on your Mac. If your antivirus software reports no problems with a piece of software, it may just be badly written. Try not using or uninstalling it to see if this solves the problem. Also, check with the manufacturer to see if there are any known issues or problems with the software.

Cable Problems   If the problem tends to involve a specific piece of hardware, chances are that a piece of hardware has become disconnected or unplugged (or is damaged). Check the cabling of the hardware in question. If you use SCSI devices on your Mac, there could also be problems with your SCSI chain (see Chapter 12) that are causing general or intermittent problems.

Prank Software   There's a fair number of shareware and freeware out there designed to play pranks on unsuspecting Mac users. If you have friends or family who are also Mac users, they may have installed one of these pieces of software on your computer as a joke. Unlike viruses, prank software is not a threat (an annoyance, perhaps, but not a threat). Prank software is almost always written as an extension or as an application designed to be placed in the Mac's Startup Items folder.

Starting your Mac with extensions off will keep both from being loaded and allow you to determine if prank software is to blame. Assuming it is, simply remove the offending extension or application (and maybe find a piece of prank software to install on the culprit's Mac in retaliation).

Choosing and Maintaining Antivirus Tools

This section contains an overview of antivirus utilities that are available for Mac users. This includes both the three primary commercial tools, as well as the various, more specific shareware/freeware options. It also includes some additional tips regarding the use of antivirus tools.

Commercial Tools

Every Mac user should own at least one commercial antivirus utility. Although there are shareware/freeware antivirus tools out there, they rarely cover all the viruses and potential virus strains that a commercial utility does. They are also not updated as regularly. This is simply because the creators of these utilities don't have the same resources that commercial developers do. Shareware/freeware tools can be good complements to commercial utilities, but they should never be used as a substitute for commercial tools.

Three major antivirus software packages are currently available for the Mac. These include the long-standing Norton AntiVirus, Virex, and relative newcomer Sophos Anti-Virus. All these tools have prices ranging between $50 and $100 for a single user license. The companies that produce each of them also all provide virus definition updates at least once a month for their respective tools. Each tool does have a different interface and may have strengths or weaknesses that separate it from the others. However, a lot of the decision between the three comes down to personal preference. In the following paragraphs, I've included an overview of each of these three utilities.

You should also be aware that antivirus utilities often need to be updated when a new version of the Mac OS is released. Chances are that one of more of the commercial utilities mentioned here will not have an update immediately following a new Mac OS release.

Norton AntiVirus Norton AntiVirus (formerly known as Symantec AntiVirus or SAM) is currently the oldest Mac antivirus utility. It offers a protection extension, can be set to scan all new files as they are downloaded from e-mail or websites, and can scan removable-media upon insertion to determine if there are any viruses or worms on the disks. Norton also includes a live update feature that automatically updates the utility whenever new virus definitions are made available (this is free for one year and available for a small fee thereafter). Some users have noted some problems with the live update technology in some versions of Norton, however.

Norton also includes the ability to scan for unknown viruses. When doing this, Norton looks at the code of files or applications to determine if the structure of the code is consistent with what a normal file should look like. If the code seems normal, then Norton will allow the file to pass. If not, it will alert you to the fact and possibly delete the offending file. Norton claims that this approach is 95 percent effective at stopping previously unknown viruses. Figure 40-5 shows Norton's interface.

Virex Virex is actually a combination of two older programs: Dr. Solomon's Virex and McAffee VirusScan. Virex includes the ability to scan downloaded files automatically once they are downloaded, the abil-

Figure 40-5
The Norton AnitVirus application interface.

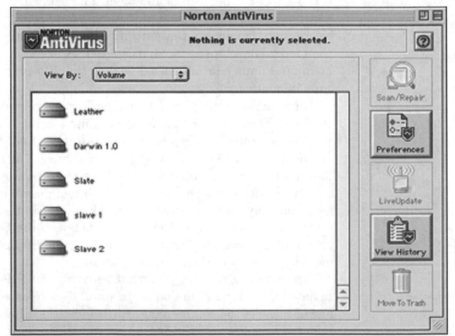

ity to scan files using a contextual menu item without needing to launch the Virex application, a protection extension, and an encyclopedia of virus information. It also includes a text listing with descriptions of all viruses currently listed in its virus definition files. New definition files are updated regularly, and for an additional fee, you can be e-mailed virus definition updates whenever they are updated (either regularly or in response to a virus threat). Virex also offers an e-update feature that lets the user set a regular schedule for Virex to automatically download new virus definition files and regularly scan individual drives or folders. Figure 40-6 shows the Virex interface.

Sophos Anti-Virus Sophos Anti-Virus is the newest Mac antivirus utility but is making a very good impression as a newcomer to the market. Sophos offers automatic updating (for monthly updates plus additional updates to major threats), contains a database of virus information, and offers support for network environments (both all-Mac and cross-platform) that has so far been lacking in previous antivirus tools. Figure 40-7 shows the Sophos antivirus interface.

Freeware/Shareware Tools

In addition to the three big commercial antivirus tools for the Mac, a large number of shareware and freeware antivirus utilities are available. These tools are very rarely full-scale antivirus software that can be used

Figure 40-6
The Virex application
interface.

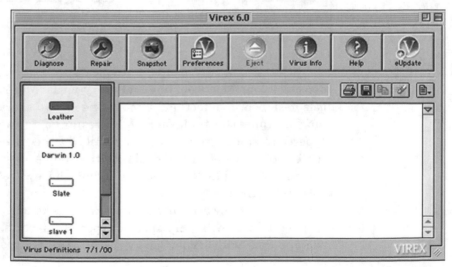

Figure 40-7
The Sophos Anti-Virus
application interface.

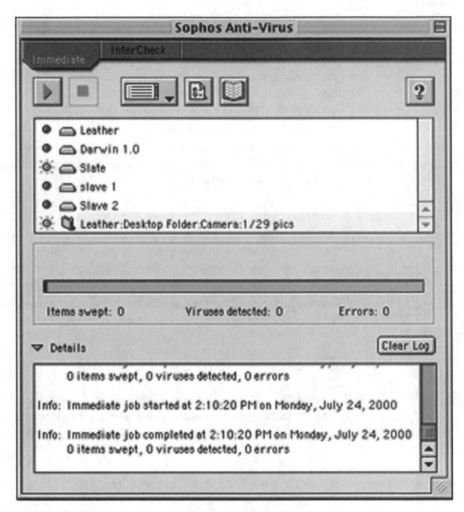

to protect your Mac from any and every virus. More commonly, they are tools designed to detect and remove one or two specific types of viruses. For example, the tool Vaccine is designed to look for and remove HyperCard stack virus infections. Similarly, the freeware Wormfood was written solely to detect and deal with the 9805 Autostart Worm virus and nothing else. Table 40-1 lists the major shareware/freeware antivirus tools and their uses.

Shareware/freeware antivirus software is usually good because it is designed to deal with very specific types of infection. Vaccine will recognize and deal with HyperCard viruses better than a commercial utility

TABLE 40-1

Shareware/
Freeware Antivirus
Utilities.

Utility	Function
Agax	Detects and removes Autostart Worm, SevenDust, and CODE9811 viruses.
Bugscan	Detects and removes the Autostart Worm and SevenDust viruses.
Disinfectant	A retired freeware antivirus utility that can protect against viruses from 1996 and earlier.
Gatekeeper	A retired antivirus utility that protected against many viruses from 1997 and earlier.
MerryXMas Vaccine	A utility to detect and deal with the MerryXMas virus.
MerryXMas Watcher	A utility to detect and deal with the MerryXMas virus.
Vaccine	Utility for dealing with HyperCard viruses.
Wormfood	Detects and removes the Autostart Worm virus.
WormGobbler	Detects and removes the Autostart Worm virus.
WormScannner	Detects and removes the Autostart Worm virus.

would because of the nature of HyperCard stack files, for example. They can also be good because they are quickly designed to deal with a specific type of infection, sometimes before commercial antivirus companies can create an update file to deal with a new threat. For example, Wormfood was made available within a very short time of the announcement of the Autostart Worm virus before commercial updates were available.

There is usually nothing wrong with using freeware/shareware antivirus tools. This is especially true if you are responding to a new virus threat and need to ensure your Mac is safe. Sometimes you may simply not have the option of waiting until you can get an update for your commercial antivirus tool (or you may not want to wait). At times you want to check your Mac for only infections of a specific type of virus, which can be done faster by a freeware tool that looks just for that virus and may not every known virus. In situations like this, running a shareware/freeware tool can be a good choice.

Always be sure that you download your freeware/shareware virus utilities from reputable sources. It is entirely possible that some malicious designer could create a Trojan horse that claims to be an antivirus tool but is actually a virus. Downloading from "safe" archives will usually prevent this from being a concern.

There Is No Such Thing as Too Much Protection

You can never be too safe. Just as having at least two disk repair utilities is a good idea, having two or more antivirus tools can be a good thing. Much for the same reason: One tool can be used to catch something another one might miss (though this is rare), or one tool can confirm the results of the other. This can mean two commercial antivirus tools—though that may not be necessary. It can, more often, mean one commercial tool and multiple freeware/shareware tools. In particular, HyperCard users should consider having a copy of Vaccine in addition to a commercial tool.

Update Your Antivirus Tools

An antivirus tool is of no use if it doesn't get updated regularly. This was mentioned in the last chapter, and earlier in this one and it bears repeating again and again. New viruses or new strains of old viruses are created all the time (this is particularly true of macro viruses). The only way your antivirus software can recognize these new threats and deal with them is if you constantly update it with information on the most recent viruses.

Commercial antivirus developers provide new virus definition files at least once a month—often twice a month. They also release updates immediately when a new virus threat is identified. You need to download and install these updates at least once a month for your antivirus software to be effective. Generally, this update is easy to accomplish because the antivirus software can check for new updates, automatically or manually at your command. When it finds new updates, it will download and install them.

For shareware/freeware antivirus tools, you will need to check the websites of the developers on your own for updates. Usually these updates require you to download a new version of the application itself rather than a definition file. You should be aware that most shareware/freeware antivirus software isn't updated as regularly as commercial tools. This is one reason you should not rely exclusively on shareware/freeware antivirus utilities. Still, check for updates to any shareware/freeware tools on a regular basis (monthly is a good idea) and immediately if a new virus threat is identified. In some cases, shareware/freeware tools may be updated more quickly after a threat is announced than commercial utilities. Or new shareware tools may be created to provide a rapid response to a new virus threat.

Beware Virus Hoaxes

I don't think there's a person alive who hasn't gotten at least one e-mail purporting to be a warning about some new and deadly virus that can destroy your computer. These warnings are usually filled with dire predictions and a warning to pass the message on to everyone that you know. Don't assume when you get these messages that they're real. In fact, the majority are nothing but hoaxes. These hoaxes frighten a lot of people and generate a lot of forwarded messages (which some people would consider spam), but most of the time, they don't do any real harm. However, the sheer amount of e-mail these e-mail chains forward can impact the performance of mail servers at thousands of ISPs, companies, and colleges. For this reason, many e-mail providers have policies in place to discourage forwarding such messages. Even if all of these virus warnings were true, most of them refer to viruses infecting PCs and not Macs.

If you do receive one, here are a few suggestions on how to deal with it. First, don't pass it on—at least not yet. Scan the warning message. If it is legitimate, the message will probably sound calm and reassuring. If it sounds panicked, it is intended to make you panic, which means it probably is nothing more than a hoax. If there seems to be a reasonable chance that the warning is real, go to one of the virus alert sites included in the resources for further study section at the end of this chapter. If there is a real threat, these sites will list it. Assuming there is a real threat, download the latest updates or definition files for your antivirus software (as pointed out in the last section, this is a good idea to do regularly anyway). Only if the threat is real should you consider passing the e-mail on. If you do pass the word on, consider writing your own message regarding the virus or at least including the URL of the alert site that you used to confirm the threat at the top of the original message.

If you go to a virus alert and don't see the virus in the e-mail you received listed, then it is almost certainly a hoax. Consider sending a polite e-mail message to the person who forwarded it to you, pointing this out to the person and suggesting that he or she might want to check with a virus alert site before forwarding such messages in the future.

TABLE 40-2

Known Mac
Viruses that May
Affect Recent Mac
OS Releases.

Virus	Symptoms/Actions
3 Tunes	A HyperCard virus that infects all HyperCard stacks and plays German folk songs and may display the messages "How are you doing?" or "Don't Panic."
ANTI	A strain of viruses that adds ANTI, ANTI-ANGE, or ANTI-0 to the code of infected applications.
Antibody	A HyperCard virus that destroys other, more malicious HyperCard viruses.
Autostart 9805	Strain of worm viruses often referred to as the Autostart Worm. Variations include Autostart 9805, 9805-B, 9805-C, 9805-D, 9805-E, and 9805-F. This worm installs as a pair of invisible files on the Mac and will periodically (usually every 6 or 30 minutes) search the hard drive for files meeting specific naming, type, and size characteristics. If the matching files are found (specifics vary depending on the strain), the worm will attempt to corrupt the files by overwriting portions of the file's code. Strains C and D do not damage files and are designed to self-destruct after specific dates during the year 1998. Strain B stops damaging files after a similar date in 1998, as does strain E after a date in 1999. Strains A and F continue damaging files regardless of date.
ChinaTalk Trojan	An extension named "female MacinTalk sound driver." When installed at startup, it will erase the contents of the hard drive and any other disks available to the Mac.
CODE-1	A virus that can cause crashes and attempts to rename the Mac's hard drive "Trent Saburo."
CODE 252	A virus that infects applications and files up until June 6th of each year. On June 6th, it will display a message saying "You are infected with a virus. Ha Ha Ha Ha Ha Ha Ha. Now erasing all disks. Ha Ha Ha Ha Ha Ha Ha (Click to continue)." However, after a user clicks the mouse, the virus self-destructs from that file (though other files will remain infected). No disks are actually erased.
CODE 32767	A virus that will infect nonexecuting applications and attempt to delete documents one day each month (the exact day and time varies each month).
CPro Trojan	A Trojan horse virus that is disguised as a file named "CPro141.sea" (supposedly an update to a compression program) that attempts to reformat all disks when launched.
Dukakis	A HyperCard virus that displays the message "Dukakis for President" and then self-destructs.
Flag	A virus that spreads to applications and Mac OS elements without doing intentional damage. Can cause serious corruption of infected files, including the Mac's System file.

TABLE 40-2

Known Mac
Viruses that May
Affect Recent Mac
OS Releases.
(Continued)

Virus	Symptoms/Actions
FontFinder	A Trojan horse that claims to be an application called FontFinder. When launched, it will destroy the directory structures of a Mac's hard drive.
HC 9507/Pickle	Known by both names, this HyperCard virus can cause erratic system behavior and may cause the HyperCard application to blink or fade and the type the word "pickle" automatically.
HC 9603	A HyperCard virus that infects other HyperCard stacks but does no deliberate damage.
INIT 17	This virus primarily just infects files and Mac OS elements (rather rapidly) and displays the message "From the depths of Cyberspace" when it first infects a Mac. It may also cause file damage when infecting files.
INIT 1984	A virus that infects only extensions and can cause serious problems, because it changes the names, type, and creator codes of files and folders to random strings of characters and can destroy files.
INIT 29	A virus that can cause crashes and printing problems but does no intentional damage.
INIT 9403/SysX	Going by both these names, this virus attempts to infect a number of files and then erase any hard drives attached to a Mac.
INIT M	A virus that is triggered on any Friday the 13th and will rename files and folders with random strings of characters. It will also scramble the creator and type codes of files and may delete files as well. When the virus is present, it creates a file called "FSV Prefs" in the Preferences folder (inside the System Folder).
MacMag	A Trojan horse that claims to be a file called "New Apple Products" but actually infects a Mac with the Peace virus.
MBDF	A Trojan horse that has two strains (A and B) and is introduced by claiming to be one of the following games: 10 Tile Puzzle, Obnoxious Tetris, or Tetricycle. This virus causes no intentional damage, but it can corrupt the Mac's System file and cause crashes.
MDEF	A collection of four virus strains (MDEF-A or Garfield, MDEF-B or Top Cat, MDEF-C, and MDEF-D). Although not malicious in intent, they can cause erratic behavior (usually garbled menus in infected applications) and crashes.
Merry XMas	A HyperCard virus that can cause irreparable damage to the Home stack of a HyperCard user's Mac.
Mosaic	A Trojan horse that claims to be a graphics utility but will actually destroy the directory structures of a Mac's hard drive.

TABLE 40-2

Known Mac
Viruses that May
Affect Recent Mac
OS Releases.
(Continued)

Virus	Symptoms/Actions
nVIR	A virus that causes the Mac to beep sporadically and to display the message "Don't Panic" occasionally. Because the source code of this virus was made publicly available, a number of derivative viruses have been created that behave similarly. These include the following viruses: AIDS, F***, Hpat, J-nVIR, MEV#, MODM, nCAM, nFLU, and prod.
NVP	A virus that infects the Mac's System file and removes the ability for the Mac to accept input from the a, e, i, o, and u keys on the keyboard.
Peace	A virus that spread only to Mac OS elements and displayed a universal message of peace on March 2, 1998 (after which it self-destructed). Spread by the MacMag Trojan horse.
Scores	This virus also goes by the names Eric and NASA and spreads to applications. Once infected, applications create several invisible files in the Mac's System Folder that can cause crashes, printing problems, and other difficulties. When infected, a Mac's Note Pad and Scrapbook icons in the Apple menu may appear as generic document icons.
SevenDust/666/ Graphics Accelerator	Going by three different names, there are several strains of this virus, some of which are harmful and some of which are not deliberately harmful. The harmful variants will attempt to delete any nonapplication documents between the hours of 6:00 a.m. and 7:00 a.m. on the 6th and 12th of each month. Some variants may also display the number "666" in a window periodically. The most common strain of the virus was delivered by means of a Trojan horse posing as a graphics accelerator extension. When infected, a Mac will contain one or more extensions with the following names: ADSP Tool, AppleTalk Library, CD-ROM Driver, Ethernet Ports, Graphics Accelerator, Internet Config, Internet Library, ISO 9661 File Access, MacLinkPlus, Monitors Plug-In, Open Transport, Photo Access, Power Enabler, PPP.Lib, TCP/IP Lib, Text Encodings, Video Picker, VideoSync, and XModem Lib. Although all of these extension names are extremely similar to those of actual extensions or other Mac OS elements, only Graphics Accelerator is the name of a true extension (an ATI video card driver extension).
Steroid Trojan	A Trojan horse that claims to be a game but is designed to destroy the directory structures of the Mac's hard drive when launched. There are four strains of this virus—A through D. Strains A, B, and C infect applications and the Mac's System file and overwrite existing code in the process, usually making the Mac unable to start up properly and applications or other files completely unusable. Strain D does not infect the System file but does successfully delete documents from the Mac's hard drive at random intervals. All strains of T4 are very dangerous, and you should reinstall the Mac OS and all applications after removing an infection of any T4 strain from your Mac.

irus	Symptoms/Actions
ZUC	There are three strains of this virus—A through C. All strains infect applications, including the Finder. When an application is infected, control of the cursor is lost from the mouse and the cursor will bounce around the screen randomly. When the Finder becomes infected, it is next to impossible to control the Mac because you will have no control of the cursor at all.

Resources for Further Study

The following URLs provide additional information on some of the concepts, issues, and products discussed in this chapter:

MacVirus—http://www.macvirus.com

Symantec AntiVirus Research Center—
http://www.symantec.com/avcenter/

F-Secure Virus Info Center—http://www.datafellows.com/vir-info/

Cert Computer Virus Resources—
http://www.cert.org/other_sources/viruses.html

Vmyths—http://www.vmyths.com/

About.com Antivirus Site—http://antivirus.about.com

Network Associates: Makers of Virex—http://www.nai.com

Sophos Anti-Virus—http://www.sophos.com

Norton—http://www.norton.com

Pure Mac: Antivirus Shareware—http://www.pure-mac.com/virus.html

Working with Other Platforms

The Macintosh is a major computing platform today, particularly in areas such as multimedia production, graphics and desktop publishing, and educational markets. Each of these professional areas is still dominated by the Mac platform. The Mac is also beginning to make significant headway in the home user markets.

Even being one of the most commonly used computing platforms today, the Mac is still a minority in the overall computer industry. PCs running one version of Windows or another by far outnumber the Macs in use today. Various individuals can, and do, argue the reasons for this, as well as which platform is the "superior" platform. The end result is that we live in a world where Mac users need to be able to interact and share data with users of Windows-based computers (and to a smaller degree users of Linux or other UNIX-based operating systems). This chapter looks at the various ways that allow Mac users to exist in a cross-platform world.

Sharing Disks and Documents

At the most basic level of cross-platform existence is the ability to share files between Macs and PCs. To accomplish this, the Mac (or PC) needs to be able to read not only the disks that are in its native file system but also those disks formatted for the other computing platforms. Beyond simply accessing a disk in a different format, you need to be able to open the files that are stored on a disk (or the files that have been sent to you as an e-mail attachment). This is a separate issue from being able to read the format of the disk. Files are created in specific types by applications. Sometimes these types are specifically designed to be opened only by a certain application. Other times they may be an industry-standard format, such as GIF or JPEG image file.

Translation Abilities Built into the Mac OS

Today's Mac OS is designed with the understanding that Mac users will have to cope with PC disks and files. It contains built-in features for accessing any type of PC-formatted disk, whether a floppy, a Zip disk, or a CD-ROM, without effort. You simply need to be certain that the File Exchange control panel (shown in Figure 41-1) is installed (in older Mac OS versions, this control panel went by other names such as PC

Figure 41-1
The File Exchange
control panel.

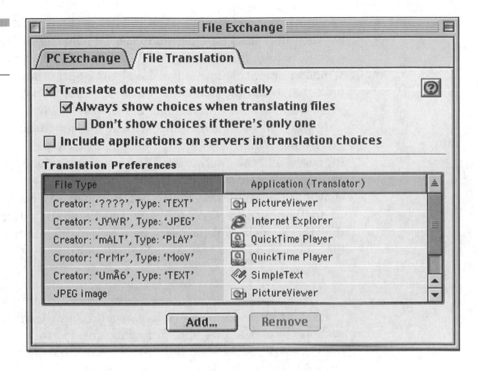

Exchange). For non-Mac CD-ROMs, additional extensions, listed in Chapter 16, may be needed as well as the File Exchange control panel.

Coping with PC files usually presents a host of issues beyond simply being able to recognize the file format used on PC disks. These issues include dealing with the differences between Mac and PC filenames, opening foreign files with appropriate applications, and dealing with the file compression schemes used by non-Mac computers. The rest of this section looks at some of these issues and how to deal with them on the Mac, while the next section looks at how to deal with these issues for the PC, as well as the ability for PCs to read Mac disks.

PC Filenames   On Macs, the file's type and the application that created a file are stored using a pair of invisible codes that are attached to a file. These creator and type codes allow the Mac OS to tell the difference between a Microsoft Word word-processing document and a JPEG image file created by Photoshop. Windows and other PC operating systems use a file extension that is appended to the end of a filename to determine what kind of file it is. A PC file must have .doc at the end of a filename for the computer to recognize it as a Word document or .jpg to recognize it as a JPEG image file. This is one of the big differences between filenames on Macs and PCs. This matter of filename extensions gets a little more confusing in Windows 95, 98, and 2000, where the Windows operating system will add the appropriate extension to a filename when the file is created but can be set to not show the extension when users are looking through the files stored on a PC's hard drive.

If you will be sharing files with a PC, get used to using these file extensions. When you create a document that you expect to share with PC users, add the appropriate file extension to the filename. Some applications will add these extensions automatically in the default name shown in the Mac's save dialog box, but many do not.

Another big difference in files is that there are a number of characters that the Mac OS will let users put in filenames that cannot be used in filenames on a PC. These include the following:

    ? [ ] \ / : ; " , * < > | = +

Each of these characters has special significance to PC operating systems like Windows and will cause the PC to react badly if used in filenames. Windows NT/2000 also doesn't like filenames that end in either a period or a space and will not allow users to open files whose names end in a period or a space. Also, there are some filenames that you should avoid using (not that most people would be likely to use them), because they are the names used by a PC when identifying its available ports. These include: com1, com2, com3, com4, com5, com6, com7, com8, com9, lpt1, lpt2, lpt3, lpt4, lpt5, lpt6, lpt7, lpt8, lpt9, con, nul, and prn.

The final major difference in terms of PC file naming is how many characters a filename can contain. Under the Mac OS, filenames can be up to 31 characters long. Windows 95, 98, 2000, and UNIX/Linux support filenames up to 256 characters long. This won't really present a problem for a Mac user giving a file to a PC user (since the PC will support longer filenames than the Mac). It may create some confusion for the Mac user getting a PC file with a long name, as the Mac will truncate the filename into something shorter that will fit within the Mac's character limits.

If you find yourself dealing with older PC operating systems that predate Windows 95, such as DOS or Windows 3.1, you will have a different character length issue to worry about. DOS and Windows 3.x only support filenames that are eight characters long (not including the file extension after the name). If you are planning on sharing a file with a user of an older PC, you should keep this in mind when naming files.

Additionally, DOS and Windows 3.x do not allow you to use a space in a filename or any of the reserved characters mentioned previously.

Manually changing all the filenames on a disk that you want to share with a PC user could be a tedious process, especially if you're talking about a large removable-media disk with hundreds of individual files. To help simplify the process, several shareware and commercial utilities are available, such A.K.A. by Miramar Systems, that will convert the names of Mac files to conform to the rules governing PC filenames. Some will even add the appropriate file extension to the name based on the file's creator and type codes if the user has not already included the extension. You can find additional information regarding these tools by visiting the "Resources for Further Study" section at the end of this chapter.

Applications and Accessing PC Files The Mac stores information about a file by using the invisible type and creator codes, as mentioned previously. A file that is created on a PC won't have a type code or creator code because the PC uses a file extension that is part of the file's name to store this information. This presents a dilemma to the Mac when you insert a disk filled with PC files (or receive files attached to an e-mail from a PC user). How does it know what type of files are on the disk? What application should it use to open the files when you double-click on them?

The answer can be supplied in one of two ways. The first is to use an application to add the appropriate creator and type codes to a file. If you open a JPEG file from within Photoshop and then save it again, the Mac will assign the JPEG type and Photoshop creator codes to it. You could do this manually with each file, but that would get tedious and boring after a while. There are also several shareware tools, such as File Buddy and A Better Finder Creators & Types (both shown in Figure 41-2), that are designed to allow you to change the creator and type codes of a file (or group of files) without opening them. This is certainly a better option than opening and resaving each file, and it is good if you want to assign files the creator code of a specific application. However, it isn't really the best method.

The second way to supply creator and type information to files is to use a Mac OS enhancement that recognizes the PC file extensions and assigns files creator and type codes based on those file extensions. For example, if you have a tool that knows .doc means a file is a Word document, it can automatically assign all files on a disk whose names end in ".doc" the creator and type codes of Word documents. The Mac OS comes with such a tool built into the File Exchange control panel.

Not only does the File Exchange control panel include the ability to assign files to the appropriate applications based on their PC file extensions, it includes an extensive database of known PC file extensions and

Figure 41-2
File Buddy (top) and
A Better Finder
Creators & Types
(bottom) both let
you assign specific
creator and type
codes to files on
the Mac.

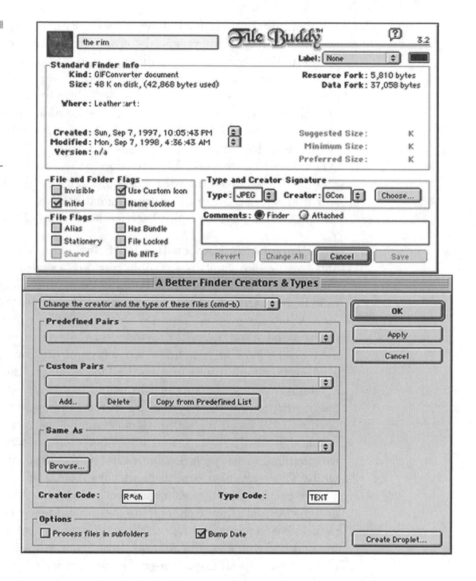

the applications that are best suited to open that sort of file. However, since there are several instances where one file type can be opened by several applications (virtually every graphics application from the free Picture Viewer to Photoshop can open JPEG image files, for example), File Exchange allows you to change the settings for each PC file extension to use whatever specific application you may want to be assigned to a specific type of file. This feature is shown in Figure 41-3.

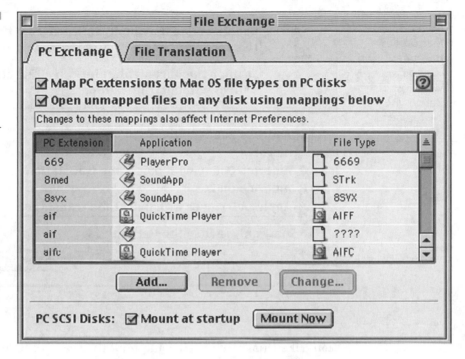

Figure 41-3
The File Exchange control panel allows you to choose which application is mapped to each PC file extension.

File Exchange also includes another powerful feature, called Mac OS Easy Open, which in versions of the Mac OS earlier than 8.5 was the domain of another control panel. This feature is for situations where there is no file extension in a file's name (or one that isn't known to the Mac OS) and no creator and type code associated with a file (or when the assigned creator code's application is not installed on a Mac). In situations like this, the Mac shouldn't be able to open a file because it has no clue what kind of file it is dealing with. However, the File Exchange control panel allows the Mac to peek inside the file and look at the data stored in it. It will then look through all the applications installed on its hard drive and list the applications that it thinks should be able to open the file. The user is then given the option of picking an application from this list to open the file with (as shown in Figure 41-4). File Exchange will remember the choices you make for opening types of files and can be set to automatically open them with your original choices rather than showing you the dialog to choose when opening them in the future.

While File Exchange allows you to open files when you have an application capable of opening a file, there are times when you may get a file that no application you have can open and display properly. For situa-

Figure 41-4
The Mac OS Easy
Open feature allows
the Mac to present
you with a list of
applications likely to
be able to open
a PC file.

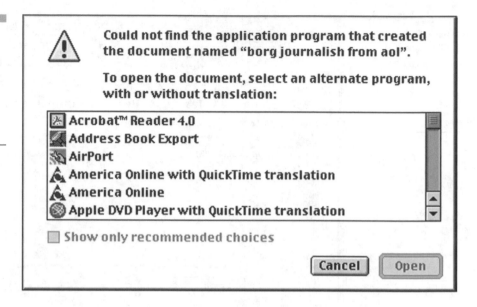

tions like this, you'll need something that can translate that file from its original format into a format that you can open. One such utility is DataViz's MacLinkPlus. MacLinkPlus can convert just about any file type into another appropriate file type. If someone gives you a PC Paintbrush file and you have no graphics program capable of opening it, MacLinkPlus can translate that file into a SimpleText PICT file that you can view, for example. And it will perform the translation by making a copy of the file, rather than changing the original file. This preserves the original file so you can send it to other users and prevents the file from being damaged in the process of translating it.

Some other utilities or applications include translators like MacLinkPlus. QuickTime can translate a number of graphics and multi-media formats in a similar manner. AppleWorks has a number of translators called the XTND system that can also be used by some other applications to translate documents. MacLinkPlus, however, tends to be the most comprehensive and full-featured translator package on the market.

PC File Compression and Encoding If you are downloading files from the Internet or receiving files as e-mail attachments, those files need to be encoded for data transfer. Encoding a file provides a framework for transferring files more easily and accurately than transferring them as raw bits of data. There are various encoding formats used today, though the most prevalent by far are Base64 (also called MIME), BinHex, MacBinary, and uuencode. These are standard formats for Windows, the Mac OS, and UNIX (and Linux), respectively.

When you are downloading files to your Mac, you may find yourself dealing with any of these encoding formats. When you are downloading files or applications designed for Mac users, you will almost certainly be dealing with BinHex or MacBinary, which are automatically decoded by most Mac FTP programs and by Microsoft's Internet Explorer. Therefore, there's little concern about decoding these. Even if your FTP program or web browser doesn't decode a BinHex or MacBinary file for you, StuffIt Expander (the ubiquitous free application for dealing with compressed files) will decode these for you.

Base64 is the default encoding method used by Windows, and you may find yourself dealing with it if you routinely extract binary files, such as pictures or movie files, from Usenet newsgroups on the Internet or if you receive e-mail attachments from PC users. Most Mac e-mail programs will decode Base64 for you when the attachment is downloaded and saved to your attachments folder. The uuencode format is the default encoding method for UNIX and is used a lot in newsgroup binary postings of all sorts. Some newsreader software will decode uuencode for you, but there are still a number of newsreaders that don't do this. If you find yourself needing to decode either a Base64 or a uuencode file, don't worry. There are plenty of shareware utilities out there that will decode the files for you, and you can find them in virtually any shareware archive.

If you are uploading a file to an FTP server and expect to have users of other platforms downloading it or if you are sending an e-mail attachment to a user of another platform, you should make sure that you are using an encoding method that the other platform can easily decode, usually Base64. Specifically, you should avoid BinHex or MacBinary, because the ability to translate these isn't common on other platforms. You can check your specific e-mail or FTP application's documentation for details on how to choose the encoding method used. For example, the popular Fetch FTP program will ask you for an encoding method whenever you upload a file, as shown in Figure 41-5. However, Microsoft's Outlook Express e-mail and newsreader application uses a preferences dialog, as shown in Figure 41-6, to determine the default encoding method for all attachments.

Beyond file encoding is the question of file compression. Compression allows you to shrink a file or collection of files for transfer over the Internet or for storage on a floppy or other removable-media disk. There are a wide variety of compression schemes for various computing plat-

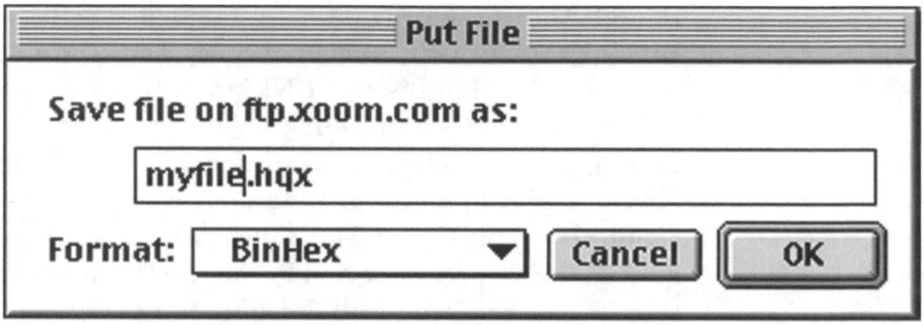

Figure 41-5
Fetch allows you to choose an encoding method whenever you upload a file.

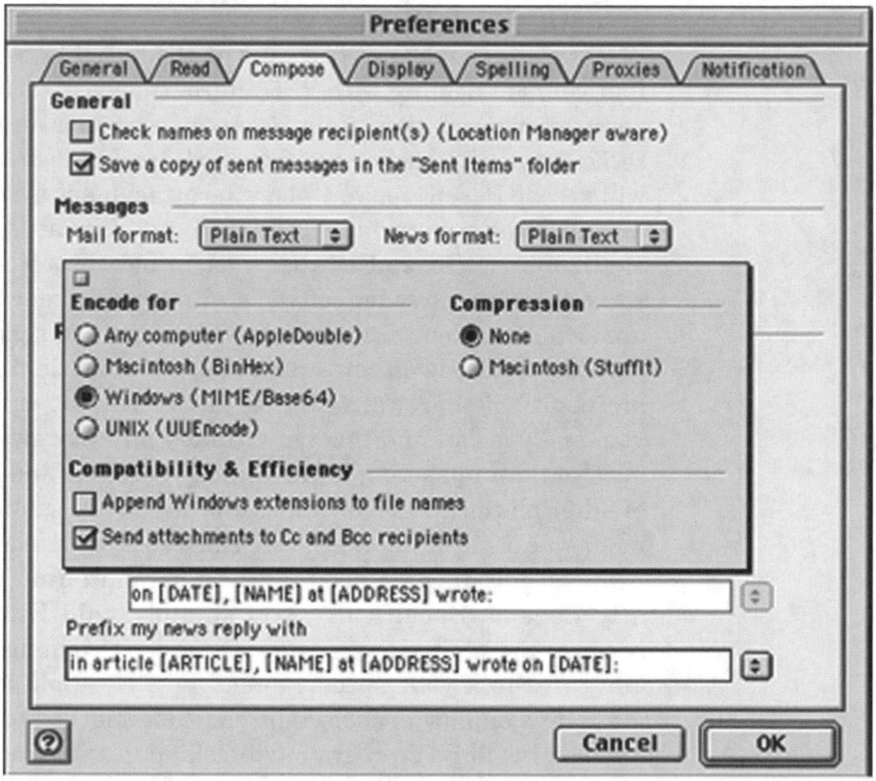

Figure 41-6
Outlook Express sets one encoding method for all e-mail and newsgroup attachments you send.

forms, but the most common are .ZIP for Windows, .SIT for Mac, and GZIP or .TAR for UNIX (TAR is technically not a compression scheme, but it does combine multiple files into a single archive). Each format requires an application that can decompress the file into its original state for use.

There are also self-expanding applications (sometimes called self-expanding archives), that are platform-specific and will decompress themselves without needing any separate decompression software. Self-expanding applications for the Mac usually end with the file suffix .sea, while self-expanding files for the PC always end in .exe. There is no way for the Mac OS to decompress a PC self-expanding application or for a PC to decompress a Mac self-expanding application.

StuffIt Expander from Aladdin Systems is the primary (almost exclusive) decompression utility for the Mac, and it is installed automatically with the current versions of the Mac OS and with most web browsers. StuffIt Expander can decompress files in a variety of compression types, including the Windows.ZIP and UNIX.TAR formats. It can also deal with a number of less common Mac and PC compression types. Self-expanding applications from the PC (which end in .exe) are about the only thing StuffIt Expander can't expand.

While StuffIt Expander will decompress cross-platform compressed files, it offers no ability to create compressed archives of files. Even its companion application, DropStuff, can only create Macintosh.SIT and self-expanding application archives. If you want to create a Windows.ZIP file, you will need to use another tool, such as the shareware ZipIt application, which can both create and expand .ZIP files.

For decompressing Mac archives on the PC, there is a Windows version of StuffIt Expander that can expand .SIT files. It also handles decoding BinHex and MacBinary files. It is not a standard part of the Windows operating system, though it is bundled with some Mac disk utilities for the PC. See the next section for more details on these utilities.

Fonts   Both Macs and Windows-based PCs use special files to store fonts that the computer can use for displaying text on-screen and for printing documents. The type of font files used on the Mac is different types of files than the Type 1 fonts usually used in Windows. You cannot use a Windows font file on a Mac and you cannot use a Mac's font on a Windows computer. However, you can convert between the two font formats. There are some shareware utilities, such as TTConverter, that can create a font file for the Mac based on a Windows font and vice versa. This can be particularly useful if you find a specialty font that you wish to use but is available for only one of the two platforms.

This does not mean that you'll have problems converting the fonts inside a document to another platform. As a rule, when a document from a PC is opened on a Mac, the Mac will use the specified font if it is installed. If not, it will either use the default font of the application used to open the document or it will use the font installed that is the most similar to the original font. Which of these two will happen depends on the application that you are using to open the document.

Mac Multimedia Files on PCs   QuickTime files intended for playback on the Mac may contain data in the same section of the file that normally only holds the creator and type codes for a file (known as the *resource fork*). Windows files do not have this part in their files, which means that multimedia files that store data in the resource fork will not play properly on a PC, because the PC will not be able to access all of the data that is part of the movie or sound recording. If you have a QuickTime file that you want to share with PC users, you may need to use the Playable on Non-Apple Computers checkbox in the QuickTime Player's save dialog box (depending on your QuickTime version) to create a version of the file that can be used on non-Mac computers.

Translation Options for PCs

While Macs have the built-in ability to deal with PC disks and documents, the same is not true of PCs. Windows does not contain the ability to cope with disks that are formatted in the Mac file systems. Nor does Windows contain the ability to readily cope with Macintosh files, primarily because Windows uses different file naming conventions that the Mac OS does, as discussed earlier.

The Ability to Use Mac Disks   If you insert a Mac formatted floppy, Zip disk, or CD-ROM into a PC and then try to access the disk, you'll receive some sort of error message telling you that the PC can't read the disk or that the disk is damaged. This is because PCs don't understand the HFS and HFS+ file systems. There are, however, software products on the market that can be installed on a PC that will allow it to read Mac-formatted disks.

Mac disk utilities for the PC all have the same general goal: to allow PC users to access files on a Mac-formatted disk. While all disk utilities allow Windows users to access a Mac disk, some do so only in a special application window. This allows you to access the files on the disk, but it is not an ideal solution because you cannot access the Mac disks from Open and Save dialogs in Windows applications. Fortunately, most commercial Mac disk utilities offer full integration, where from a user's perspective, there will be little difference between using a Mac or PC disk. Another feature to look for in a Mac disk utility for Windows is the ability to format Mac disks. Although any Mac disk utility will allow you to read Mac disks and save files on them, some may not offer the ability to format new floppies or removable-media disks in the Mac's HFS format.

The two most popular Mac disk utilities, MacDrive and MacOpener, offer both the features described above and some other interesting and useful additions. One of the most notable of these in MacOpener is the ability to append the appropriate Mac OS creator and type codes to documents when they are saved. This way, Mac users accessing the disk later will not need to worry about what file type a document is or what application will open it. MacDrive, on the other hand, offers the ability to automatically convert filenames, removing illegal characters for PC filenames and shortening long filenames to fit in the Mac's filename character limit.

One last feature to look for in a Mac disk utility for Windows is the ability to read multisession CD-ROMs. As Chapter 16 described, multisession CD-ROMs are ones where data is recorded to the CD at separate times and where each recording session is recognized and displayed as a separate CD-ROM from the others. While virtually all Mac disk utilities allow PC users to access Mac-formatted CD-ROMs, only the most recent tend to include support for multisession CD-ROMs. If you are using a utility that does not support multisession CD-ROMs, you will only be able to access the first session of the CD-ROM.

Sharing a Network between Platforms

The ability for the Mac to access PC disks is great, but more and more people are moving data between computers by network connections than they are by using individual disks. Although this is true of homes, where computers can be networked to share files and printers and an Internet connection, it is even more common in offices and schools, where the ability to access a network is essential. In a company the database you use for customer information, the spreadsheet that is used for your daily or monthly reports, or the word-processing documents that can be transformed into a publication of one sort or another are all shared among multiple users and are almost always accessed over a network. Beyond just sharing files, corporate or office networks are used for printing. Almost no office today gives a printer to every computer user; rather, they use one printer that is shared among several people in the office.

This is fine for productivity, but it presents a problem for people who want to use a Mac in a PC network or a PC in a Mac network. The problem is that each platform uses its own networking protocols and rarely natively supports other platforms. Thankfully, there are solutions that allow you to create cross-platform networks.

Quick and Easy File Transfer with an FTP Server

The TCP/IP protocol used for the Internet or an intranet is cross-platform. This means that any user can access an FTP server or web server regardless of the platform of the computer he or she is using. And just about every platform has an FTP server program that can be run on it (often these server applications are shareware or freeware), meaning that you can run a free or inexpensive FTP server on one computer in your network and then log in to it with an FTP application from another computer on the network regardless of whether each is a Mac or a PC. This is sometimes known as the "quick and dirty" way to share files between a Mac and a PC, but it is the least expensive and it does work. It also involves a little more effort to set up than some other methods, because you are essentially creating a small intranet between the two (or more) computers involved.

The first thing you need to do is create a physical network connection between the Mac and PC. The easiest choice is to use Ethernet. If an actual network already exists, simply plug both machines into it. If not, you can create a small Ethernet network as described in Chapter 32. Next, you will need to assign both computers an IP address and similar TCP/IP information. In theory, you could use any IP address if neither computer is connected to a larger network or the Internet, though it is best to stick with the 192.168.*XXX.XXX* range of private IP addresses.

Manually configuring the TCP/IP settings of the Mac is described in Chapter 32. To perform the same functions on a PC running Windows 95, 98, or 2000, follow these steps (illustrated in Figure 41-7):

1. Open the Windows control panel and double-click on the Network icon.

2. In the Network window's configuration tab, select the item labeled TCP/IP -> *XXX* (where *XXX* is the name of the PC's Ethernet card) and click on the Properties button.

3. In the resulting window, click on the IP Address tab and use the Specify IP Address radio button to enter the IP Address you wish to assign to the PC and the related subnet mask.

Once both computers have been configured in the small intranet, you will need to run an FTP server on one of them and configure the FTP server to allow access to the folders that you want to share. For the Mac, the easiest FTP server to use is NetPresenz, the operation of which was described in Chapter 34. Once the FTP server is up and running, launch an FTP application on the other computer. Use the FTP application to make a connection to the IP address of the computer running the FTP server and log in. You should now have access to the folders shared using the FTP server and can download files from the server computer or upload them to it. This works the same as if you were downloading and uploading files to a server somewhere out on the Internet.

While an FTP server on a small and personal intranet (or even a full-scale corporate intranet) will work for transferring files, it is not the most ideal situation. This is true for several reasons. First, it requires you use an FTP application to transfer files rather than simply moving the icons of files from one drive to another as you would with an actual network. Second, FTP isn't as fast as other networking protocols. Third, it only allows you transfer files. You can't open files from the other computer without first copying them to your hard drive. This means that if you want to work on the Word document TestPage.doc, which is saved on your spouse's PC, you have to copy it to your Mac using an FTP application, edit it, and then use the FTP application to put the updated copy

Figure 41-7
Setting an IP addresses on a Windows PC.

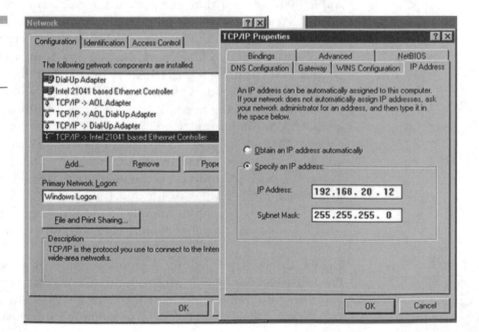

back onto his or her PC in place of the original. That's a lot more work than just opening the file over the network, editing it, and closing it, as you could with a true cross-platform network. Finally, when using FTP, you have no way to share a printer between the two computers.

Adding AppleTalk to PCs

When creating a true cross-platform network, you have two basic choices: Make the PCs understand AppleTalk, Apple's primary networking protocol (and/or Apple file sharing over TCP/IP), or make the Macs understand a PC networking protocol. Both of these approaches work and both have their advantages. Out of the box, PCs cannot understand Apple file sharing. This is true both of Windows-based PCs and those PCs that run a UNIX or Linux operating system. With the appropriate utilities, it is possible to make most PCs understand the AppleTalk protocol and allow them to access shared files and printers on a Mac network.

Windows Based PCs   There are two main products for adding Windows-based PCs to a Mac network: Miramar's PC MacLAN and Thursby's TSStalk. Either of these utilities can be installed on a Windows PC that you wish to have access to an AppleTalk network. No additional files or software needs to be installed on the Macs or AppleShare servers that are part of the AppleTalk network. From the perspective of the Windows user, the resources of the AppleTalk network are accessed through the Windows Network Neighborhood feature in the usual ways that any PC network files servers or printers are accessed.

Of the two utilities, PC MacLAN is the older and more robust, including the ability to connect to an AppleTalk Remote Access server using a phone line to join the network, as well as by a traditional Ethernet connection. More importantly, PC MacLAN includes an AppleTalk server element that allows Macs on an AppleTalk network to access shared files on the PC that has connected to the network. This feature also allows Macs to access shared resources such as file servers and networked printers on a Windows network that the connecting PC is a part of, creating a bridge between the AppleTalk and Windows network that can be used for accessing files and resources in both directions.

Linux Computers   Linux computers can comprise a wide range of hardware and can include Macintosh hardware that is running the Linux operating system, as well as PC hardware that is running Linux. In either case, Linux is not designed to communicate by AppleTalk. Linux is an open source operating system, however, which allows any Linux developer to create modifications or system additions for Linux. One such addition is Netatalk, which enables Linux computers (whatever hardware they are based on) to be able to communicate with AppleTalk servers to share files. For the popular LinuxPPC version of Linux (which can be used to install Linux on current and recent Power Mac computers), Netatalk is included with the installer. Other Linux versions may or may not include Netatalk with prepackaged installers. If not, you can locate a copy from one of the Linux resources on the Internet. Netatalk can also be used with some other UNIX versions besides Linux.

Windows NT/2000 Networks   Windows NT (now called Windows 2000 Professional) has been Microsoft's professional client/server operating system for several years. Windows NT Server (a different release from Windows NT Client or Windows 95/98) has always included an optional network package called File Services for Macintosh. As you might guess, this package was designed so that Macintosh clients could access a Windows NT network. When Services for Mac is installed and running, a Windows NT network will look to the Mac as though it were an AppleTalk network. The result is that Macs connected to such a network can access shared files and printers without any special software or settings. Services for Mac functions only in one direction, however, and will not allow Windows users connected to the NT network to access shared files on any of the Macintosh computers.

Services for Mac is a free feature included with Windows NT/2000 Server. It is not, however, part of the default Windows NT/2000 installation and must be custom-installed by the network's administrator. Unless a network administrator has a specific need or expectation to support Macs on a network, he or she usually won't include Services for Mac when setting up the network. If you will be accessing a corporate NT network, you can check to see if Macs are supported. If not, you can request that your administrator install Services for Mac.

Adding PC Networking to the Mac

The preceding solutions all looked at methods where the PC operating system was made to understand the AppleTalk protocols so that PCs could access a Mac network or so that Macs could talk to the PCs on a network. They are good solutions in a number of situations, generally where you have a larger number of Macs or an existing AppleTalk network. However, the opposite approach can also be taken, where software is installed on the Mac so that it can understand a method for file and printer sharing besides AppleTalk or Apple file sharing over TCP/IP. We'll look at three such networking methods here because they are the most common: Microsoft networking, Novell NetWare, and UNIX NFS.

Windows Networking   Although Windows NT (2000) Server supports Macintosh connections by means of Services for Mac as described earlier, these benefits are not included on other Windows versions such as Windows 95/98 or Windows NT (2000) Client. Although most large-scale Microsoft networks will use Windows NT Server, smaller office or home networks probably will not. This means that there is no built-in support for the Mac. For situations such as these, Macs need to be made to understand Microsoft's Windows networking in order to be added to such a network.

This is the aim and function of a product called DAVE by Thursby Software Systems. DAVE allows the Mac to interact with Microsoft networks that are created using the TCP/IP protocol. This is available to all current and recent versions of Windows, and it is the most popular protocol for Windows networking today. An older protocol called NetBEUI is also sometimes used for Windows networks, though it is becoming increasingly less common. NetBEUI is not supported by DAVE or any other Macintosh utility.

When Dave is installed on a Mac, the Mac can access shared resources from a Windows network. This is done through the Chooser in much the same way as accessing a Mac network. When connected to the Windows network, files on a Mac can also be accessed by Windows computers on the network through the Windows Network Neighborhood feature, just as they would access the shared files of a PC on the network would be. DAVE also allows the Mac to access shared PC printers, provided they are PostScript printers.

NetWare Networking   Novell's NetWare was one of the first networking systems used for large-scale corporate or institutional networks. NetWare is an operating system all its own that runs file and printer servers throughout the network. Computers of various platforms can connect to the file servers and shared printers through NetWare, provided that they either are equipped to understand the NetWare protocol (commonly referred to as IPX) or that the NetWare server has a module installed on it to support the platform's default networking type. The ability to communicate with a server using the IPX protocol is included with Windows. The needed software for the Mac to communicate via IPX is not included with the Mac OS.

For several years, Novell manufactured a NetWare client for the Mac that could be installed on virtually any Mac and allowed access to NetWare networks using the IPX protocol. Novell also produced a module that could be installed on a NetWare server that would allow the server to communicate with Macs through AppleTalk. When that module was installed, Macs could access NetWare servers the same as they would AppleShare servers on an AppleTalk network.

When Novell introduced NetWare 5, the most advanced version of NetWare to date, and the current version in use by almost all companies and institutions that run NetWare, they stopped supporting the Mac. NetWare 5 does not have a module with AppleTalk support, and earlier versions of the AppleTalk module for NetWare servers will not function with NetWare 5. Novell also stopped developing the NetWare client that allowed Macs to communicate with and access NetWare networks using Novell's IPX protocol.

Following Novell's decision, third-party developer Prosoft Engineering continued to develop products that would support Macs accessing a NetWare network. Prosoft produces both a NetWare (IPX) client that can be installed on any Mac and an AppleTalk module for NetWare 5. When the NetWare client is installed on an individual Mac, it allows Mac users to access NetWare servers from the Chooser in the same way that AppleTalk networks and servers can be accessed. When the AppleTalk module is installed on a NetWare server, it will appear to any Macs connected to the network as an AppleShare server and allow access to shared resources in the same way that Mac users would access any other AppleTalk resource.

UNIX/Linux NFS Networks   Although less common than the need to access Windows or NetWare networks and file servers, there may be times when a Mac user is required to access a UNIX NFS file server. Thursby's MacNFS utility can be installed on the Mac to allow access to NFS file servers using an interface similar to that of AppleTalk.

Sharing Printers over a Cross-Platform Network

Cross-platform networks can be used to share printers as well as files. As with an AppleTalk network of just Macs, printers may be connected to the network such that the computers on the network communicate directly with the printer or so that one computer on the network acts as a print server, receiving requests from other computers and then forwarding them to the printer. Cross-platform network printing is often handled by the cross-platform networking utility used to create the network. Different utilities handle print requests slightly differently, but most will simply allow shared printers to be accessed in the same manner as file requests.

The biggest challenge to cross-platform network printing can come from the fact that not all printers use the same page description language. While almost all networkable printers designed for use with the Mac use the PostScript language, many such printers for the PC use HP's PCL language, which does not support the Mac.

In addition to using a cross-platform networking utility, there is also the PowerPrint for Networks kit available from Infowave. PowerPrint for Networks allows a printer that is not normally designed to be shared to be plugged into a network using a special adapter. Once connected with PowerPrint for Networks, the printer will be accessible to both Mac and PC computers on a network.

Macs Can Run Windows (and Linux, DOS, and Even OS/2)

Even with the ability to read PC disks and files and to interact with PCs over a network, there are times when cross-platform existence requires a Mac user to go a step further and actually use PC software. This is often the case for specialized software packages that simply are not available for the Mac OS. In these situations, Mac users have three choices: buy a PC (a rather expensive proposition if you already own a Mac), install a PC compatibility card in the Mac, or buy a PC emulator.

PC compatibility cards are special expansion cards for Power Macs with PCI slots. PC emulators are applications that can be run on virtually any recent Mac. They do what their name implies: They emulate a PC or a PC operating system such as Windows 98. Both allow Mac users to run both the PC software they need to use (and the PC operating system as well) and to do so without buying another computer to run it on.

PC Compatibility Cards

A PC compatibility card is a special PCI card that has much of the same physical hardware found on a PC's motherboard built into it. This includes a PC processor (such as an Intel Pentium or AMD Athlon), memory, and other PC motherboard components. Essentially, a PC compatibility card is a PC's internals on a PCI card. About the only things not included with a PC compatibility card are a hard drive and a display, because these are shared with the Mac OS.

A special disk image file on the Mac's hard drive serves as the hard drive for the PC on the card. The compatibility card treats it as though it were a completely independent hard drive. Similarly, the display of the PC's desktop is shared with the Mac's display. This is done either by displaying the PC "screen" in a window or by using a full-screen mode, in which the monitor is used solely by the PC compatibility card while it is running (switching to another running application or the Finder will display the Mac's desktop instead).

Although a compatibility card is essentially a PC sharing space inside the Mac, it still requires a special application to access the card and to control it. This application is used to activate the PC hardware on the PCI card, as well as to generate either a window for the PC operating system and software to be displayed in or to generate a full-screen mode for PC usage. It is also used to instruct the hardware on the card to use the disk image on the Mac's hard drive as its internal hard drive and to handle other integrating functions between the PC and the Mac, such as sharing a modem and networking hardware or a single network connection.

PC compatibility cards deliver a higher level of performance than software-based emulation (see the next section) because there is no real emulation taking place. The processor on the PCI card runs at the same speed it would if it were installed in a real PC and it delivers the same level of performance. This makes hardware PC compatibility cards a choice for those users who want true, top-of-the-line PC performance along with the advantages of owning a Mac. Of course, the hardware that is part of a PC compatibility card makes these cards rather expensive, sometimes more expensive than some of the bargain PCs on the market today (though performance is usually also better than a bargain PC). Unfortunately, the only Macs that can accept a PC compatibility card today are the Power Mac G3 and G4 computers. The iMac, PowerBook, and iBook must make use of software-based emulation if the ability to run PC software is wanted or needed.

Currently, the primary developer of PC compatibility cards is Orange Micro, who manufactures the OrangePC line of cards. In the past, Apple itself developed PC compatibility cards designed to be used with specific Mac models.

Software-Based PC Emulation

Much more common, and far less expensive, than PC compatability cards is software-based emulation. In software-based emulation, the Mac mimics the action of the PC processor and other hardware. There is no Pentium processor, but the Mac pretends that there is, converting the code from the PC operating system or applications into code that the Mac's PowerPC processor can work with. The emulator then displays the results of this. The net effect is that you have the ability to run PC operating systems and applications, just as you do with a PC compatibility card, but without the excess cost or the need for a PCI card.

Software-based PC emulation is not going to provide the performance when running a PC application or operating system that a PC compatibility card would. This is because the Mac must translate the code written for one platform into code it can deal with and then return the output in a display like an actual PC. This takes a good amount of processor time and power to accomplish (and a pretty good chunk of RAM, as well). For multimedia applications and processor-intensive PC applications, you will see a definite decrease in performance compared to what a PC compatibility card or an actual PC would deliver. For general office and productivity applications, however, the performance decrease won't be as obvious, and the performance will be adequate or more than adequate for the software to be fully functional and usable.

It's difficult to give any sort of overall specifications as to what kind of performance these emulators will deliver. The results vary, depending upon factors like the Mac's processor speed and type, backside cache configuration, amount of RAM installed, what other applications or processes may be running at the same time as the emulator, and what PC applications are being run under the emulator. One rule of thumb is that you will get performance equivalent to a PC with a processor that runs at one-half to two-thirds the clock speed of the Mac's processor.

SoftWindows, Real PC, or Virtual PC   The first software-based PC emulator was SoftPC from Insignia Solutions. It was released several years ago and quickly became known as SoftWindows (because it began shipping with Windows as a default operating system). For a few years, SoftWindows dominated the software-based emulation market until Connectix released a rival product called Virtual PC. In response to the lower cost, and more versatile Virtual PC, Insignia created a utility called RealPC, which shipped without Windows and relied solely on DOS or an operating system provided by the user. Most recently, Insignia sold all of its Mac emulation technology to FWB (makers of Mac hard drive formatters and other utilities).

SoftWindows takes a different approach to PC emulation than either RealPC or Virtual PC. Virtual PC is designed to emulate the basic code of a PC's processor and other hardware and to not actually emulate anything other than the basic hardware of a PC. SoftWindows, on the other hand, is designed to emulate the hardware and to map several of the Windows functions or commands directly to the Mac OS, rather than processing them completely under emulation. This allows some functions, such as the drawing of certain items like menus to the screen, to be more efficient and potentially faster. On the other hand, this means that SoftWindows is more dependent on the Windows environment and cannot have alternate operating systems, such as Windows NT, PC versions of Linux, DOS, OS/2, or the BeOS, installed instead of Windows. This ability to run non-Windows software or operating systems was why Insignia later released RealPC (also now owned by FWB). RealPC performs emulation more similarly to Virtual PC.

Currently, the feature sets of both SoftWindows and Virtual PC are more or less comparable, and they do continue to offer similar performance. The interface of the applications that actually perform emulation differ, and they offer varying support for some devices and networking issues. They also continue to have comparable prices. SoftWindows continues to ship with the current version of Windows, while Virtual PC ships in variations that include Windows 95, Windows 98, Windows NT/2000, DOS, and Linux.

Other PC Emulators   Because they are the only fully commercial PC emulators on the market, SoftWindows and Virtual PC are the most common and full-featured PC emulators for the Mac. However, there are a number of shareware emulators out there as well. These include LisMark's Blue Label and MacBochs. None of these is very full featured, and none of them ship with a copy of a PC operating system. If you have a copy of a PC operating system, you can download and try these applications, but none of them offer as refined an interface as Virtual PC and SoftWindows do.

Running UNIX and Linux without Emulation

Linux is becoming a popular alternative for PC owners who don't want to run Windows on their computers. Linux is an open-source variation of the UNIX operating system. *Open source* means that the source code that makes up the operating system is free to anyone who wants it. It also means that anyone who chooses can take that source code, modify it, and make his or her own version of Linux, complete with whatever features he or she wants. This doesn't necessarily mean Linux is free, however. Several Linux distributions are available by companies that have designed their own commercial releases of Linux (most notably Red Hat). These releases tend to offer an easier installation and technical support to new Linux users.

Although Linux (and other UNIX variants) is primarily a PC operating system, it can easily be ported to a variety of hardware architectures (unlike the Mac OS or Windows, which are tied to specific processor and hardware designs). Several Linux distributions are available for the Mac. These are not PC emulators because they are designed to run natively on the Mac's hardware. Since they are still Linux versions, transferring files or working with PC Linux machines and Macs running Linux presents none of the problems commonly found with either PC emulators or with exchanging information between Macs and Windows PCs. However, Macs running Linux will present the same issues when working with a Mac running the Mac OS than a PC running Linux would.

Unlike running Windows under software emulators or PC compatibility cards, Macnative versions of Linux cannot run at the same time as the Mac OS. Rather, Linux replaces the Mac OS as a computer's operating system, and users must restart the computer to switch between Linux and the Mac OS. The exception to this is if you are using a PC emulator or compatibility card. You can install a PC-native version of Linux as the operating system for a PC compatibility card or the Virtual PC and RealPC emulators.

Non-Macs Can Run the Mac OS

Although most people aren't aware of it, it is possible to run the Mac OS under emulation on non-Macintosh computers. There are, in fact, a number of such emulators on the market, as listed in Table 41-1. With one exception, Ardi's Executor, Mac emulation packages work by emulating the Mac's hardware and running an actual copy of the Mac OS on that emulated hardware, much the same Virtual PC does for PC emulation on the Mac.

Mac emulation of this sort poses one problem. The ROM code that is built into a Mac's motherboard contains a required portion of the Mac OS. It is the most basic level of the operating system that controls how the Mac OS interacts with Mac hardware. Apple has never made the code in the

TABLE 41-1

Mac Emulator
Software.

Emulator Name	Non-Mac Platform(s)	Notes
Basilisk II	Windows 9x, UNIX, BeOS, Amiga	Free Open Source emulator
Fusion	Windows 9x	Commercial product
vMac	Windows 9x	Mac Plus emulation only
Gemulator Pro	Windows 9x/NT	Commercial product
Executor	Windows 3.x/9x	System 7.0 Mac OS only

Mac ROM chips available to anyone. This means that the makers of Macintosh emulation products cannot build this code into their emulators. This isn't so much because they can't locate and copy the code, but because they would be violating Apple's copyright of the code if they did so.

Of course, there is a way around this problem: Give the users of the emulation software a utility that will copy the code from an actual Macintosh computer. Since the user owns the Mac from which the ROM code is copied, he or she has a legal right or license to use that ROM code (usually just so that he or she can use that Mac). Almost all Mac emulators come with a utility that will copy the ROM code from an actual Mac (usually an older Mac based on a 68040 or earlier processor). The Mac emulator can then use the file this utility creates. The result is that to use a Mac emulator, you first need to own or get ahold of an earlier Mac to get the ROM code. The good news, though, is that you can acquire an older Mac of this type fairly inexpensively by searching Mac classifieds sites and newsgroups or checking with companies that deal in used Macs.

Another issue, as you might guess from the preceding paragraphs, is that most of these software packages can only emulate older, pre-PowerPC Macintosh computers. While this is fine for a number of uses, most software today is PowerPC native, meaning it won't run on earlier Macs (real or emulated). Similarly, emulated Macs will be limited to Mac OS 8.1 or earlier, depending upon the Mac from which the ROM code was copied. As of this writing, the major Mac emulation developers are still working on creating PowerPC Mac emulators.

Although the abilities in terms of processor code and system requirements are limited to older Macs, the actual emulated performance is not. PCs running a Mac emulator will run Mac software as fast as they can and will not be limited by the speed or other restrictions of the Mac from which the ROM code was captured. As with PC emulators for the Mac, it is hard to judge just what performance a Mac emulator will deliver, because performance depends on several factors, including the processor and RAM specifications of the PC being used, the emulator being run, the Mac OS version installed on the emulated Mac, and so forth.

Executor: A Different Emulator   The one emulator that does not actually emulate Macintosh hardware is Executor. Executor was developed in the early 1990s and was a masterpiece of reverse engineering. The developers of Executor essentially looked at how Macintosh applications interacted with the Mac OS, studying all the system calls that applications made and how the Mac responded to them. Using what they learned from doing this, they developed a PC application that responded to the same system calls in the same ways that the Mac did. The result was a piece of PC software that could run a number of Mac applications successfully but did not actually run the Mac OS at all.

Executor is still available on the Internet, but it is not overly useful to PC users today. This is because Executor was written to respond to Mac OS system calls the way the Mac OS did about 10 years ago. Originally, this was version 6.x of the Mac OS, which was an interface quite a bit different and more primitive than today's Mac OS. Executor was updated to include some of the original System (Mac OS) 7 system calls, but it has not had a major update since.

Resources for Further Study

The following URLs provide additional information on some of the concepts, issues, and products discussed in this chapter:

Orange Micro: Maker of PC Compatibility Cards—
   http://www.orangemicro.com

FWB: Makers of SoftWindows and Real PC—http://www.fwb.com

Connectix: Makers of Virtual PC—http://www.connectix.com

MacWindows—http://www.macwindows.com

About.com: Mac/Windows Integration Resources—
   http://machardware.about.com/msubmacpc.htm

About.com: PC Emulation Resources—
   http://machardware.about.com/msubemulation.htm

About.com: Mac Emulation Resources—
   http://machardware.about.com/msubmacemu.htm

CHAPTER 42

Looking Ahead: The Power Mac Cube and Mac OS X

This chapter covers Apple products that were released too close to this book's publication to be included throughout the previous chapters. It focuses on two products in particular: Apple's Power Mac G4 Cube computer (released in August of 2000) and Mac OS X (scheduled for a public beta at the time this book will hit store shelves and for a final release sometime in the first half of 2001).

The Power Mac G4 Cube

The Power Mac G4 Cube, shown in Figure 42-1, is Apple's newest desktop Mac. It is uniquely shaped and designed to contain the major components of a Macintosh computer in an 8-inch plastic cube shape. Functionally, it is very similar to the desktop Power Mac G4s, containing the same types of processor, RAM, and video cards.

The Cube's Specs

The standard G4 Cube contains a dedicated AGP slot with the same Rage 128 Pro graphics card as the Power Mac G4 computers discussed throughout this book. This is a modified 2X AGP slot (AGP is discussed in Chapters 8 and 26).

The Cube contains three standard DIMM slots for the same PC100-compliant SDRAM modules as the Power Mac G4 and slot-loading iMac computers (see Chapter 6 for details). The standard Cube comes with either 64 or 128 MB of RAM installed in a single DIMM slot and can accommodate up to 1.5 GB of RAM (using three 512-MB modules).

The Cube uses a 2.5-inch Ultra ATA/66 hard drive and can accept replacement third-party IDE hard drives if users wish to expand the internal storage, provided they are no more than 2.5 inches high (3.5 inches is the most common hard drive dimension).

The Cube also includes a slot-loading DVD-ROM drive, similar to the type used in the iMac DV models. This drive is mounted vertically, so that disks are pushed down into the computer from its upper surface.

The Cube supports Apple's AirPort wireless networking technology and can have an AirPort card installed. The installation process of the AirPort card is much the same as described in Chapter 33, though the access to the AirPort card slot is different because of the internal design of the Cube.

Figure 42-1
The Power Mac G4
Cube. Photo courtesy
of Peter Belanger.

The G4 Cube comes with two FireWire and two USB ports. It uses a nonstandard power cord and a unique external power supply. It also contains the standard 56-Kbps modem card used in every current Macintosh model (as described in Chapter 31) and a built-in 10/100Base-T Ethernet port for networking.

Table 42-1 shows the specifications for the Power Mac G4 Cube.

TABLE 42-1

Power Mac G4
Cube Specs.

Processor Type: G4

Processor Speed: 450 MHz (a 500-Mhz model can be custom-ordered from the Apple Store)

Backside Cache: 1 MB

Installed RAM: 64 MB

RAM slots: 3 (one is used by factory-installed RAM)

Maximum Possible RAM: 1.5 GB

Video RAM: 16 MB

Standard Hard Drive: 20 GB

5X DVD-ROM

Expansion Slots: Dedicated AGP slot for video card, AirPort card slot

v.90 56-Kbps internal modem

Ports: USB (2 ports), 10/100Base-T Ethernet, FireWire (2 ports), internal modem phone jack, VGA video out, ADC video out

Accessing the Cube's Internals

Accessing the G4 Cube's internal components is extremely simple:

1. Turn the Cube upside down, and press down on the panel in the center of the Cube's underside surface. This panel then extends as a plastic handle.

2. Grip the handle and pull upward. This releases the internal components of the Cube, and the entire motherboard/drive unit in the center of the Cube is released.

3. This entire unit can then be pulled free of the case, as shown in Figure 42-2.

Once free of the case, the internal component unit provides easy access to the hard drive bay, dedicated AGP slot and card, AirPort Card slot, and RAM sockets. Simply turning the unit around allows you to access each of these components. As you can see in Figure 42-3, one side contains the three RAM DIMM sockets and the AGP slot and graphics card. Another side contains the hard drive bay, and another contains the AirPort card slot.

Actually installing DIMM modules into the RAM slots is the same as with the Power Mac or slot-loading iMac computers. Installation of the

Figure 42-2
The entire inside of the Cube can be easily removed for upgrading or repair.

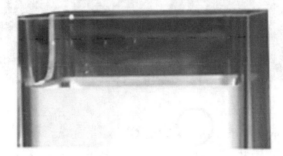

AirPort card is similar to other Mac models. Removing and replacing the graphics card is essentially the same as in the Power Mac G4, though the card is mounted vertically, which may make fully inserting the card a little more difficult. Access to the hard drive for removal and replacement is essentially the same as well, though the actual mounting process may also be slightly more difficult because of the vertical nature of the Cube's design. As mentioned earlier, the Cube can only accommodate a 2.5-inch hard drive, as opposed to the more common 3.5-inch drives. Refer to earlier chapters for installation instructions of each of these components.

Mac OS X

Mac OS X (that's a Roman numeral 10) is Apple's designation for a next-generation version of the Macintosh operating system. It is planned to include many low-level advances to improve the stability, performance,

Figure 42-3
Major components
are easily accessible
inside the Cube.

and expandability of the Mac OS, as well as several changes to the user interface that are designed to provide users more efficient and user-friendly access to important functions. It is a project that has been in development for a few years now and that Apple has repeatedly delayed from its original delivery schedule.

As of this writing, a public beta (a finished version that is not completely tested for bugs and compatibility issues) of Mac OS X is due in the fall of 2000, and the final version is due to be commercially released sometime in the beginning of 2001. Because Mac OS X is not yet a shipping product, this section is an overview of Mac OS X that relies on the public information available from Apple at the time of this writing. Changes may have been made to Mac OS X or its delivery schedule since this writing.

What Is Mac OS X?

Mac OS X is the most significant revision of the Mac OS since the Mac's introduction in 1984. It provides a number of major changes to the underlying structure and a completely new user interface of the operating system, including changing the basic foundation of the operating system to a UNIX-based foundation. It also includes removing sections of the Mac OS code that have become out-of-date but have been continually included in past releases for backward-compatibility with older software. A special layer of software in Mac OS X will allow users to run such older software, but will do so without the advantages available in the new OS.

Apple has also decided to redesign much of the Mac OS interface when releasing Mac OS X. This includes how windows and dialogs appear. It also includes the functionality of the Finder. The intention in doing this is to provide a better user experience. Although the new interface may require some acclimation time for new users, the basic functions will remain similar to that of the current Mac OS, promising a smooth transition.

The New Core of Mac OS X

The core of Mac OS X is completely new. This core operating system contains the very basic levels of code that control how the computer interacts with each piece of hardware (RAM, hard drives, expansion slots, and so on), draws items on the screen, and interacts with applications. It is at these core levels that Mac OS X is revolutionary in many ways.

Darwin Darwin is Apple's code name for the most basic layer of Mac OS X. Darwin controls the Mac's interaction with applications, RAM, and files stored on the hard drive, and it provides the foundation for Mac OS X. Darwin is based around a high-performance UNIX architecture that allows it to offer many advanced underlying features. The most important of these features include protected memory, preemptive multitasking, a modern virtual memory scheme, and integration with native UNIX disk formats and file sharing. Let's look at each of these features in more depth.

PROTECTED MEMORY Protected memory is an approach to how the Mac allocates memory to applications. It forces each application to run within predefined sections of the installed RAM. This section is completely isolated from the remaining RAM. The benefit is that when one application crashes in protected memory, it cannot have any effect on the rest of applications that are running or on the operating system itself. When a program crashes under protected memory, everything else continues running as if nothing had happened. This is a change from today's Mac OS where one application crash can cause other applications to crash and even cause the entire Mac OS to freeze up. Needless to say, this ability to keep working even after a crash is a big benefit to any computer user.

PREEMPTIVE MULTITASKING For over a decade, the Mac OS has been able to run more than one program at a time. However, it does this by letting any application use the processor for as long as it wants (called *cooperative multitasking*). This means that if you're opening a large TIFF file in Illustrator or performing a series of complex operations in Photoshop, you have to wait until this is completed before you can do anything else. In preemptive multitasking, the operating system doesn't let an application dominate the use of the processor. Instead, it continually parcels processor time to each running application. As a result, no one application can hog processor time at the expense of another. This means that there will never be a situation where you have to wait for one process to finish before you can do something else.

MODERN VIRTUAL MEMORY In the current Mac OS, you assign a specified amount of disk space to be used for virtual memory (as described in Chapter 6). When this is used up, the result is the same as if you ran out of physical RAM. In modern virtual memory, the computer decides how much hard drive space for memory as it needs it. In other words, under Mac OS X, if you don't need virtual memory, the Mac won't use it. When you run out of actual RAM, the Mac simply begins using hard drive space, taking as much hard drive space as it needs. The result is that you never need to set virtual memory or worry that you haven't set it high enough.

UNIX NATIVE FILE SYSTEMS Darwin is based on a UNIX architecture. This means that Mac OS X will have the native ability to read UNIX hard drives and other disks. This is an ability not built into the current Mac OS. It will also allow the Mac access to UNIX file sharing systems. As mentioned in the previous chapter, this is also not a built-in part of earlier Mac OS releases (although add-on products can provide it). While not as spectacular as Darwin's other advances, this is still important for people working in a UNIX environment (such as many Internet or other network providers).

Quartz: The Imaging Layer Sitting on top of the code for Darwin is Mac OS X's imaging layer. This layer consists of the operating system components that draw objects on the screen and send data to printers. Apple has code-named this layer "Quartz." Quartz relies on three imaging technologies: PDF (the PostScript format used by Adobe Acrobat documents), OpenGL, and QuickTime.

The PDF layer of Quartz controls the drawing of two-dimensional objects and replaces QuickDraw (the 2D imaging technology that has been part of the Mac OS since 1984 and was discussed in Chapter 26).

PDF offers Mac OS X the ability to render graphics on-screen using PostScript technology for increased clarity and quality. It also enables the ability for real-time anti-aliasing or smoothing of all contents on the screen for smoother, more lifelike images. Using a PDF imaging layer also gives Mac OS X the ability to easily add transparencies and similar effects to all levels of the Mac OS. All of this results in a beautiful, clear, smooth, and almost uncomputerlike display for applications and user interface elements under Mac OS X.

OpenGL and QuickTime are maintained in Mac OS X's imaging layer to provide 3D rendering and multimedia features as well. These provide the abilities and advantages that were discussed earlier in this book. See Chapters 26, 27, and 28 for more information on 3D rendering, OpenGL, multimedia, and QuickTime.

Running Applications in Mac OS X

Mac OS X includes three internal environments to run applications. These environments are part of the operating system, and running applications in each of the three should appear transparent (or nearly so) to users. These layers include Carbon (for running applications designed for Mac OS X), Classic (for running legacy Mac applications), and OS Cocoa (for running Java applications). Following is a brief look at each of these layers and what they mean for Mac users.

Carbon   When Apple began developing Mac OS X, they needed to provide a method for a smooth transition from the current Mac OS to OS X. They did this by using many of the same application program interface libraries or APIs that developers use to write current Mac applications. (APIs are the code the applications use to interact with the Mac OS to draw objects on-screen, interact with files and memory, and to do just about anything else.) By using many of the same APIs, Apple allowed developers to simply adjust their existing programs to reflect a few changes, rather than needing to write whole new application code. Apple termed the series of API libraries used by Mac OS X *Carbon*.

Carbon is the primary application environment used by Mac OS X. It provides applications access to all the new technologies in Mac OS X. When you run a native Mac OS X application, it will be in the Carbon environment. The Carbon libraries were also built into Mac OS 8.5 and 9, allowing applications adjusted for Mac OS X to also run on older Mac OS systems.

Classic   Not all applications are going to be revamped to match the Carbon APIs. This is simply a fact, particularly when you are talking about older applications or about freeware and shareware applications, in which the creators simply may not have the time or desire to update their applications. Mac OS X includes an environment to run older applications called *Classic*.

Classic is a built-in part of Mac OS X, but it functions like an application. The Classic environment relies upon a copy of the Mac OS components of the current Mac OS, and it runs like an emulator in its own protected memory space, separate from Mac OS X itself. Older applications do not directly access Mac OS X; rather, they access the earlier Mac OS elements that are part of the Classic environment.

This means that the applications can run without any problem, but they do not take advantage of the advanced features of Mac OS X. Older applications running through Classic can hog the processor and can take other applications down when they crash, for example. However, because Classic itself runs like an application in a protected memory space, these deficiencies of older applications will affect only other older applications running under Classic and not Mac OS X native applications running under Carbon.

Despite the fact that Classic runs like an emulator, older applications will open and function right alongside native Mac OS X applications.

Cocoa   *Cocoa* is a third application environment that is built into Mac OS X. It is designed to run Java applications. The advantage of Cocoa is that it allows developers to create Mac OS X programs using Java. Java is essentially a platform-transparent programming language that can be used on Windows, UNIX/Linux, and other computing platforms. Cocoa will aid in the development of new Mac OS applications and in further Java programming and development on the Mac. Because Java will be a native part of the operating system, Mac OS X will offer vastly improved Java application and applet performance over the current Mac OS.

Aqua: The New Interface

In addition to the underlying operating system advances made in Mac OS X, it will also feature a completely new user interface called *Aqua*. Aqua delivers an all-new look to windows, menus, dialog boxes, buttons, and every other facet of the Mac experience. Although Aqua does retain many similar menu options and key combinations from the current Mac OS, it still presents a very new look and experience to the Mac.

As part of the Aqua interface, menus are now translucent, allowing you to see items beneath them. Scroll bars, buttons, and window controls all feature a look that seems like drops of waters crossed with gems. Dialog boxes are tied to the windows that generate them and have a new streamlined and user-friendly look to them. Icons are given a variable size (from 16x16 pixels to 128x128 pixels), and they have a much more photo-realistic quality. All the interface elements in Aqua give a smooth, polished, and three-dimensional look to the next-generation Mac OS. Figure 42-4 shows the new Aqua interface.

Aqua also introduces some new user interface items, most notably the Dock. The Dock extends along the bottom of the screen in Mac OS X and resembles the Apple menu and Application menu from the current Mac OS and the taskbar from Windows all rolled into one. Items can be added to the Dock for easy access, as in the current Apple menu, and individual windows or running applications can be minimized to icons in the Dock to reduce clutter on the screen. Each item minimized to the Dock includes a thumbnail of the document itself. For images or multimedia files, this is a tiny version of the document.

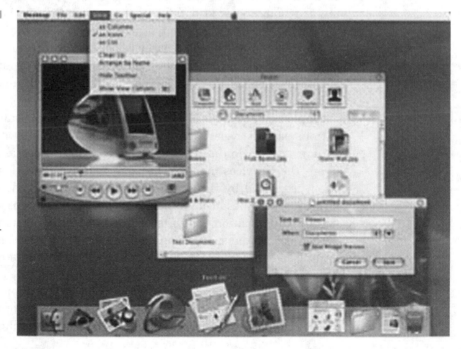

Figure 42-4
A screenshot of the Aqua interface. Note the new Finder (the window in the background), the Dock at the bottom of the screen, and the new Save dialog box attached to the window in the lower right corner. (Courtesy of Apple Computer)

The Dock can be resized to accommodate as many items as the user needs to place in it. It can also be reduced or enlarged according to personal preference. In addition, when the cursor is moved over icons in the Dock, the name of each item is displayed and the individual icon can be enlarged for easier viewing.

There are two permanent items in the Dock: the Finder icon on the leftmost end, and the Trash on the rightmost end. These items are permanently positioned in the Dock because they are no longer consistently associated with the desktop of the Mac. This is a fairly radical change from the traditional Mac OS.

In the current Mac OS, whenever you are moving items (icons, windows, and so on) around on the desktop, you are using the Finder. This is not the case in Mac OS X. The Finder is a separate application, with a separate window. This window contains icons for your hard drive, folders, and other disks (though you can drag these icons to the desktop, if you wish). To provide easy access to the Finder application, its icon is permanently part of the Dock. Similarly, the Trash is included in the Dock so that it is always easily accessible.

With the Dock serving the same functions as both the Apple menu and Application menu in the current Mac OS, Apple has removed both menus from Mac OS X (though the Apple logo still remains as a decorative feature in the middle of the menu bar). Instead, Mac OS X includes a new menu (though it is still referred to as the Application menu) that sits where the Apple menu is currently located. The new application menu displays the name of the currently active application and includes common commands including the Quit command and commands for hiding the active application, displaying the application's About box, and opening the application's preferences dialog.

Apple has also added another standard menu or submenu to all applications—the Services menu. The Services menu allows you to select data in one application and then select commands for another application (from the Services menu). The data selected in the first application is then processed by the second application, using the appropriate commands. Once these commands are completed, the results are placed in the first application. The result is as though you had copied the data, pasted it into the second application, worked with it, copied the results, and placed them back in the original application instead of the original data.

Windows are different in Mac OS X as well. A typical Mac OS X window contains three window controls on the left side of the title bar (reminiscent of Windows). These controls are shaped like glass beads and always appear in the order of red, yellow, and green. The red button serves to close the window. The yellow button minimizes the window as an item in the dock. The green button resizes the window to fill the entire screen.

On the right edge of some windows is a fourth, gray button. This button turns the Single Window Mode feature on or off. With Single Window Mode on, Mac OS X hides the current window whenever a new one is opened. This means that there will only be one window on the desktop at any time, rather than scads of windows being displayed and cluttering the desktop at once (something that is considered a fault of many operating systems today).

Dialog boxes are different in Mac OS X as well. The biggest difference is that they are tied to a window. When you use the Save command in an application, for example, the dialog extends from the title bar of the window that contains the document you are saving. This keeps it obvious which dialog boxes are associated with which windows. The Open and Save dialog boxes have also been streamlined to display only a menu of favorite and recent folders by default (though a button in the dialog does present the ability to navigate to any folder available to the computer).

The New Finder

As part of Mac OS X, Apple has redesigned the Finder. As mentioned earlier, the Finder is now a separate application from the desktop. The Finder's primary window contains icons for each disk connected to the Mac (much as disk icons now appear on the desktop), as well as an icon for browsing network drives. You can navigate through folders within the disks by using the same methods through the new Finder as with the current Finder's list and icon views (although using Mac OS X's new Single Window Mode will display the contents of only one folder in the window at once).

In addition to the traditional icon and list views, the new Finder also offers a new Browser view. In the Browser view, the Finder displays three columns, allowing you to easily view several levels of folders at once for more efficient navigation. Three small buttons in the new Finder window allow you to select between the three Finder views.

Along the top of the new Finder's window is a series of six larger buttons. These buttons allow you quick access to specific folders within the Mac. These buttons can be hidden using a command in the new Finder's View menu. They include the following:

- *Computer*. This button brings you immediately to the listing of all drives attached to the computer (the equivalent of today's Mac desktop) plus the icon for network drives and shared folders.

- *Home*. This button brings you to the home folder. Each individual user has a home folder, where their individual documents, applications, desktop items, preferences, and other files are stored. Home folders and all of their subfolders do not have to reside on a local hard drive. In fact, home folders and user preferences can reside on a network file server, allowing people to log on to any Mac OS X computer on the network and have the same settings, documents, other items, and experience regardless of which computer they are actually using.

- *Apps*. This button brings you to the Applications folder. The folder is the default install location for applications under Mac OS X.

- *Docs*. This button brings you to the Documents folder. Each user has his or her own Documents folder, though it isn't required that you store documents in this folder anymore than with the current Mac OS.

- *Favorites*. This button brings you to the Favorites folder. Again, each user has his or her own Favorites folder. The Favorites folder, as in the Favorites folder in today's Apple menu, is a place to store commonly accessed items, applications, URLs, and other items. Folders and servers in the Favorites folder are then listed in the new Open/Save dialog menu.

- *People*. This button allows you to easily access the folder containing all the individual user home folders on a given Mac.

A menu below these six navigation buttons also allows easy access to each of these folders, plus other folders you have designated as favorites and folders that you have recently accessed (much like Favorites and Recent Items menus in today's Network Browser and other Mac OS dialog boxes).

Access to Mac OS X's control panels and system preferences is made through the System Preferences Application rather than the Finder. When in the Desktop, the Application menu contains this item (much as the Apple menu does today and it is in the Dock by default).

Also for Mac users wanting to continue to keep icons for documents, folders, and drives on the desktop rather than using the new Finder, you can simply drag items from the Finder window onto the desktop. Although the icons on the desktop will actually be aliases (or the Mac

OS X equivalent) of the original items, they will continue to function like the actual items. The new Finder is displayed in Figure 42-4.

Mac OS X Server

Although Apple has yet to introduce Mac OS X itself, a special server operating system called Mac OS X Server has been available for quite some time. Mac OS X Server is a separate product entirely, although it does offer many of the core-level advantages of Mac OS X (protected memory, preemptive multitasking, modern virtual memory, and much improved network performance). Mac OS X Server contains much of the same UNIX core as Mac OS X, but it exists as a server platform, one designed for running industrial-strength file servers or Internet servers. Because it is based on UNIX, Mac OS X Server includes many high-power UNIX Internet servers, including the popular and robust Apache web server. Mac OS X Server includes a traditional Maclike interface running on top of its UNIX core, and it also includes a special Mac OS compatibility environment for running existing Mac applications.

Although a true discussion of Mac OS X Server is beyond the scope of this book, it is worth mentioning Mac OS X Server simply because it is an existing Apple product. However, Mac OS X Server is primarily a product that will be of interest to developers and to large network administrators or those providing professional-level Internet services.

High Performance Networking   The important feature of Mac OS X Server is its high-power networking abilities. Mac OS X Server is an advance of the powerful AppleShare IP server suite. It can run extremely reliable AppleShare file and print servers. Because it features protected memory, there is almost no risk that the server will crash. Likewise, preemptive multitasking helps ensure that the computer is always delivering high performance to each individual computer that connects to it.

The sheer speed at which Mac OS X Server computers can transfer data over an existing network is extremely impressive. This makes it very attractive to administrators of large Macintosh networks.

Net-Boot Support   The Macintosh computers covered by this book have the ability to use a disk image on a network as a startup disk rather than a local disk that is attached to the computer. To use this feature, a

Mac OS X Server computer needs to be on the network. No other Mac file server provides NetBoot support. Mac OS X Server allows administrators to create and configure a NetBoot disk image for any Macs on their network. This allows them to create a single, standard System Folder and to install (and later upgrade) any applications on that single disk image. NetBooted Macs will have access to that disk image and its contents as easily as their internal hard drives. The powerful network performance enabled by Mac OS X Server is one of the key elements in making NetBooting a viable option for Mac networks.

Support for Multiport Ethernet Cards   Mac OS X Server computers ordered from Apple can be configured with special multiport Ethernet cards. These special PCI cards contain more than one Ethernet port each, allowing the computer to be connected to multiple Ethernet networks and to run file servers (or other server types) for each network. Mac OS X Server is the only Macintosh environment or software to provide support for multiport Ethernet cards.

Internet Servers   As mentioned earlier, Mac OS X Server ships with the Apache web server, which is one of the most robust and configurable web servers available today, as well as one of the most popular (statistics say that half the web servers on the Internet are Apache servers). Apache is a UNIX-based server enabled on the Mac by Mac OS Server's UNIX core. It offers extreme performance for webmasters wanting to use Macintosh hardware.

Apple also includes several other Internet servers as part of Mac OS X Server, including the WebObjects environment. WebObjects is a powerful technology for integrating database functions into Internet services and provides the ability to create very powerful, dynamic sites and online stores (Apple's own online store is powered by WebObjects). Combined with the Apache server, WebObjects and Mac OS X Server offer a very powerful combination for providing high-power websites and services.

Apple also includes the QuickTime Streaming Server as a standard part of Mac OS X Server. The QuickTime Streaming Server is needed for true streaming of QuickTime movies over the Internet. It also enables the ability to broadcast live video content streams over the Internet. QuickTime Streaming Server relies on a series of standard protocols for streaming content, which makes it essentially cross-platform. Streamed QuickTime content can be viewed using the free QuickTime Player application on any supported computer (Mac or PC) with an Internet connection.

Resources for Further Study

The following URLs provide additional information on some of the concepts, issues, and products discussed in this chapter:

Apple's Power Mac G4 Cube HomePage—
http://www.apple.com/powermaccube

About.com Mac Hardware G4 Cube Resources—
http://machardware.about.com/cs/g4cube/

*Apple's Mac OS X Site—*http://www.apple.com/macosx

Apple's Mac OS X Server HomePage—
http://www.apple.com/macosx/server

About.com Mac OS X Resources—
http://macos.about.com/msubmacosx.htm

About.com Mac OS X Server Resources—
http://macos.about.com/msubxsever.htm

INDEX

ABOUT THE AUTHORS

Ryan J. Faas is a computer trainer, consultant, and Mac specialist. He is a Mac hardware expert and correspondent at About.com and the co-founder of a small consulting company that helps users choose the ideal system for their needs.

Stuart Brown and **Kim Foglia** are long-time Mac users and technicians who run a non-profit Mac users group. Mr. Foglia is the president of WriteDesign, an award-winning Web development and e-business consulting firm.